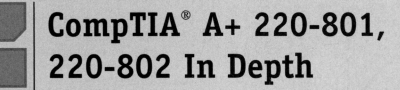

CompTIA® A+ 220-801, 220-802 In Depth

Jean Andrews, Ph.D.

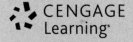 CENGAGE
Learning·

Australia • Canada • Mexico • Singapore • Spain • United Kingdom • United States

CompTIA® A+ 220-801, 220-802 In Depth, Jean Andrews

Vice President, Careers & Computing: Dave Garza

Executive Editor: Stephen Helba

Publisher and General Manager, Course Technology
    PTR: Stacy Hiquet

Associate Director of Marketing: Sarah Panella

Manager of Editorial Services: Heather Talbot

Acquisitions Editors: Nick Lombardi
    and Heather Hurley

Director, Development – Careers & Computing:
    Marah Bellegarde

Product Development Manager: Juliet Steiner

Senior Product Manager: Michelle Ruelos Cannistraci

Developmental Editor: Jill Batistick/Deb Kaufmann

Editorial Assistant: Sarah Pickering

Brand Manager: Kristin McNary

Senior Market Development Manager: Mark Linton

Senior Marketing Manager: Mark Hughes

Senior Production Director: Wendy Troeger

Production Manager: Andrew Crouth

Senior Content Project Manager: Andrea Majot

Art Director: GEX

Technology Project Manager: Joseph Pliss

Media Editor: William Overocker

Cover Designer: Mike Tanamachi

For product information and technology assistance, contact us at
Cengage Learning Customer & Sales Support, 1-800-354-9706

For permission to use material from this text or product, submit all requests online at **cengage.com/permissions**
Further permissions questions can be emailed to
permissionrequest@cengage.com

Microsoft® is a registered trademark of the Microsoft Corporation.

Library of Congress Control Number: 2013930068

ISBN-13: 978-1-285-16068-9

ISBN-10: 1-285-16068-1

Course Technology
20 Channel Center Street
Boston, MA 02210
USA

Cengage Learning is a leading provider of customized learning solutions with office locations around the globe, including Singapore, the United Kingdom, Australia, Mexico, Brazil, and Japan. Locate your local office at: **international.cengage.com/region**

Cengage Learning products are represented in Canada by Nelson Education, Ltd.

For your lifelong learning solutions, visit **courseptr.com**

Visit our corporate website at **cengage.com**.

Printed in the United States of America
1 2 3 4 5 6 7 16 15 14 13

Table of Contents

CHAPTER 15

Connecting to and Setting Up a Network 661

CHAPTER 16

Networking Types, Devices, and Cabling 721

CHAPTER 17

Windows Resources on a Network. . . . 767

CHAPTER 18

Security Strategies 827

CompTIA A+ 220-801 Exam Mapped to Chapters

A+ Guide to Managing and Maintaining Your PC, Eighth Edition fully meets all of CompTIA's A+ 220-801 and 220-802 Exam Objectives.

DOMAIN 1.0 PC HARDWARE

1.1   Configure and apply BIOS settings.

OBJECTIVES	CHAPTER	PAGE NUMBERS
◢ Install firmware upgrades – flash BIOS	Ch 4	Pages 137–156
◢ BIOS component information	Ch 4	Pages 137–156
• RAM	Ch 4	Pages 137–156
• Hard drive	Ch 4	Pages 137–156
• Optical drive	Ch 4	Pages 137–156
• CPU	Ch 4	Pages 137–156
◢ BIOS configurations	Ch 4	Pages 137–156
• Boot sequence	Ch 4	Pages 137–156
• Enabling and disabling devices	Ch 4	Pages 137–156
• Date/time	Ch 4	Pages 137–156
• Clock speeds	Ch 4	Pages 137–156
• Virtualization support	Ch 4	Pages 137–156
▪ BIOS security (passwords, drive encryption: TPM, lo-jack)	Ch 4	Pages 137–156
◢ Use built-in diagnostics	Ch 4	Pages 137–156
◢ Monitoring	Ch 4	Pages 137–156
• Temperature monitoring	Ch 4	Pages 137–156
• Fan speeds	Ch 4	Pages 137–156
• Intrusion detection/notification	Ch 4	Pages 137–156
• Voltage	Ch 4	Pages 137–156
• Clock	Ch 4	Pages 137–156
• Bus speed	Ch 4	Pages 137–156

1.2   Differentiate between motherboard components, their purposes, and properties.

OBJECTIVES	CHAPTER	PAGE NUMBERS
◢ Sizes	Ch 4	Pages 114–137, 155–160
• ATX	Ch 4	Pages 114–137, 155–160
• Micro-ATX	Ch 4	Pages 114–137, 155–160
• ITX	Ch 4	Pages 114–137, 155–160
◢ Expansion slots	Ch 4	Pages 114–137, 155–160
• PCI	Ch 4	Pages 114–137, 155–160
• PCI-X	Ch 4	Pages 114–137, 155–160
• PCIe	Ch 4	Pages 114–137, 155–160
• miniPCI	Ch 4	Pages 114–137, 155–160
• AGP2x, 4x, 8x	Ch 4	Pages 114–137, 155–160
◢ RAM slots	Ch 5	Pages 189–210
◢ CPU sockets	Ch 4	Pages 114–137, 155–160
◢ Chipsets	Ch 4	Pages 114–137, 155–160
• North Bridge	Ch 4	Pages 114–137, 155–160
• South Bridge	Ch 4	Pages 114–137, 155–160
• CMOS battery	Ch 4	Pages 114–137, 155–160

1.6 Differentiate among various CPU types and features and select the appropriate cooling method.

OBJECTIVES	CHAPTER	PAGE NUMBERS
◢ Socket types	Ch 4	Pages 116–121
• Intel: LGA, 775, 1155, 1156, 1366	Ch 4	Pages 116–121
• AMD: 940, AM2, AM2+, AM3, AM3+, FM1, F	Ch 4	Pages 116–121
◢ Characteristics	Ch 5	Pages 166–189
• Speeds	Ch 5	Pages 166–189
• Cores	Ch 5	Pages 166–189
• Cache size/type	Ch 5	Pages 166–189
• Hyperthreading	Ch 5	Pages 166–189
• Virtualization support	Ch 5	Pages 166–189
• Architecture (32-bit vs. 64-bit)	Ch 5	Pages 166–189
• Integrated GPU	Ch 5	Pages 166–189
◢ Cooling	Ch 2	Pages 67–72
• Heat sink	Ch 2	Pages 67–72
• Fans	Ch 2	Pages 67–72
• Thermal paste	Ch 2	Pages 67–72
• Liquid-based	Ch 2	Pages 67–72

1.7 Compare and contrast various connection interfaces and explain their purpose.

OBJECTIVES	CHAPTER	PAGE NUMBERS
◢ Physical connections		
• USB 1.1 vs. 2.0 vs. 3.0 speed and distance characteristics	Ch 8	Pages 314–368
▪ Connector types: A, B, mini, micro	Ch 8	Pages 314–368
• Firewire 400 vs. Firewire 800 speed and distance characteristics	Ch 8	Pages 314–368
• SATA1 vs. SATA2 vs. SATA3, eSATA, IDE speeds	Ch 6	Pages 216–229
• Other connector types	Ch 1	Pages 2–5
▪ Serial	Ch 1	Pages 2–5
▪ Parallel	Ch 1	Pages 2–5
▪ VGA	Ch 1	Pages 2–5
▪ HDMI	Ch 1	Pages 2–5
▪ DVI	Ch 1	Pages 2–5
▪ Audio	Ch 1	Pages 2–5
▪ RJ-45	Ch 1	Pages 2–5
▪ RJ-11	Ch 1	Pages 2–5
• Analog vs. digital transmission	Ch 1	Pages 2–5
▪ VGA vs. HDMI	Ch 1	Pages 2–5
◢ Speeds, distances and frequencies of wireless device connections	Ch 8	Pages 314–368
• Bluetooth	Ch 8	Pages 314–368
• IR	Ch 8	Pages 314–368
• RF	Ch 8	Pages 314–368

1.8 Install an appropriate power supply based on a given scenario.

OBJECTIVES	CHAPTER	PAGE NUMBERS
◢ Connector types and their voltages	Ch 1	Pages 2–22
• SATA	Ch 1	Pages 2–22
• Molex	Ch 1	Pages 2–22

1.9 Evaluate and select appropriate components for a custom configuration, to meet customer specifications or needs.

1.10 Given a scenario, evaluate types and features of display devices.

1.11 Identify connector types and associated cables.

1.12 Install and configure various peripheral devices.

DOMAIN 2.0 NETWORKING

2.1 Identify types of network cables and connectors.

2.2 Categorize characteristics of connectors and cabling.

2.3 Explain properties and characteristics of TCP/IP.

2.4 Explain common TCP and UDP ports, protocols, and their purpose.

• Bus	Ch 16	Pages 722–733
• Star	Ch 16	Pages 722–733
• Hybrid	Ch 16	Pages 722–733

2.9   Compare and contrast network devices, their functions, and features.

OBJECTIVES	CHAPTER	PAGE NUMBERS
◢ Hub	Ch 16	Pages 722–747
◢ Switch	Ch 16	Pages 722–747
◢ Router	Ch 16	Pages 722–747
◢ Access point	Ch 16	Pages 722–747
◢ Bridge	Ch 16	Pages 722–747
◢ Modem	Ch 16	Pages 722–747
◢ NAS	Ch 16	Pages 722–747
◢ Firewall	Ch 16	Pages 722–747
◢ VoIP phones	Ch 16	Pages 722–747
◢ Internet appliance	Ch 16	Pages 722–747

2.10   Given a scenario, use appropriate networking tools.

OBJECTIVES	CHAPTER	PAGE NUMBERS
◢ Crimper	Ch 16	Pages 748–763
◢ Multimeter	Ch 16	Pages 748–763
◢ Toner probe	Ch 16	Pages 748–763
◢ Cable tester	Ch 16	Pages 748–763
◢ Loopback plug	Ch 16	Pages 748–763
◢ Punchdown tool	Ch 16	Pages 748–763

DOMAIN 3.0 LAPTOPS

3.1   Install and configure laptop hardware and components.

OBJECTIVES	CHAPTER	PAGE NUMBERS
◢ Expansion options	Ch 19	Pages 880–928
• Express card /34	Ch 19	Pages 880–928
• Express card /54	Ch 19	Pages 880–928
• PCMCIA	Ch 19	Pages 880–928
• SODIMM	Ch 19	Pages 880–928
• Flash	Ch 19	Pages 880–928
◢ Hardware/device replacement	Ch 19	Pages 880–928
• Keyboard	Ch 19	Pages 880–928
• Hard Drive (2.5 vs. 3.5)	Ch 19	Pages 880–928
• Memory	Ch 19	Pages 880–928
• Optical drive	Ch 19	Pages 880–928
• Wireless card	Ch 19	Pages 880–928
• Mini-PCIe	Ch 19	Pages 880–928
• screen	Ch 19	Pages 880–928
• DC jack	Ch 19	Pages 880–928
• Battery	Ch 19	Pages 880–928
• Touchpad	Ch 19	Pages 880–928
• Plastics	Ch 19	Pages 880–928
• Speaker	Ch 19	Pages 880–928
• System board	Ch 19	Pages 880–928
• CPU	Ch 19	Pages 880–928

3.2   Compare and contrast the components within the display of a laptop.

OBJECTIVES	CHAPTER	PAGE NUMBERS
◢ Types	Ch 19	Pages 922–925
• LCD	Ch 19	Pages 922–925
• LED	Ch 19	Pages 922–925
• OLED	Ch 19	Pages 922–925
• Plasma	Ch 19	Pages 922–925
◢ Wi-Fi antenna connector/placement	Ch 19	Pages 922–925
◢ Inverter and its function	Ch 19	Pages 922–925
◢ Backlight	Ch 19	Pages 922–925

3.3   Compare and contrast laptop features.

OBJECTIVES	CHAPTER	PAGE NUMBERS
◢ Special function keys	Ch 19	Pages 872–896
• Dual displays	Ch 19	Pages 872–896
• Wireless (on/off)	Ch 19	Pages 872–896
• Volume settings	Ch 19	Pages 872–896
• Screen brightness	Ch 19	Pages 872–896
• Bluetooth (on/off)	Ch 19	Pages 872–896
• Keyboard backlight	Ch 19	Pages 872–896
◢ Docking station vs. port replicator	Ch 19	Pages 872–896
◢ Physical laptop lock and cable lock	Ch 19	Pages 872–896

DOMAIN 4.0 PRINTERS

4.1   Explain the differences between the various printer types and summarize the associated imaging process.

OBJECTIVES	CHAPTER	PAGE NUMBERS
◢ Laser	Ch 21	Pages 998–1006
• Imaging drum, fuser assembly, transfer belt, transfer roller, pickup rollers, separate pads, duplexing assembly	Ch 21	Pages 998–1006
• Imaging process: processing, charging, exposing, developing, transferring, fusing and cleaning	Ch 21	Pages 998–1006
◢ Inkjet	Ch 21	Pages 998–1006
• Ink cartridge, print head, roller, feeder, duplexing assembly, carriage and belt	Ch 21	Pages 998–1006
• Calibration	Ch 21	Pages 998–1006
◢ Thermal	Ch 21	Pages 998–1006
• Feed assembly, heating element	Ch 21	Pages 998–1006
• Special thermal paper	Ch 21	Pages 998–1006
◢ Impact	Ch 21	Pages 998–1006
• Print head, ribbon, tractor feed	Ch 21	Pages 998–1006
• Impact paper	Ch 21	Pages 998–1006

4.2   Given a scenario, install, and configure printers.

OBJECTIVES	CHAPTER	PAGE NUMBERS
◢ Use appropriate printer drivers for a given operating system	Ch 21	Pages 1007–1024
◢ Print device sharing	Ch 21	Pages 1007–1024

DOMAIN 5.0 OPERATIONAL PROCEDURES

5.3 Given a scenario, demonstrate proper communication and professionalism.

5.4 Explain the fundamentals of dealing with prohibited content/activity.

CompTIA A+ 220-802 Exam Objectives Mapped to Chapters

A+ Guide to Managing and Maintaining Your PC, Eighth Edition fully meets all of CompTIA's A+ 220-801 and 220-802 Exam Objectives.

DOMAIN 1.0 OPERATING SYSTEMS

1.1 Compare and contrast the features and requirements of various Microsoft Operating Systems.

OBJECTIVES	CHAPTER	PAGE NUMBERS
◢ Windows XP Home, Windows XP Professional, Windows XP Media Center, Windows XP 64-bit Professional	Ch 7, Apx C	Pages 262–280, 1084–1086
◢ Windows Vista Home Basic, Windows Vista Home Premium, Windows Vista Business, Windows Vista Ultimate, Windows Vista Enterprise	Ch 7, Apx B	Pages 262–280, 1064–1066
◢ Windows 7 Starter, Windows 7 Home Premium, Windows 7 Professional, Windows 7 Ultimate, Windows 7 Enterprise	Ch 7	Pages 262–280
◢ Features:		
• 32-bit vs. 64-bit	Ch 7	Pages 262–280
• Aero,	Ch 7	Pages 262–280
• gadgets,	Ch 7	Pages 262–280
• user account control,	Ch 7	Pages 281–283
• bit-locker,	Ch 18	Pages 828–841
• shadow copy,	Ch 10	Pages 424–435
• system restore,	Ch 10	Pages 424–435
• ready boost,	Ch 11	Pages 513–516
• sidebar,	Ch 3	Pages 87–88
• compatibility mode,	Ch 7	Pages 290–304
• XP mode,	Ch 7	Pages 290–304
• easy transfer,	Ch 7	Pages 290–304
• administrative tools,	Ch 11	Pages 468–503
• defender,	Ch 18	Pages 850–867
• Windows firewall,	Ch 18	Pages 828–841
• security center,	Ch 18	Pages 828–841
• event viewer,	Ch 11	Pages 468–503
• file structure and paths,	Ch 10	Pages 414–424
• category view vs. classic view	Ch 3	Pages 101–102
◢ Upgrade paths – differences between in place upgrades, compatibility tools, Windows upgrade OS advisor	Ch 7	Pages 262–290

1.2 Given a scenario, install and configure the operating system using the most appropriate method.

OBJECTIVES	CHAPTER	PAGE NUMBERS
◢ Boot methods	Ch 7	Pages 280–290
• USB	Ch 7	Pages 280–290
• CD-ROM	Ch 7	Pages 280–290
• DVD	Ch 7	Pages 280–290
• PXE	Ch 7	Pages 280–290, 307, 310
◢ Type of installations	Ch 7	Pages 262–290
• Creating image	Ch 7, Apx D	Pages 262–290, 1115–1123
• Unattended installation	Ch 7	Pages 307–310

1.3 Given a scenario, use appropriate command line tools.

1.4 Given a scenario, use appropriate operating system features and tools.

OBJECTIVES	CHAPTER	PAGE NUMBERS
◢ Unique to Windows 7		
• HomeGroup	Ch 7	Pages 290–304
• Action center	Ch 3	Pages 99–106
• Remote applications and desktop applications	Ch 17	Pages 768–787
• Troubleshooting	Ch 17	Pages 768–787

1.6   Setup and configure Windows networking on a client/desktop.

OBJECTIVES	CHAPTER	PAGE NUMBERS
◢ HomeGroup, file/print sharing	Ch 7	Pages 290–304
◢ WorkGroup vs. domain setup	Ch 7	Pages 262–290
◢ Network shares/mapping drives	Ch 17	Pages 787–808
◢ Establish networking connections		
• VPN	Ch 15	Pages 662–675, 682–701
• Dialups	Ch 15	Pages 662–675, 682–701
• Wireless	Ch 15	Pages 662–675, 682–701
• Wired	Ch 15	Pages 662–675, 682–701
• WWAN (Cellular)	Ch 15	Pages 662–675, 682–701
◢ Proxy settings	Ch 17	Pages 768–787
◢ Remote desktop	Ch 17	Pages 768–787
◢ Home vs. Work vs. Public network settings	Ch 7	Pages 262–290
◢ Firewall settings	Ch 18	Pages 828–841
• Exceptions	Ch 18	Pages 828–841
• Configuration	Ch 18	Pages 828–841
• Enabling/disabling Windows firewall	Ch 18	Pages 828–841
◢ Configuring an alternative IP address in Windows	Ch 15	Pages 682–701
• IP addressing	Ch 15	Pages 682–701
• Subnet mask	Ch 15	Pages 682–701
• DNS	Ch 15	Pages 682–701
• Gateway	Ch 15	Pages 682–701
◢ Network card properties		
• Half duplex/full duplex/auto	Ch 16	Pages 734–739
• Speed	Ch 16	Pages 734–739
• Wake-on-LAN	Ch 16, 17	Pages 734–739, 768–787
• PoE	Ch 16	Pages 734–739
• QoS	Ch 16, 17	Pages 734–739, 768–787

1.7   Perform preventive maintenance procedures using appropriate tools.

OBJECTIVES	CHAPTER	PAGE NUMBERS
◢ Best practices	Ch 10	Pages 414–435
• Schedules backups	Ch 10	Pages 414–435
• Scheduled check disks	Ch 10	Pages 414–435
• Scheduled defragmentation	Ch 10	Pages 414–435
• Windows updates	Ch 10	Pages 414–435
• Patch management	Ch 10	Pages 414–435
• Driver/firmware updates	Ch 8	Pages 314–319
• Antivirus updates	Ch 10	Pages 414–435
◢ Tools		
• Backup	Ch 10	Pages 414–435
• System restore	Ch 10	Pages 414–435

2.2 Compare and contrast common security threats.

2.3 Implement security best practices to secure a workstation.

2.4 Given a scenario, use the appropriate data destruction/disposal method.

2.5 Given a scenario, secure a SOHO wireless network.

3.4 **Compare and contrast hardware differences in regards to tablets and laptops.**

OBJECTIVES	CHAPTER	PAGE NUMBERS
◢ No field serviceable parts	Ch 20	Pages 946–983
◢ Typically not upgradeable	Ch 20	Pages 946–983
◢ Touch interface	Ch 20	Pages 946–983
• Touch flow	Ch 20	Pages 946–983
• Multitouch	Ch 20	Pages 946–983
◢ Solid state drives	Ch 20	Pages 946–983

3.5 **Execute and configure mobile device synchronization.**

OBJECTIVES	CHAPTER	PAGE NUMBERS
◢ Types of data to synchronize	Ch 20	Pages 950–983
• Contacts	Ch 20	Pages 950–983
• Programs	Ch 20	Pages 950–983
• Email	Ch 20	Pages 950–983
• Pictures	Ch 20	Pages 950–983
• Music	Ch 20	Pages 950–983
• Videos	Ch 20	Pages 950–983
◢ Software requirements to install the application on the PC	Ch 20	Pages 950–983
◢ Connection types to enable synchronization	Ch 20	Pages 950–983

DOMAIN 4.0 TROUBLESHOOTING

4.1 **Given a scenario, explain the troubleshooting theory.**

OBJECTIVES	CHAPTER	PAGE NUMBERS
◢ Identify the problem	Ch 12	Pages 532–544
• Question the user and identify user changes to computer and perform backups before making changes	Ch 12	Pages 532–544
• Establish a theory of probable cause (question the obvious)	Ch 12	Pages 532–544
◢ Test the theory to determine cause	Ch 12	Pages 532–544
• Once theory is confirmed determine next steps to resolve problem	Ch 12	Pages 532–544
• If theory is not confirmed re-establish new theory or escalate	Ch 12	Pages 532–544
◢ Establish a plan of action to resolve the problem and implement the solution	Ch 12	Pages 532–544
◢ Verify full system functionality and if applicable implement preventive measures	Ch 12	Pages 532–544
◢ Document findings, actions and outcomes	Ch 12	Pages 532–544

4.2 **Given a scenario, troubleshoot common problems related to motherboards, RAM, CPU and power with appropriate tools.**

OBJECTIVES	CHAPTER	PAGE NUMBERS
◢ Common symptoms	Ch 13	Pages 568–598
• Unexpected shutdowns	Ch 13	Pages 568–598
• System lockups	Ch 13	Pages 568–598
• POST code beeps	Ch 13	Pages 568–598
• Blank screen on bootup	Ch 13	Pages 568–598

4.5   Given a scenario, troubleshoot wired and wireless networks with appropriate tools.

4.6   Given a scenario, troubleshoot operating system problems with appropriate tools.

• Schedule scans and updates	Ch 18	Pages 850–867
• Enable system restore and create restore point	Ch 18	Pages 850–867
• Educate end user	Ch 18	Pages 850–867

4.8 Given a scenario, troubleshoot, and repair common laptop issues while adhering to the appropriate procedures.

OBJECTIVES	CHAPTER	PAGE NUMBERS
◢ Common symptoms	Ch 19	Pages 896–933
• No display	Ch 19	Pages 896–933
• Dim display	Ch 19	Pages 896–933
• Flickering display	Ch 19	Pages 896–933
• Sticking keys	Ch 19	Pages 896–933
• Intermittent wireless	Ch 19	Pages 896–933
• Battery not charging	Ch 19	Pages 896–933
• Ghost cursor	Ch 19	Pages 896–933
• No power	Ch 19	Pages 896–933
• Num lock indicator lights	Ch 19	Pages 896–933
• No wireless connectivity	Ch 19	Pages 896–933
• No Bluetooth connectivity	Ch 19	Pages 896–933
• Cannot display to external monitor	Ch 19	Pages 896–933
◢ Disassembling processes for proper re-assembly	Ch 19	Pages 896–933
• Document and label cable and screw locations	Ch 19	Pages 896–933
• Organize parts	Ch 19	Pages 896–933
• Refer to manufacturer documentation	Ch 19	Pages 896–933
• Use appropriate hand tools	Ch 19	Pages 896–933

4.9 Given a scenario, troubleshoot printers with appropriate tools

OBJECTIVES	CHAPTER	PAGE NUMBERS
◢ Common symptoms	Ch 21	Pages 1038–1051
• Streaks	Ch 21	Pages 1038–1051
• Faded prints	Ch 21	Pages 1038–1051
• Ghost images	Ch 21	Pages 1038–1051
• Toner not fused to the paper	Ch 21	Pages 1038–1051
• Creased paper	Ch 21	Pages 1038–1051
• Paper not feeding	Ch 21	Pages 1038–1051
• Paper jam	Ch 21	Pages 1038–1051
• No connectivity	Ch 21	Pages 1038–1051
• Garbled characters on paper	Ch 21	Pages 1038–1051
• Vertical lines on page	Ch 21	Pages 1038–1051
• Backed up print queue	Ch 21	Pages 1038–1051
• Low memory errors	Ch 21	Pages 1038–1051
• Access denied	Ch 21	Pages 1038–1051
• Printer will not print	Ch 21	Pages 1038–1051
• Color prints in wrong print color	Ch 21	Pages 1038–1051
• Unable to install printer	Ch 21	Pages 1038–1051
• Error codes	Ch 21	Pages 1038–1051
◢ Tools	Ch 21	Pages 1038–1051
• Maintenance kit	Ch 21	Pages 1038–1051
• Toner vacuum	Ch 21	Pages 1038–1051
• Compressed air	Ch 21	Pages 1038–1051
• Printer spooler	Ch 21	Pages 1038–1051

Introduction: CompTIA A+ 220-801, 220-802 In Depth

CompTIA A+ 220-801, 220-802 In Depth was written to be the very best tool on the market today to prepare you to support personal computers. Updated to include the most current hardware technologies, this book takes you from the just-a-user level to the I-can-fix-this level for PC hardware and software matters. This book achieves its goals with an unusually effective combination of tools that powerfully reinforce both concepts and hands-on, real-world experiences. It also provides thorough preparation for the hardware content on the new 2012 CompTIA A+ Certification exams. Competency in using a computer is a prerequisite to using this book. No background knowledge of electronics is assumed. An appropriate prerequisite course for this book would be a general course in microcomputer applications.

This book includes:

▲ *Comprehensive review and practice end-of-chapter material*, including a chapter summary, key terms, review questions that focus on A+ content, critical thinking questions, and real-world problems to solve.

▲ *Step-by-step instructions* on installation, maintenance, optimization of system performance, and troubleshooting.

▲ *Online video clips* featuring Jean Andrews illustrating key points from the text to aid your understanding of the material.

▲ *A wide array of photos, drawings, and screen shots* support the text, displaying in detail the exact hardware features you will need to understand to manage and maintain your PC.

In addition, the carefully structured, clearly written text is accompanied by graphics that provide the visual input essential to learning.

Coverage is balanced—while focusing on new hardware and software, the text also covers the real work of PC repair, where some older technology remains in widespread use and still needs support. For example, the book covers how to use a 64-bit operating system to support the latest processors, but also addresses how to get the most out of a 32-bit OS with limited hardware resources. At the writing of this book, Windows 7 is the current Microsoft operating systems used on desktop and laptop computers. The book focuses on supporting Windows 7 systems, while also including light coverage of Windows Vista in Appendix B, and XP in Appendix C. The book also covers other new technologies such as virtualization, quad-channel memory, home theater systems, and cellular connections, but also addresses using older technologies like PCI expansion slots, DDR2 memory, and impact printers because many individuals and businesses still use these older technologies. To rein in the physical size and weight of the book, most of the content on less significant and older technologies has been placed on the web site that accompanies the book. There you will find content on Linux, Mac OS, Windows 2000/XP, SCSI, the hexadecimal number system, electricity, multimeters, and legacy motherboards, hard drives, and processors.

This book provides thorough preparation for the CompTIA's A+ 2012 Certification examinations. This certification credential's popularity among employers is growing exponentially, and obtaining certification increases your ability to gain employment and improve your salary. To get more information on A+ certification and its sponsoring organization, the Computing Technology Industry Association, see their web site at *www.comptia.org*.

FEATURES

To ensure a successful learning experience, this book includes the following pedagogical features:

- ◢ **Learning Objectives:** Every chapter opens with a list of learning objectives that sets the stage for you to absorb the lessons of the text.
- ◢ **Comprehensive Step-by-Step Troubleshooting Guidance:** Troubleshooting guidelines are included in almost every chapter. In addition, Chapter 12 gives insights into general approaches to troubleshooting that help apply the specifics detailed in each chapter for different hardware and software problems. Chapters 13 and 14 also focus on troubleshooting hardware subsystems and Windows.
- ◢ **Step-by-Step Procedures:** The book is chock-full of step-by-step procedures covering subjects from hardware and operating system installations and maintenance to troubleshooting the boot process and optimizing system performance.
- ◢ **Art Program:** Numerous detailed photographs, three-dimensional art, and screenshots support the text, displaying hardware and software features exactly as you will see them in your work.
- ◢ **CompTIA A+ Table of Contents:** This table of contents gives the page that provides the primary content for each certification objective on the A+ 2012 exams. This is a valuable tool for quick reference.
- ◢ **Applying Concepts:** These sections offer practical applications for the material being discussed. Whether outlining a task, developing a scenario, or providing pointers, the Applying Concepts sections give you a chance to apply what you've learned to a typical PC problem.

A+ Icons: All of the content that relates to CompTIA's 2012 A+ 220-801 and A+ 220-802 Certification exams, whether it's a page or a sentence, is highlighted with an A+ icon. The icon notes the exam name and the objective number. This unique feature highlights the relevant content at a glance, so that you can pay extra attention to the material.

Notes: Note icons highlight additional helpful information related to the subject being discussed.

A+ Exam Tip Boxes: These boxes highlight additional insights and tips to remember if you are planning to take the CompTIA A+ Exams.

Caution Icons: These icons highlight critical safety information. Follow these instructions carefully to protect the PC and its data and to ensure your own safety.

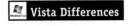

Vista Differences: These boxes point the student to Appendix B, *Windows Vista*, where Windows Vista is discussed when it differs from the coverage of Windows 7 in the chapter.

XP Differences: These boxes point the student to Appendix C, *Windows XP*, where Windows XP is discussed when it differs from the coverage of Windows 7 in the chapter.

Video Clips: Short video passages reinforce concepts and techniques discussed in the text and offer insight into the life of a PC repair technician.

End-of-Chapter Material: Each chapter closes with the following features, which reinforce the material covered in the chapter and provide real-world, hands-on testing:

◢ **Chapter Summary:** This bulleted list of concise statements summarizes all major points of the chapter.

◢ **Key Terms:** The content of each chapter is further reinforced by an end-of-chapter key-term list. The definitions of all terms are included at the end of the book in a full-length glossary.

◢ **Review Questions:** You can test your understanding of each chapter with a comprehensive set of review questions.

Companion web site: The free companion web site includes video clips that feature Jean Andrews illustrating key concepts in the text and providing advice on the real world of PC repair. Also included is less significant and older content that still might be important in some PC repair situations. The content includes the following: The Hexademical Number System and Memory Addressing, Supporting Windows XP, Introducing the Mac OS, Introducing Linux, Electricity and Multimeters, Facts about Legacy Motherboards, How an OS Uses System Resources, Facts about Legacy Processors, All about SCSI, Behind the Scenes with DEBUG, FAT Details, and Selecting and Installing Hard Drives using Legacy Motherboards. Other helpful online tools include Frequently Asked Questions, Sample Reports, Computer Inventory and Maintenance form, Troubleshooting Flowcharts, and an electronic Glossary.

CompTIA A+ and PC Repair: For additional content and updates to this book and information about our complete line of CompTIA A+ and PC Repair topics, please visit our web site at *www.cengage.com/pcrepair*.

WHAT'S NEW IN THIS EDITION

Here's a summary of what's new in this edition:

◢ Maps to all the content on CompTIA's 2012 A+ Exams.

◢ More focus on A+, with non-A+ content moved online to the companion web site or eliminated.

◢ The chapters focus on Windows 7; Vista content is in Appendix B, and XP content is in Appendix C.

◢ New content added (all new content was also new to the A+ 2012 exams).

• Windows 7 is added. Operating systems covered are now Windows 7, Vista, and XP. New content on deploring Windows 7 in an enterprise is added.

• Third Generation (Ivy Bridge) and Second Generation (Sandy Bridge) processor and chipset architectures by Intel are covered in Chapter 5.

• Enhanced content on supporting RAID and NAS.

• Designing customized systems for virtualization workstations, CAD/CAM workstations, gaming PCs, home theater systems, home servers, video editing workstations, thick clients, and thin clients is covered in Chapter 9.

• Supporting TCP/IP version 6 is added to Chapter 15.

- New content on making network cables, network wiring (T568A and T568B), and troubleshooting networks is added to Chapter 16.
- Disassembling an all-in-one computer is added to Chapter 19.
- Supporting mobile devices (including the Android OS and iOS) and client-side virtualization is covered in Chapter 20.
- New content on how printers work and how to support them is added to Chapter 21.
- How to configure motherboards and processors to support virtualization.
- Creating a standard image is added and can be found in Appendix D, *Creating a Standard Image*.
- Connecting a computer to a cellular network.

ANATOMY OF A PC REPAIR CHAPTER

This section is a visual explanation of the components that make up a PC Repair chapter. The figures identify some of our traditional instructional elements as well as the enhancements and new features we have included for the eighth edition.

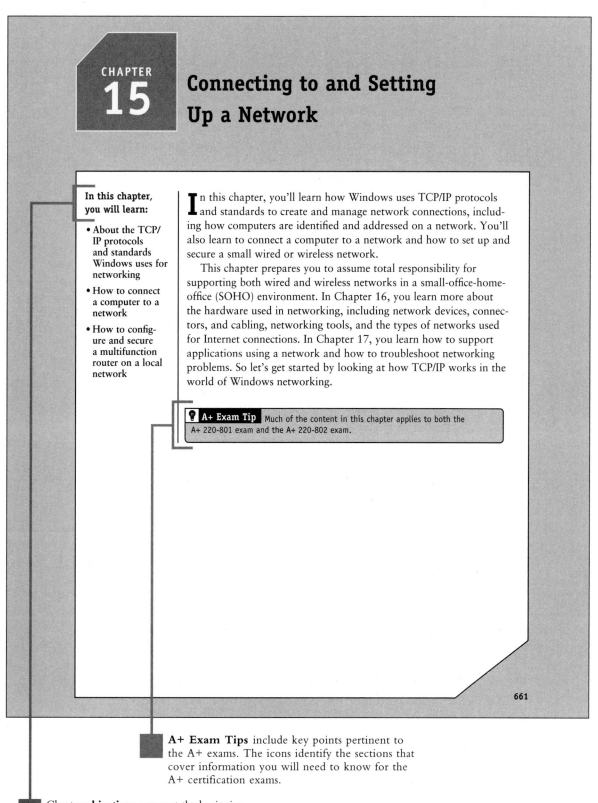

CHAPTER 15

Connecting to and Setting Up a Network

In this chapter, you will learn:

- About the TCP/IP protocols and standards Windows uses for networking
- How to connect a computer to a network
- How to configure and secure a multifunction router on a local network

In this chapter, you'll learn how Windows uses TCP/IP protocols and standards to create and manage network connections, including how computers are identified and addressed on a network. You'll also learn to connect a computer to a network and how to set up and secure a small wired or wireless network.

This chapter prepares you to assume total responsibility for supporting both wired and wireless networks in a small-office-home-office (SOHO) environment. In Chapter 16, you learn more about the hardware used in networking, including network devices, connectors, and cabling, networking tools, and the types of networks used for Internet connections. In Chapter 17, you learn how to support applications using a network and how to troubleshoot networking problems. So let's get started by looking at how TCP/IP works in the world of Windows networking.

A+ Exam Tip Much of the content in this chapter applies to both the A+ 220-801 exam and the A+ 220-802 exam.

661

A+ Exam Tips include key points pertinent to the A+ exams. The icons identify the sections that cover information you will need to know for the A+ certification exams.

Chapter **objectives** appear at the beginning of each chapter, so you know exactly what topics and skills are covered.

Cautions identify critical safety
information.

1

A+
220-801
5.1, 5.2

HOT, NEUTRAL, AND GROUND

AC travels on a hot line from the power station to a building and returns to the power station on a neutral line. When the two lines reach the building and enter an electrical device, such as a lamp, the device controls the flow of electricity between the hot and neutral lines. If an easier path (one with less resistance) is available, the electricity follows that path. This can cause a short, a sudden increase in flow that can also create a sudden increase in temperature—enough to start a fire and injure both people and equipment. Never put yourself in a position where you are the path of least resistance between the hot line and ground!

⚡ **Caution** It's very important that PC components be properly grounded. Never connect a PC to an outlet or use an extension cord that doesn't have the third ground plug. The third line can prevent a short from causing extreme damage. In addition, the bond between the neutral and ground helps eliminate electrical noise (stray electrical signals) within the PC that is sometimes caused by other electrical equipment sitting very close to the computer.

To prevent uncontrolled electricity in a short, the neutral line is grounded. Grounding a line means that the line is connected directly to the earth, so that, in the event of a short, the electricity flows into the earth and not back to the power station. Grounding serves as an escape route for out-of-control electricity because the earth is always capable of accepting a flow of current. With computers, a surge suppressor can be used to protect a computer and its components against power surges.

⚡ **Caution** Beware of the different uses of black wire. In PCs and in DC circuits, black is used for ground, but in home wiring and in AC circuits, black is used for hot!

The neutral line to your house is grounded many times along its way (in fact, at each electrical pole) and is also grounded at the breaker box where the electricity enters your house. You can look at a three-prong plug and see the three lines: hot, neutral, and ground (see Figure 1-31).

To verify that a wall outlet is wired correctly for hot, neutral, and ground, use a simple receptacle tester, as shown in Figure 1-32. Even though you might have a three-prong outlet in your home, the ground plug might not be properly grounded. To know for sure, you can test the outlet with a receptacle tester.

Notes House AC voltage in the United States is about 110–120 V, but know that in other countries, this is not always the case. In many other countries, the standard is 220 V. Outlet styles also vary from one country to the next.

Now that you know about electricity and how to protect a computer from surges and out-of-control electricity, let's turn our attention to protecting yourself against the dangers of electricity.

Notes indicate additional content that might be of student interest
or information about how best to study.

Video icons indicate content shown with video online. Videos illustrate key concepts.

A+
220-801
1.7, 1.8,
1.11

Port	Description
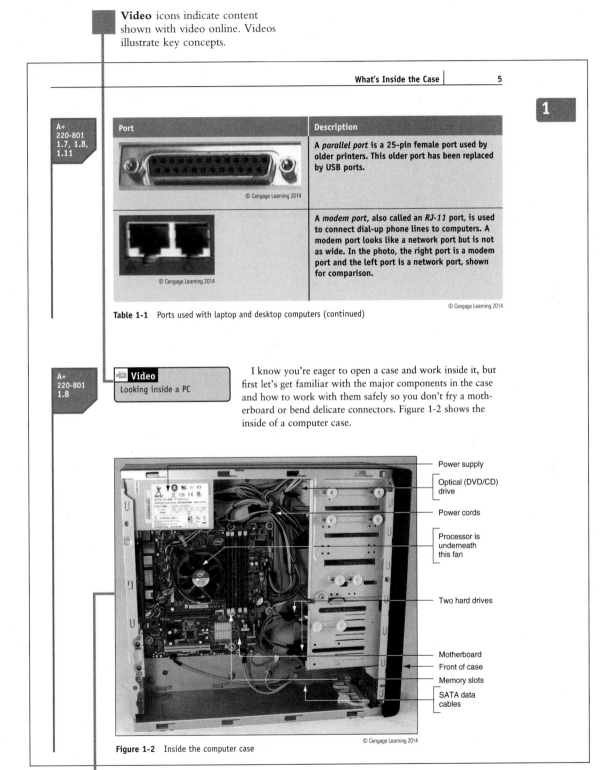© Cengage Learning 2014	A *parallel port* is a 25-pin female port used by older printers. This older port has been replaced by USB ports.
© Cengage Learning 2014	A *modem port*, also called an *RJ-11* port, is used to connect dial-up phone lines to computers. A modem port looks like a network port but is not as wide. In the photo, the right port is a modem port and the left port is a network port, shown for comparison.

© Cengage Learning 2014

Table 1-1 Ports used with laptop and desktop computers (continued)

A+
220-801
1.8

▶ **Video**
Looking inside a PC

I know you're eager to open a case and work inside it, but first let's get familiar with the major components in the case and how to work with them safely so you don't fry a motherboard or bend delicate connectors. Figure 1-2 shows the inside of a computer case.

- Power supply
- Optical (DVD/CD) drive
- Power cords
- Processor is underneath this fan
- Two hard drives
- Motherboard
- Front of case
- Memory slots
- SATA data cables

© Cengage Learning 2014

Figure 1-2 Inside the computer case

Full-color photos and screen shots accurately depict computer hardware and software components.

A+ Exam Objectives are highlighted with an icon identifying the exam and objective number to help you identify information tested on the exams. The A+ 220-801 and A+ 220-802 exams are mapped.

A+
220-801
1.9

Here are the features and hardware you need to consider when customizing a home server PC:

▲ *Use a processor with moderate power.* The Intel Core i5 or Core i3 works well. A moderate amount of RAM is sufficient, for example, 6 to 8 GB.

▲ *Storage speed and capacity need to be maximized.* Use hardware RAID implemented on the motherboard to provide fault tolerance and high performance. Make sure the motherboard supports hardware RAID. Use fast hard drives (at least 7200 RPM) with plenty of storage capacity. Make sure the case has plenty of room for all the hard drives a customer might require.

▲ *Network transfers need to be fast, especially for streaming videos and movies.* Make sure the network port is rated for Gigabit Ethernet (1000 Mbps). All other devices and computers on the LAN should also use Gigabit Ethernet.

▲ *Printer sharing.* A USB printer can be connected directly to the PC and then you can use Windows to share the printer with others on the network. How to share printers is covered in Chapter 21. Alternately, some routers and switches provide a USB port that can be used to connect a USB printer to other computers on the network.

▲ *Onboard video works well.* Recall that onboard video is a video port embedded on the motherboard and does not perform as well as a good video card. Because the PC is not likely to be used as a workstation, you don't need powerful video.

▲ *Windows 7 can be used as the OS, but Windows Home Server 2011 provides the additional security features needed to better secure a home network.* In addition, if the customer plans to use the PC to back up files on client computers, know that Windows Home Server provides a more robust backup utility than does Windows 7.

9

THICK CLIENT AND THIN CLIENT

Recall that a desktop computer can use virtual machine management software (called a hypervisor) to provide one or more VMs, and in this situation the computer is called a virtualization workstation. In a corporate environment, the VM can also be provided by a virtualization server, which serves up a virtual machine to a client computer. The **virtualization server** provides a virtual desktop for users on multiple client machines. Most, if not all, processing is done on the server, which provides to the client the Virtual Desktop Infrastructure (VDI). See Figure 9-25.

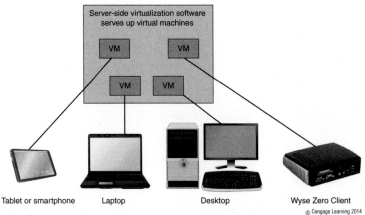

Figure 9-25 A virtualization server provides a desktop to each client computer or appliance

A+
220-801
1.6

APPLYING | CONCEPTS   SELECT A PROCESSOR

Your friend, Alice, is working toward her A+ certification. She has decided the best way to get the experience she needs before she sits for the exam is to build a system from scratch. She has purchased an Asus motherboard and asked you for some help selecting the right processor. She tells you that the system will later be used for light business needs and she wants to install a processor that is moderate in price to fit her budget. She says she doesn't want to install the most expensive processor the motherboard can support, but neither does she want to sacrifice too much performance or power.

The documentation on the Asus web site (*support.asus.com*) for the ASUS P8Z68-V LX motherboard gives this information:

▲ The ATX board contains the Z68 chipset and socket LGA1155 and uses DDR3 memory.

▲ CPUs supported include a long list of Second Generation Core i3, Core i5, and Core i7 processors and Celeron and Pentium processors. Here are five processors found in this list:

- Intel Core i7-2600, 3.4 GHz, 8 MB cache
- Intel Core i5-3450, 3.1 GHz, 6 MB cache
- Intel Core i3-2120, 3.3 GHz, 3 MB cache
- Intel Celeron G540, 2.5 GHz, 2 MB cache
- Intel Pentium G860, 3.0 GHz, 3 MB cache

Based on what Alice has told you, you decide to eliminate the most expensive processors (the Core i7) and the least-performing processors (the Celerons and Pentiums). That decision narrows your choices down to the Core i3 and Core i5. Before you select one of these processors, you need to check the list on the Asus site to make sure the specific Core i3 or Core i5 processor is in the list. Look for the exact processor number, for example, the Core i3-2120. Also double-check and make sure the processor uses the correct socket and is a Second Generation processor.

You will also need a cooler assembly. If your processor doesn't come boxed with a cooler, select a cooler that fits the processor socket and gets good reviews. You'll also need some thermal compound if it is not included with the cooler.

INSTALL A PROCESSOR

Now let's look at the details of installing a processor in an Intel LGA1155, LGA1366, LGA775, and AMD AM2+ sockets.

INSTALLING AN INTEL PROCESSOR IN SOCKET LGA1155

We're installing the Intel Core i5-2320 processor in Socket LGA1155 shown in Figure 5-8. In the photo, the socket has its protective cover in place.

Applying Concepts sections provide practical advice or pointers by illustrating basic principles, identifying common problems, providing steps to practice skills, and encouraging creating solutions.

Key Terms are defined as they are introduced and listed at the end of each chapter. Definitions can be found in the Glossary and online.

◢ DIMM and RIMM speeds are measured in MHz (for example, 1333 MHz) or PC rating (for example, PC3-10600).

◢ The memory controller can check memory for errors and possibly correct those errors using ECC (error-correcting code). Using parity, an older technology, the controller could only recognize an error had occurred, but not correct it.

◢ Buffers and registers are used to hold data and amplify a data signal. A DIMM is rated as a buffered, registered, or unbuffered DIMM.

◢ CAS Latency (CL) and RAS Latency (RL) measure access time to memory. The lower values are faster than the higher values.

◢ RIMMs require that every RIMM slot be populated. If a RIMM is not installed in the slot, install a placeholder module called a C-RIMM.

How to Upgrade Memory

◢ When upgrading memory, use the type, size, and speed the motherboard supports and match new modules to those already installed. Features to match include DDR3, DDR2, DDR, size in MB or GB, speed (MHz or PC rating), buffered, registered, unbuffered, single-sided, double-sided, CL rating, tin or gold connectors, support for dual, triple, or quad channeling, ECC, and non-ECC. Using memory made by the same manufacturer is recommended.

>> KEY TERMS

For explanations of key terms, see the Glossary near the end of the book.

CAS Latency	ECC (error-correcting code)	RAS Latency
Centrino	graphics processing unit (GPU)	RDRAM
C-RIMM (Continuity RIMM)	Hyper-Threading	RIMM
DDR	HyperTransport	SDRAM II
DDR2	Level 1 cache (L1 cache)	SIMM (single inline memory
DDR3	Level 2 cache (L2 cache)	module)
DIMM (dual inline memory	Level 3 cache (L3 cache)	single channel
module)	memory bank	single-sided
Direct Rambus DRAM	multi-core processing	SO-DIMM (small outline
Direct RDRAM	multiplier	DIMM)
Double Data Rate SDRAM	multiprocessing	static RAM (SRAM)
(DDR SDRAM)	multiprocessor platform	synchronous DRAM
double-sided	parity	(SDRAM)
dual channels	parity error	thread
dual processors	processor frequency	triple channels
dual ranked	quad channels	x86 processors
dynamic RAM (DRAM)	Rambus	x86-64 bit processor

End of Chapter Questions test understanding of fundamental concepts.

>> REVIEW QUESTIONS

1. Startup BIOS turns control over to the ____ program stored in the first sector of the hard drive.

   a) MBR

   b) BootMgr

   c) WinLoad.exe

   d) BCD

2. ____ is a lean operating system that can be launched to solve Windows startup problems after other tools available on the Advanced Boot Options menu have failed to solve the problem.

   a) System Image Recovery

   b) System Restore

   c) Last Known Good Configuration

   d) Windows Recovery Environment (Windows RE)

3. What command is used to repair a Windows 7 dual boot system?

   a) Bootsect

   b) Bcdedit

   c) Bootrec

   d) Fixmbr

4. Your best Windows tools to use for any problems that occur before the flag or progress bar appears are Startup Repair and ____.

   a) Session Manager

   b) System Image Recovery

   c) System Restore

   d) MSconfig

5. What is the most likely cause of problems that occur after the user logs onto Windows?

   a) A corrupted driver or service that is started after the kernel has finished its part of the boot.

   b) Applications or services configured to launch at startup.

   c) Hardware or startup files.

   d) A corrupted Active Directory.

6. True or false? The PC boots from the system partition and loads the Windows operating system from the boot partition.

7. True or false? The Windows startup is officially completed when the Windows 7 flag is displayed.

8. True or false? Safe Mode won't load if core Windows components are corrupted.

9. True or false? Your first decision in troubleshooting a failed boot is to decide which tool will be the least invasive to use, yet still will fix the problem.

14

STATE OF THE INFORMATION TECHNOLOGY (IT) FIELD

Computers and information technology are absolutely essential for businesses to thrive, or perhaps even exist, in today's world. In addition, the Internet makes it possible for a local or national business to go global and reach customers, suppliers, and other businesses anywhere on the planet. As technology continues to change, how we do business must also continually change. These fundamental changes in business practices have created an on-going need for skilled and certified IT workers across industries. IT workers have flooded out of traditional IT businesses into various IT-dependent industries such as banking, government, insurance, and healthcare.

Millions of individuals are self-employed in this country. Among them are the computer specialists who must keep their skills sharp as they navigate an ever-changing employment and technological landscape.

Without skilled workers in IT, businesses will struggle with the ever-changing technologies. With such a quick product life cycle, IT workers must strive to keep up with these changes to continue to bring value to their employers.

CERTIFICATIONS

Companies increasingly rely on technical certifications to identify the skills a particular job applicant possesses. Traditional degrees and diplomas are no longer sufficient to identify the education and skills needed for the many jobs in the IT industry. Technical certifications are a way for employers to ensure the quality and skill qualifications of their computer professionals, and they can offer job seekers a competitive edge. In most careers, salary and compensation are determined by experience and education, but in IT, the number and type of certifications an employee earns also factor into salary and wage increases.

As you look at certifications, note that there are two types: vendor neutral and vendor specific. Vendor neutral certifications are those that test for the skills and knowledge required in specific industry job roles and do not subscribe to a specific vendor's technology solution. Vendor neutral certifications include all of the Computing Technology Industry Association's (CompTIA) certifications, Project Management Institute's certifications, and Security Certified Program certifications. Vendor specific certifications validate the skills and knowledge necessary to be successful when using a specific vendor's technology solution. Some examples of vendor specific certifications include those offered by Microsoft, IBM, Novell, and Cisco.

Certifications provide job applicants with more than just a competitive edge over their non-certified counterparts who apply for the same IT positions. Some institutions of higher education grant college credit to students who successfully pass certification exams, moving them further along in their degree programs. Certifications also give individuals who are interested in careers in the military the ability to move into higher positions more quickly. And many advanced certification programs accept, and sometimes require, entry-level certifications as part of their exams. For example, Cisco and Microsoft accept some CompTIA certifications as prerequisites for their certification programs.

CAREER PLANNING

Finding a career that fits a person's personality, skill set, and lifestyle is challenging and fulfilling, but can often be difficult. What are the steps individuals should take to find that dream career? Is IT interesting to you? Chances are that if you are reading this book, this question has been answered. What about IT do you like? To find out, ask yourself some questions: Are you a person who likes to work alone, or do you like to work in a group? Do you like speaking directly with customers or do you prefer to stay behind the scenes? Is your lifestyle conducive to a lot of travel, or do you need to stay in one location? All of these factors influence your decision when faced with choosing the right job. A variety of web sites offer assistance with career planning and assessing an inventory of your interests, work values, and abilities.

WHAT'S NEW WITH COMPTIA A+ CERTIFICATION

In the spring of 2012, CompTIA (*www.comptia.org*) published the objectives for the 2012 CompTIA A+ Certification exams. These exams went live in the fall of 2012. However, you can still become CompTIA A+ certified by passing the older 2009 exams that are to remain available until the summer of 2013.

The A+ 2012 exams include two exams, and you must pass both to become A+ certified. The two exams are the A+ 220-801 exam and the A+ 220-802 exam.

Here is a breakdown of the domain content covered on the two A+ 2012 exams:

CompTIA A+ 220-801 Exam	
PC Hardware	40%
Networking	27%
Laptops	11%
Printers	11%
Operational Procedures	11%
Total	100%

CompTIA A+ 220-802 Exam	
Operating Systems	33%
Security	22%
Mobile Devices	9%
Troubleshooting	36%
Total	100%

HOW TO BECOME COMPTIA CERTIFIED

This training material can help you prepare for and pass a related CompTIA certification exam or exams. In order to achieve CompTIA certification, you must register for and pass a CompTIA certification exam or exams. For information on becoming CompTIA certified, please visit *http://certification.comptia.org/Training/testingcenters*.

CompTIA is a nonprofit information technology (IT) trade association. CompTIA's certifications are designed by subject matter experts from across the IT industry. Each CompTIA certification is vendor neutral, covers multiple technologies, and requires demonstration of skills and knowledge widely sought after by the IT industry.

To contact CompTIA with any questions or comments, please visit *http://certification.comptia.org/contact* or call (866) 835-8020, ext. 2.

ACKNOWLEDGMENTS

Thank you to the wonderful people at Cengage Course Technology who continue to give their best and to go the extra mile to make the books what they are: Nick Lombardi, Michelle Ruelos Cannistraci, and Andrea Majot. I'm grateful for all you've done. Thank you, Deb Kaufmann and Jill Batistick, Developmental Editors, for your careful attention to detail and your awesome commitment to excellence, and to Katherine A. Orrino, our excellent copy editor. Thank you, Serge Palladino, Susan Pedicini, Ashlee Welz Smith and Teresa Storch, for your careful attention to the technical accuracy of the book. Thank you Abigail Reip for your research efforts. Thank you to Joy Dark and Jill West who were here with me taking many photographs, researching, and helping with the many other details of the writing process.

Thank you to all the people who took the time to voluntarily send encouragement and suggestions for improvements to the previous editions. Your input and help is very much appreciated. The reviewers of this edition all provided invaluable insights and showed a genuine interest in the book's success. Thank you to:

Keith Conn – Cleveland Institute of Electronics/World College
Lee Cottrell – Bradford School, Pittsburgh, PA
Humberto Hilario – PC AGE Career Institute
Jeff McDowell – United Tribes Technical College
Carlos Miranda – Mount San Antonio College
Alicia Pearlman – Baker College
Nancy Severe-Barnett – DeVry University
Jonathan Weissman – Finger Lakes Community College
June West – Spartanburg Community College

When planning this edition, Course Technology sent out a survey to A+ and PC Repair instructors for their input to help us shape the edition. Many instructors responded, for which I am grateful. I spent much time pouring over their answers to our questions, their comments, and their suggestions. You'll find many of your ideas fleshed out in the pages of this book. Thank you so much for your help!

To the instructors and learners who use this book, I invite and encourage you to send suggestions or corrections for future editions. Please write to me at *jean.andrews@cengage.com*. I never ignore a good idea! And to instructors, if you have ideas for how to make a class in PC Repair or A+ Preparation a success, please share your ideas with other instructors! You can find me on Facebook at *http://www.facebook.com/JeanKnows*, where you can interact with me and other instructors.

This book is dedicated to the covenant of God with man on earth.

Jean Andrews, Ph.D.

ABOUT THE AUTHOR

Jean Andrews has more than 30 years of experience in the computer industry, including more than 13 years in the college classroom. She has worked in a variety of businesses and corporations designing, writing, and supporting application software; managing a PC repair help desk; and troubleshooting wide area networks. She has written numerous books on software, hardware, and the Internet, including the bestselling *A+ Guide to Hardware, Sixth Edition* and *A+ Guide to Software: Managing, Maintaining and Troubleshooting, Sixth Edition*. She lives in northern Georgia.

PROTECT YOURSELF, YOUR HARDWARE, AND YOUR SOFTWARE

When you work on a computer, it is possible to harm both the computer and yourself. The most common accident that happens when attempting to fix a computer problem is erasing software or data. Experimenting without knowing what you are doing can cause damage. To prevent these sorts of accidents, as well as the physically dangerous ones, take a few safety precautions. The text below describes the potential sources of damage and danger and how to protect against them.

POWER TO THE COMPUTER

To protect both yourself and the equipment when working inside a computer, turn off the power, unplug the computer, press the power button to drain residual power, and always use a grounding bracelet as described in Chapter 1. Consider the monitor and the power supply to be "black boxes." Never remove the cover or put your hands inside this equipment unless you know about the hazards of charged capacitors. Both the power supply and the monitor can hold a dangerous level of electricity even after they are turned off and disconnected from a power source.

PROTECT AGAINST ESD

To protect the computer against electrostatic discharge (ESD), commonly known as static electricity, always ground yourself before touching electronic components, including the hard drive, motherboard, expansion cards, processors, and memory modules. Ground yourself and the computer parts, using one or more of the following static control devices or methods:

- ▲ *Ground bracelet or static strap:* A ground bracelet is a strap you wear around your wrist. To protect components against ESD, the other end is attached to a grounded conductor such as the computer case or a ground mat.
- ▲ *Ground mats:* Ground mats can come equipped with a cord to plug into a wall outlet to provide a grounded surface on which to work. Remember, if you lift the component off the mat, it is no longer grounded and is susceptible to ESD.
- ▲ *Static shielding bags:* New components come shipped in static shielding bags. Save the bags to store other devices that are not currently installed in a PC.

The best solution to protect against ESD is to use a ground bracelet together with a ground mat. Consider a ground bracelet to be essential equipment when working on a computer. However, if you find yourself in a situation without one, touch the computer case before you touch a component. When passing a component to another person, touch the other person first so that ESD is discharged between you and the other person before you pass the component. Leave components inside their protective bags until ready to use. Work on hard floors, not carpet, or use antistatic spray on the carpets. Generally, don't work on a computer if you or the computer just came inside from the cold.

For today's computers, always unplug the power cord before working inside a computer. Even though the power switch is turned off, know that power is still getting to the system when the computer is plugged in. After you've unplugged the power, press the power button to drain the system of power. Then and only then is it safe to open the case without concern for damaging a component. And don't forget to use that ground bracelet.

There is an exception to the ground-yourself rule. Inside a monitor case, laser printer, or power supply, there is substantial danger posed by the electricity stored in capacitors. When working inside these devices, you *don't* want to be grounded, as you would provide a conduit for the voltage to discharge through your body. In this situation, be careful *not* to ground yourself.

When handling motherboards and expansion cards, don't touch the chips on the boards. Don't stack boards on top of each other, which could accidentally dislodge a chip. Hold cards by the edges, but don't touch the edge connections on the card.

Don't touch a chip with a magnetized screwdriver. When using a multimeter to measure electricity, be careful not to touch a chip with the probes. Don't touch the chips on the bottom of hard drives.

After you unpack a new device or software that has been wrapped in cellophane, remove the cellophane from the work area quickly. Don't allow anyone who is not properly grounded to touch components. Do not store expansion cards within one foot of an old CRT monitor, because the monitor can discharge as much as 29,000 volts of ESD onto the screen.

Hold an expansion card by the edges. Don't touch any of the soldered components on a card. If you need to put an electronic device down, place it on a grounded mat, inside a static shielding bag, or on a flat, hard surface. Keep components away from your hair and clothing.

PROTECT HARD DRIVES AND DISKS

Always turn off a computer before moving it, to protect the hard drive, which might be spinning. Never jar a computer while the hard disk is running. Avoid placing a PC on the floor, where the user can accidentally kick it. To keep a computer well ventilated and cool, don't place it on thick carpet.

Follow the usual precautions to protect CD, DVD, and Blu-ray discs. Keep optical discs away from heat, direct sunlight, and extreme cold, and protect them from scratches. Treat discs with care and they'll generally last for years.

First Look at Computer Parts and Tools

Like many other computer users, you have probably used your personal computer to play games, update your Facebook profile, write papers, or build Excel worksheets. This book takes you from being an end user of your computer to becoming a PC support technician. The only assumption made here is that you are a computer user—that is, you can turn on your machine, load a software package, and use that software to accomplish a task. No experience in electronics is assumed.

As a PC support technician, you'll want to become A+ certified, which is the industry standard certification for PC support technicians. This book prepares you to pass the A+ 220-801 exam and the A+ 220-802 exam by CompTIA (*www.comptia.org*). These two exams are required by CompTIA for A+ Certification. The A+ 220-801 exam is primarily about hardware and customer service. The A+ 220-802 exam is primarily about software and also includes troubleshooting both software and hardware. This book fully prepares you for both exams needed for CompTIA A+ certification.

In this chapter, you learn to recognize various hardware components you'll find inside a computer case and about the tools you'll need to work inside the case. In the next chapter, you'll learn to take a computer apart and reassemble it. Consider these two chapters your one-two punch toward becoming a hardware technician.

> **A+ Exam Tip** As you work your way through a chapter, notice the green and blue A+ mapping icons in the margins. These page elements help you know to which objectives on which exam the content applies. At the end of each chapter, take a look at the grid at the beginning of this book and make sure you understand each objective listed in the grid that is covered in the chapter.

WHAT'S INSIDE THE CASE

A+
220-801
1.7, 1.8,
1.11

Before we discuss the parts inside a computer case, let's take a quick look at the case and the ports and switches on it. The computer case, sometimes called the chassis, houses the power supply, motherboard, processor, memory modules, expansion cards, hard drive, optical drive, and other drives. A computer case can be a tower case, a desktop case that lies flat on a desk, an all-in-one case used with an all-in-one computer, or a mobile case used with laptops and tablet PCs. A **tower case** (see Figure 1-1) sits upright and can be as high as two feet and has room for several drives. Often used for servers, this type of case is also good for PC users who anticipate upgrading because tower cases provide maximum space for working inside a computer and moving components around. A **desktop case** lies flat and sometimes serves double-duty as a monitor stand. In this chapter and the next, you learn how to work inside a tower or desktop case, and in Chapter 19, you learn how to work inside a laptop case and all-in-one case.

© Courtesy of IN WIN Development Inc.

Figure 1-1   This slimline tower case supports a MicroATX motherboard

> **Notes** When a computer using a desktop case is in use, don't sit the case on its end that is designed to lie flat because the CD or DVD drive might not work properly.

Table 1-1 lists ports you might find on a laptop or desktop computer. Consider this table your introduction to these ports so that you can recognize them when you see them. Later in the book, you learn more about the details of each port.

> **💡 A+ Exam Tip** The A+ 220-801 exam expects you to know how to identify the ports shown in Table 1-1.

A+
220-801
1.7, 1.8,
1.11

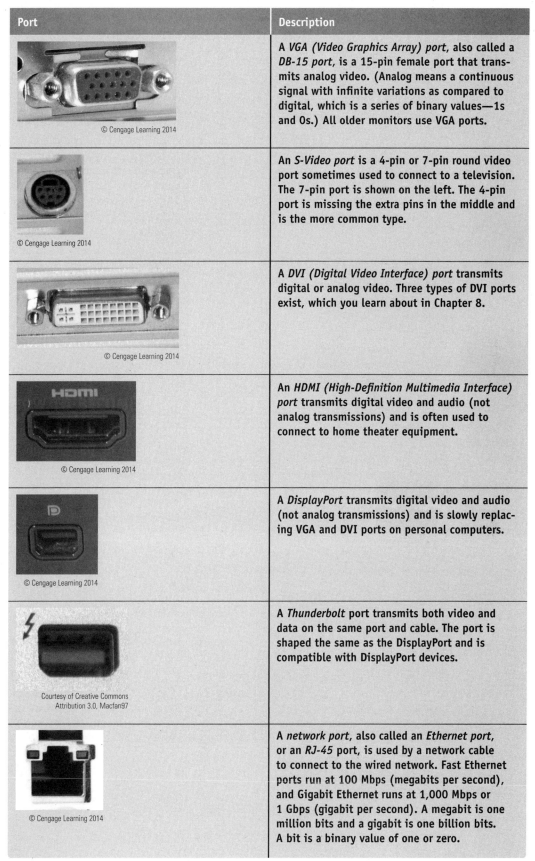

Port	Description
(VGA port image) © Cengage Learning 2014	A *VGA (Video Graphics Array) port*, also called a *DB-15 port*, is a 15-pin female port that transmits analog video. (Analog means a continuous signal with infinite variations as compared to digital, which is a series of binary values—1s and 0s.) All older monitors use VGA ports.
(S-Video port image) © Cengage Learning 2014	An *S-Video port* is a 4-pin or 7-pin round video port sometimes used to connect to a television. The 7-pin port is shown on the left. The 4-pin port is missing the extra pins in the middle and is the more common type.
(DVI port image) © Cengage Learning 2014	A *DVI (Digital Video Interface) port* transmits digital or analog video. Three types of DVI ports exist, which you learn about in Chapter 8.
(HDMI port image) © Cengage Learning 2014	An *HDMI (High-Definition Multimedia Interface) port* transmits digital video and audio (not analog transmissions) and is often used to connect to home theater equipment.
(DisplayPort image) © Cengage Learning 2014	A *DisplayPort* transmits digital video and audio (not analog transmissions) and is slowly replacing VGA and DVI ports on personal computers.
(Thunderbolt port image) Courtesy of Creative Commons Attribution 3.0, Macfan97	A *Thunderbolt* port transmits both video and data on the same port and cable. The port is shaped the same as the DisplayPort and is compatible with DisplayPort devices.
(network port image) © Cengage Learning 2014	A *network port*, also called an *Ethernet port*, or an *RJ-45 port*, is used by a network cable to connect to the wired network. Fast Ethernet ports run at 100 Mbps (megabits per second), and Gigabit Ethernet runs at 1,000 Mbps or 1 Gbps (gigabit per second). A megabit is one million bits and a gigabit is one billion bits. A bit is a binary value of one or zero.

© Cengage Learning 2014

Table 1-1 Ports used with laptop and desktop computers (continues)

A+
220-801
1.7, 1.8,
1.11

Port	Description
© Cengage Learning 2014	A system usually has three or more round *audio ports*, also called sound ports, for a microphone, audio in, audio out, and stereo audio out. If you have one audio cable to connect to a speaker or ear buds, plug it into the lime green sound port in the middle of the three ports.
© Cengage Learning 2014	An *S/PDIF (Sony-Philips Digital Interface) sound port* connects to an external home theater audio system, providing digital audio output and the best signal quality.
© Cengage Learning 2014	A *USB (Universal Serial Bus) port* is a multi-purpose I/O port used by many different devices, including printers, mice, keyboards, scanners, external hard drives, and flash drives. Some USB ports are faster than others. Hi-Speed USB 2.0 is faster than regular USB, and Super-Speed USB 3.0 is faster than USB 2.0.
© Cengage Learning 2014	A *FireWire port* (also called an *IEEE1394 port*, pronounced "I-triple-E 1394 port") is used for high-speed multimedia devices such as digital camcorders.
© Cengage Learning 2014	An *external SATA (eSATA)* port is used by an external hard drive using the eSATA interface. eSATA is faster than FireWire.
© Cengage Learning 2014	A PS/2 port, also called a mini-DIN port, is a round 6-pin port used by a keyboard or mouse. The ports look alike but are not interchangeable. On a PC, the purple port is for the keyboard, and the green port is for the mouse. Newer computers use USB ports for the keyboard and mouse rather than the older PS/2 ports.
© Cengage Learning 2014	An older *serial port*, sometimes called a DB9 port, is a 9-pin male port used on older computers. It has been mostly replaced by USB ports.

© Cengage Learning 2014

Table 1-1 Ports used with laptop and desktop computers (continues)

A+
220-801
1.7, 1.8,
1.11

Port	Description
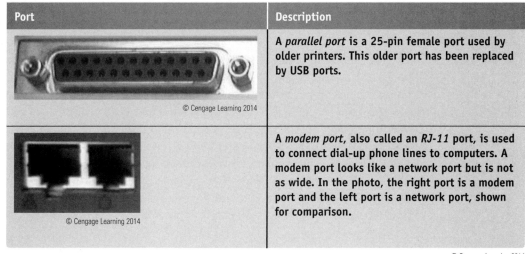 © Cengage Learning 2014	A *parallel port* is a 25-pin female port used by older printers. This older port has been replaced by USB ports.
© Cengage Learning 2014	A *modem port*, also called an *RJ-11* port, is used to connect dial-up phone lines to computers. A modem port looks like a network port but is not as wide. In the photo, the right port is a modem port and the left port is a network port, shown for comparison.

© Cengage Learning 2014

Table 1-1   Ports used with laptop and desktop computers (continued)

A+
220-801
1.8

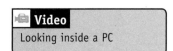

Video

Looking inside a PC

I know you're eager to open a case and work inside it, but first let's get familiar with the major components in the case and how to work with them safely so you don't fry a motherboard or bend delicate connectors. Figure 1-2 shows the inside of a computer case.

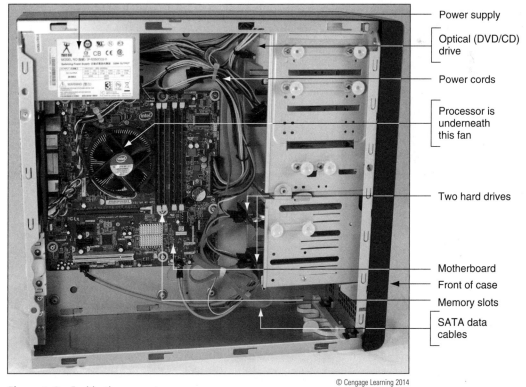

© Cengage Learning 2014

Figure 1-2   Inside the computer case

A+
220-801
1.8

Here is a quick explanation of the main components installed in the case, which are called **internal components:**

▲*The motherboard, processor, and cooler.* The **motherboard**, also called the **main board**, the **system board**, or the techie jargon term, the mobo, is the largest and most important circuit board in the computer. The motherboard contains a socket to hold the processor or CPU. The **central processing unit (CPU)**, also called the **processor** or **microprocessor**, does most of the processing of data and instructions for the entire system. Because the CPU generates heat, a fan and heat sink might be installed on top to keep it cool. A **heat sink** consists of metal fins that draw heat away from a component. The fan and heat sink together are called the processor cooler. Figure 1-3 shows the top view of a motherboard, and Figure 1-4 shows the ports on the side of a motherboard.

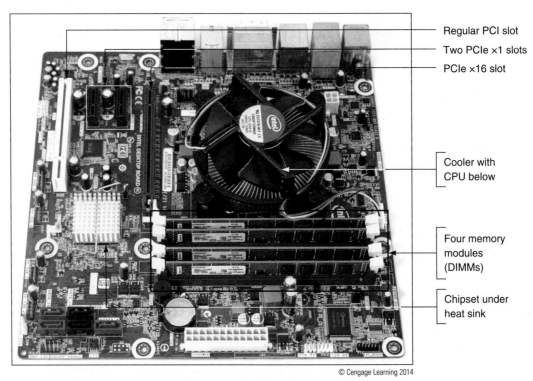

Regular PCI slot
Two PCIe ×1 slots
PCIe ×16 slot

Cooler with CPU below

Four memory modules (DIMMs)

Chipset under heat sink

© Cengage Learning 2014

Figure 1-3 All hardware components are either located on the motherboard or directly or indirectly connected to it because they must all communicate with the CPU

▲ *Expansion cards.* A motherboard has expansion slots to be used by expansion cards. An **expansion card**, also called an adapter card, is a circuit board that provides more ports than those provided by the motherboard. Figure 1-5 shows a video card that provides three video ports. Notice the cooling fan and heat sink on the card, which help to keep the card from overheating. The trend today is for most ports in a system to be provided by the motherboard (called onboard ports) and less use of expansion cards.

A+
220-801
1.8

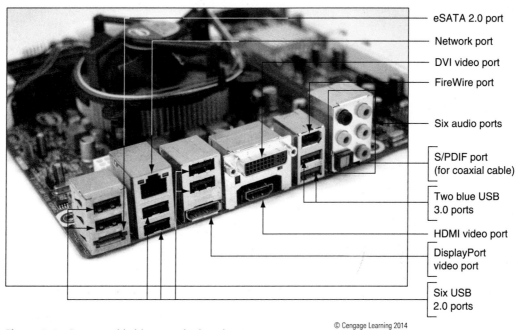

eSATA 2.0 port

Network port

DVI video port

FireWire port

Six audio ports

S/PDIF port
(for coaxial cable)

Two blue USB
3.0 ports

HDMI video port

DisplayPort
video port

Six USB
2.0 ports

© Cengage Learning 2014

Figure 1-4 Ports provided by a motherboard

Cooling fan

Heat sink

Tab used to
stabilize the card

PCI Express
x16 connector

15-pin analog
video port

TV-out connector

DVI port

© Cengage Learning 2014

Figure 1-5 The easiest way to identify this video card is to look at the ports on
the end of the card

▲ *Memory modules.* A motherboard has memory slots, called **DIMM (dual inline memory module)** slots, to hold memory modules. Figure 1-6 shows a memory module
installed in one DIMM slot and three empty DIMM slots. Memory, also called **RAM
(random access memory)**, is temporary storage for data and instructions as they are
being processed by the CPU. The memory module shown in Figure 1-6 contains several
RAM chips. Video cards also contain some embedded RAM chips for **video memory**.

A+
220-801
1.8

One installed
DIMM

Three empty
DIMM slots

© Cengage Learning 2014

Figure 1-6   A DIMM holds RAM and is mounted directly on a motherboard

▲ *Hard drives and other drives.* A system might have one or more hard drives, an optical drive, a tape drive, or, for really old systems, a floppy drive. A **hard drive**, also called a **hard disk drive (HDD)**, is permanent storage used to hold data and programs. For example, the Windows 7 operating system and applications are installed on the hard drive. All drives in a system are installed in a stack of drive bays at the front of the case. The system shown in Figure 1-2 has two hard drives and one optical drive installed. These three drives are also shown in Figure 1-7. Each drive has two connections for cables: the power cable connects to the power supply and another cable, used for data and instructions, connects to the motherboard.

© Cengage Learning 2014

Figure 1-7   Two types of hard drives (larger magnetic drive and smaller solid state drive) and a DVD drive

▲ *Power supply.* A computer **power supply**, also known as a **power supply unit (PSU)**, is a box installed in a corner of the computer case (see Figure 1-8) that receives and converts the house current so that components inside the case can use it. Most power supplies have a **dual-voltage selector switch** on the back of the computer case where you can switch the input voltage to the power supply to 115 V used in the United States or 220 V used in other countries. See Figure 1-9. The power cables can connect to and supply power to the motherboard, expansion cards, and drives.

> **Notes**   If you ever need to change the dual-voltage selector switch, be sure you first turn off the computer and unplug the power supply.

A+
220-801
1.8

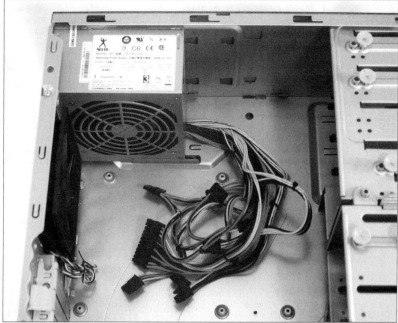

Figure 1-8 Power supply with attached power cables

© Cengage Learning 2014

Dual-voltage selector switch

Four screws hold the power supply in the case

© Cengage Learning 2014

Figure 1-9 The dual-voltage selector switch sets the input voltage to the power supply

FORM FACTORS USED BY COMPUTER CASES, POWER SUPPLIES, AND MOTHERBOARDS

The computer case, power supply, and motherboard must all be compatible and fit together as an interconnecting system. The standards that describe the size, shape, screw hole positions, and major features of these interconnected components are called **form factors**. Using a matching form factor for the motherboard, power supply, and case assures you that:

▲ The motherboard fits in the case.
▲ The power supply cords to the motherboard provide the correct voltage, and the connectors match the connections on the board.
▲ The holes in the motherboard align with the holes in the case for anchoring the board to the case.
▲ The holes in the case align with ports coming off the motherboard.

A+
220-801
1.8

▲ For some form factors, wires for switches and lights on the front of the case match up with connections on the motherboard.

▲ The holes in the power supply align with holes in the case for anchoring the power supply to the case.

The two form factors used by most desktop and tower computer cases and power supplies are the ATX and mini-ATX form factors. Motherboards use these and other form factors that are compatible with ATX or mini-ATX power supplies and cases. You learn about other motherboard form factors in Chapter 4. Following are the important details about ATX and mini-ATX.

ATX FORM FACTOR

ATX (**Advanced Technology Extended**) is the most commonly used form factor today. It is an open, nonproprietary industry specification originally developed by Intel in 1995 and has undergone several revisions since then. The original ATX form factor for cases had case fans blowing air into the case, but early revisions to the form factor had fans blowing air out of the case. Blowing air out of the case does a better job of keeping the system cool.

An ATX power supply has a variety of power connectors (see Figure 1-10). The power connectors are listed in Table 1-2 and several of them are described next.

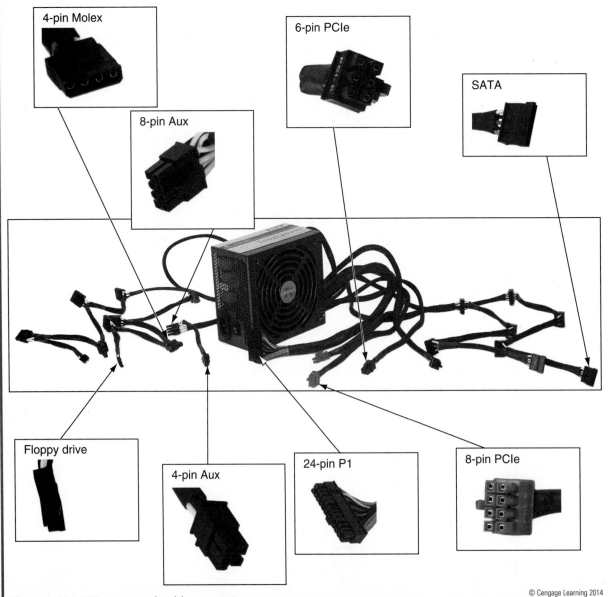

Figure 1-10 ATX power supply with connectors

A+
220-801
1.8

Connector	Description
© Cengage Learning 2014	20-pin P1 connect is the main motherboard power connector used in the early ATX systems
© Cengage Learning 2014	24-pin P1 connector, also called the 20+4 pin connector, is the main motherboard power connector used today
© Cengage Learning 2014	20+4 pin P1 connector with four pins removed so the connector can fit into a 20-pin P1 motherboard connector
© Cengage Learning 2014	4-pin auxiliary motherboard connector used for extra 12 V power to the processor
© Cengage Learning 2014	8-pin auxiliary motherboard connector used for extra 12 V power to the processor, providing more power than the older 4-pin auxiliary connector
© Cengage Learning 2014	4-pin Molex connector is used for IDE (PATA) drives
© Cengage Learning 2014	15-pin SATA connector used for SATA drives
© Cengage Learning 2014	4-pin Berg connector used by a floppy disk drive (FDD)

© Cengage Learning 2014

Table 1-2   Power supply connectors (continues)

A+
220-801
1.8

Connector	Description
© Cengage Learning 2014	6-pin PCIe connector provides an extra +12 V for high-end video cards using PCI Express, Version 1 standard
© Cengage Learning 2014	8-pin PCIe connector provides an extra +12 V for high-end video cards using PCI Express, Version 2
© Cengage Learning 2014	6-pin plus 2-pin +12 V PCIe connector is used by high-end video cards using PCIe ×16 slots to provide extra voltage to the card. To get the 8-pin connector, combine both the 6-pin and 2-pin connectors.

© Cengage Learning 2014

Table 1-2   Power supply connectors (continued)

> **🔋 A+ Exam Tip**   The A+ 220-801 exam expects you to know about each connector listed in Table 1-2.

Power connectors have evolved because components using new technologies require more power. As you read about the following types of power connectors and why each came to be, you'll also learn about the evolving expansion slots and expansion cards that drove the need for more power:

▲ *20-pin P1 connector.* The first ATX power supplies and motherboards used a single power connector called the P1 connector that had 20 pins. Figure 1-11 shows an ATX case with an ATX power supply installed, and Figure 1-12 shows the P1 connector on an ATX motherboard. The **20-pin P1 connector** used by the power supply and motherboard provided +3.3 volts, +5 volts, +12 volts, -12 volts, and an optional and rarely used -5 volts. This 20-pin power connector was sufficient for powering expansion cards installed in **PCI (Peripheral Component Interconnect)** expansion slots on the motherboard (see Figure 1-13). Several versions of PCI slots evolved over time, which you learn about in Chapter 4.

▲ *4-pin and 8-pin auxiliary connectors.* When processors began to require more power, the ATX Version 2.1 specifications added a **4-pin motherboard auxiliary connector** near the processor socket to provide an additional 12 V of power (see Figure 1-14). A power supply that provides this 4-pin 12 volt power cord is called an **ATX12V power supply**. Later boards replaced the 4-pin 12 volt power connector with an **8-pin motherboard auxiliary connector** that provided more amps for the processor.

A+
220-801
1.8

© Cengage Learning 2014

Figure 1-11 ATX power supply with connections

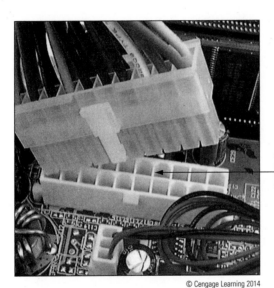

P1 connector on an
ATX motherboard

© Cengage Learning 2014

Figure 1-12 The first ATX P1 power connector used 20 pins

▲ *24-pin or 20+4-pin P1 connector.* Later, when faster **PCI Express (PCIe)** slots were
added to motherboards, more power was required and a new ATX specification (ATX
Version 2.2) allowed for a **24-pin P1 connector**, also called the 20+4 power connector.
The 20-pin power cable will still work in the new 24-pin connector. Looking back at
Figure 1-3, you can see one long blue PCIe ×16 slot (16 lanes for 16-bit transfers on
this slot) that can be used by a video card and two short black PCIe ×1 slots (for 1-bit
transfers) that can be used for other expansion cards that fit this type of slot.

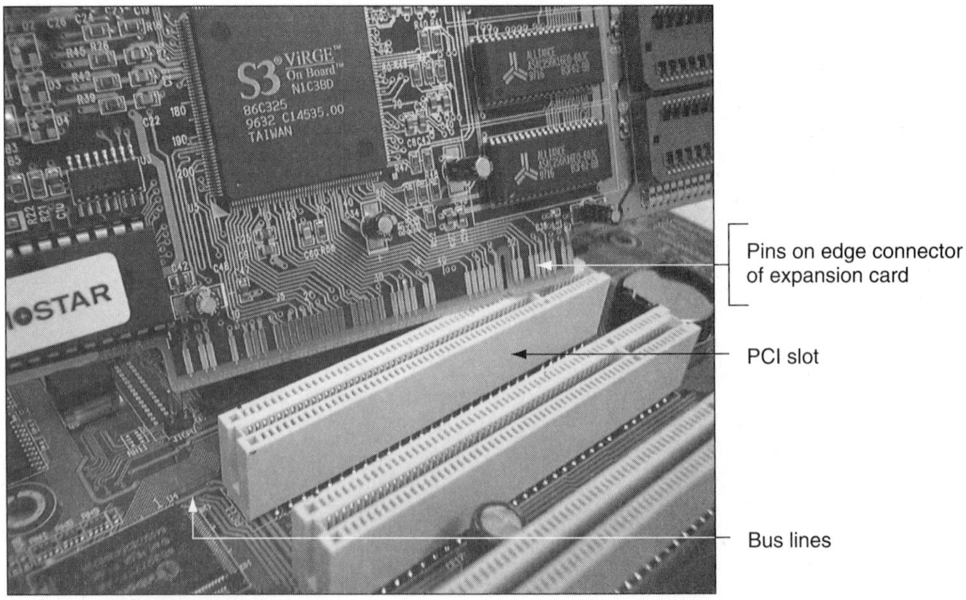

Pins on edge connector
of expansion card

PCI slot

Bus lines

© Cengage Learning 2014

Figure 1-13 A PCI expansion card about to be installed in a PCI slot

© Cengage Learning 2014

Figure 1-14 The 4-pin 12 volt auxiliary power connector on a motherboard with
power cord connected

The extra 4 pins on the 24-pin P1 connector provide +12 volts, +5 volts, and +3.3 volts pins. Motherboards that support PCI Express and have the 24-pin P1 connector are sometimes called Enhanced ATX boards. Figure 1-15 shows a 20-pin P1 power cord from the power supply and a 24-pin P1 connector on a motherboard. Figure 1-16 shows the pinouts for the 24-pin power cord connector, which is color-coded to wires from the power supply. The 20-pin connector is missing the lower four pins, which are listed in the photo and diagram.

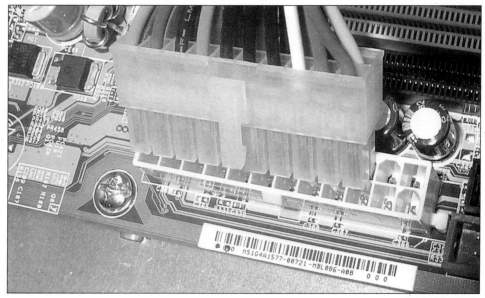

© Cengage Learning 2014

Figure 1-15 A 20-pin power cord ready to be plugged into a 24-pin P1 connector on an ATX motherboard

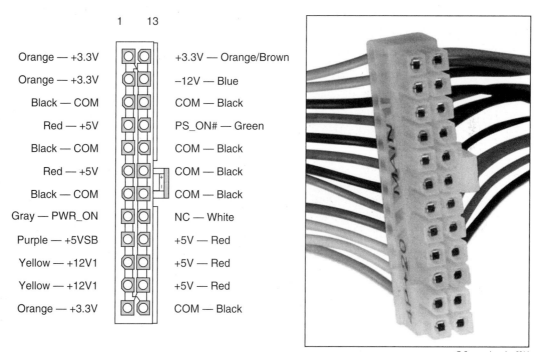

© Cengage Learning 2014

Figure 1-16 P1 24-pin power connector follows ATX Version 2.2 and higher standards

Figure 1-17 shows a PCIe ×16 video card. The edge connector has a break that fits the break in the slot. The tab at the end of the edge connector fits into a retention mechanism at the end of the slot, which helps to stabilize a heavy video card.

A+
220-801
1.8

PCIe 6-pin power connector
on the end of the video card

Edge connector

© Cengage Learning 2014

Figure 1-17   This PCIe ×16 video card has a 6-pin PCIe power connector
to receive extra power from the power supply

▲ *6-pin and 8-pin PCIe connectors.* Video cards draw the most power in a system, and
ATX Version 2.2 provides for power cables to connect directly to a video card to provide it additional power than comes through the PCIe slot on the motherboard. The
PCIe power connector might have 6 or 8 pins. PCI Express, Version 1, defined the
6-pin connector, and PCI Express, Version 2, defined the 8-pin connector. The video
card shown in Figure 1-17 has a 6-pin connector on the top of the card. A 6- or 8-pin
PCIe connector can also be located on the motherboard to supply extra power for the
video card.

> **Notes** For more information about all the form factors discussed in this chapter, check out the form
> factor web site sponsored by Intel at *www.formfactors.org*.

MICROATX FORM FACTOR

The **microATX (MATX)** form factor is a major variation of ATX and addresses some
technologies that have emerged since the original development of ATX. MicroATX reduces
the total cost of a system by reducing the number of expansion slots on the motherboard,
reducing the power supplied to the board, and allowing for a smaller case size. A micro-
ATX motherboard (see Figure 1-18) will fit into a case that follows the ATX 2.1 or higher
standard. A microATX power supply uses a 24-pin P1 connector and is not likely to have as
many extra wires and connectors as those on an ATX power supply.

A+
220-801
1.8

© Cengage Learning 2014

Figure 1-18 This MicroATX motherboard by Biostar is designed to support an AMD processor

> 💡 **A+ Exam Tip** The A+ 220-801 exam expects you to recognize and know the more important features of the ATX and micro-ATX form factors used by power supplies.

> ⚡ **Caution** Later in the chapter, you learn that you can damage a computer component with static electricity if you touch the component when you are not grounded. Before you touch a sensitive computer component, you first need to dissipate any static electricity on your body. You learn how to do that later in the chapter. For now, to protect a working component your instructor has on display, don't touch; just look.

Now let's learn about the drives you might find installed inside a system.

DRIVES, THEIR CABLES, AND CONNECTORS

A computer might have one or more hard drives, an optical drive (CD, DVD, or Blu-ray), tape drive, floppy drive, or some other type of drive. A drive receives power by a power cable from the power supply and communicates instructions and data through a cable attached to the motherboard. Two standards that hard drives, optical drives, and tape drives use for both types of connections are the faster **serial ATA (SATA)** standard and the slower and older **parallel ATA (PATA)** standard. Both standards are published by the American National Standards Institute (ANSI, see *www.ansi.org*). Most drives today use the faster SATA interface. Figure 1-19 shows a SATA cable connecting a hard drive and motherboard. SATA cables can only connect to a SATA connector on the motherboard in one direction (see Figure 1-20). SATA drives get their power from a power cable that connects to the drive using a **SATA power connector** (refer back to the photo in Table 1-2).

Serial ATA cable

Power cord

© Cengage Learning 2014

Figure 1-19 A hard drive subsystem using the SATA data cable

© Cengage Learning 2014

Figure 1-20 A SATA cable connects to a SATA connector in only one direction; use red connectors on the motherboard first

A+
220-801
1.8

The PATA interface, also called the IDE interface, uses a wide 40-pin ribbon cable and connector. The standard allows for only two connectors on a motherboard for two data cables (see Figure 1-21). Each IDE ribbon cable has a connection at the other end for an IDE drive and a connection in the middle of the cable for a second IDE drive. See Figure 1-22. Using this interface, a motherboard can accommodate up to four IDE or PATA drives in one system.

PATA drives use a 4-pin power connector called a **Molex power connector**. A Molex connector is shaped so it connects in only one direction (see Figure 1-23).

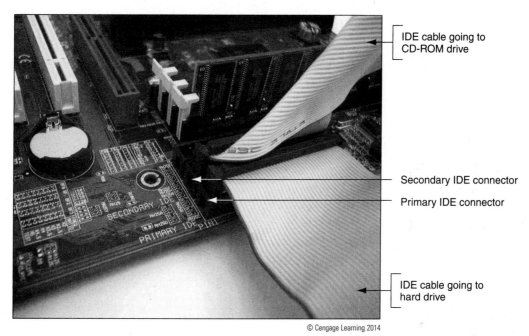

IDE cable going to CD-ROM drive

Secondary IDE connector

Primary IDE connector

IDE cable going to hard drive

© Cengage Learning 2014

Figure 1-21   Using a parallel ATA interface, a motherboard has two IDE connectors, each of which can accommodate two devices; a hard drive usually connects to the motherboard using the primary IDE connector

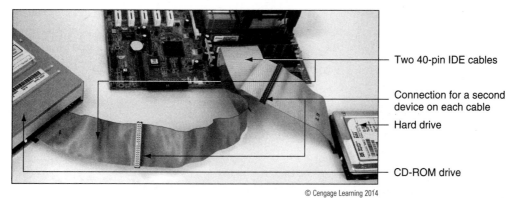

Two 40-pin IDE cables

Connection for a second device on each cable

Hard drive

CD-ROM drive

© Cengage Learning 2014

Figure 1-22   Two IDE devices connected to a motherboard using both IDE connections and two cables

A+
220-801
1.8

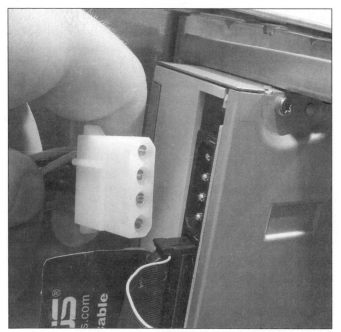

© Cengage Learning 2014

Figure 1-23 Molex power connector to a drive is shaped so that
it orients in only one direction

Older motherboards provide a connection for a floppy drive data cable (see Figure 1-24).
A **floppy drive**, also called a **floppy disk drive (FDD)**, can hold 3.5 inch disks containing
up to 1.44 MB of data. The floppy drive cable has 34 pins and a twist in the cable and can
accommodate one or two drives (see Figure 1-25). The drive at the end of the cable is drive
A, which is the drive that follows the twist in the cable. If another drive were connected to
the middle of the cable, it would be drive B in a computer system, which is the drive before
the twist. The 4-pin **Berg power connector** used by floppy drives is smaller than a Molex
connector (see the photos in Table 1-2).

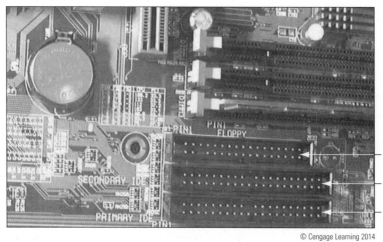

Floppy drive connector

Secondary IDE connector

Primary IDE connector

© Cengage Learning 2014

Figure 1-24 An older motherboard usually provides a connection for
a floppy drive cable

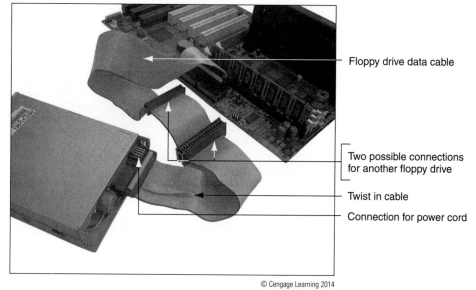

Floppy drive data cable

Two possible connections for another floppy drive

Twist in cable

Connection for power cord

© Cengage Learning 2014

Figure 1-25 One floppy drive connection on a motherboard can support one or two floppy drives

Cables used by PATA drives might be a 40-pin conductor IDE cable or a higher-quality 80-conductor IDE cable used by the Enhanced IDE (EIDE) standards. (An 80-conductor cable has 80 thin wires connected to 40 pins.) Figure 1-26 shows the two IDE cables on the right and a floppy drive cable on the left. IDE and floppy drive cables have a red color or stripe down one side of the cable. This edge color marks this side of the cable as pin 1. Pin 1 is labeled on the connector so that you can orient the cable in the connector (see Figure 1-27). The EIDE cables and some floppy drive cables have a covered pinhole and a notch in the motherboard connector, so these cables can connect in only one direction. See Figure 1-28.

And this brings us to the fact that you need to know about electricity, how a computer uses it, and how to protect yourself and the equipment against electrical dangers.

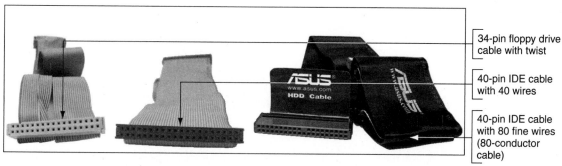

34-pin floppy drive cable with twist

40-pin IDE cable with 40 wires

40-pin IDE cable with 80 fine wires (80-conductor cable)

© Cengage Learning 2014

Figure 1-26 A system might have up to three types of ribbon cables

A+
220-801
1.8

© Cengage Learning 2014

Figure 1-27   Pin 1 for this IDE connection is clearly marked

Notch on the
floppy drive
connector

© Cengage Learning 2014

Figure 1-28   The notch on the side of this floppy drive connector allows the floppy drive
cable to connect in only one direction

PROTECTING YOURSELF AND THE EQUIPMENT AGAINST ELECTRICAL DANGERS

A+
220-801
5.1, 5.2

By the end of the next chapter, you will know how to take a working desktop computer apart and put the computer back together. When you're done, it's expected the computer will still work! That might not be the case, however, if you don't understand electricity and how to protect yourself and the equipment against it. In this part of the chapter, you learn how to keep from getting a shock or damaging a component. Let's begin with a discussion of the basics of electricity.

A+
220-801
5.1, 5.2

MEASURES AND PROPERTIES OF ELECTRICITY

In our modern world, we take electricity for granted, and we miss it terribly when it's cut off. Nearly everyone depends on it, but few really understand it. A successful PC support technician is not one who tends to encounter failed processors, fried motherboards, smoking monitors, or frizzed hair. To avoid these excitements, you need to understand how to measure electricity and how to protect computer equipment from its damaging power.

Let's start with the basics. To most people, volts, ohms, joules, watts, and amps are vague terms that simply mean electricity. All these terms can be used to measure some characteristic of electricity, as listed in Table 1-3.

Unit	Definition	Computer Example
Volt (for example, 115 V)	A measure of electrical force measured in *volts*. The symbol for volts is V.	A power supply steps down the voltage from the 115 volt house current to 3.3, 5, and 12 volts that computer components can use.
Amp or ampere (for example, 1.5 A)	An *amp* is a measure of electrical current. The symbol for amps is A.	An LCD monitor requires about 5 A to operate. A small laser printer uses about 2 A. A CD-ROM drive uses about 1 A.
Ohm (for example, 20 Ω)	An *ohm* is a measure of resistance to electricity. The symbol for ohm is Ω.	Current can flow in typical computer cables and wires with a resistance of near zero Ω (ohm).
Joule (for example, 500 joules)	A measure of work or energy. One *joule* (pronounced "jewel") is the work required to push an electrical current of one amp through a resistance of one ohm.	A *surge suppressor* (see Figure 1-29) is rated in joules—the higher the better. The rating determines how much work it can expend before it can no longer protect the circuit from a power surge.
Watt (for example, 20 W)	A measure of electrical power. One *watt* is one joule per second and measures the total electrical power needed to operate a device. Watts can be calculated by multiplying volts by amps. The symbol for watts is W.	The power consumption of an LCD computer monitor is rated at about 14 W. A DVD burner uses about 25 W when burning a DVD.

Table 1-3 Measures of electricity

© Cengage Learning 2014

Rating is 720 joules

© Cengage Learning 2014

Figure 1-29 A surge suppressor protects electrical equipment from power surges and is rated in joules

A+
220-801
5.1, 5.2

> **Notes** To learn more about how volts, amps, ohms, joules, and watts measure the properties of electricity, see the content "Electricity and Multimeters" in the online content that accompanies this book at *cengagebrain.com*. To find out how to access this content, see the Preface to this book.

Now let's look at how electricity gets from one place to another and how it is used in house circuits and computers.

AC AND DC

Electricity can be either AC, alternating current, or DC, direct current. **Alternating current (AC)** goes back and forth, or oscillates, rather than traveling in only one direction. House current in the United States is AC and oscillates 60 times in one second (60 hertz). Voltage in the system is constantly alternating from positive to negative, which causes the electricity to flow first in one direction and then in the other. Voltage alternates from +115 V to -115 V. AC is the most economical way to transmit electricity to our homes and workplaces. By decreasing current and increasing voltage, we can force alternating current to travel great distances. When alternating current reaches its destination, it is made more suitable for driving our electrical devices by decreasing voltage and increasing current.

Direct current (DC) travels in only one direction and is the type of current that most electronic devices require, including computers. A **rectifier** is a device that converts AC to DC, and an **inverter** is a device that converts DC to AC. A **transformer** is a device that changes the ratio of voltage to current. The power supply used in computers is both a rectifier and a transformer.

Large transformers reduce the high voltage on power lines coming to your neighborhood to a lower voltage before the current enters your home. The transformer does not change the amount of power in this closed system; if it decreases voltage, it increases current. The overall power stays constant, but the ratio of voltage to current changes, as illustrated in Figure 1-30.

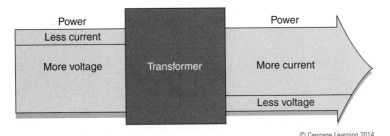

© Cengage Learning 2014

Figure 1-30   A transformer keeps power constant but changes the ratio of current to voltage

Direct current flows in only one direction. Think of electrical current like a current of water that flows from a state of high pressure to a state of low pressure or rest. Electrical current flows from a high-pressure state (called hot) to a state of rest (called ground or neutral). For a power supply, a power line may be either +5 or −5 volts in one circuit, or +12 or −12 volts in another circuit. The positive or negative value is determined by how the circuit is oriented, either on one side of the power output or the other. Several circuits coming from the power supply accommodate different devices with different power requirements.

HOT, NEUTRAL, AND GROUND

AC travels on a hot line from the power station to a building and returns to the power station on a neutral line. When the two lines reach the building and enter an electrical device, such as a lamp, the device controls the flow of electricity between the hot and neutral lines. If an easier path (one with less resistance) is available, the electricity follows that path. This can cause a short, a sudden increase in flow that can also create a sudden increase in temperature—enough to start a fire and injure both people and equipment. Never put yourself in a position where you are the path of least resistance between the hot line and ground!

⚡ **Caution** It's very important that PC components be properly grounded. Never connect a PC to an outlet or use an extension cord that doesn't have the third ground plug. The third line can prevent a short from causing extreme damage. In addition, the bond between the neutral and ground helps eliminate electrical noise (stray electrical signals) within the PC that is sometimes caused by other electrical equipment sitting very close to the computer.

To prevent uncontrolled electricity in a short, the neutral line is grounded. Grounding a line means that the line is connected directly to the earth, so that, in the event of a short, the electricity flows into the earth and not back to the power station. Grounding serves as an escape route for out-of-control electricity because the earth is always capable of accepting a flow of current. With computers, a surge suppressor can be used to protect a computer and its components against power surges.

⚡ **Caution** Beware of the different uses of black wire. In PCs and in DC circuits, black is used for ground, but in home wiring and in AC circuits, black is used for hot!

The neutral line to your house is grounded many times along its way (in fact, at each electrical pole) and is also grounded at the breaker box where the electricity enters your house. You can look at a three-prong plug and see the three lines: hot, neutral, and ground (see Figure 1-31).

To verify that a wall outlet is wired correctly for hot, neutral, and ground, use a simple receptacle tester, as shown in Figure 1-32. Even though you might have a three-prong outlet in your home, the ground plug might not be properly grounded. To know for sure, you can test the outlet with a receptacle tester.

📝 **Notes** House AC voltage in the United States is about 110–120 V, but know that in other countries, this is not always the case. In many other countries, the standard is 220 V. Outlet styles also vary from one country to the next.

Now that you know about electricity and how to protect a computer from surges and out-of-control electricity, let's turn our attention to protecting yourself against the dangers of electricity.

A+
220-801
5.1, 5.2

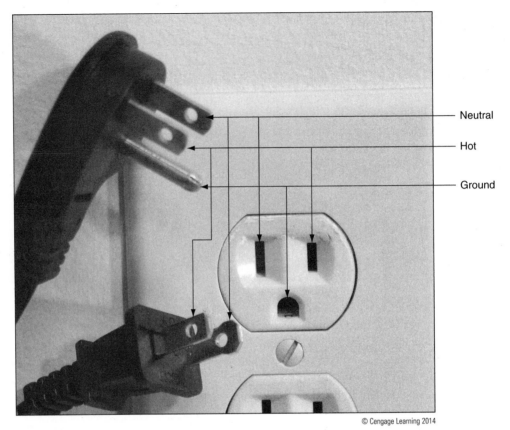

Neutral

Hot

Ground

© Cengage Learning 2014

Figure 1-31 A polarized plug showing hot and neutral, and a three-prong plug showing hot, neutral, and ground

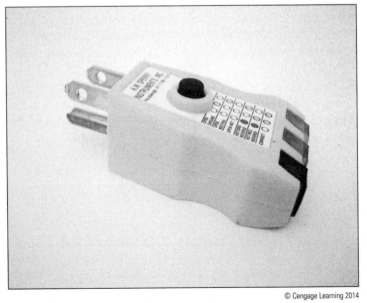

© Cengage Learning 2014

Figure 1-32 Use a receptacle tester to verify that hot, neutral, and ground are wired correctly

A+
220-801
5.1, 5.2

PROTECT YOURSELF AGAINST ELECTRICAL SHOCK AND BURNS

To protect yourself against electrical shock, when working with any electrical device, including computers, printers, scanners, and network devices, disconnect the power if you notice a dangerous situation that might lead to electrical shock or fire. When you disconnect the power, do so by pulling on the plug at the AC outlet. To protect the power cord, don't pull on the cord itself. Also, don't just turn off the on/off switch on the device; you need to actually disconnect the power. Note that any of the following can indicate a potential danger:

▲ The power cord is frayed or otherwise damaged in any way.
▲ Water or other liquid is on the floor around the device or spilled on it.
▲ The device has been exposed to excess moisture.
▲ The device has been dropped or you notice physical damage.
▲ You smell a strong electronics odor.
▲ The power supply or fans are making a whining noise.
▲ You notice smoke coming from the computer case or the case feels unusually warm.

When working inside computers, printers, and other electrical devices, remove your jewelry that might come in contact with components. Jewelry is made of metal and might conduct electricity if it touches a component.

Power supplies and CRT monitors (the old-fashioned monitors that have a large case with a picture tube) contain capacitors. A capacitor holds its charge even after the power is turned off and the device is unplugged. A ground is the easiest possible path for electricity to follow. If you are grounded and touch a charged capacitor, its charge can flow through you to the ground, which can shock you! Therefore, if you ever work inside one of these devices, be careful that you are not grounded. Later in the chapter, you will learn that being grounded while working on sensitive low-voltage electronic equipment such as a motherboard or processor is a good thing, and the best way to ground yourself is to wear an antistatic grounding bracelet connected to ground. However, when working on a CRT monitor, power supply, or laser printer, *don't* wear the antistatic bracelet because you don't want to be ground for these high-voltage devices. How to work inside a power supply or CRT monitor is not covered in this book and is not considered a skill needed by an A+ certified support technician. The power supply and monitor are both considered to be a **field replaceable unit (FRU)**. That means, as a support technician, you are expected to know how to replace one when it breaks but not how to repair one.

> 💡 **A+ Exam Tip** The A+ 220-801 exam expects you to know how to properly dispose of a CRT monitor.

Be sure a CRT monitor is discharged before you dispose of it. Most CRT monitors today are designed to discharge after sitting unplugged for 60 minutes. It can be manually discharged by using a high-voltage probe with the monitor case opened. Ask a technician trained to fix monitors to do this for you. Always follow local government regulations when disposing of computer equipment, monitors, printers, chemicals, and other substances that might be dangerous to the environment or humans.

> 📝 **Notes** Go to *www.youtube.com* and search on "discharge a CRT monitor" to see some interesting videos that demonstrate the charge inside a monitor long after the monitor is turned off and unplugged. As for proper procedures, I'm not endorsing all these videos; just watch for fun.

Never use water to put out a fire fueled by electricity because water is a conductor and you might get a severe electrical shock. A computer lab needs a fire extinguisher that is rated to put out electrical fires. Fire extinguishers are rated by the type of fires they put out:

▲ Class A extinguishers can use water to put out fires caused by wood, paper, and other combustibles.

▲ Class B extinguishers can put out fires caused by liquids such as gasoline, kerosene, and oil.

▲ **Class C fire extinguishers** use nonconductive chemicals to put out a fire caused by electricity. See Figure 1-33.

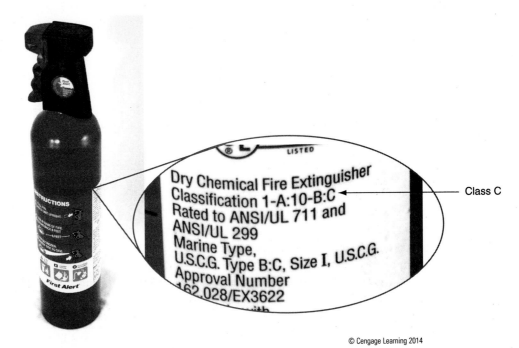

Class C

© Cengage Learning 2014

Figure 1-33 A Class C fire extinguisher is rated to put out electrical fires

PROTECT THE EQUIPMENT AGAINST STATIC ELECTRICITY OR ESD

Suppose you come indoors on a cold day, pick up a comb, and touch your hair. Sparks fly! What happened? Static electricity caused the sparks. **Electrostatic discharge (ESD)**, commonly known as **static electricity**, is an electrical charge at rest. When you came indoors, this charge built up on your hair and had no place to go. An ungrounded conductor (such as wire that is not touching another wire) or a nonconductive surface (such as your hair) holds a charge until the charge is released. When two objects with dissimilar electrical charges touch, electricity passes between them until the dissimilar charges become equal.

To see static charges equalizing, turn off the lights in a room, scuff your feet on the carpet, and touch another person. Occasionally, you can see and feel the charge in your fingers. If you can feel the charge, you discharged at least 1,500 volts of static electricity. If you hear the discharge, you released at least 6,000 volts. If you see the discharge, you released at least 8,000 volts of ESD. A charge of only 10 volts can damage electronic components! *You can touch a chip on an expansion card or motherboard, damage the chip with ESD, and never feel, hear, or see the electrical discharge.*

ESD can cause two types of damage in an electronic component: catastrophic failure and upset failure. A catastrophic failure destroys the component beyond use. An upset failure damages the component so that it does not perform well, even though it may still function to some degree. Upset failures are more difficult to detect because they are not consistent and not easily observed. Both types of failures permanently affect the device. Components are easily damaged by ESD, but because the damage might not show up for weeks or months, a technician is likely to get careless and not realize the damage he or she is doing.

> ⚡ **Caution** Unless you are measuring power levels with a multimeter, never, ever touch a component or cable inside a computer case while the power is on. The electrical voltage is not enough to seriously hurt you but more than enough to permanently damage the component.

Before touching or handling a component (for example, a hard drive, motherboard, expansion card, processor, or memory modules), to protect it against ESD, always ground yourself first. You can ground yourself and the computer parts by using one or more of the following static control devices or methods:

▲ *Ground bracelet.* A **ground bracelet**, also called an **ESD strap**, **antistatic wrist strap**, or ESD bracelet, is a strap you wear around your wrist. The strap has a cord attached with an alligator clip on the end. Attach the clip to the computer case you're working on, as shown in Figure 1-34. Any static electricity between you and the case is now discharged. Therefore, as you work inside the case, you will not damage the components with static electricity. The bracelet also contains a resistor that prevents electricity from harming you.

© Cengage Learning 2014

Figure 1-34 A ground bracelet, which protects computer components from ESD, can clip to the side of the computer case and eliminate ESD between you and the case

A+
220-801
5.1, 5.2

▲ *Ground mats.* A **ground mat**, also called an **ESD mat**, dissipates ESD and is commonly used by bench technicians (also called depot technicians) who repair and assemble computers at their workbenches or in an assembly line. Ground mats have a connector in one corner that you can use to connect the mat to ground (see Figure 1-35). If you lift a component off the mat, it is no longer grounded and is susceptible to ESD, so it's important to use a ground bracelet with a ground mat.

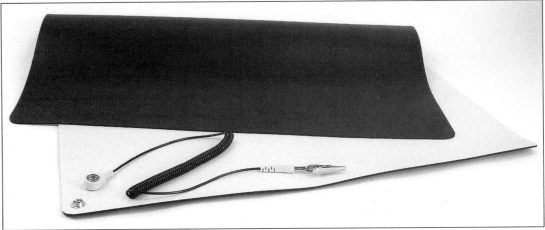

© Cengage Learning 2014

Figure 1-35   A ground mat dissipates ESD and should be connected to ground

▲ *Static shielding bags.* New components come shipped in static shielding bags, also called **antistatic bags**. These bags are a type of Faraday cage, named after Michael Faraday, who built the first cage in 1836. A Faraday cage is any device that protects against an electromagnetic field. Save the bags to store other devices that are not currently installed in a PC. As you work on a computer, know that a device is not protected from ESD if you place it on top of the bag; the protection is inside the bag (see Figure 1-36).

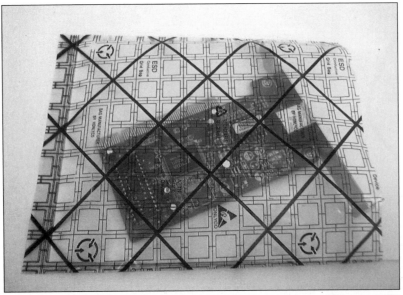

© Cengage Learning 2014

Figure 1-36   Static shielding bags help protect components from ESD

1

A+
220-801
5.1, 5.2

▲ *Antistatic gloves.* Wear **antistatic gloves**, also called **ESD gloves**, designed to prevent an ESD discharge between you and a device as you pick it up and handle it (see Figure 1-37). The gloves can be substituted for an antistatic bracelet and are good for moving, packing, or unpacking sensitive equipment. Even through these gloves tend to get in the way when working inside computer cases, Intel recommends you wear them when handling a processor.

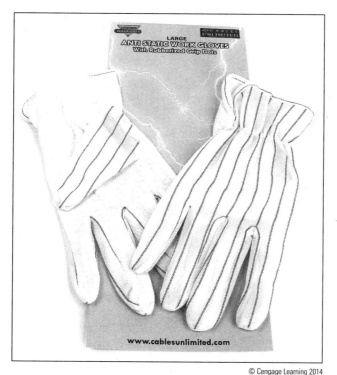

© Cengage Learning 2014

Figure 1-37 Use antistatic gloves to prevent static discharge between you and the equipment you are handling

> ⚡ **Caution** A CRT monitor can also damage components with ESD. Don't place or store expansion cards on top of or next to a CRT monitor, which can discharge as much as 29,000 volts onto the screen.

The best way to guard against ESD is to use a ground bracelet together with a ground mat or wear antistatic gloves. Consider a ground bracelet or antistatic gloves essential equipment when working on a computer. However, if you are in a situation in which you must work without one, touch the computer case or the power supply before you touch a component in the case, which is called **self-grounding**. Self-grounding dissipates any charge between you and whatever you touch. Here are some rules that can help protect computer parts against ESD:

▲ *Rule 1:* When passing a circuit board, memory module, or other sensitive component to another person, ground yourself and then touch the other person before you pass the component.

▲ *Rule 2:* Leave components inside their protective bags until you are ready to use them.

▲ *Rule 3:* Work on hard floors, not carpet, or use antistatic spray on the carpets.

▲ *Rule 4:* Don't work on a computer if you or the computer have just come in from the cold because there is more danger of ESD when the atmosphere is cold and dry.

A+
220-801
5.1, 5.2

▲ *Rule 5:* When unpacking hardware or software, remove the packing tape and cellophane from the work area as soon as possible because these materials attract ESD.
▲ *Rule 6:* Keep components away from your hair and clothing.

> 💡 **A+ Exam Tip** The A+ 220-801 exam emphasizes that you should know how to protect computer equipment as you work on it, including how to protect components against damage from ESD.

Now that you know about electrical dangers and ways to protect you and the equipment, let's discuss the tools you need.

TOOLS USED BY A PC REPAIR TECHNICIAN

A+
220-802
4.2

Every PC repair technician needs a handy toolbox with a few essential tools. Several hardware and software tools can help you maintain a computer and diagnose and repair computer problems. The tools you choose depend on the amount of money you can spend and the level of PC support you expect to provide.

Essential tools for PC hardware troubleshooting are listed here, and several of them are shown in Figure 1-38. You can purchase some of these tools in a PC toolkit, although most PC toolkits contain items you really can do without.

© Cengage Learning 2014

Figure 1-38 Tools used by PC support technicians when maintaining, repairing, or upgrading computers

Here is a list of essential tools:

▲ Ground bracelet, ground mat, or antistatic gloves to protect against ESD when working inside the computer case
▲ Flathead screwdriver
▲ Phillips-head or crosshead screwdriver
▲ Torx screwdriver set, particularly size T15
▲ Tweezers, preferably insulated ones, for picking pieces of paper out of printers or dropped screws out of tight places

A+
220-802
4.2

▲ Extractor, a spring-loaded device that looks like a hypodermic needle (When you push down on the top, three wire prongs come out that can be used to pick up a screw that has fallen into a place where hands and fingers can't reach.)

▲ Software, including recovery CD or DVD for any OS you might work on (you might need several, depending on the OSs you support), antivirus software on bootable CDs or USB flash drives, and diagnostic software

The following tools might not be essential, but they are very convenient:

▲ Cans of compressed air (see Figure 1-39), small portable compressor, or antistatic vacuum cleaner to clean dust from inside a computer case

▲ Cleaning solutions and pads such as contact cleaner, monitor wipes, and cleaning solutions for CDs, DVDs, tapes, and drives

▲ Multimeter to check cables and the power supply output

▲ Power supply tester

▲ Needle-nose pliers for removing jumpers and for holding objects (especially those pesky nuts on cable connectors) in place while you screw them in

▲ Cable ties to tie cables up and out of the way inside a computer case

▲ Flashlight to see inside the computer case

▲ AC outlet ground tester

▲ Network cable tester (You will learn to use this tool in Chapter 15.)

▲ Loopback plugs to test ports

▲ Small cups or bags to help keep screws organized as you work

▲ Antistatic bags (a type of Faraday cage) to store unused parts

▲ Chip extractor to remove chips (To pry up the chip, a simple screwdriver is usually more effective, however.)

▲ Pen and paper for taking notes

▲ POST diagnostic cards

© Cengage Learning 2014

Figure 1-39 A can of compressed air is handy to blow dust from a computer case

A+
220-802
4.2

Keep your tools in a toolbox designated for PC troubleshooting. If you put discs and hardware tools in the same box, be sure to keep the discs inside a hard plastic case to protect them from scratches and dents. In addition, make sure the diagnostic and utility software you use is recommended for the hardware and software you are troubleshooting.

Now let's turn our attention to the details of several PC support technician tools, including diagnostic cards, power supply testers, and multimeters. Then we'll finish up the chapter with some additional safety procedures you need to be aware of.

POST DIAGNOSTIC CARDS

Although not an essential tool, a **POST diagnostic card**, also called a **POST card**, or motherboard test card, can be of great help to discover and report computer errors and conflicts that occur when you first turn on a computer and before the operating system (such as Windows 7) is launched. To understand what a POST card does, you need to know about the programs and data stored on the motherboard called the **BIOS (basic input/output system)**. Some adapter cards, such as a video card, also have BIOS programs embedded on the card.

The BIOS programs are stored on a special ROM (read-only memory) chip; because these embedded programs are so closely tied to the hardware, they are called **firmware**. Figure 1-40 shows an embedded firmware chip on a motherboard that contains the BIOS programs. When the computer is not receiving power, the firmware chip is powered by a battery nearby so it does not lose the data it holds in the memory on the chip, which is called CMOS RAM. CMOS RAM holds the motherboard configuration or settings and includes the computer date and time, power-on passwords, and which devices to look to when the BIOS is searching for an operating system (OS) to launch.

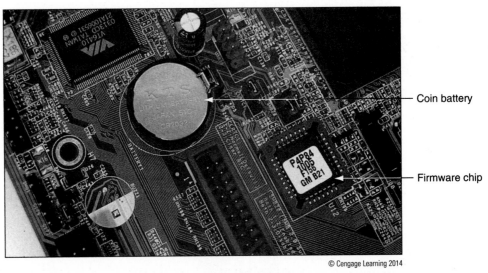

Coin battery

Firmware chip

© Cengage Learning 2014

Figure 1-40   This firmware chip contains flash ROM and CMOS RAM; CMOS RAM is powered by the coin battery located near the chip

The motherboard BIOS serves three purposes:

▲ **System BIOS** manages essential devices (such as the keyboard, mouse, hard drive, and monitor) before the OS is launched.
▲ **Startup BIOS** is used to start the computer.
▲ **BIOS setup** or **CMOS setup** is used to change the motherboard configuration or settings.

A+
220-802
4.2

So now back to the usefulness of a POST card. The **POST (power-on self test)** is a series of tests performed by the startup BIOS when you first turn on a computer. These tests determine if startup BIOS can communicate correctly with essential hardware components required for a successful boot. If you have a problem that prevents the PC from booting that you suspect is related to hardware, you can install the POST card in an expansion slot on the motherboard and then attempt to boot. The card monitors the boot process and reports errors, usually as coded numbers on a small LED panel on the card. You then look up the number online or in the documentation that accompanies the card to get more information about the error and its source.

Examples of these cards are listed below. Some manufacturers make cards for either desktop or laptop computers. The Post Code Master card is shown in Figure 1-41.

▲ PC POST Diagnostic Test Card by Elston System, Inc. (*www.elstonsystems.com*)
▲ PCI POST Diagnostic Test Card by StarTech.com (*www.startech.com*)
▲ Post Code Master by Microsystems Development, Inc. (*www.postcodemaster.com*)

© Cengage Learning 2014

Figure 1-41 Post Code Master diagnostic card by Microsystems Developments, Inc. installs in a PCI slot

Before purchasing these or any other diagnostic tools or software, read the documentation about what they can and cannot do, and read some online product reviews. Try using Google.com and searching on "PC diagnostic card reviews."

Notes Some Dell computers have lights on the case that blink in patterns to indicate a problem early in the boot before the OS loads. These blinking lights give information similar to that given by POST cards.

A+
220-802
4.2

POWER SUPPLY TESTER

A **power supply tester** is used to measure the output of each connector coming from the power supply. You can test the power supply when it is outside or inside the case. As you saw earlier in Figure 1-8, the power supply provides several cables and connectors that power various components inside the computer case. A power supply tester has plugs for each type of cable. Connect a power cable to the tester, plug up the power supply, and turn on the tester. An LCD panel reports the output of each lead (see Figure 1-42). Later in the chapter, you learn about the various power supply cables and the voltages they supply.

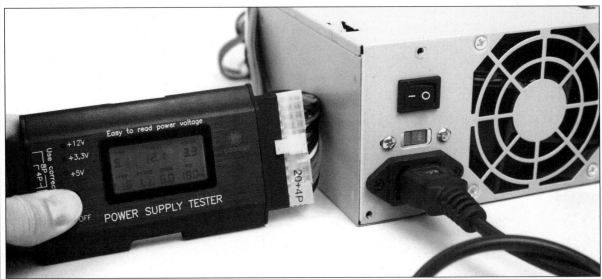

© Cengage Learning 2014

Figure 1-42   Use a power supply tester to test the output of each power connector on a power supply

MULTIMETER

A **multimeter** (see Figure 1-43) is a more general-purpose tool that can measure several characteristics of electricity in a variety of devices. Some multimeters can measure voltage, current, resistance, or continuity. (Continuity determines that two ends of a cable or fuse are connected without interruption.) When set to measure voltage, you can use it to measure output of each pin on a power supply connector. Set to measure continuity, a multimeter is useful to test fuses, to determine if a cable is good, or to match pins on one end of a cable to pins on the other end.

LOOPBACK PLUGS

A **loopback plug** is used to test a port in a computer or other device to make sure the port is working and might also test the throughput or speed of the port. Figure 1-44 shows a loopback plug testing a network port on a laptop. You know both the port and the network cable are good because the lights on either side of the port are lit. You can also buy a USB loopback plug to test USB ports.

A+
220-802
4.2

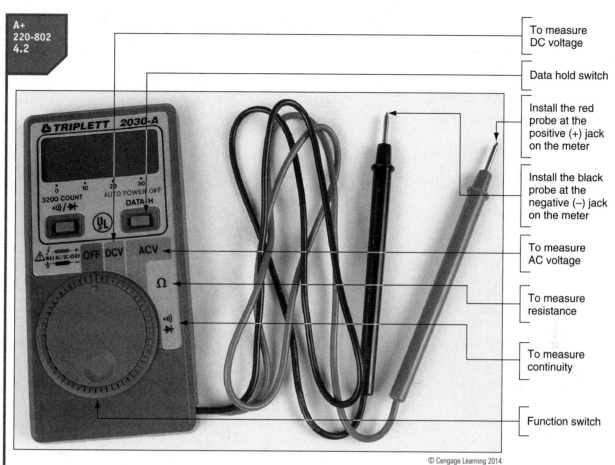

To measure
DC voltage

Data hold switch

Install the red
probe at the
positive (+) jack
on the meter

Install the black
probe at the
negative (−) jack
on the meter

To measure
AC voltage

To measure
resistance

To measure
continuity

Function switch

© Cengage Learning 2014

Figure 1-43 This digital multimeter can be set to measure voltage, resistance, or continuity

Figure 1-44 A loopback plug testing a network port and network cable © Cengage Learning 2014

A+
220-801
5.1, 5.2

PROPER USE OF CLEANING PADS AND SOLUTIONS

As a PC technician, you'll find yourself collecting different cleaning solutions and cleaning pads to clean a variety of devices, including the mouse and keyboard, CDs, DVDs, Blu-ray discs and their drives, tapes and tape drives, and CRT and LCD monitors. Figure 1-45 shows a few of these products. The contact cleaner in the figure is used to clean the contacts on the edge connectors of expansion cards; the cleaning can solve a problem with a faulty connection.

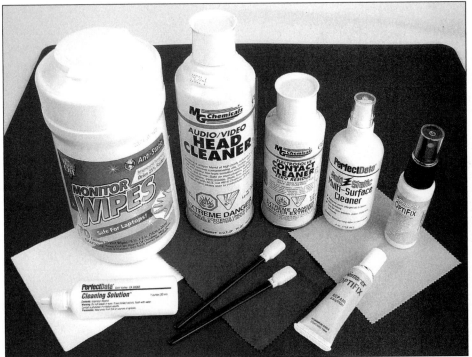

© Cengage Learning 2014

Figure 1-45 Cleaning solutions and pads

Most of these cleaning solutions contain flammable and poisonous materials. Take care when using them so that they don't get on your skin or in your eyes. To find out what to do if you are accidentally exposed to a dangerous solution, look on the instructions printed on the can or check out the material safety data sheet (see Figure 1-46). A **Material Safety Data Sheet (MSDS)** explains how to properly handle substances such as chemical solvents and how to dispose of them.

An MSDS includes information such as physical data, toxicity, health effects, first aid, storage, shipping, disposal, and spill procedures. It comes packaged with the chemical; you can order one from the manufacturer, or you can find one on the Internet (see *www .ilpi.com/msds*).

> 💡 **A+ Exam Tip** The A+ 220-801 exam expects you to know how to use MSDS documentation to find out how to dispose of chemicals so as to help protect the environment. You also need to know that you must follow all local government regulations when disposing of chemicals and other materials dangerous to the environment.

© Cengage Learning 2014

Figure 1-46 Each chemical you use should have available a material safety data sheet

If you have an accident with these or other dangerous products, your company or organization might require you to report the accident to your company and/or fill out an accident report. Check with your organization to find out how to handle reporting these types of incidents.

MANAGING CABLES

People can trip over cables or cords left on the floor, so be careful that cables are in a safe place. If you must run a cable across a path or where someone sits, use a cable or cord cover that can be nailed or screwed to the floor. Don't leave loose cables or cords in a traffic area where people can trip over them (called a **trip hazard**).

LIFTING HEAVY OBJECTS

Back injury, caused by lifting heavy objects, is one of the most common injuries that happen at work. Whenever possible, put heavy objects, such as a large laser printer, on a cart to move them. If you do need to lift a heavy object, follow these guidelines to keep from injuring your back:

1. Looking at the object, decide which side of the object to face so that the load is the most balanced.

2. Stand close to the object with your feet apart.

3. Keeping your back straight, bend your knees and grip the load.

4. Lift with your legs, arms, and shoulders, and not with your back or stomach.

5. Keep the load close to your body and avoid twisting your body while you're holding it.

6. To put the object down, keep your back as straight as you can and lower the object by bending your knees.

Don't try to lift an object that is too heavy for you. Because there are no exact guidelines for when heavy is too heavy, use your best judgment as to when to ask for help.

Now that you know about computer parts and their connections, the dangers and ways to protect you and the equipment against electricity, and the tools you need, you're ready to learn how to work inside a computer case. Have fun doing that in the next chapter, but don't forget to practice all the safety skills you learned about in this chapter.

>> CHAPTER SUMMARY

What's Inside the Case

◢ Video ports a computer might have include the VGA, S-Video, DVI, DisplayPort, and HDMI ports. Other ports include a network, sound, S/PDIF, USB, FireWire, eSATA, and PS/2 ports.

◢ Internal computer components include the motherboard, processor, expansion cards, memory modules, hard drive, optical drive, floppy drive, tape drive, and power supply.

◢ Form factors used by cases, power supplies, and motherboards are the ATX and micro-ATX form factors. The form factor determines how the case, power supply, and motherboard fit together and the cable connectors and other standards used by each.

◢ Power connectors used by the ATX and mini-ATX form factors include the 20-pin P1, 24-pin P1, 4-pin and 8-pin auxiliary motherboard, 4-pin Molex, 15-pin SATA, 4-pin FDD, 6-pin PCIe, and 8-pin PCIe connectors.

◢ Standards used by hard drives and other drives to interface with the motherboard and power supply are serial ATA (SATA) and parallel ATA (PATA). The PATA standard is also called the IDE standard.

Protecting Yourself and the Equipment against Electrical Dangers

◢ Units used to measure electricity include volts, amps, ohms, joules, and watts.

◢ Microcomputers require direct current (DC), which is converted from alternating current (AC) by the PC's power supply inside the computer case.

◢ A power supply and CRT monitor contain dangerous charges even when unplugged. PC support technicians consider them to be field replaceable units and you should not need to open one.

◢ Never use water to put out an electrical fire. Use a Class C fire extinguisher rated for electrical fires.

◢ Equipment to protect computer components against ESD includes a ground bracelet, ground mat, antistatic bags, and antistatic gloves.

Tools Used by a PC Repair Technician

◢ Special tools a PC support technician might need include a POST diagnostic card, power supply tester, multimeter, and loopback plugs.

◢ A Material Safety Data Sheet tells you how to handle chemicals and includes physical data, toxicity, health effects, first aid, storage, shipping, disposal, and spill procedures.

◢ Be careful to not lift a heavy object in a way you can hurt your back, and make sure cables are not trip hazards.

>> KEY TERMS

For explanations of key terms, see the Glossary near the end of the book.

> **A+ Exam Tip** To help you prepare for the A+ exams, the key terms in each chapter focus on the terms you need to know for the exams. Before you sit for the exams, be sure to review all the key terms in the Glossary.

4-pin motherboard auxiliary connector
8-pin motherboard auxiliary connector
20-pin P1 connector
24-pin P1 connector
alternating current (AC)
amp
antistatic bags
antistatic gloves
antistatic wrist strap
ATX (Advanced Technology Extended)
ATX12V power supply
audio port
Berg power connector
BIOS (basic input/output system)
BIOS setup
central processing unit (CPU)
Class C fire extinguisher
CMOS setup
DB-15 port
desktop case
DIMM (dual inline memory module)
direct current (DC)
DisplayPort
dual voltage selector switch
DVI (Digital Video Interface) port
electrostatic discharge (ESD)
ESD gloves
ESD mat
ESD strap
Ethernet port
expansion card

external SATA (eSATA)
field replaceable unit (FRU)
FireWire port
firmware
floppy disk drive (FDD)
floppy drive
form factors
ground bracelet
ground mat
hard disk drive (HDD)
hard drive
HDMI (High Definition Multimedia Interface) port
heat sink
IEEE1394 port
internal components
inverter
joule
loopback plug
main board
Material Safety Data Sheet (MSDS)
microATX (MATX)
microprocessor
modem port
Molex power connector
motherboard
multimeter
network port
ohm
parallel ATA (PATA)
parallel port
PCI (Peripheral Component Interconnect)
PCI Express (PCIe)
PCIe power connector

POST (power-on self test)
POST card
POST diagnostic card
power supply
power supply tester
power supply unit (PSU)
processor
PS/2 port
RAM (random access memory)
RJ-11
RJ-45
rectifier
S-Video port
S/PDIF (Sony Philips Digital Interface) sound port
SATA power connector
self-grounding
serial ATA (SATA)
serial port
startup BIOS
static electricity
surge suppressor
system BIOS
system board
Thunderbolt
tower case
transformer
trip hazard
USB (Universal Serial Bus) port
VGA (Video Graphics Array) port
video memory
volt
watt

>> REVIEW QUESTIONS

1. Which internal case component contains a socket to hold the processor or CPU?

   a) Expansion card

   b) Motherboard

   c) DIMM

   d) Heat sink

2. Which power supply connector is the main motherboard power connector used today?

   a) 24-pin P1 connector

   b) 20-pin P1 connector

   c) 20+4 pin P1 connector

   d) 15-pin SATA connector

3. A(n) ____ is a measure of electrical current.

   a) volt

   b) ohm

   c) watt

   d) amp

4. What is the best way to guard against electrostatic discharge (ESD)?

   a) Use a loopback plug.

   b) Leave the packing tape and cellophane on the hardware or software for as long as possible.

   c) Wear antistatic gloves.

   d) Work on carpet.

5. Which tool is used to test a port in a computer or other device to make sure the port is working, and might also be used to test the throughput or speed of the port?

   a) POST diagnostic card

   b) Multimeter

   c) Loopback plug

   d) Rectifier

6. True or false? A computer case can be a mobile case used with laptops and tablet PCs.

7. True or false? In the United States, the input voltage to the power supply is 220 volts.

8. True or false? Blowing air out of a computer case does a better job of keeping the system cool compared to blowing air into a case.

9. True or false? Always put yourself in a position where you are the path of least resistance between the hot line and ground.

10. True or false? When working on a CRT monitor, power supply, or laser printer, wear an antistatic grounding bracelet.

11. The standards that describe the size, shape, screw hole positions, and major features of these interconnected components are called ____.

12. ____ travels in only one direction and is the type of current that most electronic devices require, including computers.

13. Class ____ fire extinguishers use nonconductive chemicals to put out a fire caused by electricity.

14. ____ BIOS manages essential devices (such as the keyboard, mouse, hard drive, and monitor) before the OS is launched.

15. A(n) ____ explains how to properly handle substances such as chemical solvents and how to dispose of them.

Working Inside a Computer

This chapter and Chapter 1 work together as a pair to show you how to safely work inside a computer. In Chapter 1, you learned about all the safety procedures you should follow when working inside a computer. In this chapter, you apply these skills as you learn how to open a computer case and disassemble and reassemble the components in a desktop computer system. You also learn about the fans, heat sinks, and other devices needed to keep a system cool. Finally, you learn how to select a power supply to meet the wattage needs of a system.

HOW TO WORK INSIDE A COMPUTER CASE

A+
220-801
1.2, 5.1

In this part of the chapter, you'll learn how to take a computer apart and put it back together. This skill is needed in this and other chapters as you learn to add or replace computer parts inside the case and perhaps even build a system from scratch. As you read the following steps, you might want to perform the Hands-on Projects, which allow you to follow along by taking a computer apart. As you do so, be sure to follow all the safety precautions discussed in Chapter 1.

In the steps that follow, each major computer component is identified and described. You learn much more about each component later in the book. Take your time—*don't rush*—as you take apart a computer for the first time. It can be a great learning experience or an expensive disaster! As you work, pay attention to the details, and work with care.

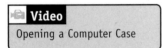

Video
Opening a Computer Case

STEP 1: PLAN AND ORGANIZE YOUR WORK

When you first begin to learn how to work inside a computer case, make it a point to practice good organization skills. If you keep your notes, tools, screws, and computer parts well organized, your work goes smoother and is more fun. Here are some tips to keep in mind:

- Make notes as you work so that you can backtrack later if necessary. (When you're first learning to take a computer apart, it's really easy to forget where everything fits when it's time to put it back together. Also, in troubleshooting, you want to avoid repeating or overlooking things to try.)
- Remove loose jewelry that might get caught in cables and components as you work.
- To stay organized and not lose small parts, keep screws and spacers orderly and in one place, such as a cup or tray.
- Don't stack boards on top of each other: You could accidentally dislodge a chip this way. When you remove a circuit board or drive from a computer, carefully lay it on an antistatic mat or in an antistatic bag in a place where it won't get bumped.
- When handling motherboards, cards, or drives, don't touch the chips on the device. Hold expansion cards by the edges. Don't touch any soldered components on a card, and don't touch the edge connectors unless it's absolutely necessary. All this helps prevent damage from static electricity. Also, your fingerprints on the edge connectors can later cause corrosion.
- To protect a microchip, don't touch it with a magnetized screwdriver.
- Never ever touch the inside of a computer that is turned on. The one exception to this rule is when you're using a multimeter to measure voltage output.
- Consider the monitor and the power supply to be "black boxes." Never remove the cover or put your hands inside this equipment unless you know about the hazards of charged capacitors and have been trained to deal with them. The power supply and monitor contain enough power to kill you, even when they are unplugged.
- As you work, remember to watch out for sharp edges on computer cases that can cut you.
- In a classroom environment, after you have reassembled everything, have your instructor check your work before you put the cover back on and power up.

Now that you've prepared your work area and tools, put on your ground bracelet and let's get started with opening the computer case.

A+
220-801
1.2, 5.1

STEP 2: OPEN THE COMPUTER CASE AND EXAMINE THE SYSTEM

Here are the steps to open a computer case:

1. **Back up important data.** If you are starting with a working computer, make sure important data is first backed up. Copy the data to an external storage device such as a flash drive or external hard drive. If something goes wrong while you're working inside the computer, at least your data will be safe.

2. **Power down the system and unplug it.** Unplug the power, monitor, mouse, and keyboard cables, and any other peripherals or cables attached and move them out of your way.

> ⚡ **Caution** When you power down a computer and even turn off the power switch on the rear of the computer case, know that residual power is still on. Some motherboards even have a small light inside the case to remind you of this fact and to warn you that power is still getting to the system. Therefore, be sure to always unplug the power cord before opening a case.

3. **Press and hold down the power button for a moment.** After you unplug the computer, press the power button for about three seconds to completely drain the power supply (see Figure 2-1). Sometimes when you do so, you'll hear the fans quickly start and go off as residual power is drained. Only then is it safe to work inside the case.

© Cengage Learning 2014

Figure 2-1   Press the power button after the computer is unplugged

4. **Have a plastic bag or cup handy to hold screws.** When you reassemble the PC, you will need to insert the same screws in the same holes. This is especially important with the hard drive because screws that are too long can puncture the hard drive housing.

A+
220-801
1.2, 5.1

5. **Open the case cover.** Sometimes I think figuring out how to open a computer case is the most difficult part of disassembling. If you need help figuring it out, check the user manual or web site of the case manufacturer. To remove the computer case cover, do the following:

▲ Many newer cases require you to start by laying the case on its side and removing the faceplate on the front of the case first. Other cases require you to remove a side panel first, and really older cases require you to first remove the entire sides and top as a single unit. Study your case for the correct approach.

▲ Most cases have panels on each side of the case that can be removed. It is usually necessary to only remove the one panel to expose the top of the motherboard. To know which panel to remove, look at where the ports are on the rear of the case. For example, in Figure 2-2, the ports on this motherboard are on the left side of the case, indicating the bottom of the motherboard is on the left. Therefore, you will want to remove the right panel to expose the top of this motherboard. Lay the case down to its left so that the ports and the motherboard are sitting on the bottom. Later, depending on how drives are installed, it might become necessary to remove the bottom panel in order to remove the screws that hold the drives in place.

Motherboard is mounted to this side of the case

© Cengage Learning 2014

Figure 2-2 Decide which side panel to remove

Locate the screws that hold the side panel in place. Be careful not to unscrew any screws besides these. The other screws probably are holding the power supply, fan, and other components in place (see Figure 2-3). Place the screws in the cup or bag used for that purpose. Some cases use clips on a side panel in addition to or instead of screws (see Figure 2-4).

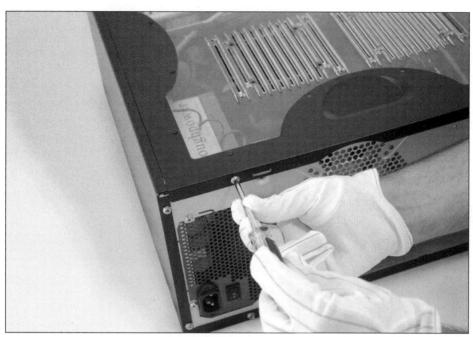

Figure 2-3 Locate the screws that hold the side panel in place

© Cengage Learning 2014

Figure 2-4 On this system, clips hold the side panel in place

© Cengage Learning 2014

A+
220-801
1.2, 5.1

◢ After the screws are removed, slide the panel toward the rear, and then lift it off the case (see Figure 2-5).

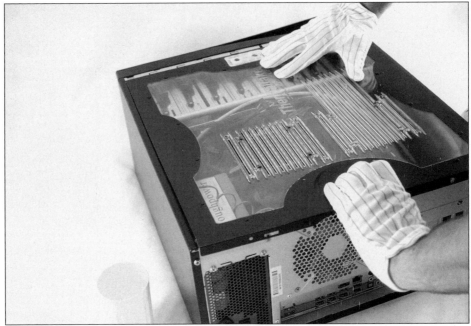

© Cengage Learning 2014

Figure 2-5   Slide the panel to the rear of the case

◢ Some cases require you to pop the front panel off the case before removing the side panels. Look for a lever on the bottom of the panel and hinges at the top. Squeeze the lever to release the front panel and lift it off the case (see Figure 2-6).

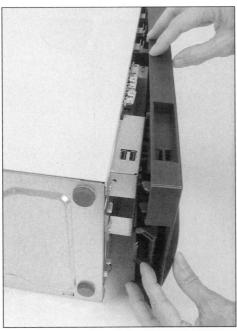

© Cengage Learning 2014

Figure 2-6   Newer cases require you to remove the front panel before removing the side panel of a computer case

Then remove a single screw (see Figure 2-7) and slide the side panel to the front and then off the case (see Figure 2-8).

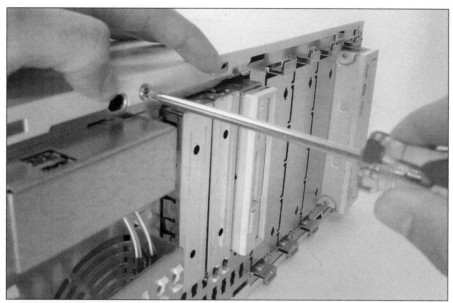

Figure 2-7   One screw holds the side panel in place

© Cengage Learning 2014

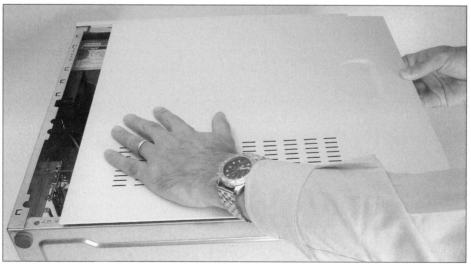

Figure 2-8   Slide the side panel to the front of the case and then lift it off the case

© Cengage Learning 2014

6. **Clip your ground bracelet to the side of the computer case.** To dissipate any charge between you and the computer, put on your ground bracelet if you have not already done so. Then clip the alligator clip on the ground bracelet to the side of the computer case (see Figure 2-9).

After you open a computer case, the main components you see inside are the power supply, motherboard, and drives installed in drive bays. You also see a lot of cables and wires connecting various components. These cables are power cables from the power supply to various components, or cables carrying data and instructions between components. The best way to know the purpose of a cable is to follow the cable from its source to destination.

A+
220-801
1.2, 5.1

© Cengage Learning 2014

Figure 2-9 Attach the alligator clip of your ground bracelet to the side of the computer case

STEP 3: REMOVE EXPANSION CARDS

If you plan to remove several components, draw a diagram of all cable connections to the motherboard, expansion cards, and drives. You might need the cable connection diagram to help you reassemble. Note where each cable begins and ends, and pay particular attention to the small wires and connectors that connect the lights, switches, and ports on the front of the case to the motherboard. It's important to be careful about diagramming these because it is so easy to connect them in the wrong position later when you reassemble. If you want, use a felt-tip marker to make a mark across components, to indicate a cable connection, board placement, motherboard orientation, speaker connection, brackets, and so on, so that you can simply line up the marks when you reassemble. This method, however, probably won't work for the front case wires because they are so small. For these, consider writing down the color of the wires and their position on the pins (see Figure 2-10).

> **Notes** A connector on a motherboard that consists of pins that stick up from the board is called a header. For example, the group of pins shown in Figure 2-10 is called the **front panel header**.

Computer systems vary in so many ways, it's impossible to list the exact order to disassemble one. Most likely, however, you need to remove the expansion cards first. Do the following to remove the expansion cards:

1. Remove any wire or cable connected to the card.

2. Remove the screw holding the card to the case (see Figure 2-11).

© Cengage Learning 2014

Figure 2-10 Diagram the pin locations of the color-coded wires that connect to the front of the case

© Cengage Learning 2014

Figure 2-11 Remove the screw holding an expansion card to the case

A+
220-801
1.2, 5.1

3. Grasp the card with both hands and remove it by lifting straight up. If you have trouble removing it from the expansion slot, you can *very slightly* rock the card from end to end (*not* side to side). Rocking the card from side to side might spread the slot opening and weaken the connection.

4. As you remove the card, don't put your fingers on the edge connectors or touch a chip, and don't stack the cards on top of one another. Lay each card aside on a flat surface, preferably in an antistatic bag.

> **Notes** Some video cards use a latch that helps to hold the card securely in the slot. To remove these cards, use one finger to hold the latch back from the slot, as shown in Figure 2-12, as you pull the card up and out of the slot.

© Cengage Learning 2014

Figure 2-12   Hold the retention mechanism back as you remove a video card from its expansion slot

STEP 4: REMOVE THE MOTHERBOARD, POWER SUPPLY, AND DRIVES

Depending on the system, you might need to remove the motherboard next or remove the drives next. My choice is to first remove the motherboard. It and the processor are the most expensive and easily damaged parts in the system. I like to get them out of harm's way before working with the drives. However, in some cases, you must remove the drives or the power supply before you can get to the motherboard. Study your situation and decide which to do first. To remove the motherboard, do the following:

1. Unplug the power supply lines to the motherboard. There might also be an audio wire from the optical drive to the motherboard. Disconnect it from the motherboard.

2. Unplug PATA, SATA, and floppy drive cables to the motherboard.

3. The next step is to disconnect wires leading from the front of the computer case to the motherboard, which are called the **front panel connectors**. If you don't have the motherboard manual handy, be very careful to diagram how these wires connect because they are never labeled well on a motherboard. Make a careful diagram and then disconnect the wires. Figure 2-13 shows five leads and the pins on the motherboard front panel header that receive these leads. The pins are color-coded and cryptically labeled on the board.

© Cengage Learning 2014

Figure 2-13   Five leads from the front panel connect to two rows of pins on the motherboard front panel header

4. Disconnect any other cables or wires connected to the motherboard. A case fan might be getting power by a small wire connected to the motherboard. In addition, USB ports on the front of the computer case might be connected by a cable to the motherboard.

5. You're now ready to remove the screws that hold the motherboard to the case. A motherboard is installed so that the bottom of the board does not touch the case. If the fine traces or lines on the bottom of the board were to touch the case, a short would result when the system is running. To keep the board from touching the case, screw holes are elevated, or you'll see **spacers**, also called **standoffs**, which are round plastic or metal pegs that separate the board from the case. Carefully pop off these spacers and/or remove the screws (up to nine) that hold the board to the case (see Figure 2-14) and then remove the board. Set it aside in a safe place. Figure 2-15 shows a motherboard sitting to the side of these spacers. One spacer is in place and the other is lying beside its case holes. Also notice in the photo the two holes in the motherboard where screws are used to connect the board to the spacers.

A+
220-801
1.2, 5.1

© Cengage Learning 2014

Figure 2-14   Remove up to nine screws that hold the motherboard to the case

© Cengage Learning 2014

Figure 2-15   This motherboard connects to a case using screws and spacers that keep the board from touching the case

> **Notes**   When you're replacing a motherboard in a case that is not the same size as the original board, you can use needle-nose pliers to unplug a standoff so you can move it to a new hole.

6. The motherboard should now be free and you can carefully remove it from the case, as shown in Figure 2-16.

Figure 2-16 Remove the motherboard from the case

© Cengage Learning 2014

> ⚡ **Caution** Some processors have heavy cooling assemblies installed on top of them. For these systems, it is best to remove the cooler before you take the motherboard out of the case because the motherboard is not designed to support this heavy cooler when the motherboard is not securely seated in the case. How to remove the cooler is covered in Chapter 4.

7. To remove the power supply from the case, look for screws that attach the power supply to the computer case, as shown in Figure 2-17. Be careful not to remove any screws that hold the power supply housing together. You do not want to take the housing apart. After you have removed the screws, the power supply still might not be free. Sometimes, it is attached to the case on the underside by recessed slots. Turn the case over and look on the bottom for these slots. If they are present, determine in which direction you need to slide the power supply to free it from the case.

8. Remove each drive next, handling the drives with care. Here are some tips:

▲ Some drives have one or two screws on each side of the drive attaching the drive to the drive bay. After you remove the screws, the drive slides to the front or to the rear and then out of the case.

A+
220-801
1.2, 5.1

© Cengage Learning 2014

Figure 2-17 Removing the power supply mounting screws

▲ Sometimes, there is a catch underneath the drive that you must lift up as you slide the drive forward.

▲ Some drive bays have a clipping mechanism to hold the drive in the bay. First release the clip and then pull the drive forward and out of the bay (see Figure 2-18). Handle the drives with care. Some drives have an exposed circuit board on the bottom of the drive. Don't touch this board.

© Cengage Learning 2014

Figure 2-18 To remove this CD drive, first pull the clip forward to release the drive from the bay

A+
220-801
1.2, 5.1

◢ Some cases have a removable bay for small drives (see Figure 2-19). These bays can hold narrow drives such as hard drives, floppy drives, and tape drives. The bay is removed first and then the drives are removed from the bay. To remove the bay, first remove the screws or release the clip holding the bay in place and then slide the bay out of the case. The drives are usually installed in the bay with two screws on each side of each drive. Remove the screws and then the drives (see Figure 2-20).

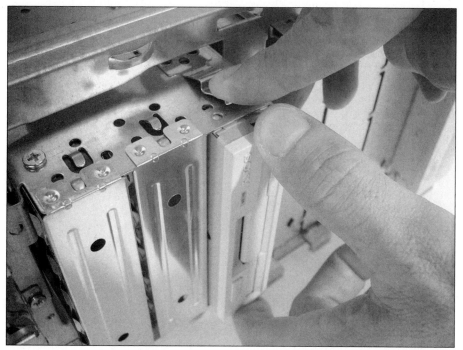

© Cengage Learning 2014

Figure 2-19 Push down on the clip and then slide the removable bay forward and out of the case

© Cengage Learning 2014

Figure 2-20 Drives in this removable bay are held in place with screws on each side of the bay

A+
220-801
1.2, 5.1

STEPS TO PUT A COMPUTER BACK TOGETHER

To reassemble a computer, reverse the process of disassembling. Here is where your diagrams will be really useful and having the screws and cables organized will also help. In the directions that follow, we're also considering the possibility that you are installing a replacement part as you reassemble the system. Do the following:

1. Install components in the case in this order: power supply, drives, motherboard, and cards. When installing drives, know that for some systems, it's easier to connect data cables to the drives and then slide the drives into the bay. If the drive is anchored to the bay with screws or latches, be careful to align the front of the drive flush with the front of the case before installing screws or pushing in the latches (see Figure 2-21).

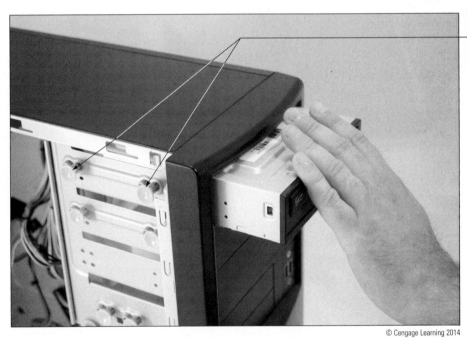

Push in two latches to secure the drive

© Cengage Learning 2014

Figure 2-21 Align the front of the drive flush with the case front and then anchor with a screw

2. Place the motherboard inside the case. Make sure the ports stick out of the I/O shield at the rear of the case and the screw holes line up with screw holes on the bottom of the case. Figure 2-22 shows how you must align the screw holes on the motherboard with those in the case. There should be at least six screw sets, and there might be as many as nine. Use as many screws as there are holes in the motherboard. Figure 2-23 shows one screw being put in place.

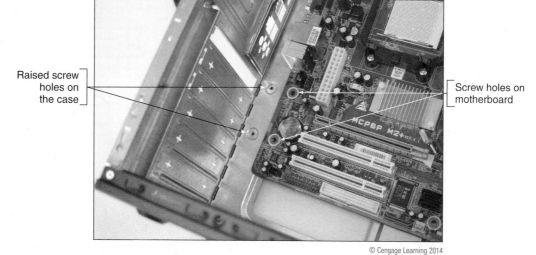

Raised screw
holes on
the case

Screw holes on
motherboard

© Cengage Learning 2014

Figure 2-22   Align screw holes in the case with those on the motherboard

© Cengage Learning 2014

Figure 2-23   Use one screw in each screw hole on the motherboard

3. Connect the power cords from the power supply to the motherboard. A system will always need the main P1 power connector and most likely will need the 4-pin auxiliary connector for the processor. Other power connectors might be needed depending on the devices you later install in the system. Here are the details:

▲ Connect the P1 power connector from the power supply to the motherboard (see Figure 2-24).

A+
220-801
1.2, 5.1

© Cengage Learning 2014

Figure 2-24 The 24-pin connector supplies power to the motherboard

▲ Connect the 4-pin auxiliary power cord coming from the power supply to the motherboard, as shown in Figure 2-25. This cord supplies the supplemental power required for the processor.

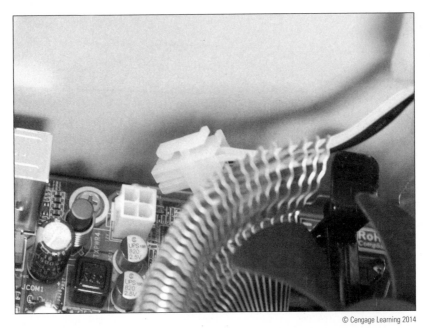

© Cengage Learning 2014

Figure 2-25 The auxiliary 4-pin power cord provides power to the processor

▲ A board might have a 6-pin or 8-pin PCIe power connector (see Figure 2-26). If the board has either connector, connect the 6-pin or 8-pin cord from the power supply to the connector. If a power supply doesn't have this connector, you can use an adapter to convert two Molex connectors to a PCIe connector.

2

A+
220-801
1.2, 5.1

8-pin connector

© Cengage Learning 2014

Figure 2-26   8-pin PCIe Version 2.0 power connector

◢ Some boards designed to support multiple PCIe video cards will have additional power connectors on the board to power these wattage-hungry cards. For example, Figure 2-27(a) shows a Molex-style connector on one board that provides auxiliary power to PCIe graphics cards. This same board offers a SATA-style connector, shown in Figure 2-27(b). The motherboard documentation says to use just one of these auxiliary power connectors to provide additional wattage for PCIe video cards.

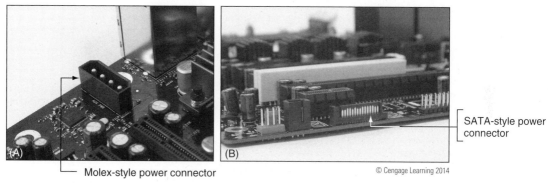

SATA-style power connector

Molex-style power connector

(A)   (B)

© Cengage Learning 2014

Figure 2-27   Auxiliary power connectors to support PCIe

◢ To power the case fan, connect the power cord from the fan to pins on the motherboard labeled Fan Header. Alternately, some case fans use a 4-pin Molex connector that connects to a power cable coming directly from the power supply.

◢ If a CPU and cooler are already installed on the motherboard, connect the power cord from the CPU fan to the pins on the motherboard labeled CPU Fan Header.

4. Connect the wire leads from the front panel of the case to the front panel header on the motherboard. These are the wires for the switches, lights, and ports on the front of the computer. Because your case and your motherboard might not have been made by the same manufacturer, you need to pay close attention to the source of the wires to determine where they connect on the motherboard. For example, Figure 2-28 shows a computer case that has seven connectors from the front panel that connect to the motherboard. Figure 2-29 shows the front panel header on the motherboard for these lights and switches. If you look closely at the board in Figure 2-29, you can see labels identifying the pins.

A+
220-801
1.2, 5.1

Figure 2-28 Seven connectors from the front panel connect to the motherboard

© Cengage Learning 2014

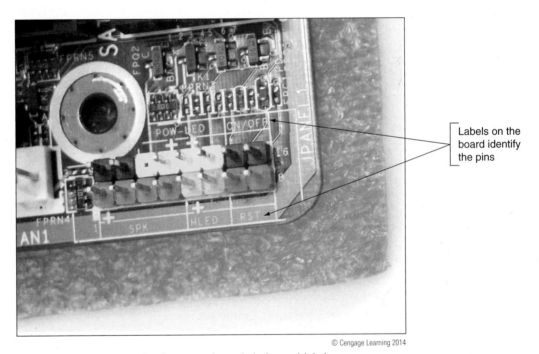

Labels on the
board identify
the pins

© Cengage Learning 2014

Figure 2-29 Front panel header uses color-coded pins and labels

The five connectors on the right side of Figure 2-28 from right to left are labeled as follows:

▲ *Power SW.* Controls power to the motherboard; must be connected for the PC to power up
▲ *HDD LED.* Controls the drive activity light on the front panel that lights up when any SATA or IDE device is in use (HDD stands for hard disk drive; LED stands for light-emitting diode; and an LED is a light on the front panel.)
▲ *Power LED+.* Positive LED controls the power light and indicates that power is on
▲ *Power LED−.* Negative LED controls the power light; the two positive and negative leads indicate that power is on
▲ *Reset SW.* Switch used to reboot the computer

2

A+
220-801
1.2, 5.1

Notes Positive wires connecting the front panel to the motherboard are usually a solid color, and negative wires are usually white or striped.

To help orient the connector on the motherboard pins, look for a small triangle embedded on the connector that marks one of the outside wires as pin 1 (see Figure 2-30). Look for pin 1 to be labeled on the motherboard as a small 1 embedded to either the right or the left of the group of pins. If the labels on the board are not clear, turn to the motherboard user guide for help. The diagram in Figure 2-31 shows what you can expect from one motherboard user guide. Notice pin 1 is identified as a square pin in the diagram, rather than round like the other pins.

Notes If the user guide is not handy, you can download it from the motherboard manufacturer's web site. Search on the brand and model number of the board, which is imprinted somewhere on the board.

Sometimes the motherboard documentation is not clear, but guessing is okay when connecting a wire to a front panel header connection. If it doesn't work, no harm is done. Figure 2-32 shows all front panel wires in place and the little speaker also connected to the front panel header pins.

© Cengage Learning 2014

Figure 2-30 Look for the small triangle embedded on the wire lead connectors to orient the connector correctly to the motherboard connector pins

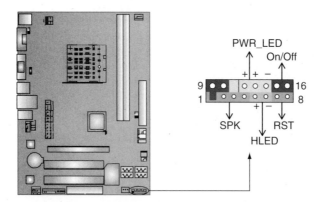

Pin	Assignment	Function	Pin	Assignment	Function
1	+5 V	Speaker connector	9	N/A	N/A
2	N/A		10	N/A	
3	N/A		11	N/A	N/A
4	Speaker		12	Power LED (+)	Power LED
5	HDD LED (+)	Hard drive LED	13	Power LED (+)	
6	HDD LED (−)		14	Power LED (−)	
7	Ground	Reset button	15	Power button	Power-on button
8	Reset control		16	Ground	

© Cengage Learning 2014

Figure 2-31 Documentation for front panel header connections

A+
220-801
1.2, 5.1

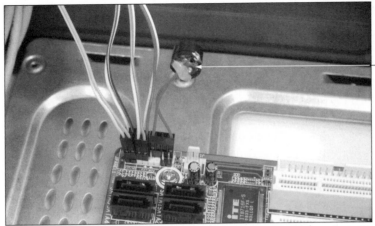

Speaker connected
to front panel
header

© Cengage Learning 2014

Figure 2-32 Front panel header with all connectors in place

5. Connect wires to ports on the front panel of the case. Depending on your motherboard and case, there might be cables to connect audio ports or USB ports on the front of the case to headers on the motherboard. Audio and USB connectors are the two left connectors shown in Figure 2-28. You can see these ports for audio and USB on the front of the case in Figure 2-33. Look in the motherboard documentation for the location of these connectors. The audio and USB connectors are labeled for one board in Figures 2-34(a) and (b).

Audio-out and
microphone ports

USB ports

© Cengage Learning 2014

Figure 2-33 Ports on the front of the computer case

Front audio header

Three USB headers

© Cengage Learning 2014

Figure 2-34 Connectors for front panel ports

A+
220-801
1.2, 5.1

6. Install the video card and any other expansion cards.

7. Take a few minutes to double-check each connection to make sure it is correct and snug. Verify all required power cords are connected correctly and the video card is seated solidly in its slot. Also verify that no wires or cables are obstructing fans. You can use cable ties to tie wires up and out of the way.

8. Plug in the keyboard, monitor, and mouse.

9. In a classroom environment, have the instructor check your work before you close the case and power up.

10. Turn on the power and check that the PC is working properly. If the PC does not work, most likely the problem is a loose connection. Just turn off the power and go back and check each cable connection and each expansion card. You probably have not solidly seated a card in the slot. After you have double-checked, try again.

Now step back and congratulate yourself on a job well done! By taking a computer apart and putting it back together, you've learned much about how computer parts interconnect and work. So now you're ready to move on to study each subsystem or major component in the computer case and how to support it. Let's begin with the pieces and parts used to keep a system from overheating.

COOLING METHODS AND DEVICES

A+
220-801
1.6

The processor, expansion cards, and other components in the case produce heat, and, if they get overheated, the system can get unstable and components can fail or be damaged. As a PC support technician, you need to know how to keep a system cool. Devices that are used to keep a system cool include CPU fans, case fans, coolers, heat sinks, liquid cooling systems, and dust-preventing tools.

In this part of the chapter, you learn about these several methods to keep the system cool. We begin with keeping the processor cool.

PROCESSOR COOLERS, FANS, AND HEAT SINKS

Because a processor generates so much heat, computer systems use a cooling assembly to keep temperatures below the Intel maximum limit of 185 degrees Fahrenheit/85 degrees Celsius. Good processor coolers maintain a temperature of 90–110 degrees F (32–43 degrees C). The **cooler** (see Figure 2-35) sits on top of the processor and consists of a fan and a heat sink. A **heat sink** uses fins that draw heat away from the processor. The fan can then blow the heat away.

© Cengage Learning 2014

Figure 2-35 A cooler sits on top of a processor to help keep it cool

A+
220-801
1.6

A cooler is made of aluminum, copper, or a combination of both. Copper is more expensive, but does a better job of conducting heat. For example, the Thermaltake (*www .thermaltake.com*) multisocket cooler shown in Figure 2-36 is made of copper and has an adjustable fan control.

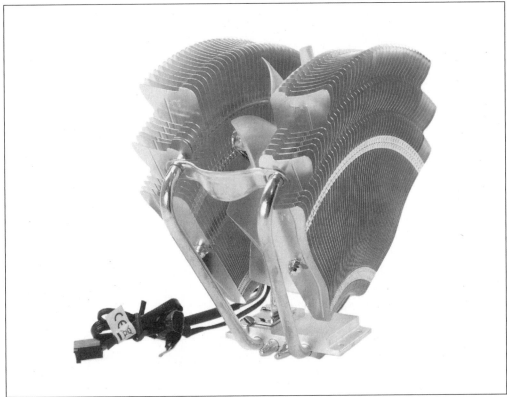

© Cengage Learning 2014

Figure 2-36   The Thermaltake V1 copper cooler fits Intel LGA1366 and LGA775 and AMD AM2 and AM2+ sockets

The cooler is bracketed to the motherboard using a wire or plastic clip. A creamlike **thermal compound** is placed between the bottom of the cooler heatsink and the top of the processor. This compound eliminates air pockets, helping to draw heat off the processor. The thermal compound transmits heat better than air and makes an airtight connection between the fan and the processor. When processors and coolers are boxed together, the cooler heatsink might have thermal compound already stuck to the bottom (see Figure 2-37).

To get its power, the fan power cord connects to a 4-pin fan header on the motherboard (see Figure 2-38). The fan connector will have three or four holes. A three-hole connector can fit onto a 4-pin header; just ignore the last pin. A 4-pin header on the motherboard supports pulse width modulation (PWM) that controls fan speed in order to reduce the overall noise in a system. If you use a fan power cord with three pins, know that the fan will always operate at the same speed. You learn how to install a processor and cooler in Chapter 4.

2

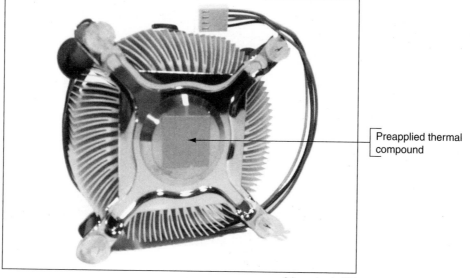

© Cengage Learning 2014

Preapplied thermal compound

Figure 2-37 Thermal compound is already stuck to the bottom of this cooler that was purchased boxed with the processor

© Cengage Learning 2014

3-pin CPU fan power cord

4-pin CPU fan header

Figure 2-38 A cooler fan gets its power from a 4-pin PWM header on the motherboard

CASE FANS AND OTHER FANS AND HEAT SINKS

To prevent overheating, you can also install additional case fans. Most cases have one or more positions on the case to hold a **case fan** to help draw air out of the case. Figure 2-39 shows holes on the rear of a case designed to hold a case fan.

A computer case might need as many as seven or eight fans mounted inside the case; however, the trend is to use fewer and larger fans. Generally, large fans tend to perform better and run quieter than small fans.

A+
220-801
1.6

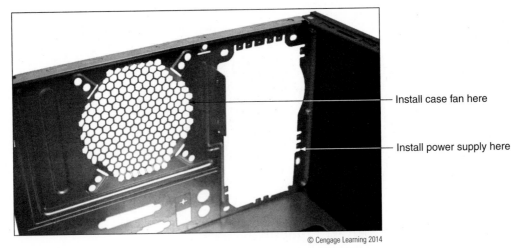

© Cengage Learning 2014

Install case fan here

Install power supply here

Figure 2-39   Install a case fan on the rear of this case to help keep the
system cool

Processors and video cards, also called graphics cards, are the two highest heat producers
in a system. Some graphics cards come with a fan on the side of the card. You can also
purchase heat sinks and fans to mount on a card to keep it cool. Another solution is to use
a fan card mounted next to the graphics card. Figure 2-40 shows a PCI fan card. Be sure
you select the fan card that fits the expansion slot you plan to use, and make sure there's
enough clearance beside the graphics card for the fan card to fit.

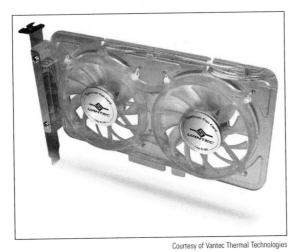

Courtesy of Vantec Thermal Technologies

Figure 2-40   A PCI fan card by Vantec can be used next
to a high-end graphics card to help keep
it cool

For additional cooling, consider a RAM cooler such as the one in Figure 2-41. It clips
over a DIMM. A fan might be powered by a SATA power connector or 4-pin Molex power
connector. The fan in Figure 2-41 uses a Molex connector. You can use an adapter to
convert a SATA or Molex connector to whichever the power supply provides.

When selecting any fan or cooler, take into consideration the added noise level and the
ease of installation. Some coolers and fans can use a temperature sensor that controls the
fan. Also consider the guarantee made by the cooler or fan manufacturer.

2

4-pin power connector

DIMM cover

© Cengage Learning 2014

Figure 2-41 A RAM cooler keeps memory modules cool

LIQUID COOLING SYSTEMS

In addition to using fans, heat sinks, and thermal compound to keep a processor cool, a liquid cooling system can be used. For the most part, they are used by hobbyists attempting to overclock to the max a processor in a gaming computer. Recently, however, Intel has recommended using a liquid cooling system with its processors that use the LGA2011 socket on a motherboard. (You learn more about this socket in Chapter 5.) Liquid cooling systems tend to run quieter than other cooling methods. They might include a PCI card that has a power supply, temperature sensor, and processor to control the cooler.

Using liquid cooling, a small pump sits inside the computer case, and tubes move liquid around components and then away from them to a place where fans can cool the liquid, similar to how a car radiator works. Figure 2-42 shows one liquid cooling system where the liquid is cooled by fans sitting inside a large case. Sometimes, however, the liquid is pumped outside the case, where it is cooled.

Courtesy of Thermaltake (USA) Inc.

Figure 2-42 A liquid cooling system pumps liquid outside and away from components where fans can then cool the liquid

A+
220-801
1.6

DEALING WITH DUST

Dust is not good for a PC because it insulates PC parts like a blanket, which can cause them to overheat. Dust inside fans can jam fans, and fans not working can cause a system to overheat (see Figure 2-43). Therefore, ridding the PC of dust is an important part of keeping a system cool and should be done as part of a regular preventive maintenance plan, at least twice a year. You can blow the dust out of the case using a can of compressed air, or you can vacuum out the dust using a special antistatic vacuum designed to be used around sensitive equipment. Whenever you open a computer case, take a few minutes to rid the inside of dust. And while you're cleaning up dust, don't forget to blow or vacuum out the keyboard.

© Cengage Learning 2014

Figure 2-43   This dust-jammed fan caused a system to overheat

> **Notes** When working in a customer's office or home, be sure you clean up any mess you create from blowing dust out of a computer case.

The motherboard BIOS records the temperatures of the processor and inside the case, and you can read this information on BIOS setup screens, which you learn to do in Chapter 4. In Chapter 13, you learn how to troubleshoot problems with overheating.

SELECTING A POWER SUPPLY

A+
220-801
1.8

To finish up this chapter about working inside a computer, let's discuss what you need to consider when purchasing a power supply. Reasons you might need to purchase a power supply are when you are building a new system from scratch, a power supply in an existing system fails, or the power supply in an existing system is not adequate for the system.

When building a new system, you can purchase a computer case with the power supply already installed (see Figure 2-44), or you can purchase a power supply separate from the case.

© Cengage Learning 2014

Figure 2-44 This case comes with a power supply, power cord, and bag of screws

A+
220-801
1.8

Let's now turn our attention to the features of a power supply.

TYPES AND CHARACTERISTICS OF POWER SUPPLIES

As you select the right power supply for a system, you need to be aware of the following power supply features:

▲ *ATX or Micro-ATX form factor.* The form factor of a power supply determines the size of the power supply and the placement of screw holes and slots used to anchor the power supply to the case.

▲ *Wattage ratings.* A power supply has wattage ratings, which are the amounts of power it can supply. These wattage capacities are listed in the documentation and on the side of a power supply, as shown in Figure 2-45. When selecting a power supply, pay particular attention to the capacity for the +12 V rail. (A rail is the term used to describe each voltage line of the power supply.) The +12 V rail is the most used, especially in high-end gaming systems. Sometimes you need to use a power supply with a higher-than-needed overall wattage to get enough wattage on this one rail. Also, a high-end PSU might have a second +12 V rail.

Power supply ratings on the label

© Cengage Learning 2014

Figure 2-45 Consider the number and type of power connectors and the wattage ratings of a power supply

▲ *Number and type of connectors.* Consider the number and type of power cables and connectors the unit provides. Connector types are shown in Table 1-2 of Chapter 1. Some power supplies include detached power cables that you can plug into connectors on the side of the unit. By using only the power cables you need, extra power cables don't get in the way of airflow inside the computer case.

> **Notes** If a power supply doesn't have the connector you need, it is likely you can buy an adapter to convert one connector to another. For example, Figure 2-46 shows an adapter that converts two Molex cables to one 12 V 6-pin PCIe connector.

▲ *Fans inside the PSU.* Every power supply has a fan inside its case; some have two fans. The fan can be mounted on the back or top of the PSU. Fans range in size from 80mm to 150mm wide. The larger the fan, the better job it does and the quieter it runs. Some PSUs can automatically adjust the fan speed based on the internal temperature of the system.

> **Notes** Some power supplies are designed without fans so that they can be used in home theater systems or other areas where quiet operation is a requirement.

© Cengage Learning 2014

Figure 2-46   This adapter converts two Molex cables to a single 12 V 6-pin PCIe connector

▲ *Extra feature.* Consider the warranty of the power supply and the overall quality. Some power supplies are designed to support two video cards used in a gaming computer. Two technologies used for dual video cards are SLI by NVIDIA and Crossfire by AMD. If you plan to use dual video cards, use a PSU that supports SLI or Crossfire used by the video cards. Know that more expensive power supplies are quieter, last longer, and don't put off as much heat as less expensive ones. Also, expect a good power supply to protect the system against overvoltage. Know that a power supply rated with Active PFC runs more efficiently and uses less electricity than other power supplies.

HOW TO CALCULATE WATTAGE CAPACITY

When deciding what wattage capacity you need for the power supply, consider the total wattage requirements of all components inside the case as well as USB and FireWire devices that get their power from ports connected to the motherboard.

> **A+ Exam Tip** The A+ 220-801 exam expects you to know how to select and install a power supply. You need to know how to decide on the wattage, connectors, and form factor of the power supply.

A+
220-801
1.8

Keep these two points in mind when selecting the correct wattage capacity for a power supply:

▲ *Video cards draw the most power.* Video cards draw the most power in a system, and they draw from the +12 V output. If your system has a video card, pay particular attention to the +12 V rating. The trend nowadays is for the motherboard to provide the video components and video port, thus reducing the overall wattage needs for a system. Video cards are primarily used in gaming computers or other systems that require high-quality graphics.

▲ *The power supply should be rated about 30 percent higher than expected needs.* Power supplies that run at less than peak performance last longer and don't overheat. In addition, a power supply loses some of its capacity over time. Also, don't worry about a higher-rated power supply using too much electricity. Components only draw what they need.

To know what size power supply you need, add up the wattage requirements of all components, and add 30 percent. Device technical documentation might give you the information you need. Table 2-1 lists appropriate wattage ratings for common devices with the 30 percent extra already added in. Alternately, you can use a wattage calculator provided on the web site of many manufacturers and vendors. Using the calculator, you enter the components in your system and then the calculator will recommend the wattage you need for your power supply.

Devices	Approximate Wattage
Moderately priced motherboard, processor, memory, keyboard, and mouse	100 watts
High-end motherboard, processor, memory, keyboard, and mouse	100 to 150 watts
Fan	5 watts
IDE (PATA) hard drive	25 watts
SATA hard drive	35 watts
CD-RW drive or tape drive	25 watts
DVD-RW or Blu-ray drive	35 watts
Low-end PCI video card	40 watts
Moderately priced video card	100 watts
High-end PCIe x16 video card	150–300 watts
PCI card (network card, Firewire card, or other PCI card)	20 watts
PCIe x16 card other than a video card	100 watts
Liquid cooling system (used in high-end gaming computers that put off a lot of heat)	50–150 watts

© Cengage Learning 2014

Table 2-1   To calculate the power supply rating you need, add up total wattage

Notes Some Dell motherboards and power supplies do not use the standard P1 pinouts for ATX, although the power connectors look the same. For this reason, never use a Dell power supply with a non-Dell motherboard, or a Dell motherboard with a non-Dell power supply, without first verifying that the power connector pinouts match; otherwise, you might destroy the power supply, the motherboard, or both. PC Power and Cooling (*www.pcpowerandcooling.com*) makes power supplies modified to work with a Dell motherboard.

A+
220-801
1.8

Table 2-2 lists a few case and power supply manufacturers.

Manufacturer	Web Site
Antec	www.antec.com
Cooler Master	www.coolermaster.com
ENlight Corporation	www.enlightcorp.com
PC Power and Cooling	www.pcpowerandcooling.com
Rosewill	www.rosewill.com
Silverstone	www.silverstonetek.com
Sunus Suntek	www.suntekgroup.com
Thermaltake	www.thermaltakeusa.com
Zalman	www.zalman.com

© Cengage Learning 2014

Table 2-2 Manufacturers of cases and power supplies for personal computers

>> CHAPTER SUMMARY

How to Work Inside a Computer Case

◢ When a PC support technician is disassembling or reassembling a computer, it is important to stay organized, keep careful notes, and follow all the safety procedures to protect the computer equipment.

◢ Before opening a computer case, shut down the system, unplug it, disconnect all cables, and press the power button to drain residual power.

◢ An expansion card fits in a slot on the motherboard and is anchored to the case by a single screw or clip.

Cooling Methods and Devices

◢ Devices that are used to keep a processor and system cool include CPU coolers and fans, case fans, heat sinks, and liquid cooling. Also, clean out the dust inside a case because dust can cause a system to overheat.

◢ Liquid cooling systems use liquids pumped through the system to keep it cool and are sometimes used by hobbyists when overclocking a system.

Selecting a Power Supply

◢ Important features of a power supply to consider when purchasing it are its form factor, wattage capacity, number and type of connectors it provides, fan size, support for dual video cards, and warranty.

◢ To decide on the wattage capacity of a power supply, add up the wattage requirements for all components in a system and then increase that total by about 30 percent.

>> KEY TERMS

For explanations of key terms, see the Glossary near the end of the book.

case fan	front panel header	spacers
cooler	heat sink	standoffs
front panel connectors	overclocking	thermal compound

>> REVIEW QUESTIONS

1. What is the first general step to complete before working inside a computer case?

    a) Demagnetize the microchip with a magnetized screwdriver.

    b) Completely drain the power supply.

    c) Remove each expansion card by rocking the cards from side to side.

    d) Plan and organize your work.

2. When is it physically safe to work inside the computer case?

    a) After all residual power is drained

    b) After you have demagnetized the microchip with a magnetized screwdriver

    c) After important data is backed up

    d) After peripherals or cables attached to the computer case are removed

3. The ____ sits on top of the processor and consists of a fan and a heat sink.

    a) power supply

    b) spacer

    c) cooler

    d) thermal compound

4. What determines the size of the power supply and the placement of screw holes and slots used to anchor the power supply to the case?

    a) The power supply wattage ratings

    b) The form factor of a power supply

    c) The number of fans inside the power supply

    d) The number and type of power cables and connectors the unit provides

5. To know what size power supply you need, add up the wattage requirements of all components, and add ____ percent.

    a) 10

    b) 20

    c) 30

    d) 40

6. True or false? Fingerprints on expansion card edge connectors can later cause corrosion.

7. True or false? The best way to know the purpose of a cable is to follow the cable from its source to destination.

8. True or false? Liquid cooling systems tend to run louder than other cooling methods.

9. True or false?   The larger the fan inside the power supply unit, the quieter it runs.

2

10. True or false? Video cards draw the least power in a system.

11. Wires leading from the front of the computer case to the motherboard are called the ____ connectors.

12. Spacers, also called ____, are round plastic or metal pegs that separate the board from the case.

13. A(n) ____ uses fins that draw heat away from the processor.

14. ____ compound transmits heat better than air and makes an airtight connection between the fan and the processor.

15. ____ is running a processor, motherboard, or video card at a higher frequency than the manufacturer recommends.

Introducing Windows Operating Systems

In this chapter, you will learn:

- How to use Windows to interface with users, files and folders, applications, and hardware

- About some Windows tools that you can use to examine and support the system

A computer needs both hardware and software to work. In Chapters 1 and 2, you learned about important hardware components and how to safely take a computer apart and put it back together. Those two chapters were your introduction to becoming a hardware technician. This chapter takes your PC support technician skills to the next level by introducing you to the operating system tools and skills you'll need to maintain, support, and troubleshoot Windows, hardware, and applications.

In this chapter, you'll learn about Microsoft Windows and how this operating system provides the interface between users and applications and between applications and hardware devices. You'll learn to use several Windows tools and utilities that are useful to change desktop settings, view and manage storage devices, examine a system, and troubleshoot simple problems with hardware and applications.

> **Notes** As a PC support technician, you should be aware of the older and current operating systems and how they have evolved over the years. Appendix A, *Operating Systems Past and Present*, gives you this quick history of operating systems.

USING WINDOWS

An **operating system (OS)** is software that controls a computer. In general, you can think of an operating system as the middleman between applications and hardware, between the user and hardware, and between the user and applications (see Figure 3-1).

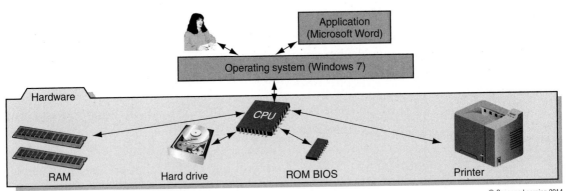

© Cengage Learning 2014

Figure 3-1 Users and applications depend on the OS to relate to all applications and hardware components

Several applications might be installed on a computer to meet various user needs, but a computer really needs only one operating system. Although there are important differences among them, all operating systems share the following four main functions:

▲ *Function 1*: Provide a user interface

- Performing housekeeping procedures requested by the user, often concerning storage devices, such as reorganizing a hard drive, deleting files, copying files, and changing the system date
- Providing a way for the user to manage the desktop, hardware, applications, and data

▲ *Function 2*: Manage files

- Managing files on hard drives, DVD drives, CD drives, USB flash drives, and other drives
- Creating, storing, retrieving, deleting, and moving files

▲ *Function 3*: Manage hardware

- Managing the BIOS (programs permanently stored on hardware devices)
- Managing memory, which is a temporary place to store data and instructions as they are being processed
- Diagnosing problems with software and hardware

3

- Interfacing between hardware and software (that is, interpreting application software needs to the hardware and interpreting hardware needs to application software)

◢ *Function 4*: Manage applications

- Installing and uninstalling applications
- Running applications and managing the interface to the hardware on behalf of an application

Windows 7 is the latest Microsoft operating system and is an upgrade to Windows XP. Every PC support technician needs to be a power user of Windows 7 and also be familiar with Vista and XP. This part of the chapter covers the two most important tools for using Windows 7/Vista/XP: The Windows desktop and Windows Explorer.

> **Notes** This chapter primarily covers Windows 7 and a little about Windows Vista and Windows XP. If you want to know more about Windows Vista, see Appendix B. If you want to learn more about Windows XP, see Appendix C. Vista and XP icons in the margin of a chapter tell you that related content about these OSs can be found in the appendices.

THE WINDOWS DESKTOP

**A+
220-802
1.1**

The **desktop** is the initial screen that is displayed after the user logs on and Windows is loaded. The Windows desktop provides a **graphical user interface** (GUI; pronounced "GOO-ee") that uses graphics as compared to a command-driven interface.

In this section, you will learn about the features of the desktop, including the Start menu and taskbar. You will also learn how to manage shortcuts and icons on the desktop. We use Windows 7 as our primary OS for learning. Minor differences about Vista and XP are noted here in the chapter. But don't forget that additional major differences about Vista are covered in Appendix B, and major differences about Windows XP are covered in Appendix C.

> **A+ Exam Tip** The A+ 220-802 exam covers Windows 7, Windows Vista, and Windows XP.

AERO USER INTERFACE

The Windows 7 and Vista desktop provides a 3-D user interface called the **Aero user interface** that gives a glassy appearance and is sometimes called Aero glass (see Figure 3-2). Windows 7 comes in several editions and each edition offers a different set of features. The Aero interface is not available for the Windows 7 Starter and Home Basic editions and is available on the Home Premium, Business, Enterprise, and Ultimate editions. To support the Aero interface, Windows 7 requires 1 GB of RAM and a video card or onboard video that supports the DirectX 9 graphics standard that has at least 128 MB of graphics memory.

THE START MENU

The Windows 7 Start menu is shown in Figure 3-3. Notice in the figure that the username for the person currently logged on is shown at the top right of the Start menu.

Figure 3-2 The Windows 7 desktop using the Aero interface has a glassy transparent look

Figure 3-3 The Windows 7 Start menu

User-oriented applications that are used often are listed in the white left columns (as shown in the figure) and can change from time to time. Items in the dark right column give access to user libraries and files and to OS utilities.

A+
220-802
1.1, 1.4

3

HOW TO LAUNCH AN APPLICATION

Let's open a few applications and then see how the Windows desktop can be used to manage these open applications. Four options to open an application are:

▲ *Use the Start menu*: Click the **Start** button, select **All Programs,** and then select the program from the list of installed software.

▲ *Use the Search box*: Click the **Start** button, and then enter the name of the program file or command in the *Search* box (see Figure 3-4). In Windows 7, the empty box is labeled the *Search programs and files* box. In Vista, the box is labeled the *Search* box, and in Windows XP, it is labeled the *Run* box. Program names you might enter in the *Search* or *Run* box include msinfo32 (to open the System Information window), Notepad (to open the Notepad text editor), and Explorer (to open Windows Explorer.) Incidentally, the Windows 7 and Vista search boxes can also find data files and folders and will search text within document files.

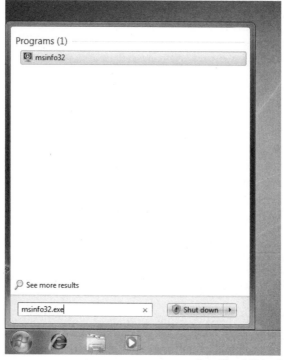

Source: Microsoft Windows 7

Figure 3-4 Use the Windows 7 *Search* box to launch a program

▲ *Use Windows Explorer or the Computer window*: Execute a program or launch an application file by double-clicking the icon beside the filename in Windows Explorer or the Computer window. (In Windows XP, the Computer window is called My Computer.) To use the Computer window in Windows 7 or Vista, click **Start, Computer.** The Computer window shown in Figure 3-5 appears. Double-click the drive on which the program file is stored. In our example, we double-clicked **Local Disk (C:).** Then we drilled down to the program file on the drive. Double-click the program file to launch it.

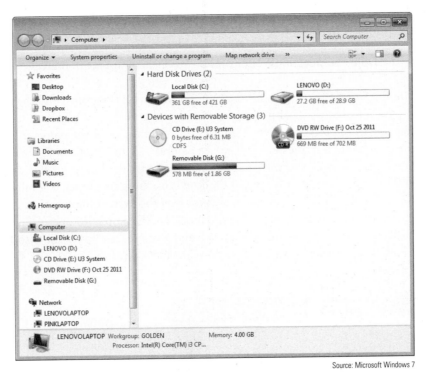

Source: Microsoft Windows 7

Figure 3-5 If you know the location of a program file, you can drill down to it and launch it from the Computer window

◢ *Use a shortcut icon*: A quick way to open an application you use often is to place a shortcut icon to the program on the desktop or place a program icon in the taskbar. A shortcut icon is a clickable item on the desktop that points to a program you can execute, or to a file or folder. One way to create a shortcut for a program is to right-click the program file in the Computer or Windows Explorer window and select **Create shortcut** from the menu that appears.

> **Notes** The difference between a window and a dialog box is a window can be resized, but a dialog box cannot. A dialog box is sometimes called a box.

When you launch a program, the program window appears on the desktop. You can close, move, or resize the window. Windows 7 Aero Snap and Aero Shake can help:

◢ **Aero Snap** automatically maximizes a window when you drag it to the top of the desktop. To restore a maximized window to its original size, drag the window downward on the screen. Drag a window to the right or left of the screen so that it snaps to the side of the screen to fill half the screen.

◢ Use **Aero Shake** to minimize all other windows except the one you shake. To shake a window, grab the title bar of the window and shake it. Shake again to restore the size of the other windows. You can also use the Maximize, Minimize, and Close buttons on a window.

> **Notes** If you are using the Aero interface, you can get a flip 3D view of applications by pressing **Win+Tab** (the Windows key and the Tab key). Then use the Tab key to move from one open application to another. Windows 7 Starter and Home Basic do not support the Aero interface, and, to conserve system resources, you can turn the feature off using other editions of Windows.

A+
220-802
1.1, 1.4

A+ Exam Tip The A+ 220-802 exam expects you to be able to use the Aero interface, including using Aero Snap and Shake.

A+
220-802
1.1

The Taskbar and Notification Area (System Tray)

The **taskbar** is normally located at the bottom of the Windows desktop, displaying information about open programs and providing quick access to others. Items displayed in the taskbar can be programs running or not running. An open application displays a program icon in the taskbar. If you are using the Aero interface, when you mouse over the icon, a thumbnail of the open application appears (see Figure 3-6).

Source: Microsoft Windows 7

Figure 3-6 Mouse over the Internet Explorer icon in the taskbar to see each open tab in IE

When you right-click an icon in the taskbar, the **Jump List** appears, which provides access to some of the major functions of the program (see Figure 3-7). When you mouse over the rectangle to the far right of the taskbar, all windows disappear so you can see the desktop and any gadgets you might have there. This feature is called **Aero Peek** because it gives you a peek at the desktop. Click the rectangle to minimize all windows. Click the rectangle again to restore all windows.

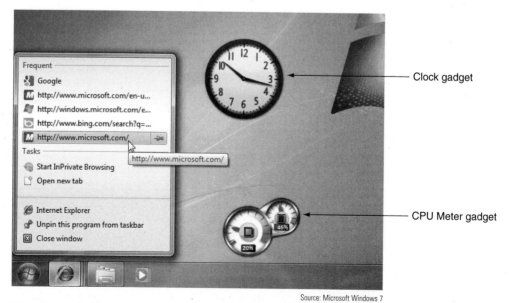

Source: Microsoft Windows 7

Figure 3-7 Right-click the Internet Explorer icon in the taskbar to see a Jump List of frequently used web pages and quickly access a page

A+
220-802
1.1

Notes A **gadget** is a mini-app that appears on the desktop. Windows 7 gadgets shown in Figure 3-7 can appear anywhere on the Windows 7 desktop. Vista gadgets appear in the Vista **sidebar** on the right side of the Vista desktop. To control Windows 7 gadgets, right-click the desktop and select **Gadgets** from the shortcut menu that appears.

The **notification area**, also called the **system tray** or **systray**, is usually on the right side of the taskbar and displays open services. A **service** is a program that runs in the background to support or serve Windows or an application. The services in the notification area include the volume control and network connectivity.

To control the Start menu, taskbar, and notification area, right-click the taskbar and click **Properties** from the shortcut menu. The Taskbar and Start Menu Properties dialog box appears (see Figure 3-8). Use it to move the taskbar on the screen, control the icons that appear in the notification area, and control Start menu items.

Notes To pin a program icon to the taskbar so that it's available to quickly launch the program, first locate the program in the Start menu. Then right-click the program and select **Pin to Taskbar** from the shortcut menu.

Source: Microsoft Windows 7

Figure 3-8 Use the Taskbar and Start Menu Properties box to control what appears in the Start menu and taskbar

Notes If you have a sluggish Windows system, one thing you can do is look at all the running services in the notification tray and try to disable the services that are taking up system resources. How to do that is covered in Chapter 11.

A+
220-802
1.1, 1.5

PERSONALIZE THE WINDOWS DESKTOP

You can also personalize the desktop. To use the Personalization window, right-click anywhere on the desktop, and choose **Personalize** from the shortcut menu (see Figure 3-9). Using this window, you can personalize the way Windows appears, including the desktop, sounds, mouse action, color themes, and display settings.

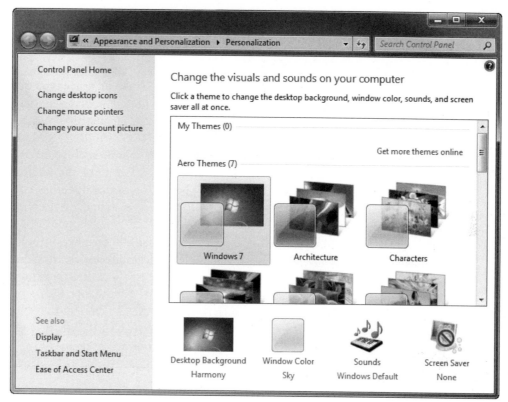

Source: Microsoft Windows 7

Figure 3-9 Use the Personalization window to change the appearance of Windows

As a support technician, you are often called on to solve problems with display settings. The most common problem with display is a problem with the screen resolution. The **screen resolution** is the number of dots or pixels on the monitor screen expressed as two numbers such as 1680 × 1050. To change the resolution, right-click anywhere on the desktop and choose **Screen resolution** from the shortcut menu. In the Screen Resolution window, make your changes and click **Apply**. You can also access the Screen Resolution window from the Control Panel or from the Personalization window.

> **XP Differences**   See Appendix C to learn about the differences in the Windows XP desktop and the Windows 7 desktop.

A+
220-802
1.1, 1.4

WINDOWS EXPLORER AND THE COMPUTER WINDOW

The two most useful tools to explore files and folders on your computer are Windows Explorer and the Computer window. (Windows XP calls the Computer window the My Computer window.) You learned to open the Computer window earlier in the chapter. For Windows 7, Windows Explorer is opened in these two ways:

▲ Click the yellow Windows Explorer icon in the taskbar. If a Windows Explorer window is already open, it becomes the active window.

A+
220-802
1.1, 1.4

▲ Right-click **Start** and select **Open Windows Explorer** from the menu. (For Vista and XP, right-click **Start** and select **Explore** from the menu.) If a Windows Explorer instance is already open, a new instance of Explorer is created. Having two instances of Explorer open makes it easy to drag and drop files and folders from one location to another.

Let's now turn our attention to how to use the Computer and Explorer windows to manage files and folders and other system resources.

FILES AND DIRECTORIES

Every OS manages a hard drive, optical drive, USB drive, or other type of drive by using directories (also called folders), subdirectories, and files. The drive is organized with a single **root directory** at the top of the top-down hierarchical structure of subdirectories, as shown in Figure 3-10. The exception to this rule is a hard drive because it can be divided into partitions that can have more than one **volume** such as drive C: and drive D: on the same physical hard drive (see Figure 3-11). For a volume, such as drive C:, the root directory is written as C:. Each volume has its own root directory and hierarchical structure of subdirectories. You can think of volumes as logical drives within the one physical drive.

As shown in Figure 3-10, the root directory can hold files or other directories, which can have names such as C:\Data. These directories, called **subdirectories**, **child directories**, or **folders**, can, in turn, have other directories listed in them. Any directory can have files and other subdirectories listed in it; for example, Figure 3-10 shows one file on drive C: is C:\Data\Business\Letter.docx. In this path to the file, the C: identifies the volume and is called the drive letter. Drive letters used for a hard drive, CD, USB drive, or DVD are C:, D:, E:, and so forth. Drive letters used for a floppy drive are A: or B:.

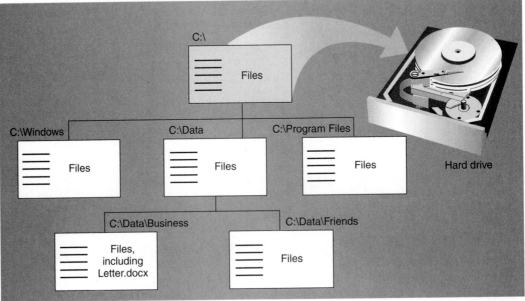

© Cengage Learning 2014

Figure 3-10 Storage devices such as a USB drive, CD, or hard drive are organized into directories and subdirectories that contain files

3

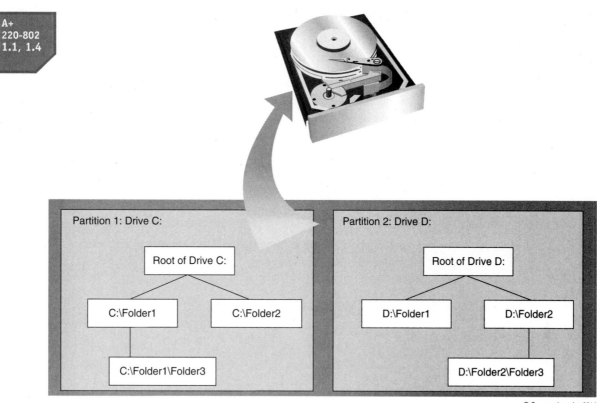

Partition 1: Drive C:

Root of Drive C:

C:\Folder1   C:\Folder2

C:\Folder1\Folder3

Partition 2: Drive D:

Root of Drive D:

D:\Folder1   D:\Folder2

D:\Folder2\Folder3

© Cengage Learning 2014

Figure 3-11   A hard drive can be divided into one or more partitions that can each contain a volume such as drive C: or drive D:

> **Notes** Technicians tend to call a directory a folder when working in Windows Explorer, but when working with a command-line interface, they call a directory a directory.

When you refer to a drive and directories that are pointing to the location of a file, as in C:\Data\Business\Letter.docx, the drive and directories are called the **path** to the file (see Figure 3-12). The first part of the name before the period is called the **filename** (Letter), and the part after the period is called the file extension (.docx). A **file extension** indicates how the file is organized or formatted, the type content in the file, and what program uses the file. For example, the .docx file extension identifies the file type as a Microsoft Word 2010 document file. By default, Windows does not display file extensions in Windows Explorer. How to display these extensions is coming up.

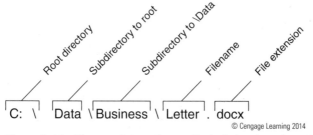

Root directory   Subdirectory to root   Subdirectory to \Data   Filename   File extension

C: \   Data \Business \ Letter . docx

© Cengage Learning 2014

Figure 3-12   The complete path to a file includes the volume letter, directories, filename, and file extension; the colon, backslashes, and period are required to separate items in the path

A+
220-802
1.1, 1.4

NAVIGATE THE FOLDER STRUCTURE

When working with the Windows Explorer or Computer window, these tips can make your work easier:

▲ *Tip 1*: Click or double-click items in the left pane, called the **navigation pane**, to drill down into these items. The folders or subfolders appear in the right pane. You can also double-click folders in the right pane to drill down. When you click the white arrow to the left of a folder in the navigation pane, its subfolders are listed underneath it in the pane. (For XP, click the plus sign to the left of a folder.)

▲ *Tip 2*: To control how files and subfolders appear in the right pane, click the View icon in the menu bar and select your view (see Figure 3-13).

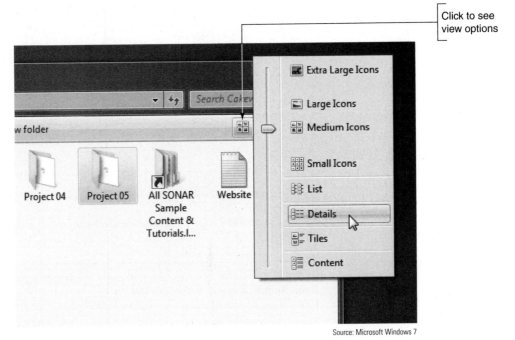

Source: Microsoft Windows 7

Figure 3-13 Click the View icon to change how files and folders display in the right pane of Windows Explorer

▲ *Tip 3*: To control the column headings that appear in the Details view, right-click a column heading and select the headings that you want to appear (see Figure 3-14). To control which column is used to sort items in the Details view, click a column heading.

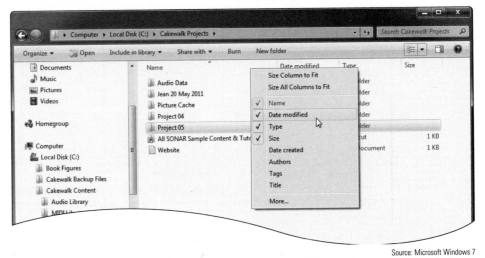

Source: Microsoft Windows 7

Figure 3-14 Right-click a column heading to select columns to display in the Details view

A+
220-802
1.1, 1.4

▲ *Tip 4*: To search for a folder or file, use the Search box in the upper-right corner of the window. (This search box is not available in Windows XP.)

▲ *Tip 5*: Use the forward and back arrows in the upper-left corner to move forward and backward to previous views. (These buttons are not available in Windows XP.)

▲ *Tip 6*: Click a right arrow in the path displayed in the address bar at the top of the Explorer window to see a drop-down list of subfolders (see Figure 3-15). Click one to move to this subfolder.

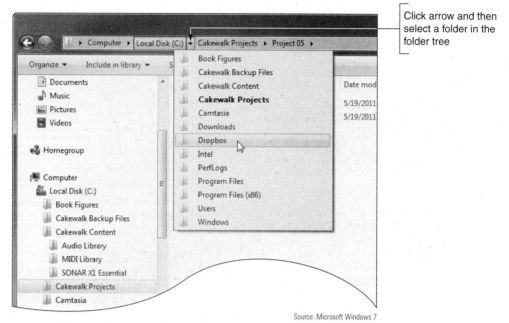

Source: Microsoft Windows 7

Figure 3-15 Click a right arrow in the address bar to move up the folder tree and down to a new folder

WINDOWS 7 LIBRARIES

A Windows 7 **library** is a collection of one or more folders, and these folders can be stored on different local drives or on the network. (Vista and XP do not support libraries.) A library is a convenient way to access several folders in different locations from one central location. When Windows is installed, it creates four default libraries: Documents, Music, Pictures, and Videos. By default, the first three libraries can be accessed from the Start menu. In addition, you can use the Computer window or Windows Explorer to access all libraries, including the four default ones and any libraries you create.

When you first open Windows Explorer, the list of libraries appears (see Figure 3-16). Use a library's Properties box to find out the folders that are contained in the library and the location of each folder. For example, right-click the Documents library and then select **Properties** from the shortcut menu. The Properties box shown on the right side of Figure 3-16 appears. The box shows that the Documents library contains two folders, the user's My Documents folder and the Public Documents folder.

When you add a new folder to a library, the files in that folder appear as though they are in the library even though they continue to be stored in the original location. When you add a file to the library, it is stored in the library's default save location folder. Which folder is that? It's the one checked as the save location in the library's Properties box. For example, in the Properties box shown in Figure 3-16, you can see the check beside the My Documents folder, indicating it is the save location folder. To create a new library, click in the white space in the right pane of Explorer and then click the **New library** command in the menu bar.

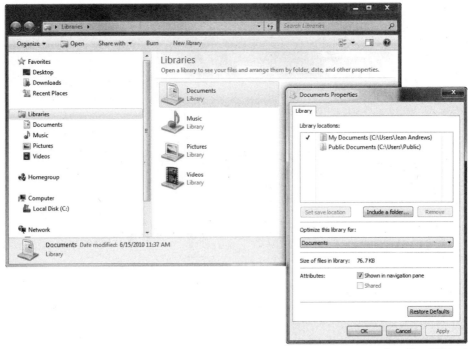

Source: Microsoft Windows 7

Figure 3-16   Windows 7 includes four default libraries

CHANGE WINDOWS EXPLORER SETTINGS AND FOLDER OPTIONS

You can view and change options assigned to folders. These options control how users view the files in the folder and what they can do with these files. In Windows Explorer and the Computer window, Windows has an annoying habit of hiding file extensions if it knows which application is associated with a file extension. For example, just after installation, it hides .exe, .com, .sys, and .txt file extensions, but does not hide .docx, .pptx, or .xlsx file extensions until the software to open these files has been installed. Also, Windows really doesn't want you to see its own system files, and it hides these files from view until you force it to show them.

APPLYING | CONCEPTS   A technician is responsible for solving problems with system files (files that belong to the Windows operating system) and file extensions. To fix problems with these files and extensions, you need to see them. To change folder options so you can view system files and file extensions, do the following:

1. To open the Control Panel, click **Start, Control Panel**. In the Control Panel, click **Appearance and Personalization**. Then click **Folder Options**. The Folder Options dialog box appears.

2. Use items on the General tab to change the way Windows Explorer works and how items appear in the navigation pane of Explorer. For Windows 7, the General tab is shown on the left in Figure 3-17. The View tab is shown on the right in Figure 3-17. (The Vista and XP Folder Options box looks and works about the same as that of Windows 7.)

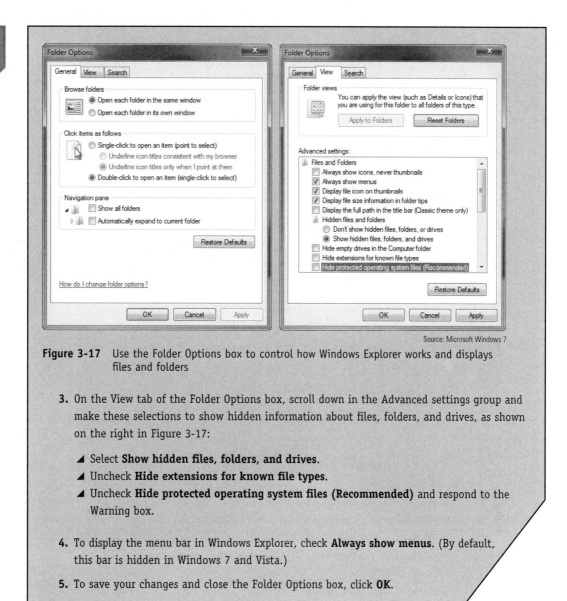

Source: Microsoft Windows 7

Figure 3-17 Use the Folder Options box to control how Windows Explorer works and displays files and folders

3. On the View tab of the Folder Options box, scroll down in the Advanced settings group and make these selections to show hidden information about files, folders, and drives, as shown on the right in Figure 3-17:

   ◢ Select **Show hidden files, folders, and drives.**
   ◢ Uncheck **Hide extensions for known file types.**
   ◢ Uncheck **Hide protected operating system files (Recommended)** and respond to the Warning box.

4. To display the menu bar in Windows Explorer, check **Always show menus.** (By default, this bar is hidden in Windows 7 and Vista.)

5. To save your changes and close the Folder Options box, click **OK.**

💡 **A+ Exam Tip** The A+ 220-802 exam expects you to know how to view hidden files and file extensions and to be able to change the layout or view of folders in Windows Explorer.

CREATE A FILE

You can create a file using a particular application, or you can create a file using Windows Explorer or the Computer window. In Explorer and the Computer window, to create a file, right-click in the unused white area in the right pane of the window and point to **New** in the shortcut menu. The menu lists applications you can use to create a file in the current folder (see Figure 3-18). Click the application and the file is created. You can then rename the filename. However, to keep the proper file association, don't change the file extension.

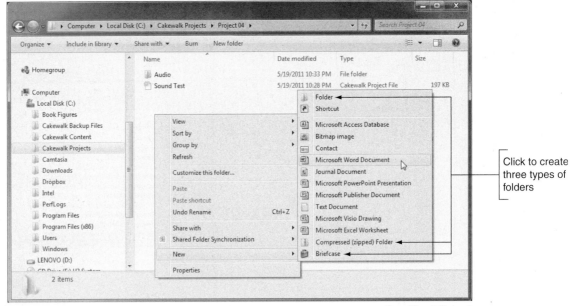

Source: Microsoft Windows 7

Figure 3-18   Create a new file or folder using Windows Explorer

CREATE A FOLDER

To create a folder, first select the folder you want to be the parent folder. (Remember that a parent folder is the folder that contains the child folder.) Right-click in the white area of the right pane and point to **New** in the shortcut menu. The menu in Figure 3-18 appears. Notice in the menu that for Windows 7 and Vista, you have three choices for folder types. These choices are explained here:

- ▲ *Folder* creates a regular folder.
- ▲ **Compressed (zipped) Folder** creates a compressed folder with a .zip extension. Any file or folder that you put in this folder will be compressed to a smaller size than normal. A compressed folder is often used to compress files to a smaller size so they can more easily be sent by email. When you remove a file or folder from a compressed folder, the file or folder is uncompressed back to its original size.
- ▲ **Briefcase** creates a Briefcase folder, which is a folder that can be used to sync up files in this folder with its corresponding Briefcase folder on another computer. (Windows offers two ways to sync files on different computers: Briefcase and Offline Files.)

Make your selection and the folder is created and highlighted so that you can rename it (see Figure 3-19).

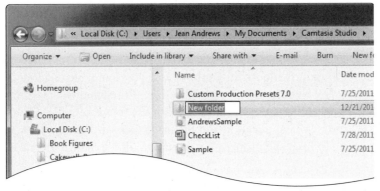

Figure 3-19   Edit the new folder's name

Source: Microsoft Windows 7

**A+
220-802
1.1, 1.4**

You can create folders within folders within folders, but there is a limitation as to the maximum depth of folders under folders; how deep you can nest folders depends on the length of the folder names themselves. The maximum length of a path and filename cannot exceed 260 characters.

Notes The Windows desktop is itself a folder and, for Windows 7 and Vista, is located at C:\Users\ *username*\Desktop. For example, if the user, Anne, creates a folder on her desktop named Downloads, this folder is located at C:\Users\Anne\Desktop\Downloads.

COPY, MOVE, RENAME, OR DELETE FILES OR FOLDERS

Use these handy tips to copy, move, and delete files or folders using Windows Explorer:

▲ To copy a file or folder, right-click it and select **Copy** from the shortcut menu. Then click in the white area of the folder where the copied item is to go and select **Paste** from the shortcut menu. You can also use the Cut and Paste commands to move an item to a new location.

▲ Drag and drop an item to move or copy it to a new location. If the location is on the same drive as the original location, the file or folder will be automatically deleted from its original location. If you don't want it deleted, hold down the **Ctrl** key while you drag and drop the item.

▲ To rename a file or folder, right-click it and select **Rename** from the shortcut menu. Change the name and click off the file or folder to deselect it.

▲ To delete a file or folder, select the item and press the **Delete** key. Or you can right-click the item and select **Delete** from the shortcut menu. Either way, a confirmation dialog box asks if you are sure you want to delete the item. If you click **Yes**, you send the file or folder and all its contents, including subfolders, to the Recycle Bin.

▲ To select multiple items to delete, copy, or move at the same time, hold down the **Shift** or **Ctrl** key as you click. To select several adjacent items in a list, click the first item and Shift-click the last item. To select nonadjacent items in a list, hold down the Ctrl key as you click each item.

Notes Appendix E lists handy keystrokes to save you time when working with Windows.

Emptying the Recycle Bin will free up your disk space. Files and folders sent to the Recycle Bin are not *really* deleted until you empty the bin. To do that, right-click the bin and select **Empty Recycle Bin** from the shortcut menu.

CHANGE FILE OR FOLDER ATTRIBUTES

Using Explorer or the Computer window, you can view and change the properties assigned to a file or folder; these properties are called the **file attributes** or **folder attributes**. Using these attributes, you can do such things as hide a file, make it a read-only file, or flag a file to be backed up. From Explorer or the Computer window, right-click a file or folder and select **Properties** from the shortcut menu. The Properties window shown on the left side of Figure 3-20 opens for the AnimalList.accdb database file.

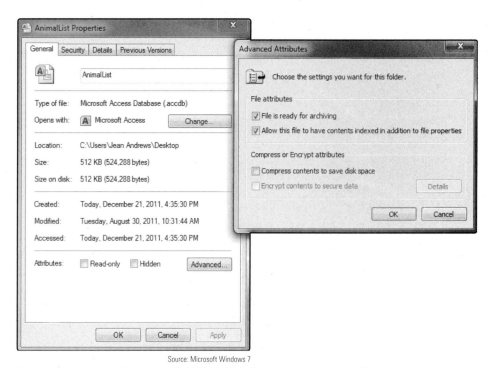

Source: Microsoft Windows 7

Figure 3-20 Use a file's Properties box to view file properties and edit file attributes

From the Properties window, you can change the read-only, hidden, archive, and indexing attributes of the file or folder. (Indexing is not used in Windows XP.) To make the file a read-only file or to hide the file so that it does not appear in the directory list, check the appropriate box and click **Apply**. The archive attribute is used to determine if a file or folder has changed since the last backup. To change its value, click **Advanced** in the Properties window (see the right side of Figure 3-20). Make your change and click **OK**.

> **Notes** In this chapter, you learn how to use Windows Explorer to create, copy, move, delete, rename, and change the attributes of files and folders. In Chapter 10, you will learn that you can do these same tasks using commands from a command prompt.

QUICK AND EASY WINDOWS SUPPORT TOOLS

As a PC support technician, you need to be able to sit down at a working computer and within five or ten minutes find the details about what software and hardware is installed on the system and the general health of the system. Within 20 minutes, you should be able to solve any minor problems the computer might have such as a broken network connection.

In this part of the chapter, you learn about the tools you need to quickly find these answers and solve some common problems. You'll learn to use the System window, System Information window, Control Panel, Action Center, User Account Control dialog box, and Windows Help and Support. In other chapters, you'll learn to use more Windows tools.

SYSTEM WINDOW

The **System window** is your friend. It can give you a quick look at what hardware and software are installed and can get you to other useful Windows tools. To open the System window, click **Start**, right-click **Computer**, and select **Properties** from the shortcut menu. (Alternately, you can open Control Panel, click System and Security, and then click System.) Figure 3-21 shows the resulting System window for one laptop.

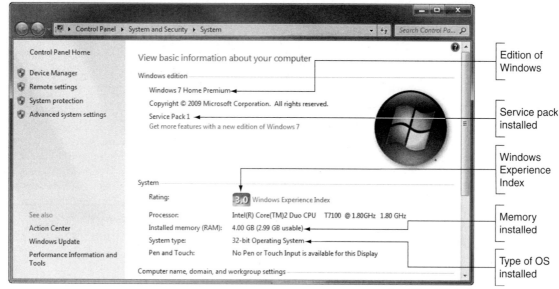

Source: Microsoft Windows 7

Figure 3-21 A 32-bit version of Windows 7 Home Premium is installed

So what technical information are you looking at? Here is the rundown:

- Windows 7 comes in several editions and you can see this system has the Windows 7 Home Premium edition installed.
- You can see that Service Pack 1 is installed. (A **service pack** is a major update or fix to an OS occasionally released by Microsoft. Minor updates or fixes that are released more frequently are called **patches**.)
- The type of OS installed is a 32-bit OS. A **32-bit operating system** processes 32 bits at a time, and a **64-bit operating system** processes 64 bits at a time. The Starter edition of Windows 7 comes in the 32-bit version and other editions come in either 32-bit or 64-bit versions. A 64-bit OS performs better than a 32-bit OS, but requires more memory. A 32-bit OS can support up to 4 GB of memory, and a 64-bit OS can support much more. The details of how much memory each edition of Windows 7 can support are covered in Chapter 7.
- The amount of installed memory is 4 GB. For a 32-bit OS, this is all the memory the system can use. If the user of this computer is thinking about upgrading RAM, you can tell him to not waste his money so long as he has a 32-bit OS installed.
- The **Windows Experience Index** is 3.0. That index is a rating of the system's overall performance on a scale from 1.0 to 7.9. Immediately, you know this system is not a snail or a blazing torch, but somewhere in the middle and probably toward the low range of performance.

That's a lot of useful information for a first look at a computer.

A+
220-802
1.4

SYSTEM INFORMATION WINDOW

Turn to the **System Information** (msinfo32.exe) window for more details about a system, including installed hardware and software, the current system configuration, and currently running programs. For example, you can use it to find out what BIOS version is installed on the motherboard, how much RAM is installed, the directory where the OS is installed, the size of the hard drive, the names of currently running drivers, a list of startup programs, print jobs in progress, currently running tasks, and much more. Because the System Information window gives so much useful information, help desk technicians often ask a user on the phone to open it and read to the technician information about the computer.

When strange error messages appear during startup, use the System Information window to get a list of drivers that loaded successfully. **Device drivers** are small programs stored on the hard drive that tell the computer how to communicate with a specific hardware device such as a printer, network card, or scanner. If you have saved the System Information report when the system was starting successfully, comparing the two reports can help identify the problem device.

To run System Information, click **Start**, and enter **Msinfo32.exe** in the *Search* box and press **Enter**. The System Information window for one computer is shown in Figure 3-22. To drill down to more information in the window, click items in the left pane.

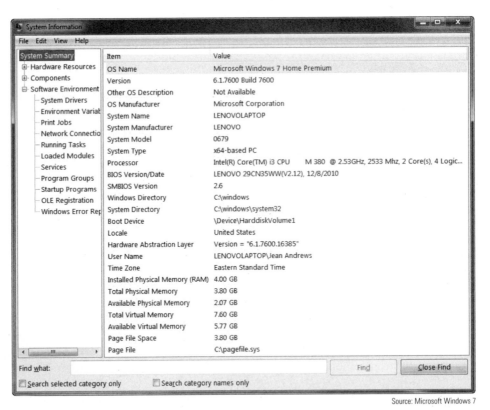

Source: Microsoft Windows 7

Figure 3-22 Use the System Information utility to examine details about a system

> **A+ Exam Tip** The A+ 220-802 exam expects you to be familiar with and know how to use the Windows 7/Vista/XP desktop, Computer, My Computer, Windows Explorer, System, System Information, Control Panel, Action Center, and Network and Sharing Center windows. All these tools are discussed in this section. If the utility can be accessed by more than one method, you are expected to know all of the methods.

THE CONTROL PANEL

The **Control Panel** is a window containing several small utility programs called applets that are used to manage hardware, software, users, and the system. (In general, a utility program is a program used to maintain a system or fix a computer problem.) To access the Control Panel, click **Start** and then click **Control Panel**.

Figure 3-23 shows the Windows 7 Control Panel in Category view. To switch to the Large icons or Small icons view, click **Category** and make your selection. (In Vista and XP, you can switch Control Panel between Category view and Classic View. Classic View looks similar to the icon views in Windows 7.) Use the search box in the title bar to help find information and utilities in Control Panel.

You can also access the utilities using one of these methods:

◢ If you know the name of the utility program file, click **Start** and type the program name in the *Search* box. For example, to open the Mouse Properties applet, type **Main.cpl** in the box, and then press **Enter**. (An applet in Control Panel sometimes has a .cpl file extension.)

◢ Type a description or title of the utility in the *Search* box. For example, type **Network and Sharing Center** to open that window.

◢ Find another path to the utility. For example, to open the System window in the System and Security group of Control Panel, click **Start**, right-click **Computer** and select **Properties**.

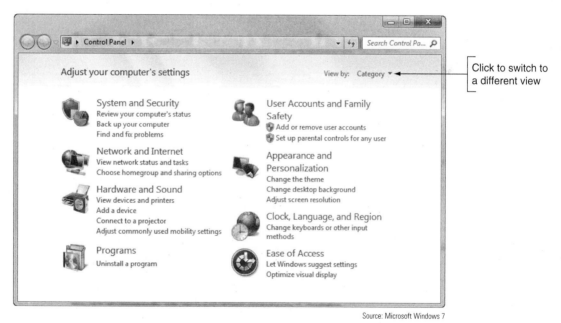

Source: Microsoft Windows 7

Figure 3-23 The Control Panel is organized by category, although you can easily switch to a list of selections

> **A+ Exam Tip** The A+ 220-802 exam expects you to be familiar with the Control Panel and its utilities. You should also know how to use the Large icons view in Windows 7 and the Classic View in Vista and XP. You are also expected to know more than one method of opening a Windows utility program.

A+
220-802
1.1, 1.5

ACTION CENTER

The Action Center is the tool to use when you want to make a quick jab at solving a computer problem. If a hardware or application problem is easy to solve, the Action Center can probably do it in a matter of minutes. The **Action Center** is new to Windows 7 and lists errors and issues that need attention. The Action Center flag appears in the notification area of the taskbar. If the flag has a red X beside it, as shown in Figure 3-24, Windows considers the system has an important issue that needs resolving immediately.

Source: Microsoft Windows 7

Figure 3-24 A red X on the Action Center flag in the taskbar indicates a critical issue needs resolving

To open the Action Center, use one of these methods:

▲ Click the **flag icon** in the taskbar. A list of issues appears (see Figure 3-25). Click **Open Action Center**.
▲ Click **Start** and type **Action Center** in the search box and press **Enter**.
▲ Click **Start** and click **Control Panel**. The Control Panel opens. Under the System and Security group, click **Review your computer's status**.

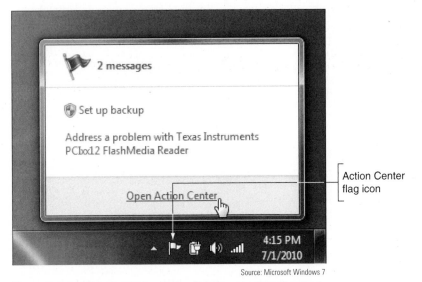

Source: Microsoft Windows 7

Figure 3-25 Click the Action Center flag to see a list of current issues and to open the Action Center

Using either method, the Action Center for one computer shown in Figure 3-26 appears. Notice the colored bar to the left of a problem. The red color indicates a critical problem that needs immediate attention. In this example, antivirus software is not installed on the system. The orange color indicates a less critical problem, such as no backups are scheduled. Click the button to the right of a problem to find a recommended solution.

A+
220-802
1.1, 1.5

3

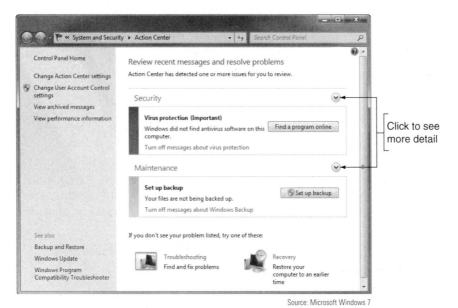

Source: Microsoft Windows 7

Figure 3-26 The Action Center shows a critical problem that needs a resolution

When you first open the Action Center, any problem that needs addressing is displayed. Looking back at Figure 3-25, you can see the Action Center reports a problem with a Texas Instruments FlashMedia Reader. When you click **View message details** in the Action Center, the screen shown in Figure 3-27 appears. Looking at Figure 3-27, you can see that the device does not have a Windows 7 driver and Windows is suggesting the problem might be solved by installing a Vista driver using compatibility mode. By clicking the links on the window, you can attempt the solution. Chapter 7 covers more about the possibility of using a Vista driver in a Windows 7 system.

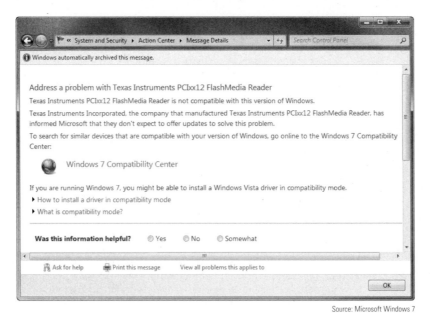

Source: Microsoft Windows 7

Figure 3-27 A problem reported in the Action Center with a possible solution

To see other information available under the Security and Maintenance groups, click the down arrow to the right of a group. For example, after the arrow to the right of Security is clicked, detailed information about Windows Firewall, Windows Update, and other security settings appears.

A+
220-802
1.1, 1.5

To see a complete list of past and current problems on this computer, click **View archived messages** in the left pane of the Action Center. This report helps understand the history of problems on a computer that you are troubleshooting. The problems in this list might or might not have a solution.

USER ACCOUNT CONTROL BOX

At some point while working with a computer to maintain or troubleshoot it, the **User Account Control (UAC) dialog box**, shown in Figure 3-28, will pop up. In Vista, this box was disruptive for power users and administrators because it appears each time a user attempts to perform an action that can be done only with administrative privileges. Windows 7 made the box less annoying and gives more options for configuring it.

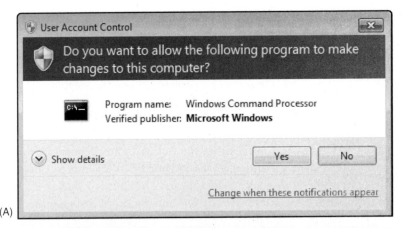

(A)

(B)

Source: Microsoft Windows 7

Figure 3-28 (a) and (b)   (a) The User Account Control box of an administrator does not require an administrative password; (b) the UAC box of a standard user requires an administrative password

In Windows, there are two types of user accounts: An **administrator account** and a **standard account**. An administrator account has more privileges than a standard account and is used by those responsible for maintaining and securing the system. When the UAC box appears, if you are logged on as an administrator, all you have to do is click Yes to close the box and move on, as shown in Figure 3-28(a). If the user account does not have

A+
220-802
1.1, 1.5

administrative privileges, you'll have the opportunity to enter a password of an administrative account to continue, as shown in Figure 3-28(b).

The purposes of the UAC box are: (1) to prevent malicious background tasks from gaining administrative privileges when the administrator is logged on, and (2) to make it easier for an administrator to log in using a less powerful user account for normal desktop activities, but still be able to perform administrative tasks while logged in as a regular user.

For example, suppose you're logged on as an administrator with the UAC box turned off and click a malicious link on a web site. Malware can download and install itself without your knowledge and might get admin privileges on the computer. If you're logged on as a standard user and the UAC box is turned off, the malware might still install without your knowledge but with lesser privileges. The UAC box stands as a gatekeeper to malware installing behind your back because someone has to click the UAC box before the installation can proceed.

APPLYING | CONCEPTS

Using Windows 7, you can control how the UAC box works. Do the following:

1. Open the Control Panel and click **User Accounts** in the User Accounts and Family Safety group.

2. In the User Accounts window, click **Change User Account Control settings**. The User Account Control Settings window appears (see Figure 3-29).

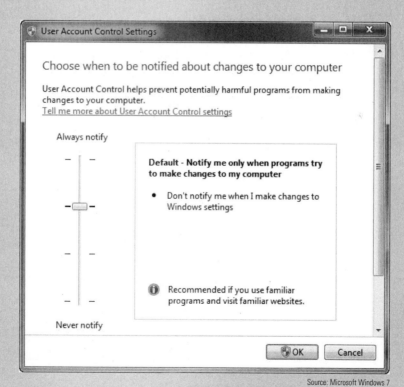

Source: Microsoft Windows 7

Figure 3-29 Windows 7 provides options to control the UAC box

3. Change when the UAC box appears. Here is a description of the four options shown in Figure 3-29:

▲ Always notify me when programs are trying to install software or make other changes to the computer and when I am making changes to Windows settings. (This is the Vista default option.)

A+
220-802
1.1, 1.5

▲ Notify me when programs are trying to make changes, but don't notify me when I am changing Windows settings. (This option is new to Windows 7 and causes the UAC box to be less annoying.)

▲ Same as the second option above but, in addition, do not dim the Windows desktop. Dimming the Windows desktop can alarm a user and take up resources. (In the Vista Business and Ultimate editions, a setting can be used to disable dimming the desktop.)

▲ Never notify me when a program is trying to change the computer or I am changing it. (This option is also available in Vista.)

4. Click **OK** and respond to the UAC box. Close the Action Center window.

Vista Differences To find out how to control the Vista User Account Control box, see Appendix B.

A+ Exam Tip The A+ 220-802 exam expects you to know how to change the settings that control when the UAC box appears.

A+
220-802
1.5

NETWORK AND SHARING CENTER

A failed network connection can sometimes quickly be resolved using the **Network and Sharing Center** available in Windows 7 and Vista. Use Control Panel or the taskbar to access the center. To use the taskbar, do the following:

1. Look for the networking icon in the taskbar. Wired networks show the icon on the left side of Figure 3-30 and wireless networks show the icon on the right side of Figure 3-30. Click the icon to see more information. An icon that indicates a problem has a red X and is shown on the left side of Figure 3-31. If wireless networks are available, the icon has a yellow star, as shown on the right side of Figure 3-31. In the pop-up bubble, click a wireless network to connect to it. If the network is secured, you must enter the wireless security key.

Notes If you don't see the networking icon in the taskbar, you can add it using the Taskbar and Start Menu Properties box you learned about earlier in the chapter. You can also access the Network and Sharing Center from the Control Panel.

Figure 3-30 shows Wired network icon and Wireless network icon. Source: Microsoft Windows 7

Figure 3-30 Wired and wireless networking icons in the taskbar

A+
220-802
1.5

Red X indicates a problem

Yellow star indicates wireless networks are available

Source: Microsoft Windows 7

Figure 3-31 The network icon in the taskbar indicates a problem or a possible new connection to a wireless network

2. To get more information about a problem, click **Open Network and Sharing Center**.

3. The Network and Sharing Center window opens (see Figure 3-32). A red X indicates a problem. Click the X to get help and resolve the problem. Windows Network Diagnostics starts looking for problems, applying solutions, and making suggestions. You can also check these things:

▲ For wired networks, is the network cable connected at both ends?

▲ Are status light indicators next to the network port on your computer lit or blinking appropriately to indicate connectivity and activity?

▲ Is the wireless switch on a laptop turned on?

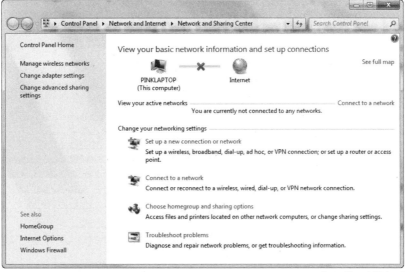

Source: Microsoft Windows 7

Figure 3-32 The Network and Sharing Center reports a problem connecting to the network

4. After Windows has resolved the problem, you should see a clear path from the computer to the Internet, as shown in Figure 3-33. To verify the problem is resolved, use Windows Explorer to try to access resources on the local network, and use Internet Explorer to try to access the Internet.

A+
220-802
1.5

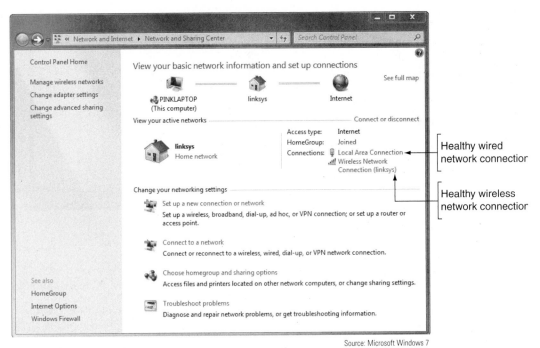

Source: Microsoft Windows 7

Figure 3-33   The Network and Sharing Center reports two healthy network connections

In Chapter 15, you learn more about the Networking and Sharing Center.

A+
220-802
1.1

WINDOWS HELP AND SUPPORT AND THE WEB

The best PC support technicians are the ones continually teaching themselves new skills. You can teach yourself to use and support Windows by using the web and the Windows Help and Support utility (see Figure 3-34). To start the utility, click **Start** and click **Help and Support**. Click links or enter a question or topic in the search box. If you are connected to the Internet, links can take you to the Microsoft web site where you can find information and watch videos about Windows.

Source: Microsoft Windows 7

Figure 3-34   Use the Help and Support tool to teach yourself about Windows

**A+
220-802
1.1**

Here are some tips for using the web and Help and Support:

◢ The Microsoft web site (*support.microsoft.com*, *windows.microsoft.com*, and *technet .microsoft.com*) has tons of useful information. Search for a device, an error message, a Windows utility, a symptom, a software application, an update version number, or keywords that lead you to articles about problems and solutions.

◢ Using a search engine such as Google (*www.google.com*), enter the error message, software application, symptom, or Windows utility in the search box to search the web for answers, suggestions, and comments. Beware, however, that you don't bump into a site that does more harm than good. Some sites are simply guessing, offering incomplete and possibly wrong solutions, and even offering a utility the site claims will solve your problem but really contains only pop-up ads or a virus. Use only reputable sites you can trust. You'll learn about several of these excellent sites in this book.

◢ To limit a Google search to the Microsoft web site, use the **site:microsoft.com** text in the search string. A Google search of the Microsoft site often gives better results than the search box on the Microsoft web site.

Other sources of help are user and installation manuals for applications and hardware devices, training materials, and the web sites of application and device manufacturers.

> **Notes** If you are serious about learning to provide professional support for Windows, each OS has a resource kit, including support software and a huge reference book containing inside information about the OS. Check out *Microsoft Windows 7 Resource Kit*, *Microsoft Windows Vista Resource Kit*, or *Microsoft Windows XP Professional Resource Kit*. All three are put out by Microsoft Press.

As you work your way through this book, try to learn to teach yourself about Windows by searching for information on the web, in Windows Help and Support, and in Microsoft documentation. The more independent a learner you are, the better support technician you will be.

>> CHAPTER SUMMARY

Using Windows

◢ An operating system manages hardware, runs applications, provides an interface for users, and stores, retrieves, and manipulates files.

◢ The Windows 7 and Vista desktop offers the Aero user interface. Vista includes the sidebar with gadgets. Gadgets are placed directly on the Windows 7 desktop.

◢ Four ways to launch an application are to use the Start menu, the search box, Windows Explorer, or a shortcut icon on the desktop or taskbar.

◢ Use Windows 7 Aero Snap and Aero Shake to manage open windows on the desktop.

◢ The right side of the taskbar is called the notification area, which some call the system tray.

▲ Windows Explorer and the Computer window are used to manage files, folders (also called directories), and libraries. Windows Vista and XP do not support libraries, and Windows XP calls the Computer window the My Computer window.

▲ The file extension indicates how the file contents are organized and formatted and what program uses the file.

▲ Use the Control Panel Folder Options box to change the way Windows Explorer works and displays files and folders.

Quick and Easy Windows Support Tools

▲ The System window gives a quick overview of the system, including which edition and version of Windows is installed and the amount of installed memory.

▲ The System Information window gives much information about the computer, including hardware, device drivers, the OS, and applications.

▲ Control Panel gives access to a group of utility programs used to manage the system.

▲ The Windows 7 Action Center is a centralized location used to solve problems with security and computer maintenance issues.

▲ The User Account Control (UAC) box is used to protect the system against malware or accidental changes to a system done by inexperienced users.

▲ Use the Network and Sharing Center to manage, secure, and troubleshoot network connections.

▲ Use the web and the Windows Help and Support utility to teach yourself about Windows and how to support it.

>> KEY TERMS

For explanations of key terms, see the Glossary near the end of the book.

32-bit operating system	filename	screen resolution
64-bit operating system	folder attributes	service pack
Action Center	folder	sidebar
administrator account	gadget	standard account
Aero Peek	graphical user interface (GUI)	subdirectory
Aero Shake	Jump List	System Information
Aero Snap	library	system tray
Aero user interface	navigation pane	System window
child directories	Network and Sharing Center	systray
Compressed (zipped) Folder	notification area	taskbar
Control Panel	operating system (OS)	User Account Control (UAC)
desktop	patches	dialog box
device driver	path	volume
file attributes	root directory	Windows Experience Index
file extension	service	

>> REVIEW QUESTIONS

1. Which term identifies the initial screen that is displayed after the user logs on and Windows is loaded?

   a) Program window

   b) Aero user interface

   c) Taskbar

   d) Desktop

2. You can use a library's ____ box to find out the folders that are contained in the library and the location of each folder.

   a) Properties

   b) Documents

   c) Information

   d) Folders

3. A(n) ____ is a major update or fix to an OS occasionally released by Microsoft.

   a) service pack

   b) applet

   c) path

   d) shell

4. Which program is used to start the System Information Window?

   a) Msinfo.exe

   b) Msinfo32.exe

   c) Sysinfo.exe

   d) Sysinfo32.exe

5. Which utility can be used to see a complete list of past and current problems on a computer?

   a) Control Panel

   b) Windows Explorer

   c) Action Center

   d) Windows Help and Support

6. True or false? When you launch a program, the program window appears on the desktop.

7. True or false? For a volume, such as drive C:, the root directory is written as C:\.

8. True or false? How deep you can nest folders depends on the length of the folder names themselves.

9. True or false? The System Window is the tool to use when you want to make a quick stab at solving a computer problem.

10. True or false? When the UAC box appears for a user logged in with an administrator account, the user must enter a password of an administrative account to continue.

11. A(n) _____ is software that controls a computer.

12. The _____ is normally located at the bottom of the Windows desktop, displaying information about open programs and providing quick access to others.

13. A(n) _____ is a program that runs in the background to support or serve Windows or an application.

14. A(n) _____ indicates how the file is organized or formatted, the type content in the file, and what program uses the file.

15. A Windows 7 _____ is a collection of one or more folders, and these folders can be stored on different local drives or on the network.

All About Motherboards

In Chapter 2, you learned how to work inside a computer and began the process of learning about each major component or subsystem in a computer case. In this chapter, we build on all that knowledge to learn about motherboards, which techies sometimes call the mobo. You'll learn about the many different features of a motherboard, including motherboard sockets, chipsets, buses, expansion slots, and onboard ports and connectors. Then you'll learn how to support a motherboard, and that includes configuring, maintaining, installing, and replacing it. A motherboard is considered a field replaceable unit, so it's important to know how to replace one, but the good news is you don't need to know how to repair one that is broken. Troubleshooting a motherboard works hand in hand with troubleshooting the processor and other components that must work to boot up a computer, so we'll leave troubleshooting the motherboard until Chapter 13, *Troubleshooting Hardware Problems*.

MOTHERBOARD TYPES AND FEATURES

A+
220-801
1.2

A motherboard is the most complicated component in a computer. When you put together a computer from parts, generally you start with deciding on which processor and motherboard you will use. Everything else follows these two decisions. Take a look at the details of Figure 4-1, which shows a microATX motherboard by Intel that can hold an Intel Core i7, Core i5, or Core i3 processor in the LGA1155 processor socket. When selecting a motherboard, generally, you'd need to pay attention to the form factor, processor socket, chipset, buses and number of bus slots, and other connectors, slots, and ports. In this part of the chapter, we'll look at the details of each of these features so that you can read a mobo ad with the knowledge of a pro and know how to select the right motherboard when replacing an existing one or when building a new system.

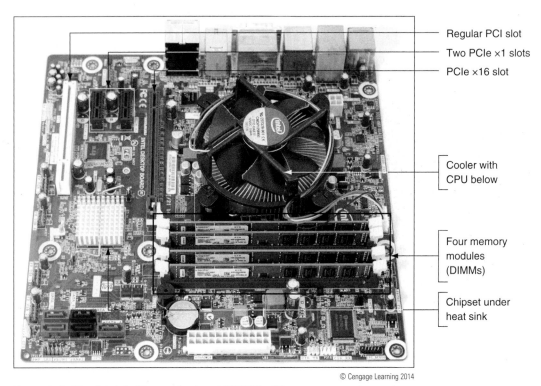

© Cengage Learning 2014

Figure 4-1   The Intel desktop motherboard DH67GD with processor, cooler, and memory modules installed

MOTHERBOARD FORM FACTORS

Recall from Chapter 1 that a motherboard form factor determines the size of the board and its features that make it compatible with power supplies and cases. The most popular motherboard form factors are ATX, microATX (a smaller version of ATX), and Mini-ITX (a smaller version of microATX). You saw a microATX motherboard in Figure 4-1. Figure 4-2 shows an ATX board, and a Mini-ITX board is shown in Figure 4-3. Also know that the Mini-ITX board is commonly referred to as an ITX board.

Table 4-1 lists the popular and not-so-popular form factors used by motherboards, and Figure 4-4 shows a comparison of the sizes and hole positions of the ATX, microATX, and Mini-ITX boards. Each of these three boards can fit into an ATX computer case and use an ATX power supply.

Four DDR3 DIMM slots

Socket LGA1366

X58 North Bridge

South Bridge

PCIe x16 slots for two video cards

© Cengage Learning 2014

Figure 4-2 Intel DX58SO motherboard is designed with the gamer in mind

4

Courtesy of ASUSTeK Computer Inc.

Figure 4-3 A Mini-ITX motherboard

Form Factor	Motherboard Size	Description
ATX, full size	Up to 12" x 9.6" (305mm × 244mm)	This popular form factor has had many revisions and variations.
MicroATX	Up to 9.6" x 9.6" (244mm × 244mm)	Smaller version of ATX.
Mini-ITX (a.k.a. ITX)	Up to 6.7" x 6.7" (170mm x 170mm)	Small form factor used in low-end computers and home theater systems. The boards are often used with an Intel Atom processor and are sometimes purchased as a motherboard-processor combo unit.
FlexATX	Up to 9" x 7.5"	Smaller version of MicroATX.
BTX	Up to 12.8" wide	The BTX boards can have up to seven expansion slots, are designed for improved airflow, and can use an ATX power supply.

Table 4-1 Motherboard form factors (continues)

© Cengage Learning 2014

A+
220-801
1.2

Form Factor	Motherboard Size	Description
MicroBTX	Up to 10.4" wide	Smaller version of BTX and can have up to four expansion slots.
PicoBTX	Up to 8" wide	Smaller than MicroBTX and can have up to two expansion slots.
NLX	Up to 9" x 13.6"	Used in low-end systems with a riser card.

© Cengage Learning 2014

Table 4-1 Motherboard form factors (continued)

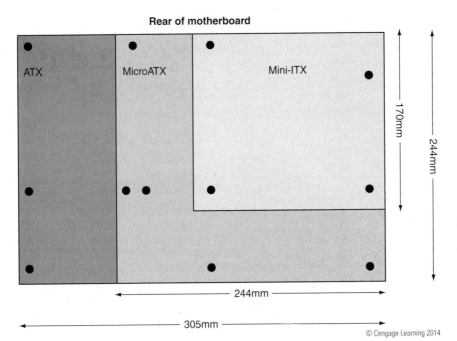

Figure 4-4 Sizes and hole positions for the ATX, microATX, and Mini-ITX motherboards

> 🔋 **A+ Exam Tip** The A+ 220-801 exam expects you to know about the ATX, MicroATX, and ITX motherboard form factors.

A+
220-801
1.2, 1.6

PROCESSOR SOCKETS

Another important feature of a motherboard is the processor socket. This socket and the chipset determine which processors a board can support. A socket for a personal computer is designed to hold either an Intel processor or an AMD processor. Some older processors were installed on the motherboard in a long narrow slot, but all processors sold today use sockets. Now let's look at sockets for Intel and AMD processors.

SOCKETS FOR INTEL PROCESSORS

Table 4-2 lists the sockets used by Intel processors for desktop systems. The first two sockets are currently used by new Intel processors. The last six sockets in the table have been discontinued by Intel, but you still need to be able to support them because you might be called on to replace a processor or motherboard using one of these legacy sockets. The types of memory listed in the table that are used with these sockets are explained in detail in Chapter 5. Also know that Intel makes several Itanium and Xeon processors designed for servers. These server processors might use different sockets than those listed in the table. Mobile processor sockets are also not included in the table.

4

Intel Socket Names	Used by Processor Family	Description
LGA2011	Second Generation (Sandy Bridge) Core i7 Extreme, Core i7, Core i5, Core i3, Pentium, and Celeron	◢ 2011 pins in the socket touch 2011 lands on the processor, which uses a flip-chip land grid array (FCLGA). ◢ Used in high-end gaming and server computers and might require a liquid cooling system.
LGA1155 and FCLGA1155	Third Generation (Ivy Bridge) Core i7, Core i5 Second Generation (Sandy Bridge) Core i7 Extreme, Core i7, Core i5, Core i3, Pentium, and Celeron	◢ 1155 pins in the socket touch 1155 lands on the processor. ◢ The LGA1155 is currently the most popular Intel socket and is shown in Figure 4-5. ◢ Works with DDR3 memory and was designed to replace the LGA1156 socket.
LGA1156 or Socket H or H1	Core i7, Core i5, Core i3, Pentium, and Celeron	◢ 1156 pins in the socket touch 1156 lands on the processor, which uses a flip-chip land grid array (FCLGA). ◢ Works with DDR3 memory.
LGA1366 or Socket B	Core i7, Core i7 Extreme	◢ 1366 pins in the socket touch 1366 lands on the processor. ◢ Works with DDR3 memory.
LGA771 or Socket J	Core 2 Extreme	◢ 771 pins in the socket touch 771 lands on the processor. ◢ Used on high-end workstations and low-end servers. ◢ Works with DDR2 memory on boards that have two processor sockets.
LGA775 or Socket T	Core 2 Extreme, Core 2 Quad, Core 2 Duo, Pentium Dual-Core, Pentium Extreme Edition, Pentium D, Pentium Pentium 4, and Celeron	◢ 775 pins in the socket touch 775 lands on the processor. ◢ Works with DDR3 and DDR2 memory.
Socket 478	Pentium 4, Celeron	◢ 478 holes in the socket are used by 478 pins on the processor. ◢ Uses a dense micro Pin Grid Array (mPGA).
Socket 423	Pentium 4	◢ 423 holes in the socket are used by 423 pins on the processor. ◢ 39 x 39 SPGA grid.

Table 4-2   Sockets for Intel processors used for desktop computers

© Cengage Learning 2014

A+ Exam Tip   The A+ 220-801 exam expects you to know about Intel LGA sockets, including the 775, 1155, 1156, and 1366 LGA sockets.

A+
220-801
1.2, 1.6

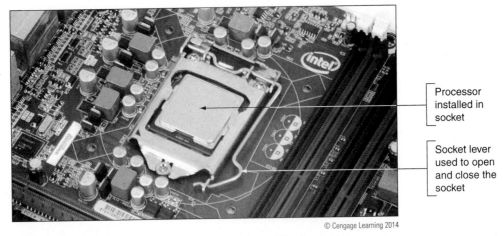

Processor installed in socket

Socket lever used to open and close the socket

© Cengage Learning 2014

Figure 4-5 The LGA1155 socket is used by a variety of Intel processors

Sockets and processors use different methods to make the contacts between them. Here is a list of the more important methods:

- ◢ A **pin grid array (PGA)** socket has holes aligned in uniform rows around the socket to receive the pins on the bottom of the processor. Early Intel processors used PGA sockets, but they caused problems because the small delicate pins on the processor were easily bent as the processor was installed in the socket. Some newer Intel mobile processors, including the Second Generation Core i3, Core i5, and Core i7 processors use the PGA988 socket or the FCPGA988 socket in laptops.
- ◢ A **land grid array (LGA)** socket has blunt protruding pins on the socket that connect with lands or pads on the bottom of the processor. The first LGA socket was the LGA775 socket. It has 775 pins and is shown with the socket lever and top open in Figure 4-6. Another LGA socket is the LGA1366 shown in Figure 4-7. LGA sockets generally give better contacts than PGA sockets, and the processor doesn't have the delicate pins so easily damaged during an installation. You learn how to use both sockets in Chapter 5.

Plastic cover protects the socket when it's not in use

© Cengage Learning 2014

Figure 4-6 Socket LGA775 is the first Intel socket to use lands rather than pins

© Cengage Learning 2014

Figure 4-7   The LGA1366 socket with socket cover removed and load level lifted ready to receive a processor

> **Notes**   Figure 4-8 shows a close-up photo of the LGA775 socket and the bottom of a Pentium processor. Can you make out the pads or lands on the processor and the pins in the socket?

© Cengage Learning 2014

Figure 4-8   Socket LGA775 and the bottom of a Pentium processor

▲ Some sockets can handle a processor using a **flip-chip land grid array (FCLGA)** processor package or a **flip chip pin grid array (FCPGA)** package. The chip is flipped over so that the top of the chip is on the bottom and makes contact with the socket. The LGA1155 socket has a flip chip version, which is called the FCLGA1155 socket. The two sockets are not compatible.

▲ A **staggered pin grid array (SPGA)** socket has pins staggered over the socket to squeeze more pins into a small space.

▲ A **ball grid array (BGA)** connection is not really a socket. The processor is soldered to the motherboard, and the two are always purchased as a unit. For example, the little Atom processors often use this technology with a Mini-ITX motherboard in low-end computers or home theater systems.

When a processor is installed in a socket, extreme care must be taken to protect the socket and the processor against ESD and from damage caused by bending the pins or scratching the socket holes during the installation. Take care to not touch the bottom of the

A+
220-801
1.2, 1.6

processor or the pins or holes of the socket, which can leave finger oil on the gold plating of the contact surfaces. This oil can later cause tarnishing and lead to a poor contact. So that even force is applied when inserting the processor in the socket, all current processor sockets have one or two levers on the sides of the socket. These sockets are called **zero insertion force (ZIF) sockets**, and this lever is used to lift the processor up and out of the socket. Push the levers down and the processor moves into its pin or hole connectors with equal force over the entire housing. Because the socket and processor are so delicate, know that processors generally should not be removed or replaced repeatedly.

SOCKETS FOR AMD PROCESSORS

Table 4-3 lists the AMD sockets for desktop systems. AMD has chosen to use the PGA socket architecture for its desktop processors. (Some of AMD's server processors use Socket F, which is an LGA socket.) Figure 4-9 shows the AM2+ socket. The lever on the

AMD Socket	Used by Processor Family	Description
FM2	Used with the Trinity line of AMD processors	◢ 904 holes for pins (PGA) ◢ Uses AMD Piledriver architecture with integrated graphics controller in the processor ◢ Works with DDR3 memory ◢ Soon to be released
FM1	AMD A4, A6, A8, E2, Athlon II	◢ 905 holes for pins (PGA) ◢ Works with DDR3 memory
AM3+	AMD FX	◢ 942 holes for pins (PGA) ◢ Uses Bulldozer architecture and is compatible with AM3 processors ◢ Works with DDR3 memory
AM3 or AMD3	Phenom II	◢ 941 holes for pins (PGA) ◢ Works with DDR3 or DDR2 memory
AM2+ or AMD2+	Phenom II, Phenom, and Athlon	◢ Works with DDR2 memory ◢ 940 holes for pins (PGA) ◢ Faster than AMD2
Socket F (1207) or F	Opteron, Athlon 64 FX	◢ 1207 pins for lands on the bottom of the processor ◢ Used with servers and high-end workstations
AM2, AMD2, or M2	Athlon 64, Athlon, Phenom, Sempron, Second Generation Opteron	◢ 940 holes for pins (PGA) ◢ Works with DDR2 memory
Socket 940	Athlon	◢ 940 holes for pins (PGA) ◢ Works with DDR memory
Socket 939	Athlon and Sempron	◢ 939 holes for pins (PGA) ◢ Works with DDR memory
Socket 754	Athlon and Sempron	◢ 754 holes for pins (PGA) ◢ Works with DDR memory
Socket A	Athlon, Sempron, and Duron	◢ 462 holes for pins (PGA) ◢ Works with DDR memory

Table 4-3 Sockets for AMD processors used for desktop computers

side of the socket is lifted, and an Athlon 64 processor is about to be inserted. If you look closely near the lower edge of the processor, you can see the small delicate pins that will seat into the holes of the socket.

© Cengage Learning 2014

Figure 4-9   AMD Athlon 64 processor to be inserted into an AM2+ socket

> **A+ Exam Tip**   The A+ 220-801 exam expects you to know about these AMD sockets: 940, AM2, AM2+, AM3, AM3+, FM1, and F.

MATCH A PROCESSOR TO THE SOCKET AND MOTHERBOARD

As you glance over Tables 4-2 and 4-3, you'll notice the same processor family listed under several different sockets. For example, the AMD Athlon family of processors offers many versions of the Athlon. Among these are the Athlon X2 Dual-Core, the Athlon Neo, and the Athlon 64 X2 Dual-Core. Because these various processors within the same processor family use different sockets, you must be careful when matching a processor to a motherboard. To be certain you have a good match, search the Intel (*www.intel.com*) or AMD (*www.amd.com*) web site for the exact processor you are buying and make sure the socket it uses is the same as the socket on the motherboard you plan to use.

Also, look at the motherboard documentation for a list of processors that the motherboard supports. It is not likely to support every processor that uses its socket because the motherboard chipset is designed to work only with certain processors.

> **A+ Exam Tip**   The A+ 220-801 exam expects you to be familiar with the desktop processor sockets in use today. You also need to know about notebook processor sockets, which are covered in Chapter 19.

THE CHIPSET

A **chipset** is a set of chips on the motherboard that works closely with the processor to collectively control the memory, buses on the motherboard, and some peripherals. The chipset must be compatible with the processor it serves. The major chipset manufacturers are Intel

A+
220-801
1.2

(*www.intel.com*), AMD (*www.amd.com*), NVIDIA (*www.nvidia.com*), SiS (*www.sis.com*), and VIA (*www.via.com.tw*).

Intel dominates the chipset market for several reasons: It knows more about its own Intel processors than other manufacturers do, and it produces the chipsets most compatible with the Intel family of processors.

INTEL CHIPSETS

Intel has produced far too many chipsets to list them here. To see a complete comparison chart of all Intel chipsets, start at the Intel link *ark.intel.com*.

Here is a list of the more significant chipset families by Intel:

▲ *North Bridge and South Bridge use a hub architecture.* Beginning with the release in 2006 of the Intel i800 series of chipsets, a hub using the Accelerated Hub Architecture is used to connect buses (see Figure 4-10). This hub has a fast and slow end, and each end is a separate chip on the motherboard. The fast end of the hub, called the **North Bridge**, contains the graphics and memory controller, and connects directly to the processor by way of a 64-bit bus, called the **Front Side Bus (FSB)**, **system bus**, or host bus. The slower end of the hub, called the **South Bridge**, contains the I/O controller hub (ICH). All I/O (input/output) devices, except video, connect to the hub by using the slower South Bridge. Notice that in Figure 4-10, the primary PCI Express slot, the

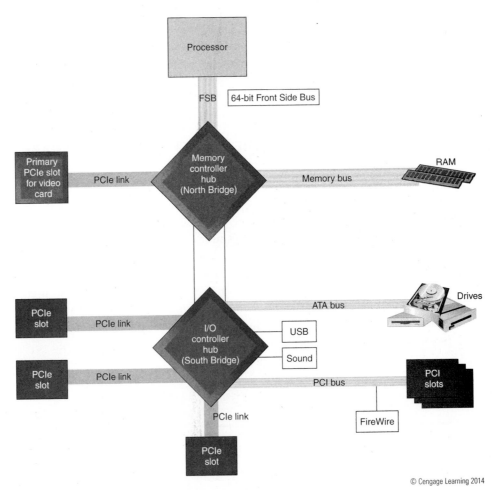

© Cengage Learning 2014

Figure 4-10 The chipset's North Bridge and South Bridge control access to the processor for all components

A+
220-801
1.2

slot designated for the video card, has direct access to the North Bridge, but other PCI Express slots must access the processor by way of the slower South Bridge. On a motherboard, when you see two major chip housings for the chipset, one is controlling the North Bridge and the other is controlling the South Bridge (refer to Figure 4-2). Other chipset manufacturers besides Intel also use the North Bridge and South Bridge architecture for their chipsets.

▲ *Nehalem chipsets with the memory controller in the processor.* The release of the X58 chipset in 2008 was significant because, with previous chipsets, the memory controller was part of the North Bridge. But beginning with the X58, the memory controller was contained in the processor housing. For example, in Figure 4-11, the Core i7 processor contains the memory controller. Notice that memory connects directly to the processor rather than to the North Bridge. Another significant change is the 64-bit Front Side Bus was replaced with a technology called the **QuickPath Interconnect (QPI)**. The QPI has 16 lanes for data packets and works similar to how PCI Express works. All Intel chipsets since the X58 use QuickPath Interconnects. A motherboard using the X58 chipset is shown in Figure 4-12. The board comes with a fan that can be clipped to the top of the North Bridge to help keep the chipset cool.

Nehalem chipsets, which Intel has begun to call the previous generation of chipsets, support the Intel LGA1366 socket, the Core i7 processors, and PCI Express Version 2. They can also support either SLI or CrossFire technologies. (SLI and CrossFire are two competing technologies that allow for multiple video cards installed in one system.)

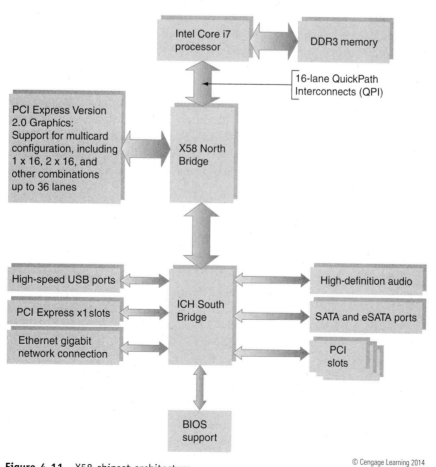

Figure 4-11 X58 chipset architecture

© Cengage Learning 2014

A+
220-801
1.2

X58 chipset

South Bridge

© Cengage Learning 2014

Figure 4-12 The X58 chipset uses heat sinks to stay cool

> **Notes** For an interesting white paper by Intel on QuickPath Interconnect, including a brief history of processor interfaces, go to *www.intel.com* and search on "An Introduction to the Intel QuickPath Interconnect."

▲ *Sandy Bridge chipsets with the memory and graphics controller in the processor.* In 2011, Intel introduced its second-generation chipsets and sockets, which it code-named Sandy Bridge technologies. Rather than using the traditional North Bridge and South Bridge, only one chipset housing is needed, which houses the Platform Controller Hub. The processor interfaces directly with the faster graphics PCI Express 2.0 bus as well as with memory (see Figure 4-13). Therefore, both the memory controller and graphics controller are contained within all Sandy Bridge processors. Sandy Bridge processors, such as the Second Generation Core i7, use the LGA1155 or the LGA2011 socket, and Sandy Bridge motherboards use DDR3 memory. Sandy Bridge chipsets for desktop computers include X79, P67, H67, Q65, Q67, and B65. The H67 chipset on an Intel motherboard is shown in Figure 4-14 and earlier in Figure 4-1.

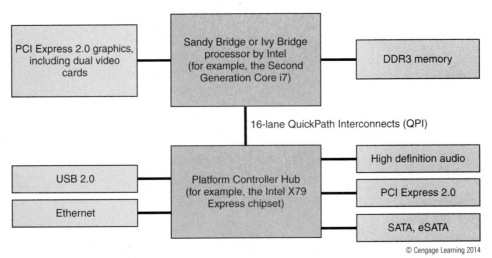

© Cengage Learning 2014

Figure 4-13 The Sandy Bridge architecture uses a single chipset hub, called the Platform Controller Hub

© Cengage Learning 2014

Figure 4-14 The Sandy Bridge H67 chipset on the Intel DH67GD motherboard sits under a heat sink to keep it cool

▲ *Ivy Bridge chipsets.* Third-generation processors and chipsets by Intel, released in 2012 and codenamed Ivy Bridge, use less power, squeeze more transistors into a smaller space, and perform better than earlier products. Ivy Bridge chipsets include B75, Q75, Q77, H77, Z75, and Z77. Several Ivy Bridge processors use the LGA1155 socket for backward compatibility with earlier motherboards. The Ivy Bridge chipset uses a single Platform Controller Hub.

AMD CHIPSETS

AMD purchased ATI Technologies, a maker of chipsets and graphics processors (called a graphics processor unit or GPU), in 2006, which increased AMD chipset and GPU offerings. Significant chipsets by AMD include the following:

▲ The AMD A-series chipsets (code named Trinity) are designed to compete with Ivy Bridge chipsets in the light notebook market.
▲ The AMD 9-series chipset supports AMD CrossFireX technologies.
▲ The AMD 9-series, 8-series, and 7-series chipsets are designed with the gamer, hobbyist, and multimedia enthusiast in mind. They focus on good graphics capabilities and support overclocking. The 9-series is the most current and supports 8-core AMD processors.
▲ The AMD 580X Crossfire chipset supports ATI CrossFire.
▲ The AMD 780V chipset is designed for business needs.
▲ The AMD 740G and 690 chipsets are designed for low-end, inexpensive systems.

NVIDIA, SIS, AND VIA CHIPSETS

NVIDIA, SiS, and VIA all make graphics processors and chipsets for both AMD and Intel processors. Recall that NVIDIA's method of connecting multiple video cards in the same system is called SLI. If you're planning a gaming computer with two video cards, check out a motherboard that supports SLI and uses the nForce chipset. In motherboard ads, look for the SLI and nForce logos.

4

A+
220-801
1.2

BUSES AND EXPANSION SLOTS

When you look carefully at a motherboard, you see many fine lines on both the top and the bottom of the board's surface (see Figure 4-15). These lines, sometimes called **traces**, are circuits or paths that enable data, instructions, and power to move from component to component on the board. This system of pathways used for communication and the protocol and methods used for transmission are collectively called the **bus**. (A **protocol** is a set of rules and standards that any two entities use for communication.) The parts of the bus that we are most familiar with are the lines of the bus that are used for data; these lines are called the **data bus**. A bus can also carry electrical power (to power components on the motherboard), control signals (to coordinate activity), and memory addresses (for one program to tell another program where to find data or instructions).

One bus line

Bottom of the
CPU socket

© Cengage Learning 2014

Figure 4-15 On the bottom of the motherboard, you can see bus lines
terminating at the CPU socket

All data and instructions inside a computer exist in binary, which means there are only two states: on and off. Binary data is put on a line of a bus by placing voltage on that line. We can visualize that bits are "traveling" down the bus in parallel, but in reality, the voltage placed on each line is not "traveling"; rather, it is all over the line. When one component at one end of the line wants to write data to another component, the two components get in sync for the write operation. Then, the first component places voltage on several lines of the bus, and the other component immediately reads the voltage on these lines. The CPU or other devices interpret the voltage, or lack of voltage, on each line on the bus as binary digits (0s or 1s).

The width of a data bus is called the **data path size**. Some buses have data paths that are 8, 16, 32, 64, 128, or more bits wide. For example, a bus that has eight wires, or lines, to transmit data is called an 8-bit bus. Figure 4-16 shows an 8-bit bus between the CPU and memory that is transmitting the letter A (binary 0100 0001). All bits of a byte are placed on their lines of the bus at the same time: no voltage for binary zero and voltage for binary one. For every eight bits of a bus, a bus might use a ninth bit for error checking. Adding a check bit for each byte allows the component reading the data to verify that it is the same data written to the bus.

4

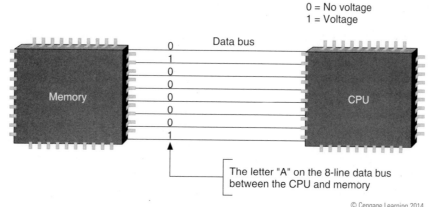

Figure 4-16   A data bus has traces or lines that carry voltage interpreted by the CPU and other devices as bits

One of the most interesting lines, or circuits, on a bus is the **system clock** or system timer, which is dedicated to timing the activities on the motherboard much like a metronome helps a musician with timing. The chipset sends out a continuous pulsating electrical signal on one line of the system bus. This one system clock line, dedicated to carrying the pulse, is read by other components on the motherboard (including the processor, bus slots, memory slots, and so forth) and ensures that all activities are synchronized. Remember that everything in a computer is binary, and this includes the activities themselves. Instead of continuously working to perform commands or move data, the CPU, bus, and other devices work in a binary fashion—do something, stop, do something, stop, and so forth. Each device works on a clock cycle or beat of the clock. Some devices, such as the CPU, do two or more operations on one beat of the clock, and others do one operation for each beat. Some devices might even do something on every other beat, but most components inside the system work according to these beats or cycles.

You can think of this as similar to children jumping rope. The system clock (child turning the rope) provides the beats or cycles, while devices (children jumping) work in a binary fashion (jump, don't jump). In the analogy, some children jump two or more times for each rope pass.

> **Notes** If the processor requests something from a slow device and the device is not ready, the device issues a **wait state**, which is a command to the processor to wait for slower devices to catch up.

The speed of memory, Front Side Bus, processor, or other component is measured in **hertz (Hz)**, which is one cycle per second; **megahertz (MHz)**, which is one million cycles per second; and **gigahertz (GHz)**, which is one billion cycles per second. Common ratings for memory are 1333 MHz and 1866 MHz. Common ratings for Front Side Buses are 2600 MHz, 2000 MHz, 1600 MHz, 1333 MHz, 1066 MHz, 800 MHz, 533 MHz, or 400 MHz. A CPU operates from 166 MHz to almost 4 GHz. The CPU can put data or instructions on its internal bus at a much higher rate than does the motherboard. Although we often refer to the speed of the CPU and memory, talking about the frequency of these devices is more accurate, because the term "speed" implies a continuous flow, while the term "frequency" implies a digital or binary flow: on and off, on and off.

> **Notes** Rather than measuring the frequency of a system bus, sometimes you see a system bus measured in performance such as the GA-990FXA-UD3 motherboard by GIGABYTE (see *www.gigabyte.us*). This system bus is rated at 5.2 GT/s or 5200 MT/s. One GT/s is one billion transfers per second, and one MT/s is one million transfers per second.

A+
220-801
1.2

A motherboard can have more than one bus, each using a different protocol, speed, data path size, and so on. Table 4-4 lists the various buses used on motherboards today, in order of throughput speed from fastest to slowest. (Throughput is sometimes called bandwidth.) Looking at the second column of Table 4-4, you can see that a bus is called an expansion bus, local bus, local I/O bus, or local video bus. A bus that does not run in sync with the system clock is called an expansion bus. For chipsets that use a South Bridge, expansion buses always connect here. Most buses today are local buses, meaning they run in sync with the system clock. If a local bus connects to the slower I/O controller hub or South Bridge of the chipset, it is called a local I/O bus. Because the video card needs to run at a faster rate than other adapter cards, this one slot always connects to the faster end of the chipset, the North Bridge, or directly to the processor when using Sandy Bridge or Ivy Bridge technology. Older boards used AGP video slots, and today's boards use PCI Express x16 slots for video. These video buses that connect to the North Bridge or to the processor are called local video buses.

Bus	Bus Type	Data Path in Bits	Address Lines	Bus Frequency	Throughput
PCI Express Version 2	Local video and local I/O	Serial with up to 32 lanes	Up to 32 lanes	2.5 GHz	Up to 500 MB/sec per lane in each direction
PCI Express Version 1.1	Local video and local I/O	Serial with up to 16 lanes	Up to 16 lanes	1.25 GHz	Up to 250 MB/sec per lane in each direction
PCI Express Version 1	Local video and local I/O	Serial with up to 16 lanes	Up to 16 lanes	1.25 GHz	Up to 250 MB/sec per lane in each direction
PCI-X	Local I/O	64	32	66, 133, 266, or 533 MHz	Up to 8.5 GB/sec
PCI	Local I/O	32 or 64	32 or 64	33, 66 MHz	133, 266, or 532 MB/sec
AGP 1x, 2x, 3x, 4x, 8x	Local video	32	NA	66, 75, 100 MHz	266 MB/sec to 2.1 GB/sec
FireWire 400 and 800	Local I/O or expansion	1	Serial	NA	Up to 3.2 Gbps (gigabits per second)
USB 1.1, 2.0, and 3.0	Expansion	1	Serial	3 MHz	12 or 480 Mbps (megabits per second) or 5.0 Gbps (gigabits per second)

© Cengage Learning 2014

Table 4-4 Buses listed by throughput

The AGP buses were developed specifically for video cards, and the PCI buses are used for many types of cards, including video cards. We'll now look at the details of the PCI and AGP buses. The FireWire and USB buses are discussed in Chapter 8.

CONVENTIONAL PCI

The first PCI bus had a 32-bit data path, supplied 5 V of power to an adapter card, and operated at 33 MHz. It was the first bus that allowed adapter cards to run in sync with the CPU. PCI Version 2.x introduced the 64-bit, 3.3 V PCI slot, doubling data throughput of the bus. Because a card can be damaged if installed in the wrong voltage slot, a notch in a PCI slot distinguishes between a 5 V slot and a 3.3 V slot. A Universal PCI card can use either a 3.3 V or 5 V slot and contains both notches (see Figure 4-17). Conventional PCI is no longer evolving and ended up with four types of slots and six possible PCI card configurations to use these slots. These slots and cards include 32-bit PCI and 64-bit PCI-X, all shown in Figure 4-18.

A+
220-801
1.2

4

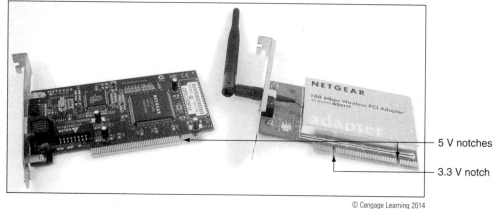

5 V notches

3.3 V notch

© Cengage Learning 2014

Figure 4-17 A 32-bit, 5 V PCI network card and a 32-bit, universal PCI wireless card show the difference in PCI notches set to distinguish voltages in a PCI slot

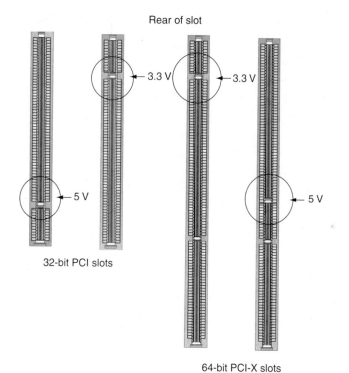

Rear of slot

3.3 V

3.3 V

5 V

5 V

32-bit PCI slots

64-bit PCI-X slots

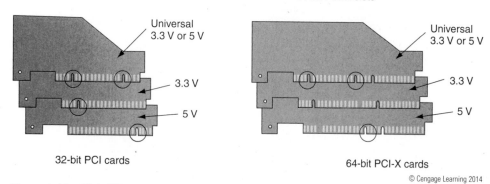

Universal
3.3 V or 5 V

3.3 V

5 V

32-bit PCI cards

Universal
3.3 V or 5 V

3.3 V

5 V

64-bit PCI-X cards

© Cengage Learning 2014

Figure 4-18 With PCI Version 2.x, there are four possible types of expansion slots and six differently configured PCI expansion cards to use these slots

Notes The miniPCI bus and slot is used in laptops and is covered in Chapter 19.

A+
220-801
1.2

PCI-X

The next evolution of PCI is PCI-X, which uses a 64-bit data path and had three major revisions; the last and final revision is PCI-X 3.0. All PCI-X revisions are backward compatible with conventional PCI cards and slots, except 5-V PCI cards are not supported. PCI-X focused on the server market; therefore, it's unlikely you'll see PCI-X slots in desktop computers. Motherboards that use PCI-X tend to have several different PCI slots with some 32-bit or 64-bit slots running at different speeds. For example, Figure 4-19 shows a server motherboard with three types of slots. The two long white slots are PCI-X; the two shorter white slots are PCI, and the two black slots are PCI-e. The two PCI-X slots can use most 32-bit and 64-bit PCI or PCI-X cards.

Courtesy of Super Micro Computer, Inc.

Figure 4-19   The two long white PCI-X slots can support PCI cards

PCI EXPRESS

PCI Express (PCIe) uses an altogether different architectural design than conventional PCI and PCI-X; PCIe is not backward compatible with either. PCI Express will ultimately replace both these buses as well as the AGP bus, although it is expected PCI Express will coexist with conventional PCI for some time to come (see Figure 4-20). Whereas PCI uses

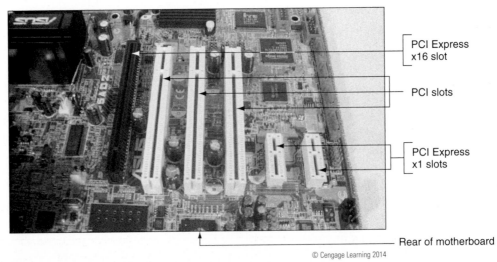

PCI Express x16 slot

PCI slots

PCI Express x1 slots

Rear of motherboard

© Cengage Learning 2014

Figure 4-20   Three PCI Express slots and three PCI slots on a motherboard

A+
220-801
1.2

a 32-bit or 64-bit parallel bus, PCI Express uses a serial bus, which is faster than a parallel bus because it transmits data in packets similar to how an Ethernet network, USB, and FireWire transmit data. A PCIe expansion slot can provide one or more of these serial lanes.

Another difference in PCI Express is how it connects to the processor. One or more PCI Express slots used for video cards have a direct link to the North Bridge or to the processor (using Sandy Bridge or Ivy Bridge architecture). Refer back to Figures 4-9, 4-10, and 4-12.

PCI Express currently comes in four different slot sizes called PCI Express ×1 (pronounced "by one"), ×4, ×8, and ×16. Figure 4-21 shows three of these slots. Notice in the photo how the PCIe slots are not as tall and the pins are closer together than the conventional PCI slot. A PCI Express ×1 slot contains a single lane for data; this lane is actually four wires. One pair of wires is used to send data and the other pair receives data, one bit at a time. The ×16 slot contains 16 lanes, with each lane timed independently of other lanes. The more lanes you have, the more data gets transmitted in a given time. Therefore, a ×16 slot is faster than a ×4 slot, which is faster than a ×1 slot. A shorter PCI Express card (such as a ×1 card) can be installed in a longer PCI Express slot (such as a ×4 slot).

Two PCIe x16 slots

PCIe x4 slot

Conventional PCI slot

Two PCIe x1 slots

© Cengage Learning 2014

Figure 4-21   Three types of PCIe slots and one conventional PCI slot

Revisions of PCIe include PCIe version 1.1, PCIe version 2.0 and 2.1, and PCIe version 3.0, which doubles the throughput of Version 2. Here are important facts about PCIe versions 1.0, 1.1, and 2.0:

▲ *PCIe version 1.0.* The original PCIe version 1.0 allowed for 150 W to PCIe cards. Pins on the expansion card provide 75 W, and a new 6-pin PCIe connector from the power supply provides an additional 75 W.

▲ *PCIe version 1.1.* PCIe version 1.1 allowed for more wattage to PCIe cards, up to 225 watts. The standard allows for two 6-pin PCIe connectors from the power supply to the card. Therefore, the total 225 W comes as 75 W from the slot and 150 W from the two connectors.

▲ *PCIe version 2.0.* PCIe version 2.0 doubled the frequency of the PCIe bus and allows for up to 32 lanes on one slot (though few motherboards or cards actually use 32 lane slots). The allowed wattage to one PCIe 2.0 card was increased to a total of 300 watts by using a new 8-pin PCIe power connector that provides 150 W (see Figure 4-22). The 300 watts to the card come from the slot (75 W), from the 8-pin connector (150 W), and an additional 75 W come from a second auxiliary connector on the motherboard. This second connector can be a 6-pin PCIe connector, a Molex-style connector, or a SATA-style connector. You'll see an example of these connectors later in the chapter.

A+
220-801
1.2

8-pin connector

© Cengage Learning 2014

Figure 4-22 8-pin PCIe Version 2.0 power connector

A+
220-801
1.2, 1.4

PCI RISER CARDS USED TO EXTEND THE SLOTS

Suppose you are installing a Mini-ITX or microATX motherboard into a low-profile or slimline case that does not give you enough room to install a PCI card standing up in an expansion slot. In this situation, a PCI riser card can solve the problem. The **riser card** installs in the slot and provides another slot at a right angle (see Figure 4-23). When you install an expansion card in this riser card slot, the card sits parallel to the motherboard, taking up less space. These riser cards come for all types of PCI slots, including PCIe, PCI-X, and conventional PCI.

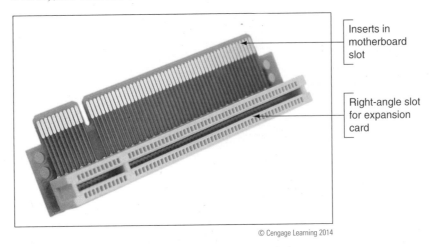

Inserts in motherboard slot

Right-angle slot for expansion card

© Cengage Learning 2014

Figure 4-23 PCI riser card provides a 3.3 V slot or 5 V slot depending on which direction the card is inserted in the PCI slot

A+
220-801
1.2

THE AGP BUSES

Motherboard video slots and video cards used the **Accelerated Graphics Port (AGP)** standards for many years, but AGP has been replaced by PCI Express. Even though AGP is a dying technology, you still need to know how to support it in case you are ever called on to replace an AGP video card or a motherboard with an AGP slot.

AGP evolved over several years, and the different AGP standards can be confusing. AGP standards include three major releases (AGP 1.0, AGP 2.0, and AGP 3.0), one major change in the AGP slot length standard (AGP Pro), four different speeds (1x, 2x, 4x, and 8x) yielding four different throughputs, three different voltages (3.3 V, 1.5 V, and 0.8 V), and six different expansion slots (AGP 3.3 V, AGP 1.5 V, AGP Universal, AGP Pro 3.3 V, APG Pro 1.5 V, and AGP Pro Universal). To help you make sense of all this, Table 4-5 sorts it all out.

A+
220-801
1.2

Standard	Speeds (Cycles Per Clock Beat)	Maximum Throughput	Voltage	Slots Supported
AGP 1.0	1x	266 MB/sec	3.3 V	Slot keyed to 3.3 V
AGP 2.0	1x, 2x, or 4x	533 MB/sec or 1.06 GB/sec	3.3 V or 1.5 V	Slot keyed to 1.5 V Slot keyed to 3.3 V Universal slot (for either 1.5 V or 3.3 V cards)
AGP Pro	Applies to all speeds	NA	3.3 V or 1.5 V	AGP Pro 3.3 V keyed AGP Pro 1.5 V keyed AGP Pro Universal (for either 1.5 V or 3.3 V cards)
AGP 3.0	4x or 8x	2.12 GB/sec	1.5 V and 0.8 V	Universal AGP 3.0 (4x/8x) slot Slot keyed to 1.5 V Slot keyed to AGP Pro 1.5 V

Table 4-5 AGP standards summarized

© Cengage Learning 2014

As you can see from Table 4-5, there are several different AGP slots and matching card connectors that apply to the different standards. When matching video cards to AGP slots, be aware of these several variations. For instance, the first two slots in Figure 4-24 are used by cards that follow the AGP 1.0 or AGP 2.0 standards. These slots have key positions so that you cannot put an AGP 3.3 V card in an AGP 1.5 V slot or vice versa. The third slot is a universal slot that can accommodate 3.3 V or 1.5 V cards. All three slots are 2.9 inches long and have 132 pins, although some pins are not used. Figure 4-25 shows a motherboard with an older AGP 3.3 V slot. Notice how the keyed 3.3 V break in the slot is near the back side of the motherboard where expansion cards are bracketed to the case.

Another AGP standard, AGP Pro, has provisions for a longer slot. This 180-pin slot has extensions on both ends that contain an additional 20 pins on one end and 28 pins on the other end, to provide extra voltage for an AGP card that consumes more than 25 watts of power. These wider slots might be keyed to 3.3 V or 1.5 V or might be a Universal Pro slot that can hold either 3.3 V or 1.5 V cards. Also, when using an AGP Pro video card, leave the PCI slot next to it empty to improve ventilation and prevent overheating.

The last AGP standard, AGP 3.0, runs at 8x or 4x speeds. AGP 3.0 cards can be installed in an AGP 1.5 V slot, but signals are put on the data bus using 0.8 V. It's best to install an AGP 3.0 card in a slot that is designed to support AGP 3.0 cards. However, if you install an AGP 3.0 card in an older AGP 1.5 V slot, the card might or might not work, but the card will not be damaged.

An AGP video card will be keyed to 1.5 V or 3.3 V, or a universal AGP video card has both keys so that it can fit into either a 1.5 V keyed slot or a 3.3 V keyed slot. A universal AGP video card also fits into a universal AGP slot. If an AGP video card does not make use of the extra pins provided by the AGP Pro slot, it can still be inserted into the AGP Pro slot if it has a registration tab that fits into the end of the Pro slot near the center of the motherboard. In Chapter 8, you'll learn about AGP video cards.

A+
220-801
1.2

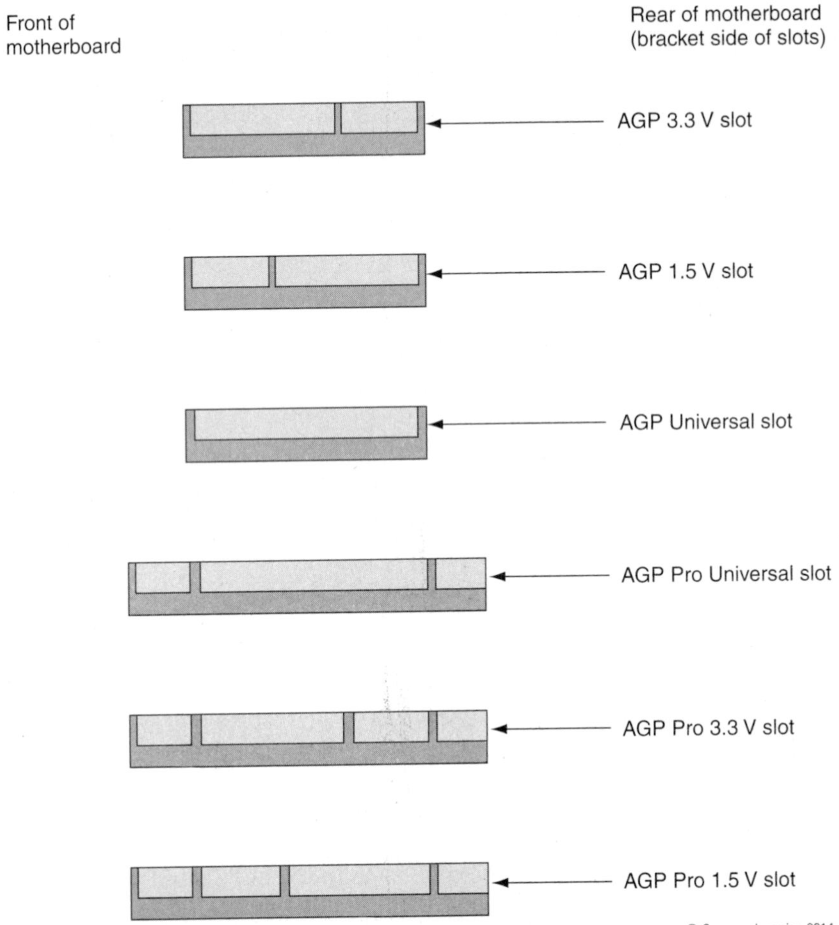

Front of
motherboard

Rear of motherboard
(bracket side of slots)

AGP 3.3 V slot

AGP 1.5 V slot

AGP Universal slot

AGP Pro Universal slot

AGP Pro 3.3 V slot

AGP Pro 1.5 V slot

© Cengage Learning 2014

Figure 4-24   Six types of AGP slots

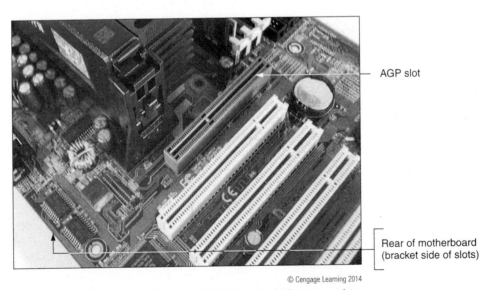

AGP slot

Rear of motherboard
(bracket side of slots)

© Cengage Learning 2014

Figure 4-25   This motherboard uses an AGP 3.3 V slot, which accommodates
an AGP 1.0 video card

Notes If you're trying to buy an AGP video card to match a motherboard slot, you have to be really careful. When reading an AGP ad, it's hard to distinguish between AGP 3.3 V and AGP 3.0, but there's a big difference in these standards, and they are not interchangeable.

A+
220-801
1.2

ON-BOARD PORTS AND CONNECTORS

In addition to expansion slots, a motherboard might also have several ports and internal connectors. Ports coming directly off the motherboard are called **on-board ports** or integrated components. Almost all motherboards have two or more USB ports and sound ports. Boards might also offer a network port, FireWire (IEEE 1394) port, video port, one or more eSATA ports (for external SATA hard drives), and a port for a wireless antenna. Older motherboards might have mouse and keyboard ports (called PS/2 ports), modem port, parallel port, and serial port. Figures 4-26 and 4-27 show ports on older motherboards. Figure 4-28 shows ports on a current high-end motherboard.

© Cengage Learning 2014

Figure 4-26 A motherboard provides ports for common I/O devices

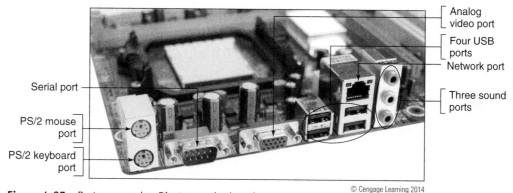

© Cengage Learning 2014

Figure 4-27 Ports on a value Biostar motherboard

© Cengage Learning 2014

Figure 4-28 Intel DX58SO motherboard on-board ports

When you purchase a motherboard, the package includes an **I/O shield**, which is the plate that you install in the computer case that provides holes for these I/O ports. The I/O shield is the size designed for the case's form factor, and the holes in the shield are positioned

A+
220-801
1.2

for the motherboard ports (see Figure 4-29). When you first install a motherboard, you might need to install the drivers that come on the CD bundled with the board before some of the motherboard ports will work. How to install the motherboard drivers is covered later in the chapter.

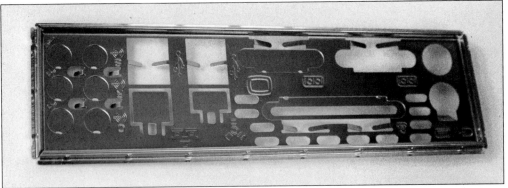

© Cengage Learning 2014

Figure 4-29   The I/O shield fits the motherboard ports to the computer case

Some motherboards come with connector modules that provide additional ports off the rear of the case. For example, Figure 4-30 shows three modules that came bundled with one motherboard. To use the ports on a module, you connect its cable to a connector on the motherboard and install the module in a slot on the rear of the case intended for an expansion card.

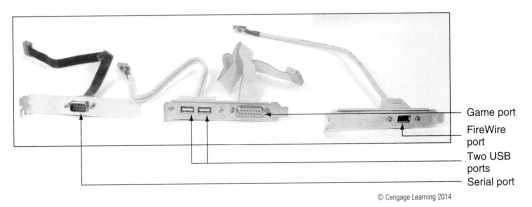

Game port
FireWire port
Two USB ports
Serial port

© Cengage Learning 2014

Figure 4-30   These modules provide additional ports off the rear of a computer case

A motherboard might have several internal connectors, including parallel ATA (PATA) connectors (also called IDE connectors), a floppy drive connector, serial ATA (SATA) connectors, SCSI connectors, a USB connector, or a FireWire (IEEE 1394) connector. When you purchase a motherboard, look in the package for the motherboard manual either printed or on CD. It will show a diagram of the board with a description of each connector. For example, the connectors for the motherboard in Figure 4-31 are labeled as the manual describes them. If a connector is a group of pins sticking up on the board, the connector is called a header. You will learn to use most of these connectors in later chapters.

S/PDIF header

High-definition
audio header

Six SATA
headers

Two USB
headers

FireWire
header

© Cengage Learning 2014

Figure 4-31 Internal connectors on a motherboard for drives and ports on the front of the case

Now that you know what to expect when examining or selecting a motherboard, let's see how to configure a board.

CONFIGURING A MOTHERBOARD

Settings on the motherboard are used to enable or disable a connector or port, set the frequency of the CPU or Front Side Bus, control security features, and control what happens when the PC first boots. In the past, configuring these and other motherboard settings was done in three different ways: jumpers, settings stored in CMOS RAM, and, for really old boards, a bank of DIP switches. Configuring the board by physically setting DIP switches or jumpers was extremely inconvenient because you had to open the computer case to make a change.

A more convenient method is to store configuration data in CMOS RAM, and today's computers store almost all configuration data there. **CMOS (complementary metal-oxide semiconductor)** is a method of manufacturing microchips, and **CMOS RAM** is a small amount of memory stored on the motherboard used to hold motherboard settings. This CMOS RAM retains the data even when the computer is turned off because it is charged by a nearby battery. A program in BIOS, called BIOS setup or CMOS setup, can easily make changes to the settings stored in CMOS RAM.

Now let's see how to configure a motherboard using jumpers, setup BIOS, and motherboard drivers. (It's unlikely you'll see a board that still uses DIP switches.) The first step in the process of configuring a motherboard is to locate the motherboard documentation.

APPLYING | CONCEPTS FIND THE MOTHERBOARD DOCUMENTATION

To know how to configure a motherboard, you need access to the motherboard user guide, which explains all the settings and how to use them. This guide can be a PDF file stored on the CD or DVD that came bundled with the motherboard. If you don't have the CD, you can download the user guide from the motherboard manufacturer's web site.

To find the correct user guide online, you need to know the board manufacturer and model. If a motherboard is already installed in a computer, you can use the Windows System Information utility (msinfo32.exe) to report the brand and model of the board. To access the utility, click **Start**, type **msinfo32.exe** in the Search box, and press **Enter**. In the System Information window, click **System Summary**. In the System Summary information in the right pane, look for the motherboard information labeled as the System Manufacturer and System Model (see Figure 4-32).

4

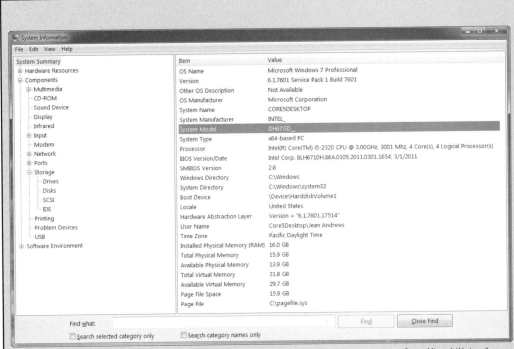

Figure 4-32   Use the System Information window to identify the motherboard brand and model

If the motherboard is not installed or the system is not working, look for the brand and model imprinted somewhere on the motherboard (see Figure 4-33). Next, go to the web site of the motherboard manufacturer and download the user guide. Web sites for several motherboard manufacturers are listed in Table 4-6. The diagrams, pictures, charts, and explanations of settings and components in the user guide will be invaluable to you when supporting this board.

Figure 4-33   The motherboard brand and model are imprinted somewhere on the board

A+
220-801
1.1

Manufacturer	Web Address
ASUS	*www.asus.com*
BIOSTAR Group	*www.biostar.com.tw*
Evga	*www.evga.com*
ASRock	*www.asrock.com*
Gigabyte Technology Co., Ltd.	*www.gigabyte.com*
Intel Corporation	*www.intel.com*
Micro-Star International (MSI)	*www.msicomputer.com*
Super Micro Computer, Inc.	*www.supermicro.com*

© Cengage Learning 2014

Table 4-6 Major manufacturers of motherboards

USING JUMPERS TO CONFIGURE A MOTHERBOARD

Older motherboards relied heavily on jumpers to configure the board, and newer motherboards still use a few important jumpers. A **jumper** is two small posts or metal pins that stick up off the motherboard that is open or closed. An open jumper has no cover, and a closed jumper has a cover on the two pins (see Figure 4-34). On older boards, a group of jumpers might be used to tell the system at what speed the CPU is running, or to turn a power-saving feature on or off. Look at the jumper cover in Figure 4-34(b) that is "parked," meaning it is hanging on a single pin for safekeeping, but is not being used to turn a jumper setting on.

© Cengage Learning 2014

Figure 4-34 A 6-pin jumper group on a circuit board: (a) has no jumpers set to on, (b) has a cover parked on one pin, and (c) is configured with one jumper setting turned on

Most motherboards today allow you to set a supervisor password (to make changes in setup BIOS) or a power-on password (to get access to the system). Know that these passwords are not the same password that can be required by a Windows OS at startup. If both passwords are forgotten, you cannot use the computer. However, jumpers can be set to clear both passwords. Also, BIOS firmware might need updating (called flashing the BIOS) to solve a problem with the motherboard or to use a new motherboard feature. If flashing BIOS fails, a jumper can be set to undo the update.

For example, Figure 4-35 shows a group of three jumpers on one board. (The tan jumper cap is positioned on the first two jumper pins on the left side of the group.) Figure 4-36 shows the motherboard documentation on how to use these jumpers. When jumpers 1 and 2 are closed, which they are in the figure, normal booting happens. When jumpers 2 and 3 are closed, passwords to BIOS setup can be cleared on the next boot. When no jumpers are closed, on the next boot, the BIOS will recover itself from a failed update. Once set for normal booting, the jumpers should be changed only if you are trying to recover when a power-up password is lost or flashing BIOS has failed. To know how to set jumpers, see the motherboard documentation.

© Cengage Learning 2014

Figure 4-35 This group of three jumpers controls the BIOS configuration

Jumper Position	Mode	Description
1 / 3	Normal (default)	The current BIOS configuration is used for booting.
1 / 3	Configure	After POST, the BIOS displays a menu in CMOS setup that can be used to clear the user and supervisor power-on passwords.
1 / 3	Recovery	Recovery is used to recover from a failed BIOS update. Details can be found on the motherboard CD.

© Cengage Learning 2014

Figure 4-36 BIOS configuration jumper settings

USING SETUP BIOS TO CONFIGURE A MOTHERBOARD

The motherboard settings stored in CMOS RAM don't normally need to be changed except, for example, when there is a problem with hardware, or a power-saving feature or security feature (such as a power-on password) needs to be disabled or enabled. In this part of the chapter, you learn about motherboard settings that you can view or change using setup BIOS.

4

A+
220-801
1.1

> 🔆 **A+ Exam Tip** The A+ 220-801 exam expects you to know about BIOS settings regarding RAM, the hard drive, optical drive, CPU, boot sequence, system date and time, virtualization support, built-in diagnostics, monitoring temperature, fan speeds, intrusion detection, voltage, and clock and bus speeds. All these settings are covered in this part of the chapter.

ACCESS THE BIOS SETUP PROGRAM

You access the BIOS setup program by pressing a key or combination of keys during the boot process. The exact way to enter setup varies from one motherboard manufacturer to another. Table 4-7 lists the keystrokes needed to access BIOS setup for some common BIOS types.

BIOS	Key to Press During POST to Access Setup
AMI BIOS	Del
Award BIOS	Del
Older Phoenix BIOS	Ctrl+Alt+Esc or Ctrl+Alt+S
Newer Phoenix BIOS	F2, F1, or Del
Dell computers using Phoenix BIOS	Press Ctrl+Alt+Enter or press F2 every few seconds until the message *Entering Setup* appears.
Compaq computers	Press the F10 key while the cursor is in the upper-right corner of the screen, which happens just after the two beeps during booting. For older Compaq computers, press F1, F2, F10, or Del.

© Cengage Learning 2014

Table 4-7 How to access setup BIOS

For the exact method you need to use to enter setup, see the documentation for your motherboard. A message such as the following usually appears on the screen near the beginning of the boot:

```
Press DEL to change Setup
```

or

```
Press F2 for Setup
```

When you press the appropriate key or keys, a setup screen appears with menus and Help features that are often very user-friendly. Although the exact menus depend on the BIOS maker, the sample screens that follow will help you become familiar with the general contents of BIOS setup screens. Figure 4-37 shows a main menu for setup. On this menu, you can view information about the BIOS version, processor model and speed, memory speed, total memory, and the amount of memory in each memory slot. You can also change the system date and time.

Now let's examine setup screens that apply to the boot sequence, virtualization, built-in diagnostics, monitoring the system, and security.

A+
220-801
1.1

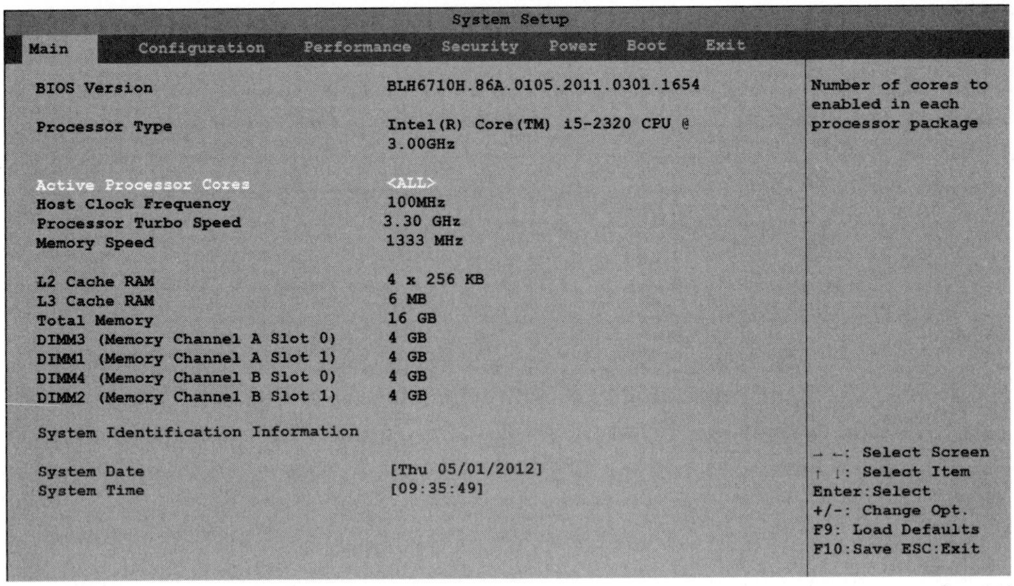

```
                              System Setup
  Main    Configuration   Performance   Security   Power   Boot   Exit

  BIOS Version                    BLH6710H.86A.0105.2011.0301.1654      Number of cores to
                                                                        enabled in each
  Processor Type                  Intel(R) Core(TM) i5-2320 CPU @       processor package
                                  3.00GHz

  Active Processor Cores          <ALL>
  Host Clock Frequency            100MHz
  Processor Turbo Speed           3.30 GHz
  Memory Speed                    1333 MHz

  L2 Cache RAM                    4 x 256 KB
  L3 Cache RAM                    6 MB
  Total Memory                    16 GB
  DIMM3 (Memory Channel A Slot 0) 4 GB
  DIMM1 (Memory Channel A Slot 1) 4 GB
  DIMM4 (Memory Channel B Slot 0) 4 GB
  DIMM2 (Memory Channel B Slot 1) 4 GB

  System Identification Information

  System Date                     [Thu 05/01/2012]             → ←: Select Screen
  System Time                     [09:35:49]                   ↑ ↓: Select Item
                                                               Enter:Select
                                                               +/-: Change Opt.
                                                               F9: Load Defaults
                                                               F10:Save ESC:Exit
```

Source: Intel

Figure 4-37 BIOS setup main menu

CHANGE THE BOOT SEQUENCE

Figure 4-38 shows an example of a boot menu in BIOS setup. Here, you can set the order in which the system tries to boot from certain devices (called the boot sequence or boot priority). Most likely when you first install a hard drive or an operating system, you will want to have the BIOS attempt to first boot from a DVD so that you can install Windows from the setup DVD. After the OS is installed, to prevent accidental boots from a DVD or other media, change setup BIOS to boot first from the hard drive.

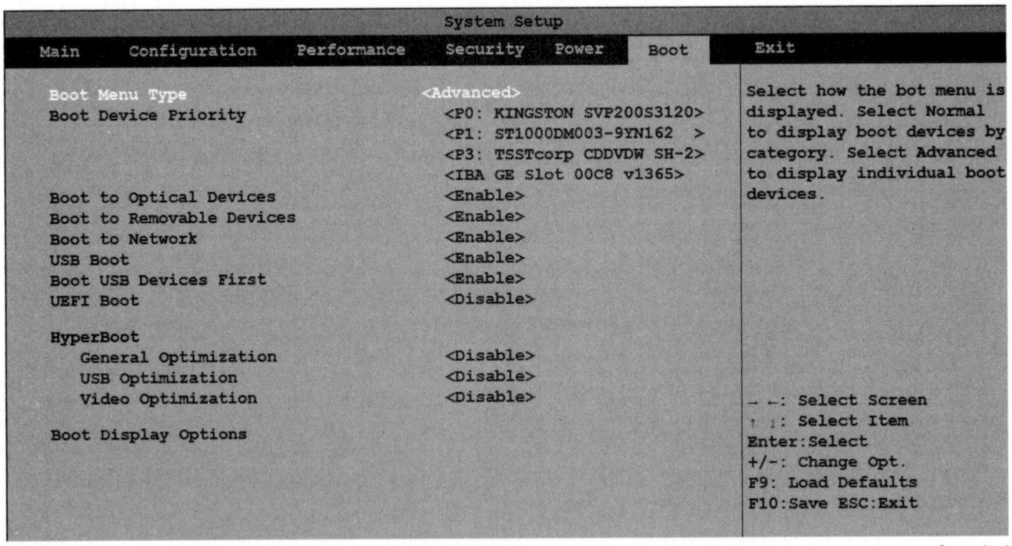

```
                              System Setup
  Main    Configuration   Performance   Security   Power   Boot      Exit

  Boot Menu Type                  <Advanced>                    Select how the bot menu is
  Boot Device Priority            <P0: KINGSTON SVP200S3120>    displayed. Select Normal
                                  <P1: ST1000DM003-9YN162  >    to display boot devices by
                                  <P3: TSSTcorp CDDVDW SH-2>    category. Select Advanced
                                  <IBA GE Slot 00C8 v1365>      to display individual boot
  Boot to Optical Devices         <Enable>                      devices.
  Boot to Removable Devices       <Enable>
  Boot to Network                 <Enable>
  USB Boot                        <Enable>
  Boot USB Devices First          <Enable>
  UEFI Boot                       <Disable>

  HyperBoot
     General Optimization         <Disable>
     USB Optimization             <Disable>
     Video Optimization           <Disable>                    → ←: Select Screen
                                                               ↑ ↓: Select Item
  Boot Display Options                                         Enter:Select
                                                               +/-: Change Opt.
                                                               F9: Load Defaults
                                                               F10:Save ESC:Exit
```

Source: Intel

Figure 4-38 Set the boot priority order in BIOS setup

Notice in Figure 4-38 the option to perform a UEFI Boot. **Unified Extensible Firmware Interface (UEFI)** is a new standard that is slowly replacing the BIOS standard. It is an interface between firmware on the motherboard and the operating system and improves on processes for booting, handing over the boot to the OS, and loading device drivers and applications before the OS loads. The UEFI Boot must be enabled in order to boot from a hard drive that is larger than 2 TB (terabytes). For more information on UEFI, see the UEFI consortium at *www.uefi.org*.

Also, the BIOS setup boot screens might give you options regarding built-in diagnostics that occur at the boot. Recall from Chapter 1 that these tests are called the POST (Power-on Self Test). You can configure some motherboards to perform a quick boot and bypass the extensive POST. For these systems, if you are troubleshooting a boot problem, be sure to set BIOS to perform the full POST.

CONFIGURE ONBOARD DEVICES

You can enable or disable some onboard devices (for example, a network port, FireWire port, USB ports, or video ports) using setup BIOS. For one system, the Configuration screen shown in Figure 4-39 does the job. On this screen, you can enable or disable a port or group of ports, and you can configure the Front Panel Audio ports for Auto, High Definition audio, and Legacy audio, or you can disable these audio ports. What you can configure on your system depends on the onboard devices the motherboard offers.

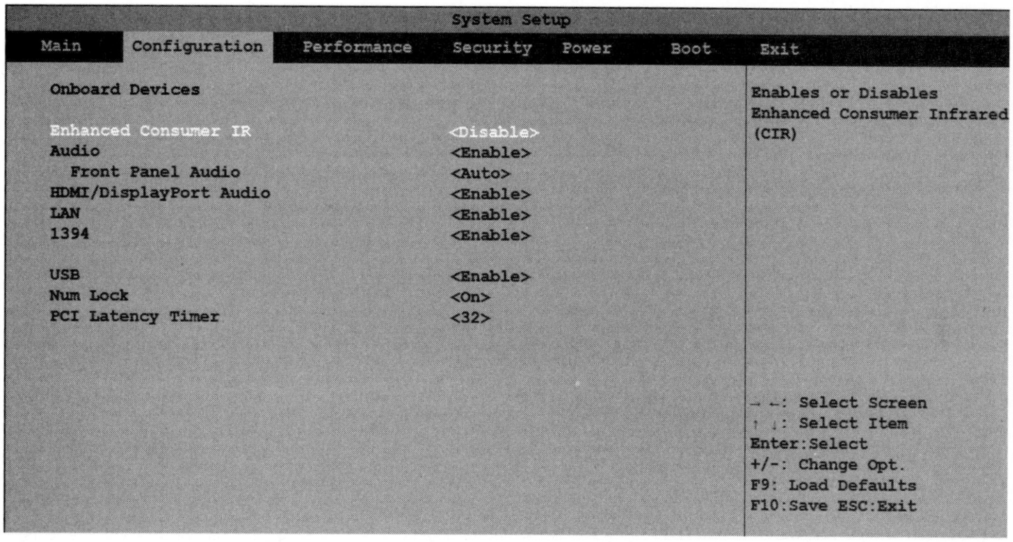

Figure 4-39 Enable and disable onboard devices

Source: Intel

Notes You don't have to replace an entire motherboard if one port fails. For example, if the network port fails, use BIOS setup to disable the port. Then use an expansion card for the port instead.

VIEW HARD DRIVE AND OPTICAL DRIVE INFORMATION

Using setup BIOS, you can view information about installed hard drives and optical drives. For example, in Figure 4-40, one system shows five internal SATA and eSATA ports and one external eSATA port. One 120 GB hard drive is installed on SATA port 0, and another 1000 GB hard drive is installed on SATA port 1. Both ports are internal SATA connectors on the motherboard. Notice the optical drive is installed on SATA port 3, also an internal connector on the motherboard.

A+
220-801
1.1

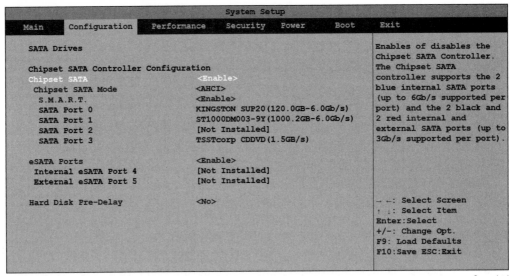

```
                                    System Setup
   Main    Configuration    Performance   Security   Power    Boot    Exit

   SATA Drives                                         Enables of disables the
                                                       Chipset SATA Controller.
   Chipset SATA Controller Configuration               The Chipset SATA
   Chipset SATA                 <Enable>                controller supports the 2
    Chipset SATA Mode           <AHCI>                 blue internal SATA ports
     S.M.A.R.T.                 <Enable>               (up to 6Gb/s supported per
     SATA Port 0                KINGSTON SUP20(120.0GB-6.0Gb/s)  port) and the 2 black and
     SATA Port 1                ST1000DM003-9Y(1000.2GB-6.0Gb/s) 2 red internal and
     SATA Port 2                [Not Installed]        external SATA ports (up to
     SATA Port 3                TSSTcorp CDDVD(1.5GB/s) 3Gb/s supported per port).

    eSATA Ports                 <Enable>
     Internal eSATA Port 4      [Not Installed]
     External eSATA Port 5      [Not Installed]

   Hard Disk Pre-Delay          <No>                   → ←: Select Screen
                                                       ↑ ↓: Select Item
                                                       Enter:Select
                                                       +/-: Change Opt.
                                                       F9: Load Defaults
                                                       F10:Save ESC:Exit
```

Source: Intel

Figure 4-40 A BIOS setup screen showing a list of drives installed on the system

PROCESSOR AND CLOCK SPEEDS

Recall from Chapter 1 that overclocking is running a processor, memory, motherboard, or video card at a higher speed than the manufacturer recommends. Some motherboards allow overclocking. If you decide to overclock a system, pay careful attention to the temperature of the processor so it does not overheat; overheating can damage the processor. Figure 4-41 shows one BIOS setup screen for adjusting performance. Notice on the screen the Host Clock Frequency. This is the basic system clock provided by the chipset, by which all other components synchronize activities. The Core Max Multiplier on this screen is 33. (This value is sometimes called the bus/core ratio.) When you multiply 100 MHz by 33, you get 3.30 GHz, which is the frequency of the processor. This board uses the QuickPath Interconnect. For older boards that use a Front Side Bus, you can change the speed of the FSB to overclock the system, which affects the processor and memory speeds. On some boards, you can change the processor multiplier to change the processor speed and/or change the memory multiplier to affect memory speed.

```
                                    System Setup
   Main    Configuration    Performance   Security   Power    Boot    Exit

                                    Proposed   Active   Default
   Host Clock Frequency             100        100      100     (MHz)
   Processor Overrides
      Intel® Turbo Boost Technology Enable     Enable   Enable
      Core Max Multiplier           33         33       33
      Speed                         3.30       3.30     3.30    (GHz)
      Graphic Max Multiplier        22         22       22
   Memory Overrides
      Multiplier                    10         10       10
      Speed                         1333       1333     1333    (MHz)
Voltage Overrides
      Memory                        <1.5000>   <1.5000> <1.5000> (V)  → ←: Select Screen
      Graphics                      <Default>  Default  Default  (V)  ↑ ↓: Select Item
                                                                      Enter:Select
                                                                      +/-: Change Opt.
                                                                      F9: Load Defaults
                                                                      F10:Save ESC:Exit
```

Source: Intel

Figure 4-41 A motherboard might give options for changing the clock speed or multipliers for the processor and memory

A+
220-801
1.1

MONITOR TEMPERATURES, FAN SPEEDS, AND VOLTAGES

Using BIOS setup screens, you can monitor temperatures inside the case, fan speeds, and voltages. One BIOS screen that allows you to monitor these values and also control fan speeds is shown in Figure 4-42. Case and CPU fans on modern computers adjust their speeds based on the temperatures of the CPU, memory, and motherboard. You can also install software (for example, SpeedFan by Alfredo Comparetti at *www.almico.com/speedfan.php*) in Windows to monitor temperatures and control fan speeds. To use the software, you might need to change a BIOS setting to allow software to control the speeds. For this system, when you select Processor Temperature, you can set the threshold temperatures that software uses to create an alert.

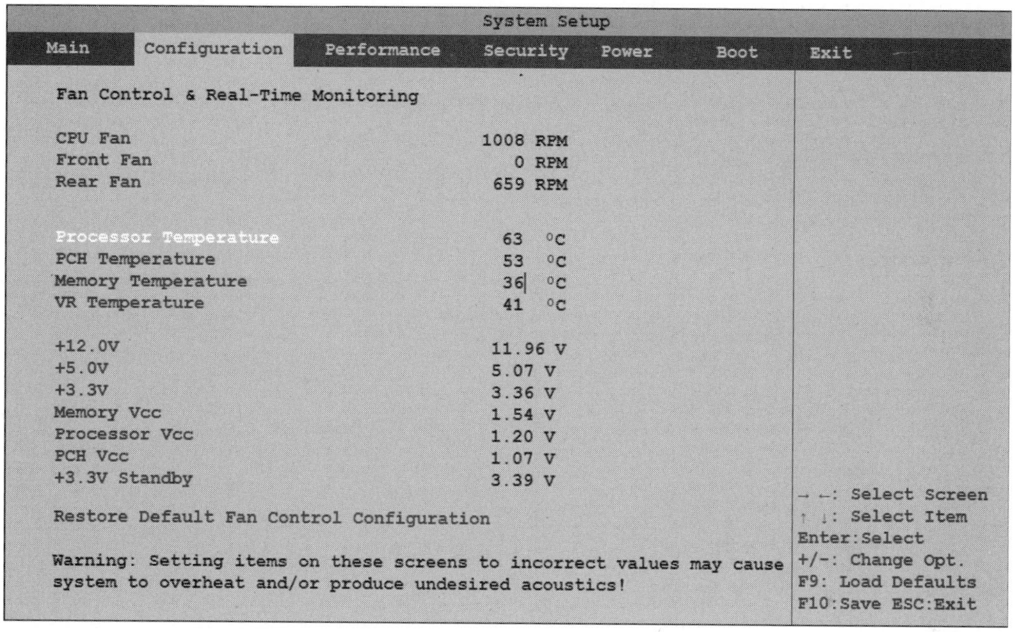

```
                                System Setup
    Main    Configuration    Performance    Security    Power    Boot    Exit

    Fan Control & Real-Time Monitoring

    CPU Fan                         1008 RPM
    Front Fan                          0 RPM
    Rear Fan                         659 RPM


    Processor Temperature            63  °C
    PCH Temperature                  53  °C
    Memory Temperature               36  °C
    VR Temperature                   41  °C

    +12.0V                         11.96 V
    +5.0V                           5.07 V
    +3.3V                           3.36 V
    Memory Vcc                      1.54 V
    Processor Vcc                   1.20 V
    PCH Vcc                         1.07 V
    +3.3V Standby                   3.39 V                  → ←: Select Screen
                                                            ↑ ↓: Select Item
    Restore Default Fan Control Configuration               Enter:Select
                                                            +/-: Change Opt.
    Warning: Setting items on these screens to incorrect values may cause    F9: Load Defaults
    system to overheat and/or produce undesired acoustics!  F10:Save ESC:Exit
```

Source: Intel

Figure 4-42 Monitor temperatures, fan speeds, and voltages in a system

INTRUSION DETECTION

BIOS settings might offer several security features, and one of these is an intrusion-detection alert. For example, for the BIOS setup screen shown in Figure 4-43, you can enable event logging, which logs when the case is opened. To use the feature, you must use a cable to connect a switch on the case to a header on the motherboard.

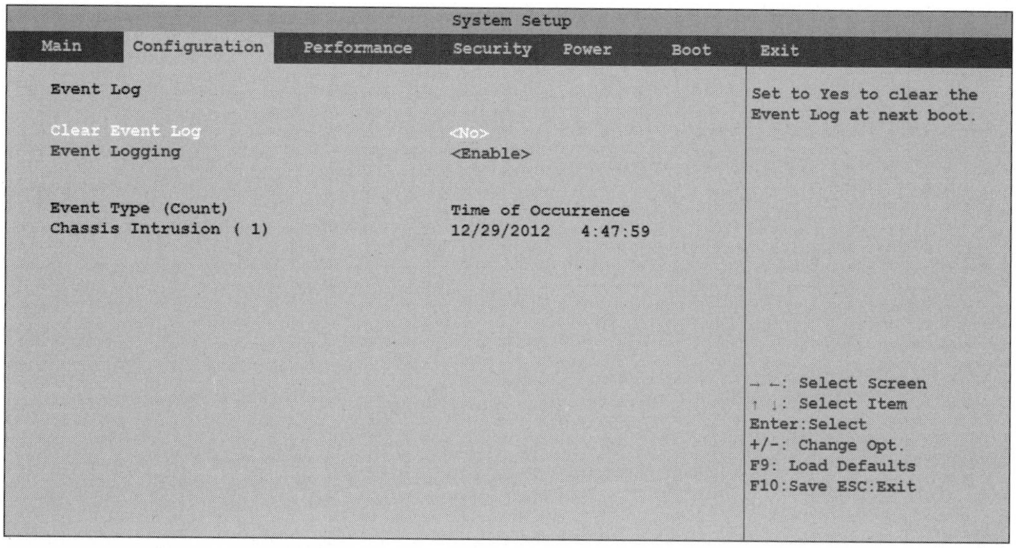

```
                                System Setup
    Main    Configuration    Performance    Security    Power    Boot    Exit

    Event Log                                               Set to Yes to clear the
                                                            Event Log at next boot.
    Clear Event Log                 <No>
    Event Logging                   <Enable>


    Event Type (Count)              Time of Occurrence
    Chassis Intrusion ( 1)          12/29/2012   4:47:59




                                                            → ←: Select Screen
                                                            ↑ ↓: Select Item
                                                            Enter:Select
                                                            +/-: Change Opt.
                                                            F9: Load Defaults
                                                            F10:Save ESC:Exit
```

Source: Intel

Figure 4-43 BIOS is enabled to log a chassis intrusion

When the security measure is in place and the case is opened, BIOS displays an alert the next time the system is powered up. For example, the alert message at startup might be "Chassis Intruded! System has halted." If you see this message, know that the case has been opened. Reboot the system and the system should start up as usual. To make sure the alert was not tripped by accident, verify that the case cover is securely in place. Also, sometimes a failed CMOS battery can trip the alert. Intrusion-detection devices are not a recommended best practice for security. False alerts are annoying, and criminals generally know how to get inside a case without tripping the alert.

POWER-ON PASSWORDS

Power-on passwords are assigned in BIOS setup and kept in CMOS RAM to prevent unauthorized access to the computer and/or the BIOS setup utility. Most likely, you'll find the security screen to set the passwords under the boot menu or security menu options. For one motherboard, this security screen looks like that in Figure 4-44, where you can set a supervisor password and a user password. In addition, you can configure how the user password works.

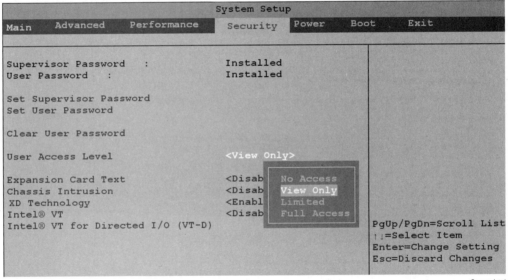

Source: Intel

Figure 4-44   Set supervisor and user passwords in BIOS setup to lock down a computer

The choices under User Access Level are **No Access** (the user cannot access the BIOS setup utility), **View Only** (the user can access BIOS setup, but cannot make changes), **Limited** (the user can access BIOS setup and make a few changes such as date and time), and **Full Access** (the user can access the BIOS setup utility and make any changes). When supervisor and user passwords are both set and you boot the system, a box to enter a password is displayed. What access you have depends on which password you enter. Also, if both passwords are set, you must enter a valid password to boot the system. By setting both passwords, you can totally lock down the computer from unauthorized access.

For another computer, BIOS setup controls how to lock down a computer on the Advanced BIOS screen shown in Figure 4-45. Under the Security Option, choices are Setup and System. If you choose Setup, the power-on passwords control access only to BIOS setup. If you choose System, a power-on password is required every time you boot the system. (The supervisor and user power-on passwords for this BIOS are set on another screen.) Also notice on the setup screen in Figure 4-45, the Virus Warning option, which is enabled.

If an attempt to write to the boot sectors of the hard drive happens, a warning message appears on-screen and an alarm beeps. (The boot sector is the first few bytes at the beginning of a hard drive that contains information needed to boot from the drive.)

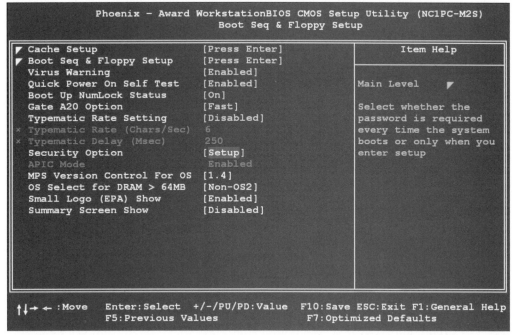

Source: Phoenix Award BIOS

Figure 4-45 Change the way a user password functions to protect the computer

A+ Exam Tip The A+ 220-801 exam expects you to know how to use BIOS setup to secure a workstation from unauthorized use.

Notes For added protection, configure the BIOS setup utility so that a user cannot boot from a removable device such as a CD, USB device, or floppy disk.

Caution In the event that passwords are forgotten, know that supervisor and user passwords to the computer can be reset by setting a jumper on the motherboard to clear all BIOS customized settings and return BIOS setup to its default settings. To keep someone from using this technique to access the computer, you can use a computer case with a lockable side panel and install a lock on the case.

LOJACK FOR LAPTOPS TECHNOLOGY

LoJack is a technology embedded in the BIOS of many laptops to protect a system against theft. When you subscribe to the LoJack for Laptops service by Absolute (*www.absolute .com*), the Computrace Agent software is installed. The software and BIOS work together to protect the system. The company can locate your laptop whenever it connects to the Internet, and you can give commands through the Internet to lock the laptop or delete all data on it.

A+
220-801
1.1

DRIVE ENCRYPTION AND DRIVE PASSWORD PROTECTION

Some motherboards and hard drives allow you to set a password that must be entered before someone can access the hard drive. This password is kept on the drive and works even if the drive is moved to another computer. Some manufacturers of storage media offer similar products. For example, Seagate (*www.seagate.com*) offers Maxtor BlackArmor, a technology that encrypts an entire external storage media that is password protected.

> **Notes** Drive lock password protection might be too secure at times. I know of a situation where a hard drive with password protection became corrupted. Normally, you might be able to move the drive to another computer and recover some data. However, this drive asked for the password, but then could not confirm it. Therefore, the entire drive, including all the data, was inaccessible.

THE TPM CHIP AND HARD DRIVE ENCRYPTION

Many high-end computers have a chip on the motherboard called the **TPM (Trusted Platform Module) chip.** BitLocker Encryption in Windows 7/Vista is designed to work with this chip; the chip holds the BitLocker encryption key (also called the startup key). If the hard drive is stolen from the computer and installed in another computer, the data would be safe because BitLocker has encrypted all contents on the drive and would not allow access without the startup key stored on the TPM chip. Therefore, this method assures that the drive cannot be used in another computer. However, if the motherboard fails and is replaced, you'll need a backup copy of the startup key to access data on the hard drive.

> **A+ Exam Tip** The A+ 220-801 exam expects you to know about drive encryption and the TPM chip.

When you use Windows to install BitLocker Encryption, the initialization process also initializes the TPM chip. Initializing the TPM chip configures it and turns it on. After BitLocker is installed, you can temporarily turn off BitLocker, which also turns off the TPM chip. For example, you might want to turn off BitLocker to test the BitLocker recovery process. Normally, BitLocker will manage the TPM chip for you, and there is no need for you to manually change TPM chip settings. However, if you are having problems installing BitLocker, one thing you can do is clear the TPM chip. *Be careful!* If the TPM chip is being used to hold an encryption key to protect data on the hard drive and you clear the chip, the encryption key will be lost. That means all the data will be lost, too. Therefore, don't clear the TPM chip unless you are certain it is not being used to encrypt data.

APPLYING | CONCEPTS   INITIALIZE OR CLEAR THE TPM CHIP

To initialize or clear the TPM chip, follow these steps:

1. Log onto Windows using an administrator account.
2. Click **Start**, type **tpm.msc**, and press **Enter**. Respond to the User Account Control box.

3. The TPM Management console opens. If there is no TPM chip present, the console displays a message that no TPM chip can be found. If your system has a TPM chip, the screen looks similar to the one in Figure 4-46.

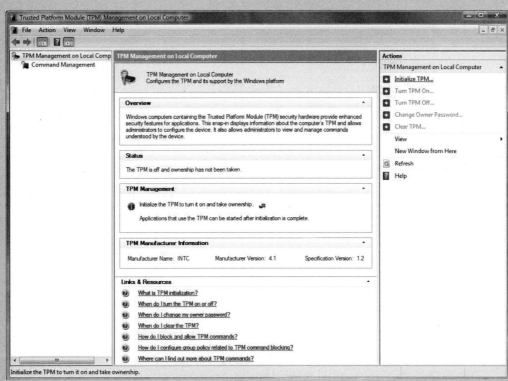

Source: Microsoft Windows Vista

Figure 4-46 Use the TPM Management console to manage the TPM chip

4. Notice in the right pane that Initialize TPM is not dimmed, which means that the TPM chip has not yet been initialized. To initialize it, click **Initialize TPM**. A dialog box (see Figure 4-47) appears, listing the steps to initialize the TPM chip, which include shutting down and restarting the system.

Source: Microsoft Windows Vista

Figure 4-47 Steps to initialize the TPM chip

A+
220-801
1.1

5. After the restart, you are given the opportunity to create the TPM owner password, save the password to a removable media, and print the password (see Figure 4-48). These steps initialize the TPM chip and assign ownership. You can then use encryption software such as BitLocker Encryption or other software embedded on the hard drive to encrypt data on the drive.

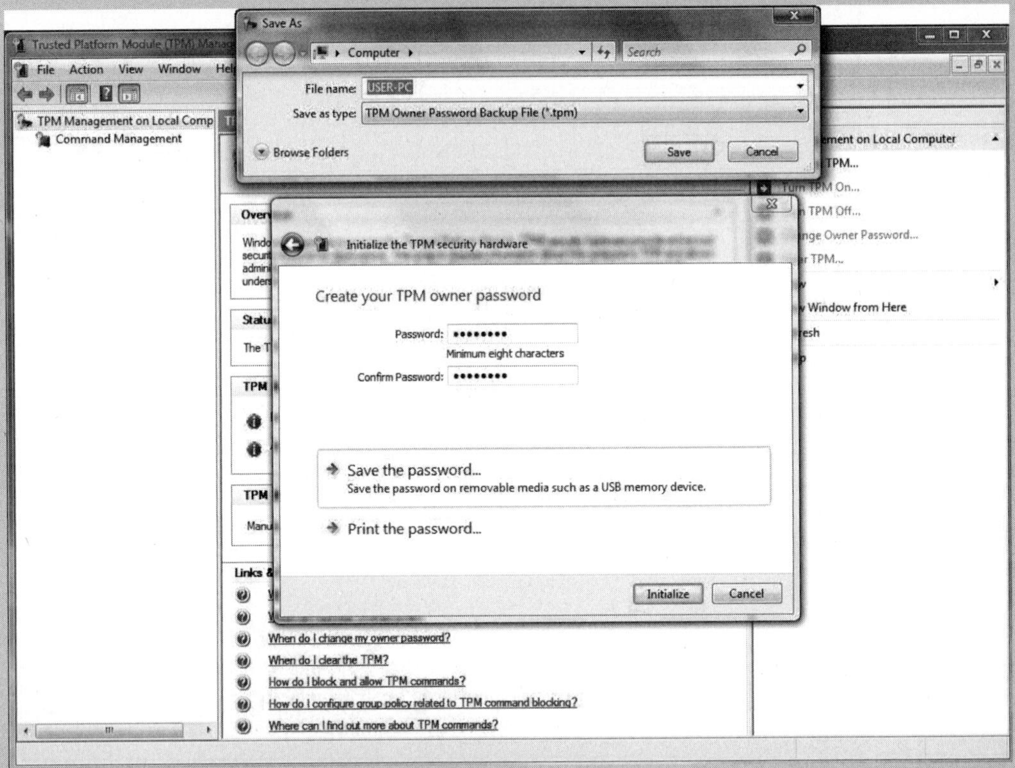

Source: Microsoft Windows Vista

Figure 4-48 Create and save the TPM owner password

6. To clear the TPM chip after it has been initialized, under Action, click **Clear TPM** and follow the directions on-screen. You will be asked to enter the owner password or provide the media where the password is stored. Clearing the TPM chip causes all encrypted data protected by the chip to be lost.

BIOS SUPPORT FOR VIRTUALIZATION

Virtualization is when one physical machine hosts multiple activities that are normally done on multiple machines. One type of virtualization is the use of virtual machines. A virtual computer or **virtual machine (VM)** is software that simulates the hardware of a physical computer. Each VM running on a computer works like a physical computer and is assigned virtual devices such as a virtual motherboard and virtual hard drive. Examples of VM software are Windows Virtual PC and Oracle Virtual Box. For VM software to work well, virtualization must be enabled in BIOS setup. Figure 4-49 shows one BIOS setup screen where Intel VT is enabled. Intel VT is the name that Intel gives to its virtualization technology.

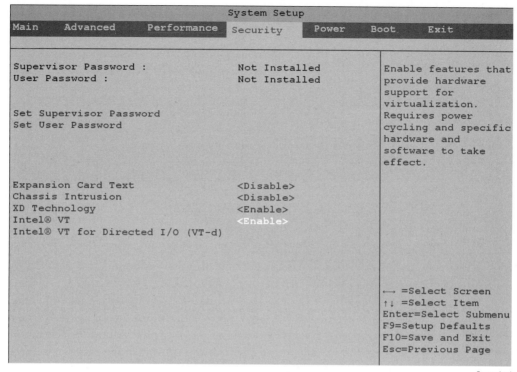

Figure 4-49 BIOS setup screen to enable hardware virtualization

Source: Intel

EXITING THE BIOS SETUP MENUS

When you finish with BIOS setup, an exit screen such as the one shown in Figure 4-50 gives you various options, such as exit and save your changes or exit and discard your changes. Notice in the figure that you also have the option to load BIOS default settings. This option can sometimes solve a problem when a user has made several inappropriate changes to the BIOS settings.

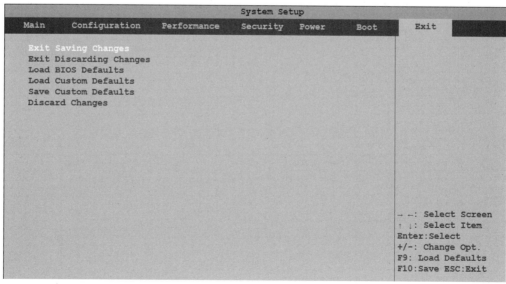

Figure 4-50 BIOS setup Exit menu

Source: Intel

Now let's see what other tasks you might need to do when you are responsible for maintaining a motherboard.

MAINTAINING A MOTHERBOARD

**A+
220-801
1.1**

To maintain a motherboard, you need to know how to update the motherboard drivers, flash BIOS, and replace the CMOS battery. All these skills are covered in this part of the chapter.

> 💡 **A+ Exam Tip** The A+ 220-801 exam expects you to know how to maintain a motherboard by updating drivers and firmware and replacing the CMOS battery.

UPDATING MOTHERBOARD DRIVERS

Device drivers are small programs stored on the hard drive and installed in Windows that tell Windows how to communicate with a specific hardware device such as a printer, network port on the motherboard, or scanner. The CD that comes bundled with the motherboard contains a user guide and drivers for its onboard components, and these drivers need to be installed in Windows. You can initially install the drivers from CD, and you can also update the drivers by downloading them from the motherboard manufacturer's web site.

The motherboard CD or DVD might also contain useful utilities, for example, a utility to monitor the CPU temperature and alert you if overheating occurs. Figure 4-51 shows the main menu for one motherboard driver CD.

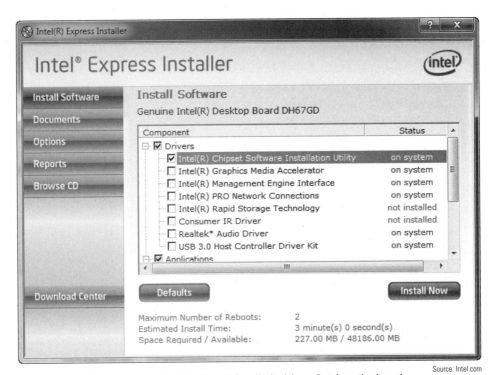

Source: Intel.com

Figure 4-51 Main menu provided by the CD bundled with an Intel motherboard

The motherboard manufacturer updates motherboard drivers from time to time. For an unstable motherboard, you can try downloading and installing updated chipset drivers and other drivers for onboard components. Figure 4-52 shows the download page for one Intel motherboard where you can download drivers and BIOS updates. Notice in the figure the choices for operating systems.

A+
220-801
1.1

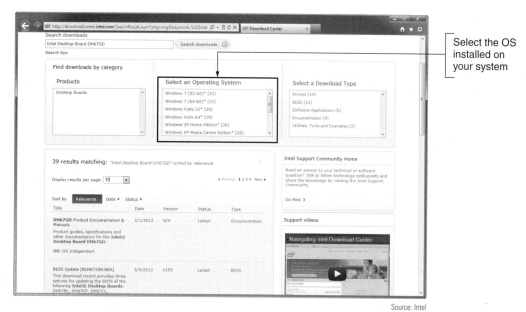

Select the OS
installed on
your system

Source: Intel

Figure 4-52 Download drivers, BIOS updates, documentation, utilities, and other help software from the motherboard manufacturer's web site

Be sure to select the correct OS (for example, Windows 7) and the correct type (32 bit or 64 bit). Always use 32-bit drivers with a 32-bit OS and 64-bit drivers with a 64-bit OS. The bit number is the number of bits the driver or OS can process at one time, and you want that to match up. To know what edition and type of Windows you are using, click **Start,** right-click **Computer,** and select **Properties.** The System window appears, giving you details about the Windows installation (see Figure 4-53).

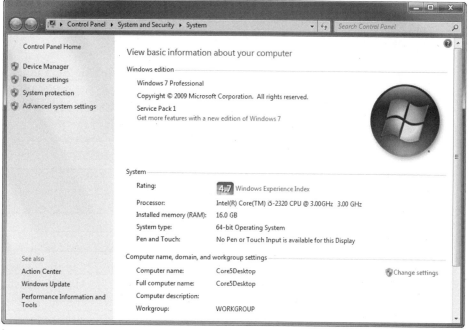

Source: Microsoft Windows 7

Figure 4-53 The System window reports the edition and type of OS installed

4

FLASHING BIOS

Recall that BIOS includes the BIOS setup program, the startup BIOS that manages the startup process, and the system BIOS that manages basic I/O functions of the system. All these programs are stored on a firmware chip. The process of upgrading or refreshing the programming stored on the firmware chip is called updating the BIOS or **flashing BIOS**. Here are some good reasons you might want to flash the BIOS:

- ▲ The system hangs at odd times or during the boot.
- ▲ Some motherboard functions have stopped working or are giving problems. For example, the onboard video port is not working.
- ▲ You want to incorporate some new features or component on the board. For example, a BIOS upgrade might be required before you upgrade the processor.

> ⚡ **Caution**   Be sure you use the correct motherboard brand and model when selecting the BIOS update on the manufacturer's web site. Trying to use the wrong update can cause problems.

The BIOS updates are downloaded from the motherboard manufacturer's web site (refer to Figure 4-52). To flash BIOS, always follow the directions that you can find in the user guide for your motherboard. Here are four methods that most motherboards can use:

- ▲ *Express BIOS update.* Some motherboards allow for an express BIOS update, which is done from Windows. Download the update file to your hard drive. Close all open applications. Double-click the file, which runs the update program, and follow the directions on-screen. The system will reboot to apply the update.
- ▲ *Update from a USB flash drive using setup BIOS.* Copy the downloaded update file to a USB flash drive. Then restart the system and press a key at startup that launches the BIOS update process. (For Intel motherboards, you press F7.) A screen appears where you can select the USB flash drive. BIOS finds the update file on the flash drive, completes the update, and restarts the system.
- ▲ *Update using a bootable CD.* You can download an ISO file from the motherboard manufacturer's web site that contains the BIOS update. An ISO file has an .iso file extension and contains an **ISO image** of a CD. You can use an ISO image to create a bootable CD with software and data on it. After you have created the bootable CD, boot from it and follow the directions on-screen to flash the BIOS.

> 📝 **Notes**   To use Windows 7 to burn a CD from an ISO file, first insert a blank CD in the optical drive. Then right-click the .iso file, select **Burn disc image**, and follow the directions on-screen.

If the BIOS update is interrupted or the update gives errors, you are in an unfortunate situation. You might be able to revert to the earlier version. To do this, generally, you download the recovery file from the web site and copy the file to a USB flash drive. Then set the jumper on the motherboard to recover from a failed BIOS update. Reboot the system and the BIOS automatically reads from the device and performs the recovery. Then reset the jumper to the normal setting and boot the system.

A+
220-801
1.1

> **Notes** To identify the BIOS version installed, look for the BIOS version number displayed on the main menu of BIOS setup. Alternately, you can use the System Information utility (Msinfo32.exe) in Windows to display the BIOS version.

Makers of BIOS code are likely to change BIOS frequently because providing the upgrade on the Internet is so easy for them. Generally, however, follow the principle that "if it's not broke, don't fix it." Update your BIOS only if you're having a problem with your motherboard or there's a new BIOS feature you want to use. Also, don't update the BIOS unless the update is a later version than the one installed. One last word of caution: it's very important the update not be interrupted while it is in progress. A failed update can make your motherboard totally unusable. Be sure you don't interrupt the update, and make sure there are no power interruptions.

> **⚡ Caution** Be very *careful* that you upgrade BIOS with the correct upgrade and that you follow the manufacturer's instructions correctly. Upgrading with the wrong file could make your system BIOS useless. If you're not sure that you're using the correct upgrade, *don't guess.* Check with the technical support for your BIOS before moving forward. Before you call technical support, have the information that identifies your BIOS and motherboard available.

A+
220-801
1.1, 1.2

REPLACING THE CMOS BATTERY

A small trickle of electricity from a nearby lithium coin-cell battery (see Figure 4-54) enables CMOS RAM to hold configuration data, even while the main power to the computer is off. If the **CMOS battery** is disconnected or fails, setup information is lost. An indication that the battery is getting weak is that the system date and time are incorrect after power has been disconnected to the PC. A message about a low battery can also appear at startup.

© Cengage Learning 2014

Figure 4-54 The coin-cell battery powers CMOS RAM when the system is turned off

A+
220-801
1.1, 1.2

> 💡 **A+ Exam Tip** The A+ 220-801 exam expects you to know about the CMOS battery.

The CMOS battery on the motherboard is considered a field replaceable unit. The battery is designed to last for years and recharges when the motherboard has power. However, on rare occasions, you might need to replace one if the system loses BIOS settings when it is unplugged. Make sure the replacement battery is an exact match to the original or is one the motherboard manufacturer recommends for the board. Power down the system, unplug it, press the power button to drain the power, and remove the case cover. Use your ground bracelet to protect the system against ESD. The old battery can be removed with a little prying using a flathead screwdriver. The new battery pops into place. For more specific directions, see the motherboard documentation.

Now let's turn our attention to installing or replacing a motherboard.

INSTALLING OR REPLACING A MOTHERBOARD

A+
220-802
4.2

A motherboard is considered a field replaceable unit, so you need to know how to replace one when it goes bad. In this part of the chapter, you learn how to select a motherboard and then how to install or replace one.

A+
220-801
1.2

HOW TO SELECT A MOTHERBOARD

Because the motherboard determines so many of your computer's features, selecting the motherboard is, in most cases, your most important decision when you purchase a computer or assemble one from parts. Depending on which applications and peripheral devices you plan to use with the computer, you can take one of three approaches to selecting a motherboard. The first approach is to select the board that provides the most room for expansion, so you can upgrade and exchange components and add devices easily. A second approach is to select the board that best suits the needs of the computer's current configuration, knowing that when you need to upgrade, you will likely switch to new technology and a new motherboard. The third approach is to select a motherboard that meets your present needs with moderate room for expansion.

Ask the following questions when selecting a motherboard:

1. What form factor does the motherboard use?

2. Which brand (Intel or AMD) and model processors does the board support? Which chipset does it use? How much memory can it hold? What memory speeds does the board support?

3. What type and how many expansion slots are on the board (for example, PCI Express 2.0 or PCI)?

4. How many and what hard drive controllers and connectors are on the board (for example, SATA, eSATA, and IDE)?

5. What are the embedded devices on the board, and what internal slots or connections does the board have? (For example, the board might provide a network port, wireless antenna port, FireWire port, two or more USB ports, video port, and so forth.)

6. Does the board fit the case you plan to use?

A+
220-802
4.2

A+
220-801
1.2

7. What are the price and the warranty on the board? Does the board get good reviews?

8. How extensive and user-friendly is the documentation?

9. How much support does the manufacturer supply for the board?

Sometimes a motherboard contains an on-board component more commonly offered as a separate device. One example is support for video. The video port might be on the motherboard or might require a video card. The cost of a motherboard with an embedded component is usually less than the combined cost of a motherboard with no embedded component and an expansion card. If you plan to expand, be cautious about choosing a proprietary board that has many embedded components. Often such boards do not easily accept add-on devices from other manufacturers. For example, if you plan to add a more powerful video card, you might not want to choose a motherboard that contains an onboard video port. Even though you can likely disable the video port in BIOS setup, there is little advantage to paying the extra money for it.

> **Notes** If you have an embedded component, make sure you can disable it so you can use another external component if needed. Components are disabled in BIOS setup.

Table 4-6 shown earlier in the chapter lists some manufacturers of motherboards and their web addresses. For motherboard reviews, check out *www.motherboards.org* and *www.pcmag.com*, or do a general search of the web.

HOW TO INSTALL OR REPLACE A MOTHERBOARD

When you purchase a motherboard, the package comes with the board, I/O shield, documentation, drivers, and various screws, cables, and connectors (see Figure 4-55). When you replace a motherboard, you pretty much have to disassemble an entire computer, install the new motherboard, and reassemble the system, which you learned to do in Chapter 2. The following list is meant to be a general overview of the process and is not meant to include the details of all possible installation scenarios, which can vary according to the components and case you are using. The best place to go for detailed instructions on installing a motherboard is the motherboard user guide.

> **Video** Motherboard Installation

Figure 4-55 A new motherboard package

© Cengage Learning 2014

A+
220-802
4.2

A+
220-801
1.2

> ⚡ **Caution** As with any installation, remember the importance of using a ground strap (ground bracelet) to ground yourself when working inside a computer case to protect components against ESD. Alternately, you can use antistatic gloves to protect components.

The general process for replacing a motherboard is as follows:

1. *Verify that you have selected the right motherboard to install in the system.* The new motherboard should have the same form factor as the case, support the RAM modules and processor you want to install on it, and have other internal and external connectors you need for your system.

2. *Get familiar with the motherboard documentation, features, and settings.* Especially important are any connectors and jumpers on the motherboard. It's a great idea to read the motherboard user guide from cover to cover. At the least, get familiar with what it has to offer and study the diagrams in it that label all the components on the board. Learn how each connector and jumper is used. You can also check the manufacturer's web site for answers to any questions you might have.

3. *Remove components so you can reach the old motherboard.* Use a ground bracelet. Turn off the system and disconnect all cables and cords. Press the power button to dissipate the power. Open the case cover and remove all expansion cards. Disconnect all internal cables and cords connected to the old motherboard. To safely remove the old motherboard, you might have to remove drives. If the processor cooler is heavy and bulky, you might remove it from the old motherboard before you remove the motherboard from the case.

4. *Set any jumpers on the new motherboard.* This is much easier to do before you put the board in the case. Verify the BIOS startup jumper is set for normal startup.

5. *Install the I/O shield.* The I/O shield is a metal plate that comes with the motherboard and fits over the ports to create a well-fitting enclosure for them. A case might come with a standard I/O shield already in place. Hold the motherboard up to the shield and make sure the ports on the board will fit the holes in the shield (see Figure 4-56).

I/O shield installed on the back of the case

© Cengage Learning 2014

Figure 4-56 Make sure the holes in the I/O shield match up with the ports on the motherboard

A+
220-802
4.2

A+
220-801
1.2

4

If the holes in the shield don't match up with the ports on the board, punch out the shield and replace it with the one that came bundled with the motherboard.

6. *Install the motherboard.* Place the motherboard into the case and, using spacers or screws, securely fasten the board to the case. Because coolers are heavy, most processor instructions say to install the motherboard before installing the processor and cooler to better protect the board or processor from being damaged. On the other hand, some motherboard manufacturers say to install the processor and cooler and then install the motherboard. Follow the order given in the motherboard user guide. The easiest approach is to install the processor, cooler, and memory modules on the board and then place the board in the case (see Figure 4-57).

7. *Install the processor and processor cooler.* The processor comes already installed on some motherboards, in which case you just need to install the cooler. How to install a processor and cooler is covered in Chapter 5.

8. *Install RAM into the appropriate slots on the motherboard.* How to install RAM is covered in Chapter 5.

9. *Attach cabling that goes from the case switches to the motherboard, and from the power supply and drives to the motherboard.* Pay attention to how cables are labeled and to any information in the documentation about where to attach them. Chapter 1 can help you identify the types of power connectors. You'll need to connect the P1 connector, the fan connectors, and the processor auxiliary power connector. Position and tie cables neatly together to make sure they don't obstruct the fans and the air flow.

© Cengage Learning 2014

Figure 4-57 Motherboard with processor, cooler, and memory modules installed is ready to go in the case

A+
220-802
4.2

A+
220-801
1.2

10. *Install the video card on the motherboard.* This card should go into the primary PCI Express x16 slot. If you plan to install multiple video cards, install only one now and check out how the system functions before installing the second one.

11. *Plug the computer into a power source, and attach the monitor, keyboard, and mouse.* Initially install only the devices you absolutely need.

12. *Boot the system and enter BIOS setup.* Make sure settings are set to the default. If the motherboard comes new from the manufacturer, it will already be at default settings. If you are salvaging a motherboard from another system, you might need to reset settings to the default. You will need to do the following while you are in BIOS setup:

   ◢ Check the time and date.

   ◢ Make sure abbreviated POST (quick boot) is disabled. While you're installing a motherboard, you generally want it to do as many diagnostic tests as possible. After you know the system is working, you can choose to abbreviate POST.

   ◢ Set the boot order to the hard drive, and then a CD, if you will be booting the OS from the hard drive.

   ◢ Leave everything else at their defaults unless you know that particular settings should be otherwise.

   ◢ Save and exit.

13. *Observe POST and verify that no errors occur.*

14. *Verify Windows starts with no errors.* If Windows is already installed on the hard drive, boot to the Windows desktop. Use Device Manager to verify that the OS recognizes all devices and that no conflicts are reported.

15. *Install the motherboard drivers.* If your motherboard comes with a CD that contains some motherboard drivers, install them now. You will probably need Internet access so that the setup process can download the latest drivers from the motherboard manufacturer's web site. Reboot the system one more time, checking for errors.

16. *Install any other expansion cards and drivers.* Install each device and its drivers, one device at a time, rebooting and checking for conflicts after each installation.

17. *Verify that everything is operating properly, and make any final OS and BIOS adjustments, such as setting power-on passwords.*

> **Notes** Whenever you install or uninstall software or hardware, keep a notebook with details about the components you are working on, configuration settings, manufacturer specifications, and other relevant information. This helps if you need to backtrack later and can also help you document and troubleshoot your computer system. Keep all hardware documentation for this system together with the notebook in an envelope in a safe place.

Video
Installing a Motherboard

>> CHAPTER SUMMARY

Motherboard Types and Features

▲ The motherboard is the most complicated of all components inside the computer. It contains the processor socket and accompanying chipset, firmware holding the BIOS, CMOS RAM, system bus, memory slots, expansion slots, jumpers, ports, and power supply connections. The motherboard you select determines both the capabilities and limitations of your system.

▲ The most popular motherboard form factors are ATX, microATX, and Mini-ITX.

▲ A motherboard will have one or more Intel sockets for an Intel processor or one or more AMD sockets for an AMD processor.

▲ Intel, AMD, NVIDIA, and SiS are the most popular chipset manufacturers. The chipset embedded on the motherboard determines what kind of processor and memory the board can support.

▲ Major advancements in Intel chipsets include the Accelerated Hub Architecture (using the North Bridge and South Bridge), Nehalem chipsets (using the memory controller on the processor), Sandy Bridge chipsets (using the memory and graphics controller on the processor), and the Ivy Bridge chipsets.

▲ Buses used on motherboards include conventional PCI, PCI-X, PCI Express, and AGP. AGP is used solely for video cards. PCI Express has been revised three times and is replacing all the other bus types.

▲ Some components can be built into the motherboard, in which case they are called on-board components. Other components can be attached to the system in some other way, such as on an expansion card.

Configuring a Motherboard

▲ The most common method of configuring components on a motherboard is BIOS setup. Some motherboards also use jumpers or DIP switches to contain configuration settings.

▲ Motherboard settings that can be configured using BIOS setup include changing the boot priority order, enabling or disabling onboard devices, support for virtualization, and security settings (for example, power-on passwords and intrusion detection). You can also view information about the installed processor, memory, and storage devices and temperatures, fan speeds, and voltages.

Maintaining a Motherboard

▲ Motherboard drivers might need updating to fix a problem with a board component or to use a new feature provided by the motherboard manufacturer.

▲ Sometimes ROM BIOS programming stored on the firmware chip needs updating or refreshing. This process is called updating BIOS or flashing BIOS. The CMOS battery that powers CMOS RAM might need replacing.

Installing or Replacing a Motherboard

▲ When selecting a motherboard, pay attention to the form factor, chipset, expansion slots, and memory slots used and the processors supported. Also notice the internal and external connectors and ports the board provides.

▲ When installing a motherboard, first study the motherboard and its manual, and set jumpers on the board. Sometimes the processor and cooler are best installed before installing the motherboard in the case. When the cooling assembly is heavy and bulky, it is best to install it after the motherboard is securely seated in the case.

>> KEY TERMS

For explanations of key terms, see the Glossary near the end of the book.

Accelerated Graphics Port (AGP)	ISO image	South Bridge
ball grid array (BGA)	jumper	staggered pin grid array (SPGA)
bus	land grid array (LGA)	
chipset	flip-chip land grid array (FCLGA)	system bus
CMOS (complementary metal-oxide semiconductor)	flip-chip pin grid array (FCPGA)	system clock
		TPM (Trusted Platform Module) chip
CMOS battery	LoJack	traces
CMOS RAM	megahertz (MHz)	Unified Extensible Firmware Interface (UEFI)
data bus	North Bridge	
data path size	on-board ports	virtual machine (VM)
device driver	PCI Express (PCIe)	virtualization
flashing BIOS	pin grid array (PGA)	wait state
Front Side Bus (FSB)	protocol	zero insertion force (ZIF) socket
gigahertz (GHz)	QuickPath Interconnect	
hertz (Hz)	riser card	
I/O shield		

>> REVIEW QUESTIONS

1. The processor socket and the ____ determine which processors a motherboard can support.

   a) firmware

   b) I/O shield

   c) chipset

   d) BIOS

2. Which socket name is currently used by new Intel processors?

   a) FM2

   b) LGA2011

   c) Sandy Bridge

   d) Crossfire

3. The speed of memory, Front Side Bus, processor, or other component is measured in ____, which is one cycle per second.

   a) ohms

   b) volts

   c) Amps

   d) hertz

4. ____ are small programs stored on the hard drive and installed in Windows that tell Windows how to communicate with a specific hardware device such as a printer, network port on the motherboard, or scanner.

   a) Firmware programs

   b) Device drivers

   c) ISO images

   d) Cookies

5. When installing a new motherboard, if the holes in the I/O shield don't match up with the ports on the board, what should you do?

   a) Return the motherboard and purchase a new one.

   b) Perform a UEFI Boot.

   c) Punch out the I/O shield and replace it with the one that came bundled with the motherboard.

   d) Use the BIOS setup program to configure the system interval timer.

6. True or false? LGA sockets generally give better contacts than PGA sockets.

7. True or false? The width of a data bus is called the data path size.

8. True or false? Ports coming directly off the motherboard are called jumpers.

9. True or false? You access the BIOS setup program by pressing a key or combination of keys during the boot process.

10. True or false? The process of upgrading or refreshing the programming stored on the firmware chip is called virtualization.

11. The fast end of the Accelerated Hub Architecture, called the ____, contains the graphics and memory controller, and connects directly to the processor by way of a 64-bit bus.

12. The many fine lines on both the top and the bottom of a motherboard's surface are sometimes called ____.

13. ____ will ultimately replace PCI and PCI-X, as well as the AGP bus.

14. ____ RAM is a small amount of memory stored on the motherboard used to hold motherboard settings.

15. ____ is a new standard that is slowly replacing the BIOS standard.

Supporting Processors and Upgrading Memory

In this chapter, you will learn:

- About the characteristics and purposes of Intel and AMD processors used for personal computers
- How to install and upgrade a processor
- About the different kinds of physical memory and how they work
- How to upgrade memory

In the last chapter, you learned about motherboards. In this chapter, you'll learn about the two most important components on the motherboard, which are the processor and memory. You'll learn how a processor works, about the many different types and brands of processors, and how to match a processor to the motherboard.

Memory technologies have evolved over the years. When you support an assortment of desktop and notebook computers, you'll be amazed at all the different variations of memory modules used in newer computers and older computers still in use. A simple problem of replacing a bad memory module can become a complex research project if you don't have a good grasp of current and past memory technologies.

The processor and memory modules are considered field replaceable units (FRU), so you'll learn how to install and upgrade a processor and memory modules. Upgrading the processor or adding more memory to a system can sometimes greatly improve performance. How to troubleshoot problems with the processor or memory is covered in Chapter 13, *Troubleshooting Hardware Problems*.

TYPES AND CHARACTERISTICS OF PROCESSORS

A+
220-801
1.6

The processor installed on a motherboard is the primary component that determines the computing power of the system (see Figure 5-1). Recall that the two major manufacturers of processors are Intel (*www.intel.com*) and AMD (*www.amd.com*).

© Cengage Learning 2014

Figure 5-1 An AMD Athlon 64 X2 installed in socket AM2+ with cooler not yet installed

In this chapter, you learn a lot of details about processors. As you do, try to keep these nine features of processors at the forefront. These features affect performance and compatibility with motherboards:

▲ *Feature 1: Clock speed the processor supports.* Current Intel and AMD processors work with system buses that run at 1.8 GHz up to more than 3.4 GHz. Recall from Chapter 4 that the smaller the processor multiplier, the faster the system bus runs in comparison to the processor speed.

▲ *Feature 2: Processor speed.* Processor core frequency is measured in gigahertz, such as 3.3 GHz.

▲ *Feature 3: Socket and chipset the processor can use.* Recall from Chapter 4 that important Intel sockets for desktop systems are the PGA988, LGA2011, LGA1155, LGA1156, LGA1366, and LGA775. AMD's important desktop sockets are AM3+, AM3, AM2+, AM2, FM1, F, and 940 sockets.

▲ *Feature 4: Processor architecture (32 bits or 64 bits).* All desktop and laptop processors sold today from either Intel or AMD are hybrid processors, which can process 64 bits or 32 bits at a time, but older processors handled only 32 bits. A hybrid processor can use a 32-bit operating system or a 64-bit OS. Most editions of Windows 7 come in either type.

A+
220-801
1.6

▲ *Feature 5: Multiprocessing abilities.* The ability of a system to do more than one thing at a time is accomplished by several means:

- *Multiprocessing.* Two processing units (called arithmetic logic units or ALUs) installed within a single processor (called **multiprocessing** and first used by Pentium processors). The Pentium was the first processor that could execute two instructions at the same time.

- *Dual processors.* A server motherboard might have two processor sockets, called **dual processors** or a **multiprocessor platform** (see Figure 5-2). A processor (for example, the Xeon processor for servers) must support this feature.

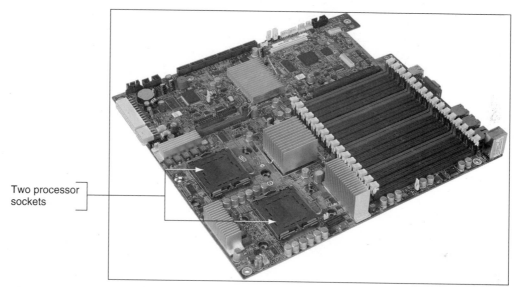

Two processor sockets

Courtesy of Intel Corporation

Figure 5-2   This motherboard for a server has two processor sockets, which allow for a multiprocessor platform

- *Multi-core processing.* Multiple processors can be installed in the same processor housing (called **multi-core processing**). A processor package might contain up to eight cores (dual-core, triple-core, quad-core, and so forth).

- *Multithreading.* Each processor or core processes two threads at the same time. When Windows hands off a task to the CPU it is called a **thread** and might involve several instructions. To handle two threads, the processor requires extra registers, or holding areas, within the processor housing that it uses to switch between threads. In effect, you have two logical processors for each physical processor or core. Intel calls this technology **Hyper-Threading** and AMD calls it **HyperTransport**. The feature must be enabled in BIOS setup.

▲ *Feature 6: Memory cache, which is the amount of memory included within the processor package.* Today's processors all have some memory on the processor chip (called a die). Memory on the processor die is called **Level 1 cache (L1 cache)**. Memory in the processor package, but not on the processor die, is called **Level 2 cache (L2 cache)**. Some processors use a third cache farther from the processor core, but still in the processor package, which is called **Level 3 cache (L3 cache)**. Memory used in a memory cache

A+
220-801
1.6

is **static RAM** or **SRAM** (pronounced "S-Ram"). Memory used on the motherboard loses data rapidly and must be refreshed often. It is, therefore, called volatile memory or **dynamic RAM** or **DRAM** (pronounced "D-Ram"). SRAM is faster than DRAM because it doesn't need refreshing; it can hold its data as long as power is available.

▲ *Feature 7: The memory features on the motherboard that the processor can support.* Current types of DRAM memory modules used on a motherboard include DDR, DDR2, or DDR3. Besides the type of memory, a processor can support certain amounts of memory, memory speeds, and number of memory channels (single, dual, triple, or quad channels). All these characteristics of memory are discussed later in the chapter.

▲ *Feature 8: Support for virtualization.* Recall from Chapter 4 that a computer can use software to create and manage multiple virtual machines that contain virtual devices. Most processors sold today support virtualization, and the feature must be enabled in BIOS setup.

▲ *Feature 9: Integrated graphics.* A processor might include an integrated GPU. A **graphics processing unit (GPU)** is a processor that manipulates graphic data to form the images on a monitor screen. The GPU might be on a video card, on the motherboard, or embedded in the CPU package. When inside the CPU package, it is called integrated graphics. Many AMD processors and all the Intel second generation (Sandy Bridge) and third generation (Ivy Bridge) processors have integrated graphics.

> **🔆 A+ Exam Tip** The A+ 220-801 exam expects you to be familiar with the characteristics of processors. Know the purposes and characteristics of Hyper-threading, core processing, types of cache, virtualization, integrated GPU, and 32-bit versus 64-bit processing.

Let's now turn our attention to a discussion of how a processor works, including several of the processor features just listed. Then you'll learn about the families of Intel and AMD processors.

HOW A PROCESSOR WORKS

Although processors continue to evolve, they all have some common elements. These elements are diagrammed in Figure 5-3 for the Pentium processor. The Pentium made several major advances in processor technologies when it was first introduced. Because of its historical significance and the foundation it created for today's processors, it's a great place to start when learning how a processor works.

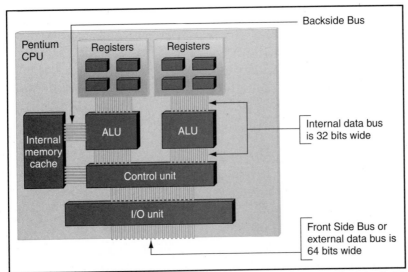

© Cengage Learning 2014

Figure 5-3 Since the Pentium processor was first released in 1993, the standard has been for a processor to have two arithmetic logic units so that it can process two instructions at once

A processor contains these basic components diagrammed in Figure 5-3 for the Pentium processor:

▲ An input/output (I/O) unit manages data and instructions entering and leaving the processor.

▲ A control unit manages all activities inside the processor itself.

▲ One or more arithmetic logic units (ALUs) do all logical comparisons and calculations inside the processor. All desktop and laptop processors sold today contain two ALUs in each processor core within the processor package.

▲ Registers, which are small holding areas on the processor chip, work much like RAM does outside the processor to hold counters, data, instructions, and addresses that the ALU is currently processing.

▲ Internal memory caches (L1, L2, and possibly L3) hold data and instructions waiting to be processed by the ALU.

▲ Buses inside the processor connect components within the processor housing. These buses run at a much higher frequency than the Front Side Bus (FSB) that connects the processor to the chipset and memory on the motherboard.

The speed at which the processor operates internally is called the **processor frequency**. For example, if the processor operates at 3.2 GHz internally but the Front Side Bus is operating at 800 MHz, the processor operates at four times the FSB speed. This factor is called the **multiplier**. As you learned in Chapter 4, you can view the actual processor frequency and the clock speed using the BIOS setup screens. You can also change the multiplier or the clock speed in order to overclock or throttle the processor.

In Figure 5-3, you can see the internal data bus for the Pentium was only 32 bits wide. More important, however, than the width of the internal bus is the fact that each ALU and register in the early Pentiums could process only 32 bits at a time. All desktop and laptop processors sold today from either Intel or AMD contain ALUs and registers that can process 32 bits or 64 bits at a time. To know which type of operating system to install, you need to be aware of three categories of processors currently used on desktop and laptop computers:

▲ *32-bit processors.* These older processors are known as **x86 processors** because Intel used the number 86 in the model number of these processors. If you are ever called on to install Windows on one of these old Pentium computers, you must use a 32-bit version of Windows. These processors can handle only 32-bit instructions from the OS.

▲ *Processors that can process 32 bits or 64 bits.* These hybrid processors are known as **x86-64 bit processors**. AMD was the first to produce one (the Athlon 64) and called the technology AMD64. Intel followed with a version of its Pentium 4 processors and called the technology Extended Memory 64 Technology (EM64T). Because of their hybrid nature, these processors can handle a 32-bit OS or a 64-bit OS. All desktop or laptop processors made after 2007 are of this type.

▲ *64-bit processors.* Intel makes several 64-bit processors for workstations or servers that use fully implemented 64-bit processing, including the Itanium and Xeon processors. Intel calls the technology IA64, but they are also called x64 processors. They require a 64-bit operating system and can handle 32-bit applications only by simulating 32-bit processing.

Notes To know which type of operating system is installed (32-bit or 64-bit) and other information about the Windows installation, recall from Chapter 4 that you can use the System window. To open the System window, click **Start**, right-click **Computer**, and select **Properties**.

A+
220-801
1.6

Each core in a processor has its own cache and can also share a cache. Figure 5-4 shows how quad-core processing can work if the processor uses an L3 cache and an internal memory controller. Each core within a processor has its own independent internal L1 and L2 caches. The L1 cache is on the die and the L2 cache is off the die. In addition, all the cores might share an L3 cache within the processor package. Recall from Chapter 4 that prior to the memory controller being in the processor package, it was part of the North Bridge chipset. Putting the controller inside the processor package resulted in a significant increase in system performance.

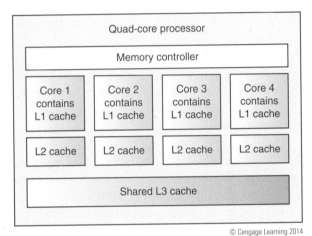

© Cengage Learning 2014

Figure 5-4   Quad-core processing with L1, L2, and L3 cache and the memory controller within the processor housing

INTEL PROCESSORS

Intel's current families of processors for the desktop include the Core, Atom, Celeron, and Pentium families of processors. In addition, Intel groups its processors into Third Generation, Second Generation, and Previous Generation processors. Each generation improves on how the processor and chipset are integrated in the system. Processors in each family are listed in Table 5-1. Some significant retired processors are also listed. Later in the chapter, I'll explain the memory technologies mentioned in the table.

Processor	Speed	Description
Third Generation (Ivy Bridge) Processors		
Core i7	Up to 3.9 GHz	8 MB cache, quad core 1333/1600 MHz DDR3 memory Dual channel memory
Core i5	Up to 3.8 GHz	6 MB cache, quad core 1333/1600 MHz DDR3 memory Dual channel memory

© Cengage Learning 2014

Table 5-1   Current Intel processors (continues)

A+
220-801
1.6

5

Processor	Speed	Description
Second Generation (Sandy Bridge) Processors		
Core i7 Extreme	Up to 3.9 GHz	15 MB cache, six cores 1066/1333/1600 MHz DDR3 memory Quad channel memory
Core i7	Up to 3.9 GHz	8 to 12 MB cache, four or six cores 1066/1333/1600 MHz DDR3 memory Dual or quad channel memory
Core i5	Up to 3.8 GHz	3 to 6 MB cache, dual or quad core 1066/1333 MHz DDR3 memory Dual channel memory
Core i3	Up to 3.4 GHz	3 MB cache, dual core 1066/1333 MHz DDR3 memory Dual channel memory
Pentium	Up to 3.0 GHz	3 MB cache 1066/1333 MHz DDR3 memory Dual channel memory
Previous Generation Processors		
Core i7 Extreme	Up to 3.4 GHz	8 or 12 MB cache 1066 MHz DDR3 memory Triple channel memory
Core i7	Up to 3.3 GHz	8 or 12 MB cache, four or six cores 800/1066/1333 MHz DDR3 memory Dual or triple channel memory
Core i5	Up to 3.3 GHz	4 or 8 MB cache, dual or quad core 1066/1333 MHz DDR3 memory Dual channel memory
Core i3	Up to 3.3 GHz	Dual core, 4 MB cache 1066/1333 MHz DDR3 memory Dual channel memory
Atom	Up to 2.1 GHz	Up to 1 MB cache, some dual core 800/1066 MHz DDR3 memory 667/800 MHz DDR2 memory Single channel memory
Celeron, Celeron Desktop, Celeron D	1.6 to 3.6 GHz 533/667/800 MHz FSB	128 KB to 1 MB cache
Core 2 Extreme, Core 2 Quad, Core 2 Duo	Up to 3.2 GHz 533 to 1600 MHz FSB	2 to 12 MB cache Dual or quad core
Pentium Extreme, Pentium, Pentium 4, Pentium D	Up to 3.7 GHz	Up to 4 MB cache, some dual core

Table 5-1 Current Intel processors (continued)

© Cengage Learning 2014

An Intel Sandy Bridge Core i5 processor is shown in Figure 5-5. You can purchase a processor with or without the cooler. When it's purchased with a cooler, it's called a boxed processor. The cooler is also shown in the photo. If you purchase the cooler separately, make sure it fits the socket you are using.

© Cengage Learning 2014

Figure 5-5   The Intel Core i5 processor (processor number i5-2320) with boxed cooler

Each processor listed in Table 5-1 represents several processors that vary in performance and functionality. To help identify a processor, Intel uses a processor number. For example, two Core i7 processors are identified as i7-940 and i7-920. To find details about an Intel processor, search the Intel ARK database at *ark.intel.com* (see Figure 5-6).

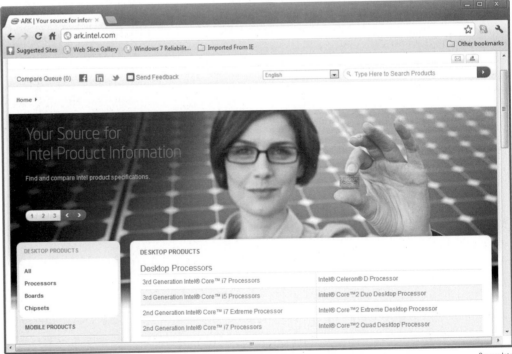

Source: Intel

Figure 5-6   The Intel ARK database at *ark.intel.com* lists details about all Intel products

Some of the Intel mobile processors are packaged in the Centrino processor technology. Using the **Centrino** technology, the Intel processor, chipset, and wireless network adapter are all interconnected as a unit, which improves laptop performance. Several Intel mobile processors have been packaged as a Centrino processor. You also need to be aware of the Intel Atom processor, which is Intel's smallest processor and is used in low-cost PCs, laptops, and netbooks.

AMD PROCESSORS

Processors by Advanced Micro Devices, Inc. or AMD (*www.amd.com*) are popular in the game and hobbyist markets, and are generally less expensive than comparable Intel processors. Recall that AMD processors use different sockets than do Intel processors, so the motherboard must be designed for one manufacturer's processor or the other, but not both. Many motherboard manufacturers offer two comparable motherboards—one for an Intel processor and one for an AMD processor.

The current AMD processor families are the FX, Phenom, Athlon, and Sempron for desktops and the Athlon, Turion, V Series, Phenom, and Sempron for laptops. Table 5-2 lists the current AMD processors for desktops. Figure 5-7 shows an FX processor by AMD.

Processor	Core Speed	Description
FX Black Edition Family		
FX 4-Core Black Edition	Up to 3.6 GHz	Quad-core uses AM3+ socket
FX 6-Core Black Edition	Up to 3.3 GHz	Six-core uses AM3+ socket
FX 8-Core Black Edition	Up to 3.6 GHz	Eight-core uses AM3+ socket
Phenom Family		
Phenom II X6	Up to 3 GHz	Six core uses AM3 socket
Phenom II X6 Black	Up to 3.2 GHz	Six core uses AM3 socket
Phenom II X4	Up to 3.2 GHz	Quad-core uses AM3 socket
Phenom II X3	Up to 2.5 GHz	Triple-core uses AM3 socket
Phenom II X2	Up to 3.1 GHz	Dual-core uses AM3 socket
Phenom X4	Up to 2.6 GHz	Quad-core uses AM2+ socket
Phenom X3	Up to 2.4 GHz	Triple-core uses AM2+ socket
Athlon Family		
Athlon II X2	Up to 3 GHz	Dual-core uses AM3 socket
Athlon X2	Up to 2.3 GHz	Dual-core uses AM3 socket
Athlon	Up to 2.4 GHz	Single-core uses AM2 socket
Sempron Family		
Sempron	Up to 2.3 GHz	Single-core uses AM2 socket

Table 5-2 Current AMD processors

© Cengage Learning 2014

5

Courtesy of Advanced Micro Devices, Inc.

Figure 5-7 The AMD FX processor can have up to eight cores

In the next part of the chapter, you'll learn the detailed steps to select and install a processor in several of the popular Intel and AMD sockets used by a desktop computer.

SELECTING AND INSTALLING A PROCESSOR

A PC repair technician is sometimes called on to assemble a PC from parts, exchange a processor that is faulty, add a second processor to a dual-processor system, or upgrade an existing processor to improve performance. In each situation, it is necessary to know how to match a processor for the system in which it is installed. And then you need to know how to install the processor on the motherboard for each of the current Intel and AMD sockets used for desktop and laptop systems. In this part of the chapter, you'll learn about selecting and installing processors in desktops. In Chapter 19, you'll learn about selecting and installing processors in laptops.

SELECT A PROCESSOR TO MATCH SYSTEM NEEDS

When selecting a processor, the first requirement is to select one that the motherboard is designed to support. Among the processors the board supports, you need to select the best one that meets the general requirements of the system and the user's needs. To get the best performance, use the highest-performing processor the board supports. However, sometimes you need to sacrifice performance for cost.

APPLYING | CONCEPTS   SELECT A PROCESSOR

Your friend, Alice, is working toward her A+ certification. She has decided the best way to get the experience she needs before she sits for the exam is to build a system from scratch. She has purchased an Asus motherboard and asked you for some help selecting the right processor. She tells you that the system will later be used for light business needs and she wants to install a processor that is moderate in price to fit her budget. She says she doesn't want to install the most expensive processor the motherboard can support, but neither does she want to sacrifice too much performance or power.

The documentation on the Asus web site (*support.asus.com*) for the ASUS P8Z68-V LX motherboard gives this information:

◢ The ATX board contains the Z68 chipset and socket LGA1155 and uses DDR3 memory.

◢ CPUs supported include a long list of Second Generation Core i3, Core i5, and Core i7 processors and Celeron and Pentium processors. Here are five processors found in this list:
- Intel Core i7-2600, 3.4 GHz, 8 MB cache
- Intel Core i5-3450, 3.1 GHz, 6 MB cache
- Intel Core i3-2120, 3.3 GHz, 3 MB cache
- Intel Celeron G540, 2.5 GHz, 2 MB cache
- Intel Pentium G860, 3.0 GHz, 3 MB cache

Based on what Alice has told you, you decide to eliminate the most expensive processors (the Core i7) and the least-performing processors (the Celerons and Pentiums). That decision narrows your choices down to the Core i3 and Core i5. Before you select one of these processors, you need to check the list on the Asus site to make sure the specific Core i3 or Core i5 processor is in the list. Look for the exact processor number, for example, the Core i3-2120. Also double-check and make sure the processor uses the correct socket and is a Second Generation processor.

You will also need a cooler assembly. If your processor doesn't come boxed with a cooler, select a cooler that fits the processor socket and gets good reviews. You'll also need some thermal compound if it is not included with the cooler.

INSTALL A PROCESSOR

Now let's look at the details of installing a processor in an Intel LGA1155, LGA1366, LGA775, and AMD AM2+ sockets.

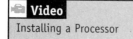
📷 **Video**
Installing a Processor

INSTALLING AN INTEL PROCESSOR IN SOCKET LGA1155

We're installing the Intel Core i5-2320 processor in Socket LGA1155 shown in Figure 5-8. In the photo, the socket has its protective cover in place.

A+
220-801
1.6

© Cengage Learning 2014

Figure 5-8 Intel socket LGA1155 with protective cover in place

> 💡 **A+ Exam Tip** The A+ 220-801 exam expects you to know how to install a processor in these Intel processor sockets: LGA775, LGA1155, LGA1156, and LGA1366 sockets.

When building a new system, if the motherboard is not already installed in the case, follow the directions of the motherboard manufacturer to install the motherboard and then the processor or to install the processor and then the motherboard. The order of installation varies among manufacturers. When replacing a processor in an existing system, power down the system, unplug the power cord, press the power button to drain the system of power, and open the case. Follow these steps to install the processor and cooler using socket LGA1155:

1. Read all directions in the motherboard user guide and carefully follow them in order.
2. Use a ground bracelet or antistatic gloves to protect the processor, motherboard, and other components against ESD.
3. Open the socket by pushing down on the socket lever and gently pushing it away from the socket to lift the lever (see Figure 5-9).

© Cengage Learning 2014

Figure 5-9 Release the lever from the socket

A+
220-801
1.6

4. As you fully open the socket lever, the socket load plate opens, as shown in Figure 5-10.

Figure 5-10   Lift the socket load plate

5. Remove the socket protective cover (see Figure 5-11). Keep this cover in a safe place. If you ever remove the processor, put the cover back in the socket to protect the socket. While the socket is exposed, be *very careful* to not touch the pins in the socket.

Figure 5-11   Remove the socket protective cover

A+
220-801
1.6

6. Remove the protective cover from the processor. You can see the processor in this clear plastic cover on the right side of Figure 5-12, which also shows the open socket. While the processor contacts are exposed, take extreme care to not touch the bottom of the processor. Hold it only at its edges. (It's best to use antistatic gloves as you work, but the gloves make it difficult to handle the processor.) Put the processor cover in a safe place and use it to protect the processor if you ever remove the processor from the socket.

© Cengage Learning 2014

Figure 5-12 Open socket LGA1155 and processor in a protective cover

7. Hold the processor with your index finger and thumb and orient the processor so that the gold triangle on the corner of the processor lines up with the right-angle mark embedded on the motherboard just outside a corner of the socket (see Figure 5-13). Gently lower the processor straight down into the socket. Don't allow the processor to tilt, slide, or shift as you put it in the socket. To protect the pads, it needs to go straight down into the socket.

Gold triangle

Right-angle mark

© Cengage Learning 2014

Figure 5-13 Align the processor in the socket using the gold triangle and the right-angle mark

A+
220-801
1.6

8. Check carefully to make sure the processor is aligned correctly in the socket. Closing the socket without the processor fully seated can destroy the socket. Figure 5-14 shows the processor fully seated in the socket. Close the socket load plate so that it catches under the screw head at the front of the socket (see Figure 5-15).

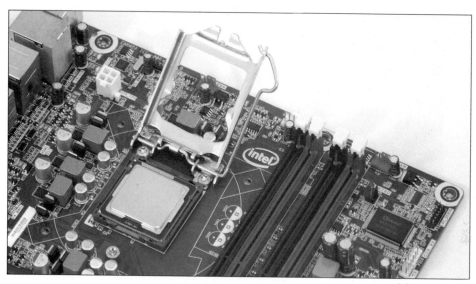

© Cengage Learning 2014

Figure 5-14   Processor in position ready to close the socket

Socket screw

© Cengage Learning 2014

Figure 5-15   The socket screw head secures the socket load plate

9. Push down on the lever and gently return it to its locked position (see Figure 5-16).

We are now ready to install the cooler. Before installing a cooler, read the directions carefully and make sure you understand them. Clips that hold the fan and heat sink to the processor frame or housing are sometimes difficult to install. The directions might give you important tips. Follow these general steps:

1. The motherboard has four holes to anchor the cooler. You can see them labeled in Figure 5-17. Examine the cooler posts that fit over these holes and the clips, screws, or wires that will hold the cooler firmly in place. Make sure you understand how this mechanism works.

A+
220-801
1.6

© Cengage Learning 2014

Figure 5-16   Return the lever to its locked position

2. If the cooler has thermal compound preapplied, remove the plastic from the compound. If the cooler does not have thermal compound applied, put a small dot of compound (about the size of a small pea) in the center of the processor (see Figure 5-17). When the cooler is attached and the processor is running, the compound spreads over the surface. Don't use too much—just enough to later create a thin layer. If you use too much compound, it can slide off the housing and damage the processor or circuits on the motherboard. To get just the right amount, you can buy individual packets that each contain a single application of the thermal compound.

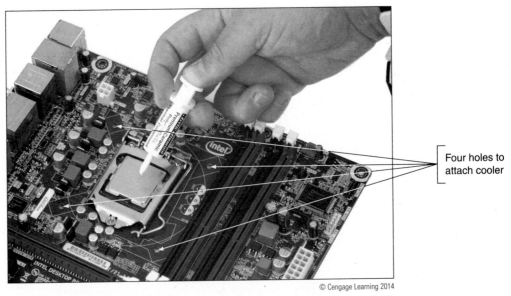

Four holes to
attach cooler

© Cengage Learning 2014

Figure 5-17   If the cooler does not have preapplied thermal compound, apply it on top of the processor

A+
220-801
1.6

Notes When removing and reinstalling a processor, use a soft dry cloth to carefully remove all the old thermal compound from both the processor and the cooler. Don't try to reuse the compound.

3. Verify the locking pins on the cooler are turned as far as they will go in a counter-clockwise direction. (Make sure the pins don't protrude into the hollow plastic posts that go down into the motherboard holes.) Align the cooler over the processor so that all four posts fit into the four holes on the motherboard and the fan power cord can reach the fan header on the motherboard (see Figure 5-18).

© Cengage Learning 2014

Figure 5-18 Align the cooler over the four holes in the motherboard

4. Push down on each locking pin until you hear it pop into the hole (see Figure 5-19). To help keep the cooler balanced and in position, push down two opposite pins and then push the remaining two pins in place. Using a flathead screwdriver, turn the locking pin clockwise to secure it. (Later, if you need to remove the cooler, turn each locking pin counterclockwise to release it from the hole.)

© Cengage Learning 2014

Figure 5-19 Push down on a locking pin to lock it into position

> **Notes** If you later notice the CPU fan is running far too often, you might need to tighten the connection between the cooler and the processor.

5. Connect the power cord from the cooler fan to the motherboard power connector near the processor, as shown in Figure 5-20.

© Cengage Learning 2014

Figure 5-20   Connect the cooler fan power cord to the motherboard CPU fan header

After the processor and cooler are installed and the motherboard is installed in the case, make sure cables and cords don't obstruct fans or airflow, especially airflow around the processor and video card. Use cable ties to tie cords and cables up and out of the way.

Make one last check to verify all power connectors are in place and other cords and cables connected to the motherboard are correctly done. You are now ready to plug back up the system, turn it on, and verify all is working. If the power comes on (you hear the fan spinning and see lights), but the system fails to work, most likely the processor is not seated solidly in the socket or some power cord has not yet been connected or is not solidly connected. Turn everything off, unplug the power cord, press the power button to drain power, open the case, and recheck your installation. If the system comes up and begins the boot process, but suddenly turns off before the boot is complete, most likely the processor is overheating because the cooler is not installed correctly. Turn everything off, unplug the power cord, press the power button to drain power, open the case, and verify the cooler is securely seated and connected.

After the system is up and running, you can check BIOS setup to verify that the system recognized the processor correctly. The setup screen for one processor is shown in Figure 5-21. Look for items on the screen that manage processor features, and make sure each is set correctly. For example, in Figure 5-21, items listed in blue can be changed. Verify the two blue items that apply to the processor; verify that all processor cores are active and Hyper-Threading Technology is enabled.

A+
220-801
1.6

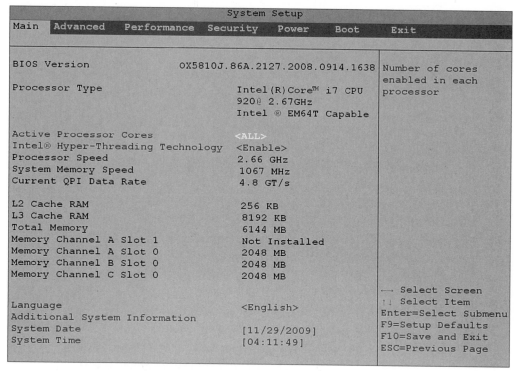

```
                                System Setup
Main   Advanced   Performance   Security   Power   Boot   Exit

BIOS Version            0X5810J.86A.2127.2008.0914.1638   Number of cores
                                                          enabled in each
Processor Type                   Intel(R)Core™ i7 CPU     processor
                                 920@ 2.67GHz
                                 Intel ® EM64T Capable

Active Processor Cores           <ALL>
Intel® Hyper-Threading Technology  <Enable>
Processor Speed                  2.66 GHz
System Memory Speed              1067 MHz
Current QPI Data Rate            4.8 GT/s

L2 Cache RAM                     256 KB
L3 Cache RAM                     8192 KB
Total Memory                     6144 MB
Memory Channel A Slot 1          Not Installed
Memory Channel A Slot 0          2048 MB
Memory Channel B Slot 0          2048 MB
Memory Channel C Slot 0          2048 MB
                                                          —→ Select Screen
                                                          ↑↓ Select Item
Language                         <English>                Enter=Select Submenu
Additional System Information                             F9=Setup Defaults
System Date                      [11/29/2009]             F10=Save and Exit
System Time                      [04:11:49]               ESC=Previous Page
```

Source: Intel

Figure 5-21 Verify the CPU is recognized correctly by BIOS setup

Also check in BIOS setup the CPU and motherboard temperatures to verify the CPU is not overheating. For one BIOS setup in another system, this screen is under the Configuration menu, Fan Control & Real-Time Monitoring window, as shown in Figure 5-22.

```
                                System Setup
Main   Configuration   Performance   Security   Power   Boot   Exit

Fan Control & Real-Time Monitoring

CPU Fan                          1008 RPM
Front Fan                           0 RPM
Rear Fan                          659 RPM


Processor Temperature            63  °C
PCH Temperature                  53  °C
Memory Temperature               36  °C
VR Temperature                   41  °C

+12.0V                           11.96 V
+5.0V                            5.07 V
+3.3V                            3.36 V
Memory Vcc                       1.54 V
Processor Vcc                    1.20 V
PCH Vcc                          1.07 V
+3.3V Standby                    3.39 V
                                                          → ←: Select Screen
Restore Default Fan Control Configuration                 ↑ ↓: Select Item
                                                          Enter:Select
Warning: Setting items on these screens to incorrect values may cause  +/-: Change Opt.
system to overheat and/or produce undesired acoustics!    F9: Load Defaults
                                                          F10:Save ESC:Exit
```

Source: Intel

Figure 5-22 Verify the processor temperature is within an acceptable range

If you see the processor temperature rising and reaching 80 degrees, open the case cover and verify the processor fan is running. Perhaps a wire is in the way and preventing the fan from turning or the fan wire is not connected. Other troubleshooting tips for processors are covered in Chapter 13.

INSTALLING AN INTEL PROCESSOR IN SOCKET LGA1366

The installations of all processors and sockets in this part of the chapter are similar to that of installing a processor in Socket LGA1155, so we will not repeat many of those steps. Listed next are the differences when installing a processor in the LGA1366 socket. These socket pins are delicate, so work slowly and take care. Here is how to work with this socket:

1. To open the socket, press down on the socket lever and gently push it away from the socket to lift the lever (see Figure 5-23). You can then lift the socket load plate, as shown in Figure 5-24. Next, remove the socket protective cover.

© Cengage Learning 2014

Figure 5-23 Release the lever from the socket

© Cengage Learning 2014

Figure 5-24 Lift the socket load plate

2. To install the processor, hold the processor with your index finger and thumb and orient the processor so that the notches on the two edges of the processor line up with the two posts on the socket. You can see the notch and post on the right side of the processor and socket in Figure 5-25. Gently lower the processor straight down into the socket. Don't allow the processor to tilt, slide, or shift as you put it in the socket. To protect the pins, it needs to go straight down into the socket.

Right notch

Right post

© Cengage Learning 2014

Figure 5-25   Orient the processor over the socket so that the notches on each side of the processor match the posts on each side of the socket

3. You can now lower the socket load plate and return the lever to its locked position (see Figure 5-26).

© Cengage Learning 2014

Figure 5-26   Return the lever to its locked position

INSTALLING AN INTEL PROCESSOR IN SOCKET LGA775

Socket LGA775 is shown in Figure 5-27 along with a Pentium processor and cooler. In the photo, the socket is open and the protective cover removed. The processor is lying upside down in front of the cooler.

© Cengage Learning 2014

Figure 5-27 A Pentium, cooler, and open socket 775

When installing a processor in socket LGA775, do the following:

1. Push down on the lever and gently push it away from the socket to lift it. Lift the socket load plate (see Figure 5-28). Remove the socket protective cover.

© Cengage Learning 2014

Figure 5-28 Lift the socket load plate

2. Orient the processor so that the notches on the two edges of the processor line up with the two notches on the socket (see Figure 5-29). Gently place the processor in the socket. Socket LGA775 doesn't have those delicate pins that Socket LGA1366 has, but you still need to be careful to not touch the top of the socket or the bottom of the processor as you work.

3. Close the socket cover. Push down on the lever and gently return it to its locked position.

Two notches on
processor package

Two notches
on socket

© Cengage Learning 2014

Figure 5-29 Place the processor in the socket, orienting the notches on two sides

INSTALLING AN AMD PROCESSOR IN SOCKET AM2+

When installing an AMD processor in AMD socket AM2, AM2+, or other AMD sockets, do the following:

1. Open the socket lever. If there's a protective cover over the socket, remove it.

2. Holding the processor very carefully so you don't touch the bottom, orient the four empty positions on the bottom with the four empty positions in the socket (see Figure 5-30). For some AMD sockets, a gold triangle on one corner of the processor matches up with a small triangle on a corner of the socket. Carefully lower the processor into the socket. Don't allow it to tilt or slide as it goes into the socket. The pins on the bottom of the processor are very delicate, so take care as you work.

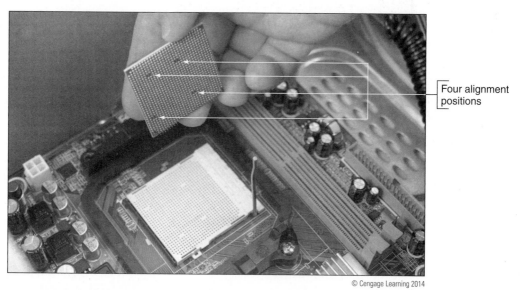

Four alignment
positions

© Cengage Learning 2014

Figure 5-30 Orient the four alignment positions on the bottom of the processor with those in the socket

A+
220-801
1.6

3. Check carefully to make sure the pins in the processor are sitting slightly into the holes. Make sure the pins are not offset from the holes. If you try to use the lever to put pressure on these pins and they are not aligned correctly, you can destroy the processor. You can actually feel the pins settle into place when you're lowering the processor into the socket correctly.

4. Press the lever down and gently into position (see Figure 5-31).

© Cengage Learning 2014

Figure 5-31   Lower the lever into place, which puts pressure on the processor

5. You are now ready to apply the thermal compound and install the cooler assembly. For one system, the black retention mechanism for the cooler is already installed on the motherboard (see Figure 5-32). Sit the cooler on top of the processor, aligning it inside the retention mechanism.

Black retention
mechanism is
preattached

© Cengage Learning 2014

Figure 5-32   Align the cooler over the retention mechanism

6. Next, clip into place the clipping mechanism on one side of the cooler. Then push down firmly on the clip on the opposite side of the cooler assembly; the clip will snap into place. Figure 5-33 shows the clip on one side in place for a system that has a yellow retention mechanism and a black cooler clip. Later, if you need to remove the cooler, use a Phillips screwdriver to remove the screws holding the retention mechanism in place. Then remove the retention mechanism along with the entire cooler assembly.

A+
220-801
1.6

Cooler clip

Retention mechanism

© Cengage Learning 2014

Figure 5-33 The clips on the cooler attach the cooler to the retention mechanism on the motherboard

7. Connect the power cord from the fan to the 4-pin fan header on the motherboard next to the CPU.

> **Notes** How to troubleshoot problems with the processor, motherboard, and RAM is covered in Chapter 13.

Now let's turn our attention to the various memory technologies used in personal computers, and how to upgrade memory.

MEMORY TECHNOLOGIES

A+
220-801
1.2, 1.3

Recall that random access memory (RAM) temporarily holds data and instructions as the CPU processes them and that the memory modules used on a motherboard are made of dynamic RAM or DRAM. DRAM loses its data rapidly, and the memory controller must refresh it several thousand times a second. RAM is stored on memory modules, which are installed in memory slots on the motherboard (see Figure 5-34).

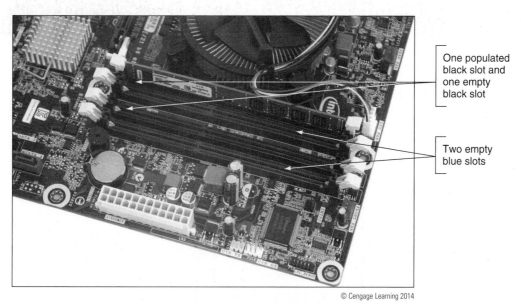

One populated black slot and one empty black slot

Two empty blue slots

© Cengage Learning 2014

Figure 5-34 RAM on motherboards today is stored in DIMMs

A+
220-801
1.2, 1.3

A+ Exam Tip The A+ 220-801 exam expects you to know the purposes and characteristics of the following memory technologies: DRAM, SRAM, SDRAM, DDR, DDR2, DDR3, and Rambus.

Several variations of DRAM have evolved over the years. Here are the four major categories of memory modules:

- All new motherboards for desktops sold today use a type of memory module called a **DIMM (dual inline memory module)**.
- Laptops use a smaller version of a DIMM called a **SO-DIMM (small outline DIMM** and pronounced "sew-dim"). MicroDIMMs are used on subnotebook computers and are smaller than SO-DIMMs. You learn about SO-DIMMs in Chapter 19.
- An older type of module is a **RIMM**, which is designed by Rambus, Inc.
- Really old computers used **SIMMs (single inline memory module)**. You're unlikely to ever see these modules in working computers.

The major differences among these modules are the width of the data path that each type of module accommodates and the way data moves from the system bus to the module. DIMMs have seen several evolutions. Four versions of DIMMs, one RIMM, and two types of SIMMs are shown in Table 5-3. Notice the notches on the modules, which prevent the wrong type of module from being inserted into a memory slot on the motherboard.

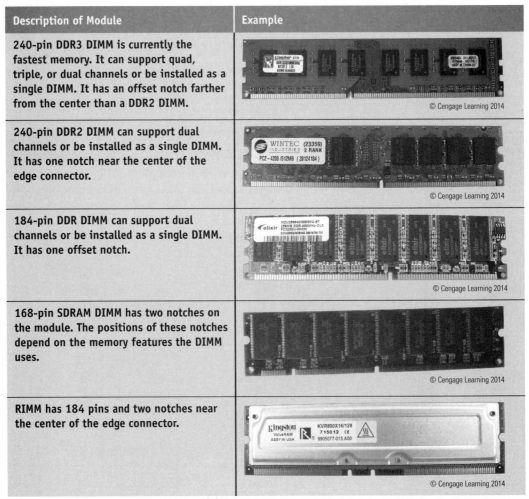

Description of Module	Example
240-pin DDR3 DIMM is currently the fastest memory. It can support quad, triple, or dual channels or be installed as a single DIMM. It has an offset notch farther from the center than a DDR2 DIMM.	© Cengage Learning 2014
240-pin DDR2 DIMM can support dual channels or be installed as a single DIMM. It has one notch near the center of the edge connector.	© Cengage Learning 2014
184-pin DDR DIMM can support dual channels or be installed as a single DIMM. It has one offset notch.	© Cengage Learning 2014
168-pin SDRAM DIMM has two notches on the module. The positions of these notches depend on the memory features the DIMM uses.	© Cengage Learning 2014
RIMM has 184 pins and two notches near the center of the edge connector.	© Cengage Learning 2014

© Cengage Learning 2014

Table 5-3 Types of memory modules (continues)

A+
220-801
1.2, 1.3

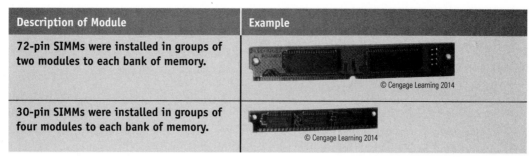

Description of Module	Example
72-pin SIMMs were installed in groups of two modules to each bank of memory.	© Cengage Learning 2014
30-pin SIMMs were installed in groups of four modules to each bank of memory.	© Cengage Learning 2014

© Cengage Learning 2014

Table 5-3 Types of memory modules (continued)

In this chapter, you'll see tons of different technologies used by RAM and so many can get a little overwhelming. You need to know about them because each motherboard you might support requires a specific type of RAM. Figure 5-35 is designed to help you keep all these technologies straight. You might find it a useful roadmap as you study each technology in the chapter. And who keeps up with all these technologies? JEDEC (*www.jedec.org*) is the organization responsible for standards used by solid state devices, including RAM technologies. The goal of each new RAM technology approved by JEDEC is to increase speed and performance without greatly increasing the cost.

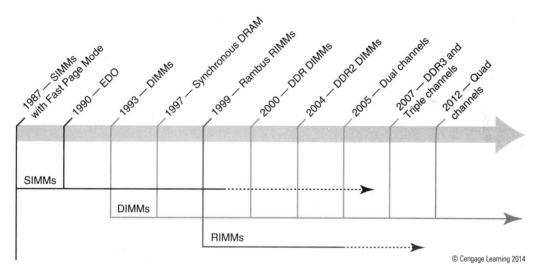

© Cengage Learning 2014

Figure 5-35 Timeline of memory technologies

Even though an older RAM technology is no longer used by new motherboards, RAM manufacturers continue to produce the older RAM because older motherboards require these replacement modules. In Figure 5-35, the dotted lines for SIMMs and RIMMs indicate these technologies are now obsolete. All new motherboards today use DIMMs. However, if you check some retail web sites, you can see that RIMMs can still be purchased.

Notes For an interesting discussion on how RAM works, complete with animation, see the web site by HowStuffWorks, Inc. at *www.howstuffworks.com/ram.htm*.

We'll now look at each of the types of DIMM and RIMM modules and wrap up the chapter section with a quick summary of the technologies.

DIMM TECHNOLOGIES

DIMMs use a 64-bit data path. (Some early DIMMs had a 128-bit data path, but they're now obsolete.) A DIMM (dual inline memory module) gets its name because it has independent pins on opposite sides of the module.

Early DIMMs did not run in sync with the system clock because they were too slow to keep up. Their speeds are measured in nanoseconds (ns), which is how long it takes for the module to read or write data. The first DIMM to run synchronized with the system clock was **synchronous DRAM (SDRAM)**, which has two notches, and uses 168 pins. (Don't confuse SDRAM with SRAM. SRAM is static RAM used in processor memory caches, and SDRAM is dynamic RAM used on DIMMs.) Synchronized memory runs in step with the processor and system clock, and its speeds are measured just as processor and bus speeds are measured in MHz.

Double Data Rate SDRAM (DDR SDRAM, or **SDRAM II,** or simply **DDR)** is an improved version of SDRAM. DDR runs twice as fast as regular SDRAM, has one notch, and uses 184 pins. Instead of processing data for each beat of the system clock, as regular SDRAM does, it processes data when the beat rises and again when it falls, doubling the data rate of memory. If a motherboard runs at 200 MHz, DDR memory runs at 400 MHz. Two other improvements over DDR are DDR2 and DDR3. **DDR2** is faster and uses less power than DDR. **DDR3** is faster and uses less power than DDR2. Both DDR2 and DDR3 use 240 pins, although their notches are not in the same position. They are not compatible, and the different notch positions keep someone from installing a DDR2 or DDR3 DIMM in the wrong memory slot.

Factors that affect the capacity, features, and performance of DIMMs include the number of channels they use, how much RAM is on one DIMM, the speed, error-checking abilities, and buffering. All these factors are discussed next.

SINGLE, DUAL, TRIPLE, AND QUAD CHANNELS

When you look at a motherboard, you might notice the DIMM slots are different colors. This color coding is used to identify the channel each slot uses. Channels have to do with how many DIMM slots the memory controller can address at a time. Early DIMMs only used a **single channel**, which means the memory controller can access only one DIMM at a time. To improve overall memory performance, **dual channels** allow the memory controller to communicate with two DIMMs at the same time, effectively doubling the speed of memory access. A motherboard that supports **triple channels** can access three DIMMs at the same time. Sandy Bridge technology introduced **quad channels** where the processor can access four DIMMs at the same time. DDR, DDR2, and DDR3 DIMMs can use dual channels. DDR3 DIMMs can also use triple channels and quad channels. For dual, triple, or quad channels to work, the motherboard and the DIMM must support the technology.

Figure 5-36 shows how dual channeling works on a board with four DIMM slots. The board has two memory channels, Channel A and Channel B. With dual channeling, the two DIMMs installed in the two slots labeled Channel A can be addressed at the same time. If two more DIMMs are installed in the Channel B slots, they can be accessed at the same time.

A+
220-801
1.2, 1.3

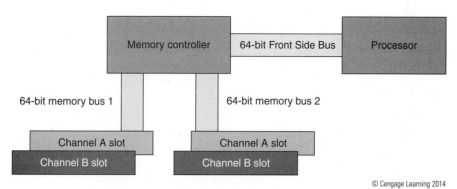

© Cengage Learning 2014

Figure 5-36 Using dual channels, the memory controller can read from two DIMMs at the same time

When setting up dual channeling, know that the pair of DIMMs in a channel must be equally matched in size, speed, and features, and it is recommended they come from the same manufacturer. A motherboard using dual channels was shown in Figure 5-34. The two black DIMM slots make up the first channel, and the two blue slots make up the second channel. To use dual channeling, matching DIMMs must be installed in the black slots and another matching pair in the blue slots, as shown in Figure 5-37. Know that the second pair of DIMMs does not have to match the first pair of DIMMs because the first channel runs independently of the second channel. If the two DIMM slots of a channel are not populated with matching pairs of DIMMs, the motherboard will revert to single channeling.

© Cengage Learning 2014

Figure 5-37 Matching pairs of DIMMs installed in four DIMM slots that support dual channeling

> **A+ Exam Tip** The A+ 220-801 exam expects you to be able to distinguish between single-channel, dual-channel, and triple-channel memory installations.

For a triple-channel installation, three DIMM slots must be populated with three matching DDR3 DIMMs (see Figure 5-38). The three DIMMs are installed in the three blue slots on the board. This motherboard has a fourth black DIMM slot. You can barely see this black slot behind the three filled slots in the photo. If the fourth slot is used, then triple channeling is disabled, which can slow down performance. If a matching pair of DIMMs is installed in the first two slots and another matching pair of DIMMs is installed in the third and fourth slots, then the memory controller will use dual channels. Dual channels are not as fast as triple channels, but certainly better than single channels.

© Cengage Learning 2014

Fourth slot
is empty

Figure 5-38 Three identical DDR3 DIMMs installed in a triple-channel configuration

The latest memory technology is quad channeling that was introduced with Intel Sandy Bridge chipsets and processors. Figure 5-39 shows an Intel motherboard that has the LGA2011 socket and eight memory slots. The processor can access four slots at the same time. The four black slots can be addressed by the processor on one memory channel and the four blue slots on another channel. Recall from Chapter 4 that Second Generation Sandy Bridge processors contain the memory controller within the processor package rather than on the chipset. To get the highest performance, memory slots are placed on either side of the processor in order to shorten the length of the memory bus. Because of the high performance of processors that use the LGA2011 socket, Intel recommends that systems using this socket use liquid cooling methods.

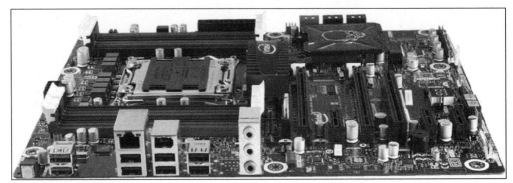

Courtesy of Intel Corporation

Figure 5-39 The Intel Desktop Board DX79TO has eight memory slots and supports two quad channels

DIMM SPEEDS

DIMM speeds are measured either in MHz (such as 1333 MHz or 800 MHz) or PC rating (such as PC6400). A PC rating is a measure of the total bandwidth of data moving between the module and the CPU. To understand PC ratings, let's take an example of a DDR DIMM module that runs at 800 MHz. The module has a 64-bit (8-byte) data path. Therefore, the transfer rate is 8 bytes multiplied by 800 MHz, which yields 6400 MB/second. This value equates to the PC rating of PC6400 for a DDR DIMM. A DDR2 PC rating is usually labeled PC2, and a DDR3 PC rating is labeled PC3. In Figure 5-40, this memory ad shows both the MHz and PC rating. Some current PC ratings for DDR3 memory are PC3-16000 (2000 MHz), PC3-14400 (1800 MHz), PC3-12800 (1600 MHz), and PC3-10600 (1333 MHz). A couple of current

Figure 5-40 Memory speed is expressed in MHz and PC rating

PC ratings for DDR2 memory are PC2-6400 (800 MHz) and PC2-5400 (667 MHz). DDR memory might be rated at PC6400 (800 MHz), PC4000 (500 MHz), PC3200 (400 MHz), or PC2700 (333 MHz). An older 168-pin SDRAM DIMM might run at PC100 or PC133.

SINGLE-SIDED AND DOUBLE-SIDED DIMMS

A DIMM can have memory chips installed on one side of the module (called **single-sided**) or both sides of the module (called **double-sided**). Most desktop and laptop processors address memory 64 bits at a time. A **memory bank** is the memory a processor addresses at one time and is 64 bits wide, and a DIMM slot provides a 64-bit data path. However, some double-sided DIMMs provide more than one bank, which means the chips on the DIMM are grouped so that the memory controller addresses one group and then addresses another. These DIMMs are said to be **dual ranked**, and don't perform as well as DIMMs where all the memory is addressed at one time. Notice in the memory ad in Figure 5-41 that the second item listed shows Dual Ranked as a feature.

Figure 5-41 Memory ad lists dual ranked DDR3 memory

A+
220-801
1.2, 1.3

ERROR CHECKING AND PARITY

Because DIMMs intended to be used in servers must be extremely reliable, error-checking technology called **ECC (error-correcting code)** is sometimes used. Some SDRAM, DDR, DDR2, and DDR3 memory modules support ECC. A DIMM normally has an even number of chips on the module, but a DIMM that supports ECC has an odd number of chips on the module. The odd extra chip is the ECC chip. ECC compares bits written to the module to what is later read from the module, and it can detect and correct an error in a single bit of the byte. If there are errors in two bits of a byte, ECC can detect the error but cannot correct it. The data path width for DIMMs is normally 64 bits, but with ECC, the data path is 72 bits. The extra 8 bits are used for error checking. ECC memory costs more than non-ECC memory, but it is more reliable. For ECC to work, the motherboard and all installed modules must support it. Also, it's important to know that you cannot install a mix of ECC and non-ECC memory on the motherboard because such a mixture causes the system to not work.

As with most other memory technologies discussed in this chapter, when buying memory to add to a motherboard, match the type of memory to the type the board supports. To see if your motherboard supports ECC memory, look for the ability to enable or disable the feature in BIOS setup, or check the motherboard documentation. Figure 5-42 shows one ad for DIMMs. The first three items are non-ECC, and the last item is ECC memory. Also notice the first two items offer DIMMs in a kit of 4 DIMMs or 2 DIMMs.

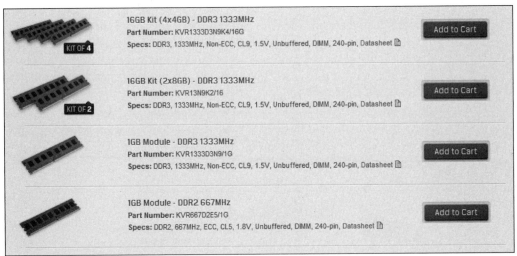

Source: kingston.com

Figure 5-42   Memory ad for DDR3 and DDR2 memory

Refer back to the memory ad shown in Figure 5-41. The first item is non-ECC memory and has ×64 in the ad. The second item is ECC memory and has ×72 in the ad. The 64 or 72 is the width of the data path for non-ECC or ECC memory.

Older SIMMs used an error-checking technology called **parity**. Using parity checking, a ninth bit is stored with every 8 bits in a byte. If memory is using odd parity, it makes the ninth or parity bit either a 1 or a 0, to make the number of ones in the nine bits odd. If it uses even parity, it makes the parity bit a 1 or a 0 to make the number of ones in the 9 bits even.

> **A+ Exam Tip**   The A+ 220-801 exam expects you to know that parity memory uses 9 bits (8 bits for data and 1 bit for parity). You also need to be familiar with ECC and non-ECC memory technologies.

Later, when the byte is read back, the memory controller checks the odd or even state. If the number of bits is not an odd number for odd parity or an even number for even parity, a **parity error** occurs. A parity error always causes the system to halt. On the screen, you see the error message "Parity Error 1" or "Parity Error 2" or a similar error message about parity. Parity Error 1 is a parity error on the motherboard; Parity Error 2 is a parity error on an expansion card.

Figure 5-43 shows a SIMM for sale. It's pricy because this old technology is hardly ever used. Notice the module is non-parity memory. In the ad, the SIMM is called EDO memory. EDO (extended data out) is a technology used by SIMMs.

Figure 5-43 A SIMM appears in a memory ad as EDO memory

Source: crucial.com

> **Notes** RAM chips that have become undependable and cannot hold data reliably can cause errors. Sometimes this happens when chips overheat or power falters.

BUFFERED AND REGISTERED DIMMS

Buffers and registers hold data and amplify a signal just before the data is written to the module. (Using buffers is an older technology than using registers.) Some DIMMs use buffers, some use registers, and some use neither. If a DIMM doesn't support registers or buffers, it's referred to as an unbuffered DIMM. Looking at the ad in Figure 5-44, you can see a kit of DDR3 unbuffered DIMMs and kits of registered DIMMs.

Figure 5-44 Kits of unbuffered or registered DIMMs

Source: crucial.com

Notches on SDRAM DIMMs are positioned to identify the technologies that the module supports. In Figure 5-45, the position of the notch on the left identifies the module as registered (RFU), buffered, or unbuffered memory. The notch on the right identifies the voltage used by the module. The position of each notch not only helps identify the type of module but also prevents the wrong kind of module from being used on a motherboard.

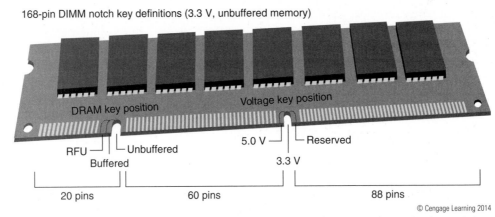

168-pin DIMM notch key definitions (3.3 V, unbuffered memory)

© Cengage Learning 2014

Figure 5-45   The positions of two notches on an SDRAM DIMM identify the type of DIMM and the voltage requirement and also prevent the wrong type from being installed on the motherboard

CAS LATENCY AND RAS LATENCY

Two other memory features are **CAS Latency** (CAS stands for "column access strobe") and **RAS Latency** (RAS stands for "row access strobe"), which are two ways of measuring access timing. Both features refer to the number of clock cycles it takes to write or read a column or row of data off a memory module. CAS Latency is used more than RAS Latency. Lower values are better than higher ones. For example, CL8 is a little faster than CL9.

> **Notes**   In memory ads, CAS Latency is sometimes written as CL, and RAS Latency might be written as RL.

Ads for memory modules sometimes give the CAS Latency value within a series of timing numbers, such as 5-5-5-15. The first value is CAS Latency, which means the module is CL5. The second value is RAS Latency. Looking back at Figure 5-44 you can see two DDR3 DIMM kits are rated at CL9 and one is rated at CL7.

> **Notes**   When selecting memory, use the memory type that the motherboard manufacturer recommends.

RIMM TECHNOLOGIES

Direct Rambus DRAM (sometimes called **RDRAM** or **Direct RDRAM** or simply **Rambus**) is named after Rambus, Inc., the company that developed it. A Rambus memory module is called a **RIMM**. RIMMs are expensive and are now slower than current DIMMs. No new motherboards are built to use RIMMs, but you might be called on to support an old motherboard that uses them.

RIMMs that use a 16-bit data bus have two notches and 184 pins (see Figure 5-46). RIMMs that use a 32-bit data bus have a single notch and 232 pins. The 232-pin RIMMs can support dual channels. RIMMs can be ECC or non-ECC and vary in size and speed. Size can vary from 64 MB to 512 MB, and speed ratings are 800 MHz or 1066 MHz.

With RIMMs, each memory slot on the motherboard must be filled to maintain continuity throughout all slots. If a slot does not hold a RIMM, it must hold a placeholder module called a **C-RIMM (Continuity RIMM)** to ensure continuity throughout all slots. The C-RIMM contains no memory chips. A C-RIMM is shown in Figure 5-46.

A+
220-801
1.2, 1.3

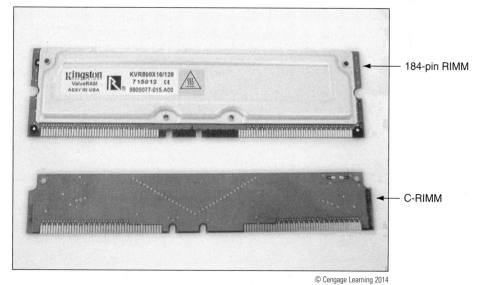

184-pin RIMM

C-RIMM

© Cengage Learning 2014

Figure 5-46 A RIMM or C-RIMM must be installed in every RIMM slot on the motherboard

MEMORY TECHNOLOGIES AND MEMORY PERFORMANCE

So now let's summarize the different memory technologies and consider how they affect overall memory performance. Factors to consider when looking at the overall performance of memory are listed below:

▲ *The total RAM installed.* The more memory there is, the faster the system. Generally use as much memory in a system as the motherboard and the OS can support and you can afford.

▲ *The memory technology used.* DDR3 is faster than DDR2. DDR2 is faster than DDR, and DDR is faster than SDRAM. When required by the motherboard, buffered or registered memory can improve performance. For all these technologies, use what the board supports.

▲ *The speed of memory in MHz or PC rating.* Use the fastest memory the motherboard supports. If you install modules of different speeds in the same system, the system will run at the slowest speed or might become unstable. Know that most computer ads give speeds in MHz or PC rating, but some ads give both values.

▲ *ECC or non-ECC.* Non-ECC is faster and less expensive but might not be as reliable. Use what the board supports.

▲ *CL or RL rating.* The lower the better. Use what the board supports, although most boards don't specify a particular CL rating. The CL rating might be expressed as a series of timing numbers.

▲ *Single, dual, triple, or quad channeling.* DIMMs that differ in capacity or speed can function on a motherboard in single channels as long as you use DIMMs that the board supports and match ECC ratings. However, to improve performance, use dual, triple, or quad channeling if the board supports the feature. To use dual, triple, or quad channeling, install matching DIMMs from the same manufacturer in each group of channel slots. These matching modules are sometimes sold as memory kits.

When selecting memory, you need to know one more fact about memory technologies. On a motherboard, the connectors inside the memory slots are made of tin or gold, as are the edge connectors on the memory modules. It used to be that all memory sockets were made of tin, but now most are made of gold. You should match tin leads to tin connectors and gold leads to gold connectors to prevent a chemical reaction between the two metals, which can cause corrosion. Corrosion can create intermittent memory errors and even make the PC unable to boot.

HOW TO UPGRADE MEMORY

To upgrade memory means to add more RAM to a computer. Adding more RAM might solve a problem with slow performance, applications refusing to load, or an unstable system. When Windows does not have adequate memory to perform an operation, it gives an "Insufficient memory" error or it slows down to a painful crawl.

When first purchased, many computers have empty slots on the motherboard, allowing you to add DIMMs to increase the amount of RAM. Sometimes a memory module goes bad and must be replaced.

When you add more memory to your computer, you need answers to these questions:

- ◢ How much RAM do I need and how much is currently installed?
- ◢ How many and what kind of memory modules are currently installed on my motherboard?
- ◢ How many and what kind of modules can I fit on my motherboard?
- ◢ How do I select and purchase the right modules for my upgrade?
- ◢ How do I physically install the new modules?

All these questions are answered in the following sections.

HOW MUCH MEMORY DO I NEED AND HOW MUCH IS CURRENTLY INSTALLED?

With the demands today's software places on memory, the answer is probably, "All you can get." Windows 7 needs at least 2 GB, but more is better. The limit for a 32-bit OS is 4 GB installed RAM. A 64-bit Windows installation can handle more. For example, a 64-bit installation of Windows 7 Home Premium can use up to 16 GB of RAM.

APPLYING | CONCEPTS HOW MUCH MEMORY IS CURRENTLY INSTALLED?

In Windows, you can use the System Information window to report the amount of physical memory installed. Click **Start**, type **Msinfo32**, and press **Enter**. The System Information window shown in Figure 5-47 reports the amount of installed physical memory. Notice on the window that 16 GB is installed, but only 14 GB is available to Windows. The other 2 GB is used by BIOS and most of that is used for video memory.

A+
220-801
1.2, 1.3

5

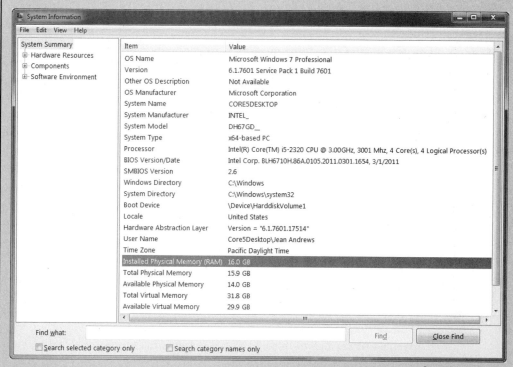

Source: Microsoft Windows 7

Figure 5-47 The System Information window reports installed physical memory

The BIOS setup screen shows more information about installed memory than does Windows. Reboot the computer and access BIOS setup (you learned how to do that in Chapter 4.) The BIOS setup main menu for one system is shown in Figure 5-48. This screen shows the number of memory slots and how much RAM is installed in each slot. Notice the system has two memory channels of two slots each. You can, therefore, conclude this system is using dual channels.

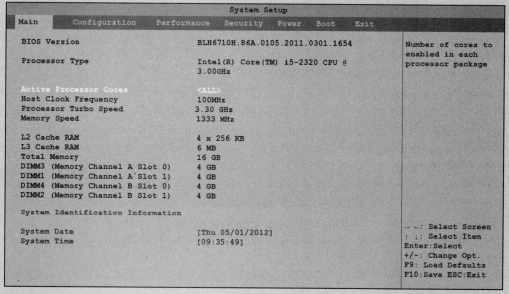

Source: Intel

Figure 5-48 BIOS setup reports memory configuration and amount

A+
220-801
1.2, 1.3

HOW MANY AND WHAT KIND OF MEMORY MODULES ARE CURRENTLY INSTALLED?

The next step to upgrading memory is to determine what type of memory modules the motherboard is currently using. If the board already has memory installed, you want to do your best to match the new modules with whatever is already installed. To learn what type of memory modules are already installed, do the following:

▲ Open the case and look at the memory slots. How many slots do you have? How many are filled? Remove each module from its slot and look on it for imprinted type, size, and speed. For example, a module might say "PC2-4200/512MB." The PC2 tells you the memory is DDR2, the 4200 is the PC rating and tells you the speed, and the 512 MB is the size. This is not enough information to know exactly what modules to purchase, but it's a start.

▲ Examine the module for the physical size and position of the notches. Compare the notch positions to those in Table 5-3 and Figure 5-45.

▲ Read your motherboard documentation. If the documentation is not clear (and some is not) or you don't have the documentation, look on the motherboard for the imprinted manufacturer and model (see Figure 5-49). With this information, you can search a good memory web site such as Kingston (*www.kingston.com*) or Crucial (*www.crucial.com*), which can tell you what type of modules this board supports.

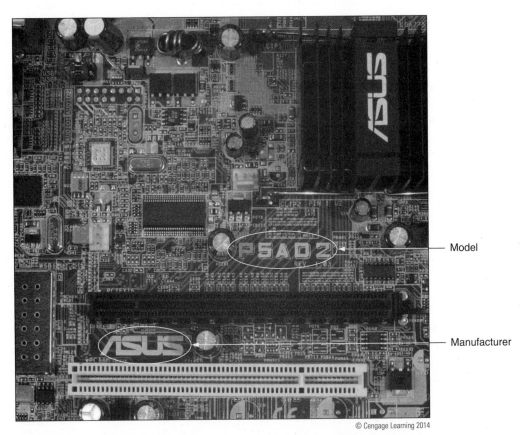

© Cengage Learning 2014

Figure 5-49 Look for the manufacturer and model of a motherboard imprinted somewhere on the board

▲ Look in the documentation to see if the board supports dual channel, triple channel, or quad channels. If it does, most likely the memory slots on the board will be color-coded in pairs (for dual channels) or groups of three slots (for triple channels) or four slots (for quad channels). If the board supports multiple channels and modules are already installed, verify that matching DIMMs are installed in each channel.

◢ If you still have not identified the module type, you can take the motherboard and the old memory modules to a good computer parts store and they should be able to match it for you.

HOW MANY AND WHAT KIND OF MODULES CAN FIT ON MY MOTHERBOARD?

Now that you know what memory modules are already installed, you're ready to decide how much and what kind of modules you can add to the board. Keep in mind that if all memory slots are full, sometimes you can take out small-capacity modules and replace them with larger-capacity modules, but you can only use the type, size, and speed of modules that the board can support. Also, if you must discard existing modules, the price of the upgrade increases.

To know how much memory your motherboard can physically hold, read the documentation that comes with the board. Next, let's look at what to consider when deciding how many and what kind of DIMMs or RIMMs to add to a system.

DIMM MODULES

You can always install DIMMs as single modules, but you might not get the best performance by doing so. For best performance, install matching DIMMs in all the slots (two, three, or four slots) on one channel. Now let's look at a few examples. The examples are ordered from a recent motherboard to an older motherboard. As you study these examples, notice that the older the board, the more complicated the configuration can be and the harder it is to understand the documentation. Is life with computers getting simpler or what?

Motherboard Using DDR3 Dual-Channel DIMMs

The Intel Desktop Board DH67GD shown earlier in Figure 5-12 has four memory slots that use dual channeling. These slots are numbered in the user guide, as shown in Figure 5-50. The slots can hold Dual Channel DDR3 1333 MHz and 1066 MHz non-ECC, 1.35 V modules for up to 32 GB of RAM on this board. To use four DIMMs and dual channeling, install matching DIMMs in the two blue slots and matching DIMMs in the two black slots.

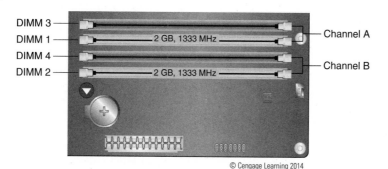

Figure 5-50 Documentation shows four DIMM slots that use dual channels

A+
220-801
1.2, 1.3

The mobo user guide says it is possible to use only three DIMMs and dual channeling if you install matching DIMMs in the two blue slots and install a third DIMM in a black slot. This third DIMM must be equal in speed and total size of the DIMMs in the blue slots. For example, you can install two 4 GB DIMMs in the two blue slots and one 8 GB DIMM in a black slot for a total of 16 GB RAM. If you install only a single DIMM on this board, it must go in the first blue slot, which is the blue slot closest to the processor.

Motherboard Using DDR3 Triple-Channel DIMMs

The Intel motherboard shown earlier in Figure 5-38 has four DDR3 memory slots that can be configured for single, dual, or triple channeling. The four empty slots are shown in Figure 5-51. If triple channeling is used, three matching DIMMs are used in the three blue slots. If the fourth slot is populated, the board reverts to single channeling. For dual channeling, install two matching DIMMs in the two blue slots farthest from the processor and leave the other two slots empty. If only one DIMM is installed, it goes in the blue slot in the farthest position from the processor.

© Cengage Learning 2014

Figure 5-51   Four DDR3 slots on a motherboard

The motherboard documentation says that these types of DIMMs can be used:

- The DIMM voltage rating no higher than 1.6 V
- Non-ECC DDR3 memory
- Serial Presence Detect (SPD) memory only
- Gold-plated contacts (some modules use tin-plated contacts)
- 1333 MHz, 1066 MHz, or 800 MHz (best to match the system bus speed)
- Unbuffered, nonregistered single- or double-sided DIMMs
- Up to 16 GB total installed RAM

A+
220-801
1.2, 1.3

The third item in the list needs an explanation. Serial Presence Detect (SPD) is a DIMM technology that declares to system BIOS at startup the module's size, speed, voltage, and data path width. If the DIMM does not support SPD, the system might not boot or boot with errors. Today's memory always supports SPD.

Motherboard Using DDR DIMMs with Dual Channeling

Let's look at another example of a DIMM installation. The Pentium motherboard allows you to use three different speeds of DDR DIMMs in one to four sockets on the board. The board supports dual channeling and has two blue slots for one channel and two black slots for the other channel. For dual channeling to work, matching DIMMs must be installed in the two blue sockets. If two DIMMs are installed in the two black sockets, they must match each other.

This board supports up to 4 GB of unbuffered, 184-pin, non-ECC memory running at PC3200, PC2700, or PC2100. The documentation says the system bus can run at 800 MHz, 533 MHz, or 400 MHz, depending on the speed of the processor installed. Therefore, the speed of the processor determines the system bus speed, which determines the speed of memory modules.

Figure 5-52 outlines the possible configurations of these DIMM modules, showing that you can install one, two, or four DIMMs and which sockets should hold these DIMMs. To take advantage of dual channeling on this motherboard, you must populate the sockets according to Figure 5-52, so that identical DIMM pairs are working together in DIMM_A1 and DIMM_B1 sockets (the blue sockets), and another pair can work together in DIMM_A2 and DIMM_B2 sockets (the black sockets).

Mode		Sockets			
		DIMM_A1	DIMM_A2	DIMM_B1	DIMM_B2
Single channel	(1)	Populated	—	—	—
	(2)	—	Populated	—	—
	(3)	—	—	Populated	—
	(4)	—	—	—	Populated
Dual channel*	(1)	Populated	—	Populated	—
	(2)	—	Populated	—	Populated
	(3)	Populated	Populated	Populated	Populated

*Use only identical DDR DIMM pairs

© Cengage Learning 2014

Figure 5-52 Motherboard documentation shows that one, two, or four DIMMs can be installed

The board has two installed DDR DIMMs. The label on one of these DIMMs is shown in Figure 5-53. The important items on this label are the size (256 MB), the speed (400 MHz or 3200 PC rating), and the CAS Latency (CL3). With this information and knowledge about what the board can support, we are now ready to select and buy the memory for the upgrade. For example, if you decide to upgrade the system to 1 GB of memory, you would buy two DDR, 400 MHz, CL3 DIMMs that support dual channeling. For best results, you need to also match the manufacturer and buy Elixir memory.

5

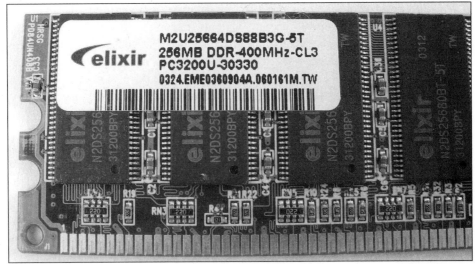

© Cengage Learning 2014

Figure 5-53 Use the label on this DIMM to identify its features

Pentium Motherboard Using SDRAM DIMMs

Our last DIMM example uses older SDRAM DIMMs. The Pentium motherboard uses 168-pin single-sided DIMM modules, and the documentation says to use unbuffered, 3.3 V, ECC, PC100 DIMM SDRAM modules. The PC100 means that the modules should be rated to work with a motherboard that runs at 100 MHz. You can choose to use ECC modules. If you choose not to, BIOS setup should show the feature disabled. Three DIMM slots are on the board, which the motherboard documentation calls sockets. Each socket holds one bank of memory. Figure 5-54 shows the possible combinations of DIMMs that can be installed in these sockets.

DIMM Location	168-Pin DIMM		Total Memory
Socket 1 (Rows 0 & 1)	SDRAM 8, 16, 32, 64, 128, 256 MB	×1	
Socket 2 (Rows 2 & 3)	SDRAM 8, 16, 32, 64, 128, 256 MB	×1	
Socket 3 (Rows 4 & 5)	SDRAM 8, 16, 32, 64, 128, 256 MB	×1	
	Total System Memory (Max 768 MB)	=	

© Cengage Learning 2014

Figure 5-54 This table is part of the motherboard documentation and is used to show possible DIMM sizes and calculate total memory on the motherboard

RIMM MODULES

Systems using RIMMs are no longer made, but you might be called on to support one. Because RIMMs are obsolete, they are really expensive. Most likely you can purchase a comparable motherboard and processor that use DIMMs for less money than you can buy the RIMMs for one of these old systems. However, if you ever find yourself needing to replace or upgrade memory using RIMMs, if possible, match the new RIMMs with one already installed on the board. Be sure to follow guidelines given in the motherboard documentation for the capacity and speeds supported.

A+
220-801
1.2, 1.3

For example, suppose you see installed a RIMM like the one shown in Figure 5-55. The important information for us is "800X16/128." The value 128 is the size of the RIMM, 128 MB. The value 800 is the speed, 800 MHz. The value X16 tells us this RIMM is a non-ECC RIMM. (If it had been ECC compliant, the value would have been X18.) That's enough information to go find a RIMM for sale that matches this one.

Figure 5-55   Use the label on this RIMM to identify its features

© Cengage Learning 2014

Recall that all RIMM slots must be filled with either RIMMs or C-RIMMs. When you upgrade, you replace one or more C-RIMMs with RIMMs.

As you can see, the motherboard documentation is essential when selecting memory. If you can't find the motherboard manual, look on the motherboard manufacturer's web site.

HOW DO I SELECT AND PURCHASE THE RIGHT MEMORY MODULES?

You're now ready to make the purchase. As you select your memory, you might find it difficult to find an exact match to DIMMs or RIMMs already installed on the board. If necessary, here are some compromises you cannot or can make:

- ◢ Mixing unbuffered memory with buffered or registered memory won't work.
- ◢ When matching memory, for best results, also match the module manufacturer. But in a pinch, you can try using memory from two different manufacturers.
- ◢ If you mix memory speeds, know that all modules will perform at the slowest speed.

Now let's look at how to use a web site or other computer ad to search for the right memory.

USING A WEB SITE TO RESEARCH YOUR PURCHASE

When purchasing memory from a web site such as Crucial Technology's site (*www.crucial.com*) or Kingston Technology's site (*www.kingston.com*), look for a search utility that will match memory modules to your motherboard (see Figure 5-56). These utilities are easy to

A+
220-801
1.2, 1.3

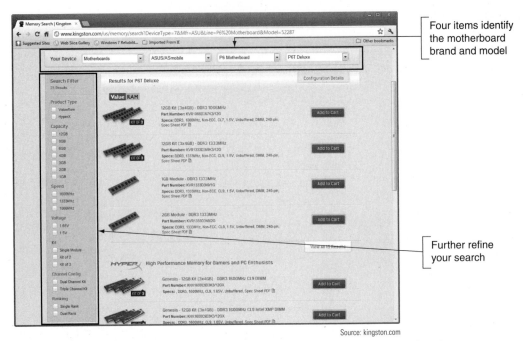

Four items identify
the motherboard
brand and model

Further refine
your search

Source: kingston.com

Figure 5-56 The Kingston web site DIMM recommendations for a particular motherboard

use and help you confirm you have made the right decisions about type, size, and speed to buy. They can also help if motherboard documentation is inadequate, and you're not exactly sure what memory to buy.

Let's look at one example on the Crucial site where we are looking to install memory in the Intel DH67GD motherboard discussed earlier in the chapter. The search results are shown in Figure 5-57. Modules faster than the board supports are listed. They will work on the board, running at a slower speed, but it's not necessary to spend the money for speed you won't use. The best buy is the second item listed; these DIMMs are rated at 1333 MHz, which is the maximum speed the board supports.

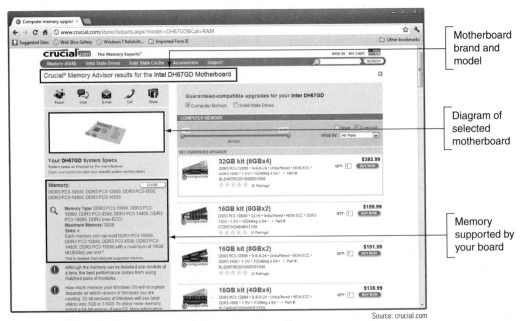

Motherboard
brand and
model

Diagram of
selected
motherboard

Memory
supported by
your board

Source: crucial.com

Figure 5-57 Selecting memory off the Crucial web site

A+
220-801
1.2, 1.3

5

HOW DO I INSTALL THE NEW MODULES?

When installing RAM modules, be careful to protect the chips against static electricity, as you learned to do in Chapter 1. Follow these precautions:

- ◢ Always use a ground bracelet as you work.
- ◢ Turn off the power, unplug the power cord, press the power button, and remove the case cover.
- ◢ Handle memory modules with care.
- ◢ Don't touch the edge connectors on the memory module or on the memory slot.
- ◢ Don't stack cards or modules because you can loosen a chip.
- ◢ Usually modules pop into place easily and are secured by spring catches on both ends. Make sure that you look for the notches on one side or in the middle of the module that orient the module in the slot.

Let's now look at the details of installing a DIMM and a RIMM.

INSTALLING DIMMS

For DIMM modules, small clips latch into place on each side of the slot to hold the module in the slot, as shown in Figure 5-58. To install a DIMM, first pull the supporting arms on the sides of the slot outward. Look on the DIMM edge connector for the notches, which help you orient the DIMM correctly over the slot, and insert the DIMM straight down into the slot. When the DIMM is fully inserted, the supporting clips should pop back into place. Figure 5-59 shows a DIMM being inserted into a slot on a motherboard. Apply pressure on both ends of the DIMM at the same time.

Clip holds module in place

Open clip on empty slot

© Cengage Learning 2014

Figure 5-58 Clips on each side of a slot hold a DIMM in place

Most often, placing memory on the motherboard is all that is necessary for installation. When the computer powers up, it counts the memory present without any further instruction and senses the features that the modules support, such as ECC or buffering. For some really old computers, you must tell BIOS setup the amount of memory present. Read the

A+
220-801
1.2, 1.3

© Cengage Learning 2014

Figure 5-59 Insert the DIMM into the slot by pressing down until the support clips lock into position

motherboard documentation to determine what yours requires. If the new memory is not recognized, power down the system and reseat the module. Most likely it's not installed solidly in the slot.

INSTALLING RIMMs

For RIMM modules, install the RIMMs beginning with bank 0, followed by bank 1. (To know which slot is bank 0, see the motherboard documentation.) If a C-RIMM is already in the slot, remove the C-RIMM by pulling the supporting clips on the sides of the socket outward and pulling straight up on the C-RIMM. When installing the RIMM, notches on the edge of the RIMM module will help you orient it correctly in the socket. Insert the module straight down in the socket (see Figure 5-60). When it is fully inserted, the supporting clips should pop back into place.

Supporting clips on
the slot are in
outward position

© Cengage Learning 2014

Figure 5-60 Install RIMM modules in banks beginning with bank 0

>> CHAPTER SUMMARY

Types and Characteristics of Processors

▲ The most important component on the motherboard is the processor, or central processing unit. The two major manufacturers of processors are Intel and AMD.

▲ Processors are rated by the speed of the system bus the processor can support, the processor speed, the socket and chipset the processor can use, processor architecture (32-bit or 64-bit), multi-core rating, how much internal memory cache the processor has, amount and type of RAM the processor can support, and the computing technologies the processor can use.

▲ A processor's memory cache inside the processor housing can be an L1 cache (contained on the processor die), L2 cache (off the die), and L3 cache (farther from the core than L2 cache).

▲ The core of a processor has two arithmetic logic units (ALUs). Multi-core processors have two, three, or more cores (called dual core, triple core, quad core, and so forth). Each core can process two threads at once if the feature is enabled in BIOS setup.

▲ The current families of Intel processors for desktops include the Core, Atom, Celeron, and Pentium families of processors. Several different processors are within each family.

▲ The current AMD desktop processor families are the FX, Phenom, Athlon, and Sempron. Several processors exist within each family.

Selecting and Installing a Processor

▲ Select a processor that the motherboard supports. A board is likely to support several processors that vary in performance and price.

▲ When installing a processor, always follow the directions given in the motherboard user guide and be careful to protect the board and processor against ESD. Current Intel sockets LGA1155, LGA1366, and LGA775 use a socket lever and socket load plate. When opening these sockets, lift the socket lever and then the socket load plate, install the processor, and then close the socket. Many AMD sockets have a socket lever, but not a socket load plate.

Memory Technologies

▲ DRAM is stored on four kinds of modules: DIMM, SO-DIMM, RIMM, and SIMM modules.

▲ Types of DIMMs are DDR3 and DDR2 DIMMs that have 240 pins, DDR DIMMs with 184 pins, and SDRAM DIMMs with 168 pins. A RIMM has 184 or 232 pins, and RIMMs are outdated technologies.

▲ DIMMs can be single-sided or double-sided. Some double-sided DIMMs provide more than one memory bank and are called dual ranked or quad ranked. A memory bank has a 64-bit data path and is accessed by the processor independently of other banks.

▲ DIMMs can work together in dual channels, triple channels, and quad channels so that the memory controller can access more than one DIMM at a time to improve performance. In a channel, all DIMMs must match in size, speed, and features. DDR3 DIMMs can use dual, triple, or quad channeling, but DDR and DDR2 DIMMs can only use dual channels.

▲ DIMM and RIMM speeds are measured in MHz (for example, 1333 MHz) or PC rating (for example, PC3-10600).

▲ The memory controller can check memory for errors and possibly correct those errors using ECC (error-correcting code). Using parity, an older technology, the controller could only recognize an error had occurred, but not correct it.

▲ Buffers and registers are used to hold data and amplify a data signal. A DIMM is rated as a buffered, registered, or unbuffered DIMM.

▲ CAS Latency (CL) and RAS Latency (RL) measure access time to memory. The lower values are faster than the higher values.

▲ RIMMs require that every RIMM slot be populated. If a RIMM is not installed in the slot, install a placeholder module called a C-RIMM.

How to Upgrade Memory

▲ When upgrading memory, use the type, size, and speed the motherboard supports and match new modules to those already installed. Features to match include DDR3, DDR2, DDR, size in MB or GB, speed (MHz or PC rating), buffered, registered, unbuffered, single-sided, double-sided, CL rating, tin or gold connectors, support for dual, triple, or quad channeling, ECC, and non-ECC. Using memory made by the same manufacturer is recommended.

>> KEY TERMS

For explanations of key terms, see the Glossary near the end of the book.

CAS Latency	ECC (error-correcting code)	RAS Latency
Centrino	graphics processing unit (GPU)	RDRAM
C-RIMM (Continuity RIMM)	Hyper-Threading	RIMM
DDR	HyperTransport	SDRAM II
DDR2	Level 1 cache (L1 cache)	SIMM (single inline memory module)
DDR3	Level 2 cache (L2 cache)	
DIMM (dual inline memory module)	Level 3 cache (L3 cache)	single channel
	memory bank	single-sided
Direct Rambus DRAM	multi-core processing	SO-DIMM (small outline DIMM)
Direct RDRAM	multiplier	
Double Data Rate SDRAM (DDR SDRAM)	multiprocessing	static RAM (SRAM)
	multiprocessor platform	synchronous DRAM (SDRAM)
double-sided	parity	
dual channels	parity error	thread
dual processors	processor frequency	triple channels
dual ranked	quad channels	x86 processors
dynamic RAM (DRAM)	Rambus	x86-64 bit processor

>> REVIEW QUESTIONS

1. Which term describes multiple processors that are installed in the same processor housing?

   a) Dual processors

   b) Multiprocessing

   c) Multithreading

   d) Multi-core processing

2. Which processor component holds data and instructions waiting to be processed by the ALU?

   a) Registers

   b) Internal memory cache

   c) Control unit

   d) Bus

3. All new motherboards for desktops sold today use a type of memory module called a(n) _____.

   a) SIMM

   b) DIMM

   c) RIMM

   d) EDO

4. _____ is a way of measuring memory access timing.

   a) DDR

   b) Frequency

   c) Parity

   d) CAS Latency

5. _____ is a DIMM technology that declares to system BIOS at startup the module's size, speed, voltage, and data path width.

   a) Serial Presence Detect (SPD)

   b) Latency

   c) Hyper-Threading

   d) Multi-core processing

6. True or false? The smaller the processor multiplier, the slower the system bus runs in comparison to the processor speed.

7. True or false? Memory used in a memory cache is dynamic RAM or DRAM.

8. True or false? Because DIMMs intended to be used in servers must be extremely reliable, error-checking technology called parity is sometimes used.

9. True or false? When measuring memory access time, lower values are better than higher ones.

10. True or false? For DIMM modules, small clips latch into place on each side of the slot to hold the module in the slot.

11. A(n) ____ is a processor that manipulates graphic data to form the images on a monitor screen.

12. The speed at which the processor operates internally is called the processor ____.

13. Using the ____ technology, the Intel processor, chipset, and wireless network adapter are all interconnected as a unit, which improves laptop performance.

14. When installing a processor, after the system is up and running, you can check ____ setup to verify that the system recognized the processor correctly.

15. A(n) ____ is the memory a processor addresses at one time and is 64 bits wide, and a DIMM slot provides a 64-bit data path.

Supporting Hard Drives

The hard drive is the most important permanent storage device
in a computer, and supporting hard drives is one of the more
important tasks of a PC support technician. This chapter introduces
the different kinds of hard drive technologies that have accounted
for the continual upward increase in hard drive capacities and speeds
over the past few years. The ways a computer interfaces with a hard
drive have also changed several times over the years as the techniques
for communication between the computer and hard drive continue to
improve.

In this chapter, you will learn about past and present methods
of communication between the computer and drive so that you can
support both older and newer drives. You'll learn how to select and
install the different types of hard drives and tape drives, and you'll
learn enough about floppy drives so that you can support these really
old storage devices.

HARD DRIVE TECHNOLOGIES AND INTERFACE STANDARDS

A+
220-801
1.5, 1.7,
1.11

A **hard disk drive (HDD)**, most often called a **hard drive**, comes in two sizes for personal computers: the 2.5″ size is used for laptop computers and the 3.5″ size is used for desktops. See Figure 6-1. In addition, a smaller 1.8″ size hard drive (about the size of a credit card) is used in some low-end laptops and other equipment such as MP3 players.

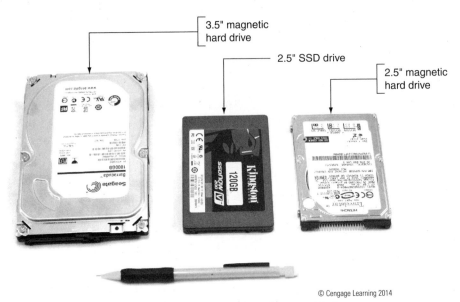

© Cengage Learning 2014

Figure 6-1 A hard drive for a desktop is larger than those used in laptops

In this part of the chapter, you learn about the technologies used inside a hard drive and about the various standards, cables, and connectors a drive might use to interface with the computer.

TECHNOLOGIES USED INSIDE A HARD DRIVE

The two types of hardware technologies used inside the drive are solid state and magnetic. In addition, some drives use a combination of both technologies. Here are important details about each:

▲ *Solid state drive.* A **solid state drive (SSD)**, also called a **solid state device (SSD)**, is called solid state because it has no moving parts. The drives are built using nonvolatile memory, which is similar to that used for USB flash drives. Recall that this type of memory does not lose its data even after the power is turned off.

In an SSD drive, flash memory is stored on EEPROM (Electronically Erasable Programmable Read Only Memory) chips inside the drive housing. The chips contain grids of rows and columns with two transistors at each intersection that hold a zero or one bit. One of these transistors is called a floating gate and accepts the zero or one state according to a logic test called NAND (stands for "Not AND"). Therefore, the memory in an SSD is called **NAND flash memory**. EEPROM chips are limited as to the number of times transistors can be reprogrammed. Therefore, the lifespan of an SSD drive is based on the number of write operations to the drive. (The number of read operations does not affect the lifespan.) For normal desktop or laptop computers, an SSD is rated to last for over 200 years. For high-use servers, the lifespan of an SSD is considerably shorter.

A+
220-801
1.5, 1.7,
1.11

Because flash memory is expensive, solid state drives are much more expensive than magnetic hard drives, but they are faster, more reliable, last longer, and use less power than magnetic drives. Figure 6-2 shows two sizes of solid state drives (2.5" and 1.8") and what the inside of an SSD hard drive looks like.

1.8" solid state drive

Inside an SSD drive

2.5" solid state drive

Courtesy of Toshiba America Electronic Components, Inc.

Figure 6-2   Solid state drives by Toshiba

◢ *Magnetic hard drive.* A **magnetic hard drive** has one, two, or more platters, or disks, that stack together and spin in unison inside a sealed metal housing that contains firmware to control reading and writing data to the drive and to communicate with the motherboard. The top and bottom of each disk have a **read/write head** that moves across the disk surface as all the disks rotate on a spindle (see Figure 6-3). All the

Actuator

Drive spindle

Platters or disks

Read-write head

Figure 6-3   Inside a magnetic hard drive

© Cengage Learning 2014

A+
220-801
1.5, 1.7,
1.11

read/write heads are controlled by an actuator, which moves the read/write heads across the disk surfaces in unison. The disk surfaces are covered with a magnetic medium that can hold data as magnetized spots. The spindle rotates at 5400, 7200, 10,000, or 15,000 RPM (revolutions per minute). The faster the spindle, the better performing the drive.

Data is organized on a magnetic hard drive in concentric circles, called tracks (see Figure 6-4). Each track is divided into segments called sectors (also called records). Older hard drives used sectors that contained 512 bytes. Most current hard drives use 4096-byte sectors.

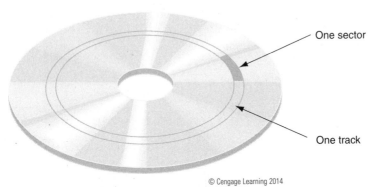

One sector

One track

© Cengage Learning 2014

Figure 6-4   A hard drive or floppy disk is divided into tracks and sectors; several sectors make one cluster

◢ *Hybrid hard drives.* Some hard drives are **hybrid hard drives,** using both technologies. The flash component is used as a buffer to improve drive performance. Some hybrid drives perform just as well as an SSD drive. For a hybrid drive to function, the operating system must support it. Windows 7/Vista technology that supports a hybrid drive is called **ReadyDrive.**

Video

Inside a Hard Drive

Before an SSD or magnetic drive leaves the factory, sector markings are written to it in a process called **low-level formatting.** (This formatting is different from the high-level formatting that Windows does after a drive is installed in a computer.) The hard drive firmware, BIOS, and the OS use a simple sequential numbering system called logical block addressing (LBA) to address all the sectors on the drive.

The size of each sector and the total number of sectors on the drive determine the drive capacity. Today's drive capacities are usually measured in GB (gigabytes) or TB (terabytes, each of which is 1024 gigabytes). Magnetic drives are generally much larger in capacity than SSD drives.

You need to be aware of one more technology supported by both SSD and magnetic hard drives called **S.M.A.R.T. (Self-Monitoring Analysis and Reporting Technology),** which is used to predict when a drive is likely to fail. System BIOS uses S.M.A.R.T. to monitor drive performance, temperature, and other factors. For magnetic drives, it monitors disk spin-up time, distance between the head and the disk, and other mechanical activities of the drive. Many SSD drives report to the BIOS the number of write operations, which is the best measurement of when the drive might fail. If S.M.A.R.T. suspects a drive failure is about to happen, it displays a warning message. S.M.A.R.T. can be enabled and disabled in BIOS setup.

A+
220-801
1.5, 1.7,
1.11

> 📝 **Notes** Malware has been known to give false S.M.A.R.T. alerts.

6

So now let's look at how the drive's firmware or controller communicates with the motherboard.

INTERFACE STANDARDS USED BY A HARD DRIVE

Video
Identifying Drives

The interface standards between the hard drive and the motherboard have evolved over time, and there are competing standards, which can make for a confusing mess of standards. To help keep them all straight, use Figure 6-5 as your guideline for the standards used by internal drives.

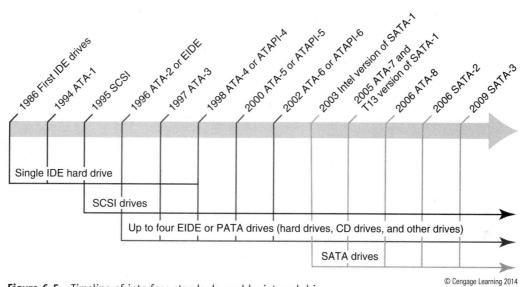

Figure 6-5 Timeline of interface standards used by internal drives
© Cengage Learning 2014

The two most popular internal drive interfaces are Parallel ATA (PATA) and Serial ATA (SATA). **Parallel ATA** or **PATA** (pronounced "pay-ta"), also called the **IDE** (**Integrated Drive Electronics**) standard, is older and slower than SATA. PATA allows for one or two IDE connectors on a motherboard, each using a 40-pin data cable (see Figure 6-6).

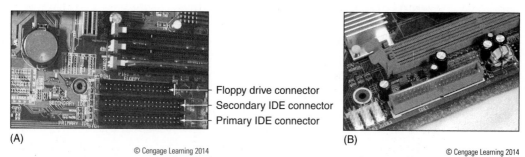

— Floppy drive connector
— Secondary IDE connector
— Primary IDE connector

(A)
© Cengage Learning 2014

(B)
© Cengage Learning 2014

Figure 6-6 (a) A really old motherboard has two IDE connectors and one floppy drive connector
(b) A not-so-old motherboard with one IDE connector

A+
220-801
1.5, 1.7,
1.11

The **serial ATA or SATA** (pronounced "say-ta") standard uses a serial data path, and a SATA data cable can accommodate only a single SATA drive (see Figure 6-7). New motherboards sold today use only SATA connections, but you still might see many older boards that use a combination of SATA and IDE on the same board or use all IDE connections. A third internal interface standard is SCSI (pronounced "scuzzy").

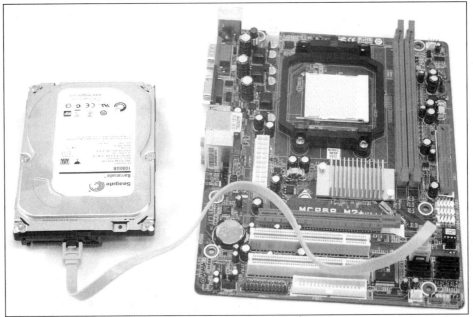

© Cengage Learning 2014

Figure 6-7   A SATA cable connects a single SATA drive to a motherboard SATA connector

External hard drives can connect to a computer by way of external SATA (eSATA), SCSI, FireWire, USB, or a variation of SCSI called Fibre Channel. The external standards are discussed in Chapter 8, and internal interface standards are covered in this chapter.

> **Notes** In technical documentation, you might see a hard drive abbreviated as HDD (hard disk drive). However, this chapter uses the term "hard drive."

Interface standards define data speeds and transfer methods between the drive controller, the BIOS, the chipset on the motherboard, and the OS. The standards also define the type of cables and connectors used by the drive and the motherboard or expansion cards.

The ATA standards are developed by Technical Committee T13 (*www.t13.org*) and published by **ANSI (American National Standards Institute**, *www.ansi.org*). As these standards developed, different drive manufacturers called them different names, which can be confusing when reading documentation or advertisements. The ATA standards have undergone several revisions, which are summarized in Table 6-1.

> **Notes** Remember from Chapter 5 that many memory standards exist because manufacturers and consortiums are always trying to come up with faster and more reliable technologies. The many ATA standards exist for the same reasons. It's unfortunate that you have to deal with so many technologies, but the old ones do stick around for many years after faster and better technologies are introduced.

A+
220-801
1.5, 1.7,
1.11

Standard (Can Have More Than One Name)	Data Transfer Rate	Description
ATA* IDE/ATA	From 2.1 MB/sec to 8.3 MB/sec	The first T13 and ANSI standard for IDE hard drives. Limited to no more than 528 MB. Supports PIO modes 0-2.
ATA-2* ATAPI, Fast ATA, Parallel ATA (PATA), Enhanced IDE (EIDE)	Up to 16.6 MB/sec	Broke the 528-MB barrier. Allows up to four IDE devices; defines the EIDE standard. Supports PIO modes 3-4 and DMA modes 1-2.
ATA-3*	Up to 16.6 MB/sec (little speed increase)	Improved version of ATA-2 and introduced S.M.A.R.T.
ATA/ATAPI-4* Ultra ATA, Fast ATA-2, Ultra DMA Modes 0-2, DMA/33	Up to 33.3 MB/sec	Defined Ultra DMA modes 0-2 and an 80-conductor cable to improve signal integrity.
ATA/ATAPI-5* Ultra ATA/66, Ultra DMA/66	Up to 66.6 MB/sec	Defined Ultra DMA modes 3-4. To use these modes, an 80-conductor cable is required.
ATA/ATAPI-6* Ultra ATA/100, Ultra DMA/100	Up to 100 MB/sec	Requires the 80-conductor cable. Defined Ultra DMA mode 5 and supports drives larger than 137 GB.
ATA/ATAPI-7* Ultra ATA/133, SATA I, SAS STP	Parallel transfer speeds up to 133 MB/sec SATA transfer speeds up to 1.5 Gb/sec	Can use the 80-conductor cable or serial ATA cable. Defines Ultra DMA mode 6, serial ATA (SATA), and Serial Attached SCSI (SAS) coexisting with SATA by using STP (SATA Tunnelling Protocol).
ATA/ATAPI-8*	N/A	Defined hybrid drives and SATA II. No new revisions of ATA/ATAPI are expected because PATA is retired.

*Name assigned by the T13 Committee

Table 6-1 Summary of ATA interface standards for storage devices

© Cengage Learning 2014

> **A+ Exam Tip** The A+ 220-801 exam expects you to know the speeds used by the IDE interfaces.

Let's now look first at the PATA or IDE standards and then we'll discuss the SATA standards. Finally, you'll learn about SCSI, a less used interface standard.

PARALLEL ATA OR EIDE DRIVE STANDARDS

PATA or IDE drives use ribbon cables that can accommodate one or two drives, as shown in Figure 6-8. A motherboard can have one or two IDE connectors for up to four PATA devices in the system using two data cables. All PATA standards since ATA-2 support this configuration of four IDE devices in a system, which is called the **Enhanced IDE (EIDE)** standard.

An optical drive must follow the **ATAPI (Advanced Technology Attachment Packet Interface)** standard in order to connect to a system using an IDE connector. Therefore, if you see ATAPI mentioned in an ad for a CD or DVD drive, know that the text means the drive connects to the motherboard using an IDE connector or header.

A+
220-801
1.5, 1.7,
1.11

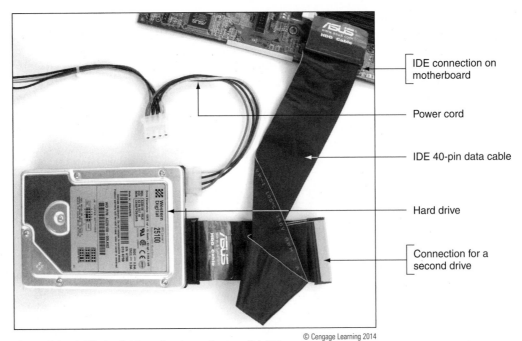

© Cengage Learning 2014

Figure 6-8 A PC's hard drive subsystem using parallel ATA

> **Notes** Acronyms sometimes change over time. Years ago, technicians knew *IDE* to mean *Integrated Drive Electronics*. As the term began to apply to other devices than hard drives, we renamed the acronym to become **Integrated Device Electronics**. Also, PATA and IDE are used interchangeably nowadays, although in the past, they had slightly different meanings. Currently, the term IDE is used more often than PATA to describe this interface standard.

Other technologies and changes mentioned in Table 6-1 that you need to be aware of are the two types of PATA data cables, DMA and PIO modes used by PATA, and Independent Device Timing. All these concerns are discussed next.

Two Types of PATA Ribbon Cables

Under parallel ATA, two types of ribbon cables are used. The older cable has 40 pins and 40 wires. The **80-conductor IDE cable** has 40 pins and 80 wires. Forty wires are used for communication and data, and an additional 40 ground wires reduce crosstalk on the cable. For maximum performance, an 80-conductor IDE cable is required by ATA/66 and above. Figure 6-9 shows a comparison between the two parallel cables. The 80-conductor cable is color-coded with the blue connector always connected to the motherboard. The connectors on each cable otherwise look the same, and you can use an 80-conductor cable in place of a 40-conductor cable in a system.

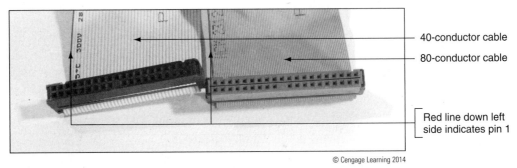

© Cengage Learning 2014

Figure 6-9 In comparing the 80-conductor cable to the 40-conductor cable, note they are about the same width, but the 80-conductor cable has many more and finer wires

The maximum recommended length of both cables is 18", although it is possible to purchase 24" cables. A ribbon cable usually comes bundled with a motherboard that has an IDE header. Because ribbon cables can obstruct airflow inside a computer case, you can purchase a smaller round PATA cable that is less obstructive to the airflow inside the case (see Figure 6-10).

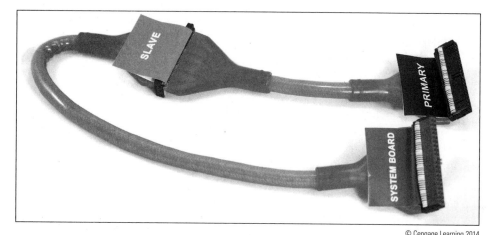

© Cengage Learning 2014

Figure 6-10 Use a smaller round PATA cable so as not to hinder airflow in a system

DMA or PIO Transfer Modes

A hard drive uses one of two methods to transfer data between the hard drive and memory: **DMA (direct memory access) transfer mode** or **PIO (Programmed Input/Output) transfer mode**. DMA transfers data directly from the drive to memory without involving the CPU. PIO mode involves the CPU and is slower and older than DMA mode.

There are different modes for PIO and DMA because both standards have evolved over the years. There are five PIO modes used by hard drives, from the slowest (PIO mode 0) to the fastest (PIO mode 4), and seven DMA modes from the slowest (DMA mode 0) to the fastest (DMA mode 6). All motherboards that use IDE today support Ultra DMA, which means that data is transferred twice for each clock beat, at the beginning and again at the end. Figure 6-11 shows a snip from an older Intel motherboard user guide that has two IDE headers. Because ATA-66/100 is mentioned rather than ATA/133, you can conclude the board supports ATA version 6 rather than version 7. (Refer to Table 6-1.)

PCI Enhanced IDE Interface

The ICH2's IDE interface handles the exchange of information between the processor and peripheral devices like hard disks, CD-ROM drives, and Iomega Zip† drives inside the computer. The interface supports:

- Up to four IDE devices (such as hard drives)
- ATAPI devices (such as CD-ROM drives)
- PIO Mode 3 and PIO Mode 4 devices
- Ultra DMA-33 and ATA-66/100 protocol
- Laser servo (LS-120) drives

Source: Intel

Figure 6-11 An older motherboard has two IDE headers using ATA-6 standards

A+
220-801
1.5, 1.7,
1.11

Most often, when installing an IDE drive, the startup BIOS autodetects the drive and selects the fastest mode that the drive and the BIOS support. After installation, you can go into BIOS setup and see which DMA mode is being used.

Independent Device Timing

As you saw in Table 6-1, there are different hard drive standards, each running at different speeds. If two hard drives share the same PATA cable but use different standards, both drives will run at the speed of the slower drive unless the motherboard chipset controlling the IDE connections supports a feature called Independent Device Timing. Most chipsets today support this feature, and with it, the two drives can run at different speeds as long as the motherboard supports those speeds.

SERIAL ATA STANDARDS

A consortium of manufacturers, called the Serial ATA International Organization (SATA-IO; see *www.sata-io.org*) and led by Intel, developed the SATA standards. These standards also have the oversight of the T13 Committee. SATA uses a serial data path rather than the traditional parallel data path. Essentially, the difference between the two is that data is placed on a serial cable one bit following the next, but with parallel cabling, all data in a byte is placed on the cable at one time. This fundamental difference is why transfer rates for PATA are expressed in bytes (MB/sec) and transfer rates for SATA are expressed in bits (Gb/sec). The three major revisions to SATA are summarized in Table 6-2.

SATA Standard	Data Transfer Rate	Comments
SATA Revision 1.x* SATA I or SATA1 Serial ATA-150 SATA/150 SATA-150	1.5 Gb/sec	First introduced with ATA/ATAPI-7.
SATA Revision 2.x* SATA II or SATA2 Serial ATA-300 SATA/300 SATA-300	3 Gb/sec	The first SATA II standards were published by the T13 Committee (t13.org) within ATA/ATAPI-8; later revisions of SATA II were published by SATA-IO (sata-io.org). The standard first came out in 2006. Most motherboards used it by 2010.
SATA Revision 3.x* SATA III or SATA3 Serial ATA-600 SATA/600 SATA-600	6 Gb/sec	SATA III was first published by SATA-IO in 2009. Most new motherboards today use this standard.

*Name assigned by the SATA-IO organization

© Cengage Learning 2014

Table 6-2 SATA standards

> **A+ Exam Tip** The A+ 220-801 exam expects you to know the speeds used by SATA1, SATA2, and SATA3, also known as SATA I, SATA II, and SATA III. These speeds apply to internal (SATA) and external (eSATA) devices.

A+
220-801
1.5, 1.7,
1.11

SATA interfaces are much faster than PATA interfaces and are used by all types of drives, including hard drives, CD, DVD, Blu-ray, and tape drives. Whereas PATA drives are not hot-swappable, SATA supports hot-swapping, also called hot-plugging. With **hot-swapping**, you can connect and disconnect a drive while the system is running. Hard drives that can be hot-swapped cost significantly more than regular hard drives.

SATA connections are much easier to configure and use than PATA connections. A SATA drive connects to one internal SATA connector on the motherboard by way of a 7-pin SATA data cable and uses a 15-pin SATA power connector (see Figure 6-12). An internal SATA data cable can be up to 1 meter in length, and is much narrower compared to the 40-pin PATA ribbon cable. The thinner SATA cables don't hinder airflow inside a case as much as the wide ribbon cables do. A motherboard might have two or more SATA connectors; use the connectors in the order recommended in the motherboard user guide. For example, for the four connectors shown in Figure 6-13, you are told to use the red ones before the black ones.

SATA power connectors

SATA data connectors

Figure 6-12 A SATA data cable and SATA power cable   © Cengage Learning 2014

Figure 6-13 This motherboard has two black and two red SATA II ports   © Cengage Learning 2014

A+
220-801
1.5, 1.7,
1.11

In addition to internal SATA connectors, the motherboard or an expansion card can provide **external SATA (eSATA)** ports for external drives (see Figure 6-14). External SATA drives use a special external shielded SATA cable up to 2 meters long. Seven-pin eSATA ports run at the same speed as the internal ports using SATA I, II, or III standards. The eSATA port is shaped differently from an internal SATA connector so as to prevent people from using the unshielded internal SATA data cables with the eSATA port.

© Cengage Learning 2014

Figure 6-14   Two eSATA ports on a motherboard

When purchasing a SATA hard drive, keep in mind that the SATA standards for the drive and the motherboard need to match. If either the drive or the motherboard uses a slower SATA standard than the other device, the system will run at the slower speed. Other hard drive characteristics to consider when selecting a drive are covered later in the chapter.

SCSI TECHNOLOGY

Other than ATA, another interface standard for drives and other devices is SCSI, which is primarily used in servers. SCSI standards can be used by many internal and external devices, including hard drives, optical drives, printers, and scanners. **SCSI** (pronounced "scuzzy") stands for **Small Computer System Interface** and is a standard for communication between a subsystem of peripheral devices and the system bus. The SCSI bus can support up to 7 or 15 devices, depending on the SCSI standard. SCSI devices tend to be faster, more expensive, and more difficult to install than similar ATA devices. Because they are more expensive and more difficult to install, they are mostly used in corporate settings and are seldom seen in the small office or used on home PCs.

The SCSI Subsystem

If a motherboard does not have an embedded SCSI controller, the gateway from the SCSI bus to the system bus is the **SCSI host adapter card**, commonly called the **host adapter**. The host adapter is inserted into an expansion slot on the motherboard and is responsible for managing all devices on the SCSI bus. A host adapter can support both internal and external SCSI devices, using one connector on the card for a ribbon cable or round cable to connect to internal devices, and an external port that supports external devices (see Figure 6-15).

A+
220-801
1.5, 1.7,
1.11

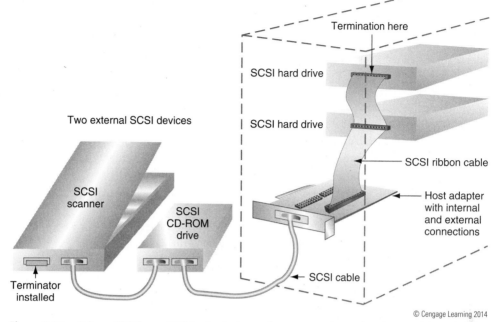

Figure 6-15 Using a SCSI bus, a SCSI host adapter card can support internal and external SCSI devices

All the devices and the host adapter form a single daisy chain. In Figure 6-15, this daisy chain has two internal devices and two external devices, with the SCSI host adapter in the middle of the chain. An example of a host adapter card is shown in Figure 6-16. It fits into a PCIe slot and provides one 68-pin internal SCSI connector and one external 68-pin connector. The host adapter manages all devices as a single SCSI chain and can support up to 15 devices.

A+ Exam Tip The A+ 220-801 exam expects you to know that a motherboard might provide a SCSI controller and connector or that the SCSI host adapter can be a card installed in an expansion slot.

Courtesy of PMC-Sierra, Inc.

Figure 6-16 This Adaptec SCSI card uses a PCIe x1 slot and supports up to 15 devices and automatic termination

A+
220-801
1.5, 1.7,
1.11

All devices go through the host adapter to communicate with the CPU or directly with each other without involving the CPU. Each device on the bus is assigned a number from 0 to 15 called the **SCSI ID**, by means of DIP switches, dials on the device, or software settings. The host adapter is assigned SCSI ID 7, which has the highest priority over all other devices. The priority order is 7, 6, 5, 4, 3, 2, 1, 0, 15, 14, 13, 12, 11, 10, 9, and 8. Cables connect the devices physically in a daisy chain, sometimes called a straight chain. The devices can be either internal or external, and the host adapter can be at either end of the chain or somewhere in the middle. The SCSI ID identifies the physical device, which can have several logical devices embedded in it. For example, a CD-ROM jukebox—a CD-ROM changer with trays for multiple CDs—might have seven trays. Each tray is considered a logical device and is assigned a **Logical Unit Number (LUN)** to identify it, such as 1 through 7 or 0 through 6. The ID and LUN are written as two numbers separated by a colon. For instance, if the SCSI ID is 5, the fourth tray in the jukebox is device 5:4.

To reduce the amount of electrical "noise," or interference, on a SCSI cable, each end of the SCSI chain has a **terminating resistor**. The terminating resistor can be a hardware device plugged into the last device on each end of the chain (see Figure 6-17), or the device can have firmware-controlled termination resistance, which makes installation simpler.

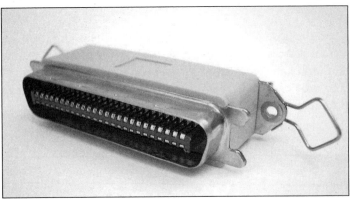

© Cengage Learning 2014

Figure 6-17 External SCSI terminator

Various SCSI Standards and Connectors

The two general categories of all SCSI standards used on PCs have to do with the width in bits of the SCSI data bus, either 8 bits (narrow SCSI) or 16 bits (wide SCSI). In almost every case, if the SCSI standard is 16 bits, the word "wide" is in the name for the standard. For 8-bit SCSI standards, the word "narrow" is usually not mentioned in names for the standard. Narrow SCSI uses a cable with a **50-pin SCSI connector** (also called an A cable), and wide SCSI uses a cable with a **68-pin SCSI connector** (also called a P cable). Narrow SCSI can also use a **25-pin SCSI connector** that looks like a parallel port connector. Figure 6-18 shows five types of SCSI connectors. The 80-pin SCA (Single Connector Attachment) connector can provide power to a SCSI device.

A SCSI bus can support more than one type of connector, and you can use connector adapters to plug a cable with one type of connector into a port using another type of connector. Figure 6-19 shows a SCSI cable. One end of the cable attaches to the host adapter, and, for best results, you should always plug a device into the last connector on the cable.

The three major versions of SCSI are SCSI-1, SCSI-2, and SCSI-3, commonly known as Regular SCSI, Fast SCSI, and Ultra SCSI. A variation of SCSI is serial SCSI, also called

6

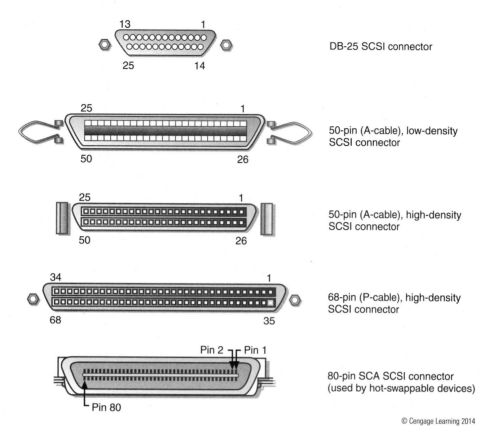

DB-25 SCSI connector

50-pin (A-cable), low-density
SCSI connector

50-pin (A-cable), high-density
SCSI connector

68-pin (P-cable), high-density
SCSI connector

80-pin SCA SCSI connector
(used by hot-swappable devices)

© Cengage Learning 2014

Figure 6-18 The most popular SCSI connectors are 50-pin, A-cable connectors for narrow SCSI
and 68-pin, P-cable connectors for wide SCSI

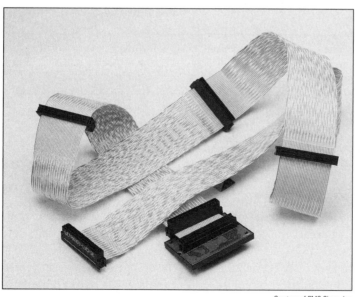

Courtesy of PMC-Sierra, Inc.

Figure 6-19 This 68-pin internal SCSI ribbon cable can connect several
SCSI devices

serial attached SCSI (SAS), which allows for more than 15 devices on a single SCSI chain,
uses smaller, longer, round cables, and uses smaller hard drive form factors that can support
larger capacities than earlier versions of SCSI. SAS can be compatible with SATA drives in
the same system and claims to be more reliable and better performing than SATA.

A+
220-801
1.5

Now that you know about the various hard drive technologies and interfaces, let's see how to select and install a hard drive.

HOW TO SELECT AND INSTALL HARD DRIVES

In this part of the chapter, you'll learn how to select a hard drive for your system. Then, you'll learn the details of installing a SATA drive and an IDE drive in a system. Next, you'll learn how to deal with using removable bays and the problem of installing a hard drive in a bay that is too wide for it. You'll also learn how to set up a RAID system.

SELECTING A HARD DRIVE

When selecting a hard drive, keep in mind that to get the best performance from the system, the system BIOS and the hard drive must support the same standard. If they don't support the same standard, they revert to the slower standard that both can use, or the drive will not work at all. There's no point in buying an expensive hard drive with features that your system cannot support.

Therefore, when making purchasing decisions, you need to know what standards the motherboard or controller card providing the drive interface can use. To find out, see the documentation for the board or the card. For the motherboard, you can look at BIOS setup screens to see which standards are mentioned. However, know that when installing a drive, you don't need to know which ATA standard a hard drive supports because the startup BIOS uses autodetection. With **autodetection**, the BIOS detects the new drive and automatically selects the correct drive capacity and configuration, including the best possible standard supported by both the hard drive and the motherboard.

> **Notes** To learn how to match up and install really old motherboards or drives, see the content "Selecting and Installing Hard Drives using Legacy Motherboards" in the online content at *cengagebrain .com* that accompanies this book. For more information, see the Preface.

When purchasing a hard drive, consider the following factors that affect performance, use, and price:

- ◢ *The capacity of the drive.* Today's hard drives for desktop systems are in the range of 60 GB for SSD drives to more than 2 TB for magnetic drives. The more gigabytes or terabytes, the higher the price. Magnetic drives have larger capacity for the money than solid state drives.
- ◢ *The spindle speed.* Magnetic hard drives for desktop systems run at 5400, 7200, 10,000, or 15,000 RPM (revolutions per minute). The most common is 7200 RPM. The higher the RPMs, the faster the drive.
- ◢ *The interface standard.* Use the standards your motherboard supports. For SATA, most likely that will be SATA II or SATA III. For a PATA IDE drive, most likely that will be Ultra ATA-100/133. For external drives, common standards are eSATA, FireWire 800 or 400, and SuperSpeed or Hi-Speed USB.

A+
220-801
1.5

▲ *The cache or buffer size.* For magnetic hard drives, buffer memory improves hard drive performance and can range in size from 2 MB to 64 MB. The more the better, though the cost goes up as the size increases. A buffer helps because the hard drive reads ahead of the requested data and stores the extra data in the buffer. If the next read is already in the buffer, the controller does not need to return to the spinning platters for the data. Buffering especially improves performance when managing large files, such as when working with videos or movies.

A hard drive manufacturer might produce both magnetic drives and solid state drives. Some hard drive manufacturers are listed in Table 6-3. Most manufacturers of memory also make solid state drives.

Manufacturer	Web Site
Crucial	*www.crucial.com*
Kingston Technology	*www.kingston.com*
Samsung	*www.samsung.com*
Seagate Technology and Maxtor	*www.seagate.com or www.maxtor.com*
Western Digital	*www.wdc.com*

© Cengage Learning 2014

Table 6-3 Hard drive manufacturers

Video

Installing a Hard Drive

Now let's turn our attention to the step-by-step process of installing a Serial ATA drive.

STEPS TO INSTALL A SERIAL ATA DRIVE

A motherboard that has SATA connectors might have an IDE header, too. An IDE header can be used for an optical drive or some other EIDE drive, including a hard drive. But SATA drives are faster than PATA drives, so it's best to use the IDE header for other types of drives than the hard drive.

> **A+ Exam Tip** The A+ 220-801 exam expects you to know how to configure IDE and SATA devices in a system. What you learn in this chapter about installing an IDE or SATA hard drive in a system also applies to installing an IDE or SATA optical drive or tape drive. Hard drives, optical drives, and tape drives all use an IDE or SATA data connector and power connector.

In Figure 6-20, you can see the back of two hard drives; one uses a SATA interface and the other uses a PATA interface. Notice the PATA drive has a bank of jumpers. These jumpers are used to determine master or slave settings on the IDE channel. Because a serial data cable accommodates only a single drive, there is no need for jumpers on the drive for master or slave settings. However, a SATA drive might have jumpers used to set features such as the ability to power up from standby mode. Most likely, if jumpers are present on a SATA drive, the factory has set them as they should be and advises you not to change them.

Some SATA drives have two power connectors, as does the one in Figure 6-20. Choose between the SATA power connector (which is the preferred connector) or the legacy 5-pin

Serial ATA
power connector

Serial ATA
hard drive

Serial ATA
data connector

Legacy power
connector

Jumper bank
set at factory

Parallel ATA
hard drive

40-pin data
connector

4-pin power
connector

Jumper bank for
master/slave
settings

© Cengage Learning 2014

Figure 6-20 (a) Rear of a SATA drive and (b) rear of a PATA drive

Molex connector, but never install two power cords to the drive at the same time because this could damage the drive.

If you have a PATA drive and a SATA connector on the motherboard, or you have a SATA drive and a PATA connector on the motherboard, you can purchase an adapter to make the hard drive connector fit your motherboard connector. Figure 6-21 shows two converters: one converts SATA drives to PATA motherboards and the other converts PATA drives to SATA motherboards. When you use a converter, know that the drive will run at the slower PATA speed.

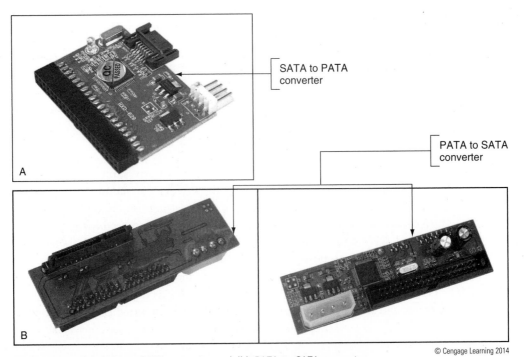

SATA to PATA
converter

PATA to SATA
converter

© Cengage Learning 2014

Figure 6-21 (a) SATA to PATA converter and (b) PATA to SATA converter

You can also purchase a SATA and/or PATA controller card that can provide internal PATA or SATA connectors and external eSATA connectors. You might want to use a controller card when (1) the motherboard drive connectors are not functioning, or (2) the motherboard does not support an ATA standard you want to implement (such as a SATA III drive). Figure 6-22 shows a storage controller card that offers one Ultra ATA-133/IDE connection, two internal SATA I connections, and one eSATA port.

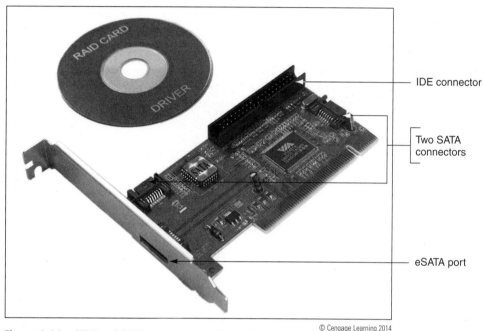

IDE connector

Two SATA connectors

eSATA port

© Cengage Learning 2014

Figure 6-22   EIDE and SATA storage controller card

Now let's look at the step-by-step process of installing a SATA drive.

STEP 1: KNOW YOUR STARTING POINT

As with installing any other devices, before you begin installing your hard drive, make sure you know where your starting point is. Do this by answering these questions: How is your system configured? Is everything working properly? Verify which of your system's devices are working before installing a new one. Later, if a device does not work, the information will help you isolate the problem. Keeping notes is a good idea whenever you install new hardware or software or make any other changes to your computer system. Write down what you know about the system that might be important later.

> **Notes** When installing hardware and software, don't install too many things at once. If something goes wrong, you won't know what's causing the problem. Install one device, start the system, and confirm that the new device is working before installing another.

STEP 2: READ THE DOCUMENTATION AND PREPARE YOUR WORK AREA

Before you take anything apart, carefully read all the documentation for the drive and controller card, as well as the part of your motherboard documentation that covers hard drive installation. Make sure that you can visualize all the steps in the installation. If you have any questions, keep researching until you locate the answer. You can also call technical support,

A+
220-801
1.5

or ask a knowledgeable friend for help. As you get your questions answered, you might discover that what you are installing will not work on your computer, but that is better than coping with hours of frustration and a disabled computer. You cannot always anticipate every problem, but at least you can know that you made your best effort to understand everything in advance. What you learn with thorough preparation pays off every time!

You're now ready to set out your tools, documentation, new hardware, and notebook. Remember the basic rules concerning static electricity, which you learned in Chapter 1. Be sure to protect against ESD by wearing a ground bracelet during the installation. You need to also avoid working on carpet in the winter when there's a lot of static electricity.

Some added precautions for working with a hard drive are as follows:

- Handle the drive carefully.
- Do not touch any exposed circuitry or chips.
- Prevent other people from touching exposed microchips on the drive.
- When you first take the drive out of the static-protective package, touch the package containing the drive to a screw holding an expansion card or cover, or to a metal part of the computer case, for at least two seconds. This drains the static electricity from the package and from your body.
- If you must set down the drive outside the static-protective package, place it component-side-up on a flat surface.
- Do not place the drive on the computer case cover or on a metal table.

If you're assembling a new system, it's best to install drives before you install the motherboard so that you will not accidentally bump sensitive motherboard components with the drives.

STEP 3: INSTALL THE DRIVE

So now you're ready to get started. Follow these steps to install the drive in the case:

1. Shut down the computer and unplug it. Then press the power button for three seconds to drain residual power. Remove the computer case cover. Check that you have an available power cord from the power supply for the drive.

> **Notes** If there are not enough power cords from a power supply, you can purchase a Y connector that can add an additional power cord.

2. Decide which bay will hold the drive. To do that, examine the locations of the drive bays and the length of the data cables and power cords. Bays designed for hard drives do not have access to the outside of the case, unlike bays for optical drives and other drives in which discs are inserted. Also, some bays are wider than others to accommodate wide drives such as a DVD drive. Will the data cable reach the drives and the motherboard connector? If not, rearrange your plan for locating the drive in a bay, or purchase a custom-length data cable. Some bays are stationary, meaning the drive is installed inside the bay because it stays in the case. Other bays are removable; you remove the bay and install the drive in the bay, and then return the bay to the case.

3. For a stationary bay, slide the drive in the bay, and secure one side of the drive with one or two short screws (see Figure 6-23). It's best to use two screws so the drive will not move in the bay, but sometimes a bay only provides a place for a single screw on each side. Some drive bays provide one or two tabs that you can pull out before you slide the drive in the bay and then push the tabs in to secure the drive. Another option

is a sliding tab (see Figure 6-24) that is used to secure the drive. Pull the tab back; slide in the drive, and push the tab forward to secure the drive.

© Cengage Learning 2014

Figure 6-23   Secure one side of the drive with one or two screws

> ⚡ **Caution**   Be sure the screws are not too long. If they are, you can screw too far into the drive housing, which will damage the drive itself.

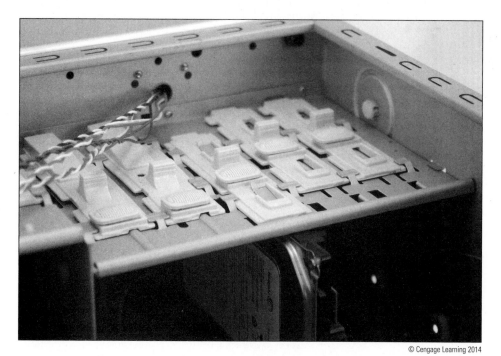

© Cengage Learning 2014

Figure 6-24   This drive bay uses tabs to secure the drive

4. When using screws to secure the drive, carefully, without disturbing the drive, turn the case over and put one or two screws on the other side of the drive (see Figure 6-25). To best secure the drive in the case, use two screws on each side of the drive.

© Cengage Learning 2014

Figure 6-25   Secure the other side of the drive with one or two screws

Notes Do not allow torque to stress the drive. In other words, don't force a drive into a space that is too small for it. Also, placing two screws in diagonal positions across the drive can place pressure diagonally on the drive.

5. Check the motherboard documentation to find out which SATA connectors on the board to use first. For example, five SATA connectors are shown in Figure 6-26. The documentation says the two blue SATA connectors support 6.0 Gb/s and slower speeds, and the two black and one red SATA connectors support 3.0 Gb/s and slower speeds. On this board, be sure to connect your fastest hard drive to a blue connector. For both the drive and the motherboard, you can only plug the cable into the connector in one direction. A SATA cable might provide a clip on the connector to secure it (see Figure 6-27).

© Cengage Learning 2014

Figure 6-26   Five SATA connectors support different SATA standards

Figure 6-27 A clip on a SATA connector secures the connection

© Cengage Learning 2014

6. Connect a 15-pin SATA power connector or 5-pin Molex power connector from the power supply to the drive (see Figure 6-28).

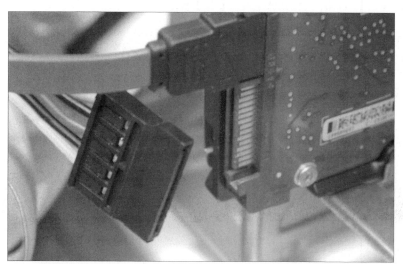

Figure 6-28 Connect the SATA power cord to the drive

© Cengage Learning 2014

7. Check all your connections and power up the system.

8. To verify the drive was recognized correctly, enter BIOS setup and look for the drive. Figure 6-29 shows a BIOS setup screen on one system that has two SATA connectors and one PATA connector. A hard drive is installed on one SATA connector and a CD drive is installed on the PATA connector.

> **Notes** If the drive light on the front panel of the computer case does not work after you install a new drive, try reversing the LED wire on the motherboard pins.

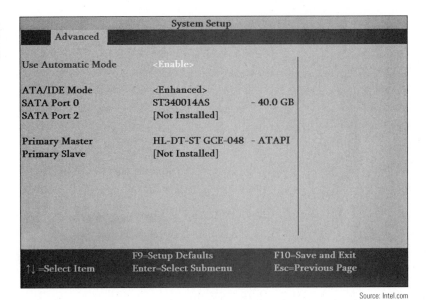

Source: Intel.com

Figure 6-29 BIOS setup screen showing a SATA hard drive and PATA CD drive installed

You are now ready to prepare the hard drive for first use. If you are installing a new hard drive in a system that is to be used for a new Windows installation, boot from the Windows setup DVD, and follow the directions on the screen to install Windows on the new drive. If you are installing a second hard drive in a system that already has Windows installed on the first hard drive, you use the Disk Management utility in Windows to prepare the drive for first use (called partitioning and formatting the drive). How to install Windows is covered in Chapter 7, and how to use Disk Management is covered in Chapter 10.

INSTALLING A DRIVE IN A REMOVABLE BAY

Now let's see how a drive installation goes when you are dealing with a removable bay. Figure 6-30 shows a computer case with a removable bay that has a fan at the front of the bay to help keep the drives cool. (The case manufacturer calls the bay a fan cage.) The bay is anchored to the case with three black locking pins. The third locking pin from the bottom of the case is disconnected in the photo.

Three locking pins used to hold the bay in the case

© Cengage Learning 2014

Figure 6-30 The removable bay has a fan in front and is anchored to the case with locking pins

A+
220-801
1.5

Video
Install a Second Hard Drive

Unplug the cage fan from its power source. Turn the handle on each locking pin counterclockwise to remove it. Then slide the bay to the front and out of the case. Insert the hard drive in the bay, and use two screws on each side to anchor the drive in the bay (see Figure 6-31). Slide the bay back into the case, and reinstall the locking pins. Plug in the cage fan power cord.

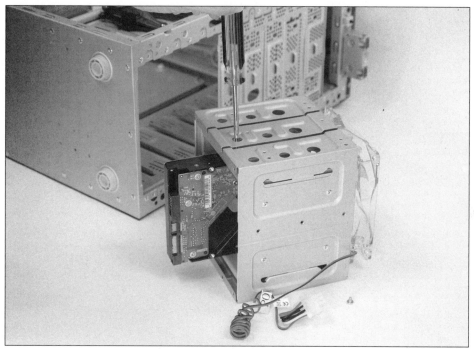

© Cengage Learning 2014

Figure 6-31 Install the hard drive in the bay using two screws on each side of the drive

INSTALLING A SMALL DRIVE IN A WIDE BAY

If you are mounting a hard drive into a bay that is too large, a universal bay kit can help you securely fit the drive into the bay. These inexpensive kits should create a tailor-made fit. In Figure 6-32, you can see how the universal bay kit adapter works. The adapter spans the

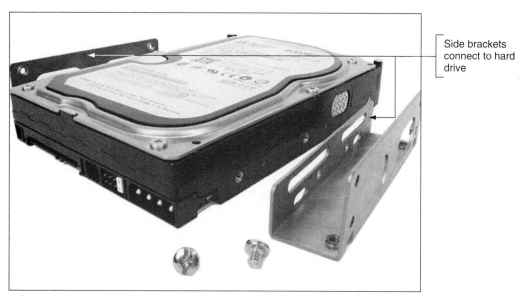

Side brackets connect to hard drive

© Cengage Learning 2014

Figure 6-32 Use the universal bay kit to make the drive fit the bay

A+
220-801
1.5

distance between the sides of the drive and the bay. Figure 6-33 shows a SATA SSD drive with the brackets connected, and Figure 6-34 shows a SATA magnetic drive installed in a wide bay. Because SSD drives are usually smaller than magnetic drives, you're likely to need a bay kit to fit these drives into most computer cases.

© Cengage Learning 2014

Figure 6-33   SSD drive with bay kit connected

© Cengage Learning 2014

Figure 6-34   Hard drive installed in a wide bay using a universal bay kit adapter

STEPS TO CONFIGURE AND INSTALL A PARALLEL ATA DRIVE

Following the PATA or EIDE standard, a motherboard can support up to four EIDE devices using either 80-conductor or 40-conductor cables. A motherboard can have one or two IDE headers (see Figure 6-35). Each header or connector accommodates one IDE channel, and each channel can accommodate one or two IDE devices. One channel is called the primary

A+
220-801
1.5

channel, while the other channel is called the secondary channel. Each IDE connector uses one 40-pin cable. The cable has two connectors on it: one connector in the middle of the cable and one at the far end. An EIDE device can be a hard drive, DVD drive, CD drive, tape drive, or another type of drive. One device is configured to act as the master controlling the channel, and the other device on the channel is the slave. There are, therefore, four possible configurations for four EIDE devices in a system:

- ◢ Primary IDE channel, master device
- ◢ Primary IDE channel, slave device
- ◢ Secondary IDE channel, master device
- ◢ Secondary IDE channel, slave device

6

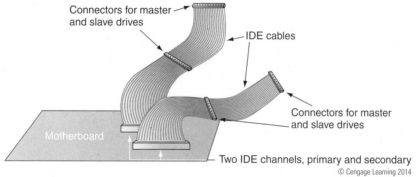

Connectors for master and slave drives

IDE cables

Connectors for master and slave drives

Motherboard

Two IDE channels, primary and secondary

© Cengage Learning 2014

Figure 6-35   A motherboard supporting PATA has two IDE channels; each can support a master and slave drive using a single EIDE cable

The master or slave designations are made by setting jumpers or DIP switches on the devices, or by using a special cable-select data cable. Documentation can be tricky. Some hard drive documentation labels the master drive setting as the Drive 0 setting and the slave drive setting as the Drive 1 setting rather than using the terms *master* and *slave*. The connectors on a PATA 80-conductor cable are color-coded (see Figure 6-36). Use the blue end to connect to the motherboard; use the black end to connect to the drive. If you only have one drive connected to the cable, put it on the black connector at the end of the cable, not the gray connector in the middle.

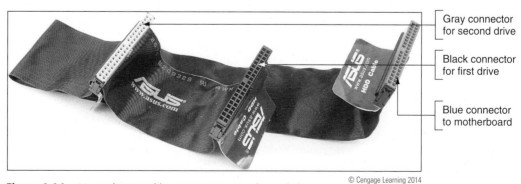

Gray connector for second drive

Black connector for first drive

Blue connector to motherboard

© Cengage Learning 2014

Figure 6-36   80-conductor cable connectors are color-coded

A+
220-801
1.5

> **Notes** When installing a hard drive on the same channel with an ATAPI drive such as a CD drive, always make the hard drive the master and make the ATAPI drive the slave. An even better solution is to install the hard drive on the primary channel and the CD drive and any other drive on the secondary channel.

The motherboard might also be color-coded so that the primary channel connector is blue (see Figure 6-37) and the secondary channel connector is black. This color-coding is intended to ensure that the ATA/66/100/133 hard drive is installed on the primary IDE channel.

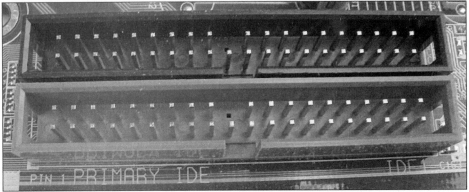

© Cengage Learning 2014

Figure 6-37 The primary IDE channel connector is often color-coded as blue

> **A+ Exam Tip** The A+ 220-801 exam expects you to know how to install a device such as a hard drive. Given a list of steps for the installation, you should be able to order the steps correctly or identify an error in a step.

As with installing SATA drives, know your starting point, read the documentation for the drive and the motherboard, prepare your work area, and be careful when handling the drive to protect it against ESD. Wear a ground bracelet as you work. Now let's look at the steps for installing a PATA drive.

STEP 1: OPEN THE CASE AND DECIDE HOW TO CONFIGURE THE DRIVES

Turn off the computer and unplug it. Press the power button to drain the power. Remove the computer case cover. Check that you have an available power cord from the power supply for the drive.

You must decide which IDE connector to use, and if another drive will share the same IDE data cable with your new drive. When possible, leave the hard drive as the single drive on one channel, so that it does not compete with another drive for access to the channel and possibly slow down performance. Use the primary channel before you use the secondary channel. Place the fastest devices on the primary channel and the slower devices on the secondary channel. This pairing helps keep a slow device from pulling down a faster device. As an example of this type of pairing, suppose you have a tape drive, CD drive, and two hard drives. Because the two hard drives are faster than the tape drive and CD drive, put the two hard drives on one channel and the tape drive and CD drive on the other.

A+
220-801
1.5

Notes If you have three or fewer devices, allow the fastest hard drive to be your boot device and the only device on the primary channel.

STEP 2: SET THE JUMPERS ON THE DRIVE

Often, diagrams of the jumper settings are printed on the top of the hard drive housing (see Figure 6-38). If they are not, see the documentation, or visit the web site of the drive manufacturer. (Hands-on Project 6-2 gives you practice researching jumper settings.)

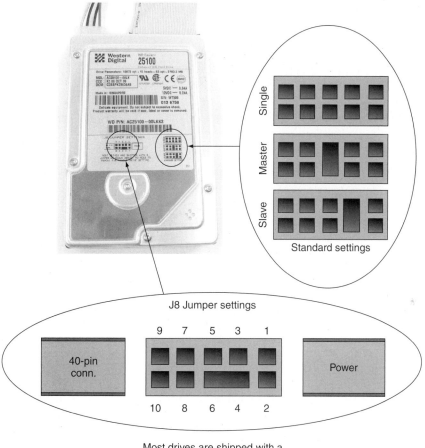

© Cengage Learning 2014

Figure 6-38 A PATA drive most likely will have diagrams of jumper settings for master and slave options printed on the drive housing

Table 6-4 lists the four choices for jumper settings, and Figure 6-39 shows a typical jumper arrangement for a drive that uses three of these settings. In Figures 6-38 and 6-39, note that a black square represents an empty pin and a black rectangle represents a pair of pins with a jumper in place. Know that your hard drive might not have the first configuration as an option, but it should have a way of indicating if the drive will be the master device. The factory default setting is usually correct for the drive to be the single drive on a system. Before you change any settings, write down the original ones. If things go wrong, you can revert to the original settings and begin again. If a drive is the only drive on a channel, set it to single. For two drives on a controller, set one to master and the other to slave.

A+
220-801
1.5

Configuration	Description
Single-drive configuration	This is the only hard drive on this EIDE channel. (This is the standard setting.)
Master-drive configuration	This is the first of two drives; it most likely is the boot device.
Slave-drive configuration	This is the second drive using this channel or data cable.
Cable-select configuration	The cable-select (CS or CSEL) data cable determines which of the two drives is the master and which is the slave.

© Cengage Learning 2014

Table 6-4   Jumper settings on a PATA hard drive

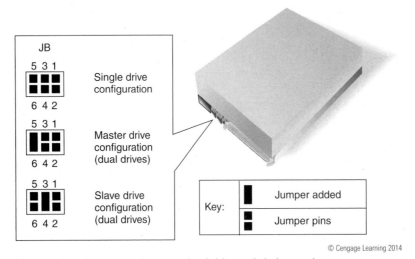

© Cengage Learning 2014

Figure 6-39   Jumper settings on a hard drive and their meanings

Some hard drives have a cable-select configuration option. If you choose this configuration, you must use a cable-select data cable and set both devices on the channel to cable-select. When using an 80-conductor cable-select cable, the drive nearest the motherboard is the master, and the drive farthest from the motherboard is the slave. You can recognize a cable-select cable by a small hole somewhere in the data cable or by labels (master or slave) on the connectors.

STEP 3: MOUNT THE DRIVE IN THE BAY

Now that you've set the jumpers, your next step is to look at the drive bay that you will use for the drive. The bay can be stationary or removable. You saw both types of bays earlier in the chapter. Follow these steps to install the drive:

1. Decide if it's best to connect the ribbon cable to the drive before or after you install the drive in the bay. Then install the drive in the bay and connect the cable in whichever order works best for your situation.

2. Connect the data cable to the IDE connector on the motherboard (see Figure 6-40). Make certain pin 1 and the edge color on the cable align correctly at both ends of the cable. Normally, pin 1 is closest to the power connection on the drive. Figure 6-41 shows three PATA drives installed in a system with data cables connected to the drives and the motherboard.

A+
220-801
1.5

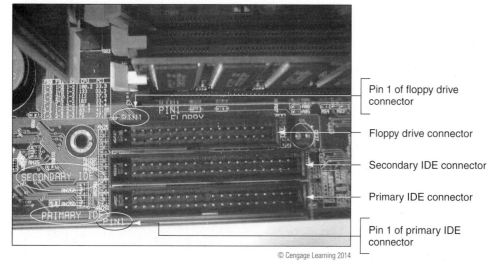

Figure 6-40 Floppy drive and two IDE connectors on the motherboard

© Cengage Learning 2014

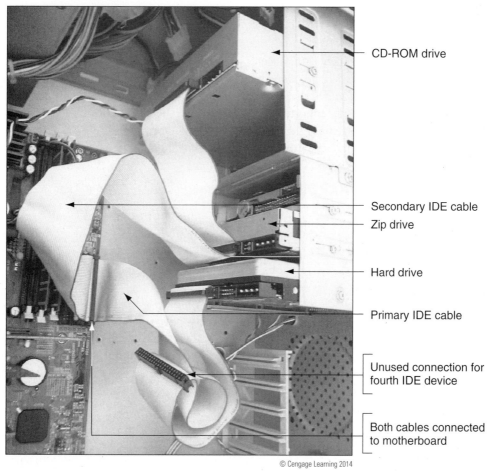

Figure 6-41 This system has a CD-ROM and a Zip drive sharing the secondary IDE cable and a hard drive using the primary IDE cable

© Cengage Learning 2014

3. You can now install a power connection to each drive (Figure 6-42). PATA drives use the Molex 5-pin power connector. The cord only goes into the connection one way.

A+
220-801
1.5

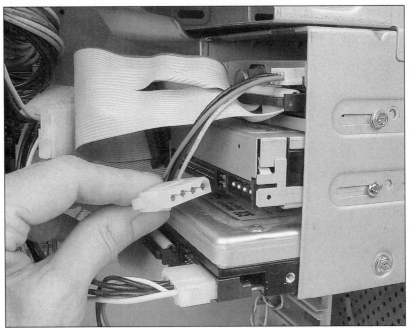

© Cengage Learning 2014

Figure 6-42 Connect a power cord to each drive

4. Before you replace the case cover, plug in the monitor and turn on the computer. (On the other hand, some systems won't power up until the front panel is installed.) After you confirm that your drive is recognized, the size of the drive is detected correctly, and supported features are set to be automatically detected, power down the system and replace the case cover. Then the next thing to do is to use an operating system to prepare the drive for first use, which is the topic of the next chapter.

SETTING UP HARDWARE RAID

For most personal computers, a single hard drive works independently of any other installed drives. A technology that configures two or more hard drives to work together as an array of drives is called **RAID (redundant array of inexpensive disks** or **redundant array of independent disks)**. Two reasons you might consider using RAID are:

◢ To improve **fault tolerance**, which is a computer's ability to respond to a fault or catastrophe, such as a hardware failure or power outage, so that data is not lost. If data is important enough to justify the cost, you can protect the data by continuously writing two copies of it, each to a different hard drive. This method is most often used on high-end, expensive file servers, but it is occasionally appropriate for a single-user workstation.

◢ To improve performance by writing data to two or more hard drives so that a single drive is not excessively used.

TYPES OF RAID

Several types of RAID exist; the four most commonly used are RAID 0, RAID 1, RAID 5, and RAID 10. Following is a brief description of each, including another method of two disks working together, called spanning. The first four methods are diagrammed in Figure 6-43:

◢ **Spanning**, sometimes called JBOD (just a bunch of disks), uses two hard drives to hold a single Windows volume, such as drive E:. Data is written to the first drive, and, when it is full, the data continues to be written to the second.

A+
220-801
1.5

▲ **RAID 0** also uses two or more physical disks to increase the disk space available for a single volume. RAID 0 writes to the physical disks evenly across all disks so that no one disk receives all the activity and therefore improves performance. Windows calls RAID 0 a **striped volume**. To understand that term, think of data striped—or written across—several hard drives. RAID 0 is preferred to spanning.

▲ **RAID 1** is a type of mirroring that duplicates data on one drive to another drive and is used for fault tolerance. Each drive has its own volume, and the two volumes are called mirrors. If one drive fails, the other continues to operate and data is not lost. Windows calls RAID 1 a **mirrored volume**.

> **Notes** In a SCSI implementation of RAID 1, if the two mirrored hard drives are sharing the same host adapter and the adapter fails, both drives go down together. To keep this from happening, each drive has its own host adapter, which is called RAID 1 with duplexing.

▲ **RAID 5** stripes data across three or more drives and uses parity checking, so that if one drive fails, the other drives can re-create the data stored on the failed drive by using the parity information. Data is not duplicated, and, therefore, RAID 5 makes better use of volume capacity. RAID 5 drives increase performance and provide fault tolerance. Windows calls these drives **RAID-5 volumes**.

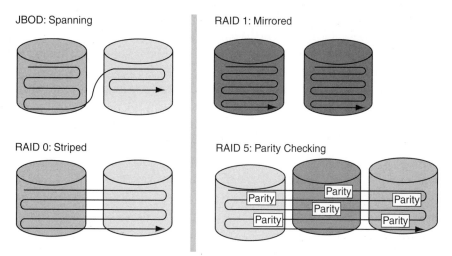

Figure 6-43 Ways that hard drives can work together

© Cengage Learning 2014

▲ **RAID 10**, also called **RAID 1+0** and pronounced "RAID one zero" (*not* "RAID ten"), is a combination of RAID 1 and RAID 0. It takes at least four disks for RAID 10. Data is mirrored across pairs of disks, as shown at the top of Figure 6-44. In addition, the two pairs of disks are striped, as shown at the bottom of Figure 6-44. To help you better understand RAID 10, in the figure notice the data labeled as A, A, B, B across the first stripe. RAID 10 is the most expensive solution that provides the best redundancy and performance.

A+
220-801
1.5

RAID 1: Two pairs of mirrored disks

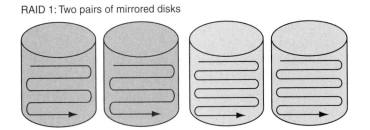

RAID 10: Mirrored and striped

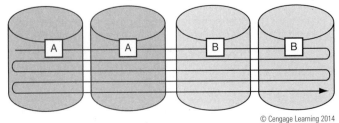

© Cengage Learning 2014

Figure 6-44　RAID 1 and RAID 10

> 💡 **A+ Exam Tip**　The A+ 220-801 exam expects you to be able to contrast RAID 0, RAID 1, RAID 5, and RAID 10.

All RAID configurations can be accomplished at the hardware level (called hardware RAID) or at the operating system level (called software RAID). Using Windows to implement software RAID, the Disk Management utility is used to configure a group of hard drives in a RAID array. However, software RAID is considered an unstable solution and not recommended by Microsoft. Configuring RAID at the hardware level is considered best practice because if Windows gets corrupted, the hardware might still be able to protect the data. Also, hardware RAID is generally faster than software RAID.

HOW TO IMPLEMENT HARDWARE RAID

Hardware RAID can be set up by using a RAID controller that is part of the motherboard BIOS or by using a RAID controller expansion card. Figure 6-45 shows a RAID controller card by Sabrent that provides four SATA ports.

> 💡 **A+ Exam Tip**　The A+ 220-801 exam expects you to be able to set up hardware RAID.

When installing a hardware RAID system, for best performance, all hard drives in an array should be identical in brand, size, speed, and other features. Also, if Windows is to be installed on a hard drive that is part of a RAID array, RAID must be implemented before Windows is installed. As with installing any hardware, first read the documentation that comes with the motherboard or RAID controller and follow those specific directions rather than the general guidelines given here. Make sure you understand which RAID configurations the board supports.

6

A+
220-801
1.5

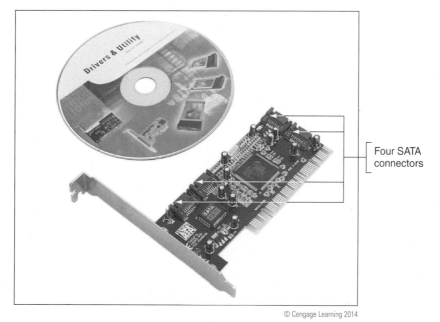

Four SATA
connectors

© Cengage Learning 2014

Figure 6-45 RAID controller card provides four SATA internal connectors

For one motherboard that has six SATA connectors that support RAID 0, 1, 5, and 10, here are the general directions to install the RAID array using three matching hard drives in a RAID 5 array:

1. Install the three SATA drives in the computer case and connect each drive to a SATA connector on the motherboard (see Figure 6-46). To help keep the drives cool, the drives are installed with an empty bay between each drive.

Three hard
drives

© Cengage Learning 2014

Figure 6-46 Install three matching hard drives in a system

2. Boot the system and enter BIOS setup. On the Advanced setup screen, verify the three drives are recognized. Select the option to configure SATA and then select RAID from the menu (see Figure 6-47).

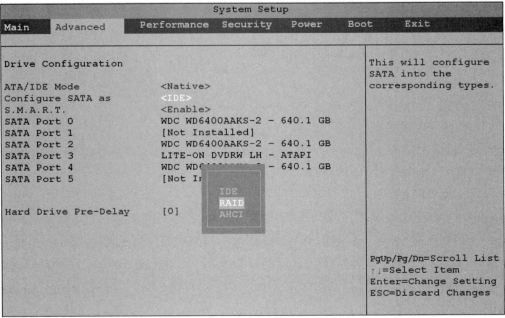

Source: Intel

Figure 6-47 Configure SATA ports on the motherboard to enable RAID

3. Reboot the system and a message is displayed on-screen: "Press <Ctrl+I> to enter the RAID Configuration Utility." Press **Ctrl** and **I** to enter the utility (see Figure 6-48). Notice in the information area that the three drives are recognized and their current status is Non-RAID Disk.

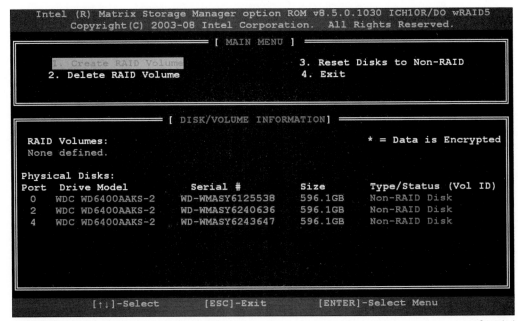

Source: Intel

Figure 6-48 BIOS utility to configure a RAID array

4. Select option 1 to "**Create RAID Volume**." On the next screen shown in Figure 6-49, enter a volume name (FileServer in our example).

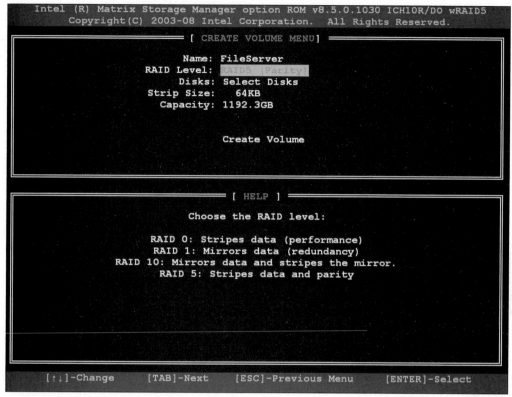

Source: Intel

Figure 6-49 Make your choices for the RAID array

5. Under RAID Level, select **RAID5 (Parity)**. Because we are using RAID 5, which requires three hard drives, the option to select the disks for the array is not available. All three disks will be used in the array.

6. Select the value for the Strip Size. (This is the amount of space devoted to one strip across the striped array. Choices are 32 KB, 64 KB, or 128 KB.)

7. Enter the size of the volume. The available size is shown in Figure 6-49 as 1192 GB, but you don't have to use all the available space. The space you don't use can later be configured as another array. (In this example, I entered 500 GB.)

8. Select **Create Volume** to complete the RAID configuration. A message appears warning you that if you proceed, all data on all three hard drives will be lost. Type **Y** to continue. The array is created and the system reboots.

You are now ready to install Windows. Windows 7/Vista automatically "sees" the RAID array as a single 500 GB hard drive because Windows 7/Vista has built-in hardware RAID drivers. For Windows XP, when you begin the XP installation, you must press F6 at the beginning of the installation to install RAID drivers. After Windows is installed on the drive, Windows will call it drive C:.

APPLYING | CONCEPTS

TROUBLESHOOTING HARD DRIVE INSTALLATIONS

Sometimes, trouble crops up during an installation. Keeping a cool head, thinking things through carefully a second, third, and fourth time, and using all available resources will most likely get you out of any mess.

Installing a hard drive is not difficult, unless you have an unusually complex situation. For example, your first hard drive installation should not involve the intricacies of installing a second SCSI drive in a system that has two SCSI host adapters. Nor should you install a second drive in a system that uses an IDE connection for one drive on the motherboard and an adapter card in an expansion slot for the other drive. If a complicated installation is necessary and you have never installed a hard drive, ask for expert help.

The following list describes the errors that cropped up during a few hard drive installations; the list also includes the causes of the errors and what was done about them. Everyone learns something new when making mistakes, and you probably will, too. You can then add your own experiences to this list.

- Shawn physically installed an IDE hard drive. He turned on the machine and accessed BIOS setup. The hard drive was not listed as an installed device. He checked and discovered that autodetection was not enabled. He enabled it and rebooted. Setup recognized the drive.
- When first turning on a previously working PC, John received the following error message: "Hard drive not found." He turned off the machine, checked all cables, and discovered that the data cable from the motherboard to the drive was loose. He reseated the cable and rebooted. POST found the drive.
- Lucia physically installed a new hard drive, replaced the cover on the computer case, and booted the PC with a Windows setup DVD in the drive. POST beeped three times and stopped. Recall that diagnostics during POST are often communicated by beeps if the tests take place before POST has checked video and made it available to display the messages. Three beeps on some computers signal a memory error. Lucia turned off the computer and checked the memory modules on the motherboard. A module positioned at the edge of the motherboard next to the cover had been bumped as she replaced the cover. She reseated the module and booted again, this time with the cover still off. The error disappeared.
- Jason physically installed a new hard drive and turned on the computer. He received the following error: "No boot device available." He forgot to insert a Windows setup DVD. He put the disc in the drive and rebooted the machine successfully.
- The hard drive did not physically fit into the bay. The screw holes did not line up. Juan got a bay kit, but it just didn't seem to work. He took a break, went to lunch, and came back to make a fresh start. Juan asked others to help view the brackets, holes, and screws from a fresh perspective. It didn't take long to discover that he had overlooked the correct position for the brackets in the bay.
- Maria set the jumpers on a PATA hard drive and physically installed the drive. She booted and received the error message "Hard drive not present." She rechecked all physical connections and found everything okay. After checking the jumper settings, she realized that she had set them as if this were the second drive of a two-drive system, when it was the only drive. She restored the jumpers to their original state. In this case, as in most cases, the jumpers were set at the factory to be correct when the drive is the only drive.

If BIOS setup does not recognize a newly installed hard drive, check the following:

- Has BIOS setup been correctly configured for autodetection?
- Are the jumpers on the drive set correctly?

A+
220-801
1.5

◢ Have the power cord and data cable been properly connected? Verify that each is solidly connected at both ends.

◢ Check the web site of the drive manufacturer for suggestions if the above steps don't solve your problem. Look for diagnostic software that can be downloaded from the web site and used to check the drive.

> ⚡ **Caution** When things are not going well, you can tense up and make mistakes more easily. Be certain to turn off the machine before doing anything inside! Not doing so can be a costly error. For example, a friend had been trying and retrying to boot for some time and got frustrated and careless. He plugged the power cord into the drive without turning the PC off. The machine began to smoke and everything went dead. The next thing he learned was how to replace a power supply!

6

ABOUT TAPE DRIVES AND FLOPPY DRIVES

A+
220-801
1.5,
1.11

Tape drives installed inside a computer case can use a SATA, PATA, or SCSI interface. Occasionally, you might be called on to support a computer with an old floppy drive. Both tape drives and floppy drives are covered in this part of the chapter.

INSTALLING TAPE DRIVES AND SELECTING TAPE MEDIA

Tape drives (see Figure 6-50) are an inexpensive way of backing up an entire hard drive or portions of it. Because tape drives are less expensive for backups than external hard drives, CDs, DVDs, or USB flash drives, they are still used for backups even though other methods are more convenient. Tapes currently have capacities up to 3.0 TB compressed and come in several types and formats. Some tape drives and tape cartridges support WORM (write once and read many). WORM drives and cartridges assure that data written on the tape will not be deleted or overwritten. Most tape drives come bundled with backup software to use them.

Courtesy of Quantum Corporation

Figure 6-50 The LTO-5 HH tape drive by Quantum writes to LTO Ultrium 5 and LTO Ultrium 4 tapes and reads from LTO Ultrium 5, LTO Ultrium 4, and LTO Ultrium 3 tapes. It provides AES 256-bit data encryption security, WORM functionality, and partitioning capability

A+
220-801
1.5,
1.11

> **A+ Exam Tip**   The A+ 220-801 exam expects you to know how to install a tape drive and how to select the right tapes for the drive.

The biggest disadvantage of using tape drives is that data is stored on tape by **sequential access**; to read data from anywhere on the tape, you must start at the beginning of the tape and read until you come to the sought-after data. Sequential access makes recovering files slow and inconvenient, which is why tapes are not used for general-purpose data storage.

Tape drives accommodate one of two kinds of tapes: full-sized **data cartridges** are $4 \times 6 \times \frac{5}{8}$ inches, and the smaller **minicartridges**, like the one in Figure 6-51, are $3\frac{1}{4} \times 2\frac{1}{2} \times \frac{3}{5}$ inches. Minicartridges are more popular because their drives can fit into a standard 3 inch drive bay of a PC case.

Here is a list of some of the more common types of tape cartridges:

1. DDS-1, DDS-2, DDS-3, DDS-4, and DDS-5 are popular types. DDS-5 holds up to 36 GB native or 72 GB compressed data. DDS-5 is also called DAT72.

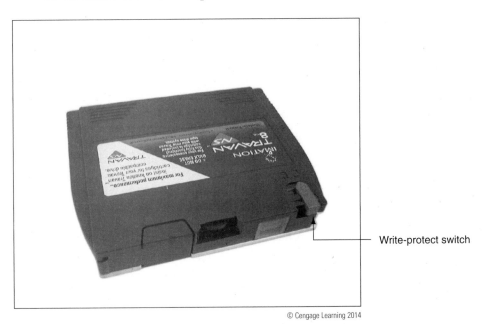

Write-protect switch

© Cengage Learning 2014

Figure 6-51   Minicartridge for a tape drive has a write-protect switch

2. LTO Ultrium 2, LTO Ultrium 3, LTO Ultrium 4, and LTO Ultrium 5 are sometimes referred to as LTO cartridges. LTO Ultrium 5 holds up to 1.5 TB native or 3.0 TB compressed data. Figure 6-52 shows an LTO Ultrium 3 tape.

3. DLT IV or DLT-4 holds up to 40 GB native or 80 GB compressed data.

4. Super DLTtape II holds up to 300 GB native or 600 GB compressed data.

5. Travan data types of cartridges vary from TR-1 through TR-7. The TR-7 holds 20 GB native and 40 GB compressed data.

6. AIT types have been around a long time and include AIT Turbo, AIT-1 through AIT-5, and S-AIT. S-AIT holds up to 1.3 TB compressed data.

7. SLR types include SLR1 through SLR140. SLR140 holds 70 GB native or 140 GB compressed data.

A+
220-801
1.5,
1.11

© Cengage Learning 2014

Figure 6-52   This Maxel LTO Ultrium 3 data tape cartridge can hold up to 800 GB of
compressed data

When selecting a tape drive, consider how many and what type of cartridges the drive
can use and how it interfaces with the computer. The drive might be able to read from more
types of cartridges than it can write to. A tape drive can be external or internal. An external
tape drive costs more but can be used by more than one computer. An internal tape drive
can interface with a computer using a SCSI, PATA, or SATA connection. An external tape
drive can connect to a computer using a USB, FireWire, SCSI, SAS, or eSATA port.

> **Notes** For an interesting photo gallery of tape media, see *www.backupworks.com*.

INSTALLING A FLOPPY DRIVE

Floppy drives: You almost never see them, but they're still covered on the A+ exam, so you
need to know about them. We'll try to make this as brief and painless as possible. A 3½"
high-density **floppy disk drive (FDD)** holds a mere 1.44 MB of data. When using floppy disks,
know that to write to the disk, the write-protect notch must be closed (see Figure 6-53).

A floppy drive might be an external or internal device. Figure 6-54 shows a USB
floppy drive. Figure 6-55 shows the floppy drive subsystem for an internal device, which
consists of the floppy drive, its 34-pin ribbon cable, power cable, and connections. The
Berg power connector has a small plastic latch that snaps in place when you connect it
to the drive.

Today's floppy drive cables have a connector at each end and accommodate a single drive,
but older cables, like the one in Figure 6-55, have an extra connector or two in the middle
of the cable for a second floppy drive. For these systems, you can install two floppy drives
on the same cable, and the drives will be identified by BIOS as drive A: and drive B:. Notice
in the figure the twist in the cable. The drive that has the twist between it and the controller
is drive A:. The drive that does not have the twist between it and the controller is drive B:.
Also notice in the figure the edge color down one side of the cable, which identifies the pin-1
side of the 34-pin connector.

> **Notes** One reason you still need to know about floppy disks and floppy disk drives is that Windows
> Server 2003 relies on floppy disks to recover from a failed installation, and Windows Server 2003 is still
> a popular server OS.

A+
220-801
1.5,
1.11

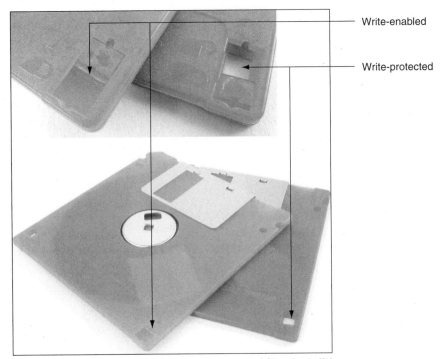

Write-enabled

Write-protected

© Cengage Learning 2014

Figure 6-53   For you to write to a disk, the write-protect notch must be closed

© Cengage Learning 2014

Figure 6-54   An external floppy drive uses a USB connection

> 💡 **A+ Exam Tip**   The A+ 220-801 exam expects you to be able to install and configure a floppy
> disk drive (FDD).

When installing a floppy drive, install the drive in a bay as you would a hard drive and connect the data cable and power cord. When connecting the data cable, align the edge color of
the ribbon cable with pin 1 on the motherboard connector. See Figure 6-56. If you connect the
cable in the wrong direction, the floppy drive light stays lit continuously and the drive does
not work. Some connectors allow you to insert the cable only in one direction. Be sure the end
of the cable with the twist connects to the drive and the other end to the motherboard.

> 📝 **Notes**   If your power supply doesn't have the smaller Berg connector for the floppy drive, you can
> buy a Molex-to-Berg converter to accommodate the floppy drive power connector.

A+
220-801
1.5,
1.11

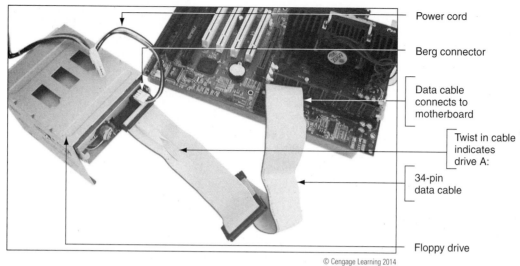

Power cord

Berg connector

Data cable
connects to
motherboard

Twist in cable
indicates
drive A:

34-pin
data cable

Floppy drive

© Cengage Learning 2014

Figure 6-55 Floppy drive subsystem: floppy drive, 34-pin data cable, and power connector

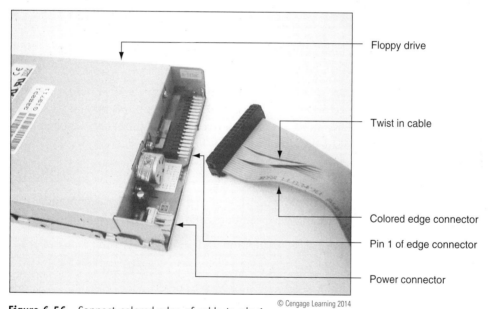

Floppy drive

Twist in cable

Colored edge connector

Pin 1 of edge connector

Power connector

© Cengage Learning 2014

Figure 6-56 Connect colored edge of cable to pin 1

Replace the cover, turn on the computer, and enter BIOS setup to verify the drive is recognized with no errors. If you are adding (not replacing) a floppy drive, you must inform BIOS setup by accessing setup and changing the drive type. Boot to the Windows desktop and test the drive by formatting a disk or copying data to a disk.

Notes Note that you can turn on the PC and test the drive before you replace the computer case cover. If the drive doesn't work, having the cover off makes it easier to turn off the computer, check connections, and try again. Just make certain that you don't touch anything inside the case while the computer is on. Leaving the computer on while you disconnect and reconnect a cable is very dangerous for the PC and will probably damage something—including you!

>> *CHAPTER SUMMARY*

Hard Drive Technologies and Interface Standards

▲ A hard disk drive (HDD) comes in two sizes: 3.5" for desktop computers and 2.5" for laptops.

▲ A hard drive can be a magnetic drive, a solid state drive, or a hybrid drive. A solid state drive contains flash memory and is more expensive, faster, more reliable, and uses less power than a magnetic drive.

▲ Most hard drives use the ATA interface standards. The two main categories of ATA are parallel ATA and serial ATA. Serial ATA is easier to configure and better performing than PATA. External SATA ports are called eSATA ports.

▲ S.M.A.R.T. is a self-monitoring technology whereby the BIOS monitors the health of the hard drive and warns of an impending failure.

▲ ATAPI standards are used by optical drives and other drives that use the ATA interface on a motherboard or controller card.

▲ Several PATA standards are Fast ATA, Ultra ATA, Ultra ATA/66, Ultra ATA/100, and Ultra ATA/133.

▲ Three SATA standards provide data transfer rates of 1.5 Gb/sec (using SATA I), 3.0 Gb/sec (using SATA II), and 6.0 Gb/sec (using SATA III).

▲ The SCSI interface standards include narrow and wide SCSI, and can use a variety of cables and connectors. Three connectors are a 50-pin, 68-pin, and 25-pin connector. A SCSI chain can contain up to 16 devices including the host adapter. Each device is identified by a SCSI ID, a number from 0 to 15.

How to Select and Install Hard Drives

▲ When selecting a hard drive, consider the storage capacity, technology (solid state or magnetic), spindle speed, interface standard, and buffer size (for hybrid drives).

▲ SATA drives require no configuration and are installed using a power cord and a single SATA data cable.

▲ PATA drives require you to set a jumper to determine if the drive will be the single drive, master, or slave on a single cable. The PATA cable can accommodate two drives. A PATA motherboard has one or two PATA connectors for up to four PATA drives in the system.

▲ RAID technology uses an array of hard drives to provide fault tolerance and/or improvement in performance. Choices for RAID are RAID 0 (striping using two drives), RAID 1 (mirroring using two drives), RAID 5 (parity checking using three drives), and RAID 10 (striping and mirroring combined using four drives).

▲ Hardware RAID is implemented using the motherboard BIOS or a RAID controller card. Software RAID is implemented in Windows. Best practice is to use hardware RAID rather than software RAID.

About Tape Drives and Floppy Drives

▲ Tape drives are an inexpensive way to back up an entire hard drive or portions of it. Tape drives are more convenient for backups than removable drives. The disadvantage of tape drives is that data can only be accessed sequentially.

▲ Today's floppy disks are 3½" high-density disks that hold 1.44 MB of data.

▲ After a floppy disk drive is installed, you must configure the drive in BIOS setup.

>> KEY TERMS

For explanations of key terms, see the Glossary near the end of the book.

25-pin SCSI connector
50-pin SCSI connector
68-pin SCSI connector
80-conductor IDE cable
ANSI (American National Standards Institute)
ATAPI (Advanced Technology Attachment Packet Interface)
autodetection
data cartridge
DMA (direct memory access) transfer mode
Enhanced IDE (EIDE)
external SATA (eSATA)
fault tolerance
floppy disk drive (FDD)
hard disk drive (HDD)
hard drive
host adapter
hot-swapping

hybrid hard drive
IDE (Integrated Drive Electronics)
Logical Unit Number (LUN)
low-level formatting
magnetic hard drive
minicartridge
mirrored volume
NAND flash memory
Parallel ATA (PATA)
PIO (Programmed Input/ Output) transfer mode
RAID (redundant array of inexpensive disks or redundant array of independent disks)
RAID 0
RAID 1
RAID 1+0
RAID 10

RAID 5
RAID-5 volume
read/write head
ReadyDrive
S.M.A.R.T. (Self-Monitoring Analysis and Reporting Technology)
SCSI (Small Computer System Interface)
SCSI host adapter card
SCSI ID
sequential access
serial ATA (SATA)
solid state device (SSD)
solid state drive (SSD)
spanning
striped volume
terminating resistor

>> REVIEW QUESTIONS

1. In an SSD drive, flash memory is stored on _____ chips inside the drive housing.

   a) S.M.A.R.T

   b) EEPROM

   c) RAID

   d) PIO

2. A motherboard can have one or two IDE connectors for up to _____ PATA devices in the system using two data cables.

   a) two

   b) four

   c) six

   d) eight

3. Which hard drive interface technology supports hot-swapping?

    a) PATA

    b) ATAPI

    c) SATA

    d) IDE

4. ____ is a type of mirroring that duplicates data on one drive to another drive and is used for fault tolerance.

    a) Spanning

    b) RAID 0

    c) RAID 1

    d) RAID 5

5. What is the biggest disadvantage of using tape drives?

    a) They are an expensive way of backing up an entire hard drive or portions of it.

    b) Data is stored on tape by sequential access.

    c) The format options are limited.

    d) They represent an older technology with small compression capacity.

6. True or false? The two most popular internal drive interfaces are Parallel ATA (PATA) and Serial ATA (SATA).

7. True or false? An optical drive must follow the ATAPI (Advanced Technology Attachment Packet Interface) standard in order to connect to a system using an IDE connector.

8. True or false? DMA transfers data directly from the hard drive to memory without involving the CPU.

9. True or false? Software RAID is generally faster than hardware RAID.

10. True or false? When writing to a floppy disk, the write-protect notch must be open.

11. A(n) ____ hard drive has one, two, or more platters, or disks, that stack together and spin in unison inside a sealed metal housing that contains firmware to control reading and writing data to the drive and to communicate with the motherboard.

12. If a motherboard does not have an embedded SCSI controller, the gateway from the SCSI bus to the system bus is the SCSI host adapter card, commonly called the ____.

13. To reduce the amount of electrical "noise," or interference, on a SCSI cable, each end of the SCSI chain has a(n) ____.

14. With____, the BIOS detects the new drive and automatically selects the correct drive capacity and configuration, including the best possible standard supported by both the hard drive and the motherboard.

15. ____ is a computer's ability to respond to a fault or catastrophe, such as a hardware failure or power outage, so that data is not lost.

Installing Windows

Windows 7, Vista, and XP all share the same basic Windows architecture, and all have similar characteristics. Windows 7 is available for purchase, but you can no longer purchase Vista or XP. However, because many individual users and corporations still rely on Vista and XP, you need to know how to support them.

At the time this book went to print, Windows 8 Beta is available. Microsoft releases beta versions of software so that the user community can test the software before retail versions become available. How to install and support Windows 8 is not covered in this book.

This chapter discusses how to plan a Windows installation and the steps to perform a Windows 7 installation, including what to do after the OS is installed. You also learn about what to expect when installing Windows on computers in a large enterprise.

> **Vista Differences** The details of a Windows 7 installation are covered in this chapter. For details about a Vista installation, see Appendix B, and for details about installing XP, see Appendix C.

HOW TO PLAN A WINDOWS INSTALLATION

A+
220-802
1.1, 1.2

As a PC support technician, you can expect to be called on to install Windows in a variety of situations. You might need to install Windows on a new hard drive, after an existing Windows installation has become corrupted, or to upgrade from one OS to another. Many decisions need to be made before the installation. Decisions to consider about Windows 7 are covered in this part of the chapter and most of these decisions apply to any Windows operating system.

CHOOSE THE EDITION, LICENSE, AND VERSION OF WINDOWS 7

When buying Windows 7, know the price is affected by the Windows edition and type of license you purchase. You also need to decide between the 32-bit and 64-bit version. In this part of the chapter, you learn about your options when purchasing Windows 7 and how to make sure your computer qualifies for Windows 7.

EDITIONS OF WINDOWS 7

Microsoft has produced several editions of Windows 7 designed to satisfy a variety of consumer needs:

- **Windows 7 Starter** has the most limited features and is intended to be used on netbooks or in developing nations. In the United States, it can only be obtained preinstalled by the manufacturer on a new netbook computer. Windows 7 Starter comes only in the 32-bit version. All other editions of Windows 7 are available in either the 32-bit or 64-bit version.
- **Windows 7 Home Basic** has limited features and is available only in underdeveloped countries and can only be activated in these countries.
- **Windows 7 Home Premium** is similar to Windows 7 Home Basic, but includes additional features.
- **Windows 7 Professional** is intended for business users. You can purchase multiple site licenses (also called volume licensing) using this edition.
- **Windows 7 Enterprise** includes additional features over Windows 7 Professional. The major additional features are BitLocker Drive Encryption used to encrypt an entire hard drive and support for multiple languages. The edition does not include Windows DVD Maker. Multiple site licenses are available.
- **Windows 7 Ultimate** includes every Windows 7 feature. You cannot purchase multiple licenses with this edition.

Notes An antitrust ruling (a ruling to break up monopolies) in Europe required that Microsoft must offer editions of Windows that do not include multimedia utilities. Windows 7, therefore, comes in N and KN editions that do not include Windows Media Player, Windows Media Center, and Windows DVD Maker. For example, Windows 7 Home Premium N, Windows 7 Ultimate N, and Windows 7 Professional KN do not include these multimedia utilities. If you have an N or KN edition of Windows 7, you can, however, legally download the utilities from the Microsoft web site.

A+
220-802
1.1, 1.2

The major features for all editions are listed in Table 7-1. You will learn how to use and support many of these features later in the book.

> **A+ Exam Tip** Before you sit for the A+ 220-802 exam, take a little time to memorize the features included in each edition of Windows 7 that are listed in Table 7-1.

Feature	Starter	Home Basic	Home Premium	Professional	Enterprise	Ultimate
Aero user interface			X	X	X	X
Create homegroups			X	X	X	X
Scheduled backups	X	X	X	X	X	X
Backup to network				X	X	X
BitLocker Drive Encryption					X	X
Encrypting File System (EFS)				X	X	X
Windows DVD Maker			X	X		X
Windows Media Center			X	X	X	X
Join a domain				X	X	X
Group Policy				X	X	X
Remote Desktop host				X	X	X
Multiple languages					X	X
Windows XP Mode				X	X	X
Processor: 32-bit or 64-bit		X	X	X	X	X

Table 7-1 Windows 7 editions and their features

© Cengage Learning 2014

> **Notes** The Windows 7 setup DVD contains only one edition of Windows 7. When you install Windows 7, setup knows which edition to install even if you do not enter the product key during the installation. On the other hand, the Vista setup DVD includes all editions of Vista. The edition of Vista that you can install depends on the product key you use.

OEM, FULL RETAIL, OR UPGRADE RETAIL LICENSE

When buying Windows 7, know that you can purchase a retail license or an **OEM (Original Equipment Manufacturer) license**. The OEM license costs less but can only be installed on a new PC for resale. The boxed retail package contains the 32-bit DVD and 64-bit DVD (see Figure 7-1). You can also purchase and download Windows 7 from the Microsoft online store at *microsoftstore.com*. The retail license costs less if you purchase a license to upgrade from Vista or XP to Windows 7. You are required to purchase the Windows 7 full license for a new computer or any computer that has an OS other than Vista and XP installed.

A+
220-802
1.1, 1.2

32-bit setup disc

64-bit setup disc

© Cengage Learning 2014

Figure 7-1 A Windows 7 DVD contains either a 32-bit version or a 64-bit version of Windows

> **Notes** The Windows 7 setup DVD is the same regardless of the full or upgrade license you purchase. This DVD can be used to perform a clean installation or an upgrade. The difference is in the product key, which is tied to the full or upgrade license you purchase. When installing Windows 7, if you use a product key purchased for an upgrade license, setup will verify that the system qualifies to use this license. You cannot use an OEM disc for an upgrade installation.

32-BIT OR 64-BIT VERSIONS

Recall that an operating system can process 32 bits or 64 bits. A 64-bit installation of Windows generally performs better than a 32-bit installation if you have enough RAM. Table 7-2 shows how much RAM each edition and version of Windows 7 can support. Another advantage of 64-bit installations of Windows is they can support 64-bit applications, which run faster than 32-bit applications. Even though you can install 32-bit applications in a 64-bit OS, for best performance, always choose 64-bit applications. Keep in mind that 64-bit installations of Windows require 64-bit device drivers.

> **Notes** All processors (CPUs) used in personal computers today are hybrid processors and can handle a 32-bit or 64-bit OS. However, the Intel Itanium and Xeon processors used in high-end workstations and servers are true 64-bit processors and require a 64-bit OS.

A+
220-802
1.1, 1.2

Operating System	32-bit Version	64-bit Version
Windows 7 Ultimate	4 GB	192 GB
Windows 7 Enterprise	4 GB	192 GB
Windows 7 Professional	4 GB	192 GB
Windows 7 Home Premium	4 GB	16 GB
Windows 7 Home Basic	4 GB	8 GB
Windows 7 Starter	2 GB	NA

© Cengage Learning 2014

Table 7-2 Maximum memory supported by Windows 7 editions and versions

7

Notes How much memory or RAM you can install in a computer depends not only on the OS installed but also on how much memory the motherboard can hold. To know how much RAM a motherboard can support, see the motherboard documentation.

VERIFY YOUR SYSTEM QUALIFIES FOR WINDOWS 7

The minimum hardware requirements for Windows 7 are listed in Table 7-3. (These minimum requirements are also the Microsoft recommended requirements.) The requirements are the same as those for Windows Vista. Know, however, that Microsoft occasionally changes the minimum and recommended requirements for an OS.

Hardware	For 32-bit Windows 7	For 64-bit Windows 7
Processor	1 GHz or faster	1 GHz or faster
Memory (RAM)	1 GB	2 GB
Free hard drive space	16 GB	20 GB
Video device and driver	DirectX 9 device with WDDM 1.0 or higher driver	DirectX 9 device with WDDM 1.0 or higher driver

© Cengage Learning 2014

Table 7-3 Minimum and recommended hardware requirements for Windows 7

The simplest way to find out if a system can be upgraded to Windows 7 is to download, install, and run the Windows 7 Upgrade Advisor. You can find the software and instructions on how to use it at *windows.microsoft.com/en-US/windows/downloads/upgrade-advisor*. Microsoft also offers the Windows 7 Compatibility Center at *www.microsoft.com/windows/ compatibility* (see Figure 7-2). You can search under both software and hardware to find out if they are compatible with Windows 7. The site sometimes offers links to patches or fixes for a program or device so that it will work with Windows 7.

A+
220-802
1.1, 1.2

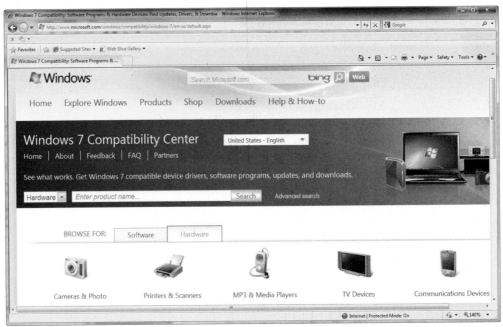

Source: Microsoft Windows 7

Figure 7-2   Use the Windows 7 Compatibility Center to find out if your hardware and software qualify for Windows 7

To understand if your system qualifies for Windows 7, it helps to understand how Windows relates to hardware by using device drivers and system BIOS, as shown in Figure 7-3. (In the figure, the kernel is that part of Windows responsible for relating to hardware.)

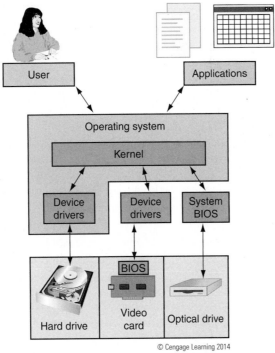

© Cengage Learning 2014

Figure 7-3   Windows relates to hardware by way of device drivers or system BIOS

A+
220-802
1.1, 1.2

When a computer is first turned on, it uses some devices such as the keyboard, monitor, and hard drive before the OS starts up. The motherboard BIOS is contained on a chip on the motherboard (see Figure 7-4) and manages these essential devices. This chip is called a firmware chip because it holds programs.

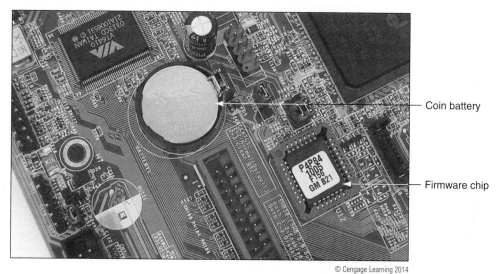

Coin battery

Firmware chip

© Cengage Learning 2014

Figure 7-4 A chip on a motherboard contains BIOS used to start the computer, hold motherboard settings, and run essential devices. The chip retains power from a nearby coin battery when the computer is turned off.

The motherboard BIOS provides three main functions:

◢ The **system BIOS (basic input/output system)** contains instructions for running essential hardware devices before an operating system is started. After the OS is started, it might continue to use system BIOS or use device drivers to communicate with these devices.

◢ The **startup BIOS** starts the computer and finds a boot device (hard drive, CD drive, or USB flash drive) that contains an operating system. It then turns the startup process over to this OS.

◢ The **setup BIOS** is used to change motherboard settings. You can use it to enable or disable a device on the motherboard (for example, network port, video port, or USB ports), change the date and time that is later passed to the OS, and select the order of boot devices for startup BIOS to search when looking for an operating system to load.

Recall that device drivers are small programs stored on the hard drive that tell the computer how to communicate with a specific hardware device such as a printer, network card, or scanner. These drivers are installed on the hard drive when the OS is first installed, or when new hardware is added to the system. A device driver is written to work for a specific OS, such as Windows 7 or Vista. In addition, a 32-bit OS requires 32-bit drivers, and a 64-bit OS requires 64-bit drivers.

Windows provides some device drivers, and the manufacturer of the hardware device provides others. When you purchase a printer, video card, digital camera, scanner, or other hardware device, a CD that contains the device drivers is usually bundled with the device along with a user manual (see Figure 7-5). You can also download the drivers for a device from the manufacturer's web site.

A+
220-802
1.1, 1.2

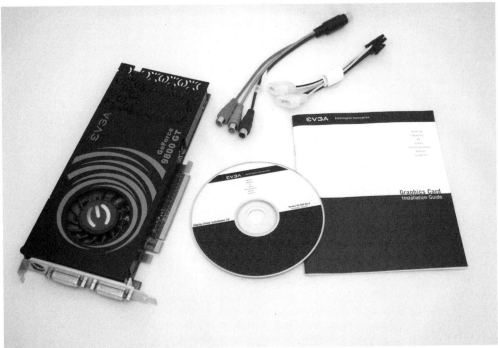

© Cengage Learning 2014

Figure 7-5 A device such as this video card comes packaged with its device drivers stored on a CD

Be sure you have Windows 7 device drivers for all your critical devices such as your network card or motherboard. To find the drivers, look on the CD that came bundled with the device or check the web site of the device manufacturer. Remember that a 64-bit OS requires all 64-bit drivers.

If you are not sure if your devices will work with Windows 7, one solution is to set up a dual boot. A **dual boot**, also called a **multiboot**, allows you to install the new OS without disturbing the old one so you can boot to either OS. After the installation, you can test your software or hardware. If they work under the new OS, you can delete the old one. If they don't work, you can still boot to the old OS and use it. How to set up a dual boot is covered later in the chapter.

If you have applications written for Vista or XP that are not compatible with Windows 7, you can use compatibility mode or Windows XP Mode to solve the problem. **Compatibility mode** is a group of settings that can be applied to older drivers or applications that might cause them to work in Windows 7. **Windows XP Mode** is a Windows XP environment installed in Windows 7 that can be used to support older applications. You learn more about compatibility mode and Windows XP Mode later in the chapter.

INSTALLATIONS WITH SPECIAL CONSIDERATIONS

Depending on the circumstances and the available hardware, you might be faced with an installation on a computer that does not have a DVD drive, a computer that needs a factory recovery, and an installation in a virtual computer. All these special considerations are discussed next.

WHEN THE COMPUTER DOES NOT HAVE A DVD DRIVE

A+
220-802
1.1, 1.2

You can buy Windows 7 on DVD or download it from the Internet. If the computer does not have a DVD drive, consider these options:

▲ *Download Windows 7 from the Microsoft web site:* Purchase Windows 7 on the Microsoft web site (*www.microsoftstore.com*) and download it to your computer's hard drive and install it from there. This option assumes the computer already has a working OS installed.

▲ *Use an external DVD drive.* Use an external DVD drive that will most likely connect to the PC by way of a USB port. If the PC does not already have an OS installed, you must boot from this USB port. To do so, access BIOS setup and set the boot order for the USB as the first boot device. The boot order is the order of devices that startup BIOS looks to for an OS. To enter BIOS setup, you press a key, such as F2 or Del, as the computer is booting and before the OS begins to load. To know which key to press, look for a message on-screen during the boot, such as *Press DEL to enter setup*. Then locate the appropriate BIOS setup screen. For example, the BIOS setup screen shown in Figure 7-6 shows a removable device as the first boot device. You can then boot from the external DVD drive and install Windows.

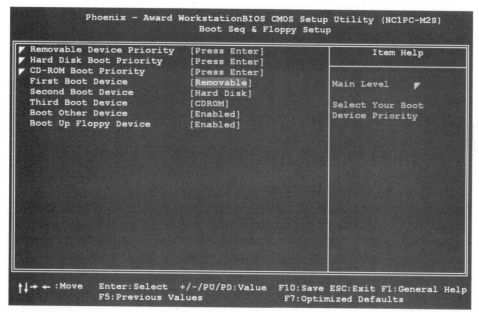

Figure 7-6 Set the boot order in BIOS setup

Source: Phoenix Technologies

▲ *Copy the installation files to a USB flash drive.* This method is easy to use if you don't need to boot from the flash drive. If you do need to boot from the flash drive, you need to install software that makes the USB flash drive bootable and also copy Windows setup files to the drive.

▲ *Use a DVD drive on another computer on the network.* Share the DVD drive on another computer on the network. Then go to the computer that is to receive the Windows installation and locate the DVD drive on the network. Double-click the

A+
220-802
1.1, 1.2

setup.exe program to run the installation across the network. Alternately, you can copy the files on the DVD from the other computer to your hard drive. Again, this option assumes the computer already has a working OS installed. How to share folders and drives on a network is covered in Chapter 17.

If you are upgrading many computers to Windows 7 in a large enterprise, more automated methods are used. Installation files are made available over the network or on bootable USB flash drives or DVDs. These automated methods are discussed later in the chapter.

FACTORY RECOVERY PARTITION

If you have a notebook computer or a brand-name computer, such as a Dell, IBM, or Gateway, and you need to reinstall Windows, follow the recovery procedures given by the computer manufacturer. A hard drive is divided into one or more **partitions,** and the hard drive on a brand-name computer is likely to have a hidden recovery partition that contains a recovery utility and installation files.

To access the utilities on the hidden partition, press a key during startup. The key to press is displayed on the screen early in the boot before the OS is loaded. If you don't see the message, search the web site of the computer manufacturer to find the key combination. For one Dell laptop, you press Ctrl and F11 to start the recovery. One Gateway computer displays the message *Press F11 to start recovery.* When you press these keys, a menu displays, giving you the opportunity to reinstall Windows from setup files kept in the hidden partition.

Sometimes a manufacturer puts a utility in this hidden partition that can be used to create recovery discs (see Figure 7-7). However, the discs must have already been created if they are to be there to help you in the event the entire hard drive fails. You might also be able to purchase these CDs or DVDs on the notebook manufacturer's web site.

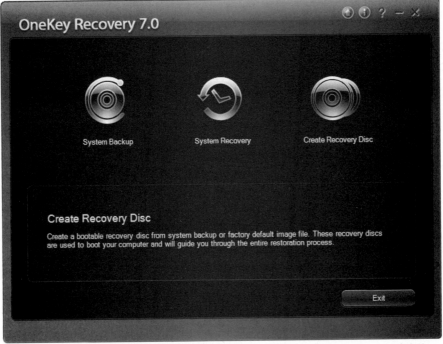

Source: Lenovo

Figure 7-7 Use the recovery utility on this laptop to create DVDs that can be used to recover the system in the event the hard drive fails

A+
220-802
1.1, 1.2

Notes In general, it's best to not upgrade an OS on a notebook unless you want to use some feature the new OS offers. For notebooks, follow the general rule, "If it ain't broke, don't fix it." Many hardware components in a notebook are proprietary, and the notebook manufacturer is the only source for these drivers. If you are considering upgrading a notebook to Windows 7, check the notebook manufacturer's web site for advice and to download Windows 7 drivers. It's very important you have a Windows 7 driver for your network port available without having to depend on the network or Internet to get one after Windows 7 is installed. Also know that many Vista drivers also work with Windows 7.

INSTALLATION IN A VIRTUAL COMPUTER

Another type of Windows installation is when you install Windows in a virtual computer. A virtual computer or **virtual machine (VM)** is software that simulates the hardware of a physical computer. Using this software, you can install and run multiple operating systems at the same time on a PC. These multiple instances of operating systems can be used to train users, run legacy software, and support multiple operating systems. For example, help-desk technicians can run a virtual machine for each OS they support on a single PC and quickly and easily switch from one OS to another by clicking a window. Another reason to use a virtual machine is that you can capture screen shots of the boot process in a virtual machine, which is the way the screen shots during the boot were made for this book.

Some popular virtual machine programs for Windows are Virtual PC by Microsoft (*www.microsoft.com*), VirtualBox by Oracle (*www.virtualbox.org*), and VMware by VMware, Inc. (*www.vmware.com*). Virtual PC, VirtualBox, and VMware Player are freeware. Be aware that virtual machine programs require a lot of memory and might slow down your system. Figure 7-8 shows two virtual machines running under Virtual PC.

XP desktop

Windows 7 logon screen

Source: Virtual PC

Figure 7-8 Two virtual machines running under Virtual PC

A+
220-802
1.1, 1.2

Windows XP Mode is a Windows XP installation that runs under Virtual PC, and can be installed on a Windows 7 Professional, Enterprise, or Ultimate computer. When you install an OS in Virtual PC, normally you must have a valid product key for the installation, but an XP product key is not required for Windows XP Mode.

To use Virtual PC, go to the Microsoft web site and download and install the software. If you plan to use Windows XP Mode, you need to download this software at the same time. To set up a new virtual machine in Virtual PC, click **Start, All Programs**, and **Windows Virtual PC**. (You might need to click Windows Virtual PC a second time.) The Explorer window shown at the top of Figure 7-9 appears. In the menu bar, click **Create virtual machine**. A wizard launches and steps you through the process of creating a new machine. During the process, you can select the name of the virtual machine, how much memory the machine has installed, and the hard drive size. The bottom of Figure 7-9 shows one window in the wizard where you select how much RAM the machine will have. When you complete the wizard, the new virtual machine is listed in the Explorer window.

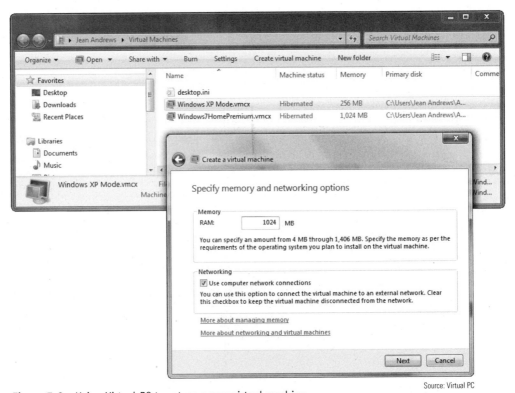

Source: Virtual PC

Figure 7-9 Using Virtual PC to set up a new virtual machine

To start this virtual machine and install an OS in it, first insert the operating system setup disc in the DVD drive. Then double-click the VM in Explorer. The VM boots up, finds the DVD, and starts the OS installation, as shown in Figure 7-10.

A+
220-802
1.1, 1.2

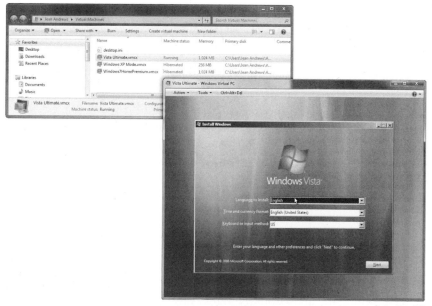

Figure 7-10 A new VM is installing Windows Vista

Source: Virtual PC

APPLYING | CONCEPTS

Windows can also be installed in a VM by using an **ISO image**. An International Organization for Standardization image, also called an ISO image or disc image, contains an image of a disc including the file system used. When downloaded from the web, an ISO image is usually stored in a file with an .iso file extension. An ISO image of the Windows setup DVD can be downloaded as an .iso file. To create a bootable Windows setup DVD from the image, right-click the .iso file and select **Burn disc image** from the shortcut menu. Using a virtual machine, you can mount an ISO image to the VM, which treats the image as though it is a disc. The ISO image file then works like a virtual disc.

To mount an ISO image to a VM, you must change the hardware configuration of the VM. For Virtual PC, first shut down the VM. Then in Explorer, select the VM and click **Settings** in the menu bar. The Settings dialog box appears (see Figure 7-11). To mount an ISO image to the VM, select DVD Drive in the figure and navigate to the ISO file. Make your changes and click **OK**.

Source: Microsoft Windows Virtual PC

Figure 7-11 Change the hardware configuration for a virtual machine in Virtual PC

CHOOSE THE TYPE OF INSTALLATION: IN-PLACE UPGRADE, CLEAN INSTALL, OR DUAL BOOT

If you are installing Windows on a new hard drive, you must perform a clean install. If an OS is already installed on the hard drive, you have three choices:

- ◢ *Clean install:* You can perform a **clean install**, overwriting the existing operating system and applications. In the Windows 7 setup program, a clean install is called a **custom installation**. The main advantage of a clean install is that problems with the old OS are not carried forward and you get a fresh start. During the installation, you will have the option to reformat the hard drive, erasing everything on the drive. If you don't format the drive, the data will still be on the drive, but the previous operating system settings and applications will be lost. After Windows is installed, you will need to install the applications.

- ◢ *In-place upgrade:* If the upgrade paths allow it, you can perform an in-place upgrade installation. An **in-place upgrade** is a Windows installation that is launched from the Windows desktop and the installation carries forward user settings and installed applications from the old OS to the new one. A Windows OS is already *in place* before you begin the new installation. An in-place upgrade is faster than a clean install and is appropriate if the system is generally healthy and does not have problems.

  In order to perform an in-place upgrade, Microsoft requires that certain editions and versions of Windows be installed. These qualifying OSs are called **upgrade paths**. Table 7-4 outlines the acceptable upgrade paths for Windows 7. Notice in the table that there is no upgrade path from Windows XP to Windows 7 or for certain editions and versions of Vista to Windows 7. Even though you can purchase an upgrade license to install Windows 7 on these systems, you must perform a clean install.

From OS	To OS
Vista Home Basic	Windows 7 Home Basic, Home Premium, or Ultimate
Vista Home Premium	Windows 7 Home Premium or Ultimate
Vista Business	Windows 7 Professional, Enterprise, or Ultimate
Vista Enterprise	Windows 7 Enterprise
Vista Ultimate	Windows 7 Ultimate
Windows 7 any edition	Can be repaired by performing an in-place upgrade of the same OS
Windows 7 Starter	Anytime Upgrade to Windows 7 Home Premium, Professional or Ultimate
Windows 7 Home Basic	Anytime upgrade to Windows 7 Home Premium, Professional or Ultimate
Windows 7 Premium	Anytime upgrade to Windows 7 Professional or Ultimate
Windows 7 Professional	Anytime upgrade to Windows 7 Ultimate

© Cengage Learning 2014

Table 7-4 In-place upgrade paths to Windows 7

A+
220-802
1.1, 1.2

▲ *Dual boot:* You can install Windows in a second partition on the hard drive and create a dual-boot situation with the other OS. Don't create a dual boot unless you need two operating systems, such as when you need to verify that applications and hardware work under Windows 7 before you delete the old OS. Windows 7/Vista/XP all require that they be the only operating system installed on a partition. So to set up a dual boot, you'll need at least two partitions on the hard drive or a second hard drive.

> **Notes** An Anytime Upgrade is used to upgrade an edition of Windows 7 to another edition, such as when you upgrade Windows 7 Starter to Windows 7 Home Premium. The upgrade is easy to do and does not require your going through the entire upgrade process.

In addition to the information given in Table 7-4, keep in mind these tips:

▲ A 64-bit version of Windows can only be upgraded to a 64-bit OS. A 32-bit OS can only be upgraded to a 32-bit OS. If you want to install a 64-bit version of Windows on a computer that already has a 32-bit OS installed, you must perform a clean install.

▲ You can only upgrade Windows Vista to Windows 7 after Vista Service Pack 1 or later has been installed in Vista.

UNDERSTAND THE CHOICES YOU'LL MAKE DURING THE INSTALLATION

While Windows is installing, you must choose which drive and partition to install Windows, the size of a new partition, and how Windows will connect to the network. These three choices are discussed next.

THE SIZE OF THE WINDOWS PARTITION

A hard drive is divided into one or more partitions. When a partition is formatted with a file system and assigned a drive letter (such as drive C:), it is called a **volume**. A **file system** is the overall structure an OS uses to name, store, and organize files on a volume, and Windows is always installed on a volume that uses the NTFS file system. For most installations, you install Windows on the only hard drive in the computer and allocate all the space on the drive to one partition that Windows setup calls drive C: and installs Windows in the C:\Windows folder.

For a clean install or dual boot, you can decide to not use all the available space on the drive for the Windows partition. Here are reasons to not use all the available space:

▲ *You plan to install more than one OS on the hard drive, creating a dual-boot system*: For example, you might want to install Windows 7 on one partition and leave room for another partition where you intend to later install Windows 8, so you can test software under both operating systems. (When setting up a dual boot, always install the older OS first.)

▲ *Some people prefer to use more than one partition or volume to organize data on their hard drives*: For example, you might want to install Windows and all your applications on one partition and your data on another. Having your data on a separate partition makes backing up easier. In another situation, you might want to set up a volume on the drive that is used exclusively to hold backups of data on another computer on the network. The size of the partition that will hold Windows 7 and its applications should be at least 20 GB, but a larger volume is preferred.

A+
220-802
1.1, 1.2

> ⚡ **Caution**   It's convenient to back up one volume to another volume on a different hard drive. However, don't back up one volume to another volume on the same hard drive, because when a hard drive fails, quite often all volumes on the drive are damaged and you will lose both your data and your backup.

Windows can handle up to four partitions on a drive. In Chapter 10, you learn to use Disk Management to create partitions from unallocated space and to resize, delete, and split existing partitions.

ADMINISTRATOR ACCOUNT

Recall from Chapter 3 that Windows supports two types of accounts, standard accounts and administrator accounts. These accounts are **local accounts**, meaning they are only recognized by the local computer. Every Windows computer has two local administrator accounts:

▲ During the Windows 7 installation, you are given the opportunity to enter an account name and password to a local user account that is assigned administrator privileges. This account is enabled by default.

▲ A built-in **administrator account** is created by default. The built-in administrator account is named Administrator, does not have a password, and is disabled by default. In Chapter 17, you learn how to enable this administrator account.

You can log on as an administrator after the OS is installed and create local user accounts that apply to this one computer. How to set up a local account is covered later in the chapter.

A+
220-802
1.1, 1.2,
1.6

NETWORK CONFIGURATION

Three ways Windows supports accessing resources on a network are to use a Windows homegroup, workgroup, or domain.

Windows Workgroup and Homegroup

A homegroup and workgroup are examples of a **peer-to-peer (P2P)** network, which is a network that is managed by each computer without centralized control. They form a logical group of computers and users that share resources (see Figure 7-12), where administration, resources, and security on a workstation are controlled by that workstation.

> 📝 **Notes**   When looking at the diagrams in Figure 7-12 and later in Figure 7-13, know that the connecting lines describe the logical connections between computers and not the physical connections. Both networks might be physically connected the same way, but logically, resources are controlled by each computer on the network or by using a centralized database. In network terminology, the arrangement of physical connections between computers is called the **physical topology**. The logical way the computers connect on a network is called the **logical topology**.

A+
220-802
1.1, 1.2,
1.6

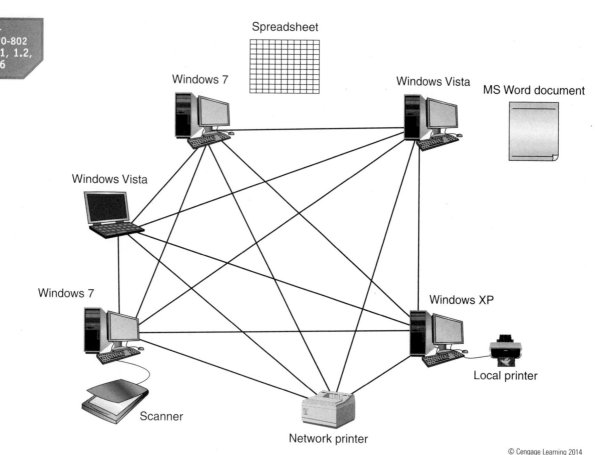

Figure 7-12 A Windows workgroup is a type of peer-to-peer network where no single computer controls the network and each computer controls its own resources

© Cengage Learning 2014

In a Windows **workgroup**, each computer maintains a list of users and their rights on that particular PC. The computer allows a user on the network to access local resources based on these rights she has been given. In a **homegroup**, each computer shares files, folders, libraries, and printers with other computers in the homegroup. A homegroup provides less security than a workgroup because any user of any computer in the homegroup can access homegroup resources.

A homegroup is new to Windows 7 and cannot be used with earlier versions of Windows. If you need to share resources with Windows Vista or XP computers or you need better security so you can share resources with specific users, use workgroup sharing rather than a homegroup. You can also use a combination of homegroup and workgroup sharing on the same computer.

During the Windows installation, if you set the network location to a home network, you are given the opportunity to create or join a homegroup. If the homegroup already exists on the network, you will need the homegroup password to join.

Notes Windows 7 Starter and Home Basic can join a homegroup, but they cannot create one.

A+
220-802
1.1, 1.2,
1.6

Windows setup automatically joins the computer to a workgroup named WORKGROUP. If necessary, you can change the workgroup name after the installation. How to change a workgroup name is covered later in the chapter. Using workgroup sharing, you must set up a user account for each user and share resources with these users. Chapter 17 covers the details of securing and managing homegroups, workgroups, user accounts, and shared resources.

Windows Domain

A Windows **domain** is a logical group of networked computers that share a centralized directory database of user account information and security for the entire group of computers (see Figure 7-13). A Windows domain is a type of **client/server** network, which is a network where resources are managed by centralized computers. Using the client/server model, the directory database is controlled by a Network Operating System (NOS). Examples of network operating systems are Windows Server 2011, UNIX, and Linux.

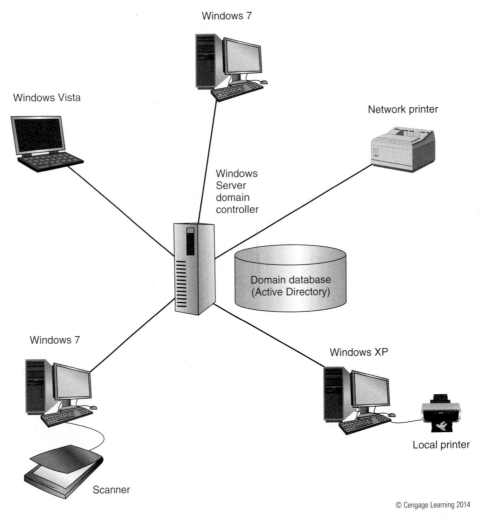

© Cengage Learning 2014

Figure 7-13 A Windows domain is a type of client/server network where security on each PC or other device is controlled by a centralized database on a domain controller

---

📝 **Notes** Windows Home Editions do not support joining a domain. If you plan to join a domain on your network, install Windows 7 Professional, Enterprise, or Ultimate editions.

A+
220-802
1.1, 1.2,
1.6

Windows Server controls a network using the directory database called **Active Directory**. Each user on the network must have his own domain-level account called a **global account**, global username or network ID, which is kept in Active Directory and assigned by the network or system administrator. If you are installing Windows on a PC that belongs to a domain, the administrator will tell you the domain name and computer name so you can join the domain during the installation. You will also need a network ID and password to the domain that you can use to log onto the network after Windows is installed.

> **Notes** If your computer is part of a domain, when Windows starts up, press Ctrl+Alt+Del to display a logon screen, and then enter your network ID and password.

The Windows installation process usually has no problems connecting to the network and the Internet without your help. However, you might need to know how the IP address is assigned. An IP address uniquely identifies a computer on the network. It might be assigned dynamically (IP address is assigned by a server each time it connects to the network) or statically (IP address is permanently assigned to the workstation). If the network is using static IP addressing, you need the IP address for the workstation.

A+
220-802
1.1, 1.2

FINAL CHECKLIST BEFORE BEGINNING THE INSTALLATION

Before you begin the installation, complete the final checklist shown in Table 7-5 to verify that you are ready.

Questions to Answer	Further Information
Does the PC meet the minimum or recommended hardware requirement?	CPU: RAM: Hard drive partition size: Free space on the partition:
Do you have in hand the Windows device drivers for your hardware devices and application setup CDs?	List hardware and software that need to be upgraded:
Do you have the product key available?	Product key:
How will users be recognized on the network?	Homegroup password: Workgroup name: Domain name: Computer name:
How will the PC be recognized on the network?	Static or dynamic IP addressing: IP address (for static addressing):
Will you do an upgrade or clean install?	Current operating system: Does the old OS qualify for an upgrade?

For a clean install, will you set up a dual boot?	List reasons for a dual boot:
	 For a dual boot
	     Size of the second partition:
	     Free space on the second partition:

Have you backed up important data on your hard drive?	Location of backup:

© Cengage Learning 2014

Table 7-5 Checklist to complete before installing Windows

A+
220-802
1.1, 1.2

> **Notes** For new installations, look for the product key written on the cover of the Windows setup DVD or affixed to the back of the Windows documentation booklet, as shown in Figure 7-14. If you are reinstalling Windows on an existing system, look for the product key displayed in the System window. Click **Start**, right-click **Computer**, and select **Properties** from the shortcut menu. If Windows will not start, look for the product key sticker mounted on the side of a desktop or bottom of a laptop.

Product key for OEM version

Product key for retail version

© Cengage Learning 2014

Figure 7-14 The Windows 7 product key found on the inside of a retail package or on the outside of an OEM

Before we get into the step-by-step instructions of installing an OS, here are some general tips about installing Windows:

- ◢ Verify that you have all application software CDs or DVDs available and all device drivers.
- ◢ Back up all important data on the drive. How to perform backups is covered in Chapter 10.
- ◢ For upgrade installations and clean installs where you do not plan to reformat the hard drive, run antivirus software to make sure the drive is free from malware. If Windows will not start and you suspect malware might be a problem, plan to reformat the hard drive during the installation so you know the hard drive is clean of malware.
- ◢ If you want to begin the installation by booting from the Windows DVD or other media such as a USB device, use BIOS setup to verify that the boot sequence is first the optical drive or USB device, and then the hard drive.
- ◢ In BIOS setup, disable any virus protection setting that prevents the boot area of the hard drive from being altered.
- ◢ For a notebook computer, connect the AC adapter and use this power source for the complete OS installation, updates, and installation of hardware and applications. You don't want the battery to fail in the middle of the installation process.

> **Notes** If your current installation of Windows is corrupted, you might be able to repair the installation rather than reinstalling Windows. Chapter 14 covers what to do to fix a corrupted Windows installation.

INSTALLING WINDOWS 7

A+
220-802
1.2, 1.6,
4.6

In this part of the chapter, you learn the steps to install Windows 7 as an in-place upgrade, clean install, and dual boot, and what to do after the installation. As you install and configure software, be sure to document what you did. This documentation will be helpful for future maintenance and troubleshooting. In a project near the end of this chapter, you will develop a documentation template.

Let's begin with how to perform an in-place upgrade of Windows Vista to Windows 7.

STEPS TO PERFORMING A WINDOWS 7 IN-PLACE UPGRADE

Recall that an in-place upgrade begins after you have booted the system to the Windows desktop. An upgrade from Windows Vista to Windows 7 carries applications and user settings forward into the new installation. Follow these steps:

1. Close any open applications. If you have not already backed up important data and used antivirus software to scan the system for viruses, do so now. After the scan is finished, close the antivirus software so that it does not run in the background. Close other third-party software such as backup software that might be running in the background.

2. Insert the Windows 7 DVD in the DVD drive. You can then launch Windows setup from the AutoPlay dialog box that appears (see Figure 7-15). If it does not appear, enter this command in the search box: **D:\setup.exe**, substituting the drive letter for your DVD drive for D. Respond to the Vista UAC (User Account Control) box.

Source: Microsoft Windows 7

Figure 7-15   Begin the Windows 7 installation from the AutoPlay box

> **Notes**   Figure 7-16 shows the error message that appears when you try to upgrade a 32-bit OS to a 64-bit version of Windows 7.

A+
220-802
1.2, 1.6,
4.6

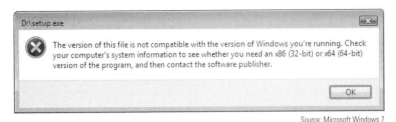

Source: Microsoft Windows 7

Figure 7-16   Error when running the 64-bit Windows 7 setup program from within a 32-bit operating system

3. The opening menu shown in Figure 7-17 appears. If you have not yet performed the Windows 7 Upgrade Advisor process, you can do so now by clicking *Check compatibility online*. To proceed with the installation, click **Install now.**

> **Notes** If your computer refuses to read from the DVD, verify that your optical drive is a DVD drive. Perhaps it is only a CD drive. If this is the case, refer to the section "When the Computer Does Not Have a DVD Drive" earlier in the chapter.

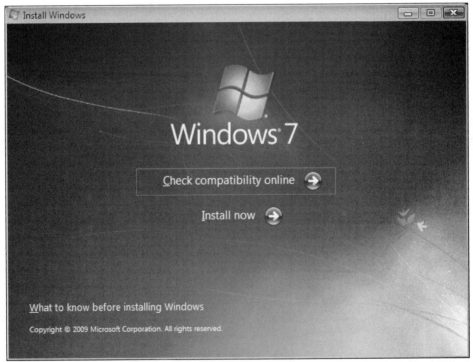

Source: Microsoft Windows 7

Figure 7-17   Opening menu when you launch Windows 7 setup from within Windows

4. On the next screen, you can choose to allow the setup program to download updates for the installation (see Figure 7-18). If you have Internet access, click **Go online to get the latest updates for installation (recommended).** Setup will download the updates. When using this option, you'll need to stay connected to the Internet throughout the installation.

A+
220-802
1.2, 1.6,
4.6

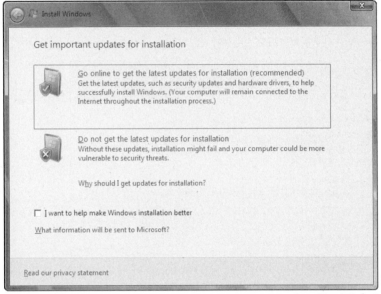

Source: Microsoft Windows 7

Figure 7-18 Allow setup to download updates for the installation process

5. On the next screen, accept the license agreement and click **Next**.

6. On the next screen, shown in Figure 7-19, select the type of installation you want, either Upgrade or Custom (advanced). The Upgrade option is only available when an existing version of Windows Vista or 7 is running. The Custom installation is a clean install. Select **Upgrade**.

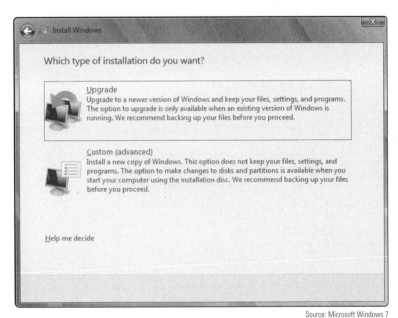

Source: Microsoft Windows 7

Figure 7-19 Select the type of installation you want

7. Setup will check for any compatibility issues. It will verify that the edition of Vista installed can be used as an upgrade path to the edition of Windows 7 you are installing according to the rules outlined earlier in Table 7-4. It will also verify that Windows Vista has a service pack applied. If setup finds a problem, an error message or a warning message appears. An error message requires that you end the installation and resolve the problem. A warning message allows you to click **Next** to continue with the installation.

A+
220-802
1.2, 1.6,
4.6

8. The installation is now free to move forward. The PC might reboot several times. At the end of this process, a screen appears asking you for the product key (see Figure 7-20). Enter the product key and click **Next**.

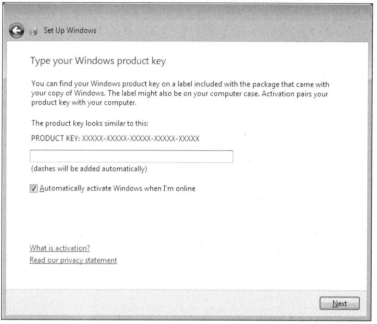

Source: Microsoft Windows 7

Figure 7-20   Enter the product key

> **Notes**   Notice in Figure 7-20 the check box *Automatically activate Windows when I'm online*. Normally, you would leave this option checked so that Windows 7 activates immediately. However, if you are practicing installing Windows 7 and intend to install it several times using the same DVD, you might choose to uncheck this box and not enter the product key during the installation. You can later decide to enter the product key and activate Windows after the installation is finished. You have 30 days before you must activate Windows.

9. On the following screen, you are asked how you want to handle Windows updates (see Figure 7-21). Unless your company has a different policy, click **Use recommended settings**.

Source: Microsoft Windows 7

Figure 7-21   Decide how to handle Windows Updates

A+
220-802
1.2, 1.6,
4.6

10. On the next screen, verify the time and date settings are correct and click **Next**.

11. On the next screen, select the network location (see Figure 7-22). Click the option that is appropriate to your network connection. If you need to change this setting later, use the Network and Sharing Center that you learned about in Chapter 3.

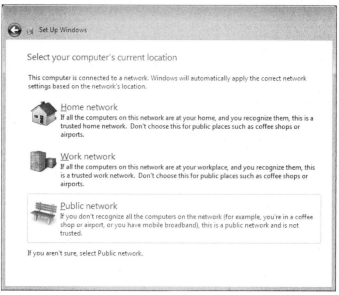

Source: Microsoft Windows 7

Figure 7-22   Select network settings

Here is an explanation of each option:

▲ *Home network.* Network Discovery is turned on and you can join a homegroup. Network Discovery is a setting that allows this computer to see other computers on the network and other computers can see this computer.

▲ *Work network.* Network Discovery is turned on, you can join a domain, but you cannot join a homegroup.

▲ *Public network.* Network Discovery is turned off and you cannot join a home-group or domain. This option is the most secure.

12. If you selected Home network in the previous step, the screen shown in Figure 7-23 appears when a homegroup already exists and allows you to configure your home-group settings. In the figure, you are told that the user, Jean Andrews, has assigned a homegroup password on the computer BLUELIGHT. If setup does not find a homeg-roup on the network, it suggests a password for the new homegroup. Check what you want to share with others in the homegroup. Enter the password for an existing home-group or verify/change the password for the new homegroup. Then click **Next** to create or join the homegroup. If you don't want to use a homegroup, click **Skip** to continue.

> **Notes** To know what password has been assigned to an existing homegroup, go to a computer on the network that belongs to this homegroup. Open Control Panel and click **Choose homegroup and sharing options** under the Network and Internet group. On the next screen, click **View or print the homegroup password**.

13. Near the end of the installation, Windows Update downloads and installs updates and the system restarts. Finally, a logon screen appears. Log in with your user account and password. The Windows 7 desktop loads and the installation is complete.

A+
220-802
1.2, 1.6,
4.6

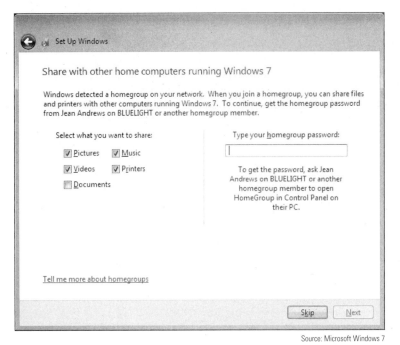

Source: Microsoft Windows 7

Figure 7-23   Configure your homegroup settings and password

STEPS TO PERFORM A CLEAN INSTALL OR DUAL BOOT

To perform a clean install of Windows 7 or a dual boot with another OS, you can begin the installation from the Windows 7 DVD or from the Windows desktop:

▲ *If no operating system is installed on the PC, begin the installation by booting from the Windows 7 DVD:* Using this method, the Upgrade option is not available and you are forced to do a Custom installation, also called a clean install.

▲ *If an operating system is already installed on the PC, you can begin the installation from the Windows desktop or by booting from the Windows 7 DVD:* Either way, you can perform a Custom installation. If you are using an upgrade license of Windows 7, setup will verify that a Windows OS is present, which qualifies you to use the upgrade license. This is the method to use when upgrading from Windows XP to Windows 7; you are required to perform a clean install even though setup verifies that Windows XP is present.

▲ *If you are installing a 64-bit OS when a 32-bit OS is already installed or vice versa, you must begin the installation by booting from the DVD:* Setup still allows you to use the less expensive upgrade license even though you are performing a clean install because it is able to verify a Windows installation is present.

> **Notes** When setting up a dual boot, you might need to shrink a partition to make room for a second partition to hold Windows 7. If so, use Disk Management in Windows Vista to shrink the partition before you begin the Windows 7 installation. You can also use Disk Management to create a new partition to hold the Windows 7 installation and format that partition. The Windows 7 volume must be formatted using the NTFS file system. How to use Disk Management is covered in Chapter 10.

Follow these steps to begin the installation by booting from the Windows 7 DVD:

1. Insert the Windows 7 DVD in the DVD drive and start the system, booting directly from the DVD. If you have trouble booting from the disc, go into BIOS setup and verify that your first boot device is the optical drive. On the first screen (see Figure 7-24), select your language and other preferences and click **Next**.

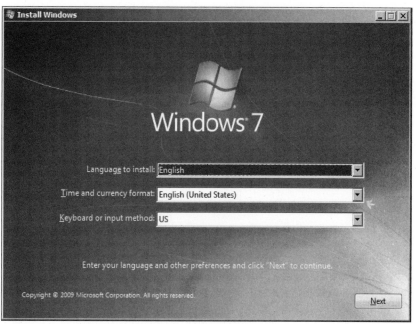

Source: Microsoft Windows 7

Figure 7-24   Select language, time, and keyboard options

> **Notes** When installing Windows XP, you have to install third-party drivers at the beginning of the XP installation if your computer is using an array of hard drives working together (called RAID) or a hard drive with a SCSI hardware interface. However, Windows 7 or Vista setup has its own drivers for these situations, so no extra third-party drivers are needed. If you encounter a problem when installing Windows 7 using RAID or SCSI drives, such as a RAID or SCSI hard drive is not detected, know that the problem is a hardware or firmware problem and not a Windows setup problem.

2. The opening menu shown in Figure 7-25 appears. Click **Install now**.

Source: Microsoft Windows 7

Figure 7-25   Screen to begin the Windows 7 installation

3. On the next screen, accept the license agreement.

4. On the next screen, shown earlier in Figure 7-19, select the type of installation you want. Choose **Custom (advanced)**.

5. On the next screen, you will be shown a list of partitions on which to install the OS. For example, the computer shown in Figure 7-26 has one partition on one hard drive. If you want to use this partition for a clean install, click **Next**, which will cause Windows 7 to replace whatever other OS might be installed on this partition. If you are performing a dual boot and need to create a new partition, click **Drive options (advanced)**; setup will step you through the process of creating a new partition.

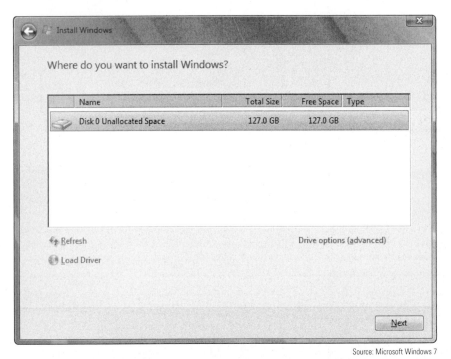

Source: Microsoft Windows 7

Figure 7-26 Select a partition to install Windows 7 in a clean install or dual-boot environment

6. The installation is now free to move forward. At the end of this process, the window in Figure 7-27 appears asking for a username and computer name. Enter these values and click **Next**. On the next screen, you can enter a password for your user account by entering the password twice followed by a password hint. Then click **Next**.

7. The installation now continues the same way as an upgrade installation. You are asked to enter the product key, Windows update settings, time and date settings, and network settings. Windows Update downloads and installs updates and you are asked to restart the system. After the restart, the logon screen appears. After you log in, the Windows 7 desktop loads and the installation is complete.

After the installation, when you boot with a dual boot, the **boot loader menu** automatically appears and asks you to select an operating system, as shown in Figure 7-28.

A+
220-802
1.2, 1.6,
4.6

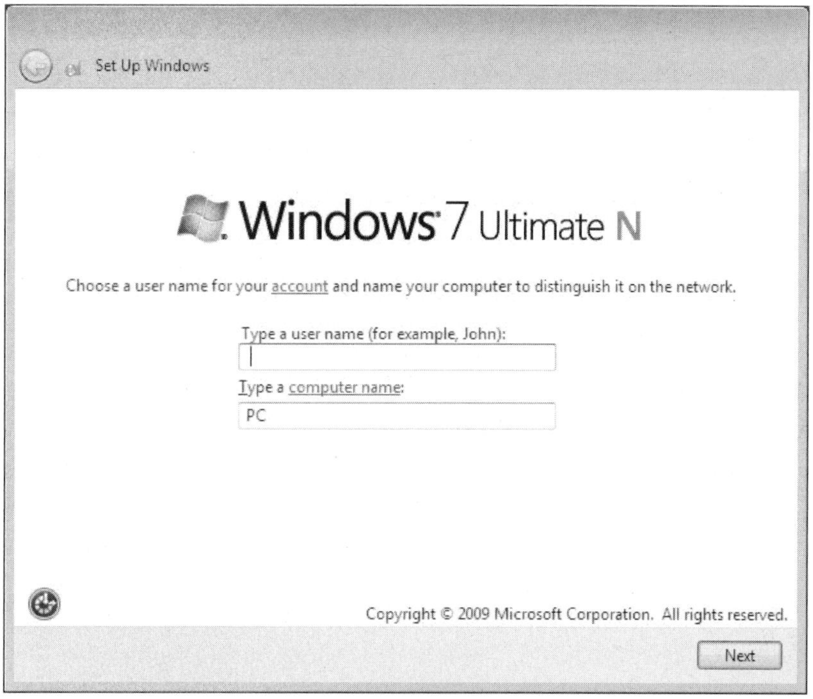

Source: Microsoft Windows 7

Figure 7-27 Choose a username and computer name

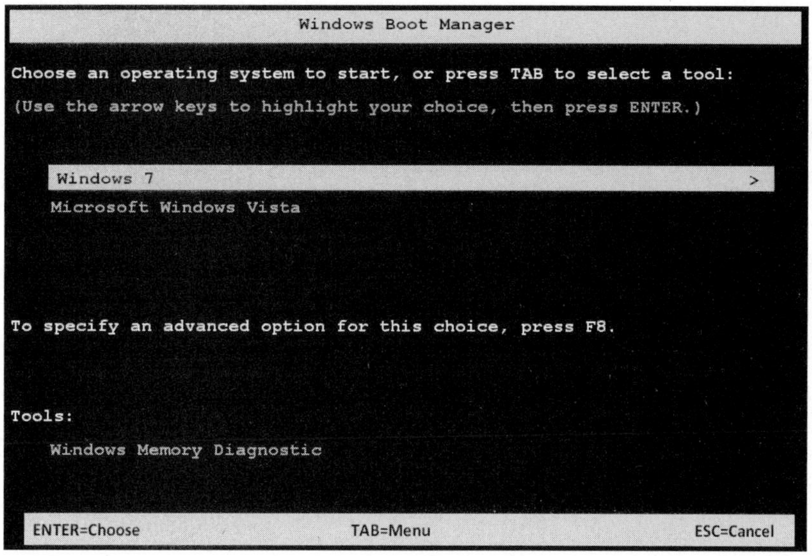

Source: Microsoft Windows 7

Figure 7-28 Boot loader menu in a dual-boot environment

When using a dual boot, you can execute an application while Windows 7 or Vista is loaded even if the application is installed under the other OS. If the application is not listed in the Start menu, locate the program file in Windows Explorer. Double-click the application to run it from Windows 7 or Vista. You should not have to install an application twice under each OS.

A+
220-802
1.2

USE THE WINDOWS 7 UPGRADE DVD ON A NEW HARD DRIVE

Windows 7 setup expects that an old OS is installed if you use the upgrade license DVD. This requirement presents a problem when you are replacing a hard drive. You have two options in this situation:

▲ *Install Vista or XP first and then install Windows 7*: You must also install a service pack under Vista or XP before you install Windows 7. This first option takes a long time!

▲ *Install Windows 7 twice*: Follow these steps:

1. Use the Windows 7 upgrade DVD to perform a clean install. When you get to the installation window that asks you to enter your product key, don't enter the key and uncheck **Automatically activate Windows when I'm online**. Complete the installation.

2. From the Windows 7 desktop, start the installation routine again, but this time as an upgrade. Enter the product key during the installation and Windows 7 will activate with no problems.

> **Notes** If you have problems installing Windows, search the Microsoft web site (*support.microsoft.com*) for solutions. Windows 7 setup creates several log files during the installation that can help you solve a problem. The list can be found in the Microsoft Knowledge Base Article 927521 at this link: *support.microsoft.com/kb/927521*.

> **Vista Differences** Editions of Windows Vista are **Windows Vista Starter, Windows Vista Home Basic, Windows Vista Home Premium, Windows Vista Business, Windows Vista Enterprise**, and **Windows Vista Ultimate**. A Vista installation works the same as a Windows 7 installation. To find out about the editions of Vista and the differences in planning a Vista installation, see Appendix B.

> **XP Differences** Windows XP comes in **Windows XP Home Edition, Windows XP Professional, Windows XP Professional x64 Edition, Windows XP Media Center Edition**, and **Windows XP Tablet PC Edition**. An XP installation begins by booting from the XP setup CD or executing the Winnt32.exe program from the Windows desktop. To find out more about the features of XP editions and how to install and configure XP, see Appendix C.

WHAT TO DO AFTER A WINDOWS INSTALLATION

A+
220-802
1.2, 1.5

After you have installed Windows, you need to do the following:

▲ Verify that you have network access.
▲ Activate Windows.
▲ Install updates and service packs for Windows
▲ Verify automatic updates are set as you want them.
▲ Install hardware.
▲ Install applications, including antivirus software.
▲ Set up user accounts and transfer or restore from backup user data and preferences to the new system.
▲ Turn Windows features on or off.

> **Notes** To protect your computer, don't surf the web for drivers or applications until you have installed Windows updates and service packs and also installed and configured antivirus software.

A+
220-802
1.2, 1.5

In addition, if you are installing Windows on a laptop, you will want to use Control Panel to configure power management settings. If you are installing an OEM (Original Equipment Manufacturer) version of Windows 7, look for a sticker on the outside of the DVD case. This sticker contains the product key and is called the **Certificate of Authenticity**. Put the sticker on the bottom of a laptop or the side or rear of a desktop computer (see Figure 7-29).

© Cengage Learning 2014

Figure 7-29 Paste the Windows 7 Certificate of Authenticity sticker on a new desktop

Now let's look at the details of the items in the preceding list.

VERIFY THAT YOU HAVE NETWORK ACCESS

When you install Windows 7, the setup process should connect you to the local network and to the Internet, if available. If you are working on a computer in a corporate environment using a Windows domain, follow these steps to join the computer to a domain:

1. Click the **Start** button, right-click **Computer**, and select **Properties** from the shortcut menu. The System window opens (see the left side of Figure 7-30).

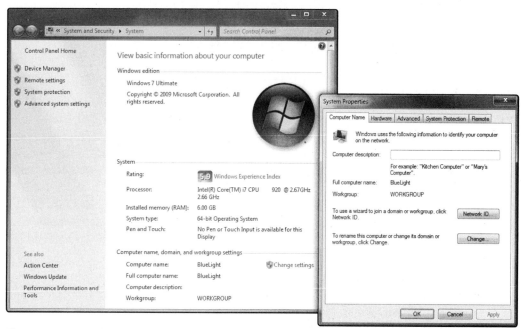

Figure 7-30 Use the System window to change computer settings

Source: Microsoft Windows 7

A+
220-802
1.2, 1.5

2. Scroll down to the *Computer name, domain, and workgroup settings* group. Click **Change settings**. The System Properties dialog box displays, as shown in the right side of Figure 7-30. (If you are installing a Windows 7 Home edition, the Network ID button in the figure will be missing because these editions cannot join a domain.)

3. To join a domain, click **Network ID** and follow the directions on-screen to join the domain. To join the domain, you will need your username and password on the domain, the computer name, and the name of the domain. Your network administrator will have all that information. You will need to restart the computer before your changes will take effect.

> **Notes** If your computer is part of a Windows domain, when Windows starts up, it displays a blank screen instead of a logon screen. To log onto the domain, press Ctrl+Alt+Del to display the logon screen. If you want to log onto the local machine instead of the domain, type **.*username*. For example, to log onto the local machine using the local user account "Jean Andrews," type **.\Jean Andrews**.

To verify that you have access to the local network and to the Internet, do the following:

1. Open Windows Explorer and verify that you can see other computers on the network (see Figure 7-31). Try to drill down to see shared resources on these computers.

Source: Microsoft Windows 7

Figure 7-31   Use Windows Explorer to access resources on your network

2. To verify that you have Internet access, open Internet Explorer and try to navigate to a couple of web sites.

3. If Windows Explorer does not show other computers on your network or you cannot access the Internet, use the Network and Sharing Center that you learned about in Chapter 3 to resolve the problem.

A+
220-802
1.2, 1.5

If the problem persists after you have tried the simple things suggested in Chapter 3, consider the problem might be the IP address, wireless network, or Network Discovery settings are wrong. How to configure network settings and troubleshoot network connections are covered in Chapters 15 and 17.

ACTIVATE WINDOWS 7

In order to make sure a valid Windows license has been purchased for each installation of Windows, Microsoft requires **product activation**. If you don't activate Windows 7 during the installation, you have 30 days to do so. To view the activation status and product key, open the System window. From this window, you can also change the product key before you activate the installation. If you fail to activate Windows after 30 days, the Windows desktop will not load and an error message appears forcing you to activate the OS.

To activate Windows 7, click the **Start** button and enter **activate** in the *Search* box and press **Enter**. The Windows Activation window opens (see Figure 7-32). Click **Activate Windows online now** to begin the process. If you have not yet entered a product key, the next screen allows you to do that.

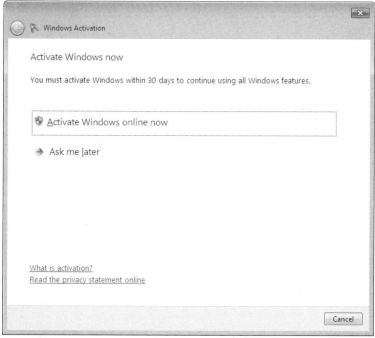

Source: Microsoft Windows 7

Figure 7-32   The system has 28 days left before you must activate the installation

Notes If you change the product key after Windows is activated, you must activate Windows again because the activation is tied to the product key and the system hardware. If you replace the motherboard or replace the hard drive and memory at the same time, you must also reactivate Windows.

If you install Windows from the same DVD on a different computer, and you attempt to activate Windows from the new PC, a dialog box appears telling you of the suspected violation of the license agreement. You can call a Microsoft operator and explain what caused the discrepancy. If your explanation is reasonable (for example, you uninstalled Windows from one PC and installed it on another), the operator can issue you a valid certificate. You can then type the certificate value into a dialog box to complete the boot process.

A+
220-802
1.2, 1.5

INSTALL WINDOWS UPDATES AND SERVICE PACKS

The Microsoft web site offers patches, fixes, and updates for known problems and has an extensive knowledge base documenting problems and their solutions. It's important to keep these updates current on your system to fix known problems and plug up security holes that might allow viruses and worms in. Be sure to install updates before you attempt to install software or hardware.

To download and apply Windows updates, click **Start**, **All Programs**, and **Windows Update**. The Windows Update window appears, as shown in Figure 7-33. If important updates are available, a message displays. Click **important updates** to select updates to install. A list of updates appears. Select the ones you want to install.

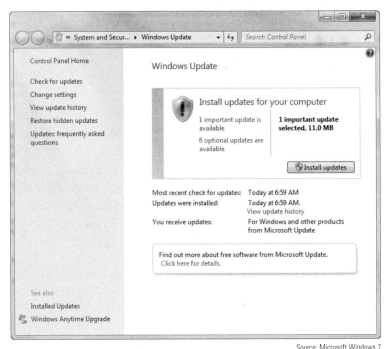

Source: Microsoft Windows 7

Figure 7-33 Download and install updates for your computer

Windows selects the updates in the order the system can receive them, and will not necessarily list all the updates you need on the first pass. After you have installed the updates listed, go back and start again until Windows Updates tells you there is nothing left to update. If Windows requests a restart after an update, do that before you install more updates. It might take two or more passes to get the PC entirely up to date.

If you see a service pack listed in the updates, install all the updates listed above it. Then install the service pack as the only update to install. It takes about 30 minutes and a reboot to download and install a service pack. Only the latest service pack for an OS will install because the latest service pack includes all the content from previous service packs.

CONFIGURE AUTOMATIC UPDATES

During the Windows installation, you were asked how you want to handle Windows updates. To verify or change this setting, in the left pane of the Windows Update window, click **Change settings**. From the Change settings window, shown in Figure 7-34, you can decide how often, when, and how you want Windows to install updates. The recommended setting is to allow Windows to automatically download and install updates daily. However, if you are not always connected to the Internet, your connection is very slow, or you want more control over which updates are installed, you might want to manage the updates differently.

Source: Microsoft Windows 7

Figure 7-34   Manage how and when Windows is updated

INSTALL HARDWARE

You're now ready to install the hardware devices that were not automatically installed during the installation. As you install each device, reboot and verify that the software or device is working before you move on to the next item. Most likely, you will need to do the following:

◢ *Install the drivers for the motherboard:* If you were not able to connect to the network earlier in the installation process, it might be because the drivers for the network port on the motherboard are not installed. Installing the motherboard drivers can solve the problem. These drivers might come on a CD bundled with the motherboard, or you can use another computer to download them from the motherboard manufacturer's web site. To start the installation, double-click a setup program on the CD or a program that was previously downloaded from the web.

◢ *Even though Windows has embedded video drivers, install the drivers that came with the video card so that you can use all the features the card offers:* These drivers are on disc or downloaded from the video card manufacturer's web site.

◢ *Install the printer:* For a network printer, run the setup program that came with the printer and this program will find and install the printer on the network. Alternately, you can click **View devices and printers** in Control Panel to open the Devices and Printers window (see Figure 7-35). Then click **Add a printer** and follow the directions on-screen. To install a local USB printer, all you have to do is plug in the USB printer, and Windows will install the printer automatically.

A+
220-802
1.2, 1.4,
1.5

◢ *For other hardware devices, always read and follow the manufacturer's directions for the installation:* Sometimes you are directed to install the drivers before you connect the device, and sometimes you will first need to connect the device.

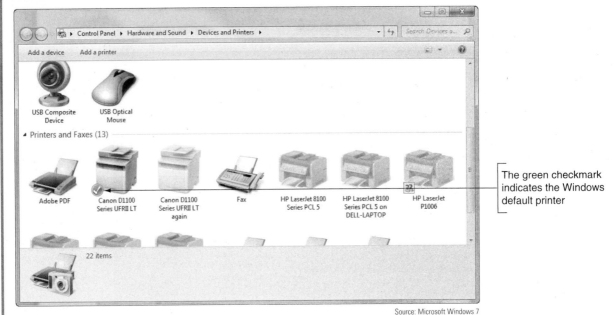

Source: Microsoft Windows 7

The green checkmark indicates the Windows default printer

Figure 7-35 Installed devices and printers

If a problem occurs while Windows is installing a device, it automatically launches the Action Center to help find a solution. For example, Figure 7-36 shows the error message window that appeared when a USB keyboard and USB printer were connected to a computer following a Windows 7 installation.

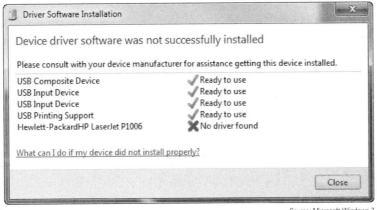

Source: Microsoft Windows 7

Figure 7-36 Windows 7 reports a problem with a driver for a USB printer

Immediately after this first window appeared, the window in Figure 7-37 appeared that is provided by the Action Center. When the user clicked **Click to download and install the new driver from the Hewlett-Packard Company website**, the driver was immediately downloaded and installed with no errors.

Recall from Chapter 3 that you can also open the Action Center at any time to see a list of problems and solutions. If the problem is still not resolved after following the solutions offered by the Action Center, turn to Device Manager.

A+
220-802
1.2, 1.4,
1.5

Source: Microsoft Windows 7

Figure 7-37 Windows offers to find the missing USB printer driver

USE DEVICE MANAGER

Device Manager (its program file is named devmgmt.msc) is your primary Windows tool for managing hardware. It lists all installed hardware devices and the drivers they use. Using Device Manager, you can disable or enable a device, update its drivers, uninstall a device, and undo a driver update (called a driver rollback).

A+ Exam Tip The A+ 220-802 exam expects you to know in what scenario it is appropriate to use Device Manager. You also need to know how to use the utility and how to evaluate its results.

To access Device Manager, use one of these methods:

▲ Click **Start**, right-click **Computer**, and select **Properties**. The System window appears. Click **Device Manager**. The Device Manager window opens.

▲ Enter **Device Manager** or **Devmgmt.msc** in the search box and press **Enter**. A Device Manager window is shown in Figure 7-38.

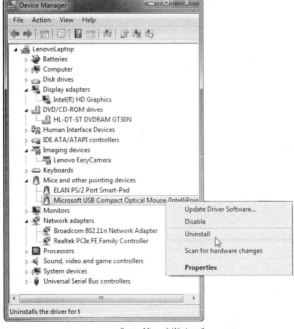

Source: Microsoft Windows 7

Figure 7-38 Use Device Manager to uninstall, disable, or enable a device

A+
220-802
1.2, 1.4,
1.5

Click a white arrow to expand the view of an item, and click a black arrow to collapse the view. Here are ways to use Device Manager to solve problems with a device:

▲ *Try uninstalling and reinstalling the device:* To uninstall the device, right-click the device and click **Uninstall** on the shortcut menu, as shown in Figure 7-38. Then reboot and reinstall the device, looking for problems during the installation that point to the source of the problem. Sometimes reinstalling a device is all that is needed to solve the problem. Notice in Figure 7-38 that the device selected is a USB mouse. Sometimes USB devices are listed in Device Manager and sometimes they are not.

▲ *Look for error messages offered by Device Manager:* To find out more information about a device, right-click the device and select **Properties** on the shortcut menu. The left side of Figure 7-39 shows the Properties box for the onboard wireless network adapter. Many times, a message shows up in this box reporting the source of the problem and suggesting a solution.

Source: Microsoft Windows 7

Figure 7-39 Use the device Properties box to solve problems with device drivers

▲ *Update the drivers:* Click the **Driver** tab (see the right side of Figure 7-39) to update the drivers and roll back (undo) a driver update.

APPLYING │ CONCEPTS

Follow these steps to use Device Manager to update device drivers:

1. For best results, locate and download the latest driver files from the manufacturer's web site to your hard drive. Be sure to use 64-bit drivers for a 64-bit OS and 32-bit drivers for a 32-bit OS. If possible, use Windows 7 drivers for Windows 7 and Vista drivers for Vista.

2. Using Device Manger, right-click the device and select **Properties** from the shortcut menu. The Properties window for that device appears. Select the **Driver** tab and click **Update Driver**. The Update Driver Software box opens (see Figure 7-40).

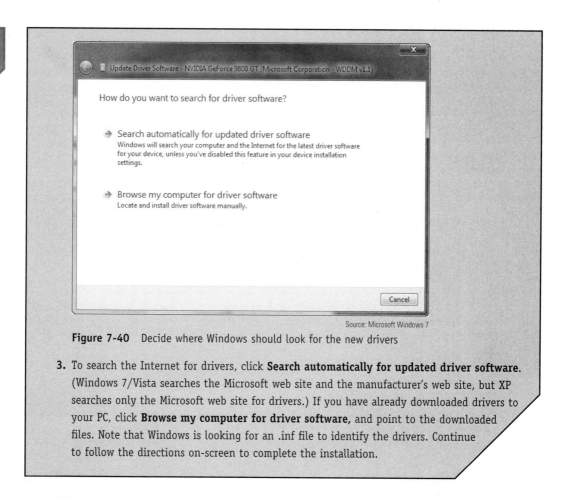

Source: Microsoft Windows 7

Figure 7-40   Decide where Windows should look for the new drivers

3. To search the Internet for drivers, click **Search automatically for updated driver software**. (Windows 7/Vista searches the Microsoft web site and the manufacturer's web site, but XP searches only the Microsoft web site for drivers.) If you have already downloaded drivers to your PC, click **Browse my computer for driver software**, and point to the downloaded files. Note that Windows is looking for an .inf file to identify the drivers. Continue to follow the directions on-screen to complete the installation.

Notes By default, Device Manager hides legacy devices that are not Plug and Play. To view installed legacy devices, click the **View** menu of Device Manager, and check **Show hidden devices** (see Figure 7-41).

Source: Microsoft Windows 7

Figure 7-41   By default, Windows does not display legacy devices in Device Manager; you show these hidden devices by using the View menu

A+
220-802
1.2, 1.4,
1.5

PROBLEMS WITH LEGACY DEVICES

Older hardware devices might present a problem. A Windows Vista driver is likely to work in the Windows 7 installation because Vista and Windows 7 are so closely related. If the driver does not load correctly or gives errors, first search the web for a Windows 7 driver. If you don't find one, try running the Vista driver installation program in compatibility mode.

APPLYING | CONCEPTS

In the example that follows, we're using the installation program for a memory card reader/writer that worked under Vista but did not load correctly when we installed Windows 7. Follow these steps to use compatibility mode with the driver installation program:

1. Using Windows Explorer, locate the program file with an .exe file extension for the driver installation program. Right-click the program file and select **Troubleshoot compatibility** from the shortcut menu (see Figure 7-42). The Program Compatibility utility launches.

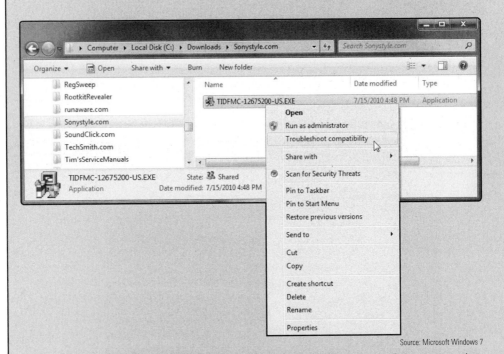

Source: Microsoft Windows 7

Figure 7-42   Run the Program Compatibility utility from the shortcut menu of the program that is giving a problem

2. On the first screen of the troubleshooter utility (see Figure 7-43), select **Troubleshoot program**.

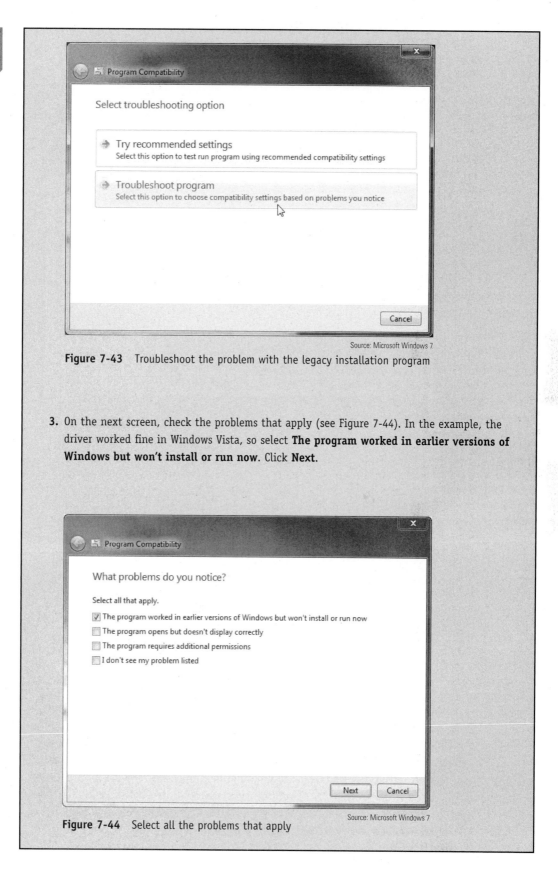

Figure 7-43 Troubleshoot the problem with the legacy installation program

3. On the next screen, check the problems that apply (see Figure 7-44). In the example, the driver worked fine in Windows Vista, so select **The program worked in earlier versions of Windows but won't install or run now**. Click **Next**.

Figure 7-44 Select all the problems that apply

A+
220-802
1.2, 1.4,
1.5

4. On the next screen, the troubleshooter asks for the OS with which the program worked (see Figure 7-45). For this example, you would select **Windows Vista (Service Pack 2)** and click **Next**.

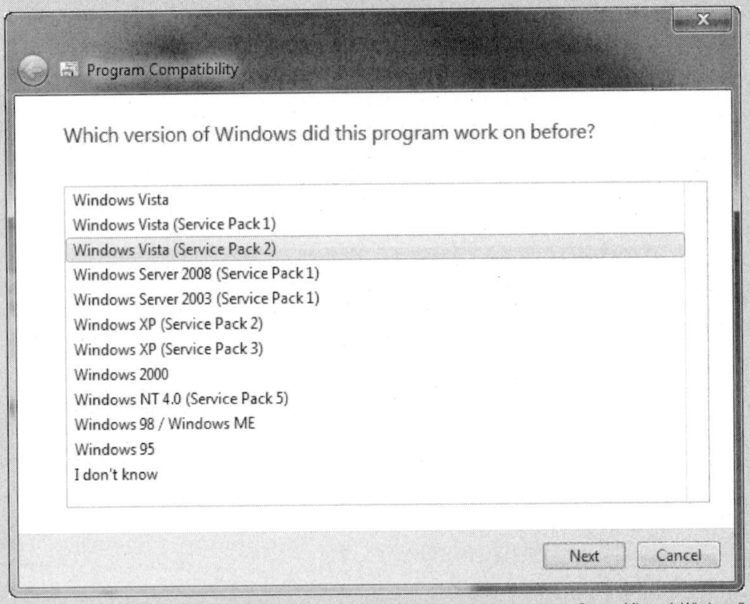

Source: Microsoft Windows 7

Figure 7-45 Select the operating system with which the program worked

5. On the next screen, click **Start the program** and respond to the UAC box. The program runs and successfully installs the drivers for the memory card device. Checking Device Manager shows no errors with the device. When you test the device, it can both read and write data to a memory card. Compatibility mode worked for this particular driver.

A+
220-802
1.2, 1.5

INSTALL APPLICATIONS

One application you want to be sure to install is antivirus software. To install applications, insert the setup CD or DVD, and follow the directions on-screen to launch the installation routine. For software downloaded from the Internet, open Windows Explorer and double-click the program filename to begin the installation. If you get errors, know that Chapter 12 covers what to do when an installation fails. After an application is installed, you might also need to install any updates available for the application on the manufacturer's web site.

If you need to uninstall an application, open Control Panel and click **Uninstall a program**. The **Programs and Features** window appears listing the programs installed on this computer where you can uninstall, change, or repair these programs. Select a program from the list. Based on the software, the buttons at the top of the list will change. For example, in Figure 7-46, the Camtasia Studio 7 software offers the option to Uninstall, Change, or Repair the software.

A+
220-802
1.2, 1.5

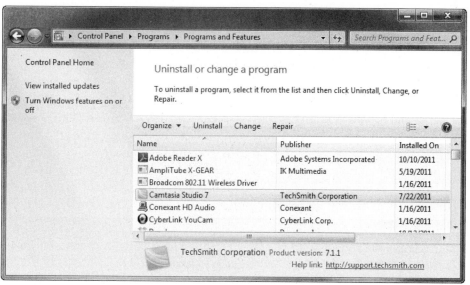

Source: Microsoft Windows 7

Figure 7-46 Select a program from the list to view your options to manage the software

A+
220-802
1.1, 1.2,
1.5

SET UP USER ACCOUNTS AND TRANSFER USER DATA

To set up a new user account, first log on using an administrator account and then do the following:

1. Open Control Panel and click **Add or remove user accounts**. In the Manage Accounts window, click **Create a new account**.

2. In the next window, enter the username (see Figure 7-47). Select if the account will be a standard user or administrator account. Click **Create Account**.

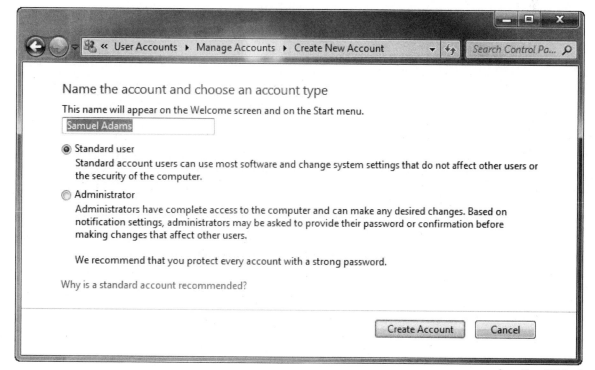

Source: Microsoft Windows 7

Figure 7-47 Decide the privilege level for the new account

3. To create a password for the account, in the Manage Accounts window, click the account icon and then click **Create a password**. Enter the new password and click **Create password**. The first time a user logs onto the account, user files and folders (called the user profile) are created in the C:\Users folder.

For individuals or small organizations, use **Windows Easy Transfer** in Windows 7/Vista or **Files and Settings Transfer Wizard** in Windows XP to copy user data and settings from one computer to another. How to use either utility can be found in Windows Help and Support for each operating system. For large corporations that use a Windows domain, a more advanced tool is required, the User State Migration Tool (USMT). This tool is discussed later in the chapter.

> **Notes** After moving user data and settings from one PC to another, the best practice is to leave the user data and settings on the original PC untouched for at least two months. This practice gives the user plenty of time to make sure everything has been moved over.

TURN WINDOWS 7 FEATURES ON OR OFF

You can save on system resources by turning off Windows features you will not use, and you might need to turn on some features that are, by default, turned off. To control Windows features, in the left pane of the Programs and Features window, click **Turn Windows features on or off** (refer to Figure 7-46). The Windows Features box opens (see Figure 7-48). Check or uncheck the features you want or don't want and then click **OK**.

Source: Microsoft Windows 7

Figure 7-48 Turn Windows features on or off

The Windows installation, devices, applications, and user accounts should now be good to go. Restart the computer and make one last check that all is well. Now would be a good time to complete your documentation and make a backup of the entire Windows volume in the event of a hard drive failure or corrupted installation. How to make backups is covered in Chapter 10.

SPECIAL CONCERNS WHEN WORKING IN A LARGE ENTERPRISE

A+
220-802
1.2, 1.4,
1.5

Working as a PC support technician in a large corporate environment is different from working as a PC support technician for a small company or with individuals. In this part of the chapter, you will learn how Windows is installed on computers in an enterprise and a little about providing ongoing technical support for Windows in these organizations.

DEPLOYMENT STRATEGIES FOR WINDOWS 7

Earlier in the chapter, you learned how to install Windows 7 using the setup DVD or using files downloaded from the Microsoft web site. You perform the installation while sitting at the computer, responding to each query made by the setup program. Then you must configure Windows and install device drivers and applications. If, however, you were responsible for installing Windows 7 on several hundred PCs in a large corporation, you might want a less time-consuming method to perform the installations. These methods are called deployment strategies. A deployment strategy is a procedure to install Windows, device drivers, and applications on a computer and can include the process to transfer user settings, application settings, and user data files from an old installation to the new installation.

Microsoft suggests four deployment strategies; the one chosen depends on the number of computers to be deployed and determines the amount of time you must sit in front of an individual computer as Windows is installed (this time is called the touch time). As a PC support technician in a large corporation, most likely you would not be involved in choosing or setting up the deployment strategy. But you need to be aware of the different strategies so that you have a general idea of what will be expected of you when you are asked to provide desk-side or help-desk support as Windows is being deployed in your organization.

The four deployment strategies are discussed next.

HIGH-TOUCH WITH RETAIL MEDIA (RECOMMENDED FOR FEWER THAN 100 COMPUTERS)

The **high-touch with retail media** strategy is the strategy used in the installations described earlier in the chapter. All the work is done by a technician sitting at the computer. To save time doing multiple installations, you can copy the setup files on the Windows setup DVD to a file server on the network and share the folder. Then at each computer, you can execute the Setup program on the server to perform a clean install or upgrade of the OS. A server used in this way is called a **distribution server**. Except for upgrade installations, applications must be manually installed after the OS is installed.

To transfer (called migrating) user settings, application settings, and user data files to a new installation, you can use Windows 7/Vista Windows Easy Transfer (a manual process that is easy to use) or the User State Migration Tool (more automated and more difficult to set up and use). Windows Easy Transfer is part of Windows 7/Vista, and XP offers a similar tool called the Files and Settings Transfer Wizard. The **User State Migration Tool (USMT)** is a command-line tool that works only when the computer is a member of a Windows domain. USMT is included in the **Windows Automated Installation Kit (AIK)** that can be downloaded from the Microsoft web site. The Windows AIK for Windows 7 contains a group of tools used to deploy Windows 7 in a large organization.

7

A+
220-802
1.2, 1.4,
1.5

HIGH-TOUCH WITH STANDARD IMAGE (RECOMMENDED FOR 100 TO 200 COMPUTERS)

To use the **high-touch using a standard image** strategy, a system administrator prepares an image called a **standard image** that includes Windows 7, drivers, and applications that are standard to all the computers that might use the image. A standard image is hardware independent, meaning it can be installed on any computer. (In Chapter 10, you learn to use Windows Backup and Restore to create another type of image, called a system image that can only be used on the computer that created it.)

> 💡 **A+ Exam Tip** The A+ 220-802 exam expects you to know about creating a standard image.

Drive-imaging software is used to clone the entire hard drive to another bootable media in a process called **drive imaging** or **disk cloning**. Tools included in the Windows AIK or third-party software can be used. Examples of third-party drive-imaging software are True Image by Acronis (*www.acronis.com*), Norton Ghost by Symantec Corp (*www.symantec.com*), and Clonezilla, freeware managed by NCHC (*www.clonezilla.org*). A standard image is usually stored on an 8 GB or larger bootable USB flash drive (UFD) or on a bootable DVD along with Windows setup files. How to create a standard image using the Windows AIK is covered in Appendix D. The process uses several tools that you will learn to use in Chapters 10 and 14.

> 📝 **Notes** To see an introduction to creating a standard image, check out this video at the Microsoft Technet site: *technet.microsoft.com/en-us/windows/ee530017.aspx*.

Installing a standard image on another computer is called **image deployment**, which always results in a clean install rather than an upgrade. To begin, boot the computer from the bootable UFD or DVD that contains the image. A menu appears to begin the Windows installation. When you finish this Windows installation, the standard image is installed. USMT can then be used to transfer user settings, user data files, and application settings to the new installation.

The high-touch using a standard image strategy takes longer to set up than the previous strategy because a system administrator must prepare the image and must set up USMT, but it takes less time to install on each computer and also assures the administrator that each computer has a standard set of drivers and applications that are configured correctly.

LITE-TOUCH, HIGH-VOLUME DEPLOYMENT (RECOMMENDED FOR 200 TO 500 COMPUTERS)

The **lite-touch, high-volume deployment** strategy uses a deployment server on the network to serve up the installation after a technician starts the process. The files in the installation include Windows, device drivers, and applications, and collectively are called the **distribution share**.

The technician starts the installation by booting the computer to Windows PE. **Windows Preinstallation Environment (Windows PE)** is a minimum operating system used to start the installation. It is included in the Windows AIK and can be installed on a USB flash drive, CD, or DVD to make the device bootable. The technician boots from the device, which might be configured to display a menu to choose from multiple distribution shares available on the deployment server.

The technician can also boot the PC directly to the network to receive Windows PE from the deployment server. To boot to the network, use BIOS setup to set the first item in the boot device priority to be Ethernet (see Figure 7-49). Then reboot the system. Startup BIOS boots to the **Preboot eXecution Environment (PXE, also known as the Pre-Execution Environment)** that is contained in the BIOS code on the motherboard. PXE searches for a server on the network to provide a bootable operating system (Windows PE on the deployment server).

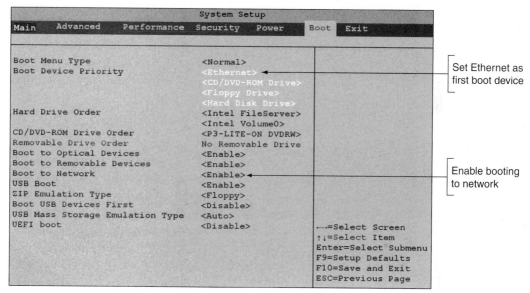

Figure 7-49 Configure BIOS setup to boot to the network

Source: Intel

After the installation begins, the technician is not required to respond to prompts by the setup program, which is called an **unattended installation**. These responses, such as the administrator password or domain name, are stored in an **answer file**. The User State Migration Tool is then used to transfer user settings, user data files, and application settings to the new installation.

For high-touch strategies, a technician would normally sit at a computer and use the Windows 7 Upgrade Advisor to determine if the system qualifies for Windows 7 before Windows 7 is installed. Using lite-touch deployments, a more automated method of qualifying a computer is preferred. The **Microsoft Assessment and Planning (MAP) Toolkit** can be used by a system administrator from a network location to query hundreds of computers in a single scan. The software automatically examines hardware and applications on each computer to verify compatibility with Windows 7. The MAP software might also be used by the system administrator before deciding to deploy a new OS to determine what computer hardware upgrades or application software upgrades are required that must be included in the overall deployment budget.

A+
220-802
1.2, 1.4,
1.5

ZERO-TOUCH, HIGH-VOLUME DEPLOYMENT (RECOMMENDED FOR MORE THAN 500 COMPUTERS)

The **zero-touch, high-volume deployment** strategy is the most difficult to set up and requires complex tools. The installation does not require the user to start the process (called **pull automation**). Rather, the installation uses **push automation**, meaning that a server automatically pushes the installation to a computer when a user is not likely to be sitting at it. The entire **remote network installation** is automated and no user intervention is required. The process can turn on a computer that is turned off and even works when no OS is installed on the computer or the current OS is corrupted.

> **Notes** PC support technicians find that large enterprises appreciate quick and easy solutions to desktop or laptop computer problems. Technicians quickly learn their marching orders are almost always "replace or reimage." Little time is given to trying to solve the underlying problem when hardware can quickly be replaced or a Windows installation can quickly be reimaged.

USING THE USMT SOFTWARE

Let's look briefly at what to expect when using the USMT software. The Windows 7 version of USMT is version 4.0, is much improved over earlier versions, and is included in the Windows AIK software. To prepare to use USMT, a system administrator must first install the AIK software on his computer. In Microsoft documentation, this computer is called the technician computer. The source computer is the computer from which the user settings, application settings, and user data files are taken. The destination computer is the computer that is to receive this data. Sometimes the source computer and the destination computer are the same computer. An example is when you perform a clean installation of Windows 7 on a computer that has Windows XP installed and you want to transfer user files and settings from the XP installation to the Windows 7 installation.

> **Notes** USMT 4.0 is the first version of USMT to use hard-link migration of user files and settings when the source computer and the destination computer are the same computer. Hard-link migration does not actually copy files and settings, but leaves them on the hard drive without copying. This method makes USMT extremely fast when the hard drive is not formatted during the Windows installation.

The USMT software uses two commands: the **scanstate** command copies settings and files from the source computer to a safe location, and the **loadstate** command applies these settings and files to the destination computer. Here are the general steps to use USMT:

1. Download and install the AIK software on the technician computer.

2. Copy the USMT program files from the technician computer to the source computer.

3. Run the scanstate command on the source computer to copy user files and settings to a file server or other safe location.

4. Install Windows 7, device drivers, and applications on the destination computer.

5. Run the loadstate command to apply user files and settings from the file server to the destination computer.

A+
220-802
1.2, 1.4,
1.5

🔘 A+ Exam Tip The A+ 220-802 exam expects you to know about the User State Migration Tool (USMT) and the scanstate and loadstate commands.

The details of the parameters for the scanstate and loadstate commands are not covered in this book. Most likely these commands are stored in batch files provided by the system administrator. A **batch file** has a .bat file extension and contains a list or batch of OS commands that are executed as a group. These batch files might be automatically executed as part of a zero-touch installation or manually executed in a lite-touch or high-touch installation. To manually execute a batch file, you type the name of the batch file at a command prompt.

📓 Notes For detailed instructions on using USMT that a system administrator might use, go to *technet.microsoft.com* and search on *using USMT for IT professionals*.

7

>> *CHAPTER SUMMARY*

How to Plan a Windows Installation

▲ The Windows 7 editions are Windows 7 Starter, Home Basic, Home Premium, Professional, Enterprise, and Ultimate.

▲ Windows can be purchased as the less expensive OEM version or the more expensive retail version. The OEM version can only be installed on a new PC for resale.

▲ Each edition of Windows 7 can be purchased using 32-bit or 64-bit code, except the Starter edition uses 32-bit code.

▲ A 32-bit OS cannot address as much memory as a 64-bit OS. A 64-bit OS performs better and requires more memory than a 32-bit OS.

▲ Before purchasing Windows, make sure your system meets the minimum hardware requirements and all the hardware and applications will work under the OS. A 64-bit OS requires 64-bit drivers.

▲ Windows can be installed from the setup DVD, from files downloaded from the Internet, from a hidden partition on the hard drive (called a factory recovery partition), or in a virtual machine.

▲ Windows can be installed as an in-place upgrade, a clean installation, or in a dual boot environment with another OS.

▲ A hard drive contains one or more partitions or volumes. Normally, Windows is installed on the C: volume in the C:\Windows folder.

▲ Windows supports two types of user accounts. An administrator account has more rights than a standard account.

▲ A Windows computer can use a homegroup, workgroup, or domain configuration to join a network. Using a workgroup or homegroup, each computer on the network is responsible for sharing its resources with other computers on the network. In a domain, the domain controller manages network resources. Windows Home editions cannot join a domain. Windows Starter and Home Basic can join a homegroup but cannot create one.

Installing Windows 7

▲ A technician needs to know how to perform Windows 7 as an in-place upgrade, a clean install, or a dual boot. In addition, you need to know how to install Windows on a new hard drive when using an upgrade license of the Windows setup DVD.

▲ Editions of Windows Vista are Vista Starter, Home Basic, Home Premium, Business, Enterprise, and Ultimate. A Vista installation works the same as a Windows 7 installation.

▲ Editions of XP are Home Edition, XP Professional, XP Professional x64 Edition, Media Center Edition, and Tablet PC Edition.

What to Do After a Windows Installation

▲ After a Windows installation, verify you have network access, activate Windows, install any Windows updates or service packs, verify automatic updates is configured correctly, install hardware and applications, create user accounts, and turn Windows features on or off.

Special Concerns When Working in a Large Enterprise

▲ Four deployment strategies for installing Windows are high-touch with retail media, high-touch with a standard image, lite-touch with high volume, and zero-touch with high volume. Which strategy to use depends on the number of computers to deploy. Zero-touch deployments require the most time to set up, but do not require a technician to be at the computer when the installation happens.

>> KEY TERMS

For explanations of key terms, see the Glossary near the end of the book.

Active Directory
administrator account
answer file
batch file
boot loader menu
Certificate of Authenticity
clean install
client/server
compatibility mode
custom installation
Device Manager
disk cloning
distribution server
distribution share
domain
drive imaging
dual boot
file system
Files and Settings Transfer Wizard
global account

high-touch using a standard image
high-touch with retail media
homegroup
image deployment
ImageX
in-place upgrade
ISO image
lite-touch, high-volume deployment
loadstate
local account
logical topology
Microsoft Assessment and Planning (MAP) Toolkit
multiboot
OEM (Original Equipment Manufacturer) license
partition
peer-to-peer (P2P)
physical topology

Preboot eXecution Environment (PXE, also known as the Pre-Execution Environment)
product activation
Programs and Features
pull automation
push automation
remote network installation
scanstate
setup BIOS
standard image
startup BIOS
system BIOS (basic input/ output system)
unattended installation
upgrade paths
User State Migration Tool (USMT)
virtual machine (VM)
volume

Windows 7 Enterprise
Windows 7 Home Basic
Windows 7 Home Premium
Windows 7 Professional
Windows 7 Starter
Windows 7 Ultimate
Windows Automated
    Installation Kit (AIK)
Windows Easy Transfer
Windows Preinstallation
    Environment (Windows PE)

Windows Vista Business
Windows Vista Enterprise
Windows Vista Home Basic
Windows Vista Home
    Premium
Windows Vista Starter
Windows Vista Ultimate
Windows XP Home Edition
Windows XP Media Center
    Edition
Windows XP Mode

Windows XP Professional
Windows XP Professional x64
    Edition
Windows XP Tablet PC
    Edition
workgroup
zero-touch, high-volume
    deployment

>> REVIEW QUESTIONS

1. Which Windows 7 version includes BitLocker Drive Encryption?

   a) Windows 7 Enterprise

   b) Windows 7 Home Premium

   c) Windows 7 Home Basic

   d) Windows 7 Professional

2. What is the simplest way to find out if a system can be upgraded to Windows 7?

   a) Run the User State Migration Tool (USMT) software.

   b) Run Device Manager.

   c) Run the startup BIOS.

   d) Run the Windows 7 Upgrade Advisor.

3. ____ is a group of settings that can be applied to older drivers or applications that might cause them to work in Windows 7.

   a) Drive imaging

   b) Home group

   c) Dual boot

   d) Compatibility mode

4. In the ____ connection option, Network Discovery is turned off and you cannot join a home-group or domain.

   a) Home network

   b) Work network

   c) Public network

   d) Private network

5. Which Windows 7 deployment strategy is the most difficult to set up and requires complex tools?

   a) Zero-touch, high-volume deployment

   b) Lite-touch, high-volume deployment

   c) High-touch using a standard image

   d) High-touch with retail media

6. True or false? A 64-bit OS can use both 32-bit drivers and 64-bit drivers.

7. True or false? There is no upgrade path from Windows XP to Windows 7.

8. True or false? A homegroup provides more security than a workgroup.

9. True or false? When selecting a network location connection, the Public network option is the most secure.

10. True or false? If you don't activate Windows 7 during the installation, you have 15 days to do so.

11. In the Windows 7 setup program, a clean install is called a(n) _____ installation.

12. In a Windows _____, each computer maintains a list of users and their rights on that particular PC.

13. Windows Server controls a network using the directory database called _____.

14. A Windows _____ is a logical group of networked computers that share a centralized directory database of user account information and security for the entire group of computers.

15. _____ is your primary Windows tool for managing hardware.

Supporting I/O
and Storage Devices

This chapter is packed full of details about the many I/O (input/ output) and mass storage devices a PC support technician must be familiar with and must know how to install and support. Most of us learn about new technologies as we need to use a device or when a client or customer requests our help with purchasing decisions or solving a problem with a device. Good technicians soon develop the skills of searching the web for explanations, reviews, and ads about a device and can quickly turn to support web sites for how to install, configure, or troubleshoot a device. This chapter can serve as your jumpstart toward learning about many computer parts and devices used to enhance a system. It contains enough information to get you started toward becoming an expert at computer devices.

We begin with the basic skills common to supporting any device, including how to use Device Manager and how to select the right port for a new peripheral device. Then you'll learn to install I/O devices and adapter cards and to support the video subsystem. Finally, you'll learn to select and install an optical drive and enough about memory cards that you'll know which type of card to buy for a particular need.

BASIC PRINCIPLES FOR SUPPORTING DEVICES

A+
220-801
1.5, 1.7,
1.10,
1.12

An I/O or storage device can be either internal (installed inside the computer case) or external (installed outside the case and called a peripheral device). These basic principles apply to supporting both internal and external devices:

▲ *Every device is controlled by software.* When you install a new device, such as a barcode reader or scanner, you must install both the device and the device drivers to control the device. These device drivers must be written for the OS you are using. Recall from earlier chapters that the exceptions to this principle are some simple devices, such as the keyboard, which are controlled by the system BIOS. Also, Windows has embedded device drivers for many devices. For example, when you install a video card, Windows can use its embedded drivers to communicate with the card, but to use all the features of the card, you can install the drivers that came bundled with it.

▲ *When it comes to installing or supporting a device, the manufacturer knows best.* In this chapter, you will learn a lot of principles and procedures for installing and supporting a device, but when you're on the job installing a device or fixing a broken one, read the manufacturer's documentation and follow those guidelines first. For example, for most installations, you install the device before you install the device driver. However, for some devices, such as a digital camera and a wireless keyboard, you might need to install the device driver first. Check the device documentation to know which to do first.

▲ *Some devices need application software to use the device.* For example, after you install a scanner and its device drivers, you might also need to install Adobe Photoshop to use the scanner.

▲ *A device is no faster than the port or slot it is designed to use.* When buying a new external device, pay attention to the type of port for which it is rated. For example, an external hard drive designed to use a USB 2.0 port will work at that speed even when it's connected to a faster USB 3.0 port. For another example, a TV tuner card in a PCI slot will not work as fast as a TV tuner card in a PCI Express slot because of the different speeds of the slots.

▲ *Use an administrator account in Windows.* When installing hardware devices under Windows, you need to be logged onto the system with a user account that has the highest level of privileges to change the system. This type of account is called an administrator account.

▲ *Problems with a device can sometimes be solved by updating the device drivers.* Device manufacturers often release updates to device drivers. Update the drivers to solve problems with the device or to add new features. You can use Device Manager in Windows to manage devices and their drivers.

▲ *Install only one device at a time.* If you have several devices to install, install one and restart the system. Make sure that device is working and all is well with the system before you move on to install another device.

A+
220-802
1.7

Now let's see how to use the Windows 7 Action Center and Windows 7/Vista/XP Device Manager. These tools can help you solve problems with installed devices.

USING THE ACTION CENTER AND DEVICE MANAGER

If a problem occurs while Windows 7 is installing a device, it automatically launches the Action Center to help find a solution. For example, Figure 8-1 shows the error message

A+
220-801
1.5, 1.7,
1.10,
1.12

A+
220-802
1.7

window that appeared when a USB keyboard and USB printer were first connected to a computer. (Windows Vista and XP do not have an Action Center.)

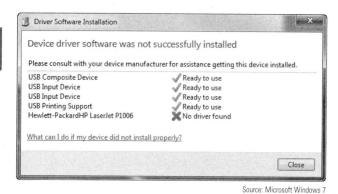

Source: Microsoft Windows 7

Figure 8-1   Windows 7 reports a problem with a driver for a USB printer

8

Immediately after this first window appeared, the Action Center provided the window shown in Figure 8-2. When the user clicked **Click to download and install the new driver from the Hewlett-Packard Company website**, the driver was immediately downloaded and installed with no errors.

Source: Microsoft Windows 7

Figure 8-2   Windows offers to find the missing USB printer driver

You can also open the Action Center at any time to see a list of problems and solutions. To open the Action Center, click **Start**, right-click **Computer**, and click **Properties**. In the System window, click **Action Center**. For example, the Action Center in Figure 8-3 shows a problem with a media reader. (A media reader is a device that can read and write to memory cards such as an SD card.) When you click a problem, you can follow on-screen directions toward a solution. If the problem is still not resolved after following the solutions offered by the Action Center, turn to Device Manager.

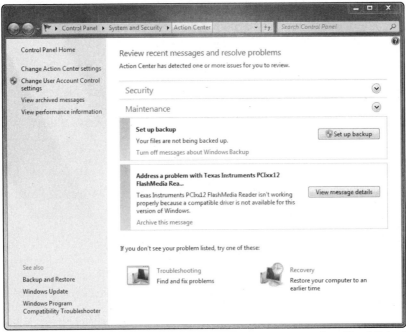

Source: Microsoft Windows 7

Figure 8-3 Use the Action Center to find a solution to a problem

Recall from Chapter 7 that **Device Manager** (its program file is named devmgmt.msc) is your primary Windows 7/Vista/XP tool for managing hardware. It lists almost all installed hardware devices and the drivers they use. (Printers and many USB devices are not listed in Device Manager.) Using Device Manager, you can disable or enable a device, update its drivers, uninstall a device, and undo a driver update (called a driver rollback).

To access Device Manager, use one of these methods, which you first learned about in Chapter 7:

▲ Click **Start**, right-click **Computer**, and select **Properties**. The System window appears. Click **Device Manager**. The Device Manager window opens.
▲ Enter **Device Manager** or **Devmgmt.msc** in the Search box and press **Enter**.

A Device Manager window is shown on the left side of Figure 8-4. Click a white arrow to expand the view of an item, and click a black arrow to collapse the view. Notice the yellow triangle beside the RAID controller, which indicates a problem with the device.

Here are ways to use Device Manager to solve problems with a device:

▲ *Look for error messages offered by Device Manager.* To find out more information about a device, right-click the device and select **Properties** on the shortcut menu. The right side of Figure 8-4 shows the properties box for the RAID controller. Many times, a message shows up in this box reporting the source of the problem and suggesting a solution.
▲ *Update the drivers or roll back (undo) a driver update.* Updating drivers can often solve a problem with a device. If a driver update creates a problem, you can roll back (undo) the driver update if the previous drivers were working. (Windows does

A+
220-801
1.5, 1.7,
1.10,
1.12

A+
220-802
1.7

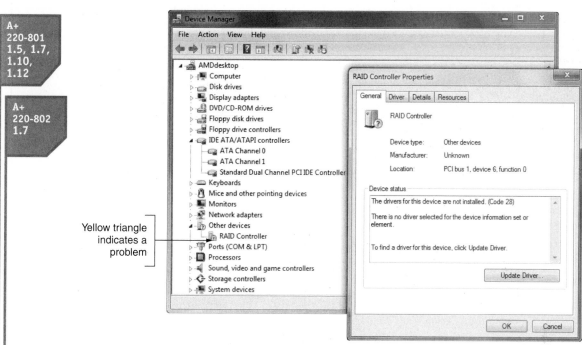

Yellow triangle
indicates a
problem

Figure 8-4 Use Device Manager to solve problems with hardware devices

not save drivers that were not working before the driver update.) Click the **Driver** tab. Figure 8-5 shows the Driver tab for one device. When you click **Update**, the box in Figure 8-6 appears.

To search the Internet for drivers, click **Search automatically for updated driver software**. (Windows 7/Vista searches the Microsoft web site and the manufacturer's

Figure 8-5 Update or roll back drivers for a device

A+
220-801
1.5, 1.7,
1.10,
1.12

A+
220-802
1.7

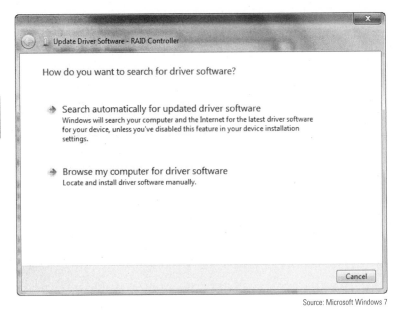

How do you want to search for driver software?

→ Search automatically for updated driver software
Windows will search your computer and the Internet for the latest driver software
for your device, unless you've disabled this feature in your device installation
settings.

→ Browse my computer for driver software
Locate and install driver software manually.

Source: Microsoft Windows 7

Figure 8-6   Decide where Windows should search to find the drivers

web site, but XP searches only the Microsoft web site for drivers.) If you have already downloaded drivers to your PC or you have the drivers on CD that came bundled with the device, click **Browse my computer for driver software,** and point to the downloaded files or to the CD. Note that Windows is looking for an .inf file to identify the drivers. Continue to follow the directions on-screen to complete the installation.

▲ *Try uninstalling and reinstalling the device.* If you are still having a problem with a device, try uninstalling it and installing it again. To uninstall the device, click **Uninstall** on the Driver tab (see Figure 8-5). Alternately, you can right-click the device and click Uninstall on the shortcut menu. Then reboot and reinstall the device, looking for problems during the installation that point to the source of the problem. Sometimes reinstalling a device is all that is needed to solve the problem.

If Windows is not able to locate new drivers for a device, locate and download the latest driver files from the manufacturer's web site to your hard drive. Be sure to use 64-bit drivers for a 64-bit OS and 32-bit drivers for a 32-bit OS. If possible, use Windows 7 drivers for Windows 7, and Vista drivers for Vista. You can double-click the downloaded driver files to launch the installation.

A few devices have firmware on the device that can be flashed similar to the way the BIOS on the motherboard is flashed. For example, after the RAID controller you saw in Figure 8-4 has its drivers installed, new tabs appear on the controller's properties box that are put there by the drivers (see Figure 8-7). To flash the firmware on this controller card, you first download the flash image file from the device manufacturer's web site. Then click **Browse** and locate the file. Next, click **Program Flash** to begin the firmware update.

Notes By default, Device Manager hides legacy devices that are not Plug and Play. To view installed legacy devices, click the **View** menu of Device Manager, and click **Show hidden devices** (see Figure 8-8).

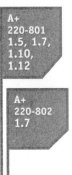

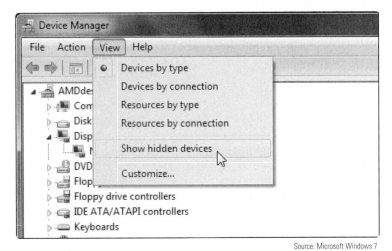

A+ 220-801 1.5, 1.7, 1.10, 1.12

A+ 220-802 1.7

Source: Microsoft Windows 7

Figure 8-7 Use the device's properties box to flash the firmware on some devices

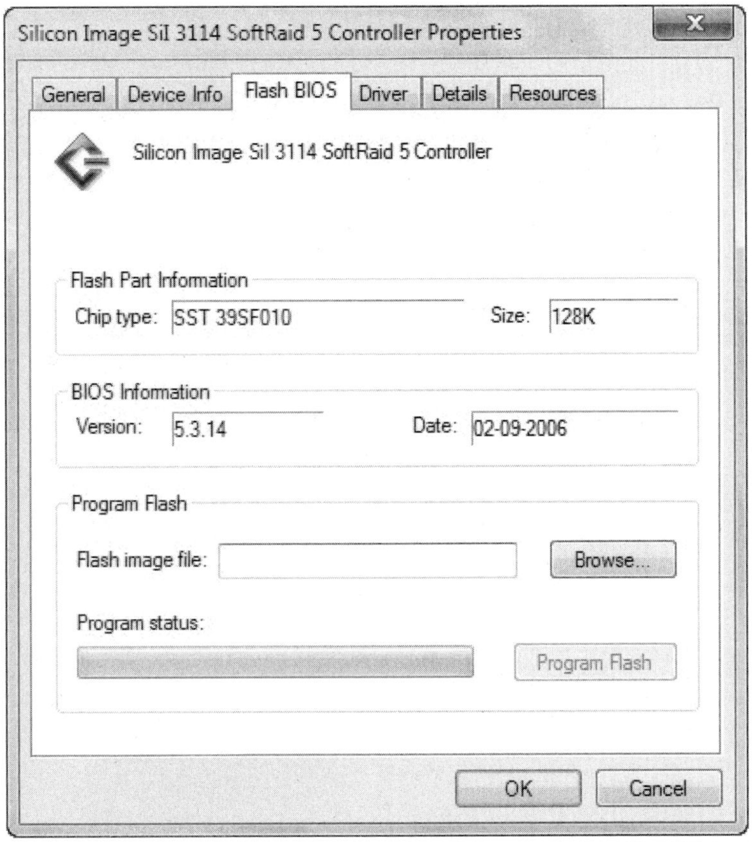

Source: Microsoft Windows 7

Figure 8-8 By default, Windows does not display legacy devices in Device Manager; you show these hidden devices by using the View menu

Before we move on to installing devices, you need to be familiar with the ports on a computer. When selecting a new device, to get the best performance, select one that uses the fastest port available on your computer.

8

A+
220-801
1.5, 1.7,
1.10,
1.12

PORTS AND WIRELESS CONNECTIONS USED BY PERIPHERAL DEVICES

Many ports used by peripheral or external devices are pictured in Table 1-1 in Chapter 1. When deciding what type of port a new device should use, the speed of the port is often a tiebreaker. Table 8-1 shows the speeds of various ports, from fastest to slowest. Because wireless connections are sometimes an option, they are also included in the table for comparison. For example, you might need to decide between a USB 2.0 printer connection and a Bluetooth wireless connection. This table can help you decide if speed should be a consideration.

> **💡 A+ Exam Tip**   The A+ 220-801 exam expects you to be able to compare the speeds and distances among USB (1.1, 2.0, and 3.0) and Firewire 400 and 800 ports and Bluetooth, Infrared, and RF wireless connections. The facts you need to know are found in Table 8-1.

Port or Wireless Type	Maximum Speed	Maximum Cable Length or Wireless Range
eSATA Version 3 (eSATA-600)	6.0 Gbps (gigabits per second)	Cable lengths up to 2 meters
SuperSpeed USB (USB 3.0)	5.0 Gbps	Cable lengths up to 3 meters
eSATA Version 2 (eSATA-300)	3.0 Gbps	Cable lengths up to 2 meters
eSATA Version 1 (eSATA-150)	1.5 Gbps or 1500 Mbps (megabits per second)	Cable lengths up to 2 meters
Firewire 800 (also called *1394b*)	1.2 Gbps or 800 Mbps	Cable lengths up to 100 meters
Wi-Fi 802.11n RF (radio frequency) of 2.4 GHz or 5.0 GHz	Up to 500 Mbps	Range up to 70 meters
Hi-Speed USB (USB 2.0)	480 Mbps	Cable lengths up to 5 meters
FireWire 400 (also called *1394a*)	400 Mbps	Cable lengths up to 4.5 meters
Original USB (USB 1.1)	12 Mbps or 1.5 Mbps	Cable lengths up to 3 meters
Parallel	1.5 Mbps	Cables up to 4.5 meters (15 feet)
Serial	115.2 Kbps (kilobits per second)	Cables up to 50 feet
Wi-Fi 802.11g RF of 2.4 GHz	Up to 54 Mbps	Range up to 100 meters
Wi-Fi 802.11a RF of 5.0 GHz	Up to 54 Mbps	Range up to 50 meters
Wi-Fi 802.11b RF of 2.4 GHz	Up to 11 Mbps	Range up to 100 meters
Bluetooth wireless RF of 2.4 GHz	Up to 3 Mbps	Range up to 10 meters
Infrared (IR) wireless Invisible light frequency range of 100 to 400 THz (terahertz or 1 trillion hertz) just above red light	Up to 4 Mbps for fast speed IR; up to 1.15 Mbps for medium speed IR, and up to 115 Kbps (kilobits per second) for slow speed IR	Range up to 5 meters

Table 8-1   Data transmission speeds for various port types and wireless connections

A+
220-801
1.5, 1.7,
1.10,
1.12

> 💡 **A+ Exam Tip** The A+ 220-801 exam expects you to know about some old technologies, including serial and parallel ports and cables. For this reason, they are listed in Table 1-1 even though you are unlikely to be called on to support these outdated technologies.

USB CONNECTIONS

Here is a summary of important facts you need to know about USB connections:

- ◢ The USB Implementers Forum, Inc. (*www.usb.org*), the organization responsible for developing USB, uses the symbols shown in Figure 8-9 to indicate SuperSpeed USB (USB 3.0), Hi-Speed USB (USB 2.0), or Original USB (USB 1.1).

Source: USB Forum

Figure 8-9 SuperSpeed, Hi-Speed, and Original USB logos appear on products certified by the USB forum

- ◢ As many as 127 USB devices can be daisy chained together using USB cables. In a daisy chain, one device provides a USB port for the next device.
- ◢ USB uses serial transmissions, and USB devices are **hot-swappable**, meaning that you can plug or unplug one without first powering down the system.
- ◢ A USB cable has four wires, two for power and two for communication. The two power wires (one is hot and the other is ground) allow the host controller to provide power to a device. Table 8-2 shows the different USB connectors on USB cables.

Cable and Connectors	Description
A-Male to B-Male cable © Cengage Learning 2014	The *A Male connector* on the left is flat and wide and connects to an A-Male USB port on a computer or USB hub. The *B Male connector* on the right is square and connects to a USB 1.x or 2.0 device such as a printer.
Mini-B to A-Male cable © Cengage Learning 2014	The *Mini-B connector* has five pins and is often used to connect small electronic devices, such as a digital camera, to a computer.

© Cengage Learning 2014

Table 8-2 USB connectors (continues)

8

A+
220-801
1.5, 1.7,
1.10,
1.12

Cable and Connectors	Description
A-Male to Micro-B cable © Cengage Learning 2014	The *Micro-B connector* has five pins and has a smaller height than the Mini-B connector. It's used on digital cameras, cell phones, and other small electronic devices.
A-Male to Micro-A cable © Cengage Learning 2014	The *Micro-A connector* has five pins and is smaller than the Mini-B connector. It's used on digital cameras, cell phones, and other small electronic devices.
USB 3.0 A-Male to USB 3.0 B-Male cable © Cengage Learning 2014	This USB 3.0 B-Male connector is used by SuperSpeed USB 3.0 devices such as printers or scanners. Devices that have this connection can also use regular B-Male connectors, but this USB 3.0 B-Male connector will not fit the connection on a USB 1.1 or 2.0 device. USB 3.0 A-Male and B-Male connectors and ports are blue.
USB 3.0 A-Male to USB 3.0 Micro-B cable © Cengage Learning 2014	The *USB 3.0 Micro-B connector* is used by SuperSpeed USB 3.0 devices. The connectors are not compatible with regular Micro-B connectors.

© Cengage Learning 2014

Table 8-2 USB connectors (continued)

> **Notes** A USB 3.0 A-Male connector or port has additional pins compared to USB 1.1 or 2.0 ports and connectors but still is backward compatible with USB 1.1 and 2.0 devices. A USB 3.0 A-Male or B-Male connector or port is usually blue. Take a close look at the blue and black USB ports shown in Figure 1-4 in Chapter 1.

FIREWIRE (IEEE 1394) CONNECTIONS

USB and FireWire competed as a solution for fast I/O connections for a few years, but USB clearly won that contest, and now FireWire is hardly used in new devices. FireWire standards are managed by the 1394 Trade Association (*www.1394ta.org*). The official name

A+
220-801
1.5, 1.7,
1.10,
1.12

of these standards is IEEE 1394, and other names used are FireWire (first used by Apple) and i.LINK (first used by Sony). The most common name used today is FireWire. Here are the key facts you need to know about FireWire:

▲ FireWire uses serial transmissions, and Firewire devices are hot-swappable.
▲ **FireWire 800 (1394b)** allows for up to 63 FireWire devices to be daisy chained together. FireWire 400 (1394a) allows for up to 16 daisy-chained devices.
▲ **FireWire 400 (1394a)** supports two types of connectors and cables: a 4-pin connector that does not provide voltage to a device and a 6-pin connector that does. Figure 8-10 shows a cable that plugs into a 6-pin FireWire port to provide a 4-pin connector for a FireWire device.

Notes IEEE 1394a ports with six pins are the most common FireWire ports on motherboards.

Video
FireWire Ports

8

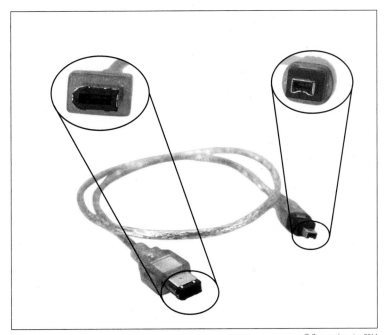

© Cengage Learning 2014

Figure 8-10   IEEE 1394a cable provides a smaller 4-pin and larger 6-pin connectors

▲ FireWire 800 (1394b) uses a 9-pin rectangular connector. Figure 8-11 shows a FireWire 800 adapter card that provides three 1394 ports: two 1394b 9-pin ports and one 1394a 6-pin port. The power cable connected to the card plugs into a 4-pin Molex power cable from the power supply to provide extra power to the card. The latest 1394 standard is 1394c, which allows FireWire 800 to use a standard network port and network cable.

A+
220-801
1.5, 1.7,
1.10,
1.12

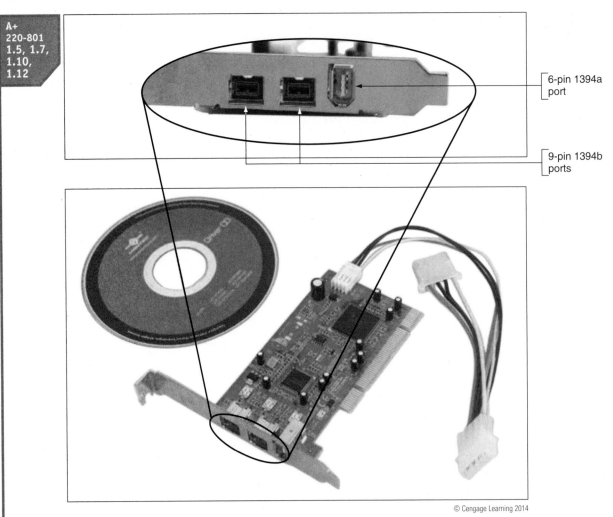

6-pin 1394a
port

9-pin 1394b
ports

© Cengage Learning 2014

Figure 8-11 This 1394 adapter card supports both 1394a and 1394b and uses a 32-bit PCI slot

INFRARED CONNECTIONS

Infrared (IR) is an outdated wireless technology that has been mostly replaced by Bluetooth to connect personal devices. IR requires an unobstructed "line of sight" between the transmitter and receiver. Today, the most common use of Infrared is by remote controls. Figure 8-12 shows a remote control that can be used with multimedia applications installed on a notebook computer. The remote communicates with the notebook by way of an IR transceiver connected to a USB port. To use the remote, the device drivers that came bundled with the device are installed and then the IR transceiver is connected to the USB port.

> **Notes** Infrared standards are defined by the Infrared Data Association (IrDA). Its web site is *www.irda.org*.

© Cengage Learning 2014

Figure 8-12   This remote control is an Infrared device that uses an IR transceiver connected to a notebook by way of a USB port

8

Now that you know about the ports and wireless connections used for external devices, let's see how to install them.

INSTALLING I/O PERIPHERAL DEVICES

Installing peripheral or external devices is easy to do and usually goes without a hitch. All devices need device drivers or BIOS to control them and to interface with the operating system. Simple input devices, such as the mouse and keyboard, can be controlled by the BIOS or have embedded device drivers built into the OS. For these devices, you don't have to install additional device drivers.

Peripheral devices you might be called on to install include a keyboard, mouse, barcode reader, biometric device (for example, a fingerprint reader), touch screen, scanner, microphone, game pad, joystick, digitizer, digital camera, web cam, camcorder, MDI-enabled devices, speakers, and display devices. These installations are similar, so learning to do one will help you do another. Here are the general procedures to install any peripheral device:

1. **Read the manufacturer's directions.** I know you don't want to hear that again, but when you follow these directions, the installation goes better. If you later have a problem with the installation and you ask the manufacturer for help, being able to say you followed their directions exactly as stated goes a long way toward getting more enthusiastic help and cooperation.

A+
220-801
1.5, 1.7,
1.10,
1.12

2. **Make sure the drivers provided with the device are written for the OS you are using.**
Recall that 64-bit drivers are required for a 64-bit operating system, and 32-bit drivers are required for a 32-bit OS. You can sometimes use drivers written for Vista in Windows 7, but for best results, use drivers written for the OS installed. You can download the drivers you need from the manufacturer's web site.

3. **Make sure the motherboard port you are using is enabled.** Most likely it is enabled, but if the device is not recognized when you plug it in, go into BIOS setup and make sure the port is enabled. In addition, BIOS setup might offer the option to configure a USB port to use SuperSpeed (USB 3.0), Hi-Speed USB (USB 2.0), or original USB (USB 1.1). Figure 8-13 shows the BIOS setup screen for one system where you can enable or disable onboard devices. In addition, if you are having problems with a motherboard port, don't forget to update the motherboard drivers that control the port.

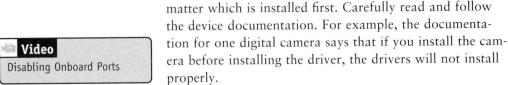

```
                                System Setup
 Main   Configuration   Performance   Security   Power   Boot   Exit

 Onboard Devices                                           If enabled,
                                                           HDMI/DisplayPort output
 Enhanced Consumer IR            <Disable>                 includes both audio and
 Audio                           <Enable>                  video. If disabled,
    Front Panel Audio            <Auto>                    HDMI/DisplayPort output i
 HDMI/DisplayPort Audio          <Enable>                  video only.
 LAN                             <Enable>
 1394                            <Enable>

 USB

 Num Lock                        <On>
 PCI Latency Timer               <32>



                                                           ← →: Select Screen
                                                           ↑ ↓: Select Item
                                                           Enter:Select
                                                           +/-: Change Opt.
                                                           F9: Load Defaults
                                                           F10:Save ESC:Exit
```

Source: Intel

Figure 8-13   Use BIOS setup to enable or disable onboard ports

4. **Install drivers or plug in the device.** Some devices, such as a USB printer, require that you plug in the device before installing the drivers, and some devices require you to install the drivers before plugging in the device. For some devices, it doesn't matter which is installed first. Carefully read and follow the device documentation. For example, the documentation for one digital camera says that if you install the camera before installing the driver, the drivers will not install properly.

▶ **Video**

Disabling Onboard Ports

If you plug in the device first, The Found New Hardware wizard appears and steps you through the installation of drivers (see Figure 8-14).

Source: Microsoft Windows 7

Figure 8-14 The Found New Hardware wizard begins installing a new device

8

If you need to install the drivers first, run the setup program on CD or DVD. If you downloaded drivers from the web, double-click the driver file and follow the directions on-screen. It might be necessary to restart the system after the installation. After the drivers are installed, plug the device into the port. The device should immediately be recognized by Windows. If you have problems using the device, turn to Device Manager or the Windows 7 Action Center for help.

5. **Install the application software to use the device.** For example, a FireWire camcorder is likely to come bundled with video-editing software. Run the software to use the device.

Now let's look at some key features and installation concerns for several peripheral devices.

MOUSE OR KEYBOARD

Plug a mouse or keyboard into a USB or older PS/2 port and Windows should immediately recognize it and install generic drivers. For keyboards with special features such as the one shown in Figure 8-15, you need to install the drivers that came with the keyboard before you can use these features.

You can later use Device Manager to uninstall, disable, or enable most devices. However, USB devices are managed differently. To uninstall a USB device such as the USB keyboard shown in Figure 8-15, in Control Panel, click **Uninstall a program**. In the Programs and Features window (see Figure 8-16), select the device and click **Change**. Follow the directions on-screen to uninstall the device.

BARCODE READERS

A **barcode reader** is used to scan barcodes on products at the point of sale (POS) or when taking inventory. The reader might use a wireless connection, a serial port, a USB port, or a keyboard port. If the reader uses a keyboard port, most likely it has a splitter (called a keyboard wedge) on it for the keyboard to use, and data read by the barcode reader is input into the system as though it were typed using the keyboard. Figure 8-17 shows a barcode reader by Intermec that is a laser scanner and uses Bluetooth to connect wirelessly to the PC.

A+
220-801
1.5, 1.7,
1.10,
1.12

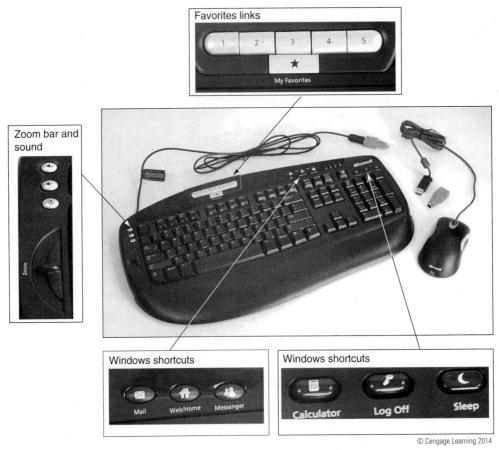

© Cengage Learning 2014

Figure 8-15 The mouse and keyboard require drivers to use the extra buttons and zoom bar

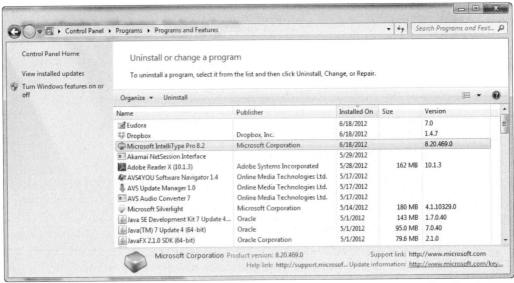

Source: Microsoft Windows 7

Figure 8-16 USB devices are listed as installed programs

A+
220-801
1.5, 1.7,
1.10,
1.12

Courtesy of Intermec Technologies

Figure 8-17 Handheld or hands-free barcode scanner by Intermec Technologies

BIOMETRIC DEVICES

A **biometric device** is an input device that inputs biological data about a person, which can be input data to identify a person's fingerprints, handprints, face, voice, eye, and handwritten signature. For example, you can use a fingerprint reader to log on to Windows. These fingerprint readers are not to be considered as the only authentication to control access to sensitive data: for that, use a strong password, which is a password that is not easy to guess.

Fingerprint readers can look like a mouse and use a wireless or USB connection, such as the one shown in Figure 8-18, or they can be embedded on a keyboard, flash drive, or laptop case. Most fingerprint readers that are not embedded in other devices use a USB connection. As with other USB devices, read the documentation to know if you should install the drivers first or the device first.

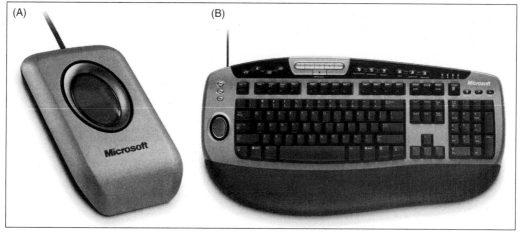

(A)   (B)

Used with permission from Microsoft

Figure 8-18 Fingerprint readers can (a) look like a mouse, but smaller, or (b) be embedded on a keyboard

8

A+
220-801
1.5, 1.7,
1.10,
1.12

DIGITAL CAMERAS AND CAMCORDERS

A digital camera or camcorder can hold images and videos both in embedded memory that cannot be removed or exchanged and in removable flash memory cards. Both of these types of memory retain data without a battery. Here are two ways to transfer images from your camera or camcorder to the PC:

▲ *Connect the camera or camcorder to the PC using a cable.* Using embedded memory or flash memory cards, you can connect the device to your computer using a USB or FireWire port and cable. To connect the device to the PC, you might need to first install the software and then connect the device, or you might need to connect the device and then install the software. Read the camera or camcorder documentation to find out which order to use. After the device and software are installed, the software displays a menu to download images or video to your PC.

▲ *Install the memory card in the PC.* If images or video are stored on a flash memory card installed in your device, you can remove the card and then insert it in a flash memory card slot on your computer. Most laptop computers have one or more of these slots (see Figure 8-19).

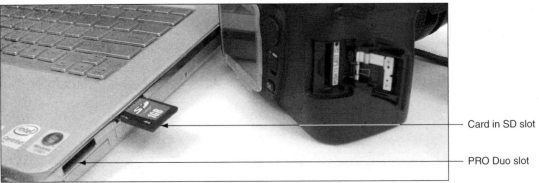

Card in SD slot

PRO Duo slot

© Cengage Learning 2014

Figure 8-19   This laptop has two flash memory card slots

If your computer doesn't have this slot, or the slot is not compatible with the type of card you are using, you have two choices:

- Perhaps you can purchase an adapter so that your smaller memory card will fit into a larger memory slot. Figure 8-20 shows examples of these adapters.
- You can install a USB memory card reader that provides a memory card slot to fit your card. Figure 8-21 shows one reader that connects to a PC using a USB port.

When the memory card is recognized by Windows, it is assigned a drive letter and you can see it listed in Windows Explorer. Use Windows Explorer to copy, move, and delete files from the card.

> **Notes**   It's interesting to know that TWAIN (Technology Without An Interesting Name) is a standard format used by scanners and digital cameras and other devices for transferring images.

> **A+ Exam Tip**   The A+ 220-801 exam expects you to know how to install the software bundled with your digital camera before attaching the camera to your PC.

A+
220-801
1.5, 1.7,
1.10,
1.12

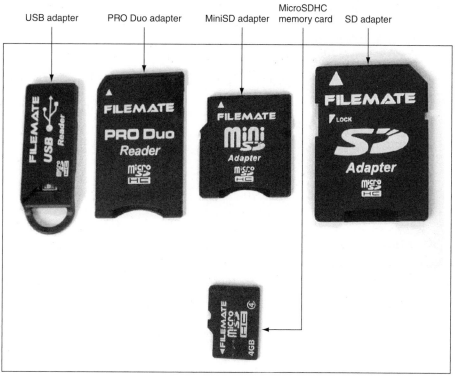

USB adapter   PRO Duo adapter   MiniSD adapter   MicroSDHC memory card   SD adapter

© Cengage Learning 2014

Figure 8-20   MicroSDHC card with four adapters

© Cengage Learning 2014

Figure 8-21   This Hi-Speed USB card reader/writer by Targus can read CompactFlash I and II, MicroDrive, SDHC, SD, MMC, xD, Memory Stick, PRO Duo, and Mini SD cards

WEBCAMS

A webcam (web camera) is embedded in most laptops and can also be installed as a peripheral device using a USB port or some other port. For example, the webcam shown in Figure 8-22 works well for personal chat sessions and videoconferencing and has a built-in microphone. First, use the setup CD to install the software and then plug in the webcam to a USB port.

A webcam comes with a built-in microphone. You can use this microphone or use the microphone port on the computer. Most software allows you to select these input devices. For example, Figure 8-23 shows the Tools Options box for Camtasia Recorder by TechSmith (*www.techsmith.com*).

A+
220-801
1.5, 1.7,
1.10,
1.12

© iStockphoto/Eric Ferfuson

Figure 8-22 This personal web camera clips to the top of your notebook and has a built-in microphone

Source: Camtasia Recorder by TechSmith

Figure 8-23 The Camtasia Recorder application allows you to change the input devices used for video and sound

GRAPHICS TABLETS

Another input device is a **graphics tablet**, also called a **digitizing tablet** or **digitizer**, that is used to hand draw and is likely to connect by a USB port (see Figure 8-24). It comes with a **stylus** that works like a pencil on the tablet. The graphics tablet and stylus can be a replacement to a mouse or touch pad on a laptop, and some graphics tablets come with a mouse. Graphics tablets are popular with graphic artists and others who use desktop publishing applications.

Install the graphics tablet the same way you do other USB devices. Additional software might be bundled with the device to enhance its functions, such as inputting handwritten signatures into Microsoft Word documents.

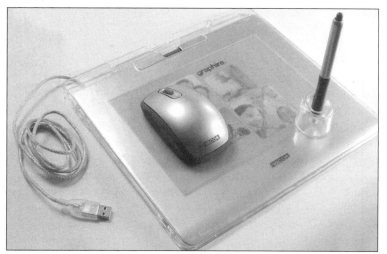

© Cengage Learning 2014

Figure 8-24 A graphics tablet and stylus are used to digitize a hand drawing

MIDI DEVICES

MIDI (musical instrument digital interface), pronounced "middy," is a set of standards that are used to represent music in digital form. Using the MIDI format, each individual note played by each individual instrument is digitally stored. MIDI standards are used to connect electronic music equipment, such as musical keyboards and mixers, or to connect this equipment to a PC for input, output, and editing. Most sound cards can play MIDI files, and most electronic instruments have MIDI ports.

A MIDI port is a 5-pin DIN port that looks like a PS/2 keyboard port, only larger. Figure 8-25 shows MIDI ports on electronic drums. A MIDI port is either an input port

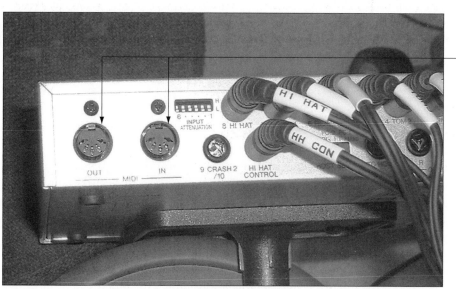

5-pin MIDI-out and MIDI-in ports

© Cengage Learning 2014

Figure 8-25 MIDI ports on an electronic drum set

or an output port, but not both. Normally, you would connect the MIDI output port to a mixer, but you can also use it to connect to a PC.

Here are ways to connect a musical instrument to a PC using the MIDI standards:

- *MIDI to MIDI:* A few sound cards provide MIDI ports. Use two MIDI cables to connect output jack to input jack and to connect input jack to output jack.
- *MIDI to USB:* If your PC does not have MIDI ports, you can use a MIDI-to-USB cable like the one in Figure 8-26. The two MIDI connectors on the cable are for input and output.
- *USB to USB:* Newer instruments have a USB port to interface with a PC using MIDI data transmissions.
- *USB to MIDI:* A USB port on an instrument can also connect to MIDI ports on a computer sound card.

> **A+ Exam Tip**   The A+ 220-801 exam expects you to know how to install and configure MIDI devices.

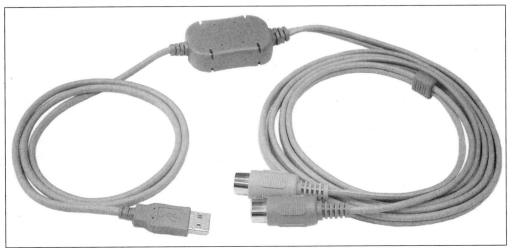

© Cengage Learning 2014

Figure 8-26   MIDI-to-USB cable lets you connect an electronic musical instrument to your computer

To mix and edit music using MIDI on your PC, you'll need MIDI editing software such as JAMMER Pro by SoundTrek (*www.soundtrek.com*). Before connecting the instrument to your PC, install the software that you intend to use to manage the music. Then, connect the instrument.

TOUCH SCREENS

A **touch screen** is an input device that uses a monitor or LCD panel as the backdrop for input options. In other words, the touch screen is a grid that senses taps, finger pinches, and slides and sends these events to the computer by way of a USB port or other type of connection. Some laptops have built-in touch screens, and you can also install a touch screen on top of a monitor screen as an add-on device. As an add-on device, the touch screen has its own AC adapter to power it. Some monitors for desktop systems have built-in touch screen capability.

For desktop monitors, clamp the touch screen over the monitor. For most installations, you install the drivers before you connect the touch screen to the computer by way of a USB port. After you install the drivers and the touch screen, you must use management software that came bundled with the device to decide how much of the monitor screen is taken up by the touch screen and to calibrate the touch screen. Later, if the monitor resolution is changed, the touch screen must be recalibrated.

KVM SWITCHES

A **KVM (Keyboard, Video, and Mouse) switch** allows you to use one keyboard, monitor, and mouse for multiple computers. A KVM switch can be useful in a server room or testing lab where you use more than one computer and want to keep desk space clear of multiple keyboards, mice, and monitors or you simply want to lower the cost of peripherals. Figure 8-27 shows a KVM switch that can connect a keyboard, monitor, mouse, microphone, and speakers to two computers. The device uses USB ports for the keyboard and mouse. Figure 8-28 shows a KVM switch that can connect up to four computers using VGA ports for the monitor and PS/2 ports for the keyboard and mouse connections. The setup for the four computers is shown in Figure 8-29.

8

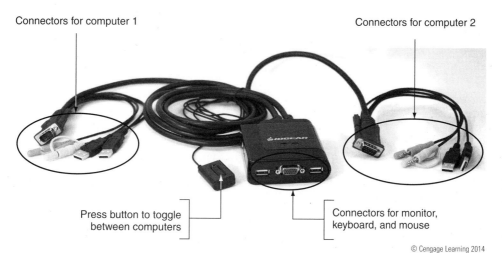

Connectors for computer 1

Connectors for computer 2

Press button to toggle between computers

Connectors for monitor, keyboard, and mouse

© Cengage Learning 2014

Figure 8-27 This KVM switch connects two computers to a keyboard, mouse, monitor, microphone, and speakers and uses USB for the keyboard and mouse

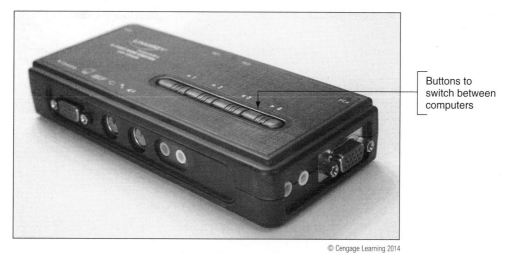

Buttons to switch between computers

© Cengage Learning 2014

Figure 8-28 This KVM switch supports up to four computers, uses PS/2 ports for the keyboard and mouse, and provides microphone and speaker ports for sound

A+
220-801
1.5, 1.7,
1.10,
1.12

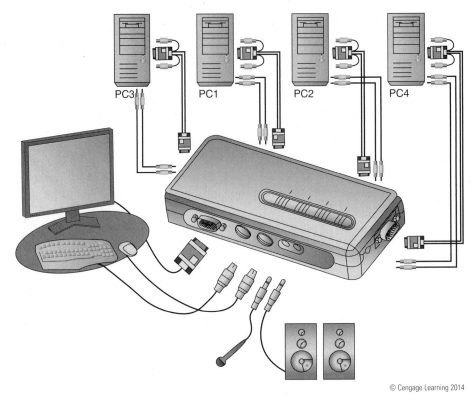

© Cengage Learning 2014

Figure 8-29   Hardware configuration for a four-port KVM switch that also supports audio

A KVM switch does not require that you install device drivers to use it. Just plug in the cables from each computer to the device. Also plug in the one monitor, mouse, keyboard, and possibly a microphone and speakers to the device. Switch between computers by using a hot key on the keyboard, buttons on the top of the KVM switch, or a wired remote such as the one shown in Figure 8-27.

INSTALLING AND CONFIGURING ADAPTER CARDS

A+
220-801
1.4, 1.5,
1.7, 1.10,
1.12

In this part of the chapter, you will learn to install and configure adapter cards. These cards include a video card, sound card, storage controller card, serial and parallel port card, FireWire card, USB card, storage card, TV tuner card, and video capture card. The purpose of adding an adapter card to a system is to have available the external ports or internal connectors the card provides.

Regardless of the type of card you are installing, when preparing to install an adapter card, be sure to verify and do the following:

▲ *Verify the card fits an empty expansion slot.* Recall from Chapter 4 that there are several AGP, PCI, and PCI Express standards. Use the details in Chapter 4 to make sure the card will fit the slot. To help with airflow, try to leave an empty slot between cards. Especially try to leave an empty slot beside the video card, which puts off a lot of heat.

▲ *Verify the device drivers for your OS are available.* Check the card documentation and make sure you have the drivers for your OS. For example, you need to install 64-bit Windows 7 drivers in a 64-bit installation of Windows 7. It might be possible to download drivers for your OS from the web site of the card manufacturer.

A+
220-801
1.4, 1.5,
1.7, 1.10,
1.12

▲ *Back up important data that is not already backed up.* Before you open the computer case, be sure to back up important data on the hard drive.

▲ *Know your starting point.* Know what works and doesn't work on the system. Can you connect to the network and the Internet, print, and use other installed adapter cards without errors?

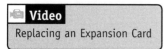

Video
Replacing an Expansion Card

Here are the general directions to install an adapter card. They apply to any type of card.

1. Read the documentation that came with the card. For most cards, you install the card first and then the drivers, but some adapter card installations might not work this way.

2. If you are installing a card to replace an onboard port, access BIOS setup and disable the port.

3. Wear a ground bracelet as you work to protect the card and the system against ESD. Shut down the system, unplug power cords and cables, and press the power button to drain the power. Remove the computer case cover.

4. Locate the slot you plan to use and remove the faceplate cover from the slot if one is installed. Sometimes a faceplate punches or snaps out, and sometimes you have to remove a faceplate screw to remove the faceplate. Remove the screw in the top of the expansion slot. Save the screw; you'll need it later.

5. Remove the card from its antistatic bag and insert it into the expansion slot. Be careful to push the card straight down into the slot, without rocking the card from side to side. Rocking it from side to side can widen the expansion slot, making it difficult to keep a good contact. If you have a problem getting the card into the slot, resist the temptation to push the front or rear of the card into the slot first. You should feel a slight snap as the card drops into the slot.

Recall from Chapter 2 that AGP and PCIe x16 slots use a retention mechanism in the slot to help stabilize a heavy card (see Figure 8-30). For these slots, you might have to use one finger to push the stabilizer to the side as you push the card into the slot. Alternately, the card might snap into the slot and then the retention mechanism snaps into position. Figure 8-31 shows a PCIe video card installed in a PCIe x16 slot.

© Cengage Learning 2014

Figure 8-30 A white retention mechanism on a PCIe x16 slot pops into place to help stabilize a heavy video card

A+
220-801
1.4, 1.5,
1.7, 1.10,
1.12

Regular PCI slots

Video card

PCI Express x16 slot

PCI Express x1 slots

© Cengage Learning 2014

Figure 8-31   A PCIe video card installed in a PCIe x16 slot

6. Insert the screw that anchors the card to the top of the slot (see Figure 8-32). Be sure to use this screw. If it's not present, the card can creep out of the slot over time.

Figure 8-32   Secure the card to the case with a single screw

© Cengage Learning 2014

A+
220-801
1.4, 1.5,
1.7, 1.10,
1.12

7. Connect any power cords or data cables the card might use. For example, a video card might have a 6-pin or 8-pin PCIe power connector for a power cord from the power supply to the card (see Figure 8-33). (If the power supply does not have the right connector, you can buy an inexpensive adapter to convert a 4-pin Molex connector to a PCIe connector.) In another example, look at Figure 8-11 shown earlier in the chapter. This FireWire card requires a power connection using a 4-pin Molex power cable from the power supply.

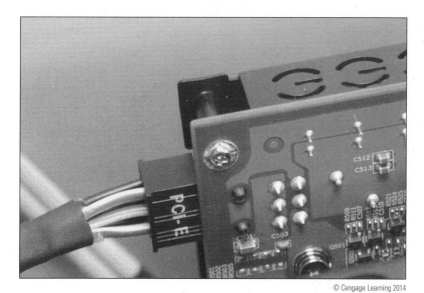

© Cengage Learning 2014

Figure 8-33   Connect a power cord to the PCIe power connector on the card

8. Make a quick check of all connections and cables, and then replace the case cover. (If you want, you can leave the case cover off until you've tested the card, in case it doesn't work and you need to reseat it.) Plug up the external power cable and essential peripherals.

9. Start the system. When Windows starts, it should detect a new hardware device is present and attempt to automatically install the drivers. As the drivers are installed, a message might appear above the taskbar (refer back to Figure 8-14). You can cancel the wizard and manually install the drivers.

10. Insert the CD that came bundled with the card and launch the setup program on the CD. The card documentation will tell you the name of the program (examples are Setup.exe and Autorun.exe). Figure 8-34 shows the opening menu for one setup program for a video card. Click **Install Video Drivers** and follow the on-screen instructions to install the drivers. If you are using downloaded driver files, double-click the file to begin the installation and follow the directions on-screen.

> **Notes** All 64-bit drivers must be certified by Microsoft to work in Windows. However, some 32-bit drivers might not be. During the driver installation, if you see a message that says 32-bit drivers have not been certified, go ahead and give permission to install the drivers if you obtained them from the manufacturer or another reliable source.

A+
220-801
1.4, 1.5,
1.7, 1.10,
1.12

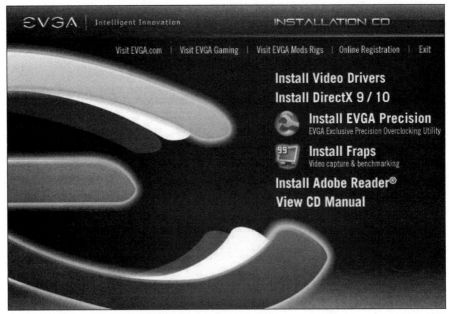

Figure 8-34 Opening menu to install video drivers

Source: EVGA

11. After the drivers are installed, you might be asked to restart the system. Then you can configure the card or use it with application software. If you have problems with the installation, turn to Device Manager and look for errors reported about the device. The card might not be properly seated in the slot.

> **Notes** Some motherboards provide extra ports that can be installed in faceplate openings off the back of the case. For example, Figure 8-35 shows a module that has a game port and two USB ports. To install the module, remove a faceplate and install the module in its place. Then connect the cables from the module to the appropriate connectors on the motherboard.

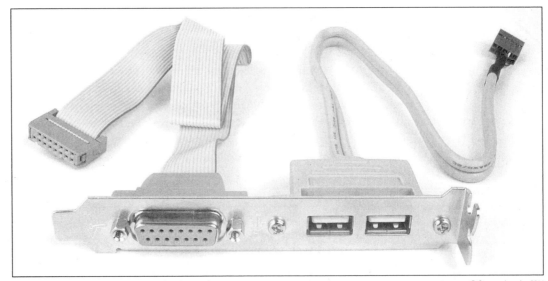

© Cengage Learning 2014

Figure 8-35 This I/O module provides two USB ports and one game port

A+
220-801
1.4, 1.5,
1.7, 1.10,
1.12

Installing a Video Card

When you install a video card, here is a list of things that can go wrong and what to do about them:

1. *When you first power up the system, you hear a whining sound.* This is caused by the card not getting enough power. Make sure a 6-pin or 8-pin power cord is connected to the card if it has this connector. The power supply might be inadequate.

2. *When you first start up the system, you see nothing but a black screen.* Most likely this is caused by the onboard video port not being disabled in BIOS setup. Disable the port.

3. *When you first start up the system, you hear a series of beeps.* BIOS cannot detect a video card. Make sure the card is securely seated. The video slot or video card might be bad.

4. *Error messages about video appear when Windows starts.* This can be caused by a conflict in onboard video and the video card. Try disabling onboard video in Device Manager.

5. *Games crash or lock up.* Try updating drivers for the motherboard, the video card, and the sound card. Also install the latest version of DirectX. (You learn about DirectX later in the chapter.) Then try uninstalling the game and installing it again. Then download all patches for the game.

Now let's turn our attention to a little information about three types of cards you might be called on to install. As with any adapter card you install, be sure to get familiar with the user guide before you start the installation so that you know the card's hardware and software requirements and what peripheral devices it supports.

SOUND CARDS AND ONBOARD SOUND

A **sound card** (an expansion card with sound ports) or onboard sound (sound ports embedded on a motherboard) can play and record sound, and save it in a file. Figure 8-36 shows a sound card by Creative (*us.creative.com*). This Sound Blaster card uses a PCIe x1 slot and supports up to eight surround sound version 7.1 speakers. The color-coded

Courtesy of Creative Technology Ltd.

Figure 8-36 Sound Blaster X-Fi Titanium sound card by Creative uses a PCIe x1 slot

A+
220-801
1.4, 1.5,
1.7, 1.10,
1.12

speaker ports are for these speakers: front left and right, front center, rear left and right, subwoofer, and two additional rear speakers. The two S/PDIF (Sony/Philips Digital Interconnect Format) ports are used to connect to external sound equipment such as a CD or DVD player.

> **Notes** If you are using a single speaker or two speakers with a single sound cable, connect the cable to the lime green sound port on the motherboard, which is usually the middle port.

TV TUNER AND VIDEO CAPTURE CARDS

A **TV tuner card** can turn your computer into a television. A port on the card receives input from a TV cable and lets you view television on your computer monitor. If the TV signal is analog, the TV tuner card can convert it to digital. A **video capture card** lets you capture this video input and save it to a file on your hard drive. Some cards are a combination TV tuner card and video capture card, making it possible for you to receive television input and save that input to your hard drive (see Figure 8-37). A high-end TV tuner/video capture card might also serve as your video card. Also, some motherboards and notebook computers have onboard TV tuners and TV captures.

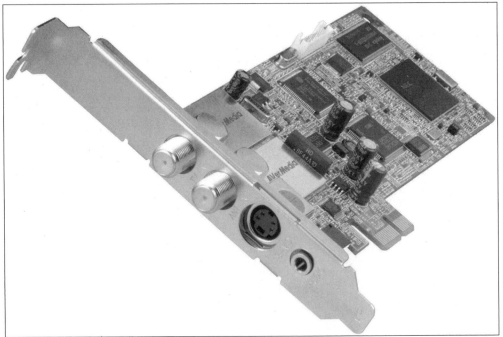

Courtesy of AVerMedia Technologies, Inc.

Figure 8-37 The AVerMedia AVerTV PVR 150 Plus TV tuner and video capture card uses a PCIe x1 slot and works alongside a regular video card

When installing a TV tuner or capture card, most likely you will install the drivers, install the card, and then install the application software that comes bundled with the card. You can then configure and manage the card using the applications.

SUPPORTING THE VIDEO SUBSYSTEM

A+
220-801
1.4, 1.5,
1.7, 1.10,
1.12

The primary output device of a computer is the monitor. The two necessary components for video output are the monitor and the video card (also called the video adapter and graphics adapter) or a video port on the motherboard. In this part of the chapter, you learn about monitors, video cards, the video connectors they use, and how to support the video subsystem.

MONITOR TECHNOLOGIES AND FEATURES

The most popular type of monitor for laptop and desktop systems is an LCD flat-screen monitor (see Figure 8-38), but you have other choices as well. Here is a list and description of each type of monitor:

▲ *CRT monitor.* The **CRT (cathode-ray tube) monitor** (see Figure 8-38) was first used in television sets, takes up a lot of desk space, and is largely obsolete. One reason to still use them is for children. The surface of a LCD monitor can easily be damaged, but CRT monitor surfaces can handle children touching them. CRT monitors use mercury, and, therefore, you must be careful when disposing of one to make sure the environment is not affected.

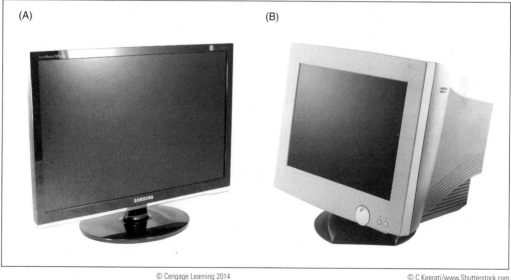

(A)   (B)

© Cengage Learning 2014   © C Keerati/www.Shutterstock.com

Figure 8-38   (a) An LCD monitor, (b) an older CRT monitor

▲ *LCD monitor.* The **LCD (liquid crystal display) monitor**, also called a **flat-panel monitor**, was first used in laptops. The monitor produces an image using a liquid crystal material made of large, easily polarized molecules. Figure 8-39 shows the layers of the LCD panel that together create the image. At the center of the layers is the liquid crystal material. Next to it is the layer responsible for providing color to the image. These two layers are sandwiched between two grids of electrodes forming columns and rows. Each intersection of a row electrode and a column electrode forms one **pixel** on the LCD panel. Software can address each pixel to create an image.

8

A+
220-801
1.4, 1.5,
1.7, 1.10,
1.12

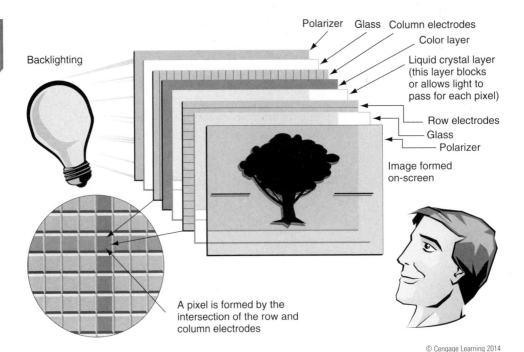

Polarizer Glass Column electrodes
Color layer
Backlighting
Liquid crystal layer
(this layer blocks
or allows light to
pass for each pixel)
Row electrodes
Glass
Polarizer
Image formed
on-screen

A pixel is formed by the
intersection of the row and
column electrodes

© Cengage Learning 2014

Figure 8-39   Layers of an LCD panel

Backlighting is used to light the LCD panel. The trend for most monitor manufacturers is to use LED backlighting, which provides a better range and accuracy of color and uses less power than earlier technologies. **LED (Light-Emitting Diode)** technology also uses less mercury, and is, therefore, kinder to the environment when an LCD monitor is disposed of. When you see a monitor advertised as an LED monitor, know the monitor is an LCD monitor that uses LED backlighting.

▲ *Plasma monitor.* A **plasma monitor** provides high contrast with better color than LCD monitors. They work by discharging xenon and neon plasma on flat glass and don't contain mercury. Plasma monitors are expensive and heavy and are generally available only in large commercial sizes.

▲ *Projector.* A **projector** (see Figure 8-40) is used to shine a light that projects a transparent image onto a large screen and is often used in classrooms or with other large groups. Several types of technologies are used by projectors, including LCD. A projector is often installed on a computer as a dual monitor, which you learn how to do later in the chapter.

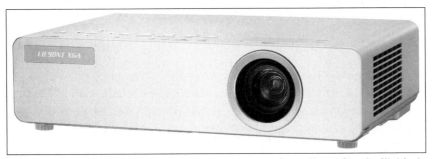

LB 90NT XGA

Courtesy of Panasonic Corporation of North America

Figure 8-40   Portable XGA projector by Panasonic

A+
220-801
1.4, 1.5,
1.7, 1.10,
1.12

◢ *OLED monitor.* An **OLED (Organic Light-emitting Diode) monitor** uses a thin LED layer or film between two grids of electrodes and does not use backlighting. It does not emit as much light as an LCD monitor does, and, therefore, can produce deeper blacks, provide better contrast, work in darker rooms, and use less power than can an LCD monitor. OLED screens are used by digital cameras, camcorders, mobile devices, and other small portable electronic devices. OLED monitors are just now appearing for desktop systems.

> 💡 **A+ Exam Tip** The A+220-801 exam expects you to know about these monitor types and technologies: CRT, LCD, LED, plasma, projector, and OLED.

In this chapter, we focus on LCD monitors—by far the most popular monitors used with desktop systems. Figure 8-41 shows an ad for one high-end LCD monitor. Table 8-3 explains the features mentioned in the ad.

8

Source: tigerdirect.com

Figure 8-41 An ad for a monitor lists cryptic monitor features

> 💡 **A+ Exam Tip** The A+ 220-801 exam expects you to know about these monitor features: refresh rate, resolution, native resolution, brightness in lumens, and analog and digital connectors used.

A+
220-801
1.4, 1.5,
1.7, 1.10,
1.12

Monitor Characteristic	Description
Screen size	Diagonal length of the screen surface in inches.
Refresh rate	The *refresh rate*, also called the response time, is the time it takes for a monitor to build one screen, measured in ms (milliseconds) or Hz (hertz). The lower the better. A monitor with a 12-ms response time can build 83 frames per second, and a 16-ms monitor can build 63 frames per second. The ad in Figure 8-41 shows a refresh rate of 6 ms.
Pixel pitch	A pixel is a spot or dot on the screen that can be addressed by software. The *pixel pitch* is the distance between adjacent pixels on the screen. An example of a pixel pitch is .283mm. The smaller the number, the better.
Resolution	The *resolution* is the number of spots or pixels on a screen that can be addressed by software. Values can range from 640 × 480 up to 1920 × 1200 for high-end monitors. Popular resolutions are 1920 × 1080 and 1366 × 768.
Native resolution	The *native resolution* is the number of pixels built into the LCD monitor. Using the native resolution usually gives the highest-quality image.
Contrast ratio	The contrast between true black and true white on the screen. The higher the *contrast ratio* the better. 1000:1 is better than 700:1. An advertised dynamic contrast ratio is much higher than the contrast ratio but not a true measurement of contrast. Dynamic contrast adjusts the backlighting to give the effect of an overall brighter or darker image. For example, in Figure 8-41, the contrast ratio is 1000:1, and the dynamic ratio is 20,000,000:1. When comparing quality of monitors, pay attention to the contrast ratio, more so than the dynamic ratio.
Viewing angle	The angle of view when a monitor becomes difficult to see. A viewing angle of 170 degrees is better than 140 degrees.
Backlighting or brightness	Brightness is measured in cd/m^2 (candela per square meter), which is the same as lumens/m^2 (lumens per square meter). In addition, the best LED backlighting for viewing photography is class IPS (in-plane switching), which provides the most accurate color.
Connectors	Options for connectors are VGA, DVI-I, DVI-D, HDMI, DisplayPort, and Thunderbolt. Some monitors offer more than one connector (see Figure 8-42). These and other connectors used by video cards and monitors are discussed later in the chapter.
Other features	LCD monitors can also provide an antiglare surface, tilt screens, microphone input, speakers, USB ports, adjustable stands, and perhaps even a port for your iPod. Some monitors are also touch screens, so they can be used with a stylus or finger touch.

Table 8-3   Important features of a monitor

⚡ **Caution**   If you spend many hours in front of a computer, you may strain your eyes. To protect your eyes from strain, look away from the monitor into the distance every few minutes. Use a good monitor with a high refresh rate or response time. The lower rates that cause monitor flicker can tire and damage your eyes. When you first install a monitor, set the rate at the highest value the monitor can support.

A+
220-801
1.4, 1.5,
1.7, 1.10,
1.12

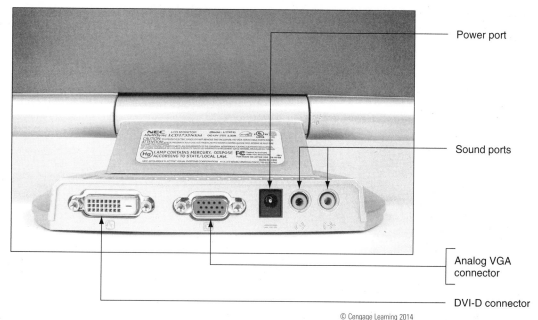

© Cengage Learning 2014

Figure 8-42 The rear of this LCD monitor shows digital and analog video ports to accommodate a video cable with either a 15-pin analog VGA connector or a digital DVI connector

VIDEO CARDS AND CONNECTORS

Video cards (see Figure 8-43) are sometimes called graphics adapters, graphics cards, or display cards. Most motherboards sold today have one or more video ports integrated into the motherboard. If you are buying a motherboard with a video port, make sure that you can disable the video port on the motherboard if it gives you trouble. You can then install a video card and use its video port rather than the port on the motherboard. Recall from Chapter 4 that a video card can use an AGP, PCI, or PCI Express slot on the motherboard. The fastest slot to use is a PCIe x16 slot.

© Cengage Learning 2014

Figure 8-43 The PCX 5750 graphics card by MSI Computer Corporation uses the PCI Express x16 local bus

A+
220-801
1.4, 1.5,
1.7, 1.10,
1.12

Recall from Chapter 1 that types of video ports include VGA, S-Video, DVI, DisplayPort, and HDMI connectors, which you can see in Table 1-1 in Chapter 1. In addition to these ports, you also need to know about a composite video, miniHDMI, miniDin-6, DVI-I, DVI-D, and DVI-A ports. All these ports are described here:

▲ *VGA.* The 15-pin VGA port is the standard analog video port and transmits three signals of red, green, and blue (RGB). A VGA port is sometimes called a **DB-15** port.

▲ *DVI ports.* DVI ports were designed to replace VGA, and variations of DVI can transmit analog and/or digital data. The five DVI standards for pinouts are shown in Figure 8-44. Three DVI connectors are shown in Figure 8-45. The DVI standards specify the maximum length for DVI cables is 5 meters, although some video cards produce a strong enough signal to allow for longer DVI cables.

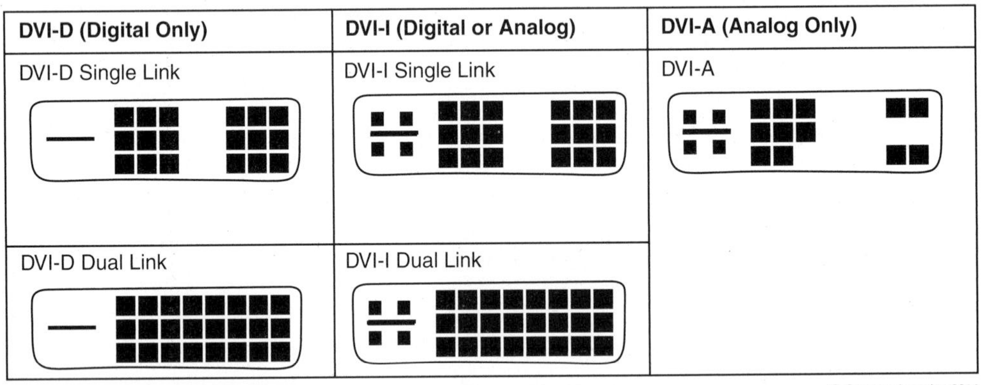

DVI-D (Digital Only)	DVI-I (Digital or Analog)	DVI-A (Analog Only)
DVI-D Single Link	DVI-I Single Link	DVI-A
DVI-D Dual Link	DVI-I Dual Link	

© Cengage Learning 2014

Figure 8-44 Five pinout arrangements for DVI ports and connectors

© Cengage Learning 2014

Figure 8-45 Three types of DVI connectors: (left) DVI-I, (middle) DVI-D, and (right) DVI-A

Here are the variations of DVI:

• *DVI-D.* The **DVI-D** port only transmits digital data. Using an adapter to convert a VGA cable to the port won't work. You can see a DVI-D port in Figure 8-46a.

• *DVI-I.* The **DVI-I** port (see Figure 8-46b) supports both analog and digital signals. If a computer has this type of port, you can use a digital-to-analog adapter to connect an older analog monitor to the port using a VGA cable (see Figure 8-47). If a video card has a DVI port, most likely it will be the DVI-I port (the one with the four extra holes) so that you can use an adapter to convert the port to a VGA port.

A+
220-801
1.4, 1.5,
1.7, 1.10,
1.12

(A) © Cengage Learning 2014 (B) © Cengage Learning 2014

Figure 8-46 Two types of DVI ports: (a) DVI-D, (b) DVI-I

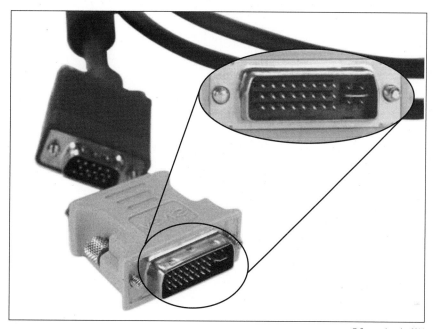

© Cengage Learning 2014

Figure 8-47 Digital-to-analog video port converter using DVI-I connector with extra four pins

- *DVI-A.* The **DVI-A** port only transmits analog data. You don't see them very often.

- *Single Link or Dual Link.* DVI digital transmissions can be Single Link or Dual Link. Dual Link transmissions double the power of the signal and can support higher screen resolutions (up to 2560 × 1600) than Single Link transmissions (up to 1920 × 1200). Most DVI-D or DVI-I ports are Dual Link.

▲ *Composite video.* Using a **composite video port**, also called an **RGB port**, the red, green, and blue (RGB) are mixed together in the same signal. This is the method used by television and can be used by a video card that is designed to send output to a TV. A composite port is round and has only a single pin in the center of the port. Figure 8-48 shows a laptop that has a composite video input port so that you can use the laptop as your display for a game box. Composite video does not produce as sharp an image as VGA video or S-Video.

▲ *S-Video (Super-Video) ports.* An S-Video port is a 4-pin or 7-pin round port used by some televisions and video equipment. An S-Video cable is shown in Figure 8-49. A few older video cameras use a 6-pin variation of S-Video. The connector is called a **MiniDin-6 connector** and looks like a PS/2 connector used by a keyboard or mouse. (In general, a Din connector is always round with multiple pins in the connector.)

A+
220-801
1.4, 1.5,
1.7, 1.10,
1.12

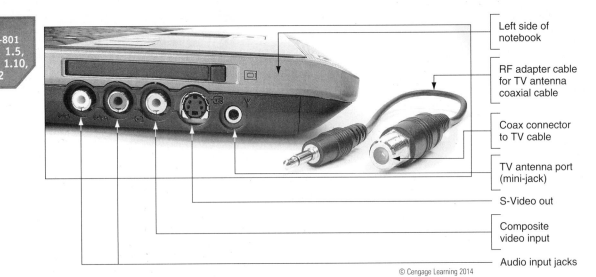

Left side of
notebook

RF adapter cable
for TV antenna
coaxial cable

Coax connector
to TV cable

TV antenna port
(mini-jack)

S-Video out

Composite
video input

Audio input jacks

© Cengage Learning 2014

Figure 8-48   This laptop designed for multimedia applications has an embedded TV tuner
and can also receive audio and video input from game boxes

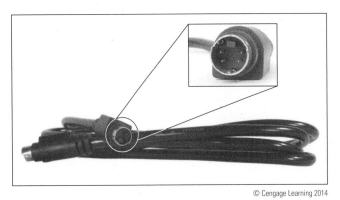

© Cengage Learning 2014

Figure 8-49   An S-Video cable used to connect a video card to an
S-Video port on a television

▲ *Component video.* Whereas composite video has the red, green, and blue mixed in the
same signal, component video has been split into different components and carried as
separate signals. Figure 8-50 shows the connectors on one component video and audio

© Cengage Learning 2014

Figure 8-50   Component video and audio cable

A+
220-801
1.4, 1.5,
1.7, 1.10,
1.12

cable. Three lines carry video (red, blue, and green), and the yellow and white connectors are used for audio (audio in and audio out).

▲ *DisplayPort.* DisplayPort was designed to replace DVI and can transmit digital (not analog) video and audio data. It uses data packet transmissions similar to those of Ethernet, USB, and PCI Express, and is expected to ultimately replace VGA, DVI, and HDMI on desktop and laptop computers. Besides the regular DisplayPort used on video cards and desktop computers, laptops might use the smaller Mini DisplayPort. Figure 8-51 shows a DisplayPort to Mini Display Port cable. Some DisplayPort controllers allow you to use a DisplayPort-to-HDMI adapter so the port can be used with an HDMI connection. Maximum length for DisplayPort cables is 15 meters.

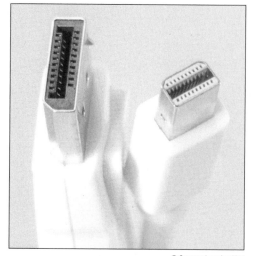

© Cengage Learning 2014

Figure 8-51 DisplayPort to Mini DisplayPort cable

BIOS setup can be used to manage onboard DisplayPort and HDMI ports. For example, look at Figure 8-13 shown earlier in the chapter, where you can enable or disable the audio transmissions of DisplayPort and HDMI ports and still use these ports for video.

▲ *HDMI and HDMI mini connectors.* HDMI transmits both digital video and audio (not analog), and was designed to be used by home theater equipment. The HDMI standards allow for several types of HDMI connectors. The best known, which is used on most computers and televisions, is the Type A 19-pin **HDMI connector**. Small mobile devices can use the smaller Type C 19-pin **HDMI mini connector**, also called the **mini-HDMI connector**. Figure 8-52 shows a cable with both connectors that is useful when connecting some devices like a smartphone to a computer. Figure 8-53 shows an HDMI to DVI-D cable. Because HDMI does not transmit analog data, the connector works only on DVI-D ports, not DVI-I ports. The maximum length of an HDMI cable depends on the quality of the cable; no maximum length has been specified.

A+
220-801
1.4, 1.5,
1.7, 1.10,
1.12

© Cengage Learning 2014

Figure 8-52 HDMI to miniHDMI cable

Courtesy of Belkin International Inc.

Figure 8-53 An HDMI to DVI cable can be used to connect a PC that has a DVI port to home theater equipment that uses an HDMI port

> **A+ Exam Tip** The A+ 220-801 exam expects you to know about these video connector types: VGA (DB-15), HDMI, miniHDMI, DisplayPort, S-Video, miniDin-6, composite (RGB), component, DVI-D, DVI-I, and DVI-A connectors.

Now let's see how to configure a monitor or dual monitors connected to a Windows computer.

A+
220-802
1.5

CHANGING MONITOR SETTINGS

Settings that apply to the monitor can be managed by using the monitor buttons and Windows utilities. Using the monitor buttons, you can adjust the horizontal and vertical position of the screen on the monitor surface and change the brightness and contrast settings. For laptops, the brightness and contrast settings can be changed using function keys on the laptop.

A+
220-801
1.4, 1.5,
1.7, 1.10,
1.12

A+
220-802
1.5

APPLYING | CONCEPTS   INSTALLING DUAL MONITORS

To increase the size of your Windows desktop, you can install more than one monitor for a single computer. To install dual monitors, you need two video ports on your system, which can come from motherboard video ports, a video card that provides two video ports, or two video cards.

To install a second monitor in a dual-monitor setup using two video cards, follow these steps:

1. Verify that the original video card works properly, determine whether it is PCIe or AGP (on really old computers), and decide whether it is to be the primary monitor.

2. Boot the PC and enter BIOS setup. If BIOS setup has the option to select the order in which video cards are initialized, verify that the currently installed card is configured to initialize first. If it does not initialize first, then, when you install the second card, video might not work at all when you first boot with two cards.

3. Install a second video card in an empty slot. A computer might have a second PCIe slot or an unused PCI slot you can use. (For a really old computer using an AGP slot, most likely you can install the second video card in an empty PCI slot.) Attach the second monitor.

4. Boot the system. Windows recognizes the new hardware and launches the Found New Hardware wizard. You can use the wizard to install the video card drivers or cancel the wizard and install them manually as you learned to do earlier in the chapter.

Here are the steps to configure dual monitors:

1. Connect two monitors to your system. Open **Control Panel**, and in the Appearance and Personalization group, click **Adjust screen resolution**. The Screen Resolution window appears (see Figure 8-54).

2. Notice the two numbered boxes that represent your two monitors. When you click one of these boxes, the drop-down menu changes to show the selected monitor, and the screen resolution and orientation (Landscape, Portrait, Landscape flipped, or Portrait flipped) follow the selected monitor. This lets you customize the settings for each monitor. If necessary, arrange the boxes so that they represent the physical arrangement of your monitors.

> **Notes** In Figure 8-54, if you arrange the two boxes side by side, your extended desktop will extend left or right. If you arrange the two boxes one on top of the other, your extended desktop will extend up and down.

3. Adjust the screen resolution according to your preferences. For the sharpest images, use the native resolution for each monitor. Most often, the native resolution is the highest resolution listed, but this is not always the case. To know for certain the native resolution, see the documentation that came with the monitor.

4. By default, Windows 7 extends your desktop onto the second monitor. However, in the Multiple displays drop-down list, you can select other options, as shown in Figure 8-54. To save the settings, click **Apply**. The second monitor should initialize and show the extended or duplicated desktop.

8

A+
220-801
1.4, 1.5,
1.7, 1.10,
1.12

A+
220-802
1.5

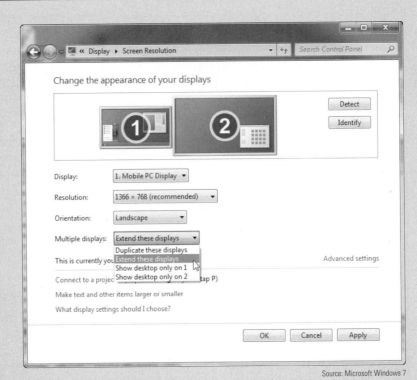

Source: Microsoft Windows 7

Figure 8-54   Configure each monitor in a dual monitor configuration

5. Close the **Screen Resolution** window. For an extended desktop, open an application and verify that you can use the second monitor by dragging the application window over to the second monitor's desktop.

After you add a second monitor to your system, you can move from one monitor to another simply by moving your mouse over the extended desktop. Switching from one monitor to the other does not require any special keystroke or menu option.

Most notebook computers are designed to be used with projectors and provide a VGA, DisplayPort, or HDMI port for this purpose. To use a projector, plug in the projector to the extra port and then turn it on. For a notebook computer, use a function key to activate the video port and toggle between extending the desktop to the projector, using only the projector, duplicating the screen on the projector, or not using the projector. When giving a presentation, most presenters prefer that they see their presentation duplicated on the LCD screen and the projector.

Notes For group presentations that require a projector, the software used for the presentations is likely to be Microsoft PowerPoint. If you configure your projector as a dual monitor, you can use PowerPoint to display a presentation to your audience on the projector at the same time you are using your LCD display to manage your PowerPoint slides. To do so, for PowerPoint 2007 and 2010, select the **Slide Show** tab. In the Set Up group, click **Set Up Slide Show**. In the Set Up Show box under Multiple monitors, check **Show Presenter View** and click **OK**.

A+
220-801
1.4, 1.5,
1.7, 1.10,
1.12

A+
220-802
1.4, 1.5

VIDEO MEMORY AND WINDOWS 7/VISTA

Video cards have their own processor called a graphics processing unit (GPU) or visual processing unit (VPU). These processors use graphics RAM installed on the card so that RAM on the motherboard is not tied up with video data. (If a motherboard offers a video port rather than using a video card, the GPU is part of the onboard video controller and is called integrated video. For integrated video, RAM on the motherboard is used for video data, or some video RAM is embedded on the motherboard.)

The more RAM installed on the card, the better the performance. Most video cards used and sold today use DDR2, DDR3, Graphics DDR3 (GDDR3), GDDR4, or GDDR5 memory. Graphics DDR memory is faster than regular DDR memory and does a better job of storing 3D images. Some video cards have as much as 2 GB of graphics memory.

Most Windows 7/Vista editions offer the Aero user interface (also called Aero glass), which has a 3D appearance. The hardware must qualify for Aero glass before Windows can enable it. These requirements include onboard video or a video card that supports DirectX 9 or higher, has at least 128 MB of video memory, and uses the Windows Display Driver Model (WDDM). The Windows Display Driver Model is a Windows component that manages graphics. **DirectX** is a Microsoft software development tool that software developers can use to write multimedia applications such as games, video-editing software, and computer-aided design software. Components of DirectX include DirectDraw, DirectMusic, DirectPlay, and Direct3D. The video firmware on the video card or motherboard chipset can interpret DirectX commands to build 3D images as presented to them by the WDDM. In addition, Windows relies on DirectX and the WDDM to produce the Aero user interface.

If an application, such as a game or desktop publishing app, that relies heavily on graphics is not performing well or giving errors, the problem might be video memory or the version of DirectX the system is using. You can use the **dxdiag.exe** command to display information about hardware and diagnose problems with DirectX. To use the command, click **Start**, type **dxdiag.exe** in the search box, and press **Enter**. The first time you use the command, a message box appears asking if you want to check if your drivers are digitally signed. Then the opening window shown in Figure 8-55 appears. Look for the version of DirectX installed (version 11 in the figure).

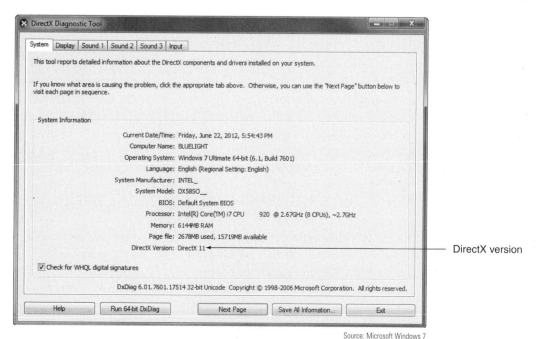

Source: Microsoft Windows 7

Figure 8-55 The DirectX Diagnostic tool reports information about DirectX components

A+
220-801
1.4, 1.5,
1.7, 1.10,
1.12

A+
220-802
1.4, 1.5

To find out the latest version of DirectX published by Microsoft, go to *www.microsoft*
.com and search on "DirectX End-User Runtime Web Installer." The download page in
Figure 8-56 appears. If you want to install a new version of DirectX, click **Download** and
follow the directions on-screen.

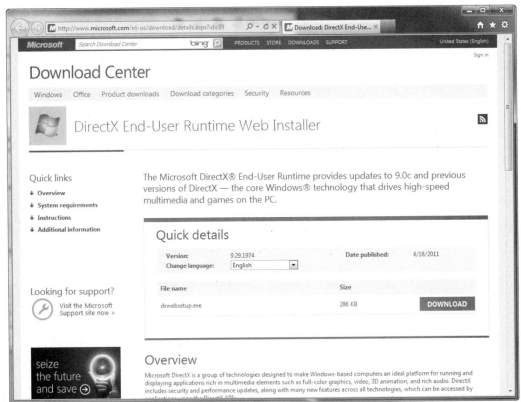

Source: Microsoft.com

Figure 8-56   Download the latest version of DirectX

Video memory available to the graphics processor can be the graphics memory embedded on the video card or on the motherboard, system memory, or a combination of both.
To see the video memory available to Windows, click **Adjust Screen Resolution** in the
Appearance and Personalization group in Control Panel. In the Screen Resolution window,
click **Advanced settings**. The video properties box appears. Figure 8-57 shows two properties boxes for two systems. Figure 8-57a is for a notebook computer, and Figure 8-57b is
for a desktop computer that has a video card.

Here is an explanation of the four entries in the dialog box that concern video memory:

▲ Total Available Graphics Memory is total memory that may be available to the video
subsystem.

▲ Dedicated Video Memory is found on a video card or embedded on the motherboard.
The motherboard in the notebook has 64 MB, and the video card in the desktop system has 512 MB of graphics memory.

▲ System Video Memory is system RAM dedicated to video. No other application or
component can use it.

▲ Shared System Memory is system RAM that might be available to video if another
application or component is not already using it.

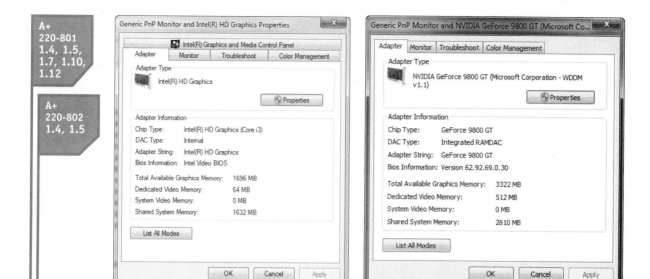

(A)   Source: Microsoft Windows 7   (B)   Source: Microsoft Windows 7

Figure 8-57 Memory allocated to video under Windows 7 (a) for a notebook computer, and (b) for a desktop computer with video card

For Windows to enable the Aero user interface, the video controller must have available at least 128 MB video memory. In other words, Total Available Graphics Memory must add up to at least 128 MB. This is true for both systems in Figure 8-57.

SUPPORTING STORAGE DEVICES

By now you must be thinking you've read in this chapter about every computer part there must be, but hold on; we have optical drives and flash memory still to go. Before we explore the details of several storage devices, including optical discs, USB flash drives, and memory cards, let's start with the file systems they might use.

FILE SYSTEMS USED BY STORAGE DEVICES

A storage device, such as a hard drive, CD, DVD, USB flash drive, or memory card, uses a file system to manage the data stored on the device. A **file system** is the overall structure the OS uses to name, store, and organize files on a drive. In Windows, each **storage** device is assigned a drive letter. In Windows Explorer, to see what file system a device is using, right-click the device and select **Properties** from the shortcut menu. The device Properties box appears, which shows the file system and storage capacity of the device (see Figure 8-58).

Installing a new file system on a device is called **formatting** the device, and the process erases all data on the device. One way to format a device is to right-click the device and select **Format** from the shortcut menu. In the box that appears, you can select the file system to use (see Figure 8-59). The NTFS file system (New Technology file system) is primarily used by hard drives. The exFAT file system is used by removable storage devices such as large-capacity USB flash drives and large-capacity memory cards. In addition, the older FAT32 and FAT file systems are used by smaller-capacity devices.

Now let's look at the types of optical drives you might be called on to support.

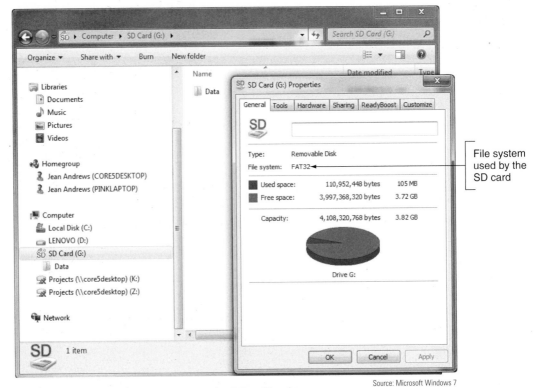

Source: Microsoft Windows 7

Figure 8-58   This 4 GB SD card is using the FAT32 file system

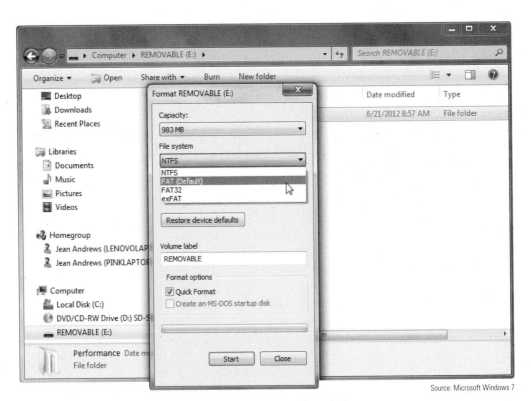

Source: Microsoft Windows 7

Figure 8-59   A storage device can be formatted using Windows Explorer

A+
220-801
1.5, 1.7,
1.10

STANDARDS USED BY OPTICAL DRIVES AND DISCS

CDs, DVDs, and Blu-ray discs use similar laser technologies. Tiny lands and pits on the surface of a disc represent bits, which a laser beam can read. This is why they are called optical storage technologies. **CD (compact disc)** drives use the **CDFS (Compact Disc File System)** or the **UDF (Universal Disk Format) file system**, while **DVD (digital versatile disc or digital video disc)** drives and **Blu-ray Disc (BD)** drives use the newer UDF file system.

Blu-ray drives are backward compatible with DVD and CD technologies, and DVD drives are backward compatible with CD technologies. Depending on the drive features, an optical drive might be able to read and write to BDs, DVDs, and CDs. An internal optical drive can interface with the motherboard by way of an IDE or SATA connection. An external drive might use an eSATA, FireWire, or USB port. Figure 8-60 shows an internal DVD drive, and Figure 8-61 shows an external DVD drive.

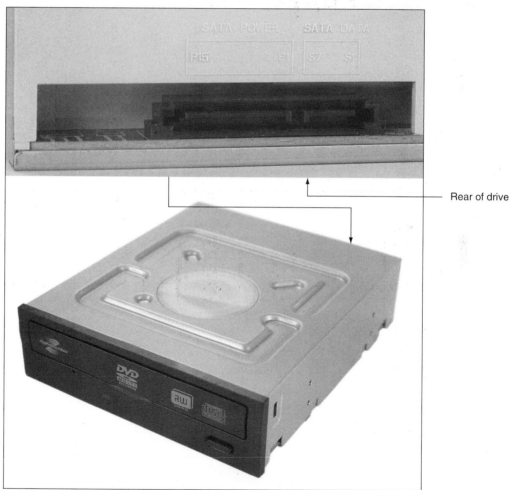

Rear of drive

© Cengage Learning 2014

Figure 8-60 This internal DVD drives uses a SATA connection

Data is written to only one side of a CD, but can be written to one or both sides of a DVD or Blu-ray disc. Also, a DVD or Blu-ray disc can hold data in two layers on each side. This means these discs can hold a total of four layers on one disc (see Figure 8-62).

The breakdown of how much data can be held on CDs, DVDs, and BDs is shown in Figure 8-63. The capacities for DVDs and BDs depend on the sides and layers used to hold the data.

A+
220-801
1.5, 1.7,
1.10

Courtesy of Plextor

Figure 8-61 The PX-610U external DVD±RW drive by Plextor uses a USB 2.0 port

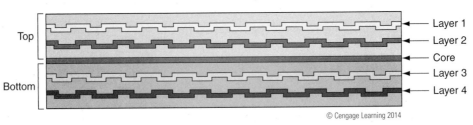

© Cengage Learning 2014

Figure 8-62 A DVD can hold data in double layers on both the top and bottom of
the disc, yielding a maximum capacity of 17 GB

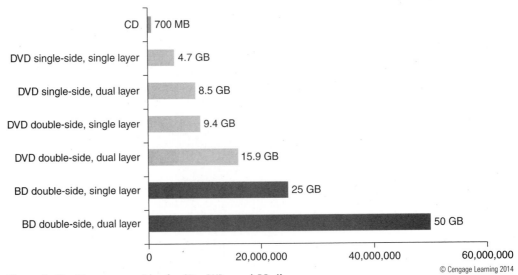

© Cengage Learning 2014

Figure 8-63 Storage capacities for CDs, DVDs, and BD discs

A+ Exam Tip The A+ 220-801 exam expects you to know the capacities of CDs, DVDs, and Blu-ray
discs. These capacities are all listed in Figure 8-63.

Notes The discrepancy in the computer industry between one billion bytes (1,000,000,000 bytes) and 1 GB (1,073,741,824 bytes) exists because 1 KB equals 1024 bytes. Even though documentation might say that a DVD holds 17 GB, in fact, it holds 17 billion bytes, which is only 15.90 GB.

When shopping for an optical drive, suppose you see a couple of ads like those shown in Figure 8-64. To sort out the mix of disc standards, Table 8-4 can help. The table lists the popular CD, DVD, and Blu-ray disc standards.

Figure 8-64 Ads for internal and external DVD burners

Source: tigerdirect.com

Disc Standard	Description
CD-ROM disc or drive	*CD-read-only memory.* A CD-ROM disc burned at the factory can hold music, software, or other data. The bottom of a CD-ROM disc is silver. A CD-ROM drive can read CDs.
CD-R disc	*CD recordable.* A CD-R disc is a write-once CD.
CD-RW disc or drive	*CD rewriteable.* A CD-RW disc can be written to many times. A CD-RW drive can write to a CD-RW or CD-R disc and also overwrite a CD-RW disc.
DVD-ROM drive	*DVD read-only memory.* A DVD-ROM drive can also read CDs or DVDs.
DVD-R disc	*DVD recordable, single layer.* A DVD-R disc can hold up to 4.7 GB of data and is a write-once disc.
DVD-R DL disc	*DVD recordable in dual layers.* Doubles storage to 8.5 GB of data on one disc surface.
DVD-RW disc or drive	*DVD rewriteable.* Also known as an erasable, recordable drive or a write-many disc. The speeds in an ad for an optical drive indicate the maximum speed supported when burning this type of disc, for example, DVD-RW 6X.
DVD-RW DL disc or drive, a.k.a. DL DVD drive	*DVD rewriteable, dual layers.* Doubles disc storage capacity to 8.5 GB.
DVD+R disc or drive	*DVD recordable.* Similar to but faster than DVD-R. Discs hold about 4.7 GB of data.
DVD+R DL disc or drive	*DVD recordable, dual layers.* Doubles disc storage to 8.5 GB on one surface.

Table 8-4 Optical discs and drive standards (continues)

Disc Standard	Description
DVD+RW disc or drive	*DVD rewriteable.* Faster than DVD-RW.
DVD-RAM disc or drive	*DVD Random Access Memory.* Rewriteable and erasable. You can erase or rewrite certain sections of a DVD-RAM disc without disturbing other sections of the disc, and the discs can handle many times over the number of rewrites (around 100,000 rewrites), compared to about a thousand rewrites for DVD-RW and DVD+RW discs. DVD-RAM discs are popular media used in camcorders and set-top boxes.
BD-ROM drive	*BD read-only memory.* A BD-ROM drive can also read DVDs, and some can read CDs.
BD-R disc or drive	*BD recordable.* A BD-R drive might also write to DVDs or CDs.
BD-RE disc or drive	*BD rewriteable.* A BD-RE drive might also write to DVDs or CDs.

© Cengage Learning 2014

Table 8-4   Optical discs and drive standards (continued)

A+ Exam Tip   The A+ 220-801 exam expects you to know about the combo optical drives and burners, including CD-RW, DVD-RW, Dual Layer DVD-RW, BD-R, and BD-RE combo drives.

One more feature that you might look for in an optical drive is the ability to burn labels on the top of a disc. Two competing technologies for this purpose are Labelflash and LightScribe. Using either technology, you flip a Labelflash or LightScribe CD or DVD upside down and insert it in the drive tray so that the drive can then burn a label on top of the disc. Both the drive and disc must support the technology for it to work, and the two technologies are not compatible. Figure 8-65 shows a LightScribe CD-R that was just labeled using LightScribe. Another way to print labels on a disc is to use special discs that have a white paper-like surface. Insert the disc into an ink-jet printer that will print the label. The printer has to be the type that will print on optical discs. It is not recommended that you glue paper labels on the top of discs because they can throw the disc off balance or clog up a drive if the labels come loose. You can use a permanent felt-tip marker to handwrite labels on a disc.

© Cengage Learning 2014

Figure 8-65   This disc label was written using a DVD burner that supports LightScribe

Notes   CDs, DVDs, and BDs are expected to hold their data for many years; however, you can prolong the life of a disc by protecting it from exposure to light.

A+
220-801
1.5, 1.7,
1.10

INSTALLING AN OPTICAL DRIVE

Internal optical drives use a SATA, IDE, or SCSI interface. You learned to install drives using these interfaces in Chapter 6. Figure 8-66 shows the front and rear of an EIDE DVD drive. Note the jumper bank that can be set to cable select, slave, or master. Figure 8-67 shows the rear of a SATA optical drive.

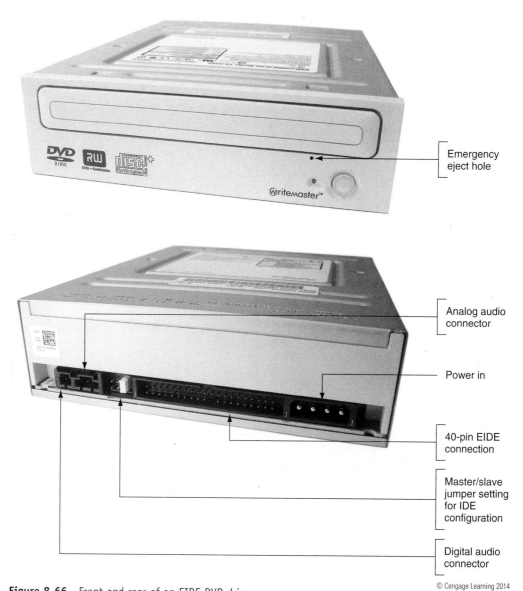

Emergency
eject hole

Analog audio
connector

Power in

40-pin EIDE
connection

Master/slave
jumper setting
for IDE
configuration

Digital audio
connector

Figure 8-66 Front and rear of an EIDE DVD drive

© Cengage Learning 2014

A+ Exam Tip The A+ 220-801 exam expects you to know how to install a CD, DVD, or Blu-ray drive.

When given the choice of putting an IDE optical drive on the same cable with an IDE hard drive or on its own cable, choose to use its own cable. An optical drive that shares a cable with a hard drive can slow down the hard drive's performance. If you must, however,

A+
220-801
1.5, 1.7,
1.10

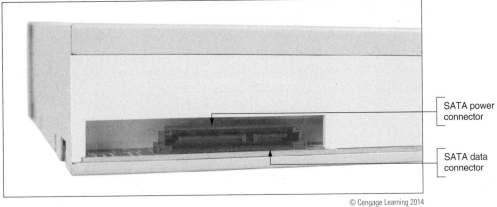

© Cengage Learning 2014

Figure 8-67   Rear of a SATA optical drive

put the optical drive and hard drive on the same IDE channel, make the hard drive the master and the optical drive the slave.

Some motherboards have one SATA connection and one IDE connection. Use SATA connections for all hard drives. The optical drive can use the one IDE connection or a SATA connection. An optical drive is usually installed in the drive bay at the top of a desktop case (see Figure 8-68). After the drive is installed in the bay, connect the data and power cables.

Optical drives might also have a connection for an audio port so that sound from audio CDs can be sent directly to the audio controller. The DVD drive in Figure 8-66 has two connectors for audio. The 4-pin connector is used for analog sound, and the 2-pin connector is used for digital sound. These connections are no longer needed because Windows 7/Vista/XP transfers digital sound from the drive to the sound card without the use of a direct cable connection.

© Cengage Learning 2014

Figure 8-68   Slide the drive into the bay flush with the front panel

Windows 7/Vista/XP supports optical drives using its own embedded drivers without add-on drivers. Therefore, after the Found New Hardware Wizard completes, Windows should recognize the drive.

And now, moving onward to solid state storage. . . . You're almost done!

A+
220-801
1.5, 1.7,
1.10

SOLID STATE STORAGE

Types of solid state storage include SSD hard drives, USB flash drives, and memory cards. You learned about SSD hard drives in Chapter 6. USB flash drives currently for sale range in size from 128 MB to 256 GB and go by many names, including a flash pen drive, jump drive, thumb drive, and key drive. Several USB flash drives are shown in Figure 8-69. Flash drives might work at USB 2.0 or USB 3.0 speed and use the FAT (for small-capacity drives) or exFAT file system (for large-capacity drives). Windows 7/Vista/XP has embedded drivers to support flash drives. To use one, simply insert the device in a USB port. It then shows in Windows Explorer as a drive with an assigned letter.

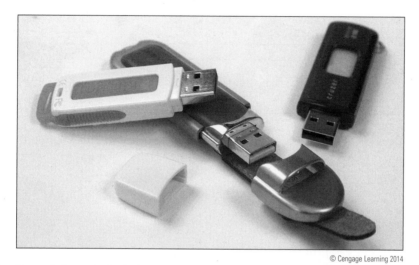

© Cengage Learning 2014

Figure 8-69   USB flash drives come in a variety of styles and sizes

To make sure that data written to a flash drive is properly saved before you remove the flash drive from the PC, double-click the **Safely Remove Hardware** icon in the notification area (see Figure 8-70). The Safely Remove Hardware box opens, also shown in Figure 8-70. After you click the device listed, it is then safe to remove it.

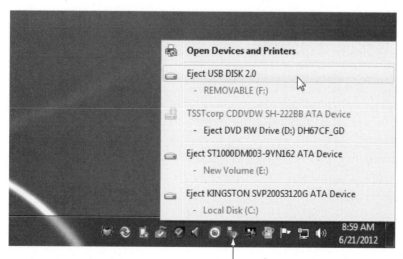

Source: Microsoft Windows 7

Safely Remove
Hardware icon

Figure 8-70   Safely Remove Hardware icon and dialog box

A+
220-801
1.5, 1.7,
1.10

Memory cards might be used in digital cameras, tablets, cell phones, MP3 players, digital camcorders, and other portable devices, and most laptops have memory card slots. The SD Association (www.sdcard.org) is responsible for standards used by the **Secure Digital (SD) cards** shown in Table 8-5. The three standards used by SD cards are 1.x (regular SD), 2.x (SD High Capacity or SDHC), and 3.x (SD eXtended Capacity or SDXC). In addition, these cards come in three physical sizes.

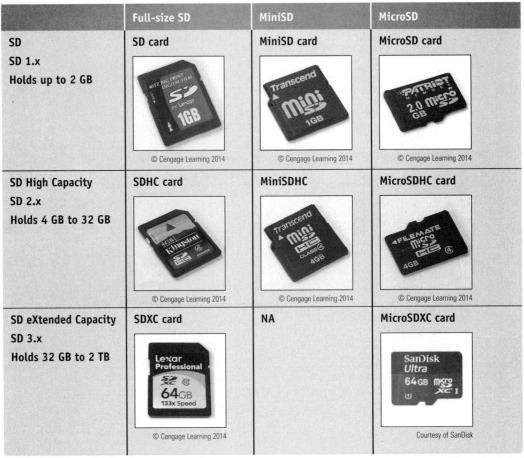

	Full-size SD	MiniSD	MicroSD
SD **SD 1.x** **Holds up to 2 GB**	SD card © Cengage Learning 2014	MiniSD card © Cengage Learning 2014	MicroSD card © Cengage Learning 2014
SD High Capacity **SD 2.x** **Holds 4 GB to 32 GB**	SDHC card © Cengage Learning 2014	MiniSDHC © Cengage Learning 2014	MicroSDHC card © Cengage Learning 2014
SD eXtended Capacity **SD 3.x** **Holds 32 GB to 2 TB**	SDXC card © Cengage Learning 2014	NA	MicroSDXC card Courtesy of SanDisk

© Cengage Learning 2014

Table 8-5 Flash memory cards that follow the SD Association standards

SDHC and SDXC slots are backward compatible with earlier standards for SD cards. However, you cannot use an SDHC card in an SD slot, and you cannot use an SDXC card in an SDHC slot or SD slot. Only use SDXC cards in SDXC slots.

SD and SDHC cards use the FAT file system, and SDXC cards use the exFAT file system. Windows 7/Vista supports both file systems, so you should be able to install an SD, SDHC, or SDXC card in an SD slot on a Windows 7/Vista laptop with no problems (assuming the slot supports the SDHC or SDXC card you are using). Windows XP can use the exFAT file system only when exFAT drivers are installed. For information about these drivers, see *support.microsoft.com/kb/955704*.

Memory cards other than SD cards are shown in Table 8-6. Some of the cards in Table 8-6 are now obsolete.

Flash Memory Device	Example
The Sony Memory Stick PRO Duo is about half the size of the Memory Stick PRO but is faster and has a higher storage capacity (up to 2 GB). You can use an adapter to insert the Memory Stick PRO Duo in a regular Memory Stick slot.	© Cengage Learning 2014
CompactFlash (CF) cards come in two types, Type I (CFI) and Type II (CFII). Type II cards are slightly thicker. CFI cards will fit a Type II slot, but CFII cards will not fit a Type I slot. The CF standard allows for sizes up to 137 GB, although current sizes range up to 32 GB. UDMA CompactFlash cards are faster than other CompactFlash cards. UDMA (Ultra Direct Memory Access) transfers data from the device to memory without involving the CPU.	© Cengage Learning 2014
MultiMedia Card (MMC) looks like an SD card, but the technology is different and they are not interchangeable. Generally, SD cards are faster than MMC cards.	© Cengage Learning 2014
The Memory Stick is used in Sony cameras and camcorders. A later version, the Memory Stick PRO, improved on the slower transfer rate of the original Memory Stick.	© Cengage Learning 2014
The *xD-Picture* Card has a compact design (about the size of a postage stamp), and currently holds up to 8 GB of data. You can use an adapter to insert this card into a PC Card slot on a notebook computer or a CF slot on a digital camera.	© Cengage Learning 2014

Table 8-6 Flash memory cards

© Cengage Learning 2014

> **A+ Exam Tip** The A+ 220-801 exam expects you to know about SD, MicroSD, MiniSD, CompactFlash, and xD memory cards

Sometimes a memory card is bundled with one or more adapters so that a smaller card will fit a larger card slot. Earlier in the chapter, Figure 8-20 shows a MicroSDHC card that came packaged with four adapters, which are labeled in the figure. Figure 8-71 shows several flash memory cards together so you can get an idea of their relative sizes.

A+
220-801
1.5, 1.7,
1.10

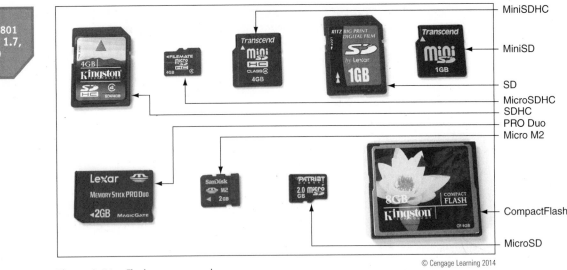

© Cengage Learning 2014

Figure 8-71 Flash memory cards

>> CHAPTER SUMMARY

Basic Principles for Supporting Devices

▲ Adding new devices to a computer requires installing hardware and software. Even if you know how to generally install an I/O device, always follow the specific instructions of the product manufacturer.

▲ Use Device Manager under Windows to manage hardware devices and to solve problems with them. The Windows 7 Action Center can also help with problem solving.

▲ Popular I/O ports on a motherboard include eSATA (Versions 1, 2, and 3), FireWire 800 and 400, and USB (Versions 1, 2, and 3). Older ports include parallel, serial, and PS/2 ports.

▲ Wireless connections can use Wi-Fi 802.11a/b/g/n, Bluetooth, and Infrared standards.

▲ USB connectors include the A-Male, B-Male, Mini-B, Micro-B, Micro-A, USB 3.0 B-Male, and USB 3.0 Micro-B connectors.

Installing I/O Peripheral Devices

▲ When installing devices, use 32-bit drivers for a 32-bit OS and 64-bit drivers for a 64-bit OS.

▲ A touch screen is likely to use a USB port. Software is installed to calibrate the touch screen to the monitor screen and receive data input.

▲ Biometric input devices, such as a fingerprint reader, collect biological data and compare it to that recorded about the person to authenticate the person's access to a system.

▲ A KVM switch lets you use one keyboard, monitor, and mouse with multiple computers.

Installing and Configuring Adapter Cards

▲ Generally, when an adapter card is physically installed in a system and Windows starts up, it detects the card and then you install the drivers using the Windows wizard. However, always follow specific instructions from the device manufacturer when installing an adapter card because the order of installing the card and drivers might be different.

▲ A TV tuner card turns your PC or notebook into a television. A video capture card allows you to capture input from a camcorder or directly from TV. Combo cards have both abilities.

Supporting the Video Subsystem

▲ Types of monitors include CRT monitor, LCD monitor, plasma monitor, projector, and OLED monitor.

▲ Technologies and features of LCD monitors include screen size, refresh rate, pixel pitch, resolution, native resolution, contrast ratio, viewing angle, backlighting, and connectors that a monitor uses.

▲ Video ports that a video card or motherboard might provide are VGA, DVI-I, DVI-D, DVI-A, composite video, S-Video, component video, DisplayPort, HDMI, and HDMI mini ports.

▲ Use the Screen Resolution window in Windows 7/Vista to configure a monitor resolution and configure dual monitors.

▲ To use the Aero user interface, Windows 7/Vista requires a video card or onboard video to have at least 128 MB of video RAM, support DirectX version 9 or higher, and use the Windows Display Driver Model (WDDM).

▲ The dxdiag.exe command is used to report information about hardware, including the video card and which version of DirectX it is using.

Supporting Storage Devices

▲ File systems a storage device might use in Windows include NTFS, exFAT, and FAT.

▲ CDs, DVDs, and BDs are optical devices with data physically embedded into the surface of the disc. Laser beams are used to read data off the disc by measuring light reflection.

▲ Optical discs can be recordable (such as a CD-R disc) or rewriteable (such as a DVD-RW disc).

▲ Types of flash memory card standards by the SD Association include SD, MiniSD, MicroSD, SDHC, MiniSDHC, MicroSDHC, SDXC, and MicroSDXC. Other memory cards include Memory Stick PRO Duo, Memory Stick PRO, Sony Memory Stick Micro M2, CompactFlash I and II, and xD-Picture Card.

>> KEY TERMS

For explanations of key terms, see the Glossary near the end of the book.

1394a	composite video port	DVI-A
1394b	contrast ratio	DVI-D
A Male connector	CRT (cathode-ray tube) monitor	DVI-I
B Male connector		dxdiag.exe
barcode reader	DB-15	file system
biometric device	Device Manager	FireWire 400
Blu-ray Disc (BD)	digitizer	FireWire 800
CD (compact disc)	digitizing tablet	flat panel monitor
CDFS (Compact Disc File System)	DirectX	formatting
	DVD (digital versatile disc or digital video disc)	graphics tablet
CompactFlash (CF) card		HDMI connector

HDMI mini connector
hot-swappable
Infrared (IR)
KVM (Keyboard, Video, and Mouse) switch
LCD (Liquid Crystal Display) monitor
LED (Light-Emitting Diode)
Micro-A connector
Micro-B connector
MIDI (musical instrument digital interface)
Mini-B connector

MiniDin-6 connector
mini-HDMI connector
native resolution
OLED (Organic Light-emitting Diode) monitor
pixel
pixel pitch
plasma monitor
projector
refresh rate
resolution
RGB port

Secure Digital (SD) card
sound card
stylus
touch screen
TV tuner card
UDF (Universal Disk Format) file system
USB 3.0 B-Male connector
USB 3.0 Micro-B connector
video capture card
xD-Picture Card

>> REVIEW QUESTIONS

1. When deciding what type of port a new device should use, the _____ of the port is often a tiebreaker.

   a) size

   b) location

   c) speed

   d) refresh rate

2. How do you uninstall a USB device such as the USB keyboard?

   a) In Control Panel, click Uninstall a program and within the Programs and Features window, select the device and click Change.

   b) Use the Firmware setup program.

   c) Use the Action Center Uninstall option.

   d) Go to Windows Explorer, right-click the device and click on Remove.

3. What is the purpose of adding an adapter card to a system?

   a) To allow a Linux device to work operate successfully within Windows

   b) To make available the external ports or internal connectors the card provides to the system

   c) To allow a 32-bit device to work within a 62-bit operating system

   d) To increase system performance within a virtual machine

4. Which DVI port supports both analog and digital signals?

   a) DVI-D Single Link

   b) DVI-D Dual Link

   c) DVI-A

   d) DVI-I Single Link

5. Why are CDs, DVDs, and Blu-ray discs called optical storage technologies?

   a) Because tiny lands and pits on the surface of a disc are written sequentially in a circular manner

   b) Because tiny lands and pits on the surface of a disc represent bits, which absorb light

   c) Because tiny lands and pits on the surface of a disc represent bits, which a laser beam can read

   d) Because tiny lands and pits on the surface of a disc represent character strings that are affected by black light

6. True or false? As many as 127 USB devices can be daisy chained together using USB cables.

7. True or false? If you hear a series of beeps when you first start up the system after installing a video card, this indicates that the card was installed successfully.

8. True or false? The primary output device of a computer is the hard disk.

9. True or false? The resolution is the number of spots or pixels on a screen that can be addressed by software.

10. True or false? An optical drive that shares a cable with a hard drive can slow down the hard drive's performance.

11. A(n) ____ device is an input device that inputs biological data about a person, which can be input data to identify a person's fingerprints, handprints, face, voice, eye, and handwritten signature.

12. A graphics tablet comes with a(n) ____ that works like a pencil on the tablet.

13. A(n) ____ is an input device that uses a monitor or LCD panel as the backdrop for input options.

14. The trend for most monitor manufacturers is to use ____ backlighting, which provides a better range and accuracy of color and uses less power than earlier technologies.

15. Installing a new file system on a device is called ____ the device, and the process erases all data on the device.

8

CHAPTER 9

Satisfying Customer Needs

In this chapter, you will learn:

- About some job roles and responsibilities of those who sell, fix, or support personal computers

- What customers want and expect beyond your technical abilities

- How to interact with customers when selling, servicing, and supporting personal computers

- How to customize a computer system to meet customer needs

In this chapter, the focus is on relating to people and your career as a professional PC support technician. As a professional PC technician, you can manage your career by staying abreast of new technology, using every available resource to do your job well, and striving for top professional certifications. There was a time when most PC support jobs had to do with simply working with hardware and software, and the perception was that people skills were not that important. But times have changed and our vocation has become much more service oriented.

Knowing how to effectively work with people in a technical world is one of the most sought-after skills in today's service-oriented work environments. Just before writing this chapter, an employer told me, "It's not hard to find technically proficient people these days. But it's next to impossible to find people who know how to get along with others and can be counted on when managers are not looking over their shoulders." I could sense his frustration, but I also felt encouraged to know that good social skills and good work ethics can take you far in today's world. My advice to you is to take this chapter seriously. It's important to be technically proficient, but the skills learned in this chapter just might be the ones that make you stand out above the crowd to land that new job or promotion.

In this chapter, you'll learn about the job roles of a professional PC support technician, including the certifications and record-keeping and informational tools you might use. Then we focus on interpersonal skills (people skills, sometimes called soft skills) needed by a technical support technician. Finally, you learn how to select appropriate parts for a customized computer system to satisfy the specifications given by your customer.

> **Notes** People respond in kind to the position of facial muscles presented to them. Try smiling when you first greet someone and watch to see what happens.

JOB ROLES AND RESPONSIBILITIES

A+
220-801
5.3

As a PC troubleshooter, you might have to solve a problem on your own PC or for someone else. As a PC technician, you might fulfill several different job roles:

© iStockphoto

Figure 9-1 Picture yourself here and think about your job role in this position

- ▲ *PC support technician.* A PC support technician works on site, closely interacting with users, and is responsible for ongoing PC maintenance. Of the job roles in this list, a PC support technician is the only one responsible for the PC before trouble occurs. Therefore, you are able to prepare for a problem by performing routine preventive maintenance, keeping good records, and making backups of important data (or teaching users how to do so). You might also be expected to provide desk-side support, helping computer users with all sorts of hardware and application concerns. Some job titles that fall into this category include enterprise technician, IT administrator, PC technician, support technician, PC support specialist, and desk-side support technician.
- ▲ *PC service technician.* A PC service technician goes to a customer site in response to a service call and, if possible, repairs the PC on site. PC service technicians are usually not responsible for ongoing PC maintenance but usually do interact with users. Other job titles might include computer repair technician, field technician, or field service technician.
- ▲ *Technical retail associate.* Those responsible for selling computers and related equipment are often expected to have technical knowledge about the products they sell. These salespeople work in somewhat of a consulting role and are expected to advise customers about the best technology to meet their needs, how to apply the technology, and maybe even how to configure entire networks and interconnected applications and equipment. Sometimes job roles involve only one stage of the sale. For instance, less technical people might make the initial contact with the customer and begin the sales process, and those who are more technically knowledgeable can act as technical sales consultants to complete the details of the sale.

A+
220-801
5.3

▲ *Bench technician.* A bench technician works in a lab environment, might not interact with users of the PCs being repaired, and is not permanently responsible for them. (The job title bench technician can also apply to someone who repairs any type of electronic equipment.) Bench technicians probably don't work at the site where the PC is kept. They might be able to interview the user to get information about the problem, or they might simply receive a PC to repair without being able to talk to the user. A bench technician who repairs computers rather than any type of electronic equipment is sometimes called a depot technician.

▲ *Help-desk technician.* A help-desk technician provides telephone or online support. Help-desk technicians, who do not have physical access to the PC, are at the greatest disadvantage of the types of technicians listed. They can interact with users over the phone, by a chat session, or by remote control of the user's computer and must obviously use different tools and approaches than technicians who are at the PC. Other job titles in this category include remote support technician, service desk technician, and call center technician.

Now let's turn our attention to the need to be certified, and then we'll look at the record-keeping and information tools needed by a technician.

© iStockphoto

Figure 9-2 PC support technicians might have limited contact with users

CERTIFICATION AND PROFESSIONAL ORGANIZATIONS

Many people work as PC technicians without any formal classroom training or certification. However, by having certification or an advanced technical degree, you prove to yourself, your customers, and your employers that you are prepared to do the work and are committed to being educated in your chosen profession. Certification and advanced degrees

A+
220-801
5.3

serve as recognized proof of competence and achievement, improve your job opportunities, create a higher level of customer confidence, and often qualify you for promotions and other training or degrees.

The most significant certifying organization for PC technicians is the Computing Technology Industry Association (CompTIA, pronounced "comp-TEE-a"). CompTIA sponsors the A+ Certification Program, and manages the exams. **A+ Certification** has industry recognition, so it should be your first choice for certification as a PC technician. CompTIA has more than 13,000 members from every major company that manufactures, distributes, or publishes computer-related products and services.

Go to the CompTIA home page at **www.comptia.org** and drill down to the information about A+ Certification, shown in Figure 9-3. Follow the *See what the exam covers* link on the page to get the list of objectives for the latest exams, which are currently the A+ 2012 exams. To become certified, you must pass the A+ 220-801 exam that covers content on hardware, soft skills (working with people), and networking and the A+ 220-802 exam that covers operating systems, security, networking, and troubleshooting hardware and software. This book covers all the content on both exams.

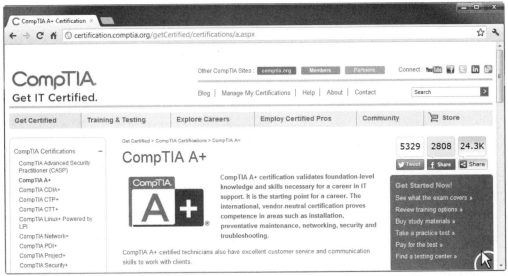

Source: comptia.org

Figure 9-3   CompTIA A+ Certification web page

Other certifications are more vendor specific. For example, Microsoft and Cisco offer certifications to use and support their products. These are excellent choices for additional certifications when your career plan is to focus on these products.

In addition to becoming certified and seeking advanced degrees, the professional PC technician must continually learn about new technologies. Helpful resources include on-the-job training, books, magazines, the Internet, trade shows, and interaction with colleagues, seminars, and workshops. Using the Internet, a convenient and inexpensive way to keep up with the latest technologies is to subscribe to newsletters by email. Newsletters I read regularly are those published by LAPTOP at *www.laptopmag.com*, *PC World* at *www.pcworld.com,* and PCstats at *www.pcstats.com*. Also, the Experts Exchange site (*www.experts-exchange.com*) is an excellent tool for learning and sharing about tech solutions.

It's important to build your professional network of technicians, co-workers, and potential employers. Focus on building good relationships on the job and maintaining these contacts even when you have moved on to another job. Trade shows, job fairs, seminars, and workshops are excellent opportunities for networking. On the web, take advantage of Facebook (*www.facebook.com*) and LinkedIn (*www.linkedin.com*) to help develop your online network.

> **Notes** Statistics show that more than 50 percent of potential employers check a person's online presence as part of the hiring process. Make sure your Facebook, blogs, and forum entries and photos present you in a favorable light. For example, don't complain online about your current job. Keep your online presence upbeat, friendly, and positive.

RECORD-KEEPING AND INFORMATION TOOLS

If you work for a service organization, it will probably have most of the tools you need to do your job, including printed forms, online record-keeping, procedures, and manuals. In some cases, help-desk support personnel might have software to help them do their jobs, such as programs that support the remote control of customers' PCs. Examples of this type of software are GoToAssist by CiTRIX at *www.netviewer.com* and LogMeIn Rescue by LogMeIn at *secure.logmeinrescue.com*.

Other types of resources, records, and information tools that can help you support PCs are:

◢ *Tool 1*. The specific application, operating system, or hardware you support must be available to you to test, observe, and study and to use to re-create a customer's problem whenever possible.

◢ *Tool 2*. You need a digital or printed copy of the same documentation the user sees and should be familiar with that documentation.

◢ *Tool 3*. Hardware and software products generally have more **technical documentation** than just a user manual. A company should make this technical documentation available to you when you support its product. If you don't find it on hand, know that you are likely to find user manuals and technical support manuals as .pdf files that can be downloaded from the product manufacturers' web sites.

◢ *Tool 4*. Online help targeted to field technicians and help-desk technicians is often available for a product. This online help will probably include a search engine that searches by topics, words, error messages, and the like.

◢ *Tool 5*. An **expert system** is software that is designed and written to help solve problems. It uses databases of known facts and rules to simulate human experts' reasoning and decision making. Expert systems for PC technicians work by posing questions about a problem to be answered by the technician or the customer. The response to each question triggers another question from the software until the expert system arrives at a possible solution or solutions. Many expert systems are "intelligent," meaning the system will record your input and use it in subsequent sessions to select more questions to ask and approaches to try. Therefore, future troubleshooting sessions on this same type of problem tend to zero in more quickly toward a solution.

◢ *Tool 6*. When someone initiates a call for help, the technician starts the process by creating a **ticket**, which is a record of the request and what is happening to resolve it. In the past, a technician kept these records on paper, but most organizations today use **call tracking** software to track the progress and resolution of a ticket. The software

A+
220-801
5.3

might track: (1) the date, time, and length of help-desk or on-site calls, (2) causes of and solutions to problems already addressed, (3) who is currently assigned to the ticket and who has already worked on it, (4) who did what and when, and (5) how each call was officially resolved. The ticket is entered into the call tracking system and stays open until the issue is resolved. Figure 9-4 shows a new ticket being created in Spiceworks (*www.spiceworks.com*), free help desk call tracking software. Support staff assigned to the ticket document their progress under this ticket in the call tracking system. As an open ticket ages, more attention and resources are assigned to it, and the ticket might be escalated, which is to assign the ticket to those higher up in the support chain until the problem is finally resolved and the ticket closed. Help-desk personnel and managers acknowledge and sometimes even celebrate those who consistently close the most tickets!

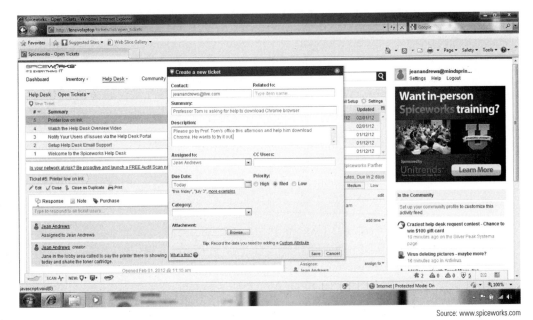

Source: www.spiceworks.com

Figure 9-4 Spiceworks Help Desk Software allows you to create, edit, and close tickets used by technicians

Now let's focus on our customers and what they expect from us beyond our technical knowledge.

WHAT CUSTOMERS WANT: BEYOND TECHNICAL KNOW-HOW

Probably the most significant indication that a PC technician is doing a good job is that customers are consistently satisfied. In your career as a support technician, commit to providing excellent service and to treating customers as you would want to be treated in a similar situation. One of the most important ways to achieve customer satisfaction is to do your best by being prepared, both technically and personally. Being prepared includes knowing what customers want, what they don't like, and what they expect from a PC technician.

Your customers can be "internal" (you both work for the same company, in which case you might consider the customer your colleague) or "external" (your customers come to you or your company for service). Customers can be highly technical or

A+
220-801
5.3

technically naive, represent a large company or simply own a home PC, be prompt or slow at paying their bills, want only the best (and be willing to pay for it) or be searching for bargain service, be friendly and easy to work with or demanding and condescending. In each situation, the key to success is always the same: don't allow circumstances or personalities to affect your commitment to excellence and to treating the customer as you would want to be treated.

The following traits distinguish a competent and helpful technician from a technician who is incompetent or unhelpful in the eyes of the customer:

▲ *Trait 1. A positive and helpful attitude.* This helps establish good customer relationships. You communicate your attitude in your tone of voice, the words you choose, how you use eye contact, your facial expressions, how you dress, and in many other subjective and subtle ways. Generally, your attitudes toward your customers stem from how you see people, how you see yourself, and how you see your job. Your attitude is a heart issue, not a head issue. To improve your attitude, you must do it from your heart. That's pretty subjective and cannot be defined with a set of rules, but it always begins with a decision to change. As you work with customers or users, make it a habit to not talk down to or patronize them. Don't make the customers or users feel inferior. People appreciate it when they feel your respect for them, even when they have made a mistake or are not knowledgeable. If a problem is simple to solve, don't make the other person feel he or she has wasted your time. Your customer or user should always be made to feel that the problem is important to you.

9

APPLYING | CONCEPTS

Josie walked into a computer parts store and wandered over to the cleaning supplies looking for Ace monitor wipes. She saw another brand of wipes, but not the ones she wanted. Looking around for help, she noticed Mary stocking software on the shelves in the next aisle. She walked over to Mary and asked her if she could help her find Ace monitor wipes. Mary put down her box, walked over to the cleaning supply aisle without speaking, picked up a can of wipes and handed them to Josie, still without speaking a word. Josie explained she was looking for Ace wipes. Mary yells over three aisles to a co-worker in the back room, "Hey, Billy! This lady says she wants Ace monitor wipes. We got any?" Billy comes from the back room and says, "No, we only carry those," pointing to the wipes in Mary's hand, and returns to the back room. Mary turns to Josie and says, "We only carry these," and puts the wipes back on the shelf. She turns to walk back to her aisle when Josie says to Mary, "Well, those Ace wipes are great wipes. You might want to consider carrying them." Mary says, "I'm only responsible for software." Josie leaves the store.

Discuss this situation in a small group of students and answer the following questions:

1. If you were Josie, how would you feel about the service in this store?

2. What would you have expected to happen that did not happen?

3. If you were Mary, how could you have provided better service?

4. If you were Billy, is there anything more you could have done to help?

5. If you were the store manager, what principles of good customer service would you want Billy and Mary to know that would have helped them in this situation?

A+
220-801
5.3

▲ *Trait 2. Listening without interrupting your customer.* When you're working with or talking to a customer, focus on him or her. Don't assume you know what your customer is about to say. Let her say it, listen carefully, and don't interrupt. Make it your job to satisfy this person, not just your organization, your boss, your bank account, or the customer's boss.

© iStockphoto

Figure 9-5 Learn to listen before you decide what a user needs or wants

▲ *Trait 3. Proper and polite language.* Speak politely and use language that won't confuse your customer. Avoid using slang or jargon (technical language that only technical people can understand). Avoid acronyms (initial letters that stand for words). For example, don't say to a nontechnical customer, "I need to ditch your KVM switch," when you could explain yourself better by saying to the customer, "I need to replace that little switch box on your desk that controls your keyboard, monitor, and mouse."

▲ *Trait 4. Sensitivity to cultural differences.* Cultural differences happen because we are from different countries and societies or because of physical disabilities. Culture can cause us to differ in how we define or judge good service. For example, culture can affect our degree of tolerance for uncertainty. Some cultures are willing to embrace uncertainty, and others strive to avoid it. Those who tend to avoid uncertainty can easily get upset when the unexpected happens. For these people, you need to make special efforts to communicate early and often when things are not going as expected. For the physically disabled, especially the deaf or sight-impaired, communication can be more difficult. It's your responsibility in these situations to do whatever is necessary to find a way to communicate. And it's especially important to have an attitude that expresses honor and patience, which you will unconsciously express in your tone of voice, your choice of words, and your actions.

▲ *Trait 5. Taking ownership of the problem.* Taking ownership of the customer's problem means to accept the customer's problem as your own problem. Doing that builds trust and loyalty because the customer knows you can be counted on. Taking ownership of a problem also increases your value in the eyes of your co-workers and boss. People who don't take ownership of the problem at hand are likely to be viewed as lazy, uncommitted, and uncaring. One way to take ownership of a problem is to not engage your boss in unproductive discussions about a situation that he expects you to handle on your own.

A+
220-801
5.3

◢ *Trait 6. Dependability and reliability.* Customers appreciate and respect those who do as they say. If you promise to be back at 10:00 the next morning, be back at 10:00 the next morning. If you cannot keep your appointment, never ignore your promise. Call, apologize, let the customer know what happened, and reschedule your appointment. Also, do your best to return phone calls the same day and email within two days.

© iStockphoto

Figure 9-6 When talking with customers, make sure they understand what to expect from you

9

APPLYING | CONCEPTS

Jack had had a bad day on the phones at the networking help desk in Atlanta. An electrical outage coupled with a generator failure had caused servers in San Francisco to be down most of the day. The entire help-desk team had been fielding calls all day explaining to customers why they did not have service and about expected recovery times. The servers were finally online, but it was taking hours to get everything reset and functioning. No one had taken a break all afternoon, but the call queue was still running about 20 minutes behind. Todd, the boss, had asked the team to work late until the queue was empty. It was Jack's son's birthday and his family was expecting Jack home on time. Jack moaned as he realized he might be late for Tyler's party. Everyone pushed hard to empty the queue. As Jack watched the last call leave the queue, he logged off, stood up, and reached for his coat.

And then the call came. Jack was tempted to ignore it, but decided it had to be answered. It was Lacy. Lacy was the executive assistant to the CEO (Chief Executive Officer over the entire company) and when Lacy calls, all priorities yield to Lacy, and Lacy knows it. The CEO was having problems printing to the laser printer in his office. Would Jack please walk down to his office and fix the problem? Jack asks Lacy to check the simple things like, "Is the printer turned on? Is it plugged in?" Lacy gets huffy and says, "Of course, I've checked that. Now come right now. I need to go." Jack walks down to the CEO's office, takes one look at the printer, and turns it on.

A+
220-801
5.3

He turns to Lacy and says, "I suppose the on/off button was just too technical for you." Lacy glares at him in disbelief. Jack says, "I'll be leaving now." As he walks out, he begins to form a plan as to how he'll defend himself to his boss in the morning, knowing the inevitable call to Todd's office will come.

In a group of two or four students, role-play Jack and Todd and discuss these questions:

1. Todd is informed the next morning of Jack's behavior. Todd calls Jack into his office. He likes Jack and wants him to be successful in the company. Jack is resistant and feels justified in what he did. As Todd, what do you think is important that Jack understand? How can you explain this to Jack so he can accept it? What would you advise Jack to do? In role-play, one student plays the role of Jack, and another the role of Todd.

2. Switch roles or switch team members and replay the roles.

3. What are three principles of relating to people that would be helpful for Jack to keep in mind?

▲ *Trait 7. Credibility.* Convey confidence to your customers. Don't allow yourself to appear confused, afraid, or befuddled. Troubleshoot the problem in a systematic way that portrays confidence and credibility. Get the job done, and do it with excellence. Credible technicians also know when the job is beyond their expertise and when to ask for help.

▲ *Trait 8. Integrity and honesty.* Don't try to hide your mistakes from your customer or your boss. Everyone makes mistakes, but don't compound them by a lack of integrity. Accept responsibility and do what you can to correct the error.

▲ *Trait 9. Know the law with respect to your work.* For instance, observe the laws concerning the use of software. Don't use or install pirated software.

▲ *Trait 10. Looking and behaving professionally.* A professional at work knows to not allow his emotions to interfere with business relationships. If a customer is angry, allow the customer to vent, keeping your own professional distance. (You do, however, have the right to expect a customer not to talk to you in an abusive way.) Dress appropriately for the environment. Take a shower each day, and brush your teeth after each meal. Use mouthwash. Iron your shirt. If you're not in good health, try as best you can to take care of the problem. Your appearance matters. And finally—don't use rough language. It is *never* appropriate.

📝 **Notes** Your customers might never remember what you said or what you did, but they will always remember how you made them feel.

PLANNING FOR GOOD SERVICE

Customers want good service. And to provide good service, you need to have a good plan when servicing customers on the phone or online, on site, or in a shop. This section surveys the entire service situation, from the first contact with the customer to closing the call. We begin with the first contact you have with the customer.

A+
220-801
5.3

> **💡 A+ Exam Tip** The A+ 220-801 exam expects you to know that when servicing a customer, you should be on time, avoid distractions, set and meet expectations and timelines, communicate the status of the solution with the customer, and deal appropriately with customer confidential materials.

INITIAL CONTACT WITH A CUSTOMER

Your initial contact with a customer might be when the customer comes to you, such as in a retail setting, when you go to the customer's site, when the customer calls you on the phone, or when the customer reaches you by chat or email. In each situation, always follow the specific guidelines of your employer. Let's look at some general guidelines when you go to the customer's site and when the customer calls you on the phone.

BEGINNING A SITE VISIT PROFESSIONALLY

When a technician makes an on-site service call, customers expect him or her to have both technical and interpersonal skills. Prepare for an on-site visit by reviewing information given you by whoever took the call. Know the problem you are going to address, the urgency of the situation, and what computer, software, and hardware need servicing. Arrive with a complete set of equipment appropriate to the visit, which might include a tool kit, flashlight, multimeter, grounding strap and mat, and bootable CDs and DVDs.

When you arrive at the customer's site, greet the customer in a friendly manner and shake his or her hand. Use Mr. or Ms. and last names or Sir or Ma'am rather than first names when addressing the customer, unless you are certain the customer expects you to use a first name. If the site is a residence, know that you should never stay at a site when only a minor is present. If a minor child answers the door, ask to speak with an adult and don't allow the adult to leave the house with only you and the child present.

© iStockphoto

Figure 9-7 If a customer permits it, begin each new relationship with a handshake

After initial greetings, the first thing you should do is listen and ask questions. As you listen, it's fine to take notes, but don't start the visit by filling out your paperwork. Save the paperwork for later, or have the essentials already filled out before you reach the site.

© iStockphoto

Figure 9-8 A frustrated customer will appreciate your confidence and friendly attitude

BEGINNING A PHONE CALL PROFESSIONALLY

When you answer the phone, identify yourself and your organization. (Follow the guidelines of your employer on what to say.) Then ask for and write down the name and phone number of the caller. Ask for spelling if necessary. If your help desk supports businesses, get the name of the business the caller represents.

Follow company policies to obtain other specific information you should take when answering an initial call. For example, your company might require that you obtain a licensing or warranty number to determine whether the customer is entitled to receive your support. Be familiar with your company's customer service policies. You might need to refer questions about warranties, licenses, documentation, or procedures to other support personnel or customer relations personnel. After you have obtained all the information you need to know that you are authorized to help the customer, open up the conversation for the caller to describe the problem.

> **Notes** If you spend many hours on the phone at a help desk, use a headset instead of a regular phone to reduce strain on your ears and neck. Investing in a high-quality headset will be worth the money.

INTERVIEW THE CUSTOMER

Troubleshooting begins by interviewing the user. As you ask the user questions, take notes and keep asking questions until you thoroughly understand the problem. Have the customer reproduce the problem, and carefully note each step taken and its results. This process gives you clues about the problem and about the customer's technical proficiency, which helps you know how to communicate with the customer.

Here are some questions that can help you learn as much as you can about the problem and its root cause:

1. Please describe the problem. What error messages, unusual displays, or failures did you see? (Possible answer: I see this blue screen with a funny-looking message on it that makes no sense to me.)

2. When did the problem start? (Possible answer: When I first booted after loading this neat little screensaver I downloaded from the web.)

3. What was the situation when the problem occurred? (Possible answers: I was trying to start up my PC. I was opening a document in MS Word. I was using the web to research a project.)

4. What programs or software were you using? (Possible answer: I was using Internet Explorer.)

5. Did you move your computer system recently? (Possible answer: Well, yes. Yesterday I moved the computer case across the room.)

6. Has there been a recent thunderstorm or electrical problem? (Possible answer: Yes, last night. Then when I tried to turn on my PC this morning, nothing happened.)

7. Have you made any hardware, software, or configuration changes? (Possible answer: No, but I think my sister might have.)

8. Has someone else used your computer recently? (Possible answer: Sure, my son uses it all the time.)

9. Is there some valuable data on your system that is not backed up that I should know about before I start working on the problem? (Possible answer: Yes! Yes! My term paper! It's not backed up! You gotta save that!)

10. Can you show me how to reproduce the problem? (Possible answers: Yes, let me show you what to do.)

After you have interviewed the user, ask him to listen while you repeat the problem to make sure you understand it correctly. If you don't understand what the customer is telling you, ask open-ended questions to try to narrow down the specifics of the problem. Re-create the circumstances that existed when the problem occurred in as much detail as you can. Make no assumptions. All users make simple mistakes and then overlook them. And before you begin work, be sure to ask the very important Question 9 listed above, "Does the system hold important data that is not backed up?" Then watch the user reproduce the problem. Or, if the user is not at the computer and you are at the computer, follow his directions to reproduce the problem yourself.

Use diplomacy and good manners when you work with a user to solve a problem. For example, if you suspect that the user dropped the PC, don't ask, "Did you drop the PC?" Put the question in a less accusatory manner: "Could the PC have been dropped?"

A+ Exam Tip The A+ 220-801 exam expects you to be able to clarify customer statements by asking open-ended questions to narrow the scope of the problem and by restating the issue or question.

A+
220-801
5.3

SET AND MEET CUSTOMER EXPECTATIONS

A professional technician knows that it is his responsibility to set and meet expectations with a customer. It's important to create an expectation of certainty with customers so that they are not left hanging and don't know what will happen next.

Part of setting expectations is to establish a timeline with your customer for the completion of a project. If you cannot solve the problem immediately, explain to the customer what needs to happen and the timeline that she should expect for a solution. Then keep the customer informed about the progress of the solution. For example, you can say to a customer, "I need to return to the office and research the cost of parts that need replacing. I'll call you tomorrow before 10:00 AM with an estimate." If later you find out you need more time, call the customer before 10:00 AM, explain your problem, and give her a new time to expect your call. This kind of service is very much appreciated by customers and, if you are consistent, you will quickly gain their confidence.

Another way to set expectations is to give the customer an opportunity to make decisions about repairs to the customer's equipment. When explaining to the customer what needs to be done to fix a problem, offer repair or replacement options if they apply. Don't make decisions for your customer. Explain the problem and what you must do to fix it, giving as many details as the customer wants. When a customer must make a choice, state the options in a way that does not unfairly favor the solution that makes the most money for you as the technician or for your company. For example, if you must replace a motherboard (a costly repair in parts and labor), explain to the customer the total cost of repairs and then help her decide if it is to her advantage to purchase a new system or repair this one.

© iStockphoto

Figure 9-9   Advise and then allow a customer to make purchasing decisions

A+
220-801
5.3

WORKING WITH A CUSTOMER ON SITE

As you work with a customer on site, avoid distractions as you work. Don't accept personal calls on your cell phone. Most organizations require that you answer calls from work, but keep the calls to a minimum. Be aware that the customer might be listening, so be careful to not discuss problems with co-workers, the boss, or other situations that might put the company, its employees, or products in a bad light with the customer. If you absolutely must excuse yourself from the on-site visit for personal reasons, explain to the customer the situation and return as soon as possible.

© iStockphoto

Figure 9-10 Consider yourself a guest at the customer's site

As you work, be as unobtrusive as possible. Consider yourself a guest in the customer's office or residence. Don't make a big mess. Keep your tools and papers out of the customer's way. Don't use the phone or sit in the customer's desk chair without permission. If the customer needs to work while you are present, do whatever is necessary to accommodate that.

Protect the customer's confidential materials. Don't read these materials. For example, if you are working on the printer and discover a budget report in the out tray, quickly turn it over so you can't read it, and hand it to the customer. If you notice a financial spreadsheet is displayed on the customer's computer screen, step away and ask the user if she wants to first close the spreadsheet before you work with the computer. If sensitive documents are lying on the customer's desk, you might let him know and ask if he would like to put them out of your view or in a safe place.

A+
220-801
5.3

When working at a user's desk, follow these general guidelines:

1. Don't take over the mouse or keyboard from the user without permission.

2. Ask permission again before you use the printer or other equipment.

3. Don't use the phone without permission.

4. Don't pile your belongings and tools on top of the user's papers, books, and so forth.

5. Accept personal inconvenience to accommodate the user's urgent business needs. For example, if the user gets an important call while you are working, don't allow your work to interfere. You might need to stop work and perhaps leave the room.

6. Also, if the user is present, ask permission before you make a software or hardware change, even if the user has just given you permission to interact with the PC.

© iStockphoto

Figure 9-11 Teaching a user how to fix her problem can prevent it from reoccurring

In some PC support situations, it is appropriate to consider yourself a support to the user as well as to the PC. Your goals can include educating the user, as well as repairing the computer. If you want users to learn something from a problem they caused, explain how to fix the problem and walk them through the process if necessary. Don't fix the problem yourself unless they ask you to. It takes a little longer to train the user, but it is more productive in the end because the user learns more and is less likely to repeat the mistake.

WORKING WITH A CUSTOMER ON THE PHONE

Phone support requires more interaction with customers than any other type of PC support. To understand the problem and also give clear instructions, you must be able to visualize what the customer sees at his or her PC. Patience is required if the customer must be told each key to press or command button to click. Help-desk support requires excellent communication skills, good phone manners, and lots of patience. As your help-desk skills improve,

Figure 9-12 Allow an irate customer to vent, and then speak calmly

© iStockphoto

9

you will learn to think through the process as though you were sitting in front of the PC yourself. Drawing diagrams and taking notes as you talk can be very helpful.

If your call is accidentally disconnected, call back immediately. Don't eat or drink while on the phone. If you must put callers on hold, tell them how long it will be before you get back to them. Speak clearly and don't talk too fast. Don't complain about your job, your boss or co-workers, your company, or other companies or products to your customers. A little small talk is okay and is sometimes beneficial in easing a tense situation, but keep it upbeat and positive.

APPLYING CONCEPTS Julie and James were good friends who worked together at the corporate help desk for internal customers. Staying on the phones all day can be tense and demanding and they had learned that good humor and occasional chit-chat can break up the day. Julie was on a long troubleshooting call and the call queue was getting backed up. James was answering one call after another trying to keep up. Julie says to her customer, "I have to check with another technician. I'll be right back," and puts the customer on hold. She turns to James and says, "You gonna go to that new movie on Saturday?" James puts his caller on hold and answers, "I sure want to. Wonder what times it's showing. Let me see." James and Julie browse through the movie listings and decide when to meet for the movie and where to eat later. About 10 minutes later, Julie and James return to their callers. Julie says to her caller, "Okay, I have the information I need. Let's continue."

In a small group, discuss this situation and answer the following questions:

1. If you were Julie's caller, how would you feel about being left on hold for 10 minutes in the middle of a long call?

2. What principles of customer service do you think Julie and James need to reconsider?

3. If you were Julie or James, how do you think you would handle this situation?

A+
220-801
5.3

DEALING WITH DIFFICULT CUSTOMERS

Most customers are polite and appreciate your help. And, if you make it a habit to treat others as you want to be treated, you'll find that most of your customers will tend to treat you well, too. However, occasionally you'll have to deal with a difficult customer. In this part of the chapter, you'll learn how to work with customers who are not knowledgeable, who are overly confident, and who complain.

WHEN THE CUSTOMER IS NOT KNOWLEDGEABLE

A help-desk call with a customer who is not knowledgeable about how to use a computer is the most difficult situation to handle. When on site, you can put a PC in good repair without depending on a customer to help you, but when you are trying to solve a problem over the phone, with a customer as your only eyes, ears, and hands, a computer-illiterate user can present a challenge. Here are some tips for handling this situation:

▲ *Tip 1.* Be specific with your instructions. For example, instead of saying, "Open Windows Explorer," say, "Using your mouse, right-click the Start button and select Open Windows Explorer from the menu."

© iStockphoto

Figure 9-13 Learn to be patient and friendly when helping users

▲ *Tip 2.* Don't ask the customer to do something that might destroy settings or files without first having the customer back them up carefully. If you think the customer can't handle your request, ask for some on-site help.

▲ *Tip 3.* Frequently ask the customer what is displayed on the screen to help you track the keystrokes and action.

▲ *Tip 4.* Follow along at your own PC. It's easier to direct the customer, keystroke by keystroke, if you are doing the same things.

▲ *Tip 5.* Give the customer plenty of opportunity to ask questions.

▲ *Tip 6.* Compliment the customer whenever you can to help the customer gain confidence.

▲ *Tip 7.* If you determine that the customer cannot help you solve the problem without a lot of coaching, you might need to tactfully request that the caller have someone with more experience call you. The customer will most likely breathe a sigh of relief and have someone take over the problem.

A+
220-801
5.3

Notes When solving computer problems in an organization other than your own, check with technical support within that organization instead of working only with the PC user. The user might not be aware of policies that have been set on the PC to prevent changes to the OS, hardware, or applications.

WHEN THE CUSTOMER IS OVERLY CONFIDENT

Sometimes customers are proud of their computer knowledge. Such customers might want to give advice, take charge of a call, withhold information they think you don't need to know, or execute commands at the computer without letting you know, so you don't have enough information to follow along. A situation like this must be handled with tact and respect for the customer. Here are a few tips:

- ▲ *Tip 1.* When you can, compliment the customer's knowledge, experience, or insight.
- ▲ *Tip 2.* Slow the conversation down. You can say, "Please slow down. You're moving too fast for me to follow. Help me catch up."
- ▲ *Tip 3.* Don't back off from using problem-solving skills. You must still have the customer check the simple things, but direct the conversation with tact. For example, you can say, "I know you've probably already gone over these simple things, but could we just do them again together?"
- ▲ *Tip 4.* Be careful not to accuse the customer of making a mistake.
- ▲ *Tip 5.* Even though the customer might be using technical jargon, keep to your policy of not using jargon back to the customer unless you're convinced he truly understands you.

A+ Exam Tip The A+ 220-801 exam expects you to know that it is important to not minimize a customer's problem and to not be judgmental toward a customer.

WHEN THE CUSTOMER COMPLAINS

When you are on site or on the phone, a customer might complain to you about your organization, products, or service or the service and product of another company. Consider the complaint to be helpful feedback that can lead to a better product or service and better customer relationships. Here are a few suggestions that can help you handle complaints and defuse customer anger:

- ▲ *Suggestion 1.* Be an active listener, and let customers know they are not being ignored. Look for the underlying problem. Don't take the complaint or the anger personally.
- ▲ *Suggestion 2.* Give the customer a little time to vent, and apologize when you can. Then start the conversation from the beginning, asking questions, taking notes, and solving problems. Unless you must have the information for problem solving, don't spend a lot of time finding out exactly whom the customer dealt with and what happened to upset the customer.
- ▲ *Suggestion 3.* Don't be defensive. It's better to leave the customer with the impression that you and your company are listening and willing to admit mistakes. No matter how much anger is expressed, resist the temptation to argue or become defensive.
- ▲ *Suggestion 4.* Know how your employer wants you to handle a situation where you are verbally abused. If this type of language is happening, you might say something like this in a very calm tone of voice: "I'm sorry, but my employer does not require me to accept this kind of talk."

9

A+
220-801
5.3

▲ *Suggestion 5.* If the customer is complaining about a product or service that is not from your company, don't start off by saying, "That's not our problem." Instead, listen to the customer complain. Don't appear as though you don't care.

▲ *Suggestion 6.* If the complaint is against you or your product, identify the underlying problem if you can. Ask questions and take notes. Then pass these notes on to people in your organization who need to know.

▲ *Suggestion 7.* Sometimes simply making progress or reducing the problem to a manageable state reduces the customer's anxiety. As you are talking to a customer, summarize what you have both agreed on or observed so far in the conversation.

▲ *Suggestion 8.* Point out ways that *you* think communication could be improved. For example, you might say, "I'm sorry, but I'm having trouble understanding what you want. Could you please slow down, and let's take this one step at a time."

© iStockphoto

Figure 9-14 When a customer is upset, try to find a place of agreement

APPLYING | CONCEPTS

Andy was one of the most intelligent and knowledgeable support technicians in his group working for CloudPool, Inc. He was about to be promoted to software engineer and today was his last day on the help desk. Sarah, a potential customer with little computer experience, calls asking for help accessing the company web site. Andy says, "The URL is www dot cloud pool dot com." Sarah responds, "What's a URL?" Andy's patience grows thin. He's thinking to himself, "Oh, help! Just two more hours and I'm off these darn phones." He answers Sarah in a tone of voice that says, hey, I really think you're an idiot! He says to her, "You know, lady! That address box at the top of your browser. Now enter www dot cloud pool dot com!" Sarah gets all flustered and intimidated and doesn't know what to say next. She really wants to know what a browser is, but instead she says, "Wait. I'll just ask someone in the office to help me," and hangs up the phone.

Discuss the situation with others in a small group and answer these questions:

1. If you were Andy's manager and overheard this call, how would you handle the situation?

2. What principles of working with customers does Andy need to keep in mind?

Two students sit back-to-back, one playing the role of Andy and the other playing the role of Sarah. Play out the entire conversation. Others in the group can offer suggestions and constructive criticism.

THE CUSTOMER DECIDES WHEN THE WORK IS DONE

When you think you've solved the problem, allow the customer to decide when the service is finished to his or her satisfaction. For remote support, generally, the customer ends the call or chat session, not the technician. If you end the call too soon and the problem is not completely resolved, the customer can be frustrated, especially if it is difficult to contact you again.

For on-site work, after you have solved the problem, complete these tasks before you close the call:

1. If you changed anything on the PC after you booted it, reboot one more time to make sure you have not caused a problem with the boot.

2. Allow the customer enough time to be fully satisfied that all is working. Does the printer work? Print a test page. Does the network connection work? Can the customer log on to the network and access data on it?

3. If you backed up data before working on the problem and then restored the data from backups, ask the user to verify that the data is fully restored.

4. Review the service call with the customer. Summarize the instructions and explanations you have given during the call. This is an appropriate time to fill out your paperwork and explain to the customer what you have written. Then ask if she has any questions.

5. Explain preventive maintenance to the customer (such as deleting temporary files from the hard drive or cleaning the mouse). Most customers don't have preventive maintenance contracts for their PCs and appreciate the time you take to show them how they can take better care of their computers. One technician keeps a pack of monitor wipes in his tool kit and ends each call by cleaning the customer's monitor screen.

It's a good idea to follow up later with the customer and ask if he is still satisfied with your work and if he has any more questions. For example, you can say to the customer, "I'll call you on Monday to make sure everything is working and you're still satisfied with the work." And then on Monday make that call.

A+ Exam Tip The A+ 220-801 exam expects you to know to follow up with the customer at a later date to verify his or her satisfaction.

A+
220-801
5.3

SOMETIMES YOU MUST ESCALATE A PROBLEM

You are not going to solve every computer problem you encounter. Knowing how to **escalate** properly so the problem is assigned to those higher in the support chain is one of the first things you should learn on a new job. Know your company's policy for escalation. What documents or entries in the ticket-tracking software do you use? Who do you contact? How do you pass the problem on (email, phone call, or an online entry in a database)? Do you remain the responsible "support" party, or does the person now addressing the problem become the new contact? Are you expected to keep in touch with the customer and the problem, or are you totally out of the picture?

For help-desk support, escalation is most likely done in the call tracking system where you keep your call notes. It's very important to include detailed information in your notes so that the next person can pick up the call without having to waste time finding out information you already knew.

When you escalate, let the customer know. Tell the customer you are passing the problem on to someone who is more experienced or has access to more extensive resources. In most cases, the person who receives the escalation will immediately contact the customer and assume responsibility for the problem. However, in some situations you should follow through, at least to confirm that the new person and the customer have made contact.

If you check back with the customer only to find out that the other support person has not called or followed through to the customer's satisfaction, don't lay blame or point fingers. Just do whatever you can to help within your company guidelines. Your call to the customer will go a long way toward helping the situation.

THE JOB ISN'T FINISHED UNTIL THE PAPERWORK IS DONE

For on-site support, a customer expects documentation about your services. Include in the documentation sufficient details broken down by cost of individual parts, hours worked, and cost per hour. Give the documentation to the customer at the end of the service and keep a copy for yourself. For phone support, the documentation stays in-house.

If your organization is using an electronic tracking system and you're providing phone support, most likely you're typing notes as the call happens. Be clear with your notes, especially if others must handle the problem. If you cannot solve the problem on this one call, the next time you talk with the customer, you'll be dependent on your notes to remember the details of the previous call. You'll also want to use the solution to help build your knowledge base about this type of problem. Make the notes detailed enough so that you can use them later when solving similar problems. Also, know that tracking-system notes are sometimes audited.

If you don't have an electronic tracking system, after the call, create a written or digital record to build your own knowledge base. Record the initial symptoms of the problem, the source of the problem you actually discovered, how you made that discovery, and how the problem was finally solved. File your documentation according to symptoms or according to solutions.

APPLYING | CONCEPTS Daniel had not been a good note taker in school, and this lack of skill was affecting his work. His manager, Jonathan, had been watching Daniel's notes in the ticketing system at the help desk he worked on and was not happy with what he saw. Jonathan had pointed out to Daniel more than once that his cryptic notes with sketchy information would one day cause major problems. On Monday morning, calls were hammering the help desk because a server had gone down over the weekend and many internal customers were not able to get to their data. Daniel escalated one call from a customer named Matt to a tier-two help desk. Later that day, Sandra, a tier-two technician, received the escalated ticket, and to her dismay the phone number of the customer was missing. She called Daniel. "How am I to call this customer? You only have his first name, and these notes about the problem don't even make sense!" Daniel apologized to Sandra, but the damage was done.

Two days later, an angry Matt calls the manager of the help desk to complain that his problem is still not solved. Jonathan listens to Matt vent and apologizes for the problem his help desk has caused. It's a little embarrassing to Jonathan to have to ask Matt for his call-back information and to repeat the details of the problem. He gives the information to Sandra and the problem gets a quick resolution.

Discuss this situation in a small group and answer the following questions:

1. If you were Daniel, what could you do to improve note taking in the ticketing system?

2. After Sandra called, do you think Daniel should have told Jonathan about the problem? Why or why not?

3. If you were Jonathan, how would you handle the situation with Daniel?

Two students play the role of Daniel and Jonathan when Jonathan calls Daniel into his office to discuss the call he just received from Matt. The other students in the group can watch and make suggestions as to how to improve the conversation.

9

WORKING WITH CO-WORKERS

Learn to be a professional when working with co-workers. A professional at work is someone who puts business matters above personal matters. In big bold letters I can say **the key to being professional is to learn to not be personally offended when someone lets you down or does not please you.** Remember, most people do the best they can considering the business and personal constraints they're up against. Getting offended leads to becoming bitter about others and about your job. Learn to keep negative opinions to yourself, and to expect the best of others. When a co-worker starts to gossip, try to politely change the subject.

Practice good organizational skills. Clean your desk before you leave work each day. Put things away. Use a good filing system. If you don't know how to organize your things, ask someone in the office for advice. Organize your time by making to-do lists and sticking with them as best you can. It's amazing the positive impression good organization makes with co-workers and the boss.

Know your limitations and be willing to admit when you can't do something. For example, Larry's boss stops by his desk and asks him to accept one more project. Larry already is working many hours overtime just to keep up. He needs to politely say to his boss, "I can accept this new project only if you relieve me of some of these tasks."

Learn how to handle conflict at work. Few of us have enough social skills to be able to effectively confront a co-worker about his faults. In almost every situation, when a co-worker disappoints us, the appropriate response is to shake it off, to not gossip to other co-workers about the problem, and move on. If you can't do that, the next best thing is to go to your boss or the co-worker's boss with the problem. Hopefully your boss has been trained in handling conflict and will take care of the problem. If you do find yourself in a situation where you want to help a co-worker with his problem, go to the co-worker with a good attitude and a sincere offer to help resolve the problem. And one more tip: Never give bad news or point out a fault by email. Using email, you are not able to communicate your tone of voice or read the facial expression of the other person. And, if miscommunication happens, you will not be able to immediately clear it up. Speak face to face, and if that is not possible, speak by telephone.

Figure 9-15   Co-workers who act professionally are fun to work with

APPLYING | CONCEPTS

Ray was new at the corporate help desk that supported hospitals across the nation. He had only had a couple weeks of training before he was turned loose on the phones. He was a little nervous the first day he took calls without a mentor sitting beside him. His first call came from Fernanda, a radiology technician who was trying to log onto her computer system to start the day. When Fernanda entered her user account and passcode, an error message appeared saying her user account was not valid. She told Ray she had tried it several times on two different computers. Ray checked his database and found her account, which appeared to be in good order. He asked her to try it again. She did and got the same results. In his two weeks of training, this problem had never occurred. He told her, "I'm sorry, I don't know how to solve this problem." She said, "Okay, well, thank you anyway," and hung up. She immediately called the help desk number back and the call was answered by Jackie, who sits across the room from Ray. Fernanda said, "The other guy couldn't fix my problem. Can you help me?"

"What other guy?" Jackie asks. "I think his name was Ray." "Oh, him! He's new and he doesn't know much and besides that he should have asked for help. Tell me the problem." Jackie resets the account and the problem is solved.

In a group of three or more students, discuss and answer the following questions:

1. What mistake did Ray make? What should he have done or said?

2. What mistake did Jackie make? What should she have done or said?

3. What three principles of relating to customers and co-workers would be helpful for Ray and Jackie to keep in mind?

DEALING WITH PROHIBITED CONTENT AND ACTIVITY

**A+
220-801
5.4**

Many organizations have documented a code of conduct that applies to its employees and/or customers. As an employee, you need to be aware of these codes of conduct and the procedures to follow when you believe these rules have been broken. Examples of prohibited content or activity might be when an employee saves pornographic photos to company computers, uses company computers and time for personal shopping, or installs pirated software on these computers.

As a PC support technician, you need to be especially aware of the issues surrounding software copyrights. When someone purchases software from a software vendor, that person has only purchased a **license** for the software, which is the right to use it. The buyer does not legally *own* the software and, therefore, does not have the right to distribute it. The right to copy the work, called a **copyright**, belongs to the creator of the work or others to whom the creator transfers this right. Copyrights are intended to legally protect the intellectual property rights of organizations or individuals to creative works, which include books, images, and software.

Making unauthorized copies of original software violates the Federal Copyright Act of 1976 and is called **software piracy** or, more officially, software copyright infringement. (This act allows for one backup copy of software to be made.) Making a copy of software and then selling it or giving it away is a violation of the law. Because it is so easy to do, and because so many people do it, many people don't realize that it's illegal. Normally, only the employee who violated the copyright law is liable for infringement; however, in some cases, an employer or supervisor is also held responsible, even when the copies were made without the employer's knowledge.

9

> **Notes** By purchasing a **site license**, a company can obtain the right to use multiple copies of software.

> **A+ Exam Tip** The A+ 220-801 exam expects you to know how to report prohibited content or activity through the proper channels and about a chain-of-custody document you might be called on to sign.

When you start a new job, find out from your employer how to deal with prohibited content or activity. Here are some things you need to know:

- When you identify what you believe to be an infringement of the law or the company's code of conduct, where do you turn to report the issue? Make sure you go only through proper channels; don't spread rumors or accusations with those who are not in these channels.
- What data or device should you immediately preserve as evidence for what you believe has happened? For example, if you believe you have witnessed a customer or employee using a company computer for a crime, should you remove and secure the hard drive from the computer or should you remove and secure the entire computer?

◢ Proper documentation surrounding the evidence of a crime is crucial to a criminal investigation. What documentation are you expected to submit and to whom is it submitted? This documentation might track the **chain of custody** for the evidence, which includes exactly what, when, and from whom evidence was collected, the condition of this evidence, and how the evidence was secured while it was in your possession. It also includes a paper trail of exactly to whom the evidence has been passed on and when. For example, suppose you suspect that a criminal act has happened and you hold a CD that you believe contains evidence of this crime. You need to carefully document exactly when and how you received the CD. Also, don't pass it on to someone else in your organization unless you have this person's signature on a chain-of-custody document so that you can later prove you handled the evidence appropriately. You don't want the evidence to not be allowed in a court of law because you have been accused of misconduct or there are allegations of tampering with the evidence.

Now let's turn our attention to a happier topic: customizing computer systems.

CUSTOMIZING COMPUTER SYSTEMS

Many computer vendors and manufacturers offer to build customized systems to meet specific needs of their customers. As a technical retail associate, you need to know how to recommend to a customer which computer components are needed for his or her specific needs. You also might be called on to select and purchase components for a customized system and perhaps even build this system from parts. In this part of the chapter, we focus on several types of customized systems you might be expected to know how to configure and what parts to consider when configuring these systems.

Here are important principles to keep in mind when customizing a system to meet customer needs:

◢ **Meet applications requirements.** Consider the applications the customer will use and make sure the hardware meets or exceeds the recommended requirements for these applications. Consider any special hardware the applications might require such as a joystick for gaming or a digital tablet for graphics applications.

◢ **Balance functionality and budget.** When working with a customer's budget, put the most money on the hardware components that are most needed for the primary intended purposes of the system. For example, if you are building a customized gaming PC, a RAID hard drive configuration is not nearly as important as the quality of the video subsystem.

◢ **Consider hardware compatibility.** When selecting hardware, start with the motherboard and processor. Then select other components that are compatible with this motherboard.

Now let's look at the components you need to consider when building these eight types of customized systems: graphics or CAD/CAM workstation, audio and video editing workstation, virtualization workstation, gaming PC, Home Theater PC, home server PC, thick client, and thin client.

A+ Exam Tip The A+ 220-801 exam expects you to know how to customize each of the eight types of computers covered in this part of the chapter.

GRAPHICS OR CAD/CAM WORKSTATION

You might be called on to configure a graphics or CAD/CAM (computer-aided design/computer-aided manufacturing) workstation. People who use these systems might be an engineer working with CAD software to design bridges, an architect who designs skyscrapers, a graphics designer who creates artistic pages for children's books, or a landscape designer who creates lawn and garden plans. Examples of the applications these people might use include AutoCAD Design Suite by Autodesk (*usa.autodesk.com*) or Adobe Illustrator by Adobe Systems (*www.adobe.com*).

These graphics-intensive, advanced applications perform complex calculations, use large and complex files, and can benefit from the most powerful of workstations. Because rendering 3D graphics is a requirement, a high-end or ultra-high-end video card is needed. Figure 9-16 shows one ultra-high-end customized CAD workstation by CAD Computers (*www.cadcomputers.com*).

Source: cadcomputers.com

Figure 9-16 A high-end CAD workstation customized for maximum performance

Here is a breakdown of the requirements for these high-end workstations:

▲ *Use a motherboard that provides quad channels for memory and plenty of memory slots and install a generous amount of RAM.* In the ad shown in Figure 9-16,

A+
220-801
1.9

the motherboard has 12 memory slots, and the system has 48 GB installed RAM. Notice the board can support up to 192 GB RAM, so there's room for upgrading RAM. For best performance, you can install the maximum amount of RAM the board supports. The board also has two processor slots, so you can install a second processor to further improve performance.

▲ *Use a powerful multicore processor with a large CPU cache.* In the ad shown in Figure 9-16, the Intel Second Generation Xeon processor, which is rated for high-end workstations and servers, has six cores and a 12 MB cache. This processor can handle the high demands of complex calculations performed by advanced software.

▲ *Use fast hard drives with plenty of capacity.* Notice the system in Figure 9-16 has two hard drives. The faster hard drive runs at 10 K RPM and holds the Windows installation. The moderately fast second hard drive has a capacity of 2 TB to accommodate large amounts of data. For best hard drive performance in any system, be sure the motherboard and hard drives are all using SATA III.

▲ *Use a high-end video card.* To provide the best 3D graphics experience, use a high-end video card. Probably the best chipset manufacturer for high-end video cards is NVIDIA (*www.nvidia.com*). The ad in Figure 9-16 mentions the Quadro 6000. The Quadro family of graphics processors has the best performing GPUs on the market, and the Quadro 6000 is the best Quadro currently sold (see Figure 9-17). It uses a PCIe ×16 slot and has 6 GB of GDDR5 video memory using a 384-bit video bus. The card can support a native screen resolution of 2560 × 1600. The card alone cost almost $4,000 and accounts for a major portion of the total system cost, which is almost $10,000.

Source: www.nvidia.com

Figure 9-17   This ultra-high-end video card by NVIDIA costs almost $4,000

Wouldn't it be fun to build this system! However, not all graphics workstations need to be this powerful or this expensive. You can still get adequate performance in a system for less than half the cost if you drop the processor down to an Intel Core i7, drop RAM down to 16 GB, and use an NVIDIA Quadro 2000 GPU on the video card along with a motherboard that supports dual-channel memory.

A+
220-801
1.9

AUDIO AND VIDEO EDITING WORKSTATION

Examples of professional applications software used to edit music, audio, video, and movies include Camtasia by TechSmith (*techsmith.com*), Adobe Production Premium by Adobe Systems (*adobe.com*), Media Composer by Avid (*avid.com*), and Final Cut Pro by Apple Computers (*apple.com*). (Final Cut Pro is used only on Macs, which are popular computers in the video editing industry.) Audio and video editing applications are not usually as power-hungry as CAD/CAM and graphics applications. The major difference in requirements is that most audio and video editing does not require rendering 3D graphics; therefore, you can get by with a not-so-expensive graphics card and processor. Customers might require a Blu-ray drive and dual monitors. Recall from Chapter 8 that the best LCD monitors that provide the most accurate color are LED monitors with a class IPS rating. Figure 9-18 shows one customized video editing workstation by ADK Media Group (*adkvideoediting.com*).

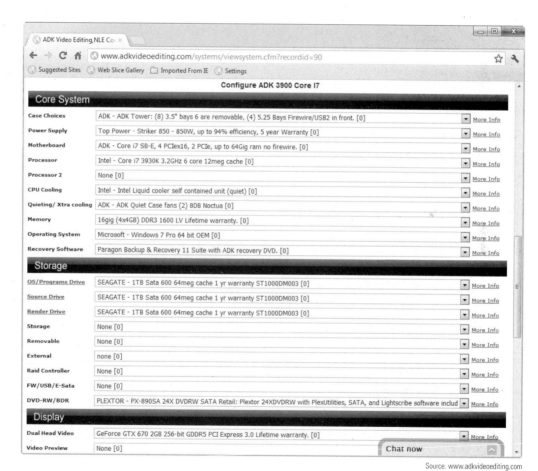

Source: www.adkvideoediting.com

Figure 9-18 This mid-range video editing workstation uses a Core i7 processor and GeForce graphics processor

Here is what you need for a mid-range to high-end audio/video editing workstation:

- Use a motherboard that supports dual, triple, or quad channel memory running at least at 1600 MHz RAM speed.
- Use a Core i7 or higher processor.
- Install at least 16 GB RAM; more is better.

A+
220-801
1.9

▲ Select a good video card that has a GeForce GTX graphics processor or better. GeForce is a family of graphics processors designed by NVIDIA that is not as high end as the Quadro graphics processors but still gives good video performance. Most users will require dual or triple monitors. You might need to consider dual video cards for optimum video performance or for more than two video ports.

▲ Use a double-sided, dual layer DVD burner and possibly a Blu-ray burner.

▲ Install one or more fast and large hard drives, running at least 7200 RPM.

VIRTUALIZATION WORKSTATION

Virtualization is when one physical machine hosts multiple activities that are normally done on multiple machines. Recall from Chapter 7 that one way to implement virtualization is to use virtual machine management software to create a virtual machine (VM) that uses simulated hardware. Each virtual machine has its own virtual hardware (virtual motherboard, processor, RAM, hard drive, and so forth) and can act like a physical computer. You can install an OS in each VM and then install applications in the VM. A program that manages VMs is called a **hypervisor**. Examples of hypervisors used on a desktop computer include XenClient by Citrix, Windows Virtual PC by Microsoft, and Oracle VirtualBox. Figure 9-19 shows a Windows 7 Professional desktop with two virtual machines running that were created by Windows Virtual PC. One VM is running Windows 7 Home Premium, and the other VM is running Windows XP. In Chapter 7, you learned how to install Windows in a VM.

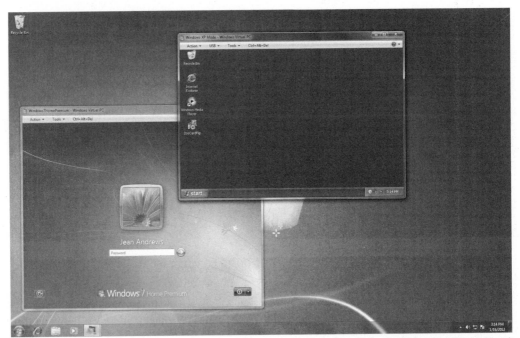

Source: Windows 7 and Windows Virtual PC, both by Microsoft

Figure 9-19   Two virtual machines running, each with its own virtual hardware and OS installed

Here are the requirements for a desktop computer that will be used to run multiple virtual machines:

▲ Each VM has its own virtual processor, so it's important the processor is a multicore processor. All dual core or higher processors and all motherboards sold today support **hardware-assisted virtualization (HAV)**. This technology enhances the processor support for virtual machines nend must be enabled in BIOS setup.

A+
220-801
1.9

◢ Some virtual machine management programs are designed so that each VM that is running ties up all the RAM assigned to it. Therefore, you need extra amounts of RAM when a computer is running several VMs.

◢ Each VM must have an operating system installed, and it takes about 20 GB for a Windows 7 installation. In addition, you need hard drive space for each application installed in each VM. Make sure you have adequate hard drive space for each VM.

When deciding how to use the overall budget for a virtualization workstation, maximize the number of CPU cores and the amount of installed RAM.

GAMING PC

Gaming computers benefit from a powerful processor and a high-end video card and sound card. Gamers who are also computer hobbyists might want to overclock their CPUs or use dual video cards for extra video performance. Take extra care to make sure the cooling methods are adequate. Because of the heat generated by multiple video cards and overclocking, liquid cooling is sometimes preferred. Also recall from Chapter 5 that when using the LGA2011 socket, liquid cooling is a Microsoft recommendation. Most gaming PCs use onboard surround sound, or you can use a sound card to improve sound. A lighted case with a clear plastic side makes for a great look.

Figure 9-20 shows a group of gaming PCs built by iBUYPOWER (*ibuypower.com*). Notice several of the PCs use liquid cooling, and all use a powerful processor with at least 8 GB of RAM. The video card uses a GeForce GTX or GT graphics processor or an AMD Radeon HD graphics processor. The Radeon line of graphics processors by AMD are comparable to the NVIDIA GeForce graphics processors.

Source: www.ibuypower.com

Figure 9-20   A group of Intel Core i5 or Core i7 gaming PCs

9

A+
220-801
1.9

HOME THEATER PC

A **Home Theater PC (HTPC)** is designed to play and possibly record music, photos, movies, and video on a television or extra-large monitor screen. Because these large screens are usually viewed from across the room, applications software is used to control output display menus and other clickable items in fonts large enough to read at a distance of 10 feet. This interface is called a **10-foot user interface.** Manufacturers such as Roku (*roku.com*) sell HTPCs as a set-top box complete with a remote control. In addition, some televisions have a built-in HTPC. An HTPC is also known as a media center appliance.

A custom-built HTPC needs to include these features:

▲ *Applications software.* The application controls the user interface and plays and records music and video. Examples of HTPC software include Windows Media Center, which is integrated into Windows, XBMC Media Center (*xbmc.org*), and Plex Media Center (*plexapp.com*).

▲ *HDMI **port to connect video output to television.*** And be sure to use a high-quality HDMI cable.

▲ *Cable TV input.* The best solution is to use a TV tuner card to connect the TV coax cable directly to the computer. Most TV tuner cards include a remote (see Figure 9-21). Some TV tuner cards are also video capture cards that offer the ability to record video and audio input. If the customer plans to use a TV cable box between the TV coax cable and the HTPC, you need to provide a way to make the connection. Most TV cable boxes have an HDMI output port. Realize this won't work with the HDMI port on a motherboard because these ports are output ports and you need an input port. To input to the PC using an HDMI port, you can use a video capture card that has an HDMI input port (see Figure 9-22).

Courtesy of Hauppauge Computer Works, Inc.

Figure 9-21   Dual TV tuner card with IR remote lets you watch and record two TV programs at the same time

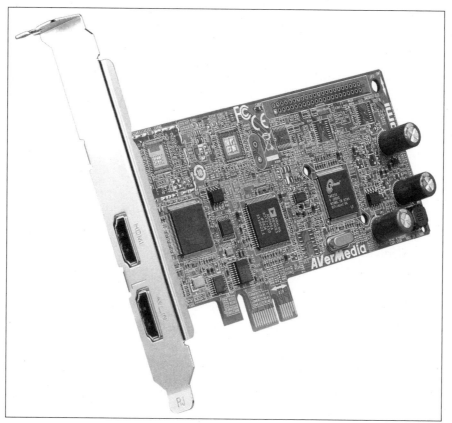

Figure 9-22 The AVerMedia AVerTV HD DVR (C027) video capture card has two HDMI input ports and uses a PCIe ×1 expansion slot

◢ *Satellite TV input.* This setup requires a satellite set-top box supplied by the company providing the satellite TV service. The best solution is to use a TV tuner card to receive input from the satellite set-top box. Make sure the types of ports on the computer and the box match up.

◢ *Internet access.* A way to receive streaming video from the Internet. To connect to the Internet, use a Gigabit Ethernet port or Wi-Fi connection.

◢ *Remote control.* A way to remotely control the HTPC because most likely the user will be sitting across the room from the computer. You can use a wireless keyboard and mouse, although the range for these devices might be too short. Some TV tuner cards include a remote. Also consider an app you can download to a smartphone to make it work as the remote.

◢ *Low background noise.* Because these computers don't perform complex calculations, you don't need as much processor or RAM power as in other systems. For example, you can use the small Intel Atom processor with 4 GB of RAM. Therefore, you won't need an extensive cooling system. You do, however, want a system that runs quietly. You can reduce noise by using SSD hard drives and low-speed fans or no fans at all.

◢ *Surround sound.* The system should support surround sound using at least six speakers located around the room. In Figure 9-23, you can see the preferred location for six speakers. Three popular variations of surround sound are 5.1 (uses up to six channels and speakers), 7.1 (uses up to eight channels and speakers), and 9.1 (uses up to 10 channels and speakers). Most sound cards and motherboards support six channels or ports for sound.

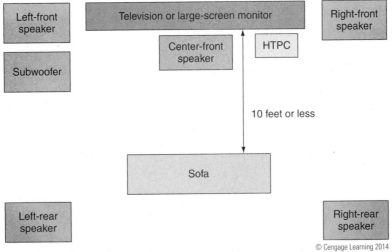

Figure 9-23   Speaker locations for surround sound

© Cengage Learning 2014

▲ *Case form factor.* An HTPC should be small enough to fit on a shelf in an entertainment center, and several companies make **HTPC cases** specifically for this purpose. The HTPC case shown in Figure 9-24 accommodates a MicroATX, mini-ITX, or mini-DTX motherboard and power supply. (A mini-DTX motherboard is slightly wider than the mini-ITX board.) The case has drive bays for 3.5 inch and 2.5 inch drives.

Courtesy of Silverstone Technology Co., Ltd.

Figure 9-24   The HTPC case by Silverstone is less than six inches high and has three silent fans

HOME SERVER PC

A home server PC is useful when you have several computers on a small home network and want to share files among them. You can use the PC to serve up these files and to stream video files and movies to client computers. One popular type of home server PC is Slingbox by Sling Media (*slingbox.com*). The device can serve up streaming media that you have stored on it not only to other computers in your home but also to a client computer anywhere on the Internet.

Here are the features and hardware you need to consider when customizing a home server PC:

▲ *Use a processor with moderate power.* The Intel Core i5 or Core i3 works well. A moderate amount of RAM is sufficient, for example, 6 to 8 GB.

▲ *Storage speed and capacity need to be maximized.* Use hardware RAID implemented on the motherboard to provide fault tolerance and high performance. Make sure the motherboard supports hardware RAID. Use fast hard drives (at least 7200 RPM) with plenty of storage capacity. Make sure the case has plenty of room for all the hard drives a customer might require.

▲ *Network transfers need to be fast, especially for streaming videos and movies.* Make sure the network port is rated for Gigabit Ethernet (1000 Mbps). All other devices and computers on the LAN should also use Gigabit Ethernet.

▲ *Printer sharing.* A USB printer can be connected directly to the PC and then you can use Windows to share the printer with others on the network. How to share printers is covered in Chapter 21. Alternately, some routers and switches provide a USB port that can be used to connect a USB printer to other computers on the network.

▲ *Onboard video works well.* Recall that onboard video is a video port embedded on the motherboard and does not perform as well as a good video card. Because the PC is not likely to be used as a workstation, you don't need powerful video.

▲ *Windows 7 can be used as the OS, but Windows Home Server 2011 provides the additional security features needed to better secure a home network.* In addition, if the customer plans to use the PC to back up files on client computers, know that Windows Home Server provides a more robust backup utility than does Windows 7.

THICK CLIENT AND THIN CLIENT

Recall that a desktop computer can use virtual machine management software (called a hypervisor) to provide one or more VMs, and in this situation the computer is called a virtualization workstation. In a corporate environment, the VM can also be provided by a virtualization server, which serves up a virtual machine to a client computer. The **virtualization server** provides a virtual desktop for users on multiple client machines. Most, if not all, processing is done on the server, which provides to the client the Virtual Desktop Infrastructure (VDI). See Figure 9-25.

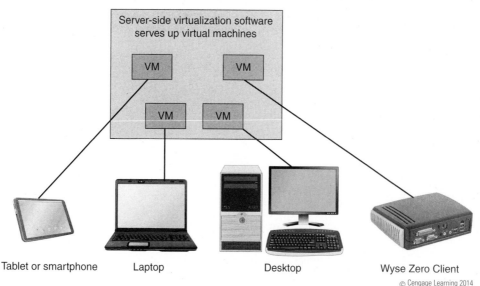

Tablet or smartphone   Laptop   Desktop   Wyse Zero Client

© Cengage Learning 2014

Figure 9-25 A virtualization server provides a desktop to each client computer or appliance

A+ 220-801 1.9

These VM clients that receive the virtual desktop from the server can be a thick client, thin client, or zero client. You might be called on to customize a thick client or thin client computer for a customer. (A zero client, also called a dumb terminal, is built by the manufacturer. It does not have an OS and is little more than an interface to the network with a keyboard, monitor, and mouse.) Here are the details for a thick client and thin client computer:

▲ A **thick client**, also called a fat client, is a regular desktop computer or laptop that is sometimes used as a client by a virtualization server. It can be a low-end or high-end desktop or laptop. It should meet the recommended requirements to run Windows 7 and any applications the user might require when it is being used as a stand-alone computer rather than a VM client. Table 9-1 lists the hardware requirements for Windows 7.

▲ A **thin client** is a computer that has an operating system but has little computer power and might only need to support a browser used to communicate with the server. The server does most of the processing for the thin client. To reduce the cost of the computer, configure it to meet only the minimum requirements for Windows.

Hardware	For 32-bit Windows 7	For 64-bit Windows 7
Processor	1 GHz or faster	1 GHz or faster
Memory	1 GB	2 GB
Free hard drive space	16 GB	20 GB
Video device and driver	Direct X 9 device with WDDM 1.0 or higher driver	Direct X 9 device with WDDM 1.0 or higher driver

© Cengage Learning 2014

Table 9-1 Minimum and recommended hardware requirements for Windows 7

>> CHAPTER SUMMARY

Job Roles and Responsibilities

▲ Five key job roles of a PC technician include PC support technician, PC service technician, technical retail associate, bench technician, and help-desk technician.

▲ A+ Certification by CompTIA is the most significant and most recognized certification for PC repair technicians.

▲ Learning about new technology can be done by attending trade shows, reading trade magazines, researching on the web, subscribing to email newsletters, and attending seminars and workshops.

What Customers Want: Beyond Technical Know-how

▲ Customers want more than just technical know-how. They want a positive and helpful attitude, respect, good communication, sensitivity to their needs, ownership of their problem, dependability, credibility, integrity, honesty, and professionalism.

Planning for Good Service

▲ Customers expect their first contact with you to be professional and friendly, and they want you to put listening to their problem or request as your first priority.

▲ Know how to ask penetrating questions when interviewing a customer about a problem or request.

▲ Set and meet customer expectations by good communication about what you are doing or intending to do and allowing the customer to make decisions where appropriate.

▲ Deal confidently and gracefully with customers who are difficult, including those who are not knowledgeable, are overly confident, or complain.

▲ When you first start a new job, find out how to escalate a problem you cannot solve.

Dealing with Prohibited Content and Activity

▲ Be aware of the documented code of conduct for your organization as it applies to any prohibited content or activity. As a PC support technician, you need to especially be aware of the problem of software piracy.

▲ A chain-of-custody document provides a paper trail of how evidence in a criminal case is handled and includes how, when, where, and by whom evidence was preserved and secured.

Customizing Computer Systems

▲ As a technician, you might be called on to customize a system for a customer including a graphics or CAD/CAM workstation, audio and video editing workstation, virtualization workstation, gaming PC, Home Theater PC (HTPC), home server PC, thick client, or thin client.

▲ A high-end video card is a requirement in a graphics, CAD/CAM, or video editing workstation or a gaming PC. These systems also need powerful processors and ample RAM.

▲ A TV tuner card is needed in a Home Theater PC.

▲ A thick client needs to meet recommended requirements for Windows and applications, and a thin client is a low-end computer that only needs to meet the minimum requirements for Windows.

>> KEY TERMS

For explanations of key terms, see the Glossary near the end of the book.

10-foot user interface	hardware-assisted	software piracy
A+ Certification	virtualization (HAV)	technical documentation
call tracking	Home Theater PC (HTPC)	thick client
chain of custody	HTPC case	thin client
copyright	hypervisor	ticket
escalate	license	virtualization server
expert system	site license	

>> REVIEW QUESTIONS

1. Which describes a PC technician who works in a lab environment, might not interact with users of the PCs being repaired, and is not permanently responsible for them?

    a) Help-desk technician

    b) PC support technician

    c) Bench technician

    d) PC service technician

2. What is the most significant certifying organization for PC technicians?

    a) ACM

    b) CompTIA

    c) Microsoft

    d) Cisco

3. What personal trait builds customer trust and loyalty and also increases a technician's value in the eyes of his co-workers and boss?

    a) A positive and helpful attitude

    b) Listening without interrupting the customer

    c) Using proper and polite language

    d) Taking ownership of a problem

4. Which type of PC support requires more interaction with customers than any other type of PC support?

    a) Phone support

    b) Onsite support

    c) Remote dial-in support

    d) Bench technician support

5. Which type of PC might require liquid cooling because of the heat generated by multiple video cards and overclocking?

    a) Home Theater PC (HTPC)

    b) Gaming computer

    c) Virtual machine (VM)

    d) Graphics or CAD/CAM workstation

6. True or false? Formal classroom training or certification is a requirement to work as a PC technician.

7. True or false? Probably the most significant indication that a PC technician is doing a good job is that customers are consistently satisfied.

8. True or false? Troubleshooting begins by interviewing the user.

9. True or false? When working with coworkers, it is best to give bad news or point out a fault by email.

10. True or false? A thin client is a regular desktop computer or laptop that is sometimes used as a client by a virtualization server.

11. A(n) _____ system is software that is designed and written to help solve problems.

12. A(n) _____ is a record of a telephone call for help request and what is happening to resolve it.

13. The right to copy the work, called a(n) _____, belongs to the creator of the work or others to whom the creator transfers this right.

14. Making unauthorized copies of original software violates the Federal Copyright Act of 1976 and is called software _____ or, more officially, software copyright infringement.

15. By purchasing a(n) _____, a company can obtain the right to use multiple copies of software.

9

Maintaining Windows

In Chapter 7, you learned how to install Windows. This chapter takes you to the next step in learning how to support a Windows operating system: maintaining the OS after it is installed. Most Windows problems stem from poor maintenance. If you are a PC support technician responsible for the ongoing support of several computers, you can make your work easier and your users happier by setting up and executing a good maintenance plan for each computer you support. A well-maintained computer gives fewer problems and performs better than one that is not maintained. In this chapter, you will learn how to schedule regular maintenance tasks, how to prepare for disaster by setting up backup routines for user data and system files, how to use commands to manage files and folders, how to manage a hard drive, and how to set up Windows to use multiple languages.

In this chapter, we use Windows 7 as our primary OS, but, as you read, know that we'll point out any differences between Windows 7 and Windows Vista/XP so that you can use this chapter to study all three operating systems. As you read, you might consider follow-ing the steps in the chapter first using a Windows 7 system, and then going through the chapter again using a Windows Vista or XP system.

Vista Differences For more details about maintaining Windows Vista and Windows XP, see the extra content, "Maintaining Windows Vista and XP," in the online content for this book at *www.cengagebrain.com*. See the Preface for more information.

SCHEDULED PREVENTIVE MAINTENANCE

A+
220-802
1.7

Regular preventive maintenance can keep a Windows computer performing well for years. At least once a month, you need to verify critical Windows settings and clean up the hard drive. These skills are covered in this part of the chapter. If you notice the system is slow as you do this maintenance, you need to dig deeper to optimize Windows. How to optimize Windows is covered in Chapter 11.

> **Notes** When you're responsible for a computer, be sure to keep good records of all that you do to maintain, upgrade, or fix the computer. When performing preventive maintenance, take notes and include those in your documentation.

VERIFY CRITICAL WINDOWS SETTINGS

Three Windows settings discussed here are critical for keeping the system protected from malware and hackers. Users sometimes change these settings without realizing their importance. Check the three settings and, if you find settings that are incorrect, take time to explain to the primary user of the computer how important these settings are. Here are the critical Windows settings you need to verify:

▲ *Windows Updates.* Install any important Windows updates or service packs that are waiting to be installed and verify that Windows Updates is configured to automatically allow updating. You learned how to configure Windows Updates in Chapter 7.

▲ *Antivirus software.* To protect a system against malicious attack, you also need to verify that antivirus software is configured to scan the system regularly and that it is up to date. If you discover it is not scanning regularly, take the time to do a thorough scan for viruses.

▲ *Network location setting.* To secure the computer against attack from the network, check that the Windows 7 network location is set correctly. How to verify the network location is covered in Chapter 7. Further details of configuring network security are discussed in Chapter 15.

CLEAN UP THE HARD DRIVE

For best performance, Windows needs about 15 percent free space on the hard drive that it uses for defragmenting the drive, for burning CDs and DVDs, and for a variety of other tasks, so it's important to delete unneeded files occasionally. In addition, you can improve drive performance and free up space by defragmenting the drive, checking the drive for errors, compressing folders, and moving files and folders to other drives. All these tasks are discussed in the following subsections. We begin by learning where Windows puts important folders on the drive.

A+
220-802
1.5, 1.7

DIRECTORY STRUCTURES

Folder or directory locations you need to be aware of include those for user files, program files, and Windows data. In the folder locations given in this discussion, we assume Windows is installed on drive C:.

User Profile Namespace

When a user first logs onto Windows 7/Vista, a **user profile** is created, which is a collection of user data and settings, and consists of two general items:

- ▲ *A user folder together with its subfolders.* These items are created under the C:\Users folder, for example, C:\Users\Jean Andrews. This folder contains a group of subfolders collectively called the **user profile namespace.** (In general, a namespace is a container to hold data, for example, a folder.)
- ▲ *Ntuser.data.* Ntuser.dat is a file stored in the C:\Users*username* folder and contains user settings. Each time the user logs on, the contents of this file are copied to a location in the registry.

Program Files

Here is where Windows stores program files unless you select a different location when a program is installed:

- ▲ Program files are stored in C:\Program Files for 32-bit versions of Windows.
- ▲ In 64-bit versions of Windows, 64-bit programs are stored in the C:\Program Files folder, and 32-bit programs are stored in the C:\Program Files (x86) folder.

Here are folders that applications and some utilities use to launch programs at startup:

- ▲ A program file or shortcut to a program file stored in the C:\Users*username*\AppData\ Roaming\Microsoft\Windows\Start Menu\Programs\Startup folder launches at startup for an individual user.
- ▲ A program file or shortcut to a program file stored in the C:\ProgramData\Microsoft\ Windows\Start Menu\Programs\Startup folder launches at startup for all users.

Folders for Windows Data

An operating system needs a place to keep hardware and software configuration information, user preferences, and application settings. This information is used when the OS is first loaded and when needed by hardware, applications, and users. Windows uses a database called the **registry** for most of this information. In addition, Windows keeps some data in text files called **initialization files**, which often have an .ini or .inf file extension.

Here are some important folder locations used for the registry and other Windows data:

- ▲ *Registry location.* The Windows registry is stored in the C:\Windows\system32\config folder.
- ▲ *Backup of the registry.* A backup of the registry is stored in the C:\Windows\system32\ config\RegBack folder.
- ▲ *Fonts.* Fonts are stored in the C:\Windows\Fonts folder.
- ▲ *Temporary files.* These files, which are used by Windows when it is installing software and performing other maintenance tasks, are stored in the C:\Windows\Temp folder.
- ▲ *Offline files.* Offline files are stored in the client-side caching (CSC) folder, which is C:\Windows\CSC. This folder is created and managed by the **Offline Files** utility, which allows users to work with files in the folder when the computer is not connected to the corporate network. Later, when a connection happens, Windows syncs up the offline files and folders stored in the C:\Windows\CSC folder with those on the network.

10

A+
220-802
1.5, 1.7

Differences for Windows XP

For Windows XP, the user profile is stored in the C:\Documents and Settings folder, for example, C:\Documents and Settings\Jean Andrews. The subfolders under the user folder are organized differently under XP than under Windows 7/Vista.

> **Notes** Most often, Windows is installed on drive C:, although in a dual boot environment, one OS might be installed on C: and another on a different drive. For example, Windows Vista can be installed on C: and Windows 7 installed on E:. If the drive letter of the Windows volume is not known, it is written in Microsoft documentation as *%SystemDrive%*. For example, the location of the Program Files folder is written as *%SystemDrive%*\Program Files.

A+
220-802
1.7

USE THE DISK CLEANUP UTILITY

Begin cleaning up the drive by finding out how much free space the drive has. Then use the Windows **Disk Cleanup** utility to delete temporary files on the drive.

APPLYING | CONCEPTS Follow these steps for Windows 7/Vista to find out how much free space is on the drive, and use Disk Cleanup. The XP Disk Cleanup utility works about the same as Windows 7/Vista.

1. Open Windows Explorer and right-click the volume on which Windows is installed, most likely drive C:. Select **Properties** from the shortcut menu. The drive Properties box appears, as shown on the left side of Figure 10-1. You can see the free space on this drive C: is 15.2 GB, which is about 11 percent of the volume.

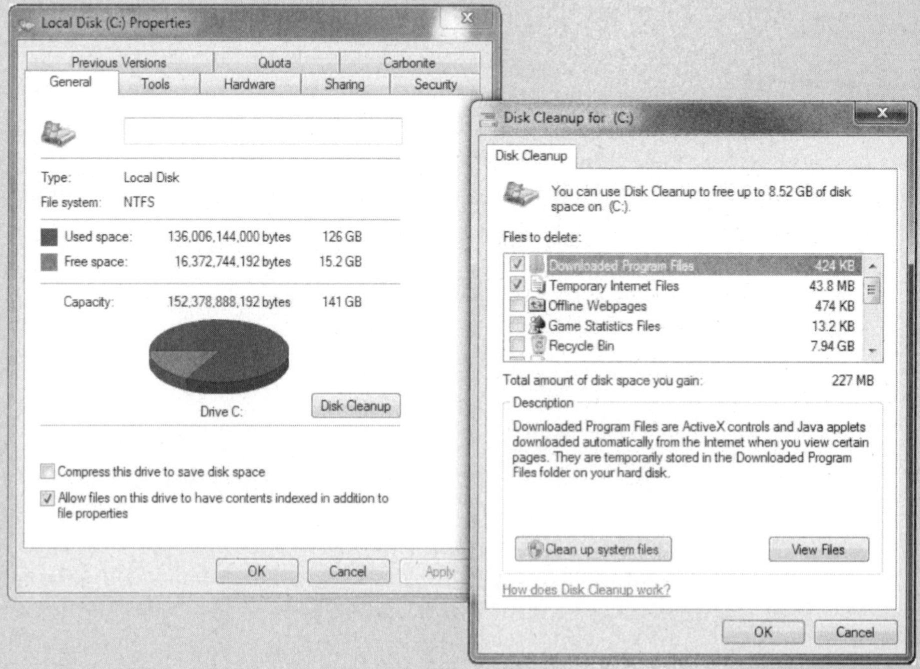

Source: Microsoft Windows 7

Figure 10-1 Use Windows Explorer to find out how much free space is on drive C

A+
220-802
1.7

2. On the General tab, click **Disk Cleanup**. (You can also access the utility by clicking **Start** and entering **cleanmgr.exe** in the *Search* box.) Disk Cleanup calculates how much space can be freed and then displays the Disk Cleanup box, shown on the right side of Figure 10-1. Select the files you want to delete.

3. Click **Clean up system files** to see temporary system files that you can also delete. The Disk Cleanup box on the left side of Figure 10-2 shows the result for one computer. Notice in the figure the option to delete files from a Previous Windows installation(s), which can free up 30.2 GB of hard drive space. This space is used by the Windows.old folder, which was created when Windows 7 was installed as an upgrade from Vista. Windows 7 setup stored the old Windows, Program Files, and User folders in the Windows.old folder. If the user assures you that no information, data, or settings are needed from the old Windows installation, it's safe to delete these files to free up the 30.2 GB.

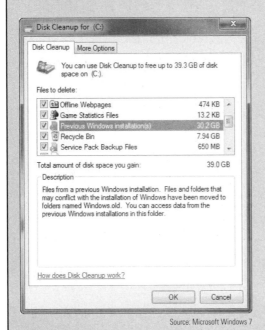
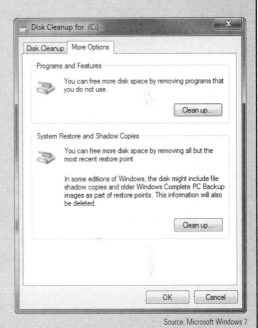

Source: Microsoft Windows 7   Source: Microsoft Windows 7

Figure 10-2 Clean up system files no longer needed in order to free up disk space

4. If you still need more free space, click the **More Options** tab (see the right side of Figure 10-2) in the Disk Cleanup box. In the Programs and Features area, click **Clean up.** You are taken to the Programs and Features window where you can uninstall unneeded software to recover that space. Also on the More Options tab in the Disk Cleanup box, when you click **Clean up** under the System Restore and Shadow Copies area, Windows will delete all but the most recent restore points that are created by System Restore. (You will learn more about System Restore later in this chapter.) In Windows XP, the More Options tab offers a third option to delete installed Windows components that you don't need.

DEFRAG THE HARD DRIVE

Two types of hard drives are magnetic hard disk drives (HDDs), which contain spinning platters, and solid state drives (SSDs), which contain flash memory. For magnetic hard drives, Windows 7/Vista automatically defragments the drive once a week. To **defragment** is to rearrange fragments or parts of files on the drive so each file is stored on the drive in contiguous clusters.

10

In a file system, a **cluster**, also called a **file allocation unit**, is a group of whole sectors. The number of sectors in a cluster is fixed and is determined when the file system is first installed. A file is stored in whole clusters, and the unused space at the end of the last cluster, called **slack**, is wasted free space. As files are written and deleted from a drive, clusters are used, released, and used again. New files written on the drive can be put in available clusters spread over the drive. Over time, drive performance is affected when the moving read/write arm of a magnetic drive must move over many areas of the drive to collect all the fragments of a file. Defragmenting a drive rewrites files in contiguous clusters and improves drive performance.

Because a solid state drive has no moving parts, defragmenting does not improve read/write time. In fact, defragmenting a solid state drive can reduce the life of the drive and is not recommended. Windows 7/Vista disables defragmenting solid state drives.

> **Notes** To find out what type of hard drive is installed, use Device Manager or the System Information window. For example, Figure 10-3 shows the System Information window where we have drilled down to the Storage Disks area, and you can see the model information for two hard drives installed in the system. A quick search on the web shows the first hard drive is an SSD and the second hard drive is a magnetic HDD.

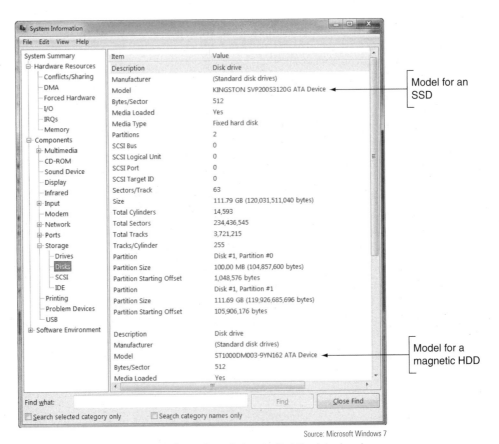

Model for an SSD

Model for a magnetic HDD

Source: Microsoft Windows 7

Figure 10-3   Use the System Information window to find the brand and model number for the hard drive

A+
220-802
1.7

APPLYING | CONCEPTS

To verify that Windows 7/Vista is defragmenting a magnetic drive and not defragmenting a solid state drive, do the following:

1. Use Windows Explorer to open the Properties box for a drive and click the **Tools** tab (see the left side of Figure 10-4), and then click **Defragment now**. In the Disk Defragmenter box (see the right side of Figure 10-4), verify the defrag settings. This system has two hard drives installed. Drive C: in this system is an SSD and is not being defragmented. Drive E: is a magnetic HDD and is scheduled for defragging. To have Windows tell you if a drive needs defragmenting, select a drive and click **Analyze disk**.

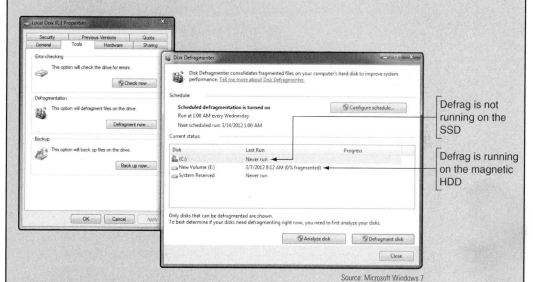

Source: Microsoft Windows 7

Figure 10-4 Windows is set to automatically defragment a magnetic hard drive once a week

2. If the drive is more than 10 percent fragmented, click **Defragment now** to defrag the drive immediately. The process can take a few minutes to several hours. If errors occur while the drive is defragmenting, check the hard drive for errors and try to defragment again.

Later in the chapter, you will learn to use the Defrag command to defrag the drive from a command prompt window.

For Windows XP, you must manually defragment the drive, and it's a good idea to do so once a week. For Windows XP, first close all open applications. Using Windows Explorer, open the Properties box for the drive. Click the **Tools** tab and then click **Defragment Now**. In the Disk Defragmenter window, click **Defragment** to start the process. Figure 10-5 shows XP defragmenting a volume. You can also use the Defrag command in XP.

10

A+
220-802
1.7

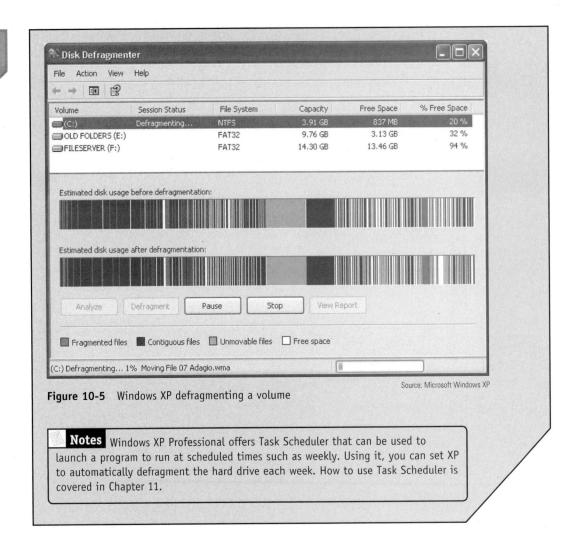

Figure 10-5 Windows XP defragmenting a volume

Source: Microsoft Windows XP

> **Notes** Windows XP Professional offers Task Scheduler that can be used to launch a program to run at scheduled times such as weekly. Using it, you can set XP to automatically defragment the hard drive each week. How to use Task Scheduler is covered in Chapter 11.

CHECK THE HARD DRIVE FOR ERRORS

Next, to make sure the drive is healthy, you need to search for and repair file system errors. The error checking utility searches for bad sectors on a volume and recovers the data from them if possible. It then marks the sector as bad so that it will not be reused.

To use the error checking utility, in Windows Explorer, right-click the drive, and select **Properties** from the shortcut menu. Click the **Tools** tab, as shown in the left side of Figure 10-6, and then click **Check now**. In the Check Disk dialog box, check **Automatically fix file system errors** and **Scan for and attempt recovery of bad sectors,** as shown in the right side of Figure 10-6, and then click **Start.** For the utility to correct errors on the drive, it needs exclusive use of all files on the drive. When Windows has exclusive use, the drive is called a locked drive. Therefore, a dialog box appears telling you about the problem and asking your permission to scan the drive the next time Windows starts. Reboot the system and let her rip.

A+
220-802
1.7

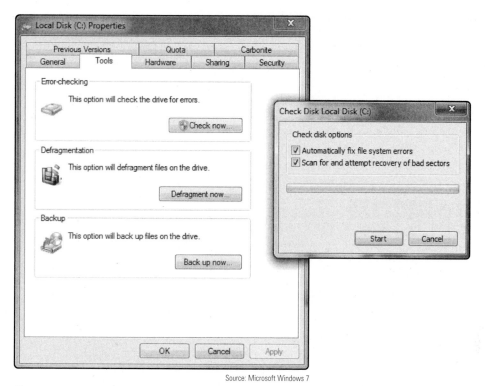

Source: Microsoft Windows 7

Figure 10-6 Windows repairs hard drive errors under the drive's Properties box using Windows Explorer

Later in the chapter, you learn how to use the Chkdsk command from the command prompt window, which also launches the error checking utility.

FREE UP SPACE ON THE DRIVE

To free up some space on the hard drive, consider these tips:

- *Uninstall software you no longer use.* Doing so will free up some space on the hard drive, and, if the software loads a service or program during Windows startup, Windows startup might see performance improvement.
- *Move data off the drive.* Consider moving home videos, movies, photos, and other data to an external hard drive or burning them to DVDs or CDs.
- **Move programs off the drive.** If your Windows volume needs more free space, you can uninstall a program and reinstall it on a second hard drive installed in the system. An installation routine usually gives you the option to point to another location to install the program other than the default C:\Program Files or C:\Program Files (x86) folder.
- *Use drive or folder compression.* Windows offers drive and folder compression that can save on hard drive space. However, it is not recommended that you compress the volume on which Windows is stored. To compress a folder or file on an NTFS drive, open the file or folder **Properties** box and click **Advanced** on the General tab. Then click **Compress contents to save disk space** and click **OK**.

> **Notes** Windows 7/Vista installs on an NTFS volume, but if a second volume on the drive is formatted using the FAT32 file system, you can convert the volume to NTFS. For large drives, NTFS is more efficient and converting might improve performance. NTFS also offers better security and file and folder compression. For two Microsoft Knowledge Base articles about converting from FAT to NTFS, go to *support.microsoft.com* and search for articles 156560 and 314097. The first article discusses the amount of free space you'll need to make the conversion, and the second article tells you how to convert.

10

A+
220-802
1.5, 1.7

MOVE THE VIRTUAL MEMORY PAGING FILE

Windows uses a file, Pagefile.sys, in the same way it uses memory. This file is called **virtual memory** and is used to enhance the amount of RAM in a system. Normally, the file, **Pagefile.sys**, is a hidden file stored in the root directory of drive C:. To save space on drive C:, you can move Pagefile.sys to another partition on the same hard drive or to a different hard drive, but don't move it to a different hard drive unless you know the other hard drive is at least as fast as this drive. If the drive is at least as fast as the drive on which Windows is installed, performance should improve. Also, make sure the new volume has plenty of free space to hold the file—at least three times the amount of installed RAM.

> **A+ Exam Tip** The A+ 220-802 exam expects you to know how to configure virtual memory for optimal performance.

APPLYING | CONCEPTS   To change the location of Pagefile.sys in Windows 7/Vista, follow these steps:

1. Open the System window and click **Advanced system settings** in the left pane. The System Properties box appears with the Advanced tab selected (see Figure 10-7).

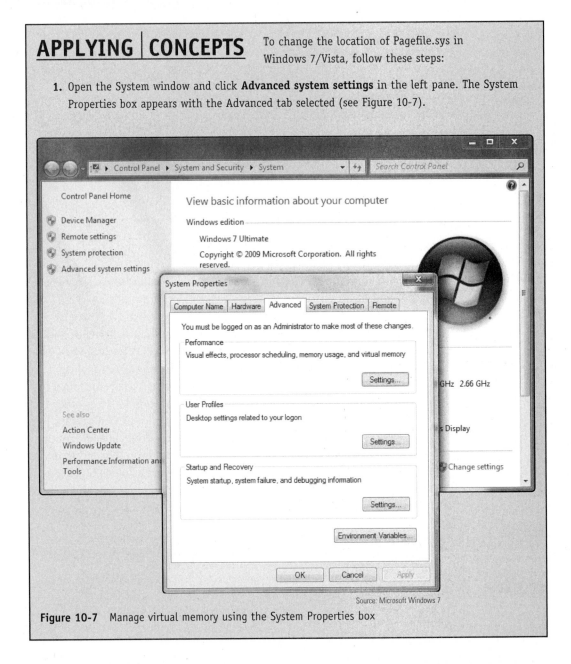

Source: Microsoft Windows 7

Figure 10-7   Manage virtual memory using the System Properties box

A+
220-802
1.5, 1.7

2. In the Performance section, click **Settings**. In the Performance Options box, select the **Advanced** tab and click **Change**. The Virtual Memory dialog box appears.

3. Uncheck **Automatically manage paging file size for all drives** (see Figure 10-8). Select the drive where you want to move the paging file. For best performance, allow Windows to manage the size of the paging file. If necessary, select **System managed size** and click **Set**.

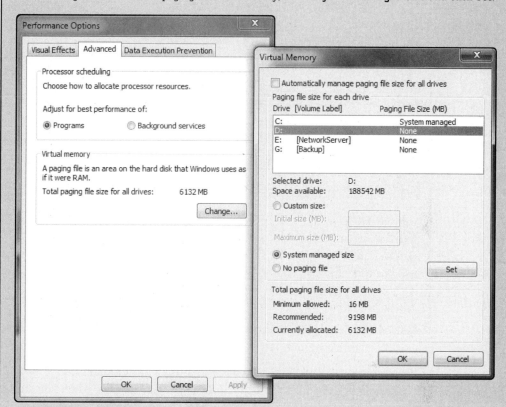

Source: Microsoft Windows 7

Figure 10-8 Move Pagefile.sys to a different drive

4. Click **OK**. Windows informs you that you must restart the system for the change to take effect. Click **OK** to close the warning box.

5. Click **Apply** and close all boxes. Then restart the system.

For Windows XP, click **Start**, right-click **My Computer**, select **Properties**, and then click the **Advanced** tab. In the Performance section, click **Settings**, click the **Advanced** tab, and then click **Change**. The Virtual Memory box that appears looks and works similarly to the Windows 7 Virtual Memory box in Figure 10-8.

If you still don't have enough free space on the Windows volume, consider adding a second hard drive to the system. In fact, if you install a second hard drive that is faster than the Windows hard drive, know that reinstalling Windows on the faster hard drive will improve performance. You can then use the slower and older hard drive for data.

Notes If the Windows system is still slow and sluggish, know that in Chapter 11 you'll learn more about how to optimize Windows so it performs better.

10

A+
220-802
1.1, 1.7

Now let's look at how to perform on-demand backups and to schedule routine backups.

BACKUP PROCEDURES

A backup is an extra copy of a data or software file that you can use if the original file becomes damaged or destroyed. Losing data due to system failure, a virus, file corruption, or some other problem really makes you appreciate the importance of having backups.

> **Notes** With data and software, here's a good rule of thumb: If you can't get along without it, back it up.

APPLYING | CONCEPTS Dave was well on his way to building a successful career as a PC repair technician. His PC repair shop was doing well, and he was excited about his future. But one bad decision changed everything. He was called to repair a server at a small accounting firm. The call was on the weekend when he was normally off, so he was in a hurry to get the job done. He arrived at the accounting firm and saw that the problem was an easy one to fix, so he decided not to do a backup before working on the system. During his repairs, the hard drive crashed and all data on the drive was lost—four million dollars' worth! The firm sued, Dave's business license was stripped, and he was ordered to pay the money the company lost. A little extra time to back up the system would have saved his whole future. True story!

Because most of us routinely write data to the hard drive, in this section, we focus on backing up from the hard drive to another media. However, when you store important data on any media—such as a flash drive, external hard drive, or CD—always keep a copy of the data on another media. Never trust important data to only one media.

In this part of the chapter, you will learn how to make a disaster recovery plan and then learn how to use Windows 7 to back up user data, critical Windows system files, and entire volumes.

PLANNING FOR DISASTER RECOVERY

The time to prepare for disaster is before it occurs. If you have not prepared, the damage from a disaster will most likely be greater than if you had made and followed disaster recovery plans. Suppose the hard drive on your PC stopped working and you lost all its data. What would be the impact? Are you prepared for this to happen? Here are decisions you need to make for your backup and recovery plans:

▲ *Decide on the backup destination.* For example, online backup, network drive, CD, DVD, Blu-Ray, SD card, USB flash drive, external hard drive, or other media. Here are points to keep in mind:

• For individuals or small organizations, an online backup service such as Carbonite (carbonite.com) or Mozy (mozy.com) is the easiest, most reliable, and most expensive solution. You pay a yearly subscription for the service, and they guarantee your backups, which are automatically done when your computer is connected to the Internet. If you decide to use one of these services, be sure to restore files from backup occasionally to make sure your backups are happening as you expect and you can recover a lost file.

A+
220-802
1.1, 1.7

- Even though it's easy to do, don't make the mistake of backing up your data to another partition or folder on your same hard drive. When a hard drive crashes, most likely all partitions go down together and you will have lost your data and your backup. Back up to another media and, for extra safety, store it at an off-site location.

▲ *Decide on the backup software.* Windows offers a backup utility. However, you can purchase third-party backup software that might offer more features. For example, the external hard drive by Western Digital shown in Figure 10-9 comes with backup software that lets you schedule backups and allows you to select the number of generations of backups you keep. However, before you decide to use an all-in-one backup system such as this one, be certain you understand the risks of not keeping backups at an off-site location and keeping all your backups on a single media.

© Cengage Learning 2014

Figure 10-9   The Western Digital My Passport Essential 750 GB external drive uses USB 3.0 and comes with backup software

▲ *Decide how simple or complex your backup strategy needs to be.* A backup and recovery plan for individuals or small organizations might be very simple. But large organizations might require backups be documented each day, scheduled at certain times of the day or night, and recovery plans tested on a regular basis. Know the requirements of your organization when creating a backup and recovery plan. As a general rule of thumb, back up data for about every 4 to 6 hours of data entry. This might mean a backup needs to occur twice a day, daily, weekly, or monthly. Find out the data entry habits of workers before making your backup schedule and deciding on the folders or volumes to back up.

After you have a backup plan working, test the recovery plan. In addition, you need to occasionally test the recovery plan to make sure all is still working as you expect. Do the following:

▲ *Test the recovery process.* Erase a file on the hard drive, and use the recovery procedures to verify that you can re-create the file from the backup. This verifies that the backup medium works, that the recovery software is effective, and that you know how to use it. After you are convinced that the recovery works, document how to perform it.

◢ *Keep backups in a safe place and routinely test them.* Don't leave a backup disc lying around for someone to steal. Backups of important and sensitive data should be kept under lock and key. In case of fire, keep enough backups off-site so that you can recover data even if the entire building is destroyed. Routinely verify that your backups are good by performing a test recovery of a backed-up file or folder. Backups are useless if the data on the backup is corrupted.

Now let's see how to back up user data, important Windows system files, and entire volumes using Windows 7/Vista/XP tools.

> 💡 **A+ Exam Tip** The A+ 220-802 exam expects you to know how to create and use backups and best practices when scheduling backups.

CREATE AND USE BACKUPS IN WINDOWS 7

Using Windows 7 Backup and Restore, you can back up user data and/or the volume on which Windows is installed. When you set up a backup schedule, you select the folders to back up and you can also choose to back up the Windows volume.

BACK UP THE WINDOWS VOLUME

The backup of the Windows 7 volume is called the **system image**. Here are points to keep in mind when creating a system image and using it to recover a failed Windows volume:

◢ *A system image includes the entire drive C: or other drive on which Windows is installed.* When you restore a hard drive using the system image, everything on the volume is deleted and replaced with the system image.

◢ *A system image must always be created on an internal or external hard drive.* When using Backup and Restore to back up your data folders, you can include the system image in the backup procedure. Even if the files and folders are being copied to a USB drive, CD, or DVD, the system image will always be copied to a hard drive.

◢ *Don't depend just on the system image as your backup.* You should also back up individual folders that contain user data. If individual data files or folders need to be recovered, you cannot rely on the system image because recovering data using the system image would totally replace the entire Windows volume with the system image.

◢ *You can create a system image any time after Windows is installed, and then you can use this image to recover from a failed hard drive.* To create the image, click **Start**, **All Programs**, **Maintenance**, and **Backup and Restore**. The Backup and Restore window opens (see Figure 10-10). Click **Create a system image** and follow the directions on-screen. Using the system image to recover a failed hard drive is called reimaging the drive. The details of how to reimage the drive are covered in Chapter 14.

> ⚡ **Caution** Before creating a system image on a laptop, plug the laptop into an AC outlet so that a failed battery will not interrupt the process.

A+
220-802
1.1, 1.7

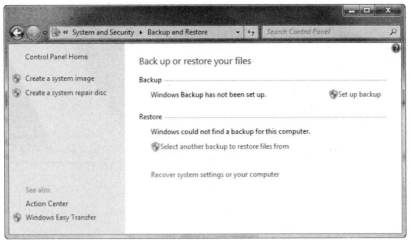

Source: Microsoft Windows 7

Figure 10-10   Use the Backup and Restore window to create a system image

10

> **Notes** The system image you create using Backup and Restore can be installed only on the computer that was used to create it. The method used to create a hardware-independent system image, called a standard image, is discussed in Chapter 7 and Appendix D.

BACK UP USER DATA

Because data on a hard drive is likely to change often, it's important to back it up on a regular schedule. Using Backup and Restore, you can create a backup schedule that can include any folder on the hard drive and the system image. The folders and volume are first backed up entirely (called a full backup). Then on the schedule you set, any file or folder is backed up that has changed or been created since the last backup (called an incremental backup). Occasionally, Windows does another full backup.

Recover a Corrupted or Lost File or Folder

If a data file or folder later gets corrupted, you can recover the file or folder using the Backup and Restore window or using the Previous Versions tab of the file or folder Properties box. To use the Backup and Restore window, follow these steps:

1. Make the backup media available to the computer by inserting the backup disc, connecting the external hard drive, or other method.

> **Notes** If the *Restore my files* button is missing from the Backup and Restore window, your backup media might not be available to Windows. You might need to plug in the media and then use Windows Explorer to verify you can access the backup folder on the media.

A+
220-802
1.1, 1.7

APPLYING │ CONCEPTS   SET UP A BACKUP SCHEDULE

Follow these steps to learn how to set up a backup schedule using Windows 7 Backup and Restore:

1. Open the Backup and Restore window. If no backup has ever been scheduled on the system, the window will look like the one in Figure 10-10. Click **Set up backup**.

> **Notes** You can open Backup and Restore using the Start, All Programs menu, using the Control Panel (in Control Panel, click **Back up your computer**), or by typing **Backup and Restore** in the *Search* box.

2. In the next dialog box (see Figure 10-11), select the media to hold the backup. In Figure 10-11, choices are volume E: (a second internal hard drive), the DVD drive, and OneTouch (an external hard drive). Make your selection and click **Next**.

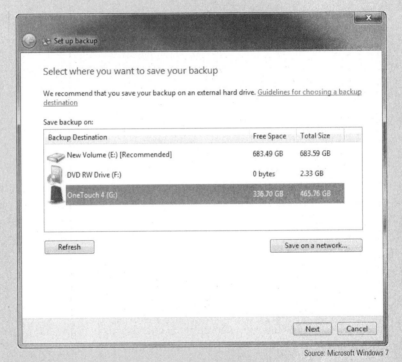

Source: Microsoft Windows 7

Figure 10-11   Select the destination media to hold the backup

> **Notes** Windows 7 Professional, Ultimate, and Enterprise editions allow you to save the backup to a network location. To use a shared folder on the network for the backup destination, click **Save on a network** (see Figure 10-11). In the resulting box (see Figure 10-12), click **Browse** and point to the folder. Also enter the username and password on the remote computer that the backup utility will use to authenticate to that computer when it makes the backup. You cannot save to a network location when using Windows 7 Home editions. For these editions, the button *Save on a network* is missing in the window where you select the backup destination.

3. In the next box, you can allow Windows to decide what to back up or decide to choose for yourself. Select **Let me choose** so that you can select the folders to back up. Click **Next**.

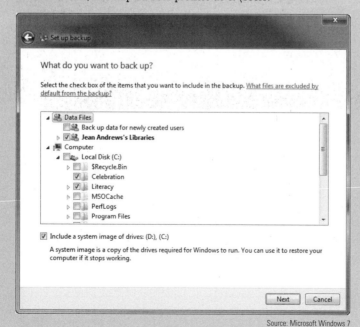

Source: Microsoft Windows 7

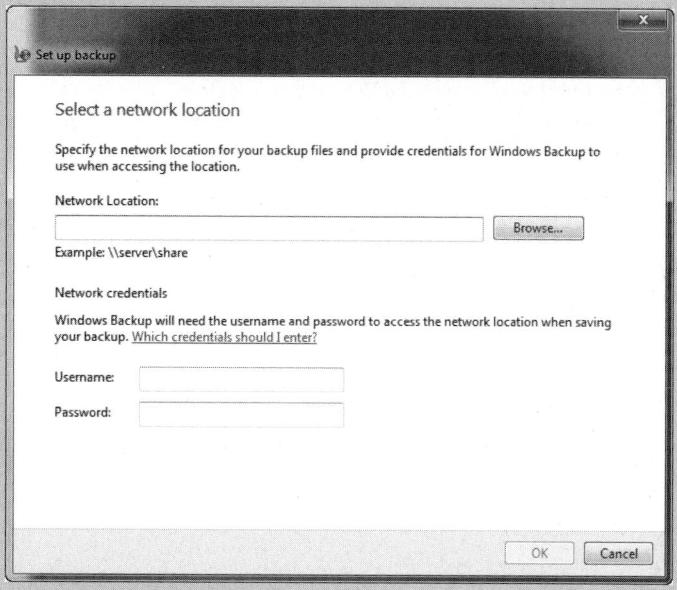

Figure 10-12 Select the folder on the network to hold the backup and enter the username and password for the remote computer

4. In the next box (see Figure 10-13), select the libraries and folders you want to back up. You can click the white triangle beside Local Disk (C:) to drill down to any folder on the hard drive for backup. Check folders or libraries to back up. If the backup media can hold the system image, the option to include the image is selected by default. If you don't want to include the image, uncheck it. Click **Next** to continue. Here are folders that might contain important user data:

▲ Application data is usually found in C:\Users*username*\AppData.

▲ Internet Explorer favorites are in C:\Users*username*\Favorites.

▲ Better still, back up the entire user profile at C:\Users*username*.

▲ Even better, back up all user profiles at C:\Users.

Source: Microsoft Windows 7

Figure 10-13 Select the folders or libraries to include in the backup

A+
220-802
1.1, 1.7

5. In the next box, verify the correct folders and libraries are selected (see Figure 10-14). Notice in the figure, the backup is scheduled to run every Sunday at 7:00 PM. To change this schedule, click **Change schedule**. In the next box, you can choose to run the backup daily, weekly, or monthly and select the time of day. Make your selections and click **OK**.

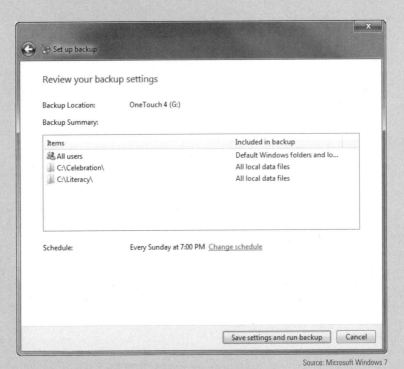

Source: Microsoft Windows 7

Figure 10-14 By default, Windows runs a backup each week at the same day and time

6. Review your backup settings and click **Save settings and run backup**. The backup proceeds. A **shadow copy** is made of any open files so that files that are currently open are included in the backup.

> 💡 **A+ Exam Tip** The A+ 220-802 exam expects you to know what a shadow copy is.

If you want to later change the settings for your scheduled backup, open the Backup and Restore window. Notice in Figure 10-15 the window has changed from that shown earlier in Figure 10-10. It now shows the details about the scheduled backup. To change the backup settings, click **Change settings**. Follow the process to verify or change each setting for the backup. Also notice in the left pane of Figure 10-15 that you can turn off the scheduled backup by clicking **Turn off schedule**.

> 📝 **Notes** One limitation of Windows Backup and Restore is that you can have only one scheduled backup routine.

A+
220-802
1.1, 1.7

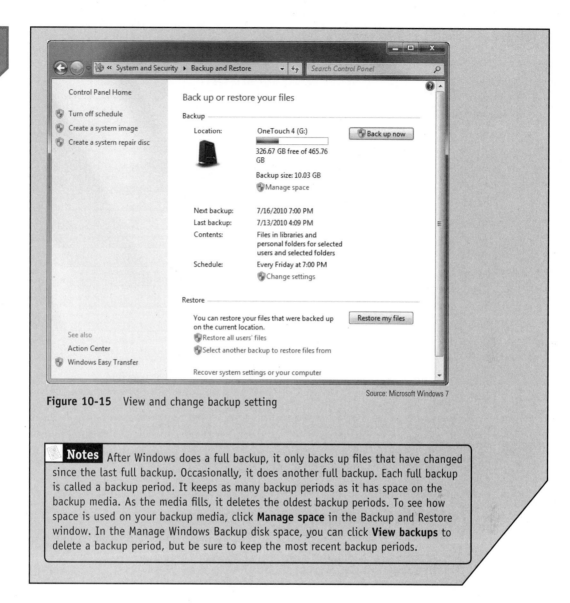

Figure 10-15 View and change backup setting

Source: Microsoft Windows 7

10

> **Notes** After Windows does a full backup, it only backs up files that have changed since the last full backup. Occasionally, it does another full backup. Each full backup is called a backup period. It keeps as many backup periods as it has space on the backup media. As the media fills, it deletes the oldest backup periods. To see how space is used on your backup media, click **Manage space** in the Backup and Restore window. In the Manage Windows Backup disk space, you can click **View backups** to delete a backup period, but be sure to keep the most recent backup periods.

2. Open the **Backup and Restore** window. Scroll down to the bottom of the window and click **Restore my files**. The Restore Files box appears (see Figure 10-16).

3. Use one of the three buttons on the window to locate the file or folder. *Search* allows you to search for a file or folder when you only know part of the filename or folder name. *Browse for files* allows you to drill down to the file to restore. *Browse for folders* allows you to search for the folder to restore. You can locate and select multiple files or folders to restore. Then follow the directions on-screen to restore all the selected items.

A previous version of a file or folder is a version that was previously created by the Backup and Restore utility or by System Protection when it created a restore point for the system. To restore a folder or file to a previous version, follow these steps:

1. Use Windows Explorer to copy (do not move) the corrupted folder or file to a new location. When you restore a file or folder to a previous version, the current file or folder can be lost and replaced by the previous version. By saving a copy of the current file or folder to a different location, you can revert to the copy if necessary.

A+
220-802
1.1, 1.7

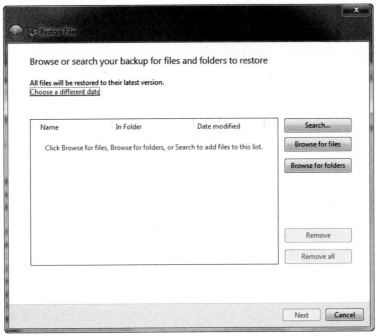

Source: Microsoft Windows 7

Figure 10-16 Locate the files and folders on the backup media to restore

2. Right-click the file or folder and select **Restore previous versions** from the shortcut menu. The Properties box for the file or folder appears with the Previous Versions tab selected. Windows displays a list of all previous versions of the file or folder it has kept (see Figure 10-17).

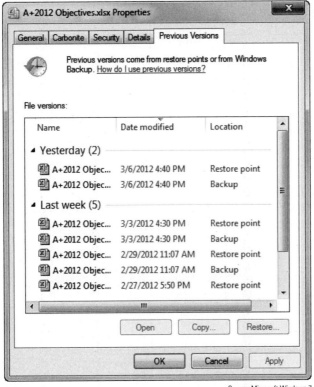

Source: Microsoft Windows 7

Figure 10-17 Restore a file or folder from a previous version

A+
220-802
1.1, 1.7

3. Select the version you want and click **Restore**. A message box asks if you are sure you want to continue. Click **Restore** and then click **OK**.

4. Open the restored file or folder and verify it is the version you want. If you decide you need another version, delete the file or folder and copy the file or folder you saved in Step 1 back into the original location. Then return to Step 2 and try again, this time selecting a different previous version.

A+
220-802
1.1, 1.5,
1.7, 1.8

BACK UP WINDOWS SYSTEM FILES

The Windows **System Protection** utility automatically backs up system files and stores them on the hard drive at regular intervals and just before you install software or hardware. These snapshots of the system are called **restore points** and include Windows system files that have changed since the last restore point was made. A restore point does not contain all user data, and you can manually create a restore point at any time.

Make Sure System Protection Is Turned On

To make sure System Protection has not been turned off, open the System window and click **System protection**. The System Protection tab of the System Properties box appears (see the left side of Figure 10-18). Make sure Protection is turned on for the drive containing Windows, which indicates that restore points are created automatically. In Figure 10-18, Protection for drive C: is on and other drives are not being protected. To make a change, click **Configure**. The System Protection box on the right side of the figure appears. If you make a change to this box, click **Apply** and then click **OK**.

Restore points are normally kept in the folder C:\System Volume Information, which is not accessible to the user. Restore points are taken at least every 24 hours, and they can use up to 15 percent of disk space. If disk space gets very low, restore points are no longer made, which is one more good reason to keep about 15 percent or more of the hard drive free.

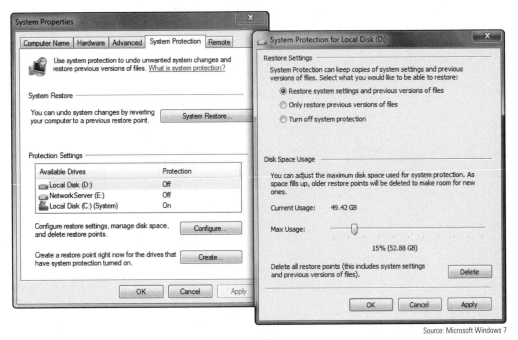

Source: Microsoft Windows 7

Figure 10-18 Make sure System Protection is turned on for the volume on which Windows is installed

A+
220-802
1.1, 1.5,
1.7, 1.8

Manually Create a Restore Point

To manually create a restore point, use the System Protection tab of the System Properties box, as shown on the left side of Figure 10-18. Click **Create**. In the System Protection box, enter a name for the restore point, such as "Before I tested software," and click **Create**. The restore point is created.

Apply a Restore Point

System Restore restores the system to its condition at the time a restore point was made. If you restore the system to a previous restore point, user data on the hard drive will not be altered, but you can affect installed software and hardware, user settings, and OS configuration settings. When you use System Restore to roll back the system to a restore point, any changes made to these settings after the restore point was created are lost; therefore, always use the most recent restore point that can fix the problem so that you make the least intrusive changes to the system.

To return the system to a previous restore point, do the following:

1. Click **Start, All Programs, Accessories, System Tools,** and **System Restore.** The System Restore box opens. Click **Next.**

2. In the next box, the most recent restore points appear. For most situations, the most recent is the one to select so as to make the least possible changes to your system. If you want to see other restore points, check **Show more restore points.** Select a restore point (see Figure 10-19) and click **Next.**

3. Windows asks you to confirm your selection. Click **Finish** and respond to the warning box. The system restarts and the restore point is applied.

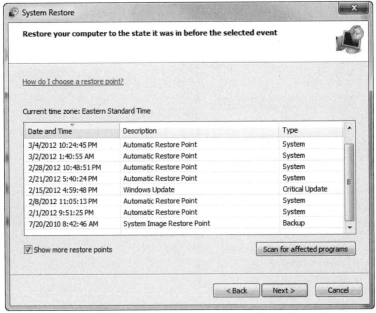

Source: Microsoft Windows 7

Figure 10-19 Select a restore point

Points to Remember About System Restore

System Restore is a great tool to try to fix a device that is not working, restore Windows settings that are giving problems, or solve problems with applications. Although it's a great tool in some situations, it does have its limitations. Keep these points in mind:

▲ *Point 1:* Restore points replace certain keys in the registry but cannot completely rebuild a totally corrupted registry. Therefore, System Restore can recover from errors only if the registry is somewhat intact.

▲ *Point 2:* The restore process cannot remove a virus or worm infection. However, it might help you start a system that is infected with a virus that launches at startup. After Windows has started, you can then use antivirus software to remove the infection.

▲ *Point 3:* System Restore might create a new problem. I've discovered that whenever I use a restore point, antivirus software gets all out of whack and sometimes even needs reinstalling. Therefore, use restore points sparingly.

▲ *Point 4:* System Restore might make many changes to a system. If you know which change caused a problem, try to undo that particular change first. The idea is to use the least invasive solution first. For example, if updating a driver has caused a problem, first try Driver Rollback to undo that change. Driver Rollback is performed using Device Manager.

▲ *Point 5:* System Restore won't help you if you don't have restore points to use. System Protection must be turned on so that restore points are automatically created.

▲ *Point 6:* Restore points are kept in a hidden folder on the hard drive. If that area of the drive is corrupted, the restore points are lost. Also, if a user turns System Protection off, all restore points are lost.

▲ *Point 7:* Viruses and other malware sometimes hide in restore points. To completely clean an infected system, you need to delete all restore points by turning System Protection off and back on.

▲ *Point 8:* If Windows will not start, you can launch System Restore using startup recovery tools, which you will learn to use in Chapter 14.

> **Vista Differences** Windows Vista uses different backup methods than Windows 7 to back up user data, system files, and the Windows volume. The backup of the Vista volume is called the **Complete PC Backup.** To find out more about Vista backups, see Appendix B.

> **XP Differences** Windows XP uses the **Automated System Recovery (ASR)** tool to back up the Windows XP volume. XP calls the backed-up system files that are critical to Windows operation the **system state data**. To find out more about XP backups, see Appendix C.

MANAGING FILES, FOLDERS, AND STORAGE DEVICES

In this part of the chapter, you learn to manage files and folders on the hard drive and other storage devices using commands in a command prompt window and to manage hard drive partitions and volumes using the Disk Management utility. We begin our discussion with how partitions and file systems work in Windows.

A+
220-802
1.2

HOW PARTITIONS AND FILE SYSTEMS WORK

A hard drive is organized using sectors, partitions, volumes, and file systems. Here's how it all works:

⊿ All data is stored on a hard drive in sectors, sometimes called records. Each **sector** on the drive is the same size, and for most hard drives, that size is 512 bytes. Sector markings used to organize the drive are done before it leaves the factory in a process called **low-level formatting**. The size of a sector and the total number of sectors on a drive determine the drive capacity. Today's drive capacities are measured in GB (gigabytes, roughly one million bytes) or TB (terabytes, roughly one trillion bytes).

> **Notes** For magnetic hard drives, each platter is divided into concentric circles called **tracks**, and each track is divided into sectors (see Figure 10-20). Magnetic drive sectors are usually 512 bytes, but sectors on SSDs can be larger: 4 KB or 16 KB.

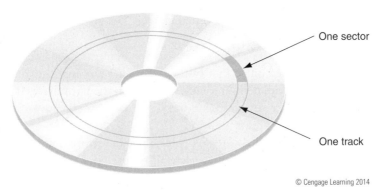

One sector

One track

© Cengage Learning 2014

Figure 10-20 A magnetic hard drive is divided into concentric circles called tracks, and tracks are divided into sectors

⊿ A drive is further divided into one or more **partitions**. Windows can track up to four partitions on a drive. It keeps a map of these partitions in a **partition table** stored in the very first sector on the hard drive called the **Master Boot Record (MBR)**.

⊿ A drive can have one, two, or three **primary partitions**, also called **volumes**. The fourth partition is called an **extended partition** and can hold one or more volumes called **logical drives**. Figure 10-21 shows how a hard drive is divided into three primary partitions and one extended partition.

> 💡 **A+ Exam Tip** The A+ 220-802 exam expects you to know the difference between a primary and extended partition and between a volume and logical drive.

⊿ Before a volume or logical drive can be used, it must be assigned a drive letter such as C: or D: and formatted using a file system. A **file system** is the overall structure an OS uses to name, store, and organize files on a drive. Windows 7 supports three types of file systems for hard drives: NTFS, FAT32, and exFAT. NTFS is the most reliable and secure and is used for the volume on which Windows is installed. Installing a drive letter, file system, and root directory on a volume is called **formatting** the drive, also called a **high-level format**, and can happen during the Windows installation.

A+
220-802
1.2

▲ One of the primary partitions can be designated the **active partition**, which is the bootable partition that startup BIOS turns to when searching for an operating system to start up.

▲ Windows assigns two different functions to hard drive partitions holding the OS (see Figure 10-22). The **system partition**, normally drive C:, is the active partition of the hard drive. This is the partition that contains the OS program to start up Windows. This boot program is called the OS boot manager or boot loader. The other partition, called the **boot partition**, is the partition where the Windows operating system is stored.

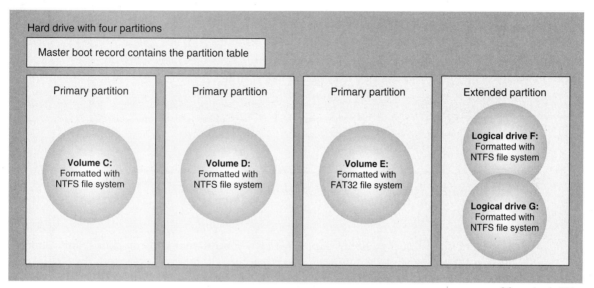

Figure 10-21 A hard drive with four partitions; the fourth partition is an extended partition

© Cengage Learning 2014

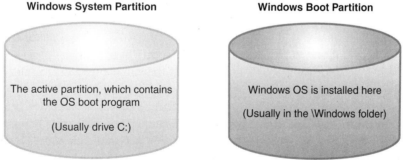

Figure 10-22 Two types of Windows hard drive partitions

© Cengage Learning 2014

> **Notes** Don't be confused by the terminology here. It is really true that, according to Windows terminology, the Windows OS is on the boot partition, and the boot program is on the system partition, although that might seem backward. The computer starts or boots from the system partition and loads the Windows operating system from the boot partition.

For most installations, the system partition and the boot partition are the same (drive C:), and Windows is installed in C:\Windows. An example of when the system partition and the boot partition are different is when Windows 7 is installed as a dual boot with Windows Vista. Figure 10-23 shows how Windows 7 is installed on drive D: and Windows Vista is installed on drive C:. For Windows 7, the system partition is drive C: and the boot partition is drive D:. (For Windows Vista on this computer, the system and boot partitions are both drive C:.)

A+
220-802
1.2

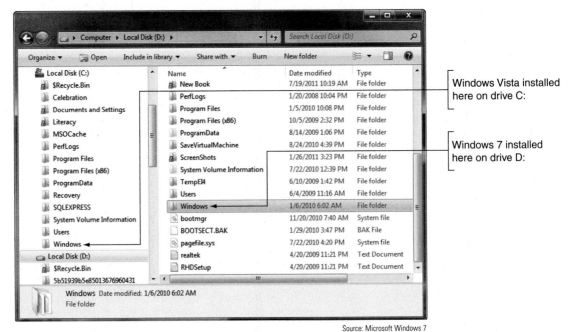

Windows Vista installed here on drive C:

Windows 7 installed here on drive D:

Figure 10-23   Windows 7 and Vista installed on the same system

Source: Microsoft Windows 7

Here is a list of file systems supported by Windows that you can choose for volumes and drives that don't hold the Windows installation:

▲ **NTFS.** Choose the NTFS file system for hard drives because it uses smaller allocation unit or cluster sizes than FAT32, which means it makes more efficient use of disk space when storing many small files. NTFS is more reliable, gives fewer errors, supports encryption, disk quotas (limiting the hard drive space available to a user), file and folder compression, and offers better security. As an example of the better security with NTFS, if you boot the system from another boot media such as a CD, you can access a volume using a FAT file system. If the volume uses NTFS, an administrator password is required to gain access.

▲ **exFAT.** Choose the exFAT file system for large external storage devices that you want to use with other operating systems. For example, you can use a smart card formatted with exFAT in a Mac or Linux computer or in a digital camcorder, camera, or smart phone. exFAT uses the same structure as the older FAT32 file system, but with a 64-bit-wide file allocation table (FAT). exFAT does not use as much overhead as the NTFS file system and is designed to handle very large files, such as those used for multimedia storage.

▲ **FAT32.** Use FAT32 for small hard drives or USB flash drives because it does not have as much overhead as NTFS.

▲ **FAT16.** The older FAT or FAT16 file system has a 16-bit file allocation table and is only recommended on volumes less than 4 GB.

💡 **A+ Exam Tip**   The A+ 220-802 exam expects you to know about the FAT, FAT32, NTFS, and CDFS file systems. It also expects you to know the difference between a quick format and a full format.

A+
220-802
1.2

▲ *CDFS and UDF.* CDFS (Compact Disc File System) is an older file system used by optical discs (CDs, DVDs, and BDs), and is being replaced by the newer **UDF** (**Universal Disc Format**) file system.

> **Notes** For Windows Vista, the exFAT file system is available if Service Pack 1 is installed. In XP, exFAT is available if Windows XP Service Packs 2 and 3 are installed and you download and install an additional update from Microsoft.

A+
220-802
1.2, 1.3,
4.6

COMMANDS TO MANAGE FILES AND FOLDERS

PC support technicians find it is much faster to manipulate files and folders using commands in a command prompt window than when using Windows Explorer. In addition, in some troubleshooting situations, you have no other option but to use a command prompt window. To open the window, enter **cmd.exe** in the search box and press **Enter**. Alternately, you can click Start, All Programs, Accessories, and Command Prompt. The Command Prompt window is shown in Figure 10-24.

C:\windows\system32\cmd.exe

Microsoft Windows [Version 6.1.7600]
Copyright (c) 2009 Microsoft Corporation.   All rights reserved.

C:\Users\Jean Andrews>msinfo32.exe

C:\Users\Jean Andrews>exit_

— Default directory

Source: Microsoft Windows 7

Figure 10-24 Use the exit command to close the command prompt window

Windows 7 and Vista have two levels of command prompt windows: a standard window and an elevated window. The standard window is shown in Figure 10-24. Notice in the figure that the default directory is the currently logged on user's folder. Commands that require administrative privileges will not work from this standard command prompt window. To get an **elevated command prompt window**, click **Start**, **All Programs**, **Accessories**, and right-click **Command Prompt**. Then select **Run as administrator** from the shortcut window. After you respond to the User Account Control (UAC) box, the Administrator: Command Prompt window appears (see Figure 10-25). Notice the word *Administrator* in the title bar, which indicates the elevated window, and the default directory, which is the C:\Windows\system32 folder.

A+
220-802
1.2, 1.3,
4.6

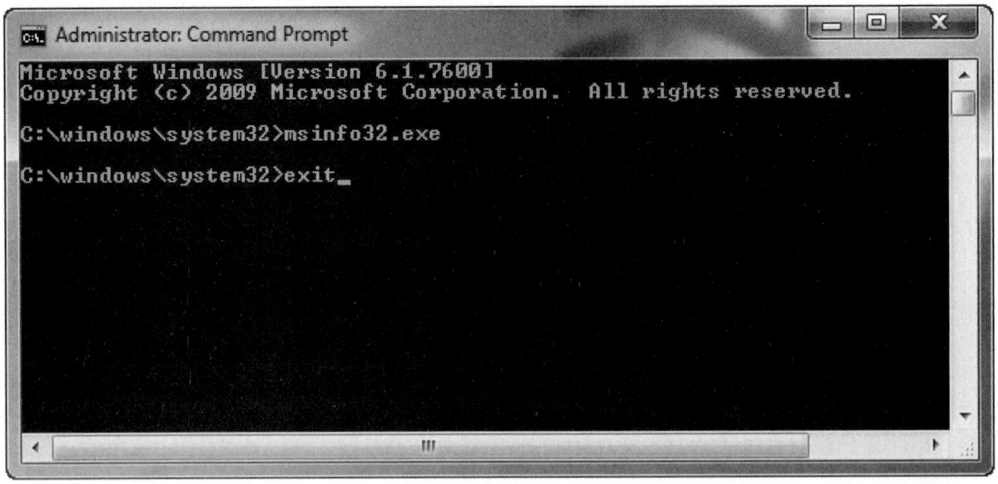

Source: Microsoft Windows 7

Figure 10-25 An elevated command prompt window has administrative privileges

Here are some tips for working in a command prompt window:

▲ Type **cls** and press **Enter** to clear the window.
▲ To retrieve the last command you entered, press the up arrow. To retrieve the last command line one character at a time, press the right arrow.
▲ To terminate a command before it is finished, press **Ctrl+Break** or **Ctrl+Pause**.
▲ To close the window, type **exit** (see Figure 10-25) and press **Enter**.

> **Notes** Many of the commands you learn about in this section can also be used from the Windows 7/ Vista Recovery Environment or the Windows XP Recovery Console. These operating systems can be loaded from the Windows setup CD or DVD to troubleshoot a system when the Windows desktop refuses to load. How to use the Recovery Environment and the Recovery Console is covered in Chapter 14.

If the command you are using applies to files or folders, the path to these files or folders is assumed to be the default drive and directory. The default drive and directory, also called the current drive and directory, shows in the command prompt. It is the drive and directory that the command will use if you don't give a drive and directory in the command line. For example, in Figure 10-24, the default drive is C: and the default path is C:\Users\Jean Andrews. If you use a different path in the command line, the path you use overrides the default path. Also know that Windows makes no distinction between uppercase and lowercase in command lines.

Now let's look at the filenaming conventions you will need to follow when creating files, wildcard characters you can use in command lines, and several commands useful for managing files and folders.

FILENAMING CONVENTIONS

When using the command prompt window to create a file, keep in mind that filename and file extension characters can be the letters a through z, the numbers 0 through 9, and the following characters:

```
_ ^ $ ~ ! # % & - { } ( ) @ ' `
```

In a command prompt window, if a path or filename has spaces in it, it is sometimes necessary to enclose the path or filename in double quotation marks.

WILDCARD CHARACTERS IN COMMAND LINES

As you work at the command prompt, you can use **wildcard** characters in a filename to say that the command applies to a group of files or to abbreviate a filename if you do not know the entire name. The question mark (?) is a wildcard for one character, and the asterisk (*) is a wildcard for one or more characters. For example, if you want to find all files in a directory that start with A and have a three-letter file extension, you would use the following command:

```
dir a*.???
```

> **A+ Exam Tip** The A+ 220-802 exam expects you to know how to use the Shutdown, MD, RD, CD, Del, Format, Copy, Xcopy, Robocopy, Defrag, Chkdsk, and Help commands, which are all covered in this section.

> **Notes** Many commands can use parameters in the command line to affect how the command will work. Parameters (also called options, arguments, or switches) often begin with a slash followed by a single character. In this chapter, you will learn about the basic parameters used by a command for the most common tasks. For a full listing of the parameters available for a command, use the Help command. Another way to learn about commands is to follow this link on the Microsoft web site: *technet .microsoft.com/en-us/library/cc772390(WS.10).aspx*.

HELP OR *<COMMAND NAME>* /?

Use the help command to get help about any command. You can enter help followed by the command name or enter the command name followed by /?. Table 10-1 lists some sample applications of this command:

Command	Result
help xcopy xcopy /?	Gets help about the Xcopy command
help	Lists all commands
help xcopy | more	Lists information one screen at a time

© Cengage Learning 2014

Table 10-1 Sample help commands

DIR [*<FILENAME>*] [/P] [/S] [/W]

Use the dir command to list files and directories. In Microsoft documentation about a command (also called the command syntax), the brackets [ ] in a command line indicate the parameter is optional. In addition, the parameter included in < >, such as <filename>, indicates that you can substitute any filename in the command. This filename can include a path or file extension. Table 10-2 lists some examples of the dir command.

10

A+
220-802
1.2, 1.3,
4.6

Command	Result
`dir /p`	Lists one screen at a time
`dir /w`	Presents information using wide format, where details are omitted and files and folders are listed in columns on the screen
`dir *.txt`	Lists all files with a .txt file extension in the default path
`dir d:\data\*.txt`	Lists all files with a .txt file extension in the D:\data folder
`dir myfile.txt`	Checks that a single file, such as myfile.txt, is present
`dir /s`	Includes subdirectory entries

© Cengage Learning 2014

Table 10-2 Sample dir commands

MD [DRIVE:]PATH

The MD command (Make Directory) creates a subdirectory under a directory. Note that in the command lines in this section, the command prompt is not bolded, but the typed command is in bold. To create a directory named \game on drive C:, you can use this command:

```
C:\> MD C:\game
```

The backslash indicates that the directory is under the root directory. If a path is not given, the default path is assumed. This command also creates the C:\game directory:

```
C:\> MD game
```

To create a directory named chess under the \game directory, you can use this command:

```
C:\> MD C:\game\chess
```

Figure 10-26 shows the result of the dir command on the directory game. Note the two initial entries in the directory table: . (dot) and . . (dot, dot). The MD command creates these two entries when the OS initially sets up the directory. You cannot edit these entries with normal OS commands, and they must remain in the directory for the directory's lifetime. The . (dot) entry points to the subdirectory itself, and the .. (dot, dot) entry points to the parent directory, which, in this case, is the root directory.

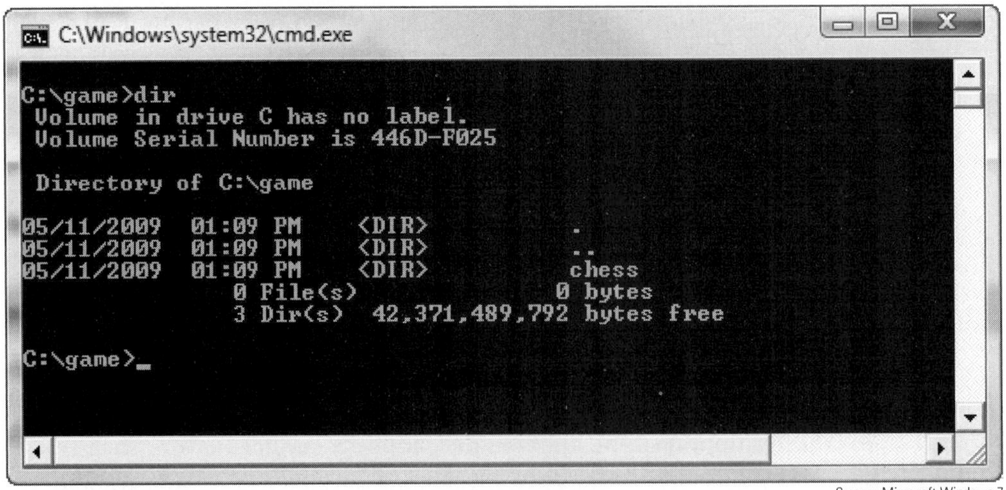

Source: Microsoft Windows 7

Figure 10-26 Results of the dir command on the game directory

A+
220-802
1.2, 1.3,
4.6

CD *[DRIVE:]PATH OR CD..*

The CD command (Change Directory) changes the current default directory. You enter CD followed by the drive and the entire path that you want to be current, like so:

```
C:\> CD C:\game\chess
```

The command prompt now looks like this:

```
C:\game\chess>
```

To move from a child directory to its parent directory, use the .. (dot, dot) variation of the command:

```
C:\game\chess> CD..
```

The command prompt now looks like this:

```
C:\game>
```

Remember that .. (dot, dot) always means the parent directory. You can move from a parent directory to one of its child directories simply by stating the name of the child directory:

```
C:\game> CD chess
```

The command prompt now looks like this:

```
C:\game\chess>
```

Remember not to put a backslash in front of the child directory name; doing so tells the OS to go to a directory named Chess that is directly under the root directory.

RD *[DRIVE:]PATH [/S]*

The RD command (Remove Directory) removes a directory. Unless you use the /s switch, three things must be true before you can use the RD command:

- The directory must contain no files.
- The directory must contain no subdirectories.
- The directory must not be the current directory.

A directory is ready for removal when only the . (dot) and .. (dot, dot) entries are present. For example, to remove the \game directory when it contains the chess directory, the chess directory must first be removed, like so:

```
C:\> RD C:\game\chess
```

Or, if the \game directory is the current directory, you can use this command:

```
C:\game> RD chess
```

10

A+
220-802
1.2, 1.3,
4.6

After you remove the chess directory, you can remove the game directory. However, it's not good to attempt to saw off a branch while you're sitting on it; therefore, you must first leave the \game directory like so:

```
C:\game> CD..
C:\> RD \game
```

When you use the /s switch with the RD command, the entire directory tree is deleted, including all its subdirectories and files.

DEL OR ERASE <FILENAME>

The del or erase command erases files or groups of files. Note that in the command lines in this section, the command prompt is not bolded, but the typed command is in bold.

To erase the file named Myfile.txt, use the following command:

```
E:\> del myfile.txt
```

To erase all files in the current default directory, use the following command:

```
E:\Docs> del *.*
```

To erase all files in the E:\Docs directory, use the following command:

```
C:\> erase e:\docs\*.*
```

A few files don't have a file extension. To erase all files that are in the current directory and that have no file extensions, use the following command:

```
E:\Docs> del *.
```

REN <FILENAME1> <FILENAME2>

The ren (rename) command renames a file. <Filename1> can include a path to the file, but <Filename2> cannot. To rename Project.docx in the default directory to Project_Hold.docx:

```
E:\Docs> ren Project.docx Project_Hold.docx
```

To rename all .txt files to .doc files in the C:\Data folder:

```
ren C:\Data\*.txt *.doc
```

COPY <SOURCE> [<DESTINATION>] [/V] [/Y]

The copy command copies a single file or group of files. The original files are not altered. To copy a file from one drive to another, use a command similar to this one:

```
E:\> copy C:\Data\Myfile.txt E:\mydata\Newfile.txt
```

The drive, path, and filename of the source file immediately follow the copy command. The drive, path, and filename of the destination file follow the source filename. If you do not specify the filename of the destination file, the OS assigns the file's original name to this copy. If you omit the drive or path of the source or the destination, then the OS uses the current default drive and path.

To copy the file Myfile.txt from the root directory of drive C: to drive E:, use the following command:

```
C:\> copy myfile.txt E:
```

Because the command does not include a drive or path before the filename Myfile.txt, the OS assumes that the file is in the default drive and path. Also, because there is no destination filename specified, the file written to drive E: will be named Myfile.txt.

To copy all files in the C:\Docs directory to the USB flash drive designated drive E:, use the following command:

```
C:\> copy c:\docs\*.* E:
```

To make a backup file named System.bak of the System file in the \Windows\system32\ config directory of the hard drive, use the following command:

```
C:\Windows\system32\config> copy system system.bak
```

If you use the copy command to duplicate multiple files, the files are assigned the names of the original files. When you duplicate multiple files, the destination portion of the command line cannot include a filename.

Here are two switches or parameters that are useful with the copy command:

▲ /V. When the /V switch is used, the size of each new file is compared to the size of the original file. This slows down the copying, but verifies that the copy is done without errors.

▲ /Y. When the /Y switch is used, a confirmation message does not appear asking you to confirm before overwriting a file.

> **Notes** When trying to recover a corrupted file, you can sometimes use the Copy command to copy the file to new media, such as from the hard drive to a USB drive. During the copying process, if the Copy command reports a bad or missing sector, choose the option to ignore that sector. The copying process then continues to the next sector. The corrupted sector will be lost, but others can likely be recovered. The Recover command can be used to accomplish the same thing.

RECOVER <FILENAME>

Use the recover command to attempt to recover a file when parts of the file are corrupted. The command is best used from the Windows 7/Vista Recovery Environment or the XP Recovery Console (discussed in Appendix C). To use it, you must specify the name of a single file in the command line, like so:

```
C:\Data> Recover Myfile.doc
```

XCOPY <SOURCE> [<DESTINATION>] [/S] [/C] [/Y] [/D:DATE]

The xcopy command is more powerful than the copy command. It follows the same general command-source-destination format as the copy command, but it offers several more options. Table 10-3 shows some of these options.

10

A+
220-802
1.2, 1.3,
4.6

Command	Result
xcopy C:\docs*.* E: /S	Use the /S switch to include subdirectories in the copy; this command copies all files in the directory C:\docs, as well as all subdirectories under \docs and their files, to drive E
xcopy C:\docs*.* E: /E	Same as /S but empty subdirectories are included in the copy
xcopy C:\docs*.* E: /D:03/14/12	The /D switch examines the date; this command copies all files from the directory C:\docs created or modified on or after March 14, 2012
xcopy C:\docs*.* E: /Y	Use the /Y switch to overwrite existing files without prompting
xcopy C:\docs*.* E: /C	Use the /C switch to keep copying even when an error occurs

© Cengage Learning 2014

Table 10-3 Xcopy commands and results

ROBOCOPY *<SOURCE>* *[<DESTINATION>]* *[/S]* *[/E]* *[/LOG:FILENAME]* *[/LOG+:*FILENAME] *[/MOVE]* *[/PURGE]*

The robocopy (Robust File Copy) command is not included in Windows XP and is similar to the xcopy command. It offers more options than xcopy and is intended to replace xcopy. A few options for robocopy are listed in Table 10-4.

Command	Result
robocopy C:\docs*.* E: /S	The /S switch includes subdirectories in the copy but does not include empty directories
robocopy C:\docs*.* E: /E	The /E switch includes subdirectories, even the empty ones
robocopy C:\docs*.* E: /LOG:Mylog.txt	Records activity to a log file and overwrites the current log file
robocopy C:\docs*.* E: /LOG+:Mylog.txt	Appends a record of all activity to an existing log file
robocopy C:\docs*.* E: /move	Moves files and directories, deleting them from the source
robocopy C:\docs*.* E: /purge	Deletes files and directories at the destination that no longer exist at the source

© Cengage Learning 2014

Table 10-4 Robocopy commands and results

CHKDSK *[DRIVE:]* *[/F]* *[/R]*

The chkdsk command (Check Disk) fixes file system errors and recovers data from bad sectors. Earlier in the chapter, you learned to check for errors using the drive properties box, which does so by launching the chkdsk command. Recall that a file is stored on the hard drive as a group of clusters. The FAT, FAT32, and exFAT file systems use a **file allocation table (FAT)** to keep a record of each cluster that belongs to a file. The NTFS file system uses a database to hold similar information called the **master file table (MFT)**. In Figure 10-27, you can see that each cell in the FAT represents one cluster and contains a pointer to the next cluster in a file.

A+
220-802
1.2, 1.3,
4.6

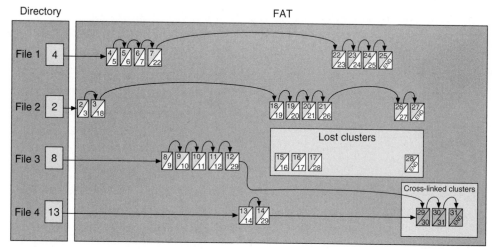

Figure 10-27 Lost and cross-linked clusters

© Cengage Learning 2014

> **Notes** For an interesting discussion of how the FAT works, see the document FAT Details.pdf on the companion web site for this book at *www.cengagebrain.com*. See the Preface for more information.

Used with the /F parameter, chkdsk searches for and fixes two types of file system errors made by the FAT or MFT:

▲ *Lost clusters (also called lost allocation units)*—Lost clusters are clusters that are marked as used clusters in the FAT or MFT, but the cluster does not belong to any file. In effect, the data in these clusters is lost.

▲ *Cross-linked clusters*—Cross-linked clusters are clusters that are marked in the FAT or MFT as belonging to more than one file.

Used with the /R parameter, chkdsk checks for lost clusters and cross-linked clusters and also checks for bad sectors on the drive. The FAT and MFT keep a table of bad sectors that they normally do not use. However, over time, a sector might become unreliable. If chkdsk determines that a sector is unreliable, it attempts to recover the data from the sector and also marks the sector as bad so that the FAT or MFT will not use it again.

Used without any parameters, the chkdsk command only reports information about a drive and does not make any repairs.

In the following sample commands, we're not showing the command prompt; the default drive and directory are not important. To check the hard drive for file system errors and repair them, use this command:

```
chkdsk C:/F
```

To redirect a report of the findings of the chkdsk command to a file that you can later print, use this command:

```
chkdsk C:>Myfile.txt
```

Use the /R parameter of the chkdsk command to fix file system errors and also examine each sector of the drive for bad sectors, like so:

```
chkdsk C:/R
```

10

If chkdsk finds data that it can recover, it asks you for permission to do so. If you give permission, it saves the recovered data in files that it stores in the root directory of the drive.

> **Notes** Use either the /F or /R parameter with chkdsk, but not both. Using both parameters is redundant. For the most thorough check of a drive, use /R.

The chkdsk command will not fix anything unless the drive is locked, which means the drive has no open files. If you attempt to use chkdsk with the /F or /R parameter when files are open, chkdsk tells you of the problem and asks permission to schedule the run the next time Windows is restarted. Know that the process will take plenty of time. For Windows 7/Vista, you must use an elevated command prompt window to run chkdsk.

> **Notes** The chkdsk command is also available from the Windows 7/Vista Recovery Environment and the Windows XP Recovery Console.

DEFRAG [*DRIVE:*] [/C]

The defrag command examines a magnetic hard drive for **fragmented files** (files written to a disk in noncontiguous clusters) and rewrites these files to the drive in contiguous clusters. You use this command to optimize a hard drive's performance. Table 10-5 shows two examples of the command. Recall that it's not a good idea to defrag solid state storage devices such as an SSD, flash drive, or smart card. Doing so can shorten the life of the drive.

Command	Result
`defrag C:`	**Defrag drive C**
`defrag /c`	**Defrag all volumes on the computer, including drive C**

© Cengage Learning 2014

Table 10-5 Defrag commands and results

The defrag command requires an elevated command prompt window in Windows 7/Vista. It is not available under the Windows 7/Vista Recovery Environment or the XP Recovery Console. Earlier in the chapter, you learned to defrag a drive using the Windows drive properties box.

FORMAT <*DRIVE:*> [/V:*LABEL*] [/Q] [FS:<*FILESYSTEM*>]

You can format a hard drive or other storage device using Disk Management. In addition, you can use the format command from a command prompt window and from the Windows 7/Vista Recovery Environment and the XP Recovery Console. This high-level format installs a file system on the device and *erases all data on the volume*. Table 10-6 lists various sample uses of the Format command.

A+
220-802
1.2, 1.3,
4.6

Command	Description
Format A: /V:mylabel	Allows you to enter a volume label only once when formatting several disks; the same volume label is used for all disks. A volume label appears at the top of the directory list to help you identify the disk.
Format A: /Q	Re-creates the root directory and FAT to quickly format a previously formatted disk that is in good condition; /Q does not read or write to any other part of the disk
Format D: /FS:NTFS	Formats drive D using the NTFS file system
Format D: /FS:FAT32	Formats drive D using the FAT32 file system
Format D: /FS:EXFAT	Formats drive D using the extended FAT file system

Table 10-6 Format commands and results

© Cengage Learning 2014

One use of the format command is to change the installed file system. For example, in Figure 10-28, the chkdsk command shows a USB flash drive is formatted using the FAT32 file system. The format command reformatted the drive using the exFAT file system.

10

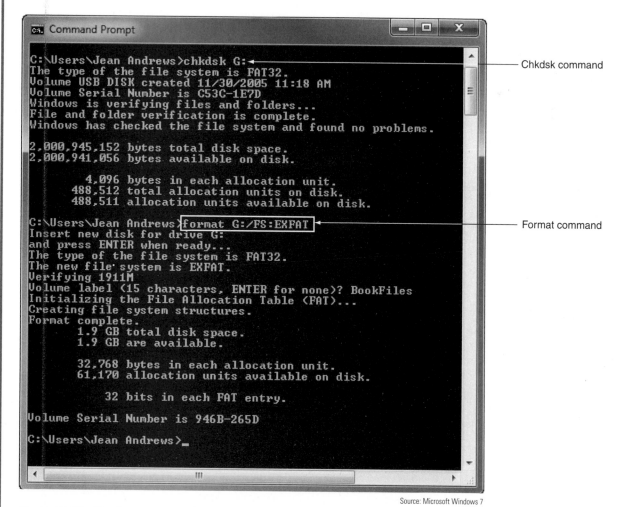

Source: Microsoft Windows 7

Figure 10-28 The format command uses the exFAT file system to format a flash drive

SHUTDOWN [/M *COMPUTERNAME*] [/I] [/R] [/S] [/F] [/T *XX*]

Use the shutdown command to shut down the local computer or a remote computer. You must be logged on with an administrator account to use this command. By default, the command gives users a 30-second warning before shutdown. To shut down a remote computer on the network, you must have an administrator account on that computer and be logged onto the local computer with that same account and password. Table 10-7 lists some shutdown commands.

Command	Description
shutdown /r	Restart the local computer
shutdown /s /m \\bluelight	Shut down the remote computer named \\bluelight
shutdown /s /m \\bluelight /t 60	Shut down the \\bluelight computer after a 60-second delay
shutdown /i	Displays the Remote Shutdown Dialog box so you can choose computers on the network to shut down

© Cengage Learning 2014

Table 10-7 Shutdown commands and results

USE DISK MANAGEMENT TO MANAGE HARD DRIVES

The primary tool for managing hard drives is Disk Management. In Chapter 7, you learned how to install Windows on a new hard drive. This installation process initializes, partitions, and formats the drive. After Windows is installed, you can use Disk Management to install and manage drives. In this part of the chapter, you will learn to use Disk Management to manage partitions on a drive, prepare a new drive for first use, mount a drive, use Windows dynamic disks, and troubleshoot problems with the hard drive.

> **Notes** In most Microsoft documentation, a partition is called a partition until it is formatted, and then it is called a volume.

RESIZE, CREATE, AND DELETE PARTITIONS

Suppose you have installed Windows 7 on a hard drive and used all available space on the drive for the one partition. Now you want to split the partition into two partitions so you can install Windows 8 in a dual boot installation with Windows 7. You can use Disk Management to shrink the original partition, which frees up some space for the new Windows 8 partition. Follow these steps:

1. To open the Disk Management window, use one of these methods:

   ▲ Click Start, right-click Computer, and select Manage from the shortcut menu. In the Computer Management window, click Disk Management.

   ▲ Click Start, type Disk Management or diskmgmt.msc in the search box and press Enter.

A+
220-802
1.2, 1.4

2. The Disk Management window opens (see Figure 10-29). To shrink the existing partition, right-click in the partition space and select **Shrink Volume** from the shortcut menu (see Figure 10-29). The Shrink dialog box appears showing the amount of free space on the partition. Enter the amount in MB to shrink the partition, which cannot be more than the amount of free space so that no data on the partition will be lost. (For best performance, be sure to leave at least 15 percent free space on the disk.) Click **Shrink**. The disk now shows unallocated space.

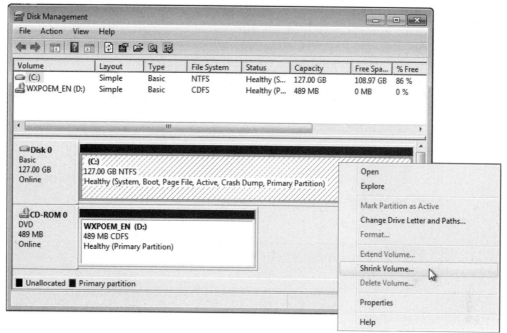

Figure 10-29 Shrink a volume to make room for a new partition

Source: Microsoft Windows 7

10

3. To create a new partition in the unallocated space, right-click in that space and select **New Simple Volume** from the shortcut menu (see Figure 10-30). The New Simple Volume Wizard opens.

4. Follow the directions on-screen to enter the size of the volume in MB and select a drive letter for the volume, a file system, and the size for each allocation unit (also called a cluster). It's best to leave the cluster size at the Default value. You can also decide to do a **quick format**, which doesn't scan the volume for bad sectors; use it only when a hard drive has been previously formatted and is in healthy condition. The partition is then created and formatted with the file system you chose.

Notice in Figure 10-29 the options on the shortcut menu that you can use to make the partition the active partition (the one the OS will boot from), change the drive letter for a volume, format the volume (erases all data on the volume), extend the volume (increase the size of the volume), and shrink and delete the volume. An option that is not available for the particular volume and situation is grayed.

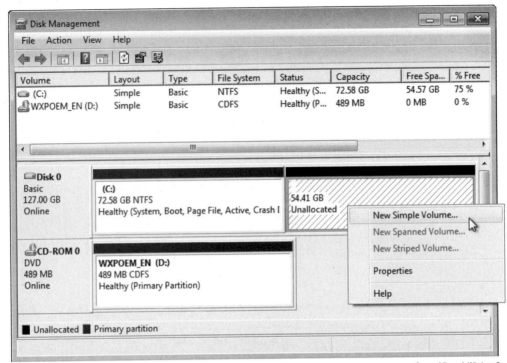

Figure 10-30 Use unallocated space to create a new partition

Source: Microsoft Windows 7

Notes The size of a partition or volume cannot be changed in Windows XP unless you use third-party software.

A+ Exam Tip The A+ 220-802 exam expects you to know how to use Disk Management to extend and split partitions and configure a new hard drive in a system.

PREPARE A DRIVE FOR FIRST USE

When you install a new, second hard drive in a computer, use Disk Management to prepare the drive for use. This happens in a two-step process:

Step 1: Initialize the Disk

When the disk is initialized, Windows identifies the disk as a basic disk. A **basic disk** is a single hard drive that works independently of other hard drives. Windows also installs a partitioning system on the hard drive. You can choose the Master Boot Record (MBR) system or the **Globally Unique Identifier Partition Table (GUID or GPT)** system. Recall that the MBR system can have up to four partitions, although one of them can be an extended partition with multiple logical drives. The GPT system can support up to 128 partitions and is recommended for drives larger than 2 TB. The GPT system is more reliable, but it can only be used by 64-bit operating systems on computers that have an EFI or UEFI chip rather than the traditional BIOS chip. In this chapter, we focus on the MBR system, which is by far the most common system.

A+
220-802
1.2, 1.4

The MBR system writes an MBR record to the first sector of the disk (512 bytes) that contains two items:

▲ *The master boot program (446 bytes).* The purpose of this program is to begin the process of finding and loading an OS installed on the drive. If you were to make this hard drive your boot device, startup BIOS would look for and execute this program. The MBR program would then look for and execute an OS boot program. (This program begins the process of loading the OS.)

▲ *The partition table.* Recall that the partition table contains the description, location, and size of each partition on the drive. For Windows-based systems, this table has space for four 16-byte entries that are used to define up to four partitions on the drive. For each partition, the 16 bytes are used to hold the beginning and ending location of the partition, the number of sectors in the partition, and whether or not the partition is bootable. Recall that the one bootable partition is called the active partition.

When you first open Disk Management after you have installed a new hard drive, the Initialize Disk box automatically appears (see Figure 10-31). If you don't see the box, right-click in the Disk area and select **Initialize Disk** from the shortcut menu (see Figure 10-32). Select the partitioning system and click **OK**. Disk Management now reports the hard drive as a Basic disk.

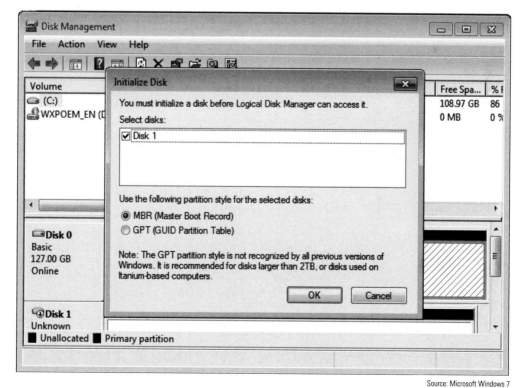

Source: Microsoft Windows 7

Figure 10-31 Use the Initialize Disk box to set up a partitioning system on a new hard drive

A+
220-802
1.2, 1.4

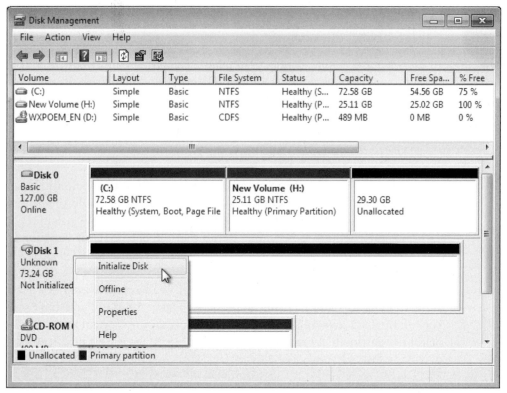

Source: Microsoft Windows 7

Figure 10-32 The first step to install a new hard drive is to initialize the disk

Step 2: Create a Volume and Format It with a File System

To create a new volume on a disk, right-click in the unallocated space, select **New Simple Volume** from the shortcut menu, and follow the directions on-screen to select the size of the volume, assign a drive letter and name to the volume, and select the file system. When the process is finished, the drive is formatted and ready for use. When you open Windows Explorer, you should see the new volume available for use.

> **Notes** In Chapter 14, you learn to use a command prompt to create and manage partitions on a hard drive.

HOW TO MOUNT A DRIVE

A **mounted drive** is a volume that can be accessed by way of a folder on another volume so that the folder has more available space. A mounted drive is useful when a folder is on a volume that is too small to hold all the data you want in the folder. In Figure 10-33, the mounted drive gives the C:\Projects folder a capacity of 30 GB. The C:\Projects folder is called the **mount point** for the mounted drive.

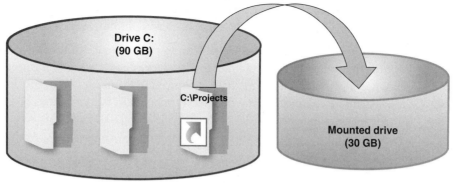

© Cengage Learning 2014

Figure 10-33 The C:\Projects folder is the mount point for the mounted drive

Follow these steps to mount a drive:

1. Make sure the volume that is to host the mounted drive uses the NTFS file system. The folder on this volume, called the mount point, must be empty. You can also create the folder during the mount process. In our example, we are mounting a drive to the C:\Projects folder.

2. Using Disk Management, right-click in the unallocated space of a disk. In our example, we're using Disk 1 (the second hard drive). Select **New Simple Volume** from the shortcut menu. The New Simple Volume Wizard launches. Using the wizard, specify the amount of unallocated space you want to devote to the volume. (In our example, we are using 30 GB, although the resulting size of the C:\Projects folder will only show about 29 GB because of overhead.)

3. As you follow the wizard, the box shown on the left side of Figure 10-34 appears. Select **Mount in the following empty NTFS folder**, and then click **Browse**. In the Browse for Drive Path box that appears (see the right side of Figure 10-34), you can drill down to an existing folder or click **New Folder** to create a new folder on drive C:.

Source: Microsoft Windows 7

Figure 10-34 Select the mount point for the new volume

10

A+
220-802
1.2, 1.4

4. Complete the wizard by selecting a file system for the new volume and an Allocation unit size (the cluster size). The volume is created and formatted.

5. To verify the drive is mounted, open Windows Explorer and then open the Properties box for the folder. In our example, the Properties box for the C:\Projects folder is shown in the middle of Figure 10-35. Notice the Properties box reports the folder type as a Mounted Volume. When you click Properties in the Properties box, the volume Properties box appears (see the right side of Figure 10-35). In this box, you can see the size of the volume, which is the size of the mounted volume, less overhead.

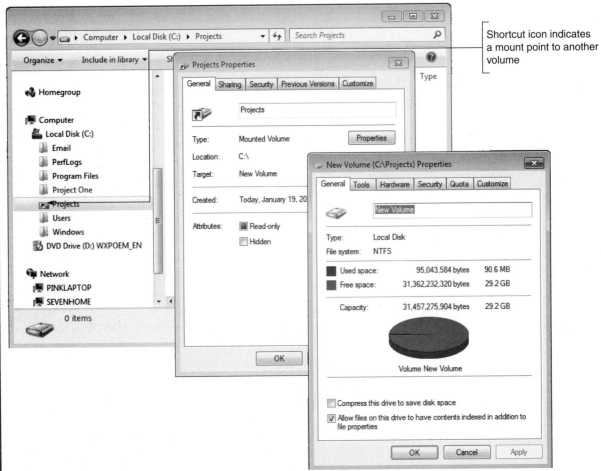

Source: Microsoft Windows 7

Figure 10-35 The mounted drive in Windows Explorer appears as a very large folder

You can think of a mount point, such as C:\Projects, as a shortcut to a volume on a second drive. If you look closely at the left window in Figure 10-35, you can see the shortcut icon beside the Projects folder.

WINDOWS DYNAMIC DISKS

A basic disk works independently of other hard drives, but a **dynamic disk** can work with other hard drives to hold data. Volumes stored on dynamic disks are called **dynamic volumes**. Several dynamic disks can work together to collectively present a single dynamic volume to the system.

A+
220-802
1.2, 1.4

When dynamic disks work together, data to configure each hard drive is stored in a disk management database that resides in the last 1 MB of storage space on each hard drive. Home editions of Windows do not support dynamic disks.

Here are four uses of dynamic disks:

▲ *For better reliability, you can configure a hard drive as a dynamic disk and allocate the space as a simple volume.* This is the best reason to use dynamic disks and is a recommended best practice. Because of the way a dynamic disk works, the simple volume is considered more reliable than when it is stored on a basic disk. A volume that is stored on only one hard drive is called a **simple volume.**

▲ *You can implement dynamic disks on multiple hard drives to extend a volume across these drives (called spanning).* This volume is called a spanned volume.

▲ *Dynamic disks can be used to piece data across multiple hard drives to improve performance.* The technology to configure two or more hard drives to work together as an array of drives is called **RAID (redundant array of inexpensive disks** or **redundant array of independent disks).** Joining hard drives together to improve performance is called **striping** or **RAID 0.** The volume is called a striped volume (see Figure 10-36). When RAID is implemented in this way using Disk Management, it is called **software RAID.** A more reliable way of configuring RAID is to use BIOS setup on a motherboard that supports RAID, which is called **hardware RAID.**

▲ *For Windows XP, you can use dynamic disks to mirror two hard drives for fault tolerance (called* **mirroring** *or* **RAID 1**). This feature is not available in Windows 7/Vista and is not considered a good practice in XP.

10

One simple volume on a single disk

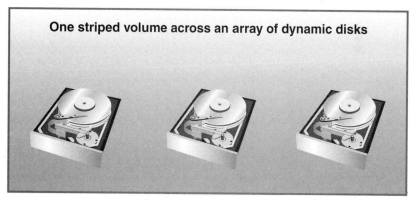
One striped volume across an array of dynamic disks

© Cengage Learning 2014

Figure 10-36 A simple volume is stored on a single disk, but a striped volume is stored on an array of dynamic disks

You can use Disk Management to convert two or more basic disks to dynamic disks. Then you can use unallocated space on these disks to create a simple, spanned, or striped volume. To convert a basic disk to dynamic, right-click the Disk area and select **Convert to Dynamic Disk** from the shortcut menu (see Figure 10-37), and then right-click free space on the disk and select **New Simple Volume, New Spanned Volume,** or **New Striped Volume** from the shortcut menu. If you were to use spanning or striping in Figure 10-37, you could make Disk 1 and Disk 2 dynamic disks that hold a single volume. The size of the volume would be the sum of the space on both hard drives.

A+
220-802
1.2, 1.4

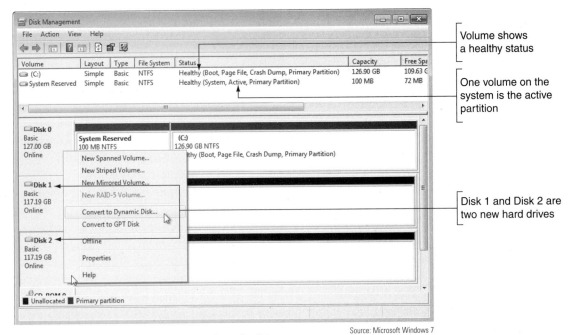

Figure 10-37   Convert a basic disk to a dynamic disk

Now for some serious cautions about software RAID where you use Windows for spanning and striping: Microsoft warns that when Windows is used for software RAID, the risk of catastrophic failure increases and can lead to data loss. Microsoft suggests you only use Windows spanning or striping when you have no other option. In other words, spanning and striping in Windows aren't very safe—to expand the size of a volume, use a mounted drive or use hardware RAID.

> **Notes** When Windows implements RAID, know that you cannot install an OS on a spanned or striped volume that uses software RAID. You can, however, install Windows on a hardware RAID drive.
> Also, after you have converted a basic disk to a dynamic disk, you cannot revert it to a basic disk without losing all data on the drive.

USE DISK MANAGEMENT TO TROUBLESHOOT HARD DRIVE PROBLEMS

Notice in Figure 10-37 that this system has three hard drives, Disk 0, Disk 1, and Disk 2, and information about the disks and volumes is shown in the window. When you are having a problem with a hard drive, it helps to know what the information in the Disk Management window means. Here are the drive and volume statuses you might see in this window:

- ▲ *Healthy*. The healthy volume status shown in Figure 10-37 indicates that the volume is formatted with a file system and that the file system is working without errors.
- ▲ *Failed*. A failed volume status indicates a problem with the hard drive or that the file system has become corrupted. To try to fix the problem, make sure the hard drive data cable and power cable are secure. Data on a failed volume is likely to be lost. For dynamic disks, if the disk status is Offline, try bringing the disk back online (how to do that is coming up in this chapter).

A+
220-802
1.2, 1.4

▲ *Online.* An online disk status indicates the disk has been sensed by Windows and can be accessed by either reading or writing to the disk.

▲ *Active.* One volume on the system will be marked as Active. This is the volume that startup BIOS looks to in order to load an OS.

▲ *Unallocated.* Space on the disk is marked as unallocated if it has not yet been partitioned.

▲ *Formatting.* This volume status appears while a volume is being formatted.

▲ *Basic.* When a hard drive is first sensed by Windows, it is assigned the Basic disk status. A basic disk can be partitioned and formatted as a stand-alone hard drive.

▲ *Dynamic.* The following status indicators apply only to dynamic disks:

• *Offline.* An offline disk status indicates a dynamic disk has become corrupted or is unavailable. The problem can be caused by a corrupted file system, the drive cables are loose, the hard drive has failed, or another hardware problem. If you believe the problem is corrected, right-click the disk and select **Reactivate Disk** from the shortcut menu to bring the disk back online.

• *Foreign drive.* If you move a hard drive that has been configured as a dynamic disk on another computer to this computer, this computer will report the disk as a foreign drive. To fix the problem, you need to import the foreign drive. To do that, right-click the disk and select **Import Foreign Disks** from the shortcut menu. You should then be able to see the volumes on the disk.

• *Healthy (At Risk).* The dynamic disk can be accessed, but I/O errors have occurred. Try returning the disk to online status. If the volume status does not return to healthy, back up all data and replace the drive.

If you are still having problems with a hard drive, volume, or mounted drive, check Event Viewer for events about the drive that might have been recorded there. These events might help you understand the nature of the problem and what to do about it. How to use Event Viewer is covered in Chapter 11.

REGIONAL AND LANGUAGE SETTINGS

A+
220-802
1.2

One more task you might be called on to do as a part of maintaining a computer is to help a user configure a computer to use a different language. Suppose a user needs to see Windows messages in Spanish and wants to use a Spanish keyboard, such as the one in Figure 10-38. Configuring a computer for another language involves downloading and installing the language pack, changing the Windows display language, changing regional settings for dates, time, and numbers, and changing the language used for keyboard input.

Two ways to install a different language in Windows are:

▲ For Windows 7/Vista Ultimate and Enterprise editions, you can use Windows Update to download and install a language pack that translates most of the Windows user interface. Microsoft offers language packs for many languages.

▲ For all editions of Windows 7/Vista/XP, you can download and install a Language Interface Pack (LIP) that translates only some of the Windows user interface.

10

Figure 10-38 Spanish keyboard

© Cengage Learning 2014

Windows 7/Vista Ultimate offers language packs through Windows Update. For other Windows editions, you can go to the Microsoft web site (*www.microsoft.com*) and download the Language Interface Pack (LIP). Then double-click the downloaded file to install the language. After the language pack is installed, use Control Panel to change the Windows display for the installed language. You also need to change the format used for numbers, currencies, dates, and time. And, if a special keyboard is to be used, you need to change the input language.

A+
220-802
1.2

APPLYING | CONCEPTS

Using Windows 7 Ultimate, follow these steps to configure the computer to use Spanish for the display:

1. To download the Spanish pack using Windows Update, click **Start**, **All Programs**, and **Windows Update**. If important updates are listed in the Windows Update window, first install any of these updates your system needs.

2. In the Windows Update window, if optional updates are not listed, click **Check for updates**. If you see optional updates listed, click **optional updates are available**.

3. In the Select updates to install window (see Figure 10-39), in the list of Windows 7 Language Packs, select the **Spanish Language Pack**. Make sure other updates that you don't want are not selected. Click **OK** and click **Install updates**.

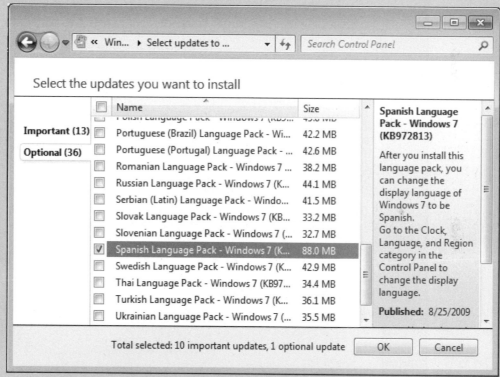

Figure 10-39 Select the language to download and install

Source: Microsoft Windows 7

4. You are now ready to configure the computer to use the new language. Open Control Panel and click **Clock, Language, and Region**. In the Clock, Language, and Region window, click **Change the date, time, or number format**. The Region and Language box opens (see Figure 10-40).

10

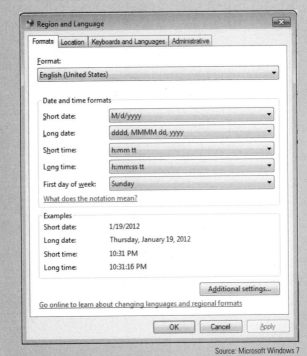

Source: Microsoft Windows 7

Figure 10-40   Use the Region and Language box to change
how dates, times, and numbers display

5. To change the format used to display dates, times, and numbers, select the language from the drop-down list under Format.

6. To change the keyboard layout, select the Keyboards and Languages tab. Click **Change keyboards**. The Text Services and Input Languages box appears. In the list of installed services, only English is listed (see the left side of Figure 10-41). Click **Add**. In the Add Input Language box, select a Spanish keyboard, as shown on the right side of Figure 10-41. Click **OK**. The Spanish keyboard is now added to the list of input languages. Under Default input language, select the Spanish language and click **Apply**. Click **OK** to close the dialog box.

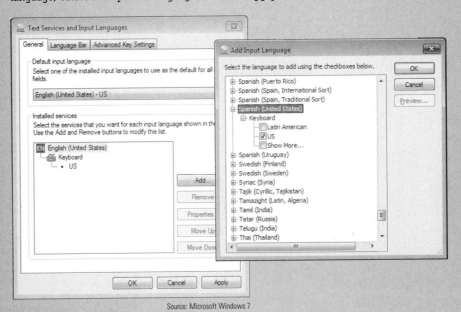

Source: Microsoft Windows 7

Figure 10-41   Add an input language

7. To change the display language on the Keyboards and Languages tab, select **español** from the drop-down menu (see Figure 10-42). The language appears in the list of installed languages because the Spanish language was installed in Step 3.

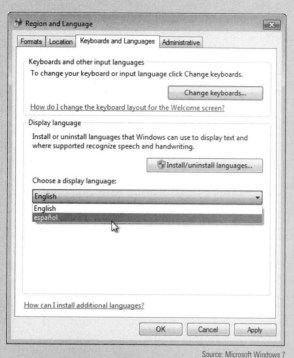

Source: Microsoft Windows 7

Figure 10-42   Select the display language

8. Click **Apply**. A message appears that says you must log off before changes will take effect. Click **Log off now**. After logging back on the system, the Windows interface is now translated into Español (see Figure 10-43).

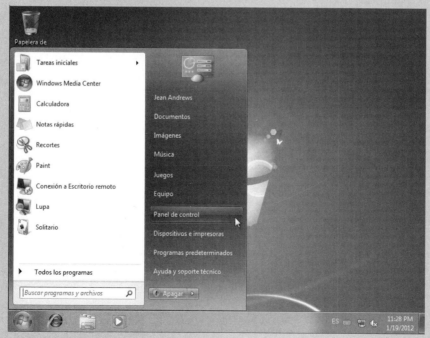

Source: Microsoft Windows 7

Figure 10-43   Display language in Spanish

10

>> CHAPTER SUMMARY

Scheduled Preventive Maintenance

▲ Regular preventive maintenance includes verifying Windows settings, cleaning up the hard drive, defragmenting the hard drive, checking the drive for errors, uninstalling unwanted software, and doing whatever else is necessary to free up enough space on the hard drive for Windows to perform well.

▲ Windows 7/Vista stores user profiles in the C:\Users folder, and XP stores them in the C:\Documents and Settings folder.

▲ For best performance, allow at least 15 percent of free space on the Windows volume. The easiest way to clean up temporary files is to use the Disk Cleanup utility in the drive properties box.

▲ You can defrag the hard drive by using the drive properties box or the Defrag command. By default, Windows 7/Vista automatically defrags weekly.

▲ Use the Chkdsk utility to check the drive for errors and recover data. The utility can be accessed from a command prompt or the drive properties box.

▲ Windows 7/Vista supports compressed (zipped) folders and NTFS folder and file compression. You can also compress an NTFS volume.

▲ Virtual memory uses hard drive space as memory to increase the total amount of memory available. Virtual memory is stored in a paging file named Pagefile.sys. To save space on drive C:, you can move the file to another volume.

Backup Procedures

▲ You need a plan for disaster recovery in the event the hard drive fails. This plan needs to include routine backups of data and system files.

▲ A system image of the Windows 7 volume can be created using the Backup and Restore utility. The Complete PC Backup in Vista is a backup of the Vista volume. Windows XP Automated System Recovery can back up the entire hard drive.

▲ Windows 7 Backup and Restore can be used to schedule routine backups of user data files.

Managing Files, Folders, and Hard Drives

▲ Commands useful to manage files, folders, and storage media include Help, Dir, Del, Copy, Recover, Xcopy, Robocopy, MD, CD, RD, Chkdsk, Defrag, and Format.

▲ Use Disk Management to manage hard drives and partitions. Use it to create, delete, and resize partitions, mount a drive, manage dynamic disks, and solve problems with hard drives. XP Disk Management cannot resize a partition.

Regional and Language Settings

▲ A language pack to display and input the Windows user interface in a language other than English can be downloaded and installed in Windows 7/Vista Ultimate and Enterprise editions. A limited Language Interface Pack (LIP) can be downloaded and installed using any edition of Windows 7/Vista.

▲ Change the display and input language and the format used for numbers, currencies, dates, and times using the Regional and Language Options dialog box accessed from Control Panel.

>> KEY TERMS

For explanations of key terms, see the Glossary near the end of the book.

active partition
Automated System Recovery (ASR)
basic disk
boot partition
cluster
Compact Disc File System (CDFS)
Complete PC Backup
defragment
Disk Cleanup
dynamic disk
dynamic volumes
elevated command prompt window
extended partition
file allocation table (FAT)
file allocation unit
file system
formatting
fragmented files
Globally Unique Identifier Partition Table (GUID or GPT)

hardware RAID
high-level format
initialization files
logical drives
low-level formatting
Master Boot Record (MBR)
master file table (MFT)
mirroring
mount point
mounted drive
Offline Files
Pagefile.sys
partition
partition table
primary partition
quick format
RAID (redundant array of inexpensive disks or redundant array of independent disks)
RAID0
RAID1
registry

restore point
sector
shadow copy
simple volume
slack
software RAID
striping
system image
system partition
System Protection
System Restore
system state data
track
Universal Disc Format (UDF)
user profile
user profile namespace
virtual memory
volume
wildcard

>> REVIEW QUESTIONS

1. What is the best way to keep a Windows 7 system protected from malware and hackers?

    a) Run the Windows Disk Cleanup utility.

    b) Check that the Windows 7 network location is set correctly.

    c) Download and install a Language Interface Pack (LIP).

    d) Use the error checking utility in Windows Explorer.

2. How can you search for bad sectors on a volume and recover the data from them if possible?

    a) Run the Windows Disk Cleanup utility.

    b) Perform the Windows update function.

    c) Defragment the drive.

    d) Use the error checking utility in Windows Explorer.

3. What is the best procedure to follow when backing up data?

    a) Keep all backups on-site so that they are readily available.

    b) As a general rule of thumb, back up data for about every 24 hours of data entry.

    c) When you store important data on any media - such as a flash drive, external hard drive, or CD - always keep a copy of the data on another media.

    d) Back up your data to another partition or folder on your same hard drive.

4. The ____ command is not included in Windows XP and is similar to the xcopy command.

   a) RD

   b) robocopy

   c) CD

   d) Recover

5. The primary tool for managing hard drives is ____.

   a) Disk Management

   b) Backup and Restore

   c) System Restore

   d) Disk Cleanup

6. True or false? For best performance, Windows needs about 15 percent free space on the hard drive that it uses for defragmenting the drive, for burning CDs and DVDs, and for a variety of other tasks, so it's important to delete unneeded files occasionally.

7. True or false? Restore points can completely rebuild a totally corrupted registry.

8. True or false? Lost clusters are clusters that are marked in the FAT or MFT as belonging to more than one file.

9. True or false? One use of the format command is to change the installed file system.

10. True or false? Microsoft warns that when Windows is used for software RAID, the risk of catastrophic failure increases and can lead to data loss.

11. The backup of the Windows 7 volume is called the ____.

12. A(n) ____ is the overall structure an OS uses to name, store, and organize files on a drive.

13. To open the command prompt window, enter ____ in the search box and press Enter.

14. A(n) ____ is a volume that can be accessed by way of a folder on another volume so that the folder has more available space.

15. A(n) ____ disk works independently of other hard drives, but a dynamic disk can work with other hard drives to hold data.

CHAPTER 1

Optimizing Windows

In the last chapter, you learned about the tools and strategies to maintain Windows and about the importance of keeping good backups. This chapter takes you one step further as a PC support technician so that you can get the best performance out of Windows. We begin the chapter learning about the Windows tools you'll need to optimize Windows. Then we turn our attention to the steps you can follow to cause a sluggish Windows system to perform at its best and how to manually remove software that does not uninstall using normal methods. As you read the chapter, you might consider following along using a Windows 7 system.

Notes Windows installed in a virtual machine is an excellent environment to use when practicing the skills in this chapter.

WINDOWS UTILITIES AND TOOLS TO SUPPORT THE OS

A+
220-802
1.4

Knowledge is power when it comes to supporting Windows. In this part of the chapter, you learn more about how Windows works and to use some Windows tools to poke around under the hood to see what is really happening that is slowing Windows down or giving other problems.

WHAT IS THE SHELL AND THE KERNEL?

Sounds like we're talking about a grain of wheat, but Windows has a shell and a kernel and you need to understand what they are and how they work so you can solve problems with each. A **shell** is the portion of an OS that relates to the user and to applications. The **kernel** is responsible for interacting with hardware. Figure 11-1 shows how the shell and kernel relate to users, applications, and hardware. In addition, the figure shows a third component of an OS, the configuration data. For Windows, this data is primarily contained in the registry.

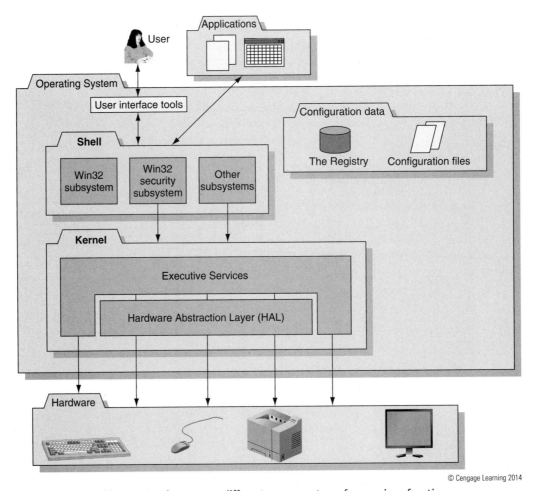

© Cengage Learning 2014

Figure 11-1 Inside an operating system, different components perform various functions

THE WINDOWS SHELL

The shell provides tools such as Windows Explorer or the Windows desktop as a way for the user to do such things as select music to burn to a CD or launch an application. For applications, the shell provides commands and procedures that applications can call on to do such things as print a document, read from a storage device, or display a photograph on-screen.

The shell is made up of several subsystems that all operate in **user mode**, which means these subsystems have only limited access to system information and can access hardware

A+
220-802
1.4

only through other OS services. One of these subsystems, the Win32 security subsystem, provides logon to the system and other security functions, including privileges for file access. All applications relate to Windows by way of the Win32 subsystem.

THE WINDOWS KERNEL

The kernel, or core, of the OS is responsible for interacting with hardware. Because the kernel operates in **kernel mode**, it has more power to communicate with hardware devices than the shell has. Applications operating under the OS cannot get to hardware devices without the shell passing those requests to the kernel. This separation of tasks provides for a more stable system and helps to prevent a wayward application from destabilizing the system.

The kernel has two main components: 1) the **HAL** (**hardware abstraction layer**), which is the layer closest to the hardware, and 2) the **executive services** interface, which is a group of services that operate in kernel mode between the user mode subsystems and the HAL. Executive services contained in the ntoskrnl.exe program file manage memory, I/O devices, file systems, some security, and other key components directly or by way of device drivers.

When Windows is first installed, it builds the HAL based on the type of CPU installed. The HAL cannot be moved from one computer to another, which is one reason you cannot copy a Windows installation from one computer to another.

HOW WINDOWS MANAGES APPLICATIONS

When an application is first installed, its program files are normally stored on the hard drive. When the application is launched, the program is copied from the hard drive into memory and there it is called a process. A **process** is a program that is running under the authority of the shell, together with the system resources assigned to it. System resources might include other programs it has started and memory addresses to hold its data. When the process makes a request for resources, this request is made to the Win32 subsystem and is called a thread. A **thread** is a single task, such as the task of printing a file that the process requests from the kernel. Figure 11-2 shows two threads in action, which is possible

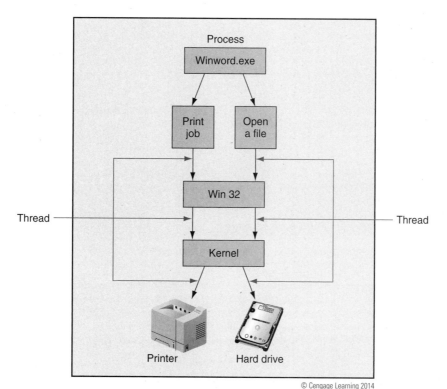

© Cengage Learning 2014

Figure 11-2 A process with more than one thread is called multithreading

11

because the process and Windows support multithreading. Sometimes a process is called an instance, such as when you say to a user, "Open two instances of Internet Explorer." Technically, you are saying to open two Internet Explorer processes.

> **A+ Exam Tip** The A+ 220-802 exam expects you to know how to use Task Manager, MSconfig, the Services console, Computer Management console, MMC, Event Viewer, Task Scheduler, the Registry Editor, and Performance Monitor. All these tools are covered in this part of the chapter.

Now that you are familiar with the concepts of how Windows works, let's see how to use some tools that can help us manage Windows components and processes.

TASK MANAGER

Task Manager (Taskmgr.exe) lets you view the applications and processes running on your computer as well as information about process and memory performance, network activity, and user activity. Several ways to access Task Manager are:

▲ Press **Ctrl+Alt+Delete**. Depending on your system, the security screen (see Figure 11-3) or Task Manager appears. If the security screen appears, click **Start Task Manager**. This method works well when the system has a problem and is frozen.
▲ Right-click a blank area in the taskbar, and select **Start Task Manager** from the shortcut menu.
▲ Press **Ctrl+Shift+Esc**.
▲ Click **Start**, enter **taskmgr.exe** in the search box, and press **Enter**.

Source: Microsoft Windows 7

Figure 11-3 Use the security screen to launch Task Manager

> **Notes** When working with a virtual machine, you cannot send the Ctrl+Alt+Delete keystrokes to the guest operating system in the VM because these keystrokes are always sent to the host operating system. To send the Ctrl+Alt+Delete keystrokes to a VM in Windows Virtual PC, click **Ctrl+Alt+Delete** in the VM menu bar (see Figure 11-4a). To send the Ctrl+Alt+Delete keystrokes to a VM in Oracle VirtualBox, click **Machine** and click **Insert Ctrl+Alt+Del** (see Figure 11-4b).

A+
220-802
1.4

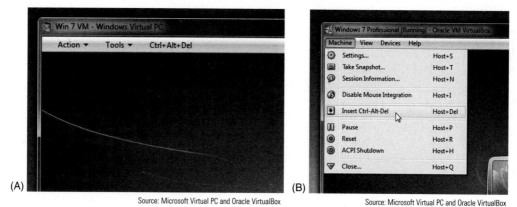

(A)   Source: Microsoft Virtual PC and Oracle VirtualBox

(B)   Source: Microsoft Virtual PC and Oracle VirtualBox

Figure 11-4   Send the Ctrl+Alt+Delete keystrokes to a VM managed by (a) Windows Virtual PC or (b) Oracle VirtualBox

Windows 7/Vista Task Manager has six tabs: Applications, Processes, Services, Performance, Networking, and Users (see Figure 11-5). Let's see how each tab of the Task Manager window works.

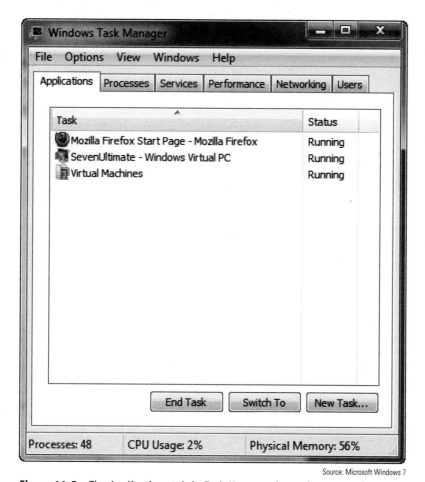

Source: Microsoft Windows 7

Figure 11-5   The Applications tab in Task Manager shows the status of active applications

APPLICATIONS TAB

On the Applications tab shown in Figure 11-5, each application loaded can have one of two states: Running or Not Responding. If an application is listed as Not Responding, you can end it by selecting it and clicking the **End Task** button at the bottom of the window.

A+
220-802
1.4

The application will attempt a normal shutdown; if data has not been saved, you are given the opportunity to save it.

PROCESSES TAB

The Processes tab of Task Manager lists system services and other processes associated with applications, together with how much CPU time and memory the process uses. This information can help you determine which applications are slowing down your system. The Processes tab for Windows 7 Task Manager (see Figure 11-6a) shows the processes running under the current user. This screen shot was taken immediately after a Windows installation and before any applications were installed.

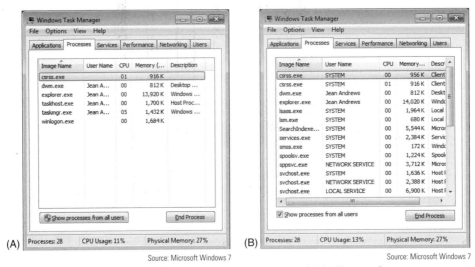

(A) Source: Microsoft Windows 7

(B) Source: Microsoft Windows 7

Figure 11-6   Processes running under (a) the current user and (b) all users, for a new Windows 7 installation

To see all processes running, click **Show processes from all users** (see Figure 11-6b). Task Manager now shows processes running under the current user, System, Local Service, and Network Service accounts. Services running under these last three accounts cannot display a dialog box on-screen or interact with the user. To do that, the service must be running under a user account. Also, a service running under the System account has more core privileges than does a service running under another account.

To stop a process using Task Manager, select the process and click **End Process**. The process is ended abruptly. If the process belongs to an application, you will lose any unsaved information in the application. Therefore, if an application is hung, try using the Applications tab to end the task before turning to the Processes tab to end its underlying process.

If you want to end the process and all related processes, right-click the process and select **End Process Tree** from the shortcut menu. Be careful to not end critical Windows processes; ending these might crash your system.

> **Notes** If your desktop locks up, you can use Task Manager to refresh it. To do so, press **Ctrl+Alt+Del** and then click **Start Task Manager**. Click the **Processes** tab. Select **Explorer.exe** (the process that provides the desktop) and then click **End Process**. Click **End process** in the warning box. Then click the **Applications** tab. Click **New Task**. Enter **Explorer.exe** in the Create New Task dialog box and click **OK**. Your desktop will be refreshed and any running programs will still be open.

APPLYING | CONCEPTS   ADJUST THE PRIORITY LEVEL OF AN APPLICATION

Each application running on your computer is assigned a priority level, which determines its position in the queue for CPU resources. You can use Task Manager to change the priority level for an application that is already loaded. If an application performs slowly, increase its priority. You should only do this with very important applications, because giving an application higher priority than certain background system processes can sometimes interfere with the operating system.

To use Task Manager to change the priority level of an open application, do the following:

1. In Task Manager, click the **Applications** tab. Right-click the application and select **Go To Process** from the shortcut menu (see Figure 11-7). The Processes tab is selected and the process that runs the application is selected.

Source: Microsoft Windows 7

Figure 11-7   Find the running process for this running application

2. Right-click the selected process. From the shortcut menu that appears, point to **Set Priority**, and set the new priority to **Above Normal** (see Figure 11-8). If that doesn't give satisfactory performance, then try **High**.

> **Notes** Remember that any changes you make to an application's priority level affect only the current session.

11

A+
220-802
1.4

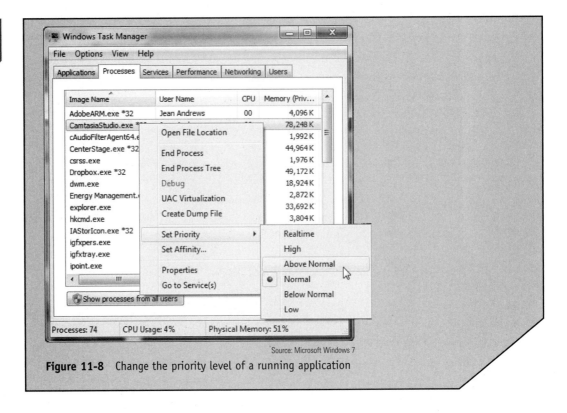

Source: Microsoft Windows 7

Figure 11-8 Change the priority level of a running application

SERVICES TAB

The third Task Manager tab, the Services tab, is shown in Figure 11-9. This tab lists the services currently installed along with the status of each service. Recall that a service is a program that runs in the background and is called on by other programs to perform a

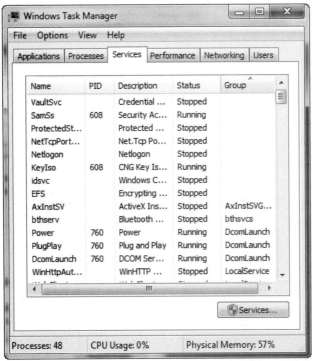

Source: Microsoft Windows 7

Figure 11-9 The Services tab of Windows 7 Task Manager gives the current status of all installed services

background task. Running services are sometimes listed in the notification area of the task-bar. To manage a service, click the **Services** button at the bottom of the window to go to the Services console. How to use this console is discussed later in the chapter.

PERFORMANCE TAB

The fourth Task Manager tab, the Performance tab, is shown in Figure 11-10. It provides graphs that can give you a quick look at how system resources are used.

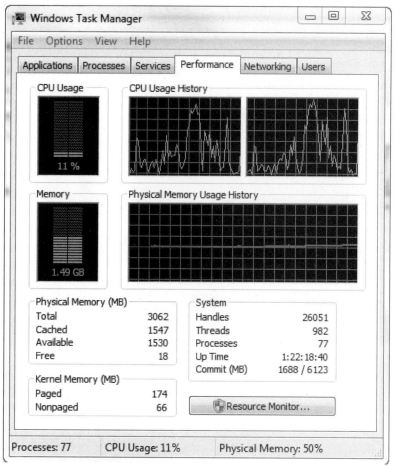

Source: Microsoft Windows 7

Figure 11-10   The Performance tab window shows details about how system resources are being used

Here is an explanation of the information in the graphs on this tab:

▲ The *CPU Usage* graph indicates the percentage of time the CPU is currently being used. If the graph indicates heavy CPU use, you need to use other tools, such as the Resource Monitor, to investigate the program(s) hogging the CPU. How to use the Resource Monitor is covered later in the chapter.

▲ The *CPU Usage History* graphs show this same percentage of use over recent time.

▲ The left *Memory* graph shows the amount of memory currently used.

▲ The right *Physical Memory Usage History* graph shows how much memory has recently been used. If this blue bar is a flat line near the top of the graph, you defi-nitely need to add more RAM to the system.

A+
220-802
1.4

NETWORKING TAB

The Networking tab lets you monitor network activity and bandwidth used. You can use it to see how heavily the network is being used by this computer. For example, in Figure 11-11, you can see that the wireless connection is running at 144 Mbps, while the local (wired) connection is running at 100 Mbps. The wired connection is slower than the wireless connection, but is used more because it is listed first. In Chapter 15, you learn how to change the order in which network connections are used.

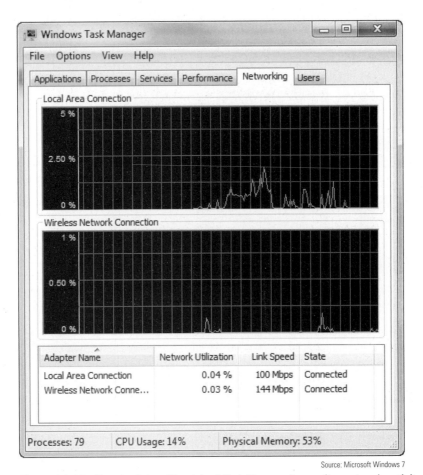

Source: Microsoft Windows 7

Figure 11-11   Use the Networking tab of Task Manager to monitor network activity

USERS TAB

The Users tab shows all users currently logged on to the system. To improve Windows performance or just before you shut down the system, you can log off a user. Before you log off another user, you can select the **Processes** tab and click **Show processes from all users** to verify no applications are running under that user account. Then return to the Users tab, select the user, and click **Logoff**. The dialog box shown in Figure 11-12 appears, warning that unsaved data might be lost. Click **Log off user** to complete the operation.

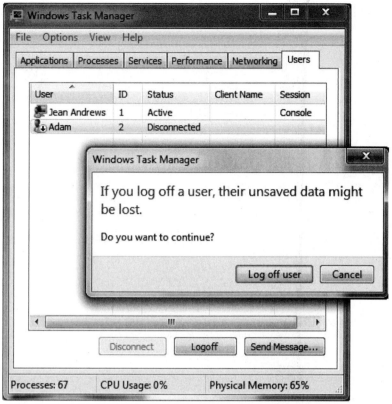

Figure 11-12 Use Task Manager to log off a user

Source: Microsoft Windows 7

11

ADMINISTRATIVE TOOLS

A+
220-802
1.1, 1.4

Windows offers a group of **Administrative tools** in the Control Panel that are used by technicians and developers to support Windows. To see the list of tools, open Control Panel and then click **Administrative Tools**. Figure 11-13 shows the Administrative Tools window for Windows 7 Ultimate. The Home editions of Windows 7 do not include the Local Security Policy (controls many security settings on the local computer) or Print Management (manages print servers on a network).

Several Administrative tools are covered next, including System Configuration, Services console, Computer Management, and Event Viewer. In Chapter 12, you learn to use more Administrative tools.

SYSTEM CONFIGURATION (MSCONFIG)

You can use the **System Configuration (Msconfig.exe)** utility, which is commonly pronounced "*M-S-config,*" to find out what processes are launched at startup and to temporarily disable a process from loading.

Using MSconfig should be a temporary fix to disable a program or service from launching at startup, but it should not be considered a permanent fix. Once you've decided you want to make the change permanent, use other methods to permanently remove that process from Windows startup. For example, you might uninstall a program, remove it

A+
220-802
1.1, 1.4

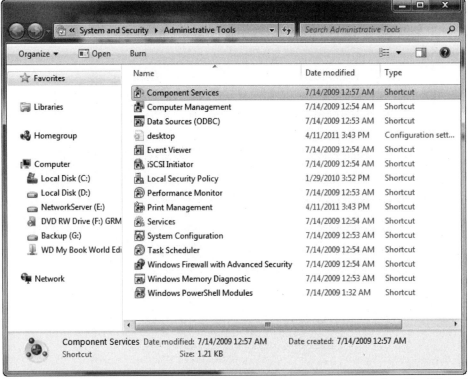

Figure 11-13 Administrative tools available in Windows 7 Ultimate

from a startup folder, or use the Services console to disable a service. Follow these steps
to learn to use MSconfig:

1. To start MSconfig, click **Start**, enter **msconfig.exe** in the search box, and press **Enter**.
   The System Configuration box opens. Click the **Boot** tab to see information about the
   boot and control some boot settings. For example, in Figure 11-14, you can see this
   computer is set for a dual boot and, using this box, you can delete one of the choices
   for a dual boot from the boot loader menu.

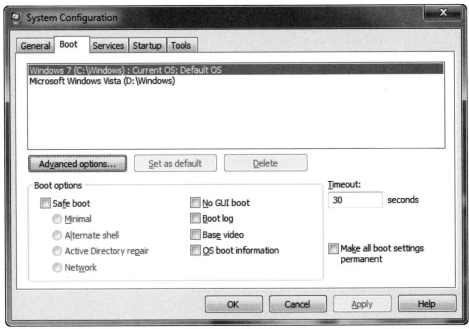

Figure 11-14 Use the Boot tab to control boot settings

A+
220-802
1.1, 1.4

2. Click the **Services** tab to see a list of all services launched at startup (see Figure 11-15). Notice that this tab has a Disable all button. If you use this button, you'll disable all nonessential Windows services as well as third-party services such as virus scan programs. Use it only for the most difficult Windows problems, because you'll disable some services that you might really want, such as Windows Task Scheduler, Print Spooler, Automatic Updates, and the System Restore service.

Source: Microsoft Windows 7

Figure 11-15   Use MSconfig to view and control services launched at startup

3. To view only those services put there by third-party software, check **Hide all Microsoft services**. If you have antivirus software running in the background (and you should), you'll see that listed as well as any service launched at startup and put there by installed software. Uncheck all services you don't want. If you don't recognize a service, try entering its name in a search string at *www.google.com* for information about the program. If the program is a service, you can permanently stop it by using the Services console or uninstalling the software.

4. Click the **Startup** tab to see a list of programs that launch at startup (see Figure 11-16). These programs launch at startup by way of a startup folder or a registry key entry. To disable all nonessential startup tasks, click **Disable all**. Or you can check and uncheck an individual startup program to enable or disable it. The Startup tab can be useful when trying to understand how a program is launched at startup because it offers the Location column. This column shows the registry key or startup folder where the startup entry is made.

A+
220-802
1.1, 1.4

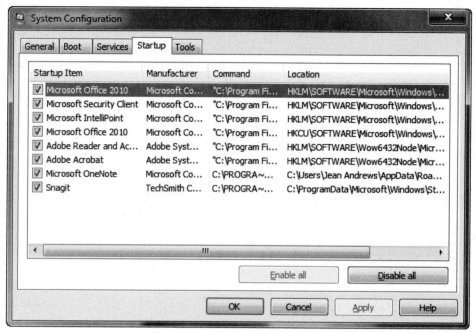

Figure 11-16   Select startup processes to enable or disable

> **Notes**   When using MSconfig to troubleshoot startup problems, keep a handwritten list of programs you enable or disable so you can backtrack, if necessary.

5. If you made changes, click **Apply**. Now click the **General** tab and you should see *Selective startup* selected, as shown in Figure 11-17. Close the MSconfig box and restart the computer.

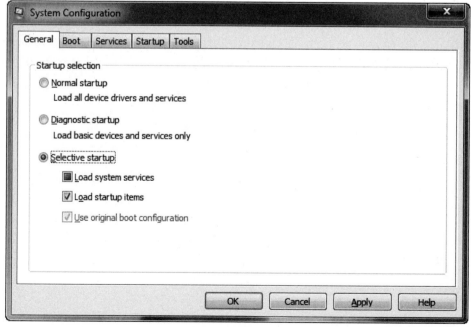

Figure 11-17   MSconfig is set to control the Windows startup programs

A+
220-802
1.1, 1.4

6. Watch for error messages during or after the boot that indicate you've created a problem with your changes. For instance, after the boot, you might find out you can no longer use that nifty little utility that came with your digital camera. To fix the problem, you need to find out which service or program you stopped that you need for that utility. Go back to the MSconfig tool and enable that one service and reboot.

The Tools tab in the System Configuration box gives you quick access to other Windows tools you might need during a troubleshooting session (see Figure 11-18).

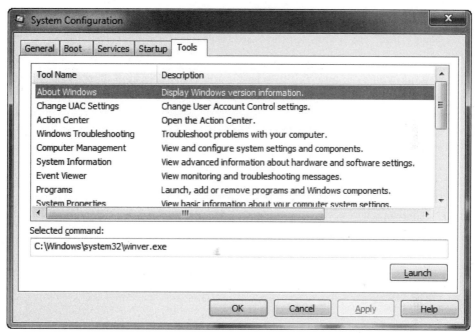

Source: Microsoft Windows 7

Figure 11-18 The Tools tab makes it easy to find troubleshooting tools

> **Notes** MSconfig reports only what it is programmed to look for when listing startup programs and services. It looks only in certain registry keys and startup folders, and sometimes MSconfig does not report a startup process. Therefore, don't consider its list of startup processes to be complete.

> **Vista Differences** Windows Vista uses the System Configuration utility to control startup programs just as does Windows 7. In addition, Vista offers Software Explorer, a user-friendly tool to control startup programs. To learn how to use Software Explorer, see Appendix B.

SERVICES CONSOLE

The **Services console** (the program file is services.msc) is used to control the Windows and third-party services installed on a system. To launch the Services console, type **Services.msc** in the search box and press **Enter**. If the Extended tab at the bottom of the window is not selected, click it (see Figure 11-19). This tab gives a description of a selected service.

A+
220-802
1.1, 1.4

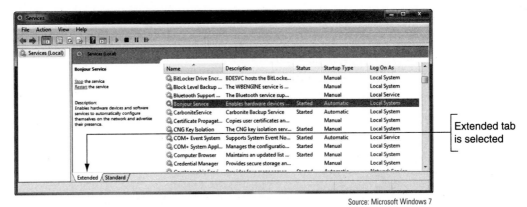

Source: Microsoft Windows 7

Figure 11-19   The Services console is used to manage Windows Services

When you click a service to select it and the description is missing, most likely the service is a third-party service put there by an installed application. To get more information about a service or to stop or start a service, right-click its name and select **Properties** from the shortcut menu. In the Properties box (see Figure 11-20), the startup types for a service are:

- ◢ *Automatic (Delayed Start).* Starts shortly after startup, after the user logs on, so as not to slow down the startup process
- ◢ *Automatic.* Starts when Windows loads
- ◢ *Manual.* Starts as needed
- ◢ *Disabled.* Cannot be started

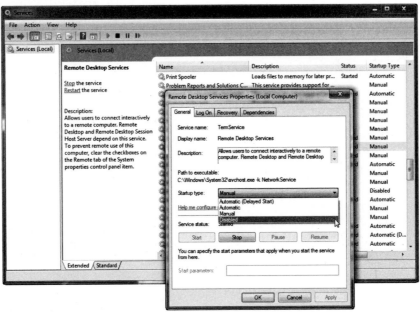

Source: Microsoft Windows 7

Figure 11-20   Manage a service with the service Properties box

> 📑 **Notes**   If you suspect a Windows system service is causing a problem, you can use MSconfig to disable the service. If this works, then try replacing the service file with a fresh copy from the Windows setup DVD.

COMPUTER MANAGEMENT

A+
220-802
1.1, 1.4

Computer Management (Compmgmt.msc) contains several tools that can be used to manage the local PC or other computers on the network. The window is called a **console** because it consolidates several Windows administrative tools. To use most of these tools, you must be logged on as an administrator, although you can view certain settings in Computer Management if you are logged on with lesser privileges.

As with most Windows tools, there are several ways to access Computer Management:

- ◢ Click **Start**, enter **Computer Management** or **compmgmt.msc** in the search box, and press **Enter**.
- ◢ Click **Start**, right-click **Computer**, and select **Manage** from the shortcut menu.
- ◢ In Control Panel, look in the **Administrative Tools** group.

The Computer Management window is shown in Figure 11-21. Using this window, you can access Task Scheduler, Event Viewer, performance monitoring tools including the Windows 7 Performance Monitor and the Vista Reliability and Performance Monitor, Device Manager, Disk Management, and the Services console. You can also manage user accounts and user groups (covered in Chapter 17). Several tools available from the Computer Management window are covered in this chapter.

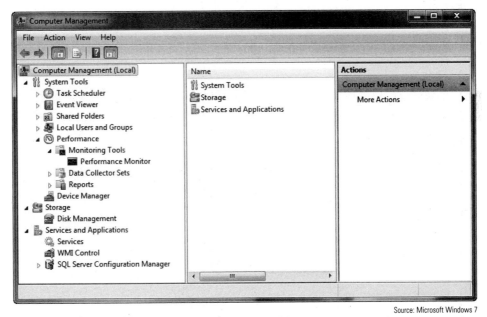

Source: Microsoft Windows 7

Figure 11-21 Windows Computer Management combines several administrative tools into a single easy-to-access window

MICROSOFT MANAGEMENT CONSOLE (MMC)

Microsoft Management Console (MMC; the program file is mmc.exe) is a Windows utility that can be used to build your own customized console windows. In a console, these individual tools are called **snap-ins**. A console is saved in a file with an .msc file extension, and a snap-in in a console can itself be a console. To use all the functions of MMC, you must be logged on with administrator privileges.

11

A+
220-802
1.1, 1.4

Notes A program that can work as a snap-in under the MMC has an .msc file extension.

APPLYING │ CONCEPTS CREATE A CONSOLE

If you find yourself often using a few Windows tools, consider putting them in a console stored on your desktop. Follow these steps to create a console:

1. Click **Start**, enter **mmc.exe** in the search box, and press **Enter**. Respond to the UAC box. An empty console window appears, as shown in Figure 11-22.

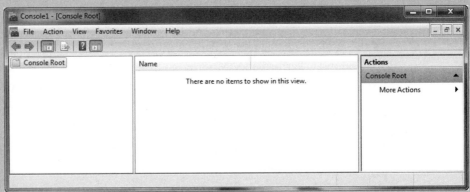

Source: Microsoft Windows 7

Figure 11-22 An empty console

2. Click **File** in the menu bar and then click **Add/Remove Snap-in**. The Add or Remove Snap-ins box opens, as shown on the left side of Figure 11-23.

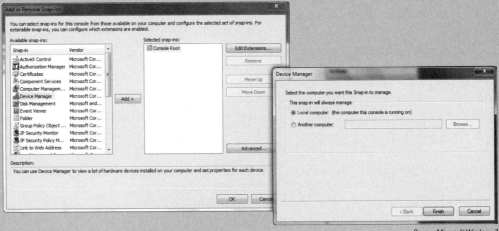

Source: Microsoft Windows 7

Figure 11-23 Add a snap-in to the new console

A+
220-802
1.1, 1.4

3. Select a snap-in from the list in the Add or Remove Snap-ins box. Notice a description of the snap-in appears at the bottom of the window. The snap-ins that appear in this list depend on the edition of Windows 7/Vista you have installed and what other components are installed on the system. Click **Add** to add the snap-in to the console. (For Windows XP, in the Add/Remove Snap-In box, click **Add**. A list of snap-ins appears. Select one and click **Add**.)

4. If parameters for the snap-in need defining, a dialog box opens that allows you to set up these parameters. The dialog box offers different selections, depending on the snap-in being added. For example, when Device Manager is selected, a dialog box appears, asking you to select the computer that Device Manager will monitor (see the right side of Figure 11-23). Select **Local computer (the computer this console is running on)** and click **Finish**. The snap-in now appears in the list of snap-ins for this console.

5. Repeat Steps 3 and 4 to add all the snap-ins that you want to the console. When you finish, click **OK** in the Add or Remove Snap-ins box.

6. To save the console, click **File** in the menu bar and then click **Save As**. The Save As dialog box opens.

7. The default location for the console file is C:\Users*username*\AppData\Roaming\\Microsoft\Windows\Start Menu\Programs\Administrative Tools. However, you can save the console to any location, such as the Windows desktop. However, if you save the file to its default location, the console will appear as an option under Administrative Tools in the Start menu. Select the location for the file, name the file, and click **Save**. Then close the console window.

Notes After you create a console, you can copy the .msc file to any computer or place a shortcut to it on the desktop.

11

EVENT VIEWER

Just about anything that happens in Windows is logged by Windows, and these logs can be viewed using **Event Viewer (Eventvwr.msc)**. You can find events such as a hardware or network failure, OS error messages, a device or service that has failed to start, or General Protection Faults.

Event Viewer is a Computer Management console snap-in, and you can open it by using the Computer Management window, by entering **Event Viewer** or **Eventvwr.msc** in the search box, or by using the Administrative Tools group in Control Panel. The Windows 7/Vista Event Viewer window is shown in Figure 11-24. The XP Event Viewer is shown in Figure 11-25. The XP Event Viewer does not keep as many logs as does the Windows 7/Vista Event Viewer.

A+
220-802
1.1, 1.4

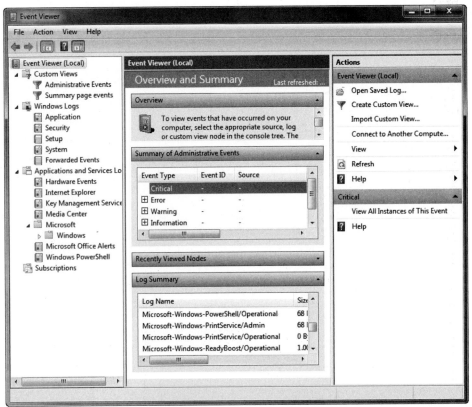

Source: Microsoft Windows 7

Figure 11-24 Use Event Viewer to see logs about hardware, Windows, security, and applications events

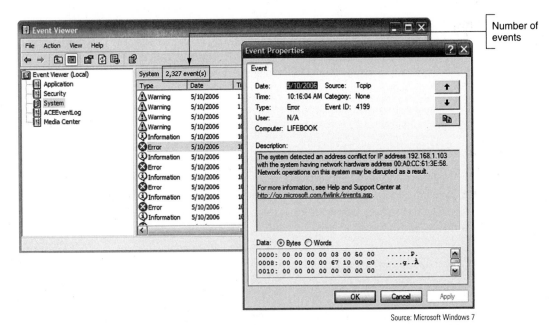

Number of events

Source: Microsoft Windows 7

Figure 11-25 Event Viewer in Windows XP works about the same way as the Windows 7/Vista Event Viewer

The different views of logs are listed in the left pane, and you can drill down into sub-categories of these logs. You can filter and sort logs to help find what you need. First select a log in the left pane and then click an event in the middle pane to see details about

A+
220-802
1.1, 1.4

the event. For example, in Figure 11-26, the Administrative Events log shows an event recorded by Windows Backup.

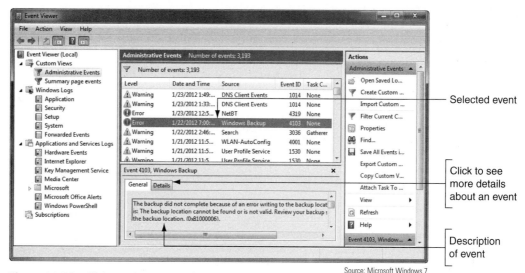

Figure 11-26 Click an event to see details about the event

Source: Microsoft Windows 7

Three main types of events are Error, Warning, and Information. Error events are the most important and indicate something went wrong with the system, such as a scheduled backup failed to work. Warning events indicate failure might occur in the future.

Here are the views of logs that are the most useful:

- ◢ *Administrative Events log.* This log is a filtered log that shows only Warning and Error events intended for the administrator. This log is in the Custom Views category and is selected in Figure 11-26.
- ◢ *Application log.* In the Windows Logs group, look in the Application log for events recorded by an application. This log might help you identify why an application is causing problems.
- ◢ *Security log.* Events in the Security log are called audits and include successful and unsuccessful logins to a user account and attempts from another computer on the network to access shared resources on this computer.
- ◢ *Setup log.* Look in the Setup log for events recorded when applications are installed.
- ◢ *System log.* Look in the System log to find events triggered by Windows components, such as a device driver failing to load or a problem with hardware.
- ◢ *Forwarded Events log.* This log receives events that were recorded on other computers and sent to this computer.

When you first encounter a Windows, hardware, application, or security problem, get in the habit of checking Event Viewer as one of your first steps toward investigating the problem. To save time, first check the Administrative Events log because it filters out all events except Warning and Error events.

If you want to create your own filtered events log, right-click any log in the left pane and select **Filter Current Log** from the shortcut menu. (For Windows XP, select **Properties** from the shortcut menu and then click the **Filter** tab.) The Filter Current Log box appears (see Figure 11-27).

The Filter Current Log box offers many ways to filter events. To view the most significant events to troubleshoot a problem, check **Critical** and **Error** under the Event level, as shown in Figure 11-27. Critical events are those errors that Windows believes are affecting critical

11

Figure 11-27 Criteria to filter events in Event Viewer

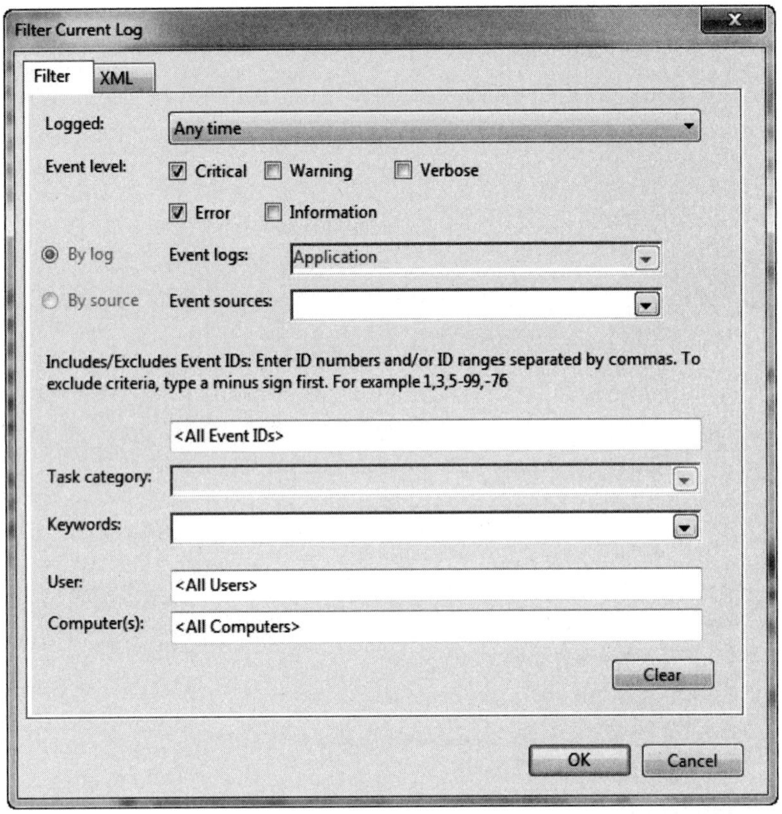

Source: Microsoft Windows 7

Windows processes. After you select the filters, click **OK**. Only the events that match your filters are listed. To remove the filter, right-click the log and select **Clear Filter**.

Besides filtering a log, here are other useful tips when dealing with logs:

- ◢ To sort a list of events, click a column heading in the middle pane.
- ◢ To save a filtered log file so you can view it later, right-click the log and select **Save Filtered Log File As** (see Figure 11-28). The log file is assigned an .evtx file extension. When you later double-click this file, it appears in an Event Viewer window. You might want to email a filtered log file to others who are helping you troubleshoot a problem.

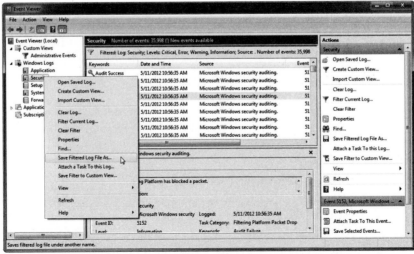

Figure 11-28 Save a filtered log file so that you can view it later

Source: Microsoft Windows 7

A+
220-802
1.1, 1.4

▲ To control the size of a log file, you can clear it. In the log's shortcut menu, select **Clear Log**. Before clearing the log, Event Viewer gives you a chance to save it.

▲ Select **Properties** in the log's shortcut menu to control the maximum size of the log file and to cause the events to be archived before they are overwritten.

APPLYING CONCEPTS

Event Viewer can be useful in solving intermittent hardware problems. For example, I once worked in an office where several people updated Microsoft Word documents stored on a file server. For weeks, people complained about these Word documents getting corrupted. We downloaded the latest patches for Windows and Microsoft Office and scanned for viruses, thinking that the problem might be with Windows or the application. Then we suspected a corrupted template file for building the Word documents. But nothing we did solved our problem of corrupted Word documents. Then one day someone thought to check Event Viewer on the file server. The Event Viewer had faithfully been recording errors when writing to the hard drive. What we had suspected to be a software problem was, in fact, a failing hard drive, which was full of bad sectors. We replaced the drive and the problem went away. That day I learned the value of checking Event Viewer very early in the troubleshooting process.

TASK SCHEDULER

Windows **Task Scheduler** can be set to launch a task or program at a future time, including at startup. When applications install, they might schedule tasks to check for and download their program updates. Task Scheduler stores tasks in a file stored in the C:\Windows\System32\Tasks folder. For example, in Figure 11-29, there are seven scheduled tasks showing and other tasks are stored in four folders.

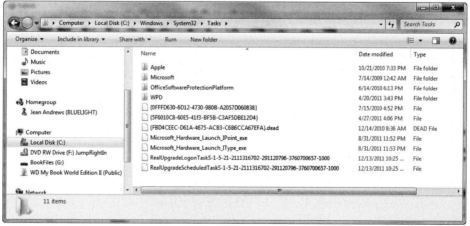

Figure 11-29 The Tasks folder contains tasks that launch at startup

Source: Microsoft Windows 7

To open Task Scheduler from the Control Panel, double-click **Task Scheduler** in the Administrative Tools group. Alternately, you can click Start, All Programs, Accessories, System Tools, and Task Scheduler. The Task Scheduler window is shown in Figure 11-30.

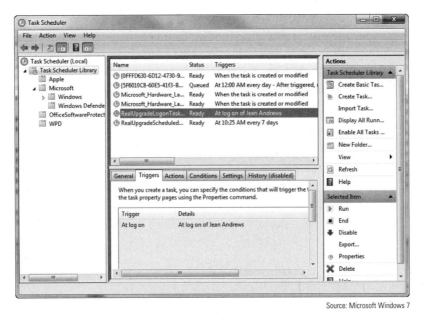

Source: Microsoft Windows 7

Figure 11-30 View and manage tasks from the Task Scheduler window

Here is what you need to know to use the Task Scheduler window:

▲ In the left pane, drill down into groups and subgroups. Tasks in a group are listed in the middle pane.

▲ To see details about a task, including what triggers it, what actions it performs, the conditions and settings related to the task, and the history of past actions, select the task and then click the tabs in the lower-middle pane. For example, in Figure 11-30, you can see that the RealUpgradeLogonTask is scheduled to run when I log on.

▲ To add a new task, first select the group for the new task and then click **Action**, **Create Basic Task**. A wizard appears to step you through creating the task.

▲ To delete, disable, or run a task, select it and in the Action menu or in the Actions pane, click Delete, Disable, or Run.

> **Notes** Tasks can be hidden in the Task Scheduler window. To be certain you're viewing all scheduled tasks, unhide them. In the menu bar, click **View**, and then **Show Hidden Tasks**.

THE REGISTRY EDITOR

Many actions, such as installing application software or hardware, can result in changes to the registry. These changes can create new keys, add new values to existing keys, and change existing values. For a few difficult problems, you might need to edit or remove a registry key. This part of the chapter looks at how the registry is organized, which keys might hold entries causing problems, and how to back up and edit the registry using the **Registry Editor (regedit.exe)**. Let's first look at how the registry is organized, and then you'll learn how to back up and edit the registry.

A+
220-802
1.1, 1.4

HOW THE REGISTRY IS ORGANIZED

The most important Windows component that holds information for Windows is the registry. The **registry** is a database designed with a treelike structure (called a hierarchical database) that contains configuration information for Windows, users, software applications, and installed hardware devices. During startup, Windows builds the registry in memory and keeps it there until Windows shuts down. During startup, after the registry is built, Windows reads from it to obtain information to complete the startup process. After Windows is loaded, it continually reads from many of the subkeys in the registry.

Windows builds the registry from the current hardware configuration and from information it takes from these files:

▲ Five files stored in the C:\Windows\System32\config folder; these files are called hives, and they are named the SAM (Security Accounts Manager), Security, Software, System, and Default hives. (Each hive is backed up with a log file and a backup file, which are also stored in the C:\Windows\System32\config folder.)

▲ For Windows 7/Vista, the C:\Users*username*\Ntuser.dat file, which holds the preferences and settings of the currently logged-on user.

▲ Windows XP uses information about the current user stored in two files:

  • C:\Documents and Settings*username*\Ntuser.dat

  • C:\Documents and Settings*username*\Local Settings\Application Data\ Microsoft\Windows\Usrclass.dat

After the registry is built in memory, it is organized into five high-level keys (see Figure 11-31). Each key can have subkeys, and subkeys can have more subkeys and can be assigned one or more values. The way data is organized in the hive files is different from the way it is organized in registry keys. Figure 11-32 shows the relationship between registry keys and hives. For example, in the figure, notice that the HKEY_CLASSES_ROOT key contains data that comes from the Software hive, and this data is also stored in the larger HKEY_ LOCAL_MACHINE key.

11

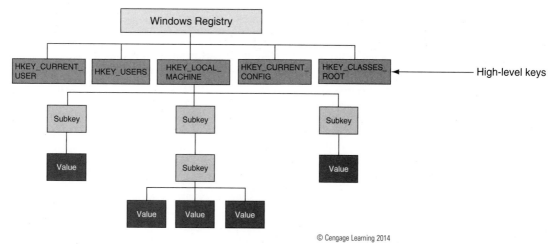

© Cengage Learning 2014

Figure 11-31 The Windows registry is logically organized in five keys with subkeys

A+
220-802
1.1, 1.4

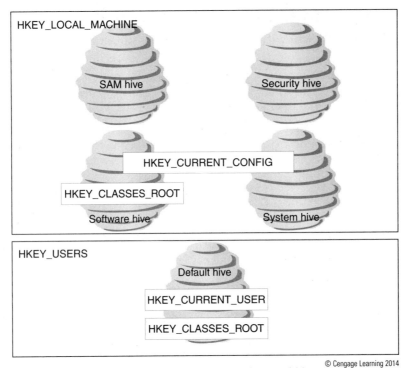

Figure 11-32 The relationship between registry keys and hives

© Cengage Learning 2014

Here are the five keys, including where they get their data and their purposes:

- **HKEY_LOCAL_MACHINE (HKLM)** is the most important key and contains hardware, software, and security data. The data is taken from four hives: the SAM hive, the Security hive, the Software hive, and the System hive. In addition, the HARDWARE subkey of HKLM is built when the registry is first loaded, based on data collected about the current hardware configuration.
- **HKEY_CURRENT_CONFIG (HKCC)** contains information that identifies each hardware device installed on the computer. Some of the data is gathered from the current hardware configuration when the registry is first loaded into memory. Other data is taken from the HKLM key, which got its data primarily from the System hive.
- **HKEY_CLASSES_ROOT (HKCR)** stores information that determines which application is opened when the user double-clicks a file. This process relies on the file's extension to determine which program to load. Data for this key is gathered from the HKLM key and the HKCU key.
- **HKEY_USERS (HKU)** contains data about all users and is taken from the Default hive.
- **HKEY_CURRENT_USER (HKCU)** contains data about the current user. The key is built when a user logs on using data kept in the HKEY_USERS key and data kept in the Ntuser.dat file of the current user.

> **Notes** Device Manager reads data from the HKLM\HARDWARE key to build the information it displays about hardware configurations. You can consider Device Manager to be an easy-to-view presentation of this HARDWARE key data.

BEFORE YOU EDIT THE REGISTRY, BACK IT UP!

When you need to edit the registry, if possible, make the change from the Windows tool that is responsible for the key—for example, by using the Programs and Features window in Control Panel. If that doesn't work and you must edit the registry, always back up the registry before attempting to edit it. Changes made to the registry are implemented immediately. *There is no undo feature in the Registry Editor, and no opportunity to change your mind once the edit is made.*

Here are the ways to back up the registry:

▲ *Use System Protection to create a restore point.* A restore point keeps information about the registry. You can restore the system to a restore point to undo registry changes, as long as the registry is basically intact and not too corrupted. Also know that, if System Protection is turned on, Windows 7/Vista automatically makes a daily backup of the registry hive files to the C:\Windows\System32\Config\RegBack folder.

▲ *Back up a single registry key just before you edit the key.* This method, called exporting a key, should always be used before you edit the registry. How to export a key is coming up in this chapter.

▲ *Make an extra copy of the C:\Window\System32\config folder.* This is what I call the old-fashioned shotgun approach to backing up the registry. This backup will help if the registry gets totally trashed. You can boot from the Windows setup DVD and use the Windows 7/Vista Recovery Environment or the XP Recovery Console to restore the folder from your extra copy. This method is drastic and not recommended except in severe cases. But, still, just to be on the safe side, I make an extra copy of this folder just before I start any serious digging into the registry.

▲ *For Windows XP, back up the system state.* Use Ntbackup in Windows XP to back up the system state, which also makes an extra copy of the registry hives. Windows XP stores the backup of the registry hives in the C:\Windows\repair folder.

In some situations, such as when you're going to make some drastic changes to the registry, you'll want to play it safe and use more than one backup method. Extra registry backups are always a good thing! Now let's look at how to back up an individual key in the registry, and then you'll learn how to edit the registry.

> **Notes** Although you can edit the registry while in Safe Mode, you cannot create a restore point in Safe Mode.

Backing Up and Restoring Individual Keys in the Registry

A less time-consuming method of backing up the registry is to back up a particular key that you plan to edit. However, know that if the registry gets corrupted, having a backup of only a particular key most likely will not help you much when trying a recovery. Also, although you could use this technique to back up the entire registry or an entire tree within the registry, it is not recommended.

To back up a key along with its subkeys in the registry, follow these steps:

1. Open the Registry Editor. To do that, click **Start** and type **regedit** in the search box, press **Enter**, and respond to the UAC box. Figure 11-33 shows the Registry Editor with the five main keys and several subkeys listed. Click the triangles on the left to see subkeys. When you select a subkey, such as KeyboardClass in the figure, the names of the values in that subkey are displayed in the right pane along with the data assigned to each value.

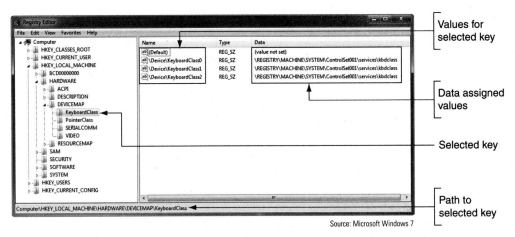

Source: Microsoft Windows 7

Figure 11-33 The Registry Editor showing the five main keys, subkeys, values, and data

> **Notes** The full path to a selected key displays in the status bar at the bottom of the editor window. If the status bar is missing, click **View** in the menu bar and make sure **Status Bar** is checked.

2. Suppose we want to back up the registry key that contains a list of installed software, which is HKLM\Software\Microsoft\Windows\CurrentVersion\Uninstall. (HKLM stands for HKEY_LOCAL_MACHINE.) First click the appropriate triangles to navigate to the key. Next, right-click the key and select **Export** from the shortcut menu, as shown in Figure 11-34. The Export Registry File dialog box appears.

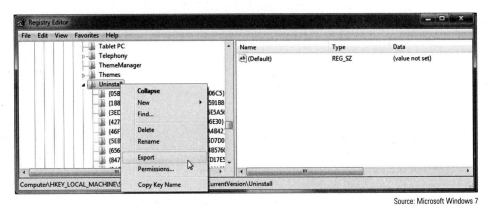

Source: Microsoft Windows 7

Figure 11-34 Using the Registry Editor, you can back up a key and its subkeys with the Export command

3. Select the location to save the export file and name the file. A convenient place to store an export file while you edit the registry is the desktop. Click **Save** when done. The file saved will have a .reg file extension.

4. You can now edit the key. Later, if you need to undo your changes, exit the Registry Editor and double-click the saved export file. The key and its subkeys saved in the export file will be restored. After you're done with an export file, delete it so that no one accidentally double-clicks it and reverts the registry to an earlier setting.

A+
220-802
1.1, 1.4

Editing the Registry

Before you edit the registry, you should use one or more of the four backup methods just discussed so that you can restore it if something goes wrong. To edit the registry, open the **Registry Editor** (**regedit.exe**), and locate and select the key in the left pane of the Registry Editor, which will display the values stored in this key in the right pane. To edit, rename, or delete a value, right-click it and select the appropriate option from the shortcut menu. For example, in Figure 11-35, I'm ready to delete the value QuickTime Task and its data. Changes are immediately applied to the registry and there is no undo feature. (However, Windows or applications might need to read the changed value before it affects their operations.) To search the registry for keys, values, and data, click **Edit** in the menu bar and then click **Find**.

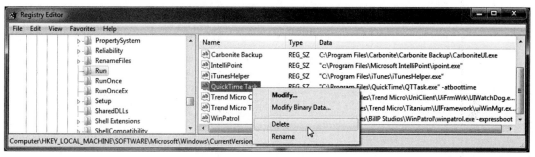

Source: Microsoft Windows 7

Figure 11-35 Right-click a value to modify, delete, or rename it

> ⚡ **Caution** Changes made to the registry take effect immediately. Therefore, take extra care when editing the registry. If you make a mistake and don't know how to correct a problem you create, then double-click the exported key to recover. When you double-click an exported key, the registry is updated with the values stored in this key.

WINDOWS 7 TOOLS TO MONITOR PERFORMANCE AND OPTIMIZE RESOURCES

The Windows 7 tools for monitoring performance and optimizing resources that differ significantly from those in Vista or XP include the Windows 7 Performance Information and Tools window, Resource Monitor, Reliability Monitor, and Performance Monitor. These Windows 7 tools are covered next.

PERFORMANCE INFORMATION AND TOOLS WINDOW

The **Performance Information and Tools** window gives information to evaluate the performance of a system and to adjust Windows for best performance.

Use one of the following methods to open the Performance Information and Tools window:

- ◢ Click **Start**, right-click **Computer**, and select **Properties**. In the System window, click **Performance Information and Tools** (in Vista, click Performance).
- ◢ In the Action Center, click **View performance information**.

The Performance Information and Tools window for Windows 7 is shown in Figure 11-36, and the Vista window is shown in Figure 11-37.

11

A+
220-802
1.1, 1.4

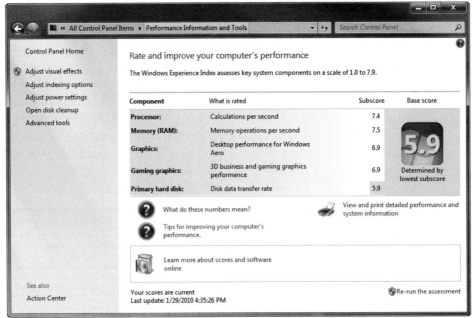

Source: Microsoft Windows 7

Figure 11-36   The Windows Experience Index gives a rating of key system components
in this Windows 7 computer

Notes   To see more detail about the Windows 7 system and to print these details, click **View and print detailed performance and system information**.

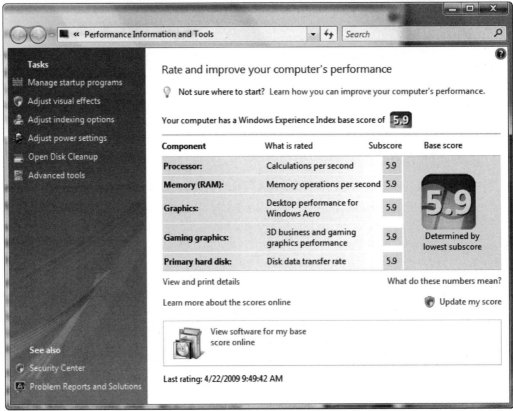

Source: Microsoft Windows 7

Figure 11-37   The Windows Experience Index for this Vista system reports no potential bottlenecks

A+
220-802
1.1, 1.4

The Windows Experience Index evaluates key system components to give a high-level view of the computer's performance. Five key components are rated on a scale of 1.0 to 7.9. The index is the lowest value of all five ratings because this component is considered the bottleneck component for overall performance.

The left pane contains links to adjusting visual effects, indexing options, and power settings and tools to clean up the hard drive. These utilities can help improve a system's performance and provide more information about the system. Follow these steps to use the tools:

1. Click **Adjust visual effects** to open the Performance Options box (see Figure 11-38). On the Visual Effects tab of this box, you can choose to adjust visual effects for best performance or best appearance. If resources are low on a system, adjusting for best performance can remove a system bottleneck hogging resources. You can also enable or disable individual visual effects to customize the visual effects, creating a balance between best performance and best appearance.

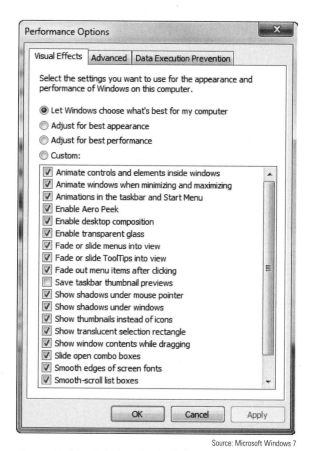

Source: Microsoft Windows 7

Figure 11-38 Balance visual effects between best performance and best appearance

> **Notes** You can also open the Performance Options box from the System Properties box. In the System Properties box, on the **Advanced** tab, click **Settings** in the Performance area.

2. Click the **Advanced** tab on the Performance Options box to choose how to allocate processor resources, adjusting for best performance between programs running in the foreground and programs running in the background (see Figure 11-39).

11

A+
220-802
1.1, 1.4

> **Notes** Reducing the CPU processing time allowed for programs is called throttling the programs.

3. Also notice on the Advanced tab the ability to adjust virtual memory. Click **Change** to move the file to a different hard drive, which can free up space on the Windows volume and might improve performance.

4. Also in the left pane in the Performance and Information Tools window (refer to Figure 11-36), you can click **Advanced tools** to see a list of performance issues and to open Task Manager, Disk Defragmenter, Event Viewer, Windows 7 Performance Monitor, Windows 7 Resource Monitor, Vista Reliability and Performance Monitor, and other tools.

Source: Microsoft Windows 7

Figure 11-39 Use the Advanced tab of the Performance Options box to adjust how processor resources are allocated to programs and background services

WINDOWS 7 RESOURCE MONITOR

Windows 7 **Resource Monitor** (resmon.exe) monitors the performance of the processor, memory, hard drive, and network. As you learned earlier in the chapter, Task Manager reports some of this information. To access Resource Monitor, use one of these methods:

- In Task Manager, click **Resource Monitor** on the Performance tab.
- In the Performance Information and Tools window, click **Advanced tools**, and then click **Open Resource Monitor**.
- In the Computer Management window, in the System Tools, Performance group, click **Monitoring Tools, More Actions,** and **Resource Monitor**.

The Resource Monitor window is shown in Figure 11-40 with the Memory tab selected.

The bar graphically showing how memory is used accounts for all the memory installed in a system. The graph shows these five ways memory is used:

- ▲ Hardware Reserved memory is used by BIOS and certain drivers such as the video drivers. Windows does not have access to this memory. For example, compare total memory reported by Task Manager in Figure 11-10 earlier in the chapter to installed memory reported by Resource Monitor in Figure 11-40 for the same system.
- ▲ In Use memory is used by other drives, the OS, and applications.
- ▲ Modified memory will be available as soon as its contents are written to disk.
- ▲ Standby memory is holding data and code that is ready to use.
- ▲ Free memory will be used as the system needs it.

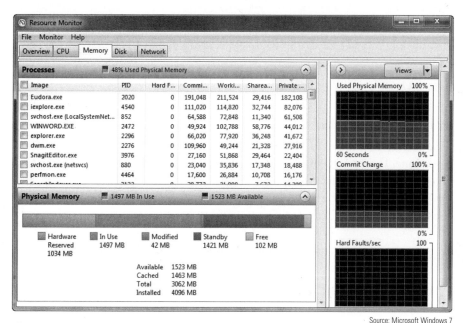

Source: Microsoft Windows 7

Figure 11-40 The Resource Monitor shows how memory is currently used

The easiest way to find out if a system would benefit from a memory upgrade (adding more memory to the system) is to watch this memory bar as a user does her work. If you consistently see Free memory disappear from this graph, the system would benefit from more installed memory.

> **Notes** To best gauge the performance of a system, ask the user to watch the Resource Monitor throughout the workday and note what the monitor shows when the system is busiest.

The Network tab of the Resource Monitor is useful if you suspect a program is hogging network resources. If you suspect a worm or other process is slowing down the network with excessive activity, look for the process in the Processes with Network Activity group on the Network tab (see Figure 11-41). (A worm is malware that can bring down a network by overwhelming it with activity.)

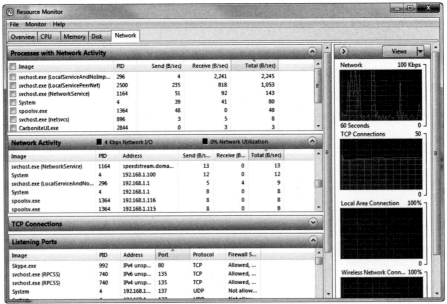

Source: Microsoft Windows 7

Figure 11-41 Look for a process using excessive networking resources

WINDOWS 7 RELIABILITY MONITOR

The Windows **Reliability Monitor** gives information about problems and errors that happen over time. Unless someone has cleared its history log, it reports problems since Windows was installed. To open the Reliability Monitor, open the **Action Center**, click the down arrow to open the Maintenance group, and click **View reliability history**. (You can also enter **Reliability** in the search box.) The Reliability Monitor window is shown in Figure 11-42.

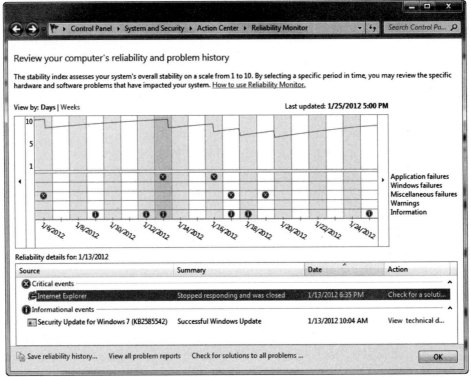

Source: Microsoft Windows 7

Figure 11-42 Use the Reliability Monitor to search for when a problem began and what else happened about that time

When you click an error in the column graph, the error and other events that happened the same day appear at the bottom of the window. Double-click one of these errors or events to see more information about it.

One important step in troubleshooting a problem is to ask what changes were made to a system at the time a problem began. If you can find out about when a performance problem started, use the Reliability Monitor to find out what happened about that same time. For example, suppose Internet Explorer locks up and the problem started around the day selected in Figure 11-42. You can see from this window that Windows received a security update on this day. The next task would be to research this security update on the Microsoft web site to see if it might be the source of the problem.

WINDOWS 7 PERFORMANCE MONITOR

Windows 7 **Performance Monitor** is a Microsoft Management Console snap-in (Perfmon.msc or Perfmon.exe) that can track activity by hardware and software to measure performance. Whereas Resource Monitor monitors activities in real time, Performance Monitor can monitor in real time and can save collected data in logs for future use. Software developers might use this tool to evaluate how well their software is performing and to identify software and hardware bottlenecks.

Use one of these methods to open the Performance Monitor window shown in Figure 11-43:

◢ Click **Start**, enter **perfmon.msc** in the search box, and press **Enter**.
◢ In the Performance Information and Tools window, click **Advanced tools**, and click **Open Performance Monitor**.
◢ In the Computer Management window in the System Tools, Performance, Monitoring Tools group, click **Performance Monitor**.

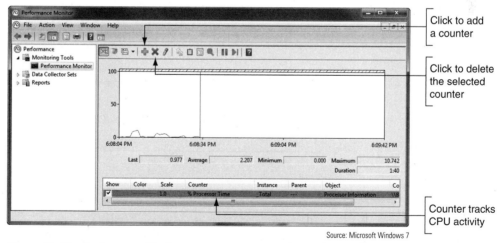

Source: Microsoft Windows 7

Figure 11-43 Performance Monitor uses counters to monitor various activities of hardware and software

Performance Monitor offers hundreds of counters used to examine many aspects of the system related to performance. The Windows default setting is to show the %Processor Time counter the first time you open the window (see Figure 11-43). This counter appears as a red line in the graph and tracks activity of the processor.

To keep from unnecessarily using system resources, only use the counters you really need. For example, suppose you want to track hard drive activity. You first remove the

A+
220-802
1.1, 1.4

%Processor Time counter. To delete a counter, select the counter from the list so that it is highlighted and click the red **X** above the graph.

Next add two counters: % Disk Time counter and Avg. Disk Queue Length counter. The % Disk Time counter tracks the percentage of time the hard drive is in use, and the Avg. Disk Queue Length counter tracks the average number of processes waiting to use the hard drive. To add a counter, click the green **plus sign** above the graph. Then, in the Add Counters box, select a counter and click **Add**. Figure 11-44 shows the Add Counters box with two counters added. After all your counters are added, click **OK**.

Allow Performance Monitor to keep running while the system is in use, and then check the counters. The results for one system are shown in Figure 11-45. Select each counter and note the average, minimum, and maximum values for the counter.

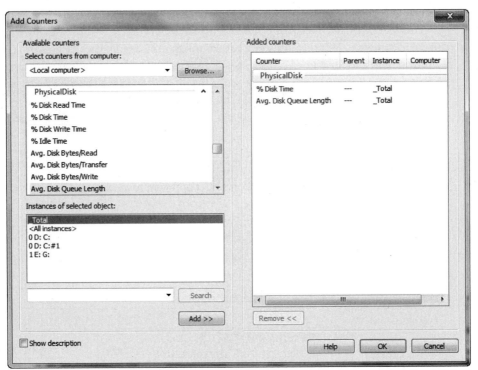

Source: Microsoft Windows 7

Figure 11-44 Add counters to set up what Performance Monitor tracks

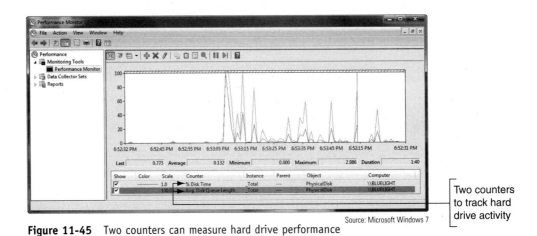

Two counters to track hard drive activity

Source: Microsoft Windows 7

Figure 11-45 Two counters can measure hard drive performance

If the Avg. Disk Queue Length is above two and the % Disk Time is more than 80 percent, you can conclude that the hard drive is working excessively hard and processes are slowed down waiting on the drive. Anytime a process must wait to access the hard drive, you are likely to see degradation in overall system performance.

Performance Monitor also offers several data collector sets. A **data collector set** is a set of counters that you can use to collect data about the system and save this data in a report or log file for future use. You can also create your own data collector sets by selecting counters to use in the set and you can decide where to save the log file when you run your customized data collector set. Data collector sets are started, stopped, and customized using the Data Collector Sets group in the left pane of the Performance Monitor window. If you want to know more about using data collector sets, click the Help button in the Performance Monitor window or search the Microsoft web site at *technet.microsoft.com*.

> **Vista Differences** The Windows Vista **Reliability and Performance Monitor (Perfmon.msc)** is an earlier version of three separate Windows 7 tools: Windows 7 Resource Monitor, Reliability Monitor, and Performance Monitor. To find out more about the Vista Reliability and Performance Monitor, see Appendix B.

> **XP Differences** The Windows XP Performance Monitor is also called the **System Monitor**. To find out more about this tool, see Appendix C.

Now let's turn our attention to the step-by-step procedures using the tools you just learned about to improve Windows performance.

IMPROVING WINDOWS PERFORMANCE

In this part of the chapter, you'll learn to search for problems affecting performance and to clean up the Windows startup process. These step-by-step procedures go beyond the routine maintenance tasks you learned about in Chapter 10. We're assuming Windows starts with no errors. If you are having trouble loading Windows, it's best to address the error first rather than to use the tools described here to improve performance. How to handle errors that keep Windows from starting is covered in Chapter 14.

> **A+ Exam Tip** The A+ 220-802 exam expects you to know how to troubleshoot and solve problems with slow system performance.

A+
220-802
4.3

Now let's look at 10 steps you can take to improve Windows performance.

STEP 1: PERFORM ROUTINE MAINTENANCE

It might seem pretty mundane, but the first things you need to do to improve performance of a sluggish Windows system are the routine maintenance tasks that you learned in Chapter 10. These tasks are summarized here:

▲ *Verify critical Windows settings.* Make sure Windows updates are current. Verify that antivirus software is updated and set to routinely scan for viruses. Make sure the network connection is secured. If the system is experiencing a marked decrease in performance, suspect a virus and use up-to-date antivirus software to perform a full scan of the system.

▲ *Clean up, defrag, and check the hard drive.* Make sure at least 15 percent of drive C: is free. For Windows 7/Vista, make sure a magnetic hard drive is being defragged weekly. If you suspect hard drive problems, use Chkdsk to check the hard drive for errors and recover data.

▲ *Uninstall software you no longer need.* Use the Windows 7/Vista Programs and Features window or the XP Add or Remove Programs window to uninstall programs you no longer need.

As always, if valuable data is not backed up, back it up before you apply any of the fixes in this chapter. You don't want to risk losing the user's data.

STEP 2: CLEAN WINDOWS STARTUP

The most important step following routine maintenance to improve performance is to verify that startup programs are kept to a minimum. Before cleaning Windows startup, you can use Safe Mode to set a benchmark for the time it takes to start Windows when only the bare minimum of programs are launched.

OBSERVE PERFORMANCE IN SAFE MODE

To find out if programs and services are slowing down Windows startup, boot the system in Safe Mode and watch to see if performance improves. Do the following:

1. Use a stopwatch or a watch with a second hand to time a normal startup from the moment you press the power button until the wait icon on the Windows desktop disappears.

2. Time the boot again, this time using Safe Mode. To boot the system in Safe Mode, press **F8** while Windows is loading and then select Safe Mode with Networking from the boot options menu (see Figure 11-46).

If the difference is significant, follow the steps in this part of the chapter to reduce Windows startup to essentials. If the performance problem still exists in Safe Mode, you can assume that the problem is with hardware or Windows settings and you can proceed to *Step 3: Check If the Hardware Can Support the OS.*

A+
220-802
4.3

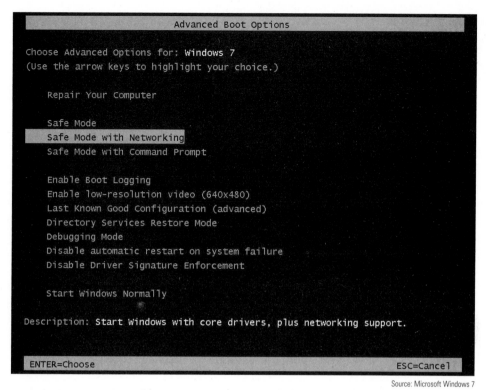

Figure 11-46 Windows Advanced Boot Options Menu allows you to launch Safe Mode

11

INVESTIGATE AND ELIMINATE STARTUP PROGRAMS

To speed up startup, search for unnecessary startup programs you can eliminate. Tools that can help are System Configuration (Msconfig.exe), startup folders, and Task Manager. Follow these steps to investigate startup:

1. Open Msconfig, select the **Startup** tab, and look for a specific startup program you don't want. If you're not sure of the purpose of a program, scroll to the right in the Command column to see the name of the startup program file (see Figure 11-47). Then search the web for information on this program. Be careful to use only reliable sites for credible information. Use the Location column to find out how the program was launched. In Figure 11-47, notice the last three items are launched from startup folders.

> ⚡ **Caution** A word of caution is important here: many web sites will tell you a legitimate process is malicious so that you will download and use their software to get rid of the process. However, their software is likely to be adware or spyware that you don't want. Make sure you can trust a site before you download from it or take its advice.

2. If you want to find out if disabling a startup entry gives problems or improves performance, temporarily disable it using Msconfig. To permanently disable a startup item, it's best to uninstall the software or remove the entry from a startup folder. See Appendix G for a list of startup folders.

A+
220-802
4.3

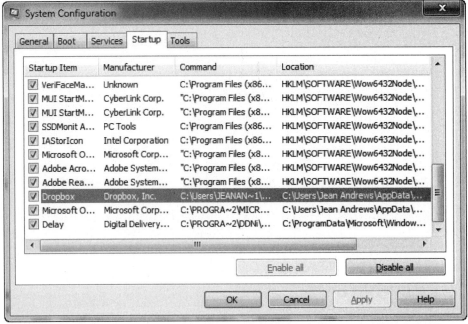

Source: Microsoft Windows 7

Figure 11-47 Find the path and name of the program file in the Command column of System Configuration

> **Notes** The startup folder for all users is hidden by default. In Chapter 3, you learned how to unhide folders that are hidden.

3. As you research startup processes, Task Manager can tell you what processes are currently running. Open Task Manager and select the **Processes** tab. If you see a process and want to know its program file location, click **View** and click **Select Columns**. In the Select Process Page Columns, check **Image Path Name** and click **OK**. The Image Path Name column is added (see Figure 11-48).

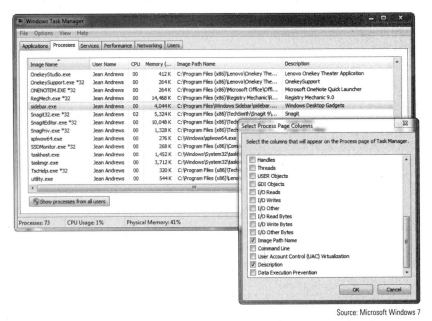

Source: Microsoft Windows 7

Figure 11-48 Use the Image Path Name column on the Processes tab to locate a program file

For extremely slow systems that need a more drastic fix, do the following:

▲ Using Msconfig, disable all startup items on the Startup tab. Then restart the system and see what problems you get into with a program disabled that you really need. Then enable just the ones you decide you need.

▲ An even more drastic approach for extremely slow startups is to disable all non-Microsoft services. On the Services tab, check **Hide all Microsoft services**, and then click **Disable all**.

Regardless of the method you use, be sure to restart the system after each change and note what happens. Do you get an error message? Does a device or application not work? If so, you have probably disabled a service or program you need.

Has performance improved? If performance does not improve by disabling services or startup programs, go back and enable them again. If no non-Microsoft service or startup program caused the problem, then you can assume the problem is caused by a Microsoft service or startup program. Start disabling them one at a time.

> ⚡ **Caution**   You might be tempted to disable all Microsoft services. If you do so, you are disabling Networking, Event Logging, Error Reporting, Windows Firewall, Windows Installer, Windows Backup, Print Spooler, Windows Update, System Protection, and other important services. These services should be disabled only when testing for performance problems and then immediately enabled when the test is finished. Also, know that if you disable the Volume Shadow Copy service, all restore points kept on the system will be lost. If you intend to use System Restore to fix a problem with the system, don't disable this service. If you are not sure what a service does, read its description in the Services console before you change its status.

Remember that you don't want to permanently leave MSconfig in control of startup. After you have used MSconfig to identify the problem, use other tools to permanently remove them from startup. Use the Services console to disable a service, use the Programs and Features window to uninstall software, and remove program files from startup folders. After the problem is fixed, return MSconfig to a normal startup.

Don't forget to restart the computer after making a change to verify that all is well.

CHECK FOR UNWANTED SCHEDULED TASKS

When applications install, they often schedule tasks to check for and download their program updates, and malware sometimes hides as a scheduled task. Scheduled tasks might be unnecessary and can slow a system down. The best way to uninstall a scheduled task is to uninstall the software that is responsible for the task. Open the Task Scheduler window and search through tasks looking for those you think are unnecessary or causing trouble. Research the software the task works with and then you might decide to uninstall the software or disable the task.

Don't forget to restart the system to make sure all is well before you move on.

MONITOR THE STARTUP PROCESS

Now that you have the startup process clean, you will want to keep it that way. You can use several third-party tools to monitor any changes to startup. A good one is WinPatrol by BillP Studios (*www.winpatrol.com*). Download and install the free version of the

11

A+
220-802
4.3

program to run in the background to monitor all sorts of things, including changes to the registry, startup processes, Internet Explorer settings, and system files. In Figure 11-49, you can see how WinPatrol gave an alert when it detected an Internet Explorer plug-in is placing an entry in the registry. WinPatrol displays a little black Scotty dog in the notification area of the taskbar to indicate it's running in the background and guarding your system. Also, many antivirus programs monitor the startup process and inform you when changes are made.

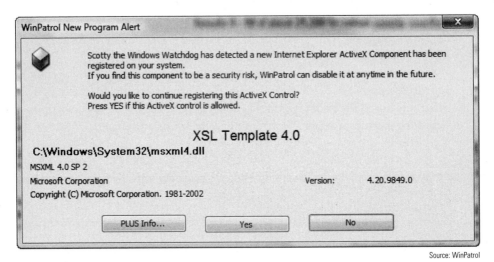

Source: WinPatrol

Figure 11-49 WinPatrol by BillP Studios alerts you when a program is making a system change

STEP 3: CHECK IF THE HARDWARE CAN SUPPORT THE OS

The system might be slow because the OS does not have the hardware resources it needs. Use the Windows 7/Vista Windows Experience Index to quickly zero in on a hardware component that might be a bottleneck. If you suspect that the processor, hard drive, or memory is a bottleneck, consider using the Windows 7 Resource Monitor, the Vista Reliability and Performance Monitor, or the XP Performance Monitor to get more detailed information. If the bottleneck appears to be graphics, the problem might be solved by updating the graphics drivers or by updating Windows.

> **Notes** Use the System Information Utility (msinfo32.exe) to find information about the installed processor and its speed, how much RAM is installed, and free space on the hard drive. Compare all these values to the minimum and recommended requirements for Windows listed in Chapter 7.

If you find that the system is slow because of a hardware component, discuss the situation with the user. You might be able to upgrade the hardware or install another OS that is compatible with the hardware that is present. Upgrading from Vista to Windows 7 can often improve performance in a computer that has slow hardware components. Better still, perform a clean installation of Windows 7 so that you get a fresh start with installed applications, plug-ins, and background services that might be slowing down the system.

A+
220-802
4.3

STEP 4: CHECK FOR PERFORMANCE WARNINGS

Windows 7/Vista tracks issues that are interfering with performance. To see these warnings, open the Performance Information and Tools window and click **Advanced tools**. The Advanced Tools window appears, as shown in Figure 11-50. If Windows knows of performance issues, they are listed at the top of this window. Click an issue to see a recommended solution.

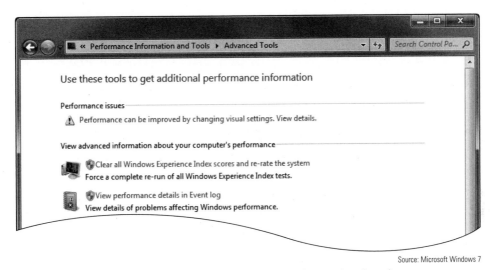

Source: Microsoft Windows 7

Figure 11-50 Windows 7/Vista provides performance warnings and tools to improve Windows performance

For example, when you click the one issue reported in Figure 11-50, a box appears describing the problem and offering solutions (see Figure 11-51). If you make a change to the system while resolving the issue, restart Windows before tackling the next fix or issue. After you have resolved an issue or have decided to live with it, you can click **Remove from list** so that it will no longer appear in the list of issues. If you need more information about an issue, click **View details in the event log** and Event Viewer opens, displaying the appropriate logs.

Windows XP does not offer the Advanced Tools window. For XP, open Event Viewer and view the System log. Look for events that might indicate a performance problem.

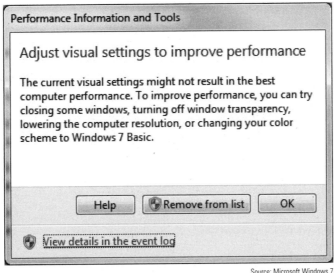

Source: Microsoft Windows 7

Figure 11-51 Windows reports that current visual settings are affecting performance.

A+
220-802
4.3

STEP 5: CHECK FOR A HISTORY OF PROBLEMS

Try to identify when the slow performance problem began, and then use the Windows 7 or Vista Reliability Monitor to find out what changes were made to the system around that time and what other problems occurred. If you don't know when the problem started, skim through the line graph at the top of the Reliability Monitor window and look for drops in the graph. Also look for critical events indicated by a red X (refer to Figure 11-42).

STEP 6: DISABLE THE INDEXER FOR WINDOWS SEARCH

The Windows 7/Vista indexer is responsible for maintaining an index of files and folders on a hard drive to speed up Windows searches. The indexing service has a low priority and only works when it senses that the hard drive is not being accessed by a service with a higher priority. However, it might still slow down performance. Do the following to find out if this service is causing a performance problem:

1. Find out if the indexing service is currently indexing the system. To do that, click **Adjust indexing options** in the left pane of the Performance and Information Tools window. (You can also enter **Indexing Options** in the search box.) The Indexing Options box appears (see Figure 11-52).

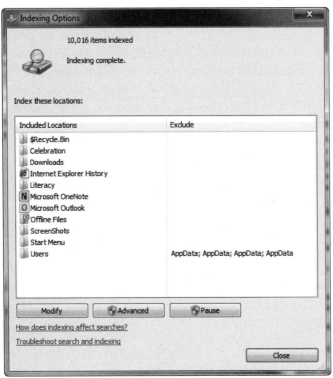

Source: Microsoft Windows 7

Figure 11-52 Indexing is enabled on this system

2. If you see *Indexing speed is reduced due to user activity* at the top of the box, wait while indexing is in progress and the status changes to *Indexing complete.* You can now stop the indexing service.

3. To stop the indexing service, open the Services console. Then stop and disable the **Windows Search** service (see Figure 11-53).

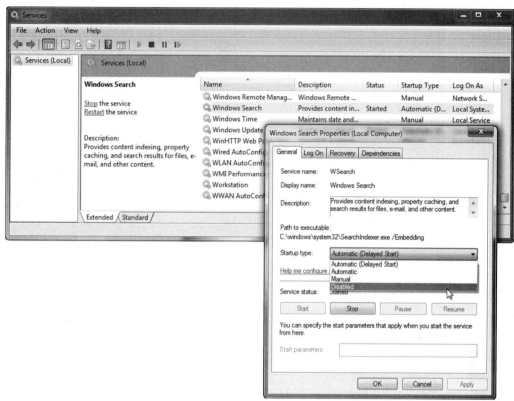

Figure 11-53 Disable the Windows Search service

Source: Microsoft Windows 7

4. Restart the computer. Run the system for a while and see if performance improves.

5. If performance does not improve, restart the indexing service. To do that, use the Services console to set the status of the Windows Search service to **Automatic (Delayed Start)** and start the service. Then move on to the next section of this chapter, *Step 7: Plug Up Any Memory Leaks.*

6. If performance does improve, it is possible that the problem was caused by a corrupted index database. To rebuild the database, first use the Services console to set the Windows Search service status back to **Automatic (Delayed Start)** and to start the service.

7. Open the Indexing Options box and click **Advanced**. The Advanced Options box opens (see Figure 11-54).

A+
220-802
4.3

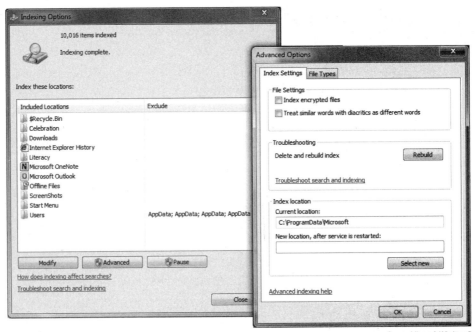

Source: Microsoft Windows 7

Figure 11-54 Rebuild the indexing database

8. To rebuild the indexing database, click **Rebuild**. A dialog box appears warning you that this can take some time. Click **OK**. Close the Indexing Options box.

9. After running the system for a while, if the performance problem returns, you can disable the Windows Search service and leave it disabled. However, know that searching will not be as fast without indexing.

STEP 7: PLUG UP ANY MEMORY LEAKS

If you notice that performance slows after a system has been up and running without a restart for some time, suspect a memory leak. A memory leak is caused when an application does not properly release memory allocated to it that it no longer needs and continually requests more memory than it needs.

To see how much memory an application has allocated to it that is not available to other programs, open Task Manager and click the **Processes** tab. In the menu bar, click **View, Select Columns**. Verify that the Memory Private Working Set, Handles, and Threads columns are checked and click **OK**. If you observe that the values in these three columns increase over time for a particular program, suspect the program has a memory leak. To sort the data by one column, click the column label. For example, the Task Manager window shown in Figure 11-55 is sorted by Memory. It shows the memory-hungry applications on this system are Eudora (an email client) and Skype (an Internet voice and video program).

Note that the Windows 7 Resource Monitor and the Vista Reliability and Performance Monitor give similar information about how memory is used. If you decide a program has a memory leak, try to get an update or patch from the program manufacturer's web site.

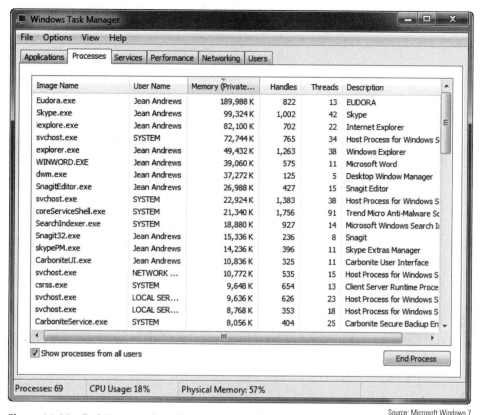

A+
220-802
4.3

Figure 11-55 Task Manager shows how memory is allocated for an application
Source: Microsoft Windows 7

A+
220-802
1.1, 4.3

STEP 8: CONSIDER USING READYBOOST

Windows 7/Vista **ReadyBoost** uses a flash drive or secure digital (SD) memory card to boost hard drive performance. The faster flash memory is used as a buffer to speed up hard drive access time. You see the greatest performance increase using ReadyBoost when you have a slow magnetic hard drive (running at less than 7200 RPM). To find out what speed your hard drive is using, use System Information (Msinfo32.exe) and drill down into the Components, Storage group, and select Disks (see Figure 11-56). The model of the hard drive appears in the right pane. Use Google to search on this brand and model; a quick search shows this drive runs at 5400 RPM. It's, therefore, a good candidate to benefit from ReadyBoost.

> 💡 **A+ Exam Tip** The A+ 220-802 exam expects you to know how to use ReadyBoost to improve performance.

When you first connect a flash device, Windows will automatically test it to see if it qualifies for ReadyBoost. To qualify, it must have a capacity of 256 MB to 4 GB with at least 256 MB of free space, and run at about 2 MB/sec of throughput. If the device qualifies,

11

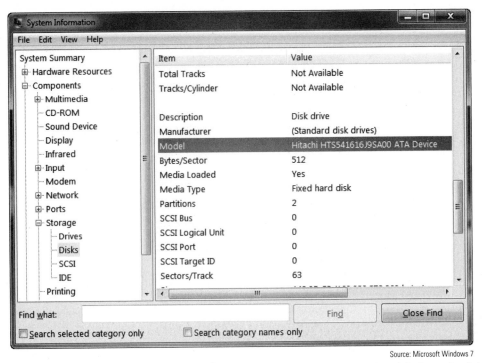

Source: Microsoft Windows 7

Figure 11-56 Use the System Information window to find out the brand and model of your hard drive

Windows displays a dialog box that can be used to activate ReadyBoost (see Figure 11-57a). When you click **Speed up my system**, the device properties box appears with the ReadyBoost tab selected (see Figure 11-57b). Here you can decide how much of the device memory to allot for ReadyBoost. You can manually have Windows test a memory card or flash drive for ReadyBoost by right-clicking the device and selecting **Properties** from the shortcut menu. On the device properties window, click the **ReadyBoost** tab.

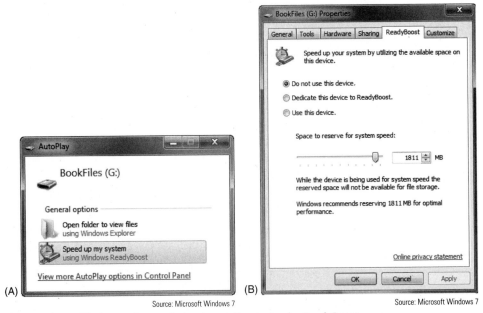

(A)

Source: Microsoft Windows 7

(B)

Source: Microsoft Windows 7

Figure 11-57 Windows asks permission to use the device for ReadyBoost

The best flash devices to use for ReadyBoost are the ones that can take advantage of the faster ports. For example, a SuperSpeed USB (USB 3.0) device and port is about 10 times faster than a Hi-Speed USB (USB 2.0) device and port. Incidentally, when you remove the device, no data is lost because the device only holds a copy of the data.

STEP 9: DISABLE THE AERO INTERFACE

The Windows Aero interface might be slowing down the system because it uses memory and computing power. Try disabling it. If performance improves, you can conclude that the hardware is not able to support the Aero interface. At that point, you might want to upgrade memory, upgrade the video card, or leave the Aero interface disabled.

To disable the Aero interface using Windows 7, do the following:

1. Right-click the desktop and select **Personalize** from the shortcut menu. The Personalization window opens (see Figure 11-58).

2. Scroll down to and click **Windows 7 Basic** and close the window.

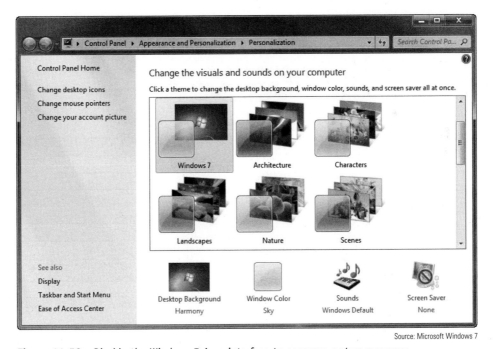

Source: Microsoft Windows 7

Figure 11-58 Disable the Windows 7 Aero interface to conserve system resources

To disable the Aero interface using Windows Vista, follow these steps:

1. Open the Personalization window and click **Window Color**. Then click **Open classic appearance properties for more color options**. The Appearance Settings box opens, shown on the right side of Figure 11-59.

2. Under Color scheme, select **Windows Vista Basic** and click **Apply**. Close the dialog box and window.

A+
220-802
4.3

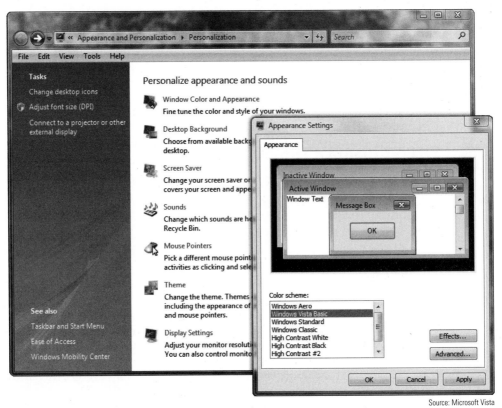

Source: Microsoft Vista

Figure 11-59 Disable the Windows Vista Aero interface to conserve system resources

STEP 10: DISABLE THE VISTA SIDEBAR

Recall that the Vista sidebar appears on the Windows desktop to hold apps called gadgets. The sidebar uses system resources and disabling it can improve performance. To do that, right-click the sidebar and select **Properties** from the shortcut menu. The Windows Sidebar Properties box appears (see Figure 11-60). Uncheck **Start Sidebar when Windows starts**. Then click **Apply** and **OK** to close the box.

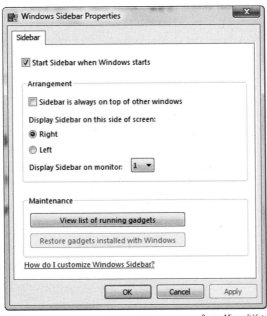

Source: Microsoft Vista

Figure 11-60 Disable the Vista sidebar to improve performance

MANUALLY REMOVING SOFTWARE

**A+
220-802
4.3**

In this part of the chapter, we focus on getting rid of programs that refuse to uninstall or give errors when uninstalling. In these cases, you can manually uninstall a program. Doing so often causes problems later, so use the methods discussed in this section only as a last resort after normal uninstall methods have failed.

This part of the chapter discusses the following steps to manually remove software:

1. First try to locate and use an uninstall routine provided by the software. If this works, you are done and can skip the next steps.

2. Delete the program folders and files that hold the software.

3. Delete the registry entries used by the software.

4. Remove the entries in the Start menu and delete any shortcuts on the desktop.

5. Remove any entries that launch processes at startup.

> **Notes** Before uninstalling software, make sure it's not running in the background. For example, antivirus software cannot be uninstalled if it's still running. You can use Task Manager to end all processes related to the software, and you can use the Services console to stop services related to the software. Then remove the software.

Now let's step through the process of manually removing software.

STEP 1: FIRST TRY THE UNINSTALL ROUTINE

Most programs written for Windows have an uninstall routine that can be accessed from the Windows 7/Vista Programs and Features window, the XP Add Remove Programs window, or an uninstall utility in the All Programs menu. For example, in Figure 11-61, you can see in the All Programs menu that an uninstall item is listed for the Registry Mechanic software installation. (Registry Mechanic is utility software that can clean the registry of unused keys.) Click this option and follow the directions on-screen to uninstall the software. Alternately, you can use the Programs and Features window to uninstall the software.

Source: Microsoft Windows 7

Figure 11-61 Most applications have an uninstall utility included with the software

11

STEP 2: DELETE PROGRAM FILES

If the uninstall routine is missing or does not work, the next step is to delete the program folders and files that contain the software. In our example, we'll delete the Registry Mechanic software without using its uninstall routine.

Look for the program folder in one of these folders:

▲ C:\Program Files
▲ C:\Program Files (x86)

In Figure 11-62, you can see the Registry Mechanic folder under the C:\Program Files (x86) folder. Keep in mind, however, that the program files might be in another location that was set by the user when the software was installed. Delete the **Registry Mechanic** folder and all its contents.

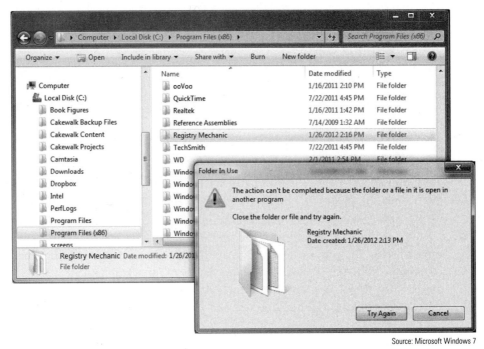

Source: Microsoft Windows 7

Figure 11-62   Program files are usually found in the Program Files or Program Files (x86) folder

As you do, you might see the warning box shown on the right side of Figure 11-62 saying the program is in use. In this situation, do the following:

1. Look for the program file reported on the Processes tab of Task Manager. If you see it listed, end the process. The Command Line column can help you find the right program.

2. If you don't find the program on the Processes tab, check the **Services** tab. If you find it there, select it and click **Services** (see Figure 11-63). The Services console opens where you can stop the service. (Note in the figure the Registry Mechanic software by PC Tools is running under the PC Tools name.)

3. After the program or service is stopped, try to delete the program folder again. If you still cannot delete the folder, look for other running programs or services associated with the software.

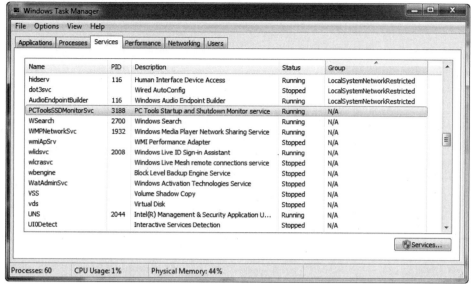

Figure 11-63 Task Manager shows a service is running and needs to be stopped before the program files can be deleted

STEP 3: DELETE REGISTRY ENTRIES

Editing the registry can be dangerous, so do this with caution and be sure to back up first! Do the following to delete registry entries that cause a program to be listed as installed software in the Windows 7/Vista Programs and Features window or the XP Add or Remove Programs window of Control Panel:

1. To be on the safe side, back up the entire registry using one or more of the methods discussed earlier in the chapter.

2. Open the Registry Editor by using the **regedit** command in the search box.

3. Locate a key that contains the entries that make up the list of installed software. Use this criteria to decide which key to locate:

   ◢ For a 32-bit program installed in a 32-bit OS or for a 64-bit program installed in a 64-bit OS, locate this key:
   HKEY_LOCAL_MACHINE\Software\Microsoft\Windows\CurrentVersion\Uninstall

   ◢ For a 32-bit program installed in a 64-bit OS, locate this key:
   HKEY_LOCAL_MACHINE\SOFTWARE\Wow6432Node\Microsoft\Windows\CurrentVersion\Uninstall

> **Notes** Recall that 32-bit programs are installed the \Program Files (x86) folder on a 64-bit system. These 32-bit programs use the Wow6432Node subkey in the registry of a 64-bit OS.

4. Back up the Uninstall key to the Windows desktop so that you can backtrack, if necessary. To do that, right-click the Uninstall key and select **Export** from the shortcut menu (see Figure 11-34 earlier in the chapter).

5. In the Export Registry File dialog box, select the **Desktop**. Enter the filename as **Save Uninstall Key,** and click **Save.** You should see a new file icon on your desktop named Save Uninstall Key.reg.

A+
220-802
4.3

6. The Uninstall key can be a daunting list of all the programs installed on your PC. When you expand the key, you see a long list of subkeys in the left pane, which might have meaningless names that won't help you find the program you're looking for. Select the first subkey in the Uninstall key and watch as its values and data are displayed in the right pane (see Figure 11-64). Step down through each key, watching for a meaningful name of the subkey in the left pane or meaningful details in the right pane until you find the program you want to delete.

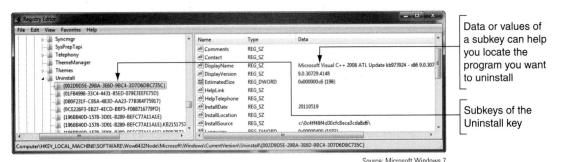

Source: Microsoft Windows 7

Figure 11-64 Select a subkey under the Uninstall key to display its values and data in the right pane

7. To delete the key, right-click the key and select **Delete** from the shortcut menu (see Figure 11-65) and confirm the deletion. Be sure to search through all the keys in this list because the software might have more than one key. Delete them all and exit the Registry Editor.

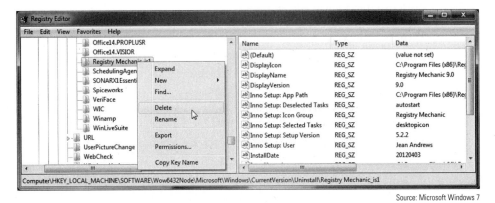

Source: Microsoft Windows 7

Figure 11-65 Delete the registry key that lists the software as installed software

8. Open the Windows 7/Vista Programs and Features window or the XP Add or Remove Programs window and verify that the list of installed software is correct and the software you are uninstalling is no longer listed.

9. If the list of installed software is not correct, to restore the Uninstall registry key, double-click the **Save Uninstall Key.reg** icon on your desktop.

10. As a last step when editing the registry, clean up after yourself by deleting the Save Uninstall Key.reg file on your desktop. Right-click the icon and select **Delete** from the shortcut menu.

STEP 4: REMOVE THE PROGRAM FROM THE ALL PROGRAMS MENU AND THE DESKTOP

**A+
220-802
4.3**

To remove the program from the All Programs menu, right-click it and select **Delete** from the shortcut menu (see Figure 11-66). If the program has shortcuts on the desktop, delete these.

Source: Microsoft Windows 7

Figure 11-66   Delete the program from the All Programs menu

STEP 5: REMOVE STARTUP PROCESSES

Restart the PC and watch for any startup errors about a missing program file. The software might have stored startup entries in the registry, in startup folders, or as a service that is no longer present and causing an error. If you see an error, use MSconfig to find out how the program is set to start. This entry point is called an orphaned entry. You'll then need to delete this startup entry by editing the registry, deleting a shortcut in a startup folder, or disabling a service using the Services console.

It's unlikely you will be able to completely remove all keys in the registry that the software put there. A registry cleaner can help you find these orphaned keys, but if no errors appear at startup, you can just leave these keys untouched. Also, an installation might put program files in the C:\Program Files\Common Files or the C:\Program Files (x86)\Common Files folder. Most likely you can just leave these untouched as well. Address all error messages you encounter and stop there.

A+
220-802
4.3

REGISTRY KEYS THAT AFFECT STARTUP AND LOGON EVENTS

You have just seen how you can edit the registry to remove the entries left there by software that you have manually removed. If a system is giving repeated startup errors or you have just removed several programs, you might want to search through registry keys where startup processes can be located. See Appendix G for a list of these registry keys and startup folders. As you read through this list of registry keys to search, know that the list is not exhaustive. With experience, you'll learn that the registry is an ever-changing landscape of keys and values.

>> CHAPTER SUMMARY

Windows Utilities and Tools to Support the OS

- ◢ The Windows OS is made up of two main components, the shell and the kernel. The shell provides an interface for users and applications. The kernel is responsible for interacting with hardware.

- ◢ A process is a program running under the shell, together with all the resources assigned to it. A thread is a single task that a process requests from the kernel.

- ◢ Task Manager (Taskmgr.exe) lets you view services and other running programs, CPU and memory performance, network activity, and user activity. It is useful to stop a process that is hung.

- ◢ Tools listed in the Administrative Tools group of Control Panel are used by technicians and developers to support Windows and applications.

- ◢ System Configuration (Msconfig.exe) can be used to temporarily disable startup processes to test for performance improvement and find a startup program causing a problem.

- ◢ The Services console (Services.msc) is used to manage Windows and application services. When and if a service starts can be controlled from this console.

- ◢ The Computer Management console (Compmgmt.msc) contains a group of Windows administrative tools useful for managing a system.

- ◢ The Microsoft Management Console (MMC) can be used to build your own custom consoles from available snap-ins.

- ◢ The Event Viewer (Eventvwr.msc) console displays a group of logs kept by Windows that are useful for troubleshooting problems with software and hardware. You can also use Event Viewer to view security audits made by Windows.

- ◢ The Registry Editor (Regedit.exe) is used to edit the registry in real time. There is no way to use the Registry Editor to undo changes you make to the registry. Therefore, you should always make a backup before editing it.

- ◢ The Performance Information and Tools window displays the Windows Experience Index that rates the overall performance of the system. You can reach tools to optimize performance from this window.

- ◢ Windows 7 Resource Monitor monitors the performance of the processor, memory, hard drive, and network in real time.

◢ The Windows 7 Reliability Monitor can be used to get historical data about problems on the computer since Windows was installed.

◢ The Windows 7 Performance Monitor uses counters to track activity by hardware and software to evaluate performance.

◢ The Vista Reliability and Performance Monitor (Perfmon.msc) is an earlier version of the three separate tools in Windows 7: the Resource Monitor, Reliability Monitor, and Performance Monitor.

◢ The XP Performance Monitor (also called the System Monitor) uses counters and is an earlier version of the Windows 7 Performance monitor.

Improving Windows Performance

◢ The 10 high-level steps to improve Windows performance are (1) routine maintenance, (2) clean Windows startup, (3) check if hardware can support the OS, (4) check for performance warnings, (5) check for a history of problems to find the source of a problem, (6) disable indexing for Windows search, (7) plug up memory leaks, (8) consider using ReadyBoost to improve a slow hard drive's performance, (9) disable the Aero interface, and (10) disable the Vista sidebar.

◢ Tools that can be used to investigate and clean up the Windows start process include Safe Mode, startup folders, MSconfig, Task Scheduler, Task Manager, and Services console.

Manually Removing Software

◢ If software does not uninstall using the Windows 7/Vista Programs and Features window or the XP Add or Remove Programs window, you can manually uninstall the software.

◢ To manually delete software, delete the program files, entries in the Start, All Programs menu, registry keys, and items in startup folders.

11

>> KEY TERMS

For explanations of key terms, see the Glossary near the end of the book.

Administrative tools

Computer Management (Compmgmt.msc)

console

data collector set

Event Viewer (Eventvwr.msc)

executive services

HAL (hardware abstraction layer)

HKEY_CLASSES_ROOT (HKCR)

HKEY_CURRENT_CONFIG (HKCC)

HKEY_CURRENT_USER (HKCU)

HKEY_LOCAL_MACHINE (HKLM)

HKEY_USERS (HKU)

kernel

kernel mode

Microsoft Management Console (MMC)

Performance Information and Tools

Performance Monitor

process

ReadyBoost

registry

Registry Editor (regedit.exe)

Reliability and Performance Monitor (Perfmon.msc)

Reliability Monitor

Resource Monitor

Services console

shell

snap-ins

System Configuration (Msconfig.exe)

System Monitor

Task Manager (Taskmgr.exe)

Task Scheduler

thread

user mode

>> REVIEW QUESTIONS

1. ____ lets you view the applications and processes running on your computer as well as information about process and memory performance, network activity, and user activity.

   a) Task Manager

   b) System Configuration

   c) Registry Editor

   d) Performance Monitor

2. You can use the ____ utility to find out what processes are launched at startup and to temporarily disable a process from loading.

   a) Resource Monitor

   b) Performance Monitor

   c) System Configuration

   d) Task Manager

3. ____ contains several tools that can be used to manage the local PC or other computers on the network.

   a) System Configuration

   b) Computer Management

   c) Performance Monitor

   d) Resource Monitor

4. Which registry key is the most important key and contains hardware, software, and security data?

   a) HKEY_CURRENT_CONFIG (HKCC)

   b) HKEY_LOCAL_MACHINE (HKLM)

   c) HKEY_CURRENT_USER (HKCU)

   d) HKEY_CLASSES_ROOT (HKCR)

5. The Windows ____ gives information about problems and errors that happen over time.

   a) Reliability Monitor

   b) Resource Monitor

   c) Performance Monitor

   d) Registry Editor

6. True or false? Using MSconfig is the best way to provide a permanent fix to disable a program or service at startup.

7. True or false? In a console, the individual tools are called gadgets.

8. True or false? Look in the System log to find events triggered by Windows components, such as a device driver failing to load or a problem with hardware.

9. True or false? The most important step following routine maintenance to improve performance is to verify that startup programs are kept to a minimum.

10. True or false? Upgrading from Vista to Windows 7 can often improve performance in a computer that has slow hardware components.

11. A(n) _____ is a program that is running under the authority of the shell, together with the system resources assigned to it.

12. The _____ is a database designed with a treelike structure (called a hierarchical database) that contains configuration information for Windows, users, software applications, and installed hardware devices.

13. The _____ evaluates key system components to give a high-level view of the computer's performance.

14. A(n) _____ is caused when an application does not properly release memory allocated to it that it no longer needs and continually requests more memory than it needs.

15. Windows 7/Vista _____ uses a flash drive or secure digital (SD) memory card to boost hard drive performance.

11

Troubleshooting Windows and Applications

When a computer gives you problems, a good plan for solving that problem can help you to not feel so helpless. This chapter is designed to give you just that—a plan with all the necessary details and tools so that you can determine just what has gone wrong and what to do about it.

In this chapter, you learn about Windows tools for problem solving and troubleshooting strategies to help solve any computer problem. You learn what to do when a computer freezes or gives a blue screen error (also called the blue screen of death) and when applications give problems. This chapter focuses on problems that occur after the Windows desktop has loaded. In Chapter 13, you'll learn how to solve hardware problems, including those that cause the system to not boot. In Chapter 14, you'll learn how to solve problems when Windows refuses to start.

OVERVIEW OF WINDOWS TROUBLESHOOTING TOOLS

Table 12-1 is a summary of the Windows tools covered in this and other chapters and is given to you as a quick-and-easy reference of these tools. When you're stuck on a problem, take a quick glance through this list to remind you of tools that might help. In Chapter 14, you learn about more tools that are used to troubleshoot a failed boot.

Tool	Description
Action Center Windows 7	◢ Accessed from the System window or Action Center flag in the taskbar. ◢ Use it to solve problems when installing a device or application, to solve problems with software or hardware, and to get a history of past and current problems.
Advanced Boot Options Menu Windows 7 Windows Vista Windows XP	◢ Accessed by pressing the F8 key when Windows first starts to load. ◢ Use several options on this menu to help you troubleshoot boot problems. ◢ In XP, the menu is called the Boot Options Menu.
Backup and Restore Windows 7 Windows Vista Windows XP	◢ Accessed from the Start menu. In Windows 7, use it to back up and restore user data and the system image and to make a rescue disc. ◢ In Vista, the tool is called the Backup and Restore Center. Use it to back up and restore data and make a Complete PC Backup. ◢ In XP, the program name is ntbackup.exe. Use it to back up and restore data and the system state.
Chkdsk (Chkdsk.exe) Windows 7 Windows Vista Windows XP	◢ At a command prompt, enter Chkdsk with parameters. ◢ Use it to check and repair errors on a drive. If critical system files are affected by these errors, repairing the drive might solve a startup problem.
Cipher (Cipher.exe) Windows 7 Windows Vista Windows XP	◢ At a command prompt, enter Cipher with parameters. ◢ Log in as an administrator and use this command to decrypt a file that is not available because the user account that encrypted the file is no longer accessible.
Compatibility Mode Windows 7 Windows Vista Windows XP	◢ Accessed from the Action Center or the program file's shortcut menu. Use it to resolve issues that prevent legacy applications or drivers from working. ◢ Vista calls the tool the Program Compatibility Wizard.
Component Services Windows 7 Windows Vista Windows XP	◢ A tool in the Administrative Tools list in Control Panel. ◢ Registers a component of an application with the system.
Computer Management (Compmgmt.msc) Windows 7 Windows Vista Windows XP	◢ Accessed from Control Panel, or you can enter Compmgmt .msc at a command prompt. ◢ Use it to access several snap-ins to manage and troubleshoot a system.

© Cengage Learning 2014

Table 12-1 Windows 7/Vista/XP maintenance and troubleshooting tools (continues)

Tool	Description
Data Sources (ODBC) Windows 7 Windows Vista Windows XP	▲ A tool in the Administrative Tools list in Control Panel. ▲ Installs drivers so that an application can open a foreign data source.
Device Driver Roll Back Windows 7 Windows Vista Windows XP	▲ Accessed from Device Manager. ▲ Use it to replace a driver with the one that worked before the current driver was installed.
Device Manager (Devmgmt.msc) Windows 7 Windows Vista Windows XP	▲ Accessed from the System window or XP System Properties window. ▲ Use it to solve problems with hardware devices, to update device drivers, and to disable and uninstall a device.
Disk Cleanup (Cleanmgr.exe) Windows 7 Windows Vista Windows XP	▲ Accessed from a drive's properties box or by entering cleanmgr at a command prompt. ▲ Use it to delete unused files to make more disk space available. Not enough free hard drive space can cause boot problems.
Disk Defragmenter (Dfrg.msc or Defrag.exe) Windows 7 Windows Vista Windows XP	▲ Accessed from a drive's properties box, or use Defrag.exe with parameters at a command prompt. ▲ Use it to defragment a volume on a magnetic hard drive to improve performance.
Disk Management (Diskmgmt.msc) Windows 7 Windows Vista Windows XP	▲ Accessed from the Computer Management console, or enter Diskmgmt.msc at a command prompt. ▲ Use it to view and modify partitions on hard drives and to format drives.
File Signature Verification Tool (Sigverif.exe) Windows 7 Windows Vista Windows XP	▲ At a command prompt, enter Sigverif with parameters. ▲ The tool searches for installed drivers that are unsigned and stores results in \Windows\sigverif.txt. ▲ When a device driver or other software is giving problems, use it to verify that the software has been approved by Microsoft.
Driver Verifier (verifier.exe) Windows 7 Windows Vista Windows XP	▲ Enter verifier.exe at a command prompt. ▲ Use it to identify a driver that is causing a problem. The tool puts stress on selected drivers, which causes the driver with a problem to crash. ▲ The tool can be used to solve system lock-up errors or blue screen errors caused by a corrupted I/O device driver.
Error Reporting or Archived Messages Windows 7 Windows Vista Windows XP	▲ This automated Windows service displays error messages when an application error occurs. In Windows 7, see these messages in the Action Center. ▲ Windows 7 and Vista keep a history of past problems and solutions, but XP does not. ▲ Vista calls the tool Problem Reports and Solutions.

Table 12-1 Windows 7/Vista/XP maintenance and troubleshooting tools (continues)

12

Tool	Description
Event Viewer (Eventvwr.msc) Windows 7 Windows Vista Windows XP	◢ Accessed from the Computer Management console or in Administrative Tools. ◢ Check the Event Viewer logs for error messages to help you investigate all kinds of hardware, security, and system problems.
Group Policy (Gpedit.msc) Windows 7 Windows Vista Windows XP	◢ At a command prompt, enter Gpedit.msc, or use the Computer Management console. Only available in Business and Professional editions of Windows. ◢ Use it to display and change policies controlling users and the computer.
Last Known Good Configuration Windows 7 Windows Vista Windows XP	◢ Press F8 at startup and select from the Advanced Boot Options menu. ◢ Use this tool when Windows won't start normally and you want to revert the system to before a Windows setting, driver, or application that is causing problems was changed.
Memory Diagnostics (mdsched.exe) Windows 7 Windows Vista	◢ Enter mdsched.exe in a command prompt window or find it on the System Recovery Options menu after booting the computer into the Windows Recovery Environment (Windows RE). ◢ Use it to test memory.
Network and Sharing Center Windows 7 Windows Vista	◢ Accessed from the taskbar or Control Panel. ◢ Centralized location to manage network connections and network security.
Performance Monitor (Perfmon.msc) Windows 7 Windows Vista Windows XP	◢ At a command prompt, enter Perfmon.msc. Use it to view information about performance to help you identify a performance bottleneck. ◢ Vista embeds the tool in the Reliability and Performance Monitor window.
Programs and Features window Windows 7 Windows Vista Windows XP	◢ Accessed from Control Panel. ◢ Use it to uninstall, repair, or update software or certain device drivers that are causing a problem. ◢ XP calls the tool the Add or Remove Programs window.
Registry Editor (Regedit.exe) Windows 7 Windows Vista Windows XP	◢ At a command prompt, enter regedit. ◢ Use it to view and edit the registry.
Reliability Monitor Windows 7 Windows Vista	◢ Accessed in Windows 7 by way of the Action Center, and in Vista, find it in the Reliability and Performance Monitor window. ◢ Use it to get a history of past problems with a computer.
Resource Monitor (Resmon.exe) Windows 7 Windows Vista	◢ Accessed from Windows 7 Task Manager or Action Center. In Vista, find it in the Reliability and Performance Monitor window. ◢ Use it to view performance of the CPU, memory, hard drive, and network.

Table 12-1   Windows 7/Vista/XP maintenance and troubleshooting tools (continues)

Tool	Description
Runas (Runas.exe) Windows 7 Windows Vista Windows XP	◢ At a command prompt, enter Runas with parameters, or press shift-right-click and choose *Run as administrator* or *Run as different user* from the shortcut menu. ◢ Use it to run a program using different permissions from those assigned to the currently logged-on user.
Safe Mode Windows 7 Windows Vista Windows XP	◢ At startup, press F8 and select the option from the Advanced Boot Options menu. ◢ Use it when Windows does not start or starts with errors. Safe Mode loads the Windows desktop with a minimum configuration. In this minimized environment, you can solve a problem with a device driver, display setting, or corrupted or malicious applications.
SC (Sc.exe) Windows 7 Windows Vista Windows XP	◢ At a command prompt, enter Sc with parameters. ◢ Use it to stop or start a service that runs in the background.
Services (Services.msc) Windows 7 Windows Vista Windows XP	◢ At a command prompt, enter Services.msc. ◢ Graphical version of SC.
Software Explorer Windows Vista	◢ Accessed from the Windows Defender window. ◢ Use it to view and change programs launched at startup.
System Configuration (Msconfig.exe) Windows 7 Windows Vista Windows XP	◢ Enter Msconfig.exe in the Search box. ◢ Troubleshoot the startup process by temporarily disabling startup programs and services.
System File Checker (Sfc.exe) Windows 7 Windows Vista Windows XP	◢ At a command prompt, enter Sfc with parameters. ◢ Use it to verify the version of all system files when Windows loads. Useful when you suspect system files are corrupted, but you can still access the Windows desktop.
System Information (Msinfo32.exe) Windows 7 Windows Vista Windows XP	◢ Enter Msinfo32.exe in the Search box. ◢ Use it to display information about hardware, applications, and Windows.
System Information (Systeminfo.exe) Windows 7 Windows Vista Windows XP	◢ At a command prompt, enter Systeminfo. ◢ A text-only version of the System Information window. To direct that information to a file, use the command System-info.exe >Myfile.txt. Later the file can be printed and used to document information about the system.
System Restore (Rstrui.exe) Windows 7 Windows Vista Windows XP	◢ Accessed from the Start menu, when loading Safe Mode, or from the System Recovery Options menu after booting the computer into Windows RE. ◢ Use it to restore the system to a previously working condition called a restore point; it restores the registry, some system files, and some application files. ◢ Restore points are automatically created when Windows System Protection is turned on.

12

© Cengage Learning 2014

Table 12-1   Windows 7/Vista/XP maintenance and troubleshooting tools (continues)

Tool	Description
Task Killing Utilities (Tskill.exe or Taskkill.exe) Windows 7 Windows Vista Windows XP	▲ At a command prompt, enter Taskkill or Tskill with parameters. Tskill is available only in business and professional editions of Windows. ▲ Use it to stop or kill a process or program currently running. Useful when managing background services such as an email server or web server.
Task Lister (Tasklist.exe) Windows 7 Windows Vista Windows XP	▲ At a command prompt, enter Tasklist. ▲ Use it to list currently running processes similar to the list provided by Task Manager.
Task Manager (Taskman.exe) Windows 7 Windows Vista Windows XP	▲ Right-click the taskbar and select Start Task Manager. ▲ Use it to list and stop currently running processes. ▲ Useful when you need to stop a locked-up application.
Windows Defender Windows 7 Windows Vista	▲ Accessed from Control Panel. ▲ Monitors activity and alerts you if a running program appears to be malicious or damaging the system.
Windows File Protection Windows 7 Windows Vista Windows XP	▲ Windows service that runs in the background to protect system files and restore overwritten system files as needed.
Windows Firewall Windows 7 Windows Vista Windows XP	▲ Service that runs in the background to prevent or filter uninvited communication from another computer.
Windows Update (Wupdmgr.exe) Windows 7 Windows Vista Windows XP	▲ Accessed from the Start menu. ▲ Use it to update Windows by downloading the latest patches from the Microsoft web site.
Windows XP Mode Windows 7	▲ Download and install on Windows 7 Professional and Ultimate editions to run legacy applications that won't work using Compatibility mode.

Table 12-1 Windows 7/Vista/XP maintenance and troubleshooting tools (continued)

© Cengage Learning 2014

> **💡 A+ Exam Tip** If an often-used Windows utility can be launched from a command prompt, the A+ 220-802 exam expects you to know the program name of that utility.

STRATEGIES TO TROUBLESHOOT ANY COMPUTER PROBLEM

A+ 220-802 4.1

When a computer doesn't work and you're responsible for fixing it, you should generally approach the problem first as an investigator and discoverer, always being careful not to compound the problem through your own actions. If the problem seems difficult, see it as an opportunity to learn something new. Ask questions until you understand the source of

A+
220-802
4.1

the problem. Once you understand it, you're almost done because most likely the solution will be evident. If you take the attitude that you can understand the problem and solve it, no matter how deeply you have to dig, you probably *will* solve it.

One systematic method to solve a problem used by most expert troubleshooters is the six steps diagrammed in Figure 12-1, which can apply to both software and hardware problems.

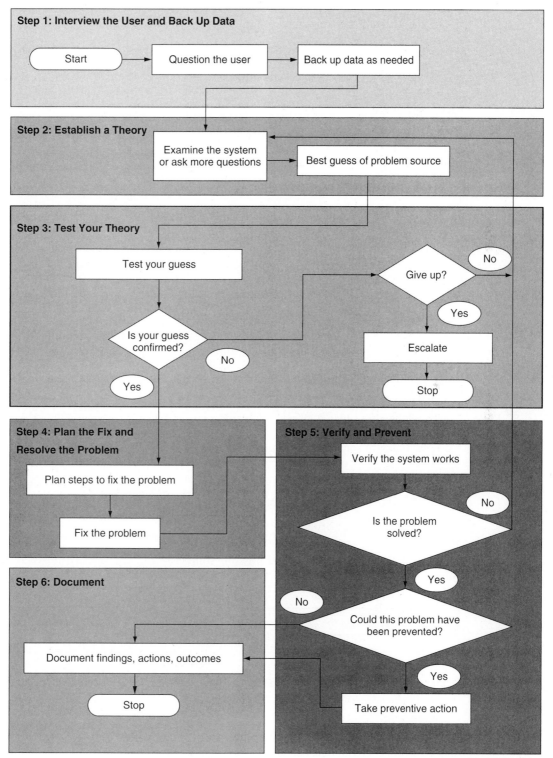

Figure 12-1 General approach to problem solving

12

> **A+ Exam Tip** The A+ 220–802 exam expects you to know about all the aspects of troubleshooting theory and strategy and how to apply the troubleshooting procedures and techniques described in this section. At the front of the book, read over A+ 220–802 Objective 4.1 and compare it to Figure 12-1.

Here are the steps:

1. Interview the user and back up data before you make any changes to the system.

2. Examine the system, analyze the problem, and make an initial determination of what is the source of the problem.

3. Test your theory. If the theory is not confirmed, form another theory or escalate the problem to someone higher in your organization with more experience or resources.

4. After you know the source of the problem, plan what to do to fix the problem and then fix it.

5. Verify the problem is fixed and that the system works. Take any preventive measures to make sure the problem doesn't happen again.

6. Document activities, outcomes, and what you learned.

Now let's examine the process step by step. As you learn about these six steps, you'll also learn about 13 rules useful when troubleshooting. Here's the first rule.

Rule 1: Approach the Problem Systematically

When trying to solve the problem, start at the beginning and walk through the situation in a thorough, careful way. This one rule is invaluable. Remember it and apply it every time. If you don't find the explanation to the problem after one systematic walkthrough, then repeat the entire process. Check and double-check to find the step you overlooked the first time. Most problems with computers are simple, such as a loose cable or incorrect Windows setting. Computers are logical through and through. Whatever the problem is, it's also very logical. Also, if you are faced with more than one problem on the same computer, work on only one problem at a time. Trying to solve multiple problems at the same time can get too confusing.

STEP 1: INTERVIEW THE USER AND BACK UP DATA

Every troubleshooting situation begins with interviewing the user if he or she is available. If you have the opportunity to speak with the user, ask questions to help you identify the problem, how to reproduce it, and possible sources of the problem. Also ask about any data on the PC that is not backed up.

> **A+ Exam Tip** The A+ 220–801 exam expects you to know how to interact with a user and know what questions to ask, given a troubleshooting scenario.

Here are some questions that can help you learn as much as you can about the problem and its root cause:

1. Please describe the problem. What error messages, unusual displays, or failures did you see? (Possible answer: I see this blue screen with a funny-looking message on it that makes no sense to me.)

2. When did the problem start? (Possible answer: When I first booted after loading this neat little screensaver I downloaded from the web.)

3. What was the situation when the problem occurred? (Possible answers: I was trying to start up my PC. I was opening a document in MS Word. I was using the web to research a project.)

4. What programs or software were you using? (Possible answer: I was using Internet Explorer.)

5. What changes have recently been made to the system? For example, did you recently install new software or move your computer system? (Possible answer: Well, yes. Yesterday I moved the computer case across the room.)

6. Has there been a recent thunderstorm or electrical problem? (Possible answer: Yes, last night. Then when I tried to turn on my PC this morning, nothing happened.)

7. Have you made any hardware, software, or configuration changes? (Possible answer: No, but I think my sister might have.)

8. Has someone else used your computer recently? (Possible answer: Sure, my son uses it all the time.)

9. Is there some valuable data on your system that is not backed up that I should know about before I start working on the problem? (Possible answer: Yes! Yes! My term paper! It's not backed up! You gotta save that!)

10. Can you show me how to reproduce the problem? (Possible answers: Yes, let me show you what to do.)

Based on the answers you receive, ask more penetrating questions until you feel the user has given you all the information he or she knows that can help you solve the problem. As you talk with the user, keep in mind rules 2, 3, and 4.

Rule 2: Establish Your Priorities
This rule can help make for a satisfied customer. Decide what your first priority is. For example, it might be to recover lost data or to get the PC back up and running as soon as possible. When practical, ask the user or customer for help deciding on priorities.

Rule 3: Beware of User Error
Remember that many problems stem from user error. If you suspect this is the case, ask the user to show you the problem and carefully watch what the user is doing.

Rule 4: Keep Your Cool and Don't Rush
In some situations, you might be tempted to act too quickly and to be drawn into the user's sense of emergency. But keep your cool and don't rush. For example, when a computer stops working, if unsaved data is still in memory or if data on the hard drive has not been backed up, look and think carefully before you leap! A wrong move can be costly. The best advice is not to hurry. Carefully plan your moves. Research the problem using documentation or the web if you're not sure what to do, and don't hesitate to ask for help. Don't simply try something, hoping it will work, unless you've run out of more intelligent alternatives!

12

After you have talked with the user, be sure to back up any important data that is not currently backed up before you begin work on the PC. If the PC is working well enough to boot to the Windows desktop, you can use Windows Explorer to copy data to a flash drive, another computer on the network, or other storage media.

> **A+ Exam Tip**   The A+ 220–802 exam expects you to know the importance of making backups before you make changes to a system.

If the computer is not healthy enough to use Windows Explorer, don't do anything to jeopardize the data. If you must take a risk with the data, let it be the user's decision to do so, not yours. Try to boot the system. If the system will not boot to the Windows desktop, know that you can remove the hard drive from the system and use a converter to connect the drive to a USB port on another computer. You can then copy the data to the other computer. Next, return the hard drive to the original computer so you can begin troubleshooting the problem.

If possible, have the user verify that all important data is safely backed up before you continue to the next troubleshooting step. If you're new to troubleshooting and don't want the user looking over your shoulder while you work, you might want to let him or her know you'd prefer to work alone. You can say something like, "Okay, I think I have everything I need to get started. I'll let you know if I have another question."

STEP 2: EXAMINE THE SYSTEM AND MAKE YOUR BEST GUESS

You're now ready to start solving the problem. Rules 5 and 6 can help.

Rule 5: Make No Assumptions
This rule is the hardest to follow because there is a tendency to trust anything in writing and assume that people are telling you exactly what happened. But documentation is sometimes wrong, and people don't always describe events as they occurred, so do your own investigating. For example, if the user tells you that the system boots up with no error messages but that the software still doesn't work, boot for yourself. You never know what the user might have overlooked.

Rule 6: Try the Simple Things First
Most problems are so simple and obvious that we overlook them because we expect the problem to be difficult. Don't let the complexity of computers fool you. Most problems are easy to fix. Really, they are! To save time, check the simple things first, such as whether a power switch is not turned on or a cable is loose. Generally, it's easy to check for a hardware problem before you check for a software problem. For example, if a USB drive is not working, verify the drive works on another computer before verifying the drivers are installed correctly.

Follow this process to form your best guess (best theory) and test it:

1. *Reproduce the problem and observe for yourself what the user has described.* For example, if the user tells you the system is totally dead, find out for yourself. Plug in the power and turn on the system. Listen for fans and look for lights and error messages. As another example, suppose the user tells you that Internet Explorer will not open.

Try opening it yourself to see what error messages might appear. As you investigate the system, refrain from making changes until you've come up with your theory as to what the source of the problem is. Can you duplicate the problem? Intermittent problems are generally more difficult to solve than problems that occur consistently.

2. *Decide if the problem is hardware or software related.* Sometimes you might not be sure, but make your best guess. For example, if the system fails before Windows starts to load, chances are the problem is a hardware problem. If the user tells you the system has not worked since the lightning storm the night before, chances are the problem is electrical. If the problem is that Windows Explorer will not open even though the Windows desktop loads, you can assume the problem is software related. In another example, suppose a user complains that his Word documents are getting corrupted. Possible sources of the problem might be that the user does not know how to save documents properly, the application or the OS might be corrupted, the PC might have a virus, or the hard drive might be intermittently failing. Investigate for yourself, and then decide if the problem is caused by software, hardware, or the user.

3. *Make your best guess as to the source of the problem, and don't forget to question the obvious.* Here are some practical examples of questioning the obvious and checking the simple things first:

   ▲ The video does not work. Your best guess is the monitor cables are loose or the monitor is not turned on.
   ▲ Excel worksheets are getting corrupted. Your best guess is the user is not saving the workbook files correctly.
   ▲ The DVD drive is not reading a DVD. Your best guess is the DVD is scratched.
   ▲ The system refuses to boot and gives the error that the hard drive is not found. Your best guess is internal cables to the drive are loose.

Rule 7: Become a Researcher
Following this rule is the most fun. When a computer problem arises that you can't easily solve, be as tenacious as a bulldog. Search the web, ask questions, read more, make some phone calls, and ask more questions. Take advantage of every available resource, including online help, documentation, technical support, and books such as this one. Learn to perform advanced searches using a good search engine on the web, such as *www.google.com*. What you learn will be yours to take to the next problem. This is the real joy of computer troubleshooting. If you're good at it, you're always learning something new.

If you're having a problem deciding what might be the source of the problem, keep in mind Rule 7 and try searching these resources for ideas and tips:

   ▲ User manuals and installation manuals for a device or software often list symptoms of problems with possible solutions and troubleshooting tips.
   ▲ Use a search engine to search the web for help. Use, in your search string, an error message, symptom, hardware device, or description of the problem. For the most reliable information about a hardware device or application, see the web site of the manufacturer (see Figure 12-2). These sites might offer troubleshooting and support pages, help forums, chat sessions, and email support. For Windows problems, the best web sites to search are *technet.microsoft.com* or *support.microsoft.com*. The chances are always good that someone has had exactly the same problem, presented the problem online, and someone else has presented a step-by-step solution. All you have to do is

12

find it! As you practice this type of web research, you'll get better and better at knowing how to form a search string and which web sites are trustworthy and present the best information. If your first five minutes of searching doesn't turn up a solution, please don't give up! It might take patience and searching for 20 minutes or more to find the solution you need. As you search, most likely you'll learn more and more about the problem, and you'll slowly zero in on a solution.

◢ Training materials, technical books, reference manuals, and textbooks like this one can all be good sources of help.

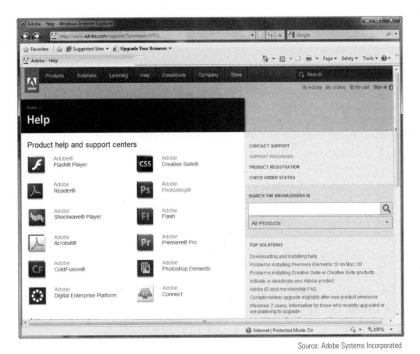

Source: Adobe Systems Incorporated

Figure 12-2 Search manufacturer web sites for help with a hardware or software product

> **Notes** To limit your search to a particular site when using *www.google.com*, use the site parameter in the search box. For example, to search only the Microsoft site for information about the defrag command, enter this search string: **defrag site:microsoft.com**.

STEP 3: TEST YOUR THEORY

For simple problems, you can zip right through Steps 3, 4, and 5 in Figure 12-1. Here are two examples where Steps 3, 4, and 5 go very fast:

◢ The video does not work and you suspect loose cables or the monitor is not turned on. You check the video cable connection (Step 3) and discover it's loose. As you connect it (Step 4), the video display works. Problem solved. You now can take the time to screw the video cable to the connection (Step 5) so that the problem won't happen again.

◢ Excel worksheets are getting corrupted. As you watch the user save a file, you discover he is saving files in an incorrect format that other software in the office cannot read (Step 3). You step the user through saving the file correctly and then verify that others can open the file (Step 4). You explain to the user which format to use (Step 5). The problem is then solved, and it's not likely to happen again.

A+
220-802
4.1

Here are two examples of Step 3 that include testing a guess that is not correct:

- ◢ The CD drive won't read a CD and you suspect the CD is scratched. When you check the disc, it looks fine. Your next guess is the CD drive is not recognized by Windows. You check Device Manager, and it reports errors with the drive. Your next guess is that drivers are corrupted.
- ◢ The system refuses to boot and gives the error message that the hard drive is not found. Internal cable connections are solid. Your next guess is the drive is not getting power.

Here are two examples of Step 3 where your guess is correct, and then you move on toward Step 4 to plan a solution:

- ◢ Word files are getting corrupted. After eliminating several simple causes, you guess that the hard drive is going bad. You check Event Viewer and discover Windows has recorded write errors to the drive multiple times (Step 3). Your theory is confirmed that the drive is bad and needs replacing (Step 4).
- ◢ Video does not work. You check cables and power and verify monitor settings controlled by buttons on the front of the monitor are all okay, but still no video. You guess the video cable might be bad and exchange it with one you know is good, but still no video. Therefore, you guess that the monitor is bad. You move the monitor to a working PC and it still does not work. You try a good monitor on the first PC, and it works fine. Your guess that the monitor is bad has been confirmed (Step 3). Next, you plan how to purchase a new monitor (Step 4).

As you test your guesses, keep in mind rules 8 through 11.

12

Rule 8: Divide and Conquer

This rule is the most powerful. Isolate the problem. In the overall system, remove one hardware or software component after another until the problem is isolated to a small part of the whole system. As you divide a large problem into smaller components, you can analyze each component separately. You can use one or more of the following to help you divide and conquer on your own system:

- ◢ In Windows, stop all nonessential services running in the background to eliminate them as the problem.
- ◢ Boot from a bootable CD or DVD to eliminate the OS and startup files on the hard drive as the problem.
- ◢ Start Windows in Safe Mode to eliminate unnecessary startup programs as a source of the problem.

Rule 9: Write Things Down

Keep good notes as you're working. They'll help you think more clearly. Draw diagrams. Make lists. Clearly and precisely write down what you're learning. If you need to leave the problem and return to it later, it's difficult to remember what you have observed and already tried. When the problem gets cold like this, your notes will be invaluable.

> **Rule 10: Don't Assume the Worst**
> When it's an emergency and your only copy of data is on a hard drive that is not working, don't assume that the data is lost. Much can be done to recover data. If you want to recover lost data on a hard drive, don't write anything to the drive; you might write on top of lost data, eliminating all chances of recovery.

> **Rule 11: Reboot and Start Over**
> This is an important rule. Fresh starts are good, and they uncover events or steps that might have been overlooked. Take a break! Get away from the problem. Begin again.

By the time you have finished Step 3, the problem might already be solved or you will know the source of the problem and will be ready to plan a solution.

STEP 4: PLAN YOUR SOLUTION AND THEN FIX THE PROBLEM

Some solutions, such as replacing a hard drive or a motherboard, are expensive and time consuming. You need to carefully consider what you will do and the order in which you will do it. When planning and implementing your solution, keep rules 12 and 13 in mind.

> **Rule 12: Use the Least Invasive Solution First**
> As you solve computer problems, always keep in mind that you don't want to make things worse, so you should use the least invasive solution. Keep in mind that you want to fix the problem in such a way that the system is returned to normal working condition with the least amount of effort. For example, don't format the hard drive until you've first tried to fix the problem without having to erase everything on the drive. In another example, don't reinstall Microsoft Office until you have tried applying patches to the existing installation.

> **Rule 13: Know Your Starting Point**
> Find out what works and doesn't work before you take anything apart or try some possible fix. Suppose you decide to install a Windows 7 service pack to solve a problem with USB devices not working. After the installation, you discover Microsoft Office gives errors and you cannot print to the network printer. You don't know if the service pack is causing problems or the problems existed before you began work. As much as possible, find out what works or what doesn't work before you attempt a fix.

Do the following to plan your solution and fix the problem:

1. Consider different solutions and select the least invasive one. In other words, choose the solution that fixes the problem by making as few changes to the system as possible. Some solutions are obvious, such as updating a device driver, but others might not be so obvious. For example, if Windows is corrupted and your options are to reinstall Windows or repair it, it's better to repair it so there's less work to do to restore the system to good working order and to return it to the configuration the user had before the problem occurred.

2. Before applying your solution, as best you can, determine what works and doesn't work about the system so you know your starting point.

3. Fix the problem. This might be as simple as plugging up a new monitor. Or it might be as difficult as reinstalling Windows and applications software and restoring data from backups.

STEP 5: VERIFY THE FIX AND TAKE PREVENTIVE ACTION

After you have fixed the problem, reboot the system and verify all is well. Can you reach the Internet, use the printer, or use Microsoft Office? If possible, have the user check everything and verify that the job is done satisfactorily. If either of you find a problem, return to Step 2 in the troubleshooting process to examine the system and form a new theory as to the cause of the problem.

After you and the user have verified all is working, ask yourself the question, "Could this problem have been prevented?" If so, go the extra mile to instruct the user, set Windows to automatically install updates, or do whatever else is appropriate to prevent future problems.

STEP 6: DOCUMENT WHAT HAPPENED

Good documentation helps you take what you learned into the next troubleshooting situation, train others, develop effective preventive maintenance plans, and satisfy any audits or customer or employer queries about your work. Be sure to write down the initial symptoms, the source of the problem, and what you did to fix it. Many companies use call tracking software to record this type of information. Figure 12-3 shows a window in Spiceworks Help Desk Software, which is popular and free call tracking software.

So now let's see how to handle some Windows problems. We'll begin with blue screen stop errors and improper shutdowns.

Source: Spiceworks, Inc.

Figure 12-3 Help Desk Software allows you to create, edit, and close tickets used by technicians

TROUBLESHOOTING BLUE SCREEN ERRORS AND IMPROPER SHUTDOWNS

A+
220-802
4.6

A **blue screen error**, also called a stop error or a **blue screen of death (BSOD)**, happens when processes running in kernel mode encounter a problem and Windows must stop the system. In such situations, a blue screen appears with a cryptic error message such as the one in Figure 12-4. Look on the blue screen for the stop error at the top and the specific number of the error near the bottom of the screen, as labeled in Figure 12-4.

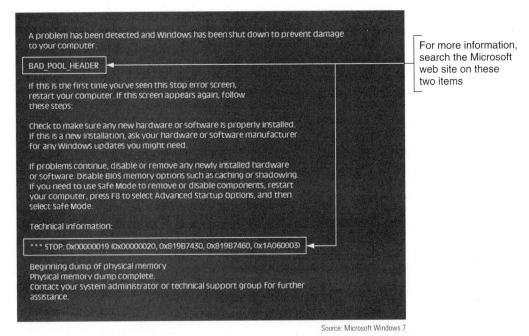

A problem has been detected and Windows has been shut down to prevent damage to your computer.

BAD_POOL_HEADER

If this is the first time you've seen this stop error screen,
restart your computer. If this screen appears again, follow
these steps:

Check to make sure any new hardware or software is properly installed.
If this is a new installation, ask your hardware or software manufacturer
for any Windows updates you might need.

If problems continue, disable or remove any newly installed hardware
or software. Disable BIOS memory options such as caching or shadowing.
If you need to use Safe Mode to remove or disable components, restart
your computer, press F8 to select Advanced Startup Options, and then
select Safe Mode.

Technical information:

*** STOP: 0x00000019 (0x00000020, 0x819B7430, 0x819B7460, 0x1A060003)

Beginning dump of physical memory
Physical memory dump complete.
Contact your system administrator or technical support group for further
assistance.

For more information, search the Microsoft web site on these two items

Source: Microsoft Windows 7

Figure 12-4   A blue screen of death (BSOD) is definitively not a good sign; time to start troubleshooting

How to deal with blue screen errors that happen at startup is covered in Chapter 14. Here's what to do when you get a blue screen error after startup:

1. As for the tools useful in solving blue screen errors, put the web at the top of your list! (But don't forget that some sites are unreliable and others mean you harm.) Search the Microsoft web site on the two items labeled in Figure 12-4.

2. If the blue screen names the device driver or service that caused the problem, use Windows Explorer to locate the program file. Driver files are stored in the C:\Windows\System32\drivers folder. Right-click the file and select **Properties** from the shortcut menu. The Details tab of the Properties box tells you the purpose of the file (see Figure 12-5). You can then reinstall the device or program that caused the problem.

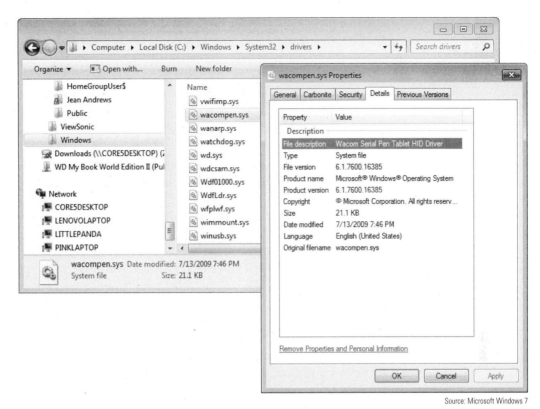

Source: Microsoft Windows 7

Figure 12-5 Use the Details tab of a driver's Properties box to identify the purpose of the driver

12

3. Immediately after you restart the system, a Windows error message box or bubble might appear with useful information. Follow the links in the bubble.

4. Check Event Viewer, which might provide events it has logged. Recall that critical errors and warnings are recorded in the Administrative Events log.

5. Also check Archived Messages in the Action Center, and, in Vista, check the Problem Reports and Solutions window for clues.

6. Use Windows Updates to apply patches.

7. Undo any recent changes to the system. If you are not sure which changes to undo, consider using System Restore to restore the system to the point in time before the problem started.

8. Use the Memory Diagnostics tool to check memory and use Chkdsk with the /r parameter to check the hard drive for errors. If the problem is still not resolved, you might need to repair Windows system files by using System File Checker, Safe Mode, or other Windows startup repair tools you will learn about in Chapter 14.

Here are some common blue screen errors, the source of the problem, and what to do about it. Following this list, you learn to use the new tools mentioned in the list.

▲ **BAD_POOL_HEADER.** This is the error shown in Figure 12-4 and can occur for a variety of reasons, including a corrupted Windows update, bad memory, or a corrupted application. Start troubleshooting by suspecting the most recent change to the

A+
220-802
4.6

system and try undoing that change. For example, try to roll back a driver or uninstall a Windows update. If there have been several recent changes, you might consider using System Restore to apply a restore point to a point in time just before the problem started.

Next, suspect memory is bad. Use Memory Diagnostics to test memory. Events logged in Event Viewer might give more clues.

▲ **NTFS_FILE_SYSTEM.** The hard drive is most likely corrupted. Try running Chkdsk with the /r parameter.

▲ **KERNEL_DATA_INPAGE_ERROR.** The immediate problem is Windows could not read the paging file (Pagefile.sys). The file might be corrupted because of bad memory, a corrupted hard drive, or a failing processor. Begin troubleshooting by rebuilding Pagefile.sys. If the error reoccurs, then you must dig deeper to solve the root problem.

▲ **UNEXPECTED_KERNEL_MODE_TRAP.** This error is most likely caused by bad memory. Run Memory Diagnostics to test memory.

▲ **DIVIDE_BY_ZERO_ERROR.** This error is most likely caused by an application. Begin troubleshooting by identifying what application was running when the error occurred.

WINDOWS 32-BIT AND 64-BIT PATCHES

When researching a problem, suppose you discover that Microsoft or a manufacturer's web site offers a fix or patch you can download and apply. To get the right patch, you need to make sure you get a 32-bit patch for a 32-bit installation of Windows, a device driver, or an application. For a 64-bit installation of Windows, make sure you get a 64-bit device driver. An application installed in a 64-bit OS might be a 32-bit application or a 64-bit application.

The documentation on the Microsoft or other web sites might be cryptic about the type of patch. Follow these guidelines when reading error messages or documentation:

▲ The term x86 refers to 32-bit CPUs or processors and to 32-bit operating systems. For example, you need to download a patch from Microsoft to fix a Windows 7 problem you are having with USB devices. The article on the Microsoft web site that applies to your problem says to download the patch if you are using a Windows 7, x86-based version. Take that to mean you can use this patch if you are using a 32-bit version of Windows 7.

▲ All CPUs installed in personal computers today are hybrid processors that can process either 32 bits or 64 bits. The term x86-64 refers to these processors, such as the Intel Core2 Duo or an AMD Athlon processor. (AMD64 refers specifically to these hybrid AMD processors.) The term x86-64 can also refer to a 64-bit OS. For example, a Windows message might say, "You are attempting to load an x86-64 operating system." Take that to mean you are attempting to load a 64-bit OS onto a computer that has a hybrid 32-bit/64-bit processor installed, such as the Athlon 64 or Intel Core2 Duo.

▲ The term IA64 refers specifically to 64-bit Intel processors such as the Xeon or Itanium used in servers or high-end workstations. For example, you are selecting a utility to download from the Microsoft web site. One choice for the utility specifies an IA64 platform. Only select this choice if you have installed an Itanium or Xeon processor. (By the way, a techie often uses the word *platform* to mean the processor and operating system on which other software is running. However, in this context, the operating system's platform is the processor.)

▲ The term x64 refers to 64-bit operating systems. For example, Microsoft offers two versions of Windows 7 Home Premium: the x86 version and the x64 version.

A+
220-802
4.6

> **A+ Exam Tip** The A+ 220-802 exam expects you to know the difference between Windows 32-bit and 64-bit versions. You are also expected to be familiar with the terms 32-bit, 64-bit, x86, and x64.

Now let's learn to use the Memory Diagnostics and System File Checker tools, which can be useful when troubleshooting blue screen errors.

A+
220-802
1.4, 4.6

MEMORY DIAGNOSTICS

Errors with memory are often difficult to diagnose because they can appear intermittently and might be mistaken as application errors, user errors, or other hardware component errors. Sometimes these errors cause the system to hang, a blue screen error might occur, or the system continues to function with applications giving errors or data getting corrupted. You can quickly identify a problem with memory or eliminate memory as the source of a problem by using the Windows 7/Vista **Memory Diagnostics** tool. It tests memory for errors and works before Windows is loaded and can be used on computers that don't have Windows 7 or Vista installed. Use one of these three methods to start the utility:

▲ *Method 1:* In a command prompt window, enter **mdsched.exe** and press **Enter**. A dialog box appears (see Figure 12-6) asking if you want to run the test now or on the next restart.

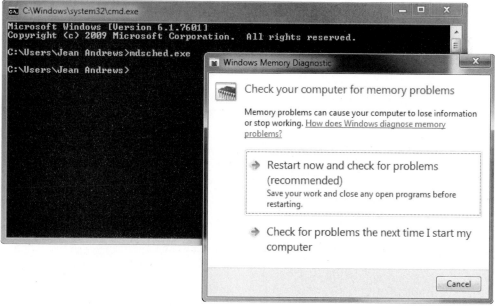

Source: Microsoft Windows 7

Figure 12-6 Use the mdsched.exe command to test memory

▲ *Method 2:* If you cannot load the Windows desktop, press the Spacebar during the boot. The Windows Boot Manager screen appears (see Figure 12-7). Select **Windows Memory Diagnostic** and press **Enter**.

A+
220-802
1.4, 4.6

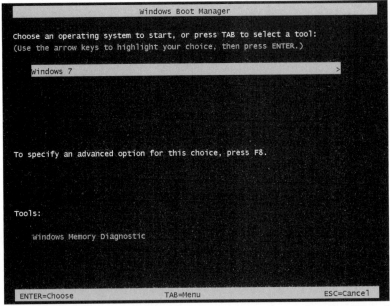

Source: Microsoft Windows 7

Figure 12-7   Force the Windows Boot Manager menu to display by pressing the
Spacebar during the boot

▲ *Method 3:* If you cannot boot from the hard drive, boot the computer from the
Windows setup DVD. On the opening screen, select your language. On the next screen
(see Figure 12-8), click **Repair your computer**. In the next box, select the Windows
installation to repair. The System Recovery Options window appears (see Figure 12-9).
Click **Windows Memory Diagnostic** and follow the directions on-screen.

Source: Microsoft Windows 7

Figure 12-8   Opening menu when you boot from the Windows 7 setup DVD

A+
220-802
1.4, 4.6

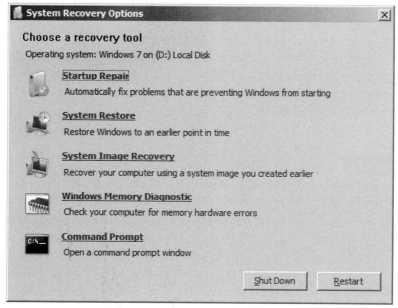

Source: Microsoft Windows 7

Figure 12-9 Test memory using the System Recovery Options menu

If the tool reports memory errors, replace all memory modules installed on the motherboard.

SYSTEM FILE CHECKER

A+
220-802
1.3, 4.6

A Windows application or hardware problem might be caused by a corrupted Windows system file. That's where System File Checker might help. **System File Checker (SFC)** protects system files and keeps a cache of current system files in case it needs to refresh a damaged file. To use the utility to scan all system files and verify them, first close all applications and then enter the command **sfc /scannow** in an elevated command prompt window (see Figure 12-10). If corrupted system files are found, you might need to provide the Windows setup DVD to restore the files. If you have problems running the utility, try the command **sfc/ scanonce**, which scans files immediately after the next reboot.

12

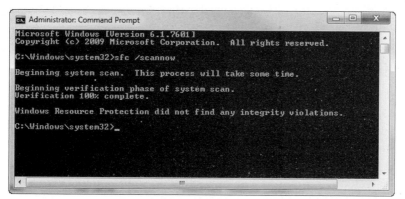

Source: Microsoft Windows 7

Figure 12-10 Use System File Checker to verify Windows system files

> **Notes** Recall from Chapter 10 that you can get an elevated command prompt window in Windows 7/ Vista by clicking **Start**, **All Programs**, and **Accessories**. Then right-click **Command Prompt** and select **Run as administrator** from the shortcut menu.

DEALING WITH IMPROPER SHUTDOWNS

Improper shutdowns and a system lockup that cause a computer to freeze and require that it be restarted are most likely caused by hardware. Hardware that can cause these errors include memory, the motherboard, CPU, video card, or the system overheating. I/O devices such as the keyboard, mouse, or monitor or application errors don't usually cause these types of catastrophic problems.

> 💡 **A+ Exam Tip** The 220-802 exam expects you to know how to solve problems when the system shuts down improperly.

When these types of errors occur, try and check these things:

1. Check Event Viewer to see if it has reported a hardware failure.

2. Apply any Windows patches.

3. Use Memory Diagnostics and Chkdsk with the /r parameter to check memory and the hard drive for errors.

4. If you suspect overheating is a problem, immediately after the lockup, go into BIOS setup and check the temperature of the CPU, which should not exceed 38 degrees C. Alternately, you can install a freeware utility, such as SpeedFan by Alfredo Comparetti (*www.almico.com*) to monitor the temperature of the motherboard or hard drive.

When solving problems with any kind of hardware, it's important that you check for physical damage to the device. If you feel excessive heat coming from the computer case or a peripheral device, immediately unplug the device or power down the system. Don't turn the device or system back on until the problem is solved; you don't want to start a fire! Other symptoms that indicate potential danger are strong electrical odors, unusual noises, no noise (such as when the fan is not working to keep the system cool), liquid spills on a device, and visible damage such as a frayed cable, melted plastic, or smoke. In these situations, turn off the equipment immediately.

DEALING WITH ENDLESS SHUTDOWNS AND RESTARTS

With normal Windows settings, if a blue screen error occurs, the system displays the error screen for a moment and then automatically restarts the system, which can result in an endless cycle of restarts. If you're caught in this situation, you can do the following:

1. Try to boot into Safe Mode where the endless shutdowns might not occur. In Safe Mode, you can change the Windows setting to control automatic restarts. Follow these steps:

   a. To boot to Safe Mode, press **F8** before Windows loads. The Advanced Boot Options Menu appears (see Figure 12-11). In the Advanced Boot Options Menu, select **Safe Mode**. The Windows desktop in Safe Mode is shown in Figure 12-12.

A+
220-802
4.6

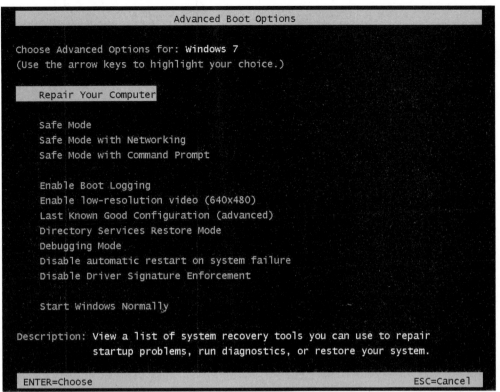

```
                        Advanced Boot Options

Choose Advanced Options for: Windows 7
(Use the arrow keys to highlight your choice.)

   Repair Your Computer

     Safe Mode
     Safe Mode with Networking
     Safe Mode with Command Prompt

     Enable Boot Logging
     Enable low-resolution video (640x480)
     Last Known Good Configuration (advanced)
     Directory Services Restore Mode
     Debugging Mode
     Disable automatic restart on system failure
     Disable Driver Signature Enforcement

     Start Windows Normally

Description: View a list of system recovery tools you can use to repair
            startup problems, run diagnostics, or restore your system.

ENTER=Choose                                              ESC=Cancel
```

Source: Microsoft Windows 7

Figure 12-11 Press F8 during the boot to launch the Advanced Boot Options menu

12

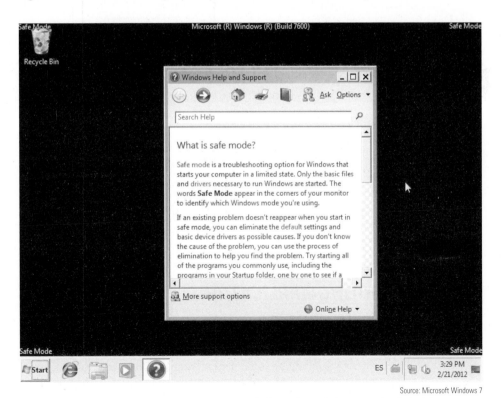

Source: Microsoft Windows 7

Figure 12-12 The Safe Mode black desktop reminds us that Windows was loaded with a minimum configuration

b. Click **Start**, right-click **Computer**, and select **Properties** from the shortcut menu. The System window opens.

c. In the left pane of the System window, click **Advanced system settings**. (For Windows XP, in the System Properties window, click the **Advanced** tab.)

d. In the System Properties box (see the left side of Figure 12-13) in the Startup and Recovery section, click **Settings**.

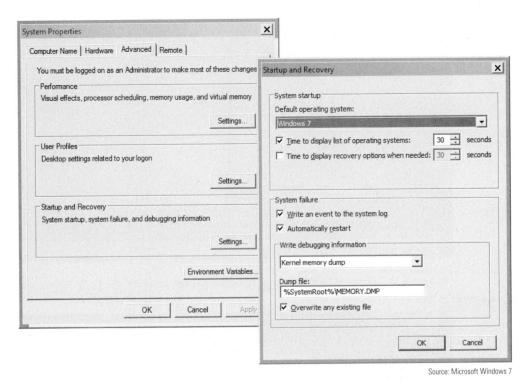

Source: Microsoft Windows 7

Figure 12-13 Use the Startup and Recovery box to change the way Windows responds to a stop error

e. In the Startup and Recovery box (see the right side of Figure 12-13), uncheck **Automatically restart**. Click **OK** twice to close both boxes. Then close the System window.

2. If you cannot boot the system to Safe Mode, press **F8** at startup and select **Disable automatic restart on system failure** on the Advanced Boot Options menu (refer to Figure 12-11).

TROUBLESHOOTING APPLICATIONS

A problem with an application might be caused by the application, the hardware, the operating system, the data, other applications in conflict with this one, or the user. We begin this part of the chapter by looking at some general steps to help you solve a problem with an application, and then we look at some specific error messages and what to do about them.

> **Notes** As you are troubleshooting a problem and make a change to the system, be sure to restart Windows and check to see if the problem is resolved before you move on to the next fix.

A+
220-802
4.6

GENERAL STEPS FOR SOLVING APPLICATION ERRORS

Here are a bunch of things to do and try that might solve a problem with an application. As you work your way through these steps, keep in mind where each step fits in the overall strategy given earlier in the chapter for solving any computer problem.

STEP 1: INTERVIEW THE USER AND BACK UP DATA

Worth saying again: Start with interviewing the user:

1. *Interview the user and back up data.* Find out as much information as you can from the user about the problem, when it started, and what happened to the system around the time the problem started. Also ask if valuable data is on the system. If so, back it up.

2. *Ask the user to reproduce the problem while you watch.* Many problems with applications are caused by user error. Watch carefully as the user shows you the problem. If you see him making a mistake, be tactful and don't accuse. Just explain the problem and its solution. It's better to explain and teach rather than fix the problem yourself; that way, the user learns from the experience.

3. *Try a reboot.* Reboots solve a lot of application problems and one might be a shortcut to your solution. If that doesn't work, no harm is done and you're ready to begin investigating the system.

STEP 2: ERROR MESSAGES, THE WEB, AND LOGS MIGHT HELP

Windows might display an error message and offer a solution. Logs kept by Windows can offer clues. Here are a few examples of how to get help from Windows and the web:

▲ *Error messages and the Action Center.* For Windows 7, the Action Center tracks problems with applications, hardware, and Windows (see Figure 12-14). In the Action Center, click **View archived messages** to see a history of past problems (see Figure 12-15). Double-click a problem to read the details about it.

12

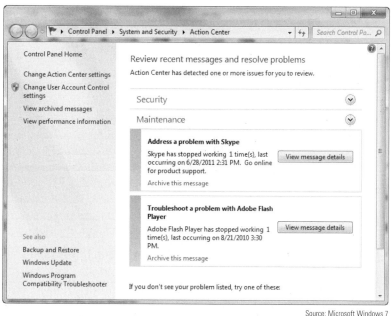

Source: Microsoft Windows 7

Figure 12-14 Windows 7 reports problems with two applications

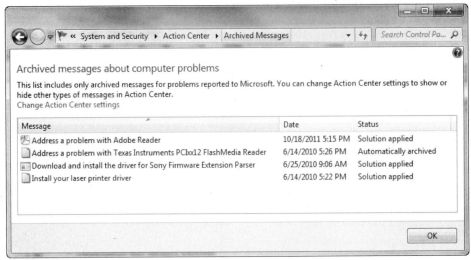

Figure 12-15 Archived messages of past and current problems

Source: Microsoft Windows 7

▲ *Vista Problem Reports and Solutions window.* For Vista, click **Start**, click **All Programs**, click **Maintenance**, and click **Problem Reports and Solutions**. In the **Problem Reports and Solutions** window (see Figure 12-16), click **View problem history** to see a list of current and past problems. Click a problem to see details.

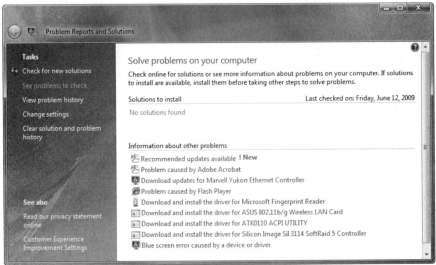

Figure 12-16 Known Vista problems and solutions

Source: Microsoft Windows Vista

▲ *XP error messages.* For XP, an error message appears in a dialog box similar to that in Figure 12-17. When you click Send Error Report and follow the links, your browser opens and displays information from Microsoft about the problem and might offer a solution.

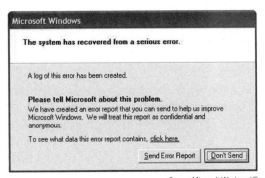

Source: Microsoft Windows XP

Figure 12-17 A serious Windows XP error sometimes generates this Microsoft Windows error reporting box

▲ *Search the web for help.* You might find more information about a problem by searching the web site of the application manufacturer for support and help. Also, search the web on the error message, application, or description of the problem. Look for forums where others have posted the same problem with the same app. Someone else has likely posted a solution. However, be careful and don't take the advice unless you trust the web site.

▲ *Use Event Viewer and Reliability Monitor to look for clues.* The Event Viewer logs might give clues about applications and the system. Hard drive errors often appear as application errors. Use Reliability Monitor to look for errors with other applications or with key hardware components such as the hard drive.

STEP 3: CONSIDER THE DATA OR THE APPLICATION IS CORRUPTED

Now that you've interviewed the user, backed up important data, and examined the system, it's time to come up with a theory as to the cause of the problem. Consider and do these things:

▲ *Consider data corruption.* For applications that use data files such as Microsoft Office, it might appear that the application has a problem when the problem is really a corrupted data file. Try creating an entirely new data file. If that works, then suspect that previous errors might be caused by corrupted data. You might be able to recover part of a corrupted file by changing its file extension to .txt and importing it into the application as a text file.

▲ *Application settings might be wrong.* Maybe a user has made one too many changes to the application settings, which can cause a problem with missing toolbars and other functions. Write down each setting the user has changed and then restore all settings back to their default values. If the problem is solved, restore each setting to the way the user had it until you find the one causing the problem. The process will take some time, but users can get upset if you change their application settings without justification.

▲ *The application might be corrupted.* The application setup might have the option to repair the installation. Look for it in the Programs and Features window, on the setup CD for the application, or on the manufacturer's web site.

▲ *Uninstall and reinstall the application.* Do so with caution because you might lose any customized settings, macros, or scripts. Also know this still might not solve a problem with a corrupted application because registry entries might not be properly reset during the uninstall process.

12

STEP 4: CONSIDER OUTSIDE INTERFERENCE

The problem might be caused by a virus, Windows, other applications, or hardware. Check these things:

- *Suspect a virus is causing a problem.* Scan for viruses and check Task Manager to make sure some strange process is not interfering with your applications.
- *You might be low on system resources or another application might be interfering.* Close all other applications.
- *Maybe a service failed to start.* Research the application documentation and find out if the app relies on a service to work. Use the Services console to make sure the service has started. If the service has failed to start, make sure it has an Automatic or Manual setting.
- *The problem might be bad memory.* Following the directions given earlier in the chapter, use the Memory Diagnostics tool (mdsched.exe) to test memory. If it finds errors, replace the memory modules.
- *The problem might be a corrupted hard drive.* To eliminate the hard drive as the source of an application error, use the Chkdsk command with the /r parameter to check the drive and recover data in bad sectors.
- *A background program might be conflicting with the application.* To eliminate background programs or services as a source of the problem, run the application after booting into Safe Mode. Press **F8** at startup to display the Advanced Boot Options menu, and select **Safe Mode with Networking** from the menu. If the application works in Safe Mode, then you can assume the problem is not with the application but with the operating system, device drivers, or other applications that load at startup and are conflicting with the application.

STEP 5: CONSIDER WINDOWS MIGHT BE THE PROBLEM

A problem with an application can sometimes be solved by updating or restoring Windows system files. Do the following:

- *Download Windows updates.* Make sure all critical and important Windows updates are installed. Microsoft Office updates are included in Windows updates.
- *Use System File Checker.* For essential hardware devices, use the System File Checker (SFC) to verify and replace system files. Use the command **sfc /scannow** or **sfc /scanonce**.
- *Use System Restore.* If you can identify the approximate date the error started and that date is in the recent past, use System Restore. Select a restore point just before the problem started. Reverting to a restore point can solve problems with registry entries the application uses that have become corrupted. However, System Restore can cause problems of its own, so use it with caution.

> 💡 **A+ Exam Tip**   The 220-802 exam expects you to know when and how to use System Restore to solve a Windows, hardware, or application problem.

RESPONDING TO SPECIFIC ERROR MESSAGES

In this part of the chapter, we look at some specific error messages that relate to problems with applications.

A+
220-802
1.3, 4.6

WHEN AN APPLICATION HANGS

If an application is locked up and not responding, use Task Manager to end it. If Task Manager can't end a process, use the Tasklist and Taskkill commands. The **Tasklist** command returns the process identify (PID), which is a number that identifies each running process. The **Taskkill** command uses the process ID to kill the process. Do the following:

1. Open a Command Prompt window and use the **Tasklist | more** command to get a list of processes currently running. Note the PID of the process you want to end. For example, suppose you see that its PID is 2212.

2. Enter the command **taskkill /f /pid:2212**, using the PID you noted in Step 1. The /f parameter forcefully kills the process. Be careful using this command; it is so powerful that you can end critical system processes that will cause the system to shut down.

> 💡 **A+ Exam Tip** For the A+ 220-802 exam, the Kill and Tlist commands are listed in the objectives. These older Windows 2000 commands have been replaced by the Tasklist and Taskkill commands.

A+
220-802
4.6

WHEN A FILE FAILS TO OPEN

When you double-click a data file and get an error message that Windows cannot open the file (see Figure 12-18), Windows is unable to identify the application used to read the data file. This problem happens because the application is not installed or the file extension is wrong. The **file association** between a data file and an application is determined by the file extension. A program associated with a file extension is called its **default program**.

12

Source: Microsoft Windows 7

Figure 12-18 Windows does not know which application to use to open the data file

Follow these steps to use the Default Programs window to change the program associated with a file extension:

1. Click **Start** and then click **Default Programs**. The Default Programs window opens. Click **Associate a file type or protocol with a program**. The list of current associations appears in the Set Associations window (see the left side of Figure 12-19).

A+
220-802
4.6

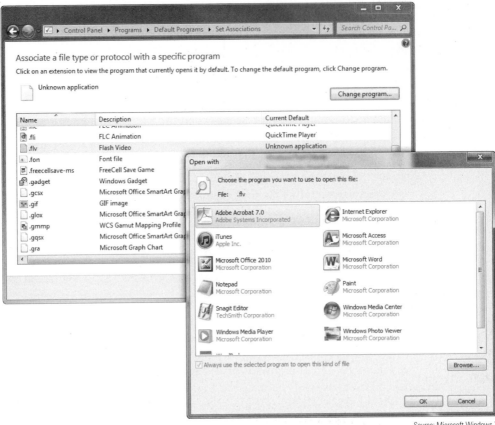

Figure 12-19 Select the default program to associate with a file extension

2. Select the file extension you want to change and click **Change program**. The Open with dialog box appears (see the right side of Figure 12-19).

3. The box displays installed programs that can handle the selected file extension. If you don't see the program you want, click **Browse** to find it in the Program Files or Program Files (x86) folder on your hard drive. Otherwise, make your selection and click **OK**. Then close all windows.

If a file extension is not listed in the Set Associations window, the **Data Sources Open Database Connectivity (ODBC)** tool in the Administrative Tools group of Control Panel can help. This tool can be used to allow data files (called data sources) to be connected to applications they normally would not use.

APPLYING | CONCEPTS USING THE ODBC DATA SOURCE TOOL

Suppose a user has some old dBASE database files, which have a .dbf file extension, and she wants to use Microsoft Access installed on her PC to manage these files. Do the following to make this work:

1. In the Administrative Tools group in Control Panel, double-click **Data Sources (ODBC)**. The ODBC Data Source Administrator box opens, as shown in Figure 12-20.

A+
220-802
4.6

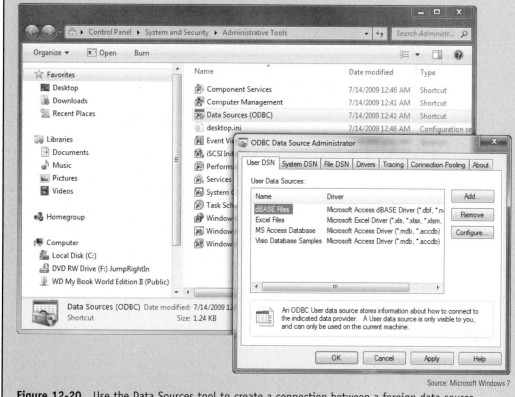

Figure 12-20 Use the Data Sources tool to create a connection between a foreign data source and an application

12

2. Make sure the **User DSN** tab is selected. (DSN stands for Data Source Name.) The connections made on this tab apply only to the current user. Click **Add**. The Create New Data Source box appears (see Figure 12-21). Select the dBASE driver and click **Finish**.

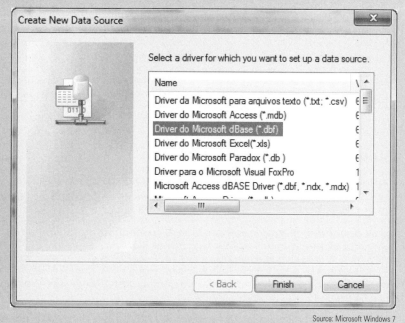

Figure 12-21 Select a driver to interface between the application and the data source

Notes If you don't see the driver you need in the Create New Data Source box, close all windows and use Explorer to locate the C:\Windows\SysWOW64\Odbcad32.exe program file. When you double-click this file, the ODBC Data Source Administrator box appears and will have all ODBC drivers available.

3. The ODBC dBASE Setup box appears. Uncheck **Use Current Directory**. Then click **Select Directory** and navigate to the folder that contains the dBASE files and click **OK**. Enter a name for the Data Source Name, as shown in Figure 12-22, and click **OK**. The new data source is now listed in the ODBC Data Source Administrator box, and Windows knows which ODBC driver to use to manage this data source.

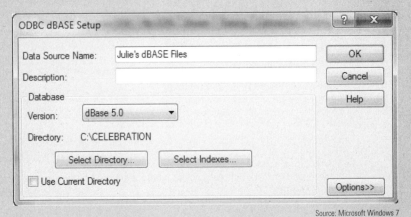

Source: Microsoft Windows 7

Figure 12-22   Locate the data source files and assign a name to the data source

4. Now you need to establish the file association. Go to the Default Programs window and associate the .dbf file extension with Microsoft Access. Because you have identified an ODBC driver for these .dbf files, this file extension is now listed in the Set Associations box.

5. Test the association by double-clicking a .dbf file in Windows Explorer. The file should open in a Microsoft Access window.

WHEN A SERVICE FAILS TO START

A message about a service failing to start can be caused by a corrupted or missing service program, or the service might not be configured to launch at startup. Recall from Chapter 11 that you can use the Services console to enable, disable, start, or stop a service. A service can be disabled at startup using the System Configuration tool, and the System Information window can give you a list of all running services.

If you get an error message that a service has failed to start, check the Service console to make sure the service is set to start automatically. Make sure the Startup type is set to Automatic or Automatic (Delayed Start). Use the service's Properties box in the console to find the path and filename to the executable program. Then use Windows Explorer to make sure the program file is not missing. You might need to reinstall the service or the application that uses the service.

A+
220-802
1.4, 4.6

WHEN A DLL IS MISSING OR A COMPONENT IS NOT REGISTERED

Most applications have a main program file that uses a collection of many small programs called components or objects that serve the main program. The main program for an application has an .exe file extension and relies on several component services that often have a .DLL file extension. (DLL stands for Dynamic Link Library.) Problems with applications can be caused by a missing DLL program or a broken association between the main program and a component.

If you get an error message about a missing DLL, the easiest way to solve this problem might be to reinstall the application. However, if that is not advisable, you can identify the path and name of the missing DLL file and recover it from backup or from the application installation files.

> **A+ Exam Tip** The A+ 220-802 exam expects you to know how to handle missing DLL errors and to know when it's appropriate to use the Component Services, Regsvr32, and Data Sources tools.

On the other hand, the file might be present and undamaged, but the application cannot find it because the relationship between the two is broken. Relationships between a main program and its components are normally established by entries in the registry when the application is installed. The process is called registering a component. In addition, the **Component Services (also called COM+)** tool, which is a Microsoft Management Console snap-in, can be used to register components. The tool is often used by application developers and system administrators when developing and deploying an application. For example, a system administrator might use COM+ when installing an application on servers or client computers where an application on one computer calls an application on another computer on the network. COM+ is more automated than the older and more manual **Regsvr32_** utility that is also used to register component services.

The Regsvr32.exe program is stored in the C:\Program Files or C:\Program Files (x86) folder and requires an elevated command prompt. Note in Figure 12-23, the first regsvr32 command uses the /u parameter to unregister a component. The second regsvr32 command registers the component again. Also notice that you need to include the path to the DLL file in the command line.

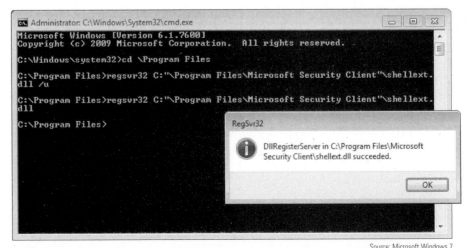

Source: Microsoft Windows 7

Figure 12-23 Use the regsvr32 command to register or unregister an application component

A+
220-802
1.4, 4.6

As a PC support technician, you might be asked by a system administrator or software provider to use the COM+ or Regsvr32 tool to help solve a problem with an application giving errors. Suppose you get this error when installing an application:

```
Error 1928 "Error registering COM+ application."
```

When you contact the help desk of the application provider, you might be instructed to use the COM+ tool to solve the problem. To open the tool, open the **Administrative Tools** group in Control Panel. Then double-click **Component Services**. The Component Services window is shown in Figure 12-24. To learn how to use the tool, click **Help** in the menu bar.

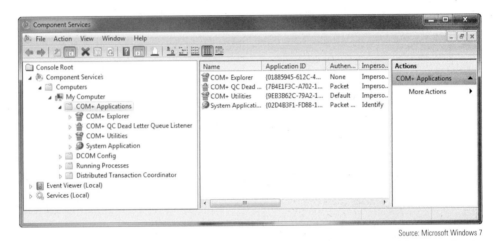

Source: Microsoft Windows 7

Figure 12-24   Use the Component Services window to register components used by an application

A+
220-802
4.6

WHEN THE APPLICATION HAS NEVER WORKED

If the application has never worked, follow these steps:

1. *Update Windows and search the web.* Installing all important and critical Windows updates can sometimes solve a problem with an application that won't install. Also check the web site of the software manufacturer and the Microsoft support site (*support.microsoft.com*) for solutions. Search on the application name or the error message you get when you try to run it.

2. *Run the installation program or application as an administrator.* The program might require that the user have privileges not assigned to the current user account. Try running the application with administrator privileges, which Windows calls a **secondary logon**. If the installation has failed, use Windows Explorer to locate the installation executable file. Right-click it and select **Run as administrator** from the shortcut menu (see Figure 12-25).

> **Notes** To run a program using a user account other than administrator, hold down the Shift key and right-click the program file. Then select **Run as different user** from the shortcut menu. You must then enter the username and password of another user account in the Windows Security box.

A+
220-802
4.6

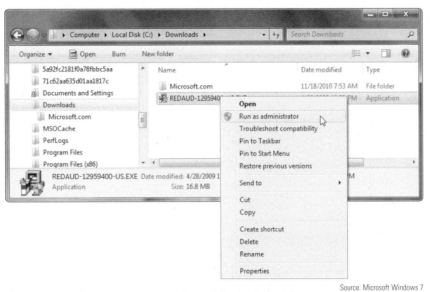

Figure 12-25 Execute a program using administrative privileges

If the application has failed after it is installed, locate the installed program. Look for it in a subfolder of the Program Files or Program Files (x86) folder. If the program works when you run it with administrative privileges, you can make that setting permanent. To do so, right-click it and select **Properties** from the shortcut menu. Then click the **Compatibility** tab and check **Run this program as an administrator** (see Figure 12-26). Click **Apply** and then close the Properties box.

12

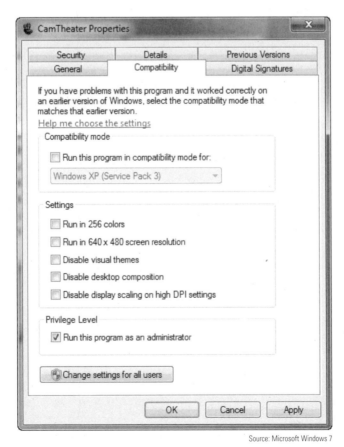

Figure 12-26 Permanently change the privilege level of an application

A+
220-802
4.6

3. *Consider whether an older application is having compatibility problems with Windows.* Some older applications cannot run under Windows 7 or run with errors. Here are some steps you can take to fix the problem:

a. Go to the Windows 7 Compatibility Center site at *www.microsoft.com/windows/compatibility* and search for the application. The site reports problems and solutions for known legacy software. For example, when you search on the application WinPatrol, you find that Microsoft recommends Version 16 for Windows 7 (see Figure 12-27). Use the 32-bit or 64-bit type appropriate for your system. If the version and type you are using are not compatible, try to replace or upgrade the software.

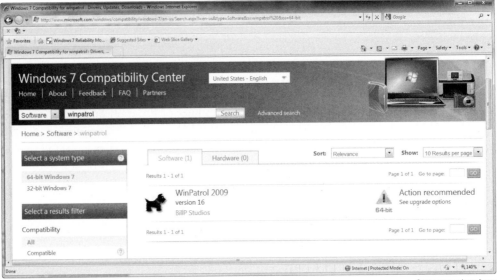

Source: www.microsoft.com

Figure 12-27 Microsoft tracks software and hardware compatible with Windows 7

b. Try running the application in compatibility mode. To do that, on the Compatibility tab of the program file Properties box shown earlier in Figure 12-26, check **Run this program in compatibility mode for:**. Then, from the drop-down menu, select the operating system that the application was written to run under. Click **Apply** and close the **Properties** box.

c. For Windows 7 Professional and Ultimate editions, try running the program in Windows XP Mode. Recall from Chapter 7 that Windows XP Mode can be used to install XP in a virtual machine under Windows 7. Applications installed in XP Mode work in the XP environment. Only use this option as a last resort because XP Mode takes up a lot of system resources.

4. *Verify that the application is digitally signed.* Although applications that are not digitally signed can still run on Windows, a digital signature does verify that the application is not a rogue application and that it is certified as Windows-compatible by Microsoft. To view the digital signature, select the **Digital Signatures** tab of the program file's Properties box. Select a signer in the list and click **Details** (see Figure 12-28). If the Digital Signatures tab is missing, the program is not digitally signed.

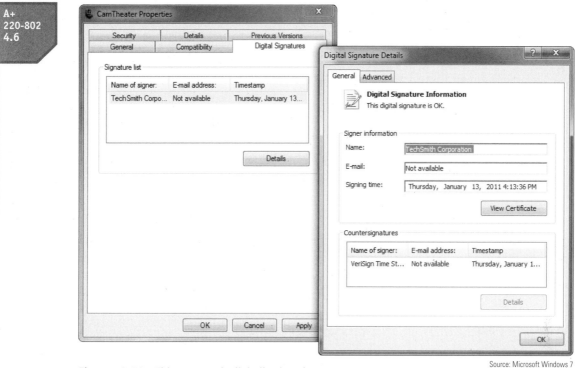

A+
220-802
4.6

Figure 12-28 This program is digitally signed

Source: Microsoft Windows 7

12

>> CHAPTER SUMMARY

Overview of Windows Troubleshooting Tools

◢ In solving Windows problems, it helps to have a handy reference of available Windows tools to remind you of what you might check or do toward finding a solution.

Strategies to Troubleshoot Any Computer Problem

◢ The six steps in the troubleshooting process are: 1) Interview the user and back up data, 2) Examine the system and form a theory of probable cause (your best guess), 3) Test your theory, 4) Plan a solution and implement it, 5) Verify that everything works and take appropriate preventive measures, and 6) Document what you did and the final outcome.

Troubleshooting Blue Screen Errors

◢ To solve blue screen stop errors after Windows startup, use the web to research the error message or symptom, and use Windows error-reporting tools, Event Viewer, Windows updates, System Restore, Memory Diagnostics, and Chkdsk to examine the system and solve the problem.

◢ Operating systems process either 32 bits or 64 bits. Microsoft calls 32-bit operating systems x86-based OSs. The term x64 applies to 64-bit OSs.

◢ 64-bit operating systems require 64-bit drivers and can support 32-bit and 64-bit applications.

◢ Use the Memory Diagnostics tool to test memory during the boot.

◢ Use the System File Checker (SFC) tool to verify and restore system files.

◢ Use the Startup and Recovery section in the System Properties box to keep Windows from automatically restarting after a stop error. Automatic restarts can put the boot into an endless loop.

Troubleshooting Applications

◢ Windows error messages and logs can help you examine a system looking for the source of an application problem.

◢ Applying Windows patches and repairing system files can sometimes solve an application problem. Use System File Checker and System Restore to repair system files.

◢ Other tools that can help you fix a problem with an application include the Default Programs window, Data Sources (ODBC) and Component Services administrative tools, the Services console, a secondary logon, Compatibility Mode, Windows 7 XP Mode, Task Manager, antivirus software, Windows updates, Windows 7 archived messages, Vista Problem Reports and Solutions, XP Error Reporting, Chkdsk, Memory Diagnostics, Safe Mode, and the web site of the application developer.

>> KEY TERMS

For explanations of key terms, see the Glossary near the end of the book.

blue screen error	default program	secondary logon
blue screen of death (BSOD)	file association	System File Checker (SFC)
Component Services (also called COM+)	Memory Diagnostics	Taskkill
	Problem Reports and Solutions	Tasklist
Data Sources Open Database Connectivity (ODBC)	Regsvr32	

>> REVIEW QUESTIONS

1. How should you begin every troubleshooting procedure?

   a) Try to boot the system.

   b) Stop all nonessential services running in the background.

   c) Interview the user to see if he or she is available.

   d) Run Windows Update.

2. Which tool should be at the top of the list when solving blue screen errors?

   a) System File Checker

   b) Memory Checker

   c) Check Disk

   d) The Web

3. The term ____ refers to processors such as the Intel Core2 Duo or an AMD Athlon processor.

   a) x86-64

   b) x86

   c) x64

   d) IA64

4. If an application is locked up and not responding, use ____ to end it.

   a) The Action Center

   b) System BIOS

   c) Task Manager

   d) Resource Monitor

5. The ____ tool is a Microsoft Management Console snap-in that can be used to register components.

   a) Registry Editor

   b) COM+

   c) DLL

   d) System File Checker

6. True or false? Most problems with computers are simple, such as a loose cable or incorrect Windows setting.

7. True or false? Generally, it's easy to check for a software problem before you check for a hardware problem.

8. True or false? Improper shutdowns and a system lockup that cause a computer to freeze and require that it be restarted are most likely caused by software.

9. True or false? Many problems with applications are caused by user error.

10. True or false? Only applications that are digitally signed will run on Windows.

11. A(n) ____ error happens when processes running in kernel mode encounter a problem and Windows must stop the system.

12. ____ protects system files and keeps a cache of current system files in case it needs to refresh a damaged file.

13. If you suspect overheating is a problem, go into BIOS setup and check the temperature of the CPU, which should not exceed ____ degrees C.

14. The ____ command uses the process ID to kill the process.

15. A program associated with a file extension is called its ____.

12

Troubleshooting Hardware Problems

In the first chapters of this book, you have learned much about the hardware components of a system, including features and characteristics of the power supply, motherboard, processor, RAM, hard drive, I/O devices, and storage devices. You've learned how to select, install, and configure each device.

This chapter focuses on troubleshooting these various hardware subsystems and components. I've gathered troubleshooting techniques and procedures into a single chapter so you can get the full picture of what it's like to have the tools and knowledge in hand to solve any computer hardware-related problem. By the end of this chapter, you should feel confident that you can face a problem with hardware and understand how to zero in on the source of the problem and its solution. The best support technicians are good at preventing a problem from happening in the first place, so in this chapter, you'll learn some tips for protecting a computer from damage.

We begin the chapter with a general strategy for facing a computer problem and a strategy for quickly isolating the source of a problem related to booting up a computer. Then we tackle the problems and solutions for each major hardware component and subsystem.

HOW TO APPROACH A HARDWARE PROBLEM

A+
220-802
4.2

When an end user brings any computer problem to you, begin the troubleshooting process by interviewing the user. When you interview the user, you might want to include these questions:

▲ Can you describe the problem and describe when the problem first started and when it occurs?
▲ Was the computer recently moved?
▲ Was any new hardware or software recently installed?
▲ Was any software recently reconfigured or upgraded?
▲ Did someone else use your computer recently?
▲ Does the computer have a history of similar problems?
▲ Is there important data on the drive that is not backed up?
▲ Can you show me how to reproduce the problem?

After you gather this basic information, you can prioritize what to do and begin diagnosing and addressing the problem. If the computer will not start or starts with errors so that you cannot reach the Windows desktop, setting priorities helps focus your work. For most users, data is the first priority unless they have a recent backup.

A good PC technician builds over time a strong network of resources he or she can count on when solving computer problems. Here are some resources to help you get started with your own list of reliable and time-tested sources of help:

▲ *User manuals* often list error messages and their meanings. They also might contain a troubleshooting section and list any diagnostic tools available.
▲ *The web* can also help you diagnose computer problems. Go to the web site of the product manufacturer, and search for a support forum. It's likely that others have encountered the same problem and posted the question and answer. If you search and cannot find your answer, you can post a new question. Use a search engine such as *www.google.com* to search for the error, the hardware device, the problem, the technology used, and other keywords that can help you find useful information. *Youtube.com* videos might help. Many technicians enjoy sharing what they know online, and the web can be a rich source of all kinds of technical information and advice. Be careful, however. Not all technical advice is correct or well intentioned.
▲ *Chat, telephone, or email technical support* from the hardware and software manufacturers can help you interpret an error message, or it can provide general support in diagnosing a problem. Most technical support is available during working hours by way of an online chat session.
▲ *Manufacturer's diagnostic software* is available for download from the web sites of many hardware device manufacturers. For example, you can download SeaTools for Windows (must be installed in Windows) or SeaTools for DOS (used to create a bootable CD that contains the software) and use the software to diagnose problems with Seagate and Maxtor drives. See Figure 13-1. Search the support section of a manufacturer's web site to find diagnostic software and guidelines for using it.

> **Notes** Always check compatibility between utility software and the operating system with which you plan to use it.

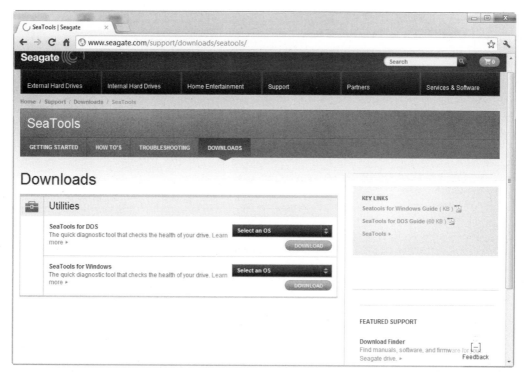

Figure 13-1 Download diagnostic software from a manufacturer's web site

▲ *Technical associates in your organization can help.* Be sure to ask for advice when you're stuck. Also, after making a reasonable and diligent effort to resolve a problem, getting the problem fixed could become more important than resolving it yourself. There comes a time when you might need to turn the problem over to a more experienced technician. (In an organization, this process is called escalating the problem.)

Most PC problems are simple and can be simply solved, but you do need a game plan. That's how Figure 13-2 can help. The flowchart focuses on problems that affect the boot. As we work our way through it, you're eliminating one major computer subsystem after another until you zero in on the problem. After you've discovered the problem, many times the solution is obvious.

As Figure 13-2 indicates, troubleshooting a computer problem is divided into problems that occur during the boot and those that occur after the Windows desktop has successfully loaded. Problems that occur during the boot might happen before Windows starts to load or during Windows startup. Read the flowchart in Figure 13-2 very carefully to get an idea of the symptoms you might be faced with that would cause you to suspect each subsystem. Also, Table 13-1 can help as a general guideline for the primary symptoms and what are likely to be the sources of a problem.

> **💡 A+ Exam Tip** The A+ 220-802 exam might give you a symptom and expect you to select a probable source of a problem from a list of sources. These examples of what can go wrong can help you connect problem sources to symptoms.

A+
220-802
4.2

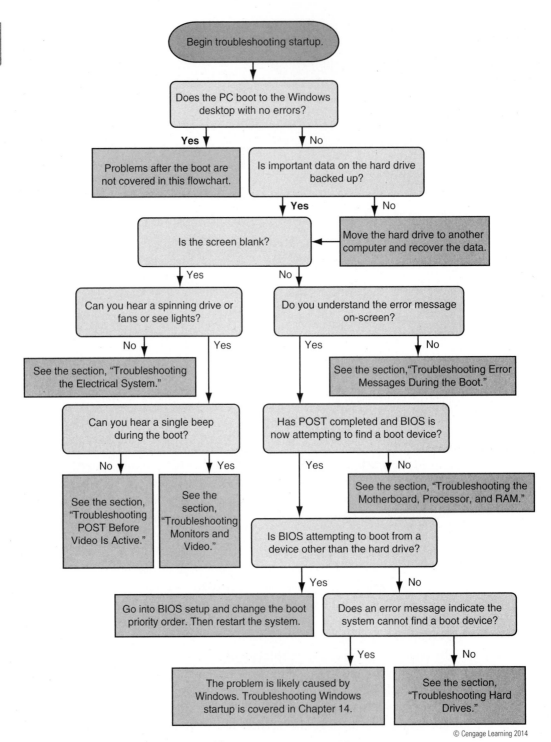

© Cengage Learning 2014

Figure 13-2 Use this flowchart when first facing a computer problem

If the hard drive has important data on it that has not been backed up, your first priority is most likely to recover the data. If a system won't boot from the hard drive, consider removing the drive and installing it as a second drive in a working system. If the file system on the problem drive is intact, you might be able to copy data from the drive to the primary drive in the working system.

A+
220-802
4.2

Symptom or Error Message	What to Do About the Problem
The system shuts down unexpectedly	Try to find out what was happening at the time of the shutdowns to zero in on an application or device causing the problem. Possible sources of the problem are overheating or faulty RAM, motherboard, or processor.
Error messages appear on a blue screen called a *blue screen of death (BSOD)*	Figure 13-3 shows an example of a BSOD error screen. These Windows errors are caused by problems with devices, device drivers, or a corrupted Windows installation. Begin troubleshooting by searching the Microsoft web site for the error message and a description of the problem.
Error messages on a black screen	These error messages, such as the one shown in Figure 13-4, are most likely caused by an error at POST. Begin by troubleshooting the device mentioned in the error message.
The system freezes or locks up	If the system locks up immediately after a BSOD error screen, begin troubleshooting by investigating the error messages on the blue screen. If the system freezes while still displaying the Windows desktop, the problem is most likely caused by Windows or an application.
POST code beeps	Startup BIOS communicates POST errors as a series of beeps before it tests video. Search the web site of the motherboard or BIOS manufacturer to know how to interpret a series of beep codes.
Blank screen when you first power up the computer, and no noise or indicator lights	Is power getting to the system? If power is getting to the computer, address the problem as an electrical problem with the computer. Make sure the power supply is good and power supply connectors are securely connected.
Blank screen when you first power up the computer, and you can hear the fans spinning and see indicator lights	Troubleshoot the video subsystem. Is the monitor turned on? Is the monitor data cable securely connected at both ends? Is the indicator light on the front of the monitor on?
BIOS loses its time and date settings	This problem happens when the CMOS battery fails. Replace the battery.
The system attempts to boot to the wrong boot device	Go into BIOS setup and change the boot device priority order.
Continuous reboots	Continuous reboots can be caused by overheating, a failing processor, motherboard, or RAM, or a corrupted Windows installation. Begin by checking the system for overheating. Is the processor cooler fan working? Go to BIOS setup and check the temperature of the processor.
No power	If you see no lights on the computer case and hear no spinning fans, make sure the surge protector or wall outlet has power. Is the switch on the rear of the case on? Is the dual voltage selector switch set correctly? Are power supply connectors securely connected? Is the power supply bad?

Table 13-1 Symptoms or error messages caused by hardware problems and what to do about them (continues)

13

Symptom or Error Message	What to Do About the Problem
Fans spin but no power gets to other devices	Begin by checking the power supply. Are connectors securely connected? Use a power supply tester to check for correct voltage outputs.
Smoke or burning smell	Consider this a serious electrical problem. Immediately unplug the computer.
Loud whining noise	Most likely the noise is made by the power supply or a failing hard drive. There might be a short. The power supply might be going bad or is underrated for the system.
Intermittent device failures	Failures that come and go might be caused by overheating or failing RAM, the motherboard, processor, or hard drive. Begin by checking the processor temperature for overheating. Then check RAM for errors and run diagnostics on the hard drive.

© Cengage Learning 2014

Table 13-1   Symptoms or error messages caused by hardware problems and what to do about them (continued)

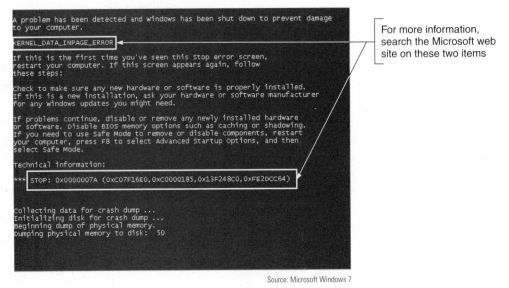

For more information, search the Microsoft web site on these two items

Source: Microsoft Windows 7

Figure 13-3   Search the Microsoft web site for information about a BSOD error

To move the hard drive to a working computer, you don't need to physically install the drive in the drive bay. Open the computer case. Carefully lay the drive on the case and connect a power cord and data cable (see Figure 13-5). Then turn on the PC. While you have the PC turned on, be *very careful* to not touch the drive or touch inside the case. Also, while a tower case is lying on its side like the one in Figure 13-5, don't use the optical drive.

Start the computer and log onto Windows using an Administrator account. (If you don't sign in with an Administrator account, you must provide the password to an Administrator account before you can access the files on the newly connected hard drive.) When Windows finds the new drive, it assigns it a drive letter. Use Windows Explorer to copy files from this drive to the primary hard drive in this system or to another storage media. Then return the drive to the original system and turn your attention to solving the original problem.

A+
220-802
4.2

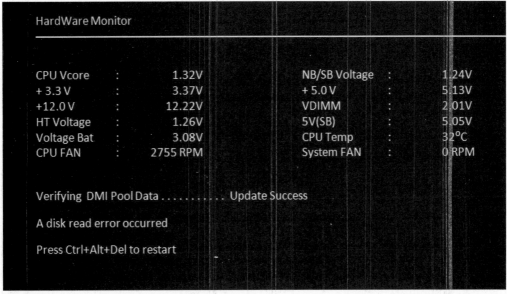

HardWare Monitor

CPU Vcore	:	1.32V	NB/SB Voltage	:	1.24V
+ 3.3 V	:	3.37V	+ 5.0 V	:	5.13V
+12.0 V	:	12.22V	VDIMM	:	2.01V
HT Voltage	:	1.26V	5V(SB)	:	5.05V
Voltage Bat	:	3.08V	CPU Temp	:	32°C
CPU FAN	:	2755 RPM	System FAN	:	0 RPM

Verifying DMI Pool Data . . . . Update Success

A disk read error occurred

Press Ctrl+Alt+Del to restart

Source: Intel

Figure 13-4 A POST error message on a black screen shown early in the boot

© Cengage Learning 2014

Figure 13-5 Move a hard drive to a working computer to recover data on the drive

Notes An easier way to temporarily install a hard drive in a system is to use a USB port. For a PATA hard drive, use a PATA-to-USB converter. The converter kit in Figure 13-6 includes a converter for a PATA desktop and PATA laptop hard drive. Figure 13-7 shows a SATA-to-USB converter kit. The SATA connector can be used for desktop or laptop hard drives because a SATA connector is the same for both. These ATA-to-USB converters are really handy when recovering data and troubleshooting problems with hard drives that refuse to boot.

13

A+
220-802
4.2

© Cengage Learning 2014

Figure 13-6 Use an IDE-to-USB converter for diagnostic testing and to recover data from a failing PATA hard drive

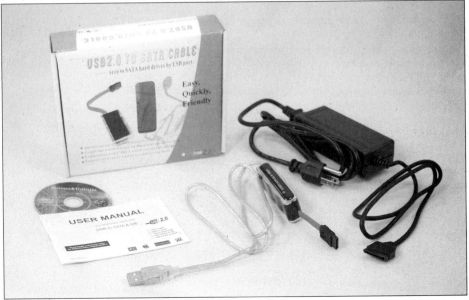

© Cengage Learning 2014

Figure 13-7 Use a USB-to-SATA converter to recover data from a drive using a SATA connector

Now that you have a general idea as to how to troubleshoot hardware errors during the boot, you're ready to look at how to troubleshoot each subsystem that is critical to booting up the computer. We begin with the electrical system.

TROUBLESHOOTING THE ELECTRICAL SYSTEM

Electrical problems can occur before or after the boot and can be consistent or intermittent. Many times PC repair technicians don't recognize the cause of a problem to be electrical because of the intermittent nature of some electrical problems. In these situations, the hard drive, memory, the OS, or even user error might be suspected as the source of the problem and then systematically eliminated before the electrical system is suspected. This section will help you to be aware of symptoms of electrical problems so that you can zero in on the source of an electrical problem as quickly as possible.

A+
220-802
4.2

APPLYING | CONCEPTS   FOUR TROUBLESHOOTING RULES

Here are four important rules that can help you solve many hardware problems:

Rule 1: Check the Obvious and Check Simple Things First

Check for obvious and simple solutions first. Here are some tips:

- Is the external device plugged in and turned on? Are the data cable connections solid at both ends? Is there a wall light switch controlling the power, and is it turned on? Is the power strip you're using plugged in and turned on?
- For expansion cards and memory modules, are they seated solidly in their slots? For sound, is the volume knob turned up? For video, is the monitor getting power, turned on, connected, and is the screen resolution correct?
- Consider the application using the device. For example, if you are having problems trying to use a USB scanner, try scanning using a different application.

Rule 2: Trade Known Good for Suspected Bad

When diagnosing hardware problems, this method works well if you can draw from a group of parts that you know work correctly. Suppose, for example, video does not work. The parts of the video subsystem are the video card, the power cord to the monitor, the cord from the monitor to the PC case, and the monitor itself. Also, don't forget that the video card is inserted into an expansion slot on the motherboard, and the monitor depends on electrical power. As you suspect each of these five components to be bad, you can try them one at a time beginning with the easiest one to replace: the monitor. Trade the monitor for one that you know works. If this theory fails, trade the power cord, trade the cord to the PC video port, move the video card to a new slot, and trade the video card. When you're trading a good component for a suspected bad one, work methodically by eliminating one component at a time.

Rule 3: Trade Suspected Bad for Known Good

An alternate approach works well in certain situations. If you have a working computer that is configured similarly to the one you are troubleshooting (a common situation in many corporate or educational environments), rather than trading good for suspected bad, you can trade suspected bad for good. Take each component that you suspect is bad and install it in the working computer. If the component works on the good computer, then you have eliminated it as a suspect. If the working computer breaks down, then you have probably identified the bad component.

Rule 4: Divide and Conquer

Isolate the problem. In the overall system, remove one hardware or software component after another, until the problem is isolated to a small part of the whole system. As you divide a large problem into smaller components, you can analyze each component separately. You can use one or more of the following to help you divide and conquer on your own system:

- In Windows, stop all nonessential services running in the background to eliminate them as the problem.
- Boot from a bootable CD or DVD to eliminate the OS and startup files on the hard drive as the problem.
- Remove any unnecessary hardware devices, such as a second video card, optical drive, and even the hard drive.

Once down to the essentials, start exchanging components you know are good for those you suspect are bad, until the problem goes away. You don't need to physically remove the optical drive or hard drive from the bays inside the case. Simply disconnect the data cable and the power cable.

13

A+
220-802
4.2

APPLYING | CONCEPTS

Your friend Sharon calls to ask for your help with a computer problem. Her system has been working fine for over a year, but now strange things are happening. Sometimes the system powers down for no apparent reason while she is working, and sometimes Windows locks up. As you read this section, look for clues as to what the problem might be. Also, as you read, think of questions to ask your friend that will help you.

Possible symptoms of a problem with the electrical system are:

▲ The PC appears "dead"—no indicator lights and no spinning drive or fan.
▲ The PC sometimes locks up during booting. After several tries, it boots successfully.
▲ Error codes or beeps occur during booting, but they come and go.
▲ You smell burnt parts or odors. (Definitely not a good sign!)
▲ The PC powers down at unexpected times.
▲ The PC appears dead except you hear a whine coming from the power supply.

Without opening the computer case, the following list contains some questions you can ask and things you can do to solve a problem with the electrical system. The rule of thumb is "try the simple things first." Most PC problems have simple solutions.

▲ If you smell any burnt parts or odors, don't try to turn the system on. Identify the component that is fried and replace it.
▲ When you first plug up power to a system and hear a whine coming from the power supply, the power supply might be inadequate for the system or there might be a short. Don't press the power button to start up the system. Unplug the power cord so that the power supply will not be damaged. The next step is to open the case and search for a short. If you don't find a short, consider upgrading the power supply.
▲ Is the power cord plugged in? If it is plugged into a power strip or surge suppressor, is the device turned on and also plugged in?
▲ Is the power outlet controlled by a wall switch? If so, is the switch turned on?
▲ Are any cable connections loose?
▲ Is the circuit breaker blown? Is the house circuit overloaded?
▲ Are all switches on the system turned on? Computer? Monitor? Surge suppressor or UPS (uninterruptible power supply)?
▲ Is there a possibility the system has overheated? If so, wait a while and try again. If the system comes on, but later turns itself off, you might need additional cooling fans inside the unit. How to solve problems with overheating is covered later in the chapter.
▲ Older computers might be affected by electromagnetic interference (EMI). Check for sources of electrical or magnetic interference such as fluorescent lighting or an electric fan or copier sitting near the computer case.

The next step is to open the computer case and then do the following:

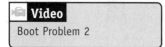
Video
Boot Problem 2

▲ Turn off the computer, unplug it, press the power button to drain residual power, and open the case. Check all power connections from the power supply to the motherboard and drives. Also, some cases require the case's front panel be in place before the power-on button will work. Are all cards securely seated?

A+
220-802
4.2

▲ If you smell burnt parts, carefully search for shorts and frayed and burnt wires. Disassemble the parts until you find the one that is damaged.

▲ If you suspect the power supply is bad, test it with a power supply tester.

> ⚡ **Caution** Before opening the case of a brand name computer, such as a Gateway or Dell, consider the warranty. If the system is still under warranty, sometimes the warranty is voided if the case is opened. If the warranty prevents you from opening the case, you might need to return the system to a manufacturer's service center for repairs.

PROBLEMS THAT COME AND GO

If a system boots successfully to the Windows desktop, you still might have a power system problem. Some problems are intermittent; that is, they come and go. Generally, intermittent problems are more difficult to solve than a dead system. There can be many causes of intermittent problems, such as an inadequate power supply, overheating, and devices and components damaged by ESD. Here are some symptoms that might indicate an intermittent problem with the electrical system after the boot:

▲ The computer stops or hangs for no reason. Sometimes it might even reboot itself.

▲ Memory errors appear intermittently.

▲ Data is written incorrectly to the hard drive.

▲ The keyboard stops working at odd times.

▲ The motherboard fails or is damaged.

▲ The power supply overheats and becomes hot to the touch.

▲ The power supply fan whines and becomes very noisy or stops.

Here is what to do to eliminate the electrical system as the source of an intermittent problem:

1. ***Consider the power supply is inadequate.*** If the power supply is grossly inadequate, it will whine when you first plug up the power. If you have just installed new devices that are drawing additional power, follow the directions given in Chapter 2 to make sure the wattage rating of the power supply is adequate for the system.

   You can also test the system to make sure you don't have power problems by making all the devices in your system work at the same time. For instance, you can make two hard drives and the DVD drive work at the same time by copying files from one hard drive to the other while playing a movie on the DVD. If the new drive and the other drives each work independently, but data errors occur when all work at the same time, suspect a shortage of electrical power.

2. ***Suspect the power supply is faulty.*** You can test it using either a power supply tester (the easier method) or a multimeter (the more tedious method). However, know that a power supply that gives correct voltages when you measure it might still be the source of problems because power problems can be intermittent. Also be aware that an ATX power supply monitors the range of voltages provided to the motherboard and halts the motherboard if voltages are inadequate. Therefore, if the power supply appears "dead," your best action is to replace it.

3. ***The power supply fan might not work.*** Don't operate the PC if the fan does not work because computers without cooling fans can quickly overheat. Usually just before a fan stops working, it hums or whines, especially when the PC is first turned on. If this has just happened, replace the power supply. After you replace the power supply, if the new fan does not work, you have to dig deeper to find the source of the problem.

13

You can now assume the problem wasn't the original fan. A short somewhere else in the system drawing too much power might cause the problem. To troubleshoot a non-functional fan, which might be a symptom of another problem and not a problem of the fan itself, follow these steps:

a. Turn off the power and remove all power cord connections to all components except the motherboard. Turn the power back on. If the fan works, the problem is with one of the systems you disconnected, not with the power supply, the fan, or the motherboard.

b. Turn off the power and reconnect one card or drive at a time until you identify the device with the short.

c. If the fan does not work when all devices except the motherboard are disconnected, the problem is the motherboard or the power supply. Because you have already replaced the power supply, you can assume the problem is the motherboard and it's time to replace it.

POWER PROBLEMS WITH THE MOTHERBOARD

A short might occur if some component on the motherboard makes improper contact with the chassis. This short can seriously damage the motherboard. For some cases, check for missing standoffs (small plastic or metal spacers that hold the motherboard a short distance away from the bottom of the case). A missing standoff most often causes these improper connections. Also check for loose standoffs or screws under the board that might be touching a wire on the bottom of the board and causing a short.

Shorts in the circuits on the motherboard might also cause problems. Look for damage on the bottom of the motherboard. These circuits are coated with plastic, and quite often damage is difficult to spot. Also look for burned-out capacitors that are spotted brown or corroded. You'll see examples of burned-out capacitors later in the chapter.

APPLYING | CONCEPTS

Back to Sharon's computer problem. Here are some questions that will help you identify the source of the problem:

- ◢ Have you added new devices to your system? (These new devices might be drawing too much power from an overworked power supply.)
- ◢ Have you moved your computer recently? (It might be sitting beside a heat vent or electrical equipment.)
- ◢ Does the system power down or hang after you have been working for some time? (This symptom might have more than one cause, such as overheating or a power supply, processor, memory, or motherboard about to fail.)
- ◢ Has the computer case been opened recently? (Someone working inside the case might not have used a ground bracelet and components are now failing because of ESD damage.)
- ◢ Are case vents free so that air can flow? (The case might be close to a curtain covering the vents.)

Intermittent problems like the one Sharon described are often heat related. If the system only hangs but does not power off, the problem might be caused by faulty memory or bad software, but because it actually powers down, you can assume the problem is related to power or heat.

If Sharon tells you that the system powers down after she's been working for several hours, you can probably assume overheating. Check that first. If that's not the problem, the next thing to do is replace the power supply.

> ⚡ **Caution** Never replace a damaged motherboard with a good one without first testing or replacing the power supply. You don't want to subject another good board to possible damage.

PROBLEMS WITH OVERHEATING

A+
220-802
4.2

As a PC repair technician, you're sure to eventually face problems with computers overheating. Overheating can happen as soon as you turn on the computer or after the computer has been working a while. Overheating can cause intermittent errors, the system to hang, or components to fail or not last as long as they normally would. (Overheating can significantly shorten the lifespan of the CPU and memory.) Overheating happens for many reasons, including improper installations of the CPU cooler or fans, overclocking, poor air flow inside the case, an underrated power supply, a component going bad, or the computer's environment (for example, heat or dust).

Here are some symptoms that a system is overheating:

- ▲ The system hangs or freezes at odd times or freezes just a few moments after the boot starts.
- ▲ A Windows BSOD error occurs during the boot.
- ▲ You cannot hear a fan running or the fan makes a whining sound.
- ▲ You cannot feel air being pulled into or out of the case.

If you suspect overheating, know that processors can sense their operating temperatures and report that information to BIOS. You can view that information in BIOS setup. To protect the expensive processor and other components, you can also purchase a temperature sensor. The sensor plugs into a power connection coming from the power supply and mounts on the side of the case or in a drive bay. The sensor sounds an alarm when the inside of the case becomes too hot. To decide which temperature sensor to buy, use one recommended by the case manufacturer. You can also install utility software that can monitor the system temperatures. For example, SpeedFan by Alfredo Comparetti is freeware that can monitor fan speeds and temperatures (see Figure 13-8). A good web site to download the freeware is *www.filehippo.com/download_speedfan*.

Here are some simple things you can do to solve an overheating problem:

1. If the system refuses to boot or hangs after a period of activity, suspect overheating. Immediately after the system hangs, go into BIOS setup and find the CPU screen that reports the temperature. The temperature should not exceed 38 degrees C.

2. Use compressed air, a blower, or an antistatic vacuum to remove dust from the power supply, the vents over the entire computer, and the processor cooler fan (see Figure 13-9). Excessive dust insulates components and causes them to overheat.

3. Check airflow inside the case. Are all fans running? You might need to replace a fan. Is there an empty fan slot on the rear of the case? If so, install a case fan in the slot (see Figure 13-10). Orient the fan so that it blows air out of the case. The power cord to the fan can connect to a fan header on the motherboard or to a power connector coming directly from the power supply.

4. If there are other fan slots on the side or front of the case, you can also install fans in these slots. However, don't install more fans than the case is designed to use.

5. Can the side of the case hold a chassis air guide that guides outside air to the processor? If it has a slot for the guide and the guide is missing, install one. However, don't install a guide that obstructs the CPU cooler. How to install an air guide is covered later in this section.

6. A case is generally designed for optimal airflow when slot openings on the front and rear of the case are covered and when the case cover is securely in place. To improve airflow, replace missing faceplates over empty drive bays and replace missing slot covers over empty expansion slots. See Figure 13-11.

13

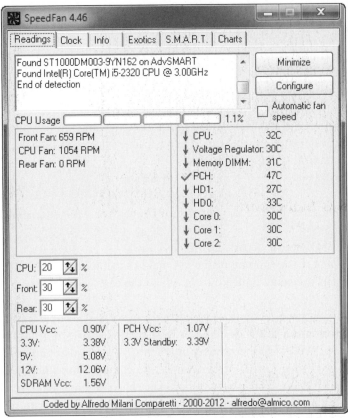

Figure 13-8 SpeedFan monitors fan speeds and system temperatures

Figure 13-9 Dust in this cooler fan can cause the fan to fail and the processor to overheat

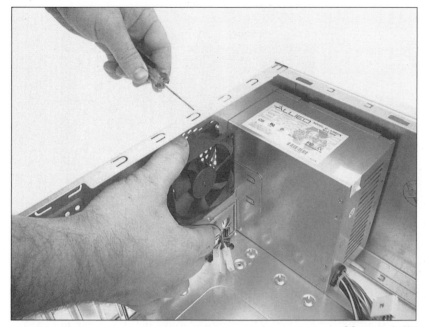

© Cengage Learning 2014

Figure 13-10 Install one exhaust fan on the rear of the case to help pull air through the case

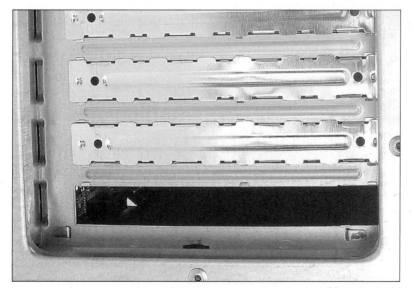

© Cengage Learning 2014

Figure 13-11 For optimum airflow, don't leave empty expansion slots and bays uncovered

7. Are cables in the way of airflow? Use tie wraps to secure cables and cords so that they don't block airflow across the processor or get in the way of fans turning. Figure 13-12 shows the inside of a case where cables are tied up and neatly out of the way of air flow from the front to the rear of the case.

8. A case needs some room to breathe. Place it so there are at least a few inches of space on both sides and the top of the case. If the case is sitting on carpet, put it on a computer stand so that air can circulate under the case and also to reduce carpet dust inside the case. Many

A+
220-802
4.2

© Cengage Learning 2014

Figure 13-12 Use cable ties to hold cables out of the way of fans and airflow

© Cengage Learning 2014

Figure 13-13 Keep a tower case off carpet to allow air to flow into the bottom air vent

cases have a vent on the bottom front of the case and carpet can obstruct airflow into this vent (see Figure 13-13). Make sure drapes are not hanging too close to fan openings.

9. Verify the cooler is connected properly to the processor. If it doesn't fit well, the system might not boot and certainly the processor will overheat. If the cooler is not tightly connected to the motherboard and processor or the cooler fan is not working,

A+
220-802
4.2

the processor will quickly overheat as soon as the computer is turned on. Has thermal compound been installed between the cooler and processor?

10. After you close the case, leave your system off for at least 30 minutes. When you power up the computer again, let it run for 10 minutes, go into BIOS setup, check the temperature readings, and reboot. Next, let your system run until it shuts down. Power it up again and check the temperature in BIOS setup again. A significant difference in this reading and the first one you took after running the computer for 10 minutes indicates an overheating problem.

11. Check BIOS setup to see if the processor is being overclocked. Overclocking can cause a system to overheat. Try restoring the processor and system bus frequencies to default values.

12. Have too many peripherals been installed inside the case? Is the case too small for all these peripherals? Larger tower cases are better designed for good airflow than smaller slimline cases. Also, when installing cards, try to leave an empty slot between each card for better airflow. The same goes for drives. Try not to install a group of drives in adjacent drive bays. For better airflow, leave empty bays between drives. Take a close look at Figure 13-12, where you can see space between each drive installed in the system.

13. Flash BIOS to update the firmware on the motherboard. How to flash BIOS is covered in Chapter 4.

14. Thermal compound should last for years, but eventually it will harden and need replacing. If the system is several years old, replace the thermal compound.

> 💡 **A+ Exam Tip** The A+ 220-802 exam expects you to recognize that a given symptom is possibly power or heat related.

If you try the above list of things to do and still have an overheating problem, it's time to move on to more drastic solutions. Consider the case design is not appropriate for good air-flow, and the problem might be caused by poor air circulation inside the case. The power supply fan in ATX cases blows air out of the case, pulling outside air from the vents in the front of the case across the processor to help keep it cool. Another exhaust fan is usually installed on the back of the case to help the power supply fan pull air through the case. In addition, most processors require a cooler with a fan installed on top of the processor. Figure 13-14 shows a good arrangement of vents and fans for proper airflow and a poor arrangement.

13

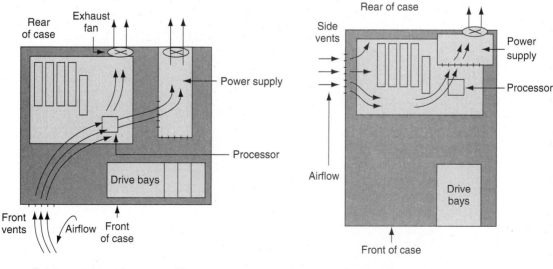

Good arrangement for proper airflow   Poor arrangement for proper airflow

Figure 13-14 Vents and fans need to be arranged for best airflow

A+
220-802
4.2

For better ventilation, use a power supply that has vents on the bottom and front of the power supply. Note in Figure 13-15 airflow is coming into the bottom of the power supply because of these bottom vents. The power supply in Figure 13-10 has vents only on the front and not on the bottom. Compare that to the power supply in Figure 13-15, which has vents on both the front and bottom.

An intake fan on the front of the case might help pull air into the case. Intel recommends you use a front intake fan for high-end systems, but AMD says a front fan for ATX systems is not necessary. Check with the processor and case manufacturers for specific instructions as to the placement of fans and what type of fan and heat sink to use.

Intel and AMD both recommend a **chassis air guide (CAG)** as part of the case design. This air guide is a round air duct that helps to pull and direct fresh air from outside the case to the cooler and processor (see Figure 13-16). The guide should reach inside the case

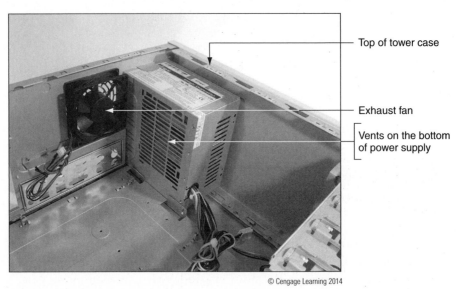

Top of tower case

Exhaust fan

Vents on the bottom of power supply

© Cengage Learning 2014

Figure 13-15   This power supply has vents on the bottom to provide better airflow inside the case

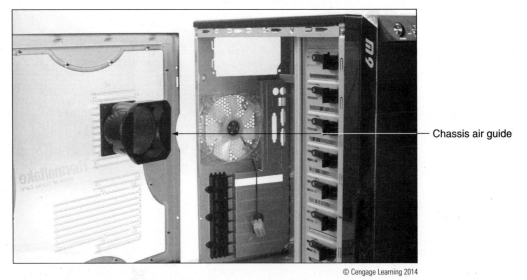

Chassis air guide

© Cengage Learning 2014

Figure 13-16   Use a chassis air guide to direct outside air over the cooler

very close to the cooler, but not touch it. Intel recommends the clearance be no greater than 20 mm and no less than 12 mm. If the guide obstructs the cooler, you can remove the guide, but optimum airflow will not be achieved.

Be careful when trying to solve an overheating problem. Excessive heat can damage the CPU and the motherboard. Never operate a system if the case fan, power-supply fan, or cooler fan is not working.

TROUBLESHOOTING POST BEFORE VIDEO IS ACTIVE

Error messages on the screen indicate that video and the electrical system are working. If you observe that power is getting to the system (you see lights and hear fans or beeps) but the screen is blank, turn off the system and turn it back on and carefully listen to any beep codes or BIOS speech messages. Recall that, before BIOS checks video, POST reports any error messages as beep codes. When a PC boots, one beep or no beep indicates that all is well after POST. If you hear more than one beep, look up the beep code in the motherboard or BIOS documentation or on the web sites of these manufacturers. Each BIOS manufacturer has its own beep codes, and Table 13-2 lists the more common meanings.

Video
Beep Codes

Beeps During POST	Description
One short beep or no beep	The computer passed all POST tests
1 long and 2 short beeps	Award BIOS: A video problem, no video card, bad video memory Intel BIOS: A video problem
Continuous short beeps	Award BIOS: A memory error Intel BIOS: A loose card or short
1 long and 1 short beep	Intel BIOS: Motherboard problem
1 long and 3 short beeps	Intel BIOS: A video problem
3 long beeps	Intel BIOS: A keyboard controller problem
Continuous 2 short beeps and then a pause	Intel BIOS: A video card problem
Continuous 3 short beeps and then a pause	Intel BIOS: A memory error
8 beeps followed by a system shutdown	Intel BIOS: The system has overheated
Continuous high and low beeps	Intel BIOS: CPU problem

© Cengage Learning 2014

Table 13-2 Common beep codes and their meanings for Intel and Award BIOS

TROUBLESHOOTING ERROR MESSAGES DURING THE BOOT

If video and the electrical systems are working, then most boot problems show up as an error message displayed on-screen. These error messages that occur before Windows starts to load apply to hardware components that are required to boot the system. Some possible error messages are listed in Table 13-3, along with their meanings. For other error messages, look in your motherboard user guide or on the manufacturer's web site. You can also search the web on the motherboard brand and model and the error message.

A+
220-802
4.2

Error Message Before Windows Starts	Meaning of the Error Message
CMOS battery low	The CMOS battery needs replacing.
CMOS checksum bad	CMOS RAM might be corrupted. Run BIOS setup and reset BIOS to default settings. If the problem occurs again, try flashing the BIOS.
Memory size decreased	Startup BIOS recognized that the amount of installed RAM is less than that of the previous boot. A memory module might be bad. Begin troubleshooting memory.
Processor thermal trip error	The processor overheated and the system has restarted.
Intruder detection error	An intrusion detection device installed on the motherboard has detected that the computer case was opened.
Overclocking failed. Please enter setup to reconfigure your system.	Overclocking should be discontinued. However, this error might not be related to overclocking; it can occur when the power supply is failing.
No boot device available Hard drive not found Fixed disk error Invalid boot disk Inaccessible boot device or drive Invalid drive specification	Startup BIOS did not find a device to use to load the operating system. Make sure the boot device priority order is correct in BIOS setup. Then begin troubleshooting the hard drive.
Missing BOOTMGR Missing NTLDR Missing operating system Error loading operating system	The Windows program needed to start Windows is missing or corrupted. This program is called the OS boot manager program. How to trouble-shoot Windows startup is covered in Chapter 14.

© Cengage Learning 2014

Table 13-3   Error messages that occur before Windows starts

If the Windows boot manager program has problems loading Windows, it gives a different set of error messages than the ones listed in Table 13-3. For example, a Windows error that occurred early in the boot is shown in Figure 13-17.

When these errors are related to hardware that is necessary for the boot, they are likely to be a BSOD error message on a blue screen such as the one shown earlier in Figure 13-3. Sometimes Windows is configured to restart immediately after a BSOD. This setting can lead to continuous reboots, and the error message might fly by so fast you can't read it. To disable these automatic restarts, press **F8** as Windows starts up. The Advanced Boot Options menu appears. Figure 13-18 shows the Windows 7 menu; the Vista and XP menus are similar.

Select **Disable automatic restart on system failure**. When you restart Windows, the error message stays on-screen long enough for you to read it. Search the Microsoft web sites (*support.microsoft.com* and *technet.microsoft.com*) for information about the hardware component causing the problem and what to do about it. BSOD errors might apply to the motherboard, video card, RAM, processor, hard drive, or some other device for which Windows is trying to load device drivers.

A+
220-802
4.2

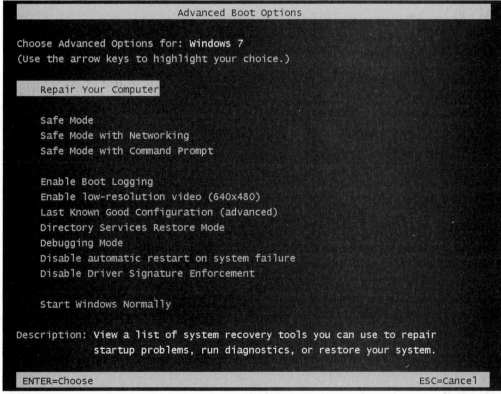

```
                         Windows Boot Manager

Windows failed to start. A recent hardware or software change might be the
cause. To fix the problem:

  1. Insert your Windows installation disc and restart your computer.
  2. Choose your language settings, and then click "Next."
  3. Click "Repair your computer."

If you do not have this disc, contact your system administrator or computer
manufacturer for assistance.


    File: \windows\system32\boot\winload.exe


    Status: 0xc000035a


    Info: Attempting to load a 64-bit application, however this CPU is not
          compatible with 64-bit mode.




ENTER=Continue                                                    ESC=Exit
```

Source: Microsoft Windows 7

Figure 13-17 A Windows error early in the boot that is related to software

13

```
                         Advanced Boot Options

Choose Advanced Options for: Windows 7
(Use the arrow keys to highlight your choice.)

  Repair Your Computer

    Safe Mode
    Safe Mode with Networking
    Safe Mode with Command Prompt

    Enable Boot Logging
    Enable low-resolution video (640x480)
    Last Known Good Configuration (advanced)
    Directory Services Restore Mode
    Debugging Mode
    Disable automatic restart on system failure
    Disable Driver Signature Enforcement


    Start Windows Normally

Description: View a list of system recovery tools you can use to repair
             startup problems, run diagnostics, or restore your system.

ENTER=Choose                                                      ESC=Cancel
```

Source: Microsoft Windows 7

Figure 13-18 Press F8 during the boot to see the Advanced Boot Options menu

TROUBLESHOOTING THE MOTHERBOARD, PROCESSOR, AND RAM

A+
220-802
4.2

The field replaceable units (FRUs) on a motherboard are the processor, the processor cooler assembly, RAM, and the CMOS battery. Also, the motherboard itself is an FRU. As you troubleshoot the motherboard and discover that some component is not working, such as a network port, you might be able to disable that component in BIOS setup and install a card to take its place.

> **A+ Exam Tip** The A+ 220-802 exam expects you to know how to troubleshoot problems with motherboards, processors, and RAM.

When you suspect a bad component, a good troubleshooting technique is to substitute a known-good component for the one you suspect is bad. Be cautious here. A friend once had a computer that would not boot. He replaced the hard drive, with no change. He replaced the motherboard next. The computer booted up with no problem; he was delighted, until it failed again. Later he discovered that a faulty power supply had damaged his original motherboard. When he traded the bad one for a good one, the new motherboard also got zapped! If you suspect problems with the power supply, check the voltage coming from the power supply before putting in a new motherboard.

Symptoms that a motherboard, processor, or memory module is failing can appear as:

- The system begins to boot but then powers down.
- An error message is displayed during the boot. Investigate this message.
- The system becomes unstable, hangs, or freezes at odd times. (This symptom can have multiple causes, including a failing power supply, RAM, hard drive, motherboard or processor, Windows errors, and overheating.)
- Intermittent Windows or hard drive errors occur.
- Components on the motherboard or devices connected to it don't work.

Remember the troubleshooting principle to check the simple things first. The motherboard and processor are expensive and time consuming to replace. Unless you're certain the problem is one of these two components, don't replace either until you first eliminate other components as the source of the problem.

If you can boot the system, follow these steps to eliminate Windows, software, RAM, BIOS settings, and other software and hardware components as the source of the problem:

1. The problem might be a virus. If you can boot the system, run a current version of antivirus software to check for viruses.

2. A memory module might be failing. In Windows 7/Vista, use the **Memory Diagnostics** tool to test memory. Even if Windows 7/Vista is not installed, you can still run the tool by booting the system from the Windows setup DVD. How to use the Memory Diagnostics tool is coming up later in the chapter.

A+
220-802
4.2

Notes Other than the Windows 7/Vista Memory Diagnostics tool, you can use the Memtest86 utility to test installed memory modules. Check the site *www.memtest86.com* to download this program.

3. Suspect the problem is caused by an application or by Windows. In Windows, the best tool to check for potential hardware problems is Device Manager.

4. In Windows, download and install any Windows updates or patches. These updates might solve a hardware or application problem.

Notes Another useful Windows tool for troubleshooting hardware problems that reports logs of hardware and applications errors is Event Viewer. For a thorough discussion of how to use Event Viewer, see Chapter 11. A Real Problems, Real Solutions activity at the end of this chapter gives you experience using Event Viewer.

5. Ask yourself what has changed since the problem began. If the problem began immediately after installing a new device or application, uninstall the device or applications.

6. A system that does not have enough RAM can sometimes appear to be unstable. Using the System window, find out how much RAM is installed, and compare that to the recommended amounts. Consider upgrading RAM.

7. The BIOS might be corrupted or have wrong settings. Check BIOS setup. Have settings been tampered with? Is the system bus speed set incorrectly or is it overclocked? Reset BIOS setup to restore default settings.

8. Disable any quick booting features in BIOS so that you get a thorough report of POST. Then look for errors reported on the screen during the boot.

9. Following the procedures in Chapter 4, flash BIOS to update the firmware on the board.

10. Look on the CD that came bundled with the motherboard. It might have diagnostic tests on it that might identify a problem with the motherboard.

11. Update all drivers of motherboard components that are not working. For example, if the USB ports are not working, try updating the USB drivers with those downloaded from the motherboard manufacturer's web site. This process can also update the chipset drivers. For example, for one Intel motherboard, Figure 13-19 shows updates available for the board.

12. If an onboard port or connector isn't working, but the motherboard is stable, follow these steps:

    a. Verify the problem is not with the device using the port. Try moving the device to another port on the same computer or move the device to another computer. If it works there, return it to this port. The problem might have been a bad connection.

    b. Go into BIOS setup and verify the port is enabled.

    c. Check Device Manager and verify Windows recognizes the port with no errors. For example, Device Manager shown in Figure 13-20 reports a problem with the onboard Wi-Fi adapter. Uninstall and reinstall the drivers for the device using the port.

    d. Update the motherboard drivers for this port from the motherboard manufacturer's web site.

    e. If you have a loop-back plug, use it to test the port.

    f. If the problem is still not solved, disable the port in BIOS setup and install an expansion card to provide the same type of port or connector.

13

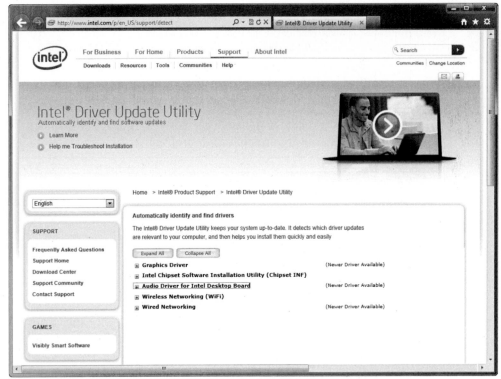

Source: Intel at www.intel.com

Figure 13-19 Update all motherboard drivers using the motherboard manufacturer's web site

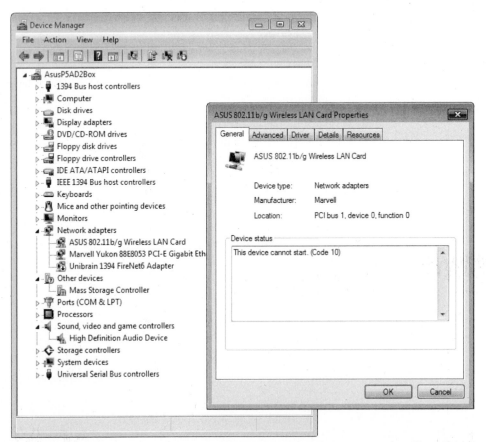

Source: Microsoft Windows 7

Figure 13-20 Device Manager reports a problem with an onboard port

A+
220-802
4.2

13. Suspect the problem is caused by a failing hard drive. How to troubleshoot a failing drive is covered later in the chapter.

14. Suspect the problem is caused by overheating. How to check for overheating is covered earlier in the chapter.

15. Search the support section of the web sites of the motherboard and processor manufacturers for things to do and try. Then do a general search of the web using a search engine such as *www.google.com*. Search on the error message, symptom, motherboard model, processor model, or other text related to the problem. Most likely, you'll find a forum where someone else has posted the same problem, and others have posted a solution.

16. Verify the installed processor is supported by the motherboard. Perhaps someone has installed the wrong processor.

APPLYING | CONCEPTS HOW TO USE WINDOWS MEMORY DIAGNOSTICS

Errors with memory are often difficult to diagnose because they can appear intermittently and might be mistaken as application errors, user errors, or other hardware component errors. Sometimes these errors cause the system to hang, a blue screen error might occur, or the system continues to function with applications giving errors or data getting corrupted. You can quickly identify a problem with memory or eliminate memory as the source of a problem by using the Windows 7/Vista Memory Diagnostics tool. It tests memory for errors and works before Windows is loaded and can be used on computers that don't have Windows 7 or Vista installed. Use one of these three methods to start the utility:

▲ *Method 1:* In a command prompt window, enter **mdsched.exe** and press **Enter**. A dialog box appears (see Figure 13-21) asking if you want to run the test now or on the next restart.

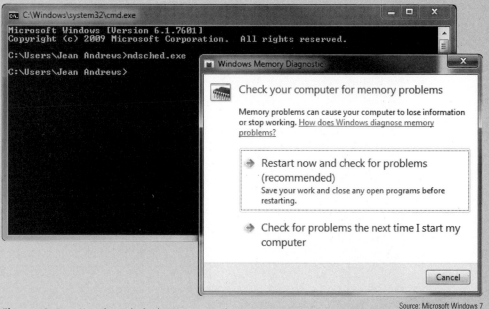

Source: Microsoft Windows 7

Figure 13-21 Use the mdsched.exe command to test memory

13

A+
220-802
4.2

▲ *Method 2:* If you cannot load the Windows desktop, press the Spacebar during the boot. The Windows Boot Manager screen appears (see Figure 13-22). Select **Windows Memory Diagnostic** and press **Enter**.

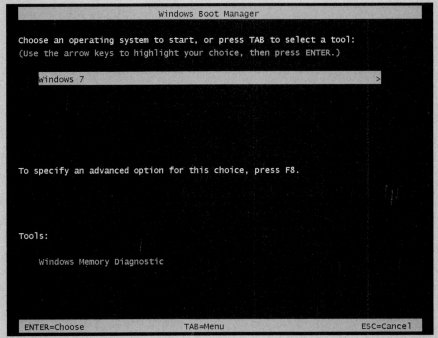

Source: Microsoft Windows 7

Figure 13-22   Force the Windows Boot Manager menu to display by pressing the Spacebar during the boot

▲ *Method 3:* If you cannot boot from the hard drive, boot the computer from the Windows setup DVD. On the opening screen, select your language. On the next screen (see Figure 13-23), click **Repair your computer**. In the next box, select the Windows installation

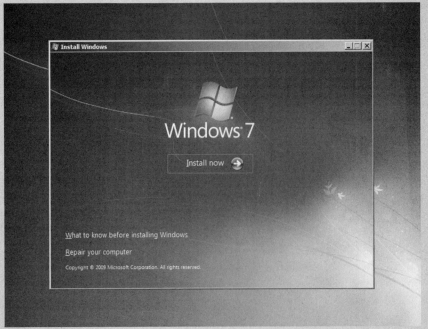

Source: Microsoft Windows 7

Figure 13-23   Opening menu when you boot from the Windows 7 setup DVD

A+
220-802
4.2

to repair. The System Recovery Options window appears (see Figure 13-24). Click **Windows Memory Diagnostic** and follow the directions on-screen.

If the tool reports memory errors, replace all memory modules installed on the motherboard.

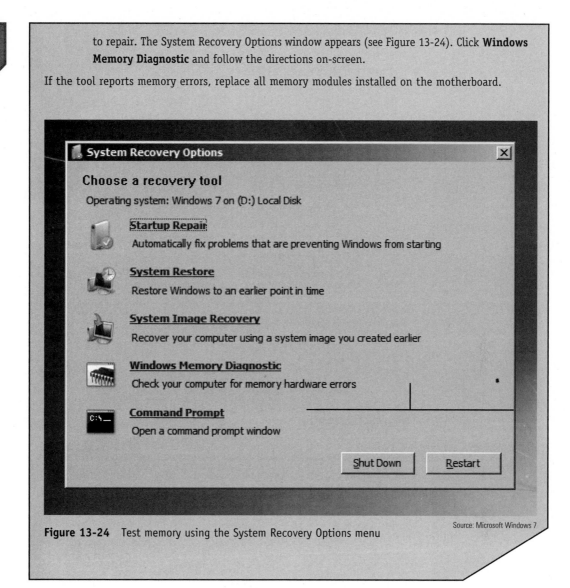

Figure 13-24 Test memory using the System Recovery Options menu

Source: Microsoft Windows 7

13

APPLYING | CONCEPTS USE DEVICE MANAGER TO DELETE THE DRIVER STORE

One thing you can do to solve a problem with a device is to uninstall and reinstall the device. When you first install a device, Windows stores a copy of the driver software in a **driver store**. When you uninstall the device, you can tell Windows to also delete the driver store. If you don't delete the driver store, Windows uses it when you install the device again. That's why the second time you install the same device Windows does not ask you for the location of the drivers. Windows might also use the driver store to automatically install the device on the next reboot without your involvement.

All this is convenient unless there is a problem with the driver store. To get a true fresh start with an installation, you need to delete the driver store. To do that in Device Manager, open the **Properties** box for the device, click the **Driver** tab, and click **Uninstall**. In the Confirm Device Uninstall box (see Figure 13-25), check **Delete the driver software for this device**, and click **OK**. The installed drivers and the driver store are both deleted. When you reinstall the device, you'll need the drivers on CD or downloaded from the web.

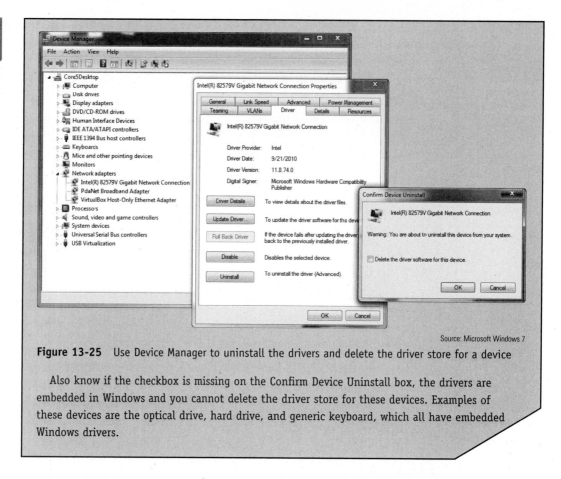

Source: Microsoft Windows 7

Figure 13-25   Use Device Manager to uninstall the drivers and delete the driver store for a device

Also know if the checkbox is missing on the Confirm Device Uninstall box, the drivers are embedded in Windows and you cannot delete the driver store for these devices. Examples of these devices are the optical drive, hard drive, and generic keyboard, which all have embedded Windows drivers.

We're working our way through what to do when the system locks up, gives errors, or generally appears unstable. After you have checked Windows and BIOS settings and searched the web for help and still not identified the source of the problem, it's time to open the case and check inside. As you do so, be sure to use an antistatic bracelet and follow other procedures to protect the system against ESD. With the case open, follow these steps:

1. Check that all the power and data cables the system is using are securely connected. Try reseating all expansion cards and DIMM modules.

2. Look for physical damage on the motherboard. Look for frayed traces on the bottom of the board or brown or burnt capacitors on the board.

3. Reduce the system to essentials. Remove any unnecessary hardware, such as expansion cards, and then watch to see if the problem goes away. If the problem goes away, replace one component at a time until the problem returns and you have identified the component causing the trouble.

4. Try using a POST diagnostic card. It might offer you a clue as to which component is giving a problem.

5. Suspect the problem is caused by a failing power supply. It's less expensive and easier to replace than the motherboard or processor, so eliminate it before you move on to the motherboard or processor.

6. Exchange the processor.

7. Exchange the motherboard, but before you do, measure the voltage output of the power supply or simply replace it, in case it is producing too much power and has damaged the board.

A+ 220-802 4.2

APPLYING | CONCEPTS

Jessica complained to Wally, her PC support technician, that Windows was occasionally giving errors, data would get corrupted, or an application would not work as it should. At first, Wally suspected Jessica might need a little more training in how to open and close an application or save a file, but he discovered user error was not the problem. He tried reinstalling the application software Jessica most often used, and even reinstalled Windows, but the problems persisted.

> **Notes** Catastrophic errors (errors that cause the system to not boot or a device to not work) are much easier to resolve than intermittent errors (errors that come and go).

Then he began to suspect a hardware problem. Carefully examining the motherboard revealed the source of the problem: failing capacitors. Look carefully at Figure 13-26 and you can see five bad capacitors with bulging and discolored heads. (Know that sometimes a leaking capacitor can also show crusty corrosion at the base of the capacitor.) When Wally replaced the motherboard, the problems went away.

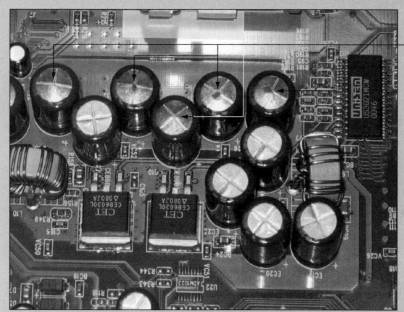

Bad capacitors

© Cengage Learning 2014

Figure 13-26 These five bad capacitors have bulging and discolored heads

PROBLEMS WITH INSTALLATIONS

If you have just installed a new processor, DIMM, or other component and the system does not boot, do the following:

1. When troubleshooting an installation, it's easy to forget to check the simple things first. Are the system and monitor plugged in and turned on? Are the monitor, keyboard, and mouse connected to the system? Is the case front cover securely in place?

2. As you work inside the case, don't forget to use your antistatic bracelet. Open the case and check the installation of the new component:

   ◢ When installing DIMMs, verify each DIMM is securely seated in the memory socket. Make sure a new DIMM sits in the socket at the same height as other modules and clips on each side of the slot are in latched positions.

A+
220-802
4.2

▲ For a new processor, did you install thermal compound between the processor and the heat sink? Is the cooler securely fastened to the frame on the motherboard? If the cooler and thermal compound are not installed correctly, the CPU can overheat during the boot, causing BIOS to immediately power down the system. Is the power cable from the cooler fan connected to the correct fan header on the motherboard? Look in the motherboard documentation for the correct header.

▲ For all types of installations, did other components or connectors become dislodged during the installation? Check memory modules, the P1 power connector, the 4-pin CPU auxiliary power connector, hard drive connectors, and auxiliary PCIe power connectors.

3. Try rebooting the system. If you still have a problem, verify you have installed a component that is compatible with the system. For a processor, double-check that the motherboard supports the processor installed. For memory, check that you have the right memory modules supported by your motherboard. Can your OS support all the memory installed?

4. For a processor installation, remove the processor from its socket and look for bent or damaged pins or lands on the socket and processor. For memory, remove the newly installed memory and check whether the error message disappears. Try the memory in different sockets. Try installing the new memory without the old installed. If the new memory works without the old, the problem is that the modules are not compatible.

5. Consider whether the case does not have enough cooling. Is a case fan installed and running at the rear of the case? Are cables and cords tied up out of the way of airflow?

6. For memory modules or expansion cards, clean the edge connectors with a soft cloth or contact cleaner. Blow or vacuum dust from the slot. Don't touch the edge connectors or the slot.

7. When upgrading a processor, reinstall the old processor, flash BIOS, and then try the new processor again.

Here are additional things to check if you have just installed a new motherboard that is not working:

1. If the system can boot into Windows, install all motherboard drivers on the CD that came bundled with the board.

2. Open the computer case and check the following:

▲ Study the motherboard documentation and verify all connections are correct. Most likely this is the problem. Remember the Power Switch lead from the front of the case must be connected to the header on the motherboard. Check all connectors from the front of the case to the front panel header.

▲ Is the BIOS jumper group set for a normal boot?

▲ Are cards seated firmly in their slots? Is the screw in place that holds the card to the back of the case?

▲ Are DIMMs seated firmly in their slots? Remove the DIMMs and reseat them.

▲ Are all I/O cables from the front panel connected to the right connector on the motherboard? Check the USB cable and the audio cable.

▲ Verify the processor, thermal compound, and cooler are all installed correctly.

▲ Are standoffs or spacers in place? Verify that a standoff that is not being used by the motherboard is not under the motherboard and causing a short.

3. Check the motherboard web site for other things you can check or try.

APPLYING | CONCEPTS

Lance is putting together a computer from parts for the first time. He has decided to keep costs low and is installing an AMD processor on a microATX motherboard, using all low-cost parts. He installed the hard drive, optical drive, and power supply in the computer case. Then he installed the motherboard in the case, followed by the processor, cooler, and memory. Before powering up the system, he checked all connections to make sure they were solid and read through the motherboard documentation to make sure he did not forget anything important. Next, he plugs in the monitor to the onboard video port and then plugs in the keyboard and power cord. He takes a deep breath and turns on the power switch on the back of the computer. Immediately, he hears a faint whine, but he's not sure what is making the noise. When he presses the power button on the front of the case, nothing happens. No fans, no lights. Here are the steps Lance takes to troubleshoot the problem:

1. He turns off the power switch and unplugs the power cord. He remembers to put on his ground bracelet and carefully checks all power connections. Everything looks okay.

2. He plugs in the system and presses the power button again. Still all he hears is the faint whine.

3. He presses the power button a second and third time. Suddenly a loud pop followed by smoke comes from the power supply, and the strong smell of electronics fills the room! Lance jumps back in dismay.

4. He removes a known-good power supply from another computer, disconnects the blown power supply, and connects the good one to the computer. When he turns on the power switch, he hears that same faint whine. Quickly he turns off the switch and unplugs the power cord. He does not want to lose another power supply!

5. Next, Lance calls technical support of the company that sold him the computer parts. A very helpful technician listens carefully to the details and tells Lance that the problem sounds like a short in the system. He explains that a power supply might whine if too much power is being drawn. As Lance hangs up the phone, he begins to think that the problem might be with the motherboard installation.

6. He removes the motherboard from the case, and the source of the problem is evident: he forgot to install spacers between the board and the case. The board was sitting directly on the bottom of the case, which had caused the short.

7. Lance installs the spacers and reinstalls the motherboard. Using the good power supply, he turns on the system. The whine is gone, but the system is dead.

8. Lance purchases a new power supply and motherboard, and this time, carefully uses spacers in every hole used by the motherboard screws. Figure 13-27 shows one installed spacer and one ready to be installed. The system comes up without a problem.

In evaluating his experience with his first computer build, Lance declares the project a success. He was grateful he had decided to use low-cost parts for his first build. He learned much from the experience and will never, ever forget to use spacers. He told a friend, "I made a serious mistake, but I learned from it. I feel confident I know how to put a system together now, and I'm ready to tackle another build. When you make mistakes and get past them, your confidence level actually grows because you learn you can face a serious problem and solve it."

A+
220-802
4.2

© Cengage Learning 2014

Figure 13-27   Spacers installed in case holes keep the motherboard from causing a short

TROUBLESHOOTING HARD DRIVES

A+
220-802
4.3

In this part of the chapter, you'll learn how to troubleshoot problems with hard drives. Problems caused by the hard drive during the boot can be caused by the hard drive subsystem, by the file system on the drive, or by files required by Windows when it begins to load. When trying to solve a problem with the boot, you need to decide if the problem is caused by hardware or software. All the problems discussed in this section are caused by hardware.

Hardware problems usually show up at POST, unless there is physical damage to an area of the hard drive that is not accessed during POST. Hardware problems often make the hard drive totally inaccessible. If BIOS cannot find a hard drive at POST, it displays an error message similar to these:

```
No boot device available

Hard drive not found

Fixed disk error

Invalid boot disk

Inaccessible boot device

Inaccessible boot drive

Numeric error codes in the 1700s or 10400s
```

The reasons BIOS cannot access the drive can be caused by the drive, the data cable, the electrical system, the motherboard, the SCSI host adapter (if one is present), or a loose connection. Here is a list of things to do and check before you open the case:

1. If BIOS displays numeric error codes or cryptic messages during POST, check the Web site of the BIOS manufacturer for explanations of these codes or messages.

2. Check BIOS setup for errors in the hard drive configuration. If you suspect an error, set BIOS to default settings, make sure autodetection is turned on, and reboot the system.

3. Try booting from another bootable media such as the Windows setup DVD or a USB flash drive or CD with the Linux OS and diagnostics software installed (for example, Hiren's BootCD software at *www.hirensbootcd.org*). If you can boot using another media, you

have proven that the problem is isolated to the hard drive subsystem. You can also use the bootable media to access the hard drive, run diagnostics on the drive, and possibly recover its data. A Hands-on Project later in the chapter gives you practice doing that.

4. For a RAID array, use the firmware utility to check the status of each disk in the array and to check for errors. Recall from Chapter 6 that you press a key at startup to access the RAID BIOS utility. This utility lists each disk in the array and its status. You can search the web site of the motherboard or RAID controller manufacturer for an interpretation of the messages on this screen and what to do about them. If one of the disks in the array has gone bad, it might take some time for the array to rebuild using data on the other disks. In this situation, the status for the array is likely to show as Caution.

   After the array has rebuilt, your data should be available. However, if one of the hard drives in the array has gone bad, you need to replace the hard drive. After you have replaced the failed drive, you must add it back to the RAID array. This process is called rebuilding a RAID volume. How to do this depends on the RAID hardware you are using. For some motherboards or RAID controller cards, you use the RAID firmware. For others, you use the RAID management software that came bundled with the motherboard or controller. You install this software in Windows and use the software to rebuild the RAID volume using the new hard drive.

If the problem is still not solved, open the case and check these things. Be sure to protect the system against ESD as you work:

1. Remove and reattach all drive cables. For IDE drives, check for correct pin-1 orientation.

2. If you're using a RAID, SATA, PATA, or SCSI controller card, remove and reseat it or place it in a different slot. Check the documentation for the card, looking for directions for troubleshooting.

3. For new installations, check the jumper settings on an IDE drive.

4. Inspect the drive for damage, such as bent pins on the connection for the cable.

5. Determine if the hard drive is spinning by listening to it or lightly touching the metal drive (with the power on).

6. Check the cable for frayed edges or other damage.

7. Check the installation manual for things you might have overlooked. Look for a section about system setup, and carefully follow all directions that apply.

8. Windows includes several tools for checking a hard drive for errors and repairing a corrupted Windows installation that are covered in Chapter 14. Without getting into these details of supporting Windows, here are a few simple things you can try:

   a. Following directions given earlier in the chapter, boot from the Windows setup DVD and load the System Recovery Options menu shown earlier in Figure 13-24. Select Startup Repair. This option restores many of the Windows files needed for a successful boot.

   b. To make sure the hard drive does not have bad sectors that can corrupt the file system, you can use the chkdsk command. To use the command, select Command Prompt from the System Recovery Options menu. At the command prompt that appears, enter the **chkdsk C: /r** command to search for and recover data from bad sectors on drive C:.

9. Check the drive manufacturer's web site for diagnostic software. Sometimes this software can be run from a bootable CD. Run the software to test the drive for errors.

13

A+
220-802
4.3

10. If it is not convenient to create a bootable CD with hard drive diagnostic software installed, you can move the drive to a working computer and install it as a second drive in the system. Then you can use the diagnostic software installed on the primary hard drive to test the problem drive. While you have the drive installed in a working computer, be sure to find out if you can copy data from it to the good drive, so that you can recover any data not backed up. Remember that you sit the drive on the open computer case (see Figure 13-28) or use a PATA-to-USB converter or SATA-to-USB converter to connect the drive to a USB port. If you have the case open with the PC turned on, be *very careful* to not touch the drive or touch inside the case.

© Cengage Learning 2014

Figure 13-28 Temporarily connect a faulty hard drive to another system to diagnose the problem and try to recover data

11. If the drive still does not boot, exchange the three field replaceable units—the data cable, the adapter card (optional), and the hard drive itself—for a hard drive subsystem. Do the following, in order:

   a. Reconnect or swap the drive data cable.

   b. Reseat or exchange the drive controller card, if one is present.

   c. Exchange the hard drive for a known good drive.

12. Sometimes older drives refuse to spin at POST. Drives that have trouble spinning often whine at startup for several months before they finally refuse to spin altogether. If your drive whines loudly when you first turn on the computer, never turn off the computer and replace the drive as soon as possible. One of the worst things you can do for a drive that is having difficulty starting up is to leave the computer turned off for an extended period of time. Some drives, like old cars, refuse to start if they are unused for a long time.

13. A bad power supply or a bad motherboard also might cause a disk boot failure.

A+
220-802
4.3

If the problem is solved by exchanging the hard drive, take the extra time to reinstall the old hard drive to verify that the problem was not caused by a bad connection.

Hard drives are sometimes stored in external enclosures such as the one shown in Figure 13-29. These enclosures make it easy to expand the storage capacity of a single computer or to make available hard drive storage to an entire network. For network attached storage (NAS), the enclosure connects to the network using an Ethernet port. When the

Courtesy of D-Link Corporation

Figure 13-29   The NAS ShareCenter Pro 1100 by D-Link can hold four hot-swappable SATA hard drives totalling 12 TB storage, has a dual core processor and 512 MB RAM, and supports RAID

storage is used by a single computer, the connection is made using a USB or eSATA port. Regardless of how the enclosure connects to a computer or network, the hard drives inside the enclosure might use a SATA or PATA connection.

Here is what you need to know about supporting these external enclosures:

1. An enclosure might contain firmware that supports RAID. For example, a switch on the rear of one enclosure for two hard drives can be set for RAID 0, RAID 1, or stand-alone drives. Read the documentation for the enclosure to find out how to manage the RAID volumes.

2. To replace a hard drive in an enclosure, see the documentation for the enclosure to find out how to open the enclosure and replace the drive.

3. If a computer case is overheating, one way to solve this problem is to remove the hard drives from the case and install them in an external enclosure. However, it's better to leave in the case the hard drive that contains the Windows installation.

TROUBLESHOOTING MONITORS AND VIDEO

A+
220-802
4.4

For monitor and video problems, as with other devices, if you have problems, try doing the easy things first. For instance, try to make simple hardware and software adjustments. Many monitor problems are caused by poor cable connections or bad contrast/brightness adjustments. Typical monitor and video problems and how to troubleshoot them are described next. In Chapter 19, you learn more about troubleshooting video problems on notebook computers.

> **Notes** A user very much appreciates a PC support technician who takes a little extra time to clean a system being serviced. When servicing a monitor, take the time to clean the screen with a soft dry cloth or monitor wipe.

MONITOR INDICATOR LIGHT IS NOT ON; NO IMAGE ON-SCREEN

If you hear one beep during the boot and you see a blank screen, then BIOS has successfully completed POST, which includes a test of the video card or onboard video. You can then assume the problem must be with the monitor or the monitor cable. Ask these questions and try these things:

1. Is the monitor power cable plugged in?

2. Is the monitor turned on? Try pushing the power button on the front of the monitor. An indicator light on the front of the monitor should turn on, indicating the monitor has power.

3. Is the monitor cable plugged into the video port at the back of the PC and the connector on the rear of the monitor?

4. Try a different monitor and a different monitor cable that you know are working.

> **Notes** When you turn on your computer, the first thing you see on the screen is the firmware on the video card identifying itself. You can use this information to search the web, especially the manufacturer's web site, for troubleshooting information about the card.

MONITOR INDICATOR LIGHT IS ON; NO IMAGE ON-SCREEN

For this problem, try the following:

1. Make sure the video cable is securely connected at the computer and the monitor. Most likely the problem is a bad cable connection.

2. If the monitor displays POST but goes blank when Windows starts to load, the problem is Windows and not the monitor or video. Try booting Windows in Safe Mode, which you learned to do earlier in the chapter. Safe Mode allows the OS to select a generic display driver and low resolution. If this works, change the driver and resolution. Other tools for troubleshooting Windows are covered in Chapter 14.

3. The monitor might have a switch on the back for choosing between 110 volts and 220 volts. Check that the switch is in the right position.

4. The problem might be with the video card. If you have just installed the card and the motherboard has onboard video, go into BIOS setup and disable the video port on the motherboard.

5. Verify that the video cable is connected to the video port on the video card and not to a disabled onboard video port.

6. Using buttons on the front of the monitor, check the contrast adjustment. If there's no change, leave it at a middle setting.

7. Check the brightness or backlight adjustment. If there's no change, leave it at a middle setting.

8. If the monitor-to-computer cable detaches from the monitor, exchange it for a cable you know is good, or check the cable for continuity. If this solves the problem, reattach the old cable to verify that the problem was not simply a bad connection.

9. Test a monitor you know is good on the computer you suspect to be bad. If you think the monitor is bad, make sure that it also fails to work on a good computer.

10. Open the computer case and reseat the video card. If possible, move the card to a different expansion slot. Clean the card's edge connectors, using a contact cleaner purchased from a computer supply store.

11. If there are socketed chips on the video card, remove the card from the expansion slot and then use a screwdriver to press down firmly on each corner of each socketed chip on the card. Chips sometimes loosen because of temperature changes; this condition is called chip creep.

12. Trade a good video card for the video card you suspect is bad. Test the video card you think is bad on a computer that works. Test a video card you know is good on the computer that you suspect is bad. Whenever possible, do both.

13. Test the RAM on the motherboard with memory diagnostic software.

14. For a motherboard that is using a PCI-Express or AGP video card, try using a PCI video card in a PCI slot or a PCIe ×1 video card in a PCIe ×1 slot. A good repair technician keeps an extra PCI video card around for this purpose.

15. Trade the motherboard for one you know is good. Sometimes, though rarely, a peripheral chip on the motherboard can cause the problem.

16. For notebook computers, is the LCD switch turned on? Function keys are sometimes used for this purpose.

17. For notebook computers, try connecting a second monitor to the notebook and use the function key to toggle between the LCD panel and the second monitor. If the second monitor works, but the LCD panel does not work, the problem might be with the LCD panel hardware. How to solve problems with notebook computers is covered in Chapter 19.

SCREEN GOES BLANK 30 SECONDS OR ONE MINUTE AFTER THE KEYBOARD IS LEFT UNTOUCHED

A Green motherboard (one that follows energy-saving standards) used with an Energy Saver monitor can be configured to go into standby or sleep mode after a period of inactivity. To wake up the computer, press any key on the keyboard or press the power button. How to configure sleep mode settings is covered in Chapter 19.

13

A+
220-802
4.4

> **Notes** Problems might occur if the motherboard power-saving features are turning off the monitor, and Windows screen saver is also turning off the monitor. If the system hangs when you try to get the monitor going again, try disabling one or the other. If this doesn't work, disable both.

POOR DISPLAY

In general, you can solve problems with poor display by using controls on the monitor and using Windows settings. Do the following:

▲ *LCD monitor controls.* Use buttons on the front of an LCD monitor to adjust color, brightness, contrast, focus, and horizontal and vertical positions.

▲ *Windows display settings.* Use Windows settings to adjust font size, screen resolution, brightness, color, and Clear Type text. Open Control Panel and in the Appearance and Personalization group, click **Display**. Use these settings to adjust the display:

- To make sure Clear Type text is selected, click **Adjust ClearType text** and turn on ClearType (see Figure 13-30). Then follow the steps in the wizard to improve the quality of text displayed on the screen.

- To adjust screen resolution, click **Change display settings** in the Display window.

- To calibrate colors, click **Calibrate color** and follow the directions on-screen. As you do so, color patterns appear (see Figure 13-31). Use these screens to adjust the gamma settings, which define the relationships among red, green, and blue as well as other settings that affect the display.

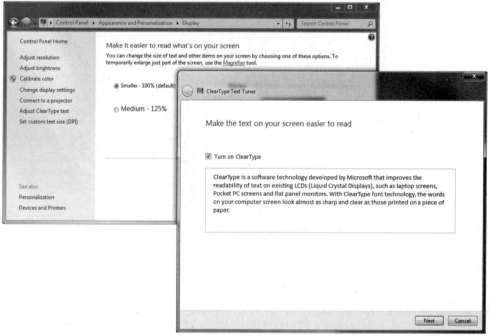

Source: Microsoft Windows 7

Figure 13-30 ClearType in Windows improves the display of text on the screen

A+
220-802
4.4

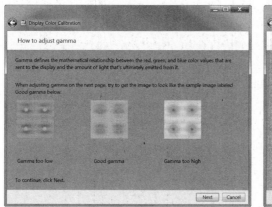
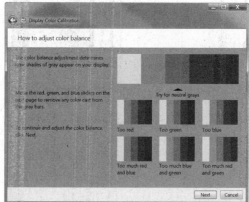

Source: Microsoft Windows 7

Source: Microsoft Windows 7

Figure 13-31 Two screens in the Windows 7 color calibration wizard

▲ *Update the video drivers.* How to do that is covered in Chapter 8. The latest video drivers can solve various problems with the video subsystem, including poor display.

Here are a few other display problems and their solutions:

▲ *Dead pixels.* An LCD monitor might have pixels that are not working called **dead pixels**, which can appear as small white, black, or colored spots on your screen. A black or white pixel is likely to be a broken transistor, which cannot be fixed. Having a few dead pixels on an LCD monitor screen is considered acceptable and usually not covered under the manufacturer's warranty.

> **Notes** A pixel might not be a dead pixel (a hardware problem), but only a stuck pixel (a software problem). You might be able to use software to fix stuck pixels. For example, run the online software at *www.flexcode.org/lcd2.html* to fix stuck pixels. The software works by rapidly changing all the pixels on the screen. (Be aware the screen flashes rapidly during the fix.)

▲ *Dim image.* A notebook computer dims the LCD screen when the computer is running on battery to conserve the charge. You can brighten the screen using the Windows display settings. To do so, open **Control Panel**, and click **Display** in the Appearance and Personalization group and then click **Adjust brightness** (see Figure 13-32). To check if settings to conserve power are affecting screen brightness, note the power plan that is selected. Click **Change plan settings** for this power plan. On the next screen, you can adjust when or if the screen will dim (see Figure 13-33). If the problem is still not resolved, it might be a hardware problem. How to troubleshoot hardware in laptops is covered in Chapter 19.

A dim image in a desktop monitor might be caused by a faulty video card or a faulty monitor. To find out which is the problem, connect a different monitor. If the monitor is the problem, most likely the backlighting in the LCD monitor is faulty and the monitor needs replacing.

▲ *Artifacts.* Horizontally torn images on-screen are called **artifacts** (see Figure 13-34), and happen when the video feed from the video controller gets out of sync with the refresh

A+
220-802
4.4

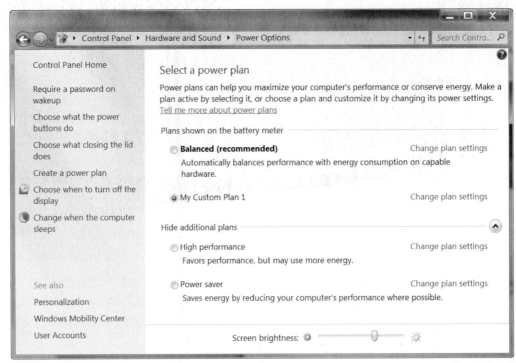

Source: Microsoft Windows 7

Figure 13-32 Adjust screen brightness

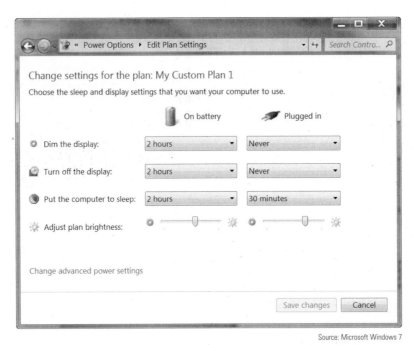

Source: Microsoft Windows 7

Figure 13-33 Change power plan options to affect how or if the screen dims

of the monitor screen. The problem can be caused by hardware or software. A common cause is when the GPU on the video card overheats. You can test that possibility by downloading and running freeware to monitor the temperature of the CPU and the GPU while you're playing a video game. If you notice the problem occurs when the GPU temp is high, install extra fans around the video card to keep it cool. Two freeware programs to monitor temperatures are CPU-Z by CPUID (*www.cpuid.com/softwares/cpu-z .html*) and GPU-Z by TechPowerUp (*www.techpowerup.com/gpuz*). See Figure 13-35.

A+
220-802
4.4

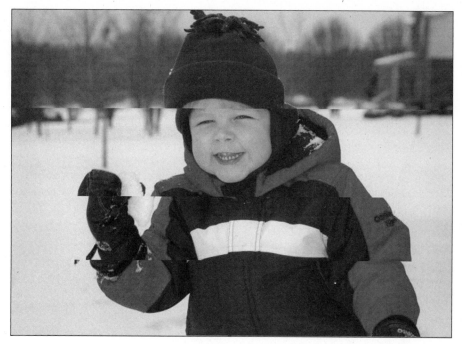

© Cengage Learning 2014

Figure 13-34 A simulation of horizontal tears on an image called artifacts

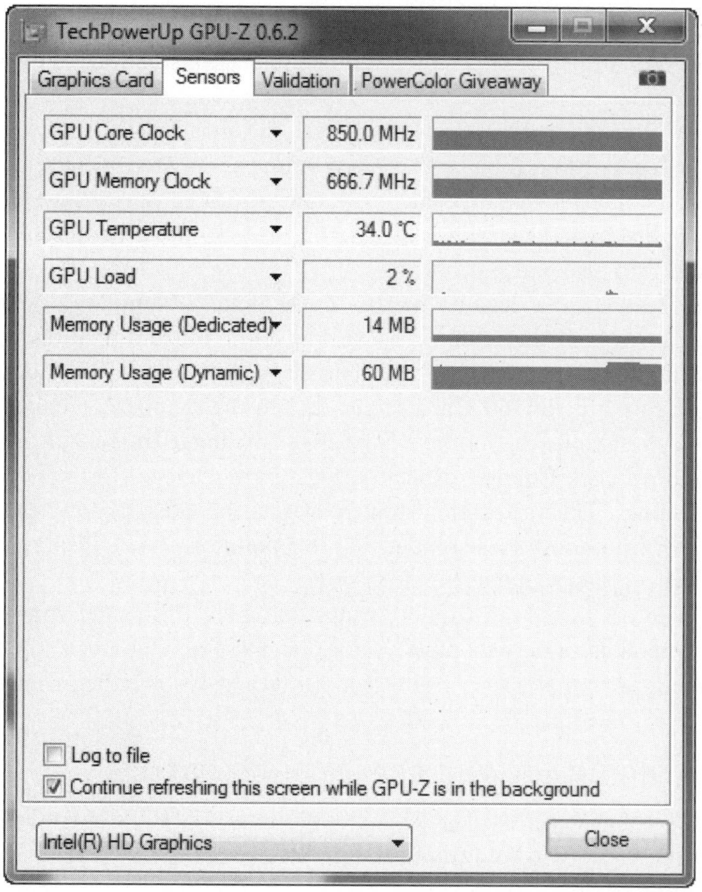

Source: GPU-Z by TechPowerUp

Figure 13-35 GPU-Z monitors the GPU temperature

13

A+
220-802
4.4

> **Notes** In this book, I've given several options for various freeware utilities. It's a good idea to know about your options for several reasons. Each freeware utility has different options; owners of freeware might not update their utility in a timely manner, and web sites might decide to include adware with their downloads.

Try updating the video drivers. However, if you see artifacts on the screen before Windows loads, then you know the problem is not caused by the drivers. The problem might be caused by the monitor. Try using a different monitor to see if the problem goes away. If so, replace the monitor.

Overclocking can cause artifacts. Other causes of artifacts are the motherboard or video card going bad, which can happen if the system has been overheating or video RAM on the card is faulty. Try replacing the video card. The power supply also might be the problem.

In general, to improve video quality, upgrade the video card and/or monitor. Poor display might be caused by inadequate video RAM. Your video card might allow you to install additional video RAM. See the card's documentation.

PROBLEMS WITH CRT MONITORS

If a CRT monitor makes a crackling sound, dirt or dust inside the monitor might be the cause. Someone at a computer monitor service center trained to work on the inside of the monitor can vacuum inside it. Recall from Chapter 1 that a monitor holds a dangerous charge of electricity, and you should not open one unless trained to do so.

If the monitor flickers or has wavy lines, a distorted image, or discoloration, try the following:

- ▲ Monitor flicker can be caused by poor cable connections. Check that the cable connections are snug.
- ▲ Odd-colored blotches on the screen or a screen flicker might indicate a device such as a speaker or fan is sitting too close to the monitor and emitting electrical noise called electromagnetic interference or EMI. Move any suspected device such as a fan, bad fluorescent lights, or large speakers away from the monitor. Two monitors placed very close together can also cause problems.
- ▲ Does the monitor have a **degauss button** to eliminate accumulated or stray magnetic fields? If so, press it. If the monitor doesn't have the button, turn the monitor on and off several times to trigger a built-in degausser, which some CRT monitors have.
- ▲ If the refresh rate is below 60 Hz, a screen flicker might appear. Change the refresh rate to the highest value the monitor supports. To change the refresh rate, in the Display window, click **Change display settings**. In the Screen Resolution window, click **Advanced settings**. Then select the **Monitor** tab on the video properties box (see Figure 13-36). Make sure **Hide modes that this monitor cannot display** is selected. Then select the largest value in the drop-down list.
- ▲ For older monitors that don't support a high enough refresh rate, your only cure might be to purchase a new monitor. Before buying a new monitor, try a second available monitor to make sure a different monitor will solve the problem.

DISPLAY SETTINGS MAKE THE SCREEN UNREADABLE

When the display settings don't work, you can easily return to standard VGA settings called **VGA mode**, which includes a resolution of 640 × 480. Do the following:

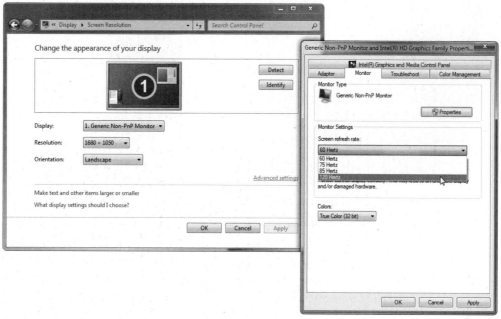

A+
220-802
4.4

Figure 13-36 Set the refresh rate high to avoid screen flicker

Source: Microsoft Windows 7

▲ Reboot the system and press the **F8** key after the first beep. The Advanced Boot Options menu appears (refer to Figure 13-18).

▲ Select **Safe Mode** to boot up with minimal configurations of Windows, which includes standard VGA mode. To boot to the regular Windows environment and use VGA mode, select **Enable low-resolution video** (640 × 480).

▲ After you have changed the display settings, restart Windows.

Now let's turn our attention to the final topic of this chapter: protecting a computer and the environment.

PROTECTING A COMPUTER AND THE ENVIRONMENT

A+
220-801
5.1, 5.2

As you learn to troubleshoot and solve computer problems, you gradually begin to realize that many problems you face could have been avoided by good computer maintenance that includes protecting the computer against environmental factors such as humidity, dust, and out-of-control electricity. In addition, computer technicians need to be aware that we can do damage to the environment if we carelessly dispose of used computer equipment improperly. Both these concerns are covered in this part of the chapter.

PHYSICALLY PROTECT YOUR EQUIPMENT

Preventive maintenance can prevent certain computer problems from occurring in the first place. The more preventive maintenance work you do initially, the fewer problems you are likely to have later, and the less troubleshooting and repair you will have to do. Here is my

13

list of dos and don'ts (you can probably add your own tips to the list) that you can do to physically protect a computer:

▲ *Don't move or jar your desktop computer while the hard drive is working.* Don't put the computer case under your desk where it might get bumped or kicked. Although modern hard drives are tougher than earlier ones, it's still possible to crash a drive by banging into it while it's reading or writing data.

> **Notes** The read/write heads on a hard drive get extremely close to the platters, but do not actually touch them. A "hard drive crash" can happen when a computer is bumped while the hard drive is operating, and a head bumps against the platter and scratches the surface. Most likely, this hard drive is now unusable.

▲ *Protect a computer against dust and other airborne particles.* Here are some things you can do to protect a computer when it must sit in a dusty environment, around those who smoke, or where pets might leave hair:

• You can purchase a plastic keyboard cover to protect the keyboard. When the computer is turned off, cover the entire system with a protective cover or enclosure.

• Install air filters over the front or side vents of the case where air flows into the case. Put your hand over the case of a running computer to feel where the air flows in. For most systems, air flows in from the front vents (refer to Figure 13-14) or vents on the side of the case that is near the processor cooler (refer to Figure 13-16). The air filter shown in Figure 13-37 has magnets that hold the filter to the case when screw holes are not available.

• Whenever you have the case cover open, be sure to use compressed air or an anti-static vacuum (see Figure 13-38) to remove dust from inside the case. Figure 13-39 shows a case fan that jammed because of dust and caused a system to overheat. And while you're cleaning up dust, don't forget to blow or vacuum out the keyboard.

> **Notes** When working at a customer site, be sure to clean up any mess you created by blowing dust out of a computer case or keyboard.

▲ *Allow for good ventilation inside and outside the system.* Proper air circulation is essential to keeping a system cool. Don't block air vents on the front and rear of the computer case or on the monitor. Inside the case, make sure cables are tied up and out of the way so as to allow for air flow and not obstruct fans from turning. Put covers on expansion slot openings on the rear of the case and put faceplates over empty bays on the front of the case. Don't set a tower case directly on thick carpet because the air vent on the bottom front of the case can be blocked. If you are concerned about overheating, monitor temperatures inside and outside the case.

> **A+ Exam Tip** The A+ 220–801 exam expects you to know how to keep computers and monitors well ventilated and to use protective enclosures and air filters to protect the equipment from airborne particles.

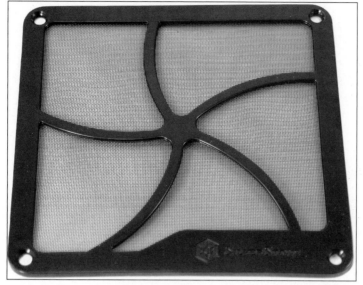

© Cengage Learning 2014

Figure 13-37   This air filter is designed to fit over a case fan, power supply fan, or panel vent on the case

13

Courtesy of Metropolitan Vacuum Cleaner Company, Inc.

Figure 13-38   An antistatic vacuum designed to work inside sensitive electronic equipment such as computers and printers

▲ *High temperatures and humidity can be dangerous for hard drives.* I once worked in a basement with PCs, and hard drives failed much too often. After we installed dehumidifiers, the hard drives became more reliable. If you suspect a problem with humidity, you can use a hygrometer to monitor the humidity in a room. High temperatures can also damage computer equipment, and you should take precautions to not allow a computer to overheat.

© Cengage Learning 2014

Figure 13-39 This dust-jammed case fan caused a system to overheat

> **Notes** A server room where computers stay and people generally don't stay for long hours is set to balance what is good for the equipment and to conserve energy. Low temperature and moderate humidity are best for the equipment, although no set standards exist for either. Temperatures might be set from 65 to 70 degrees F, and humidity between 30 percent and 50 percent, although some companies keep their server rooms at 80 degrees F to conserve energy. A data center where both computers and people stay is usually kept at a comfortable temperature and humidity for humans.

▲ *In BIOS setup, disable the ability to write to the boot sector of the hard drive.* This alone can keep boot viruses at bay. However, before you upgrade your OS, such as when you upgrade Windows XP to Windows 7, be sure to enable writing to the boot sector, which the OS setup will want to do.

▲ *Protect your CDs, DVDs, BDs, and other storage media.* To protect discs, keep them away from direct sunlight, heat, and extreme cold. Don't allow a disc to be scratched.

▲ *Don't leave a computer turned off for weeks or months at a time.* Once my daughter left her computer turned off for an entire summer. At the beginning of the new school term, the computer wouldn't boot. We discovered that the boot record at the beginning of the hard drive had become corrupted. PCs, like old cars, can give you problems after long spans of inactivity.

▲ *Don't unpack and turn on a computer that has just come in from the cold.* If your new laptop has just arrived and sat on your doorstep in freezing weather, don't bring it in and immediately unpack it and turn it on. Wait until a computer has had time to reach room temperature to prevent damage from condensation and static

A+
220-801
5.1, 5.2

electricity. In addition, when unpacking hardware or software, to help protect against static electricity, remove the packing tape and cellophane from the work area as soon as possible.

▲ *Protect electrical equipment from power surges.* Lightning and other electrical power surges can destroy computers and other electrical equipment. If the house or office building does not have surge protection equipment installed at the breaker box, be sure to install a protective device at each computer. The least expensive device is a power strip that is also a surge protector, although you might want to use a line conditioner or UPS for added protection.

Lightning can also get to your equipment across network cabling coming in through your Internet connection. To protect against lightning, use a surge protector such as the one shown in Figure 13-40 in line between the DSL modem or cable modem and the computer or home router to protect it from spikes across the network cables. Notice the cord on the surge protector, which connects it to ground.

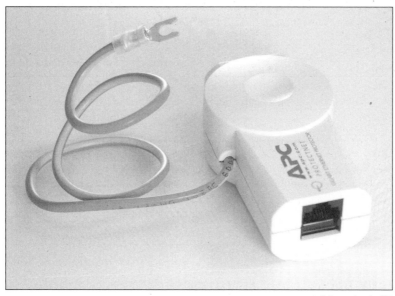

© Cengage Learning 2014

Figure 13-40 Surge protector by APC for Ethernet lines

An **uninterruptible power supply (UPS)** is a device that raises the voltage when it drops during **brownouts** or **sags** (temporary voltage reductions). A UPS also does double-duty as a surge protector to protect the system against power surges or spikes. In addition, a UPS can provide power for a brief time during a total blackout long enough for you to save your work and shut down the system. A UPS is not as essential for a laptop computer as it is for a desktop because a laptop has a battery that can sustain it during a blackout.

A common UPS device is a rather heavy box that plugs into an AC outlet and provides one or more outlets for the computer and the monitor (see Figure 13-41). It has an on/off switch, requires no maintenance, and is very simple to install. Use it to provide uninterruptible power to your desktop computer and monitor. It's best not to connect it to nonessential devices such as a laser printer or scanner.

13

A+
220-801
5.1, 5.2

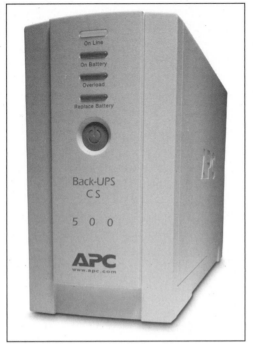

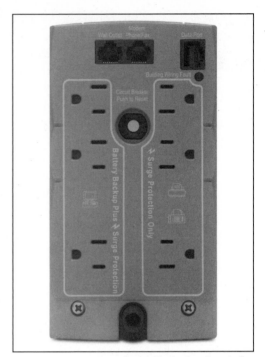

Courtesy of American Power Conversion Corp.

Courtesy of American Power Conversion Corp.

Figure 13-41 Uninterruptible power supply (UPS)

> **Notes** Whenever a power outage occurs, unless you have a reliable power conditioner installed at the breaker box in your house or building, unplug all power cords to the computers, printers, monitors, and the like. Sometimes when the power returns, sudden spikes are accompanied by another brief outage. You don't want to subject your equipment to these surges. When buying a surge suppressor, look for those that guarantee against damage from lightning and that reimburse for equipment destroyed while the surge suppressor is in use.

DOCUMENT PREVENTIVE MAINTENANCE

When you first set up a new computer, start a record book about this computer, using either a file on a removable storage device or a handwritten notebook dedicated to this machine. In this notebook or file, record any changes in setup data as well as any problems you experience or maintenance that you do on this computer. Be diligent in keeping this notebook up to date because it will be invaluable in diagnosing problems and upgrading equipment. Keep a printed or handwritten record of all changes to BIOS setup data and jumpers on the motherboard, and store the record with the hardware and software documentation.

If you are not the primary user of the computer, you might want to keep the hardware documentation separate from the computer itself. Label the documentation so that you can easily identify that it belongs to this computer. Keep this hardware documentation and your notes in a safe place. Some support people tape a large envelope inside the computer case; the envelope contains important documentation and records specific to that computer. On the other hand, if you're also responsible for software reference manuals, know that these manuals need to be kept in a location that is convenient for users.

A+
220-801
5.1, 5.2

> **Notes** We've provided the document, "Computer Inventory and Maintenance," that you can use to take an inventory of the hardware and software installed on a computer and record the ongoing maintenance, upgrades, and troubleshooting you do to the computer. To download the document, go to *www.cengagebrain.com*. For more information, see the Preface.

HOW TO DISPOSE OF USED EQUIPMENT

As a PC technician, one day you're sure to face an assortment of useless equipment and consumables (see Figure 13-42). Before you decide to trash it all, take a moment and ask yourself if some of the equipment can be donated or at least recycled. Think about fixing up an old computer and donating it to a needy middle school student. If you don't have the time for that, consider donating to the local computer repair class. The class can fix the computers up as a class project and donate them to young students.

© iStockphoto

Figure 13-42   Keep, trash, recycle, or donate?

13

If you do decide to give away a computer, first uninstall any applications software that you intend to use on another computer and delete any private data. To completely wipe a hard drive clean without destroying it, you can use a **zero-fill utility** downloaded from the hard drive manufacturer. For Windows or other software still installed on the drive, be sure to include documentation and installation CDs or DVDs with the computer.

If you're trashing a computer or hard drive, you can use special equipment called a degausser to erase *everything* on a magnetic hard drive or you can do physical damage (such as drilling holes through the drive). For SSDs, download and use a Secure Erase utility from the drive manufacturer. When disposing of any type of equipment or consumables, make sure to comply with local government environmental regulations. Table 13-4 lists some items and how to dispose of them.

A+
220-801
5.1, 5.2

Part	How to Dispose
Alkaline batteries, including AAA, AA, A, C, D, and 9-volt	Dispose of these batteries in the regular trash. First check to see if there are recycling facilities in your area.
Button batteries used in digital cameras and other small equipment; battery packs used in notebooks	These batteries can contain silver oxide, mercury, lithium, or cadmium and are considered hazardous waste. Dispose of them by returning them to the original dealer or by taking them to a recycling center. To recycle, pack them separately from other items. If you don't have a recycling center nearby, contact your county for local regulations for disposal.
Laser printer toner cartridges	Return these to the manufacturer or dealer to be recycled.
Ink-jet printer cartridges, computer cases, power supplies, and other computer parts, monitors, chemical solvents, and their containers	Check with local county or environmental officials for laws and regulations in your area for proper disposal of these items. The county might have a recycling center that will receive them. Discharge a CRT monitor before disposing of it. See the MSDS documents for chemicals to know how to dispose of them.
Storage media such as hard drives, CDs, DVDs, and BDs	Do physical damage to the device so it is not possible for sensitive data to be stolen. Then the device can be recycled or put in the trash. Your organization might be required to meet legal requirements to destroy data. If so, make sure you understand these requirements and how to comply with them.

© Cengage Learning 2014

Table 13-4 Computer parts and how to dispose of them

> **A+ Exam Tip** The A+ 220–801 exam expects you to know to follow environmental guidelines to dispose of batteries, CRTs, chemical solvents, and containers. If you're not certain how to dispose of a product, see its MSDS document.

>> CHAPTER SUMMARY

How to Approach a Hardware Problem

- ◢ If possible, always begin troubleshooting a computer problem by interviewing the user. Find out when the problem started and what happened about the time it started. You also need to know if important data on the computer is not backed up. When troubleshooting, set your priorities based on user needs.

- ◢ Sources that can help with hardware troubleshooting are user manuals, the web, online technical support and forums, diagnostic software, and your network of technical associates.

- ◢ Decide if a computer problem occurs before or after a successful boot and if it is caused by hardware or software.

Troubleshooting the Electrical System

◢ To determine if a system is getting power, listen for spinning fans or drives and look for indicator lights.

◢ Use a power supply tester to test the power supply.

◢ Intermittent problems that come and go are the most difficult to solve and can be caused by hardware or software. The power supply, motherboard, RAM, processor, hard drive, and overheating can cause intermittent problems.

◢ Removing dust from a system, providing for proper ventilation, and installing extra fans can help to keep a system from overheating.

Troubleshooting POST Before Video Is Active

◢ BIOS gives beep codes when a POST error occurs during the boot before it tests video.

Troubleshooting Error Messages During the Boot

◢ Error messages on a black screen during the boot are usually put there by startup BIOS during POST.

◢ Error messages on a blue screen during or after the boot are put there by Windows and are called the blue screen of death (BSOD).

◢ Search the web site of the BIOS or motherboard manufacturer or the Microsoft web site to find an error message and what to do about it.

Troubleshooting the Motherboard, Processor, and RAM

◢ The motherboard, processor, RAM, processor cooler assembly, and CMOS battery are field replaceable units.

◢ An unstable system that freezes or hangs at odd times can be caused by a faulty power supply, RAM, hard drive, motherboard, or processor, Windows error, or overheating.

◢ When troubleshooting, check the simple things first. For example, you can scan for viruses, test RAM, and run diagnostic software before you begin the process of replacing expensive components.

◢ A POST diagnostic card can troubleshoot problems with the motherboard.

Troubleshooting Hard Drives

◢ Problems caused by the hard drive during the boot can be caused by the hard drive subsystem, by the file system on the drive, or by files required by Windows when it begins to load. After the boot, bad sectors on a drive can cause problems with corrupted files.

◢ To determine if the hard drive is the problem when booting, try to boot from another media, such as the Windows setup DVD.

◢ For problems with a RAID volume, use the RAID controller firmware (on the motherboard or on the RAID controller card) or RAID management software installed in Windows to report the status of the array and to rebuild the RAID volume.

13

◢ To determine if a drive has bad sectors, use the chkdsk command. You can run the command after booting to the System Recovery Options menu using the Windows setup DVD.

Troubleshooting Monitors and Video

◢ Video problems can be caused by the monitor, video cable, video card, onboard video, video drivers, or Windows display settings.

◢ To bypass Windows display settings, boot the system to the Advanced Boot Options menu and select Safe Mode or Enable low-resolution video (640 × 480).

◢ A few dead pixels on an LCD monitor screen are considered acceptable by the manufacturer.

◢ Artifacts on the monitor screen can be caused by hardware, software, overheating, or overclocking. Try updating video drivers and checking for high temperatures.

◢ A CRT monitor might have a degauss button to eliminate stray EMI.

Protecting a Computer and the Environment

◢ Protect a computer against dust and other airborne particles using protective enclosures and air filters, and ridding the inside of a computer from dust.

◢ To further protect a computer, use good ventilation, keep temperatures and humidity from getting too high, and use a surge protector or UPS. To conserve energy, a company keeps a balance between cool temperatures and the cost of air conditioning.

◢ To protect the environment, make sure you dispose of used equipment and consumables, including batteries, printer toner cartridges, hard drives, and monitors, according to local government environmental guidelines.

>> KEY TERMS

For explanations of key terms, see the Glossary near the end of the book.

artifacts	dead pixel	sags
blue screen of death (BSOD)	degauss button	uninterruptible power supply (UPS)
brownouts	driver store	VGA mode
chassis air guide (CAG)	Memory Diagnostics	zero-fill utility

>> REVIEW QUESTIONS

1. When an end user brings any computer problem to you, how should you begin the troubleshooting process?

   a) Prioritize what to do.

   b) Interview the user.

   c) Go to the web site of the product manufacturer, and search for a support forum.

   d) Boot the system to obtain problem symptoms.

2. During the system boot process, what is the meaning of the error message "Invalid drive specification"?

   a) CMOS RAM is corrupted.

   b) The processor overheated.

   c) There is a bad memory module.

   d) Startup BIOS did not find a device to use to load the operating system.

3. For better ventilation, use a power supply that has vents on the ____ of the power supply.

   a) bottom and front

   b) top and bottom

   c) front and back

   d) top and back

4. What symptom indicates that a motherboard, processor, or memory module is failing?

   a) A "CMOS battery low" message appears during system startup.

   b) You cannot feel air being pulled into or out of the case.

   c) The system begins to boot but then powers down.

   d) The PC appears dead except for a whining noise coming from the power supply.

5. An LCD monitor might have pixels that are not working called ____, which can appear as small white, black, or colored spots on your screen.

   a) dead points

   b) dead pixels

   c) ghost points

   d) gauss points

6. True or false? Startup BIOS communicates POST errors as a series of beeps before it tests video.

7. True or false? When a PC boots, three short beeps indicate that all is well after POST.

8. True or false? Even if Windows 7/Vista is not installed, you can still run the Memory Diagnostics tool by booting the system from the Windows setup DVD.

9. True or false? Hardware problems usually show up at POST, unless there is physical damage to an area of the hard drive that is not accessed during POST.

10. True or false? The best place to store a desktop is under the desk.

11. A(n) ____ is a round air duct that helps to pull and direct fresh air from outside the case to the cooler and processor.

12. Horizontally torn images on-screen are called ____, and happen when the video feed from the video controller gets out of sync with the refresh of the monitor screen.

13. A monitor's ____ button can be used to eliminate accumulated or stray magnetic fields.

14. A(n) ____ is a device that raises the voltage when it drops during brownouts or sags (temporary voltage reductions).

15. To completely wipe a hard drive clean without destroying it, you can use a(n) ____ utility downloaded from the hard drive manufacturer.

Troubleshooting Windows Startup Problems

In Chapter 12, you learned how to deal with Windows and application problems that occur after Windows has started. In Chapter 13, you learned about troubleshooting hardware problems, including problems with hardware that prevented a system from booting. In this chapter, you take your troubleshooting skills one step further by learning to deal with startup problems caused by Windows. When Windows fails to start, it can be stressful if important data has not been backed up or the user has pressing work to do with the computer. What helps more than anything else is a cool head and a good plan so you don't feel so helpless.

We begin the chapter with a discussion of what happens when you first turn on a computer and Windows starts. The more you understand about startup, the better your chances of fixing startup problems. Then you learn about Windows tools specifically designed to handle startup problems. Finally, you learn a step-by-step strategy for solving startup problems and recovering data on a hard drive when Windows is corrupted beyond repair.

UNDERSTANDING THE BOOT PROCESS

A+
220-802
4.6

Knowledge is power. The better you understand what happens when you first turn on a computer until Windows is loaded and the Windows desktop appears, the more likely you will be able to solve a problem when Windows cannot start. Let's begin by noting the differences between a hard boot and a soft boot.

> **Notes** Most techies use the terms "boot" and "startup" interchangeably. However, in general, the term "boot" refers to the hardware phase of starting up a computer. Microsoft consistently uses the term "startup" to refer to how its operating systems are booted, well, started, I mean.

CHOOSING BETWEEN A HARD BOOT AND A SOFT BOOT

The term **booting** comes from the phrase "lifting yourself up by your bootstraps" and refers to the computer bringing itself up to a working state without the user having to do anything but press the on button. This boot can be a hard boot or soft boot. A **hard boot**, or **cold boot**, involves turning on the power with the on/off switch. A **soft boot**, or **warm boot**, involves using the operating system to reboot.

A hard boot takes more time than a soft boot because in a soft boot, the initial steps of a hard boot don't happen. To save time in most circumstances, you should use the soft boot to restart. A hard boot initializes the processor and clears memory. If a soft boot doesn't work or you want to make certain you get a fresh start, use a hard boot. If you cannot boot from the operating system, look for power or reset buttons on the front or rear of the case. For example, one computer has three power switches: a power button and a reset button on the front of the case and a power switch on the rear of the case (see Figure 14-1).

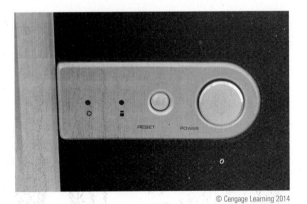

© Cengage Learning 2014   © Cengage Learning 2014

Figure 14-1 This computer case has two power buttons on the front and one power switch on the rear of the case

They work like this:

▲ The power button in front can be configured as a "soft" power button, causing a normal Windows shutdown and restart.

▲ The reset button initializes the CPU so that it restarts at the beginning of the BIOS startup program. The computer behaves as though the power were turned off and back on and then goes through the entire boot process.

▲ The switch on the rear of the case simply turns off the power abruptly and is a "hard" power button. If you use this switch, wait 30 seconds before you press the power button on the front of the case to boot the system. This method gives you the greatest assurance that memory will clear. However, if Windows is abruptly stopped, it might give an error message when you reboot.

How the front two buttons work can be controlled in BIOS setup. Know, however, that different cases offer different options.

STARTUP BIOS CONTROLS THE BEGINNING OF THE BOOT

Recall that the startup BIOS is programming contained on the firmware chip on the motherboard that is responsible for getting a system up and going and finding an OS to load. A successful boot depends on the hardware, the BIOS, and the operating system all performing without errors. If errors occur, they might stall or lock up the boot. Errors are communicated as beeps, as text messages on-screen, or as recorded voice messages.

Startup BIOS is responsible for these early steps in the boot process:

1. *Startup BIOS reads* motherboard settings *and runs the POST.* Here are a few important details:

    a. A small amount of RAM on a firmware chip on the motherboard holds an inventory of hardware devices, hardware settings, security passwords, date and time, and startup settings. Startup BIOS reads this information and then surveys the hardware devices it finds present, comparing it to the list kept in this RAM.

    b. Startup BIOS runs **POST (power-on self test)**, which is a series of tests used to find out if startup BIOS can communicate correctly with essential hardware components required for a successful boot.

    c. Before the video controller on the motherboard or video card is tested and configured, startup BIOS communicates any errors as a series of beeps or recorded speech. Short and long beeps indicate an error; the coding for the beeps depends on the BIOS. After startup BIOS has checked the video controller (note that it does not check to see if a monitor is present or working), it can use video to display its progress on-screen.

2. *Setup BIOS might be run.* The keyboard is checked, and if the key is pressed to request BIOS setup, the BIOS setup program is run. For example, for one system, when you press Del, the BIOS setup opening menu shown in Figure 14-2 appears. You can use the menus and items on these screens to verify hardware devices recognized by the system, enable and disable devices, set the date and time, set security passwords to the computer, change the boot device order, and make other changes to BIOS settings. Know that the screens provided by different motherboard manufacturers might be organized differently.

14

A+
220-802
4.6

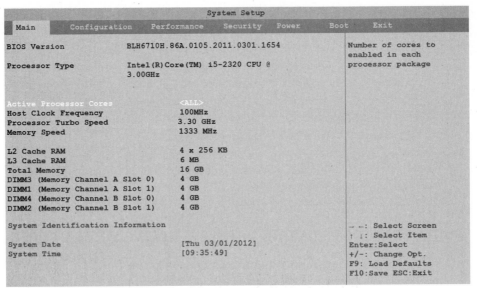

Source: Intel

Figure 14-2   Use BIOS setup screens to change the hardware configuration for a system

3. ***Startup BIOS searches for a bootable device.*** The boot sequence stored in CMOS RAM tells startup BIOS which device to use to launch an OS. Most BIOSs support booting from the hard drive, a CD or DVD, a USB device, or another computer on the network. (Older computers could also boot from a floppy disk.) The BIOS turns to the specified device and turns control over to it. Next let's see what happens if the device is the hard drive.

> 📄 **Notes** Future desktop and notebook systems are likely to use replacement technologies for the BIOS firmware on the motherboard. EFI (Extensible Firmware Interface) and UEFI (Unified EFI) are two standards for the interface between firmware on the motherboard and the operating system. The standards replace the legacy BIOS standards and improve on processes for booting, handing over the boot to the OS, and loading device drivers and applications before the OS loads. For more information on either standard, see the UEFI consortium at *www.uefi.org*.

STEPS TO START WINDOWS 7/VISTA

Table 14-1 lists the components and files necessary to start Windows 7/Vista

Component or File	Path*	Description
MBR	**First sector of the hard drive called the master boot record**	**Contains the partition table and the master boot program used to locate and start the BootMgr program.**
OS boot record	**First sector of the system partition (most likely drive C:)**	**Windows XP uses this sector, but Windows 7/Vista does not use it.**

© Cengage Learning 2014

Table 14-1   Software components and files needed to start Windows 7/Vista (continues)

A+
220-802
4.6

Component or File	Path*	Description
BootMgr	Root directory of system partition (C:\)	Windows Boot Manager manages the initial startup of the OS.
BCD	Boot folder of the system partition (C:\Boot)	The Boot Configuration Data file is organized the same as a registry hive and contains boot settings that control BootMgr, WinLoad.exe, WinResume.exe (when resuming from hibernation), MemTest.exe (when memory is tested), and dual boots.
WinLoad.exe	C:\Windows\System32	Windows Boot Loader loads and starts essential Windows processes.
Ntoskrnl.exe	C:\Windows\System32	Windows kernel.
Hal.dll	C:\Windows\System32	Dynamic link library handles low-level hardware details.
Smss.exe	C:\Windows\System32	Sessions Manager program responsible for starting user sessions.
Csrss.exe	C:\Windows\System32	Win32 subsystem manages graphical components and threads.
Winlogon.exe	C:\Windows\System32	Logon process.
Services.exe	C:\Windows\System32	Service Control Manager starts and stops services.
Lsass.exe	C:\Windows\System32	Authenticates users.
System registry hive	C:\Windows\System32\Config	Holds data for the HKEY_LOCAL_MACHINE key of the registry.
Device drivers	C:\Windows\System32\Drivers	Drivers for required hardware.

*It is assumed that Windows is installed in C:\Windows.

Table 14-1   Software components and files needed to start Windows 7/Vista (continued)

© Cengage Learning 2014

14

> **Notes** Take a moment to distinguish between the system partition and the boot partition. The PC boots from the system partition and loads the Windows operating system from the boot partition. The system partition is the active partition that is used first when finding and loading an operating system. The boot partition contains the \Windows folder where system files are located. Most of the time the boot partition and the system partition are the same partition (drive C:). The only time they are different is in a dual-boot configuration. For example, if Windows 7 has been installed in a dual-boot configuration with Windows XP, the system partition is most likely drive C: (where Windows XP is installed), and Windows 7 is installed on another drive, such as drive E:, which Windows 7 calls the boot partition. The PC boots from drive C: and then loads Windows 7 system files stored on drive E: in the E:\Windows folder.

Now let's look at the steps to start a Windows 7/Vista computer. Several of these steps are diagrammed in Figures 14-3 and 14-4 to help you visually understand how the steps work.

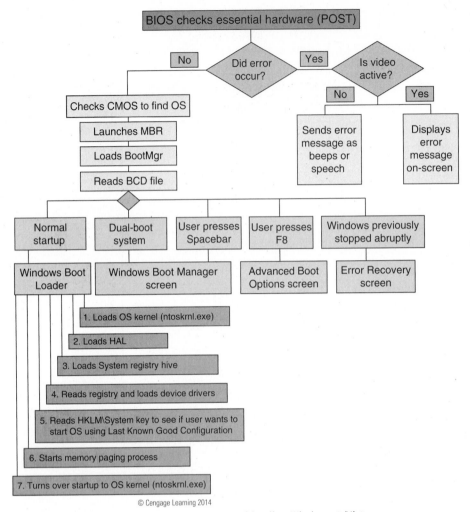

Figure 14-3   Steps to booting the computer and loading Windows 7/Vista

Study these steps carefully because the better you understand startup, the more likely you'll be able to solve startup problems:

1. Startup BIOS turns control over to the MBR program stored in the first sector of the hard drive.

> **Notes** Future desktop and notebook systems are likely to use a different method than the MBR for organizing the hard drive. Even now, in Windows 7/Vista, you can choose between two disk-partitioning systems: MBR and GPT. Using the MBR system, you can have up to four partitions on a hard drive, although one of them can have multiple volumes, which are called logical drives. The GPT (Globally Unique Identifier Partition Table) disk-partitioning system can support up to 128 partitions, and these partitions are more stable and can be larger than MBR partitions. To use the GPT system for your bootable hard drive, your computer motherboard must contain an EFI or UEFI chip rather than the traditional BIOS chip. For more information on the GPT method of organizing a hard drive, go to the *www.microsoft.com* site and search on GPT.

2. The MBR program searches the partition table looking for the active partition, which Windows calls the system partition. It finds and loads the **Windows Boot Manager (BootMgr)** program in the root directory of this partition. (Note that the BootMgr

A+
220-802
4.6

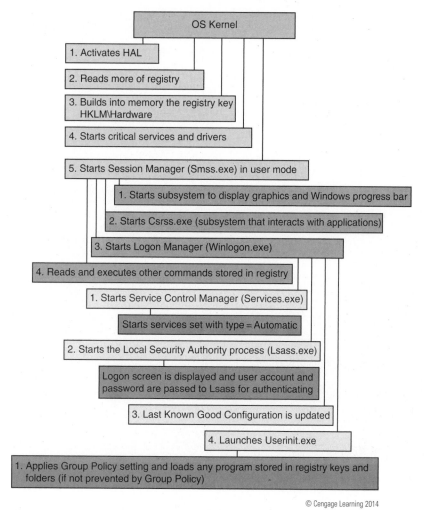

© Cengage Learning 2014

Figure 14-4 Steps to complete loading Windows 7/Vista

14

program file has no file extension.) If the MBR program cannot find BootMgr or cannot turn over operation to it, one of these error messages appears:

```
Missing operating system

Error loading operating system

Windows failed to load

Invalid partition table
```

> **XP Differences**   When starting XP, the MBR looks for the first sector in the active partition, which is called the **OS boot record**. This sector contains a small program that finds the Windows XP boot program named **Ntldr**. Ntldr reads XP settings used for the boot stored in **Boot.ini**. For more detail about starting Windows XP, see Appendix C.

3. BootMgr does the following:

   a. It reads the settings in the **Boot Configuration Data (BCD) file**.

   b. The next step, one of five, depends on entries in the BCD and these other factors:

   ◢ *Option 1:* For normal startups that are not dual booting, no menu appears and BootMgr finds and launches **Windows Boot Loader (WinLoad.exe)** stored in the \Windows\System32 folder.

A+
220-802
4.6

▲ *Option 2:* If the computer is set up for a dual-boot environment, BootMgr displays the Windows Boot Manager screen, as shown in Figure 14-5.

▲ *Option 3:* If the user presses the Spacebar, the Windows Boot Manager screen appears.

▲ *Option 4:* If the user presses F8, BootMgr displays the Advanced Boot Options screen, as shown in Figure 14-6.

▲ *Option 5:* If Windows was previously stopped abruptly or another error occurs, the Windows Error Recovery screen (see Figure 14-7) appears.

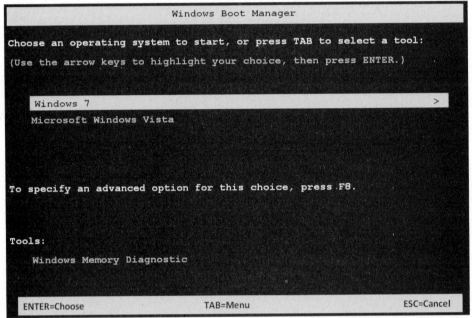

Source: Microsoft Windows 7

Figure 14-5   Boot loader menu in a dual-boot environment

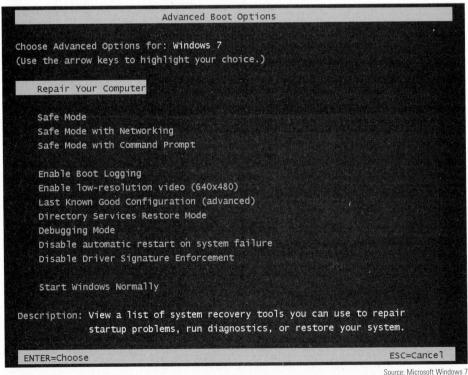

Source: Microsoft Windows 7

Figure 14-6   Press F8 during the boot to launch the Windows 7 Advanced Boot Options menu

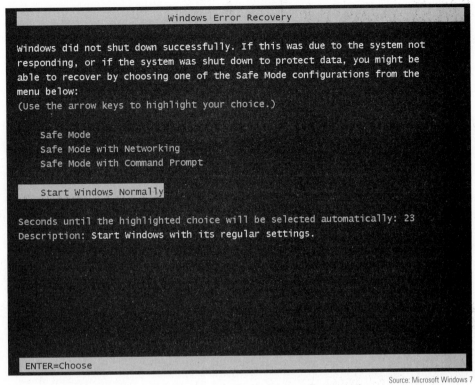

A+
220-802
4.6

Figure 14-7 This window appears if Windows has been abruptly stopped

Source: Microsoft Windows 7

4. **WinLoad** is responsible for loading Windows components. It does the following:

   a. For normal startups, WinLoad loads into memory the OS kernel, Ntoskrnl.exe, but does not yet start it. WinLoad also loads into memory the Hardware Abstraction Layer (Hal.dll), which will later be used by the kernel.

   b. WinLoad loads into memory the system registry hive (C:\Windows\System32\ Config\System).

   c. WinLoad then reads the registry key just created, HKEY_LOCAL_ MACHINE\ SYSTEM\Services, looking for and loading into memory device drivers that must be launched at startup. The drivers are not yet started.

   d. WinLoad reads data from the HKEY_LOCAL_MACHINE\SYSTEM key that tells the OS if the user wants to start the OS using the Last Known Good Configuration.

   e. WinLoad starts up the memory paging process and then turns over startup to the OS kernel (Ntoskrnl.exe).

5. The kernel (Ntoskrnl.exe) does the following:

   a. It activates the HAL, reads more information from the registry, and builds into memory the registry key HKEY_LOCAL_ MACHINE\HARDWARE, using information that has been collected about the hardware.

   b. The kernel then starts critical services and drivers that are configured to be started by the kernel during the boot. Recall that drivers interact directly with hardware and run in kernel mode, while services interact with drivers. Most services and drivers are stored in C:\Windows\System32 or C:\Windows\System32\Drivers and have an .exe, .dll, or .sys file extension.

   c. After the kernel starts all services and drivers configured to load during the boot, it starts the Session Manager (Smss.exe), which runs in user mode.

14

A+
220-802
4.6

6. The Session Manager (Smss.exe) does the following:

   a. It starts the part of the Win32 subsystem that displays graphics, and the Windows 7 flag or the Vista progress bar is displayed (see Figure 14-8). When you see the flag or progress bar, you know the Windows kernel has loaded successfully.

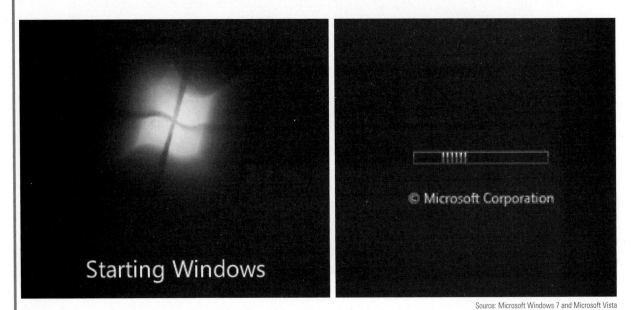

Source: Microsoft Windows 7 and Microsoft Vista

Figure 14-8 The Windows 7 flag on the left or the Vista progress bar on the right indicates that the Windows graphics subsystem is running and the kernel has successfully loaded

   b. Smss.exe then starts the client/server run-time subsystem (Csrss.exe), which also runs in user mode. Csrss.exe is the Win32 subsystem component that interacts with applications.

   c. Smss.exe starts the Logon Manager (Winlogon.exe) and reads and executes other commands stored in the registry, such as a command to replace system files placed there by Windows Update.

7. Winlogon.exe does the following:

   a. It starts the Service Control Manager (Services.exe). Services.exe starts all services listed with the startup type of Automatic in the Services console.

   b. Winlogon.exe starts the Local Security Authority process (Lsass.exe). The logon screen appears (see Figure 14-9), and the user account and password are passed to the Lsass.exe process for authenticating. The Last Known Good Configuration information in the registry is updated.

   c. Winlogon.exe launches Userinit.exe and the Windows desktop (Explorer.exe).

8. Userinit.exe applies Group Policy settings and any programs not trumped by Group Policy that are stored in startup folders and startup registry keys. See Appendix G for a list of these folders and registry keys.

The Windows startup is officially completed when the Windows desktop appears and the wait circle disappears.

With this basic knowledge of the boot in hand, let's turn our attention to the Windows tools that can help you solve problems when Windows refuses to load.

Figure 14-9 Windows 7 logon screen

Source: Microsoft Windows 7

WINDOWS 7/VISTA TOOLS FOR SOLVING STARTUP PROBLEMS

Before we begin troubleshooting Windows startup, it helps to first survey the Windows tools so you are familiar with how they can help and how they work. These tools include the Advanced Boot Options menu, the Windows Recovery Environment (Windows RE), and the command prompt window in Windows RE.

As you learn to use each tool, keep in mind that you want to use the tool that makes as few changes to the system as possible to fix the problem.

> **⚡ Caution** This chapter often refers to the Windows setup DVD. If you have a notebook computer or a brand-name computer such as a Dell, IBM, Lenovo, or Gateway, be sure to use the hidden recovery partition on the hard drive of these computers or the manufacturer's recovery discs rather than the regular Windows setup DVD. These recovery media are likely to contain proprietary drivers needed for installed devices.

ADVANCED BOOT OPTIONS MENU

The Advanced Boot Options menu (refer back to Figure 14-6) appears when a user presses F8 as Windows is loading. You need to be familiar with each option on this menu and know how to use it.

> **XP Differences** The XP **Advanced Options menu** is similar to the Windows 7/Vista Advanced Boot Options menu and has many of the same items on its menu. See Figure 14-10.

A+
220-802
4.6

```
Windows Advanced Options Menu
Please select an option:

    Safe Mode
    Safe Mode with Networking
    Safe Mode with Command Prompt

    Enable Boot Logging
    Enable VGA Mode
    Last Known Good Configuration (your most recent settings that worked)
    Directory Services Restore Mode (Windows domain controllers only)
    Debugging Mode
    Disable automatic restart on system failure

    Start Windows Normally
    Reboot
    Return to OS Choices Menu

Use the up and down arrow keys to move the highlight to your choice.
```

Source: Microsoft Windows 7

Figure 14-10   Windows XP Advanced Options menu

REPAIR YOUR COMPUTER

This option is available only in Windows 7 and launches the Windows Recovery Environment (Windows RE) that provides a variety of tools to solve Windows startup problems. You learn to use Windows RE later in the chapter.

SAFE MODE

Safe Mode boots the OS with a minimum configuration and can be used to solve problems with a new hardware installation, a corrupted Windows installation, or problems caused by user settings. Safe Mode boots with the mouse, monitor (with basic video), keyboard, and mass storage drivers loaded. It uses the default system services (it does not load any extra services) and does not provide network access. It uses a plain VGA video driver (Vga.sys) instead of the video drivers specific to your video card.

When you boot in Safe Mode, you will see "Safe Mode" in all four corners of your Windows desktop screen. The screen resolution is 800 × 600 and the desktop wallpaper (background) is black. Figure 14-11 shows Windows 7 in Safe Mode.

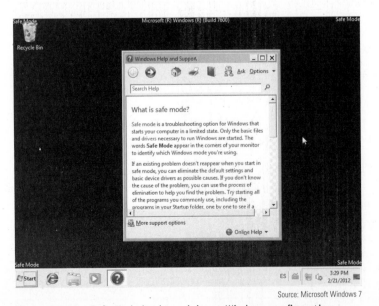

Source: Microsoft Windows 7

Figure 14-11   Safe Mode loads a minimum Windows configuration

Here's what you can do in Safe Mode to recover the system:

1. When Safe Mode first loads, if Windows senses the problem is drastic, it gives you the opportunity to go directly to System Restore. Use System Restore unless you know exactly what it is you need to do to solve your problem. You can also start System Restore from within Safe Mode as you do from the regular Windows desktop.

> **Notes** When using System Restore, you run the risk of undoing *desired* changes to the Windows environment and software installations. Before using one of these fixes, consider what recent changes will be lost when you apply the fix.

2. If you suspect a virus, scan the system for viruses. Use Memory Diagnostics to verify memory and use Chkdsk to fix hard drive problems. Your hard drive might be full; if so, make some free space available.

3. Use Device Manager to uninstall or disable a device with problems or to roll back a driver.

4. Use System Configuration to disable unneeded services or startup processes. If you don't know which one is causing the problem, disable all non-Microsoft services and processes. If the problem goes away, enable one at a time until you discover the one causing the problem.

5. If you suspect a software program you have just installed is the issue, use the Programs and Features window to uninstall it.

6. Use Event Viewer and other error-reporting logs to find information saved during previously failed startups that can help you identify the source of a problem.

> **A+ Exam Tip** The A+ 220-802 exam expects you to know how to use Safe Mode and Chkdsk to help resolve a Windows startup problem.

Here are some tips about loading Safe Mode that you need to be aware of:

- From the Advanced Boot Options menu, first try Safe Mode with Networking. If that doesn't work, try Safe Mode. And if that doesn't work, try Safe Mode with Command Prompt.
- Know that Safe Mode won't load if core Windows components are corrupted.
- When you load Windows in Safe Mode, all files used for the load are recorded in the C:\Windows\Ntbtlog.txt file. Use this file to identify a service, device driver, or application loaded at startup that is causing a problem.

SAFE MODE WITH NETWORKING

Use this option when you are solving a problem with booting and need access to the network to solve the problem. For example, you might need to download updates to your antivirus software. Another example is when you have just attempted to install a printer, which causes the OS to hang when it boots. You can boot into Safe Mode with Networking and download new printer drivers from the network. Uninstall the printer and then install it again from the network. Also use this mode when the Windows installation files are available on the network, rather than the Windows setup DVD, and you need to access those files.

A+
220-802
4.6

SAFE MODE WITH COMMAND PROMPT

If the first Safe Mode option does not load the OS, then try Safe Mode with the command prompt. At the command prompt, use the **sfc /scannow** command to verify system files (see Figure 14-12). Also use the **chkdsk /r** command to check for file system errors. If the problem is still not solved, you can use this command to launch System Restore: **C:\Windows\system32\ rstrui.exe**. Then follow the directions on-screen to select a restore point (see Figure 14-13).

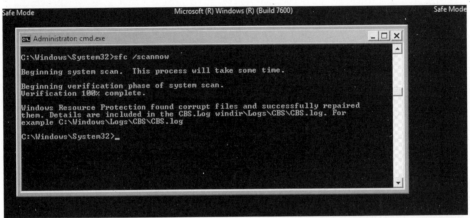

Source: Microsoft Windows 7

Figure 14-12   SFC finds and repairs corrupted system files

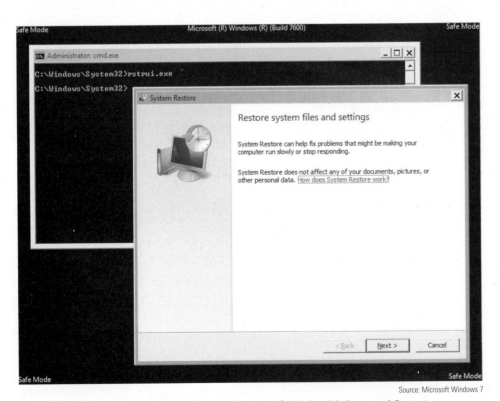

Source: Microsoft Windows 7

Figure 14-13   Use System Restore after booting to Safe Mode with Command Prompt

ENABLE BOOT LOGGING

When you boot with this option, Windows loads normally and you access the regular desktop. However, all files used during the load process are recorded in a file, C:\Windows\ Ntbtlog.txt (see Figure 14-14). Thus, you can use this option to see what did and did not load during the boot. For instance, if you have a problem getting a device to work, check Ntbtlog.txt to see what driver files loaded. Boot logging is much more effective if you have a copy of Ntbtlog.txt that was made when everything worked as it should. Then you can compare the good load to the bad load, looking for differences.

> **Notes** The Ntbtlog.txt file is also generated when you boot into Safe Mode.

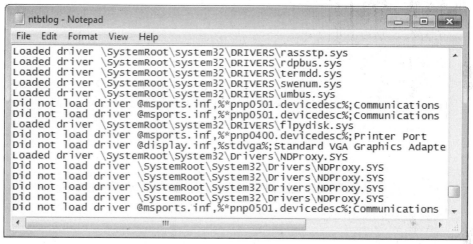

Figure 14-14   Sample Ntbtlog.txt file

Source: Microsoft Windows 7

> **Notes** If Windows hangs during the boot, try booting using the option Enable Boot Logging. Then look at the last entry in the Ntbtlog.txt file. This entry might be the name of a device driver causing the system to hang.

ENABLE LOW-RESOLUTION VIDEO (640 × 480)

Use this option when the video setting does not allow you to see the screen well enough to fix a bad setting. This can happen when a user creates a desktop with black fonts on a black background, or something similar that makes it impossible to see the desktop. Booting in this mode gives you a very plain, standard VGA video. You can then go to the Display settings, correct the problem, and reboot normally. You can also use this option if your video drivers are corrupted and you need to update, roll back, or reinstall your video drivers. In Windows XP, this option is called "Enable VGA Mode."

14

A+
220-802
4.6

LAST KNOWN GOOD CONFIGURATION

Registry settings collectively called the **Last Known Good Configuration** are saved in the registry each time the user successfully logs onto the system. If your problem is caused by a bad hardware or software installation and you get an error message the first time you restart the system after the installation, using the Last Known Good can, in effect, undo your installation and solve your problem.

Remember, the Last Known Good registry settings are saved each time a user logs on to Windows. Therefore, it's important to try the Last Known Good early in the troubleshooting session before it's overwritten. (However, know that if you log onto the system in Safe Mode, the Last Known Good is not saved.)

DIRECTORY SERVICES RESTORE MODE (WINDOWS DOMAIN CONTROLLERS ONLY)

This option applies only to domain controllers and is used as one step in the process of recovering from a corrupted Active Directory. Recall that Active Directory is the domain database managed by a domain controller that tracks users and resources on the domain.

DEBUGGING MODE

This mode gives you the opportunity to move system boot logs from the failing computer to another computer for evaluation. To use this mode, both computers must be connected to each other by way of the serial port. Then, you can reboot into this mode and Windows on the failing computer will send all the boot information through the serial port and on to the other computer. For more details, see the *Windows 7 Resource Kit* by Microsoft Press.

DISABLE AUTOMATIC RESTART ON SYSTEM FAILURE

By default, Windows automatically restarts immediately after a blue screen stop error. The error can cause the system to continually reboot rather than shut down. To stop the rebooting, choose **Disable automatic restart on system failure**. Recall from Chapter 12 that you can use the System Properties box to make this setting permanent.

THE WINDOWS RECOVERY ENVIRONMENT (WINDOWS RE)

Windows Recovery Environment (Windows RE) is a lean operating system that can be launched to solve Windows startup problems after other tools available on the Advanced Boot Options menu have failed to solve the problem. It provides a graphical and command-line interface.

In Windows 7 or Vista, you can launch Windows RE from the Windows setup DVD. In Windows 7, Windows RE is installed on the hard drive and available on the Advanced Boot Options menu. In addition, you can create a Windows 7 **system repair disc** and use it to launch Windows RE.

To create a Windows 7 system repair disc, click **Create a system repair disc** in the Windows 7 Backup and Restore window (see Figure 14-15). A 32-bit Windows 7 installation will create a 32-bit version of the repair disc, and a 64-bit Windows 7 installation will create a 64-bit version of the repair disc. A repair disc created on one computer can be used on a different computer even if they are using different editions of Windows 7, but be sure to use a 32-bit disc for a 32-bit installation and a 64-bit disc for a 64-bit Windows installation.

A+
220-802
4.6

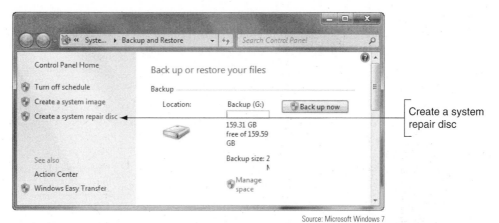

Create a system
repair disc

Source: Microsoft Windows 7

Figure 14-15 Use Backup and Restore to create a system repair disc to use instead of the Windows setup DVD

Notes To launch Windows RE from a Windows setup DVD or Windows 7 repair disc, be sure to use a 64-bit DVD for a 64-bit installation of Windows and a 32-bit DVD for a 32-bit installation of Windows. To boot from a DVD, you might have to change the boot sequence in BIOS setup to put the optical drive first above the hard drive.

APPLYING | CONCEPTS EXPLORE WINDOWS RE

Follow these steps to start Windows RE and explore what it has to offer:

1. Use one of the following methods to start Windows RE:

   ▲ For Windows 7 or Vista, boot from the Windows setup DVD. Select your language preference and click **Next**. The Install Windows screen appears, as shown in Figure 14-16. Click **Repair your computer**.

Source: Microsoft Windows 7

Figure 14-16 Launch Windows RE after booting from the Windows DVD

14

▲ For Windows 7, press **F8** during the boot and on the Advanced Boot Options menu, select **Repair Your Computer**. In the dialog box that appears, select your keyboard input method.

▲ For Windows 7, boot from the Windows 7 repair disc. Select your language preference and click **Next**. The Install Windows screen appears, as shown in Figure 14-16. Click **Repair your computer**.

Regardless of the method you use, the System Recovery Options box appears.

2. Depending on the situation, the System Recovery Options box might ask you to select your language preference (when you have booted from a disc) or the Windows installation to repair (in a dual boot system). Make your selection and click **Next**.

3. The System Recovery Options box then asks you to select your user account that has administrative privileges (see Figure 14-17). Select your user account, enter your password, and click **OK**. Without this account and password you will not be allowed to access the volume where Windows is installed.

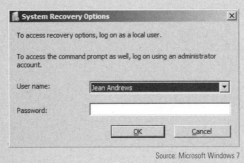

Source: Microsoft Windows 7

Figure 14-17   Select an account with administrative privileges

4. The System Recovery Options box appears, where you can select a recovery tool (see Figure 14-18).

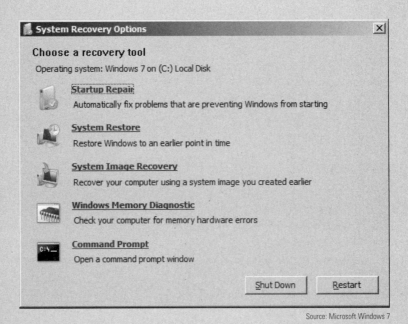

Source: Microsoft Windows 7

Figure 14-18   Recovery tools in Windows RE for a Windows 7 installation

When deciding which tool to use in Figure 14-18, always use the least intrusive tool first. In other words, fix the problem while making as few changes to the system as possible.

> **Notes** As you use a tool in the System Recovery Options window, be sure to reboot after each attempt to fix the problem to make sure the problem has not been resolved before you try another tool. To exit the Recovery Environment, click **Shut Down** or **Restart**.

Use the Windows RE tools in the order listed so as to fix the system using the least intrusive method:

1. *Startup Repair.* This option is the least intrusive. It does not change user data or installed applications and can sometimes fix a startup problem, including those caused by corrupted or missing system files. You can't cause any additional problems by using it and it's easy to use. Follow these steps:

   a. Click **Startup Repair** and the tool will examine the system for errors (see Figure 14-19). Based on what it finds, it will suggest various solutions such as using System Restore (see Figure 14-20). If it cannot fix the problem, the box in Figure 14-21 appears. For the system in Figure 14-22, Startup Repair has made repairs and suggests a reboot.

   b. To see a list of items examined and actions taken by Startup Repair, click **Click here for diagnostic and repair details**. A dialog box appears showing the list of repairs accomplished. In addition, a log file can be found at C:\Windows\System32\LogFiles\SRT\SRTTrail.txt.

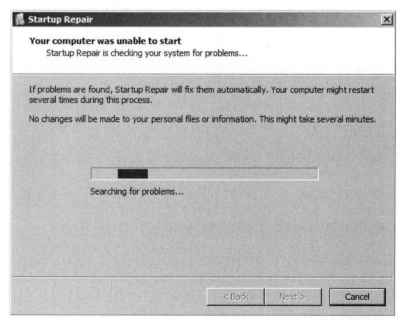

Source: Microsoft Windows 7

Figure 14-19 Startup Repair searches the system for problems it can fix

A+
220-802
4.6

Source: Microsoft Windows 7

Figure 14-20 Startup Repair suggests you use System Restore

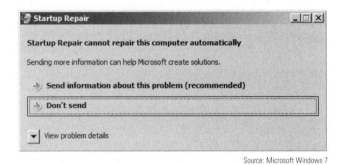

Source: Microsoft Windows 7

Figure 14-21 Startup Repair has decided it cannot fix the system

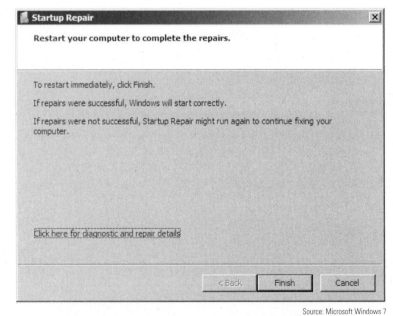

Source: Microsoft Windows 7

Figure 14-22 Startup Repair has attempted to fix the problem

2. *Windows Memory Diagnostic.* If you suspect memory might be a problem, click this option to identify a corrupted memory module.

3. *System Restore.* Use System Restore to restore the system to a previously saved restore point. This option can sometimes fix a problem with a corrupted device driver,

A+
220-802
4.6

corrupted Windows settings, or corrupted programs. The process will not affect user data. Click **System Restore** and then select a restore point. Select the most recent restore point to make the least intrusive changes to the system.

4. *Command Prompt.* If you suspect the hard drive is corrupted, use the Command Prompt option to open a command prompt window and then use Chkdsk with the /r parameter to check the hard drive for errors. You can also use commands in the Command Prompt window to restore a corrupted registry from a backup. How to use the Windows RE command prompt window is covered later in the chapter.

5. *System Image Recovery.* Use the System Image Recovery as a last resort. It uses a previously created system image to restore the entire Windows volume to this image. Be aware that everything on the Windows volume will be erased and replaced with the system image. Before you use this option, make every attempt to recover from the hard drive any data files that have not yet been backed up. Recall from Chapter 10 that the system image is created and updated using the Backup and Restore window. Also know that your organization might use a standard image or a deployment image rather than a system image to recover a failed Windows volume.

> **Vista Differences**   In Vista, the System Image Recovery option is replaced with the Complete PC Restore option (see Figure 14-23). Use it to completely restore the Windows Vista volume and possibly other drives to their state when the last backups of the drives were made. The backups are made using Complete PC Backup, which you learned about in Chapter 10.

Source: Microsoft Vista

Figure 14-23   Recovery tools in Windows RE for Windows Vista

Now let's see how to use the Windows RE command prompt window.

THE COMMAND PROMPT WINDOW IN WINDOWS RE

A+
220-802
1.3, 4.6

Use the command prompt window in Windows RE when graphical tools available in Windows RE fail to solve the Windows problem. Using this command prompt, you have full read and write access to all files on all drives. Many commands you learned about in

A+
220-802
1.3, 4.6

Chapter 10 can be used at this command prompt. Here are some examples of how to use the Windows RE command prompt to repair a system:

▲ *Repair a hard drive or other drive.* Use the chkdsk and format commands to repair a hard drive. Use the **diskpart** command to manage hard drives, partitions, and volumes. When you enter diskpart at a command prompt, the DISKPART> prompt appears where you can enter diskpart commands. Some important diskpart commands are listed in Table 14-2. Figure 14-24 shows the diskpart commands used to partition and format a USB flash drive. Diskpart can also be used in a normal command prompt window.

Diskpart Command	Description
`list disk`	Lists installed hard disk drives.
`select disk`	Selects a hard disk or other storage device. For example: *select disk 0*
`list partition`	Lists partitions on selected disk.
`select partition`	Selects a partition on the selected disk. For example: *select partition 1*
`clean`	Removes any partition or volume information from the selected disk. Can be useful to remove dynamic disk information or a corrupted partition table or if you just want a fresh start when partitioning a hard disk. All data and partition information on the disk are deleted.
`create partition primary`	Creates a primary partition on the currently selected hard disk.
`assign`	Assigns a drive letter to a new partition. For example: *assign letter=H*
`format`	Formats the currently selected partition. For example: *format fs=ntfs quick* *format fs=fat32*
`active`	Makes the selected partition the active partition.
`inactive`	Makes the selected partition inactive.
`exit`	Exits the Diskpart utility.

Table 14-2   Important diskpart commands used at the DISKPART> prompt

© Cengage Learning 2014

> **Notes** For a complete list of Diskpart commands, go to the Microsoft support site (*support.microsoft.com*) and search on "DiskPart Command-Line Options."

▲ *Enable networking.* Networking is not normally available from this command prompt. Use the wpeinit command to enable networking.

▲ *Repair the file system and key boot files.* Use the **bootrec** command to repair the BCD and boot sectors. Use the **bcdedit** command to manually edit the BCD. Use the **bootsect** command to repair a dual boot system. Some examples of each command are listed in Table 14-3. To get helpful information about these commands, enter the command followed by /?, such as **bcdedit /?**.

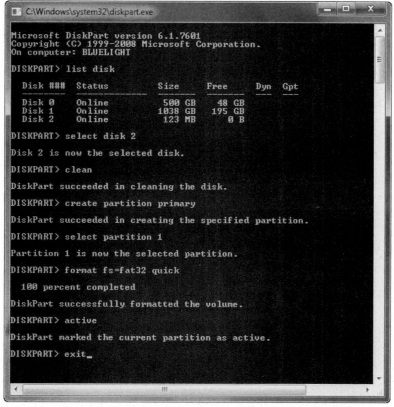

A+
220-802
1.3, 4.6

Source: Microsoft Windows 7

Figure 14-24 Use commands in diskpart to partition and format a USB flash drive

Command Line	Description
bootrec /scanOS	Scans the hard drive for Windows installations not stored in the BCD
bootrec /rebuildBCD	Scans for Windows installations and rebuilds the BCD
bcdedit	Manually edits BCD; be sure to make a copy of the file before you edit it
bootrec /fixboot	Repairs the boot sector of the system partition
bootrec /fixmbr	Repairs the MBR

© Cengage Learning 2014

Table 14-3 Commands used in the command prompt window of Windows RE to repair system files and the file system

14

A+ Exam Tip The A+ 220-802 exam expects you to know how to use the bootrec and diskpart commands. In addition, it expects you to know about the **FDISK** command, which was part of Windows 9x and was used to create and manage partitions on a hard drive. The FDISK command was launched after booting a computer using a Windows 9x startup floppy disk. The FDISK /MBR command was used to repair a damaged MBR program.

XP Differences The XP **Recovery Console** is similar to the command prompt window in Windows RE. The XP Recovery Console uses the **fixmbr** command to repair the MBR and uses the **fixboot** command to repair the boot sector of the system partition. For more information, see Appendix C.

A+
220-802
1.3, 4.6

▲ *Manage data files and system files.* Use cd, copy, rename, and delete commands to manage data and system files. For example, if key registry files are corrupted or deleted, the system will not start. You can restore registry files using those saved in the C:\Windows\System32\Config\RegBack folder. This RegBack folder contains partial backups of the registry files put there after a successful boot. Use the commands in Table 14-4 to restore the registry files.

Command Line	Description
1. c:	Makes drive C: the current drive.
2. cd \windows\system32\config	Makes the Windows registry folder the current folder.
3. ren default default.save 4. ren sam sam.save 5. ren security security.save 6. ren software software.save 7. ren system system.save	Renames the five registry files.
8. cd regback	Makes the registry backup folder the current folder.
9. copy system c:\windows\system32\config	For hardware problems, first try copying just the System hive from the backup folder to the registry folder and then reboot.
10. copy software c:\windows\system32\config	For software problems, first try copying just the Software hive to the registry folder, and then reboot.
11. copy system c:\windows\system32\config 12. copy software c:\windows\system32\config 13. copy default c:\windows\system32\config 14. copy sam c:\windows\system32\config 15. copy security c:\windows\system32\config	If the problem is still not solved, try copying all five hives to the registry folder and reboot.

© Cengage Learning 2014

Table 14-4 Steps to restore the registry files

After you try each fix, reboot the system to see if the problem is solved before you do the next fix.

> **XP Differences** Windows XP uses an **emergency repair disk** (a floppy disk) to solve problems with missing system files needed for the boot. XP startup error messages that indicate missing system files include "Missing NTLDR" and "Missing Boot.ini." How to create an emergency repair disk and use it to deal with these errors are covered in Appendix C.

> **A+ Exam Tip** The A+ 220-802 exam expects you to know how to use the Windows XP emergency repair disk to repair boot files on an XP system.

TROUBLESHOOTING WINDOWS 7/VISTA STARTUP

A+
220-802
4.3, 4.6

This section is written as step-by-step instructions for problem solving, so that you can use it to solve a boot problem with Windows 7/Vista by following the steps. Each step takes you sequentially through the boot process and shows you what to do when the boot fails at that point in the process. Therefore, your first decision in troubleshooting a failed boot is to decide at what point in the boot the failure occurred. Next, you have to decide which tool will be the least invasive to use, yet still will fix the problem. The idea is to make as few changes to your system as possible in order to solve the problem without having to do a lot of work to return the system to normal (such as having to reinstall all your applications). And, as with every computer problem, if user data is at risk, you need to take steps to back up the data as soon as possible in the troubleshooting process.

To determine where in the boot process the failure occurred, we'll focus on these three startup stages of the boot:

- *Stage 1: Before the Windows 7 flag or Vista progress bar.* When you see the flag or progress bar appear, you know the Windows kernel, including all critical services and drivers, has loaded. Any problems that occur before this graphic appears are most likely related to corrupt or missing system files or hardware. Your best Windows tools to use for these problems are Startup Repair and System Restore.
- *Stage 2: After the flag or progress bar and before logon.* After the flag or progress bar appears, user mode services and drivers are loaded and then the logon screen appears. Problems with these components can best be solved using Startup Repair, the Last Known Good Configuration, System Restore, Safe Mode, Device Manager, and MSconfig.
- *Stage 3: After logon.* After the logon screen appears, problems can be caused by startup scripts, applications set to launch at startup, and desktop settings. Use MSconfig to temporarily disable startup programs. Safe Mode can also be useful.

> 💡 **A+ Exam Tip** The A+ 220-802 exam expects you to know how to deal with errors that occur when the graphical interface fails to load.

Now let's take a closer look at how to address problems at each of the three stages of Windows startup.

PROBLEMS AT STAGE 1: BEFORE THE FLAG OR PROGRESS BAR APPEARS

These problems might be caused by hardware or startup files. Hardware that might be failing includes the power supply, motherboard, CPU, memory, hard drive, video, or keyboard. If any one of these devices is not working, the error is communicated using beep codes, or using on-screen or voice error messages—and then the computer halts.

> 💡 **A+ Exam Tip** The A+ 220-802 exam expects you to know how to troubleshoot problems with hardware, including how to replace the motherboard, memory modules, hard drive, CPU, and power supply. Chapter 13 covers troubleshooting hardware problems.

14

As you perform each troubleshooting step, be sure to restart the system to see if the problem is solved before you apply the next step.

IS THE SCREEN BLANK?

If you see absolutely nothing on the screen, check these things:

◢ Is the monitor totally without lights, or is the screen blank but the LED light on front of the monitor is lit? If the LED light is lit, try rebooting the system. If the LED light is not lit, check that power is getting to the monitor. Is it turned on?

◢ Can you hear the spinning fan or hard drive inside the computer case? Are lights lit on the front of the case? If not, suspect that power is not getting to the system or the system might have overheated.

◢ Check that the system is not in standby mode or hibernation: try waking up the system by pressing any key or a special standby key on laptops or by pressing the power-on button.

◢ Try trading the monitor for one you know is good. If you can hear a spinning drive and see lights on the front of the computer case and know the monitor works, the video card might be bad or not seated properly in its slot, the memory might be bad, the video cable might be bad or loosely connected, or a component on the motherboard might have failed.

DOES THE COMPUTER APPEAR TO HAVE POWER?

If you can't hear the spinning drive or see lights on the front of the case, suspect the electrical system. Check power connections and switches. The power supply might be bad or connections inside the case might be loose.

DOES AN ERROR MESSAGE APPEAR BEFORE WINDOWS STARTS?

Recall that when you first turn on a system, startup BIOS takes control, checks essential hardware devices, and searches for an OS to load. If it has a problem while doing all that and the video system is working, it displays an error message on-screen. If video is not working, it might attempt to communicate an error with a series of beep codes or speech (for speech-enabled BIOS). Restart the system and carefully listen for and count the beeps. Then you can look up what they mean on the web site of the motherboard manufacturer.

For messages displayed on-screen that apply to nonessential hardware devices such as a DVD drive, you might be able to bypass the error by pressing a key and moving forward in the boot. However, for errors with essential hardware devices such as the one shown in Figure 14-25, focus your attention on the error message, beep code, or voice message describing the problem. If you don't know what the error message or beep codes mean, you can search the web site of the motherboard manufacturer or do a general search of the web using a search engine such as Google.

CAN STARTUP BIOS ACCESS THE HARD DRIVE?

Error messages generated by startup BIOS that pertain to the hard drive can be caused by a variety of things. Here is a list of text error messages that indicate that BIOS could not find a hard drive:

◢ Hard drive not found
◢ Fixed disk error
◢ Disk boot failure, insert system disk and press enter
◢ No boot device available

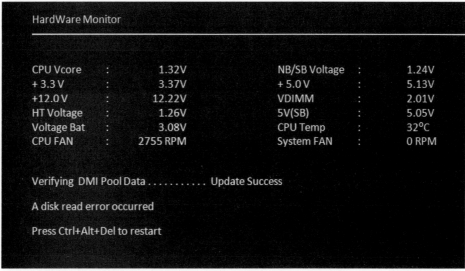

```
HardWare Monitor
_____

CPU Vcore      :      1.32V          NB/SB Voltage   :      1.24V
+ 3.3 V        :      3.37V          + 5.0 V         :      5.13V
+12.0 V        :     12.22V          VDIMM           :      2.01V
HT Voltage     :      1.26V          5V(SB)          :      5.05V
Voltage Bat    :      3.08V          CPU Temp        :      32°C
CPU FAN        :   2755 RPM          System FAN      :      0 RPM


Verifying  DMI Pool Data . . . . . . . . . .  Update Success

A disk read error occurred

Press Ctrl+Alt+Del to restart
```

Source: Intel

Figure 14-25 This error message at POST indicates a hardware problem

The problem might be a physical problem with the drive, the data cable, power, or the motherboard. Start with checking BIOS setup to verify that BIOS detected the drive correctly. If the drive was not detected, check the autodetection setting in BIOS setup. If autodetection is turned off, turn it on and reboot. Your problem might be solved. If startup BIOS still doesn't find the drive, power down the system, unplug it, and open the case. Physically check the hard drive power and data cable connections at both ends. Sometimes cables work their way loose. Be careful not to touch circuit boards or the processor as you work, and to protect the system against static electricity, wear an antistatic bracelet that is clipped to the computer case.

Here is a list of error messages that indicate the BIOS was able to find the hard drive but couldn't read what was written on the drive or could not find what it was looking for:

◢ A disk read error occurred
◢ Drive not recognized
◢ Invalid boot disk
◢ Invalid partition table
◢ Inaccessible boot device
◢ Invalid drive specification
◢ Invalid partition table
◢ Operating system not found, No operating system found, Missing operating system, Error loading operating system
◢ Couldn't find bootmgr or bootmgr is missing

A+ Exam Tip The A+ 220-802 exam expects you to be able to resolve a problem that gives the error messages "Drive not recognized" or "OS not found."

For these types of error messages, try the following:

1. Try to press **F8** at startup and launch the Advanced Boot Options menu. This menu cannot load if the system cannot access the hard drive. But at least give it a try before you move on to the tools on the Windows setup DVD.

2. Check BIOS setup to make sure the boot sequence lists the DVD drive before the hard drive, and then boot from the Windows setup DVD.

14

A+
220-802
4.3, 4.6

Notes To access BIOS setup, reboot the PC and look on-screen for a message such as "Press DEL for setup," "Press F2 for BIOS settings," or something similar. Press that key and the BIOS setup utility loads. Find the screen, such as the one in Figure 14-26, that lets you set the boot sequence. (If you cannot find the key to press to access BIOS setup, search the web using the computer's brand and model.)

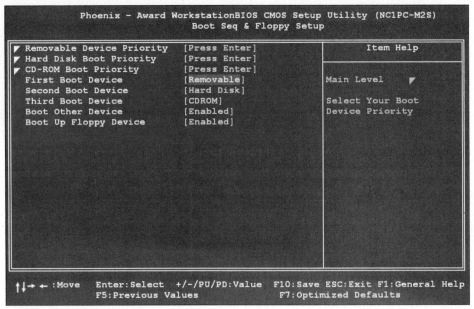

Source: Phoenix Award BIOS

Figure 14-26 Set the boot order in BIOS setup

CAN YOU BOOT FROM THE WINDOWS SETUP DVD?

Try to boot from the Windows setup DVD. If you cannot boot from this disc, the problem is not just the hard drive. Study the error message and solve the immediate hardware problem. It's possible the hard drive and the optical drive have failed, but a USB port might still work. If you have a bootable USB flash drive, you can try booting from it. If you can boot from the flash drive, you have proven the problem is with both the hard drive and the optical drive.

If you are able to boot from the Windows setup DVD, the window shown in Figure 14-27 appears. If you see this window, you have proven that the problem is isolated to the hard drive. Now the trick is to find out exactly what is wrong with the drive and fix it.

CAN WINDOWS RE FIND THE WINDOWS INSTALLATION?

At this point, click **Next** in Figure 14-27 and then click **Repair your computer** to attempt to launch Windows RE. The first thing Windows RE does is attempt to locate a Windows installation on the hard drive. If it cannot locate the installation, but BIOS setup recognizes the drive, then the drive partitions and file systems might be corrupted. If Windows RE does locate the installation, the problem is more likely to be limited to corrupted or missing system files or drivers.

A+
220-802
4.3, 4.6

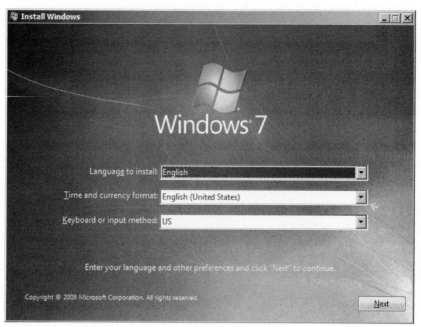

Source: Microsoft Windows 7

Figure 14-27 Select your language preference

14

As you attempt each fix in the following list, be sure to restart the system after each step to find out if the problem still exists or has changed:

1. Run Startup Repair. This process can sometimes fix drastic problems with system files and boot records.

2. Run System Restore. The process won't help if the file system is corrupted.

3. Restart the system and press **F8** during the boot to launch the Advanced Boot Options menu, as shown earlier in Figure 14-6. If the boot menu does not appear, chances are the problem is a corrupted boot sector. If the boot menu appears, chances are the BCD file or other startup files are the problem. If you do see the menu, enable boot logging and reboot. Then check the boot log (\Windows\ntbtlog.txt) for the last entry, which might indicate which system file is missing or corrupt. (If the hard drive is at all accessible, your best chance of viewing the boot log file is to use the command prompt window and the Type command.)

4. If the boot menu does not appear, return to Windows RE, launch the command prompt window, and attempt to repair the boot sector. Try these commands: **bootrec /fixmbr** and **bootrec /fixboot**. Also try the **diskpart** command followed by the **list volume** command. Does the OS find the system volume? If not, the entire partition might be lost.

5. If the boot menu does appear, return to Windows RE, launch the command prompt window, and attempt to repair the BCD file. Try this command: **bootrec /rebuildbcd**.

6. Try to repair a corrupted file system by using the command prompt window and the **chkdsk c: /r** command.

7. When startup files are missing or corrupt, sometimes Windows displays an error message similar to the one shown in Figure 14-28, which names the file giving the problem. You can replace the file by going to a healthy Windows computer and copying

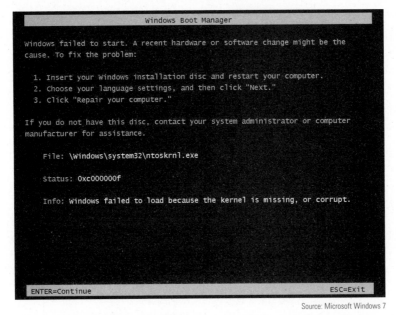

Source: Microsoft Windows 7

Figure 14-28 Windows might display a screen similar to this one when a critical startup file is missing or corrupt

the file to a removable media. Then, on the problem computer, boot to Windows RE, open the command prompt window, and rename the original file so you will not overwrite it with the replacement and you can backtrack, if necessary. Then copy the replacement file to the hard drive.

8. Try using the command prompt window to access drive C:. If you can get to a C: prompt, use the **dir** command to list folders and files. If you see a good list, check the log file, C:\Windows\System32\LogFiles\SRT\SRTTrail.txt, for clues. (Recall this log file is kept by the Startup Repair process of Windows RE.) If you cannot get a good list of contents of drive C:, most likely the Windows installation is destroyed beyond repair. Before you address the problem of a corrupted Windows installation, make every effort to copy data to another media. You can use copy commands in the Windows RE command prompt window or move the drive to a working computer to copy files.

OPTIONS TO RECOVER FROM A CORRUPTED WINDOWS INSTALLATION

If you are not able to repair the corrupted installation using the techniques in the previous list, your next step is to consider what options are available to restore the system. Your options depend on backups available, including a backup of user data and a backup of the Windows 7 system image or a Vista Complete PC backup. The system image or Complete PC backup is a backup of the Windows volume and is called a **recovery image**. Here are your choices to restore a corrupted installation:

◢ *Option 1:* If you have a recovery image, use it to restore the system to the last backup. If data is on the hard drive that has not been backed up, make every effort to copy this data to a safe place before you restore the system. To start the recovery, boot into Windows RE. For Windows 7, on the System Recovery Options screen, click **System Image Recovery** and follow the directions on-screen. (For Vista, click **Windows Complete PC Restore** on the System Recovery Options screen.)

◢ *Option 2:* If you don't have a recovery image but you do have backups of the data on the hard drive, reinstall Windows, formatting the hard drive during the installation. You'll need to install all applications again and then restore the data.

A+
220-802
1.7, 4.3,
4.6

▲ *Option 3:* If you don't have a recovery image and you also don't have backups of the data on the drive (worst-case scenario), try to copy the data and then reinstall Windows. Even if you cannot copy the data, you might be able to recover it after the reinstallation. If you have data on the Windows volume, don't format during the Windows installation.

> **Notes** If you cannot start Windows and there is important data on the drive, consider moving the hard drive to another computer and installing it as a second device. Then boot the computer and copy data from the drive to another storage device. You can then return the hard drive to its original computer and reinstall Windows, formatting the drive during the installation process.

> **XP Differences** Windows XP can make a backup of the entire Windows volume using the Automated System Recovery tool. To restore the Windows volume, you need the ASR floppy disk, the ASR backup, and the XP setup CD. For details, see Appendix C.

STEPS TO REINSTALL WINDOWS

Recall from Chapter 7 that you can install Windows from the Windows setup DVD, from a standard image, or from a deployment image. For a network deployment of Windows, recall that you must boot the computer to the network where it finds and loads Windows PE on the deployment server. To boot to the network, go into BIOS setup and set the first boot device to be Ethernet. The PC then boots to the Pre-Execution Environment (PXE) and then PXE searches for a server on the network for Windows PE and the deployment image.

> **A+ Exam Tip** The A+ 220-802 exam expects you to know how to use a preinstallation environment and a recovery image to help resolve a Windows startup problem.

14

Follow these steps to reinstall Windows using the Windows setup DVD when the OS refuses to boot and there is important data on the drive:

1. Boot from the Windows setup DVD, and follow the directions on-screen to perform a clean installation of Windows, but do not format the hard drive. Windows setup will move all folders of the old installation into the \Windows.Old folder, including the \Windows, \Users, and \Program Files folders. A fresh, clean installation of Windows is installed in the \Windows folder.

2. If you suspect the hard drive might be failing or need reformatting, immediately save all important data to another media and reinstall Windows a second time, this time reformatting the hard drive. If you believe the hard drive is healthy, then follow these steps to get things back to their original order:

   a. Run Chkdsk to fix errors on the drive.

   b. Install all applications and device drivers.

   c. Create all user accounts and customize Windows settings. How to create user accounts is covered in Chapter 7. Then copy all user data and other folders from the \Windows.Old folder to the new installation.

   d. To free up disk space, delete the \Windows.Old folder. To do that, using the Disk Cleanup utility in the Properties box for drive C:, select **Previous Windows installation(s)** (see Figure 14-29). Note that this option will not be available if the \Windows.Old folder does not exist.

A+
220-802
1.7, 4.3,
4.6

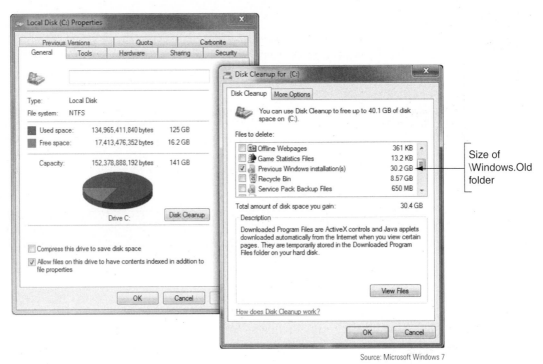

Source: Microsoft Windows 7

Figure 14-29   Free up disk space by deleting the \Windows.Old folder, which is labeled as Previous Windows installation(s)

Notes Remember that when reinstalling Windows on a laptop or brand-name computer, use the hidden recovery partition on the hard drive or recovery discs so that you have access to proprietary device drivers the system might use.

Caution When you first become responsible for a laptop computer, it's extremely important that you create or obtain the recovery DVD or CDs that you will need in case the hard drive crashes. Without this recovery media, it's almost impossible to recover the system using a new hard drive. And, laptop manufacturers don't make these media available to customers after the laptop is a few years old. Get the recovery media in hand while it is still available! You might be able to create the media from the hard drive while the system is still healthy. See the laptop documentation for instructions.

A+
220-802
4.3, 4.6

PROBLEMS AT STAGE 2: AFTER THE FLAG OR PROGRESS BAR APPEARS AND BEFORE LOGON

When you see the Windows 7 flag or the Vista progress bar appear during the boot, you know the Windows kernel has loaded successfully and critical drivers and services configured to be started by the kernel are running. You also know the Session Manager (Smss.exe) running in user mode has started the Win32 subsystem necessary to provide the graphics of the flag or progress bar. If the flag or progress bar has appeared and the logon screen has not yet been displayed, most likely the problem is caused by a corrupted driver or service that is started after the kernel has finished its part of the boot. Your general attack plan to fix the problem is to isolate and disable the Windows component, service, or application causing trouble. However, if user data on the hard drive is not backed up, do what you can to copy that data to another media before you focus on the problem at hand.

Follow these steps:

1. Press F8 at startup to launch the Advanced Boot Options menu and then try to boot into **Safe Mode**. If you don't know the source of the problem, here are some things you can try in Safe Mode to discover the source and hopefully solve the problem:

   ◢ *Tip 1:* Immediately run antivirus software to eliminate a virus as the problem.

   ◢ *Tip 2:* Run **chkdsk c: /r** to check and repair the hard drive.

   ◢ *Tip 3:* Examine the logs in Event Viewer for errors that might point to the problem.

   > **Notes** The Last Known Good Configuration is updated after you log on normally to Windows. However, logging onto a computer when booting into Safe Mode does not update the Last Known Good.

   ◢ *Tip 4:* Use MSconfig to stop any applications just installed. Then uninstall and reinstall the application. You can also disable all nonessential programs and services.

   ◢ *Tip 5:* Use Device Manager to check for hardware errors and disable any devices just installed. If you have just updated a driver, roll back the driver.

   ◢ *Tip 6:* In Safe Mode, use System Information (msinfo32.exe) to find the program filenames of drivers and services. Useful information can be found at these locations: Services in the Software Environment group and Problem Devices in the Components group.

   > **A+ Exam Tip** The A+ 220-802 exam expects you to know how to use System Information to help you resolve a Windows startup problem.

   ◢ *Tip 7:* Open an elevated command prompt window and use the System File Checker (SFC) tool to search for and replace corrupted system files. The command **sfc /scannow** searches for and replaces corrupted system files. Be sure to restart the system after this command is finished.

   ◢ *Tip 8:* If you have an Ntbtlog.txt file from a normal boot, compare the entries in the Ntbtlog.txt file when booting in Safe Mode to the entries when booting normally. Consider that the culprit might be any item that is loaded for a normal boot but not loaded for Safe Mode. Disable each driver one at a time until the problem goes away.

   ◢ *Tip 9:* Rename the Ntbtlog.txt file so it will not be overwritten during a normal boot and you can read it later.

2. If you cannot boot into Safe Mode, select the **Last Known Good Configuration** on the Advanced Boot Options menu. It's important to try this option early in the troubleshooting process because you might accidentally overwrite a good Last Known Good with a bad one as you attempt to log on with the problem still there.

3. Launch Windows RE from the Windows setup DVD and run **Startup Repair** from the System Recovery Options menu shown earlier in Figure 14-18. It can't do any harm, it's easy to use, and it might fix the problem.

4. In Windows RE, run **System Restore**. Select the latest restore point. If that doesn't fix the problem, try an earlier one.

14

A+
220-802
4.3, 4.6

5. Boot to the Advanced Boot Options menu and select **Enable Boot Logging**. Windows starts logging information to the log file WindowsNtbtlog.txt. Every driver that is loaded or not loaded is written to the file (see Figure 14-14 shown earlier in the chapter).

6. Compare the Ntbtlog.txt file to one that was created in Safe Mode. If the boot failed, look at the last entry in the Ntbtlog.txt file that was generated. Find that entry in the one created while booting into Safe Mode. The next driver listed in the Safe Mode Ntbtlog.txt file is likely the one giving problems.

7. After you believe you've identified the problem service or device, if you can boot into Safe Mode, first use Device Manager to disable the device or use the Services console to disable the service. Then reboot, and, if the problem goes away, replace the driver or service program file and then enable the driver or service.

8. If you cannot boot into Safe Mode, open the command prompt window in Windows RE. Then back up the registry and open the Registry Editor using the regedit command. Drill down to the service or device key. The key that loads services and drivers can be found in this location:

> HKEY_LOCAL_MACHINE\System\CurrentControlSet\Services

9. Disable the service or driver by changing the Start value to 0x4. Close the Registry Editor and reboot. If the problem goes away, use the copy command to replace the service or driver program file, and restart the service or driver.

PROBLEMS AT STAGE 3: AFTER WINDOWS LOGON

Problems that occur after the user logs onto Windows are caused by applications or services configured to launch at startup. Programs can be set to launch at startup by placing their shortcuts in startup folders, by Scheduled Tasks, or by software installation processes that affect registry entries. If you see an error message at startup that gives you a clue as to which service or program is at fault, test your theory by using MSconfig to disable that program. You can also disable all non-Microsoft services and programs and enable them one at a time until you find the one causing the problem.

Table 14-5 summarizes some symptoms and error messages, including blue screen stop errors you might encounter during the boot and what to do about them. Remember that stop errors most likely point to a hardware or driver problem.

Symptom or Error Message	Description and What to Do
A disk read error occurred Non-system disk or disk error Invalid boot disk	Startup BIOS could not communicate with the hard drive. Check BIOS setup for the boot sequence and try to boot from another device. Check drive cables and connections. The drive might be failing. To recover data from the drive, move it to another computer and install it as a second hard drive.
Loud clicking noise	The hard drive is likely failing. Make it your first priority to back up any data on the drive.
Invalid partition table Invalid drive specification Error loading operating system Missing operating system Drive not recognized	MBR record is damaged or the active partition is corrupt or missing. Use the repair commands from the Windows RE command prompt window.

© Cengage Learning 2014

Table 14-5 Error messages during Windows startup and what to do about them (continues)

A+
220-802
4.3, 4.6

Symptom or Error Message	Description and What to Do
Operating system not found Missing operating system Missing bootmgr	Windows system files are missing or corrupted. Boot to Windows RE and use tools there. First try Startup Repair. Use Chkdsk to fix hard drive errors.
RAID not found	Hardware RAID is managed by BIOS on the motherboard. Check the web site of the motherboard manufacturer for help with the exact error message. You might need to update BIOS.
Automatically boots into Safe Mode	This action can occur when Windows recognizes a problem with the registry or other startup files. Attempt to use Last Known Good on the Advanced Boot Options menu, or use System Restore to apply a restore point.
No graphics appear when Windows is started	An error that occurs before the Graphical Interface is started is caused by hardware or the Windows kernel failing to load. To solve problems with critical startup files that load the Windows kernel, use the tools in Windows RE.
An application launched at startup that gives errors or takes up resources	Use Msconfig to remove it from the list of startup programs.
Stop error (BSOD) that occurs during startup	A Stop error can be caused by a corrupted registry, a system file that is missing or damaged, a device driver that is missing or damaged, bad memory, or a corrupted or failing hard drive. Use the Microsoft web site to research the exact error message and error code. Use the Startup Repair tool and then examine the log file it creates at C:\Windows\System32\LogFiles\Srt\Srttrail.txt.

Table 14-5 Error messages during Windows startup and what to do about them (continued)

© Cengage Learning 2014

HOW TO RECOVER LOST DATA

When data is lost or corrupted, you might be able to recover it using Windows tools, third-party file recovery software, or commercial data recovery services. This section discusses your options to recover lost data.

RECOVER A DELETED OR CORRUPTED DATA FILE

Here are some things to try to recover a deleted or corrupted data file:

- If you have accidentally deleted a data file, to get it back, look in the Recycle Bin. Drag and drop the file back to where it belongs, or right-click the file and click **Restore** on the shortcut menu.
- If a data file is corrupted, you can restore it from backup using the Backup and Restore window or using the Previous Versions tab on the file's Properties box, as you learned to do in Chapter 10.
- You might recover a corrupted file using the Recover command. To use the command, the volume on which the file is located cannot be in use. The easiest way to do that is to boot into Windows RE and open a command prompt window. For example, Figure 14-30 shows the command **recover C:\Data\Mydata.txt**. Notice in the figure that the C: drive is not the current drive. The drive is not used when you load Windows RE, and drive C: is not the current or default drive.

14

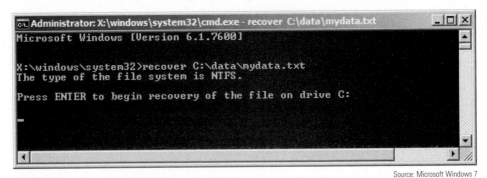

Source: Microsoft Windows 7

Figure 14-30 Use the Recover command to recover a corrupted file while the volume on which it is stored is not in use

▲ If an application's data file gets corrupted, go to the web site of the application's manufacturer and search the support section for what to do to recover the file. For example, if an Excel workbook file gets corrupted, search the Knowledge Base at *support.microsoft.com* for solutions.

▲ Third-party software can help recover deleted and corrupted files. On the Internet, do a search on "data recovery" for lots of examples. One good product is GetDataBack by Runtime Software (*www.runtime.org*), which can recover data and program files even when Windows cannot recognize the drive. It can read FAT and NTFS file systems and can solve problems with a corrupted partition table, boot record, or root directory.

RECOVER DATA FROM A COMPUTER THAT WILL NOT BOOT

If Windows is corrupted and the system will not boot, recovering your data might be your first priority. One way to get to the data is to remove your hard drive from your computer and install it as a second nonbooting hard drive in another system. After you boot up the system, you should be able to use Windows Explorer to copy the data to another medium. If the data is corrupted, try to use data recovery software.

For less than $30, you can purchase an IDE-to-USB converter kit (see Figure 14-31) or a SATA-to-USB converter kit (see Figure 14-32) that includes a data cable and power adapter. (For notebook hard drives, the IDE-to-USB kit needs to include an adapter for these smaller drives. This extra adapter is not needed for SATA notebook hard drives because these SATA connectors are the same size as those used for desktop drives.) You can use one of these

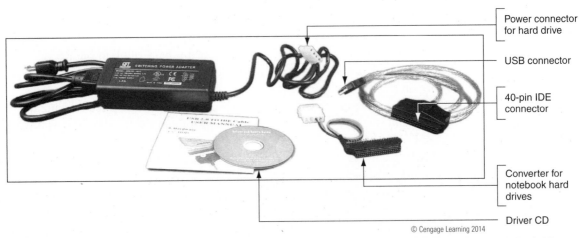

© Cengage Learning 2014

Figure 14-31 Use an IDE-to-USB converter for diagnostic testing and to recover data from a failing IDE hard drive

A+
220-802
4.3, 4.6

kits to temporarily connect a desktop or notebook hard drive to a USB port on a working computer. Set the drive beside your computer and plug one end of the data cable into the drive and the other into the USB port. (For an IDE drive, a jumper on the drive must be set to the master setting.) The AC adapter supplies power to the drive. While power is getting to the drive, be careful to not touch the circuit board on the drive.

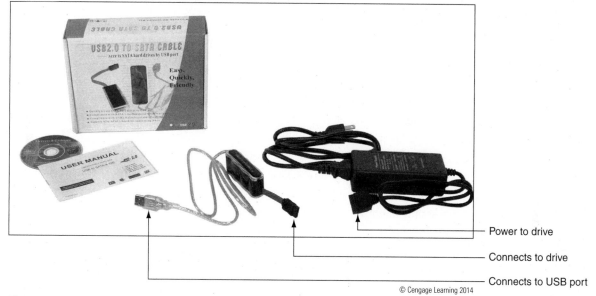

© Cengage Learning 2014

Power to drive

Connects to drive

Connects to USB port

Figure 14-32   Use a SATA-to-USB converter to recover data from a drive using a SATA connector

Using Windows Explorer, you can browse the drive and copy data to other media. After you have saved the data, use Disk Management to try to repartition and reformat the drive. You can also use diagnostic software from the hard drive manufacturer to examine the drive and possibly repair it.

USE A DATA RECOVERY SERVICE

If your data is extremely valuable and other methods have failed, you might want to consider a professional data recovery service. They're expensive, but getting the data back might be worth it. To find a service, use *Google.com* and search on "data recovery." Before selecting a service, be sure to read up on reviews, understand the warranty and guarantees, and perhaps get a recommendation from a satisfied customer.

>> CHAPTER SUMMARY

Understanding the Boot Process

▲ When you first turn on a system, startup BIOS on the motherboard takes control to examine hardware components and find an operating system to load.

▲ Windows 7/Vista startup is managed by the Windows Boot Manager (BootMgr) and the Windows Boot Loader (WinLoad.exe). The Boot Configuration Data (BCD) file contains Windows startup settings.

14

Windows 7/Vista Tools for Solving Startup Problems

◢ The Advanced Boot Options menu offers the options to repair your computer, Safe Mode, Safe Mode with networking, Safe Mode with command prompt, enable boot logging, enable low-resolution video (enable VGA mode in Windows XP), Last Known Good Configuration, directory services restore mode, debugging mode, and disable automatic restart on system failure.

◢ The Windows Recovery Environment (Windows RE) can be started from the Windows 7/Vista setup DVD, the Windows 7 Advanced Boot Options menu, and by booting from a Windows 7 repair disc.

◢ Startup Repair in Windows RE can automatically fix many Windows problems, including those caused by a corrupted BCD file and missing system files. You can't cause any additional problems by using it and it's easy to use. Therefore, it should be your first recovery option when Windows refuses to load.

◢ Other tools in Windows RE include Memory Diagnostics, System Restore, a command prompt window, and System Image Recovery. This last tool is used to restore Windows using a system image.

◢ Commands that might be useful when repairing Windows include Bootrec, Bcdedit, Diskpart, Bootsect, and Chkdsk.

Troubleshooting Windows 7/Vista Startup

◢ Windows tools and techniques used to troubleshoot a failed boot include Last Known Good Configuration, Startup Repair, System Restore, Safe Mode, Command Prompt, in-place upgrade of Windows, reimaging the hard drive, and reinstalling Windows.

◢ Last Known Good Configuration can solve problems caused by a bad hardware or software installation by undoing the install.

◢ Use the command prompt window in Windows RE when the other RE tools fail to solve the problem.

◢ Your first decision in troubleshooting a failed Windows boot is to decide at what point in the boot the failure occurred. Determine if the failure occurred before the Windows 7 flag or Vista progress bar appears, after the flag or progress bar and before logon, or after logon.

◢ If a hard drive contains valuable data but will not boot, you might be able to recover the data by installing the drive in another system as the second, nonbooting hard drive in the system.

>> KEY TERMS

For explanations of key terms, see the Glossary near the end of the book.

Advanced Options menu	emergency repair disk	recovery image
bcdedit	FDISK	soft boot
Boot Configuration Data (BCD) file	fixboot	system repair disc
	fixmbr	warm boot
booting	hard boot	Windows Boot Loader (WinLoad.exe)
Boot.ini	Last Known Good Configuration	Windows Boot Manager (BootMgr)
bootrec	Ntldr	
bootsect	OS boot record	Windows Recovery Environment (Windows RE)
cold boot	POST (power-on self test)	
diskpart	Recovery Console	

>> REVIEW QUESTIONS

1. Startup BIOS turns control over to the ____ program stored in the first sector of the hard drive.

   a) MBR

   b) BootMgr

   c) WinLoad.exe

   d) BCD

2. ____ is a lean operating system that can be launched to solve Windows startup problems after other tools available on the Advanced Boot Options menu have failed to solve the problem.

   a) System Image Recovery

   b) System Restore

   c) Last Known Good Configuration

   d) Windows Recovery Environment (Windows RE)

3. What command is used to repair a Windows 7 dual boot system?

   a) Bootsect

   b) Bcdedit

   c) Bootrec

   d) Fixmbr

4. Your best Windows tools to use for any problems that occur before the flag or progress bar appears are Startup Repair and ____.

   a) Session Manager

   b) System Image Recovery

   c) System Restore

   d) MSconfig

5. What is the most likely cause of problems that occur after the user logs onto Windows?

   a) A corrupted driver or service that is started after the kernel has finished its part of the boot.

   b) Applications or services configured to launch at startup.

   c) Hardware or startup files.

   d) A corrupted Active Directory.

6. True or false? The PC boots from the system partition and loads the Windows operating system from the boot partition.

7. True or false? The Windows startup is officially completed when the Windows 7 flag is displayed.

8. True or false? Safe Mode won't load if core Windows components are corrupted.

9. True or false? Your first decision in troubleshooting a failed boot is to decide which tool will be the least invasive to use, yet still will fix the problem.

14

10. True or false? If you have accidentally deleted a data file, to get it back, look in the Recycle Bin.

11. To save time in most circumstances, you should use the ____ boot to restart a computer.

12. ____ is responsible for loading Windows components.

13. The Advanced Boot Options menu appears when a user presses ____ as Windows is loading.

14. Use the ____ command to manage hard drives, partitions, and volumes.

15. The system image or Complete PC backup is a backup of the Windows volume and is called a(n) ____.

Connecting to and Setting Up a Network

In this chapter, you'll learn how Windows uses TCP/IP protocols and standards to create and manage network connections, including how computers are identified and addressed on a network. You'll also learn to connect a computer to a network and how to set up and secure a small wired or wireless network.

This chapter prepares you to assume total responsibility for supporting both wired and wireless networks in a small-office-home-office (SOHO) environment. In Chapter 16, you learn more about the hardware used in networking, including network devices, connectors, and cabling, networking tools, and the types of networks used for Internet connections. In Chapter 17, you learn how to support applications using a network and how to troubleshoot networking problems. So let's get started by looking at how TCP/IP works in the world of Windows networking.

> **A+ Exam Tip** Much of the content in this chapter applies to both the A+ 220-801 exam and the A+ 220-802 exam.

UNDERSTANDING TCP/IP AND WINDOWS NETWORKING

When two computers communicate using a local network or the Internet, communication happens at three levels (hardware, operating system, and application). The first step in communication is one computer must find the other computer. The second step is both computers must agree on the methods and rules for communication (called **protocols**). Then one computer takes on the role of making requests from the other computer. A computer making a request from another is called the client and the one answering the request is called the server. Most communication between computers on a network or the Internet uses this **client/server** model. For example, in Figure 15-1, someone uses a web browser to request a web page from a web server. To handle this request, the client computer must first find the web server, the protocols for communication are established, and then the request is made and answered. Hardware, the OS, and the applications on both computers are all involved in this process.

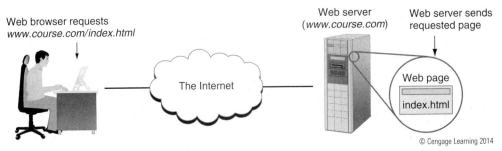

Web browser requests
www.course.com/index.html

The Internet

Web server
(*www.course.com*)

Web server sends
requested page

Web page
index.html

© Cengage Learning 2014

Figure 15-1 A web browser (client software) requests a web page from a web server (server software); the web server returns the requested data to the client

Let's first look at the layers of communication that involve hardware, the OS, and applications and then see how computers are addressed and found on a network or the Internet. Then we'll see how a client/server request is made by the client and answered by the server.

LAYERS OF NETWORK COMMUNICATION

When your computer at home is connected to your Internet Service Provider (ISP) off somewhere in the distance, your computer and a computer on the Internet must be able to communicate. When two devices communicate, they must use the same protocols so that the communication makes sense. For almost all networks today, including the Internet, the group or suite of protocols used is called **TCP/IP (Transmission Control Protocol/Internet Protocol)**.

Before data is transmitted on a network, it is first broken up into segments. Each data segment is put into a **packet**. The packet contains the data (called the payload) and information at the beginning of the packet (called the IP header) that identifies the type of data, where it came from, and where it's going. If the data to be sent is large, it is first divided into several packets, each small enough to travel on the network.

Part of the information included in a packet header is the address information needed to find the computer that is to receive the packet. The address information includes three levels: the address at the hardware level (called a MAC address), the address at the OS level (called an IP address), and the address at the application level (called a port address).

Communication between two computers happens in layers. In Figure 15-2, you can see how communication starts with an application (browser) passing a request to the OS, which

A+
220-801
2.3

A+
220-802
1.6

passes the request to the network card and then onto the network. When the request reaches the network card on the server, the network card passes it on to the OS and then the OS passes it on to the application (the web server).

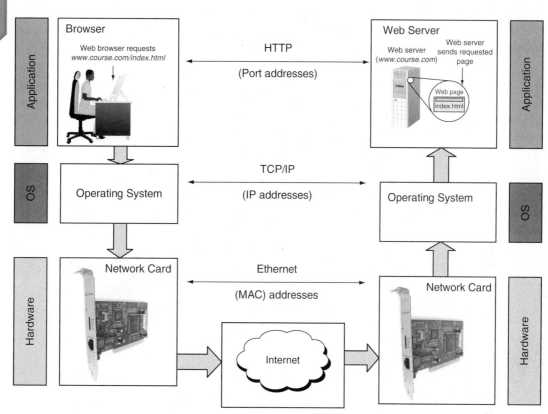

Figure 15-2 Network communication happens in layers

© Cengage Learning 2014

15

Listed next is a description of each level of communication:

◢ *Level 1: Hardware level.* At the root level of communication is hardware. The hardware or physical connection might be wireless or might use network cables, phone lines (for DSL or dial-up), or TV cable lines (for a cable modem). For local wired or wireless networks, a **network adapter** (also called a network card, a network interface card, or a NIC) inside your computer is part of this physical network. Every network adapter (including a network card, network port on a motherboard, onboard wireless, or wireless NIC) has a 48-bit (6-byte) number hard-coded on the card by its manufacturer that is unique for that device (see Figure 15-3). The number is written in hex, and is called the **MAC (Media Access Control) address, hardware address, physical address, adapter address,** or Ethernet address. Part of the MAC address identifies the manufacturer that is responsible for making sure that no two network adapters have the same MAC address. MAC addresses are used to locate a computer on a local area network (LAN). A **local area network (LAN)** is a network bound by routers or other gateway devices. A **router** is a device that manages traffic between two or more networks and can help find the best path for traffic to get from one network to another. A **gateway** is any device or computer that network traffic can use to leave one network and go to a different network.

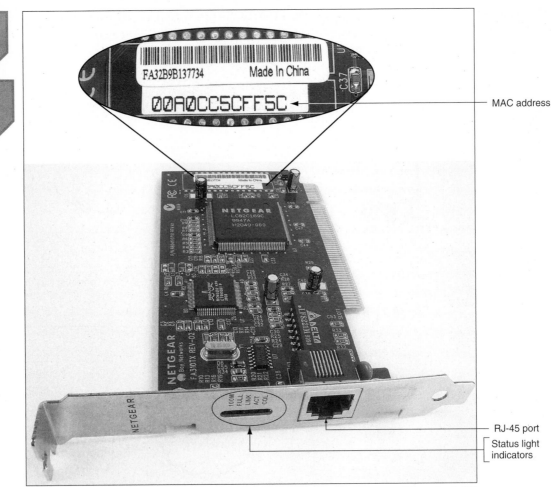

MAC address

RJ-45 port

Status light indicators

© Cengage Learning 2014

Figure 15-3 Ethernet network card showing its MAC address

▲ *Level 2: Operating system level.* Operating systems use IP addresses to find other computers on a network. An **IP address** is a 32-bit or 128-bit string that is assigned to a network connection when the connection is first made. Whereas a MAC address is only used to find a computer on a local network, an IP address can be used to find a computer anywhere on the Internet (see Figure 15-4) or on an intranet. An **intranet** is

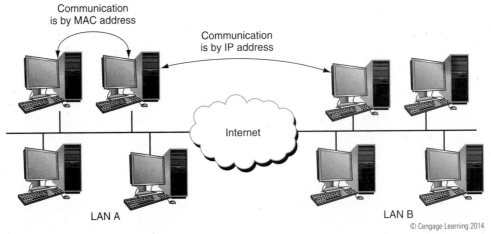

© Cengage Learning 2014

Figure 15-4 Computers on the same LAN use MAC addresses to communicate, but computers on different LANs use IP addresses to communicate over the Internet

A+
220-801
2.3

A+
220-802
1.6

any private network that uses TCP/IP protocols. A large enterprise might support an intranet that is made up of several local networks. When several local networks are tied together in a subsystem of the larger intranet, this group of small local networks is called a subnetwork or **subnet**. IP addresses are used to find computers on subnets, an intranet, or the Internet.

▲ *Level 3: Application level*. Most applications used on the Internet or a local network are client/server applications. Client applications, such as Internet Explorer, Google Chrome, or Outlook, communicate with server applications such as a web server or email server. Each client and server application installed on a computer listens at a predetermined address that uniquely identifies the application on the computer. This address is a number and is called a **port number, port,** or **port address**. For example, you can address a web server by entering into a browser address box an IP address followed by a colon and then the port number. These values are known as a socket. For example, an email server waiting to send email to a client listens at port 25, and a web server listens at port 80. Suppose a computer with an IP address of 136.60.30.5 is running both an email server and a web server application. If a client computer sends a request to 136.60.30.5:25, the email server that is listening at that port responds. On the other hand, if a request is sent to 136.60.30.5:80, the web server listening at port 80 responds (see Figure 15-5).

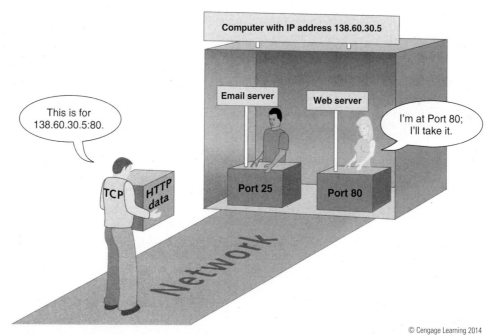

© Cengage Learning 2014

Figure 15-5 Each server running on a computer is addressed by a unique port number

Figure 15-6 shows how communication moves from a browser to the OS to the hardware on one computer and on to the hardware, OS, and web server on a remote computer. As you connect a computer to a network, keep in mind that the connection must work at all three levels. And when things don't work right, it helps to understand that you must solve the problem at one or more levels. In other words, the problem might be with the physical equipment, with the OS, or with the application.

A+
220-801
2.3

A+
220-802
1.6

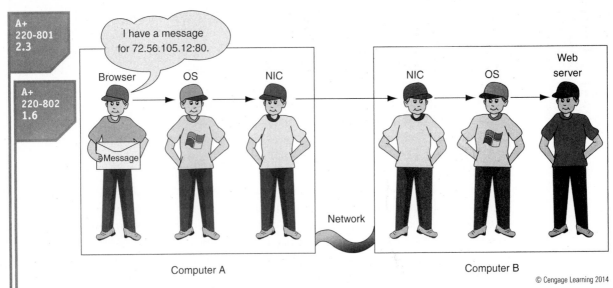

Figure 15-6 How a message gets from a browser to a web server using three levels of communication

© Cengage Learning 2014

HOW IP ADDRESSES GET ASSIGNED

A MAC address is embedded on a network adapter at the factory, but IP addresses are assigned manually or by software. In Chapter 7, you learned that an IP address can be a **dynamic IP address** (IP address is assigned by a server each time it connects to the network) or a **static IP address** (IP address is permanently assigned to the computer or device).

> **A+ Exam Tip** The A+ 220-801 and A+ 220-802 exams expect you to know what a DHCP server is and understand how to use static and dynamic IP addressing.

For dynamic IP addresses, a **DHCP (dynamic host configuration protocol)** server gives an IP address to a computer when it first attempts to initiate a connection to the network and requests an IP address. A computer or other device (such as a network printer) that requests an address from a DHCP server is called a **DHCP client**. It is said that the client is leasing an IP address. How to configure a Windows computer to use dynamic or static IP addressing is covered later in the chapter.

An IP address has 32 bits or 128 bits. When the Internet and TCP/IP were first invented, it seemed that 32 bits were more than enough to satisfy any needs we might have for IP addresses because this standard, called **Internet Protocol version 4 (IPv4)**, created about four billion potential IP addresses. Today we need many more than four billion IP addresses over the world. Partly because of a shortage of 32-bit IP addresses, **Internet Protocol version 6 (IPv6)**, which uses an IP address with 128 bits, was developed. Currently, the Internet uses a mix of 32-bit and 128-bit IP addresses. The Internet Assigned Numbers Authority (IANA at *iana.org*) is responsible for keeping track of assigned IP addresses and has already released all its available 32-bit IP addresses. IP addresses leased from IANA today are all 128-bit addresses.

A+
220-801
2.3

> **Notes** Now that all of the four billion IPv4 addresses are leased, companies that own these addresses are selling them. Recently, Microsoft purchased over 600,000 IP addresses from Nortel for 7.5 million dollars.

A+
220-802
1.6

Next, let's see how IPv4 IP addresses are used, and then you'll learn about IPv6 addresses.

HOW IPV4 IP ADDRESSES ARE USED

A 32-bit IP address is organized into four groups of eight bits each, which are presented as four decimal numbers separated by periods, such as 72.56.105.12. The largest possible 8-bit number is 11111111, which is equal to 255 in decimal, so the largest possible IP address in decimal is 255.255.255.255, which in binary is 11111111.11111111.11111111.11111111. Each of the four numbers separated by periods is called an **octet** (for 8 bits) and can be any number from 0 to 255, making a total of about 4.3 billion IP addresses (256 × 256 × 256 × 256). Some IP addresses are reserved, so these numbers are approximations.

The first part of an IP address identifies the network, and the last part identifies the host. When data is routed over the Internet, the network portion of the IP address is used to locate the right network. After the data arrives at the local network, the host portion of the IP address is used to identify the one computer on the network that is to receive the data. Finally, the IP address of the host must be used to identify its MAC address so the data can travel on the host's LAN to that host. The next section explains this in detail.

CLASSES OF IP ADDRESSES

IPv4 IP addresses are divided into three classes: Class A, Class B, and Class C. IP addresses belong in each class according to the scheme outlined in Table 15-1. When IPv4 addresses were available from IANA, a company would lease a Class A, Class B, or Class C license from IANA and from this license could generate multiple IP addresses.

Class	Network Octets*	Approximate Number of Possible Networks or Licenses	Total Number of Possible IP Addresses in Each Network
A	1.x.y.z to 126.x.y.z	126	16 million
B	128.0.x.y to 191.255.x.y	16,000	65,000
C	192.0.0.x to 223.255.255.x	2 million	254

*An x, y, or z in the IP address stands for an octet used to identify hosts.

Table 15-1 Classes of IP addresses

Recall that the first part of an IP address identifies the network, and the last part identifies the host. Figure 15-7 shows how each class of IP addresses is divided into the network and host portions.

Looking back at Table 15-1, you can see that a **Class A** license is for a single octet, which is the network portion of the IP addresses in that license. The remaining octets can be used for host addresses or to identify subnetworks in the larger network. For example, if a company is assigned 87 as its Class A license, then 87 is the network address and is used as the first octet for every host using this license (87.0.0.1, 87.0.0.2, 87.0.0.3, and so forth).

15

A+
220-801
2.3

A+
220-802
1.6

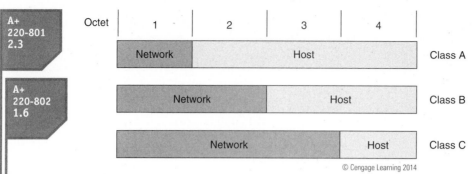

Figure 15-7 The network portion and host portion for each class of IP addresses

(In practice, such a large network is divided into subnets.) Because three octets can be used for Class A host addresses, one Class A license can have approximately 256 × 256 × 254 host addresses, or about 16 million IP addresses. Only very large corporations with heavy communication needs were able to obtain a Class A license.

> **🔍 A+ Exam Tip** The A+ 220-801 exam expects you to know how to identify the class of any given IP address. For the exam, memorize these facts: IP addresses that begin with 1 through 126 are Class A addresses; addresses that begin with 128 through 191 are Class B addresses, and addresses that begin with 192 through 223 are Class C addresses.

A **Class B** license leases the first two octets, and these first two octets are used for the network portion and the last two can be used for the host address or for subnetting the network. An example of a Class B license is 150.35, and examples of IP addresses in this network are 150.35.0.1, 150.35.0.2, and 150.35.0.3. How many host addresses are there in one Class B license? The number of possible values for two octets is about 256 × 254, or about 65,000 host addresses in a single Class B license.

A **Class C** license assigns three octets as the network address. With only one octet used for the host addresses, there can be only 254 host addresses on a Class C network or its subnetworks. For example, if a company is assigned a Class C license for its network with a network address of 200.80.15, some IP addresses on the network would be 200.80.15.1, 200.80.15.2, and 200.80.15.3.

Class D and Class E IP addresses are not available for general use. Class D addresses begin with octets 224 through 239 and are used for **multicasting**, in which one host sends messages to multiple hosts, such as when the host transmits a video conference over the Internet. Class E addresses begin with 240 through 254 and are reserved for research.

In addition to classes of IP addresses, a few IP addresses were reserved for special use by TCP/IP and should not be assigned to a device on a network. Table 15-2 lists these reserved IP addresses.

IP Address	How It Is Used
255.255.255.255	Used for broadcast messages by TCP/IP background processes
0.0.0.0	Currently unassigned IP address
127.0.0.1	Indicates your own computer and is called the *loopback address*

Table 15-2 Reserved IP addresses

© Cengage Learning 2014

A+
220-801
2.3

A+
220-802
1.6

SUBNETS USING IPV4

Looking back at Table 15-1, you can see that a single class license network might have millions of hosts. Managing a network with so many hosts is not practical unless you divide the network into subnets. To divide a network into subnets, you designate part of the host portion of the IP address as a subnet. For example, suppose you have a Class A license of 69. Without using subnets, you have one network: the first octet of all the IP addresses in this network is 69; the last three octets are used for host addresses; and the number of hosts in this one network is about 16 million. Suppose you divide this one network into 256 subnets by using the second octet for the subnet address. (The subnets are 69.0.x.y through 69.255.x.y.) The last two octets are used for host addresses in each subnet with a potential of about 65,000 hosts in each subnet (256 x 254).

The **subnet mask** used with IPv4 identifies which part of an IP address is the network portion and which part is the host portion. Using a subnet mask, a computer or other device can know if an IP address of another computer is on its network or another network (see Figure 15-8).

© Cengage Learning 2014

Figure 15-8 A host (router, in this case) can always determine if an IP address is on its network

A subnet mask is a string of ones followed by a string of zeros. The ones in a subnet mask say, "On our network, this part of an IP address is the network part," and the group of zeros says, "On our network, this part of an IP address is the host part."

If you don't divide a network into subnets, the default subnet mask is used, which is called a **classful subnet mask** because the network portion of the IP address aligns with the class license. For example, Table 15-3 shows the default subnet masks used for three IP addresses. In the table, the green numbers identify the network and the red numbers identify the host.

15

A+
220-801
2.3

A+
220-802
1.6

Class	Subnet Mask	Address	Network ID	Host ID
Class A	11111111.00000000.00000000.00000000	89.100.13.78	89	100.13.78
Class B	11111111.11111111.00000000.00000000	190.78.13.250	190.78	13.250
Class C	11111111.11111111.11111111.00000000	201.18.20.208	201.18.20	208

© Cengage Learning 2014

Table 15-3 Default subnet masks for classes of IP addresses

These three subnet masks would be displayed in a TCP/IP configuration window like this:

▲ Subnet mask of 11111111.00000000.00000000.00000000 is displayed as 255.0.0.0
▲ Subnet mask of 11111111.11111111.00000000.00000000 is displayed as 255.255.0.0
▲ Subnet mask of 11111111.11111111.11111111.00000000 is displayed as 255.255.255.0

A network is divided into subnets when the subnet mask takes some of the host portion of the IP address for the network ID. This **classless subnet mask** does not align the network ID with the network octets assigned by the class license. Using our earlier example, the classless subnet mask for a Class A license of 69 that uses two octets for the network ID rather than the one octet assigned by the class license would be 11111111.1111111 1.00000000.00000000 or 255.255.0.0. A classless subnet mask can also have a mix of zeros and ones in one octet such as 11111111.11111111.11110000.00000000, which can be written as 255.255.240.0. These classless subnet masks are used to subnet large corporate networks.

APPLYING | CONCEPTS   Larry is setting up a new computer on a network. He creates TCP/IP settings to use static IP addressing. He assigns a subnet mask of 255.255.240.0 and an IP address of 15.50.212.59 to this computer. Suppose this computer wants to communicate with a computer assigned an IP address of 15.50.235.80. Are these two computers in the same subnet? To find out, you can first compare the binary values of the first two octets and determine if they match. Then compare the binary values of the third octet, like this:

```
212 = 11010100
235 = 11101011
```

To be in the same subnet, the first four bits must match, which they don't. Therefore, these two computers are not in the same subnet. However, an IP address that is in the same subnet as 15.50.212.59 is 15.50.220.100 because the first two octets match and the first four bits of the third octet match (comparing 11010100 to 11011100).

> **Notes** Sometimes an IP address and subnet mask are written using a shorthand notation like 15.50.212.59/20, where the /20 means that the subnet mask is written as 20 ones followed by enough zeros to complete the full 32 bits.

A+
220-801
2.3

A+
220-802
1.6

That brings us to a fun way of explaining subnet masks. Suppose all the tall sticks shown in Figure 15-9 belong to the same network, and the short stick is the subnet mask for this network. How many subnets are in the network? Which sticks belong in the same subnet as Stick 5? As Stick 6?

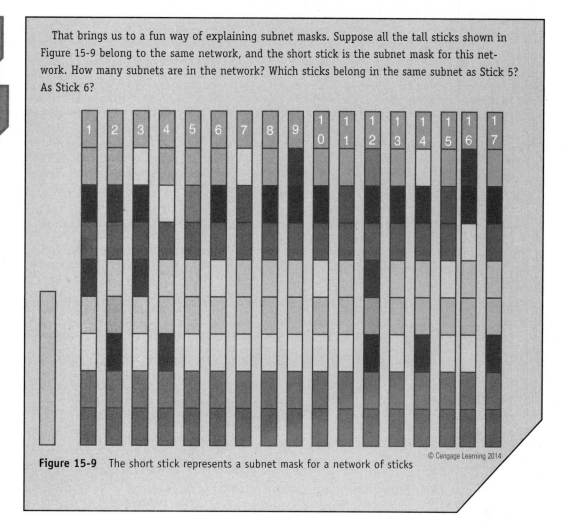

Figure 15-9 The short stick represents a subnet mask for a network of sticks

© Cengage Learning 2014

PUBLIC, PRIVATE, AND AUTOMATIC PRIVATE IP ADDRESSES

When a company applied for a Class A, B, or C license, it was assigned a group of IP addresses that are different from all other IP addresses and are available for use on the Internet. The IP addresses available to the Internet are called **public IP addresses**.

A company conserves its public IP addresses by using **private IP addresses** that are not allowed on the Internet. Within the company network, computers communicate with one another using these private IP addresses. A computer using a private IP address on a private network can still access the Internet if a router or other device that stands between the network and the Internet is using **NAT (Network Address Translation)**. NAT is a TCP/IP protocol that substitutes the public IP address of the router for the private IP address of the other computer when these computers need to communicate on the Internet.

Because of NAT, a small company can rely solely on private IP addresses for its internal network and use only the one public IP address assigned to it by its ISP for Internet communication. IEEE recommends that the following IP addresses be used for private networks:

- 10.0.0.0 through 10.255.255.255
- 172.16.0.0 through 172.31.255.255
- 192.168.0.0 through 192.168.255.255

15

A+
220-801
2.3

Notes IEEE, a nonprofit organization, is responsible for many Internet standards. Standards are proposed to the networking community in the form of an RFC (Request for Comment). RFC 1918 outlines recommendations for private IP addresses. To view an RFC, visit the web site *www.rfc-editor.org*.

A+
220-802
1.6

If a computer first connects to the network and is unable to lease an IP address from the DHCP server, it uses an **Automatic Private IP Address (APIPA)** in the address range 169.254.*x.y*.

HOW IPV6 IP ADDRESSES ARE USED

Using the IPv6 standards, more has changed than just the number of bits in an IP address. To improve routing capabilities and speed of communication, IPv6 changed the way IP addresses are used to find computers on the Internet. Let's begin our discussion of IPv6 by looking at how IPv6 IP addresses are written and displayed:

- An IPv6 address has 128 bits that are written as 8 blocks of hexadecimal numbers separated by colons, like this: 2001:0000:0B80:0000:0000:00D3:9C5A:00CC.
- Each block is 16 bits. For example, the first block in the address above is 2001 in hex, which can be written as 0010 0000 0000 0001 in binary.
- Leading zeros in a 4-character hex block can be eliminated. For example, the IP address above can be written as 2001:0000:B80:0000:0000:D3:9C5A:CC.
- If blocks contain all zeros, they can be written as double colons (::). The IP address above can be written two ways:
  - 2001::B80:0000:0000:D3:9C5A:CC
  - 2001:0000:B80::D3:9C5A:CC

To avoid confusion, only one set of double colons is used in an IP address. In this example, the preferred method is the second one: 2001:0000:B80::D3:9C5A:CC because the address is written with the fewest zeros.

The way computers communicate using IPv6 has changed the terminology used to describe TCP/IP communication. Here are a few terms used in the IPv6 standards:

- A **link**, sometimes called the **local link**, is a local area network (LAN) or wide area network (WAN) bounded by routers.
- An **interface** is a node's attachment to a link. The attachment can be a logical attachment or a physical attachment using a network adapter or wireless connection. For example, a logical attachment can be used for tunneling. Tunnels are used by IPv6 to transport IPv6 packets over an IPv4 network.
- The last 64 bits or 4 blocks of an IP address identify the interface and are called the **interface ID** or interface identifier. These 64 bits uniquely identify an interface on the local link.
- **Neighbors** are two or more nodes on the same link.

Three tunneling protocols have been developed for IPv6 packets to travel over an IPv4 network:

- **ISATAP** (pronounced "eye-sa-tap") stands for Intra-Site Automatic Tunnel Addressing Protocol).
- **Teredo** (pronounced "ter-EE-do") is named after the Teredo worm that bores holes in wood. IPv6 addresses intended to be used by this protocol always begin with the same

A+
220-801
2.3

A+
220-802
1.6

32 bit-prefix (called fixed bits). Teredo IP addresses begin with 2001, and the prefix is written as 2001::/32.

▲ **6TO4** is an older tunneling protocol being replaced by the more powerful Teredo or ISATAP protocols.

IPv6 classifies IP addresses differently from that of IPv4. IPv6 supports these three types of IP addresses:

▲ Using a **unicast address**, packets are delivered to a single node on a network.

▲ Using a **multicast address**, packets are delivered to all nodes on a network.

▲ An **anycast address** is used by routers. The address identifies multiple destinations, and packets are delivered to the closest destination.

A unicast address identifies a single interface on a network. The three types of unicast addresses are global, link-local, and unique local addresses, which are graphically shown in Figure 15-10.

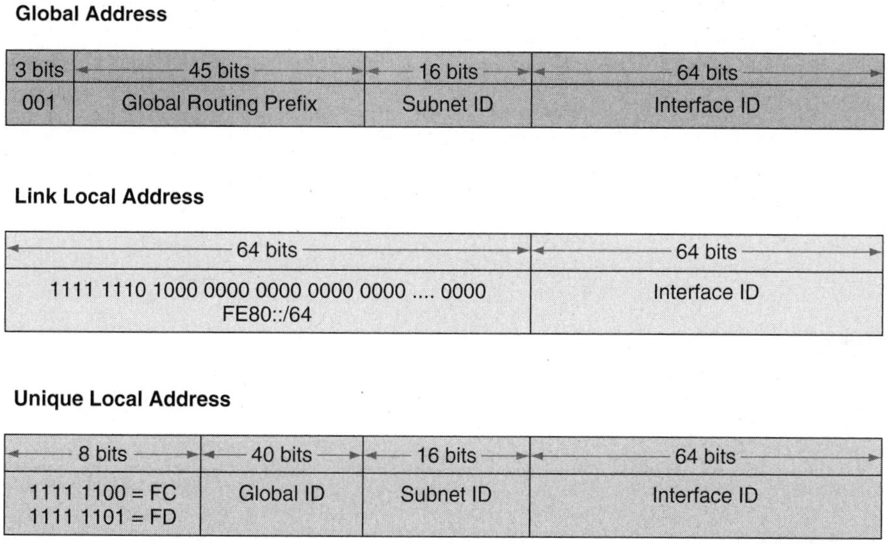

Global Address

3 bits	45 bits	16 bits	64 bits
001	Global Routing Prefix	Subnet ID	Interface ID

Link Local Address

64 bits	64 bits
1111 1110 1000 0000 0000 0000 0000 .... 0000 FE80::/64	Interface ID

Unique Local Address

8 bits	40 bits	16 bits	64 bits
1111 1100 = FC 1111 1101 = FD	Global ID	Subnet ID	Interface ID

© Cengage Learning 2014

Figure 15-10 Three types of IPv6 addresses

Here is a description of each of the three types:

▲ A **global unicast address**, also called a **global address**, can be routed on the Internet. These addresses are similar to IPv4 public IP addresses. Most global addresses begin with the prefix 2000::/3, although other prefixes are being released. The /3 indicates that the first three bits are fixed and are always 001.

▲ A **link-local unicast address**, also called a **link-local address** or local address, can be used for communicating with nodes in the same link. These addresses are similar to IPv4 private IP addresses and are sometimes called link-local addresses or local addresses and most begin with FE80::/64. (This prefix notation means the address begins with FE80 followed by enough zeros to make 64 bits.) Link-local addresses are not allowed on the Internet.

▲ A **unique local unicast address**, also called a **unique local address (ULA)**, is used to identify a specific site within a large organization. For example, an organization might have these two sites: *employee.mycompany.com* and *support.mycompany.com*. The

15

address prefixes used for unique local addresses are FC00::/7 and FD00::/8. The Global ID portion of the address is assigned by the organization. Unique local addresses are not allowed on the Internet. They are hybrid addresses between a global unicast address that works on the Internet and a link-local address that works on only one link.

Notice in Figure 15-10 that global and unique local addresses contain a block labeled the **Subnet ID**, which is the last block in the 64-bit prefix of an IP address. Recall that when using IPv4, the subnet could be identified by any number of bits at the beginning of the IP address. Using IPv6, a subnet is identified using some or all of the 16 bits in the Subnet ID block. Using IPv6, a subnet is, therefore, identified as one or more links that have the same 64 bits in the IP address prefix. This definition implies that a local link is itself a subnet.

Table 15-4 lists the currently used address prefixes for these types of IP addresses. In the future, we can expect more prefixes to be assigned as they are needed.

IP Address Type	Address Prefix
Global unicast	2000::/3 (First 3 bits are always 001)
Link-local unicast	FE80::/64 (First 64 bits are always 1111 1110 1000 0000 0000 0000 ..... 0000)
Unique local unicast	FC00::/7 (First 7 bits are always 1111 110) FD00::/8 (First 8 bits are always 1111 1101)
Multicast	FF00::/8 (First 8 bits are always 1111 1111)

© Cengage Learning 2014

Table 15-4 Address prefixes for types of IPv6 addresses

A+ Exam Tip The A+ 220-801 exam expects you to know the prefixes listed in Table 15-4.

Notes An excellent resource for learning more about IPv6 and how it works is the ebook, *TCP/IP Fundamentals for Microsoft Windows*. To download the free PDF, search for it at *www.microsoft.com/download*.

VIEW IP ADDRESS SETTINGS

The Ipconfig command can be used in a command prompt window to show the IPv4 and IPv6 IP addresses assigned to all network connections (see Figure 15-11).

Notice in the figure the four IP addresses that have been assigned to the physical connections:

◢ Windows has assigned the wireless connection two IP addresses, one using IPv4 and one using IPv6.
◢ The Ethernet LAN connection has also been assigned an IPv4 address and an IPv6 address.

The IPv6 addresses are followed by a % sign and a number; for example, %13 follows the first IP address. This number is called the zone ID or scope ID and is used to identify the interface in a list of interfaces for this computer.

A+
220-801
2.3

A+
220-802
1.6

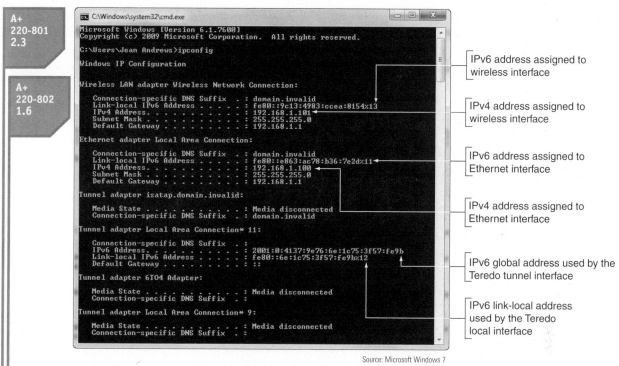

Source: Microsoft Windows 7

Figure 15-11 The ipconfig command showing IPv4 and IPv6 addresses assigned to this computer

IPv6 addressing is designed so that a computer can autoconfigure its own link-local IP address, which is similar to how IPv4 uses an Automatic Private IP Address (APIPA). Here's what happens when a computer using IPv6 first makes a network connection:

1. The computer creates its IPv6 address by using the FE80::/64 prefix and randomly generating an Interface ID for the last 64 bits.

2. It then performs a duplicate address detection process to make sure its IP address is unique on the network.

3. Next, it asks if a router is present on the network to provide configuration information. If a router responds with DHCP information, the computer uses whatever information this might be, such as the IP addresses of DNS servers or its own IP address. Because a computer can generate its own link-local IP address, a DHCPv6 server usually serves up only global IPv6 addresses.

A+
220-801
2.4

CHARACTER-BASED NAMES IDENTIFY COMPUTERS AND NETWORKS

Remembering an IP address is not always easy, so character-based names are used to substitute for IP addresses. Here are the possibilities:

▲ A **host name**, also called a **computer name**, is the name of a computer and can be used in place of its IP address. Examples of host names are www, ftp, Jean's Computer, TestBox3, and PinkLaptop. You assign a host name to a computer when you first configure it for a network connection. The name can have up to 63 characters, including letters, numbers, and special characters. On a local network, you can use the computer name in the place of an IP address to identify a computer. To find out and change the computer name in Windows 7/Vista, click **Start**, right-click **Computer**, and select

15

A+
220-801
2.4

Properties from the shortcut menu. In the System window, click **Advanced system settings**. In the System Properties box, click the **Computer Name** tab (see Figure 15-12). To rename a computer, click **Change**. (For XP, click **Start**, right-click **My Computer**, and select **Properties** from the shortcut menu. Then click the **Computer Name** tab.)

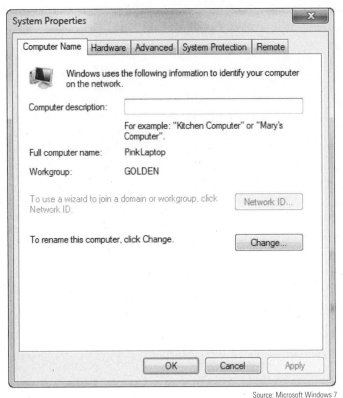

Source: Microsoft Windows 7

Figure 15-12   View and change the computer name

- ▲ A workgroup is a group of computers on a peer-to-peer network that are sharing resources. The workgroup name assigned to this group is only recognized within the local network.
- ▲ A **domain name** identifies a network. Examples of domain names are the names that appear before the period in *microsoft.com*, *course.com*, and *mycompany.com*. The letters after the period are called the top-level domain and tell you something about the domain. Examples are .com (commercial), .org (nonprofit), .gov (government), and .info (general use).
- ▲ A **fully qualified domain name (FQDN)** identifies a computer and the network to which it belongs. An example of an FQDN is *www.course.com*. The host name is *www* (a web server), *course* is the domain name, and *com* is the top-level domain name of the Course Technology network. Another FQDN is *joesmith.mycompany.com*.

On the Internet, a fully qualified domain name must be associated with an IP address before this computer can be found. This process of associating a character-based name with an IP address is called **name resolution**. The DNS (**Domain Name System or Domain Name Service**) protocol is used by a **DNS server** to find an IP address for a computer when the fully qualified domain name is known. Your ISP is responsible for providing you access to one or more DNS servers as part of the service it provides for Internet access. When a

A+
220-801
2.4

web-hosting site first sets up your web site, IP address, and domain name, it is responsible for entering the name resolution information into its primary DNS server. This server can present the information to other DNS servers on the web and is called the authoritative name server for your site.

> **A+ Exam Tip** The A+ 220-802 exam expects you to be familiar with client-side DNS.

> **Notes** When you enter a fully qualified domain name such as *www.cengage.com* in a browser address bar, that name is translated into an IP address followed by a port number. It's interesting to know that you can skip the translation step and enter the IP address and port number in the address box. See Figure 15-13.

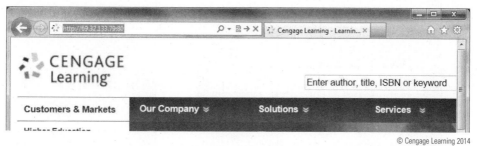

© Cengage Learning 2014

Figure 15-13 A web site can be accessed by its IP address and port number: http://69.32.133.79:80

When Windows is trying to resolve a computer name to an IP address, it first looks in the DNS cache it holds in memory. Information in this cache includes what it loaded at startup from the **Hosts file** in the C:\Windows\System32\drivers\etc folder. This file, which has no file extension, contains computer names and their associated IP addresses on the local network. An administrator is responsible for manually editing the hosts file when the association is needed on the local network. If the computer name is not found in the hosts file, Windows then turns to a DNS server if it has the IP address of the server. When Windows queries the DNS server for a name resolution, it is called the **DNS client**.

> **Notes** For an entry in the Hosts file to work, the remote computer must always use the same IP address. One way to accomplish this is to assign a static IP address to the computer. Alternately, if your DHCP server supports this feature, you can configure it to assign the same IP address to this computer each time if you tell the DHCP server the computer's MAC address. This method of computer name resolution is often used for intranet web servers, Telnet servers, and other servers.

TCP/IP PROTOCOL LAYERS

Recall that a protocol is an agreed-to set of rules for communication between two parties. Operating systems and client/server applications on the Internet all use protocols that are supported by TCP/IP. The left side of Figure 15-14 shows these different layers of protocols and how they relate to one another. As you read this section, this figure can serve as your road map to the different protocols.

15

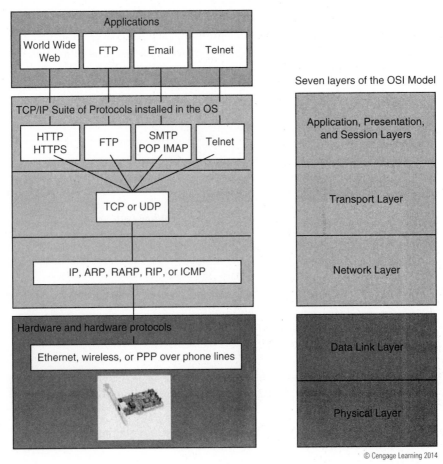

Figure 15-14 How software, protocols, and technology on a TCP/IP network relate to each other

> **Notes** When studying networking theory, the OSI Model is used, which divides network communication into seven layers. In the OSI Model, protocols used by hardware are divided into two layers (data link and physical), and TCP/IP protocols used by the OS are divided into five layers (network, transport, session, presentation, and application). These seven layers are shown on the right side of Figure 15-14.

In the following sections, the more significant applications and operating system protocols are introduced. However, you should know that the TCP/IP protocol suite includes more protocols than just those mentioned in this chapter; only some of them are shown in Figure 15-14.

TCP/IP PROTOCOLS USED BY THE OS

Looking back at Figure 15-14, you can see three layers of protocols between the applications and the hardware protocols. These three layers make up the heart of TCP/IP communication. In the figure, TCP or UDP manages communication with the applications protocols above them as well as the protocols shown underneath TCP and UDP, which control communication on the network.

Remember that all communication on a network happens by way of packets delivered from one location on the network to another. In TCP/IP, the protocol that guarantees packet delivery is **TCP (Transmission Control Protocol)**. TCP makes a connection, checks whether the data is received, and resends it if it is not. TCP is, therefore, called a **connection-oriented protocol**. TCP is used by applications such as web browsers and email. Guaranteed delivery takes longer and is used when it is important to know that the data reached its destination.

For TCP to guarantee delivery, it uses protocols at the IP layer to establish a session between client and server to verify that communication has taken place. When a TCP packet reaches its destination, an acknowledgment is sent back to the source (see Figure 15-15). If the source TCP does not receive the acknowledgment, it resends the data or passes an error message back to the higher-level application protocol.

© Cengage Learning 2014

Figure 15-15 TCP guarantees delivery by requesting an acknowledgment

> 💡 **A+ Exam Tip** The A+ 220-801 exam expects you to be able to contrast the TCP and UDP protocols.

On the other hand, **UDP (User Datagram Protocol)** does not guarantee delivery by first connecting and checking whether data is received; thus, UDP is called a **connectionless protocol** or **best-effort protocol**. UDP is used for broadcasting, such as streaming video or sound over the web, where guaranteed delivery is not as important as fast transmission. UDP is also used to monitor network traffic.

TCP/IP PROTOCOLS USED BY APPLICATIONS

Some common applications that use the Internet are web browsers, email, chat, FTP, Telnet, Remote Desktop, and Remote Assistance. Here is a bit of information about several of the protocols used by these and other applications:

◢ *HTTP*. HTTP (Hypertext Transfer Protocol) is the protocol used for the World Wide Web and used by web browsers and web servers to communicate. You can see when a browser is using this protocol by looking for http at the beginning of a URL in the address bar of a browser, such as *http://www.microsoft.com*.

◢ *HTTPS*. HTTPS (HTTP secure) is the HTTP protocol working with a security protocol such as Secure Sockets Layer (SSL) or Transport Layer Security (TLS), which is better than SSL, to create a secured socket. HTTPS is used by web browsers and servers to encrypt the data before it is sent and then decrypt it before the data is processed. To know a secured protocol is being used, look for https in the URL, as in *https://www.wellsfargo.com*.

◢ *SMTP*. SMTP (Simple Mail Transfer Protocol) is used to send an email message to its destination (see Figure 15-16). An improved version of SMTP is **SMTP AUTH (SMTP Authentication)**. This protocol is used to authenticate a user to an email server when the email client first tries to connect to the email server to send email. Using SMTP AUTH, an extra dialogue between the client and server happens before the client can fully connect that proves the client is authorized to use the service. After authentication, the client can then send email to the email server. The email server that takes care of sending email messages (using the SMTP protocol) is often referred to as the SMTP server.

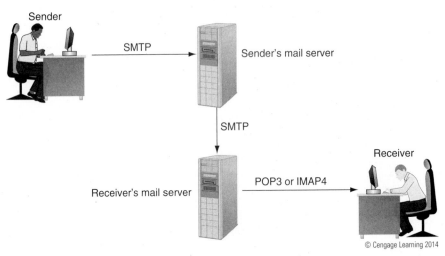

© Cengage Learning 2014

Figure 15-16   The SMTP protocol is used to send email to a recipient's mail server, and the POP3 or IMAP4 protocol is used by the client to receive email

- ◢ *POP and IMAP.* After an email message arrives at the destination email server, it remains there until the recipient requests delivery. The recipient's email server uses one of two protocols to deliver the message: **POP3 (Post Office Protocol, version 3)** or **IMAP4 (Internet Message Access Protocol, version 4)**. Using POP, email is downloaded to the client computer. Using IMAP, the client application manages the email stored on the server.
- ◢ *Telnet.* The **Telnet** protocol is used by the Telnet client/server applications to allow an administrator or other user to control a computer remotely. Telnet is not considered secure because transmissions in Telnet are not encrypted.
- ◢ *LDAP.* **Lightweight Directory Access Protocol (LDAP)** is used by various client applications when the application needs to query a database. For example, an email client on a corporate network might query a database that contains the email addresses for all employees. Another example is when an application looks for a printer by querying a database of printers supported by an organization on the corporate network or Internet. Data sent and received using the LDAP protocol is not encrypted; therefore, an encryption layer is sometimes added to LDAP transmissions.
- ◢ *SMB.* **Server Message Block (SMB)** is the protocol used by Windows to share files and printers on a network.
- ◢ *FTP.* **FTP (File Transfer Protocol)** is used to transfer files between two computers. Web browsers can use the protocol. Also, special FTP client software such as CuteFTP by GlobalSCAPE (*www.cuteftp.com*), can be used, which offers more features for file transfer than does a browser. To use FTP in Internet Explorer version 9, enter the address of an FTP site in the address box, for example, *ftp.cengage.com*. A logon dialog box appears where you can enter a username and password (see Figure 15-17). When you click **Log on**, you can see folders on the

A+
220-801
2.4

FTP site and the FTP protocol displays in the address bar, as in *ftp://ftp.cengage .com*. It's easier to use Windows Explorer to transfer files rather than Internet Explorer. After you have located the FTP site, to use Windows Explorer for file transfers, press **Alt**, which causes the menu bar to appear. In the menu bar, click **View, Open FTP site in Windows Explorer** (see Figure 15-18). Then click **Allow** in the Internet Explorer Security box. Windows Explorer opens, showing files and folders on the FTP site. You can copy and paste files and folders from your computer to the site.

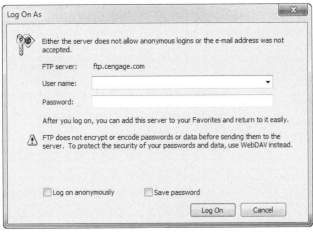

Source: Microsoft Windows 7

Figure 15-17   Log on to an FTP site

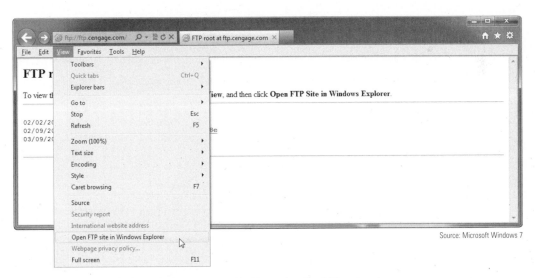

Source: Microsoft Windows 7

Figure 15-18   Use Windows Explorer to transfer files using the FTP protocol

15

- ▲ *SSH.* The **Secure Shell (SSH)** protocol is used to pass login information to a remote computer and control that computer over a network. Transmissions are encrypted so they cannot be intercepted by a hacker.
- ▲ *SFTP.* **Secure FTP (SFTP)** is used to transfer files from an FTP server to an FTP client using encryption. The encryption layer of the protocol used by Secure FTP is a variation of the SSH (Secure Shell) protocol.

A+
220-801
2.4

▲ *SNMP.* Simple Network Management Protocol (SNMP) is used to monitor network traffic. It is used by the Microsoft SNMP Agent application that monitors traffic on a network and helps balance that traffic.

▲ *RDP.* Remote Desktop Protocol (RDP) is used by the Windows Remote Desktop and Remote Assistance utilities to connect to and control a remote computer.

> 💡 **A+ Exam Tip** The A+ 220-801 exam expects you to know about the following application protocols: FTP, Telnet, SMTP, DNS, HTTP, POP3, IMAP, HTTPS, RDP, DHCP, LDAP, SNMP, SMB, SSH, and SFTP.

Recall that client/server applications use ports to address each other. Table 15-5 lists the port assignments for common applications.

Port	Protocol and App	Description
20	FTP client	The FTP client receives data on port 20 from the FTP server.
21	FTP server	The FTP server listens on port 21 for commands from an FTP client.
22	SSH server	A server using the SSH protocol listens at port 22.
23	Telnet server	A Telnet server listens at port 23.
25	SMTP email server	An email server listens at port 25 to receive email from a client computer.
53	DNS server	A DNS server listens at port 53.
67	DHCP client	A DHCP client receives data from a DHCP server at port 67.
68	DHCP server	A DHCP server listens for requests at port 68.
80	Web server using HTTP	A web server listens at port 80 when receiving HTTP requests.
110	POP3 email client	An email client using POP3 receives email at port 110.
143	IMAP email client	An email client using IMAP receives email at port 143.
443	Web server using HTTPS	A web server listens at port 443 when receiving HTTPS transmissions.
3389	RDP apps, including Remote Desktop and Remote Assistance	Remote Desktop and Remote Assistance listen at port 3389.

© Cengage Learning 2014

Table 15-5 Common TCP/IP port assignments for client/server applications

> 💡 **A+ Exam Tip** The A+ 220-801 expects you to know the common port assignments of the FTP, Telnet, SMTP, DNS, HTTP, POP3, IMAP, HTTPS, and RDP protocols. Before sitting for this exam, be sure to memorize the ports listed in Table 15-5.

Now that you have an understanding of TCP/IP and Windows networking, let's apply that knowledge to making network connections.

CONNECTING A COMPUTER TO A NETWORK

A+
220-802
1.5, 1.6

Connecting a computer to a network is quick and easy in most situations. In this part of the chapter, you'll learn to connect a computer to a network using Ethernet, wireless, and dial-up connections.

A+
220-802
1.5, 1.6

CONNECT TO A WIRED NETWORK

To connect a computer to a network using a wired (Ethernet) connection, follow these steps:

1. If the network adapter is not yet installed, install it now. These steps include physically installing the card, installing drivers, and using Device Manager to verify that Windows recognizes the adapter without errors.

2. Connect a network cable to the Ethernet port (called an RJ-45 port) and to the network wall jack or directly to a switch or router. Indicator lights near the network port should light up to indicate connectivity and activity. If you connected the cable directly to a switch or router, verify the light at that port is also lit.

3. By default, Windows assumes dynamic IP addressing and automatically configures the network connection. To find out if the connection is working, open Windows Explorer and drill down into the Network group (see Figure 15-19). (For Windows XP, click **Start, My Network Places** to open the My Network Places window.) You should see icons that represent other computers on the network. Double-click a computer and drill down to shared folders and files to verify you can access these resources.

4. To verify you have Internet connectivity, open Internet Explorer and browse to a few web sites.

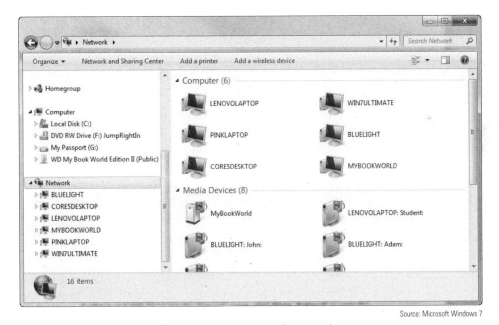

Source: Microsoft Windows 7

Figure 15-19 Windows Explorer shows resources on the network

If the connection does not work, it's time to verify that network settings are configured correctly. Follow these steps using Windows 7:

1. Verify that Device Manager recognizes the network adapter without errors. If you find an error, try updating the network adapter drivers. If that doesn't work, then try uninstalling and reinstalling the drivers. Make sure Device Manager recognizes the network adapter without errors before you move on to the next step.

2. To open the Network and Sharing Center, open **Control Panel** and click **Network and Sharing Center**. (You can also click the network icon in the taskbar.) The Network and Sharing Center window opens (see Figure 15-20).

15

A+
220-802
1.5, 1.6

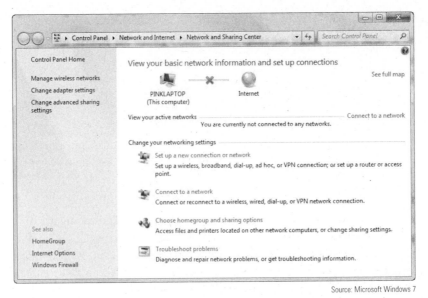

Source: Microsoft Windows 7

Figure 15-20   The Network and Sharing Center reports a problem connecting to the network

3. A red X indicates a problem. Click the **X** to get help and resolve the problem. Windows Network Diagnostics starts looking for problems, applying solutions, and making suggestions. You can also check these things:

   ◢ Is the network cable connected?

   ◢ Are status light indicators on the network port and router or switch lit or blinking appropriately to indicate connectivity and activity?

4. After Windows has resolved the problem, you should see a clear path from the computer to the Internet, as shown in Figure 15-21. Use Windows Explorer to try again to access resources on the local network, and use Internet Explorer to try to access the Internet.

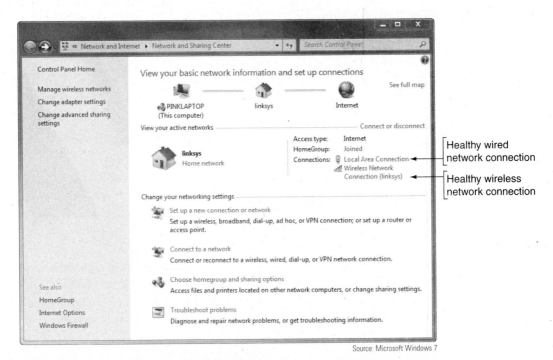

Source: Microsoft Windows 7

Figure 15-21   The Network and Sharing Center reports two healthy network connections

If you still do not have connectivity, follow these steps to verify and change TCP/IP settings:

1. In the Network and Sharing Center, click **Change adapter settings**. In the Network Connections window, right-click the local area connection and select **Properties** from the shortcut menu. The properties box appears (see Figure 15-22).

2. Select **Internet Protocol Version 4 (TCP/IPv4)** and click **Properties**. The properties box shown in Figure 15-23 (a) appears. Settings are correct for dynamic IP addressing.

> **Notes** Notice in Figure 15-22 that you can uncheck Internet Protocol Version 6 (TCP/IPv6) to disable it. For most situations, you need to leave it enabled. A bug in Windows 7 prevents you from joining a homegroup if IPv6 is disabled.

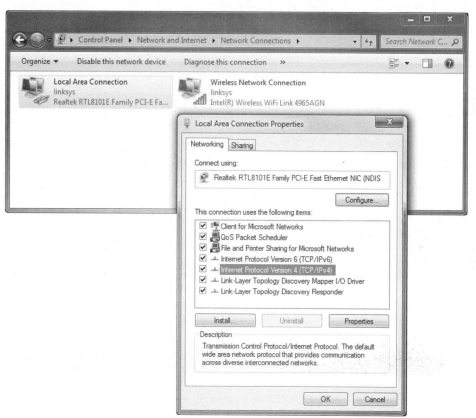

Source: Microsoft Windows 7

Figure 15-22 Verify and change TCP/IP settings

15

3. To change the settings to static IP addressing, select **Use the following IP address**. Then enter the IP address, subnet mask, and default gateway. (A **default gateway** is the gateway a computer uses to access another network if it does not have a better option.)

4. If you have been given the IP addresses of DNS servers, check **Use the following DNS server addresses** and enter up to two IP addresses. If you have other DNS IP addresses, click **Advanced** and enter them on the **DNS** tab of the Advanced TCP/IP Settings box.

5. If the computer you are using is a laptop that moves from one network to another and one network uses static IP addressing, you can click the **Alternate Configuration** tab and configure an **alternate IP address** (see Figure 15-23 [b]). On this tab, select

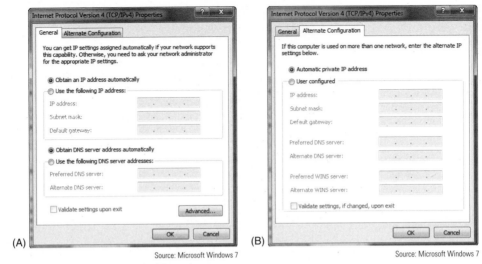

(A)   (B)

Source: Microsoft Windows 7   Source: Microsoft Windows 7

Figure 15-23 Configure TCP/IP settings

User configured. Then enter a static IP address, subnet mask, default gateway, and DNS server addresses. When you configure the General tab to use dynamic IP addressing, the computer will first try to use dynamic IP addressing. If that is not available on the network, it then applies the static IP address settings entered on the Alternate Configuration tab. If static IP address settings are not available on this tab, the computer uses an automatic private IP address (APIPA). This setup works well for a computer to receive a dynamic IP address while traveling, but use a static IP address when connected to the company network that uses static IP addressing.

> 🔆 **A+ Exam Tip** The A+ 220-802 exam expects you to know how to configure an alternate IP address, including setting the static IP address, subnet mask, DNS addresses, and gateway.

6. Close all boxes and windows and again try to access network resources. If you still don't have connectivity, try to disable and enable the network connection. To do that, right-click the connection in the Network Connections window and select **Disable** (see Figure 15-24). For dynamic IP addressing, the IP address is released. Then right-click again and select **Enable**. The connection is remade and a new IP address is leased.

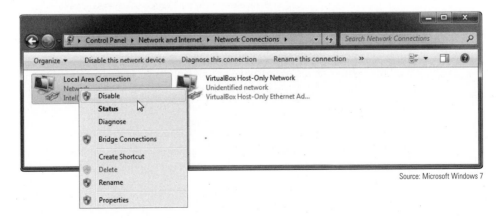

Source: Microsoft Windows 7

Figure 15-24 To reset a network connection, disable and enable the connection

A+
220-802
1.5, 1.6

If you still don't have local or Internet access, it's time to dig a little deeper into the source of the problem. Troubleshooting network connections is covered in Chapter 17.

Vista Differences   To find out how to connect a Vista computer to a wired network, see Appendix B.

XP Differences   To find out how to connect an XP computer to a wired network and how to verify TCP/IP settings for the connection, see Appendix C.

CONNECT TO A WIRELESS NETWORK

Wireless networks are either unsecured public hotspots or secured private hotspots. Even if you connect to a secured private hotspot, still be careful to protect your data and other Windows resources from attack. In this part of the chapter, you learn how to connect to unsecured and secured wireless networks.

Here are the steps to connect to a wireless network using Windows 7 and how to protect your computer on that network:

1. If necessary, install the wireless adapter. For external adapters such as the one shown in Figure 15-25, be sure to follow the manufacturer's instructions for the installation. Most likely you'll be asked to first install the software before installing the device. During the installation process, you will be given the opportunity to use the manufacturer's configuration utility to manage the wireless adapter or to use Windows to do the job. For best results, use the utility provided by the manufacturer. In the following steps, we're using the Windows utility.

© Cengage Learning 2014

Figure 15-25   Plug the wireless USB adapter into the USB port

2. For embedded wireless, turn on your wireless device. For some laptops, that's done by a switch on the keyboard (see Figure 15-26) or on the side of the laptop. The wireless antenna is usually in the lid of a notebook and gives best performance when the lid is fully raised. For a desktop computer, make sure the antenna is in an upright position (see Figure 15-27).

15

A+
220-802
1.5, 1.6

© Cengage Learning 2014

Figure 15-26 Turn on the wireless switch on your laptop

© Cengage Learning 2014

Figure 15-27 Raise the antenna on a NIC to an upright position

3. A yellow star in the network icon in the taskbar indicates hotspots are available. Double-click the network icon to see a list of networks. Click one to select it and then click **Connect** (see Figure 15-28).

4. If the network is secured, Windows asks for the security key the first time you connect (see Figure 15-29). Enter the security key or password to the network and click **OK**.

5. If the network is unsecured or you don't trust all the users of the network, verify that Windows has configured the network as a Public network. To do so, open the Network and Sharing Center window (see Figure 15-30). If the network location says

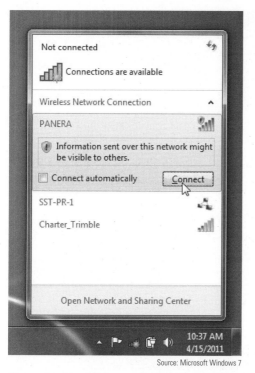

Source: Microsoft Windows 7

Figure 15-28 Windows orders the list of wireless networks in the area from strongest to weakest signals

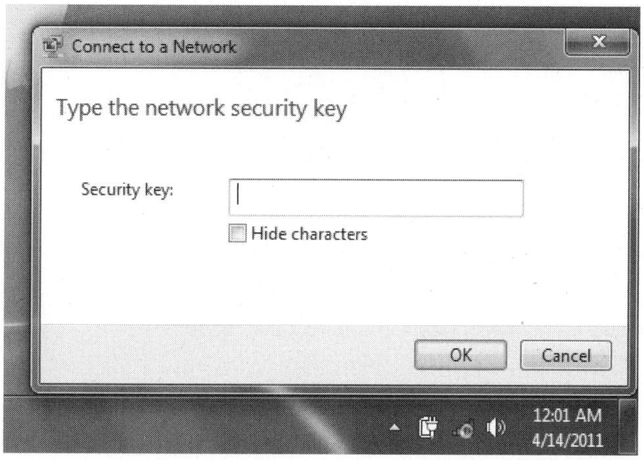

Source: Microsoft Windows 7

Figure 15-29 Enter the security key to connect to a secured wireless network

Home network or Work network, click it. The Set Network Location box appears (see Figure 15-31). Click **Public network** and click **Close**. The Network and Sharing Center reports the network location as Public network.

6. Open your browser to test the connection. For some hotspots, a home page appears and you must enter a code or agree to the terms of use before you can use the network.

In addition to a security key used to access a secured wireless network, the network might be set up for even more security. A wireless network is created by a wireless device known

A+
220-802
1.5, 1.6

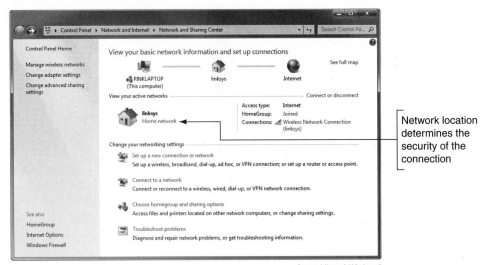

Source: Microsoft Windows 7

Figure 15-30 Verify that your connection is secure

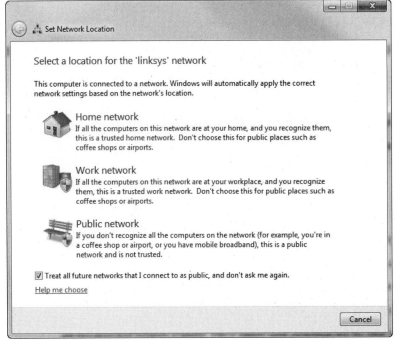

Source: Microsoft Windows 7

Figure 15-31 For best protection on a network, use the Public network location

as the **wireless access point.** Here is a list of methods that the wireless access point might use to secure the wireless network:

▲ *A security key is required.* This is the most common method of securing a wireless network. A network that uses a security key encrypts data on the network using an encryption standard. You learn about these standards later in the chapter.

▲ *The SSID is not broadcasted.* The wireless device might not be broadcasting its name, which is called the **Service Set Identifier (SSID).** If the SSID is not broadcasting, the name of the wireless network will appear as Unnamed or Unknown Network. When you select this network, you are given the opportunity to enter the name. If you don't enter the name correctly, you will not be able to connect.

▲ *Only computers with registered MAC addresses are allowed to connect.* If MAC address filtering is used, you must give the network administrator the MAC address of your wireless adapter. This address is entered into a table of acceptable MAC addresses kept by the wireless access point.

To know the MAC address of your wireless adapter, for an external adapter, you can look on the back of the adapter itself (see Figure 15-32) or in the adapter documentation. Also, if the adapter is installed on your computer, you can open a command prompt window and enter the command **ipconfig /all**, which displays your TCP/IP configuration for all network connections. In the results displayed, the MAC address is called the Physical Address (see Figure 15-33).

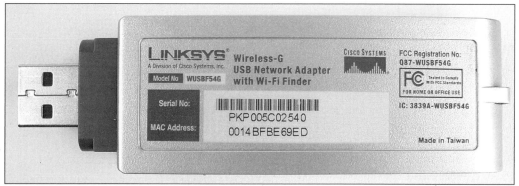

© Cengage Learning 2014

Figure 15-32 The MAC address is printed on the back of this USB wireless adapter

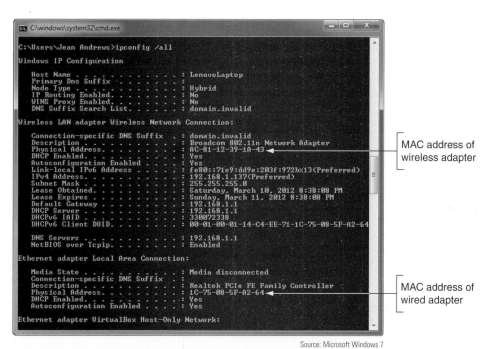

Source: Microsoft Windows 7

Figure 15-33 Use the ipconfig /all command to display TCP/IP configuration data

A+
220-802
1.5, 1.6

If you have problems connecting to a wireless network, here are the steps to follow to verify the network settings:

1. In the left pane of the Network and Sharing Center, click **Manage wireless networks**. The Manage Wireless Networks window appears (see the left side of Figure 15-34).

2. Using this window, you can change the order of networks that Windows uses to try to make a wireless connection. To view security settings, double-click a network in the list. The Properties box for the wireless network appears.

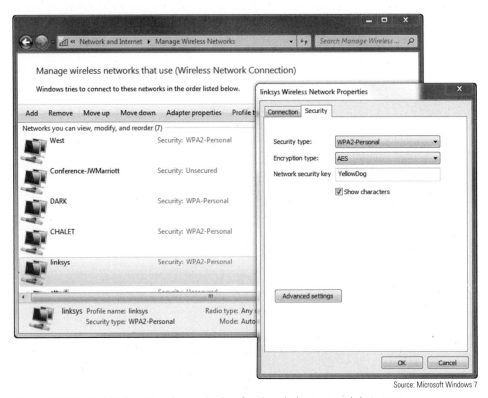

Source: Microsoft Windows 7

Figure 15-34   Verify the Network security key for the wireless network is correct

3. On the Properties box, click the **Security** tab, which is shown in the right side of Figure 15-34. Check **Show characters** so that you can verify the Network security key is correct. Windows 7 should automatically sense the Security type and Encryption type for the wireless network, and these values should be correct. Change the Network security key, if necessary.

4. Click **OK** to close the Properties box. Windows should automatically connect to the network. If you still cannot connect, know that troubleshooting network connections is covered in Chapter 17.

Vista Differences   To find out how to connect a Vista computer to a wireless network, see Appendix B.

XP Differences To find out how to connect an XP computer to a wireless network, see Appendix C.

CONNECT TO A WIRELESS WAN (CELLULAR) NETWORK

To connect a computer using mobile broadband to a **wireless wide area network (WWAN)**, also called a cellular network, such as those provided by Verizon or AT&T, you need the hardware and software to connect and a SIM card. A **SIM (Subscriber Identification Module) card** is a small flash memory card that contains all the information you need to connect to a cellular network, including a password and other authentication information needed to access the network, encryption standards used, and the services that your subscription includes. SIM cards are used in cell phones, mobile broadband modems, and other devices that use a cellular network (see Figure 15-35).

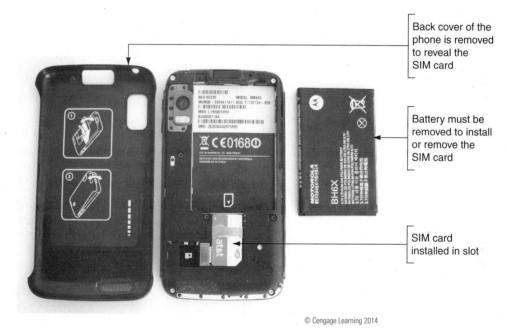

Back cover of the phone is removed to reveal the SIM card

Battery must be removed to install or remove the SIM card

SIM card installed in slot

© Cengage Learning 2014

Figure 15-35 A SIM card contains proof that your device can use a cellular network

Here are your options for hardware and software:

▲ *Use an embedded mobile broadband modem.* A laptop might have an embedded broadband modem. In this situation, you still need to subscribe to a mobile operator, which will provide you with a SIM card for your laptop.

▲ *Tether your cell phone to your computer.* You can tether your cell phone to your computer by way of a cable that connects your cell phone to a USB port. See Figure 15-36. (Some cell phones don't have a USB port; in this situation, you have to purchase a special cable that works with your proprietary phone connector and a USB port on your computer.) A cell phone with Wi-Fi capabilities can be used to provide a Wi-Fi hotspot that your computer and other devices can connect to. In this situation, the cell phone acts like a wireless router. An app installed on the phone is used to configure the WLAN created by the phone.

15

A+
220-802
1.5, 1.6

© Cengage Learning 2014

Figure 15-36   Tether your cell phone to your laptop using a USB cable

▲ *Use a USB broadband modem.* For any computer, you can use a USB broadband modem (sometimes called an air card), such as the one shown in Figure 15-37. If you purchase the device from your mobile operator, a SIM card is included. If you purchase the modem from another source, you need to go to your mobile operator (for example, AT&T, Verizon, or Sprint) to obtain the SIM card the device will use to verify your subscription to the cellular network. A USB broadband modem is likely to give you access to a cellular network as well as a Wi-Fi network.

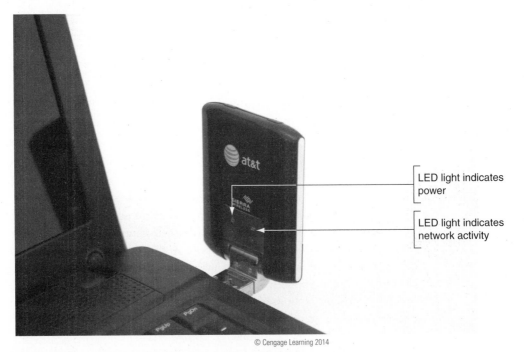

LED light indicates power

LED light indicates network activity

© Cengage Learning 2014

Figure 15-37   A USB broadband modem by Sierra Wireless

A+
220-802
1.5, 1.6

Mobile operators and laptop manufacturers with embedded modems provide software and instructions for connecting to the cellular network. Follow those instructions rather than the generic ones presented here. Generally, here's how you can connect to a cellular network:

▲ *Using an embedded broadband modem.* For a laptop with an embedded broadband modem, you must insert the SIM card provided by your mobile operator in the SIM card slot on the laptop. For some laptops, this slot might be in the battery bay, and you must remove the battery to find the slot. Then use a program installed on the laptop by the laptop manufacturer to connect to the cellular network. Look for a shortcut on the desktop or a program in the Start menu. In addition, the mobile operator might provide software for you to use.

▲ *Using your cell phone.* To tether your cell phone to your computer to use a cellular network, know that you need a subscription from your mobile operator to use this service. The mobile operator is likely to provide you software on CD, or you can download the software from the operator's web site. Install the software first and then tether your cell phone to your computer. Use the software to make the connection.

▲ *Use a USB broadband modem.* When using a USB broadband modem, make sure the SIM card is inserted in the device (see Figure 15-38). When you insert the modem into a USB port, Windows finds the device, and the software stored on the device automatically installs and runs. A window then appears provided by the software that allows you to connect to the cellular network.

Here are more details of how to connect to a WWAN. In this example, we are using the Sierra Wireless modem shown earlier in Figure 15-37. Do the following to make the connection:

1. For best results, connect your computer to a wired network during the first part of the installation.

2. Insert the device into the USB port, and Windows automatically installs the device drivers stored on the device as well as the management software to use the device. Then the management software launches where you must accept the licensing agreement. A shortcut is added to your desktop and programs in the Start menu.

3. You must go to the web site of your mobile operator (AT&T in our example) and activate the phone number used by the modem. Then for best results, remove the modem and restart your computer.

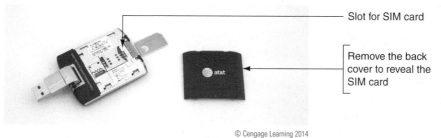

Slot for SIM card

Remove the back cover to reveal the SIM card

© Cengage Learning 2014

Figure 15-38   A SIM card with subscription information on it is required to use a cellular network

A+
220-802
1.5, 1.6

4. After your computer restarts, plug in the modem. Wait until LED lights on the modem indicate the modem has found a network and is ready to connect. For this device, a solid blue light on the left indicates power is on, and a blinking green light on the right indicates the device has found a network and is ready to connect.

5. Start the Communication Manager software. When the software starts, it automatically connects to the network (see Figure 15-39). Note that if your computer is connected to a cellular network, it disconnects from a Wi-Fi network.

Source: AT&T Communications Manager

Figure 15-39   Use the management software to connect and disconnect from the Mobile (cellular) or Wi-Fi network

6. To test the connection, unplug your network cable and try to surf the web. The speed of the connection depends on the type of cellular network you are using, 2G, 3G, or 4G. The 4G networks are the fastest. For the device we are using, the color of the LED indicates the type of network (solid amber is 2G, solid blue is 3G or 4G, solid green is 4G LTE, which currently is the fastest type of cellular network).

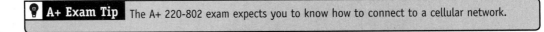
A+ Exam Tip   The A+ 220-802 exam expects you to know how to connect to a cellular network.

To manage the broadband modem and the WWAN connection, you can do the following:

1. Open the **Network and Sharing Center**. You should see the Mobile Broadband Connection (see Figure 15-40). Make sure the network location is set to Public network.

2. Use Ipconfig to see the IP address assigned to the connection. In Figure 15-41, you can see the IPv4 IP address is a public IP address.

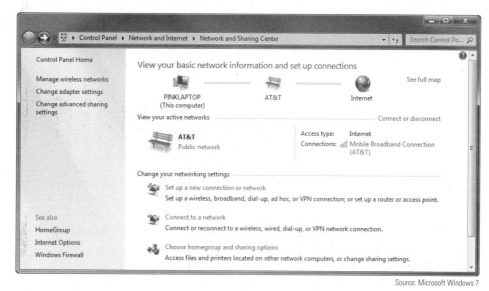

Source: Microsoft Windows 7

Figure 15-40 Make sure your WWAN connection is secured with a Public network location

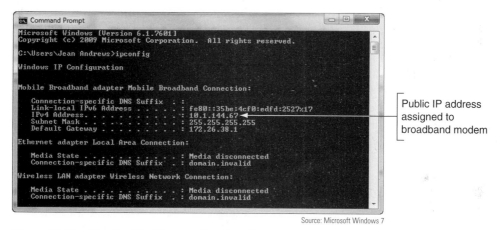

Source: Microsoft Windows 7

Figure 15-41 View the IP address assigned to the WWAN connection by the mobile operator

15

3. Device Manager should report the modem is installed with no errors. If you are having problems making the connection, start by checking Device Manager. If errors are reported here, update the device drivers.

CREATE A DIAL-UP CONNECTION

You never know when you might be called on to support an older dial-up connection. Here are the bare-bones steps you need to set up and support this type of connection:

1. Install an internal or external dial-up modem. Make sure Device Manager recognizes the card without errors.

2. Plug the phone line into the modem port on your computer and into the wall jack.

3. Open the Network and Sharing Center window and click **Set up a new connection or network**. In the dialog box that appears, select **Set up a dial-up connection** and click **Next**.

4. In the next box (see Figure 15-42), enter the phone number to your ISP, your ISP username and password, and the name you decide to give the dial-up connection, such as the name and city of your ISP. Then click **Connect**.

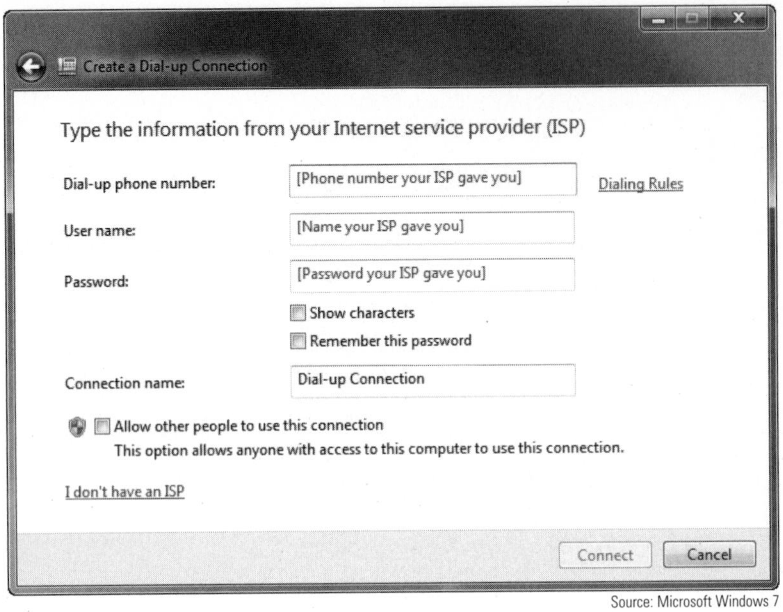

Create a Dial-up Connection

Type the information from your Internet service provider (ISP)

Dial-up phone number: [Phone number your ISP gave you]   Dialing Rules

User name: [Name your ISP gave you]

Password: [Password your ISP gave you]

☐ Show characters
☐ Remember this password

Connection name: Dial-up Connection

☐ Allow other people to use this connection
This option allows anyone with access to this computer to use this connection.

I don't have an ISP

Connect   Cancel

Source: Microsoft Windows 7

Figure 15-42   Configure a dial-up connection

To use the connection, go to the Network and Sharing Center and click **Connect to a network** (see Figure 15-40). Alternately, you can click your network icon in the taskbar. A bubble appears above your taskbar (see Figure 15-43). Select the dial-up connection, and click **Connect**. The Connect dialog box appears, where you can enter your password (see Figure 15-44). Click **Dial**. You will hear the modem dial up the ISP and make the connection. (For XP, double-click the connection icon in the Network Connections window, and then click **Dial**.)

Currently connected to:

LittlePanda
Internet access

Dial-up and VPN   ^

My Dial-up to my IPS

Wireless Network Connection   ^

LittlePanda

LittlePanda-guest

Open Network and Sharing Center

2:57 PM
3/9/2012

Source: Microsoft Windows 7

Figure 15-43   Select the dial-up connection
and then click the Connect
button that appears

A+
220-802
1.5, 1.6

Source: Microsoft Windows 7

Figure 15-44 Enter the password to your ISP

> 💡 **A+ Exam Tip** The A+ 220-802 exam expects you to be able to establish a dial-up connection.

If the dial-up connection won't work, here are some things you can try:

- Is the phone line working? Plug in a regular phone and check for a dial tone. Is the phone cord securely connected to the computer and the wall jack?
- Does the modem work? Check Device Manager for reported errors about the modem. Does the modem work when making a call to another phone number (not your ISP)?
- Check the Dial-up Connection Properties box for errors. To do so, click **Change adapter settings** in the Network and Sharing Center, and then right-click the dial-up connection and select **Properties** from the shortcut menu. Is the phone number correct? Does the number need to include a 9 to get an outside line? Has a 1 been added in front of the number by mistake? If you need to add a 9, you can put a comma in the field like this "9,4045661200", which causes a slight pause after the 9 is dialed.
- Try dialing the number manually from a phone. Do you hear beeps on the other end? Try another phone number.
- When you try to connect, do you hear the number being dialed? If so, the problem is most likely with the phone number, the phone line, or the username and password.
- Try removing and reinstalling the dial-up connection.

15

A+
220-802
1.5, 1.6

CREATE A VPN CONNECTION

A **virtual private network (VPN)** is often used by employees when they work away from the corporate network to connect to that network by way of the Internet. A VPN protects data by encrypting it from the time it leaves the remote computer until it reaches a server on the corporate network. The encryption technique is called a tunnel or tunneling (see Figure 15-45).

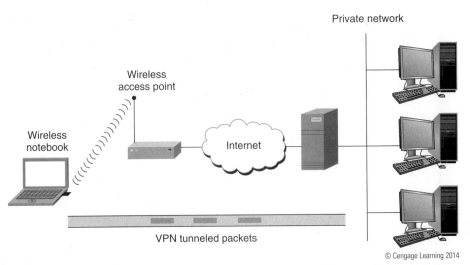

© Cengage Learning 2014

Figure 15-45 With a VPN, tunneling is used to send encrypted data over wired and wireless networks and the Internet

The VPN is often managed by client/server software such as Citrix Access Gateway by Citrix Systems (*www.citrix.com*). Also, Windows can create a VPN connection rather than using third-party software. A VPN connection is a virtual connection, which means you are really setting up the tunnel over an existing connection to the Internet. When creating a VPN connection on a personal computer, always follow directions given by the network administrator who set up the VPN. The company web site might provide VPN client software to download and install on your PC.

Here are the general steps to use Windows 7 to connect to a VPN:

1. In the Network and Sharing Center, click **Set up a new connection or network**. In the set up box, click **Connect to a workplace** and click **Next**.

2. In the Connect to a Workplace box, click **Use my Internet connection (VPN)**. In the next box, enter the IP address or domain name of the network (see Figure 15-46). Name the VPN connection and click **Next**.

3. Enter your username and password to the VPN and click **Connect**. If you want to just set up the connection without connecting to the VPN, in the next box, click **Skip**. The connection is ready to use. Click **Close** to close the wizard.

A+
220-802
1.5, 1.6

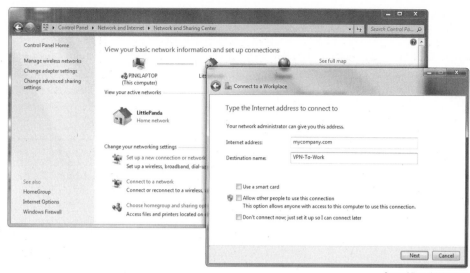

Source: Microsoft Windows 7

Figure 15-46   Enter login information to the VPN network

Whenever you want to use the VPN connection, click the network icon in the taskbar. In the list of available networks, click the VPN connection (see Figure 15-47) and then click **Connect**. A box similar to the one shown earlier in Figure 15-44 appears where you can enter your username and password and click **Connect**. After the connection is made, you can use your browser to access the corporate secured intranet web sites or other resources. The resources you can access depend on the permissions assigned the user account.

Source: Microsoft Windows 7

Figure 15-47   Select the VPN connection

SETTING UP A MULTIFUNCTION ROUTER FOR A SOHO NETWORK

A+
220-801
2.6

A PC support technician is likely to be called on to set up a small office or home office network. As part of setting up a small network, you need to know how to configure a multipurpose router to stand between the network and the Internet. You also need to know how to set up and secure a wireless access point. Most SOHO routers are also a wireless access point.

A+
220-802
2.5

> 💡 **A+ Exam Tip** The A+ 220-801 and A+ 220-802 exams expect you to be able to install, configure, and secure a SOHO wired and wireless router.

FUNCTIONS OF A SOHO ROUTER

Routers can range from small ones designed to manage a SOHO network connecting to an ISP (costing around $75 to $150) to those that manage multiple networks and extensive traffic (costing several thousand dollars). On a small office or home network, a router stands between the ISP network and the local network (see Figure 15-48), and the router is the gateway to the Internet. Note in the figure that computers can connect to the router using wired or wireless connections.

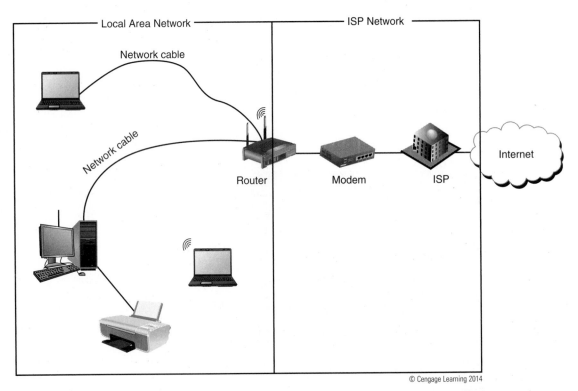

© Cengage Learning 2014

Figure 15-48 A router stands between a local network and the ISP network and manages traffic between them

This router is typical of many SOHO routers and is several devices in one:

▲ *Function 1:* As a router, it stands between the ISP network and the local network, routing traffic between the two networks.
▲ *Function 2:* As a switch, it manages several network ports that can be connected to wired computers or to a switch that provides more ports for more computers.
▲ *Function 3:* As a DHCP server, all computers can receive their IP address from this server.

▲ *Function 4:* As a wireless access point, a wireless computer can connect to the network. This wireless connection can be secured using wireless security features.

▲ *Function 5:* As a firewall, it blocks unwanted traffic initiated from the Internet and provides Network Address Translation (NAT) so that computers on the LAN can use private or link local IP addresses. Another firewall feature is to restrict Internet access for computers behind the firewall. Restrictions can apply to days of the week, time of day, keywords used, or certain web sites.

▲ *Function 6:* As an FTP server, you can connect an external hard drive to the router, and the FTP firmware on the router can be used to share files with network users.

> **Notes** The speed of a network depends on the speed of each device on the network and how well a router manages that traffic. Routers, switches, and network adapters currently run at three speeds: Gigabit Ethernet (1000 Mbps or 1 Gbps), Fast Ethernet (100 Mbps), or Ethernet (10 Mbps). If you want your entire network to run at the fastest speed, make sure all your devices are rated for Gigabit Ethernet.

An example of a multifunction router is the Linksys E4200 by Cisco shown in Figures 15-49 and 15-50. It has one port for the broadband modem (cable modem or DSL modem) and four ports for computers on the network. The USB port can be used to plug in a USB external hard drive for use by any computer on the network. The router is also a wireless access point having multiple antennas to increase speed and range using Multiple In, Multiple Out (MIMO) technology. The antennas are built in.

© Cengage Learning 2014

Figure 15-49 The Linksys E4200 router by Cisco has built-in wireless antennas and can be used with a DSL or cable modem Internet connection

15

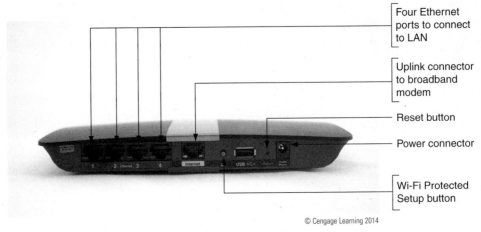

Four Ethernet
ports to connect
to LAN

Uplink connector
to broadband
modem

Reset button

Power connector

Wi-Fi Protected
Setup button

© Cengage Learning 2014

Figure 15-50 Connectors and ports on the back of the Cisco router

INSTALL AND CONFIGURE THE ROUTER ON THE NETWORK

To install a router on the network, always follow the directions of the manufacturer rather than the general directions given here. Using the Linksys E4200 as our example router, here is how to install it on the network:

1. On one of your computers on the network (it doesn't matter which one), launch the setup program on the CD that came bundled with the router. The setup program instructs you to use one network cable to connect the computer to the router and a second network cable to connect the router to the DSL or cable modem box using the Internet port on the router. After you have made the connections, click **Next** on the setup screen.

2. On the next screen, you are given the opportunity to change the SSID and password to the router. Be sure to change the password. On the next screen, you can decide to allow or not allow the router to receive automatic updates from Cisco.

3. The setup program says you should be connected to the Internet. Verify the connection by opening your browser and surfing the web. You can then close the router setup program.

> ⚡ **Caution** Changing the router password is especially important if the router is a wireless router. Unless you have disabled or secured the wireless access point, anyone outside your building can use your wireless network. If they guess the default password to the router, they can change the password to hijack your router. Also, your wireless network can be used for criminal activity. When you first install a router, before you do anything else, change your router password and disable the wireless network until you have time to set up and test the wireless security. And, to give even more security, change the default name to another name if the router utility allows that option.

Using any computer on the network, you can use your browser and the firmware on the router to configure it at any time. To do so, follow these steps:

1. Open your browser and enter the IP address of the router, 192.168.1.1, in the address box. The Windows Security box appears (see Figure 15-51). Enter **admin** as the username and the password is the one you set up when installing the router.

2. The main setup page of the router firmware appears in your browser window (see Figure 15-52). Use the menus near the top of the screen and items on each menu to change your router's configuration. Each router utility is different, but you should be able to poke around and find the setting you need. When finished, click **Save Settings** and close the browser window.

A+
220-801
2.6

A+
220-802
2.5

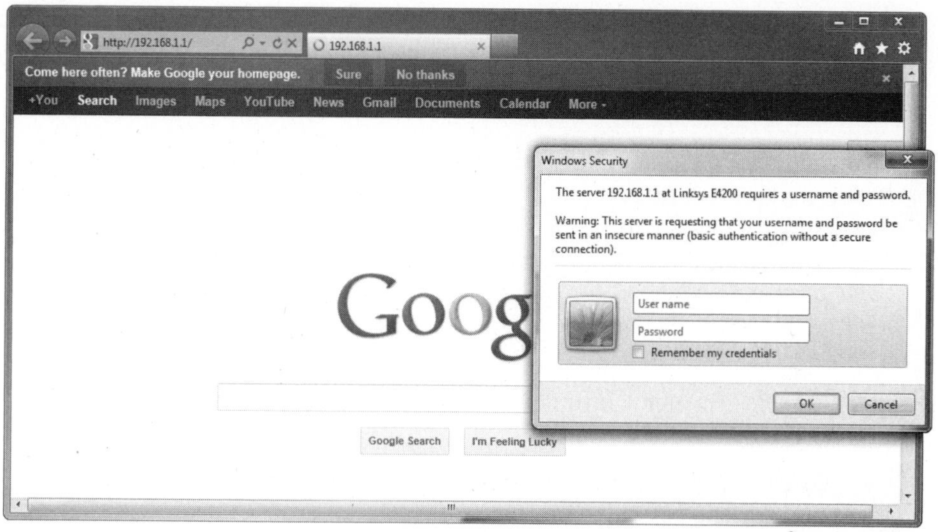

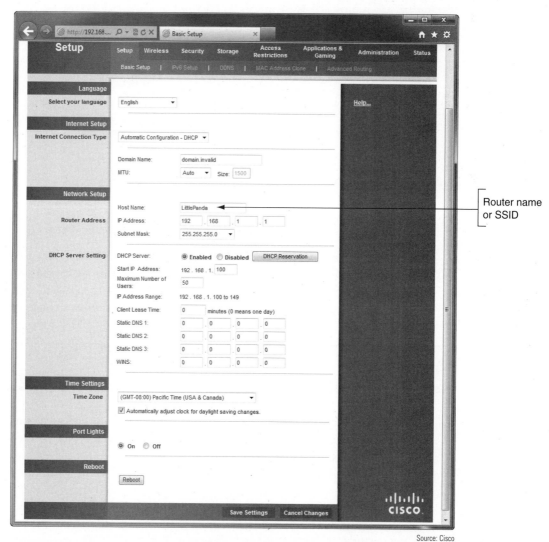

Source: www.google.com

Figure 15-51 Enter the username and password to your router firmware utility

15

Router name
or SSID

Source: Cisco

Figure 15-52 Use menus on the router firmware mutility screens to configure your router

A+
220-801
2.6

A+
220-802
2.5

Following are some changes that you might need to make to the router's configuration. If you make changes on a page, be sure to click **Save Settings** to save your changes. The first setting should always be done:

▲ *Change the router password.* It's extremely important to protect access to your network and prevent others from hijacking your router. If you have not already done so, change the default password to your router firmware. If the firmware offers the option, disable the ability to configure the router from over the wireless network (see Figure 15-53).

▲ *Change the SSID and configure the DHCP server.* On the Basic Setup menu shown earlier in Figure 15-52, you can change the name of the router (the SSID), and you can enable or disable the DHCP server. For the DHCP server, you set the start IP address and set the number of IP addresses DHCP can serve up.

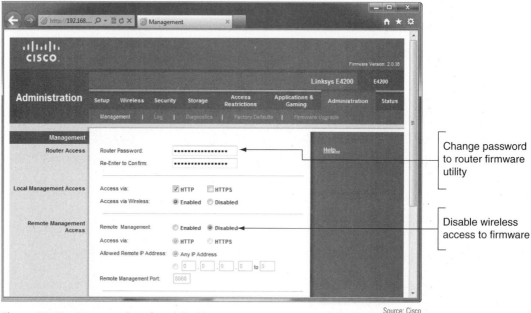

Source: Cisco

Figure 15-53 Prevent others from hijacking your router

▲ *View assignments made by the ISP.* The router belongs to both the local network and the ISP network. On the Status page shown in Figure 15-54, you can see the ISP has assigned the router a private IP address on its network. You can also use this page to release and renew this IP address, which might help solve a problem when you cannot connect to the ISP.

> **Notes** If you are running a web server on the Internet, the web server must use a public and static IP address. For this situation, you can lease a public IP address from your ISP at an additional cost.

▲ *Assign static IP addresses.* A computer or network printer might require a static IP address. For example, when a computer is running a web server on the local network, it needs a static IP address that you can add to the Hosts file for each computer on the network that needs to access this intranet web site. A network printer also needs a static IP address so computers will always be able to find the printer. To assign a static IP address to a client, click **DHCP Reservation** on the Setup page shown earlier in Figure 15-52. In the DHCP Reservation box, select a client from the DHCP table and click **Add Clients**. Then click **Save Settings**. In Figure 15-55, a Canon network printer is set to receive the IP address 192.168.1.118 each time it connects to the network.

A+
220-801
2.6

A+
220-802
2.5

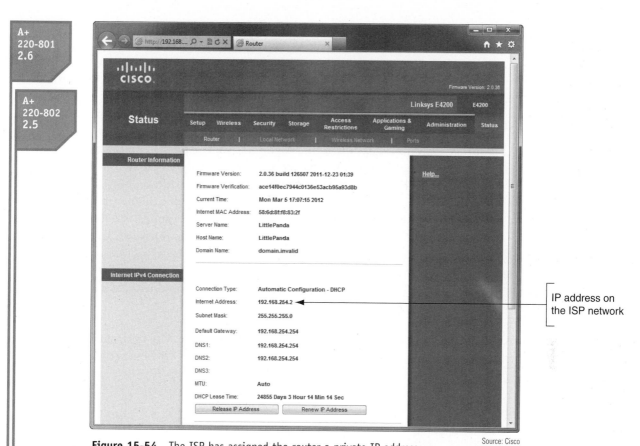

IP address on
the ISP network

Figure 15-54 The ISP has assigned the router a private IP address

Source: Cisco

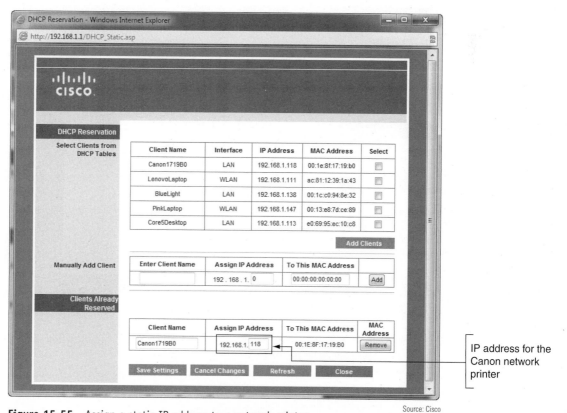

IP address for the
Canon network
printer

Figure 15-55 Assign a static IP address to a network printer

Source: Cisco

▲ *Configure the firewall to disable all ports.* On the Security page, you can enable SPI Firewall Protection (see Figure 15-56). SPI (stateful packet inspection) examines each data packet and rejects those unsolicited by the local network. Using this setting, all ports are disabled (closed) and no activity initiated from the Internet can get in. You can allow exceptions to this firewall rule by using port forwarding, port triggering, or a DMZ. How to do so is coming up in the next section.

▲ *Improve QoS for an application.* As you use your network and notice that one application is not getting the best service, you can improve network performance for this application using the **Quality of Service (QoS)** feature. For example, suppose you routinely use Skype to share your desktop with collaborators over the Internet. To assign a high priority to Skype, go to the **Applications & Gaming** tab (see Figure 15-57). Under Internet Access Priority, select **Enabled**. Under Category, in the drop-down list of Applications, select **Skype**. Under Priority, select **High** and click **Apply**. Skype is added in the Summary area. If you don't see your application listed, you can click **Add a New Application** in the drop-down list of applications and enter its name.

Now let's look at the concepts and steps to allow certain activity initiated from the Internet past your firewall. Then we'll look at how to set up a wireless network.

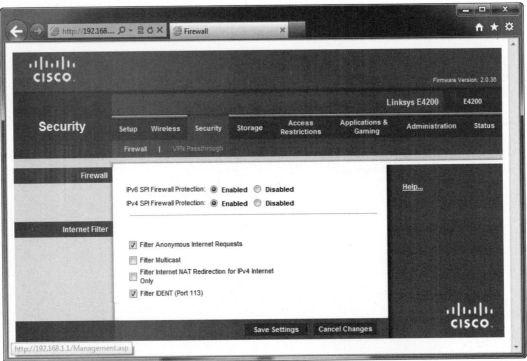

Source: Cisco

Figure 15-56 Configure the router's firewall to prevent others on the Internet from seeing or accessing your network

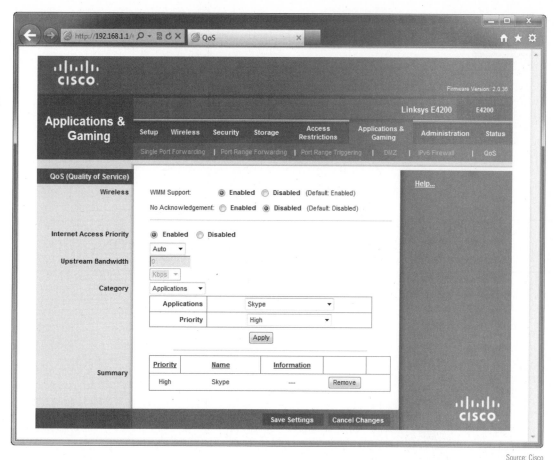

Source: Cisco

Figure 15-57 Use the QoS feature to assign a high priority to an application to improve its network service

PORT FORWARDING, PORT TRIGGERING, AND A DMZ

Suppose you're hosting an Internet game or want to use Remote Desktop to access your home computer from the Internet. In both situations, you need to enable (open) certain ports so that activity initiated from the Internet can get past your firewall.

Recall that a router uses NAT redirection to present its own IP address to the Internet in place of IP addresses of computers on the local network. The NAT protocol is also responsible for passing communication to the correct port on the correct local computer.

Here are the ways a router can use NAT to open or close certain ports:

▲ **Port filtering** is used to open or close certain ports so they can or cannot be used. Remember that applications are assigned these ports. Therefore, in effect, you are filtering or controlling what applications can or cannot get through the firewall. For example, in Figure 15-58a, all requests from the Internet to ports 20, 443, 450, and 3389 are filtered or disabled. These ports are closed.

▲ **Port forwarding** means that when the firewall receives a request for communication from the Internet to a specific computer and port, the request will be allowed and forwarded to that computer on the network. The computer is defined to the router by its static IP address. For example, in Figure 15-58a, port 80 is open and requests to port 80 are forwarded to the web server that is listening at that port. This one computer on the network is the only one allowed to receive requests at port 80.

15

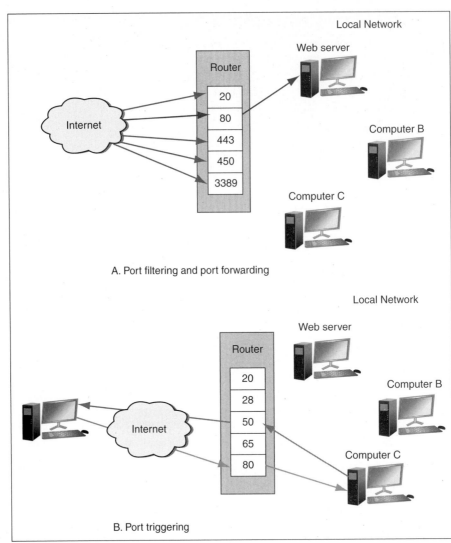

© Cengage Learning 2014

Figure 15-58 Port filtering, port forwarding, and port triggering

▲ **Port triggering** opens a port when a PC on the network initiates communication through another port. For example, in Figure 15-58b, Computer C sends data to port 50 to a computer on the Internet. The router is configured to open port 80 for communication from this remote computer. Port 80 is closed until this trigger occurs. Port triggering does not require a static IP address for the computer inside the network, and any computer can initiate port triggering. The router will leave port 80 open for a time. If no more data is received from port 50, then it closes port 80.

> 🔎 **A+ Exam Tip** The A+ 220-801 exam expects you to know how to implement port forwarding and port triggering.

To configure port forwarding or port triggering, use the Applications & Gaming tab shown in Figure 15-59. In the figure, the Remote Desktop application outside the network can use port forwarding to communicate with the computer whose IP address is 192.168.1.90 using port 3389. The situation is illustrated in Figure 15-60. This computer is set to support the Remote Desktop server application. You will learn to use Remote Desktop in Chapter 17.

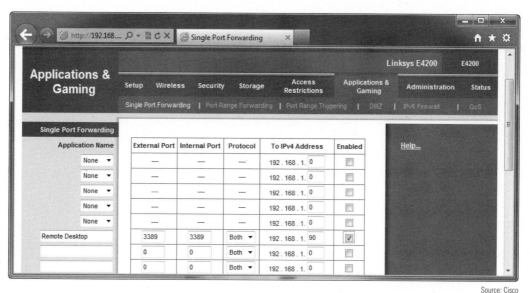

Figure 15-59 Using port forwarding, activity initiated from the Internet is allowed access to a computer on the network

To configure port triggering, click the **Port Range Triggering** tab and enter the two ranges of ports. For example, in Figure 15-61, the Triggered Range of ports will trigger the event to open the ports listed under Forwarded Range.

Here are some tips to keep in mind when using port forwarding or port triggering:

▲ You must lease a static IP address from your ISP so that people on the Internet can find you. Most ISPs will provide you a static IP address for an additional monthly fee.

▲ For port forwarding to work, the computer on your network must have a static IP address so that the router knows where to send the communication.

▲ If the computer using port triggering stops sending data, the router might close the triggered port before communication is complete. Also, if two computers on the network attempt to trigger the same port, the router will not allow data to pass to either computer.

▲ Using port forwarding, your computer and network are more vulnerable because you are allowing external users directly into your private network. For better security, turn on port forwarding only when you know it's being used.

Figure 15-60 With port forwarding, a router allows requests initiated outside the network

15

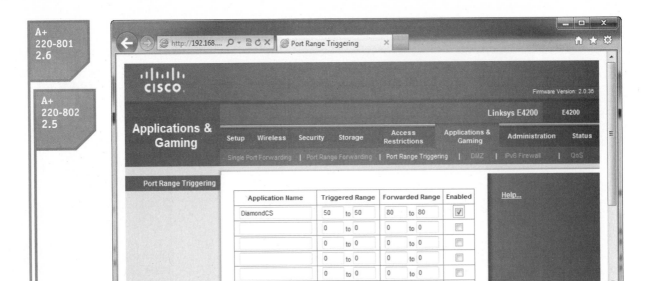

Source: Cisco

Figure 15-61   Port triggering opens a range of ports when data is sent from inside the network

A demilitarized zone (DMZ) in networking is a computer or network that is not protected by a firewall. You can drop all your shields protecting a computer by putting it in a **DMZ** and the firewall no longer protects it. If you are having problems getting port forwarding or port triggering to work, putting your computer in a DMZ can free it to receive any communication from the Internet. Enter its IP address or MAC address on the DMZ page of the router utility (see Figure 15-62) under Destination. You can also specify that any IP address on the Internet is allowed access or you can limit access to a specific IP address. It goes without saying to not leave the DMZ enabled unless you are using it.

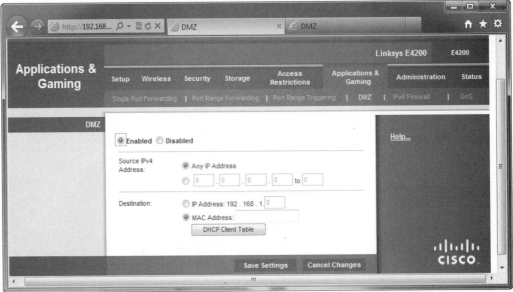

Source: Cisco

Figure 15-62   Put a computer in a DMZ so that the router firewall does not prevent it from receiving communication from the Internet

> **Notes**   By the way, if you want to use a domain name rather than an IP address to access a computer on your network from the Internet, you'll need to purchase the domain name and register it in the Internet name space to associate it with your static IP address assigned by your ISP. Several web sites on the Internet let you do both; one site is by Network Solutions at *www.networksolutions.com*.

A+
220-801
2.5, 2.6

A+
220-802
2.5

SET UP A WIRELESS NETWORK

The standards for a local wireless network are called **Wi-Fi (Wireless Fidelity)**, and their technical name is IEEE 802.11. The IEEE 802.11 standards, collectively known as the **802.11 a/b/g/n** standards, have evolved over the years and are summarized in Table 15-6.

> 💡 **A+ Exam Tip** The A+ 220-801 exam expects you to know about 802.11 a/b/g/n standards, their speeds, distances, and frequencies.

Wi-Fi Standard	Speeds, Distances, and Frequencies
IEEE 802.11a	• Speeds up to 54 Mbps (megabits per second). • Short range up to 50 meters with radio frequency of 5.0 GHz. • 802.11a is no longer used.
IEEE 802.11b	• Up to 11 Mbps with a range of up to 100 meters. (Indoor ranges are less than outdoor ranges.) • The radio frequency of 2.4 GHz experienced interference from cordless phones and microwaves.
IEEE 802.11g	• Same as 802.11b, but with a speed up to 54 Mbps.
IEEE 802.11n	• Up to 500 Mbps depending on the configuration. • Indoor range up to 70 meters and outdoor range up to 250 meters. • Can use either 5.0 GHz or 2.4 GHz radio frequency.

© Cengage Learning 2014

Table 15-6 Older and current Wi-Fi standards

The latest Wi-Fi standard, 802.11n, uses **multiple input/multiple output (MIMO)**, which means a device can use two or more antennas to improve performance (see Figure 15-63). Most wireless devices today are 802.11 b/g/n compatible.

© Cengage Learning 2014

Figure 15-63 Wireless network adapter with two antennas supports 802.11 b/g/n Wi-Fi standards

When setting up a wireless network, position your router or the stand-alone wireless access point in the center of where you want your hotspot and know that a higher position (near the ceiling) works better than a lower position (on the floor). Be sure to set the device in a physically secure place and not in a public area where it can be stolen.

15

A+
220-801
2.5, 2.6

A+
220-802
2.5

When configuring an 802.11n network, consider these options:

▲ *The radio frequency (RF) the network will use.* Choices for **radio frequency (RF)** are 5 GHz and 2.4 GHz. The 5 GHz frequency yields faster speeds than the 2.4 GHz frequency, but the range is shorter. For best performance in a small space, use 5 GHz. Use 2.4 GHz if your hotspot must reach a longer distance. Use both frequencies so they can share the network traffic.

▲ *The older wireless devices that will use the network.* If your network must support older 802.11 b/g wireless devices, you must support the 2.4 GHz frequency.

▲ *The RF interference the network will experience.* Interference for 2.4 GHz frequency might come from cordless phones, microwaves, and other Wi-Fi networks. The 5 GHz frequency is less likely to experience this interference.

▲ *The channel the network will use.* A **channel** is a specific radio frequency within a broader frequency. For example, two channels in the 5 GHz band are 5.180 GHz and 5.200 GHz channels. In the United States, eleven channels are allowed for 5 GHz or 2.4 GHz bands (Channels 1 through 11). For most networks, you can allow auto channel selection so that any channel in the frequency range (5 GHz or 2.4 GHz) will work. The device scans for the least-busy channel. However, if you are trying to solve a problem with interference from a nearby wireless network, you can set each network to a different channel; make the channels far apart to reduce interference. For example, set one network to Channel 1 and set the other to Channel 11.

▲ *The channel width the network will use.* For a 5 GHz network, choices are 40 MHz and 20 MHz channel widths. For best performance, use 40 MHz. For less interference, use 20 MHz.

▲ *The radio power level the device will use.* Some high-end access points allow you to adjust the radio power levels the device can use. To reduce interference, limit the range of the network, or to save on electricity, reduce the power level.

For the firmware utility of the Linksys E4200 wireless router, you can change wireless settings on the Wireless tab when you click **Manual** (see Figure 15-64). Notice in the figure the two wireless setting groups; one is for the 5 GHz range and the other is for the 2.4 GHz range. Unless you have a reason to do otherwise, you can leave the Network Mode for each group set to Mixed, which allows 801.11 b/g/n connections in the 5 GHz or 2.4 GHz band. Notice in the figure that the Channel and Channel Width for each band are set to Auto. If necessary, you can specify a channel or channel width. To force a device to use one band or the other, set a different passphrase for each band.

It is important to secure a wireless network from outside attack. Recall that securing a wireless network is generally done in three ways:

▲ *Method 1: Requiring a security key and using data encryption*—If encryption is used when you connect to a wireless network, a security key is required. If no security key is required, the data on the wireless network is not encrypted. The three main protocols for encryption for 802.11 wireless networks are:

   o *WEP.* WEP (**Wired Equivalent Privacy**) is no longer considered secure because the key used for encryption is static (it doesn't change).

   o *WPA.* WPA (**Wi-Fi Protected Access**) also called **TKIP** (**Temporal Key Integrity Protocol**) encryption, is stronger than WEP and was designed to replace it. With WPA encryption, encryption keys are constantly changing.

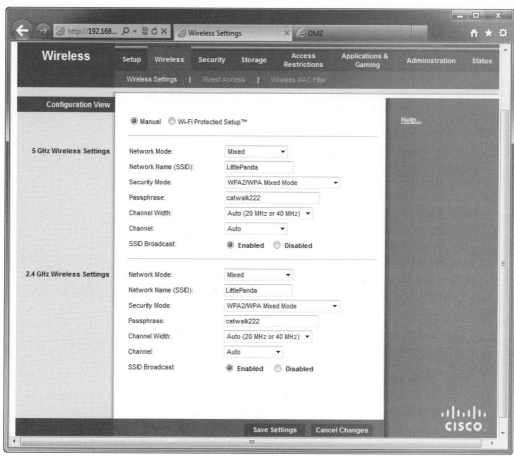

Source: Cisco

Figure 15-64 Configure settings for the wireless network

> o **WPA2.** **WPA2 (Wi-Fi Protected Access 2)**, also called the 802.11i standard, is the latest and best wireless encryption standard. It is based on the **AES (Advanced Encryption Standard)**, which improved on the way TKIP generated encryption keys. All wireless devices sold today support the WPA2 standard.

To configure encryption for the Cisco router, select **Manual** in the Wireless Settings page shown in Figure 15-64 and select the Security Mode from the drop-down menu. For best security, enter a passphrase (security key) to the wireless network that is different from the password you use to the router utility.

> **Notes** To make the strongest passphrase or security key, use a random group of numbers, uppercase and lowercase letters, and, if allowed, at least one symbol. Also use at least eight characters in the passphrase.

> ▲ *Method 2: Disable SSID broadcasting*—You can disable SSID broadcasting and change the SSID on the Wireless page shown in Figure 15-64. This security method is not considered strong security because software can be used to discover an SSID that is not broadcasted.
> ▲ *Method 3: Filter MAC addresses*—A wireless access point can filter the MAC addresses of wireless adapters to either allow or not allow these MAC addresses access to the wireless network (see Figure 15-65). MAC address filtering is considered a weak security measure and does not use encryption.

A+
220-801
2.5, 2.6

A+
220-802
2.5

15

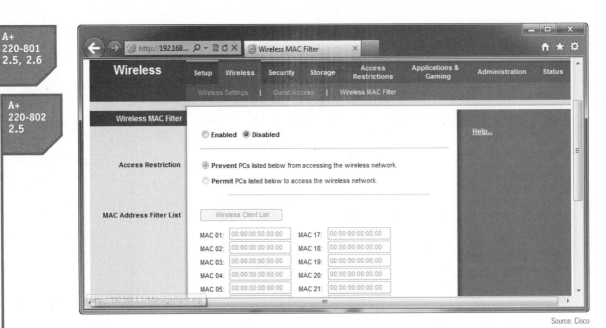

Source: Cisco

Figure 15-65 Configure how the router will filter MAC addresses

You also need to know about **Wi-Fi Protected Setup (WPS)**, which is designed to make it easier for users to connect their computers to a wireless network when a hard-to-remember SSID and security key are used. WPS generates the SSID and security key using a random string of hard-to-guess letters and numbers. The SSID is not broadcasted, so both the SSID and security key must be entered to connect. Rather than having to enter these difficult strings, a user presses a button on a wireless computer or the router's PIN or computer's PIN is used. All computers on the wireless network must support WPS for it to be used. WPS is enabled on the Wireless page of the router utility shown in Figure 15-66.

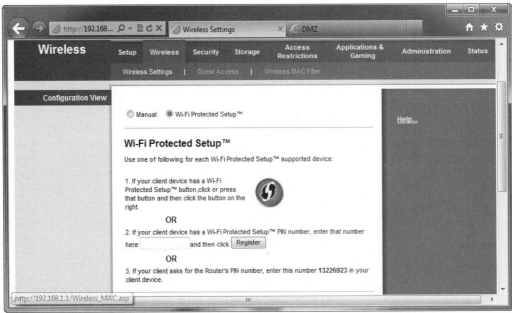

Source: Cisco

Figure 15-66 Using WPS, it is easy for users to connect to a wireless network with strong security

A+
220-801
2.5, 2.6

A+
220-802
2.5

> **💡 A+ Exam Tip** The A+ 220-801 exam expects you to know about installing and configuring a wireless network, including MAC filtering, Wi-Fi channels (1–11), SSID broadcasting, WEP, WPA, WPA2, TKIP, AES, and WPS.
> The A+ 220-802 exam expects you to know about installing and configuring a wireless network, including changing default usernames and passwords, disabling and changing the SSID, using MAC filtering, antenna and access point placements, radio power levels, and assigning static IP addresses.

>> CHAPTER SUMMARY

Understanding TCP/IP and Windows Networking

▲ Networking communication happens at three levels: hardware, operating system, and application levels.

▲ At the hardware level, a network adapter has a MAC address that uniquely identifies it on the network.

▲ Using the TCP/IP protocols, the OS identifies a network connection by an IP address. At the application level, a port address identifies an application.

▲ IP addresses can be dynamic or static. A dynamic IP address is assigned by a DHCP server when the computer first connects to a network. A static IP address is manually assigned.

▲ An IP address using IPv4 has 32 bits, and an IP address using IPv6 has 128 bits.

▲ Classes of IPv4 IP addresses used by the public are Class A, Class B, and Class C addresses. Some IP addresses are private IP addresses that can be used only on intranets.

▲ If a computer is unable to obtain an IP address from a DHCP server, Windows uses Automatic Private IP Addressing (APIPA) to assign the computer an IP address unless an alternate static IP address has been configured for the computer.

▲ Using IPv6, three types of IP addresses are a unicast address (used by a single node on a network), multicast address (used for one-to-many transmissions), and anycast address (used by routers).

▲ Three types of unicast addresses are a global unicast address (used on the Internet), a link local unicast address (used on a private network), and a unique local unicast address (used on subnets in a large enterprise).

▲ A computer can be assigned a computer name (also called a host name), and a network can be assigned a domain name. A fully qualified domain name (FQDN) includes the computer name and the domain name. An FQDN can be used to find a computer on the Internet if this name is associated with an IP address kept by DNS servers.

▲ TCP/IP uses protocols at the application level (such as FTP, HTTP, and Telnet) and at the operating system level (such as TCP and UDP).

Connecting a Computer to a Network

▲ A PC support person needs to know how to configure TCP/IP settings and make a wired or wireless connection to an existing network.

▲ The best method to secure a wireless network is to use encryption (which requires you enter a security key to connect). Two other methods that are sometimes used to secure a network are to not broadcast the SSID (which requires you enter the SSID to connect) and MAC address

15

filtering (which requires the network administrator enter the MAC address of your wireless adapter in a table). These last two methods provide weak security and are not recommended.

▲ To connect to a wireless WAN or cellular network, you need a mobile broadband modem, a SIM card, and a subscription to the cellular network. The mobile operator provides you a SIM card with your subscription. Your cell phone can serve as the mobile broadband modem when you tether it to your computer.

▲ A dial-up connection uses a telephone modem to make a connection to an ISP.

Setting Up a Multifunction Router for a SOHO Network

▲ A multifunction router for a small-office-home-office network might serve several functions, including a router, a switch, a DHCP server, a wireless access point, a firewall using NAT, and an FTP server.

▲ It's extremely important to change the password to configure your router as soon as you install it, especially if the router is also a wireless access point.

▲ To allow certain network traffic initiated on the Internet past your firewall, you can use port forwarding, port triggering, and a DMZ.

▲ To secure a wireless access point, you can enable MAC address filtering, disable SSID broadcasting, and enable encryption (WPA2, WPA, or WEP).

>> KEY TERMS

For explanations of key terms, see the Glossary near the end of the book.

6TO4
802.11 a/b/g/n
adapter address
AES (Advanced Encryption Standard)
alternate IP address
anycast address
Automatic Private IP Address (APIPA)
best-effort protocol
channel
Class A
Class B
Class C
classful subnet mask
classless subnet mask
client/server
computer name
connectionless protocol
connection-oriented protocol
default gateway
DHCP (dynamic host configuration protocol)
DHCP client
DMZ
DNS (Domain Name System or Domain Name Service)

DNS client
DNS server
domain name
dynamic IP address
FTP (File Transfer Protocol)
fully qualified domain name (FQDN)
gateway
global address
global unicast address
hardware address
host name
Hosts file
HTTP (Hypertext Transfer Protocol)
HTTPS (HTTP secure)
IMAP4 (Internet Message Access Protocol, version 4)
interface
interface ID
Internet Protocol version 4 (IPv4)
Internet Protocol version 6 (IPv6)
intranet
IP address

ISATAP
Lightweight Directory Access Protocol (LDAP)
link
link-local address
link-local unicast address
local area network (LAN)
local link
loopback address
MAC (Media Access Control) address
multicast address
multicasting
multiple input/multiple output (MIMO)
name resolution
NAT (Network Address Translation)
neighbors
network adapter
octet
packet
physical address
POP3 (Post Office Protocol, version 3)
port

port address
port filtering
port forwarding
port number
port triggering
private IP addresses
protocols
public IP addresses
Quality of Service (QoS)
radio frequency (RF)
Remote Desktop Protocol (RDP)
router
Secure FTP (SFTP)
Secure Shell (SSH)
Server Message Block (SMB)
Service Set Identifier (SSID)

SIM (Subscriber Identification Module) card
Simple Network Management Protocol (SNMP)
SMTP (Simple Mail Transfer Protocol)
SMTP AUTH (SMTP Authentication)
static IP address
subnet
subnet ID
subnet mask
TCP (Transmission Control Protocol)
TCP/IP (Transmission Control Protocol/Internet Protocol)
Telnet
Teredo

TKIP (Temporal Key Integrity Protocol)
UDP (User Datagram Protocol)
unicast address
unique local address (ULA)
unique local unicast address
virtual private network (VPN)
WEP (Wired Equivalent Privacy)
Wi-Fi (Wireless Fidelity)
Wi-Fi Protected Setup (WPS)
wireless access point
wireless wide area network (WWAN)
WPA (Wi-Fi Protected Access)
WPA2 (Wi-Fi Protected Access 2)

>> REVIEW QUESTIONS

1. What is used by the OS to find other computers on a network?

   a) MAC address

   b) Port address

   c) IP address

   d) Private address

2. A(n) _____ identifies a network.

   a) domain name

   b) workgroup

   c) host name

   d) computer name

3. Which protocol is used by various client applications when the application needs to query a database?

   a) SMB

   b) Telnet

   c) SNMP

   d) LDAP

4. When setting up a wireless router, which action is considered to be the strongest security measure?

   a) Disabling SSID broadcasting

   b) Changing the default password to the router firmware

   c) Configuring MAC address filtering

   d) Using WEP encryption

15

5. Which wireless radio frequency should be used for the best performance in a small space?

   a) 20 MHz

   b) 40 MHz

   c) 2 GHz

   d) 5 GHz

6. True or false? IP addresses leased from IANA today are all 128-bit addresses.

7. True or false? A Class C license assigns three octets as the host address.

8. True or false? A classless subnet mask aligns the network ID with the network octets assigned by the class license.

9. True or false? IPv6 classifies IP addresses differently from that of IPv4.

10. True or false? A channel is a specific radio frequency within a broader frequency.

11. IP addresses that begin with 192 through 223 are class ____ addresses.

12. The ____ used with IPv4 identifies which part of an IP address is the network portion and which part is the host portion.

13. A(n) ____ card is a small flash memory card that contains all the information you need to connect to a cellular network, including a password and other authentication information needed to access the network, encryption standards used, and the services that your subscription includes.

14. Port ____ is used to open or close certain ports so they can or cannot be used.

15. The latest Wi-Fi standard, 802.11n, uses ____, which means a device can use two or more antennas to improve performance.

Networking Types, Devices, and Cabling

In this chapter, you will learn:

- About network types and topologies
- About the hardware used to build local networks
- How to set up and troubleshoot the wiring in a small network

In the last chapter, you learned how to connect a computer to a network and how to set up and secure a wired and wireless router for a small network. This chapter takes you one step further in supporting networks. You'll learn about the types of networks and the technologies used to build these networks. You'll also learn about the hardware devices, cables, and connectors used to construct a network. Finally, you'll learn about networking tools, how to terminate network cables, and how to troubleshoot problems with network hardware.

In the next chapter, we continue our discussion of supporting networks. In Chapter 17, you'll learn how to support Windows applications on a network, how to share and secure resources on a network, and how to troubleshoot network connections.

NETWORK TYPES AND TOPOLOGIES

A computer network is created when two or more computers can communicate with each other. Networks can be categorized by several methods, including the technology used and the size of the network. When networks are categorized by size or physical area they cover, these are the categories used:

- ▲ *PAN.* A **PAN (personal area network)** consists of personal devices communicating at close range such as a cell phone and notebook computer. PANs can use wired connections (such as USB or FireWire) or wireless connections (such as Bluetooth or infrared).
- ▲ *LAN.* A **LAN (local area network)** covers a small local area such as a home, office, other building, or small group of buildings. LANs can use wired (most likely Ethernet) or wireless (most likely Wi-Fi, also called 802.11) technologies. A LAN is used for workstations, servers, printers, and other devices to communicate and share resources.
- ▲ *Wireless LAN.* A **wireless LAN (WLAN)** covers a limited geographical area, and is popular in places where networking cables are difficult to install, such as outdoors, in public places, and in homes that are not wired for networks. They are also useful in hotel rooms.
- ▲ *MAN.* A **MAN (metropolitan area network)** covers a large campus or city. (A small MAN is sometimes called a CAN or campus area network.) Network technologies used can be wireless (most likely LTE or WiMAX) and/or wired (for example, Ethernet with fiber-optic cabling).
- ▲ *WAN.* A **WAN (wide area network)** covers a large geographical area and is made up of many smaller networks. The best-known WAN is the Internet. Some technologies used to connect a single computer or LAN to the Internet include DSL, cable Internet, satellite, cellular WAN, and fiber optic.

 **A+ Exam Tip** The A+ 220-801 exam expects you to know about a LAN, WAN, PAN, and MAN.

The physical arrangement of the connections between computers is called the network **topology** or the physical topology. Here are the possibilities:

- ▲ *A mesh network.* In a **mesh network**, each node (a computer or other device that uses the network) on the network is responsible for sending and receiving transmissions to any other node to which it wants to communicate without a central point of communication. Figure 16-1a shows one configuration for a mesh network. Notice there might be more than one path from one node to another. One example of a wireless mesh network is when wireless computers connect to each other in ad hoc mode. In **ad hoc mode**, each wireless computer serves as its own wireless access point and is responsible for securing each connection. When several wireless computers each set up their own ad hoc mode network, the group of networked computers are a mesh network. When each node connects to every node on the network, the network is called a **fully connected mesh topology** (see Figure 16-1b).
- ▲ *A ring network.* In a **ring network** (see Figure 16-1c), nodes form a ring. Really old IBM Token Ring networks worked by passing a token around the ring. This topology is seldom used today because one down computer or a broken cable can halt all communication on the ring.

A+
220-801
2.7, 2.8

▲ *A bus network.* Another really old topology is a **bus network** (see Figure 16-1d) whereby all computers are connected in a sequential line. The bus network worked better than a ring network because one down computer does not prevent other computers from communicating on the bus. However, a broken cable can still bring down an entire bus network.

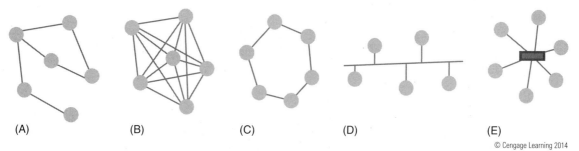

(A)	(B)	(C)	(D)	(E)

© Cengage Learning 2014

Figure 16-1 Network topologies: (a) mesh, (b) fully connected mesh, (c) ring, (d) bus, and (e) star

▲ *A star network.* A **star network** uses a centralized device to manage traffic on the network (see Figure 16-1e). This centralized device can be a switch or hub that offers multiple network ports or wireless connections. (Hubs are not as efficient as switches and no longer sold even though you might still see a hub in use.) Star networks are almost totally used for LANs today. An advantage of a star network is that one down computer or one broken cable does not bring down the entire network. When a star network uses multiple switches in sequence, the switches form a bus network, and the network topology is called a star bus network or a **hybrid network** (see Figure 16-2).

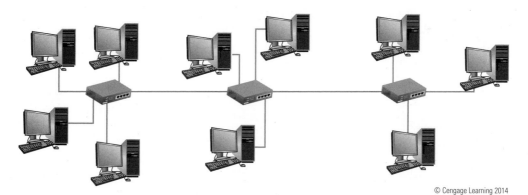

© Cengage Learning 2014

Figure 16-2 A hybrid network formed by nodes connected to multiple switches

16

APPLYING | CONCEPTS   SET UP AN AD HOC NETWORK

Suppose you are sitting in a meeting with a friend and you want to share some files on your laptops but you are not within range of a public Wi-Fi hotspot. If the two laptops are within 30 feet of each other, one of you can set up an ad hoc network so the two laptops can communicate wirelessly. Do the following:

1. Open the Network and Sharing Center. Click **Set up a new connection or network**. Then click **Set up a wireless ad hoc (computer-to-computer) network** and click **Next**.

A+
220-801
2.7, 2.8

2. If a message appears saying you are already connected to the Internet (for example, when your cell phone is tethered to your laptop and the cell phone is providing an Internet connection), click **Set up a new connection anyway** and then click **Wireless**.

3. You can then give the network a name and select a security type and security key (see Figure 16-3). Recall from Chapter 15 that the best security is WPA2-Personal.

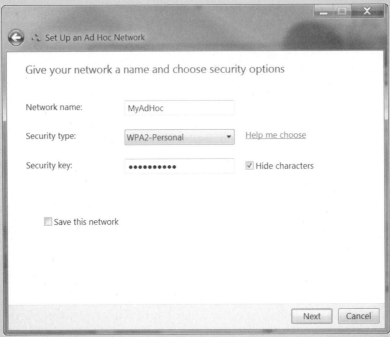

Source: Microsoft Windows 7

Figure 16-3   Set up security for the ad hoc network

4. The next box (see Figure 16-4) asks if you want to share your Internet connection with others on the ad hoc network. If so, click **Turn on Internet connection sharing**. Click **Close**.

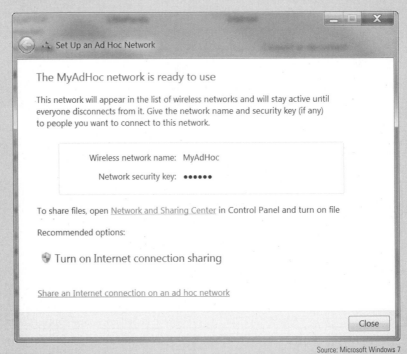

Source: Microsoft Windows 7

Figure 16-4   You can share an Internet connection with others on your ad hoc network

A+
220-801
2.7, 2.8

5. On the other computer, the new network is listed when the user clicks the network icon in the taskbar (see Figure 16-5). The user must enter your security key to connect.

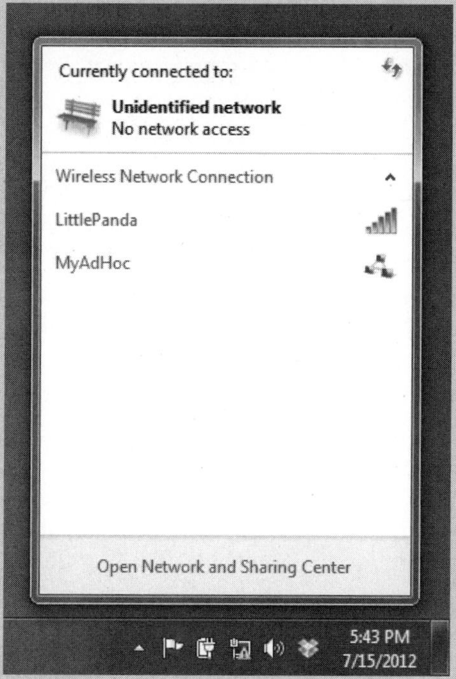

Figure 16-5 Other users can see and connect to your ad hoc network

By default, an ad hoc network is deleted after you or all users disconnect from the network.

Now let's look at network technologies used for Internet connections.

NETWORK TECHNOLOGIES USED FOR INTERNET CONNECTIONS

To connect to the Internet, a network first connects to an **Internet Service Provider (ISP)**, such as Earthlink or Comcast. The most common type of connections are DSL and cable Internet (commonly called cable or cable modem). See Figure 16-6. When connecting to an ISP, know that upload speeds are generally slower than download speeds. These rates differ because users generally download more data than they upload. Therefore, an ISP devotes more of the available bandwidth to downloading and less of it to uploading.

Networks are built using one or more technologies that provide varying degrees of bandwidth. **Bandwidth** (the width of the band) is the theoretical number of bits that can be transmitted over a network at one time, similar to the number of lanes on a highway. In practice, however, the networking industry refers to bandwidth as a measure of the maximum rate of data transmission in bits per second (bps), thousands of bits per second (Kbps), millions of bits per second (Mbps), or billions of bits per second (Gbps). Bandwidth is the theoretical or potential speed of a network, whereas **data throughput** is the average of the actual speed. In practice, network transmissions experience delays that result in slower network performance. These delays in network transmissions are

16

A+
220-801
2.7, 2.8

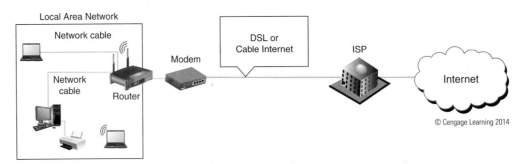

Figure 16-6   An ISP stands between a LAN and the Internet

called **latency**. Latency is measured by the round-trip time it takes for a data packet to travel from source to destination and back to source.

Table 16-1 lists network technologies used to connect to the Internet. The table is more or less ordered from slowest to fastest maximum bandwidth, although latency (time delays) can affect the actual bandwidth of a particular network. For comparison, the table includes the more common Ethernet and Wi-Fi standards used for LANs as well as the faster technologies used for Internet backbones.

Currently, cable Internet and DSL are the two most popular ways to make an Internet connection. Let's first compare these two technologies and then we'll look at satellite, fiber-optic dedicated lines, WiMAX, and cellular WANs.

Technology Wireless or Wired	Maximum Speed	Common Uses
2G cellular (second-generation cellular) ✓ Wireless	Up to 50 Kbps	Uses the mobile phone service on a cellular network for voice and data (digital) transmissions. Most 2G networks use an improved version of the GSM mobile phone service, although some use CDMA, which is a competing service.
Dial-up or regular telephone (POTS, for plain old telephone service) ✓ Wired	Up to 56 Kbps	Slow access to an ISP using a modem and dial-up connection over phone lines.
ISDN ✓ Wired	64 Kbps or 128 Kbps	*ISDN (Integrated Services Digital Network)* is an outdated business-use access to an ISP over dial-up phone lines.
2G EDGE or 2G E cellular ✓ Wireless	Up to 230 Kbps	Improved over 2G and uses the GSM mobile phone service. (EDGE stands for Enhanced Data for GSM Evolution.)
3G cellular (third-generation cellular) ✓ Wireless	At least 200 Kbps, but can be up to 2.4 Mbps	Improved over 2G EDGE and allows for transmitting data and video. Uses either CDMA or GSM mobile phone services. Speeds vary widely according to the revision standards used.
Satellite ✓ Wireless	Up to 1.5 Mbps	Requires a dish to send and receive from a satellite, which is in a relative fixed position with earth.

© Cengage Learning 2014

Table 16-1   Networking technologies (continues)

A+
220-801
2.7, 2.8

Technology Wireless or Wired	Maximum Speed	Common Uses
SDSL (Symmetric Digital Subscriber Line) ✓ Wired	Up to 2.3 Mbps	Equal bandwidth in both directions. SDSL is a type of broadband technology. (*Broadband* refers to a networking technology that carries more than one type of signal, such as DSL and telephone or cable Internet and TV.) DSL uses regular phone lines and is an always-up or always-on connection that does not require a dial-up.
ADSL (Asymmetric DSL) ✓ Wired	640 Kbps upstream and up to 24 Mbps downstream	Most bandwidth is from ISP to user. Slower versions of ADSL are called ADSL Lite or DSL Lite. ISP customers pay according to a bandwidth scale.
Cable Internet ✓ Wired	Up to 30 Mbps, depends on the type of cable	Connects a home or small business to an ISP, and usually comes with a cable television subscription and shares cable TV lines. Fiber-optic cable gives highest speeds.
T3 ✓ Wired	44 Mbps	Dedicated lines used by large companies that require a lot of bandwidth.
Dedicated line using fiber optic ✓ Wired	Up to 20 Mbps upstream and 50 Mbps downstream	Dedicated line from ISP to business or home. Speeds vary with price.
VDSL (very-high-bit-rate DSL) ✓ Wired	Up to 52 Mbps	A type of asymmetric DSL that works only a short distance.
Wi-Fi 802.11g wireless ✓ Wireless	Up to 54 Mbps	Compatible with and has replaced 802.11b.
802.16 wireless (WiMAX) WiMAX 2.0 ✓ Wireless	Up to 75 Mbps Up to 1 Gbps	Ranges up to 6 miles and is used to provide wireless access to an ISP in rural areas.
Fast Ethernet (100BaseT) ✓ Wired	100 Mbps	Used for local networks.
802.11n wireless ✓ Wireless	Up to 160 Mbps	Latest Wi-Fi technology.
4G cellular (fourth-generation cellular) ✓ Wireless	100 Mbps to 1 Gbps	Higher speeds are achieved when the client stays in a fixed position. A 4G network uses either LTE (Long Term Evolution) or WiMAX technology. LTE is more popular and faster.
Gigabit Ethernet (1000BaseT) ✓ Wired	1000 Mbps or 1 Gbps	Fastest Ethernet standard for a local network.
OC-1, OC-3, OC-24, up to OC-3072 ✓ Wired	52 Mbps, 155 Mbps, 1.23 Gbps, 160 Gbps	Optical Carrier levels (OCx) used for Internet backbones; they use fiber-optic cabling.

16

Table 16-1 Networking technologies (continues)

A+
220-801
2.7, 2.8

Technology Wireless or Wired	Maximum Speed	Common Uses
10-gigabit Ethernet (10GBaseT) ✓ Wired	10 Gbps	Newest Ethernet standard expected to largely replace SONET, OC, and ATM because of its speed, simplicity, and lower cost.
SONET (Synchronous Optical Network) ✓ Wired	Up to 160 Gbps	Major backbones built using fiber-optic cabling make use of different OC levels.

© Cengage Learning 2014

Table 16-1 Networking technologies (continued)

> **⚲ A+ Exam Tip** The A+ 220-801 exam expects you to be able to compare these network types used for Internet connections: Cable, dial-up, DSL, fiber, satellite, ISDN, cellular (mobile hotspot), and WiMAX.

COMPARE CABLE INTERNET AND DSL

Here are the important facts about cable Internet and DSL:

- ▲ **Cable Internet** is a broadband technology that uses cable TV lines and is always connected (always up). With cable Internet, the TV signal to your television and the data signals to your PC or LAN share the same coaxial (coax) cable. The cable modem converts a computer's digital signals to analog when sending them and converts incoming analog data to digital.
- ▲ **DSL (Digital Subscriber Line)** is a group of broadband technologies that covers a wide range of speeds. DSL uses ordinary copper phone lines and a range of frequencies on the copper wire that are not used by voice, making it possible for you to use the same phone line for voice and DSL at the same time. When you make a regular phone call, you dial in as usual. However, the DSL part of the line is always connected (always up) for most DSL services.

When deciding between cable Internet and DSL, consider these points:

- ▲ Both cable Internet and DSL can sometimes be purchased on a sliding scale, depending on the bandwidth you want to buy. Subscriptions offer residential and the more-expensive business plans. Business plans are likely to have increased bandwidth and better support when problems arise.
- ▲ With cable Internet, you share the TV cable infrastructure with your neighbors, which can result in service becoming degraded if many people in your neighborhood are using cable Internet at the same time. I once used cable Internet in a neighborhood where I found I needed to avoid web surfing between 5:00 and 7:00 P.M. when folks were just coming in from work and using the Internet. With DSL, you're using a dedicated phone line, so your neighbors' surfing habits are not important.
- ▲ With DSL, static over phone lines in your house can be a problem. The DSL company provides filters to install at each phone jack (see Figure 16-7), but still the problem might not be fully solved. Also, your phone line must qualify for DSL; some lines are too dirty (too much static or noise) to support DSL.
- ▲ Setup of cable and DSL works about the same way, using either a cable modem or a DSL modem for the interface between the broadband jack (TV jack or phone jack) and the computer. Figure 16-8 shows a DSL modem. In most cases, cable Internet and DSL

A+
220-801
2.7, 2.8

use a network port or a USB port on the computer to connect to the cable modem or DSL modem. Alternately, you can use a small router between the modem and the LAN (refer to Figure 16-6), such as the one you learned to configure in Chapter 15.

© Cengage Learning 2014

Figure 16-7 When DSL is used in your home, filters are needed on every phone jack except the one used by the DSL modem

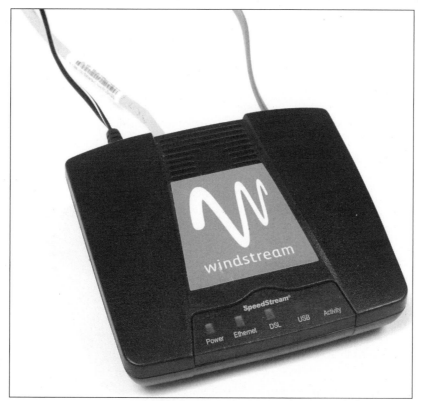

© Cengage Learning 2014

Figure 16-8 This DSL modem connects to a phone jack and a computer or router to provide a broadband connection to an ISP

16

A+
220-801
2.7, 2.8

SATELLITE

People who live in remote areas and want high-speed Internet connections often are limited in their choices. DSL and cable options might not be available where they live, but satellite access is available from pretty much anywhere. Internet access by satellite is available even on airplanes. Passengers can connect to the Internet using a wireless hotspot and satellite dish on the plane. A satellite dish mounted on top of your house or office building communicates with a satellite used by an ISP offering the satellite service (see Figure 16-9). One disadvantage of satellite is that it requires **line-of-sight connectivity** without obstruction from mountains, trees, and tall buildings. Another disadvantage is that it experiences delays in transmission (called latency), especially when uploading, and is, therefore, not a good solution for an Internet connection that is to be used for video conferencing or voice over Internet.

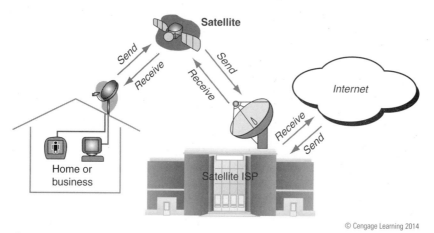

© Cengage Learning 2014

Figure 16-9 Communication by satellite can include television and Internet access

DEDICATED LINE USING FIBER OPTIC

Another broadband technology used for Internet access is **fiber optic**. The technology uses a dedicated line from your ISP to your place of business or residence. This dedicated line is called a point-to-point (PTP) connection because no other business or residence shares the line with you. Many types of cabling can be used for dedicated lines, but fiber-optic cabling is becoming popular. Television, Internet data, and voice communication all share the broadband **fiber-optic cable**. Verizon calls the technology FiOS (Fiber Optic Service), and the fiber-optic cabling is used all the way from the ISP to your home. Other providers can provide fiber-optic cabling up to your neighborhood and then use coaxial cable (similar to that used in cable Internet connections) for the last leg of the connection to your business or residence. Upstream and downstream speeds and prices vary.

WIMAX OR 802.16 WIRELESS

WiMAX is defined under IEEE 802.16d and 802.16e. WiMAX supports up to 75 Mbps with a range up to several miles and uses 2- to 11-GHz frequency. WiMAX version 2.0, defined under IEEE 802.16m, is not widely available and can support up to 1 Gbps for fixed-position users and up to 100 Mbps for mobile users. The WiMAX range in miles depends on many factors. For a wide-area network, WiMAX cellular towers are generally placed 1.5 miles apart to assure complete coverage. It is sometimes used as a last-mile solution for DSL and cable Internet technologies, which means that the DSL or cable connection goes into a central point in an area, and WiMAX is used for the final leg to the consumer. WiMAX was

A+
220-801
2.7, 2.8

first used for 4G transmissions in cell phones, but LTE has taken over this market. Some laptops have a built-in WiMAX modem to connect to 4G networks that use WiMAX.

Figure 16-10 shows a WiMAX external modem used to create an Internet connection for a single computer or LAN. The modem communicates wirelessly with a WiMAX tower within range. You connect the computer or local network to the modem using its one Ethernet port. To configure the modem, enter its IP address (192.168.15.1) in your browser address box and enter its default password. The firmware page that appears in your browser is used to configure the modem. You must have a subscription with the WiMAX carrier to use the modem.

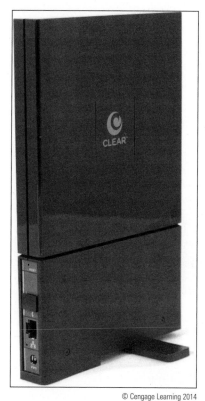

© Cengage Learning 2014

Figure 16-10 WiMAX modem by Motorola used to create a WiMAX Internet connection for a computer or network

16

CELLULAR WAN

A **cellular network** or **cellular WAN** consists of cells, and each cell is controlled by a base station (see Figure 16-11). The **base station** might include more than one transceiver and antenna on the same tower to support multiple technologies (such as WiMAX, LTE, and GSM). Cell phones are called that because they use a cellular network.

Cell phone networks use one of these two competing technologies:

▲ **GSM (Global System for Mobile Communications)** is an open standard that uses digital communication of data, and is accepted and used worldwide. GSM networks require that a cellular device have a **SIM (Subscriber Identity Module) card** that contains a microchip to hold data about the subscription you have with your cellular carrier. Figure 16-12 shows the slot on the side of an iPad where you can insert a SIM card.

A+
220-801
2.7, 2.8

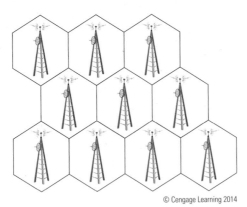

© Cengage Learning 2014

Figure 16-11 A cellular WAN is made up
of many cells that provide
coverage over a wide area

▲ **CDMA (Code Division Multiple Access)** was more popular than GSM in the United States for many years, but GSM is overtaking the market. CDMA networks do not require a SIM card in a cellular device.

© Cengage Learning 2014

Figure 16-12   A SIM card is required for a device to use a GSM cellular network

The ability to use your cell phone to browse the web, stream music and video, play online games, and use instant messaging and video conferencing is called 2G, 3G, or 4G. **4G (Fourth Generation)** offers the fastest speeds for cellular data. To use 2G, 3G, or 4G, both the client and cellular network must support it, and you must have a subscription for data transmissions.

Look back at Table 16-1 to see where 4G cellular fits in the list of technologies ordered from slow to fast; 4G is faster than both DSL and cable. 4G is not yet widely available but is expected to ultimately replace both DSL and cable as a solution for connecting homes and small businesses to the Internet. Where 4G coverage is available, you can use it to connect a mobile computer, desktop computer, or network to the Internet, and this connection is faster than DSL or cable.

Some laptops and tablets have embedded broadband modems. Figure 16-13 shows four other ways a computer or network can connect to the Internet by way of a cellular network connection.

A+
220-801
2.7, 2.8

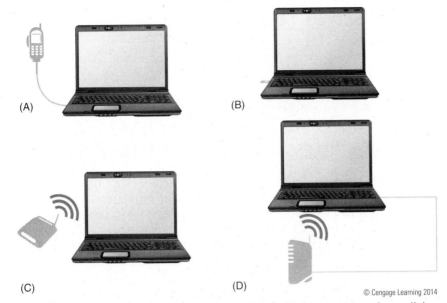

(A)

(B)

(C)

(D)

© Cengage Learning 2014

Figure 16-13 Four external devices a computer or network can use to make a cellular Internet connection

Here is an explanation of the four methods shown in Figure 16-13:

▲ *Cell phone tethered to computer.* A cell phone connected to a computer by way of a USB port (see Figure 16-13a) communicates with the cellular network. Software must be installed on the computer to use the connection and your subscription with the cellular carrier must include the option to tether your phone.

▲ *Mobile broadband modem.* An external mobile broadband modem, also called an Internet card or air card, can be a small USB device (see Figure 16-13b), a Wi-Fi portable broadband modem that creates a Wi-Fi hotspot for one or more computers (see Figure 16-13c), or a wired stationary broadband modem that is part of a wired LAN (see Figure 16-13d). Figure 16-14 shows a USB broadband modem that you learned to configure in Chapter 15. An example of a stationary wired broadband modem is the WiMAX modem shown in Figure 16-10.

16

© Cengage Learning 2014

Figure 16-14 A USB broadband modem by Sierra Wireless

HARDWARE USED BY LOCAL NETWORKS

A+
220-801
1.4, 1.11,
2.1, 2.2,
2.9

A+
220-802
1.6

In this part of the chapter, you will learn about the hardware devices that create and connect to networks. In Chapter 15, you learned about routers, firewalls, and wireless access points. In the following subsections, we discuss desktop and laptop devices, hubs, switches, bridges, and other network devices, and the cables and connectors these devices use.

WIRED AND WIRELESS NETWORK ADAPTERS

A PC makes a direct connection to a local wired network by way of a **network adapter**, which might be a network port embedded on the motherboard or a **network interface card (NIC)** installed in an expansion slot on the motherboard. In addition, the adapter might also be an external device plugged into a USB port (see Figure 16-15). The wired network adapter provides an **RJ-45** port (RJ stands for registered jack) that looks like a large phone jack.

© Cengage Learning 2014

Figure 16-15 USB device provides an Ethernet port

> 💡 **A+ Exam Tip** The A+ 220-801 exam expects you to know the features of a network adapter, including the slot it uses, speeds, half duplex, full duplex, MAC address, status indicator lights, Wake on LAN, QoS, and PoE.

Video
PCI Express and Wireless

Here are the features you need to be aware of that might be included with a network adapter. You learned about several of these features in Chapter 15:

▲ *The slot a NIC uses.* For expansion cards, consider the slot (PCI Express or PCI) the network adapter card uses. Figure 16-16 shows a network adapter that uses a PCI Express ×1 slot. Before installing a network adapter, be sure to first go to Device Manager and uninstall any network adapters already present. You might also need to go to BIOS setup and disable an onboard network port.

A+
220-801
1.4, 1.11,
2.1, 2.2,
2.9

A+
220-802
1.6

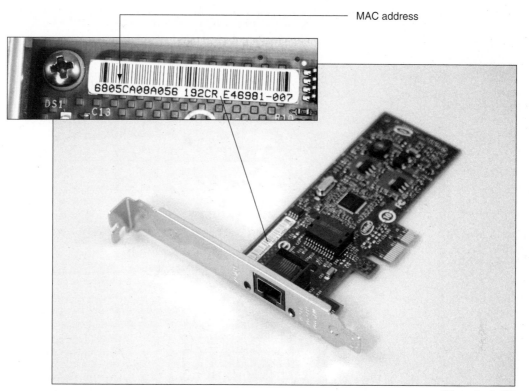

MAC address

© Cengage Learning 2014

Figure 16-16 Gigabit Ethernet adapter by Intel uses a PCIe ×1 slot

▲ *Ethernet speeds.* For wired networks, the four speeds for Ethernet are 10 Mbps, 100 Mbps (Fast Ethernet or 100BaseT), 1 Gbps (Gigabit Ethernet or 1000BaseT), and 10 Gbps (10-gigabit Ethernet or 10GBaseT). Most network cards sold today for local networks use Gigabit Ethernet and also support the two slower speeds. To see the speeds supported, open the network adapter's properties box in Device Manager. The speed is usually included in the name of the adapter (see the left side of Figure 16-17). If the adapter connects with slower network devices on the network, the adapter works at the slower speed. The properties box might offer the Link Speed tab (see the right side of Figure 16-17) where you can manually adjust the speed to correct a problem when the adapter is not connecting to an older device. Notice in the drop-down list that the choices include the three speeds at half duplex or full duplex. **Full duplex** sends and receives transmissions at the same time. **Half duplex** works in only one direction at a time. Select Auto Negotiation for Windows to use the best possible speed and duplex. Also notice on the Link Speed tab the Diagnostics button, which you can use to run diagnostics on the adapter when you suspect it's giving problems.

▲ *MAC address.* Every network adapter (including a wired or wireless) has a 48-bit (6-byte) identification number, called the MAC address or physical address, hard-coded on the card by its manufacturer that is unique for that adapter, and this number is used to identify the adapter on the network. An example of a MAC address is 00-0C-6E-4E-AB-A5. Most likely the MAC address is printed on the device. You can also have Windows tell you the MAC address by entering the **ipconfig /all** command in a command prompt window (see Figure 16-18).

▲ *Status indicator lights.* A wired network adapter might provide indicator lights on the side of the RJ-45 port that indicate connectivity and activity (see Figure 16-19). When you first discover you have a problem with a computer not connecting to a network, be sure to check the status indicator lights to verify you have connectivity and activity. If not, then the problem is related to hardware. Next, check the cable connections to make sure they are solid.

16

A+
220-801
1.4, 1.11,
2.1, 2.2,
2.9

A+
220-802
1.6

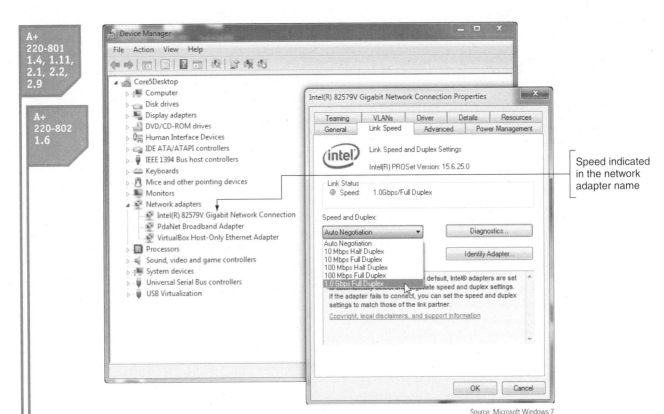

Source: Microsoft Windows 7

Figure 16-17   Set the speed and duplex for the network adapter

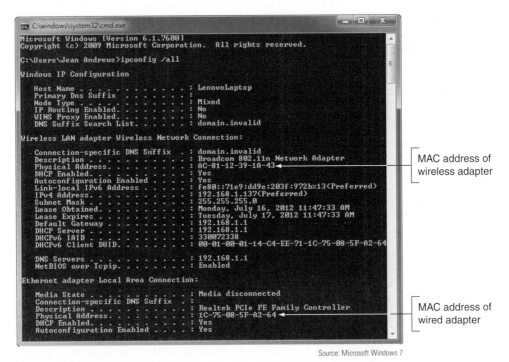

Source: Microsoft Windows 7

Figure 16-18   Use the ipconfig /all command to show the MAC address of a
network adapter

▲ *Wake-on-LAN.* A network adapter might support Wake-on-LAN, which allows the
adapter to wake up the computer when it receives certain communication on the
network. To use the feature, it must be enabled on the network adapter. To do that, use
the Power Management tab on the network adapter properties box (see Figure 16-20).
It is not recommended that you enable Wake on LAN for a wireless network adapter.

A+
220-801
1.4, 1.11,
2.1, 2.2,
2.9

A+
220-802
1.6

© Cengage Learning 2014

Figure 16-19   Status indicator lights for the embedded network port

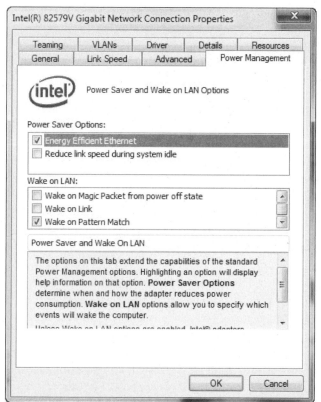

Source: Microsoft Windows 7

Figure 16-20   Enable variations of Wake on LAN based on what type of software is allowed to wake up the computer

16

Source: Microsoft Windows 7

Figure 16-21 Select Priority Enabled to allow the network adapter to support QoS on the network

▲ *Quality of Service (QoS).* Another feature of a network adapter is the ability to control which applications have priority on the network. The feature must be enabled and configured on the router and also enabled on the network adapters and configured in Windows for every computer on the network using the high-priority applications. To enable the network adapter to use QoS, use the Advanced tab on the network adapter properties box (see Figure 16-21). Make sure **Priority Enabled** is selected. (If the option is not listed, the adapter does not support QoS.) In Chapter 15, you learned how to configure a router to use QoS. How to configure Windows to prioritize an application on the network is covered in Chapter 17.

▲ *Power over Ethernet (PoE).* **Power over Ethernet (PoE)** is a feature that might be available on high-end wired network adapters that allow power to be transmitted over Ethernet cable. Using this feature, you can place a wireless access point, webcam, IP phone, or other device that needs power in a position in a building where you don't have an electrical outlet. The Ethernet cable to the device provides both power and data transmissions. Some devices, such as a webcam, are designed to receive both power and data from the Ethernet cable. For other devices, you must use a splitter that splits the data transmission and the power transmission. Then use both a power cable and Ethernet data cable to run from the splitter to the device. PoE can provide up to 25.5 W from a single Ethernet port. The amount of power that reaches a device degrades with the length of the cable. Most high-quality switches provide PoE. Figure 16-22 shows a PoE switch and a splitter used to provide power to a non-PoE access point. When setting up a device to receive power by PoE, make sure the

A+
220-801
1.4, 1.11,
2.1, 2.2,
2.9

A+
220-802
1.6

device sending the power, the splitter, and the device receiving the power are all compatible. Pay special attention to the voltage and wattage requirements and the type of power connector of the receiving device.

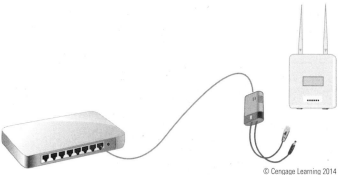

© Cengage Learning 2014

Figure 16-22   Use a PoE splitter if the receiving device is not PoE compatible

DIAL-UP MODEMS

Of all the types of networking connections, dial-up or POTS (Plain Old Telephone Service) is the least expensive and slowest connection to the Internet. Dial-up connections are painfully slow, but many times we still need them when traveling, and they're good at home when our broadband connection is down or when we just plain want to save money.

Modem cards in desktop computers provide two phone jacks, called **RJ-11 jacks**, so that one can be used for dial-up networking and the other jack can be used to plug in an extension telephone. Figure 16-23 shows a modem card that comes bundled with drivers on CD and a phone cord. Phone cords are a type of twisted-pair cable and use an RJ-11 connector. **Twisted-pair cabling** uses pairs of wires twisted together to reduce crosstalk. The RJ-11 jack has four connectors, and a phone cord can have one or two twisted pairs for a total of two or four wires in the cord. The cord carries power on the lines that can be used to power a simple telephone. Laptop computers that have embedded modem capability generally have only a single phone jack. Dial-up standards are no longer being revised, and the last dial-up modem standard is the V.92 standard.

© Cengage Learning 2014

Figure 16-23   This 56K V.92 PCI modem card comes bundled with a phone cord and setup CD

When installing a modem card, be sure to follow manufacturer directions. Most directions say to install the drivers on CD before you physically install the modem. How to configure a modem card and set up a dial-up connection are covered in Chapter 15.

16

A+
220-801
1.11,
2.1, 2.2,
2.9

SWITCHES AND HUBS

Recall that today's Ethernet networks use a star bus topology whereby nodes are connected to one or more centralized devices (refer to Figure 16-2). This centralized device can be a switch or a hub. Each device handles a network packet or frame differently.

> **Notes** In Chapter 15, you learned about packets, which are segments of data sent over a TCP/IP network with IP address header information added. Just before a packet is put on the network, the network adapter adds additional information to the beginning and end of the packet, and this information includes the source and destination MAC addresses. The packet, with this additional information, is now called a frame.

Here are the differences between a hub and a switch:

▲ An Ethernet **hub** transmits the data frame to every device, except the device that sent the frame, as shown in Figure 16-24. A hub is just a pass-through and distribution point for every device connected to it, without regard for what kind of data is passing through and where the data might be going. Hubs are outdated technology, having been replaced by switches. Figure 16-25 shows a hub that supports 10 Mbps and 100 Mbps Ethernet speeds.

▲ A **switch** (see Figure 16-26) is smarter and more efficient than a hub because it keeps a table of all the MAC addresses for devices connected to it. When the switch receives a frame, it searches its MAC address table for the destination MAC address of the frame and sends the frame only to the device or interface using this MAC address. At first, a switch does not know the MAC addresses of every device connected to it. It learns this information as it receives frames and records the source MAC addresses in its MAC address table. When it receives a frame destined to a MAC address not in its table, the switch acts like a hub and broadcasts the frame to all devices except the one that sent it.

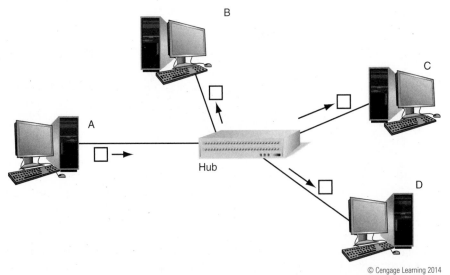

© Cengage Learning 2014

Figure 16-24 Any data received by a hub is replicated and passed on to all other devices connected to it

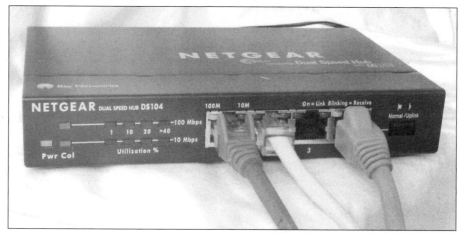

© Cengage Learning 2014

Figure 16-25 A hub is a pass-through device to connect nodes on a network

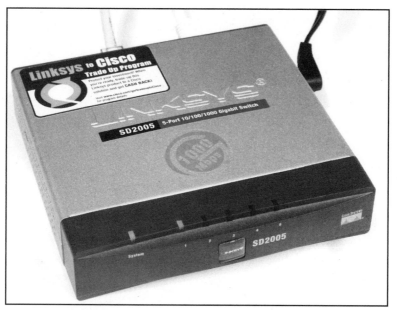

© Cengage Learning 2014

Figure 16-26 A five-port Gigabit Ethernet switch by Linksys

16

Figure 16-2, shown earlier in the chapter, uses three switches in sequence. Physically, the network cables that run between two switches or a switch and a computer might be inside a building's walls with a network jack on the wall providing an RJ-45 connector. You plug a network cable into the jack to make the connection. In practice, a small network might begin as one switch and three or four computers. As the need for more computers grows, new switches are added to provide these extra connections.

Another reason to add a switch to a network is to regenerate the network signal. An Ethernet cable should not exceed 100 meters (about 328 feet) in length. If you need to reach distances greater than that, you can add a switch in the line, which regenerates the signal.

WIRELESS ACCESS POINTS AND BRIDGES

In Chapter 15, you learned that a router can also be a wireless access point. In addition, a wireless access point can be a dedicated device. The wireless access point, such as the one shown in Figure 16-27, can also be a bridge. A **bridge** is a device that stands between

A+
220-801
1.11,
2.1, 2.2,
2.9

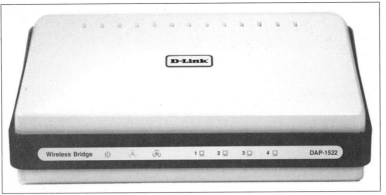

Courtesy of D-Link Corporation

Figure 16-27   Xtreme N Duo Wireless Bridge/Access Point by D-Link

two segments of a network and manages network traffic between them. For example, one network segment might be a wireless network and the other segment might be a wired network; the wireless access point (AP) connects these two segments. Functioning as a bridge, the AP helps to reduce the overall volume of network traffic by not allowing data frames across the bridge if it knows that the frame is addressed to a destination on its own segment. Figure 16-28 demonstrates the concept of a network bridge. (Logically, you can think of a switch as a multiport bridge.)

© Cengage Learning 2014

Figure 16-28   A bridge is an intelligent device making decisions concerning network traffic

Similar to a switch, a bridge at first does not know which nodes are on each network segment. It learns that information by maintaining a table of MAC addresses from information it collects from each frame that arrives at the bridge. Eventually, it learns which nodes are on which network segment and becomes more efficient at preventing frames from getting on the wrong segment, which can bog down network traffic.

> **A+ Exam Tip** The A+ 220-801 exam expects you to know the functions and features of a hub, switch, router, access point, bridge, modem, NAS, firewall, VoIP phone, and Internet appliance.

OTHER NETWORK DEVICES

Here are a few more network devices that you might encounter as you support small networks:

- ◢ *Network Attached Storage (NAS) device.* You saw an example of a **Network Attached Storage (NAS)** device in Chapter 13 in Figure 13-29. The enclosure provides four bays for hard drives and an Ethernet port to connect to the network and supports RAID. NAS enclosures might provide many more drive bays and almost always support RAID.
- ◢ *VoIP phone.* VoIP (**Voice over Internet Protocol**) is a TCP/IP protocol that manages voice communication over the Internet. A **VoIP phone** connects directly to a network by way of an Ethernet port or an embedded Ethernet cable (see Figure 16-29). A VoIP phone uses firmware to configure its TCP/IP settings (including its IP address) and the phone number assigned to the phone.
- ◢ *Internet appliance.* An **Internet appliance** is a type of thin client that is designed to make it easy for a user to connect to the Internet, browse the web, use email, and perform other simple chores on the Internet. They were sold several years ago, but are hard to find today, primarily because a low-end netbook or tablet doesn't cost that much compared to what an Internet appliance would cost today.

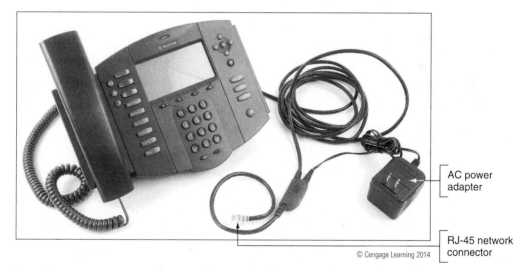

© Cengage Learning 2014

AC power adapter

RJ-45 network connector

Figure 16-29 This VoIP digital telephone connects to a local network and to the Internet by way of a network cable

16

ETHERNET CABLES AND CONNECTORS

Several variations of Ethernet cables and connectors have evolved over the years and are primarily identified by their speeds and the types of connectors used to wire these networks. Table 16-2 compares cable types and Ethernet versions.

> **A+ Exam Tip** The A+ 220-801 exam expects you to know the details shown in Table 16-2.

A+
220-801
1.11,
2.1, 2.2,
2.9

Cable System	Speed	Cables and Connectors	Example of Connectors	Maximum Cable Length
10Base2 (ThinNet)	10 Mbps	Coaxial cable uses a BNC connector.	© Albert Lozano/Shutterstock.com	185 meters or 607 feet
10Base5 (ThickNet)	10 Mbps	Coaxial uses an AUI 15-pin D-shaped connector.	Courtesy of Black Box Network Service	500 meters or 1,640 feet
10BaseT, 100BaseT (Fast Ethernet), 1000BaseT (Gigabit Ethernet), and 10GBaseT (10-Gigabit Ethernet)	10 Mbps, 100 Mbps, 1 Gbps, or 10 Gbps	Twisted pair (UTP or STP) uses an RJ-45 connector.	© Olga Lipatova/Shutterstock.com	100 meters or 328 feet
10BaseF, 10BaseFL, 100BaseFL, 100BaseFX, 1000BaseFX, or 1000BaseX (fiber optic)	10 Mbps, 100 Mbps, 1 Gbps, or 10 Gbps	Fiber-optic cable uses ST or SC connectors (shown to the right) or LC and MT-RJ connectors (not shown).	Courtesy of Black Box Network Services	Up to 2 kilometers (6,562 feet)

© Cengage Learning 2014

Table 16-2 Variations of Ethernet and Ethernet cabling

Video

Ethernet Cables

As you can see from Table 16-2, the three main types of cabling used by Ethernet are twisted-pair, coaxial, and fiber optic. Coaxial cable is older and almost never used today. Within each category, there are several variations:

▲ *Twisted-pair cable*. Twisted-pair cable is the most popular cabling method for local networks and uses an RJ-45 connector. The cable comes in two varieties: **unshielded twisted pair (UTP) cable** and **shielded twisted pair (STP) cable**. UTP cable is the least expensive and is commonly used on LANs. UTP is rated by category: **CAT-3** (**Category 3**) is less expensive than the more popular **CAT-5** cable or **enhanced CAT-5** (**CAT-5e**). **CAT-6** has less crosstalk than CAT-5 or CAT-5e because it has a plastic core that keeps the twisted pairs separated. Always use CAT-5e or CAT-6 for Gigabit Ethernet. **CAT-6a** is thicker than CAT-6 and used by 10GBase-T (10-Gigabit Ethernet).

Figure 16-30 shows unshielded twisted pair cables and the RJ-45 connector. Twisted-pair cable has four pairs of twisted wires for a total of eight wires. You learn more about how the eight wires are arranged later in the chapter.

A+
220-801
1.11,
2.1, 2.2,
2.9

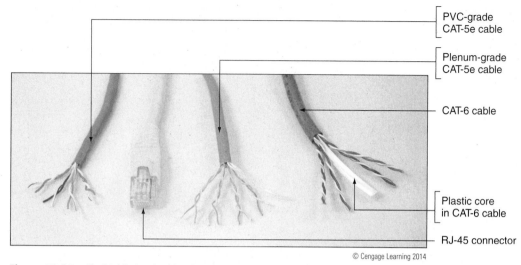

PVC-grade
CAT-5e cable

Plenum-grade
CAT-5e cable

CAT-6 cable

Plastic core
in CAT-6 cable

RJ-45 connector

© Cengage Learning 2014

Figure 16-30   Unshielded twisted-pair cables and RJ-45 connector used for local wired networks

STP cable uses a covering or shield around each pair of wires inside the cable that protects it from electromagnetic interference caused by electrical motors, transmitters, or high-tension lines. It costs more than unshielded cable, so it's used only when the situation demands it.

> **Notes** Normally, the plastic covering of a cable is made of PVC (polyvinyl chloride), which is not safe when used inside plenums (areas between the floors of buildings). In these situations, plenum cable covered with Teflon is used because it does not give off toxic fumes when burned. Plenum cable is two or three times more expensive than PVC cable. Figure 16-30 shows plenum cable and PVC cable, which are unshielded twisted-pair cables.

▲ *Coaxial cable.* **Coaxial cable** has a single copper wire down the middle and a braided shield around it (see Figure 16-31). The cable is stiff and difficult to manage, and is no longer used for networking. **RG-6 coaxial cable** is used for cable TV, having replaced the older and thinner **RG-59 coaxial cable** once used for cable TV. RG-6 cables use an **F connector** shown in Figure 16-32.

© Cengage Learning 2014

Figure 16-31   Coaxial cable and a BNC connector are used with ThinNet Ethernet

16

A+
220-801
1.11,
2.1, 2.2,
2.9

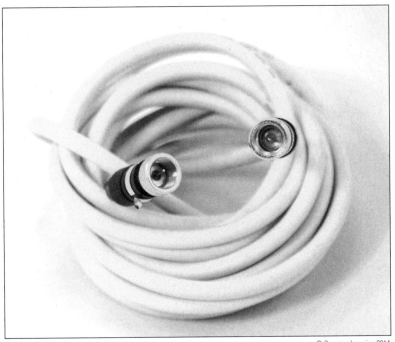

© Cengage Learning 2014

Figure 16-32 An RG-6 coaxial cable with an F connector used for connections to TV has a single copper wire

> 💡 **A+ Exam Tip** The A+ 220-801 exam expects you to know about these cables and connectors: BNC, RJ-45, coaxial, SC, ST, LC, RJ-11, F-connector, STP, UTP, CAT-3, CAT-5, CAT-5e, CAT-6, plenum, PVC, RG-6, and RG-59.

▲ *Fiber optic.* **Fiber-optic cables** transmit signals as pulses of light over glass or plastic strands inside protected tubing, as illustrated in Figure 16-33. Fiber-optic cable comes in two types: single-mode (thin, difficult to connect, expensive, and best performing) and multimode (most popular). A single-mode cable uses a single path for light to travel in the cable and multimode cable uses multiple paths for light. Both single-mode and multimode fiber-optic cables can be constructed as loose-tube cables for outdoor use or tight-buffered cables for indoor or outdoor use. Loose-tube cables are filled with gel to prevent water from soaking into the cable, and tight-buffered cables are filled with yarn to protect the fiber-optic strands, as shown in Figure 16-33.

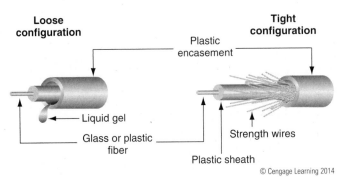

Loose configuration

Tight configuration

Plastic encasement

Liquid gel

Glass or plastic fiber

Strength wires

Plastic sheath

© Cengage Learning 2014

Figure 16-33 Fiber-optic cables contain a glass or plastic core for transmitting light

A+
220-801
1.11,
2.1, 2.2,
2.9

Fiber-optic cables can use one of four connectors, all shown in Figure 16-34. The two older types are **ST** (**straight tip**) **connectors** and **SC** (**subscriber connector or standard connector**) **connectors**. Two newer types are **LC** (**local connector**) **connectors** and **MT-RJ** (**mechanical transfer registered jack**) **connectors**. Any one of the four connectors can be used with either single-mode or multimode fiber-optic cable.

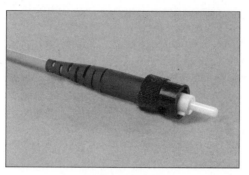

(A) ST (straight tip)

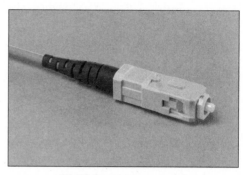

(B) SC (standard connector)

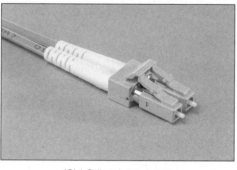

(C) LC (local connector)

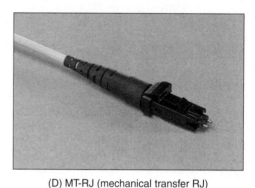

(D) MT-RJ (mechanical transfer RJ)

Courtesy Fiber Communications, Inc.

Figure 16-34   Four types of fiber-optic connectors: (a) ST, (b) SC, (c) LC, and (d) MT-RJ

Recall that Ethernet can run at four speeds. Each version of Ethernet can use more than one cabling method. Here is a brief description of the transmission speeds and the cabling methods they use:

▲ *10-Mbps Ethernet.* This first Ethernet specification was invented by Xerox Corporation in the 1970s, and later became known as Ethernet.

▲ *100-Mbps Ethernet or Fast Ethernet.* This improved version of Ethernet (sometimes called **100BaseT** or **Fast Ethernet**) operates at 100 Mbps and uses STP or UTP cabling rated CAT-5 or higher. 100BaseT networks can support slower speeds of 10 Mbps so that devices that run at either 10 Mbps or 100 Mbps can coexist on the same LAN. Two variations of 100BaseT are 100BaseTX and 100BaseFX. The most popular variation is 100BaseTX. 100BaseFX uses fiber-optic cable.

▲ *1000-Mbps Ethernet or Gigabit Ethernet.* This version of Ethernet operates at 1000 Mbps and uses twisted-pair cable and fiber-optic cable. **Gigabit Ethernet** is becoming the most popular choice for LAN technology. Because it can use the same cabling and connectors as Fast Ethernet, a company can upgrade from Fast Ethernet to Gigabit without rewiring the network.

▲ *10-Gigabit Ethernet.* This version of Ethernet operates at 10 billion bits per second (10 Gbps) and uses fiber-optic cable. It can be used on LANs, MANs, and WANs, and is also a good choice for backbone networks. (A backbone network is a channel whereby local networks can connect to wide area networks or to each other.)

16

SETTING UP AND TROUBLESHOOTING NETWORK WIRING

A+
220-801
1.11,
2.1, 2.10

A+
220-802
4.5

To set up a small network, you'll need computers, switches, network cables, a router, and whatever device (for example, a DSL or cable modem) that provides Internet access. Some network cables might be wired inside walls of your building with wall jacks that use RJ-45 ports. These cables might converge in an electrical closet or server room. If network cables are lying on the floor, be sure to install them against the wall so they won't be a trip hazard. Take care that cables don't exceed the recommended length (100 meters for twisted pair). For best results, always use twisted-pair cables rated at CAT-5e or higher. (CAT-6 gives better performance than CAT-5e for Gigabit Ethernet, but it is a lot harder to wire and also more expensive.) To connect multiple computers, use switches rated at the same speed as your router and network adapters. For Gigabit speed on the entire network, you need to use all Gigabit switches and network adapters and a Gigabit router. However, if some devices run at slower speeds, most likely a switch or router can still support the higher speeds for other devices on the network.

If your router is also your wireless access point, take care in planning where to place it. Place the wireless access point near the center of the area where you want your wireless hotspot. The router also needs to have access to your cable modem or DSL modem. The modem needs access to the cable TV or phone jack where it receives service. Figure 16-35 shows a possible inexpensive wiring job where two switches and a router are used to wire two rooms for five workstations and a network printer. The only inside-wall wiring that is required is two back-to-back RJ-45 wall jacks on either side of the wall between the two rooms. The plan allows for all five desktop computers and a network printer to be wired with cabling neatly attached to the baseboards of the office without being a trip hazard.

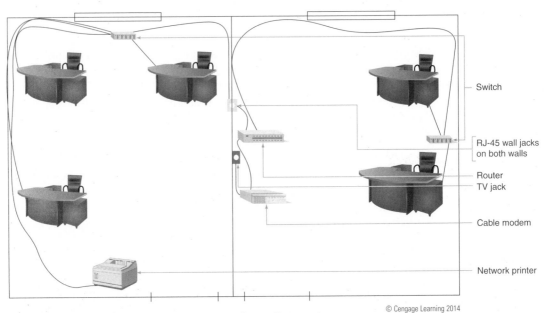

© Cengage Learning 2014

Figure 16-35 Plan the physical configuration of a small network

Let's look at the tools you need to solve problems with network cabling, the details of how a network cable is wired, and how you can create your own network cables by installing RJ-45 connectors on twisted-pair cables.

A+
220-801
1.11,
2.1, 2.10

A+
220-802
4.5

TOOLS USED BY NETWORK TECHNICIANS

Here's a list of tools a network technician might want in his or her toolbox:

◢ *Loopback plug.* A **loopback plug** can be used to test a network cable or port. To test a port or cable, connect one end of the cable to a network port on a computer or other device, and connect the loopback plug to the other end of the cable (see Figure 16-36). If the LED light on the loopback plug lights up, the cable and port are good. Another way to use a loopback plug is to find out which port on a switch in an electrical closet matches up with a wall jack. Plug the loopback plug into the wall jack. The connecting port on the switch in the closet lights up. When buying a loopback plug, pay attention to the Ethernet speeds it supports. Some only support 100 Mbps; others support 100 Mbps and 1000 Mbps.

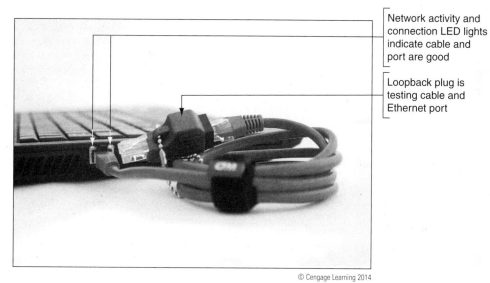

Network activity and connection LED lights indicate cable and port are good

Loopback plug is testing cable and Ethernet port

© Cengage Learning 2014

Figure 16-36 A loopback plug verifies the cable and network port are good

◢ *Cable tester.* A **cable tester** is used to test a cable to find out if it is good or to find out what type of cable it is if the cable is not labeled. You can also use a cable tester to locate the ends of a network cable in a building. A cable tester has two components, the remote and the base (see Figure 16-37).

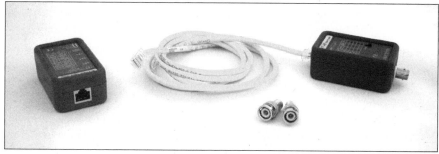

© Cengage Learning 2014

Figure 16-37 Use a cable tester pair to determine the type of cable and/or if the cable is good

16

A+
220-801
1.11,
2.1, 2.10

A+
220-802
4.5

To test a cable, connect each component to the ends of the cable and turn on the tester. Lights on the tester will show you if the cable is good and what type of cable you have. You'll need to read the user manual that comes with the cable tester to know how to interpret the lights.

You can also use the cable tester to find the two ends of a network cable installed in a building. Suppose you see several network jacks on walls in a building, but you don't know which jacks connect. Install a short cable in each of the two jacks or a jack and a port in a patch panel. Then use the cable tester base and remote to test the continuity, as shown in Figure 16-38. Whereas a loopback plug works with live cables and ports, a cable tester works on cables that are not live. You might damage a cable tester if you connect it to a live circuit, so before you start connecting the cable tester to wall jacks, be sure that you turn off all devices on the network.

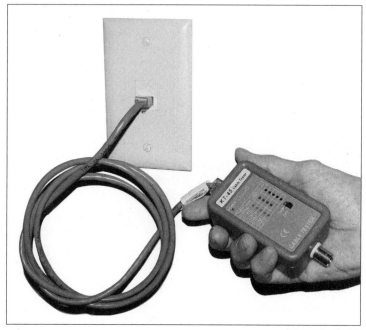

© Cengage Learning 2014

Figure 16-38   Use cable testers to find the two ends of a network cable in a building

▲ *Network multimeter.* You learned about multimeters in Chapter 1. A **network multimeter** (see Figure 16-39) is a multifunctional tool that can test cables, ports, and network adapters. When you connect it to your network, it can also detect the Ethernet speed, duplex status, default router on the network, length of a cable, voltage levels of PoE, and other network statistics and details. Many network multimeters can document test results and upload results to a PC. Good network multimeters can cost several hundred dollars.

▲ *Toner probe.* A **toner probe**, sometimes called a **tone probe**, is a two-part kit that is used to find cables in the walls of a building. See Figure 16-40. The toner connects to one end of the cable and puts out a continuous or pulsating tone on the cable. While the toner is putting out the tone, you use the probe to search the walls for the tone. The probe amplifies the tone so you hear it as a continuous or pulsating beep. The beeps get louder when you are close to the cable and weaker when you move the probe away from the cable. With a little patience, you can trace the cable through the walls. Some toners can put out tones up to 10 miles on a cable and offer a variety of ways to connect to the cable, such as clips and RJ-45 and RJ-11 connectors.

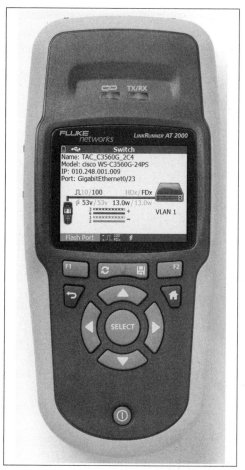

Courtesy of Fluke Corporation

Figure 16-39 The LinkRunner Pro network
multimeter by Fluke Corporation
works on Gigabit Ethernet networks
using twisted-pair copper cabling

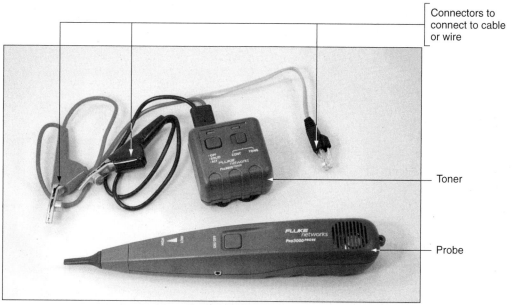

Connectors to
connect to cable
or wire

Toner

Probe

16

Figure 16-40 A toner probe kit by Fluke Corporation

© Cengage Learning 2014

A+
220-801
1.11,
2.1, 2.10

A+
220-802
4.5

▲ *Wire stripper.* A **wire stripper** is used to build your own network cable or repair a cable. Use the wire stripper to cut away the plastic jacket or coating around the wires inside a twisted-pair cable so that you can install a connector on the end of the cable. How to use wire strippers is covered later in the chapter.

▲ *Crimper.* A **crimper** is used to attach a terminator or connector to the end of a cable. It applies force to pinch the connector to the wires in the cable to securely make a solid connection. Figure 16-41 shows a multifunctional crimper that can crimp a RJ-45 or RJ-11 connector. It also serves double-duty as a wire cutter and wire stripper.

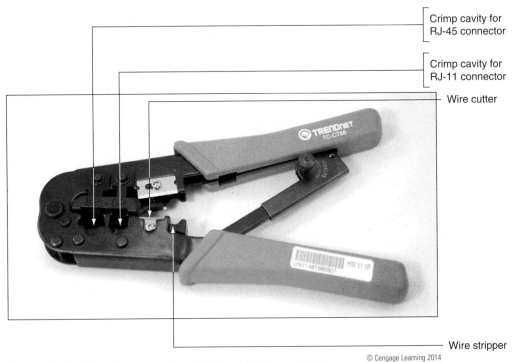

Crimp cavity for
RJ-45 connector

Crimp cavity for
RJ-11 connector

Wire cutter

Wire stripper

© Cengage Learning 2014

Figure 16-41 This crimper can crimp RJ-45 and RJ-11 connectors

▲ *Punchdown tool.* A **punchdown tool**, also called an impact tool (see Figure 16-42), is used to punch individual wires in a network cable into their slots in a **keystone RJ-45 jack** that is used in an RJ-45 wall jack. Later in the chapter, you'll learn how to use the tool with a keystone jack.

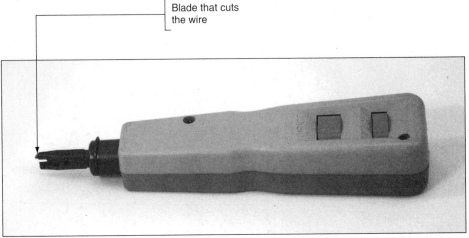

Blade that cuts
the wire

© Cengage Learning 2014

Figure 16-42 A punchdown tool forces a wire into a slot and cuts off the wire

A+
220-801
1.11,
2.1, 2.10

A+
220-802
4.5

Another use of a punchdown tool is to terminate network cables in a patch panel. A **patch panel** (see Figure 16-43) provides multiple network ports for cables that converge in one location such as an electrical closet or server room. Each port is numbered on the front of the panel. On the back side, keystone jacks are color-coded for the wires to be inserted.

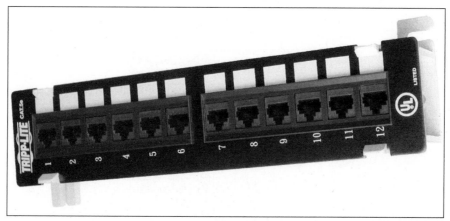

Courtesy of Tripp Lite

Figure 16-43 A patch panel provides Ethernet ports for cables converging in an electrical closet

When terminating a cable in a keystone jack, you first gently push each wire down into the color-coded slot of the keystone jack and then you use the punchdown tool to punch the wire down all the way into the slot. A small blade on the tip of one prong cuts off the wire at the side of the slot.

Now that you know about the tools you'll need to wire networks, let's see how the cables and connectors are wired.

HOW TWISTED-PAIR CABLES AND CONNECTORS ARE WIRED

Recall from Chapter 15 that two types of network cables can be used when building a network: a straight-through cable and a crossover cable. A **straight-through cable** (also called a **patch cable**) is used to connect a computer to a switch or other network device. A **crossover cable** is used to connect two like devices such as a hub to a hub or a PC to a PC (to make the simplest network of all).

The difference between a straight-through cable and a crossover cable is the way the transmit and receive lines are wired in the connectors at each end of the cables. A crossover cable has the transmit and receive lines reversed so that one device receives off the line to which the other device transmits. Before the introduction of Gigabit Ethernet, 10BaseT and 100BaseT required that a crossover cable be used to connect two like devices such as a switch to a switch. Today's devices that support Gigabit Ethernet use auto-uplinking, which means you can connect a switch to a switch using a straight-through cable. Crossover cables are seldom used today except to connect a PC to a PC to create this simple two-node network.

16

A+
220-801
1.11,
2.1, 2.10

A+
220-802
4.5

Twisted-pair copper wire cabling uses an RJ-45 connector that has eight pins, as shown in Figure 16-44. 10BaseT and 100BaseT Ethernet use only four of these pins: pins 1 and 2 for transmitting data and pins 3 and 6 for receiving data. The other pins can be used for phone lines or for power (PoE). Gigabit Ethernet uses all eight pins to transmit and receive data and can also transmit power on these same lines.

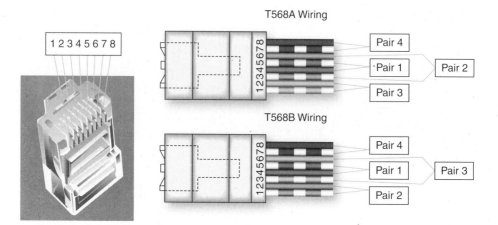

© Cengage Learning 2014

Figure 16-44 Pinouts for an RJ-45 connector

Twisted-pair cabling used with RJ-45 connectors is color-coded in four pairs, as shown in Figure 16-44. Pair 1 is blue; pair 2 is orange; pair 3 is green, and pair 4 is brown. Each pair has one solid wire and one striped wire. Two standards have been established in the industry for wiring twisted-pair cabling and RJ-45 connectors: T568A and T568B standards. Both are diagrammed in Figure 16-44 and listed in Table 16-3. The **T568A** standard has the green pair connected to pins 1 and 2 and the orange pair connected to pins 3 and 6. The **T568B** standard has the orange pair using pins 1 and 2 and the green pair using pins 3 and 6, as shown in the diagram and the table. For both standards, the blue pair uses pins 4 and 5, and the brown pair uses pins 7 and 8.

It doesn't matter which standard you use so long as you're *consistent*. The important thing is that the wiring on one end of the cable match the wiring on the other end, be it T568A or T568B standards. Either way, you have a straight-through cable.

> **Notes** The T568A and T568B standards as well as other network wiring standards and recommendations are overseen by the Telecommunications Industry Association (TIA), Electronics Industries Alliance (EIA), and American National Standards Institute (ANSI).

For 10BaseT and 100BaseT networks, if you use T568A wiring on one end of the cable and T568B on the other end of the cable, you have a crossover cable (see the diagram on the left side of Figure 16-45). For Gigabit Ethernet (1000BaseT) that transmits data on all four pairs, you must not only cross the green and orange pairs but also cross the blue and brown pairs to make a crossover cable (see the diagram on the right

A+
220-801
1.11,
2.1, 2.10

A+
220-802
4.5

Pin	100BaseT Purpose	T568A Wiring	T568B Wiring
1	Transmit+	Pair 3: White/green	Pair 2: White/orange
2	Transmit–	Pair 3: Green	Pair 2: Orange
3	Receive+	Pair 2: White/orange	Pair 3: White/green
4	(Used only on Gigabit Ethernet)	Pair 1: Blue	Pair 1: Blue
5	(Used only on Gigabit Ethernet)	Pair 1: White/blue	Pair 1: White/blue
6	Receive–	Pair 2: Orange	Pair 3: Green
7	(Used only on Gigabit Ethernet)	Pair 4: White/brown	Pair 4: White/brown
8	(Used only on Gigabit Ethernet)	Pair 4: Brown	Pair 4: Brown

© Cengage Learning 2014

Table 16-3 The T568A and T568B Ethernet standards for wiring RJ-45 connectors

side of Figure 16-45). Recall, however, that crossover cables are seldom used on Gigabit Ethernet. When you buy a crossover cable, most likely it is wired only for 10BaseT or 100BaseT networks. If you ever find yourself needing to make a crossover cable, be sure to cross all four pairs so the cable will work on 10BaseT, 100BaseT, and 1000BaseT networks. You can also buy an adapter to convert a straight-through cable to a crossover cable. But most likely the adapter only crosses two pairs and works only for 10BaseT or 100BaseT networks, such as the adapter shown in Figure 16-46.

When you are wiring a network in a building that already has network wiring, be sure to find out if the wiring is using T568A or T568B. And then be sure you always use that standard. If you don't know which to use, use T568B because it's the most common, unless, however, you are working for the U.S. government, which requires T568A for all its networking needs.

16

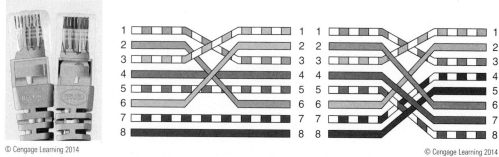

© Cengage Learning 2014

© Cengage Learning 2014

Figure 16-45 Two crossed pairs in a crossover cable is compatible with 10BaseT or 100BaseT Ethernet; four crossed pairs in a crossover cable is compatible with Gigabit Ethernet

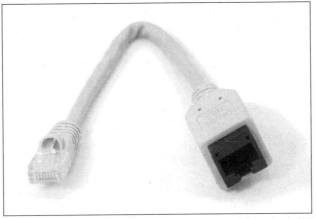

© Cengage Learning 2014

Figure 16-46   A crossover adapter converts a patch cable to a crossover cable for a 10BaseT or 100BaseT network

APPLYING | CONCEPTS   MAKE A STRAIGHT-THROUGH CABLE USING T568B WIRING

It takes a little practice to make a good network straight-through cable, but you'll get the hang of it after doing only a couple of cables. Figure 16-47 shows the materials and tools you'll need to make a network cable.

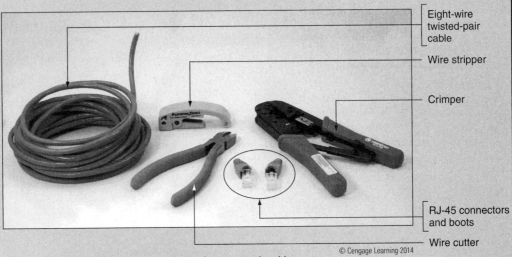

Eight-wire twisted-pair cable

Wire stripper

Crimper

RJ-45 connectors and boots

Wire cutter

© Cengage Learning 2014

Figure 16-47   Tools and materials to make a network cable

Here are the steps to make a straight-through cable using the T568B standard.

1. Use wire cutters to cut the twisted-pair cable the correct length plus a few extra inches.

2. If your RJ-45 connectors include boots, slide two boots onto the cable.

3. Use wire strippers to strip off about two inches of the plastic jacket from the end of the wire. To do that, put the wire in the stripper and rotate the stripper around the wire to score the jacket (see Figure 16-48). You can then pull off the jacket.

A+
220-801
1.11,
2.1, 2.10

A+
220-802
4.5

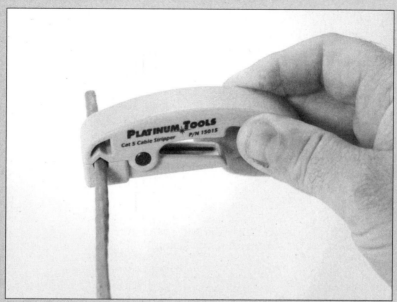

© Cengage Learning 2014

Figure 16-48 Rotate a wire stripper around the jacket to score it so you can slide it off the wire

4. Use wire cutters to start a cut into the jacket, and then use the rip cord to pull the jacket back a couple of inches (see Figure 16-49). Next, cut off the rip cord and the jacket. You take this extra precaution of removing the jacket because you might have nicked the wires with the wire strippers.

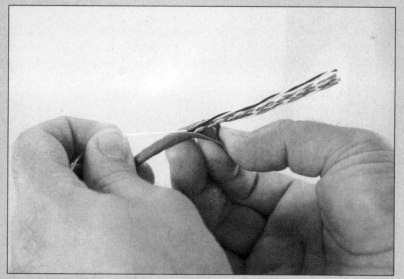

© Cengage Learning 2014

Figure 16-49 Rip back the jacket, and then cut off the extra jacket and rip cord

5. Untwist each pair of wires so you have the eight separate wires. Smooth each wire out, straightening out the kinks. Line up the wires in the T568B configuration (refer to Table 16-3).

6. Holding the tightly lined-up wires between your fingers, use wire cutters to cut the wires off evenly, leaving a little over an inch of wire. See Figure 16-50. To know how short to cut the wires, hold the RJ-45 connector up to the wires. The wires must go all the way to the front of the connector. The jacket must go far enough into the connector so that the crimp at the back of the connector will be able to solidly pinch the jacket.

16

A+
220-801
1.11,
2.1, 2.10

A+
220-802
4.5

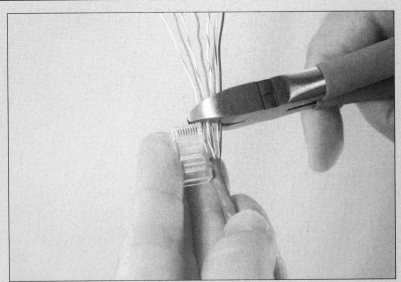

© Cengage Learning 2014

Figure 16-50   Evenly cut off wires measured to fit in the RJ-45 connector with the jacket protruding into the connector

7. Be sure you have pin 1 of the connector lined up with the orange and white wire. Then insert the eight wires in the RJ-45 connector. Guide the wires into the connector, making sure they reach all the way to the front. (It helps to push up a bit as you push the wires into the connector.) You can jam the jacket firmly into the connector. Look through the clear plastic connector to make sure the wires are lined up correctly and they all reach the front and that the jacket goes past the crimp.

8. Insert the connector into the crimper tool. Use one hand to push the connector firmly into the crimper as you use the other hand to crimp the connector. See Figure 16-51. Use plenty of force to crimp. The eight blades at the front of the connector must pierce through to each copper wire to complete each of the eight connections, and the crimp at the back of the connector must solidly crimp the cable jacket to secure the cable to the connector (see Figure 16-52). Remove the connector from the crimper and make sure you can't pull the connector off the wire.

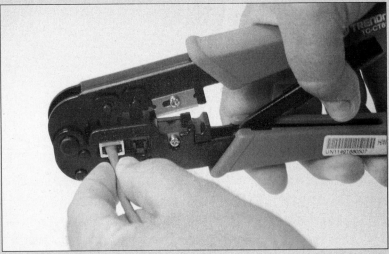

© Cengage Learning 2014

Figure 16-51   Use the crimper to crimp the connector to the cable

A+
220-801
1.11,
2.1, 2.10

A+
220-802
4.5

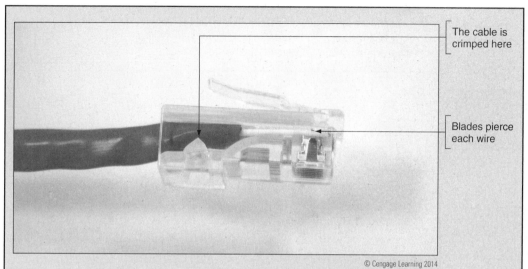

The cable is crimped here

Blades pierce each wire

© Cengage Learning 2014

Figure 16-52 The crimper crimps the cable and cable jacket, and eight blades pierce the jacket of each individual copper wire

9. Slide the boot into place over the connector. Now you're ready to terminate the other end of the cable. Configure it to also use the T568B wiring arrangement. Figure 16-53 shows the straight-through cable with only one boot in place.

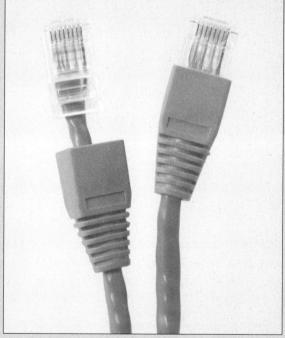

© Cengage Learning 2014

Figure 16-53 Finished patch cable with one boot in place

10. Use a cable tester to make sure the cable is good.

Notes You'll find several YouTube videos on network wiring. An excellent one of making a straight-through cable by CableSupply.com is posted at *www.youtube.com/watch?v=h7TjqnRl3QQ*.

16

Notes Networking standards that apply to wiring a keystone RJ-45 jack and a straight-through panel say that, to avoid crosstalk, the cable jacket should be removed to expose no more than three inches of twisted-pair wires, and that exposed twisted-pair wires should be untwisted no more than a half inch.

APPLYING | CONCEPTS   WIRE A KEYSTONE JACK

A keystone RJ-45 jack is used in a network wall jack. Here are the instructions to wire one:

1. Using a wire stripper and wire cutter, strip and trim back the jacket from the twisted-pair wire, leaving about two inches of wire exposed. Untwist the wires only so far as necessary so each wire can be inserted in the color-coded slot in the jack. The twists are needed to prevent crosstalk, and the untwisted wire should be no longer than a half inch. Figure 16-54 shows the wires in position for T568B wiring. Notice how the cable jacket goes into the keystone jack.

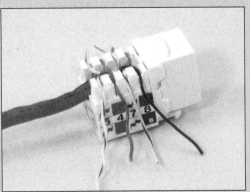 

© Cengage Learning 2014   © Cengage Learning 2014

Figure 16-54   Eight wires are in position in a keystone jack for T568B wiring

2. Using the punchdown tool, make sure the blade side of the tool is on the outside of the jack. (The punchdown tool has Cut embedded on the blade side of the tool.) Push down with force to punch each wire into its slot and cut off the wire on the outside edge of the slot. It might take a couple of punches to do the job. See the left side of Figure 16-55. Place the jack cover over the jack, as shown in the right side of Figure 16-55.

3. The jack can now be inserted into the back side of a wall faceplate (see Figure 16-56). Make sure the wires in the jack are at the top of the jack. If you look closely at the faceplate, you can see the arrow pointing up. It's important the wires in the jack be at the top so that over the years dust doesn't settle on these wires. Use screws to secure the faceplate to the wall receptacle. Be sure to use a cable tester to check the network cable from its jack to the other end to make sure the wiring is good. When wiring a building, testing the cable and its two connections is called certifying the cable.

A+
220-801
1.11,
2.1, 2.10

A+
220-802
4.5

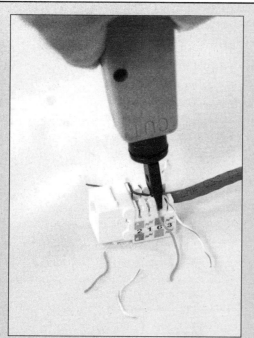 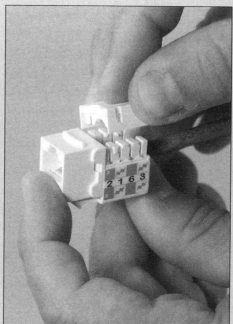

© Cengage Learning 2014   © Cengage Learning 2014

Figure 16-55 Use a punchdown tool to punch the wires into the keystone jack, and then place the cover in position

© Cengage Learning 2014

Figure 16-56 Insert the jack in the faceplate, making sure the wire connectors are at the top of the jack

Notes To see a video by CableSupply.com of using a punchdown tool to make an RJ-45 keystone jack, see *www.youtube.com/watch?v=sHy8mtW9eak*.

16

A+
220-801
1.11,
2.1, 2.10

A+
220-802
4.5

Let's wrap up the chapter with some guidelines to follow when troubleshooting a network problem related to hardware. The process is outlined in Figure 16-57 and listed here:

1. First check the status indicator lights on the network ports for connectivity and activity.

2. Use a loopback plug to verify each port. The loopback plug can work on ports provided by a computer, wall jack, patch panel, switch, router, or other device that is turned on. If you find a bad port, try a different port on a switch, router, or patch panel. You might need to replace the device.

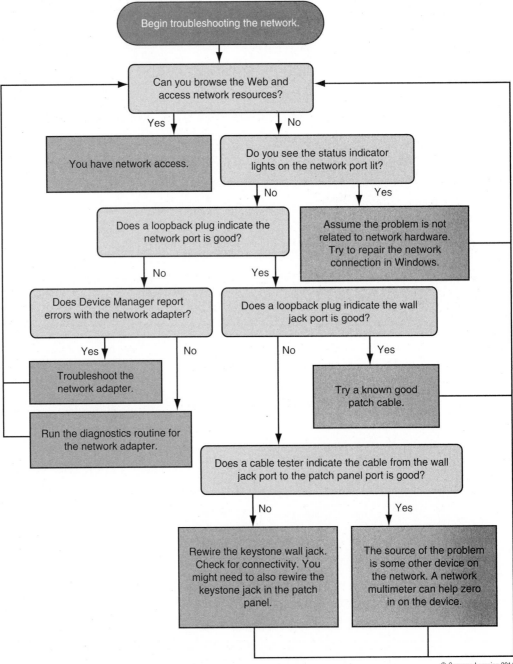

© Cengage Learning 2014

Figure 16-57   Flowchart to troubleshoot networking problems related to hardware

3. For short straight-through cables connecting a computer to a wall jack or other nearby device, exchanging the straight-through cable for a known good one is easier and quicker than using a cable tester to test the cable.

4. Use a cable tester to verify a cable permanently installed alongside or inside a wall is good. To test the cable, you have to first disconnect it from a computer, patch panel, switch, or other device at both ends of the cable. Common problems with networks are poorly wired termination in patch panels and wall jacks. If the cable proves bad, first try reinstalling the two jacks before you replace the cable.

>> CHAPTER SUMMARY

Network Types and Topologies

▲ Networks are categorized in size as a PAN, LAN, Wireless LAN, MAN, or WAN.

▲ Topologies used by a network include a mesh, ring, bus, star, and hybrid network topology. Ethernet that is used to create a LAN uses the star or hybrid (star bus) topology.

▲ Performance of a network technology is measured in bandwidth and latency.

▲ The two most popular ways to connect to the Internet are cable Internet and DSL. Other methods used include satellite, dedicated fiber optic, dial-up, and wireless technologies (a cellular WAN using 2G, 3G, 4G, WiMAX, and/or LTE).

▲ Technology used by cell phones that allows us to browse the web, stream music and video, play online games, and use chat and video conferencing is called 3G or 4G.

Hardware Used by Local Networks

▲ Networking hardware used on local networks includes network adapters, dial-up modems, hubs, switches, routers, wireless access points, bridges, cables, and connectors.

▲ Features used and supported by a network adapter include the slot a NIC uses, Ethernet speeds, MAC address, status indicator lights, Wake on LAN, Quality of Service (QoS), and Power over Ethernet (PoE).

▲ The most popular Ethernet cable is twisted pair using an RJ-45 connector. Phone lines use an RJ-11 connector.

▲ Switches and older hubs are used as a centralized connection for devices on a wired network. A bridge stands between two network segments and controls traffic between them.

▲ Other network devices include a NAS (Network Attached Storage), a VoIP phone, and older and outdated Internet appliances.

▲ Most wired local networks use twisted-pair cabling that can be unshielded twisted-pair (UTP) cable or shielded twisted-pair (STP) cable. UTP is rated by category: CAT-3, CAT-5, CAT-5e, CAT-6, and CAT-6a.

Setting Up and Troubleshooting a Small Network

▲ Tools used to manage and troubleshoot network wiring and connectors are a loopback plug, cable tester, multimeter, tone probe, wire stripper, crimper, and punchdown tool.

▲ The RJ-45 connector has eight pins. Four pins (pins 1, 2, 3, and 6) are used to transmit and send data using the 10BaseT and 100BaseT speeds. Using 1000BaseT speed, all eight pins are used for transmissions.

16

◢ Two standards used to wire network cables are T568A and T568B. The difference between the T568A and T568B standards is the orange twisted-pair wires are reversed in the RJ-45 connector from the green twisted-pair wires.

◢ A straight-through cable uses the T568A or T568B standard on both connectors. A crossover cable for 10BaseT or 100BaseT uses T568A for one connector and T568B for the other connector. Crossover cables are generally not used on Gigabit Ethernet networks.

◢ Either T568A or T568B can be used to wire a network. To avoid confusion, don't mix the two standards in a building.

◢ Use wire strippers, wire cutters, and a crimper to make network cables. A punchdown tool is used to terminate cables in a patch panel or keystone RJ-45 jack. Be sure to use a cable tester to test or certify a cable you have just made.

◢ When troubleshooting network wiring, tools that can help are status indicator lights, loopback plug, cable testers, and a network multimeter.

>> KEY TERMS

For explanations of key terms, see the Glossary near the end of the book.

100BaseT
4G (Fourth Generation)
ad hoc mode
bandwidth
base station
BNC connector
bridge
broadband
bus network
cable Internet
cable tester
CAT-3 (Category 3)
CAT-5 (Category 5)
CAT-6
CAT-6a
CDMA (Code Division Multiple Access)
coaxial cable
cellular network
cellular WAN
crimper
crossover cable
data throughput
DSL (Digital Subscriber Line)
enhanced CAT-5 (CAT-5e)
F connector
Fast Ethernet
fiber optic
fiber-optic cable
full duplex

fully connected mesh topology
Gigabit Ethernet
GSM (Global System for Mobile Communications)
half duplex
hub
hybrid network
Internet appliance
Internet Service Provider (ISP)
ISDN (Integrated Services Digital Network)
keystone RJ-45 jack
LAN (local area network)
latency
LC (local connector) connector
line-of-sight connectivity
loopback plug
MAN (metropolitan area network)
mesh network
MT-RJ (mechanical transfer registered jack) connector
network adapter
Network Attached Storage (NAS)
network interface card (NIC)
network multimeter
PAN (personal area network)
patch cable
patch panel
Power over Ethernet (PoE)

punchdown tool
RG-6 coaxial cable
RG-59 coaxial cable
ring network
RJ-11 jack
RJ-45
SC (subscriber connector or standard connector) connector
shielded twisted pair (STP) cable
SIM (Subscriber Identity Module) card
ST (straight tip) connector
star network
straight-through cable
switch
T568A
T568B
tone probe
toner probe
topology
twisted-pair cabling
unshielded twisted pair (UTP) cable
VoIP (Voice over Internet Protocol)
VoIP phone
WAN (wide area network)
wire stripper
wireless LAN (WLAN)

>> REVIEW QUESTIONS

1. A(n) _____ covers a large geographical area and is made up of many smaller networks.

   a) WAN

   b) MAN

   c) LAN

   d) PAN

2. What technology offers the fastest speeds for cellular data?

   a) CAT-5

   b) Gigabit Ethernet

   c) 4G

   d) Full duplex

3. A(n) _____ is a type of thin client that is designed to make it easy for a user to connect to the Internet, browse the web, use email, and perform other simple chores on the Internet.

   a) Network Attached Storage (NAS) device

   b) bridge

   c) VoIP phone

   d) Internet appliance

4. Which version of Ethernet is becoming the most popular choice for LAN technology?

   a) 10-Mbps Ethernet

   b) Gigabit Ethernet

   c) 10-Gigabit Ethernet

   d) Fast Ethernet

5. Which tool is a two-part kit that is used to find cables in the walls of a building?

   a) Cable tester

   b) Loopback plug

   c) Network multimeter

   d) Toner probe

6. True or false? Data throughput is the theoretical number of bits that can be transmitted over a network at one time.

7. True or false? One disadvantage of satellite is that it requires line-of-sight connectivity without obstruction from mountains, trees, and tall buildings.

8. True or false? A switch is smarter and more efficient than a hub because it keeps a table of all the MAC addresses for devices connected to it.

9. True or false? Shielded twisted pair (STP) cable is the least expensive and is commonly used on LANs.

16

10. True or false? A crossover cable is used to connect a computer to a switch or other network device.

11. A(n) ____ network uses a centralized device to manage traffic on the network.

12. ____ duplex sends and receives transmissions at the same time.

13. An Ethernet ____ transmits a data frame to every device, except the device that sent the frame.

14. A(n) ____ is used to attach a terminator or connector to the end of a cable.

15. A(n) ____ provides multiple network ports for cables that converge in one location such as an electrical closet or server room.

chapter 17

Windows Resources on a Network

In Chapter 15, you learned how to connect to a network and set one up, and in Chapter 16, you learned about networking hardware. This chapter focuses on using a network for client/server applications and for sharing files and folders with network users. You also learn how to troubleshoot network connections and what to do when you cannot reach resources on the network.

Security is always a huge concern when dealing with networks. In this chapter, you learn how to share resources on the network and still protect these resources from those who should not have access. In the next chapter, we take security to a higher level and discuss all the many tools and techniques you can use to protect a computer or a SOHO network.

SUPPORTING CLIENT/SERVER APPLICATIONS

Client/server applications you will likely be expected to support include Internet Explorer, Remote Desktop, and other remote applications. You also need to know how to configure network settings to improve performance for client/service applications using Wake on LAN, Quality of Service techniques, and Group Policy. All these skills are covered in this part of the chapter.

A+
220-802
1.5, 1.6

INTERNET EXPLORER

By far, the most popular client/server applications on the Internet are a browser and web server. At the time of this writing, Internet Explorer (IE) version 9 is the latest browser released by Microsoft. Windows 7 comes with IE version 8, but you can upgrade to version 9 using Windows Updates. To upgrade, open Windows Updates and find and install the Internet Explorer 9 update. You can also go to the *Microsoft.com* web site and follow links to download and install IE 9.

If you later have a problem with IE9, you can uninstall it and install it again. Go to the Programs and Features window in Control Panel. Then click **View installed updates**. Select the update (see Figure 17-1) and click **Uninstall**.

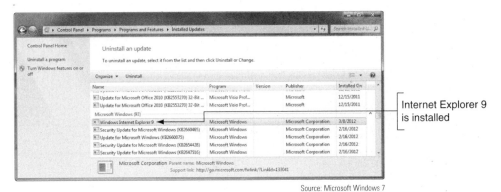

Source: Microsoft Windows 7

Figure 17-1 Use the Programs and Features window to uninstall Internet Explorer 9, which was installed as a Windows update

Here are some tips when using the Internet Explorer window:

▲ To show the menu bar, press the **Alt** key. The menu appears long enough for you to make one selection from the menu. If you want the menu bar to be permanent, right-click a blank area in the title bar and check **Menu bar** from the shortcut menu (see Figure 17-2). Notice in Figure 17-2 you can also add the command bar to the IE window.

▲ To get help using IE, press **F1** to open Windows Help and Support. Alternately, you can click **Help** on the menu bar and click **Internet Explorer Help**, or you can click the question mark on the command bar and click **Internet Explorer Help**.

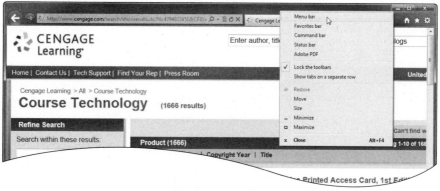

Figure 17-2 Access the shortcut menu from the title bar to control the Internet Explorer window

Some web servers use the HTTP with SSL or TLS protocols to secure transmissions to and from the web server. To find out if HTTPS is being used in IE 9, look for https and a padlock in the browser address box. Click the padlock to get information about the site security (see Figure 17-3).

Https and padlock indicate a secure connection

Figure 17-3 A secured connection from browser to web server assures all transmissions are encrypted

Use the **Internet Options** box to manage Internet Explorer settings. To open the box, click the Tools icon on the right side of the IE title bar and click **Internet Options**. Another method is to press **Alt**, which causes the menu bar to appear; then click **Tools, Internet Options**. And still a third method is to click **Internet Options** in the Network and Internet group of Control Panel. The Internet Options box appears. Whenever you make changes in the box, click **Apply** to apply these changes without closing the box. Alternately, you can click **OK** to save your changes and close the box.

Now let's see how to use each tab on the Internet Options box.

A+ Exam Tip The A+ 220-802 exam expects you to know how to use the General, Security, Privacy, Connections, Programs, and Advanced tabs on the Internet Options box.

A+
220-802
1.5, 1.6

GENERAL TAB

The General tab on the Internet Options box is shown on the left side of Figure 17-4.

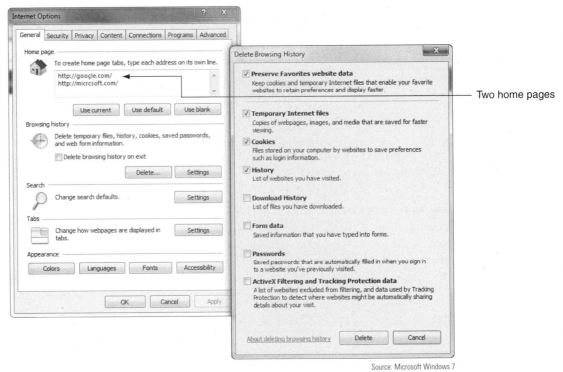

Source: Microsoft Windows 7

Figure 17-4 Use the General tab of the Internet Options box to delete your browsing history

Here's what you can do using the General tab:

▲ Change the home page or add a second home page. To add a second home page, insert the URL on a second line in the Home page area, as shown on the left side of Figure 17-4.

▲ To protect your identity and surfing records, it's a good idea to delete all your browsing history each time you use IE on a computer that is not your own. To delete this history, click **Delete**. In the Delete Browsing History box (see the right side of Figure 17-4), notice the item at the top. When you leave this item checked, any cookies used by web sites in your Favorites list are *not* deleted. Select the items to delete and click **Delete**.

▲ If you want to delete your browsing history each time you close Internet Explorer, check **Delete browsing history on exit** on the General tab.

▲ Internet Explorer holds a cache containing previously downloaded content in case it is requested again. The cache is stored in several folders named Temporary Internet Files. To manage the IE cache, click **Settings** under Browsing history. The Temporary Internet Files and History Settings box appears (see Figure 17-5). Use this box to change the maximum allowed space used for temporary Internet files and to control the location of these files.

SECURITY TAB

Set the security level on the Security tab (see the left side of Figure 17-6). Medium-high is the default value, which prompts before downloading content and does not download ActiveX controls that are not signed by Microsoft. An **ActiveX control** is a small app or add-on that

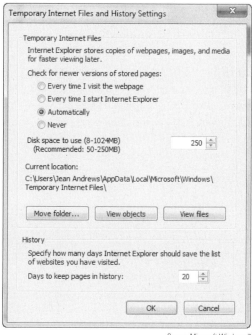

Source: Microsoft Windows 7

Figure 17-5 Control the size and location of temporary files used by Internet Explorer

can be downloaded from a web site along with a web page and is executed by IE to enhance the web page (for example, add animation to the page). A virus can sometimes hide in an ActiveX control, but IE is designed to catch them by authenticating each ActiveX control it downloads. To customize security settings, click **Custom level**. In the Security Settings box (see the right side of Figure 17-6), you can decide exactly how you want to handle downloaded content. For example, you can disable file downloads.

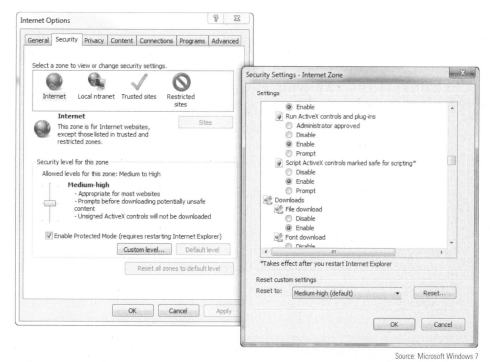

Source: Microsoft Windows 7

Figure 17-6 Use the Security tab to control what type of content is downloaded and how it is managed

17

A+
220-802
1.5, 1.6

PRIVACY TAB AND CONTENT TAB

Use the Privacy tab (see the left side of Figure 17-7) to block cookies that might invade your privacy or steal your identity. You can also use the tab to control the Pop-up Blocker, which prevents annoying pop-ups as you surf the Web. To allow a pop-up from a particular web site, click **Settings** and enter the URL of the web site in the Pop-up Blocker Settings box (see the right side of Figure 17-7). Some pop-ups are useful, such as when you're trying to download a file from a web site and the site asks permission to complete the download.

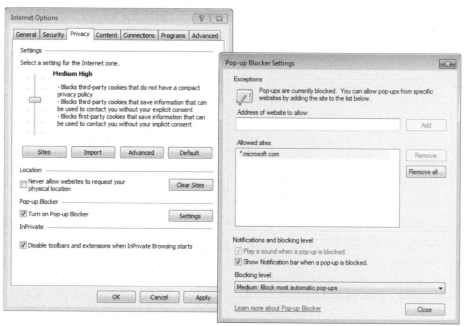

Source: Microsoft Windows 7

Figure 17-7   Use the Privacy tab to control pop-ups and cookies

The Content tab contains settings for parental controls, allowed content based on ratings, certificates used by web sites, and how AutoComplete and Feeds are handled.

CONNECTIONS TAB AND PROXY SETTINGS

The Connections tab allows you to configure proxy server settings and create a VPN connection. Many large corporations and ISPs use proxy servers to speed up Internet access. A **proxy server** is a computer that intercepts requests that a browser makes of a server. The proxy server substitutes its own IP address for the request using NAT protocols. Then, when it receives the content, it caches it and passes it on to the browser. If another browser requests the same content, the proxy server can provide the content that it has cached. In addition, proxy servers sometimes act as a gateway to the Internet, a firewall to protect the network, and to restrict Internet access by employees in order to force those employees to follow company policies.

A web browser does not have to be aware that a proxy server is in use. However, one reason you might need to configure Internet Explorer to be aware of and use a proxy server is when you are on a corporate network and are having a problem connecting to a secured web site (one using HTTP over SSL or another encryption protocol). The problem might be caused by Windows trying to connect using the wrong proxy server on the network. Check with your network administrator to find out if a specific proxy server should be used to manage secure web site connections.

A+
220-802
1.5, 1.6

> 💡 **A+ Exam Tip** The A+ 220-802 exam expects you to know how to configure proxy settings on a client desktop.

If you need to configure Internet Explorer to use a specific proxy server, on the Connections tab, click **LAN settings**. In the settings box, check **Use a proxy server for your LAN** and enter the IP address of the proxy server (see Figure 17-8). If your organization uses more than one proxy server, click **Advanced** and enter IP addresses for each type of proxy server on your network (see Figure 17-9). You can also enter a port address for each server. If you are trying to solve a problem of connecting to a server using HTTP over SSL or other secured protocol, enter the IP address of the proxy server that is used to manage secure connections in the Secure field of this box.

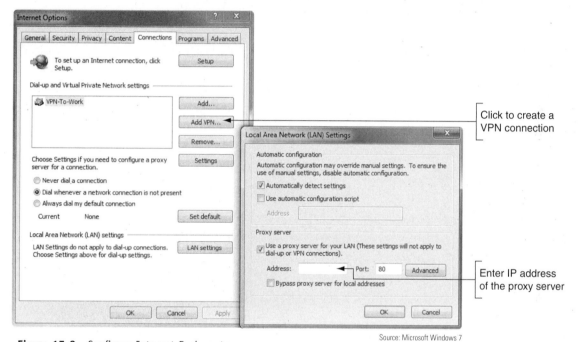

Click to create a
VPN connection

Enter IP address
of the proxy server

Source: Microsoft Windows 7

Figure 17-8   Configure Internet Explorer to use one or more proxy servers

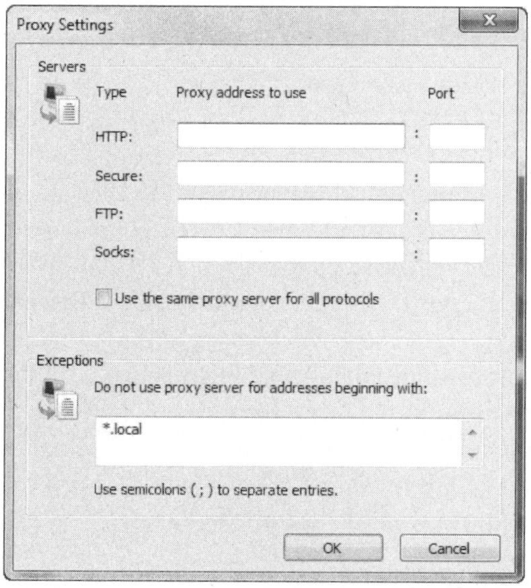

Source: Microsoft Windows 7

Figure 17-9   Enter the IP addresses of all proxy
servers on your corporate network

17

A+
220-802
1.5, 1.6

Also notice on the Connections tab of the Internet Options box that you can create a VPN connection. To do so, click **Add VPN** (refer back to the left side of Figure 17-8) and follow the steps of the connection wizard. Recall from Chapter 15 that you can also create a VPN connection using the Network and Sharing Center.

PROGRAMS TAB

Add-ons, also called plug-ins, are small apps that help Internet Explorer to display multimedia content, manage email, translate text, or other actions. The Programs tab (see Figure 17-10) is used to manage add-ons.

Source: Microsoft Windows 7

Figure 17-10 Use the Programs tab to manage add-ons and default applications used for Internet services

Click **Manage add-ons** to open the Manage Add-ons box (see the left side of Figure 17-11). In the left pane under Show, you can display All add-ons, Currently loaded add-ons (default view), Run without permission, and Downloaded controls. Click an add-on to select it and see information about it in the lower pane. To disable an add-on, click **Disable**. To enable a disabled one, click **Enable**.

Downloaded ActiveX controls can be uninstalled using this window. To delete a selected ActiveX control, click **More information**. In the More Information box (see the right side of Figure 17-11), click **Remove**. To see only the add-ons you can delete, select **Downloaded controls** in the Show drop-down list of the Manage Add-ons window. You can delete other add-ons using the Programs and Features window in Control Panel.

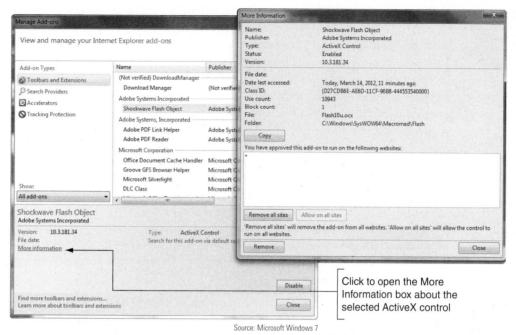

Source: Microsoft Windows 7

Figure 17-11 Manage Internet Explorer add-ons and delete downloaded ActiveX controls

> **Notes** If you open the Internet Options box through the Control Panel, the box is called the Internet Properties box. Also, when you use the Internet Properties box to open the Manage Add-ons box, the *Currently loaded add-ons* option is missing in the drop-down list under Show.

ADVANCED TAB

The Advanced tab (see the left side of Figure 17-12) contains several miscellaneous settings used to control Internet Explorer. One setting is useful when IE is giving problems. If you suspect problems are caused by wrong settings, you can click **Reset** to return IE to all default settings. In the Reset Internet Explorer Settings box shown on the right side of Figure 17-12, make your decision about how to handle personal settings and then click **Reset**.

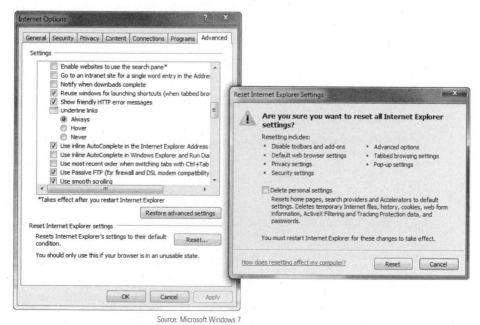

Source: Microsoft Windows 7

Figure 17-12 Solve problems with Internet Explorer by resetting it to default settings

17

A+
220-802
1.4, 1.5,
1.6

REMOTE DESKTOP

Remote Desktop gives a user access to a Windows desktop from anywhere on the Internet. As a software developer, I find Remote Desktop extremely useful when I work from a remote location (my home office) and need to access a corporate network to support software on that network. Using the Internet, I can access a file server on these secured networks to make my software changes. Remote Desktop is easy to use and relatively safe for the corporate network. To use Remote Desktop, the computer you want to remotely access (the server) must be running business or professional editions of Windows 7/Vista/XP, but the computer you're using to access it (the client) can be running any version of Windows.

 **A+ Exam Tip** The A+ 220-802 exam expects you to know how to use Remote Desktop.

In this section, you'll first see how to set up Remote Desktop for first use, and then you'll learn how to use it.

APPLYING | CONCEPTS   HOW TO SET UP REMOTE DESKTOP FOR FIRST USE

The host or server computer is the computer that is serving up Remote Desktop to client computers. To prepare your host computer, you need to configure the computer for static IP addressing and also configure the Remote Desktop service. Here are the steps needed:

1. Configure the computer for static IP addressing. How to assign a static IP address is covered in Chapter 15.

2. If your computer is behind a firewall, configure the router for port forwarding and allow incoming traffic on port 3389. Forward that traffic to the IP address of your desktop computer. You learned how to set up port forwarding in Chapter 15.

3. To turn on the Remote Desktop service, open the System window and click **Remote settings** in the left pane. The System Properties box appears with the Remote tab selected (see Figure 17-13). On this window you can control settings for Remote Assistance and Remote Desktop. In the Remote Desktop area, check **Allow connections from computers running any version of Remote Desktop (less secure)**.

4. Users who have administrative privileges are allowed to use Remote Desktop by default, but other users need to be added. If you need to add a user, click **Select Users** and follow the directions on-screen. Then close all windows.

5. Verify that Windows Firewall is set to allow Remote Desktop activity to this computer. To do that, open the **Network and Sharing Center** and click **Windows Firewall**. The Windows Firewall window appears (see Figure 17-14). In the left pane, click **Allow a program or feature through Windows Firewall**.

A+
220-802
1.4, 1.5,
1.6

Source: Microsoft Windows 7

Figure 17-13 Configure a computer to run the Remote Desktop service

Source: Microsoft Windows 7

Figure 17-14 Windows Firewall can block or allow activity on the network to your computer

6. The Allowed Programs window appears. Scroll down to Remote Desktop and adjust the settings as needed (see Figure 17-15). Click **OK** to apply any changes. You will learn more about Windows Firewall in Chapter 18.

You are now ready to test Remote Desktop using your local network. Try to use Remote Desktop from another computer somewhere on your local network. Verify you have Remote Desktop working on your local network before you move on to the next step of testing the Remote Desktop connection from the Internet.

17

A+
220-802
1.4, 1.5,
1.6

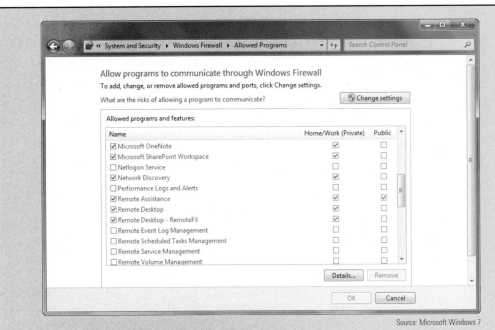

Source: Microsoft Windows 7

Figure 17-15 Allow Remote Desktop communication through Windows Firewall on your local computer

HOW TO USE REMOTE DESKTOP

On the client computer, you can start Remote Desktop to remote in to your host computer by using the **mstsc** command in the search box or using the Start, All Programs menu. Follow these steps to use Remote Desktop:

1. Click **Start**, enter **mstsc** in the search box, and press **Enter**. Alternately, you can click **Start**, **All Programs**, **Accessories** and **Remote Desktop Connection**. The Remote Desktop Connection box opens (see Figure 17-16).

Source: Microsoft Windows 7

Figure 17-16 The IP address of the remote computer can be used to connect to it

A+
220-802
1.4, 1.5,
1.6

XP Differences To start Remote Desktop in XP, click **Start**, **All Programs**, **Accessories**, **Communications**, and **Remote Desktop Connection**. (After Service Pack 3 is applied to Windows XP, the location of Remote Desktop on the Start menu might change to **Start**, **All Programs**, **Accessories**.)

2. Enter the IP address or the host name of the computer to which you want to connect. If you decide to use a host name, begin the host name with two backslashes, as in *CompanyFileServer*.

Notes To use the host name when making a Remote Desktop connection on a local network, the host name and IP address of the remote computer must be entered in the Hosts file of the client computer.

3. If you plan to transfer files from one computer to the other, click **Options** and then click the **Local Resources** tab, as shown in the left side of Figure 17-17. Click **More**. The box on the right side of Figure 17-17 appears. Check **Drives**. Click **OK**. Click **Connect** to make the connection. If a warning box appears, click **Connect** again. If another warning box appears, click **Yes**.

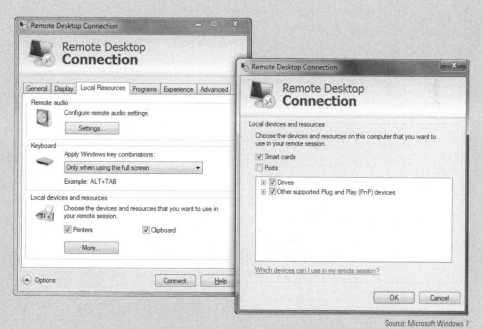

Source: Microsoft Windows 7

Figure 17-17 Allow drives and other devices to be shared using the Remote Desktop Connection

4. A Windows security box appears that is displayed by the remote computer (see Figure 17-18). Log on using a username and password for the remote computer. If a warning box appears saying the remote computer might not be secure, click **Yes** to continue the connection.

17

A+
220-802
1.4, 1.5,
1.6

Source: Microsoft Windows 7

Figure 17-18   Enter your username and password on the
remote computer

5. The desktop of the remote computer appears in a window, as shown in Figure 17-19. When you click this window, you can work with the remote computer just as if you were sitting in front of it, except response time is slower. To move files back and forth between computers, use Windows Explorer on the remote computer. Files on your local computer and on the remote computer will appear in Windows Explorer on the remote computer in the Computer group. For example, in Figure 17-19, you can see drive C on each computer labelled in the figure. To close the connection to the remote computer, log off the remote computer or close the desktop window.

Source: Microsoft Windows 7

Figure 17-19   The desktop of the remote computer is available on your local computer

> **Notes** Even though Windows normally allows more than one user to be logged on at the same time, this is not the case with Remote Desktop. When a Remote Desktop session is opened, all local users on the remote computer are logged off.

A+
220-802
1.4, 1.5,
1.6

Is your host computer as safe as it was before you set it to serve up Remote Desktop and enabled port forwarding to it? Actually, no, because a port has been opened, so take this into account when you decide to use Remote Desktop. In a project at the end of this chapter, you'll learn how you can take further steps to protect the security of your computer when using Remote Desktop. Alternately, you can consider using software that does not require you to open ports. Examples of this type of software, some of which are free, are TeamViewer (*www.teamviewer.com*), GoToMyPC by Citrix (*www.gotomypc.com*), and LogMeIn (*www.logmein.com*).

A+
220-802
1.5

REMOTE APPLICATIONS

A **remote application** is an application that is installed and executed on a server and is presented to a user working at a client computer. Windows Server includes the software to manage these remote applications. The software, **Remote Desktop Services** (included in Windows Server 2008 and later) or **Terminal Services** (included in versions of Windows Server prior to 2008), uses the RDP protocol to present the remote app and its data to the client. Remote applications are becoming popular because most of the computing power (memory and CPU speed) and technical support (for application installations and updates and backing up data) are focused on the server in a centralized location, which means the client computers in the field don't require as much computing power or support.

As a PC support technician, you need to know how to set up a client computer so that a user sitting at the client computer can access a remote application on a server. Setting the client up is actually pretty easy to do because the client computer only needs a small client program installed that is used to connect to the remote application on the server.

> **Notes** The difference between a client computer using Remote Desktop and using a remote application is that in the first case, the host computer is serving up its entire desktop, and in the second case, the host computer is only serving up a single application.

Windows 7 **RemoteApp and Desktop Connection** is used to install the small client program using one of two methods. The method used depends on how the system administrator has set up the remote application, which determines what she provides to you to complete the setup on the client end. She might give you a file or a URL:

▲ *The system administrator provides an application proxy file.* An **application proxy** file has an .msi file extension and is intended to work on a client computer when the complete application is on a server. If you were given an application proxy file, install the proxy by double-clicking this .msi file in Windows Explorer. In the box that appears, click **Ready to set up the connection** and click **Next**.

▲ *The system administrator provides a URL to the server application.* If you were given a URL, follow these steps to make the connection to this URL:

1. Open the Control Panel and in the search box, enter **RemoteApp** and click **Set up a new connection with RemoteApp and Desktop Connections**. A wizard appears to step you through the installation (see Figure 17-20).

2. In the Connection URL field, enter the URL for the connection provided by your system administrator (include https:// at the beginning). Click **Next** twice and then close all windows.

17

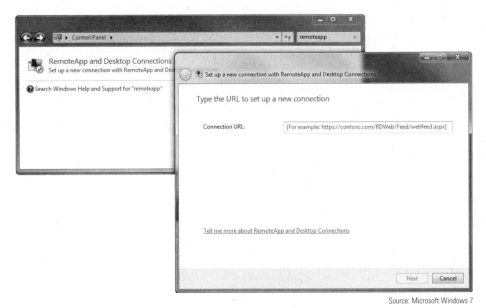

Source: Microsoft Windows 7

Figure 17-20   Follow the wizard to step through installing the client program to use a remote application

To launch the application, click **Start, All Programs,** and **RemoteApp and Desktop Connections,** and then click the name of the remote application. The user must sign onto the remote application using dialog boxes also used by Remote Desktop (refer back to Figures 17-16 and 17-18).

NETWORK SETTINGS TO SUPPORT APPLICATIONS

Two network settings that can be used to support client/server applications on the network are Wake on LAN and Quality of Service. Both are discussed in this part of the chapter.

WAKE ON LAN

Server applications such as Remote Desktop listen for network activity from clients. If you want these server applications to be available at all times, you can set your network adapter properties to Wake on LAN. **Wake on LAN (WoL)** causes the host computer to turn on even from a powered-off state when a specific type of network activity happens. When a computer is powered off or asleep, the network adapter retains power and listens for network activity. When it receives a specific type of network activity, it wakes up or powers up the computer. Two types of network activity that can trigger Wake on LAN are a wake pattern and a magic packet.

System administrators might use utilities to remotely wake a computer to perform routine maintenance. In a project at the end of this chapter, you learn to use one of these utilities. Some applications, such as media-sharing apps, can be configured to remotely wake a server that has been configured for Wake on LAN.

Don't use Wake on LAN on a laptop because it can drain the battery. Wake on LAN must be supported by your motherboard and network adapter and must be enabled in both Windows and BIOS setup. To enable Wake on LAN, follow these steps:

1. In Windows, go to the Network and Sharing Center and click **Change adapter settings.** In the Network Connections window, right-click the network connection and select **Properties.** The Properties box for the network connection opens.

2. In the Properties box, click **Configure** on the Networking tab. The Properties box for the network adapter opens. Select the **Power Management** tab (see Figure 17-21).

Source: Microsoft Windows 7

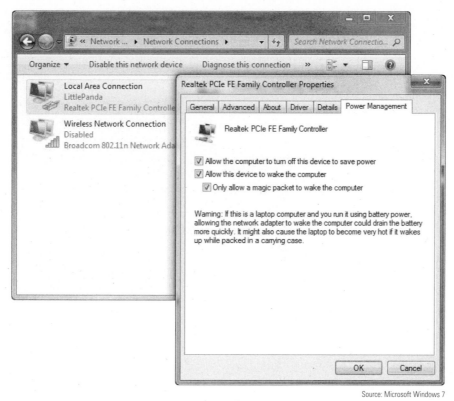

Figure 17-21 Configure Windows for Wake on LAN when the network adapter receives a magic packet

> **Notes** Using these steps to enable Wake on LAN, notice you are using two properties boxes: Step 1 uses the Network Connections properties box, and Step 2 uses the network adapter properties box. The network adapter properties box is also available in Device Manager.

3. To enable Wake on LAN, check **Allow this device to wake the computer**. (If this option is not listed, your network adapter does not support WoL.) To limit a wake up only to magic packets, check **Only allow a magic packet to wake the computer**. Click **OK** to close the box. Close all windows.

4. Wake on LAN must also be enabled in BIOS setup. To do so, shut down and boot up the computer. As it boots up, press a key at the beginning of the boot to access BIOS setup. Then locate the screen to manage power. One power management screen to control Wake on LAN is shown in Figure 17-22, but yours might look different. In this BIOS setup, to enable Wake on LAN, choose **Power On – Normal Boot**.

QUALITY OF SERVICE

Recall from Chapter 15 that Quality of Service (QoS) can improve network performance for an application by raising its priority for allotted network bandwidth. In Chapter 15, you saw how a SOHO router can improve QoS for an application. For Windows to enable QoS for installed applications, the network adapter must support QoS. To configure Windows

17

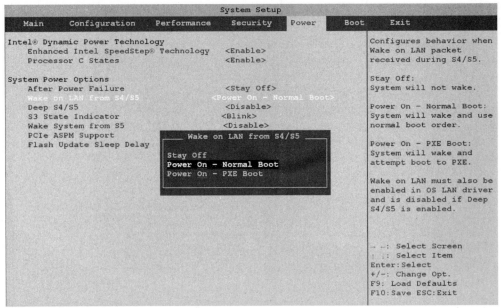

Figure 17-22 Use the Power screen in the BIOS setup to enable Wake on LAN

Source: Intel

to provide QoS for applications, you must (1) enable QoS for the network connection and adapter, and (2) set the QoS priority level for applications. Some applications, such as Microsoft Office 365, have QoS priority levels set automatically.

Follow these steps in Windows to enable QoS for the network connection and network adapter:

1. Using the Network and Sharing Center, go to the Network Connections window, and open the Properties box for the network connection. Verify QoS Packet Scheduler is checked (see Figure 17-23).

2. Click **Configure** to open the Properties box for the network adapter, and click the **Advanced** tab (see Figure 17-24). The exact property for QoS might vary by manufacturer. For example, look for Priority & VLAN, Priority, or QoS Packet Tagging and make sure the property is enabled. Click **OK** and close all windows.

To set the priority level for applications, you must use Group Policy.

USE GROUP POLICY TO IMPROVE QOS FOR APPLICATIONS

Group Policy (gpedit.msc) is a console available only in Windows professional and business editions (not home editions) that is used to control what users can do and how the system can be used. Group Policy works by making entries in the registry, applying scripts to Windows startup, shutdown, and logon processes, and affecting security settings. Policies can be applied to the computer or to a user. Computer-based polices are applied just before the logon screen appears, and user-based policies are applied after logon.

A+
220-802
1.4, 1.6,
1.8, 2.1

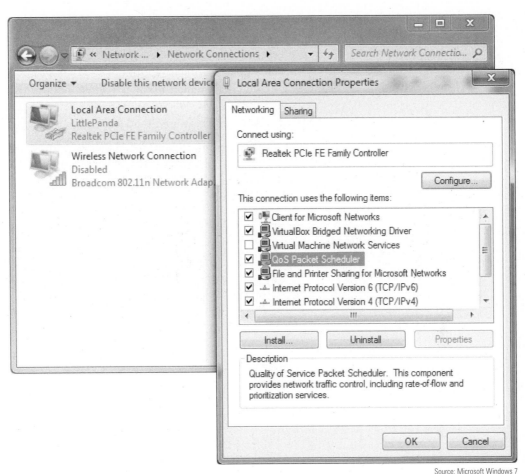

Figure 17-23   QoS Packet Scheduler enabled for the network connection

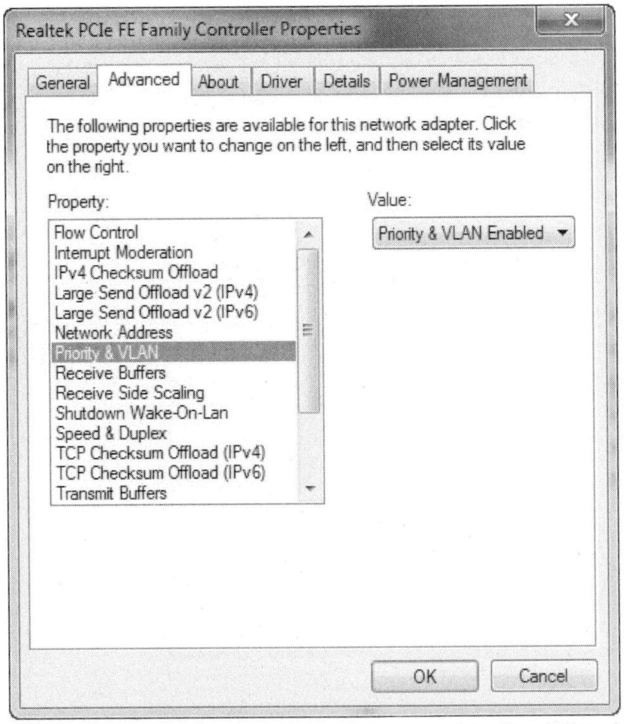

Figure 17-24   Enable the QoS property for the network adapter

17

A+
220-802
1.4, 1.6,
1.8, 2.1

Follow these steps to use Group Policy to set the QoS level for an application:

1. Click **Start,** type **gpedit.msc** in the search box, and press **Enter.** The Group Policy console opens. On the left side of Figure 17-25, notice the two groups of policies are Computer Configuration and User Configuration. To apply a policy to all users, create it under Computer Configuration. Also notice at the top of the list is Local Computer Policy, which means all policies apply only to the local computer.

2. In the Computer Configuration group, expand the Windows Settings group. Right-click **Policy-based QoS** and click **Create new policy,** as shown in Figure 17-25. A wizard opens to step you though the options for the policy (see Figure 17-26).

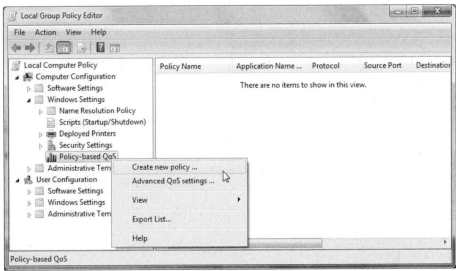

Source: Microsoft Windows 7

Figure 17-25 Use Group Policy to create a new QoS policy

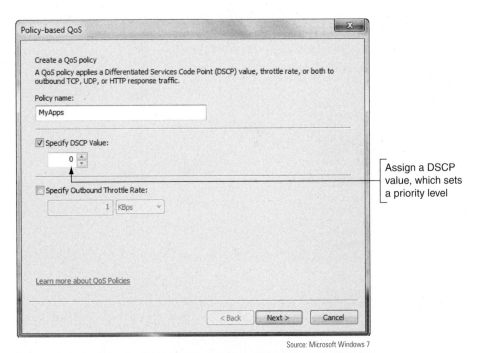

Source: Microsoft Windows 7

Figure 17-26 Name the QoS policy and enter a DSCP value that determines the priority level of the program(s) to which the policy applies

A+
220-802
1.4, 1.6,
1.8, 2.1

When creating a policy, here are important options that appear on different screens as you step through the wizard, but know you only need to use the ones that apply to your situation:

◢ The priority level is determined by a DSCP (Differentiated Services Code Point) value, which is a number from 0 to 63. The higher the number, the higher the priority.

◢ Outbound traffic can be throttled to limit the bandwidth assigned an application.

◢ The policy can apply to all applications or a specific program. (The program name must have an .exe file extension.)

◢ You can specify the source IP address and/or destination IP address.

◢ You can select the protocol (TCP or UDP) and port numbers for the policy.

3. When the wizard is finished, you are returned to the Group Policy console. Close the console. To apply the new policy, you can restart the computer or enter **gpupdate.exe** at a command prompt.

To get the most out of QoS, configure each router and computer on the network to use QoS. Now let's turn our attention to managing another resource on the network: folders and files.

CONTROLLING ACCESS TO FOLDERS AND FILES

Responsibility for a small network can include controlling access to folders and files for users of a local computer and for remote users accessing shared resources over the network. Managing shared resources is accomplished by (1) assigning rights to user accounts and (2) assigning permissions to folders and files.

> **Notes** In Windows, the two terms, rights and permissions, have different meanings. Rights (also called privileges) refer to the tasks an account is allowed to do in the system (for example, installing software or changing the system date and time). **Permissions** refer to which user accounts or user groups are allowed access to data files and folders. *Rights are assigned to an account, and permissions are assigned to data files and folders.*

Let's first look at the strategies used for controlling rights to user accounts and controlling permissions to folders and files. Then you'll learn the procedures in Windows for assigning these rights and permissions.

CLASSIFY USER ACCOUNTS AND USER GROUPS

Computer users should be classified to determine the rights they need to do their jobs. For example, some users need the right to log onto a system remotely and others do not. Other rights granted to users might include the right to install software or hardware, change the system date and time, change Windows Firewall settings, and so forth. Generally, when a new employee begins work, that employee's supervisor determines what rights the employee needs to perform his job. You, as the support technician, will be responsible to make sure the user account assigned to the employee has these rights and no more. This approach is called the **principle of least privilege**.

17

A+
220-802
1.4, 1.6,
1.8, 2.1

In Windows, the rights or privileges assigned to an account are established when you first create a user account, which is when you decide the account type. You can later change these rights by changing the user groups to which the account belongs. User accounts can be created from the Control Panel (using any edition of Windows) or by using the Computer Management console (using business and professional editions of Windows). User accounts can be assigned to different user groups using the Computer Management console (using business and professional editions of Windows). (Home editions of Windows, therefore, cannot be used to manage user groups.)

TYPE OF USER ACCOUNT

When you first create a user account, Windows 7/Vista supports these two types of user accounts:

▲ *Administrator account.* An administrator account has complete access to the system and can make changes that affect the security of the system and other users. Recall from Chapter 7 that Windows has a built-in administrator account named Administrator. By default, this account is disabled in Windows 7/Vista.

▲ *Standard user account.* A standard user account (sometimes called a user account) can use software and hardware and make some system changes but cannot make changes that affect the security of the system or other users.

> **XP Differences** Windows XP offers two account types for new accounts: an administrator account and a limited account. A **limited account** has read-write access only on its own folders, read-only access to most system folders, and no access to other users' data. Using a Limited account, a user cannot install applications or carry out any administrative responsibilities.

Recall from Chapter 7 that when you use Control Panel to create a user account, you are given the opportunity to select the account type (see Figure 17-27).

When you use Computer Management to create an account, the account type is automatically a standard user account. To create a user account using Computer Management, first open the Computer Management console. Then right-click **Users** under **Local Users and Groups** and select **New User** from the shortcut menu. (Windows Home editions don't include the Local Users and Groups option in the Computer Management console.) Enter information for the new user and click **Create** (see Figure 17-28).

> **A+ Exam Tip** The A+ 220-802 exam expects you to know about the administrator, standard user, power user, and guest accounts and groups.

BUILT-IN USER GROUPS

A user account can belong to one or more user groups. Windows offers several built-in user groups and you can create your own. Here are important built-in user groups:

▲ *Administrators and Users groups.* By default, administrator accounts belong to the **Administrators group,** and standard user accounts belong to the **Users group.** If you want to give administrator rights to a standard user account, use the Computer Management console to add the account to the Administrators group.

Source: Microsoft Windows 7

Figure 17-27 Using Control Panel to create a user account, the account type can be Standard user or Administrator

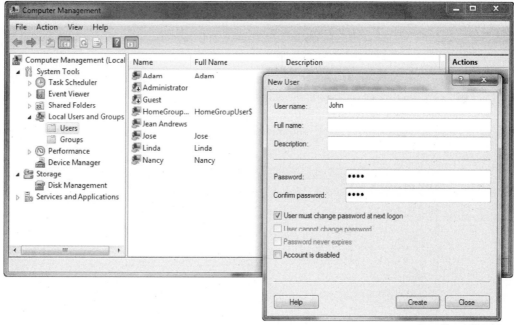

Source: Microsoft Windows 7

Figure 17-28 Creating a new user

▲ *Guests group.* The **Guests group** has limited rights on the system and is given a temporary profile that is deleted when the user logs off. Windows automatically creates one account in the Guests group named the Guest account, which is disabled by default.

▲ *Backup Operators group.* An account in the **Backup Operators** group can back up and restore any files on the system regardless of its access permissions to these files.

A+
220-802
1.4, 1.6,
1.8, 2.1

▲ *Power Users group.* Windows XP has a **Power Users group** that can read from and write to parts of the system other than its own user profile folders, install applications, and perform limited administrative tasks. Windows 7/Vista offers a Power Users group only for backward compatibility with XP to be used with legacy applications that were designed to work in XP.

To view user groups installed on a system, open the Computer Management console and click **Groups** under Local Users and Groups (see Figure 17-29).

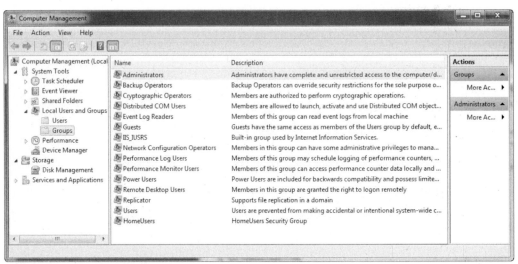

Source: Microsoft Windows 7

Figure 17-29   Users groups installed on a system

To change the groups a user account is in, click **Users**. The list of user accounts appears in the right pane of the console window (see the left side of Figure 17-30). Right-click the user account and select **Properties** from the shortcut menu. On the user account properties box, click the **Member Of** tab (see the middle of Figure 17-30). Click **Add** and enter the user group name.

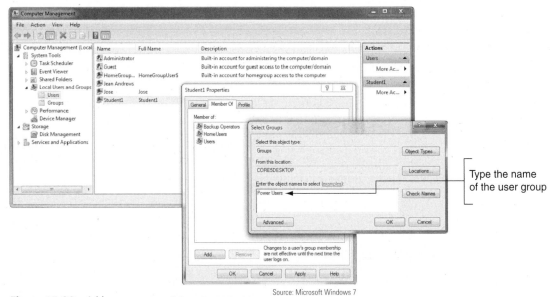

Source: Microsoft Windows 7

Figure 17-30   Add a user account to a user group

A+
220-802
1.4, 1.6,
1.8, 2.1

You must type the user group name exactly as it appears in the list of user groups that you saw earlier in the list of groups (see Figure 17-29). (Alternately, you can click **Advanced**, click **Find Now**, and select the group name from the list of groups that appears.) Click **OK** twice to close both boxes.

In addition to the groups you can assign to an account, Windows might automatically assign one of these built-in user groups to an account when it is determining permissions assigned to a file or folder:

▲ The **Authenticated Users group** includes all user accounts that can access the system except the Guest account. These accounts include domain accounts (used to log onto the domain) and local accounts (used to log onto the local computer). The accounts might or might not require a password. When you create a folder or file that is not part of your user profile, by default, Windows gives access to all Authenticated Users.

▲ The **Everyone group** includes the Authenticated Users group as well as the Guest account. When you share a file or folder on the network or to a homegroup, by default, Windows gives access to the Everyone group.

▲ **Anonymous users** are those users who have not been authenticated on a remote computer. If you log onto a computer using a local account and then attempt to access a remote computer, you must be authenticated on the remote computer. You will be authenticated if your user account and password match on both computers. If you logged onto your local computer with an account and password that do not match one on the remote computer, you are considered an anonymous user on the remote computer. As an anonymous user, you might be allowed to use Windows Explorer to view shared folders and files on the remote computer, but you cannot access them.

CUSTOMIZED USER GROUPS

Using the Management Console in business and professional editions of Windows, you can create your own user groups. When managing several user accounts, it's easier to assign permissions to user groups rather than to individual accounts. First create a user group and then assign permissions to this user group. Any user account that you put in this group then acquires these permissions.

User groups work especially well when several users need the same permissions. For example, you can set up an Accounting group and a Medical Records group for a small office. Users in the Accounting department and users in the Medical Records department go into their respective user groups. Then you only need to manage the permissions for two groups rather than multiple user accounts.

17

METHODS TO ASSIGN PERMISSIONS TO FOLDERS AND FILES

A+
220-802
1.4, 1.5,
1.6, 1.8,
2.1

Here are the three general strategies for managing shared folders and files in Windows:

▲ *Windows 7 homegroup sharing.* When all users on a network require the same access to all resources, you can use a Windows homegroup. Folders, libraries, files, and printers shared with the homegroup are available to all users on the network whose computers have joined the homegroup. You learned how to set up a homegroup in Chapter 7. (Recall that homegroups are not supported by Vista and XP.) After the

A+
220-802
1.4, 1.5,
1.6, 1.8,
2.1

homegroup is set up, to share a file or folder with the homegroup, use the Sharing Wizard. To do so, right-click the item and select **Share with** from the shortcut menu. The wizard lists four options for sharing (see Figure 17-31). Click **Homegroup (Read)** or **Homegroup (Read/Write)** to assign this permission to the homegroup. To see share permissions, select the folder or file in Windows Explorer. The two-person share icon appears in the status bar (see Figure 17-32). Notice in the status bar the permission is assigned to the Everyone group.

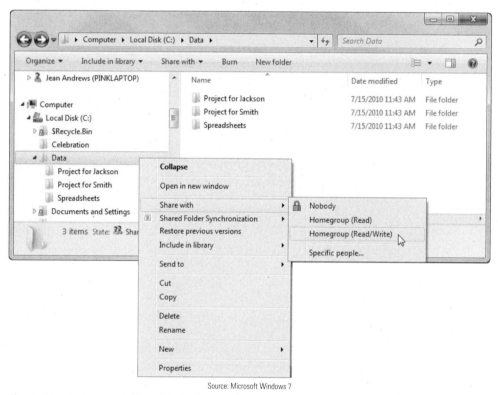

Source: Microsoft Windows 7

Figure 17-31   Share a folder with the homegroup

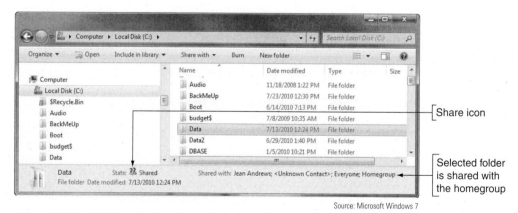

Source: Microsoft Windows 7

Figure 17-32   A folder shared with the homegroup shows the two-person shared icon in the status bar of Windows Explorer

A+
220-802
1.4, 1.5,
1.6, 1.8,
2.1

Notes If the Sharing Wizard is disabled, the four sharing options shown in Figure 17-31 will not appear when you click *Share with*. To enable the Sharing Wizard, using Control Panel, open the Folder Options box and, on the View tab, select **Use Sharing Wizard (Recommended)**. See Figure 17-33. If the Sharing Wizard is not used, you must use advanced sharing methods covered later in the chapter.

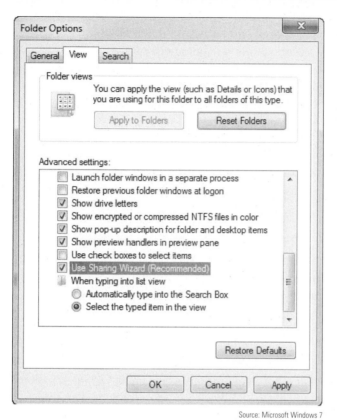

Source: Microsoft Windows 7

Figure 17-33 The Folder Options box shows the Sharing Wizard is enabled

A+ Exam Tip The A+ 220-802 exam expects you to know how to use the Folder Options box to enable or disable the Sharing Wizard.

▲ *Workgroup sharing.* For better security than a homegroup, use workgroup sharing. Using this method, you decide which users on the network have access to which shared folder and the type of access they have. All rights and permissions are set up on each local computer so that each computer manages access to its files, folders, and printers shared on this peer-to-peer network.

▲ *Domain controlling.* If a Windows computer belongs to a domain instead of a workgroup or homegroup, all security is managed by the network administrator for the entire network.

In this chapter, we focus on workgroup sharing, which might use a file server. A **file server** is a computer dedicated to storing and serving up data files and folders. Here are some tips on which folders to use to hold shared data on a file server or personal computer:

▲ Private data for individual users is best kept in the C:\Users folder or the XP C:\Documents and Settings folder for that user. User accounts with limited or standard privileges cannot normally access these folders belonging to another user account. However, accounts with administrative rights do have access.

17

A+
220-802
1.4, 1.5,
1.6, 1.8,
2.1

⬧ The C:\Users\Public folder is intended to be used for folders and files that all users share. It is not recommended you use this folder for controlled access to data.
⬧ For best security, create a folder not in the C:\Users or C:\Documents and Settings folder and assign permissions to that folder and its subfolders. You can allow all users access or only certain users or user groups.

Some applications can be shared with others on the network. If you share a folder that has a program file in it, a user on another computer can double-click the program file and execute it remotely on his or her desktop. This is a handy way for several users to share an application that is installed on a single computer. However, know that not all applications are designed to work this way.

Using workgroup sharing, Windows offers two methods to share a folder over the network:

⬧ *Share permissions*. **Share permissions** grant permissions only to network users and these permissions do not apply to local users of a computer. Share permissions work on NTFS, FAT32, and exFAT volumes and are configured using the Sharing tab on a folder's Properties box. Share permissions apply to a folder and its contents, but not to individual files.
⬧ *NTFS permissions*. **NTFS permissions** apply to local users and network users and apply to both folders and individual files. NTFS permissions work on NTFS volumes only and are configured using the Security tab on a file or folder Properties box. (The Security tab is missing on the Properties box of a folder or file on a FAT volume.)

Here are some tips when implementing share permissions and NTFS permissions:

⬧ If you use both share permissions and NTFS permissions on a folder, the most restrictive permission applies. For NTFS volumes, use only NTFS permissions because they can be customized better. For FAT volumes, your only option is share permissions.
⬧ If NTFS permissions are conflicting, for example, when a user account has been given one permission and the user group to which this user belongs has been given a different permission, the more liberal permission applies.
⬧ **Permission propagation** is when permissions are passed from parent to child. **Inherited permissions** are permissions that are attained from a parent object. For example, when you create a file or folder in a folder, the new object takes on the permissions of the parent folder.
⬧ When you move or copy an object to a folder, the object takes on the permissions of that folder. The exception to this rule is when you move (not copy) an object from one location to another on the same volume. In this case, the object retains its permissions from the original folder.

> **Notes** You can use the xcopy or robocopy command with switches to change the rules for how inherited permissions are managed when copying and moving files. For more information, see the Microsoft Knowledge Base Article 310316 at *support.microsoft.com*.

> **A+ Exam Tip** The A+ 220-802 exam expects you to know about NTFS and share permissions, including how allow and deny conflicts are resolved and what happens to permissions when you move or copy a file or folder.

A+
220-802
1.4, 1.6,
1.8, 2.1

HOW TO SHARE FOLDERS AND FILES

Now that you know about the concepts and strategies for sharing folders and files, let's look at the details of how to use Windows to manage user rights and file and folder permissions.

A+
220-802
1.4, 1.6,
1.8, 2.1

APPLYING | CONCEPTS

Nicole is responsible for a peer-to-peer network for a medical doctor's office. Four computers are connected to the small company network; one of these computers acts as the file server for the network. Nicole has created two classifications of data, Financial and Medical. Two workers (Nancy and Adam) require access to the Medical data, and two workers (Linda and Jose) require access to the Financial folder. In addition, the doctor, John, requires access to both categories of data. Here is what Nicole must do to set up the users and data:

1. Create folders named Financial and Medical on the file server. Create five user accounts, one for John, Nancy, Adam, Linda, and Jose. All the accounts belong to the Windows standard user group. Create two user groups, Financial and Medical.

2. Using NTFS permissions, set the permissions on the Financial and Medical folders so that only the members of the appropriate group can access each folder.

3. Test access to both folders using test data and then copy all real data into the two folders and subfolders. Set up a backup plan for the two folders as you learned to do in Chapter 10.

Let's look at how each of these three steps is done.

> **XP Differences** The steps you're about to see apply to Windows 7/Vista. To find out how to share a folder or file in Windows XP, see Appendix C.

STEP 1: CREATE FOLDERS, USER ACCOUNTS, AND USER GROUPS

Follow these steps to create the folders, user accounts, and user groups on the file server computer that is using Windows 7 Professional:

1. Log onto the system as an administrator.

2. Using an NTFS volume, create these two folders: **C:\Medical** and **C:\Financial**.

3. Open the Computer Management console and create user accounts for **John**, **Nancy**, **Adam**, **Linda**, and **Jose**. The account types are automatically a standard user account.

4. To create the Medical user group, right-click **Groups** under Local Users and Groups and select **New Group** from the shortcut menu. The New Group box appears. Enter the name of the group (**Medical**) and its description (**Users have access to the Medical folder**), as shown in Figure 17-34.

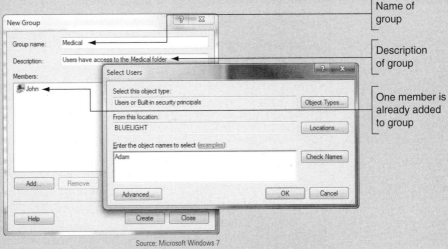

Source: Microsoft Windows 7

Figure 17-34 Setting up a new user group

A+
220-802
1.4, 1.6,
1.8, 2.1

5. Add all the users that need access to medical data (John, Adam, and Nancy). To add members to the Medical group, click **Add**. The Select Users box opens, as shown on the right side of Figure 17-34. Under *Enter the object names to select*, enter the name of a user and click **OK**. As each user is added, his name appears under Members in the New Group box, as shown in Figure 17-34. To create the group, click **Create** in the New Group box.

6. In the same way, create the Financial group and add John, Linda, and Jose to the group. Later, you can use the Computer Management console to add or remove users from either group.

7. Close the Computer Management console.

> **⛯ A+ Exam Tip** The A+ 220–802 exam expects you to be able to set up a user account or group and know how to change the group to which an account is assigned.

> **⊞ XP Differences** By default, when you share a folder in Windows XP, it is shared with Everyone because XP uses **simple file sharing**. Before you can share an XP folder with specific users or user groups, you must turn off simple file sharing. See Appendix C to find out how.

STEP 2: SET FOLDER PERMISSIONS FOR USER GROUPS

Follow these steps to set the permissions for the two folders:

1. Open Windows Explorer, right-click the **Medical** folder, and select **Properties** from the shortcut menu. The Properties box for the folder appears.

2. Click the **Security** tab (see Figure 17-35). Notice in the box that Authenticated Users, SYSTEM, Administrators, and Users all have access to the C:\Medical folder. When you select a user group, the type of permissions assigned to that group appears in the *Permissions for*

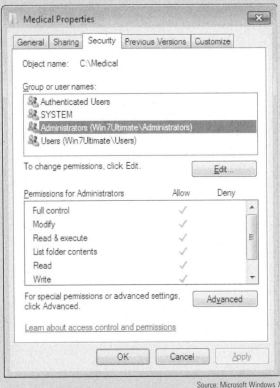

Source: Microsoft Windows 7

Figure 17-35 Permissions assigned to the Medical folder

A+
220-802
1.4, 1.6,
1.8, 2.1

users area. Table 17-1 gives an explanation of the more significant types of permission. Note that the Administrators group has full control of the folder. Also notice the checks under Allow are dimmed. These permissions are dimmed because they have been inherited from the parent object. In this case, the parent object is Windows default settings.

Permission Level	Description
Full control	Can read, change, delete, and create files and subfolders, read file and folder attributes, read and change permissions, and take ownership of a file or folder.
Modify	Can read, change, and create existing files and subfolders, but cannot delete existing ones. Can read and change attributes. Can view permissions but not change them.
Read & execute	Can read folders and contents and run programs in a folder.
List folder contents	Can read folders and contents and run programs in a folder.
Read	Can read folders and contents.
Write	Can create a folder or file and change attributes, but cannot read data. This permission is used for a drop folder where users can drop confidential files that can only be read by a manager. For example, an instructor can receive student homework in a drop folder.

© Cengage Learning 2014

Table 17-1 Permission levels for files and folders

A+ Exam Tip The A+ 220-802 exam expects you to know that NTFS permissions can customize permissions better than share permissions.

3. To remove the inherited status from these permissions so we can change them, click **Advanced**. The Advanced Security Settings box appears (see the left side of Figure 17-36). Click **Change Permissions**. In the new Advanced Security Settings box (see the middle of Figure 17-36), you can now uncheck **Include inheritable permissions from this object's parent**. A Windows Security warning box appears, also shown in the figure. To keep the current permissions, but remove the inherited status placed on them, click **Add** (in Vista, click **Copy**).

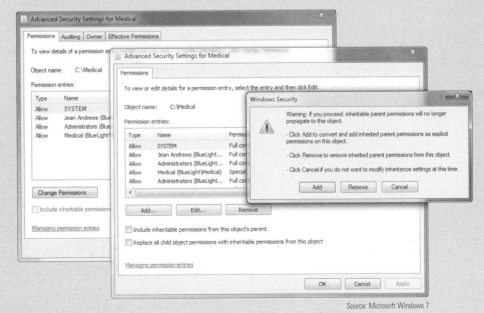

Source: Microsoft Windows 7

Figure 17-36 Remove the inherited status from the current permissions

17

A+
220-802
1.4, 1.6,
1.8, 2.1

4. Click **OK** twice to close the Advanced Security Settings box.

5. In the Medical Properties box, notice the permissions are now checked in black, indicating they are no longer inherited permissions and can be changed. Click **Edit** to change these permissions.

6. The Permissions box opens (see Figure 17-37). Select the **Authenticated Users** group and click **Remove**. Also remove the **Users** group. Don't remove the SYSTEM group, which gives Windows the access it needs. Also, don't remove the Administrators group. You need to leave the group as-is so that administrators can access the data.

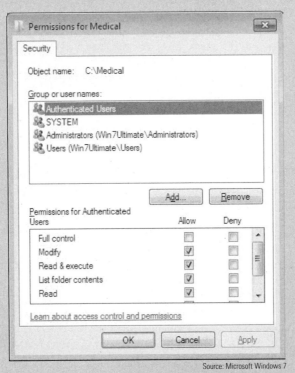

Source: Microsoft Windows 7

Figure 17-37 Change the permissions to a folder

7. To add a new group, click **Add**. The Select Users or Groups box opens. Under *Enter the object names to select*, type **Medical**, as shown in Figure 17-38, and click **OK**. The Medical group is added to the list of groups and users for this folder.

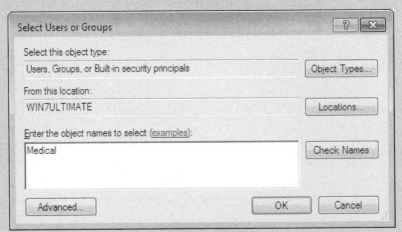

Source: Microsoft Windows 7

Figure 17-38 Add a user or group to shared permissions

8. Using the check box under Permissions for Medical, check **Allow** under *Full control* to give that permission to this user group. Click **OK** twice to close the Properties box.

A+
220-802
1.4, 1.6,
1.8, 2.1

9. Change the permissions of the C:\Financial folder so that Authenticated Users and Users are not allowed access and the Financial group is allowed full control.

STEP 3: TEST AND GO LIVE

It's now time to test your security measures. Do the following to test the share permissions and implement your shared folders:

1. Test a user account in each user group to make sure the user can read, write, and delete in the folder he needs but cannot access the other folder. Put some test data in each folder. Then log onto the system using an account you want to test and try to access each folder. Figure 17-39 shows the box that appears when an unauthorized user attempts to access a folder. When you click **Continue**, entering an administrator password in the resulting UAC box gives you access.

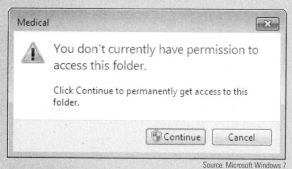

Source: Microsoft Windows 7

Figure 17-39 Access to a folder is controlled

2. Now that NTFS permissions are set correctly for each local and network user, you are ready to allow access over the network. To do that, both NTFS and share permissions must allow network access. (Share permissions apply only to network access, not local access.) Best practice is to allow full access using share permissions and restrictive access using NTFS permissions. The most restrictive permissions apply. To allow full access using share permissions, click the Sharing tab of the folder properties box, and click Share. In the drop-down list, select Everyone and click Add. Then give Read/Write access to the Everyone group. Click Share and close all boxes.

3. Now that you have the security working on the one computer, go to each computer on the network and create the user accounts that will be using this computer. Then test the security and make sure each user can access or cannot access the \Financial and \Medical folders as you intend. To access shared folders, you can drill down into the Network group in Windows Explorer. Another method is to type the computer name—as in \\bluelight—in the address bar of the Explorer window (see Figure 17-40).

Source: Microsoft Windows 7

Figure 17-40 Use the computer name to access shared folders on that computer

4. After you are convinced the security works as you want it to, copy all the company data to subfolders in these folders. Check a few subfolders and files to verify that each has the permissions that you expect. And don't forget to put in place on the file server the backup procedures you learned about in Chapter 10.

17

A+
220-802
1.4, 1.6,
1.8, 2.1

HOW TO USE SHARE PERMISSIONS

Although you can mix NTFS permissions and share permissions on the same system, life is simpler if you use one or the other. For NTFS volumes, NTFS permissions are the way to go because they can be customized better than share permissions. However, you must use share permissions on FAT volumes. To do so, follow these steps:

1. Open the Properties box for the folder (*Financial* in this case) and go to the **Sharing** tab. Then click **Advanced Sharing**. The Advanced Sharing box opens (see Figure 17-41).

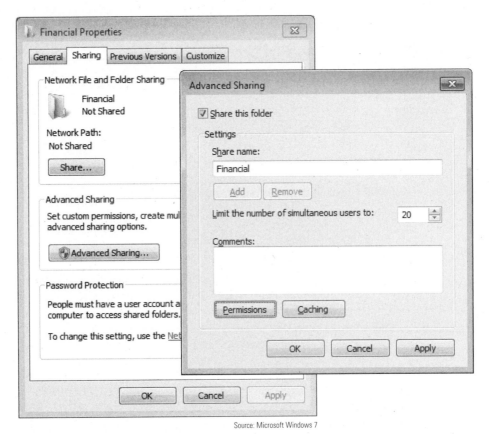

Source: Microsoft Windows 7

Figure 17-41 Use the Sharing tab of a folder Properties box to set up share permissions

2. Click **Share this folder**. Then click **Permissions**. The Permissions box opens (see the left side of Figure 17-42). Initially, the folder is shared with Everyone. Also notice that share permissions offer only three permission levels, Full Control, Change, and Read.

3. Click **Add**. The Select Users or Groups box appears (see the right side of Figure 17-42). Enter a user account or user group and click **OK**.

4. To delete the Everyone group, select it in the Permissions box and click **Remove**. Click **OK** to close each open box in turn.

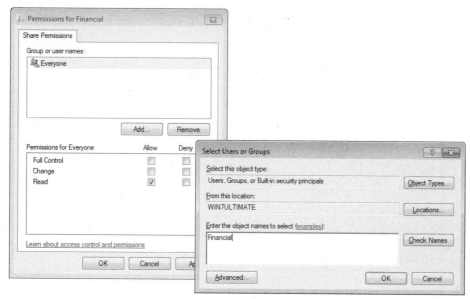

Source: Microsoft Windows 7

Figure 17-42 Add a user or user group to assign share permissions

SUPPORT AND TROUBLESHOOT SHARED FOLDERS AND FILES

You have just seen how to set up user groups and folder permissions assigned to these groups. If you have problems accessing a shared resource, follow these steps:

1. Open the Network and Sharing Center. Make sure your network location is set to Home or Work.

2. In the left pane, click **Change advanced sharing settings**. The Advanced sharing settings, window opens (see Figure 17-43). Verify the settings here are the default settings for a Home or Work network profile:

- Select **Turn on network discovery**.
- Select **Turn on file and printer sharing**.
- If you want to share the Public folder to the network, under Public folder sharing, select **Turn on sharing so anyone with network access can read and write files in the Public folders**.
- If you want the added protection of requiring that all users on the network must have a valid user account and password on this computer, select **Turn on password protected sharing**.
- For a Home network, if you want user accounts and passwords to be required in order to access Homegroup resources, under HomeGroup connections, select **Use user accounts and passwords to connect to other computers**.

After you have made your changes, click **Save changes** at the bottom of the window.

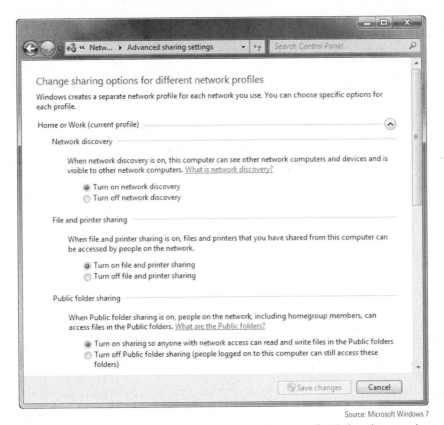

Source: Microsoft Windows 7

Figure 17-43   Use the Advanced sharing settings window to verify Windows is set to share resources

3. In the Network and Sharing Center, click **Change adapter settings**. Right-click the network connection icon, and select **Properties** from the shortcut menu. In the Properties box, verify that **File and Printer Sharing for Microsoft Networks** is checked (see Figure 17-44).

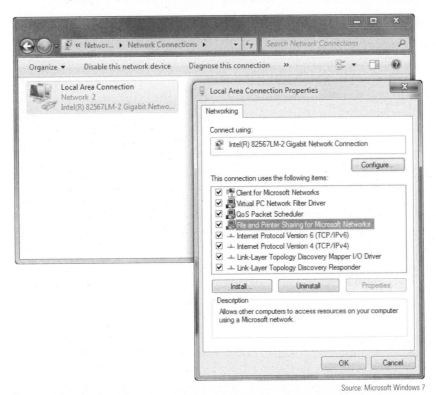

Source: Microsoft Windows 7

Figure 17-44   Verify the properties for the network connection are set for sharing resources over the connection

A+
220-802
1.4, 1.6,
1.8, 2.1

4. Verify the user account and password on the remote computer match the user account and password on the host computer. If these accounts and passwords don't match, the user is considered an anonymous user and is denied access to resources shared on the remote computer.

Vista Differences The Vista Network and Sharing Center works a little differently from that of Windows 7. To find out how to verify settings that apply to shared files and folders in Vista using its Network and Sharing Center, see Appendix B.

XP Differences For Windows XP to share resources, two services, Client for Microsoft Networks and File and Printer Sharing for Microsoft Networks, must be installed and enabled for the network connection. To find out how to verify these settings using Windows XP, see Appendix C.

Here are a few tips about managing shared folders and files:

▲ *Use advanced permissions settings.* If you need further control of the permissions assigned a user or group, click **Advanced** on the Security tab of a folder's Properties box. The Advanced Security Settings box appears (see the left side of Figure 17-45). On the Permissions tab, click **Change Permissions**. In the next box (see the middle of Figure 17-45), you can see that the Medical user group was given full control. To change these permission details, select the user group and click **Edit**. In our example, we're editing the Medical group. The Permission Entry box opens (see the right side of Figure 17-45).

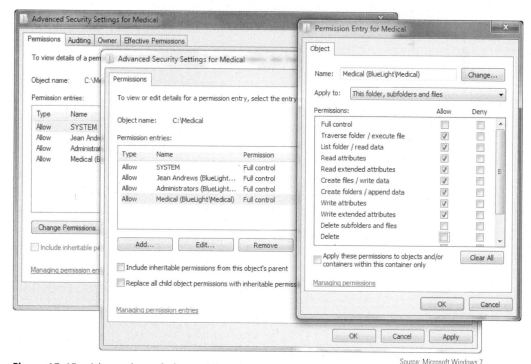

Figure 17-45 Advanced permissions settings

Source: Microsoft Windows 7

We now can change detailed permissions. Notice that the right to delete subfolders and files has been set to Deny, and the right to delete the folder itself has been set to Deny. Click **OK** to close each box. The resulting change means that users of the Medical group cannot delete or move a file or folder. (They can, however, copy the file or folder.)

> 💡 **A+ Exam Tip** The A+ 220–802 exam expects you to be able to implement permissions so that a user can copy but not move a file or folder and understand how to apply Allow and Deny permissions.

▲ *Manage permissions using the parent folder.* When a subfolder is created, it is assigned the permissions of the parent folder. Recall that these inherited permissions appear dimmed, indicating they are inherited permissions. The best way to change inherited permissions is to change the permissions of the parent object. In other words, to change the permissions of the C:\Financial\QuickBooks folder, change the permission of the C:\Financial folder. Changing permissions of a parent folder affects all subfolders in that folder.

▲ *Check the effective permissions.* Permissions manually set for a subfolder or file can override inherited permissions. Permissions that are manually set are called explicit permissions. When a folder or file has inherited an explicit permission set, it might be confusing as to exactly which permissions are in effect. To know for sure exactly which permissions for a file or folder are in effect, see the Effective Permissions tab of the Advanced Security Settings box. (Look back at the leftmost box in Figure 17-45.)

▲ *Take ownership of a folder.* The owner of a folder always has full permissions for the folder. If you are having a problem changing permissions and you are not the folder owner, try taking ownership of the folder. To do that, click **Advanced** on the Security tab of the folder's Properties box. The Advanced Security Settings box appears. Click the **Owner** tab (see the left side of Figure 17-46). Click **Edit**. The owner can then be edited (see the right side of Figure 17-46). Select a user from the *Change owner to* list and click **Apply** to make that user the new owner. If a user is not listed, click **Other users or groups** and add the user. Close the Advanced Security Settings box and the Properties box, and reopen the Properties box for the change to take effect.

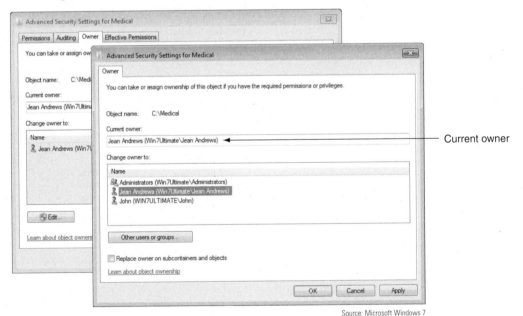

Source: Microsoft Windows 7

Figure 17-46   Change the owner of a folder

▲ *Use only one workgroup.* It is not necessary that all computers belong to the same workgroup in order to share resources. However, performance improves when they are all in the same workgroup.

▲ *Require passwords for all user accounts.* Don't forget that for best security, each user account needs a password. How to use Group Policy to require that all accounts have passwords is covered in Chapter 18.

▲ *Use a mapped network drive.* For the convenience of remote users, map network drives for shared folders that are heavily used. How to do that is coming up next.

HOW TO MAP A NETWORK DRIVE

A **network drive map** is one of the most powerful and versatile methods of communicating over a network. A network drive map makes one computer (the client) appear to have a new hard drive, such as drive E, that is really hard drive space on another host computer (the server). This client/server arrangement is managed by a Windows component, the Network File System (NFS), which makes it possible for files on the network to be accessed as easily as if they are stored on the local computer. NFS is a type of distributed file system (DFS), which is a system that shares files on a network. Even if the host computer uses a different OS, such as UNIX, the drive map still functions.

> **Notes** A network-attached storage (NAS) device provides hard drive storage for computers on a network. Computers on the network can access this storage using a mapped network drive.

To set up a network drive, follow these steps:

1. On the host computer, share the folder or entire volume to which you want others to have access.

2. On the remote computer that will use the network drive, open Windows Explorer and press **Alt** to display the menu bar. Click the **Tools** menu and select **Map network drive**.

> **Notes** By default, Windows does not show the menu bar in Windows Explorer. To cause the menu to always display, click **Organize** and then click **Folder and search options**. In the Folder Options box, click the **View** tab. Under Advanced settings, check **Always show menus**. Click **OK** to close the box.

3. The Map Network Drive dialog box opens, as shown in Figure 17-47. Select a drive letter from the drop-down list.

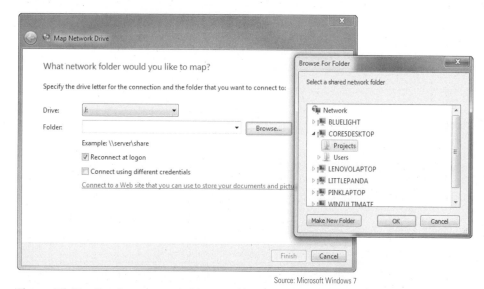

Source: Microsoft Windows 7

Figure 17-47 Mapping a network drive to a host computer

4. Click the **Browse** button and locate the shared folder or drive on the host computer (see the right side of Figure 17-47). Click **OK** to close the Browse For Folder dialog box, and click **Finish** to map the drive. The folder on the host computer now appears as one more drive in Explorer on your computer.

A+
220-802
1.4, 1.6,
1.8, 2.1

> **Notes** When mapping a network drive, you can type the path to the host computer rather than clicking the Browse button to navigate to the host. To enter the path, in the Map Network Drive dialog box, use two backslashes, followed by the name of the host computer, followed by a backslash and the drive or folder to access on the host computer. For example, to access the Projects folder on the computer named Core5Desktop, enter **\\Core5Desktop\Projects** and then click **Finish**.

If a network drive does not work, go to the Network and Sharing Center, and verify that the network connection is good. You can also use the net use command discussed later in the chapter to solve problems with mapped network drives.

> **Notes** A host computer might be in sleep mode or powered down when a remote computer attempts to make a mapped drive connection at startup. To solve this problem, configure the host computer for Wake on LAN.

HIDDEN NETWORK RESOURCES AND ADMINISTRATIVE SHARES

Sometimes your goal is to assure that a folder or file is not accessible from the network or by other users or is secretly shared on the network. When you need to protect confidential data from users on the network, you can do the following:

- ◢ *Disable File and Printer Sharing.* If no resources on the computer are shared, use the Network and Sharing Center (or the XP Network Connections window) to disable File and Printer Sharing for Microsoft Networks.
- ◢ *Hide a shared folder.* If you want to share a folder, but don't want others to see the shared folder in Windows Explorer, add a $ to the end of the folder name. This shared and hidden folder is called a **hidden share**. Others on the network can access the folder only when they know its name. For example, if you name a shared folder Financial$ on the computer named Fileserver, in order to access the folder, a user must enter *Fileserver*\Financial$ in the search box (see Figure 17-48) on the remote computer and press **Enter**.

Source: Microsoft Windows 7

Figure 17-48 Accessing a hidden, shared folder on the network

> **XP Differences** To find out how to make your user profile private using Windows XP, see Appendix C.

Folders and files on a computer that are shared with others on the network using local user accounts are called **local shares**. For computers that belong to a domain, you need to be aware of another way folders are shared, called administrative shares. **Administrative shares**

A+
220-802
1.4, 1.6,
1.8, 2.1

are the folders that are shared by default that administrator accounts at the domain level can access. You don't need to manually share these folders because Windows automatically does so by default. Two types of administrative shares are:

▲ *The %systemroot% folder.* Enter the path *computername*\admin$ to access the %*systemroot*% folder (most likely the C:\Windows folder) on a remote computer. For example, in Figure 17-49, the entry in the Explorer address bar is *bluelight*\admin$. Windows requests that the user authenticate with an administrator account to access this administrative share. The admin$ administrative share is called the **Remote Admin** share.

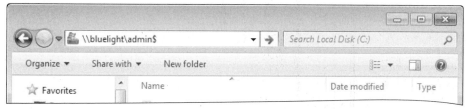

Figure 17-49   Access an administrative share on a domain

Source: Microsoft Windows 7

▲ *Any volume or drive.* To access the root level of any volume or drive on the network, enter the computer name and drive letter followed by a $, for example, \\\\bluelight\C$.

🔘 A+ Exam Tip   The A+ 220–802 exam expects you to understand the difference between administrative shares and local shares.

📝 Notes   To see a list of all shares on a computer, open the **Computer Management** console and drill down to **System Tools**, **Shared Folders**, **Shares** (see Figure 17-50).

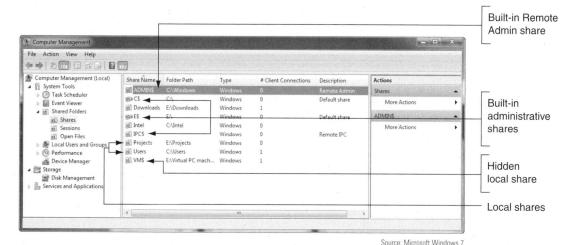

Figure 17-50   Use the Computer Management console to view all shares

Source: Microsoft Windows 7

When supporting a workgroup, you might be tempted to share all the drives on all computers so that you can have easy access remotely. However, to use local shares in this way is not a good security practice. Don't share the \Windows folder or an entire drive or volume on the network. These local shares appear in everyone's Explorer window. You don't want your system files and folders exposed like this.

TROUBLESHOOTING NETWORK CONNECTIONS

A+
220-802
4.5

When troubleshooting network connections, both hardware and software tools can help. Some hardware tools are a cable tester, loopback plug, and wireless locator. Windows offers several TCP/IP utilities that can help you troubleshoot a network problem. Let's first take a look at the tools you'll need, and then we'll discuss troubleshooting strategies using these tools.

CABLE TESTER, LOOPBACK PLUG, AND WIRELESS LOCATOR

A **cable tester** can be used to test a cable to find out if it is good or to find out what type of cable it is if the cable is not labeled. You can also use a cable tester to trace a network cable through a building. A cable tester has two components, as shown in Figure 17-51.

© Cengage Learning 2014

Figure 17-51   Use a cable tester pair to determine the type of cable and if the cable is good

To test a cable, connect each component to the ends of the cable and turn on the tester. Lights on the tester will show you if the cable is good and what type of cable you have. You'll need to read the user manual that comes with the cable tester to know how to interpret the lights.

You can also use cable testers to trace a network cable through a building. Suppose you see several network jacks on walls in a building, but you don't know which jacks connect. Install a short cable in each of two jacks and then use the cable tester to test the continuity, as shown in Figure 17-52. You might damage a cable tester if you connect it to a live circuit, so before you start connecting the cable tester to wall jacks, be sure that you turn off all devices on the network.

A **loopback plug** can be used to test a network cable or port. Whereas a cable tester works on cables that are not live, a loopback plug works with live cables. To test a port or cable, connect one end of the cable to a network port on a router or computer, and connect the loopback plug to the other end of the cable (see Figure 17-53). If the LED light on the loopback plug lights up, the cable and port are good. Another way to use a loopback plug is to find out which port on a switch in a server closet matches up with a wall jack. Plug the loopback plug into the wall jack. The connecting port on the switch in the closet lights up. When buying a loopback plug, pay attention to the Ethernet speeds it supports. Some only support 100 Mbps; others support 100 Mbps and 1000 Mbps.

A+
220-802
4.5

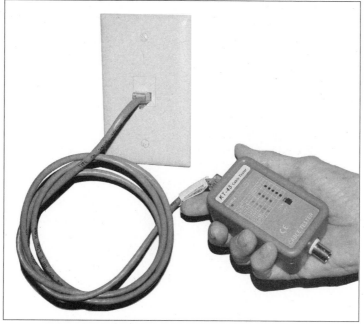

© Cengage Learning 2014

Figure 17-52 Use cable testers to trace network cables through a building

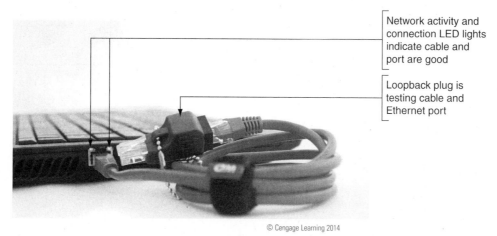

Network activity and connection LED lights indicate cable and port are good

Loopback plug is testing cable and Ethernet port

© Cengage Learning 2014

Figure 17-53 A loopback plug verifies the cable and network port are good

A **wireless locator** helps you find a Wi-Fi hotspot and tells you the strength of the RF signal (see Figure 17-54). If you're in a public place looking for a strong hotspot to connect your laptop, walk around with your wireless locator until you find one. Wireless locators are also helpful when mapping out where you need to position your wireless access points so that all areas have a strong RF signal. When buying a wireless locator, look for one that tells you if a hotspot is encrypted (requires a security key to connect) and make sure it supports all the Wi-Fi standards (802.11 b/g/n).

17

A+
220-802
4.5

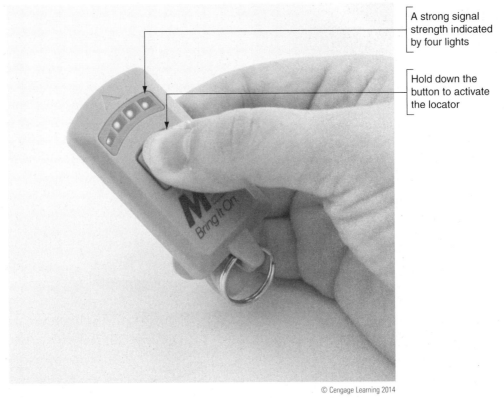

A strong signal strength indicated by four lights

Hold down the button to activate the locator

© Cengage Learning 2014

Figure 17-54 Use a wireless locator to measure the strength of an RF signal

💡 **A+ Exam Tip** The A+ 220-802 exam expects you to know how to use a cable tester, loopback plug, and wireless locator to troubleshoot network problems.

A+
220-802
1.3, 4.5

TCP/IP UTILITIES USED FOR TROUBLESHOOTING

Windows includes several TCP/IP utilities you can use to troubleshoot networking problems. In this part of the chapter, you learn to use ping, ipconfig, nslookup, tracert, net use, net user, nbtstat, and netstat. Most of these program files are found in the \Windows\System32 folder.

💡 **A+ Exam Tip** The A+ 220-802 exam expects you to know about these TCP/IP utilities: ping, tracert, netstat, ipconfig, net, nslookup, and nbtstat. You need to know when and how to use each utility and how to interpret results.

📝 **Notes** Only the more commonly used parameters or switches for each command are discussed. For several of these commands, you can use the /? or /help parameter to get more help with the command. And for even more information about each command, search the *technet.microsoft.com* site.

Now let's see how to use each utility.

A+
220-802
1.3, 4.5

PING [-A] [-T] [*TARGETNAME*]

The **Ping (Packet InterNet Groper)** command tests connectivity by sending an echo request to a remote computer. If the remote computer is online, detects the signal, and is configured to respond to a ping, it responds. (Responding to a Ping is the default Windows setting.) Use ping to test for connectivity or to verify name resolution is working. A few examples of ping are shown in Table 17-2. Two examples are shown in Figure 17-55.

Ping Command	Description
Ping 69.32.142.109	To test for connectivity using an IP address. If the remote computer responds, the round-trip times are displayed.
Ping -a 69.32.142.109	The –a parameter tests for name resolution. Use it to display the host name and verify DNS is working.
Ping -t 69.32.142.109	The –t parameter causes pinging to continue until interrupted. To display statistics, press Ctrl+Break. To stop pinging, press Ctrl+C.
Ping 127.0.0.1	A loopback address test. The IP address 127.0.0.1 always refers to the local computer. If the local computer does not respond, you can assume there is a problem with the TCP/IP configuration.
Ping www.course.com	Use a host name to find out the IP address of a remote computer. If the computer does not respond, assume there is a problem with DNS. On the other hand, some computers are not configured to respond to pings.

© Cengage Learning 2014

Table 17-2   Examples of the ping command

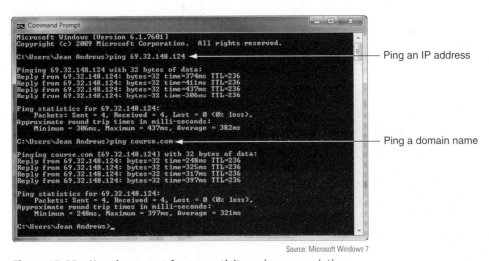

Source: Microsoft Windows 7

Figure 17-55   Use ping to test for connectivity and name resolution

17

IPCONFIG [/ALL] [/RELEASE] [/RENEW] [/DISPLAYDNS] [/FLUSHDNS]

The **Ipconfig (IP configuration)** command can display TCP/IP configuration information and refresh the TCP/IP assignments to a connection including its IP address. Some examples of the command are listed in Table 17-3.

Ipconfig Command	Description
Ipconfig /all	Displays TCP/IP information.
Ipconfig /release	Releases the IP address when dynamic IP addressing is being used.
Ipconfig /release6	Releases an IPv6 IP address.
Ipconfig /renew	Leases a new IP address from a DHCP server.
Ipconfig /renew6	Leases a new IPv6 IP address from a DHCP IPv6 server.
Ipconfig /displaydns	Displays information about name resolutions that Windows currently holds in the DNS resolver cache.
Ipconfig /flushdns	Flushes the name resolver cache, which might solve a problem when the browser cannot find a host on the Internet.

© Cengage Learning 2014

Table 17-3   Examples of the ipconfig command

NSLOOKUP [*COMPUTERNAME*]

Nslookup (**name space lookup**) lets you read information from the Internet name space by requesting information about domain name resolutions from the DNS server's zone data. Zone data is information about domain names and their corresponding IP addresses kept by a DNS server. For example, to find out what your DNS server knows about the domain name *www.microsoft.com*, use this command:

```
nslookup www.microsoft.com
```

Figure 17-56 shows the results. Notice in the figure that the DNS server reports one IP address assigned to *www.microsoft.com*. It also reports that this information is non-authoritative, meaning that it is not the authoritative, or final, name server for the *www .microsoft.com* computer name.

Source: Microsoft Windows 7

Figure 17-56   The Nslookup command reports information about the Internet name space

A **reverse lookup** is when you use the Nslookup command to find the host name when you know a computer's IP address, such as:

```
nslookup 192.168.1.102
```

To find out the default DNS server for a network, enter the Nslookup command with no parameters.

TRACERT *TARGETNAME*

The **Tracert** (**trace route**) command can be useful when you're trying to resolve a problem reaching a destination host such as an FTP site or web site. The command sends a series of requests to the destination computer and displays each hop to the destination. (A hop happens when a packet moves from one router to another.) For example, to trace the route to the *www.course.com* site, enter this command in a command prompt window:

```
tracert www.course.com
```

The results of this command are shown in Figure 17-57. A packet is assigned a Time To Live (TTL), which is the number of hop counts it can make before a router drops the packet and sends an ICMP message back to the host that sent the packet (see Figure 17-58). Internet

```
Command Prompt

Copyright (c) 2009 Microsoft Corporation.  All rights reserved.

C:\Users\Jean Andrews>tracert www.course.com

Tracing route to www.course.com [69.32.148.124]
over a maximum of 30 hops:

  1    <1 ms    <1 ms    <1 ms  LittlePanda.domain.invalid [192.168.1.1]
  2    <1 ms     1 ms    <1 ms  192.168.254.254
  3   177 ms   173 ms   173 ms  h1.20.29.71.dynamic.ip.windstream.net [71.29.20.
1]
  4   245 ms   297 ms   237 ms  h228.112.186.173.static.ip.windstream.net [173.1
86.112.228]
  5   318 ms   237 ms   203 ms  h114.72.102.166.static.ip.windstream.net [166.10
2.72.114]
  6   194 ms   199 ms   196 ms  h80.72.102.166.static.ip.windstream.net [166.102
.72.80]
  7   207 ms   203 ms   241 ms  xe-8-0-0.edge4.Atlanta2.Level3.net [4.59.12.41]
  8   218 ms   206 ms   215 ms  vlan52.ebr2.Atlanta2.Level3.net [4.69.150.126]
  9   154 ms   166 ms   171 ms  ae-3-3.ebr2.Chicago1.Level3.net [4.69.132.73]
 10   119 ms   158 ms   195 ms  ae-5-5.ebr2.Chicago2.Level3.net [4.69.140.194]
 11     *      170 ms     *     ae-2-52.edge4.Chicago3.Level3.net [4.69.138.166]

 12   202 ms   203 ms   221 ms  TIME-WARNER.edge4.Chicago3.Level3.net [4.53.98.4
6]
 13    54 ms    54 ms    54 ms  cnc1-ar3-xe-0-0-0-0.us.twtelecom.net [66.192.244
.202]
 14   195 ms   199 ms   196 ms  69.32.144.42
 15   217 ms   223 ms   226 ms  tluser.thomsonlearning.com [69.32.128.159]
 16     *        *        *     Request timed out.
 17   231 ms   229 ms   238 ms  www.course.com [69.32.148.124]

Trace complete.

C:\Users\Jean Andrews>_
```

Figure 17-57 The Tracert command traces a path to a destination computer

Figure 17-58 A router eliminates a packet that has exceeded its TTL

A+
220-802
1.3, 4.5

Control Message Protocol (ICMP) messages are used by routers and hosts to communicate error messages and updates, and some routers don't send this information. The tracert command creates its report from these messages. If a router doesn't respond, the *Request timed out* message appears.

THE NET COMMANDS

The net command is several commands in one, and most of the net commands require an elevated command prompt window. In this section, you learn about the net use and net user commands. The **net use** command connects or disconnects a computer from a shared resource or can display information about connections. For example, the following command makes a new connection to a remote computer and to a shared folder on that computer:

```
net use \\bluelight\Medical
```

> **Notes** Other important net commands are net accounts, net config, net print, net share, and net view. You might want to do a Google search on each of these commands to find out how they work.

Use the following command to pass a username and password to the \\bluelight remote computer and then map a network drive to the \Medical folder on that computer:

```
net use \\bluelight\Medical /user:"Jean Andrews" mypassword
```

```
net use z: \\bluelight\Medical
```

The double quotation marks are needed in the first command above because the username has a space in it.

A persistent network connection is one that happens at each logon. To make the two commands persistent, add the /persistent parameter like this:

```
net use \\bluelight\Medical /user:"Jean Andrews" mypassword
/persistent:yes
```

```
net use z: \\bluelight\Medical /persistent:yes
```

The **net user** command manages user accounts. For example, recall that the built-in administrator account is disabled by default. To activate the account, use this net user command:

```
net user administrator /active:yes
```

NBTSTAT [-N] [-R] [-RR]

The **nbtstat** (NetBIOS over TCP/IP Statistics) command is used to display statistics about the NetBT (NetBIOS over TCP/IP) protocol. NetBIOS is an older network protocol suite used before TCP/IP. Occasionally, you find a legacy application still in use that relies on NetBIOS and NetBIOS computer names. The NetBT protocol was developed to allow NetBIOS to work over a TCP/IP network.

Whereas TCP/IP uses a Hosts file on the local computer and a DNS server to resolve computer names, NetBIOS uses an Lmhosts file on the local computer and a WINS

(Windows Internet Name Service) server to resolve NetBIOS computer names. Table 17-4 lists some nbtstat commands that you might use when a legacy application cannot access resources on the network.

Command	Description
nbtstat –n	Displays the NetBIOS name table on the local computer
nbtstat –r	Purges and rebuilds the NetBIOS name cache on the local computer using entries in the Lmhosts file
nbtstat –RR	Releases and renews the NetBIOS names kept by the WINS server

Table 17-4 Nbtstat commands

© Cengage Learning 2014

NETSTAT [-a] [-b] [-o]

The **netstat** (**network statistics**) command gives statistics about TCP/IP and network activity and includes several parameters. Table 17-5 lists a few Netstat commands.

Command	Description
netstat	Lists statistics about the network connection, including the IP addresses of active connections and the ports the computer is listening on.
netstat >>netlog.txt	Directs output to a text file.
netstat –b	Lists programs that are using the connection (see Figure 17-59) and is useful for finding malware that might be using the network. The –b switch requires an elevated command prompt.
netstat –b –o	Includes the process ID of each program listed. When you know the process ID, you can use the taskkill command to kill the process.
netstat –a	Lists statistics about all active connections.

Table 17-5 Netstat commands

© Cengage Learning 2014

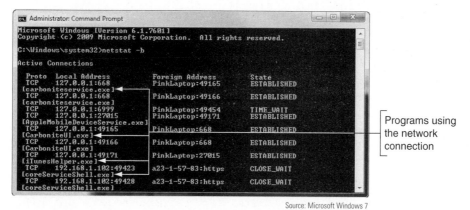

Source: Microsoft Windows 7

Figure 17-59 Netstat –b lists programs and their ports that are using a network connection

Notes Many commands other than netstat can use the >> parameter to redirect output to a text file. For example, try the ping or tracert command with this parameter.

17

A+
220-802
4.5

STRATEGIES FOR TROUBLESHOOTING NETWORK CONNECTIONS

With tools in hand, you're now ready to tackle network troubleshooting, including problem solving when there is no connectivity and limited or intermittent connectivity. Here is how to find out the extent of the problem:

1. To check for local connectivity, use Windows Explorer to try to access shared folders on the network. No connectivity might be caused by the network cable or its connection, a wireless switch not turned on, a bad network adapter, or TCP/IP settings in Windows.

2. Determine whether other computers on the network are having trouble with their connections. If the entire network is down, the problem is not isolated to the computer you are working on.

3. If you can access some, but not all, shared resources on the network, this limited connectivity problem might be caused by cables or a switch on the network or a problem at the computer sharing the resources you're trying to reach.

4. To test for Internet access, use a browser to surf the web. Problems with no Internet access can be caused by cables, a SOHO router, a broadband modem, or problems at the ISP.

5. To find out if a computer with limited or no connectivity was able to initially connect to a DHCP server on the network, check for an Automatic Private IP Address (APIPA). Recall from Chapter 15 that a computer assigns itself an APIPA if it is unable to find a DHCP server at the time it first connects to the network. Use the ipconfig command to find out the IP address (see Figure 17-60). In the results, an APIPA presents itself as the Autoconfiguration IPv4 Address, and the address begins with 169.254.

Source: Microsoft Windows 7

Figure 17-60   The network connection was not able to lease an IP address

Now let's see how to handle problems with no or intermittent connectivity and then we'll look at problems with Internet access.

PROBLEMS WITH NO CONNECTIVITY OR INTERMITTENT CONNECTIVITY

When a computer has no network connectivity or intermittent connectivity, begin by checking hardware and then move on to checking Windows network settings.

A+
220-802
4.5

Follow these steps to solve problems with hardware:

1. Check the status indicator lights on the NIC or the motherboard Ethernet port. A steady light indicates connectivity and a blinking light indicates activity (see Figure 17-61). Check the indicator lights on the router or switch at the other end. Try a different port on the device. If the router or switch is in a server closet and the ports are not well labelled, you can use a loopback plug to find out which port the computer is using. If you don't see either light, this problem must be resolved before you consider OS or application problems.

© Cengage Learning 2014

Figure 17-61   Status indicator lights verify connectivity for a network port

2. Check the network cable connection at both ends. Is the cable connected to a port on the motherboard that is disabled? It might need to be connected to the network port provided by a network card. A cable tester can verify the cable is good or if it is the correct cable (patch cable or crossover cable). Try a different network cable.

3. For wireless networking, make sure the wireless switch on a laptop is turned on. If you have no connectivity, limited connectivity, or intermittent connectivity, move the laptop to a new position in the hotspot. Use a wireless locator to find the best position. Rebooting a laptop might solve the problem of not receiving a signal. Problems with a low RF signal can sometimes be solved by moving the laptop or connecting to a different wireless access point with a stronger RF signal.

4. After you've checked cable connections and the wireless switch and the problem still persists, turn to Windows to repair the network connection. Use one of these methods:

   ◢ In an elevated command prompt window, use these two commands: **ipconfig /release** followed by **ipconfig /renew**.
   ◢ For Windows 7, in the Network and Sharing Center, click a yellow triangle or red **X** to launch Windows diagnostics (see Figure 17-62). If that doesn't work, click **Change adapter settings**, right-click the connection, and click **Disable** followed by **Enable**.
   ◢ For Vista, open the Network and Sharing Center window and click **Diagnose and repair**.
   ◢ For XP, in the Network Connections window, right-click the network icon and select **Repair** from the shortcut window.

17

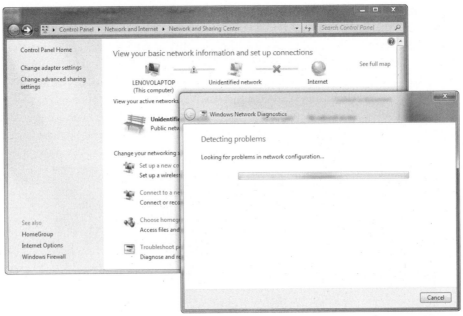

Source: Microsoft Windows 7

Figure 17-62 Windows indicates a network connectivity problem

If the problem is still not resolved, you need to dig deeper. Perhaps the problem is with the network adapter drivers. To solve problems with device drivers, which might also be related to a problem with the NIC, follow these steps:

1. Make sure the network adapter and its drivers are installed by checking for the adapter in Device Manager. Device Manager should report the device is working with no problems.

2. If errors are reported, try updating the device drivers. (Use another computer to download new drivers to a USB flash drive and then move the flash drive to this computer.) If the drivers still install with errors, look on the manufacturer's web site or installation CD that came bundled with the adapter for diagnostic software that might help diagnose the problem.

3. If Device Manager still reports errors, try running antivirus software and updating Windows. Then try replacing your network adapter. If that does not work, the problem might be a corrupted Windows installation.

Intermittent connectivity on a wired network might happen when a network device such as a VoIP phone is sensitive to electrical interference. You can solve this problem by attaching a **ferrite clamp** (see Figure 17-63) on the network cable near the phone port. This clamp helps to eliminate electromagnetic interference (EMI). Some cables come with preinstalled clamps, and you can also buy ferrite clamps to attach to other cables.

⚡ A+ Exam Tip The A+ 220-802 exam expects you to be able to troubleshoot network problems that present themselves as no connectivity or limited, local, or intermittent connectivity.

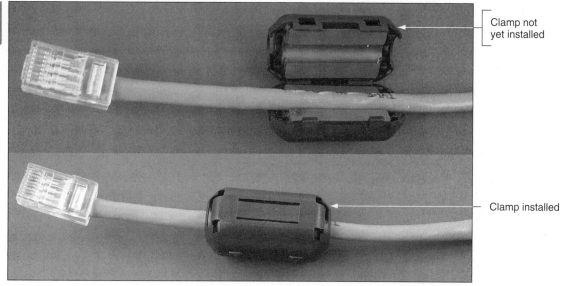

Clamp not
yet installed

Clamp installed

© Cengage Learning 2014

Figure 17-63 Install a ferrite clamp on a network cable to protect against electrical interference

PROBLEMS WITH INTERNET CONNECTIVITY

If you have local connectivity, but not Internet access, do the following:

1. Try recycling the connection to the ISP. Follow these steps:

   a. Unplug from the power source the cable modem, DSL modem, or other device that you use to connect to your ISP. Unplug the router. Wait about five minutes for the connection to break at the ISP.

   b. Plug in the cable modem, DSL modem, or other ISP device. Wait until the lights settle. Then plug in your router.

   c. On any computer on your network, use the Network and Sharing Center to repair the network connection. Open your browser and try to browse some web sites.

2. For a cable modem, check to make sure your television works. The service might be down. For a DSL connection, check to make sure your phone gives a dial tone. The phone lines might be down.

3. To eliminate the router as the source of the problem, connect one computer directly to the broadband modem. If you can access the Internet, you have proven the problem is with the router or cables going to it. Connect the router back into the network and check all the router settings. The problem might be with DHCP, the firewall settings, or port forwarding. Try updating the firmware on the router. If you are convinced all settings on the router are correct, but the connection to your ISP works without the router and does not work with the router, it's time to replace the router.

4. To eliminate DNS as the problem, follow these steps:

   a. Try substituting a domain name for the IP address in a ping command:

   ```
   ping www.course.com
   ```

   If this ping works, then you can conclude that DNS works. If an IP address works, but the domain name does not work, the problem lies with DNS.

   b. Try pinging your DNS server. To find out the IP address of your DNS server, open the firmware utility of your router and look on a status screen.

17

5. If you're having a problem accessing a particular computer on the Internet, try using the tracert command, for example:

```
tracert www.course.com
```

The results show computers along the route that might be giving delays.

6. If one computer on the network cannot access the Internet but other computers can, make sure MAC address filtering is disabled or this computer is allowed access.

7. Perhaps the problem is with your router firewall or Windows Firewall. How to verify router firewall settings is covered in Chapter 15, and Windows Firewall is covered in Chapter 18.

8. If you still cannot access the Internet, contact your ISP.

If some computers on the network have both local and Internet connectivity, but one computer does not, move on to checking problems on that computer, which can include TCP/IP settings and problems with applications.

USE TCP/IP UTILITIES TO SOLVE CONNECTIVITY PROBLEMS

No connectivity or no Internet access can be caused by Windows TCP/IP configuration and connectivity. Follow these steps to verify that the local computer is communicating over the network:

1. Using the Network and Sharing Center or the ipconfig command, try to release the current IP address and lease a new address. This process solves the problem of an IP conflict with other computers on the network or your computer's failure to connect to the network.

2. To find out if you have local connectivity, try to ping another computer on the network. To find out if you have Internet connectivity and DNS is working, try to ping a computer on the Internet using its host address. Try **ping www.course.com**. If this last command does not work, try the tracert command to find out if the problem is outside or inside your local network. Try **tracert www.course.com**.

3. In a command prompt window, enter **ipconfig /all**. Verify the IP address, subnet mask, and default gateway. For dynamic IP addressing, if the computer cannot reach the DHCP server, it assigns itself an APIPA, which is listed as an Autoconfiguration IPv4 Address that begins with 169.254 (refer back to Figure 17-60). In this case, suspect that the PC is not able to reach the network or the DHCP server is down.

4. Next, try the loopback address test. Enter the command **ping 127.0.0.1** (with no period after the final 1). Your computer should respond. If you get an error, assume the problem is TCP/IP settings on your computer. Compare the configuration to that of a working PC on the same network.

5. If you're having a problem with slow transfer speeds, suspect a process is hogging network resources. Use the **netstat –b** command to find out if the program you want to use to access the network is actually running.

6. Firewall settings might be wrong. Are port forwarding settings on the router and in Windows Firewall set correctly? You learn to configure Windows Firewall in the next chapter.

A+
220-802
4.5

7. Two computers on the network might have the same computer name. This command reports the error:

```
net view \\computername
```

8. If you can ping a computer, but cannot access it in Windows Explorer, verify the NTFS permissions and share settings on the remote computer. For help, see "Support and Troubleshoot Shared Folders and Files" earlier in the chapter. Also verify that the user account and password are the same on both computers.

9. Use this command to view a list of shared folders on the remote computer:

```
net view \\computername
```

If the command gives an error about access being denied, the problem is with permissions. Make sure the account you are using is an account recognized by the remote computer. Try this command to pass a new account to the remote computer:

```
net use \\computername /user:username
```

In this last command, if there is a space in the username, enclose the username in double quotation marks, as in:

```
net use \\computername /user:"Jean Andrews"
```

10. If the net view command using a computer name does not work, try the command using the remote computer's IP address, as in:

```
net view 192.168.1.102
```

If this command works, the problem is likely with name resolution. Make sure the computer name you are using is correct.

11. If you're having problems getting a network drive map to work, try making the connection with the net use command like this:

```
net use z: \\computername\folder
```

To disconnect a mapped network drive, use this command:

```
net use z: /delete
```

For slow network connections, try these things:

1. If a computer uses both a wireless and wired connection to the network, you can control the priority order of the connections. To see the priority order and find out which connection is faster, use the Networking tab of Task Manager (see Figure 17-64). Notice the wired connection graph is listed first, followed by the wireless connection graph. Windows is using the wired connection at the top the most, although it's slower than the wireless connection. (To compare connection speeds, compare 100 Mbps to 144 Mbps in the list at the bottom of the window.)

17

A+
220-802
4.5

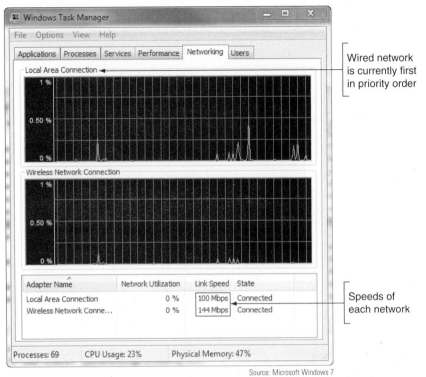

Wired network
is currently first
in priority order

Speeds of
each network

Source: Microsoft Windows 7

Figure 17-64 Use Task Manager to find out network connection speeds and
priority order

2. To change the priority order, open the Network and Sharing Center and click **Change**
adapter settings in the left pane. The Network Connections window appears (see the
left side of Figure 17-65). Press **Alt** to display the menu bar and, on the menu bar,
click **Advanced** and click **Advanced Settings**. The Advanced Settings box appears (see
the right side of Figure 17-65). Select the connection you want to move up in the priority order and then click the green up arrow, as shown in the figure. Then return to
the Task Manager window and confirm the priority order has changed.

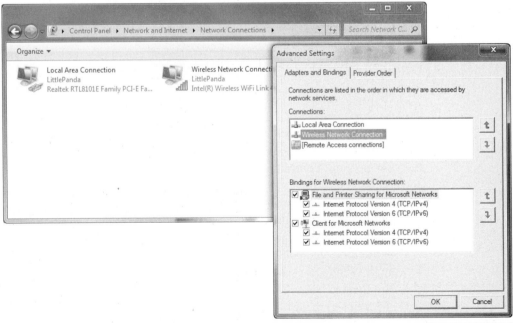

Source: Microsoft Windows 7

Figure 17-65 Change the priority order of the network connections

A+
220-802
4.5

> **Notes** Figure 17-64 reports the wired network is running at 100 Mbps (called Fast Ethernet), rather than 1000 Mbps (called Gigabit Ethernet). Most network adapters, switches, and routers sold today use Gigabit Ethernet. For best performance, the network adapters, switches, and routers on this network should be converted to Gigabit Ethernet so the entire network runs at the faster speed.

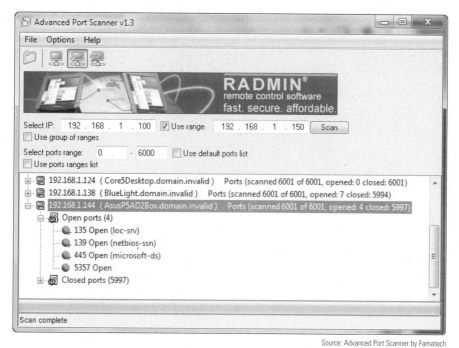

Source: Advanced Port Scanner by Famatech

Figure 17-66 Advanced Port Scanner shows open ports on networked computers

>> CHAPTER SUMMARY

Supporting Client/Server Applications

▲ The Internet Options dialog box is used to manage many Internet Explorer settings. Proxy settings are managed using the Connections tab, and add-ons are managed using the Programs tab.

▲ Remote Desktop gives you access to your Windows desktop from anywhere on the Internet. To turn on the Remote Desktop service, use the Remote tab on the System Properties box. The service listens at port 3389.

▲ The RemoteApp and Desktop Connection tool in Control Panel is used to install the client portion of a remote application that runs on a server in a corporate environment.

▲ Configure the Windows network adapter properties and BIOS setup to use Wake on LAN so that a computer can be powered up by specific network activity.

▲ A policy can be set using Group Policy to improve Quality of Service (QoS) for an application so that it gets a higher priority on the network.

17

Controlling Access to Folders and Files

◢ Controlling access to folders and files on a network is done by assigning rights to user accounts and assigning permissions to folders and files.

◢ Apply the principle of least privilege when assigning rights to users. Types of user accounts that can be used when creating a new user account in Windows 7/Vista are administrative and standard accounts. You can change the rights an account has by adding or removing it from a user group.

◢ Customized user groups that you create make it easier to manage rights to multiple user accounts.

◢ Three ways to share files and folders on the network are to use homegroup sharing, workgroup sharing, and domain controllers. With workgroup sharing, you can use share permissions and/or NTFS permissions.

◢ A mapped network drive makes it easier for users to access drives and folders on the network.

◢ Peer-to-peer networks use local shares, and a Windows domain supports administrative shares.

Troubleshooting Network Connections

◢ Cable testers are used to test cables and trace network cables through a building. A loopback plug is used to test network cables and ports. A wireless locator can help find a wireless hotspot with a strong RF signal.

◢ Useful Windows TCP/IP utilities are ping, ipconfig, nslookup, tracert, net use, net user, nbtstat, and netstat.

◢ When troubleshooting network problems, check hardware, device drivers, Windows, and the client or server application, in that order.

>> KEY TERMS

ActiveX control
administrative shares
Administrators group
anonymous users
application proxy
Authenticated Users group
Backup Operators
cable tester
Everyone group
ferrite clamp
file server
Group Policy (gpedit.msc)
Guests group
hidden share
inherited permissions
Internet Options
Ipconfig (IP configuration)

limited account
local shares
loopback plug
mstsc
nbtstat (NetBIOS over TCP/IP Statistics)
net use
net user
netstat (network statistics)
network drive map
Nslookup (name space lookup)
NTFS permissions
permission propagation
permissions
Ping (Packet InterNet Groper)
Power Users group
principle of least privilege

proxy server
Remote Admin
remote application
Remote Desktop
Remote Desktop Services
RemoteApp and Desktop Connection
reverse lookup
share permissions
simple file sharing
Terminal Services
Tracert (trace route)
Users group
Wake on LAN (WoL)
wireless locator

>> REVIEW QUESTIONS

1. Which IE Options tab would you use if you are on a corporate network and are having a problem connecting to a secured web site (one using HTTP over SSL or another encryption protocol)?

   a) Privacy tab

   b) Connections tab

   c) Advanced tab

   d) Security tab

2. If you were given a URL, how would you begin the process of installing the small client program used to connect to the remote application on the server?

   a) Enter the URL in the browser address box and press ENTER.

   b) Open the IE browser Options tab followed by the Connections tab; Copy the URL into the proxy area.

   c) Double-click the URL's associated .msi file in Windows Explorer.

   d) Within the Set up a new connection with RemoteApp and Desktop Connections wizard, enter the URL in the Connection URL field and click NEXT.

3. The ____ group includes all user accounts that can access the system except the Guest account.

   a) Authenticated Users

   b) Everyone

   c) Power Users

   d) Home Users

4. ____ occurs when permissions are passed from parent to child.

   a) Principle of least privilege

   b) Share permissions

   c) Permission propagation

   d) Network drive mapping

5. When troubleshooting problems with Internet connectivity, how can you eliminate DNS as a problem?

   a) Try substituting a domain name for the IP address in a ping command.

   b) Make sure MAC address filtering is disabled.

   c) Verify router firewall settings.

   d) Try the loopback address test by entering the command ping 127.0.0.1.

6. True or false? For Windows to enable QoS for installed applications, the network adapter must support QoS.

7. True or false? Policies can be applied to the computer or to a user.

8. True or false? Rights refer to which user accounts or user groups are allowed access to data files and folders.

9. True or false? If you want to share a folder, but don't want others to see the shared folder in Windows Explorer, add a $ to the end of the folder name.

17

10. True or false? A cable tester works on live cables.

11. ____ causes the host computer to turn on even from a powered-off state when a specific type of network activity happens.

12. ____ permissions are granted only to network users; these do not apply to local users of a computer.

13. By default, standard user accounts belong to the ____ group.

14. Folders and files on a computer that are shared with others on the network using local user accounts are called ____.

15. A(n) ____ is when you use the Nslookup command to find the host name when you know a computer's IP address.

Security Strategies

In Chapter 17, you learned the concepts and principles of classifying users and data and protecting that data by applying appropriate permissions to the data so that only the authorized users can access it. In this chapter, you'll learn about additional Windows tools and techniques to secure a workstation. You'll also learn how to use hardware and other physical security tools and techniques to secure a workstation and small network. Finally, you'll learn how to recognize that a system is infected with malware and how to clean an infected system and keep it clean.

As you learn about these and other security strategies, keep in mind that when implementing a security plan, be sure you know about and follow any security guidelines established by your organization or by government regulations that control your organization.

This chapter gives you the basics of securing a personal computer. Later in your career as a support technician, you can build on the skills of this chapter to implement even more security such as controlling how Windows stores its passwords. However, keep in mind that even the best security will eventually fail. As a thief once said, "Locks are for honest people," and a thief will eventually find a way to break through. Security experts tell us that security measures basically make it more difficult and time consuming for a thief to break through so that she gets discouraged and moves on to easier targets.

SECURING A WINDOWS WORKSTATION

Where you have a choice in the security that you use, keep in mind two goals, which are sometimes in conflict. One goal is to protect resources, and the other goal is to not interfere with the functions of the system. A computer or network can be so protected that no one can use it, or so accessible that anyone can do whatever they want with it. The trick is to provide enough security to protect your resources while still allowing users to work unhindered. Also, too much security can sometimes force workers to find nonsecure alternatives. For example, if you require users to change their passwords weekly, some of them might start writing their passwords down to help remember them.

© Phil Marden/Getty Images

Figure 18-1 Security measures should protect resources without hindering how users work

A+
220-802
2.1

> **Notes** The best protection against attacks is layered protection. If one security method fails, the next might stop an attacker. When securing a workstation, use as many layers of protection as is reasonable for the situation and are justified by the value of the resources you are protecting.

USE WINDOWS TO AUTHENTICATE USERS

Recall from Chapter 17 that controlling access to computer resources is done by authenticating and authorizing a user or process. A user is authenticated when he proves he is who he says he is. Recall that when a computer is on a Windows domain, the domain is responsible for authentication. For a peer-to-peer network, authentication must happen at the local computer. Normally, Windows authenticates a user with a Windows password.

As an administrator, when you first create an account, be sure to assign a password to that account. It's best to give the user the ability to change the password at any time. As an administrator, you can control how a user logs on, require a workstation be locked when the user steps away, disable the guest account, and reset a password if a user forgets it. Now let's see how to do all these chores to bring added security to a Windows workstation.

CONTROLLING HOW A USER LOGS ON

Normally, when a computer is first booted or comes back from a sleep state, Windows provides a welcome screen that shows all active user accounts (see Figure 18-2). Malware can sometimes display a false welcome screen to trick users into providing user account passwords. A more secure method of logon is to require the user to press **Ctrl+Alt+Delete** to get to a logon window.

Figure 18-2 Windows 7 Welcome screen

Source: Microsoft Windows 7

Use the netplwiz command to change the way Windows logon works:

◢ Using Windows 7/Vista, enter **netplwiz** in the search box and press **Enter**. The User Accounts box appears. On the Users tab (see the left side of Figure 18-3), you can add and remove users, change the groups a user is in, and reset a password. Click the **Advanced** tab (see the right side of Figure 18-3). Check **Require users to press Ctrl+Alt+Delete**. Click **Apply** and close the box.

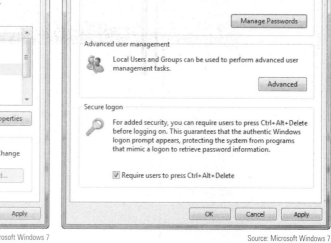

Source: Microsoft Windows 7

Source: Microsoft Windows 7

Figure 18-3 Change the way users log onto Windows

XP Differences To find out how to change the way Windows XP users log onto a system, see Appendix C.

When Crtl+Alt+Delete is required, the Welcome screen looks like that in Figure 18-4. When a user presses Ctrl+Alt+Delete, the Windows Welcome screen that appears has not been known to be intercepted by malware.

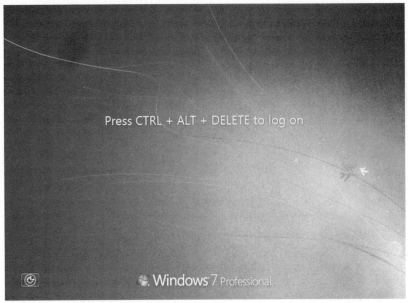

Source: Microsoft Windows 7

Figure 18-4 Windows 7 screen after the boot or returning from sleep state

POWER SETTINGS USED TO LOCK A WORKSTATION

To keep a system secure, users need to practice the habit of locking down their workstation each time they step away from their desks. The quickest way to do this is to press the **Windows key + L**. Another method is to press **Ctrl+Alt+Delete**. If the user is already logged on when she presses these keys, the login screen in Figure 18-5 appears. When the user clicks **Lock this computer**, Windows locks down. To unlock Windows, the user must enter her password. For this method to be effective, all user accounts need a password. Later in the chapter, you learn to use Group Policy to make passwords a requirement.

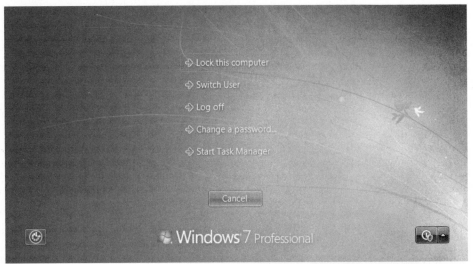

Source: Microsoft Windows 7

Figure 18-5 Results of pressing Ctrl-Alt-Del when a user is already logged on

A+
220-802
2.1, 2.3

APPLYING | CONCEPTS   REQUIRE A PASSWORD TO WAKE UP A COMPUTER

An unauthorized user might get access to a system when a user steps away from her workstation and forgets to lock it. To better secure the workstation, you can activate the screensaver (turn off the display) after a short period of inactivity and require a password be used to turn on the display and wake up the computer. Follow these steps:

1. In the Control Panel, click **Power Options** in the Hardware and Sound group.

2. In the Power Options window (see Figure 18-6), click **Change when the computer sleeps**.

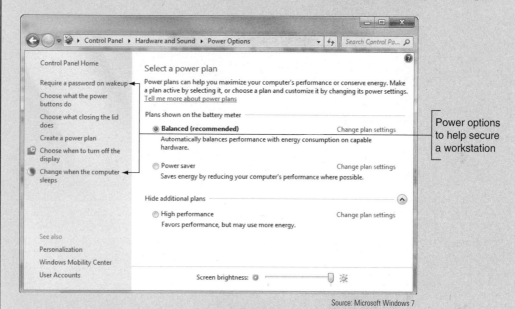

Source: Microsoft Windows 7

Figure 18-6   Windows power options available on the Power Options window to help lock down a workstation

3. In the Edit Plan Settings window, set when the display turns off and when the computer goes to sleep (see Figure 18-7). Click **Save changes**.

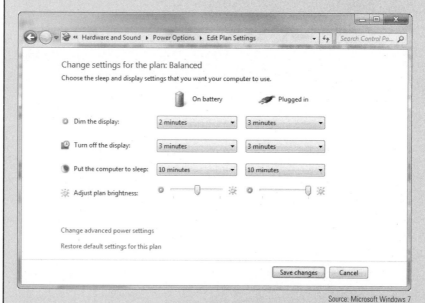

Source: Microsoft Windows 7

Figure 18-7   To protect the computer's resources from uninvited users, put the computer to sleep after a short period of inactivity

18

A+
220-802
2.1, 2.3

4. In the Power Options window, click **Require a password on wakeup**. In the System Settings window, make sure **Require a password (recommended)** is selected (see Figure 18-8). If you need to change this setting, first click **Change settings that are currently unavailable**. Save your changes and close all windows.

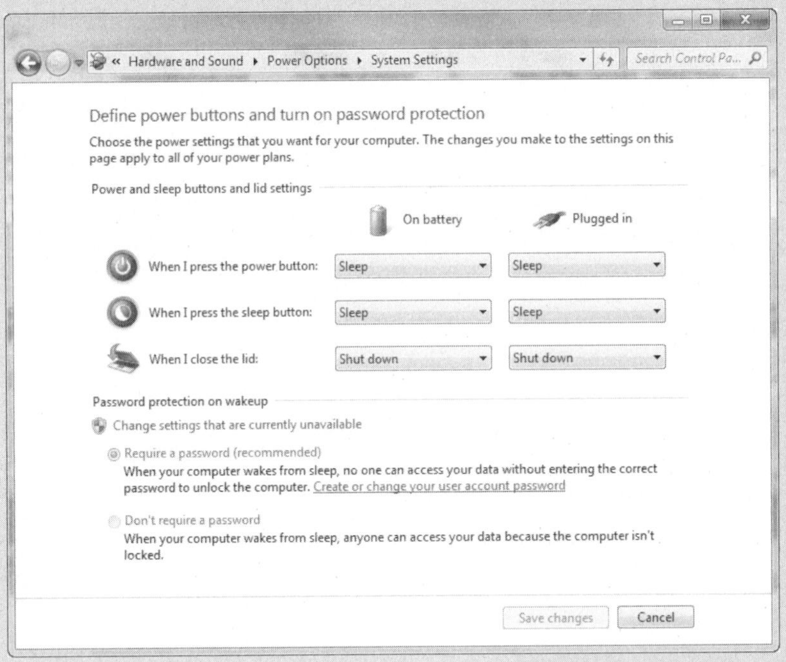

Figure 18-8   Require a password when the computer wakes up

Source: Microsoft Windows 7

A+
220-802
2.1

DISABLE THE GUEST ACCOUNT

The Guest account is disabled by default and should remain disabled. If you want to set up an account for visitors, create a standard account and name it Visitor. To make sure the Guest account is disabled, in Control Panel, click **Add or remove user accounts** in the User Accounts and Family Safety group. In the list of accounts, verify the Guest account is turned off. If it is not, double-click it and click **Turn off the guest account** (see Figure 18-9).

Figure 18-9   For best security, turn off the Guest account

Source: Microsoft Windows 7

RESET A USER PASSWORD

Sometimes a user forgets his or her password or the password is compromised. If this happens, as an administrator, you can reset the password. Keep in mind, however, that resetting a password causes the OS to lock the user out from using encrypted files or email and from

A+
220-802
2.1

using Internet passwords stored on the computer. For business and professional editions of Windows, reset a password using the Computer Management console. For all editions of Windows, you can use the netplwiz command or the Control Panel to reset a password for another user. Follow these steps:

1. In Control Panel, click **Add or remove user accounts** in the User Accounts and Family group. Double-click the account and then click **Change the password**. The Change Password window opens (see Figure 18-10).

2. Enter the new password twice and a password hint. Click **Change password**. Close the window.

Source: Microsoft Windows 7

Figure 18-10 Reset a user's password

A+
220-802
2.1, 2.3

CREATE STRONG PASSWORDS

A password needs to be a **strong password**, which means it should not be easy to guess by both humans and computer programs designed to hack passwords.

A strong password, such as @y&kK1ff, meets all of the following criteria:

- ◢ Use eight or more characters (14 characters or longer is better).
- ◢ Combine uppercase and lowercase letters, numbers, and symbols.
- ◢ Use at least one symbol in the second through sixth position of your password.
- ◢ Don't use consecutive letters or numbers, such as "abcdefg" or "12345."
- ◢ Don't use adjacent keys on your keyboard, such as "qwerty."
- ◢ Don't use your logon name in the password.
- ◢ Don't use words in any language. Don't even use numbers for letters (as in "p@ssw0rd") because programs can now guess those as well.
- ◢ Don't use the same password for more than one system.

> **Notes** To keep from having to write down a password, create one that is easy to remember, for example, mF1dI8iC. The letters in the password stand for "My favorite dessert is ice cream." If you must keep track of lots of different passwords, password management software can hold your passwords safely so that you don't forget them.

18

A+
220-802
2.1, 2.3

In some situations, a blank Windows password might be more secure than an easy-to-guess password such as "1234." That's because you cannot authenticate to a Windows computer from a remote computer unless the user account has a password. A criminal might be able to guess an easy password and authenticate remotely. For this reason, if your computer is always sitting in a protected room such as your home office and you don't intend to access it remotely, you might choose to use no password. However, if you travel with a laptop, always use a strong password.

If you write your password down, keep it in as safe a place as you would the data you are protecting. Don't send your passwords over email or chat. Change your passwords regularly, and don't type your passwords on a public computer. For example, computers in hotel lobbies or Internet cafes should only be used for web browsing—not for logging on to your email account or online banking account. These computers might be running keystroke-logging software put there by criminals to record each keystroke. Several years ago, while on vacation, I entered credit card information on a computer in a hotel lobby in a foreign country. Months later, I was still protesting $2 or $3 charges to my credit card from that country. Trust me. Don't do it—I speak from experience.

FILE AND FOLDER ENCRYPTION

In Windows, files and folders can be encrypted using the Windows **Encrypted File System (EFS)**. This encryption works only with the NTFS file system and business and professional editions of Windows. If a folder is marked for encryption, every file created in the folder or copied to the folder will be encrypted. An encrypted file remains encrypted if you move it from an encrypted folder to an unencrypted folder on the same or another NTFS volume. To encrypt a folder or file, right-click it and open its Properties box (see Figure 18-11).

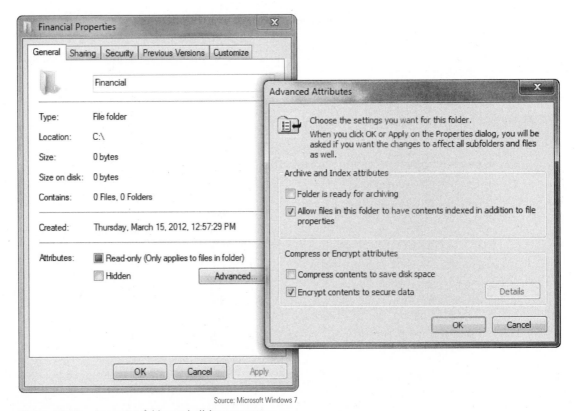

Source: Microsoft Windows 7

Figure 18-11 Encrypt a folder and all its contents

On the General tab, click **Advanced**. On the Advanced Attributes tab, check **Encrypt contents to secure data** and click **OK**. In Windows Explorer, encrypted file and folder names are displayed in green.

WINDOWS FIREWALL SETTINGS

A+
220-802
1.1, 1.4,
1.5, 1.6,
2.1

Recall from Chapter 15 that a router can serve as a hardware firewall to protect its network from attack over the Internet. Recall that the best protection from attack is layered protection (see Figure 18-12). In addition to a hardware network firewall, a large corporation might use a software firewall, also called a corporate firewall, installed on a computer that stands between the Internet and the network to protect the network. This computer has two network cards installed, and the installed corporate firewall filters the traffic between the two cards.

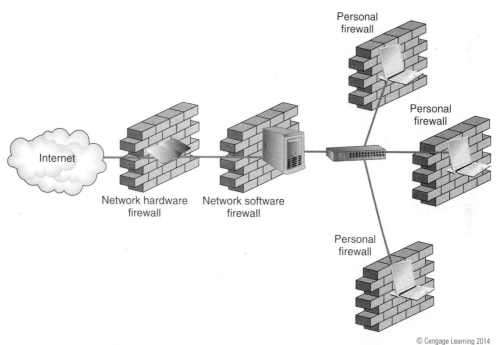

© Cengage Learning 2014

Figure 18-12   Three types of firewalls used to protect a network and individual computers on the network

18

A personal firewall, also called a host firewall, is software installed on a computer to protect this computer. A personal firewall provides redundant protection from attacks over the Internet and also protects a computer from attack from other computers on the same network. When setting up a SOHO network or a personal computer, configure a personal firewall on each computer.

Windows Firewall is a personal firewall that protects a computer from intrusion and is automatically configured when you set your network location in the Network and Sharing Center. However, you might want to customize these settings. For example, recall from Chapter 17 that you customized Windows Firewall to allow access through Remote Desktop connections.

A+
220-802
1.1, 1.4,
1.5, 1.6,
2.1

APPLYING | CONCEPTS CONFIGURE WINDOWS FIREWALL

Follow these steps to find out how to configure Windows Firewall:

1. Use one of these methods to open Windows Firewall:

   ◢ Open the **Network and Sharing Center** and in the lower part of the left pane, click **Windows Firewall**.

   ◢ In Control Panel, click **System and Security** and then click **Windows Firewall**.

   The Windows Firewall window is shown in Figure 18-13.

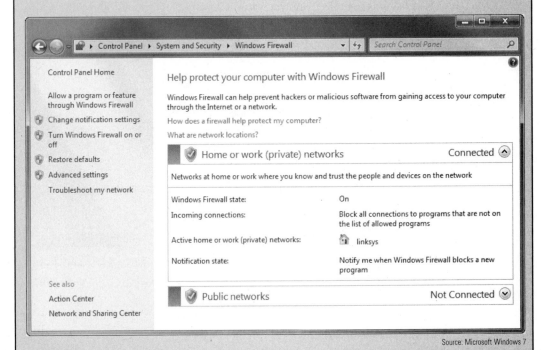

Source: Microsoft Windows 7

Figure 18-13 Windows Firewall shows the computer currently connected to a private network

2. To control firewall settings for each type of network location, click **Turn Windows Firewall on or off** in the left pane. The Windows Firewall Customize Settings window appears (see Figure 18-14). Notice in the figure Windows Firewall is turned on for each network location.

3. To allow no exceptions though the firewall on a home or work (private) network or public network, check **Block all incoming connections, including those in the list of allowed programs**. After you have made your changes, click **OK**.

4. You can allow an exception to your firewall rules. To change the programs allowed through the firewall, in the Windows Firewall window shown in Figure 18-13, click **Allow a program or feature through Windows Firewall**. The Allowed Programs window appears (see Figure 18-15).

5. Find the program you want to allow to initiate a connection from a remote computer to this computer. In the right side of the window, click either **Home/Work (Private)** or **Public** to indicate which type of network location the program is allowed to use. If you don't see your program in the list, click **Allow another program** to see more programs or to add your own. (If the option is gray, click **Change settings** to enable it.) When you are finished making changes, click **OK** to return to the Windows Firewall window.

A+
220-802
1.1, 1.4,
1.5, 1.6,
2.1

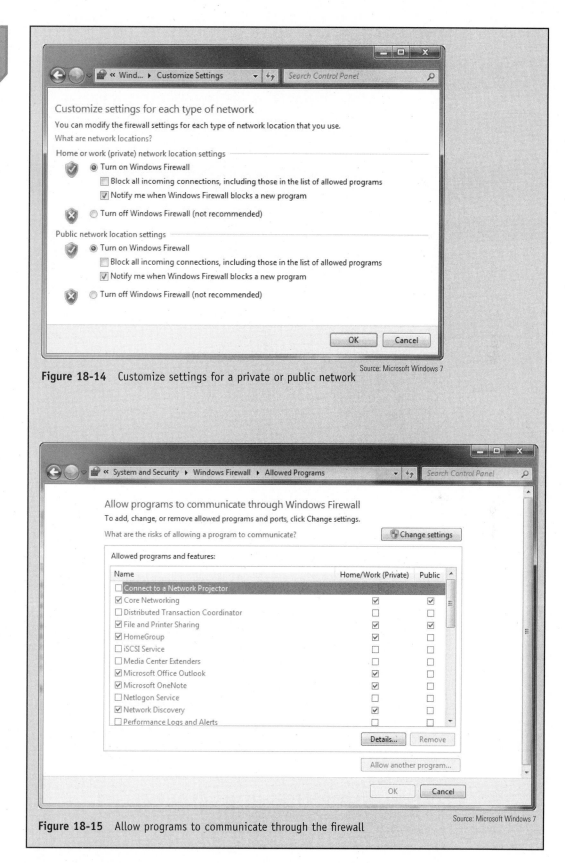

Figure 18-14 Customize settings for a private or public network

Source: Microsoft Windows 7

Figure 18-15 Allow programs to communicate through the firewall

Source: Microsoft Windows 7

18

A+
220-802
1.1, 1.4,
1.5, 1.6,
2.1

6. For even more control over firewall settings, in the Windows Firewall window, click **Advanced settings**. The Windows Firewall with Advanced Security window opens. In the left pane, select Inbound Rules or Outbound Rules. A list of programs appears. Right-click a program and select **Properties** from the shortcut menu. Using the Properties box, you have full control of how exceptions work to get through the firewall, including which users, protocols, ports, and remote computers can use it (see Figure 18-16).

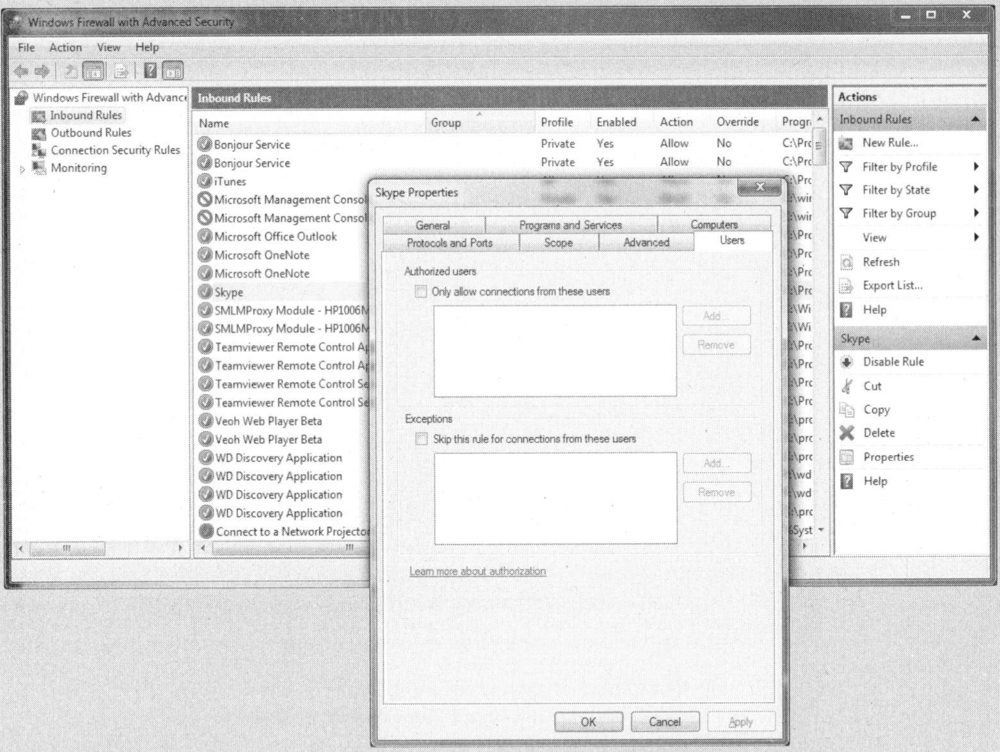

Source: Microsoft Windows 7

Figure 18-16 Use advanced settings to control exactly how a program can get through Windows Firewall

> **Vista Differences** In Vista, you can allow exceptions to Windows Firewall by program name or port number. To see how the Vista Windows Firewall works differently from Windows 7, see Appendix B.

> **XP Differences** To see how Windows Firewall in Windows XP works differently from Windows 7, see Appendix C.

A+
220-802
1.8, 2.3

LOCAL SECURITY POLICES USING GROUP POLICY

Recall from Chapter 17 that the Group Policy utility controls what users can do with a system and how the system is used and is available with business and professional editions of Windows. Using Group Policy, you can set security policies to help secure a workstation. For example, you can set policies to require all users to have passwords and to rename default user accounts.

A+
220-802
1.8, 2.3

APPLYING | CONCEPTS APPLY LOCAL SECURITY POLICIES

Follow these steps to set a few important security policies:

1. Log onto Windows using an administrator account on a system using Windows 7 Professional, Ultimate, or Enterprise.

2. To start Group Policy, use the **gpedit.msc** command in the search box. The Local Group Policy Editor console opens.

3. To change a policy, first use the left pane to drill down into the appropriate policy group and then use the right pane to view and edit a policy. Here are important security policies you might want to change:

   ▲ *Change default usernames.* A hacker is less likely to hack into the built-in Administrator account or Guest account if you change the names of these default accounts. To change the name of the Administrator account, drill down in the **Computer Configuration**, **Windows Settings**, **Security Settings**, **Local Policies**, **Security Options** group (see the left side of Figure 18-17). In the right pane, double-click **Accounts: Rename administrator account**. In the Properties box for this policy (see the right side of Figure 18-17), change the name and click **OK**. To change the name of the Guest account, use the policy **Account: Rename guest account**.

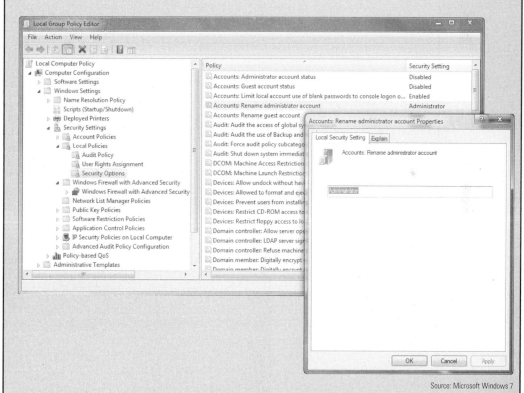

Source: Microsoft Windows 7

Figure 18-17   Use Group Policy to rename a default user account

> **Notes** The Properties box for many policies offers the Explain tab. Use this tab to read more about a policy and how it works.

18

A+
220-802
1.8, 2.3

▲ *Require user passwords.* To require that all user accounts have passwords, drill down to the **Computer Configuration**, **Windows Settings**, **Security Settings**, **Account Policies**, **Password Policy** group (see the left side of Figure 18-18). Use the **Minimum password length** policy and set the minimum length to six or eight characters (see the right side of Figure 18-18).

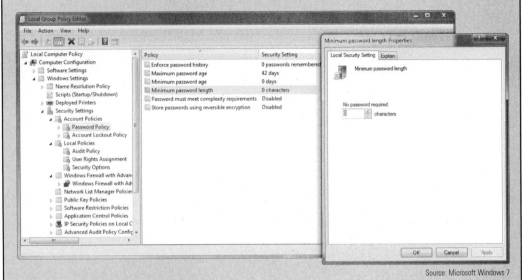

Source: Microsoft Windows 7

Figure 18-18 Require that each user account have a password by setting the minimum password length policy

▲ *Allow only a single logon.* By default, Windows allows fast user switching, which means multiple users can log onto Windows. To disable this feature and allow only a single logon, drill down to the **Computer Configuration**, **Administrative Templates**, **System**, **Logon** group. Then use the **Hide entry points for Fast User Switching** policy. Enable this policy so that the *Switch user* option is dimmed and not available on the Shut down menu on the Start menu.

▲ *Audit logon failures.* Group Policy offers several auditing policies that monitor and log security events. These Security logs can then be viewed using Event Viewer. To set an audit policy to monitor a failed logon event, drill down to the **Computer Configuration**, **Windows Settings**, **Security Settings**, **Local Policies**, **Audit Policy** group. Use the **Audit logon events** policy. You can audit logon successes and failures. To keep the log from getting too big, you can select **Failure** to only log these events.

▲ *Disable logon and shutdown scripts.* Policies can run scripts for the computer or user during logon or shutdown. These scripts can contain programs, which might contain malware. To manage logon scripts, in the Computer Configuration or User Configuration group, drill down to the **Administrative Templates**, **System**, **Logon** group. Use the **Run these programs at user logon** policy. To manage shutdown scripts, drill down to the **Administrative Templates**, **System**, **Scripts** group. For a list of folders where Group Policy stores these scripts, see Appendix G.

4. When you finish setting your local security policies, close the Local Group Policy Editor console. To put into effect the changes you have made, reboot the system or enter the command **Gpupdate.exe** in a command prompt window.

> **Notes** Sometimes policies overlap or conflict. To find out the resulting policies for the computer or user that are currently applied to the system, you can use the **Gpresult** command in a command prompt window with parameters. To find out more about this command, search the *technet.microsoft.com* web site.

A+
220-802
1.8, 2.3

Notes The group of policies in the Local Computer Policy, Computer Configuration, Windows Settings, Security Settings group can also be edited from the Control Panel. In the Control Panel, open the **Administrative Tools** and double-click **Local Security Policy**.

A+
220-802
1.1

USE BITLOCKER ENCRYPTION

BitLocker Encryption in Windows professional and business editions locks down a hard drive by encrypting the entire Windows volume and any other volume on the drive. It's a bit complicated to set up and has some restrictions that you need to be aware of before you decide to use it. It is intended to work in partnership with file and folder encryption to provide data security.

A+ Exam Tip The A+ 220–802 exam expects you to know about the features and benefits of BitLocker Encryption.

The three ways you can use BitLocker Encryption depend on the type of protection you need and the computer hardware available:

- *Computer authentication.* Many notebook computers have a chip on the motherboard called the TPM (Trusted Platform Module) chip. The TPM chip holds the BitLocker encryption key (also called the startup key). If the hard drive is stolen from the notebook and installed in another computer, the data would be safe because BitLocker would not allow access without the startup key stored on the TPM chip. Therefore, this method authenticates the computer. However, if the motherboard fails and is replaced, you'll need a backup copy of the startup key to access data on the hard drive. (You cannot move the TPM chip from one motherboard to another.)
- *User authentication.* For computers that don't have TPM, the startup key can be stored on a USB flash drive (or other storage device the computer reads before the OS is loaded), and the flash drive must be installed before the computer boots. This method authenticates the user. For this method to be the most secure, the user must never leave the flash drive stored with the computer. (Instead, the user might keep the USB startup key on his key ring.)
- *Computer and user authentication.* For *best* security, a PIN or password can be required at every startup in addition to TPM. Using this method, both the computer and the user are authenticated.

BitLocker Encryption provides great security, but security comes with a price. For instance, you risk the chance your TPM will fail or you will lose all copies of the startup key. In these events, recovering the data can be messy. Therefore, use BitLocker only if the risks of BitLocker giving problems outweigh the risks of stolen data. And, if you decide to use BitLocker, be sure to make extra copies of the startup key and/or password and keep them in a safe location.

For detailed instructions on how to set up BitLocker Encryption, see the Microsoft Knowledge Base article 933246 at *support.microsoft.com*.

18

USE BIOS FEATURES TO PROTECT THE SYSTEM

Many motherboards for desktop and laptop computers offer several BIOS security features, including power-on passwords, support for intrusion-detection devices, and support for a TPM chip. Power-on passwords include a supervisor password (required to change BIOS setup), user password (required to use the system or view BIOS setup), and a drive lock password (required to access the hard drive). The drive lock password is stored on the hard drive so that it will still control access to the drive in the event the drive is removed from the computer and installed on another system. Figure 18-19 shows one BIOS setup Security screen where you can set the hard drive password. This screen can also be used to set the supervisor and user passwords to the system.

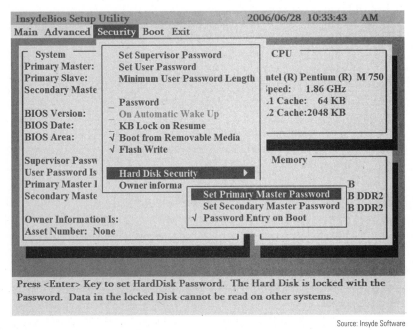

Source: Insyde Software

Figure 18-19   Submenu shows how to set a hard drive password that will be written on the drive

Some laptops contain the **LoJack** technology on the motherboard to support the laptop-tracking software Computrace LoJack by Absolute Software (*www.absolute.com*). When you install the software on your laptop and if the laptop is ever stolen, Absolute can lock down your hard drive and track down the laptop.

ADDITIONAL METHODS TO PROTECT RESOURCES

Securing data and other computer resources might seem like a never-ending task. Come to think of it, that's probably true. In this part of the chapter, you'll learn even more ways to securely authenticate users on a large network, physically protect computer resources, destroy data before you toss out a storage device, and educate users to not unintentionally compromise the security measures you've put in place.

A+
220-802
2.1

AUTHENTICATE USERS FOR LARGE NETWORKS

Normally, Windows authenticates a user with a Windows password. However, the best authentication happens when a user (1) knows something (such as a Windows password) and (2) possesses something, which is called the security token (such as a smart card or biometric data; for example, a fingerprint scan). This extra authentication is sometimes used to secure access to a corporate network. In this part of the chapter, you learn about smart cards and biometric data used to add this extra authentication. One warning to keep in mind is a smart card or biometric data should be used in addition to, and not as a replacement to a Windows password.

SMART CARDS

The most popular type of token used to authenticate a user is a **smart card**, which is any small device that contains authentication information. The information on the smart card can be keyed into a logon window by a user, read by a **smart card reader** (when the device is inserted in the reader), or transmitted wirelessly. (You also need to know that some people don't consider a card to be a smart card unless it has an embedded microprocessor.)

> **A+ Exam Tip** The A+ 220-802 exam expects you to know about biometric data, badges, key fobs, RFID badges, retinal scans, and RSA tokens used to authenticate to a computer system or network.

Here are some variations of smart cards:

▲ *Key fob*. A key fob is a smart card that fits conveniently on a keychain. RSA Security (*www.rsasecurity.com*), a leader in authentication technologies, makes several types of smart cards, called SecurIDs or **RSA tokens**. One SecurID key fob by RSA Security is shown in Figure 18-20. The number on the key fob changes every 60 seconds. When a user logs onto the network, she must enter the number on the key fob, which is synchronized with the network authentication service. Entering the number proves that the user has the smart card in hand. Because the device does not actually make physical contact with the system, it is called a contactless token.

Courtesy of RSA, The Security Division of EMC

Figure 18-20 A smart card such as this SecurID key fob is used to authenticate a user gaining access to a secured network

18

▲ *Wireless token.* Another type of contactless token uses wireless technology to transmit information kept by the token to the computer system. A Radio Frequency Identification (RFID) token transmits authentication to the system when the token gets in range of a query device. For example, an **RFID badge** worn by an employee can allow the employee entrance into a locked area of a building.

▲ *Memory stripe card.* An example of a contact token is an employee badge or other smart card with a magnetic stripe that can be read by a smart card reader (see Figure 18-21). Because these cards don't contain a microchip, they are sometimes called memory cards. They can be read by a smart card reader, such as the one shown in Figure 18-22, which connects to a computer using a USB port. Used in this way, they are part of the authentication process into a network. The magnetic stripe can contain information about the user to indicate their rights on the system. The major disadvantage of this type of smart card is that each computer used for authentication must have one of these smart card reader machines installed. Also, in the industry, because a card with a magnetic stripe does not contain a microchip, some in the industry don't consider it to fit into the category of a smart card, but rather simply call it a magnetic stripe card.

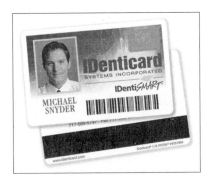 

Courtesy of IDenticard Systems

Figure 18-21   A smart card with a magnetic stripe can be used inside or outside a computer network

Courtesy of Athena-SCS, Inc.

Figure 18-22   This smart card reader by Athena Smartcard Solutions (*www.athena-scs.com*) uses a USB connection

▲ *Cell phone with token.* An app installed on a cell phone can hold the user's token, which includes a digital signature or digital certificate. A **digital certificate** is assigned by a Certification Authority (for example, VeriSign—*www.verisign. com*) and is used to prove you are who you say you are. The authentication can be sent to the network via a USB connection, text message, phone call, or Bluetooth connection. This method is sometimes used when an employee authenticates to a VPN connection to the corporate network.

A+
220-802
2.1

BIOMETRIC DATA

As part of the authentication process, some systems use biometric data to validate the person's physical body, which, in effect, becomes the token. A **biometric device** is an input device that inputs biological data about a person, which can identify a person's fingerprints, handprints, face, voice, retinal, iris, and handwritten signatures. Figure 18-23 shows one biometric input device, an iris reader, that scans your iris. Iris scanning is one of the most accurate ways to identify a person using biological data. **Retinal scanning** scans the blood vessels on the back of the eye and is considered the most reliable of all biometric data scanning. However, the equipment is more expensive and it takes more time to make a retinal scan than other scans. Retinal scanning is used for the highest level of security by the government and military.

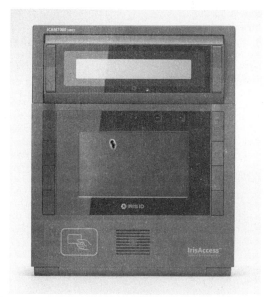

Courtesy of Iris ID, Inc.

Figure 18-23 The iCAM7000 iris recognition camera
by Iris ID Systems, Inc.

PHYSICAL SECURITY METHODS AND DEVICES

Physically protecting your computer and data might be one of the security measures you will implement when on the job. Here are some suggestions:

▲ *If your data is really private, keep it behind a locked door or under lock and key.* You can use all kinds of security methods to encrypt, password protect, and hide data, but if it really is that important, one obvious thing you can do is to keep the computer behind a locked door. You can also store the data on a removable storage device such as an external hard drive and, when you're not using the data, put the drive in a fireproof safe. And, of course, keep two copies. Sounds simple, but it works. And don't forget printouts of sensitive documents should also be kept under lock and key.

▲ *Lock down the computer case.* Some computer cases allow you to add a lock so that you can physically prevent others from opening the case (see Figure 18-24). Some motherboards have a BIOS feature that alerts you when an intrusion has been detected.

18

A+
220-802
2.1

Courtesy of Innovative Security Products Inc.

Figure 18-24 This computer case allows you to use a lock and key to keep intruders from opening the case

▲ *Lock and chain.* You can also use a lock and chain to physically tie a computer to a desk or other permanent fixture so someone can't walk away with it. Figure 18-25 shows a cable lock system for a laptop. Most laptops have a security slot on the case to connect the cable lock.

Courtesy of Kensington Computer Group

Figure 18-25 Use a cable lock system to secure a notebook computer to a desk to help prevent it from being stolen

▲ *Privacy filters.* To keep other people from viewing a monitor screen, you can install a **privacy filter** that fits over the screen to prevent it from being read from a wide angle.

A+
220-802
2.1

▲ *Theft-prevention plate.* As an added precaution, physically mark a computer case or laptop so it can be identified if it is later stolen. You embed a theft-prevention plate into the case or engrave your ID information into it. The identifying numbers or bar code identify you, the owner, and can also clearly establish to police that the notebook has been stolen. Two sources of theft-prevention plates and cable locks are Computer Security Products, Inc. (*www.computersecurity.com*) and Flexguard Security System (*www.flexguard.com*). To further help you identify stolen equipment, record serial numbers and model numbers in a safe place separate from the equipment.

A+
220-802
2.1, 2.4

DATA DESTRUCTION

Don't throw out a hard drive, CD, DVD, tape, or other media that might have personal or corporate data on it unless you know the data can't be stolen off the device. Trying to wipe a drive clean by deleting files or even using Windows to format the drive does not completely destroy the data. Here are some ways to destroy printed documents and sanitize storage devices:

▲ *Use a paper shredder.* Use a paper shredder to destroy all documents that contain sensitive data.

> **🔦 A+ Exam Tip** The A+ 220-802 exam expects you to know about data-destruction techniques, including a low-level format, drive wipe, shredder, degausser, and drill, which can do physical damage to a hard drive.

▲ *Overwrite data on the drive.* You can perform a low-level format of a drive to overwrite the data with zeroes. (A low-level format is different from a Windows format. A device receives a low-level format at the factory, which writes sector markings on the drive. You can obtain a low-level format utility from the device manufacturer.) You can also use a zero-fill utility that overwrites all data on the drive with zeroes. Either method works for most low-security situations, but professional thieves know how to break through this type of destruction. If you use one of these utilities, run it multiple times to write zeroes on top of zeroes. Data recovery has been known to reach 14 levels of overwrites because each bit is slightly offset from the one under it.

▲ *Physically destroy the storage media.* Use a drill to drill many holes through the drive housing all the way through to the other side of the housing. Break CDs and DVDs in half and do similar physical damage to flash drives or tapes. Again, expert thieves can still recover some of the data.

▲ *For magnetic devices, use a degausser.* A **degausser** exposes a storage device to a strong magnetic field to completely erase the data on a magnetic hard drive or tape drive (see Figure 18-26). For best destruction, use the degausser and also physically destroy the drive. Degaussing does not erase data on a solid state hard drive or other flash media because these devices don't use a magnetic surface to hold data.

▲ *For solid state devices, use a Secure Erase utility.* As required by government regulations for personal data privacy, the American National Standards Institute (ANSI) developed the **ATA Secure Erase** standards for securely erasing data from solid state devices such as a USB flash drive or SSD drive. You can download a Secure Erase utility from the manufacturer of the device and run it to securely erase all data on the device.

▲ *Use a secure data-destruction service.* For the very best data destruction, consider a secure data-destruction service. To find a service, search the web for "secure data destruction." However, don't use a service unless you have thoroughly checked its references and guarantees of legal compliance that your organization is required to meet.

18

A+
220-802
2.1, 2.4

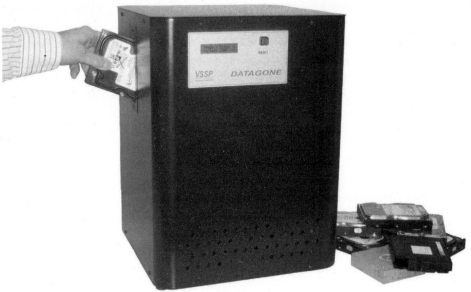

Courtesy of VS Security Products, Ltd.

Figure 18-26 Use a degausser to sanitize a magnetic hard drive or tape

A+
220-802
2.1, 2.2

EDUCATE USERS

Generally speaking, the weakest link in setting up security in a computer environment is people. That's because people can often be tricked into giving out private information. Even with all the news and hype about identity theft and criminal web sites, it's amazing how well these techniques still work. Many users naively download a funny screen saver, open an email attachment, or enter credit card information on a web site without regard to security. In the computer arena, **social engineering** is the practice of tricking people into giving out private information or allowing unsafe programs into the network or computer.

A good support technician is aware of the criminal practices used, and is able to teach users how to recognize this mischief and avoid it. Here is a list of important security measures that users need to follow to protect passwords and the computer system:

- ◢ Never give out your passwords to anyone, not even a supervisor or tech support person who calls and asks for it.
- ◢ Don't store your passwords on a computer. Some organizations even forbid employees from writing down their passwords.
- ◢ Don't use the same password on more than one system (computer, network, application, or web site).
- ◢ Be aware of **shoulder surfing** when other people secretly peek at your monitor screen as you work. A privacy filter can help.
- ◢ Lock down your workstation each time you step away from your desk.
- ◢ Users need to be on the alert for **tailgating**, which is when someone who is unauthorized follows the employee through a secured entrance to a room or building. Another form of tailgating is when a user steps away from her computer and another person continues to use the Windows session when the system is not properly locked.

Beware of online social engineering techniques. For example, don't be fooled by scam email or an **email hoax** such as the one shown in Figure 18-27. When the user who received this email scanned the attached file using antivirus software, the software reported the file contained malware.

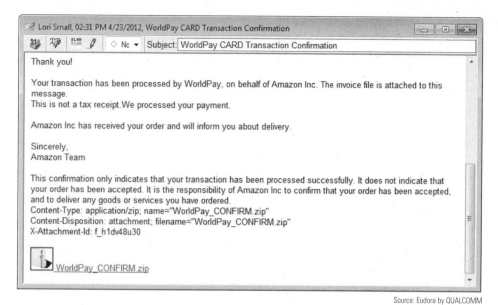

Figure 18-27   This phishing technique using an email message with an attached file is an example of social engineering

A+ Exam Tip   The A+ 220-802 exam expects you to be aware of social engineering situations such as tailgating, phishing, and shoulder surfing that might compromise security.

Here are some good sites to help you debunk a virus hoax or email hoax:

- *www.snopes.com* by Barbara and David Mikkelson
- *www.viruslist.com* by Kaspersky Lab
- *www.vmyths.com* by Rhode Island Soft Systems, Inc.

Don't forward an email hoax. When you get a hoax, if you know the person who sent it to you, do us all a favor and send that person some of these links!

Here are some other types of online social engineering situations:

- **Phishing** (pronounced "fishing") is a type of identity theft where the sender of an email message scams you into responding with personal data about yourself. The scam artist baits you by asking you to verify personal data on your bank account, ISP account, credit card account, or something of that nature. Often you are tricked into clicking a link in the email message, which takes you to an official-looking site complete with corporate or bank logos where you are asked to enter your user ID and password to enter the site.
- An email message might contain a link that leads to a malicious script. To keep the script from running, copy and paste the link to your browser address bar instead.

A study by Dell showed that 65 percent of business travelers have not secured the corporate data on their hard drives, and 42 percent don't back up that data. Here are some commonsense rules to help protect a laptop when traveling:

- When traveling, always know where your laptop is. If you're standing at an airport counter, tuck your laptop case securely between your ankles. At security checkpoints, pay attention to your belongings; tell yourself to stay focused. When flying, never check in your laptop as baggage, and don't store it in airplane overhead bins; keep it at your feet.

18

- ◢ Never leave a laptop in an unlocked car. If you leave your laptop in a hotel room, use a laptop cable lock to secure it to a table.
- ◢ When at work, lock your laptop in a secure place or use a laptop cable lock to secure it to your desk.

A PC support technician will most certainly be called on to help a user rid a system of malware. Let's turn our attention to how to deal with that problem.

DEALING WITH MALICIOUS SOFTWARE

Malicious software, also called **malware**, or a **computer infestation**, is any unwanted program that means you harm and is transmitted to your computer without your knowledge. **Grayware** is any annoying and unwanted program that might or might not mean you harm. In this part of the chapter, you'll learn about the different types of malware and grayware, what to do to clean up an infected system, and how to protect a system from infection.

WHAT ARE WE UP AGAINST?

You need to know your enemy! Different categories of malicious software and scamming techniques are listed next:

- ◢ A **virus** is a program that replicates by attaching itself to other programs. The infected program must be executed for a virus to run. The program might be an application, a macro in a document, a Windows system file, or a boot loader program.
- ◢ A **boot sector virus** is a virus that hides in the MBR program in the boot sector of a hard drive or in an OS boot loader program.
- ◢ **Adware** produces all those unwanted pop-up ads.
- ◢ **Spyware** spies on you to collect personal information about you that it transmits over the Internet to web-hosting sites.
- ◢ A **keylogger** tracks all your keystrokes and can be used to steal a person's identity, credit card numbers, Social Security number, bank information, passwords, email addresses, and so forth.
- ◢ A **worm** is a program that copies itself throughout a network or the Internet without a host program. A worm creates problems by overloading the network as it replicates and can even hijack or install a server program such as a web server.
- ◢ A **Trojan** does not need a host program to work; rather, it substitutes itself for a legitimate program. In most cases, a user launches it thinking she is launching a legitimate program. A Trojan is often downloaded from a web site when a user is tricked into thinking it is legitimate software, or a user is tricked into opening an email attachment (refer back to Figure 18-27).
- ◢ A **rootkit** is a virus that loads itself before the OS boot is complete. Because it is already loaded when the antivirus software loads, it is sometimes overlooked by the software. A rootkit can hide folders that contain software it has installed and can hijack internal Windows components so that it masks information Windows provides to user mode utilities such as Task Manager, Windows Explorer, the registry editor, and antivirus software. This last trick helps it remain undetected.

> 💡 **A+ Exam Tip** The A+ 220-802 exam expects you to be able to compare and contrast viruses, Trojans, worms, spyware, and rootkits.

A+
220-802
2.1

STEP-BY-STEP ATTACK PLAN

This section is a step-by-step attack plan to clean up an infected system. We'll use **antivirus (AV) software** to remove all types of general malware and then use **antispyware software** to remove spyware and adware. Then we'll use some Windows tools to check out the system to make sure all remnants of malware have been removed and the system is in tip-top order.

> ⚡ **Caution** If a system is highly infected and will later hold sensitive data, consider backing up the data, reformatting the hard drive, and reinstalling the OS and applications. In fact, Microsoft recommends this to be the safest way to deal with highly infected systems.

A+
220-802
2.1, 4.7

STEP 1: IDENTIFY MALWARE SYMPTOMS

A PC support technician needs to know how to recognize that a system is infected with malware and how to clean an infected system. Here are some warnings that suggest malicious software is at work:

◢ Pop-up ads plague you when surfing the web. Your browser home page has changed and you see new toolbars you didn't ask for. Your browser might be redirected to a web site you didn't ask for. This last type of attack is called browser hijacking. Figure 18-28 shows a web page that appeared as the user tried to access another page. This bogus page is phishing for login information to the DSL service or home router. Also notice in the figure the uninvited toolbars.

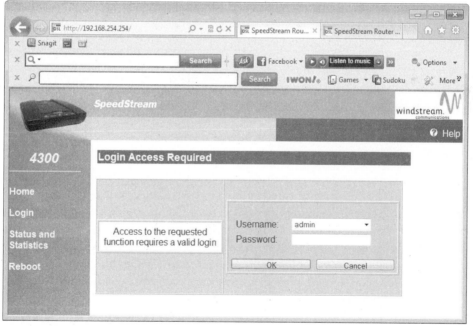

Source: Windstream Communications

Figure 18-28 Uninvited toolbars and a redirected web page indicate an infected system

◢ Generally, the system works much slower than it used to. Programs take longer than normal to load. Strange or bizarre error messages appear. Programs that once worked now give errors. Task Manager shows unfamiliar processes running.
◢ The number and length of disk accesses seem excessive for simple tasks. The number of bad sectors on the hard drive continues to increase. The system might even lock up.
◢ You have problems making a network connection or accessing the web.
◢ Your antivirus software displays one or more messages.

18

A+
220-802
2.1, 4.7

- ◢ Windows updates fail to install correctly or give errors during installation.
- ◢ The system cannot recognize the CD or DVD drive, although it worked earlier.
- ◢ In Windows Explorer, filenames now have weird characters or their file sizes seem excessively large. Executable files have changed size or file extensions change without reason. Files mysteriously disappear or appear. Windows system files are renamed. Files constantly become corrupted. Files you could once access now give access denied messages, and file permissions change.
- ◢ The OS begins to boot, but hangs before getting a Windows desktop.
- ◢ You receive email messages telling you that you have sent someone spam or an infected message. This type of attack indicates your email address or email client software on your computer has been hijacked.
- ◢ Even though you can browse to other web sites, you cannot access AV software sites such as *www.symantec.com* or *www.mcafee.com*, and you cannot update your AV software. A window appears telling you that antivirus software you didn't ask for is installed (called rogue antivirus software).
- ◢ A message appears that a downloaded document contains macros, or an application asks whether it should run macros in a document. (It is best to disable macros if you cannot verify that they are from a trusted source and that they are free of viruses or worms.)

> **💡 A+ Exam Tip** The A+ 220-802 exam expects you to know about the common symptoms of malware listed previously and how to quarantine and remediate an infected system.

> **Notes** Malicious software is designed to do varying degrees of damage to data and software, although it does not damage PC hardware. However, when boot sector information is destroyed on a hard drive, the hard drive can appear to be physically damaged.

STEP 2: QUARANTINE AN INFECTED SYSTEM

If an infected computer is connected to a network (wired or wireless), immediately disconnect the network cable or turn off the wireless adapter. You don't want to spread a virus or worm to other computers on your network. A **quarantined computer** is not allowed to use the regular network that other computers use. If you need to use the Internet to download AV software or its updates, take some precautions first. Consider your options. Can you disconnect other computers from the network while this one computer is connected? Can you isolate the computer from your local network, connecting it directly to the ISP or a special quarantined network? If neither option is possible, try downloading the AV software updates while the computer is booted into Safe Mode with Networking. Malware might still be running in Safe Mode, but is less likely to do so than when the system is started normally.

Always keep in mind that data might be on the hard drive that is not backed up. Before you begin cleaning up the system, back up data to another media.

STEP 3: RUN AV SOFTWARE

Table 18-1 lists popular antivirus software for personal computers and web sites that also provide information about viruses. Before selecting a product, be sure to read some reviews about it and check out some reliable web sites that rate AV software.

A+
220-802
2.1, 4.7

Notes Be aware of web sites that appear as sponsored links at the top of search results for AV software. These sites might make you think they are the home site for the software, but are really trying to lure you into downloading adware or spyware.

Antivirus Software	Web Site
AntiVirus + AntiSpyware by Trend Micro (for home use)	www.trendmicro.com
Avast by ALWIL Software (home edition is free)	www.avast.com
AVG Anti-Virus by AVG Technologies	www.avg.com
Bitdefender Antivirus	www.bitdefender.com
ClamWin Free Antivirus by ClamWin (open source and free)	www.clamwin.com
F-Secure Anti-Virus by F-Secure Corp.	www.f-secure.com
Kaspersky Anti-Virus	www.kaspersky.com
Malwarebytes Anti-Malware (free version available)	www.malwarebytes.org
McAfee AntiVirus Plus by McAfee, Inc.	www.mcafee.com
Norton AntiVirus by Symantec, Inc.	www.symantec.com
Panda Antivirus Pro	www.pandasecurity.com
SUPERAntiSpyware	www.superantispyware.com
Microsoft Security Essentials (free)	windows.microsoft.com

© Cengage Learning 2014

Table 18-1 Antivirus software and web sites

Notes It's handy to have AV software on CD so that you don't need Internet access to download the software, but recognize that this AV software won't have the latest updates. You'll need these updates downloaded from the Internet before the software will catch newer viruses.

Now let's look at different situations you might encounter when attempting to run AV software.

Run AV Software Already Installed

If AV software is already installed and you suspect an infection, update the software and perform a full scan on the system. Do the following:

1. Make sure the AV software is up to date. These updates download the latest **virus definitions**, also called **virus signatures**, which the software uses to define or detect new viruses as they get into the wild.

2. Use the AV software to perform a full scan of the system. As it scans, the software might ask you what to do with an infected program or it might log this event in an event viewer or history log it keeps. The logs are likely to contain a history of quarantined items and programs that you've allowed to run. Use the event viewer and the logs to decide what to do with each item. In most situations, choose to delete any suspicious file. Take notes of any program files the software is not able to delete. You can manually delete them later. Figure 18-29 shows the history of events kept by Microsoft Security Essentials.

18

A+
220-802
2.1, 4.7

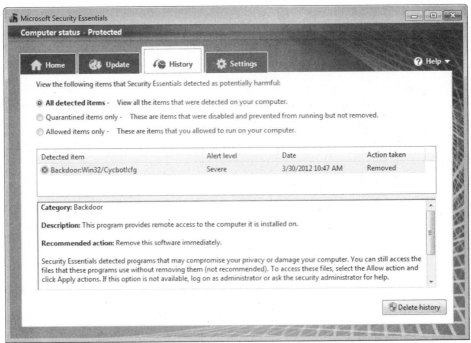

Source: Microsoft Security Essentials

Figure 18-29   History of events kept by Microsoft Security Essentials

3. After the scan is complete and you have decided what to do with each suspicious file, reboot the system and allow the software to update itself again and then scan the system again. Most likely, some new malware will be discovered. Keep rebooting and rescanning until a scan comes up clean.

If you have problems running the AV software, try running it in Safe Mode. In Safe Mode, a virus might not load that is keeping the AV software from working or from detecting the virus.

> **Notes** If you ever encounter a virus that your updated AV software did not find, be sure to let the manufacturer of the software know so they can research the problem.

Run AV Software from a Networked Computer

If AV software is not already installed, the most effective way to clean the computer is to run the software from another computer. Follow these steps:

1. Make sure the remote computer has its software firewall set for maximum protection and its installed AV software is up to date and running.

2. Network the two computers and share drive C on the infected computer. (Don't connect the infected computer to the entire network. If necessary, you can connect the two computers using a crossover cable or using a small switch and network cables.)

3. To make your work easier, you can map a network drive from the remote computer to drive C on the infected computer.

4. Perform a virus scan on the remote computer, pointing the scan to drive C on the infected computer.

A+
220-802
2.1, 4.7

Install and Run AV Software on the Infected Computer

If you don't have another computer available to scan the infected computer, you can purchase the AV software on CD, or use another computer to download the AV software from its web site and then burn the downloaded files to a CD. Don't make the mistake of using the infected PC to purchase and download AV software because keyloggers might be spying and collecting credit card information. During the installation process, the AV software updates itself and performs a scan. You can also run free online AV software without downloading and installing it, but be careful to use only reputable web sites.

Install and Run AV Software in Safe Mode

Some malware prevents AV software from installing. In this situation, try booting the system in Safe Mode with Networking and installing the AV software. Some viruses still load in Safe Mode, and some AV programs will not install in Safe Mode.

In either situation, while you are in Safe Mode, use System Restore to apply a restore point that was taken before the infection. Applying a restore point cannot be counted on to completely remove an infection, but it might remove startup entries the malware is using, making it possible to install the AV software from the normal Windows desktop or run the AV software in Safe Mode.

> **Notes** If viruses are launched even after you boot in Safe Mode and you cannot get the AV software to work, try searching for suspicious entries in the subkeys under HKLM\System\CurrentControlSet\Control\SafeBoot. Subkeys under this key control what is launched when you boot into Safe Mode. How to edit the registry is covered in Chapter 11.

Run AV Software from a Bootable Rescue Disc or Flash Drive

If the system is so infected you cannot install the AV software, know that some AV software products, such as the AVG Rescue CD software, offer the option to create a bootable USB flash drive or CD. You can then use this device to boot the system and run the AV software from the device in this preinstallation environment. Most of the products listed earlier in Table 18-1 offer the option on their web site to download software to create the bootable CD or drive. Be sure to use a healthy computer to create the rescue CD or flash drive. In addition, you might need to create a 32-bit version to scan a 32-bit Windows system or a 64-bit version to scan a 64-bit system. When selecting a product to create a bootable device, find one that can store the latest updates on the CD or flash drive so you don't need Internet access when you scan the infected system.

After you've scanned the system using this method, reboot and install AV software on the hard drive. Update the AV software, and then keep scanning and rebooting until the scan report is clean.

A+
220-802
1.1, 2.1,
4.7

STEP 4: RUN ADWARE OR SPYWARE REMOVAL SOFTWARE

To completely clean a badly infected system, experience says use more than one anti-malware product. Almost all AV software products today also search for adware and spyware. However, software specifically dedicated to removing this type of malware generally does a better job of it than does AV software. The next step in the removal process is to use antispyware software. Table 18-2 lists some products that can catch adware, spyware, cookies, browser hijackers, dialers, keyloggers, and Trojans.

18

A+
220-802
1.1, 2.1,
4.7

Adware and Spyware Removal Software	Description
Ad-Aware by Lavasoft (*www.lavasoft.com*)	One of the most popular and successful adware and spyware removal products. It can be downloaded without support for free.
Spybot Search & Destroy by Safer Networking, Ltd. (*www.safer-networking.org*)	Does an excellent job of removing malicious software and it's free.
Spy Sweeper by Webroot Software, Inc (*www.webroot.com*)	Very good antivirus and antispyware software but does require that you pay a yearly subscription.
Windows Defender (*windows.microsoft.com*)	Free antispyware software embedded in Windows.

© Cengage Learning 2014

Table 18-2   Anti-adware and antispyware software

Windows Defender is antispyware included in Windows 7/Vista. To perform a scan using Windows Defender, open Control Panel and enter **Windows Defender** in the Control Panel search box. Then click **Windows Defender**. The Windows Defender window appears (see Figure 18-30). To check for updates, click the down arrow to the right of the help question mark and then click **Check for updates**. After updates are installed, click **Scan** to perform a scan. If Defender is not turned on, when you first open the Defender window you are given the opportunity to turn it on. However, if Microsoft Security Essentials is running, it does not allow Defender to also be on.

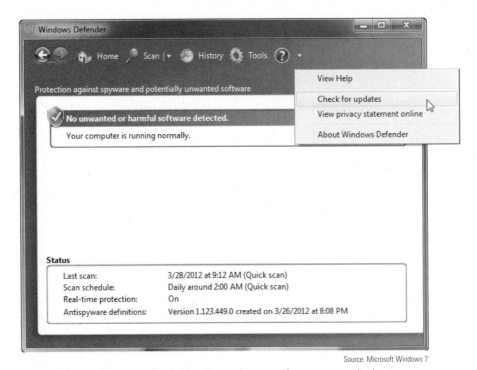

Source: Microsoft Windows 7

Figure 18-30   Windows Defender can be used to scan for spyware and adware

🔘 A+ Exam Tip   The A+ 220-802 exam expects you to know how to use Windows Defender.

A+
220-802
2.1, 4.7

STEP 5: PURGE RESTORE POINTS

Some malware hides its program files in restore points stored in the System Volume Information folder maintained by System Protection. If System Protection is on, AV software can't clean this protected folder. To get rid of that malware, you can turn off System Protection and run the AV software again so it can clean the System Volume Information folder (see Figure 18-31). Realize that when you turn off System Protection, all your restore points are lost. To turn off System Protection, open the System window and click **System protection**. After your AV software has scanned the system again, turn System Protection back on. Later, when you are sure the system is clean, create a new restore point that you can use in the future if problems arise.

Source: McAffee VirusScan

Figure 18-31 Malware found in a restore point

STEP 6: CLEAN UP WHAT'S LEFT OVER

Next, you'll need to clean up anything the anti-malware software left behind. Sometimes AV software tells you it is not able to delete a file, or it deletes an infected file but leaves behind an orphaned entry in the registry or startup folders. If the AV software tells you it was not able to delete or clean a file, first check the AV software web site for any instructions you might find to manually clean things up. In this section, you'll learn about general things you can do to clean up what might be left behind.

Respond to Any Startup Errors

On the first boot after anti-malware software has declared a system clean, you might still find some startup errors caused by incomplete removal of the malware. Recall from Chapter 11 that you can use Msconfig.exe to find out how a startup program is launched. If the program is launched from the registry, you can back up and delete the registry key. If the program is launched from a startup folder, you can move or delete the shortcut or program in the folder. See Chapter 11 for the details of how to remove unwanted startup programs. Appendix G lists registry keys and folders that are known to contain startup entries.

Research Malware Types and Program Files

Your AV software might alert you to a suspicious program file that it quarantines and then ask you to decide if you want to delete it. Also, Task Manager and other tools might find processes you suspect are malware. The web is your best tool to use when making your

18

A+
220-802
2.1, 4.7

decision about a program. Here are some web sites that offer **virus encyclopedias** that are reliable and give you symptoms and solutions for malware:

◢ Process Library by Uniblue Systems Limited at *www.processlibrary.com*
◢ DLL Library by Uniblue Systems Limited at *www.liutilities.com*
◢ All the antivirus software sites listed earlier in the chapter in Table 18-1

Beware of using other sites! Much information on the web is written by people who are just guessing, and some of the information is put there to purposefully deceive. Check things out carefully, and learn which sites you can rely on.

Delete Files

For each program file the AV software told you it could not delete, delete the program file yourself following these steps:

1. First try Windows Explorer to locate a file and delete it. For peace of mind, don't forget to empty the Recycle Bin when you're done.

2. If the file is hidden or access is denied, open an elevated command prompt window and use the commands listed in Table 18-3 to take control of a file so you can delete it. If the commands don't work using an elevated command prompt window, use the commands in a command prompt in Windows RE or the XP Recovery Console.

Command	Description
attrib –h –s filename.ext	Remove the hidden and system attributes to a file.
tasklist |more taskkill /f /pid:9999	To stop a running process, first use the Tasklist command to find out the process ID for the process. Then use the Taskkill command to forcefully kill the process with the given process ID.
takeown /f filename.ext	Take ownership of a file.
icacls filename.ext /GRANT ADMINISTRATORS:F	Take full access of a file.

© Cengage Learning 2014

Table 18-3   Commands used to take control of a malware file so you can delete it

3. To get rid of other malware files, delete all Internet Explorer temporary Internet files. To do so, use the Disk Cleanup process in the Drive C: properties box, or delete the browsing history using the Internet Options box.

Clean the Registry

Appendix G lists registry keys that can affect startup. You can search these keys and delete entries you don't want. You can also use Autoruns at Microsoft TechNet (*technet .microsoft.com*) to help you search for orphaned registry entries. Figure 18-32 shows a screen shot where Autoruns is displaying an orphaned entry in the HKLM\Software\ Microsoft\Windows\CurrentVersion\Run registry key used to launch the OsisOijw.dll malware program. AV software had already found and deleted this DLL file, but it left the registry key untouched.

A+
220-802
2.1, 4.7

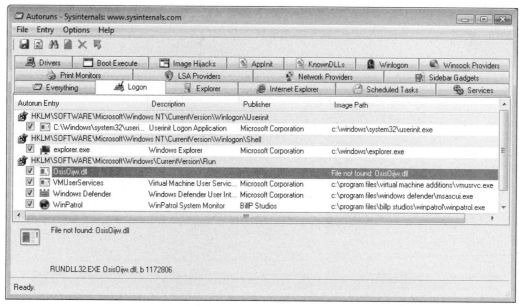

Figure 18-32 Autoruns finds orphan registry entries left there by AV software

Scan through the Autoruns window looking for suspicious entries. Research any entries that you think might be used by malware. To get rid of these entries, back up the registry and then use Regedit to delete unwanted keys or values.

After you have finished cleaning the registry, don't forget to restart the system to make sure all is well before you move on.

Clean Up Internet Explorer

Adware and spyware might install add-ons to Internet Explorer (including toolbars you didn't ask for), install cookie trackers, and change your IE security settings. Antiadware and antivirus software might have found all these items, but as a good defense, take a few minutes to find out for yourself. Chapter 17 covers how to use the Internet Options box to search for unwanted add-ons and delete ActiveX controls. You can uninstall unwanted toolbars and plug-ins using the Programs and Features window (see Figure 18-33).

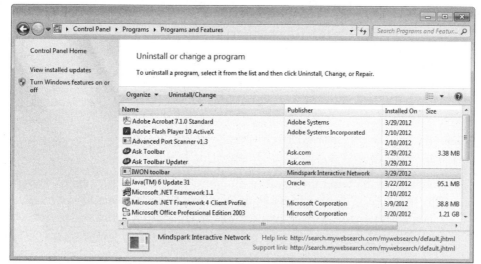

Figure 18-33 Browser toolbars can be uninstalled using the Programs and Features window

18

STEP 7: DIG DEEPER TO FIND MALWARE PROCESSES

It is my hope you won't need this section! Hopefully, by now the system is malware free. However, occasionally you'll need to deal with a really nasty infection that won't be found or deleted by conventional means. In this situation, use Task Manager or Process Explorer by Sysinternals and Microsoft TechNet to find running malware processes.

Use Task Manager to Search for Malware Processes

Open Task Manager and search for unknown processes. On the Processes tab, check **Show processes from all users** (see Figure 18-34). You can also click in the Image Name column to sort processes alphabetically, as shown in the figure. Recall from Chapter 11 that a process can run under a user (in this case, Jean Andrews), System, Local Service, or Network Service account.

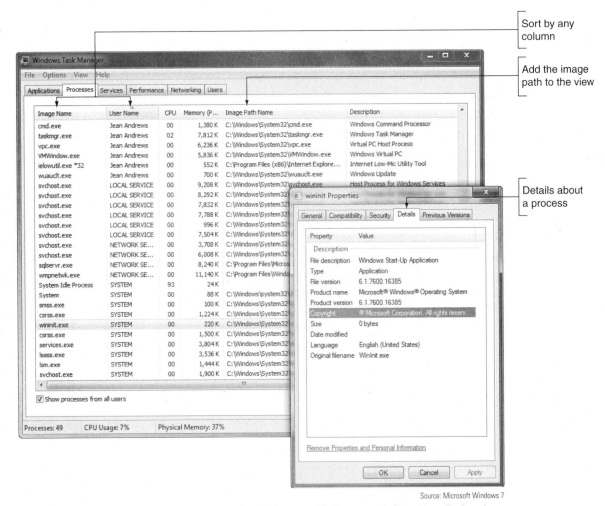

Source: Microsoft Windows 7

Figure 18-34 Processes currently running under Windows 7 with important information displayed

To find out the path to a process, click **View** on the Task Manager menu and select **Select Columns**. In the Select Process Page Columns dialog box, check **Image Path Name** and click **OK**. In Figure 18-34, the Image Path Name column is showing.

Sometimes a virus will disguise itself as a legitimate Windows core process such as svchost.exe or lsass.exe. Here are some tips to help you find malware processes:

▲ You can recognize a program as a counterfeit process if it's not running under System, Local Service, or Network Service. For example, if you spot a svchost.exe process running under a username, suspect a rat.

A+
220-802
2.1, 4.7

▲ If you notice the svchost.exe program file is located somewhere other than C:\Windows\system32, this most likely means it's a counterfeit version put there to make trouble.

▲ To find out more about a process, right-click it and select **Properties** from the shortcut menu. In the Properties box for the process, click the **Details** tab. Figure 18-34 shows the details for the Wininit.exe process.

▲ As you research each process listed by Task Manager, know the most reliable sites about Windows processes are the Microsoft support sites (*support.microsoft.com* or *technet.microsoft.com*). A search on a process name, an error message, a description of a process or problem with a process, or other related information can turn up a Knowledge Base article with the information you need.

To help you with researching a process, Table 18-4 lists core Windows processes that are likely to be listed by Task Manager. If you suspect a core Windows process is corrupted or has been hijacked by a virus, use an SFC command to restore the corrupted program. If you suspect a program is masquerading as a Windows program and it is not in the Windows folder or subfolders, kill it and delete it. Stomp that bug.

Process and Path	Description
Csrss.exe (C:\Windows\System32)	Client/server run-time server subsystem; manages many commands in Windows that use graphics.
Explorer.exe (C:\Windows)	Windows graphical shell that manages the desktop, Start menu, taskbar, and file system.
Lsass.exe (C:\Windows\System32)	Manages local security and logon policies.
Lsm.exe (C:\Windows\System32)	Manages user services for the currently logged-on users.
SearchIndexer.exe (C:\Windows\System32)	Manages indexes used for fast searches.
Services.exe (C:\Windows\System32)	Starts and stops services.
Smss.exe (C:\Windows\System32)	Windows sessions manager; essential Windows process.
Spoolsv.exe (C:\Windows\System32)	Handles Windows print spooling. Stopping and starting this process can sometimes solve a print spooling problem.
Svchost.exe (C:\Windows\System32)	Manages each process that is executed by a DLL. One instance of Svchost runs for each process it manages. To see a list of services managed by Svchost, enter this command in a command-prompt window: `tasklist /SVC`
System Idle Process	Appears in the Task Manager window to show how CPU usage is allotted. It is not associated with a program file.
System	Windows system counter that shows up as a process, but has no program file associated with it.
Taskmgr.exe (C:\Windows\System32)	Task Manager utility itself.
Wininit.exe (C:\Windows\System32)	Starts Windows background services and applications.
Winlogon.exe (C:\Windows\System32)	Manages logon and logoff events.

Table 18-4 Core Windows processes and their purposes

18

A+
220-802
2.1, 4.7

Use Process Explorer at Microsoft TechNet

Process Explorer by Mark Russinovich, which is available at Microsoft TechNet (*technet .microsoft.com*), works like Task Manager, but takes us to another level of information. When you look at all the processes and services running in Task Manager, it's difficult, if not impossible, to know how these processes are related to each other. Understanding these relationships can help you identify a process that is launching other processes, which is called a process tree. By identifying the original process, which is the one handling other processes, you can lay the axe to the root of the tree rather than swinging at branches.

When you go to the web site *technet.microsoft.com*, search for and download Process Explorer, and run it, the window in Figure 18-35 appears.

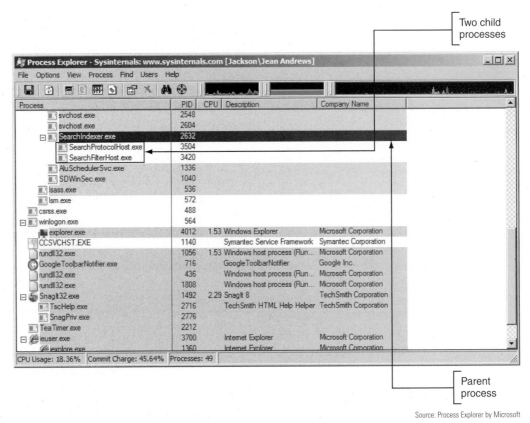

Source: Process Explorer by Microsoft

Figure 18-35 Process Explorer color codes child-parent relationships among processes and gives information about processes

On this system monitored by Process Explorer, a browser hijacker is at work changing web pages and producing pop-ups. As I watched the browser jump from one web page to another without my involvement, Process Explorer showed me what was happening with the related processes. From the information in Figure 18-35, we see that the process, SearchIndexer.exe, has called two other processes shown in the figure. As the browser jumped from one web page to another, these two processes completed and started up again. I was watching live malware in action!

As you can see, Process Explorer gives much information about a process and is a useful tool for software developers when writing and troubleshooting problems with their software, installation routines, and software conflicts. You can use the tool to smoke out processes, DLLs, and registry keys that elude Task Manager.

A+
220-802
2.1, 4.7

STEP 8: REMOVE ROOTKITS

A rootkit uses unusually complex methods to hide itself, and many spyware and adware programs are also rootkits. The term rootkit applies to a kit or set of tools used originally on UNIX computers. In UNIX, the lowest and most powerful level of UNIX accounts is called the root account; therefore, this kit of tools was intended to keep a program working at this root level without detection.

Rootkits can prevent Task Manager from displaying the running rootkit process, or may cause Task Manager to display a different name for this process. The program filename might not be displayed in Windows Explorer, the rootkit's registry keys might be hidden from the registry editor, or the registry editor might display wrong information. All this hiding is accomplished in one of two ways, depending on whether the rootkit is running in user mode or kernel mode (see Figure 18-36). A rootkit running in user mode intercepts the API calls between the time when the API retrieves the data and when it is displayed in a window. A rootkit running in kernel mode actually interferes with the Windows kernel and substitutes its own information in place of the raw data read by the Windows kernel.

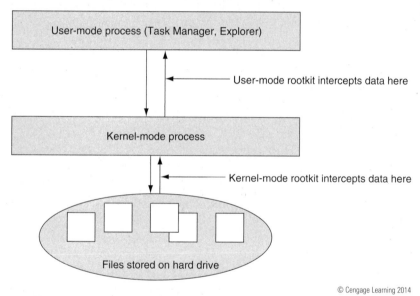

© Cengage Learning 2014

Figure 18-36 A rootkit can run in user mode or kernel mode

Because most AV software to one degree or another relies on Windows tools and components to work, the rootkit is not detected if the Windows tools themselves are infected. Rootkits are also programmed to hide from specific programs designed to find and remove them.

> **Notes** The Windows UAC box has been known to catch a rootkit before it installs itself.

18

The best-known anti-rootkit product is Blacklight by F-Secure (*www.f-secure.com*). Generally, anti-rootkit software works to identify a rootkit using these methods:

- ◢ The software looks for hidden files and folders or for running processes that don't match up with the underlying program filenames.
- ◢ The software compares files, registry entries, and processes provided by the OS to the lists it generates from the raw data. If the two lists differ, a rootkit is suspected.

If the software suspects a rootkit, it reports that to you. If you believe your system has a rootkit, the best solution is to immediately disconnect the computer from the network (if you have not already done so), back up your important data, format your hard drive, and reinstall Windows.

STEP 9: REPAIR BOOT BLOCKS

If an infected computer will not boot, it might be that the boot sectors of the hard drive are infected or damaged or the BIOS code might be corrupted. Here are the methods to deal with these problems:

- ◢ Launch the Windows RE command prompt and use the command **bootrec /fixmbr** to repair the MBR. The command **bootrec /fixboot** repairs the OS boot record. For Windows XP, launch the Recovery Console and use these two commands: **fixmbr** and **fixboot**. Chapter 14 gives more information about solving boot problems.
- ◢ A virus is rarely able to attack startup BIOS code stored on the motherboard. BIOS contains a boot block, which is a small program stored on the BIOS firmware chip that attempts to recover the BIOS when updating (flashing) the BIOS has failed. If you see an error at POST, such as "Award BootBlock BIOS ROM checksum error" or a similar error, you can suspect BIOS has become corrupted. The solution is to treat the problem as you would if flashing the BIOS has failed. See the motherboard manufacturer's web site for more information. Again, however, know that viruses are unlikely to be able to gain access to BIOS programs.

STEP 10: ENABLE SYSTEM PROTECTION AND EDUCATE THE USER

Now that the system is clean, if System Protection is still turned off, turn it back on and create a restore point. Now would be a good time to go over with the user some tips presented earlier in the chapter to keep the system free from malware. Sometimes the most overlooked step in preventing malware infections is to educate the user.

STEP 11: PROTECT AGAINST MALICIOUS SOFTWARE

Once your system is clean, you'll certainly want to keep it that way. The best practices you need to follow to protect a system against malware are listed next. The first three methods are the most important ones:

- ◢ *Always use a software firewall.* Never, ever connect your computer to an unprotected network without using a firewall. Windows Firewall is turned on by default. Recall that you can configure Windows Firewall to allow no uninvited communication in or to allow in the exceptions that you specify (see Figure 18-37).

Figure 18-37 A software firewall protecting a computer

A+
220-802
1.1, 1.5,
2.1, 4.7

Notes To avoid conflicts, don't run more than one personal firewall program on the same computer.

◢ *Use anti-malware software.* As a defensive and offensive measure to protect against malware, install and run AV software and keep it current. Configure the AV software so that it (1) runs in the background, (2) automatically scans incoming email attachments, and (3) automatically downloads updates to the software. Most AV software is also antispyware and protects the system from spyware. To avoid conflicts and not slow down performance, it's best to run only one anti-malware program on a computer. Do the following to find out what AV software or antispyware is installed and turned on:

- For Windows 7, open the Security group in the Action Center. Figure 18-38 shows one system that has Microsoft Security Essentials installed, which automatically disabled Windows Defender. When you click **View installed antispyware programs**, you can see three programs installed (see the lower part of Figure 18-38).

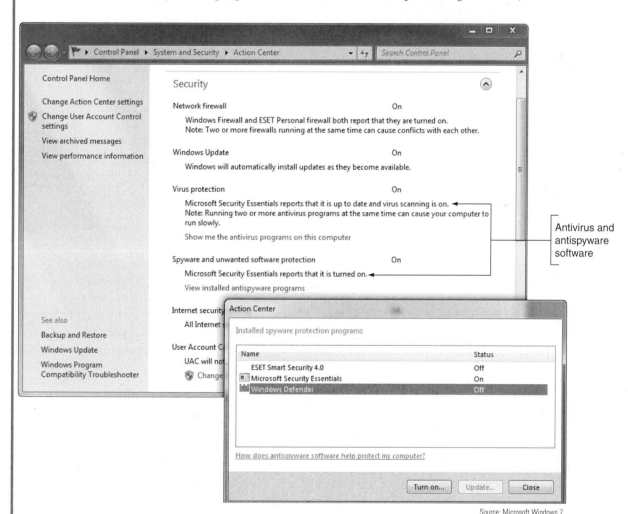

Figure 18-38 Microsoft Security Essentials installed

Source: Microsoft Windows 7

- For Vista, in the Control Panel, click **Security** and then click **Security Center**. The Vista **Security Center** is shown in Figure 18-39. Using this window, you can confirm Windows Firewall, Windows Update, anti-malware settings, including that of Windows Defender, and other security settings.

18

A+
220-802
1.1, 1.5,
2.1, 4.7

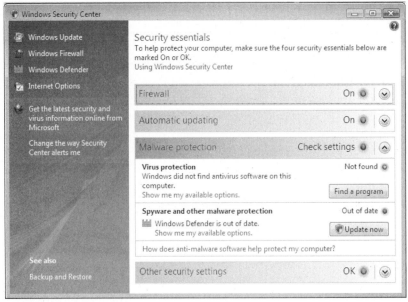

Source: Microsoft Windows Vista

Figure 18-39 Use the Windows Security Center in Vista to confirm security settings to protect a computer against malware

▲ *Keep Windows updates current.* Windows updates are continually being released to plug up vulnerable entrances in Windows where malware might attack and to update Microsoft Security Essentials or Windows Defender. Recall you can verify Windows Update settings by clicking **Start, All Programs,** and **Windows Update.**

▲ *Keep good backups.* One of the more important tasks in securing a computer is to prepare in advance for disaster to strike. One of the most important things you can do to prepare for disaster is to make good backups of user data.

▲ *Keep the User Account Control box enabled.* The UAC box is one of your best defenses against malware installing itself. When software attempts to install, the UAC box appears. If you don't respond to the box, Windows aborts the installation.

▲ *Limit the use of administrator accounts.* If malware installs itself while you're logged on as an administrator, it will most likely be running under this account with more privileges and the ability to do more damage than if you had been logged on under a less powerful account. Use a standard user account with lesser privileges for your everyday normal computer activities.

▲ *Set Internet Explorer for optimum security.* Internet Explorer includes the pop-up blocker, the ability to manage add-ons, the ability to block scripts and disable scripts embedded in web pages, and the ability to set the general security level. You learned how to configure IE in Chapter 17.

Notes You might want to consider using an alternate browser other than Internet Explorer and an alternate email client other than Outlook because these programs are often attacked by malware. Using an alternate email address might also be wise. When you have to give an email address to companies that you suspect might sell your address to spammers, use a second email address that you don't use for normal emailing.

A+
220-802
1.1, 1.5,
2.1, 4.7

Large corporations generally have additional plans in place so that malware is quickly detected and does not take down the entire network. Here is what these plans might look like:

▲ *Use a hard drive image.* Each computer is built using a hard drive image. If a system gets infected, a technician simply reinstalls the image. Reinstalling from a standard image or deployment image is much faster than going through the detailed process of removing malware from a system.

▲ *No data is kept on a personal computer.* Company policy says that all data must be installed on network drives and not on the local hard drive. The purpose of this policy is so that (1) an infected system can be restored from an image without having to deal with data on the hard drive, and (2) data on network drives are backed up on a regular basis and, therefore, safer than when stored on a local hard drive. Recall that reinstalling a hard drive image erases everything on the drive. Because all user data is stored on network drives, no user data is lost when the image is used.

▲ *Use network-monitoring software.* Network-monitoring software (for example, Big Brother Professional at *www.bb4.com*) is constantly monitoring the network for unusual activity. If the software discovers a computer on the network is acting suspiciously, the computer will be quarantined. The monitoring software alerts a technician about the problem. If the technician believes the system is infected, he will reimage the hard drive. All this can take place within an hour of malware becoming active on a computer.

>> CHAPTER SUMMARY

Securing a Windows Workstation

▲ The netplwiz command can be used to require the user to press Ctl+Alt+Delete to log onto Windows.

▲ Windows power settings can be used to lock down the workstation after a short period of inactivity and to require a password to unlock the workstation.

▲ An administrator might be called on to reset a forgotten password.

▲ A strong password is not easy to guess and contains uppercase and lowercase letters, numbers, and symbols.

▲ The Encrypted File System (EFS) is used with an NTFS volume for Windows business and professional editions.

▲ Windows Firewall can block all communication initiated outside the workstation and can allow exceptions for certain programs, protocols, ports, and remote computers.

▲ Group Policy is used in Windows professional and business editions to set policies that can secure the local computer.

▲ BitLocker Encryption with Windows professional or business editions can lock down the entire hard drive. It can be set to authenticate the computer, authenticate the user, or authenticate both the computer and the user.

▲ BIOS security features include passwords, drive lock passwords, and support for a TPM chip and an intrusion-detection device.

18

Additional Methods to Protect Resources

◢ Large networks might use a security token in addition to a Windows password to authenticate a user.

◢ Tokens include a smart card (key fob, RSA token, or RFID badge) and biometric data (iris scan, retinal scan, or fingerprint scan). The most secure biometric data is a retinal scan.

◢ Physical security can include a locked door, lock and chain, or privacy filter.

◢ Data can be partly or completely destroyed using a paper shredder, low-level format, drill, degausser, or Secure Erase utility.

◢ Security methods include educating users against social engineering and how to best protect a laptop when traveling.

Dealing with Malicious Software

◢ Malware includes a virus, adware, spyware, keylogger, worm, Trojan, and rootkit.

◢ Symptoms that malware is present include pop-up ads, slow performance, error messages, file errors, spam, and strange processes running.

◢ When you suspect a computer is infected, immediately quarantine it. Then scan the system with up-to-date antivirus software. If necessary, you can scan the infected computer using AV software installed on another computer or use a rescue disc for the scan. Some systems become so highly infected, the only solution is to reinstall Windows.

◢ To protect a computer against malware, use a software firewall, keep AV software up to date and running, and maintain Windows updates.

>> KEY TERMS

For explanations of key terms, see the Glossary near the end of the book.

adware	keylogger	smart card reader
antispyware software	LoJack	social engineering
antivirus (AV) software	malicious software	spyware
ATA Secure Erase	malware	strong password
biometric device	phishing	tailgating
BitLocker Encryption	privacy filter	Trojan
boot sector virus	quarantined computer	virus
computer infestation	retinal scanning	virus definition
degausser	RFID badge	virus encyclopedia
digital certificate	rootkit	virus signature
email hoax	RSA tokens	Windows Defender
Encrypted File System (EFS)	Security Center	Windows Firewall
grayware	shoulder surfing	worm
key fob	smart card	

>> REVIEW QUESTIONS

1. Which action is considered to be a good Windows security practice?

   a) Allow fast user switching.

   b) Enable logon and shutdown scripts.

   c) Use a minimum password length policy and set the minimum length to five.

   d) Require users to press CTRL+ALT+DELETE to get to a logon window.

2. What BIOS security feature is stored on the hard drive so that it will still control access to the drive in the event the drive is removed from the computer and installed on another system?

   a) Supervisor password

   b) Drive lock password

   c) TPM chip support

   d) Power-on password

3. What is the best way to sanitize a solid-state device?

   a) Download a Secure Erase utility from the manufacturer of the device and run it.

   b) Delete all the files on the drive.

   c) Use Windows to format the drive.

   d) Use a degausser.

4. What is the first step to take after discovering a computer infected with malware?

   a) Update and run antivirus software.

   b) Reboot the computer.

   c) Purge all system restore points.

   d) Quarantine the computer.

5. What is one of the best defenses against malware installing itself?

   a) Use a screen saver.

   b) Enable the Guest account for visitors.

   c) Keep the User Account Control box enabled.

   d) Use BitLocker for all of your data.

6. True or false? An encrypted file will become decrypted if you move it from an encrypted folder to an unencrypted folder on the same or another NTFS volume.

7. True or false? Using Group Policy, you can set security policies to help secure a workstation.

8. True or false? A smart card or biometric data should be used as a replacement to a Windows password.

9. True or false? Generally speaking, the weakest link in setting up security in a computer environment is people.

18

10. True or false? To avoid conflicts and not slow down performance, it's best to run only one anti-malware program on a computer.

11. ____ in Windows professional and business editions locks down a hard drive by encrypting the entire Windows volume and any other volume on the drive.

12. The most popular type of token used to authenticate a user is a(n) ____, which is any small device that contains authentication information.

13. In the computer arena, ____ is the practice of tricking people into giving out private information or allowing unsafe programs into the network or computer.

14. ____ is any annoying and unwanted program that might or might not mean you harm.

15. A(n) ____ is a virus that loads itself before the OS boot is complete.

Supporting Notebooks

More than half of personal computers purchased today are note-book computers, and almost 30 percent of personal computers currently in use are notebooks. As a PC service technician, you need to know how to support notebooks. In this chapter, you'll learn about supporting, upgrading, and troubleshooting notebooks and all-in-one computers.

There was a time that a notebook was considered a "black box" to PC support technicians. If it needed servicing inside, the notebook was taken to an authorized service center supported by the notebook manufacturer. These technicians were all trained by the manufacturer to service its products. However, taking apart and servicing a notebook computer are now seen as tasks that every A+ certified technician needs to know how to do. As part of your preparation to be A+ certified, try to find an old notebook computer you can take apart. If you can locate the service manual, you should be able to take it apart, repair it (assuming the parts are still available and don't cost more than the notebook is worth), and get it up and running again. Have fun with this chapter and enjoy tinkering with that old notebook!

SPECIAL CONSIDERATIONS WHEN SUPPORTING NOTEBOOKS

A **notebook**, also called a **laptop**, is designed for portability (see Figure 19-1 a and b) and can be just as powerful as a desktop computer. Notebooks use the same technology as desktops, but with modifications to use less power, take up less space, and operate on the move. Notebooks come in several varieties, including tablet PCs and netbooks. A tablet PC has more features than a notebook, including a touch screen that also allows you to handwrite on it with a stylus. Another variation of a notebook is a **netbook** that is smaller and less expensive than a notebook and has fewer features. An **all-in-one computer** (Figure 19-1c) has the monitor and computer case built together and uses components that are common to both a notebook and a desktop computer. Because all-in-one computers use many notebook components and are serviced in similar ways, we include them in this chapter.

A+ 220-801 3.3

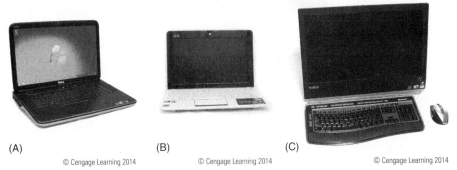

(A)   (B)   (C)
© Cengage Learning 2014   © Cengage Learning 2014   © Cengage Learning 2014

Figure 19-1 A laptop, netbook, and all-in-one computer

A notebook provides ports on its sides, back, or front for connecting peripherals (see Figure 19-2). Ports common to notebooks as well as desktop systems include USB (A male and/or B male), FireWire, network, dial-up modem (seldom seen on newer

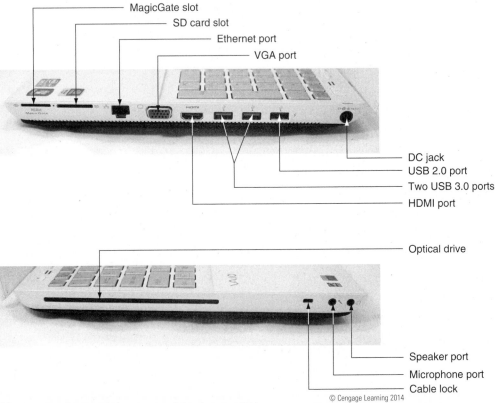

- MagicGate slot
- SD card slot
- Ethernet port
- VGA port
- DC jack
- USB 2.0 port
- Two USB 3.0 ports
- HDMI port
- Optical drive
- Speaker port
- Microphone port
- Cable lock

© Cengage Learning 2014

Figure 19-2 Ports and slots on a notebook computer

A+
220-801
3.3

notebooks), and audio ports (for a microphone, headset, or external speakers). Video ports might include one or more VGA, HDMI, DisplayPort, or S-Video ports to connect to a projector, second monitor, or television. On the side or back of the notebook, you'll see a lock connector that's used to physically secure the laptop with a cable lock (see Figure 19-3) and a DC jack to receive power from the AC adapter.

Slots you might find on a notebook include one or more flash memory and ExpressCard slots. Also, a notebook is likely to have an optical drive, but netbooks usually don't have optical drives. The notebook shown in Figure 19-2 has two slots for flash memory: a MagicGate slot and an SD slot. The MagicGate slot is used for memory sticks and can support Memory Stick Duo, Memory Stick PRO Duo, Memory Stick PRO-HG Duo, and Memory Stick Micro. The SD slot supports SD, SDHC, and SDXC cards. Be sure the flash memory slots on a notebook support the type of card you're trying to use in a slot.

Notebooks and their replacement parts cost more than desktop PCs with similar features because their components are designed to be more compact and stand up to travel. They use compact hard drives, small memory modules, and CPUs that require less power than regular components. Whereas a desktop computer is often assembled from parts made by a variety of manufacturers, notebook computers are almost always sold by a vendor that either manufactured the notebook or had it manufactured as a consolidated system. Factors to consider that generally apply more to notebook computers than desktop computers are the original equipment manufacturer's warranty, the service manuals and diagnostic software provided by the manufacturer, the customized installation of the OS that is unique to notebooks, and the advantage of ordering replacement parts directly from the notebook manufacturer or other source authorized by the manufacturer.

In many situations, the tasks of maintaining, upgrading, and troubleshooting a notebook require the same skills, knowledge, and procedures as when servicing a desktop computer.

Source: Kensington Technology Group

Figure 19-3 Use a cable lock system to secure a notebook computer to a desk to help prevent it from being stolen

19

A+
220-801
3.3

However, you should take some special considerations into account when caring for, supporting, upgrading, and troubleshooting notebooks. These same concerns apply to netbooks and all-in-one computers. Let's begin with warranty concerns.

WARRANTY CONCERNS

Most manufacturers or retailers of notebooks offer at least a one-year warranty and the option to purchase an extended warranty. Therefore, when problems arise while the notebook is under warranty, you are dealing with a single manufacturer or retailer to get support or parts. After the notebook is out of warranty, this manufacturer or retailer can still be your one-stop shop for support and parts.

> ⚡ **Caution** The warranty often applies to all components in the system, but it can be voided if someone other than an authorized service center services the notebook. Therefore, you, as a service technician, must be very careful not to void a warranty that the customer has purchased. Warranties can be voided by opening the case, removing part labels, installing other-vendor parts, upgrading the OS, or disassembling the system unless directly instructed to do so by the authorized service center help desk personnel.

Before you begin servicing a notebook, to avoid problems with a warranty, always ask the customer, "Is the notebook under warranty?" If the notebook is under warranty, look at the documentation to find out how to get technical support. Options are chat sessions on the web, phone numbers, and email. Use the most appropriate option. Before you contact technical support, have the notebook model and serial number ready (see Figure 19-4).

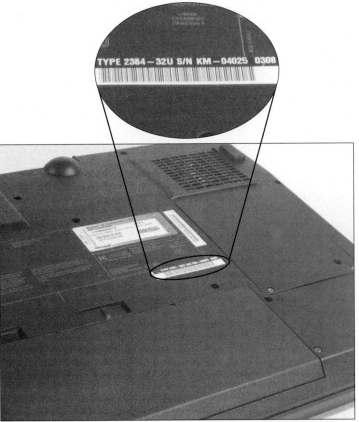

Figure 19-4 The model and serial number stamped on the bottom of a notebook are used to identify the notebook to service desk personnel

A+
220-801
3.3

You'll also need the name, phone number, and address of the person or company that made the purchase. Consider asking the customer for a copy of the receipt and warranty so that you'll have the information you need to talk with support personnel.

Based on the type of warranty purchased by the notebook's owner, the manufacturer might send an on-site service technician, ask you to ship or take the notebook to an authorized service center, or help you solve the problem by an online chat session or over the phone. Table 19-1 lists some popular manufacturers of notebooks, netbooks, tablet PCs, and all-in-ones. Manufacturers of notebooks typically also produce all-in-ones because of the features they have in common.

Manufacturer	Web Site
Acer	us.acer.com and support.acer.com
Apple Computer	www.apple.com and www.apple.com/support
ASUS	usa.asus.com and www.service.asus.com
Dell Computer	www.dell.com and support.dell.com
Fujitsu/Fuji	www.fujitsu.com and www.fujitsu.com/support
Gateway	www.gateway.com and support.gateway.com
Hewlett Packard (HP)	www.hp.com www8.hp.com/us/en/support-drivers.html
Lenovo (formerly IBM ThinkPads)	www.lenovo.com and support.lenovo.com
Samsung	www.samsung.com and www.samsung.com/support
Sony (VAIO)	store.sony.com and esupport.sony.com
Toshiba America	www.csd.toshiba.com

© Cengage Learning 2014

Table 19-1 Notebook, netbook, tablet PC, and all-in-one manufacturers

SERVICE MANUALS AND OTHER SOURCES OF INFORMATION

Desktop computer cases tend to be similar to one another, and components in desktop systems tend to be interchangeable among manufacturers. Not so with notebooks. Notebook manufacturers tend to take great liberty in creating their own unique computer cases, buses, cables, connectors, drives, circuit boards, fans, and even screws, all of which are likely to be proprietary in design.

Every notebook model has a unique case. Components are installed in unique ways and opening the case for each notebook model is done differently. Because of these differences, servicing notebooks can be very complicated and time consuming. For example, a hard drive on one notebook is accessed by popping open a side panel and sliding the drive out of its bay. However, to access the hard drive on another model notebook, you must remove the keyboard. If you are not familiar with a particular notebook model, you can damage the case as you pry and push trying to open it. Trial and error is likely to damage a case. Even though you might successfully replace a broken component, the damaged case will result in an unhappy customer.

Fortunately, a notebook service manual can save you much time and effort—if you can locate one (see Figure 19-5). Most notebook manufacturers closely guard these service manuals and release them only to authorized service centers. Two notebook manufacturers, Lenovo (formally IBM ThinkPad) and Dell, provide their service manuals online free of charge. HP also does an excellent job of offering online support. For example, in Figure 19-6, you can see a video in progress showing you the steps to replace the optical drive in an HP notebook. I applaud Lenovo, Dell, and HP for the generous documentation

19

A+
220-801
3.3

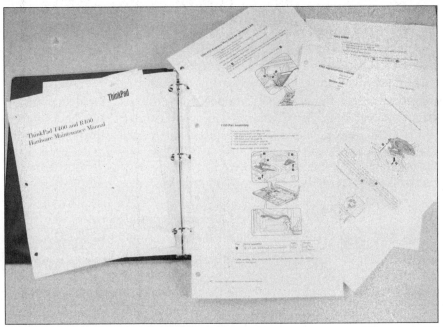

© Cengage Learning 2014

Figure 19-5 A notebook service manual tells you how to use diagnostic tools, troubleshoot a notebook, and replace components

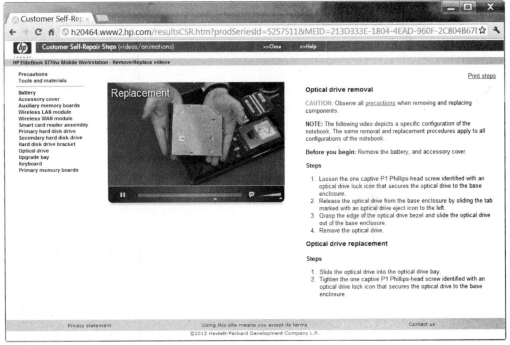

Source: hp.com

Figure 19-6 The HP web site (*www.hp.com*) provides detailed instructions and videos for troubleshooting and replacing components

about how their notebooks are disassembled and the options to purchase proprietary parts without first being an authorized service center.

For all notebook manufacturers, check the Support or FAQ pages of their web sites for help in tasks such as opening a case without damaging it and locating and replacing a component. Be aware that some manufacturers offer almost no help at all. Sometimes, you can

A+
220-801
3.3

find service manuals on the web. To find your manual, search on the model of notebook, for example, search on "Sony VGN-CR120E notebook service manual."

Don't forget about the user manuals. They might contain directions for upgrading and replacing components that do not require disassembling the case, such as how to upgrade memory or install a new hard drive. User manuals also include troubleshooting tips and procedures and possibly descriptions of BIOS settings. In addition, you can use a web search engine to search on the computer model, component, or error message, which might give you information about the problem and solution.

DIAGNOSTIC TOOLS PROVIDED BY MANUFACTURERS

Most notebook manufacturers provide diagnostic software that can help you test components to determine which component needs replacing. As one of the first steps when servicing a notebook, check the user manual, service manual, or manufacturer's web site to determine if diagnostic software exists and how to use it. Use the software to pinpoint the problem component, which can then be replaced.

> **Notes** When you purchase a replacement part for a notebook from the notebook's manufacturer, most often the manufacturer also sends you detailed instructions for exchanging the part.

Check the manufacturer's web site for diagnostics software that can be downloaded for a particular model notebook or stored on the hard drive or on CDs bundled with the notebook. Figure 19-7 shows a window provided by the diagnostics program installed on the hard drive of one laptop.

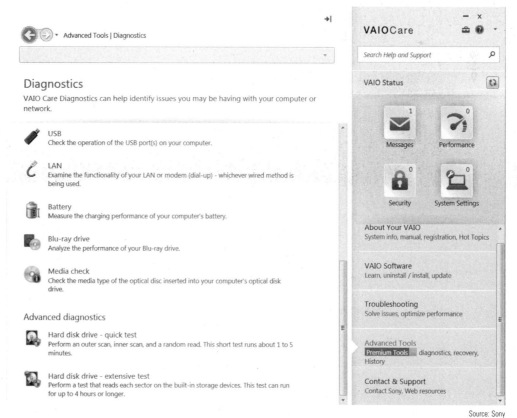

Source: Sony

Figure 19-7 Use diagnostics software provided by a notebook manufacturer to troubleshoot hardware problems

19

A+
220-801
3.3

One example of diagnostic software is PC-Doctor, which is used by several manufacturers, including Lenovo, Fujitsu, and HP notebooks. The diagnostic software is stored on the hard drive or on CD. If stored on CD, you can boot from the CD to run the tests. If the software is stored on the hard drive, you can run it from the Windows Start menu or by pressing a function key at startup before Windows loads. Either way, PC-Doctor can run tests on the keyboard, video, speakers, touchpad, optical drive, wireless LAN, motherboard, processor, ports, hard drive, and memory. To learn how to use the software, see the notebook's service manual or user manual.

Lenovo offers PC-Doctor for DOS that you can download from their web site at *www.lenovo.com/support* and burn to a CD. Boot from the CD to run the tests. You can also find a stand-alone version of PC-Doctor at *www.pc-doctor.com*. You can purchase it at this site; it's expensive but might be worth it if you plan to service many notebooks.

THE OEM OPERATING SYSTEM BUILD

Notebook computers are sold with an operating system preinstalled at the factory. The OS installation is tailored by the manufacturer to satisfy the specific needs of the notebook. In this situation, the manufacturer is called the OEM (original equipment manufacturer) and the customized installation of the OS is called the operating system build or OS build. Drivers installed are also specific to proprietary devices installed in the notebook. Diagnostic software is often written specifically for a notebook and its installed OS. For all these reasons, use caution when deciding to upgrade to a new OS and know that, if you have problems with a device, in most circumstances, you must turn to the OEM for solutions and updates for device drivers.

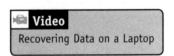
Video
Recovering Data on a Laptop

Now let's look at some considerations to be aware of when repairing or upgrading a notebook operating system.

RECOVERY PARTITION AND RECOVERY CDS

Most notebook computers come with a recovery partition on the hard drive that contains a copy of the OS build, device drivers, and preinstalled applications needed to restore the system to its factory state. The partition is likely to also contain diagnostics programs for troubleshooting and perhaps a backup program to back up the hard drive at any time. This partition might or might not be hidden.

The Disk Management utility in Windows can be used to see a list of hard drives installed in a system and the partitions on each drive. The easiest way to get to Disk Management is to click **Start**, type **Disk Management** in the search box, and press **Enter**. Figure 19-8 shows the Disk Management information for a hard drive on one notebook that has a 16.38 GB

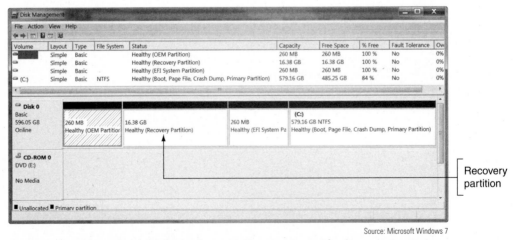

Source: Microsoft Windows 7

Figure 19-8 This notebook hard drive has a 16 GB recovery partition that can be used to recover the system

A+
220-801
3.3

recovery partition. Notice in the figure the 596 GB hard drive is labeled Disk 0. Most of the space on the hard drive is used by drive C:.

To know how to access the recovery tools stored on a recovery partition, see the user manual. Most likely, you'll see a message at the beginning of the boot, such as "Press ESC for diagnostics" or "Press F12 to recover the system." For one Sony laptop, you press the red **Assist** button during the boot (see Figure 19-9). When you press the key or button, a menu appears giving you options to diagnose the problem, to repair the current OS installation, or to completely rebuild the entire hard drive to its state when the notebook was first purchased.

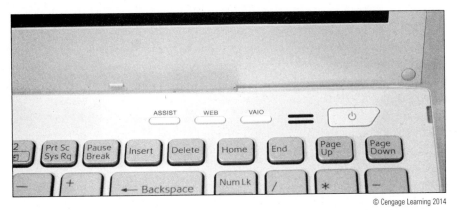

© Cengage Learning 2014

Figure 19-9 For this laptop, press the Assist button during the boot to launch programs on the recovery partition

The recovery partition won't be any help at all if the hard drive is broken or corrupted. In this situation, you're dependent on other recovery media. Older laptops came bundled with the full recovery on CDs, but today's laptops only provide a way for you to create the recovery media. It's important to create the recovery media *before* a problem occurs. To do so, you launch a program preinstalled in Windows. For one Lenovo laptop, the program's window is shown in Figure 19-10. When you click Create Recovery Disc, you are given the option to create recovery discs using the current system or the factory default recovery.

Source: Lenovo

Figure 19-10 Create recovery discs *before* a problem occurs

A+
220-801
3.3

Notes When you first become responsible for a notebook, make sure you have recovery discs containing the installed OS so you can recover from a failed hard drive. If you cannot create them, you can purchase the discs from the notebook manufacturer. (The price should be less than $30.) Do this before problems arise. If the notebook is more than three years old, the manufacturer might no longer provide the recovery media.

You can also download all the device drivers for the notebook from the manufacturer's web site and burn them to CD.

OPERATING SYSTEM UPGRADES

For desktop systems, upgrading the operating system is usually a good thing to do if the desktop system has the power and hard drive space to support the new OS. Not so with notebooks. Unless a specific need to upgrade arises, the operating system preinstalled on the notebook should last the life of the notebook.

As an example of a specific reason to upgrade, consider a situation in which a notebook holds private data, and you need to provide the best possible security on the notebook. In this situation, it might be appropriate to upgrade from Windows XP to Windows 7 so that you can use BitLocker Encryption.

If at all possible, always upgrade the OS using an OS build purchased from the notebook manufacturer, which should include the OS and device drivers specific to your notebook. In addition, carefully follow their specific instructions for the installation.

If you decide to upgrade the OS using an off-the-shelf version of Windows, first determine that all components in the system are compatible with the upgrade. Be certain to have available all the device drivers you need for the new OS before you upgrade. Download the drivers from the notebook manufacturer's web site and store them in a folder on the hard drive. After you upgrade the OS, install the drivers from this folder. The notebook manufacturer might also suggest you first flash the BIOS before you perform the upgrade. And, if applications are installed on the notebook, find out if you have the applications' setup CDs, and if they will install under the new OS.

Now let's turn our attention to how to maintain a notebook.

MAINTAINING NOTEBOOKS AND NOTEBOOK COMPONENTS

A+
220-801
3.1, 3.3

Notebook computers tend to not last as long as desktop computers because they are portable and, therefore, subjected to more wear and tear. A notebook's user manual gives specific instructions on how to care for the notebook. Those instructions follow these general guidelines:

▲ LCD panels on notebooks are fragile and can be damaged fairly easily. Take precautions against damaging a notebook's LCD panel. Don't touch it with sharp objects like ballpoint pens.

▲ Don't pick up or hold the notebook by the lid. Pick it up and hold it by the bottom. Keep the lid closed when the notebook is not in use.

▲ Only use battery packs recommended by the notebook manufacturer. Keep the battery pack away from moisture or heat, and don't attempt to take the pack apart. When it no longer works, dispose of it correctly. Chapter 13 covers how to dispose of batteries.

A+
220-801
3.1, 3.3

▲ Don't tightly pack the notebook in a suitcase because the LCD panel might get damaged. Use a good-quality carrying case and make it a habit of always transporting the notebook in the carrying case. Don't place heavy objects on top of the notebook case.

▲ Don't move the notebook while the hard drive is being accessed (the drive indicator light is on). Wait until the light goes off.

▲ Don't put the notebook close to an appliance such as a TV, large audio speakers, or refrigerator that generates a strong magnetic field, and don't place your cell phone on a notebook while the phone is in use.

▲ Never, ever connect to the Internet using a public network without setting the network location to a Public network or using a software firewall.

▲ Always use passwords with each Windows user account so that the laptop is better protected when connected to a public network, stolen, or used by an unauthorized person.

▲ Keep your notebook at room temperature. For example, never leave it in a car overnight when it is cold, and don't leave it in a car during the day when it's hot. Don't expose your notebook to direct sunlight for an extended time.

▲ Don't leave the notebook in a dusty or smoke-filled area. Don't use it in a wet area such as near a swimming pool or in the bathtub. Don't use it at the beach where sand can get in it.

▲ Don't power it up and down unnecessarily.

▲ Protect the notebook from overheating by not running it when it's still inside the case, resting on a pillow, or partially covered with a blanket or anything else that would prevent proper air circulation around it.

▲ If a notebook has just come indoors from the cold, don't turn it on until it reaches room temperature. In some cases, condensation can cause problems. Some manufacturers recommend that when you receive a new notebook shipped to you during the winter, you should leave it in its shipping carton for several hours before you open the carton to prevent subjecting the notebook to a temperature shock.

▲ Protect a notebook against ESD. If you have just come in from the cold on a low-humidity day when there is the possibility that you are carrying ESD, don't touch the notebook until you have grounded yourself.

▲ Before placing a notebook in a carrying case for travel, remove any CDs, DVDs, or USB flash drives, and put them in protective covers. Verify that the system is powered down and not in suspend or standby mode.

▲ If a notebook gets wet, you can follow steps given later in the chapter to partially disassemble it to allow internal components to dry. Give the notebook several days to dry before attempting to turn it on. Don't use heat to speed up the drying time.

▲ When you first become responsible for a notebook, take the time to locate or create the recovery media in case the hard drive ever crashes and needs replacing.

A well-used notebook, especially one that is used in dusty or dirty areas, needs cleaning occasionally. Here are some cleaning tips:

▲ Clean the LCD panel with a soft dry cloth. If the panel is very dirty, you can use monitor wipes to clean it or dampen the cloth with water. Some manufacturers recommend using a mixture of isopropyl alcohol and water to clean an LCD panel. Be sure the LCD panel is dry before you close the lid.

19

A+
220-801
3.1, 3.3

◢ Use a can of compressed air meant to be used on computer equipment to blow dust and small particles out of the keyboard, track ball, and touchpad. Turn the notebook at an angle and direct the air into the sides of the keyboard. Then use a soft, damp cloth to clean the key caps and touch pad.

◢ Use compressed air to blow out all air vents on the notebook to make sure they are clean and unobstructed.

◢ If keys are sticking, remove the keyboard so you can better spray under the key with compressed air. If you can remove the key cap, remove it and clean the key contact area with contact cleaner. One example of a contact cleaner you can use for this purpose is Stabilant 22 (*www.stabilant.com*). Reinstall the keyboard and test it. If the key still sticks, replace the keyboard.

◢ Remove the battery and clean the battery connections with a contact cleaner.

Now let's look at the special keys and buttons a notebook might have, how to support the slots and peripherals used on notebooks, how to manage power on a notebook, and how to use port replicators or docking stations.

SPECIAL KEYS, BUTTONS, AND INPUT DEVICES ON A NOTEBOOK

A+
220-802
1.5

Buttons or switches might be found above the keyboard, and a **keyboard backlight** might light up the keyboard. Here are the purposes of a few keys and buttons. Some of them change Windows settings. Know that these same settings can also be changed using Windows tools:

◢ *Volume setting.* You can set the volume using the volume icon in the Windows taskbar. In addition, some notebooks offer buttons or function keys to control the volume (see Figure 19-11).

◢ *Screen brightness.* The Fn key and F5 or F6 control the screen brightness on many notebooks. Screen brightness can also be controlled in Windows display settings.

© Cengage Learning 2014

Figure 19-11 Use the Fn and the F2, F3, or F4 key to control volume; use the Fn key and the F5 or F6 key to control screen brightness; and use the Fn key and the F7 key to manage dual displays

A+
220-801
3.1, 3.3

A+
220-802
1.5

▲ *Dual displays.* Most laptops use a function key to control dual displays. For example, for one laptop, the combination of the Fn key and the F7 key (see Figure 19-11) displays the box shown in Figure 19-12. Use arrow keys to use only the LCD panel, duplicate or extend output to the external monitor, or use only the external monitor. Dual displays can also be managed using Windows display settings.

▲ *Bluetooth or Wi-Fi on or off.* Some notebooks use function keys such as Fn with F5 or F6 to toggle Bluetooth or Wi-Fi on or off, or a notebook might have a switch for this purpose. You can also control Bluetooth and Wi-Fi using Windows settings or software utilities provided by the manufacturer.

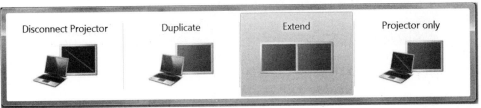

Source: Microsoft Windows 7

Figure 19-12   Control dual monitors on a laptop

Notes Later in the chapter, you learn how to exchange a notebook keyboard. If the keyboard fails and you're not able to immediately exchange it, know that you can plug in an external keyboard to a USB port to use in the meantime.

The most common pointing device on a notebook is a **touchpad** (see Figure 19-13). IBM and Lenovo ThinkPad notebooks use a unique and popular pointing device embedded in the keyboard (see Figure 19-14) called a **TrackPoint** or **pointing stick**. Some people prefer to use a USB wired or wireless mouse instead of a touchpad or TrackPoint.

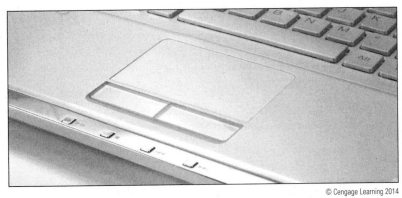

© Cengage Learning 2014

Figure 19-13   The touch pad is the most common pointing device on a notebook

You can adjust the way the touchpad or TrackPoint works on a laptop using the Mouse Properties box. Click **Mouse** in the Hardware and Sound group of Control Panel to open the box shown in Figure 19-15. The tabs on this box vary depending on the pointing devices installed. Use the Mouse Properties box to adjust pointer speed, mouse trails, pointer size, how the touchpad buttons work, and other settings for pointing devices.

19

© Cengage Learning 2014

Figure 19-14   An IBM ThinkPad TrackPoint

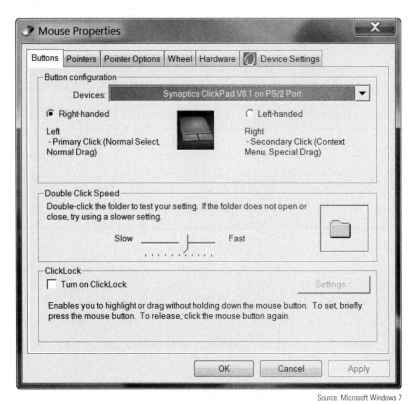

Source: Microsoft Windows 7

Figure 19-15   Use the Mouse Properties box to control a mouse, touch pad,
or other pointing device

For tablet PCs, the stylus can be controlled from the Pen and Input Devices box. The box can be accessed from Control Panel, and allows you to control stylus clicks and motion.

PCMCIA AND EXPRESSCARD SLOTS

Most peripheral devices on today's notebooks use a USB port to connect to the notebook. Before USB devices became so popular, a notebook offered ExpressCard slots and even older PC Card and CardBus slots to connect peripheral devices. These slot and card standards were designed and supported by the PCMCIA (Personal Computer Memory Card International Association). **PCMCIA cards** include one or more variations of PC Card, CardBus, and ExpressCard. The cards were used by many devices, including modems, network cards for wired or wireless networks, sound cards, SCSI host adapters, FireWire (IEEE 1394) controllers, USB controllers, flash memory adapters, TV tuners, and hard disks. Most new notebooks don't have these slots, but you still need to know how to support them because you'll see them on older notebooks.

You need to be aware of the different standards for PCMCIA cards, which are summarized here, listed in the order they were introduced into the market:

1. A **PC Card** that uses a PC Card slot is about the size of a credit card, but thicker. The slot used a 16-bit bus called the ISA bus. Originally, PC Cards were called PCMCIA Cards and the first of these cards were used to add memory to a notebook. Figure 19-16 shows a PC Card being inserted into a PC Card slot. Three standards for PC Cards and PC Card slots that pertain to size are Type I, Type II, and Type III. Generally, the thicker the PC Card or slot, the higher the standard. You're unlikely to see PC Card slots on notebooks today.

© Cengage Learning 2014

Figure 19-16 Many peripheral devices are added to a notebook using a PC Card slot; here, a Microdrive (a tiny hard drive) adapter PC Card is inserted in a PC Card slot

2. **CardBus** slots improved PC Card slots by increasing the bus width to 32 bits, while maintaining backward compatibility with earlier standards. The slot uses the 32-bit PCI bus standards. CardBus slots can support the older 16-bit PC Card devices. You cannot, however, insert a CardBus card into an older 16-bit PC Card slot. A PC Card has a smooth edge, and a CardBus has a bumpy strip on the edge. This bumpy strip prevents a CardBus card from being inserted into a 16-bit PC Card slot.

Figure 19-17 shows a TV tuner CardBus card. If you look closely at the edge, you can see the gold, bumpy strip that prevents a CardBus card from being inserted into an older PC Card slot. PC Card and CardBus slots look alike on a notebook computer, and you

19

A+
220-801
3.1, 3.3

can recognize these slots by the eject button on the side of the slot (see Figure 19-18). One way to know which type of slot you have is to look in Device Manager. If Device Manager shows a controller with "CardBus" in the controller title, then the slot is a 32-bit CardBus slot (see Figure 19-19).

Gold, bumpy
strip identifies
a CardBus card

Source: AVerMedia Technologies, Inc.

Figure 19-17 AVerMedia AVerTV CardBus Plus (E501R) TV tuner card connects to a notebook by way of a PCMCIA CardBus slot

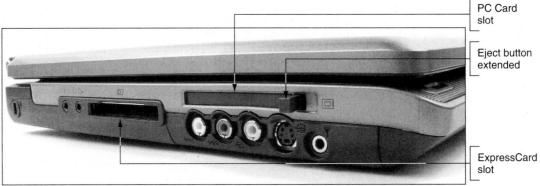

PC Card
slot

Eject button
extended

ExpressCard
slot

© Cengage Learning 2014

Figure 19-18 This notebook has one CardBus slot and one ExpressCard slot

Source: Microsoft Windows XP

Figure 19-19 Device Manager recognizes a PCMCIA slot as a CardBus slot

A+
220-801
3.1, 3.3

> **A+ Exam Tip** The A+ 220-801 exam expects you to know about PCMCIA cards and slots and ExpressCard/34 and ExpressCard/54 cards and slots.

3. The last PCMCIA standard is ExpressCard, which uses the PCI Express bus standard or the USB 2.0 standard. Two sizes of ExpressCards exist: **ExpressCard/34** is 34mm wide and **ExpressCard/54** is 54mm wide. Both of these types of cards are 75mm long and 5mm high. Figure 19-20 compares a CardBus card to each of the two ExpressCard cards. An ExpressCard/34 card can fit into an ExpressCard/54 slot, but not vice versa. ExpressCard slots are not backward compatible with PC Card or CardBus cards. An ExpressCard slot is fully hot-pluggable (add a card while the system is on), hot-swappable (exchange or add a card while the system is on), and supports autoconfiguration, just as does a USB port. Figure 19-21 shows an ExpressCard/54 card that provides two eSATA ports for external SATA drives.

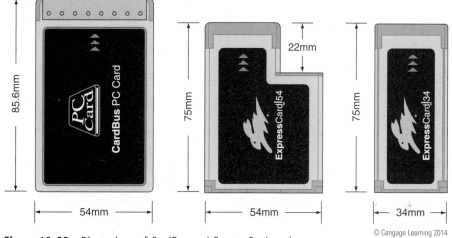

© Cengage Learning 2014

Figure 19-20 Dimensions of CardBus and ExpressCard cards

Courtesy of SIIG, Inc.

Figure 19-21 This ExpressCard/54 card supports two eSATA drives

19

Windows must provide two services for a PC Card or ExpressCard: a socket service and a card service. The socket service establishes communication between the card and the notebook when the card is first inserted. The card service provides the device driver to interface with the card after the socket is created.

A+
220-801
3.1, 3.3

The first time you insert a PCMCIA card in a notebook, the Found New Hardware Wizard starts and guides you through the installation steps in which you can use the drivers provided by the hardware manufacturer or use Windows drivers. The next time you insert the card in the notebook, the card is detected and starts without help.

ExpressCards and PC Cards can be hot-swapped (inserted or removed while the system is on), but you must stop one card before inserting another. To stop the card, use the Safely Remove Hardware icon in the notification area, which is similar to how you stop a USB device before unplugging it.

After you have stopped the card, press the eject button beside the PC Card slot, which causes the button to pop out. You can then press the button again to eject the card. For an ExpressCard, push on the card, which causes it to pop out of the slot. Then you can remove the card.

> ⚡ **Caution** Inserting a card in a PCMCIA slot while the notebook is shutting down or booting up can cause damage to the card and/or to the notebook. Also, a card might give problems when you insert or remove the card while the system is in hibernation or sleep mode.

UPDATING PORT OR SLOT DRIVERS

If you ever have a problem with a port or slot on a notebook not working, first turn to Device Manager to see if errors are reported and to update the drivers for the port or slot. The notebook manufacturer has probably stored backups of the drivers on the hard drive under support tools and on the recovery media if the recovery media is available. You can also download the latest drivers from the manufacturer's web site. For some laptops, you can launch the support tools from the Windows **Start, All Programs** menu. Figure 19-22 shows a dialog box available in the support tools for one laptop where you select which drivers to update. If the problem is still not solved after updating the drivers, try using Device Manager to uninstall the port or slot drivers and then use the support tools to reinstall the drivers.

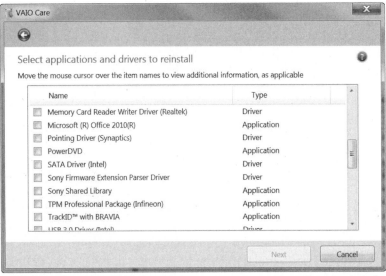

Source: Sony

Figure 19-22 Update drivers to solve a problem with a port or slot not working

POWER AND ELECTRICAL DEVICES

A notebook can be powered by an **AC adapter** (which uses regular house current to power the notebook) or an installed battery pack. Battery packs today use **Lithium Ion** technology. Most AC adapters today are capable of **auto-switching** from 110 V to 220 V AC power. Figure 19-23 shows an AC adapter that has a green light that indicates the adapter is receiving power.

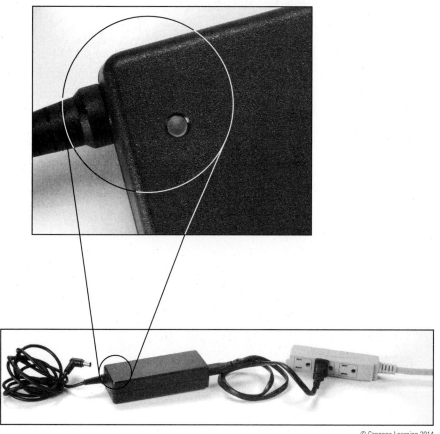

© Cengage Learning 2014

Figure 19-23 AC adapter for a notebook uses a green light to indicate power

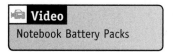

Video
Notebook Battery Packs

Some mobile users like to keep an extra battery on hand in case the first one uses up its charge. When the notebook signals that power is low, shut down the system, remove the old battery, and replace it with a charged one. To remove a battery, generally, you release a latch and then remove the battery, as shown in Figure 19-24.

For best battery charge times, some notebooks can use two batteries. For example, the notebook in Figure 19-25 uses a second battery called a **sheet battery** that fits on the bottom of the notebook. The two batteries together give about 12 hours of use between charges. The sheet battery comes with an adapter so you can charge it when it's disconnected from the notebook.

A DC adapter to provide power while in a car can be handy. Figure 19-26 shows an inexpensive one that plugs into a cigarette lighter in a vehicle to provide AC power. The device is a type of inverter. (An **inverter** is an electrical device that changes DC to AC.) You can plug your AC adapter into the inverter to power a laptop in your car. If you are using an inverter, be sure to purchase one that supplies enough power (measured in watts) to meet the needs of your notebook.

19

A+
220-801
3.1, 3.3

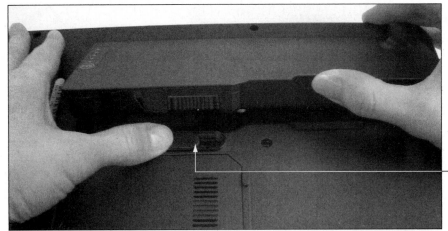

Thumb latch
releases
the battery

© Cengage Learning 2014

Figure 19-24 Release a latch to remove the battery from a notebook

© Cengage Learning 2014

Figure 19-25 The second battery for this notebook is a sheet battery that attaches to
the bottom of the notebook and adds up to six hours to the battery charge

© Cengage Learning 2014

Figure 19-26 An inverter changes DC to AC and provides an outlet for your laptop's
AC adapter

A+
220-801
3.1, 3.3

> **Notes** If you're using the AC adapter to power your notebook when the power goes out, the installed battery serves as a built-in UPS. The battery immediately takes over as your uninterruptible power supply (UPS). Also, a notebook has an internal surge protector. However, for extra protection, you might want to use a power strip that provides surge protection.

A+
220-802
1.5

POWER MANAGEMENT

Use power management settings to conserve power and to increase the time before a battery pack needs recharging. Power is managed by putting the computer into varying degrees of suspend or sleep modes.

> **A+ Exam Tip** The A+ 220–801 exam expects you to know how to manage power, including using sleep (suspend), hibernate, and standby modes.

Here are the different power-saving states:

◢ *Sleep mode.* Using Windows 7/Vista, you can put the computer into **sleep mode**, also called **suspend mode**, to save power when you're not using the computer. If applications are open or other work is in progress, Windows first saves the current state including open files to memory and saves some of the work to the hard drive. Then everything is shut down except memory and enough of the system to respond to a wake-up. In sleep mode, the power light on the notebook might blink from time to time. (A notebook generally uses about 1 to 2 percent of battery power for each hour in sleep mode.) To wake up the computer, press the power button or, for some computers, press a key or touch the touchpad. Windows wakes up in about two seconds. When Windows is in sleep mode, it can still perform Windows updates and scheduled tasks. Windows can be configured to go to sleep after a period of inactivity, or you can manually put it to sleep. To put the system to sleep manually, click **Start**, click the arrow to the right of Shut down, and then click **Sleep** (see Figure 19-27). Notebooks are usually configured to go to sleep when you close the lid.

> **Notes** In Windows XP, **standby mode** is similar to Windows 7/Vista sleep mode. Work is saved to memory and a trickle of power preserves that memory. In hibernation, all work in memory is saved to the hard drive and then the power is turned off.

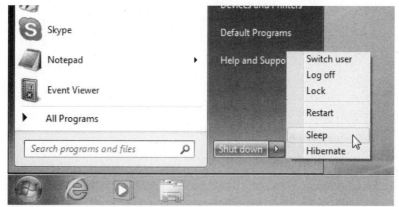

Source: Microsoft Windows 7

Figure 19-27 Put Windows to sleep using the Start menu

19

A+
220-801
3.1, 3.3

▲ *Hibernation.* **Hibernation** saves all work to the hard drive and powers down the system. When you press the power button, Windows reloads its state, including all open applications and documents. When Windows is in sleep mode on a notebook and senses the battery is critically low, it will put the system into hibernation.

A+
220-802
1.5

> **Notes** Recall that hard drives are permanent or nonvolatile storage and memory is temporary or volatile storage. A hard drive does not require power to hold its contents, but memory, on the other hand, is volatile and loses its contents when it has no power. In hibernation, the computer has no power and everything must, therefore, be stored on the hard drive.

APPLYING | CONCEPTS   CONFIGURE WINDOWS POWER MANAGEMENT SETTINGS

Follow these steps to configure power in Windows 7:

1. In Control Panel, click **Power Options** in the Hardware and Sound group. The Power Options window opens. Figure 19-28 shows the window for one laptop. The plans might be different for other laptops.

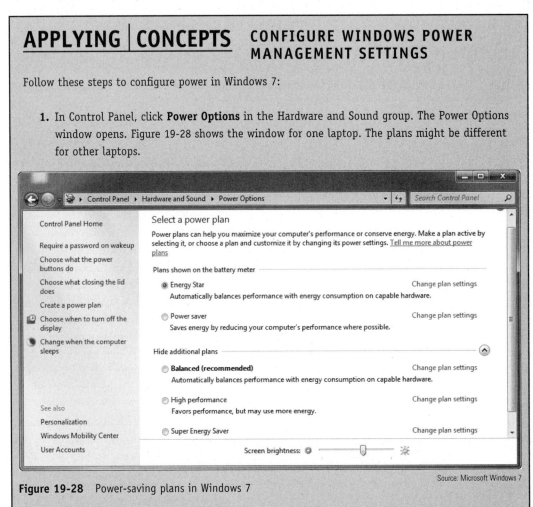

Source: Microsoft Windows 7

Figure 19-28   Power-saving plans in Windows 7

2. You can customize each plan. For example, under Balanced (recommended), click **Change plan settings**. The Edit Plan Settings window appears (see the left side of Figure 19-29). Notice in the figure the various times of inactivity before the computer goes into sleep mode, which are called **sleep timers**.

3. To see other changes you can make, click **Change advanced power settings**. Using this Power Options box (see the right side of Figure 19-29), you can do such things as control the minutes before the hard drive turns off, control what happens when you close the lid, press the sleep button, or press the power button, or set the brightness level of the LCD panel to conserve power. You can also use this box to set what happens when the battery gets low or critically low. Make your changes and click **OK** to close the box.

A+
220-801
3.1, 3.3

A+
220-802
1.5

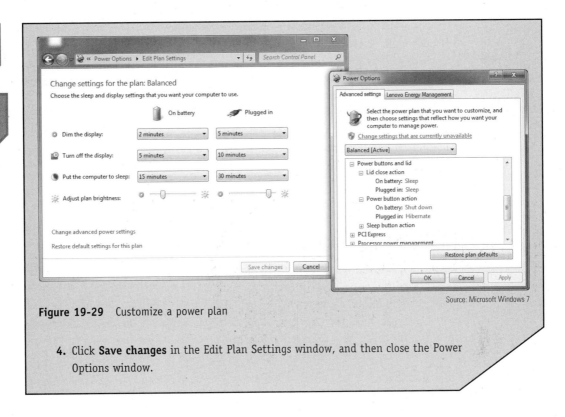

Figure 19-29 Customize a power plan

4. Click **Save changes** in the Edit Plan Settings window, and then close the Power Options window.

With older computers, power settings could be configured in Windows and in BIOS setup and the two settings could create a conflict. Newer BIOS does not control power settings that might be in conflict with Windows settings, such as when the computer goes to sleep. If you are having a problem with a computer refusing to go into sleep mode or hibernation or to wake up from sleep mode, check the BIOS power settings. Figure 19-30 shows the BIOS Power screen for one newer system. These settings apply primarily to how or when the system can wake up.

Let's cover a little of what you might see on the BIOS power screen. Using the **Advanced Configuration and Power Interface (ACPI)** power standards, BIOS might refer to five S states,

19

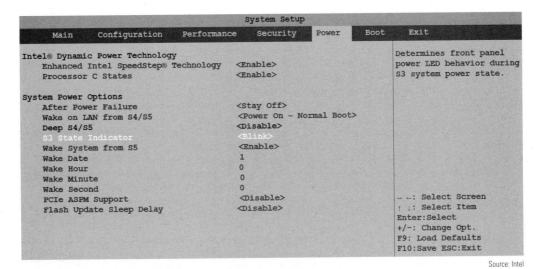

Figure 19-30 BIOS setup screen to configure power options

A+
220-801
3.1, 3.3

A+
220-802
1.5

S1 through S5, used to indicate different levels of power-saving functions. In **S1 state**, the hard drive and monitor are turned off and everything else runs normally. In **S2 state**, the processor is also turned off. In **S3 state**, everything is shut down except RAM and enough of the system to respond to a wake-up. S3 state is sleep mode. **S4 state** is hibernation. **S5 state** is the power off state after a normal shutdown.

C states in setup BIOS refer to various degrees of shutting down the CPU. In C0 state, a CPU can work, executing instructions. In C1 though C6 states, the CPU shuts down various internal components (for example, the core clock, buffers, cache, and core voltage) to conserve power. The deeper the C state, the longer it takes for the processor to wake up. Mobile processors usually offer more C states than desktop processors.

So, onward to port replicators and docking stations.

PORT REPLICATORS AND DOCKING STATIONS

Some notebooks have a connector, called a **docking port,** on the bottom of the notebook (see Figure 19-31) to connect to a port replicator or docking station. A **port replicator** provides ports to allow a notebook to easily connect to a full-sized monitor, keyboard, AC power adapter, and other peripheral devices. See Figure 19-32. A **docking station** provides the same functions as a port replicator but provides additional slots for adding secondary storage devices and expansion cards. Laptop manufacturers usually offer a port replicator or docking station as additional options.

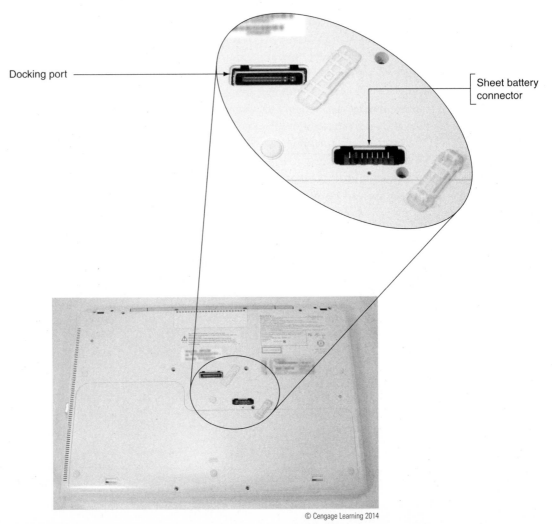

Docking port

Sheet battery connector

© Cengage Learning 2014

Figure 19-31   The docking port and sheet battery connector on the bottom of a laptop

A+
220-801
3.1, 3.3

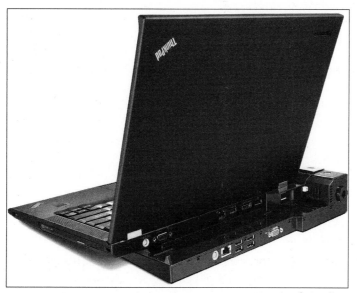

Courtesy of Lenovo

Figure 19-32 Port replicator for a Lenovo ThinkPad

Video

Port Replicators

To use a port replicator or docking station, plug all the peripherals into the port replicator or docking station. Then connect your notebook to the device. No software needs installing. When you need to travel with your notebook, rather than having to unplug all the peripherals, all you have to do is disconnect the notebook from the port replicator or docking station.

> 💡 **A+ Exam Tip** The A+ 220-801 exam expects you to know the difference between a port replicator and a docking station.

A+
220-802
1.5

APPLYING | CONCEPTS   HARDWARE PROFILES AND WINDOWS XP

A **hardware profile** is a group of settings that Windows keeps about a specific hardware configuration. If a notebook using Windows XP has a docking station, you can set up one hardware profile to use the docking station and another when you are on the road and don't have access to the docking station. Windows 7/Vista doesn't require you to set up hardware profiles, because it automatically senses when a docking station is present.

> 💡 **A+ Exam Tip** The A+ 220-802 exam expects you to know about Windows XP hardware profiles and how to use Control Panel to create one.

To create a hardware profile in Windows XP, do the following:

1. Open the **System Properties** window and click the **Hardware** tab.

2. Click the **Hardware Profiles** button at the bottom of the Hardware tab. The Hardware Profiles dialog box opens (Figure 19-33).

3. Select a profile from the list of available hardware profiles, and then click the **Copy** button.

4. Type a new name for the profile, and then click **OK**.

19

A+
220-801
3.1, 3.3

A+
220-802
1.5

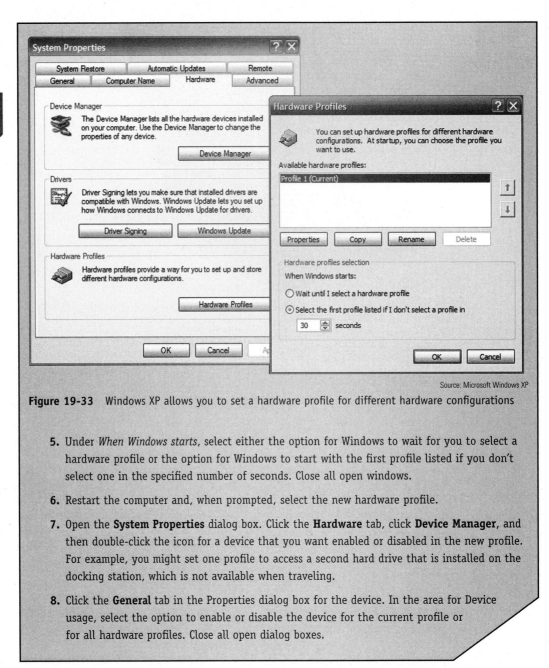

Source: Microsoft Windows XP

Figure 19-33   Windows XP allows you to set a hardware profile for different hardware configurations

5. Under *When Windows starts*, select either the option for Windows to wait for you to select a hardware profile or the option for Windows to start with the first profile listed if you don't select one in the specified number of seconds. Close all open windows.

6. Restart the computer and, when prompted, select the new hardware profile.

7. Open the **System Properties** dialog box. Click the **Hardware** tab, click **Device Manager**, and then double-click the icon for a device that you want enabled or disabled in the new profile. For example, you might set one profile to access a second hard drive that is installed on the docking station, which is not available when traveling.

8. Click the **General** tab in the Properties dialog box for the device. In the area for Device usage, select the option to enable or disable the device for the current profile or for all hardware profiles. Close all open dialog boxes.

REPLACING AND UPGRADING INTERNAL PARTS

A+
220-801
3.1

A+
220-802
4.8

Sometimes it is necessary to open a notebook case so you can upgrade memory, exchange a hard drive, or replace a failed component such as the LCD panel, video inverter, keyboard, touchpad, processor, optical drive, DC jack, fan, motherboard, CMOS battery, Mini-PCIe card, wireless card, or speaker. Most notebooks sold today are designed so that you can easily purchase and exchange memory modules or hard drives. However, replacing a broken LCD panel or motherboard can be a complex process, taking several hours. In this section, we'll first look at the alternatives you need to consider before you decide to take on complex repair projects, and then we'll look at how to upgrade memory, exchange a drive, and perform other complex repair projects, such as exchanging an LCD panel or motherboard.

THREE APPROACHES TO DEALING WITH A BROKEN INTERNAL DEVICE

When a component on a notebook needs replacing or upgrading, first you need to consider the warranty and how much time the repair will take. Before you decide to upgrade or repair an internal component, take into consideration these three alternatives:

▲ *Return the notebook to the manufacturer or another service center for repair.* If the notebook is under warranty, you need to return it to the manufacturer to do any serious repair work such as fixing a broken LCD panel. However, for simple repair and upgrade tasks, such as upgrading memory or exchanging a hard drive, most likely you can do these simple jobs by yourself without concern for voiding a warranty. Manufacturers allow a user to exchange the hard drive or memory when these components are accessible by way of a door or cover on the bottom of the notebook and it's not necessary to open the case. If you're not sure about the possibility of voiding the warranty, check with the manufacturer before you begin working on the notebook. If the notebook is not under warranty and you don't have the experience or time to fix a broken component, find out how much the manufacturer will charge to do the job. Also, consider using a generic notebook repair service. Know that some notebook manufacturers refuse to sell internal components or service manuals that explain how to take the notebook apart except to authorized service centers. In this case, you have few options but to use the service center for repairs.

> ⚡ **Caution** Before you send a notebook for repairs, if possible, back up any important data on the hard drive. It's possible the service center will format the hard drive or install a new drive.

▲ *Substitute an external component for an internal component.* As you'll see later in the chapter, replacing components on notebooks can be time consuming and require a lot of patience. If the notebook is not under warranty, sometimes it's wiser to simply avoid opening the case and working inside it. Instead, you could simply use BIOS setup to disable an internal component and then use an external device in its place. For example, if a keyboard fails, you can use a wireless keyboard with an access point connected to the USB port. Also, if the Ethernet port fails, the simplest solution might be to disable the port and use a USB network adapter to provide the Ethernet port.

▲ *Replace the internal device.* Before deciding to replace an internal device that is not easy to get to, such as an LCD panel, first find out if you can get the manufacturer documentation necessary to know how to open the notebook case and exchange the component. How to find this documentation was discussed earlier in the chapter. Without the instructions or a lot of experience servicing notebooks, the project could be very frustrating and result in a notebook useful only as a paperweight. Also consider if the cost of parts and labor is worth more than the value of the notebook. Buying a new notebook might be the best solution.

19

> **Notes** Before making the decision to replace an internal part, ask the question, "Can an external device substitute?" Many customers appreciate these solutions because most often they are much less labor intensive and less costly.

Before attempting to replace or upgrade a component installed in a notebook, always do the following:

1. If the computer is working, have the user back up any important data stored on the notebook.
2. Ground yourself by using an antistatic ground strap.
3. Remove any ExpressCards, CDs, DVDs, flash memory cards, or USB devices and then shut down the notebook.
4. Disconnect the AC adapter from the computer and from the electrical outlet.
5. If the notebook is attached to a port replicator or docking station, release it to undock the computer.
6. Remove the battery pack.

> ⚡ **Caution** It is very important to unplug the AC adapter and remove the battery pack before working inside a notebook case. If the battery is still in the notebook, power provided by the battery could damage components as you work on them.

You are now ready to follow specific instructions for your particular notebook model to replace or upgrade an internal component. Some components can easily be accessed by either removing a panel to expose the component or by removing a screw or two and then sliding the component out the side of the case. When a component can be accessed this easily, most users can do the job if given detailed instructions.

Now let's see how to upgrade memory and exchange a hard drive. Then we'll look at more complicated replacements that require you to disassemble the notebook.

UPGRADING MEMORY

In this section, you'll learn about the different types of memory modules used with notebook computers and how to upgrade memory.

TYPES OF MEMORY USED IN NOTEBOOKS

Today's notebooks all use DDR3 or DDR2 SO-DIMM (small outline DIMM) memory. You might encounter older notebooks that use SO-RIMM (small outline RIMM) memory. Table 19-2 lists current and outdated SO-DIMMs and SO-RIMMs. All of these memory modules are smaller than regular DIMMs or RIMMs.

> 💡 **A+ Exam Tip** The A+ 220-801 exam expects you to know that DDR3, DDR2, DDR, and SDRAM memory can be found on SO-DIMMs. You also need to be aware of SO-RIMMs by Rambus.

A+
220-801
3.1

A+
220-802
4.8

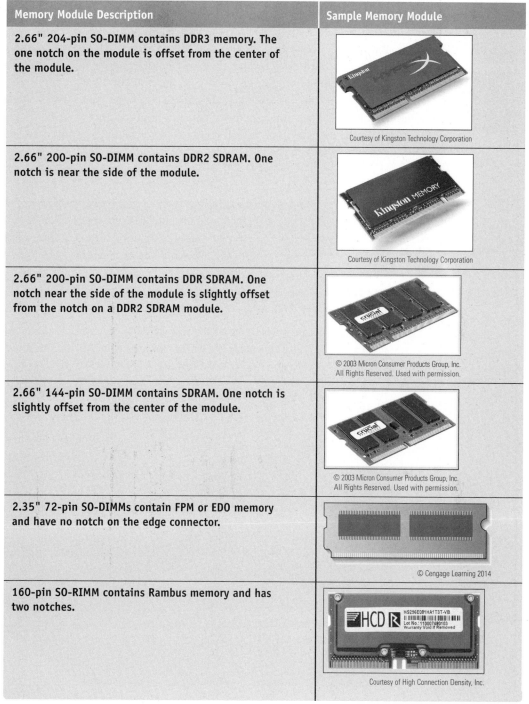

Memory Module Description	Sample Memory Module
2.66" 204-pin SO-DIMM contains DDR3 memory. The one notch on the module is offset from the center of the module.	Courtesy of Kingston Technology Corporation
2.66" 200-pin SO-DIMM contains DDR2 SDRAM. One notch is near the side of the module.	Courtesy of Kingston Technology Corporation
2.66" 200-pin SO-DIMM contains DDR SDRAM. One notch near the side of the module is slightly offset from the notch on a DDR2 SDRAM module.	© 2003 Micron Consumer Products Group, Inc. All Rights Reserved. Used with permission.
2.66" 144-pin SO-DIMM contains SDRAM. One notch is slightly offset from the center of the module.	© 2003 Micron Consumer Products Group, Inc. All Rights Reserved. Used with permission.
2.35" 72-pin SO-DIMMs contain FPM or EDO memory and have no notch on the edge connector.	© Cengage Learning 2014
160-pin SO-RIMM contains Rambus memory and has two notches.	Courtesy of High Connection Density, Inc.

© Cengage Learning 2014

Table 19-2 Memory modules used in notebook computers

Just as with memory modules used in desktop computers, you can only use the type of memory the notebook is designed to support. The number of pins and the position of the notches on a SO-DIMM keep you from inserting the wrong module in a memory slot.

19

HOW TO UPGRADE MEMORY ON A NOTEBOOK

Before upgrading memory, make sure you are not voiding your warranty. Search for the best buy, but make sure you use memory modules made by or authorized by your notebook's manufacturer and designed for the exact model of your notebook. Installing generic memory might save money but might also void the notebook's warranty.

Upgrading memory on a notebook works about the same way as with upgrading memory on a desktop: Decide how much memory you can upgrade and what type of memory you need, purchase the memory, and install it. As with a desktop computer, be sure to match the type of memory to the type the notebook supports.

APPLYING | CONCEPTS

Most notebooks are designed for easy access to memory. Follow these steps to exchange or upgrade memory for one notebook.

1. Back up data and shut down the system. Remove peripherals, including the AC adapter. Remove the battery. Be sure to use a ground bracelet as you work.

2. Many notebooks have a RAM door on the bottom of the notebook. For some notebooks, this door is in the battery cavity. Turn the notebook over and loosen the two screws on the RAM door. (It is not necessary to remove the screws.)

3. Raise the door (see Figure 19-34) and remove the door from its hinges. The two memory slots are exposed.

© Cengage Learning 2014

Figure 19-34 Raise the DIMM door on the bottom of the notebook

4. Notice in Figure 19-35 that one slot is filled and one is available for a memory upgrade. Also notice in the figure that when you remove the RAM door, the CMOS battery is exposed. This easy access to the battery makes exchanging it very easy. To remove a SO-DIMM, pull the clips on the side of the memory slot apart slightly (see Figure 19-36). The SO-DIMM will pop up out of the slot and can then be removed. If it does not pop up, you can hold the clips apart as you pull the module up and out of the slot.

A+
220-801
3.1

A+
220-802
4.8

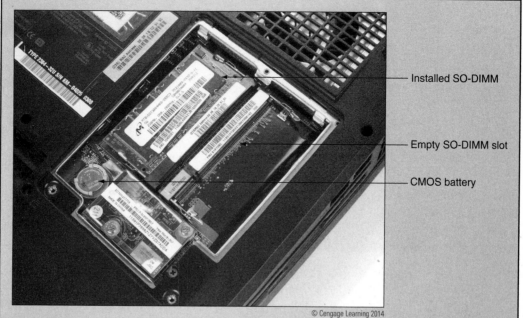

© Cengage Learning 2014

Installed SO-DIMM

Empty SO-DIMM slot

CMOS battery

Figure 19-35 SO-DIMM slots, one installed SO-DIMM, and the CMOS battery are exposed

© Cengage Learning 2014

Figure 19-36 Pull apart the clips on the memory slot to release the SO-DIMM

5. To install a new SO-DIMM, insert the module at an angle into the slot (see Figure 19-37) and gently push it down until it snaps into the clips (see Figure 19-38). Replace the RAM door.

19

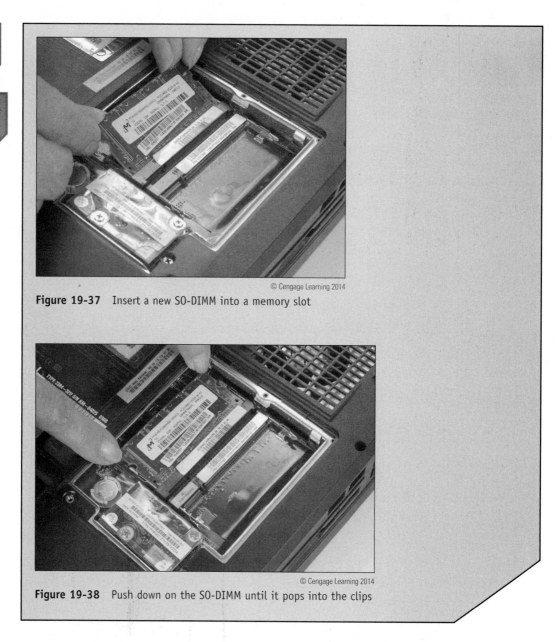

© Cengage Learning 2014

Figure 19-37   Insert a new SO-DIMM into a memory slot

© Cengage Learning 2014

Figure 19-38   Push down on the SO-DIMM until it pops into the clips

REPLACING A HARD DRIVE

When purchasing and installing an internal hard drive or optical drive, see the notebook manufacturer's documentation about specific sizes and connectors that will fit the notebook. Also be aware of voiding a warranty if you don't follow the notebook manufacturer's directions. Here is what you need to know when shopping for a notebook hard drive:

▲ A desktop hard drive is 3.5 inches wide and a notebook drive is 2.5 inches wide. Because the form factor of a notebook drive is more compact, it costs more than a desktop drive holding the same amount of data. Some notebook hard drives use SSD (solid state device) technology.

▲ Notebook hard drives use either a SATA or PATA interface. A SATA connector on a notebook looks the same as that on a desktop. PATA or IDE connectors on a desktop

A+
220-801
3.1

A+
220-802
4.8

motherboard use 40 pins, but notebook IDE connectors use 44 pins. Figure 19-39 shows interfaces for IDE and SATA drives for desktop and notebook systems. Check your notebook manual to know which type of hard drive to buy, or remove the old drive and see which interface it uses.

3.5 inch SATA hard drive
3.5 inch IDE hard drive
2.5 inch SATA hard drive
2.5 inch IDE hard drive

© Cengage Learning 2014

Figure 19-39 SATA and IDE interfaces used by drives in notebook and desktop systems

▲ For IDE drives, some notebooks use an adapter to interface between the 44-pin IDE connector on the hard drive and a proprietary connector on the notebook mother-board. You'll need to remove the old drive and see how it's connected to know if an adapter is used. If you find an adapter, you can remove it from the old hard drive and connect it to the new drive.

Before deciding to replace a hard drive, consider these issues:

▲ If the old drive has crashed, you'll need the recovery media to reinstall Windows and the drivers. Make sure you have the recovery media before you start.

▲ If you are upgrading from a low-capacity drive to a higher-capacity drive, you need to consider how you will transfer data from the old drive to the new one. One way to do that is to use a USB-to-IDE or USB-to-SATA converter that you first learned about in Chapter 13 (refer back to Figures 13-6 and 13-7). Using this converter, both drives can be up and working on the notebook at the same time, so you can copy files.

To replace a hard drive, older notebook computers required that you disassemble the notebook. With newer notebooks, you should be able to easily replace a drive. For exam-ple, for one notebook, first power down the system, remove peripherals, including the AC adapter, and remove the battery pack. Then remove a screw that holds the drive in place (see Figure 19-40). Open the lid of the notebook slightly so that the lid doesn't obstruct your removing the drive. Turn the notebook on its side and push the drive out of its bay (see Figure 19-41). Then remove the plastic cover from the drive. Move the cover to the new drive, and insert the new drive in the bay. Next, replace the screw and power up the system.

When the system boots up, if BIOS setup is set to autodetect hard drives, BIOS recog-nizes the new drive and searches for an operating system. If the drive is new, boot from the Windows recovery DVD and install the OS.

19

© Cengage Learning 2014

Figure 19-40 This one screw holds the hard drive in position

© Cengage Learning 2014

Figure 19-41 Push the drive out of its bay

> **Notes** In other chapters, it is possible to give general directions on PC repair that apply to all kinds of brands, models, and systems. Not so with notebooks. Learning to repair notebooks involves learning unique ways to assemble, disassemble, and repair notebook components for specific brands and models of notebooks.

For some laptops, such as the one shown in Figure 19-42, you remove a cover on the bottom of the computer to expose the hard drive. Then remove one screw that anchors the drive. You can then remove the drive.

DISASSEMBLING AND REASSEMBLING A NOTEBOOK COMPUTER

Working on notebooks requires special tools and extra patience. Just as when you are working with desktop systems, before opening the case of a notebook or touching sensitive components, you should always use a ground strap to protect the system against ESD. You can attach the alligator clip end of the ground strap to an unpainted metallic surface on the notebook. This surface could be, for instance, a port on the back of the notebook (see Figure 19-43). If a ground strap is not available, first dissipate any ESD between you and the notebook by touching a metallic unpainted part of the notebook, such as a port on the back, before you touch a component inside the case.

A+
220-801
3.1

A+
220-802
4.8

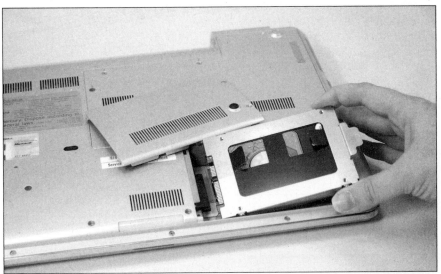

© Cengage Learning 2014

Figure 19-42 Remove a cover on the bottom of the laptop to exchange the hard drive, which is attached to a proprietary bracket

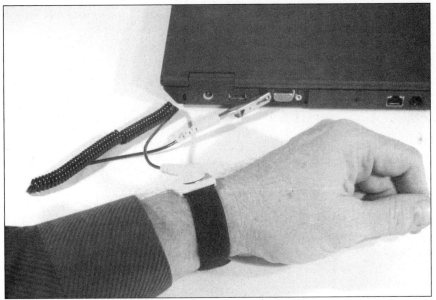

© Cengage Learning 2014

Figure 19-43 To protect the system against ESD, attach the alligator clip of a ground strap to an I/O port on the back of the notebook

19

Screws and nuts on a notebook are smaller than a desktop system and therefore require smaller tools. Figure 19-44 shows a display of several tools used to disassemble a notebook, although you can get by without several of them. Here's the list:

- Antistatic ground strap
- Small flat head screwdriver
- Number 1 Phillips head screwdriver
- Dental pick (useful for prying without damaging plastic cases, connectors, and screw covers such as the one in Figure 19-45)
- Torx screwdriver set, particularly size T5
- Something such as a pillbox to keep screws and small parts organized

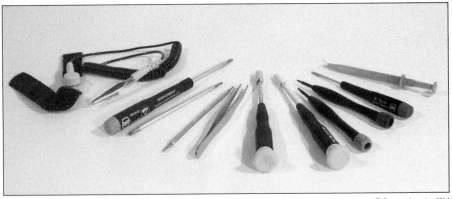

© Cengage Learning 2014

Figure 19-44 Tools for disassembling a notebook computer

© Cengage Learning 2014

Figure 19-45 Use a small screwdriver or dental pick to pry up the plastic
cover hiding a screw

▲ Notepad for note taking or digital camera (optional)
▲ Flashlight (optional)
▲ Three-prong extractor to pick up tiny screws (optional)

Notebooks contain many small screws of various sizes and lengths. When reassembling, put screws back where they came from so that when you reassemble the system, you won't use screws that are too long and that can protrude into a sensitive component and damage it. As you remove a screw, store or label it so you know where it goes when reassembling. One way to do that is to place screws in a pillbox with each compartment labeled. Another way is to place screws on a soft padded work surface and use white labeling tape to label each set of screws. A third way to organize screws is to put them on notebook paper and write beside them where the screw belongs (see Figure 19-46). My favorite method of keeping up with all those screws is to tape the screw beside the manufacturer documentation that I'm following to disassemble the notebook (see Figure 19-47). Whatever method you use, work methodically to keep screws and components organized so you know what goes where when reassembling.

A+
220-801
3.1

A+
220-802
4.8

© Cengage Learning 2014

Figure 19-46   Using a notepad can help you organize screws so you
know which screw goes where when reassembling

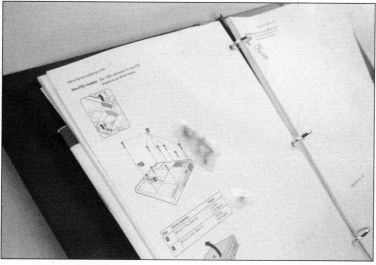

© Cengage Learning 2014

Figure 19-47   Tape screws beside the step in the manufacturer
documentation that told you to remove the screw

> **💡 A+ Exam Tip**   The A+ 220-802 exam expects you to know the importance of keeping parts organized when disassembling a notebook as well as the importance of having manufacturer documentation to know the steps to disassembly.

   As you disassemble the computer, if you are not following directions from a service manual, keep notes as you work to help you reassemble later. Draw diagrams and label things carefully. Include in your drawings cable orientations and screw locations. You might consider using a digital camera. Photos that you take at each step in the disassembly process will be a great help when it's time to put the notebook back together.

19

A+
220-801
3.1

A+
220-802
4.8

When disassembling a notebook, consider the following tips:

▲ Make your best effort to find the hardware service manual for the particular note-book model you are servicing. The manual should include all the detailed steps to disassemble the notebook and a parts list of components that can be ordered from the notebook manufacturer. If you don't have this manual, your chances of success-fully replacing an internal component are greatly reduced! And, if you don't have much experience disassembling a notebook, it is not wise to attempt to do so without this manual.

▲ Consider the warranty that might still apply to the notebook. Remember that open-ing the case of a notebook under warranty most likely will void the warranty. Make certain that any component you have purchased to replace an internal component will work in the model of notebook you are servicing.

▲ Take your time. Patience is needed to keep from scratching or marring plastic screw covers, hinges, and the case.

▲ As you work, don't force anything. If you find yourself forcing something, you're likely to break it.

▲ Always wear a ground strap or use other protection against ESD.

▲ When removing cables, know that sometimes cable connectors are ZIF connectors. To disconnect a cable from a ZIF connector, first pull up on the connector and then remove the cable, as shown in Figure 19-48. Figure 19-49 shows a notebook using three ZIF connectors that hold the three keyboard cables in place.

▲ Again, use a dental pick or very small screwdriver to pry up the plastic cover hiding a screw.

▲ Some notebooks use plastic screws that are intended to be used only once. The service manual will tell you to be careful to not overtighten these screws and to always use new screws when reassembling a notebook.

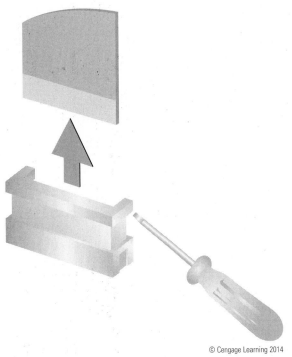

© Cengage Learning 2014

Figure 19-48 To disconnect a ZIF connector, first push up on the connector to release the latch, and then remove the cable

A+
220-801
3.1

A+
220-802
4.8

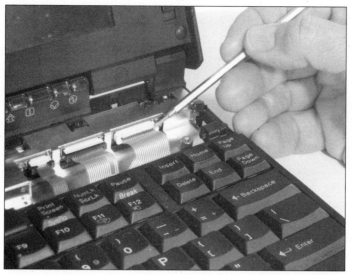

© Cengage Learning 2014

Figure 19-49   Three ZIF connectors hold the three keyboard cables in place

◢ Disassemble the notebook by removing each field replaceable unit (FRU) in the order given by the service manual for your notebook. For example, one manufacturer says that to replace the motherboard for a notebook, remove components in this order: battery pack, RAM door, keyboard, middle cover, hinge cover, DVD drive and bracket, mini PCIe adapter, keyboard bezel assembly, fan assembly, CPU, CPU fixture, and DVD drive bracket. After all these components are removed, you can then remove the motherboard. Follow the steps to remove each component in the right order.

When reassembling a notebook, consider these general tips:

◢ Reassemble the notebook in the reverse order of the way you disassembled it. Follow each step carefully.
◢ Be sure to tighten, but not overtighten, all screws. Loose screws or metal fragments in a notebook can be dangerous; they might cause a short as they shift about inside the notebook.
◢ Before you install the battery or AC adapter, verify there are no loose parts inside the notebook. Pick it up and shake it. If you hear anything loose, open the case and find the loose component, screw, spring, or metal flake, and fix the problem.

Now let's look at the specific situations where you are disassembling a notebook to replace an LCD panel, mini PCIe card, and other internal components.

REPLACING THE KEYBOARD AND TOUCHPAD

Replacing the keyboard is pretty easy to do. Here are typical steps that are similar to many models of notebooks:

1. Power down the notebook and remove the AC adapter and the battery pack.

2. Remove two or more screws on the bottom of the notebook (see Figure 19-50). (Only the documentation can tell you which ones because there are probably several of them used to hold various components in place.)

3. Turn the notebook over and open the lid. Gently push the keyboard toward the lid while pulling it up to release it from the case (see Figure 19-51).

19

A+
220-801
3.1

A+
220-802
4.8

Figure 19-50 Remove screws on the bottom of the notebook

© Cengage Learning 2014

Figure 19-51 Pry up and lift the keyboard out of the notebook case

© Cengage Learning 2014

4. Bring the keyboard out of the case and forward to expose the keyboard ribbon cable attached underneath the board. Use a screwdriver to lift the cable connector up and out of its socket (see Figure 19-52).

5. Replace the keyboard following the steps in reverse order.

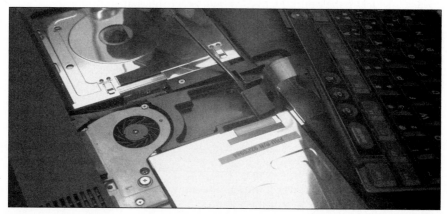

Figure 19-52 Disconnect the keyboard cable from the motherboard

© Cengage Learning 2014

A+
220-801
3.1

Sometimes the touchpad and keyboard are one complete field replaceable unit. If the touchpad is a separate component, if might be part of the keyboard bezel, also called the palm rest. This bezel is the flat cover that surrounds the keyboard. Most likely you have to remove the keyboard before you can remove the keyboard bezel.

A+
220-802
4.8

REPLACING OPTICAL DRIVES

For some systems you'll need to first remove the keyboard to expose an optical drive. Follow along as we remove the DVD drive from one system:

1. Remove the keyboard.

2. Remove the screw that holds the DVD drive to the notebook (see Figure 19-53).

3. Slide the drive out of the bay (see Figure 19-54).

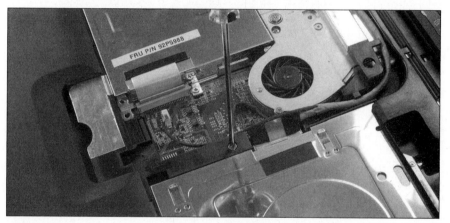

© Cengage Learning 2014

Figure 19-53 Remove the screw that holds the DVD drive

© Cengage Learning 2014

Figure 19-54 Slide the drive out of the bay

19

4. When you slide the new drive into the bay, make sure you push it far enough into the bay that it solidly connects with the drive connector at the back of the bay. Replace the screw.

For other systems, the optical drive can be removed by first removing a cover from the bottom of the notebook. Then you remove one screw that secures the drive. Next, push the optical drive out of the case (see Figure 19-55).

A+
220-801
3.1

A+
220-802
4.8

Screw was
removed from this
screw hole to free
the optical drive

© Cengage Learning 2014

Figure 19-55   Push the optical drive out the side of the case

REPLACING EXPANSION CARDS

A notebook does not contain the normal PCI Express or PCI slots found in desktop systems. Newer notebooks are likely to use the **Mini PCI Express** slots (also called **Mini PCIe** slots) that use the PCI Express standards applied to notebooks. Mini PCI Express slots use 52 pins on the edge connector. These slots can be used by many kinds of Mini PCIe cards. These cards are often used to enhance communications options for a notebook, including Wi-Fi wireless, cellular WAN, and Bluetooth Mini PCIe cards. Figure 19-56 shows a Mini PCI

Courtesy of Sierra Wireless

Figure 19-56   MC8775 PCI Express Mini card
by Sierra Wireless used for
voice and data transmissions
on 3G networks

A+
220-801
3.1

A+
220-802
4.8

Express Sierra Wireless mobile broadband Internet card. Older notebooks use a **Mini PCI** slot (see Figure 19-57), which uses PCI standards. Mini PCI cards are about twice the size of Mini PCI Express cards. Figure 19-58 shows a Wi-Fi Mini PCI card by MikroTik.

© Cengage Learning 2014

Figure 19-57 A Mini PCI slot follows PCI standards applied to notebooks

Courtesy of MikroTik

Figure 19-58 Wireless IEEE 802.11a/b/g/n Mini PCI card by MikroTik

19

For many laptops, you can remove a cover on the bottom of the laptop to expose expansion cards so that you can exchange them without an extensive disassemble. For example, to remove the cover on the bottom of one Lenovo laptop, first remove several screws and then lift the laptop cover up and out. Several internal components are exposed, as shown in Figure 19-59.

The half-size Mini PCIe wireless Wi-Fi card shown in Figure 19-60 has two antennas. To remove the card, first remove the one screw shown in the photo and disconnect the two black and white antenna wires. Then slide the card forward and out of the slot. You can then install a new card.

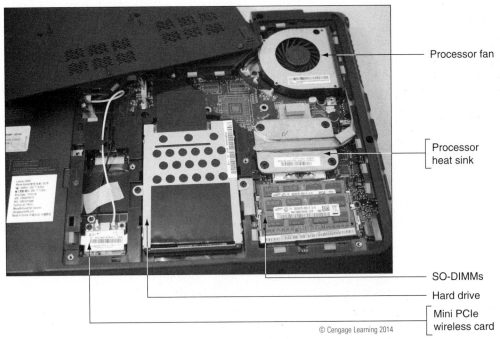

Processor fan

Processor
heat sink

SO-DIMMs

Hard drive

Mini PCIe
wireless card

© Cengage Learning 2014

Figure 19-59 Removing the cover from the bottom of a laptop exposes several
internal components

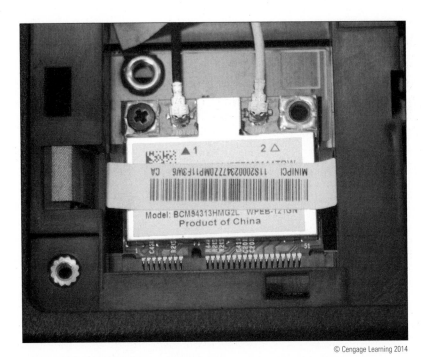

© Cengage Learning 2014

Figure 19-60 This half-size Mini PCIe wireless card is anchored in the
expansion slot with one screw

Figure 19-61 shows a full-size Mini PCIe card installed in a different laptop. First disconnect the one antenna and remove the one screw at the top of the card, and then pull the
card forward and out of the slot.

A+
220-801
3.1

A+
220-802
4.8

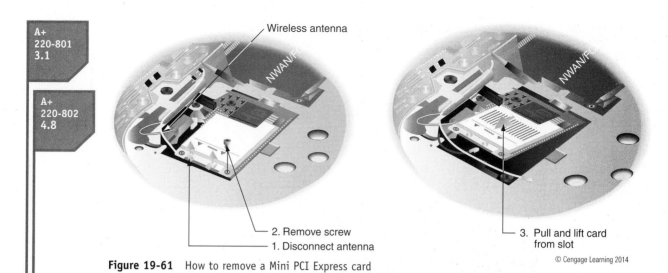

Figure 19-61 How to remove a Mini PCI Express card

© Cengage Learning 2014

> **💡 A+ Exam Tip** The A+ 220–801 exam expects you to be able to replace a Mini PCIe card in a notebook.

After you have installed a Mini PCIe card that is a Bluetooth, cellular WAN, or other wireless adapter, try to connect the notebook to the wireless network. If you have problems making a connection, verify that Device Manager reports the device is working properly and that Event Viewer has not reported error events about the device.

REPLACING THE PROCESSOR

When replacing or upgrading the processor in a laptop, be sure to select a processor supported by the notebook manufacturer for this particular notebook. The range of processors supported by a notebook does not usually include as many options as those supported by a desktop motherboard. Some significant Intel mobile processor sockets include FCPGA988, PPGA988, and the older PPGA478. Currently the FCPGA988 is the most popular Intel mobile socket. AMD sockets for mobile processors include sockets S1, AM2+, and ASB1. By far, the most used AMD mobile socket is the 638-pin S1 socket.

For many laptops, removing the cover on the bottom of a laptop exposes the processor fan and heat sink assembly. When you remove this assembly, you can then open the socket and remove the processor. For example, looking back at the laptop shown in Figure 19-59, you can see the processor heat sink and fan assembly exposed. To remove the assembly, remove the seven screws and the fan power connector (see Figure 19-62). Then lift the assembly straight up, being careful not to damage the processor underneath.

For another laptop, the heat sink and fan assembly is also exposed when you remove the cover on the bottom of the laptop (see Figure 19-63). Notice the heat sink on this laptop extends to the processor and chipset. You remove several screws and then lift the entire assembly out as a unit. For both laptops, the heat sink fits on top of the processor and the fan sits to the side of the processor. This design is typical of many laptops. However, some laptops require you to remove the keyboard and the keyboard bezel to reach the fan assembly and processor under the bezel.

Figure 19-64 shows the heat sink and fan assembly removed in one laptop, exposing the processor. Notice the thermal compound on the processor. To remove the processor, turn the CPU socket screw 90 degrees to open the socket, as shown in the figure. Most Intel and AMD sockets have this socket screw on the side of the socket, as shown in Figure 19-64, although other sockets have the screw on the corner of the socket.

Seven screws
secure the fan
and heat sink
assembly

© Cengage Learning 2014

Figure 19-62 Seven screws hold the processor heat sink and
fan assembly in place

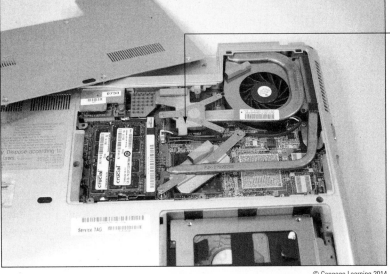

Processor socket
is under this
portion of the
heat sink

© Cengage Learning 2014

Figure 19-63 Remove the cover from the bottom of the laptop to expose the
heat sink and fan assembly and to reach the processor

A+
220-801
3.1

A+
220-802
4.8

Figure 19-64   Open the CPU socket

© Cengage Learning 2014

Lift the CPU from the socket. Be careful to lift straight up without bending the CPU pins. Figure 19-65 shows the processor out of the socket. If you look carefully, you can see the missing pins on one corner of the processor and socket. This corner is used to correctly orient the processor in the socket, which is socket 478B.

Figure 19-65   The processor removed from socket 478B

© Cengage Learning 2014

Before you place the new processor into the socket, be sure the socket screw is in the open position. Then delicately place the processor into its socket. If it does not drop in completely, consider that the screw might not be in the full open position. Be sure to use thermal compound on top of the processor. Intel recommends 0.2 grams of compound, which is about the size of a small pea. To make sure you use just the right amount of compound, consider buying it in individual packets that are measured for a single application.

REPLACING THE MOTHERBOARD

Replacing the motherboard probably means you'll need to fully disassemble the entire notebook except the LCD assembly. Therefore, before you tackle the job, consider alternatives. If a port or component on the motherboard fails, consider installing an external device

19

rather than replacing the motherboard (also called the system board). Also, before you decide to replace the motherboard, check if the notebook manufacturer has diagnostic software you can download and use to verify the problem is the motherboard. Search the site for information about the error message or symptom. Replacing the motherboard is a big deal, so consider that the cost of repair, including parts and labor, might be more than the laptop is worth. A new laptop might be your best solution.

Here is the general procedure for replacing the motherboard in one notebook:

1. Remove the keyboard, optical drive, and mini PCIe card.

2. The next step is to remove the notebook lid and keyboard bezel assembly. To do this, first remove two screws on the back of the notebook (see Figure 19-66) and the screws on the bottom of the notebook. You can then crack the case by lifting the notebook lid and keyboard bezel from the case (see Figure 19-67).

© Cengage Learning 2014

Figure 19-66 Remove two screws on the back of the notebook

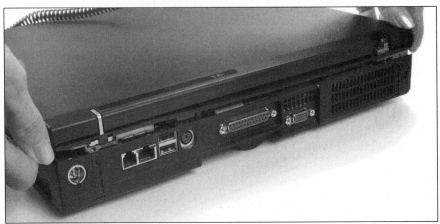

© Cengage Learning 2014

Figure 19-67 Cracking the notebook case

3. Lift up the assembly and look underneath to see two cables connecting the assembly to the motherboard (see Figure 19-68). Disconnect these two cables and set the assembly aside.

4. Figure 19-69 shows the open case. To remove the CPU fan assembly, remove screws (see Figure 19-70) and then lift the fan assembly up. Then open the CPU socket and remove the CPU.

© Cengage Learning 2014

Figure 19-68   Lift the assembly to locate the two cable connections

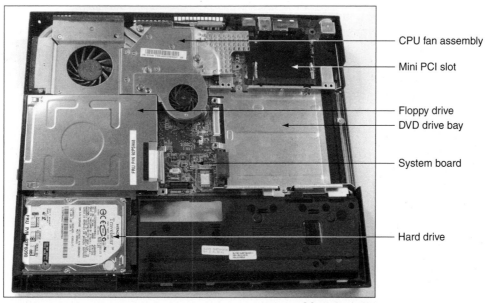

CPU fan assembly

Mini PCI slot

Floppy drive
DVD drive bay

System board

Hard drive

© Cengage Learning 2014

Figure 19-69   Components inside the open case

19

© Cengage Learning 2014

Figure 19-70   Remove the screws holding the CPU fan assembly in place

5. The DVD drive can now be removed, and the motherboard is fully exposed.

6. Remove a single screw that holds the motherboard in place (see Figure 19-71) and lift the board out of the case. Figure 19-72 shows the top of the board, and Figure 19-73 shows the bottom. Both top and bottom are packed with components. When reassembling the system, all steps are done in reverse.

© Cengage Learning 2014

Figure 19-71   Remove the single screw attaching the motherboard to the case

A+
220-801
3.1

A+
220-802
4.8

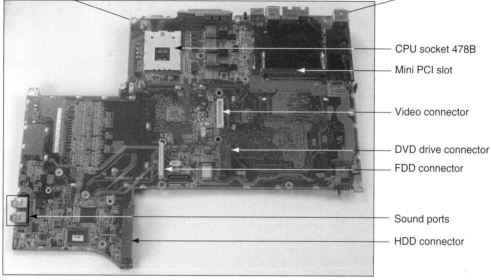

Ports on back of motherboard

CPU socket 478B

Mini PCI slot

Video connector

DVD drive connector

FDD connector

Sound ports

HDD connector

© Cengage Learning 2014

Figure 19-72 Top of the motherboard

Chipset

SO-DIMM slots
(one populated)

CardBus bay

© Cengage Learning 2014

Figure 19-73 Bottom of the motherboard

19

REPLACING THE LCD PANEL

A notebook display almost always uses LCD technology, although Samsung recently released a notebook that uses OLED display. It is expected that laptops will one day use plasma display because plasma is expected to use only about 20 percent as much power as LCD and gives better quality display than LCD. Some laptop LCD panels use LED backlighting to improve display quality and conserve power.

Because the LCD panel is so fragile, it is one component that is likely to be broken when a notebook is not handled properly. If the LCD panel is dim or black when the notebook is running, first try to use the video port on the notebook to connect it to an external monitor. After you connect the monitor, use a function key to toggle between the LCD panel, the external monitor, and both the panel and monitor. If the external monitor works, but the LCD panel does not work, then most likely the problem is with the LCD panel assembly.

> **A+ Exam Tip** The A+ 220-801 exam expects you to know about the components within the display of a laptop, including LCD, LED, OLED, and plasma types. You also need to know about backlighting and the function of an inverter.

If the LCD display is entirely black, most likely you'll have to replace the entire LCD assembly. However, if the screen is dim, but you can make out that some display is present, the problem might be the inverter. The inverter converts DC to AC used to power the backlighting of the LCD panel (see Figure 19-74). Check with the notebook manufacturer to confirm that it makes sense to first try replacing just the relatively inexpensive inverter board before you replace the more expensive entire LCD panel assembly. If the entire assembly needs replacing, the cost of the assembly might exceed the value of the notebook. You also need to know that LCD panels that use LED backlighting don't use an inverter because the LED backlight uses DC power directly from the motherboard.

© Cengage Learning 2014

Figure 19-74 A ThinkPad inverter board

Sometimes, a notebook LCD panel, including the entire cover and hinges, is considered a single field replaceable unit, and sometimes components within the LCD assembly are considered FRUs. For example, the field replaceable units for the display panel in Figure 19-75 are the LCD front bezel, the hinges, the LCD panel, the inverter card, the LCD interface cables, the LCD USB cover, and the rear cover. Also know that an LCD assembly might include a microphone, webcam, or speakers that are embedded in the laptop lid. For other laptops, the microphone and speakers are inside the case. In addition, a Wi-Fi antenna might be in the lid of the notebook. When you disassemble the lid, you must disconnect the antenna from the bottom part of the notebook.

Some high-end notebooks contain a video card that has embedded video memory. This video card might also need replacing. In most cases, you would replace only the LCD panel and perhaps the inverter card.

A+
220-801
3.1, 3.2

A+
220-802
4.8

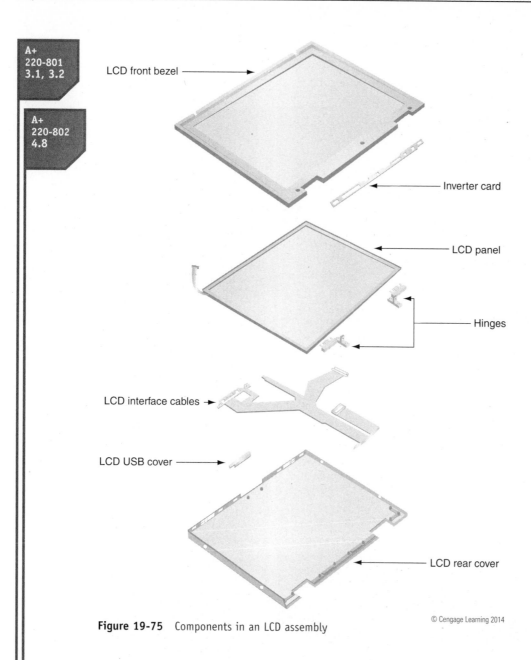

LCD front bezel

Inverter card

LCD panel

Hinges

LCD interface cables

LCD USB cover

LCD rear cover

© Cengage Learning 2014

Figure 19-75 Components in an LCD assembly

The following are some general directions to replace an LCD panel:

1. Remove the AC adapter and the battery pack.

2. Remove the keyboard.

3. Remove the screws holding the hinge in place and remove the hinge cover. Figure 19-76 shows a notebook with a metal hinge cover, but some notebooks use plastic covers that you can easily break as you remove them. Be careful with the plastic ones.

4. Remove the screws holding the LCD panel to the notebook.

5. You're now ready to remove the LCD panel from the notebook. Be aware there might be wires running through the hinge assembly, cables, or a pin connector. Cables might be connected to the motherboard using ZIF connectors. As you remove the LCD top cover, be careful to watch for how the panel is connected. Don't pull on wires or cables as you remove the cover, but first carefully disconnect them.

19

A+
220-801
3.1, 3.2

A+
220-802
4.8

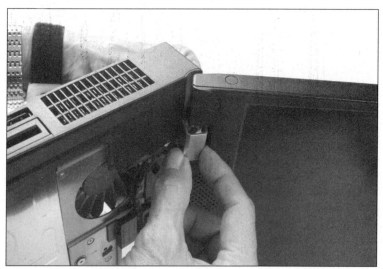

© Cengage Learning 2014

Figure 19-76 Remove the hinge cover from the notebook hinge

6. Next, remove screws that hold the top cover and LCD panel together. Sometimes, these screws are covered with plastic or rubber circles or pads that match the color of the case. First use a dental pick or small screwdriver to pick off these covers. You should then be able to remove the front bezel and separate the rear cover from the LCD panel. For one LCD panel, when you separate the LCD assembly from the lid cover, you can see the inverter card. Figure 19-77 shows the inverter card being compared to the new one to make sure they match. The match is not identical but should work.

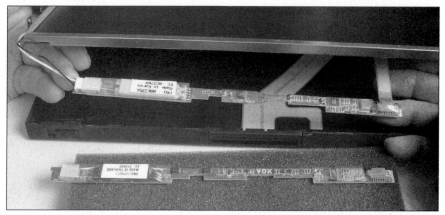

© Cengage Learning 2014

Figure 19-77 The inverter is exposed and is compared to the new one

7. Disconnect the old inverter and install the new one. When disconnecting the ribbon cable from the old inverter, notice you must first lift up on the lock holding the ZIF connector in place, as shown in Figure 19-78.

8. Install the new inverter. Reassemble the LCD panel assembly. Make sure the assembly is put together with a tight fit so that all screws line up well.

9. Reattach the LCD panel assembly to the notebook.

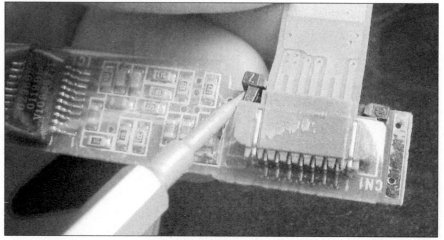

© Cengage Learning 2014

Figure 19-78 Lift up on the ZIF connector locking mechanism before removing the ribbon cable

WORKING INSIDE AN ALL-IN-ONE COMPUTER

An all-in-one computer uses a mix of components sized for a desktop computer and a notebook. Just as with notebooks, you'll need the service manual to know how to crack the case and replace internal components. Also, for some components, such as the motherboard and power supply, you'll need to buy the replacement component from the all-in-one manufacturer because these components are likely to be proprietary as with many notebook components.

For specific directions about replacing parts in an all-in-one, see the service manual. Let's get the general idea by looking inside the case of the Lenovo ThinkCentre all-in-one shown earlier in Figure 19-1. First remove all discs and other devices, shut down the computer, and disconnect all cables. Lay the computer flat with the LCD panel down on a soft cloth or other surface that will not scratch the screen. An antistatic pad works well. To open the case, push the two clips on either side of the case cover outward as you push the back of the case upward toward the top of the computer. See Figure 19-79. The case cover can then be removed and laid to the side.

Figure 19-80 shows the computer with the case cover removed. Notice in the figure the hard drive is a 3.5 inch drive appropriate for a desktop system, and the memory modules

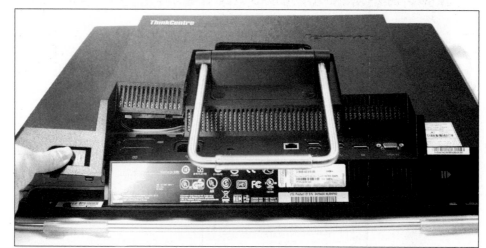

© Cengage Learning 2014

Figure 19-79 Push back on release tabs to open the case of an all-in-one computer

19

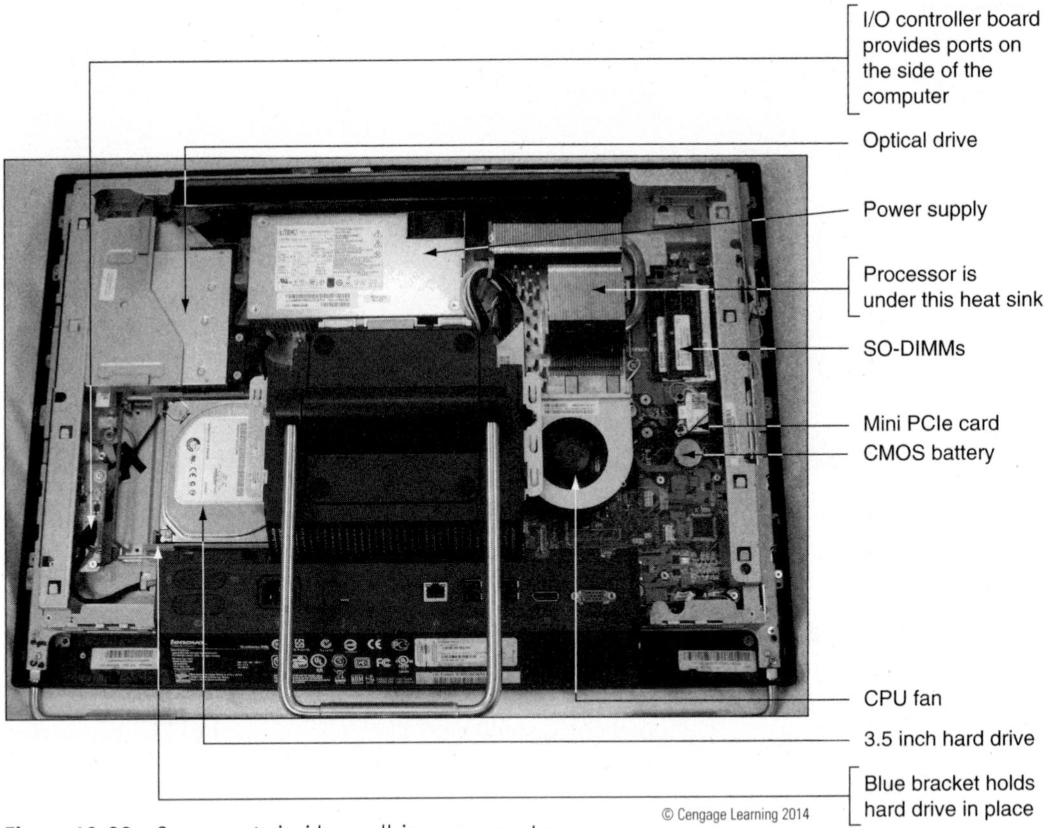

I/O controller board provides ports on the side of the computer

Optical drive

Power supply

Processor is under this heat sink

SO-DIMMs

Mini PCIe card
CMOS battery

CPU fan

3.5 inch hard drive

Blue bracket holds hard drive in place

© Cengage Learning 2014

Figure 19-80 Components inside an all-in-one computer

are SO-DIMMs appropriate for a notebook. So goes the hybrid nature of an all-in-one. The fan and heat sink look more like that of a notebook computer, but the processor socket on the motherboard is a desktop processor socket, another hybrid design.

Several components are easy to exchange in this all-in-one without further disassembly. For example, the Mini PCIe card for wireless connectivity, shown in Figure 19-81, is easy to get to as is the CMOS battery that you can see to the left of the card.

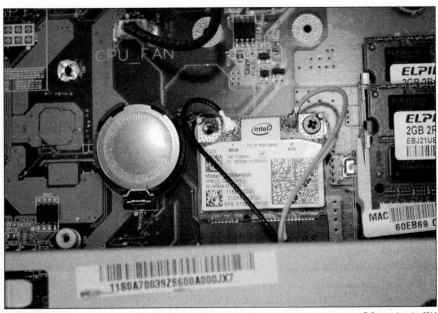

© Cengage Learning 2014

Figure 19-81 CMOS battery and Mini PCIe wireless card

A+
220-801
3.1

A+
220-802
4.8

To remove the hard drive, simply lift up on the blue handle shown in Figure 19-82 and slide the drive attached to the blue bracket out of the case. You then have to remove the bracket from the old drive, install it on the new drive, and reinsert the bracket with the new drive.

Blue handle

© Cengage Learning 2014

Figure 19-82 Lift up on the blue handle to release the 3.5 inch hard drive

The optical drive is removed by pressing a release button at the back of the optical drive and then sliding it out of the case. After the hard drive and optical drive are removed, you can get to the video inverter, which is secured to the case with two screws (see Figure 19-83).

Optical drive

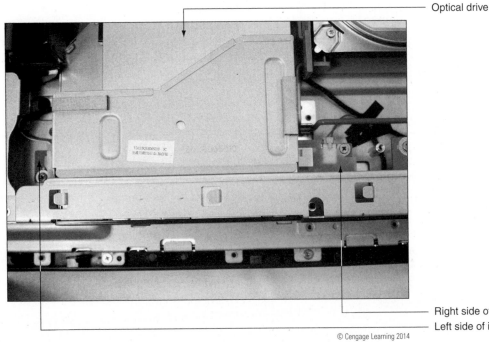

Right side of inverter
Left side of inverter

© Cengage Learning 2014

Figure 19-83 Optical drive above the inverter

19

The SO-DIMMs shown in Figure 19-84 are to the right of the Mini PCIe card. The processor is underneath the heat sink, and the heat sink is held in place with four screws shown in Figure 19-84. Remove the four screws and lift the heat sink up and out exposing the processor. The desktop processor socket works like the ones you saw in Chapter 5.

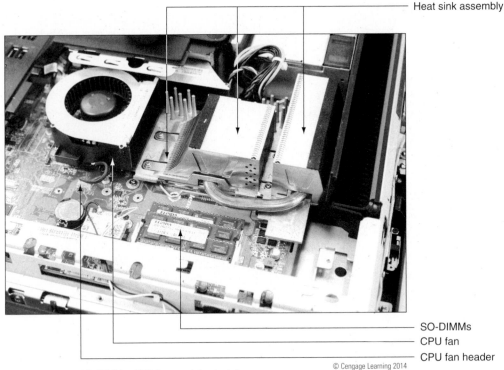

Heat sink assembly

SO-DIMMs
CPU fan
CPU fan header

© Cengage Learning 2014

Figure 19-84   SO-DIMMs, CPU fan, and heat sink

To exchange the LCD panel is not as difficult as you might expect. The motherboard, power supply, drives, and other components are secured to a front bezel. This bezel is secured to the case with 13 screws along the four edges of the case. You can see several of these screws just inside the outer edge of the case in Figure 19-80. When you remove the 13 screws, you can lift out the bezel like a tray holding all its installed components. The LCD panel is then exposed, which is held in place with four screws.

TROUBLESHOOTING NOTEBOOKS

When troubleshooting problems with notebook ports, slots, or other devices, don't forget to use the diagnostics software installed on the hard drive or available on the notebook manufacturer's web site to help with troubleshooting components. Now let's look at some common problems with notebooks and how to solve them.

Video
Troubleshooting Notebooks

PROBLEMS LOGGING ONTO WINDOWS

If a user complains she cannot log onto Windows even when she's certain she is entering the correct password, ask her to make sure the NumLock key is off. Notebooks use this key to toggle between the keys interpreted as letters and numbers. Most notebooks have a NumLock indicator light near the keyboard.

NO WIRELESS CONNECTIVITY

In a notebook, an internal wireless adapter uses an internal antenna, and the notebook might have a switch to turn on the internal wireless adapter or might use a key combination for that purpose. Look for the switch near the keyboard or on the side of the notebook (see Figure 19-85). Make sure the switch is set to the on position when you want to use wireless. The internal antenna might be embedded in the lid of the notebook. Raising the lid to a vertical position can sometimes improve the signal and solve a problem with intermittent connectivity. For intermittent wireless connectivity, check that the laptop is within range of the wireless access point.

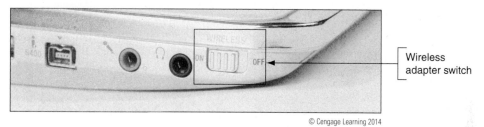

© Cengage Learning 2014

Figure 19-85 This switch controls an internal wireless adapter

If your notebook supports Bluetooth, you need to read the documentation for configuring the Bluetooth connection that came with the notebook because Bluetooth setups differ from one notebook to another. Following the directions for your notebook, turn on Bluetooth. After Bluetooth is turned on, you should be able to make a connection with your Bluetooth device when it is set close to the notebook.

If you are having problems getting the Bluetooth connection to work, try the following:

◢ Make sure Bluetooth is turned on (for some notebooks, Bluetooth and Wi-Fi wireless is controlled by a function key or a wireless switch).

◢ Verify that Windows sees Bluetooth enabled. You might do this by using an applet in Control Panel, by using a program on the Start menu, or by using the Bluetooth icon in the notification area of the taskbar.

Notes Be aware that a notebook might show the Bluetooth icon in the taskbar even when the notebook does not support Bluetooth.

◢ Be sure you have downloaded all Windows updates. (Windows XP Service Pack 2 is required for Bluetooth.)

◢ Look in Device Manager to make sure the Bluetooth component is recognized with no errors. For some notebooks, even though the component is an internal device, it is seen in Device Manager as a USB device.

◢ Make sure the other device has Bluetooth turned on. For example, when trying to communicate with a cell phone, you must use the menu on the phone to activate Bluetooth connections. Windows should see the Bluetooth device when you use the Bluetooth icon in the taskbar and then click **Add a device,** as shown in Figure 19-86.

◢ The Bluetooth software on the notebook might have a high level of security enabled. If so, you can lower the security mode or follow directions in the documentation to pair up the two devices. Pairing up is the term used to allow the other device to use your secured Bluetooth connection and involves entering a password before the connection is established.

◢ You can also try uninstalling and reinstalling the Bluetooth drivers that come bundled with your notebook.

19

A+
220-802
4.8

◢ You can also try uninstalling and reinstalling the drivers for your Bluetooth device. For example, if you are trying to connect to a printer using a Bluetooth wireless connection, try first turning on Bluetooth and then uninstalling and reinstalling the printer. During the printer installation, select the Bluetooth connection for the printer port, which might be called Bluetooth COM or something similar.

For more ideas for solving a Bluetooth problem, try the web site of the notebook manufacturer or the web site of the device you are trying to connect to your notebook using Bluetooth.

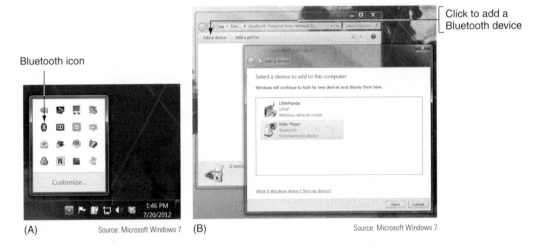

Bluetooth icon

Click to add a Bluetooth device

(A)   Source: Microsoft Windows 7   (B)   Source: Microsoft Windows 7

Figure 19-86   (a) Bluetooth icon used to control Bluetooth devices and settings, and (b) connect to a Bluetooth device

POWER OR BATTERY PROBLEMS

If power is not getting to the system or the battery indicator light is lit when the AC adapter should be supplying power, verify the AC adapter is plugged into a live electrical outlet. Is the light on the AC adapter lit? Check if the AC adapter's plug is secure in the electrical outlet. Check the connections on both sides of the AC adapter transformer. Check the connection at the notebook. Try exchanging the AC adapter for one you know is good.

If the battery is not charging when the AC adapter is plugged in, the problem might be with the battery or the motherboard. A hot battery might not charge until it cools down. If the battery is hot, remove it from the computer and allow it to cool to room temperature. Then try to recharge it.

APPLYING | CONCEPTS   TEST AN AC ADAPTER

If the system fails only when the AC adapter is connected, it might be defective. Try a new AC adapter, or, if you have a multimeter, use it to verify the voltage output of the adapter. Do the following for an adapter with a single center pin connector:

1. Unplug the AC adapter from the computer, but leave it plugged into the electrical outlet.

2. Using a multimeter set to measure voltage in the 1 to 20 V DC range, place the red probe of the multimeter in the center of the DC connector that would normally plug into the DC outlet on the notebook. Place the black probe on the outside cylinder of the DC connector (see Figure 19-87).

3. The voltage range should be plus or minus 5 percent of the accepted voltage. For example, if a notebook is designed to use 16 V, the voltage should measure somewhere between 15.2 and 16.8 V DC.

A+
220-802
4.8

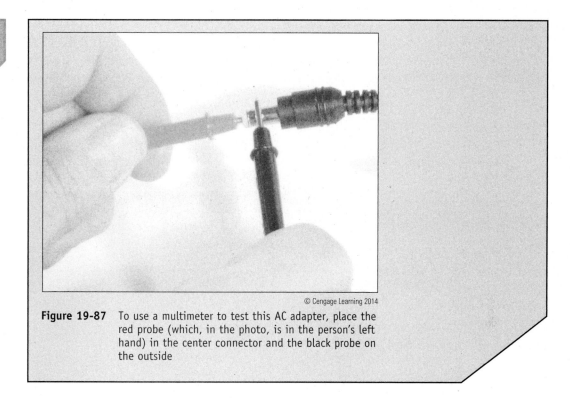

© Cengage Learning 2014

Figure 19-87 To use a multimeter to test this AC adapter, place the red probe (which, in the photo, is in the person's left hand) in the center connector and the black probe on the outside

NO DISPLAY

If the LCD panel shows a black screen, but the power light indicates that power is getting to the system, the video subsystem might be the source of the problem. Do the following:

1. Look for an LCD cutoff switch or button on the laptop (see Figure 19-88). The switch must be on for the LCD panel to work.

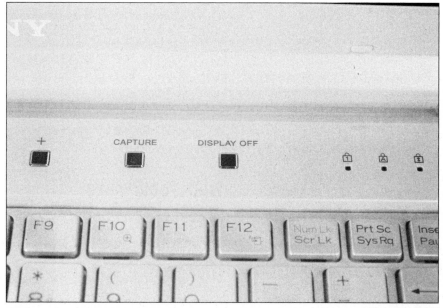

© Cengage Learning 2014

Figure 19-88 LCD cutoff button on a laptop

19

2. Try to use the video port on the notebook to connect it to an external monitor. After you connect the monitor, use a function key to toggle between the LCD panel, the external monitor, and both the panel and monitor. If the external monitor works, but the LCD panel does not work, try these things using the external monitor:

▲ Check Device Manager for warnings about the video controller and to update the video drivers. See Figure 19-89 for an example of the dedicated video card installed on the motherboard of one laptop.

▲ Check Event Viewer for reported problems with the video subsystem.

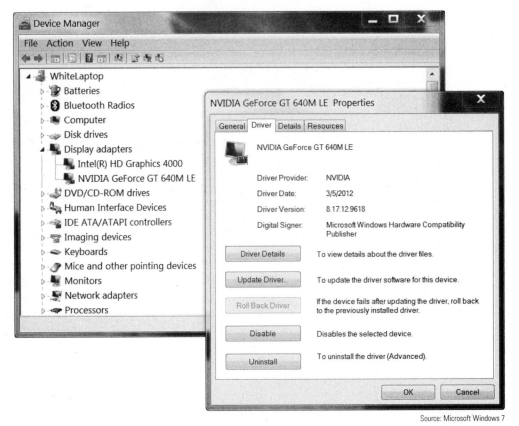

Source: Microsoft Windows 7

Figure 19-89 Use Device Manager to check for errors and update the video drivers

3. If you still can't get the LCD panel to work, but the external monitor does work, you have proven the problem is with the LCD panel assembly. Recall from earlier in the chapter, a dim screen or no display can be caused by a bad inverter. If replacing the inverter does not help, the next task is to replace the LCD panel. Be aware the replacement components might cost more than the laptop is worth.

FLICKERING, DIM, OR OTHERWISE POOR VIDEO

Use these tips to solve problems with bad video:

▲ Verify Windows display settings. Try using the native resolution for the LCD panel. This resolution will be the highest resolution available unless the wrong video drivers are installed.

▲ Try adjusting the brightness, which is a function of the backlight component of the LCD panel.

▲ Try updating the video drivers. Download the latest drivers from the notebook manufacturer's web site. Bad drivers can cause an occasional ghost cursor on-screen. A **ghost cursor** is a trail left behind when you move the mouse.

▲ A flickering screen can be caused by bad video drivers, a low refresh rate, a bad inverter, or loose connections inside the laptop. To adjust the refresh rate, use Control Panel to open the Display window. In the Display window, click **Change display settings**. In the Screen Resolution window, click **Advanced settings**. On the Monitor tab, select the highest refresh rate available (see Figure 19-90).

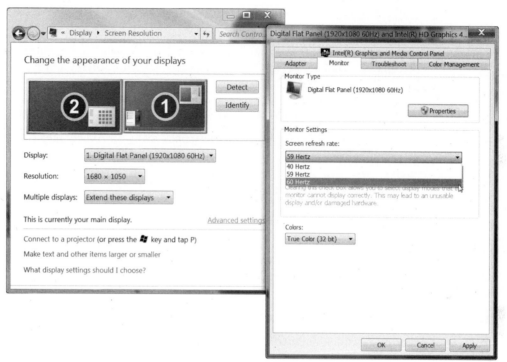

Figure 19-90   Use the highest refresh rate the system supports

Source: Microsoft Windows 7

>> CHAPTER SUMMARY

Special Considerations when Supporting Notebooks

▲ Notebook computers are designed for travel. They use the same technology as desktop computers, with modifications for space, portability, and power conservation. A notebook generally costs more than a desktop with comparable power and features. Special concerns when supporting a notebook also apply to supporting a netbook or all-in-one computer.

▲ When supporting notebooks, pay careful attention to what the warranty allows you to change on the computer.

▲ The notebook manufacturer documentation, including the service manual, diagnostic software, and recovery media are useful when disassembling, troubleshooting, and repairing a notebook.

▲ A notebook uses a customized installation of the Windows OS, customized by the notebook manufacturer. For most situations, the OS does not need upgrading for the life of the notebook unless you need to use features of a new OS. To perform an upgrade, you might need to obtain a customized version of the new OS from the notebook manufacturer.

19

◢ A notebook hard drive is likely to contain a recovery partition or the notebook might come bundled with recovery CDs. You might be able to create recovery media by using a program installed on the hard drive. Use the media to diagnose problems with the notebook, create system backups, and reimage the hard drive if the hard drive is replaced or becomes corrupted.

Maintaining Notebooks and Notebook Components

◢ Use special keys or buttons on a notebook to manage volume, dual displays, screen brightness, and Bluetooth.

◢ PC Cards, CardBus, and ExpressCard slots are a popular way to add peripheral devices to notebooks. ExpressCard slots are faster and newer than PC Card or CardBus slots. All three slots are sometimes called PCMCIA slots. ExpressCard/34 and ExpressCard/54 cards do not work in PC Card slots.

◢ Updating the drivers for a port or slot can sometimes solve problems with the port or slot.

◢ A notebook can be powered by its battery pack or by an AC adapter connected to a power source. Some notebooks have two battery packs, one of which can be a sheet battery.

◢ Windows 7/Vista uses sleep mode and hibernation to conserve power. Windows XP uses standby mode and hibernation. Use Control Panel to change power settings for a notebook to conserve power and make the battery charge last longer.

◢ Port replicators and docking stations can make it easier to connect a notebook to peripherals. Docking stations can provide additional slots and bays for components.

Replacing and Upgrading Internal Parts

◢ Field replaceable units in a notebook can include the memory modules, hard drive, LCD panel, video inverter, keyboard, touchpad, processor, optical drive, DC jack, fan, motherboard, CMOS battery, Mini-PCIe card, wireless card, or speakers.

◢ When an internal component needs replacing, consider the possibility of disabling the component and using an external peripheral device in its place. Don't jeopardize the warranty on a notebook by opening the case or using components not authorized by the manufacturer.

◢ When disassembling a notebook, the manufacturer's service manual is essential.

◢ Current notebooks use SO-DIMMs for memory. SO-DIMMs can have DDR, DDR2, or DDR3 memory. An older notebook might use SO-RIMMs.

◢ When upgrading components on a notebook, including memory, use components that are the same brand as the notebook, or use only components recommended by the notebook's manufacturer.

◢ Hard drives use a SATA or 44-pin IDE connection on a notebook. Notebooks use 2.5 inch magnetic or SSD hard drives.

◢ Follow the directions in a service manual to disassemble a notebook. Keep small screws organized as you disassemble a notebook because the notebook will have a variety of sizes and lengths of screws. Some manufacturers use plastic screws and require you to use new screws rather than reuse the old ones.

Troubleshooting Notebooks

◢ Use diagnostics software from the notebook manufacturer to troubleshoot problems with notebook slots, ports, or devices.

◢ Use a multimeter to check the voltage output of an AC adapter.

◢ Use an external monitor to verify that a video problem is with the LCD panel rather than the internal video card or motherboard.

>> KEY TERMS

For explanations of key terms, see the Glossary near the end of the book.

AC adapter	inverter	S1 state
Advanced Configuration and Power Interface (ACPI)	keyboard backlight	S2 state
	laptop	S3 state
all-in-one computer	Lithium Ion	S4 state
auto-switching	Mini PCI	S5 state
CardBus	Mini PCIe	sheet battery
docking port	Mini PCI Express	sleep mode
docking station	netbook	sleep timers
ExpressCard/34	notebook	standby mode
ExpressCard/54	PC Card	suspend mode
ghost cursor	PCMCIA card	touchpad
hardware profile	pointing stick	TrackPoint
hibernation	port replicator	

>> REVIEW QUESTIONS

1. What is one variation of a notebook that is smaller and less expensive than a notebook and has fewer features?

   a) netbook

   b) smartphone

   c) all-in-one computer

   d) laptop

2. _____ mode saves all work to the hard drive and powers down the system.

   a) Standby

   b) Sleep

   c) Hibernation

   d) Suspend

19

3. When a component on a notebook needs replacing or upgrading, you first need to ____ and consider how much time the repair will take.

   a) determine repair costs

   b) obtain the manufacturer documentation

   c) back up any important data stored on the notebook

   d) consider the warranty

4. What should you do if a ground strap is not available to dissipate any ESD between you and a notebook?

   a) Touch a metallic painted part of the notebook.

   b) Touch a metallic unpainted part of the notebook.

   c) Touch the laptop cover for three seconds.

   d) Unplug the AC power supply connected to the laptop.

5. What is the first step you should take to verify that a video problem is with the LCD panel rather than with the internal video card or motherboard?

   a) Test using an external monitor.

   b) Test using the internal video card.

   c) Test using the motherboard.

   d) Test using Windows software tools.

6. True or false? Unless a specific need to upgrade arises, the operating system preinstalled on the notebook should last the life of the notebook.

7. True or false? The most common pointing device on a notebook is a mouse.

8. True or false? Most new notebooks have PCMCIA slots.

9. True or false? A notebook drive is 2.5 inches wide.

10. True or false? If a notebook LCD screen is dim, but you can make out that some display is present, you will most likely have to replace the entire LCD assembly.

11. A(n) ____ is an electrical device that changes DC to AC.

12. A(n) ____ provides the same functions as a port replicator but provides additional slots for adding secondary storage devices and expansion cards.

13. A hardware ____ is a group of settings that Windows keeps about a specific hardware configuration.

14. Today's notebooks all use ____ or DDR2 SO-DIMM (small outline DIMM) memory.

15. A(n) ____ cursor is a trail left behind when you move the mouse.

Mobile Devices and Client-side Virtualization

Previous chapters have focused on supporting personal computers. This chapter deviates from this topic as we discuss mobile devices and client-side virtualization. As mobile devices become more common, many people use them to surf the web, access email, and manage apps and data. As a computer support technician, you need to know about the operating systems and hardware used with mobile devices and how to help a user configure and secure a mobile device. The data, settings, and apps stored on mobile devices need to be backed up and synchronized to other storage locations. In this chapter, you learn how you can synchronize content on mobile devices to a personal computer or to storage in the cloud (on the Internet). Finally, in this chapter, you learn about server-side and client-side virtualization and the various ways client-side virtualization is implemented.

OPERATING SYSTEMS USED ON MOBILE DEVICES

The operating system for a mobile device is installed at the factory. Here are the two most popular ones in the United States:

- Android OS by Google (*android.com*) is based on Linux and is used on various smartphones and tablets. Currently, Android is the most popular OS for smartphones. About 60 percent of the smartphones sold today use the Android OS.
- iOS by Apple (*apple.com*) is based on Mac OS X and is currently used on the iPhone, iPad, and iPod touch by Apple. About 30 percent of smartphones sold today are made by Apple and use the iOS.

The remaining 10 percent of the current market share for smartphones in the United States is shared by these mobile OSs:

- Blackberry OS by RIM (*rim.com*) is a proprietary OS used on devices built by RIM.
- Windows Phone by Microsoft (*microsoft.com*) is based on Windows and is used on devices made by Dell, Fujitsu, Nokia, Samsung, and others.
- The Symbian OS from the Symbian Foundation (*symbian.org*) is popular outside the United States and is used on devices made by multiple manufacturers, including Nokia, Samsung, Sony, and others.

This chapter focuses on the Android and iOS operating systems used on smartphones and tablets.

> 💡 **A+ Exam Tip** The A+ 220-802 exam expects you to know how to support the Android and iOS operating systems used with mobile devices.

A+
220-802
3.1

ANDROID OS BY THE OPEN HANDSET ALLIANCE AND GOOGLE

The **Android** operating system is based on the Linux OS and uses a Linux kernel. Linux and Android are **open source**, which means the source code for the operating system is available for free and anyone can modify and redistribute the source code. Open source software is typically developed as a community effort by many contributors. Android was originally developed by the Open Handset Alliance (*www.openhandsetalliance.com*), which is made up of many technology and mobile phone companies and led by Google, Inc.

In 2005, Google acquired this source code. Google does not own Android, but it has assumed a leadership role in development, quality control, and distributions of the Android OS and Android apps. Ongoing development of the Android OS code made by Google and other contributors is released to the public as open source code.

GETTING TO KNOW AN ANDROID DEVICE

Releases of Android are named after desserts and include Froyo or frozen yogurt (version 2.2.x), Gingerbread (version 2.3.x), Honeycomb (version 3.x), and Ice Cream Sandwich (version 4.x). (Future releases of Android will follow in alphabetic order: G, H, I, and J.) Most smartphones currently sold use Gingerbread, and most tablets use Honeycomb. It is expected that most new phones and tablets will ship with Ice Cream Sandwich installed.

Android supports windows, panes, and 3D graphics. It can use an embedded browser, manage a database using SQLite, and connect to Wi-Fi, Bluetooth, and cellular networks. Current Android phones have four physical buttons on the front of the device for Menu, Home, Go Back, and Search (see Figure 20-1).

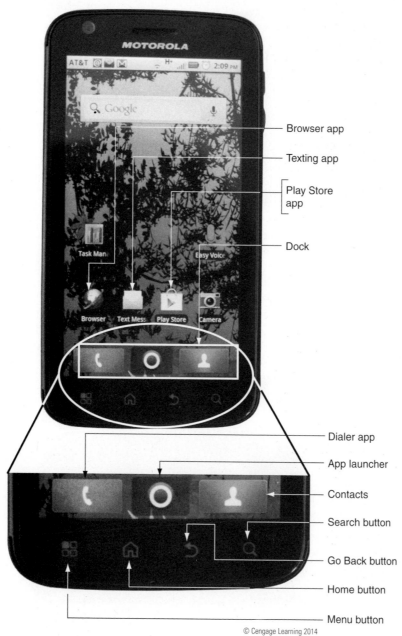

© Cengage Learning 2014

Figure 20-1 The Atrix smartphone by Motorola comes with Android Froyo installed

The Menu button changes functions (depending on the app in use) to give you settings and options for that app. On Android phones, up to four apps can be pinned to the **dock** at the bottom of the screen. The pinned apps shown in Figure 20-1 are the Dialer (for making phone calls), the App launcher (lists and manages all your apps), and Contacts. Apps in the dock stay put as you move from home screen to home screen. All but the App launcher

A+
220-802
3.1

can be replaced by third-party apps. For example, Figure 20-2 shows the home screen on an Android Gingerbread smartphone. On this phone, the apps pinned to the dock are the Dialer app, Email app, Web app (a browser to surf the web), and App launcher.

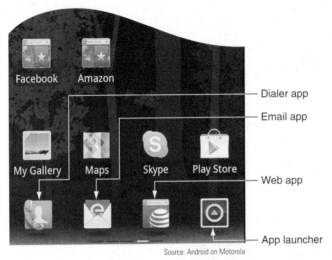

Source: Android on Motorola

Figure 20-2 This Android smartphone has four apps pinned to the dock

Android tablets have software buttons at the bottom of the screen. For example, the Android Thrive by Toshiba shown in Figure 20-3 in landscape view has the Back button, Home button, and Recent apps button in the bar at the bottom of the screen called the System bar or Action bar. Buttons in the System bar stay put as you move from home screen to home screen (up to seven screens).

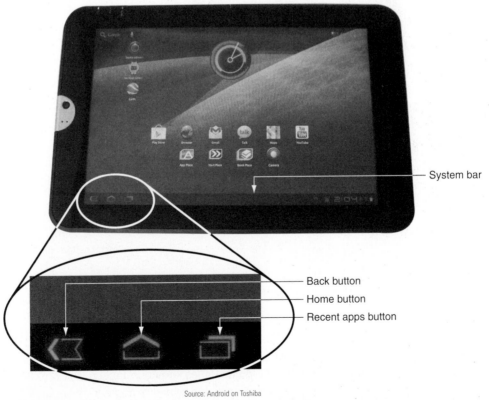

Source: Android on Toshiba

Figure 20-3 The Thrive tablet by Toshiba comes with Android Honeycomb installed

A+
220-802
3.1

ANDROID APPS

Android apps are sold or freely distributed from any source or vendor. However, the official source for apps, called the Android marketplace, is **Google Play** at *play.google.com*. To download content, you need a **Google account**, which you can set up using the web site or your device. The account is associated with any valid email address. Associate a credit card with the account to make your purchases at Google Play. Then you can purchase or download free music, books, movies, and Android apps from Google Play to your mobile device.

Android Market was renamed Google Play in March 2012. To download an app using newer versions of Android, use the Play Store app. For older versions of Android, use the Market app.

To download an app, tap the **Play Store** app or the **Market** app on the home screen of your device. (If you don't see the app icon on your home screen, tap the **App launcher** and then tap **Play Store** or **Market**.) The app takes you to Google Play, where you can search for apps, music, books, and movies (see Figure 20-4). In addition, you can get apps and data from other sources, such as the Amazon Appstore at *Amazon.com* or directly from a developer.

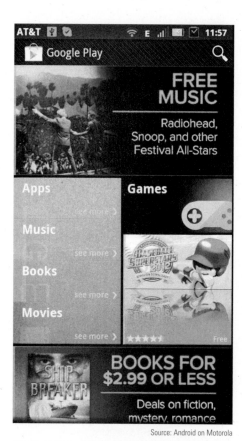

Source: Android on Motorola

Figure 20-4 Use the Play Store app to search Google Play for apps, music, books, and movies that you can download

20

Google maintains the Android web site at *android.com* where an app developer can download the Android Software Development Kit (SDK) from *developer.android.com*. An SDK is a group of tools that developers use to write apps. The Android SDK is free and is released as open source. Most Android apps are written using the Java programming language.

A+
220-802
3.1

IOS BY APPLE

Apple, Inc. (*www.apple.com*) owns, manufactures, and sells the Apple **iPhone** (a smartphone), **iPad** (a handheld tablet), and **iPod touch** (a multimedia recorder and player *and* a game player). These devices all use the **iOS** operating system, also developed and owned by Apple. The iOS is based on OS X, the operating system used by Apple desktop and laptop computers. There have been five major releases of the iOS; the latest is iOS version 5.

GETTING TO KNOW AN IOS DEVICE

Because Apple is the sole owner and distributor of the iOS, the only devices that use it are Apple devices (currently the iPhone, iPad, and iPod touch). Figure 20-5 shows an iPhone and Figure 20-6 shows an iPad. Each device has a Wake/sleep button and a Home button. Apps pinned to the bottom of the iPhone screen are the Phone, Mail, Safari, and Music apps. (The Music app is also called the iPod app.) Apps pinned to the bottom of the iPad screen are the Safari, Mail, Photos, and Music apps.

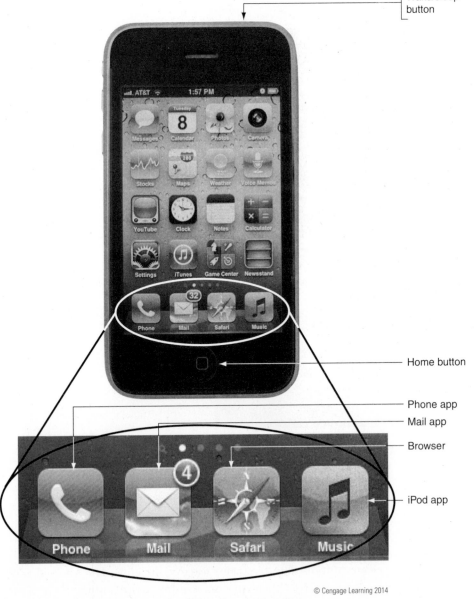

© Cengage Learning 2014

Figure 20-5   An iPhone by Apple has iOS version 5.1 installed

Figure 20-6 An iPad by Apple has iOS version 5.1 installed

Also, because Apple is the sole developer and manufacturer, it can maintain strict standards on its products, which means the iOS is extremely stable and bug free. The iOS is also a very easy and intuitive operating system to use. The iOS can have up to 11 home screens. (Use your finger to swipe screens to the left or right.) As with OS X, the iOS makes heavy use of icons.

IOS APPS AVAILABLE THROUGH ITUNES

You can get Android apps from many sources, but the only place to go for an iOS app is Apple. Apple is the sole distributer of iOS apps at its iTunes App Store (*itunes.apple.com*). Other developers can write apps for the iPhone, iPad, or iPod, but these apps must be sent to Apple for their close scrutiny. If they pass muster, they are distributed by Apple on its web site. One requirement is that an app be written in the Objective-C, C, or C++ programming language.

A+
220-802
3.1

Not only does Apple scrutinize an app for quality, it also filters apps for inappropriate content, such as pornography. What content is judged to be inappropriate? That decision is made solely by Apple.

All downloads of iOS updates and patches, apps, and multimedia content are by way of the iTunes web site. First, you set up an **Apple ID** or user account using a valid email address and password and associate this account with a credit card number. Then you can use the iTunes web site to:

▲ Use the **App Store** app on your mobile device (see Figure 20-7 for an iPhone example) to purchase and download (or download for free) content from the **iTunes Store**, including apps, music, TV shows, movies, books, podcasts, and iTunes U content. (**iTunes U** contains lectures and even complete courses from many schools, colleges, and universities.)

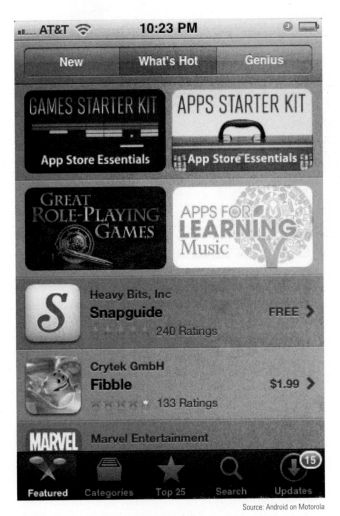

Source: Android on Motorola

Figure 20-7 Use the App Store app to download content from the iTunes Store

▲ Download and install the iTunes software on a Mac or Windows personal computer. Then connect your mobile device to the computer by way of a USB port. iTunes can then sync the device to iOS updates downloaded from *iTunes.com* and to content on your computer. You can also purchase content that is downloaded to your device by way of iTunes on your computer. Figure 20-8 shows the iTunes window when an iPhone is connected to the PC. How to use iTunes to sync data and apps on your device is covered later in the chapter.

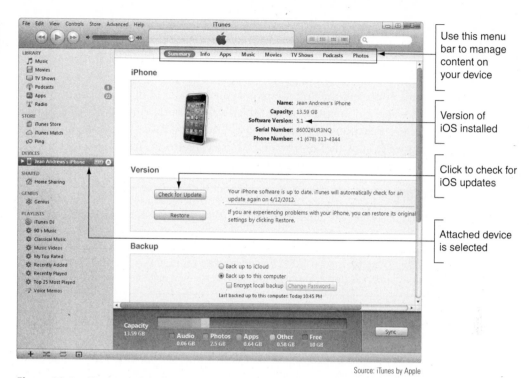

Figure 20-8 iTunes window shows summary information for an attached iPhone

When you first purchase an iPad or an iPod touch, you must activate it by connecting it to a computer that has iTunes installed. iTunes then downloads the latest updates to the iOS and you can then use the device. Therefore, the iPad and iPod touch are considered peripheral devices to a personal computer. iPhone version 5 (not iOS version 5) is to be released in late 2012, and Apple has announced that this iPhone will be capable of activating itself and directly downloading OS updates without your first connecting the device to a computer. (After activation, current iPhones and iPads can receive iOS updates without a PC connection.)

> **Notes** If you ask, a retail associate at an Apple store will activate your new iPad or iPod touch for you before you leave the store.

Recall that apps can be downloaded to an iOS device only from the iTunes Store. People have discovered that it is possible to break through this restriction in a process called jailbreaking. **Jailbreaking** gives you root or administrative privileges to the operating system and the entire file system (all files and folders) and complete access to all commands and features. Jailbreaking was once illegal, but in 2010, the U.S. Copyright Office and the Library of Congress made a copyright ruling that a user has the right to download and use software that will jailbreak his iOS device.

COMPARING OPEN SOURCE AND CLOSED SOURCE OPERATING SYSTEMS

Open source (such as the Android) and closed source (such as the iOS) operating systems have their advantages and disadvantages. Here are some key points to consider about releasing or not releasing source code:

▲ Apple carefully guards its iOS source code and internal functions of the OS. Third-party developers of apps only have access to APIs, which are calls to the OS. An app must be tested and approved by Apple before it can be sold in its online App Store. These policies assure users that apps are high quality. It also assures developers they have a central point of contact for users to buy their apps.

A+
220-802
3.1

◢ The Android source code and the development and sale of apps are not closely guarded. Apps can be purchased or downloaded from Google Play, but they can also be obtained from other sources such as *Amazon.com* or directly from a developer. This freedom comes with a cost because users are not always assured of high-quality, bug-free apps, and developers are not always assured of a convenient market for their apps.

◢ Because any smartphone or tablet manufacturer can modify the Android source code, many variations of Android exist. These variations can make it difficult for developers to write apps that port to any Android platform. It can also make it difficult for users to learn to use new Android devices because of these inconsistencies.

> **Notes** Apple iOS does not support Adobe Flash, which is used by many web sites to present graphics, animation, and other multimedia content. By comparison, the Android OS does support Flash.

> 💡 **A+ Exam Tip** The A+ 220-802 exam expects you to understand the advantages and disadvantages of open-source and closed-source operating systems on mobile devices.

COMPARING MOBILE DEVICE HARDWARE TO LAPTOPS

A+
220-802
3.1, 3.4

Besides the operating system, you need to know about hardware used with smartphones and handheld tablets and how this hardware differs from that which is used with laptops. A **smartphone** is primarily a cellphone and also includes abilities to send text messages (using a technology called **Short Message Service** or **SMS**), send text messages with photos, videos, or other multimedia content attached (using a technology called **Multimedia Messaging Service** or **MMS**), surf the web, manage email, play games, take photos and videos, and download and use small apps. A smartphone uses a cellular network (for voice or data) and is likely to have the ability to use a Wi-Fi local wireless network or make a Bluetooth wireless connection to other nearby Bluetooth devices. Earlier in the chapter, you saw smartphones that use touch screens. Figure 20-9 shows a smartphone that uses a physical keyboard and a touch screen.

© Oleksiy/www.Shutterstock.com

Figure 20-9 This smartphone uses a physical keyboard and a touch screen

A **handheld tablet** is a computing device with a touch screen that is larger than a smartphone and has functions similar to a smartphone. Most tablets can connect to Wi-Fi networks and use Bluetooth to wirelessly connect to nearby Bluetooth devices. Many tablets have the ability to use a cellular network for data transmissions. A few tablets, such as the Samsung Galaxy Tab and the Viewsonic ViewPad 7, have the ability for texting and making phone calls. You can also install apps such as a Skype app on a tablet so that you can make voice phone calls, send text, and make video calls. When you can use your tablet to make a phone call, the distinction between a smartphone and a tablet is almost nonexistent.

You can buy all kinds of accessory devices for smartphones and tablets, such as wireless keyboards, speakers, ear buds, headphones, printers, extra batteries, USB adapters, and chargers. Figure 20-10 shows a wireless keyboard and an iPad that use a Bluetooth connection. Figure 20-11 shows a car dock for a smartphone. Using this car dock, the smartphone is a GPS device giving driving directions.

© Cengage Learning 2014

Figure 20-10   An iPad and a wireless keyboard can connect using Bluetooth

Figure 20-11   A smartphone and a car dock

© Cengage Learning 2014

20

A+
220-802
3.1, 3.4

TOUCH INTERFACE

Mobile devices rely on touch screens more so than do laptops. Mobile device touch screens can work by the touch of a finger or a stylus, and the touch on the screen can be a tap, long-press, slide, or two-finger pinch. A touch screen that can handle a two-finger pinch is called a **multitouch** screen. High Tech Computer (HTC), Inc., a manufacturer of smartphones and tablets, developed one type of multitouch technology called **TouchFLO**. HTC now incorporates the older TouchFLO technology into a more comprehensive user interface called **HTC Sense**.

A touch screen uses resistive or capacitive technologies. A **capacitive touch screen** uses electrodes that sense the conductive properties of skin. A **resistive touch screen** has two sheets of glass covered with a resistive coating (see Figure 20-12). The two sheets are kept from touching by spacers between them. When pressure is placed on the top glass, the glass bends and makes contact with the lower glass.

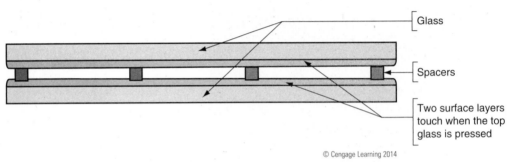

Glass

Spacers

Two surface layers touch when the top glass is pressed

© Cengage Learning 2014

Figure 20-12   Pressure causing contact between two surfaces is used on a resistive touch screen

Capacitive touch screens don't respond to pressure, but resistive touch screens do. The trend for all smartphones and tablets is to move toward capacitive touch screens, which are generally more responsive than resistive touch screens. iPhone, iPad, and iPod touch devices use capacitive touch screens, which is why you should not wear gloves when you use them. With some laptops and monitors, touch screens need to be calibrated so that the software that controls touch input is in alignment with the hardware. Because of the way a touch screen is integrated into a mobile device, screen calibration is not required. When a mobile device appears as though the touch of a finger is not aligned with data input (such as when you touch a P on the touch keyboard and an O appears on-screen), the problem most likely can be resolved by updating the operating system.

STORAGE DEVICES

Most smartphones use a SIM (Subscriber Identity Module) card that contains a microchip to hold data about the subscription you have with your cellular carrier. The SIM card is purchased from the cellular carrier, and the carrier is responsible for loading it with your subscription information. The SIM card must be inserted in the phone or tablet for the device to make a connection to a cellular network. Figure 20-13 shows the slot on the side of the iPad where you can insert a SIM card so that the iPad can send and receive data transmissions (not voice transmissions) over the cellular network.

A+
220-802
3.1, 3.4

© Cengage Learning 2014

Figure 20-13 A SIM card is required for a tablet or smartphone to use most cellular networks

> **Notes** Two types of cellular networks are GSM (Global System for Mobile Communication) and CDMA (Code Division Multiple Access). GSM is by far the most popular and is replacing CDMA. GSM networks require that a cellular device have a SIM card, but CDMA networks do not require a SIM card.

The internal storage used by Android and iOS for their apps and data is a solid state device (SSD), a type of flash memory. In addition, an Android device might have an external slot where you can plug in a smart card such as an SD card to provide extra storage (see Figure 20-14). The iPhone, iPad, and iPod touch don't have these external slots for a smart card.

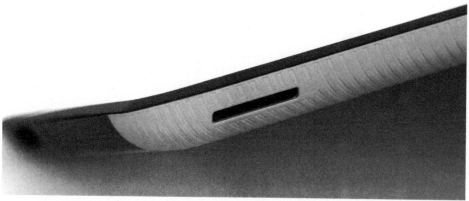

© Cengage Learning 2014

Figure 20-14 An Android device might provide a memory card slot to allow for extra storage

An Android device might also have a USB port that you can use to plug in a USB flash drive to provide extra storage or transfer files and folders to other devices. Apple devices don't have USB ports.

FIELD-SERVICEABLE PARTS

For the purposes of PC support technicians supporting mobile devices, know that there are no field-replaceable units (FRU) in mobile devices, and it is not possible to upgrade or replace internal components. (Although it is possible to replace the screens in some

20

mobile devices, a support technician is not expected to have this skill.) SIM cards and batteries can be replaced, and accessories such as a battery charger or ear buds can be attached.

OTHER HARDWARE COMPONENTS

Other internal hardware components of a mobile device include a small gyroscope, called an accelerometer, and a GPS component. Here are brief details about each:

▲ A **gyroscope** is a device that contains a disc that is free to move and can respond to gravity as the device is moved (see Figure 20-15). Three axes in the device sense how the disc moves and, therefore, can tell the direction of motion. An **accelerometer** is a type of gyroscope used in mobile devices to sense the physical position of the device. The accelerometer is used by the OS and apps to adjust the **screen orientation** from portrait to landscape as the user rotates the device. Apps such as a Compass, Carpenter's Leveler, and some game apps use the accelerometer to sense how the user is moving the device.

© Cengage Learning 2014

Figure 20-15 A gyroscope uses gravity to sense its relative position to the earth

▲ Mobile devices might contain a **GPS (Global Positioning System) receiver**. The Global Positioning System is a system of 24 or more satellites orbiting the earth, and a GPS receiver can locate four or more of these satellites at any time and from these four locations, calculate its own position in a process called triangulation. A smartphone can determine its position by using the GPS satellite data or data from the position of nearby cellular towers in its cellular network. A phone with a GPS receiver is likely to use both types of data to find its position. A mobile device routinely reports its position to Apple or Google at least twice a day, and usually more often, which makes it possible for these companies to track your device's whereabouts, which is called **geotracking**. Law enforcement agencies sometimes use this data to reconstruct a person's travels.

CONFIGURING, SYNCING, AND SECURING IOS DEVICES

In this part of the chapter, you learn to configure network connections, update, secure, and back up data, content, and settings on an iOS device. (We cover the iPad and iPhone but not the iPod touch.) Later in the chapter, you learn similar skills using Android devices.

This chapter is intended to show you how to support a device that you might not own or normally use. Technicians are often expected to do such things! If you don't have an iPhone or iPad to use as you read through these sections, you can still follow along paying careful attention to the screen shots taken on each device. Learning to use an iOS device is fun, and supporting one is equally easy.

Most of the settings you need to know to support an iOS device are contained in the Settings app, which you can find on the home screen (see Figure 20-16a). Basically, you can

A+
220-802
3.2

Source: iOS by Apple

Source: iOS by Apple

Figure 20-16 (a) Use the Settings app to configure the iOS and apps, (b) Airplane mode turns off all three antennas that connect the iPhone to networks

tap the Settings app and search through its menus and submenus until you find what you need. So let's get started.

CONFIGURING NETWORK CONNECTIONS

A mobile device can contain up to four antennas (Wi-Fi, GPS, Bluetooth, and cellular). The device uses a Wi-Fi, Bluetooth, or cellular antenna to connect to each type of network, and settings on the device allow you to enable or disable each antenna. One setting, called **airplane mode**, disables all three antennas so the device can neither transmit nor receive signals. To use Airplane Mode, tap the **Settings** app and turn **Airplane Mode** on or off (see Figure 20-16b).

A cellular network provided by a carrier (for example, AT&T or Verizon) is used by cell phones for voice communication and text messaging. A smartphone or tablet might also contain the technology to connect to a cellular network for data transmission. These cellular data networks are called 2G, EDGE (an earlier version of 3G), 3G, 4G, or 4G LTE (the latest and fastest version of 4G). For example, the iPad shown earlier in Figure 20-16 contains 3G technology and is able to connect to this type of network for data transmissions (not voice transmissions). To make a cellular data connection, the subscription with your carrier must include an activated cellular data plan.

> 💡 **A+ Exam Tip** The A+ 220-802 exam expects you to know how to configure a Wi-Fi, cellular data, and Bluetooth connection using the iOS and Android operating systems.

20

A+
220-802
3.2

Here is how to manage connections with the iOS using cellular, Wi-Fi, and Bluetooth:

▲ *Cellular connection.* To enable a cellular data network connection, tap **Settings**, **General**, **Network**. On the Network screen (see Figure 20-17a), enable the Cellular Data connection. The device used in the figure supports 3G. When you enable 3G, data transmissions are faster. Also notice in Figure 20-17a you can enable or disable Data Roaming. Using data roaming might mean additional charges if you are in a foreign country.

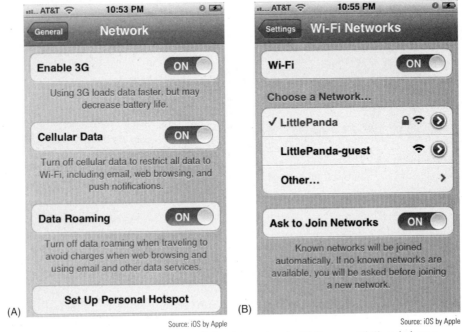

(A)   Source: iOS by Apple

(B)   Source: iOS by Apple

Figure 20-17   (a) Enable access to a cellular data network, (b) Turn on Wi-Fi and show a Wi-Fi network

▲ *Wi-Fi connection.* To configure a Wi-Fi connection, tap **Settings, Wi-Fi**. On the Wi-Fi Networks screen (see Figure 20-17b), you can view available Wi-Fi hotspots, see which Wi-Fi network you are connected to, turn Wi-Fi off and on, and decide whether the device needs to ask before joining a Wi-Fi network. When the device is within range of a Wi-Fi network, it displays the list of networks. Select one to connect. If the Wi-Fi network is secured, enter the security key to complete the connection.

▲ *Bluetooth connection.* To configure a Bluetooth connection, first turn on the other Bluetooth device you want to connect to. Then on your mobile device, tap **Settings, General, Bluetooth**. On the Bluetooth screen, turn on Bluetooth. The device searches for Bluetooth devices. If it discovers a Bluetooth device, tap it to connect. The two Bluetooth devices now begin the **pairing** process. The devices might require a **Bluetooth PIN code** to complete the Bluetooth connection. For example, in Figure 20-18, an iPad and Bluetooth keyboard are pairing. To complete the connection, enter the 4-digit PIN on the keyboard. To test the connection, enter text on the keyboard and make sure the text appears on the iPad screen in the active app.

A+
220-802
3.2

Source: iOS by Apple

Figure 20-18 A PIN code is required to pair the two Bluetooth devices

If you have a problem connecting to a Bluetooth device, try turning the device off and back on. The device might also offer a pairing button to enable pairing. When you press this button, a pairing light blinks, indicating the device is ready to receive a Bluetooth connection.

CONFIGURING EMAIL

Using a personal computer or mobile device, email can be managed in one of two ways:

- ◢ *Use a browser.* Using a browser, go to the web site of your email provider and manage your email on the web site. In this situation, your email is never downloaded to your computer or mobile device, and your messages remain on the email server until you delete them.
- ◢ *Use an email client.* An email client, such as Microsoft Outlook, can be installed on your personal computer, or you can use an email app on your mobile device. The client or app can either download email messages to your device (using the POP protocol) or can manage email on the server (using the IMAP protocol). When the client or app downloads the email, you can configure the server to continue to store the email on the server for later use or delete the email from the server. The built-in Mail app for managing email is available on smartphones and tablets.

Here is the information you'll need to configure the Mail app on an iOS device:

- ◢ *Your email address and password.* If your email account is with iCloud, Microsoft Exchange, MobileMe (Apple's email service), Gmail, Yahoo!, Hotmail, or AOL, your email address and password are all you need because the iOS can automatically set up these accounts.

20

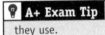

▲ *The names of your incoming and outgoing email servers.* To find this information, check the support page of your email provider's web site. For example, the server you use for incoming mail might be pop.mycompany.com, and the server you use for outgoing mail might be smtp.mycompany.com. The two servers might have the same name.

▲ *The type of protocol your incoming server uses.* This server will use POP or IMAP. Using IMAP, you are managing your email on the server. For example, you can move a message from one folder to another and that change happens on the server. Using POP, the messages are downloaded to your device where you manage them. Using POP, the Mail app leaves the messages on the server (does not delete them), but you can change this setting if you like.

▲ *Security used.* Most likely, if email is encrypted during transmission using the SSL protocol, the configuration will happen automatically without your involvement. However, if you have problems, you need to be aware of these possible settings:

- An IMAP server uses port 143 unless it is secured and using SSL. IMAP over SSL (IMAPS) uses port 993.

- A POP server uses port 110 unless it is secured and using SSL. POP over SSL uses port 995.

> 💡 **A+ Exam Tip**   The A+ 220-802 exam expects you to know about POP, IMAP, SSL, and the ports they use.

Follow these steps to configure the email client on an iOS device:

1. Tap **Settings** and then tap **Mail, Contacts, Calendars**. In the Mail, Contacts, Calendars screen, you can add a new email account and decide how email is handled. To add a new email account, tap **Add Account**. On the next screen, select the type of account (see Figure 20-19a) and enter your email address and password. If your email account type is not in the list, slide the screen up and tap **Other** at the bottom of the list.

2. On the Other screen, tap **Add Mail Account**. On the New Account screen, enter your name, email address, password, and description (optional). Tap **Next**.

3. On the next screen, tap IMAP or POP (see Figure 20-19b). Enter the Host Name for your incoming mail server. Enter your User Name and Password if they are different from your email address and its password. Slide the screen up and enter the Host Name for your outgoing mail server. Tap **Next**.

4. The Mail app assumes it is using SSL (to secure email in transit using encryption) and attempts to make the connection. If it cannot, it asks if you want it to try to make the connection without using SSL. Click **OK** to make that attempt.

5. To use the account, tap the **Mail** app on your Home screen.

A+
220-802
3.2

(A) Source: iOS by Apple

(B) Source: iOS by Apple

Figure 20-19 (a) The iOS can automatically set up several types of email accounts
(b) An email account is set up to use IMAP or POP for incoming mail

If you later need to verify the email account settings or delete the account, follow these steps.

1. Tap **Settings**, and then tap **Mail, Contacts, Calendars**. In the list of Accounts, tap the account. On the account screen, you can enable and disable the account and change the account settings.

2. To delete the account, slide the screen up and tap **Delete Account** at the bottom of the screen (see Figure 20-20a).

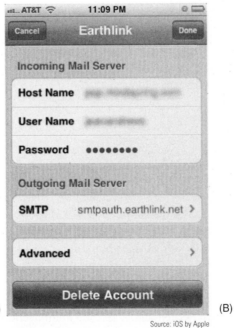

(A) Source: iOS by Apple

(B) Source: iOS by Apple

20

Figure 20-20 (a) Delete an email account or use Advanced settings, (b) Decide how messages are handled on the server after you receive them

3. To see advanced settings, tap **Advanced**. On the Advanced screen (see Figure 20-20b), tap **Delete from server** to decide how to handle mail you have downloaded using the POP protocol. Choices are Never, Seven Days, or When removed from inbox.

4. Also notice on the Advanced screen that you can enable and disable SSL. When you do so, notice that the port the app addresses is also changed.

You need to know about an exception in how email is managed when using a Gmail account. **Gmail** is an email service provided by Google at *mail.google.com*. Normally, when you use the Mail app, you can delete a message by selecting it and tapping **Delete** (see Figure 20-21a). However, using Gmail, by default, you archive a message rather than delete it (see Figure 20-21b).

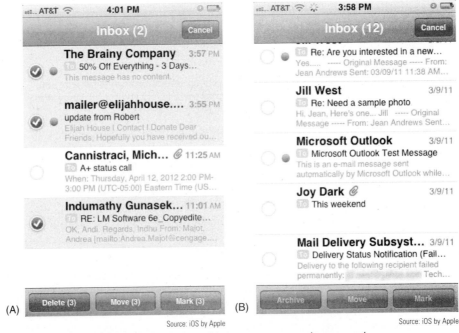

(A)   Source: iOS by Apple

(B)   Source: iOS by Apple

Figure 20-21   Two methods for dealing with messages you no longer need:
a) Using most email, delete a message, or b) Using Gmail, archive a message

Using most email services, a message arrives in your Inbox, which is a folder on the email server. You organize these messages by moving them to other folders or deleting them. Deleted messages are placed in the Trash folder and permanently deleted after a period of time. Using Gmail, a message remains in the Inbox and you organize these messages by assigning each message one or more labels. When you archive a message, you move the message from the Inbox to the All Mail folder out of sight but still accessible. Therefore, when using the Mail app on an Apple device with a Gmail account, the Delete button is replaced with the Archive button.

To change the Gmail account so that you can delete messages, go to the Home screen and tap **Settings** and then tap **Mail, Contacts, Calendars**. Tap the Gmail account. On the account screen (see Figure 20-22), turn off the **Archive Messages** switch. The Mail app will now have a Delete button for Gmail.

Source: iOS by Apple

Figure 20-22 Decide if Gmail messages are archived or deleted

Microsoft Exchange is a server application that can handle email, contacts, and calendars, and is a popular application used by large corporations for their employee email, contacts, and calendars. When you set up a Microsoft Exchange email account, the Mail app automatically enables ActiveSync, which causes all email, contacts, and calendar updates made on the Exchange server or on your mobile device to stay in sync. Any changes at either location are automatically and immediately transmitted to the other. You can change the ActiveSync settings by doing the following:

1. On the Home screen, tap **Settings**, and tap **Mail, Contacts, Calendars**.

2. Select your Exchange email account. On the account screen, you can turn on or off the Mail (to sync email), Contacts (to sync contacts) and Calendars (to sync your calendar) settings. You can also set the number of days, weeks, or months of email you want to stay in sync. You can also decide whether you want folders in addition to the Inbox folder to be pushed to you from the Exchange server.

> **A+ Exam Tip** The A+ 220-802 exam expects you to know about special considerations when configuring Gmail and Exchange email accounts.

SYNCING, UPDATING, BACKING UP, AND RESTORING FROM BACKUP

To protect your data and apps in the event your mobile device is destroyed, lost, or stolen, you will want to keep backups of this content. For Apple devices, you can back up app data, iOS settings, email, contacts, wallpaper, and multimedia content, including photos,

20

A+
220-802
3.5

music, and videos, by syncing this content using iTunes or iCloud. iTunes backs up to your computer, and iCloud backs up to storage on the Apple web sites at *www.icloud.com*. In the following subsections, you learn to use both iTunes and iCloud to back up your data and to use iTunes to install iOS updates and patches.

USE ITUNES TO SYNC IOS APPS AND CONTENT

To sync data and install iOS updates using iTunes, you first must install the iTunes software on your computer. Follow these steps:

1. Make sure your computer qualifies for iTunes. For a Windows PC, iTunes can install under Windows 7/Vista/XP and needs 200 MB of free hard drive space. Install a 64-bit version of iTunes on a 64-bit OS and a 32-bit version of iTunes on a 32-bit OS.

2. Go to **www.apple.com/itunes/download** and download and install the software. After the software is installed, restart your computer.

3. Connect your device to your computer by way of a USB port. iTunes automatically launches and displays the window shown in Figure 20-23.

Source: iTunes by Apple

Figure 20-23 Opening window when you first connect a new device to iTunes

4. Step through each window to register your Apple device and set up or enter an existing Apple ID (see Figure 20-24).

5. One window in the process asks which types of data to sync (contacts, calendars, bookmarks, notes, and email). After you make your selections, the sync starts and the *Sync in Progress* message appears on your device. If you must interrupt the sync, don't worry. When the device is next connected, syncing picks up where it left off.

A+
220-802
3.5

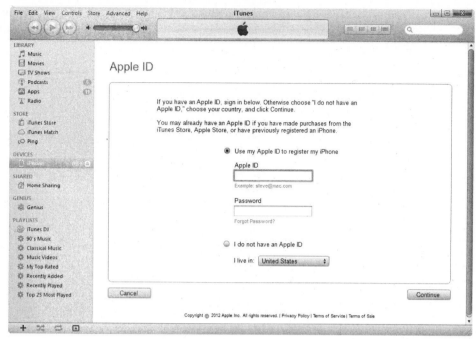

Source: iTunes by Apple

Figure 20-24 An Apple ID is required to sync a device with iTunes

iTunes automatically syncs the contacts, app data and app settings, documents, calendar, call history, photos and videos taken by the iPhone, Wi-Fi and email passwords, Microsoft Exchange information, bookmarks, text messages and pictures, and voice messages. To verify and customize exactly what iTunes is syncing, do the following:

1. With your device connected to your computer, select your device in the DEVICES list in the left pane of the iTunes window. To see what apps are synced, click **Apps** in the menu bar under the apple icon (see Figure 20-25). In this pane, you can view your apps and decide how they are synced.

Click to manage apps on your device

Source: iTunes by Apple

Figure 20-25 View apps and configure how apps are synced

20

A+
220-802
3.5

2. Also click other types of content (Music, Movies, TV Shows, Podcasts, and Photos) in the menu bar under the apple icon to view that content and to configure how to sync the content.

3. On the Info pane (see Figure 20-26), you can decide how to sync contacts, calendars, email, and bookmarks. This type of content can be synced with Microsoft Outlook and Internet Explorer installed on your computer.

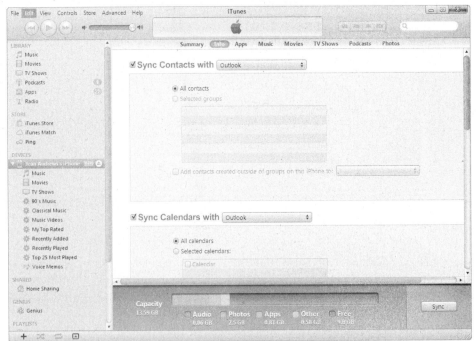

Source: iTunes by Apple

Figure 20-26   Decide how to sync contacts, calendars, email, and bookmarks

4. If you have made changes to the content to sync, click **Sync** at the bottom of the iTunes window to sync content immediately.

When you sync content with iTunes, the backup is stored on your computer at this location using Windows 7/Vista:

C:\Users*username*\AppData\Roaming\Apple Computer\MobileSync\Backup

If you have more than one Apple device, the next time the second device is connected to iTunes, content is synced to it. Using iTunes, any content on any device makes its way to the other devices and to your computer for backup.

> **Notes**   For best protection, be sure you make routine backups of the user profile folder. The user profile folder contains user settings and data, and part of this data is your iOS device backups.

After iTunes is set up for your new device, the next time you plug the device into your computer, iTunes does one of the following:

▲ When iTunes recognizes the device, it automatically syncs up unless you have iCloud backup turned on. (If you have iCloud backup turned on, iTunes backup is automatically disabled.)

▲ To manually sync with iTunes, right-click the device in the DEVICES list and click **Back Up** in the shortcut menu.

A+
220-802
3.5

To restore from backup, connect the device to iTunes, right-click the device in the DEVICES list, and select **Restore from Backup** in the shortcut menu (see Figure 20-27). Also, when you are setting up a new device and you first connect it to iTunes on your computer, it will ask if you want to restore from backup.

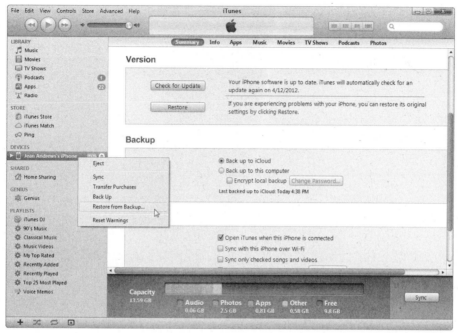

Source: iTunes by Apple

Figure 20-27   iTunes can restore from backup to your iPhone or iPad

USE ITUNES TO INSTALL IOS UPDATES AND PATCHES

The operating system on a mobile device is installed on firmware at the factory. Before iOS version 5, a device must be connected to iTunes to receive iOS updates and patches, which can happen automatically when a device is connected. With iOS version 5, these updates can be received without an iTunes connection. You can use iTunes to upgrade a device to iOS version 5. Follow these steps:

1. For an iPhone, set the device to Airplane Mode so it will not be interrupted while the OS upgrade is in progress.

2. Connect the Apple device to your computer.

3. Select the phone in the DEVICES list and back up all your content and settings.

4. Click the **Summary** tab. iTunes reports new updates are available. To download the updates, click **Update**. A message box appears (see Figure 20-28). To start the update, click **Update**.

5. The update process can take an hour or longer and it's best to not interrupt it. When the process is finished, disconnect your device. When iTunes installs a new version of iOS, you must go through the process of configuring your device for the new OS. Follow the directions on the device screen to do so. One of these setup screens is shown in Figure 20-29a, where you are asked to sign in with your Apple ID.

With iOS version 5, updates can happen at any time. You can manually request updates by tapping **Settings**, **General**. On the General screen, tap **Software Update**, as shown in Figure 20-29b.

20

Source: iTunes by Apple

Figure 20-28 Update the operating system to a newer version

(A)

Source: iOS by Apple

(B)

Source: iOS by Apple

Figure 20-29 (a) Each of your Apple devices uses your Apple ID to connect to iTunes and iCloud, (b) Use the General screen to request iOS updates

USE ICLOUD TO SYNC IOS CONTENT

A+
220-802
3.5

Another option for syncing content on your Apple device is to use **iCloud** storage at *www.icloud.com*. You can set up a free iCloud account to hold all your apps, music, movies, videos, books, and iTunes U course curriculum and push this content to any iOS device you have. The first 5 GB of storage is free. iCloud syncing happens every day if the screen is locked and the device is connected to a cellular or Wi-Fi network and is plugged into an electrical outlet (such as when you recharge your iPhone while you sleep).

To use iCloud, follow these steps:

1. iCloud requires iOS 5 or higher. To verify your Apple device is updated to iOS 5, tap **Settings**, **General**, **About** (see Figure 20-30 for an iPhone screen).

Source: iOS by Apple

Figure 20-30 Verify your iOS is using version 5 or higher

2. To configure iCloud, tap **Settings, iCloud**. Using the iCloud screen (see Figure 20-31 for an iPad screen), you can turn on or off items to sync to iCloud. These items include Mail, Contacts, Calendars, and so forth. Note that iCloud does not back up movies, podcasts, audio books, photos that came from your computer, and music and TV shows not purchased from the iTunes Store. (You can, however, sync these items using iTunes.)

3. To have your device report its position to iCloud, turn on **Find My iPad** or **Find My iPhone**. Later, if you lose your device, sign in to iCloud and there you can see its position on a map.

20

Source: iOS by Apple

Figure 20-31 Decide what type of content to sync to iCloud

4. Tap **Storage & Backup.** On the Storage and Backup screen (see Figure 20-32), make sure iCloud Backup is turned on.

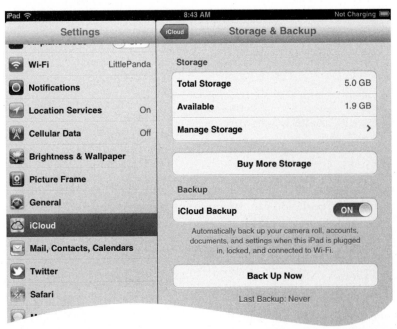

Source: iOS by Apple

Figure 20-32 Manage iCloud backup and view available storage on iCloud

5. To back up manually to iCloud at any time, on the Storage & Backup screen shown in Figure 20-32, you can tap **Back Up Now.**

A+
220-802
3.5

6. To view and manage your backups, on the Storage & Backup screen, tap **Manage Storage**. On the Manage Storage screen, you can see a list of devices backed up. Figure 20-33a shows that iPhone and iPad backups exist. Tap one to view a list of what's backed up and to manage the backup (see Figure 20-33b).

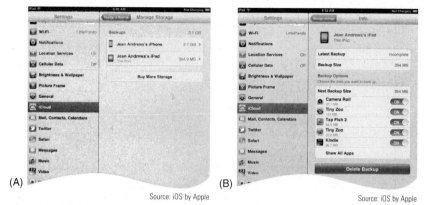

(A)   Source: iOS by Apple   (B)   Source: iOS by Apple

Figure 20-33   Manage your backups kept in iCloud

Later, if you need to restore your data from iCloud backup, here are your options:

▲ When you are setting up a new iOS device, the Setup process provides a screen asking if you want to restore from backup. Tap **Restore from iCloud Backup**.

▲ If you lose the content and settings on a device, to restore from backup, connect the device to your computer. In the iTunes window, select the device in the DEVICES list. Right-click the device and click **Restore from Backup** (refer to Figure 20-27).

Apps, music, and books you have previously downloaded from iTunes can be downloaded again to this and other devices tied to your Apple ID. To automatically sync this content, tap **Settings** on the home screen and tap **Store**. On the Store screen (see Figure 20-34 for an iPhone), turn on and configure Automatic Downloads.

Source: iOS by Apple

Figure 20-34   Decide how to handle Automatic Downloads

20

A+
220-802
3.3

SECURING AN IOS MOBILE DEVICE

Smartphones and tablets are with us everywhere and most of us keep much personal and professional information on our smartphones. Here's a list of what might be stored on a smartphone and would be at risk if the phone is lost, stolen, or damaged:

▲ Data kept by apps can reveal much about our lives. Consider data kept on these iPhone apps: Email, Calendar, Call Logs, Voicemail, Text Messages, Google Maps, YouTube, Videos, Photos, Notes, Contacts, Bookmarks, and Web History.
▲ Videos and photos we have taken might be tagged with date and time stamps and GPS locations.
▲ Network connection settings, including Wi-Fi security keys, email configuration settings, usernames, and email addresses.

To protect this data, consider using passcode locks, locator applications, and remote wipes discussed in this part of the chapter.

PASSCODE LOCKS AND FAILED LOGINS

To protect your device in case it is stolen, you can set a passcode. For iOS devices, tap **Settings, General, Passcode Lock, Turn Passcode On,** and enter a four-digit code. When you wake up your iPhone or iPad, you must enter the passcode to proceed (see Figure 20-35). Notice in the figure that you can tap **Emergency Call** to bypass entering the passcode. This feature takes you to the keypad to make a call and protects you in the event you need to make an emergency call and don't want to take the time to enter your passcode.

Source: iOS by Apple

Figure 20-35 Enter your four-digit passcode to unlock your iPhone

A+
220-802
3.3

You can set the iOS to erase your data after it receives 10 failed logins (incorrect attempts at entering the passcode). This setting protects you from someone repeatedly guessing until she finally enters the correct passcode. After you have set a passcode, to set the device to erase data, tap **Settings, General, Passcode Lock**. You are required to enter your passcode to proceed. On the Passcode Lock screen (see Figure 20-36), tap **Erase Data** to turn it on and then tap **Enable**.

Source: iOS by Apple

Figure 20-36   Set the iOS to erase your data after 10 failed logons

If your device is ever lost or stolen and the erase feature is used, you can restore your data from backup assuming you get your device back.

LOCATOR APPLICATIONS AND REMOTE WIPES

To cover the possibility that you might one day lose your mobile device, you can configure it to send its position to you. To do so, use the iCloud setting to turn on Find My iPhone or Find My iPad. How to do that was covered earlier in the chapter. If you lose your device, you can do the following:

1. Using a browser on any computer, go to **iCloud.com/find** and sign in with your Apple ID. If iCloud requests permission to install an add-on, allow the installation. Next, a map appears showing your device's reported position as a green dot on the map (see Figure 20-37).

2. Click the dot to see more options. The Info box appears, which is shown in Figure 20-37. If you see the device is close by, but you still can't find it, click **Play Sound or Send Message**, and have it play a sound. This sound overrides a low volume setting.

20

A+
220-802
3.3

Figure 20-37 Use the iCloud web site to locate a lost Apple device

Source: www.apple.com

3. If you still cannot find the device, you can have it display a message on-screen such as, "This device is lost. Please call me at 444-555-1234."

4. If you believe the device is stolen and you want to protect its contents, you can click **Remote Lock** to remotely set a passcode lock. Someone must key in this four-digit code to unlock the device.

5. If you decide the device cannot be found, you might want to click **Remote Wipe** to perform a **remote wipe**, which remotely erases all contacts, email, photos, and other data from the device to protect your privacy. Later, if you find the device, you can restore this data from backup.

Besides using a browser on a computer to find your device, you can also download the free app, Find My iPhone or Find My iPad, to another Apple device and use it to locate your lost device.

TROUBLESHOOTING IOS DEVICES

Common problems with iOS devices include the touch screen not working properly, iOS settings cannot be changed, buttons don't work, or an app does not work. For the iPhone or iPad, which use the iOS and a capacitive touch screen, recall that Apple says that the screen does not get out of alignment unless there is a hardware problem. Here are some tips to try when a touch screen is giving you problems:

▲ Clean the screen with a soft, damp cloth.
▲ Don't use the touch screen when your hands are wet or you are wearing gloves.
▲ Remove any plastic sheet or film protecting the touch screen.

For iPhones or iPads, you can sometimes solve an apparent touch screen alignment problem or other problems with the iOS by restarting, resetting, updating, or restoring the device.

A+
220-802
3.3

Try the first step that follows and if that does not solve the problem, move on to the next step. The steps are ordered so as to solve the problem while making the least changes to the system (least-intrusive solution). After you try one step, check to see if the problem is solved before you move on to the next step. Do the following:

1. *Restart the phone.* To restart the phone, press and hold the Wake/sleep button until the red slider bar appears and then drag the slider. Then press and hold the Wake/sleep button until the Apple logo appears.

2. *Reset the phone.* To reset the phone, press and hold the Wake/sleep button and the Home button at the same time for at least 10 seconds until the Apple logo appears.

3. *Update the iOS.* To update the iOS with the latest patches, first make sure the latest version of iTunes is installed on your computer. Connect the iPhone to your computer and select it in the DEVICES list. If possible, back up content and settings. Then click the **Summary** tab, and click **Updates**.

4. *Reset all settings.* If you have not already done so, back up the data and settings. Then to erase settings, tap **Settings**, **General** and **Reset**. On the Reset screen (see Figure 20-38), tap **Reset All Settings**.

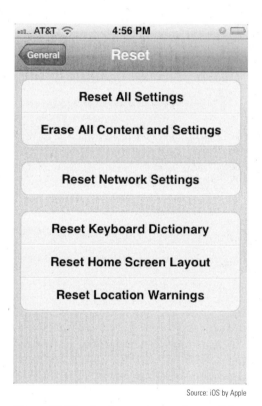

Source: iOS by Apple

Figure 20-38   Erasing settings and content can sometimes solve problems with the iOS

20

5. *Erase all data and settings.* To erase all data and settings, tap **Settings**, **General** and **Reset**. On the Reset screen (see Figure 20-38), tap **Erase All Content and Settings**.

A+
220-802
3.3

6. *Restore the phone.* This process reinstalls the iOS and you will lose all your data on the device. The device is restored to its factory condition. Before you do this, try to back up all your data and settings. Then follow these steps:

   a. Make sure the latest version of iTunes is installed on your computer. Connect the iPhone to your computer and make sure it appears in the DEVICES list. Click the **Summary** tab and click **Restore**. You are given the opportunity to back up settings and data (see Figure 20-39). If you have not already done a backup, do so now.

   b. Don't unplug or interrupt the device during the restore. The iOS is reinstalled and all data and settings are lost.

   c. Next, restore your data and settings from backup. How to do that was covered earlier in the chapter.

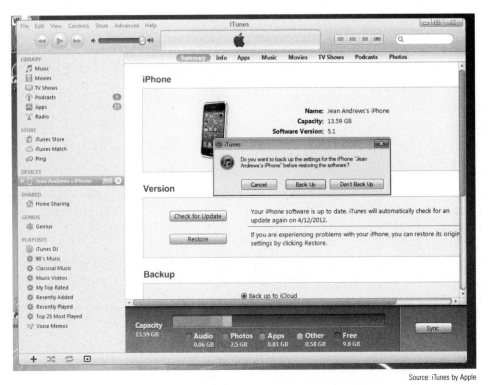

Source: iTunes by Apple

Figure 20-39   Back up data and settings and restore the device to factory condition

7. *Recover the device.* This process might work to restore the device to factory state when the restore process fails or you cannot start the restore process. The process does a firmware upgrade. All content and data are lost and the OS is refreshed. Follow these steps:

   a. Turn off the device. If you have trouble turning off the device, press and hold the Wake/sleep button and the Home button at the same time.

   b. While holding down the Home button, connect the device to your computer. If you see the device charging, wait a few minutes while it charges. Do not release the Home button while it is charging. When you see the Connect to iTunes screen, release the Home button.

c. Use the Start menu to start iTunes. iTunes should recognize the device and display a message saying the device is in recovery mode and ask if you want to restore the device. Follow the directions on-screen to restore the device to factory state.

d. Restore data and settings using the most recent backups.

If the device is still not working properly, search for more troubleshooting tips on the Apple web site at *support.apple.com* or take the device to an Apple store for repair.

CONFIGURING, SYNCING, AND SECURING ANDROID DEVICES

Because the Android operating system is open source, manufacturers can customize the OS and how it works in many variations. Therefore, it is not always possible to give specific step-by-step directions similar to those given for the iOS. In this part of the chapter, you learn about general procedures you can follow to support an Android device. And we give a few examples for specific Android devices so that you can see how the step-by-step directions might work on an Android device.

When you are assigned responsibility for supporting an Android device, begin with the user guide for the device, which you can download from the device manufacturer's web site. The user guide is likely to tell you the detailed steps of how to connect to a network, configure email, update the OS, sync and back up settings and data, secure the device, and what to do when things go wrong.

> **Notes** Most of us rarely follow step-by-step directions when learning to use a new device unless when "all else fails, read the directions." This part of the chapter can give you an idea of what to look for on an Android device, and you can likely figure out the steps for yourself.

Most of the settings you need to support an Android device are found in the Settings app. However, not all settings are there and the Settings app is not always easy to find. In addition, Android is not as intuitive as the iOS and relies more on third-party apps to do administrative chores than does the iOS.

On the other hand, Android is usually fun to use and support because it offers so much flexibility and the potential to customize. Once you get comfortable with Android, you can do amazing things with it. Technicians who love to tinker with devices tend to gravitate to Android, and those who just want a quick and easy tool to use without a hassle choose the iOS.

Now let's look at what to expect when supporting an Android device.

CONFIGURING NETWORK CONNECTIONS

20

To configure settings on an Android device, use the Settings app, which can always be found in the App launcher. For many Android phones, the App launcher is an app in the dock at the bottom of the screen (see Figure 20-40). Use it to access all installed apps, including the Settings app. For many Android tablets, the App launcher is the Apps icon in the upper-right corner of the screen (see Figure 20-41).

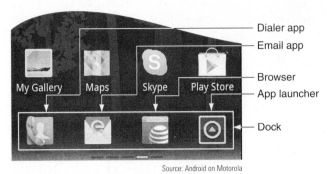

Dialer app
Email app
Browser
App launcher
Dock

Source: Android on Motorola

Figure 20-40 Up to four apps stay pinned to the dock at the bottom of the Android home screens

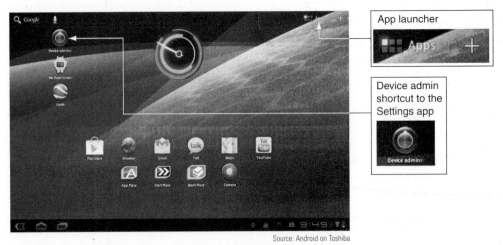

App launcher

Device admin shortcut to the Settings app

Source: Android on Toshiba

Figure 20-41 Use the Apps icon in the upper-right corner of a tablet to view and manage installed apps

Devices also have other methods that lead to the Settings app. For Android phones, tap the **Menu** button and tap **Settings**. For the tablet screen shown in Figure 20-41, tap the **Device admin** shortcut on the home screen. Figure 20-42 shows the Settings screen for one Android tablet.

To configure network connections using the Settings screen, tap **Wireless & networks**, as shown in Figure 20-42. Use the Wireless & networks screen to change these network settings:

▲ *Turn Airplane mode on or off.* Recall that airplane mode disables all wireless network antennas and is required in the United States during travel on airplanes. It's also convenient when you want to disable your device's data network access to conserve data usage or battery power when your battery is low. Some devices, such as Motorola smartphones, come preinstalled with a shortcut button on the home screen to toggle Airplane mode, Bluetooth, Wi-Fi, and GPS connections.

▲ *Turn Wi-Fi on or off and configure Wi-Fi access points.* Tap **Wi-Fi settings**. On the Wi-Fi settings screen, you can request to be notified of available networks, determine whether to auto-connect to Wi-Fi hot spots, determine when to disconnect from Wi-Fi, add a Wi-Fi network, and manage existing networks (see Figure 20-43). When you first attempt to connect to a secured Wi-Fi network, you need the security key.

Source: Android on Toshiba

Figure 20-42 In the Wireless & networks group of the Settings menu, change Airplane mode, Wi-Fi, Bluetooth, and VPN settings

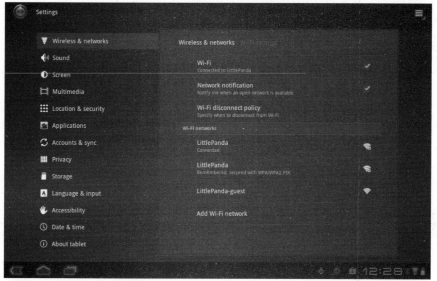

Source: Android on Toshiba

Figure 20-43 Configure Wi-Fi settings

Notes Searching for a Wi-Fi network can drain the battery power. To make a battery charge last longer, disable Wi-Fi when you're not using it.

20

◢ *Turn Bluetooth on or off.* To configure Bluetooth settings, tap **Bluetooth settings** on the Wireless & networks screen. On the Bluetooth settings screen, you can make the device discoverable by Bluetooth devices and pair with these devices (see Figure 20-44). You can also determine how long the Android device can be discovered.

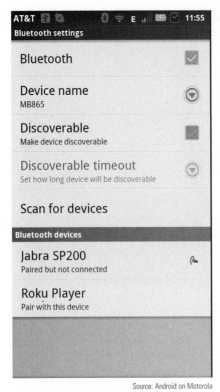

Source: Android on Motorola

Figure 20-44 Configure Bluetooth settings and pair with Bluetooth devices

▲ *View cellular settings.* Figure 20-45 shows the top and bottom of the Wireless & network settings screen on an Android phone. To view settings for the cellular network connection, tap **Mobile networks.** Some systems offer the option on this screen to switch on or off the cellular data connection; this system does not. For this system, if you want to turn off cellular data and use Wi-Fi for data transmissions, first turn on Airplane mode, which disables cellular, Wi-Fi, and Bluetooth, and then enable Wi-Fi.

Notes The advantage of disabling cellular data and using Wi-Fi for data transmissions is data transmissions over Wi-Fi are not charged against your cellular data subscription plan with your carrier. Also, Wi-Fi is generally faster than most cellular connections.

▲ *Set up tethering.* To set up tethering so that your computer can use the cellular network that your phone is connected to, tap **Tethering & Mobile Hotspot.** (A tablet that does not have cellular capability will not have these last two options for Mobile networks and Tethering.)

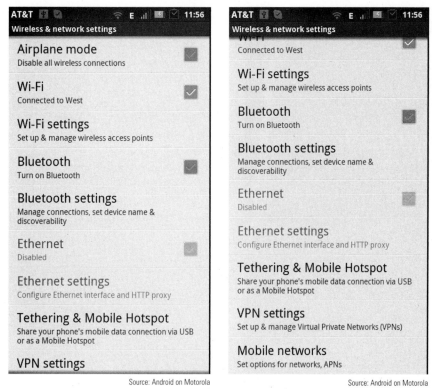

Figure 20-45 Top and bottom of the Wireless & network settings screen on an Android phone

CONFIGURING EMAIL

Because Google owns Gmail, Google makes it very easy to configure a Gmail account on an Android device. To set up a Gmail account, tap the **Gmail** app on the home screen and enter your email account and password. (If you don't see the app on your home screen, tap the App launcher, and then tap Gmail.) The app then gives you the opportunity to sync books, calendars, contacts, Gmail, and Google Photos with Google. Make your selections and tap **Done**. If you want to later change what type of data is synced, go to the Settings app, tap **Accounts & sync**, and select your Gmail account. The Data & synchronization screen appears (see Figure 20-46 for an Android phone).

Here are the steps to set up email accounts other than Gmail or any other type of account such as Skype, YouTube, Photobucket, Dropbox, or Facebook accounts:

1. Tap **Settings, Accounts & sync, Add account**. On the Setup accounts screen (see Figure 20-47a), select the type of account. For an email account, tap **Email**. On the next screen (see Figure 20-47b), enter your email account and password. Note on this screen that *Automatically configure account* is checked. Android can automatically configure several types of accounts. First try to set up the account with this item checked.

2. If you get errors using automatic configuration, then try again with **Automatically configure account** unchecked. You can then manually configure the account. When you manually configure an email account, you are given the opportunity to select the type of account (POP, IMAP, or Exchange), enter incoming and outgoing mail server addresses, POP or IMAP protocols, port addresses, and email encryption.

20

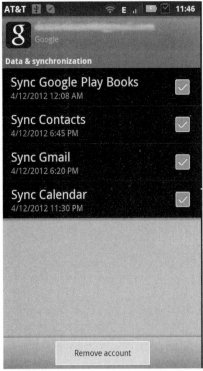

Source: Android on Motorola

Figure 20-46 Sync content tied to your Gmail account

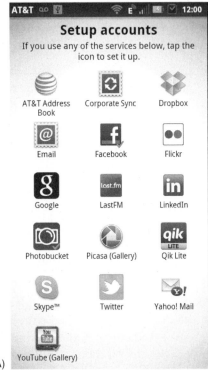

(A)

Source: Android on Motorola

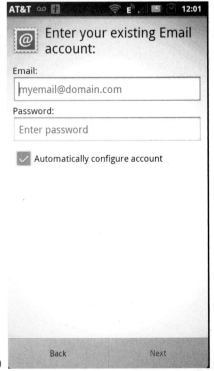

(B)

Source: Android on Motorola

Figure 20-47 Android can automatically configure several types of accounts

A+
220-802
3.5

SYNCING, BACKING UP, AND RESTORING FROM BACKUP

Syncing, backing up, and restoring from backup with Android is not quite as simple as it is with the iOS because Android offers more methods and options for these chores, and third-party apps are usually involved. In this part of the chapter, you learn to sync with online accounts (using third-party apps for syncing), sync all your apps to an app store, and back up any content to external storage connected to your device.

SYNC USING ONLINE ACCOUNTS

As you saw earlier, when you set up a Gmail account on your device, Google provides automatic syncing of books, contacts, Gmail, calendars, and Google photos (refer to Figure 20-46). You can also sync contacts and other data with other online accounts, including Facebook, Twitter, Dropbox, LinkedIn, and more that you have set up on your device (refer to Figure 20-47). With some online accounts, be aware that syncing might be automatic only from the online account, not the other way around.

USE THIRD-PARTY SYNCING APPS

For other content, including pictures, music and videos, third-party apps are normally used. Some Android devices come preinstalled with sync apps. Motorola's Phone Portal, for example, can sync music, pictures, and videos from a computer's iTunes program. Some apps require a USB connection to sync, and others sync wirelessly at set intervals. Some apps like SugarSync will sync entire folders in the background with no user intervention required, while others like Dropbox only sync files placed in the app's own folder. Some apps sync between a mobile device and computer, while others maintain those files in the cloud and the service is linked to the user's account.

SYNC APPS WITH YOUR APP SOURCE

Google Play maintains records of all apps for a particular Google account. A Google account is associated with an email address (Gmail or some other email address). To tie a Google account to your device, tap **Settings, Accounts & sync, Add account, Google Accounts**, and follow the directions on-screen. The process allows you to create a Google account if you don't already have one.

You can sometimes solve a problem with an app by uninstalling it and then installing it again. To uninstall an app, open the Settings app (refer to Figure 20-42) and tap **Applications, Manage applications**. Tap the app you want to uninstall and then tap **Uninstall**.

To update an app or restore an app you uninstalled, follow these steps:

1. On the home screen, tap **Play Store**. The Google Play screen appears (see Figure 20-48 for an Android tablet). Apps are tied to the Google account you used when you downloaded the app. If you have more than one Google account, tap the Menu icon on the far-right corner (for a tablet) or the Menu button (for a phone). Tap **Accounts** (see Figure 20-48) and select your Google account.

2. On the Google Play screen, tap the download icon (for a tablet), or tap **Menu** and My Apps (for a phone). On the next screen (see Figure 20-49), tap **INSTALLED** to see a list of apps. To update an app, select it and tap **Update**. To reinstall an app that has been uninstalled, tap **ALL** at the top of the screen. In the list of apps that you have previously downloaded, select the app and tap **Install**. The app installs again. Notice on these screens that you can control permissions assigned to each app, including how it can use storage, the network, GPS locator service, and other hardware controls.

20

A+
220-802
3.5

Download (to see all downloaded content under current account)

Search Google Play

Submenu under Google Play menu

Menu (to change the Google account and how updates are handled)

Source: Android on Toshiba

Figure 20-48   Manage apps you have downloaded from Play Store and search for more content

You can control how an app is updated. To do so, return to the Google Play screen and tap **Menu** (refer to Figure 20-48). Then tap **Settings**. The Settings screen appears (see Figure 20-50). To conserve battery charge and use of the cellular data network, check **Update over Wi-Fi only**. To manually control your updates, uncheck **Auto-update apps**. To manually update an app, go to the apps store, select the app, and tap **Update,** as shown earlier in Figure 20-49.

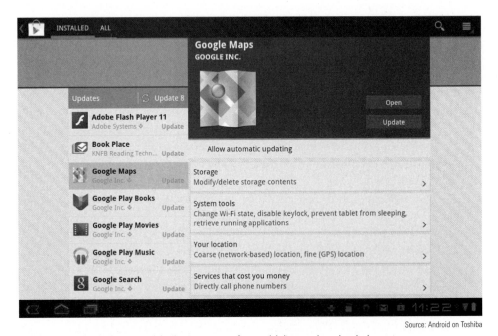

Source: Android on Toshiba

Figure 20-49   Sync apps with the app store from which you downloaded your apps

In addition to the Play Store, each device manufacturer provides an app store, and you can purchase apps from other sites like *Amazon.com*. When you purchase an app from another source than the Play Store, make sure the site provides the opportunity to restore the app if that becomes necessary.

A+
220-802
3.5

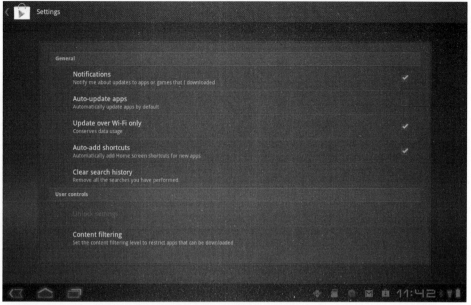

Source: Android on Toshiba

Figure 20-50 Configure how to update your apps

BACK UP TO A USB DEVICE OR SMART CARD

If an Android device has a slot for a smart card (for example, an SD card slot) or a USB port, most likely the manufacturer has preinstalled an app to back up your data to the smart card or USB flash drive. For example, Toshiba provides the File Manager app for this purpose. To use the app, follow these steps:

1. Tap **File Manager** on the home screen. The TOSHIBA File Manager screen appears (see Figure 20-51). The three storage devices listed at the top of the screen are Internal Storage (currently selected), SD card, and USB storage. Tap **Internal Storage** to select it.

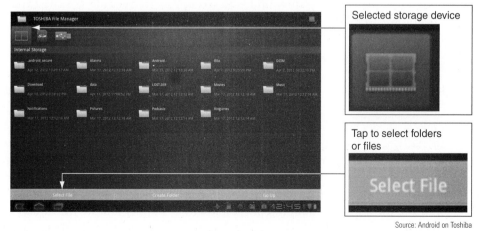

Source: Android on Toshiba

Figure 20-51 The File Manager app allows you to copy files and folders to an SD card or USB device

20

2. Tap **Select File** at the bottom of the screen. New buttons appear (see Figure 20-52). Select the folders to back up or tap **Select All**. A red check mark indicates the folder is selected. Tap **Copy**.

Source: Android on Toshiba

Figure 20-52 Use the menu at the bottom of the screen to manage selected files and folders

3. Tap the device that is to receive the backup (SD card or USB storage). Then tap **Paste**. The files and folders are copied to the device.

Restoring data and settings from backup can be quite a production because no one app backs up all the data on an Android device. Basically, you have to go to wherever you have synced or backed up (an online account, app store, SD card, USB flash drive, or other location) and retrieve the contents from each location. The key to making this restoration process flow smoothly is to use apps with reliable syncing capabilities in both directions.

UPDATING THE ANDROID OS

Updates to the Android OS are automatically pushed to the device from the manufacturer. Because each manufacturer maintains its own versions of Android, these updates might not come at the same time Google announces a major update. When the device receives notice of an update, it displays a message asking permission to install the update. You can also manually check for updates at any time. To do so, go to the **Settings** app and tap **About tablet** or **About phone**. On the About screen (see Figure 20-53 for a phone), tap **System updates**. The device turns to the manufacturer's web site for information and reports updates available. Follow the directions on-screen to install these updates.

A+
220-802
3.5

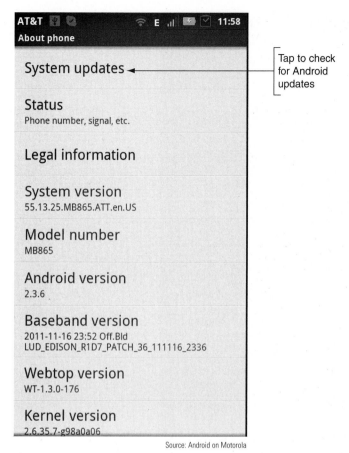

Source: Android on Motorola

Figure 20-53 Manually check for Android updates

SECURING AN ANDROID MOBILE DEVICE

The Android OS includes some security features and relies on third-party applications for other security needs. Here is an overview of how to secure an Android device:

▲ *Passcode protection.* To set a passcode for an Android, tap **Settings, Location & security**. On the Location & security screen (see Figure 20-54), tap **Configure lock screen**. On the next screen, you can set a Pattern, PIN, or Password that must be entered to unlock the device. A pattern is the most secure, which requires you to use your finger to connect at least four dots on the screen (see Figure 20-55).

▲ *Failed login restrictions.* Android automatically locks down the device after five attempts at the pattern. You are then given an opportunity to unlock the device by entering your Google account and password.

▲ *Remote wipes and locator applications.* The Android OS contains native code to remote wipe data from an Android device, but there is no native app on the device to access this feature. Microsoft Exchange server and similar systems implement this feature so that system administrators can wipe a device in an emergency to prevent the loss of corporate data. Google offers Google Apps Mobile Management software, which an administrator can use to secure Android devices used in their organization. This software includes the ability to remote wipe a device. Third-party apps can be used to locate a device. However, the app must be installed before the device is lost. Read several reviews about these apps before you choose one.

20

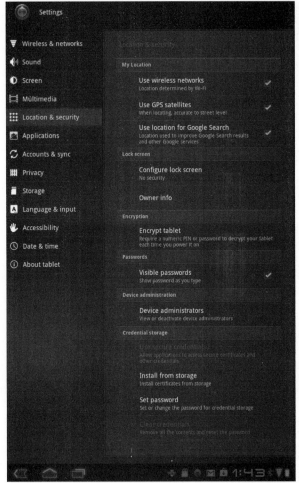

Source: Android on Toshiba

Figure 20-54 Secure a mobile device

◢ *Antivirus protection.* Because Apple closely protects the iOS and iOS apps, it's unlikely an Apple device will need antivirus software. The Android OS and apps are not so closely guarded. Even so, Android devices don't normally get malware. Before installing an Android antivirus app, be sure to read reviews about it. Most of the major antivirus software companies provide Android antivirus apps.

TROUBLESHOOTING ANDROID DEVICES

Follow these general tips to solve problems with Android devices. For more specific instructions, search the web site of the device manufacturer:

◢ You can forcefully reboot the device by pressing a combination of buttons on the device. Turn to the manufacturer's web site to find out this combination. As a last resort, you can open the back cover of the device, remove the battery, and then reinstall the battery.

◢ If you suspect an app is giving a problem, uninstall it and use the app store to reinstall it. How to do this was covered earlier in the chapter.

◢ Try installing Android updates.

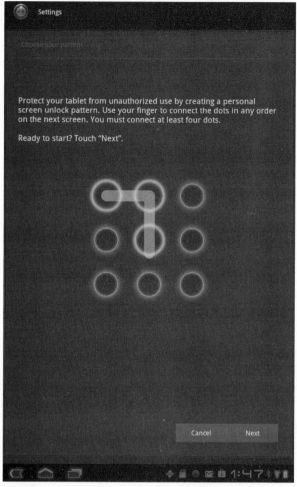

Source: Android on Toshiba

Figure 20-55 Create a pattern that must be entered in order to unlock the device

▲ Take the device into Recovery mode. To do so, look for instructions on the manufacturer's web site. Most likely, you need to hold down a combination of buttons. Once there, Android presents a menu where you can reboot the system or restore the system to factory state. Try the reboot before you try the factory state, because this last option causes all your apps and data to be lost.

If you find you are unable to do all you want to do with your Android device (such as install a powerful app or download the latest Android release before your device manufacturer makes it available), you can root your device. **Rooting** is the process of obtaining root or administrator privileges to an Android device, which then gives you complete access to the entire file system (all folders and files) and all commands and features. To root a device, you download and use third-party software. The process takes some time and might even involve restoring the device to factory state.

The process of rooting might corrupt the OS, and after the device is rooted, installed apps that require root access can corrupt the OS. For some manufacturers, rooting will void your warranty, and some carriers refuse to provide technical support for a rooted device. Avoid it if you can; if you decide to root a device, do so with caution!

Now let's turn our attention away from mobile devices and toward an entirely different topic, virtualization.

20

VIRTUALIZATION BASICS

In Chapter 7, you learned about using a virtual machine to hold an installation of Windows on a personal computer along with installed applications. In this chapter, we explore the many ways virtualization can be implemented, including using a virtual machine. **Virtualization** is when one physical machine hosts multiple activities that are normally done on multiple machines. Two general types of virtualization are server-side virtualization and client-side virtualization. The basic difference between the two is where the virtualizing takes place. Let's see how each can be implemented.

SERVER-SIDE VIRTUALIZATION

Server-side virtualization provides a virtual desktop for users on multiple client machines. Most, if not all, processing is done on the server, which provides to the client the **Virtual Desktop Infrastructure (VDI)**. See Figure 20-56.

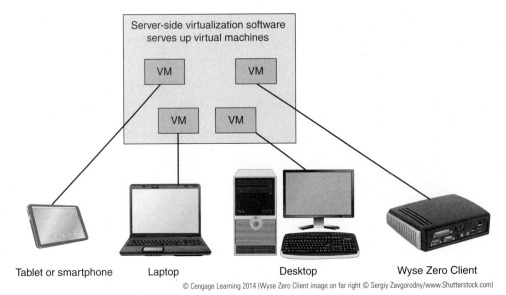

Figure 20-56 Server-side virtualization provides a virtual desktop to each user

The advantages or main purposes of using server-side virtualization are to:

▲ *Maximize a company's investment in hardware.* In recent years, processor computing power and hard drive storage capacity have exponentially increased compared to cost. Today, a server using the latest multi-core processor and hard drives can easily support multiple virtual machines on the same platform. This fact makes it more cost effective to run VMs on a single server rather than pay for hardware at each client computer. The trend, therefore, is to use virtualization with a high-power central server and inexpensive client machines that do very little processing, but are often reduced to merely sending commands to a VM running on the central server.

▲ *Centralize support for hardware, software, and users.* As the cost of labor increases, corporations can save money by centralizing technical support for hardware, software, and users. With virtualization, most hardware and software are installed at a central corporate office or even outsourced to another company, which means technical support is also centralized. Less onsite technical support is needed because a client computer needs less software installed and users can often be supported from a centralized help desk.

The disadvantages of using server-side virtualization are:

▲ *High-end servers are required and network load increases.* Therefore, the data center and network infrastructure are likely to need hardware improvements when implementing server-side virtualization.

▲ *User experience might suffer.* Remote users cannot work offline and are, therefore, totally dependent on the server and the network. What users can do at their local computers cannot be easily modified for unique user needs. Remote support rather than desk-side support is sometimes frustrating for users.

Now let's look at the types of clients and third-party services used with server-side virtualization.

CLIENTS USED WITH SERVER-SIDE VIRTUALIZATION

Using server-side virtualization, three categories of clients might be used, based on the computing power of the client:

▲ *Thick client or fat clients.* The client computer can be a regular desktop computer or laptop. In this case, the client is called a **thick client** or **fat client**. The main advantage of using thick clients is the personal computer can be used for other purposes than server-side virtualization.

▲ *Thin clients.* Because the client does little or no processing with server-side virtualization, a thin client can be used. A **thin client** is a computer that has an operating system, but has little computing power and might only need to support a browser used to communicate with the server. The main advantage of using thin clients is the reduced cost of the client machine.

▲ *Zero clients.* To even further reduce the cost of the client machine, a **zero client**, also called a **dumb terminal** or **ultra-thin client**, can be used. A zero client, such as a Wyse Zero Client, does not have an operating system and merely provides an interface between the user and the server. A zero client might contain little more than a keyboard, mouse, monitor, and network connection.

SERVER-SIDE VIRTUALIZATION USING CLOUD COMPUTING

Many small organizations that want to use server-side virtualization are turning to cloud computing services to reduce the cost of hardware, software, and technical support. **Cloud computing** is when server-side virtualization is delegated to a third-party service, and the Internet is used to connect server and client machines. Cloud computing can vary by the degree of service provided:

▲ **Infrastructure as a Service (IaaS).** Using IaaS, the cloud-computing service provides only the hardware, which can include servers, Network-attached Storage (NAS) devices, and networks. The organization is responsible for the operating systems and applications installed on the servers.

▲ **Platform as a Service (PaaS).** Using PaaS, the cloud-computing service provides hardware and the operating systems and is responsible for updating and maintaining both. The organization is responsible for the applications installed on these machines.

▲ **Software as a Service (SaaS).** Using SaaS, you guessed it, the service is responsible for the hardware, the operating systems, and the applications installed. These turnkey services are the most expensive, but for a small organization that does not have the technical expertise or other resources, this option is sometimes the most cost effective.

20

A+
220-802
1.9

CLIENT-SIDE VIRTUALIZATION

Using **client-side virtualization**, a personal computer provides multiple virtual environments for applications. Client-side virtualization can be implemented using several methods, including these three, which are presented from the least amount of computing done on the client machine to the most computing done on the client machine:

▲ *Presentation virtualization.* Using **presentation virtualization**, a remote application running on a server is controlled by a local computer. You learned to set up these remote applications in Chapter 17 using Remote App and Desktop Connection. The user remotely controls the application running on the server and the application data is also stored on the server (see Figure 20-57).

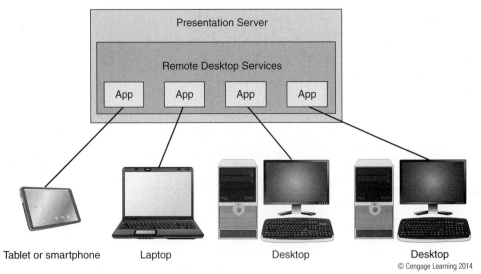

Presentation Server

Remote Desktop Services

| App | App | App | App |

Tablet or smartphone   Laptop   Desktop   Desktop

© Cengage Learning 2014

Figure 20-57   Microsoft Remote Desktop Services presents applications to the user at a local computer

▲ *Application virtualization.* Using **application virtualization**, a virtual environment is created in memory for an application to virtually install itself. An example of software used for application virtualization is Microsoft **Application Virtualization** (**App-V**). The App-V software is installed on the client computer and is responsible for virtually installing an instance of an application whenever the user selects the application from a list provided by App-V. When the application installs and launches, it does not make changes to the Windows registry. An application managed by App-V can be permanently stored on the local hard drive or on an application server.

▲ *Client-side desktop virtualization.* Using **client-side desktop virtualization**, software installed on a desktop or laptop manages virtual machines. Each VM has its own operating system installed. In Chapter 7, you learned that Windows Virtual PC and Oracle VirtualBox are two examples of freeware that can be installed on a computer and used to manage virtual machines. This type of software is called a hypervisor or virtual machine manager (VMM).

Now let's take a closer look at different types of hypervisors and how each can be used to create virtual machines.

VIRTUAL MACHINES AND HYPERVISORS

Both server-side and client-side virtualization can be used to create a virtual machine (VM). The VM can exist on the server and be presented to a remote user (server-side desktop virtualization), or the VM can be created on the local machine to be used locally (client-side desktop virtualization). Software to create and manage virtual machines on a server or on a local computer is called a **virtual machine manager (VMM)** or **hypervisor**.

Now let's look at the different types of hypervisors, the hardware requirements needed for client-side virtualization, and how to secure a virtual machine.

TYPE 1 AND TYPE 2 HYPERVISORS

Hypervisor software can be a Type 1 or Type 2 hypervisor. The differences are diagrammed in Figure 20-58.

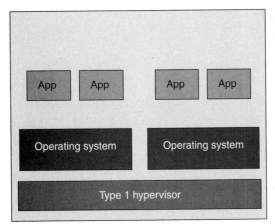
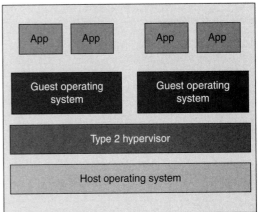

© Cengage Learning 2014

Figure 20-58 Type 1 and Type 2 hypervisors

Here is an explanation of the two types of hypervisors:

▲ A **Type 1 hypervisor** installs on a computer before any operating system, and is, therefore, called a bare-metal hypervisor. After it installs, it partitions the hardware computing power into multiple VMs. An OS is installed in each VM. Examples of Type 1 hypervisors are XenServer by Citrix, ESXi by VMware, and Hyper-V by Microsoft. Most server-side desktop virtualization is done using a Type 1 hypervisor.

Some Type 1 hypervisors are designed for client-side desktop virtualization on personal computers. For example, XenClient by Citrix installs on a personal computer and then you can install Windows or other operating systems in the VMs provided by XenClient. One major advantage of a local computer running a Type 1 hypervisor is added security because each OS and its applications are isolated from the others. For example, employees can install one OS in a VM for business use and another OS in a VM for personal use. The VM used for business can be locked down for secured VPN connections, and the personal VM does not require so much security.

> **Notes** To see some interesting videos of how XenClient by Citrix works and what it can do, go to *www.citrix.com/xenclient*.

▲ A **Type 2 hypervisor** installs in a host operating system as an application. Virtual PC, VirtualBox, and VMware Player are examples of Type 2 hypervisors. A Type 2 hypervisor is not as powerful as a Type 1 hypervisor because it is dependent on the host OS

20

to allot its computing power. A VM in a Type 2 hypervisor is not as secure or as fast as a VM in a Type 1 hypervisor. Type 2 hypervisors are typically used on desktops and laptops when performance and security are not significant issues. Here are some ways that virtual machines provided by Type 2 hypervisors might be used:

▲ Developers often use VMs to test applications. If you save a copy of a virtual hard drive (VHD) that has a fresh installation of Windows installed, you can easily build a new and fresh VM to test an application.

▲ Help desk technicians use VMs so they can easily switch from one OS to another when a user asks for help with a particular OS.

▲ Honeypots are a single computer or a network of computers that lure hackers to them so as to protect the real network. Virtual machines can be used to give the impression to a hacker that he has found a computer or entire network of computers. Administrators can monitor the honeypot for unauthorized activity.

HARDWARE REQUIREMENTS

When preparing to install a hypervisor and virtual machines, you need to be aware of the hardware requirements:

▲ *The motherboard BIOS.* The motherboard BIOS and the processor should support **hardware-assisted virtualization (HAV)**. For Intel processors, this feature is called Intel-VT. For AMD processors, the technology is called AMD-V. The feature must be enabled in BIOS setup. Figure 20-59 shows the BIOS setup screen for one motherboard where the feature is called Intel® VT. When you enable the feature, also verify that all subcategories under the main category for hardware virtualization are enabled.

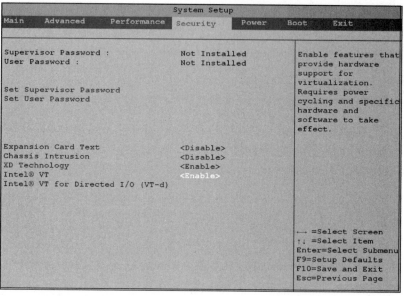

Source: Intel

Figure 20-59 BIOS setup screen to enable hardware virtualization

▲ *Hard drive space.* See the requirements provided by the hypervisor manufacturer for hard drive space for the hypervisor. Each VM has its own virtual hard drive (VHD), which is a file stored on the physical hard drive and acts like a hard drive complete with its own boot sectors and file systems. You can configure this VHD to be a fixed size or dynamically expanding. The fixed size takes up hard drive space whether the VM uses the space or not. An expanding VHD increases in capacity as the VM uses the space. Remember that about 15 GB is required for a Windows installation. Therefore, you'll need at least 15 GB for each VM.

A+
220-802
1.9

◢ *Processor and memory.* All processors sold today support hardware-assisted virtualization. Plan on using at least a dual-core processor or better. A system needs lots of memory when running multiple virtual machines. Some hypervisors tie up all the memory you have configured for a VM from the time the VM is opened until the VM is closed.

When setting up a virtual machine, be aware of emulators that might be required by an application or user. A hypervisor emulates hardware and presents this virtual hardware to each VM, which can include a virtual processor, memory, motherboard, hard drive, optical drive, keyboard, mouse, monitor, network adapter, SD card, USB device, printer, and other components and peripherals. For example, all VMs have a virtual motherboard. When you press a key at startup to access setup BIOS on the VM under Windows Virtual PC, the BIOS setup main menu shown in Figure 20-60 appears. Using this virtual BIOS setup, you can configure the virtual motherboard and other hardware components in the VM.

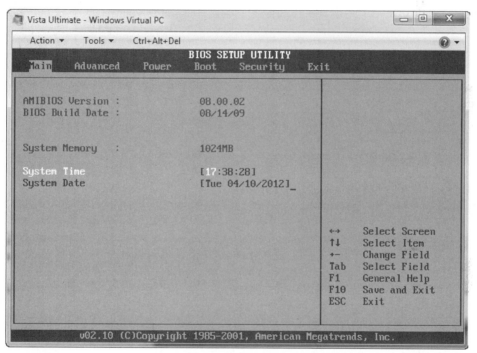

Source: Intel

Figure 20-60   An emulated motherboard provides setup BIOS screens in the VM

A hypervisor offers a way to configure each VM, including which virtual hardware is installed. For example, when you launch Windows Virtual PC, the Virtual Machines window shown on the left side of Figure 20-61 appears. To configure a VM, select the VM in the right pane and click **Settings**. The Settings box shown on the right side of Figure 20-61 appears. You can use this box to install and uninstall virtual hard drives and other virtual devices in the VM.

Using Virtual PC, a VM must have Integrated Components software installed in the VM before it can share some hardware components with the host OS. This software is installed from the virtual DVD drive in the VM. After it is installed, the Integration Features selected in the Virtual PC Settings box become available. Notice on the right side of this box in Figure 20-61 that the VM can share audio, a printer, smart cards, USB drives, and other drives later plugged into the physical computer.

Also notice in the Settings box in Figure 20-61 that this VM has two hard drives installed. Hard Disk 1 is the virtual hard drive stored in the Win 7 VM.vhd file, and Hard Disk 2 is installed in the HDD4.vhd file.

20

A+
220-802
1.9

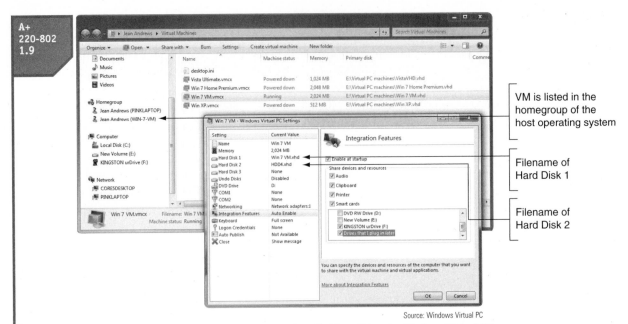

VM is listed in the
homegroup of the
host operating system

Filename of
Hard Disk 1

Filename of
Hard Disk 2

Source: Windows Virtual PC

Figure 20-61   Emulated (virtual) hardware is installed in a VM under Windows Virtual PC

> **Notes**   It's interesting to know that a Windows 7 system image and a Vista Complete PC Backup are
> each stored in a VHD file.

Recall that an .iso file holds the image of a CD. You can mount an .iso image file to the
optical drive in a VM. To do so, first close the VM. Then select it in the Virtual Machines
window and click **Settings** in the menu bar. The Settings box opens. Select the DVD Drive.
Then on the right side of the Settings box, select **Open an ISO image** and click **Browse** to
point to the .iso file (see Figure 20-62). Windows setup files can be downloaded from the
Microsoft web site in an .iso file. When you mount this file to the VM, you can install
Windows in the VM from this virtual CD.

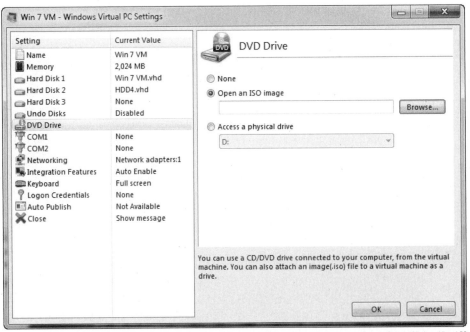

Source: Windows Virtual PC

Figure 20-62   Mount an .iso file to the optical drive in a VM

A+
220-802
1.9

Also consider network requirements for the VM. A VM can have one or more virtual network adapters. A VM connects to a local network the same as other computers and can share and use shared resources on the network. Looking back at Figure 20-61, you can see the VM named Win 7 VM is running and is available in the Homegroup on this network. To change the virtual network adapters for this VM, first close the VM. Then select it in the Virtual Machines window and click **Settings** in the menu bar. The Settings box opens (see Figure 20-63). Select **Networking**, as shown in the figure. On the right side of the Settings box, you can control the number and type of installed network adapters up to four adapters.

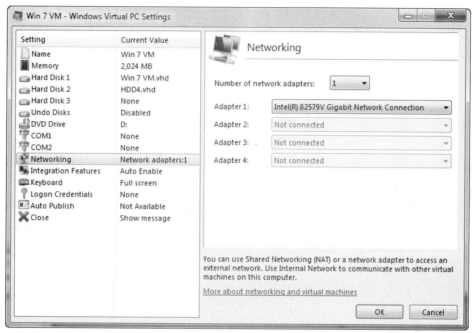

Figure 20-63   Emulate the network adapters in the VM

Source: Windows Virtual PC

In one more example, Oracle VirtualBox can also emulate up to four network adapters in a VM. Figure 20-64 shows the Oracle VM VirtualBox Manager window on the left, which has two installed VMs listed in the left pane of this window. To manage the virtual hardware for a VM, first select it and then click **Settings**. The Settings box appears (see the right side of Figure 20-64). When you click **Network**, you can see the four tabs where each tab can be used to emulate a network adapter.

> 💡 **A+ Exam Tip**   The A+ 220-802 exam expects you to be able to explain methods used to secure a virtual machine installed on a client computer.

SECURE A VIRTUAL MACHINE

A virtual machine is susceptible to hackers and malware just as is a physical machine. Keep these points in mind when securing the resources in a VM:

◢ *Secure the VM within the VM.* When supporting a VM that has network and Internet connectivity or is located in a public area, be sure to configure Windows Firewall in the VM, keep Windows updates current, install and run antivirus software, and perform other security chores discussed in Chapters 17 and 18 to protect the virtual machine and its resources.

20

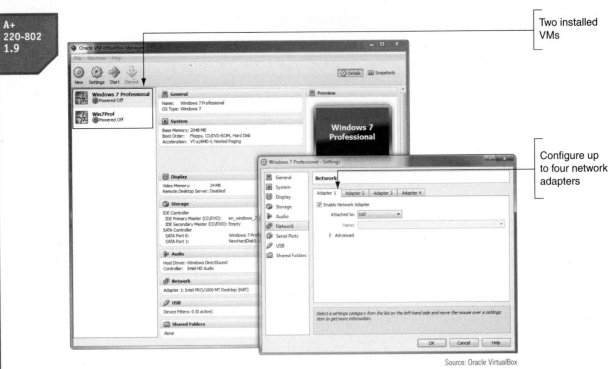

Two installed VMs

Configure up to four network adapters

Source: Oracle VirtualBox

Figure 20-64 Configure up to four network adapters for a VM using Oracle VirtualBox

▲ *VMs should be isolated for best security.* One major advantage of using VMs on a desktop computer is that VMs running under a Type 1 hypervisor are isolated from each other. If one VM gets infected, the other VMs will not be affected.

▲ *Secure permissions to the files that hold a VM.* You can move a VM from one computer to another by moving the files that contain the VM. Be sure these files that hold the VM are secured with permissions that allow access only to specific local or network users.

>> CHAPTER SUMMARY

Operating Systems Used on Mobile Devices

▲ Operating systems used on mobile devices include Android by Google, iOS by Apple, Blackberry by RIM, Windows Phone by Microsoft, and Symbian by the Symbian Foundation.

▲ Android is an open-source OS, and anyone can develop and sell Android apps or variations in the Android OS. Google is the major distributor of Android and Android apps from its Google Play web site.

▲ The iOS by Apple is used only on Apple devices, including the iPhone, iPad, and iPod touch. Apps for the iOS are distributed solely by Apple from its online iTunes App Store.

Comparing Mobile Device Hardware to Tablets and Laptops

▲ Smartphones and handheld tablets use multitouch screens and SSD storage, and they contain no field-serviceable parts. Because some tablets can make phone calls and send text messages, there is little distinction between a tablet and a smartphone.

▲ An accelerometer in a mobile device is used to sense the position of the device and can be used to change the screen orientation.

▲ A device can know its location because of its GPS receiver. Geotracking can be done as the device reports its position.

Configuring, Syncing, and Securing iOS Devices

▲ Using the iOS, the Settings app is used to manage network connections, configure email, manage content on the device, and configure many iOS settings.

▲ Content on an Apple device can be synced and backed up using iTunes to a personal computer or using iCloud to sync to online storage at *icloud.com*.

▲ iTunes installed on a personal computer is used to update the iOS and can restore the iOS to its factory state.

▲ iCloud can be used to sync content to all your iOS devices associated with an Apple ID. iCloud can also be used to locate a lost iOS device if the feature is enabled on the device.

▲ An iOS device can be secured using a passcode. In addition, you can use iCloud to perform a remote wipe to protect sensitive data.

▲ To troubleshoot an iOS device, you can restart, reset, update, erase, restore, and recover the iOS on the device.

Configuring, Syncing, and Securing Android Devices

▲ The Settings app on an Android device can be used to manage network connections, email, online accounts, updates to Android, and security.

▲ Syncing and backing up content on an Android device are done with online accounts, using third-party apps for syncing, syncing all your apps to an app store, and backing up content to external storage connected to the device.

Virtualization Basics

▲ Server-side virtualization happens on the server, and client-side virtualization happens on the client machine.

▲ Three ways to implement client-side virtualization include presentation virtualization, application virtualization, and client-side desktop virtualization.

▲ Client-side desktop virtualization is done by creating multiple virtual machines on a physical machine using a hypervisor.

▲ A Type 1 hypervisor installs before any OS is installed and is called a bare-metal hypervisor. A Type 2 hypervisor is an application that installs in an OS. A Type 1 hypervisor is faster and more secure than a Type 2 hypervisor.

20

>> KEY TERMS

accelerometer
airplane mode
Android
App Store
Apple ID
application virtualization
Application Virtualization (App-V)
Bluetooth PIN code
capacitive touch screen
client-side desktop virtualization
client-side virtualization
cloud computing
dock
dumb terminal
fat client
geotracking
Gmail
Google account
Google Play
GPS (Global Positioning System) receiver

gyroscope
handheld tablet
hardware-assisted virtualization (HAV)
HTC Sense
hypervisor
iCloud
Infrastructure as a Service (IaaS)
iOS
iPad
iPhone
iPod touch
iTunes Store
iTunes U
jailbreaking
Microsoft Exchange
Multimedia Messaging Service (MMS)
multitouch
open source
pairing
Platform as a Service (PaaS)

presentation virtualization
remote wipe
resistive touch screen
rooting
screen orientation
server-side virtualization
Short Message Service (SMS)
smartphone
Software as a Service (SaaS)
thick client
thin client
TouchFLO
Type 1 hypervisor
Type 2 hypervisor
ultra-thin client
Virtual Desktop Infrastructure (VDI)
virtual machine manager (VMM)
virtualization
zero client

>> REVIEW QUESTIONS

1. The Android operating system is based on the ____ OS.

   a) Symbian

   b) Google

   c) Android

   d) Linux

2. What feature is common to Android and iOS devices?

   a) A solid-state device for internal storage of apps and data.

   b) An external slot where you can plug in a smart card such as an SD card to provide extra storage.

   c) A USB port that you can use to plug in a USB flash drive to provide extra storage or transfer files and folders to other devices.

   d) The ability to purchase apps from Amazon.com.

3. Most of the settings you need to know to support an iOS device are contained in the ____ app.

   a) Personal

   b) Settings

   c) Setup

   d) Configure

4. What feature provides the best passcode protection security for an Android device?

   a) Using a pattern

   b) Using a pin

   c) Using a password

   d) Using a watermark

5. ____ is when server-side virtualization is delegated to a third-party service, and the Internet is used to connect server and client machines.

   a) Cloud computing

   b) Rooting

   c) Geotracking

   d) Presentation virtualization

6. True or false? Google owns Android.

7. True or false? The trend for all smart phones and tablets is to move toward resistive touch screens.

8. True or false? When using the Mail app on an Apple device with a Gmail account, the Delete button is replaced with the Archive button.

9. True or false? On an Android device, restoring data and settings from backup can be quite a production because no one app backs up all the data on an Android device.

10. True or false? A virtual machine is susceptible to hackers and malware just as is a physical machine.

11. ____ gives you root or administrative privileges to the operating system and the entire file system (all files and folders) and complete access to all commands and features.

12. A touch screen that can handle a two-finger pinch is called a(n) ____ screen.

13. A(n) ____ is a type of gyroscope used in mobile devices to sense the physical position of the device.

14. A(n) ____ is a computer that has an operating system, but has little computing power and might only need to support a browser used to communicate with the server.

15. A(n) ____ hypervisor installs on a computer before any operating system, and is, therefore, called a bare-metal hypervisor.

Supporting Printers

This chapter discusses the most popular types of printers and how to support them. As you work through the chapter, you'll learn about printer types and features, how to install a local or network printer, and how to share a printer with others on a network. You'll learn how to manage printer features, add-on devices, shared printers, and print jobs. Then, you'll learn about maintaining and troubleshooting printers.

PRINTER TYPES AND FEATURES

A+
220-801
4.1

You need to be aware of the types of printers and know about features a printer might have that you could be called on to configure, repair, or maintain. We begin with a discussion of how data is sent from Windows to a printer and then how each type of printer works. Understanding how a printer works will help you fix printer problems when they arise.

PRINTER LANGUAGES

The language or method that Windows uses to send a page to a printer depends on what the printer is designed to support and the printer drivers installed. If the printer has sophisticated firmware, it might be able to support more than one method. In this case, the installed printer drivers determine which methods can be used:

▲ *The printer uses PostScript commands to build the page.* Windows can send the commands and data needed to build a page to the printer using the **PostScript** language by Adobe Systems. The printer firmware then interprets and processes these commands to produce a bitmap of the page, which is stored in the printer memory. (A **bitmap** is just a bunch of bits in rows and columns. Each row in the bitmap is called a **raster line**.) PostScript is popular with desktop publishing, the typesetting industry, and the Mac OS.

▲ *The printer uses PCL commands to build the page.* A printer language that competes with PostScript is **PCL** (**Printer Control Language**). PCL was developed by Hewlett-Packard but is considered a de facto standard in the printing industry. Many printer manufacturers use PCL.

▲ *The Windows GDI builds the page and then sends it to the printer.* A less-sophisticated method of communicating to a printer is to use the **GDI** (**Graphics Device Interface**) component of Windows. GDI draws and formats the page, converting it to bitmap form, and then sends the almost-ready-to-print bitmap to the printer. Because Windows, rather than the printer, does most of the work of building the page, a GDI printer needs less firmware and memory, and, therefore, generally costs less than a PCL or PostScript printer. The downside of using the GDI method is that Windows performance can suffer when printing a lot of complicated pages. Most low-end inkjet and laser printers are GDI printers. If the printer specifications don't say PCL or PostScript, you can assume it's a GDI printer.

▲ *Windows 7/Vista uses XML Paper Specification (XPS) to build the page and then sends it to the printer.* XPS (**XML Paper Specification**) was introduced with Windows Vista and was designed to ultimately replace GDI as the method Windows uses to prepare (render) the page before sending it to the printer. Windows 7/Vista uses either GDI or XPS for rendering based on the type of printer driver installed. Generally, PostScript and PCL are used with high-end printers, and GDI and XPS are used with low-end printers. Many high-end printers support more than one protocol and can handle GDI, XPS, PCL, or PostScript printing.

▲ *Raw data is printed with little-to-no formatting.* Text data that contains no graphics or embedded control characters is sent to the printer as is, and the printer can print it without any processing. The data is called **raw data**.

TYPES OF PRINTERS

The major categories of printer types include laser, inkjet (ink dispersion), thermal printers, and impact printers. In the following sections, we'll look at the different types of printers for desktop computing.

> **Notes** For heavy business use, the best practice is to purchase one machine for one purpose, instead of bundling many functions into a single machine. For example, if you need a scanner and a printer, purchase a good printer and a good scanner rather than a combo machine. Routine maintenance and troubleshooting are easier and less expensive on single-purpose machines, although the initial cost is higher. On the other hand, for home or small office use, a combo device can save money and counter space.

LASER PRINTERS

A **laser printer** is a type of electrophotographic printer that can range from a small, personal desktop model to a large, network printer capable of handling and printing large volumes continuously. Figure 21-1 shows an example of a typical laser printer for a small office.

© Cengage Learning 2014

Figure 21-1 Oki Data C3200n color laser printer

> **A+ Exam Tip** The A+ 220-801 exam expects you to be familiar with these types of printers: laser, inkjet, thermal, and impact.

Laser printers require the interaction of mechanical, electrical, and optical technologies to work. Laser printers work by placing toner on an electrically charged rotating drum (sometimes called the **imaging drum**) and then depositing the toner on paper as the paper moves through the system at the same speed the drum is turning. Figure 21-2 shows the seven steps of laser printing.

21

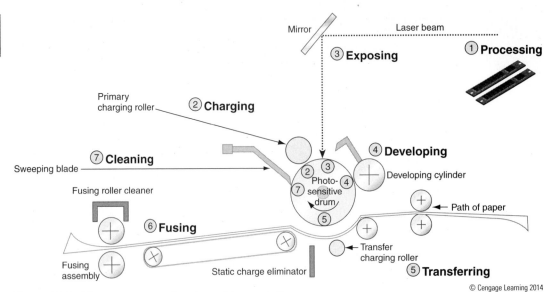

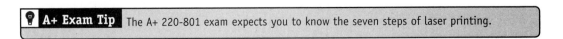

© Cengage Learning 2014

Figure 21-2 The seven progressive steps of laser printing

Note that Figure 21-2 shows only a cross-section of the drum, mechanisms, and paper. Remember that the drum is as wide as a sheet of paper. The mirror, blades, and rollers in the drawing are also as wide as paper. Also know that toner responds to a charge and moves from one surface to another if the second surface has a more positive charge than the first.

> **A+ Exam Tip** The A+ 220-801 exam expects you to know the seven steps of laser printing.

The seven steps of laser printing are listed next:

1. *Processing the image.* A laser printer processes and prints an entire page at one time. The page comes to the printer encoded in a printer language and the firmware inside the printer processes the incoming data to produce a bitmap of the final page, which is stored in the printer's memory. One bitmap image is produced for monochrome images. For color images, one bitmap is produced for each of four colors. (The colors are blue, red, yellow, and black, better known as cyan, magenta, yellow, and black, and sometimes written as CMYK.)

2. *Charging or conditioning.* The drum is conditioned by a roller that places a high uniform electrical charge of −600 V on the surface of the drum. The roller is called the primary charging roller or primary corona, which is charged by a high-voltage power supply assembly. For some printers, a corona wire is used instead of the charging roller to charge the drum.

3. *Exposing or writing.* A laser beam controlled by motors and a mirror scans across the drum until it completes the correct number of passes. The laser beam is turned on and off continually as it makes a single pass down the length of the drum, once for each raster line, so that dots are exposed only where toner should go to print the image. For example, for a 1200 dots per inch (dpi) printer, the beam makes 1200 passes for every one inch of the drum circumference. For a 1200-dpi printer, 1200 dots are exposed or not exposed along the drum for every inch of linear pass. The 1200 dots per inch down this single pass, combined with 1200 passes per inch of drum circumference, accomplish the resolution of 1200 × 1200 dots per square inch of many laser printers. The laser beam writes an image to the drum surface as a −100 V charge. The −100 V charge on this image area will be used in the developing stage to transmit toner to the drum surface.

A+
220-801
4.1

> **Notes** A laser printer can produce better quality printouts than a dot matrix printer, even when printing at the same dpi, because it can vary the size of the dots it prints, creating a sharp, clear image. Hewlett-Packard (HP) calls this technology of varying the size of dots **REt (Resolution Enhancement technology)**.

4. *Developing.* The developing cylinder applies toner to the surface of the drum. The toner is charged and sticks to the developing cylinder because of a magnet inside the cylinder. A control blade prevents too much toner from sticking to the cylinder surface. As the cylinder rotates very close to the drum, the toner is attracted to the part of the surface of the drum that has a −100 V charge and repelled from the −600 V part of the drum surface. The result is that toner sticks to the drum where the laser beam has hit and is repelled from the area where the laser beam has not hit.

5. *Transferring.* In the transferring step (shown in Figure 21-2), a strong electrical charge draws the toner off the drum onto the paper. This is the first step that takes place outside the cartridge and the first step that involves the paper. The soft, black **transfer roller** puts a positive charge on the paper to pull the toner from the drum onto the paper. Then the static charge eliminator (refer again to Figure 21-2) weakens the charges on both the paper and the drum so that the paper does not stick to the drum. The stiffness of the paper and the small radius of the drum also help the paper move away from the drum and toward the fusing assembly. Very thin paper can wrap around the drum, which is why printer manuals usually instruct you to use only paper designated for laser printers.

6. *Fusing.* The **fuser assembly** uses heat and pressure to fuse the toner to the paper. Up to this point, the toner is merely sitting on the paper. The fusing rollers apply heat to the paper, which causes the toner to melt, and the rollers apply pressure to bond the melted toner into the paper. The temperature of the rollers is monitored by the printer. If the temperature exceeds an allowed maximum value (410 degrees F for some printers), the printer shuts down.

7. *Cleaning.* A sweeper strip cleans the drum of any residual toner, which is swept away by a sweeping blade. The charge left on the drum is then neutralized. Some printers use erase lamps in the top cover of the printer for this purpose. The lamps use red light so as not to damage the photosensitive drum.

For color laser printers, the writing process repeats four times, one for each toner color of cyan, magenta, yellow, and black. Each color requires a separate image drum. Then, the paper passes to the fusing stage, when the fuser bonds all toner to the paper and aids in blending the four tones to form specific colors.

The charging, exposing, developing, and cleaning steps use the printer components that undergo the most wear. To make the printer last longer, these steps are done inside removable cartridges that can be replaced. For older printers, all four steps were done inside one cartridge. For newer printers, the cleaning, charging, and exposing steps are done inside the image drum cartridge. The developing cylinder is located inside the toner cartridge. The transferring is done using a **transfer belt** that can be replaced, and the fusing is done inside a fuser cartridge. By using these multiple cartridges inside laser printers, the cost of maintaining a printer is reduced. You can replace one cartridge without having to replace them all. The toner cartridge needs replacing the most often, followed by the image drum, the fuser cartridge, and the transfer assembly, in that order.

Other printer parts that might need replacing include the **pickup roller** that pushes forward a sheet of paper from the paper tray and the **separation pad** that keeps more than one sheet of paper from moving forward. If the pickup roller is worn, paper misfeeds into the printer. If the separation pad is worn, multiple sheets of paper will be drawn into the printer. Sometimes you can clean a pickup roller or separation pad to prolong its life before it needs replacing.

21

A+
220-801
4.1

> **Notes** Before replacing expensive parts in a printer, consider whether a new printer might be more cost effective than repairing the old one.

A printer that is able to print on both sides of the paper is called a **duplex printer** or a double-sided printer. After the front of the paper is printed, a **duplexing assembly,** which contains several rollers, turns the paper around and draws it back through the print process to print on the back of the paper. Alternately, some high-end printers have two print engines so that both sides of the paper are printed at the same time.

INKJET PRINTERS

An **inkjet printer** (see Figure 21-3) uses a type of ink-dispersion printing and doesn't normally provide the high-quality resolution of laser printers. Inkjet printers are popular because they are small and can print color inexpensively. Most inkjet printers today can print high-quality photos, especially when used with photo-quality paper.

Courtesy of EPSON America, Inc.

Figure 21-3 An example of an inkjet printer

An inkjet printer contains firmware that processes the image. The more expensive inkjet printers can process PostScript or PCL, and the less expensive ones can process GDI and XPS print jobs. An inkjet printer uses a **print head** that moves across the paper, creating one line of the image with each pass. The printer puts ink on the paper using a matrix of small dots. Different types of inkjet printers form their droplets of ink in different ways. Printer manufacturers use several technologies, but the most popular is the bubble-jet. Bubble-jet printers use tubes of ink that have tiny resistors near the end of each tube. These resistors heat up and cause the ink to boil. Then, a tiny air bubble of ionized ink (ink with an electrical charge) is ejected onto the paper. A typical bubble-jet print head has 64 or 128 tiny nozzles, all of which can fire a droplet simultaneously. (High-end printers can have as many as 3,000 nozzles.) Plates carrying a magnetic charge direct the path of ink onto the paper to form shapes.

Inkjet printers include one or more **ink cartridges** to hold the different colors of ink for the printer. Figure 21-4 shows two ink cartridges. A black cartridge is on the left and a three-color cartridge is on the right. For this printer, a print head is built into each ink cartridge.

A stepper motor moves the print head and ink cartridges across the paper using a belt to move the assembly and a stabilizing bar to control the movement (see Figure 21-5). A paper tray can hold a stack of paper, or a paper feeder on the back of the printer can hold a few

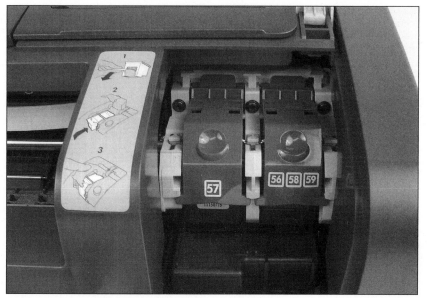

Figure 21-4 The ink cartridges of an inkjet printer

© Cengage Learning 2014

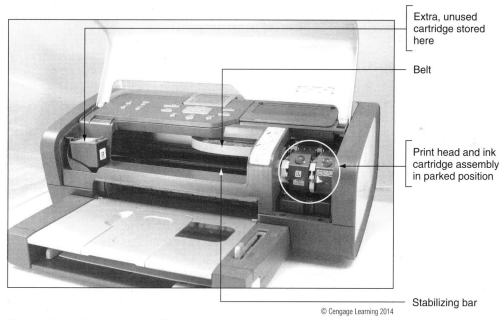

Extra, unused cartridge stored here

Belt

Print head and ink cartridge assembly in parked position

Stabilizing bar

© Cengage Learning 2014

Figure 21-5 The belt and stabilizing bar used to move the print head across the page

sheets of paper. The sheets stand up in the feeder and are dispensed one at a time. Rollers pull a single sheet into the printer from the paper tray or paper feeder. A motor powers these rollers and times the sheet going through the printer in the increments needed to print the image. When the printer is not in use, the assemblage sits in the far-right position shown in Figure 21-4, which is called the home position or parked position. This position helps protect the ink in the cartridges from drying out.

Some inkjet printers offer duplex printing. These printers are larger than normal inkjet printers because of the added space required for the duplexing assembly. For duplex printing, be sure to use heavy paper (rated at 24-pound paper or higher) so the ink doesn't bleed through.

21

A+
220-801
4.1

> **Notes** Weight and brightness are the two primary ways of measuring paper quality. The rated weight of paper (for example, 20 pounds to 32 pounds) determines the thickness of the paper. Brightness is measured on a scale of 92 to 100.

When purchasing an inkjet printer, look for the kind that uses two or four separate cartridges. One cartridge is used for black ink. Three cartridges, one for each color, give better quality color than one cartridge that holds all three colors. Some low-end inkjet printers use a single three-color cartridge and don't have a black ink cartridge. These printers must combine all colors of ink to produce a dull black. Having a separate cartridge for black ink means that it prints true black and, more important, does not use the more expensive colored ink. To save money, you should be able to replace an empty cartridge without having to replace all cartridges.

> **Notes** To save money, you can refill an ink cartridge, and many companies will sell you the tools and ink you need as well as show you how to do it. You can also purchase refilled cartridges at reduced prices. When you purchase ink cartridges, make sure you know if they are new or refilled. Also, for best results, don't refill a cartridge more than three times.

Inkjet printers tend to smudge on inexpensive paper, and they are slower than laser printers. If a printed page later gets damp, the ink can run and get quite messy. The quality of the paper used with inkjet printers significantly affects the quality of printed output. You should use only paper that is designed for an inkjet printer, and you should use a high-grade paper to get the best results.

> **Notes** Photos printed on an inkjet printer tend to fade over time, more so than photos produced professionally. To make your photos last longer, use high-quality paper (rated at high gloss or studio gloss) and use fade-resistant ink (such as Vivera ink by HP). Then protect these photos from exposure to light, heat, humidity, and polluted air. To best protect photos made by an inkjet printer, keep them in a photo album rather than displayed and exposed to light.

IMPACT PRINTERS

An **impact printer** creates a printed page by using some mechanism that touches or hits the paper. The best-known impact printer is a dot matrix printer, which prints only text that it receives as raw data. It has a print head that moves across the width of the paper, using pins to print a matrix of dots on the page. The pins shoot against a cloth ribbon, which hits the paper, depositing the ink. The ribbon provides both the ink for printing and the lubrication for the pinheads. The quality of the print is poor compared to other printer types. However, three reasons you see impact printers still in use are: (1) they use continuous **tractor feeds** and fanfold paper (also called computer paper) rather than individual sheets of paper, making them useful for logging ongoing events or data, (2) they can use carbon paper to print multiple copies at the same time, and (3) they are extremely durable, give little trouble, and seem to last forever.

Maintaining a dot matrix impact printer is easy to do. The **impact paper** used by impact printers comes as a box of fanfold paper or in rolls (used with receipt printers). When the paper is nearing the end of the stack or roll, a color on the edge alerts you to replace the paper. Occasionally, you should replace the ribbon of a dot matrix printer. If the print head fails, check on the cost of replacing the head versus the cost of buying a new printer. Sometimes, the cost of the head is so high it's best to just buy a new printer. Overheating

A+
220-801
4.1

can damage a print head (see Figure 21-6), so keep it as cool as possible to make it last longer. Keep the printer in a cool, well-ventilated area, and don't use it to print more than 50 to 75 pages without allowing the head to cool down.

Print head

© Cengage Learning 2014

Figure 21-6 Keep the print head of a dot matrix printer as cool as possible so that it will last longer

THERMAL PRINTERS

Thermal printers use heat to create an image. Two types of thermal printers are a direct thermal printer and a thermal transfer printer. The older **direct thermal printer** burns dots onto special coated paper, called **thermal paper**, as was done by older fax machines. The process requires no ink and does not use a ribbon. Direct thermal printers are often used as receipt printers that use rolls of thermal paper (see Figure 21-7). The printed image can fade over time.

Courtesy of EPSON America, Inc.

Figure 21-7 The TM-T88V direct thermal printer by EPSON

21

A+
220-801
4.1

A **thermal transfer printer** uses a ribbon that contains wax-based ink. The heating element melts the ribbon (also called foil) onto special thermal paper so that it stays glued to the paper as the feeder assembly moves the paper through the printer. Thermal transfer printers are used to print receipts, bar code labels, clothing labels, or container labels. Figure 21-8 shows a thermal transfer printer used to make bar codes and other labels.

Courtesy of Zebra Technologies

Figure 21-8 The GC420 printer by Zebra is both a thermal transfer printer and a direct thermal printer

Thermal printers are reliable and easy to maintain. When you are responsible for a thermal printer, you know it's time to replace the paper roll when the roll shows the color down one edge. It's important to regularly clean the print head because build-up can harden over time and permanently damage the head. Follow the printer manufacturer's directions to clean the print head. Some thermal printer ribbons have a print head cleaning stripe at the end of the ribbon, and it's a good idea to clean the head each time you replace the ribbon. Additionally, some manufacturers suggest cleaning the head with isopropyl alcohol wipes.

When cleaning, remove any dust and debris that gets down in the print head assembly. As you work, ground yourself to protect the sensitive heating element against static electricity. Don't touch the heating element with your fingers. Also, to prolong the life of the print head, use the lowest heat setting for the heating element that still gives good printing results.

Table 21-1 lists some printer manufacturers.

Printer Manufacturer	Web Site
Brother	www.brother-usa.com
Canon	usa.canon.com
Hewlett-Packard	www.hp.com
Konica Minolta	kmbs.konicaminolta.us
Lexmark	www.lexmark.com
Oki Data	www.okidata.com
Samsung	www.samsung.com
Seiko Epson	www.epson.com
Xerox	www.xerox.com
Zebra Technologies	www.zebra.com

© Cengage Learning 2014

Table 21-1 Printer manufacturers

Now let's turn our attention to using Windows to install, share, and manage printers.

USING WINDOWS TO INSTALL, SHARE, AND MANAGE PRINTERS

A+
220-801
1.11,
1.12,
4.2

A printer connects to a single computer or to the network. A **local printer** connects directly to a computer by way of a USB port, parallel port, serial port, or wireless connection (Bluetooth, infrared, or Wi-Fi). Some printers support more than one method. A **network printer** has an Ethernet port to connect directly to the network or uses Wi-Fi to connect to a wireless access point. Some printers have both an Ethernet port and a USB port (see Figure 21-9). These printers can be installed as either a network printer (connecting directly to the network) or a local printer (connecting directly to a computer) depending on which port you use.

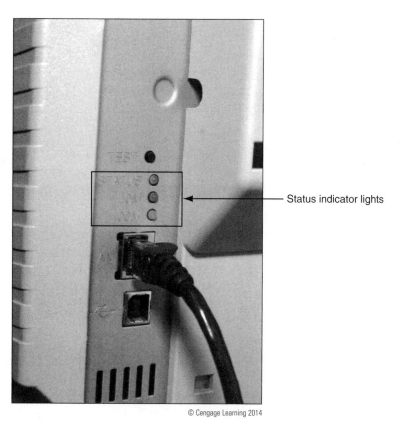

Status indicator lights

© Cengage Learning 2014

Figure 21-9 This printer has an Ethernet and USB port

The two ways to install a printer and make it available on a network are listed here:

▲ A local printer can be attached to a computer using a port (for example, USB, parallel, or wireless) on the computer (see Computer A in Figure 21-10). The printer can be dedicated to only this one computer, or you can share the printer for network users. For a shared local printer to be available to other computers on the network, the host computer must be turned on and not in sleep or standby mode. For another computer on the network to use the shared printer, the printer drivers must be installed on the remote computer.

▲ A network printer can connect directly to a network with its own NIC (see the network printer in Figure 21-10). A network printer is identified on the network by its IP address. To use the printer, any computer on the network can install drivers for this printer.

21

A+
220-801
1.11,
1.12,
4.2

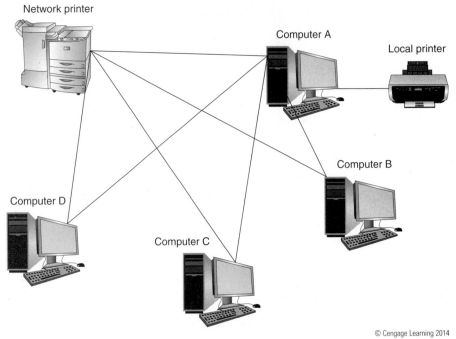

Figure 21-10 A shared local printer and a network printer

© Cengage Learning 2014

> **Notes** A computer can have several printers installed. Of these, Windows designates one printer to be the **default printer**, which is the one Windows prints to unless another is selected.

When you install a printer, printer drivers are required that are compatible with the installed operating system. Be sure to use 32-bit drivers for a 32-bit OS and 64-bit drivers for a 64-bit OS. Windows 7 has many printer drivers built in. The drivers also come on a CD bundled with the printer or you can download them from the printer manufacturer's web site.

In this part of the chapter, you will learn to install local and network printers, share an installed printer, and remotely use a shared printer. You'll also learn how to configure printer add-ons and features and to manage the printer queue in Windows. We begin with learning how to install a printer under Windows 7 or Vista.

INSTALLING A LOCAL OR NETWORK PRINTER

To install a local USB printer, all you have to do is plug in the USB printer and Windows 7/Vista installs the printer automatically. Also, for some types of printers, you can launch the installation program that came bundled on CD with the printer or downloaded from the printer manufacturer's web site. On the other hand, you can use the Windows 7 **Devices and Printers window**, the Vista **Printers window**, or the XP **Printers and Faxes window** to install a printer. These windows are also used to manage and uninstall printers. Printer installations in Windows 7/Vista work differently than XP installations. You first learn how to install a printer in Windows 7/Vista and then in XP.

A+
220-801
1.11,
1.12,
4.2

INSTALL A PRINTER USING WINDOWS 7/VISTA

Follow these steps to use Windows 7 or Vista to install a non-USB local printer or a network printer:

1. For a network printer, make sure the printer is connected to the network and turned on. For a wireless printer, turn on the printer and set the printer within range of the access point or computer. For a parallel port or serial port printer, connect the printer to the computer and turn it on.

2. In the Windows 7 Control Panel, using the Large or Small icon view, click **Devices and Printers**. (Alternately, you can click Start, Devices and Printers.) The Devices and Printers window opens, as shown on the left side of Figure 21-11. (For Windows Vista, in Control Panel, click **Printers** to open the Printers window, which works the same as the Windows 7 Devices and Printers window.)

> **Notes** By default, the Devices and Printers option is listed in the Start menu. If you don't find it there, you can add it by right-clicking the taskbar and selecting **Properties**. In the Taskbar and Start Menu Properties box, click the **Start Menu** tab and then click **Customize**. Check **Devices and Printers** and click **OK** twice.

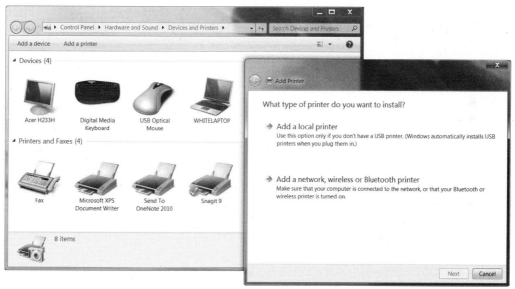

Source: Microsoft Windows 7

Figure 21-11 Use the Devices and Printers window to install a printer

> **Notes** Notice in Figure 21-11 that Windows includes the Microsoft XPS Document Writer as an installed printer. When you print to this printer, the **XPS Document Writer** creates an .xps file. The file is similar to a .pdf file and can be viewed, edited, printed, faxed, emailed, or posted on web sites. In Windows, the file is viewed in a browser window.

21

A+
220-801
1.11,
1.12,
4.2

3. Click **Add a printer**. In the Add Printer window that appears (see the right side of Figure 21-11), select the type of printer.

4. Windows searches for available printers and lists them. Figure 21-12 shows a list when installing a network printer. Select the printer from the list and click **Next**. If your printer is not listed, click **The printer that I want isn't listed**, and, on the next screen, point to the port or IP address of the printer. In Figure 21-12, we are installing a network printer identified by its IP address, which is 192.168.1.101.

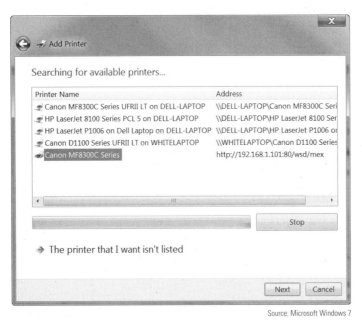

Source: Microsoft Windows 7

Figure 21-12 Select the printer from the list of available printers

> **Notes** To know the IP address of a network printer, direct the printer to print a configuration page, which should include its IP address. To print the page, use buttons, keys, or other controls on the front of the printer. The printer documentation shows you how to use these controls. Some printers have a control panel on the front of the printer. For these printers, scroll through the menu to display the IP address in the panel window.

5. In the next box (see the far left of Figure 21-13), you tell Windows where to find the printer drivers. To select the drivers kept by Windows, select the printer brand and model. To use drivers stored on CD or previously downloaded from the web, click **Have Disk**. The Install From Disk box appears (see the middle of Figure 21-13). Click **Browse** to locate the drivers; Windows is looking for an .inf file. Notice the choice of folders for this particular printer listed in the Locate File box on the far-right side of Figure 21-13. Use the 32bit or x64 folder depending on which type of OS you are using.

> **Notes** Use the System window to find out if a 32-bit or 64-bit OS is installed. To open the System window, click **Start**, right-click **Computer**, and select **Properties**.

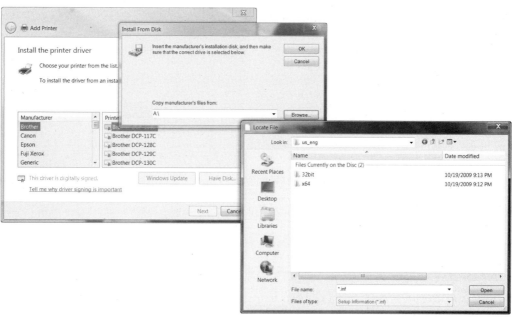

Figure 21-13 Locate printer drivers on CD or downloaded from the web

Source: Microsoft Windows 7

6. Continue to follow the wizard to install the printer. Dialog boxes give you the opportunity to change the name of the printer and designate the printer as the default printer. You are also given the opportunity to test the printer. It's always a good idea to print a test page when you install a printer to verify the installation works.

You can also send a test page to the printer at any time. To do so, right-click the printer in the Devices and Printers window and select **Printer properties**. See Figure 21-14. On the General tab of the Properties box, click **Print Test Page** (see Figure 21-15).

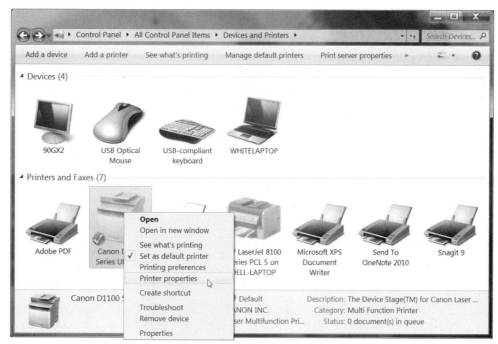

Figure 21-14 Select Printer properties to open the printer Properties box

Source: Microsoft Windows 7

21

A+
220-801
1.11,
1.12,
4.2

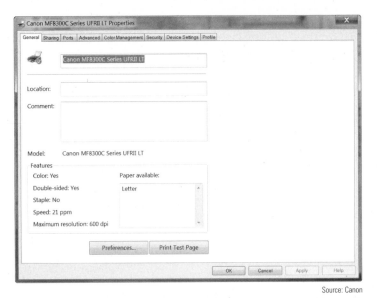

Source: Canon

Figure 21-15 Send a test page to the printer to test connectivity to the printer, the printer, and the printer installation

Rather than using the Windows Devices and Printers window to start a printer installation, you can also start the installation using the setup program on the CD that came bundled with the printer or using the setup program downloaded from the printer manufacturer's web site. For one Canon printer, when you launch that setup program, the menu shown in Figure 21-16 appears. Follow the directions to install the printer. This method might work when the first method fails.

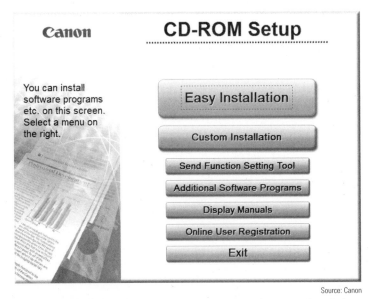

Source: Canon

Figure 21-16 Menu provided by a setup program that came bundled with a printer

INSTALL A LOCAL PRINTER USING WINDOWS XP

Installing a local printer using Windows XP begins differently depending on the type of port you are using. For local printers that use a FireWire, USB, or wireless connection, you might need to first install the software before connecting the printer or connect the printer before installing the software. See the documentation to know which order to use.

A+
220-801
1.11,
1.12,
4.2

A+ Exam Tip The A+ 220-801 exam expects you to know how to install a local and network printer using Windows 7, Vista, or XP.

Follow these steps to install a local printer using FireWire, USB, or a wireless connection:

1. Log onto the system as an administrator. Run the setup program stored on CD or downloaded from the printer manufacturer's web site before you install the printer. The setup program installs the drivers.

2. At one point in the setup, you will be told to connect the printer. Figure 21-17 shows this step for one HP printer installation routine. Connect the printer to the port. For this printer, a USB port is used. For wireless printers, verify the wireless connection is enabled. For infrared wireless printers, place the printer in the line of sight of the infrared port on the computer. (Most wireless printers have a status light that stays lit when a wireless connection is active.) Turn on the printer.

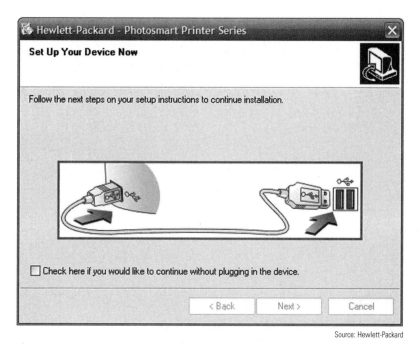

Source: Hewlett-Packard

Figure 21-17 The printer setup program tells you when to connect the printer

3. The setup program detects the printer. If Windows launches the Found New Hardware Wizard, it should close quickly. If not, cancel the wizard.

4. The setup program asks if you want this printer to be the default printer. Click Yes or No to make your selection. The setup program finishes the installation.

5. You can now test the printer. Open the Printers and Faxes window by clicking **Start**, **Control Panel**, and **Printers and Faxes** (in Classic view). For Category view, click **Printers and Other Hardware** and then click **Printers and Faxes**. Either way, the Printers and Faxes window opens (see the top of Figure 21-18). Right-click the printer and select **Properties** from the shortcut menu. Click the **General** tab and then click the **Print Test Page** button, as shown in Figure 21-18.

21

A+
220-801
1.11,
1.12,
4.2

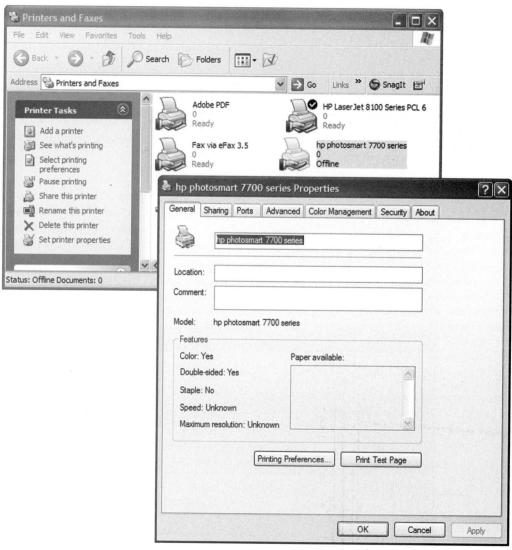

Source: Microsoft Windows 7 and Hewlett-Packard

Figure 21-18 To verify a printer installation, always print a test page as the last step in the installation

> **A+ Exam Tip** The A+ 220-801 exam expects you to know how to install a printer using older technologies, including how to install a local printer using a serial or parallel port in Windows XP.

PRINTER INSTALLATIONS USING A PARALLEL PORT

Serial and parallel printer ports are not hot pluggable. Here are the directions to install a local printer using a serial or parallel port in Windows XP:

1. Plug in the printer to the port and turn on the printer. Now, you must decide how you want to install the drivers. You can use the setup program from the printer manufacturer or use the Windows installation process. First try using the setup program that came on the printer's setup CD or downloaded from the manufacturer's web site. If you have problems with the installation, you can then try the Windows approach.

2. To use the printer's setup program, launch the program and follow the directions on-screen to install the printer.

3. Alternately, you can use the Windows installation process to install the printer drivers. Open the Printers and Faxes window and click **Add a printer**. The Add Printer Wizard launches, as shown in Figure 21-19. Follow the directions on-screen to install the printer drivers. After the printer is installed, print a test page to verify the installation works.

Source: Microsoft Windows 7

Figure 21-19 Use the Add Printer Wizard to install a printer

> 💡 **A+ Exam Tip** The A+ 220-801 exam expects you to be able to configure a parallel port and install a printer that uses a parallel port.

If you have a problem with the installation that is using a parallel port, consider the port might not be configured correctly in BIOS setup or there is a problem with the parallel cable.

Parallel ports, commonly used by older printers, transmit data in parallel, eight bits at a time. Parallel ports fall into three categories: **Standard Parallel Port (SPP)** that transmits in only one direction (the computer can communicate with the printer, but the printer cannot communicate with the computer), **EPP (Enhanced Parallel Port)** that transmits in both directions, and **ECP (Extended Capabilities Port)** that is faster than an EPP port. A parallel port is sometimes called a Centronics port, named after the 36-pin Centronics connection used by printers (see Figure 21-20). Both EPP and ECP are covered under the **IEEE 1284** specifications of the Institute of Electrical and Electronics Engineers (IEEE). A parallel cable should not exceed 10 feet and should be IEEE 1284 compliant; look for the IEEE 1284 label on the cable.

21

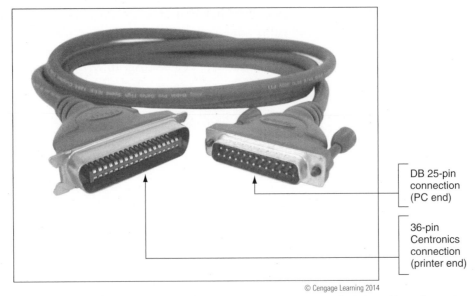

DB 25-pin
connection
(PC end)

36-pin
Centronics
connection
(printer end)

© Cengage Learning 2014

Figure 21-20 A parallel cable has a DB25 connection at the PC end of the cable and a
36-pin Centronics connection at the printer end of the cable

If you're having a problem with a parallel port, check BIOS setup to make sure the port
is enabled and configured correctly. For example, the BIOS setup on one system is shown in
Figure 21-21. Unless you are having a problem with the port or suspect a conflict with other
hardware, keep the default setting of ECP.

Also check Device Manager to make sure it recognizes the port without an error.
In Device Manager, a parallel port is known as LPT1: or LPT2:. The **LPT (Line Printer
Terminal)** assignments refer to the system resources a parallel port will use to manage a
print job.

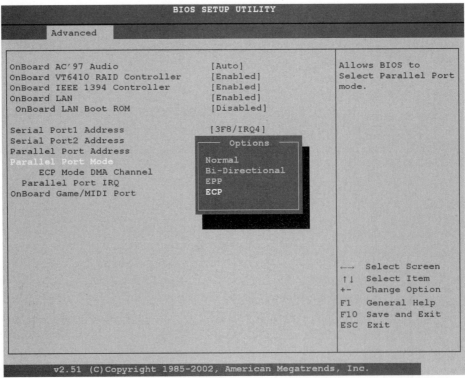

Source: Microsoft Windows 7

Figure 21-21 BIOS settings for a parallel port on one motherboard

A+
220-801
1.11,
1.12,
4.2

STEPS TO INSTALL A NETWORK PRINTER USING WINDOWS XP

Always follow the manufacturer's directions when installing a printer. If you don't have these instructions, here are the general steps to install a network printer using Windows XP:

1. Open the XP Printers and Faxes window and start the wizard to add a new printer. Select the option to install a local printer but do not ask Windows to automatically detect the printer.

2. On the next window shown in Figure 21-22, choose **Create a new port**. From the list of port types, select **Standard TCP/IP Port**. Click **Next** twice.

Source: Microsoft Windows 7

Figure 21-22   Configure a local printer to use a standard TCP/IP port

3. On the next window shown in Figure 21-23, you need to identify the printer on the network. If you know the IP address of the printer, enter it in the first box on this window and click **Next**. Alternately, you can enter the printer name.

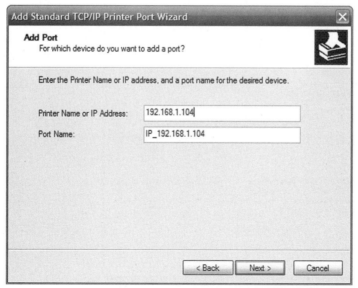

Source: Microsoft Windows 7

Figure 21-23   Enter the printer name or IP address to identify the printer on the network

21

A+
220-801
1.11,
1.12,
4.2

4. On the next window, click **Have Disk** so you can point to and use the downloaded driver files that will then be used to complete the printer installation.

SHARING AN INSTALLED PRINTER

Before you share an installed local or network printer, verify these Windows settings for shared resources:

◢ Using Windows 7, make sure **Turn on file and printer sharing** is selected, which is the default setting for a Home or Work network. To check the setting, click **Change advanced sharing settings** in the Network and Sharing Center.

◢ Using Windows Vista, Printer sharing must be turned on in the Network and Sharing Center.

◢ Using Windows XP, to share an installed printer, File and Printer Sharing must be installed. To use a printer shared by a remote computer, Client for Microsoft Networks must be installed. In most cases, it is easiest to simply install both XP components on all computers on the network. To install the components, open the Windows XP Network Connections window and use the Properties box for the Local Area Connection icon.

> **Notes** Remote users will not be able to use a shared printer if the computer sharing the printer is asleep. You can configure the Wake-on-LAN feature of the computer's network adapter to cause network activity to wake up the sleeping computer. The feature must be enabled in BIOS setup and also in the network adapter's properties box. How to do that is covered in Chapters 16 and 17.

To share an installed local or network printer using Windows 7/Vista/XP with others on the network, follow these steps:

1. In the printer Properties box, click the **Sharing** tab. Check **Share this printer**, as shown in Figure 21-24 for Windows 7. (For Vista or XP, you must click the **Change sharing options** button on the Sharing tab before you can make changes. This button is missing in Windows 7.)

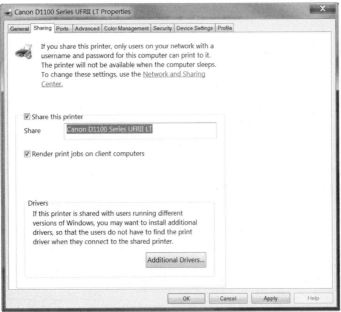

Source: Canon

Figure 21-24   Share the printer and make decisions as to how printer sharing is handled

A+
220-801
1.11,
1.12,
4.2

2. You can then change the share name of the printer. Notice in Figure 21-24 the option to control where print jobs are rendered. A print job can be prepared (rendered) on the remote computer (client computer) or this computer (print server). Your choice depends on which computer you think should carry this burden. You can test several print jobs on remote computers with rendering done at either location and see which method best uses computing resources on the network.

> **Notes** Group Policy under Windows 7/Vista can be used to limit and control all kinds of printer-related tasks, including the number of printers that can be installed, how print jobs are sent to print servers (rendered or not rendered), which print servers the computer can use, and which printers on a network the computer can use.

3. If you want to make drivers for the printer available to remote users who are using an operating system other than the OS on this computer, click **Additional Drivers**.

4. The Additional Drivers box opens, as shown in Figure 21-25. For 32-bit operating systems, select **x86**. For 64-bit operating systems, select **x64**. Click **OK** to close the box. You might be asked for the Windows setup DVD or other access to the installation files. (For Windows XP, the Additional Drivers box lists specific operating systems for drivers to be made available to remote computers.)

Source: Microsoft Windows 7

Figure 21-25 Select additional drivers you want available for other operating systems that will use the shared printer

5. Click **OK** to close the Properties box. A shared printer shows a two-friends icon (for Windows 7/Vista) or a hand icon (for XP) under it in the Devices and Printers window, and the printer is listed in the Network windows of other computers on the network.

A+
220-801
1.11,
1.12,
4.2

INSTALLING A SHARED PRINTER

You can install a shared printer on a remote computer using one of two methods: (1) Use the Windows 7 Devices and Printers window, the Vista Printer window, or the XP Printers and Faxes window, or (2) use Windows Explorer or the Network or My Network Places window. Here are the general steps to follow when using the first method:

1. On a remote computer, open the Windows 7 Devices and Printers window, the Vista Printer window, or the XP Printers and Faxes window. Click **Add a printer** and follow the directions on-screen to add a network printer.

2. As you follow the wizard, select the shared printer from the list of available printers. Windows attempts to use printer drivers found on the host computer. If it doesn't find the drivers, you will be given the opportunity to provide them on CD or another media. Follow the directions on-screen to complete the installation wizard.

Another way to install a shared printer is to first use Windows Explorer or the Network window or XP My Network Places to locate the printer on the network. Do the following:

1. On a remote computer, open **Windows Explorer**. In the Network resources, select the computer that is sharing the printer. Double-click the computer to reveal the resources it is sharing, which include the printer. See Figure 21-26. Right-click the printer and select **Connect** from the shortcut menu and follow the directions on-screen. A warning box that appears during the process is shown in Figure 21-26.

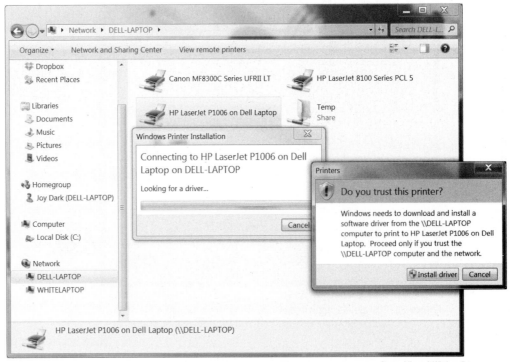

Source: Microsoft Windows 7

Figure 21-26 Install a shared printer using Windows Explorer

A+
220-801
1.11,
1.12,
4.2

2. If the host computer is sharing the right drivers, you can use those drivers for the installation. If Windows cannot find the right drivers, it sends you an error message and gives you the opportunity to install the drivers using the printer manufacturer's CD or downloaded from the web. Be sure to send a test page to the printer to verify the installation is successful.

MANAGING PRINTER FEATURES AND ADD-ON DEVICES

After the printer is installed, use the printer Properties box to manage printer features and hardware devices installed on the printer. To open the box, right-click the printer and choose **Printer properties**. On the Properties box, click the **Device Settings** tab. The options on this tab depend on the installed printer. Figure 21-27 shows the box for an HP printer, and the box for a Canon printer is shown in Figure 21-28. For the printer in Figure 21-27, duplex printing is available, as shown in the figure. You can also control the size of the paper installed in each input tray bin and various add-on devices for this printer, such as a stapler or stacker unit.

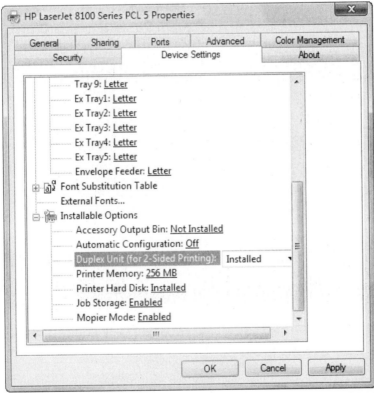

Source: Microsoft Windows 7

Figure 21-27   The Device Settings for an HP printer

After you have installed new printer add-on equipment or a feature, the equipment or feature is listed as an option in the Printing Preferences box when a user is printing a document. The users of this printer need to know how to use the option. For example, if you install duplexing and a user attempts to print from an application, the user needs to know how to print on both sides of the paper. When printing from Notepad, the Print window shown on the left side of Figure 21-29 appears. To print on both sides of the paper, the user can select the printer and click **Preferences**, select the **Finishing** tab in the Printing Preferences box, and select **2-sided Printing** from the drop-down list (see the right side of Figure 21-29).

21

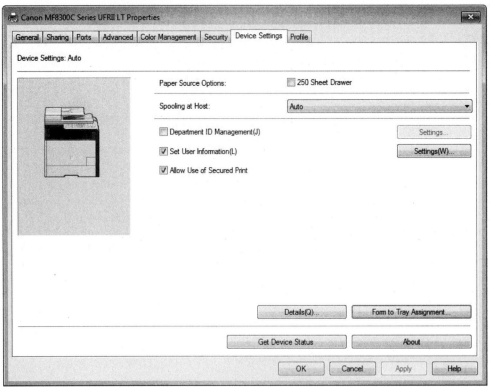

Source: Canon

Figure 21-28 The Device Settings for a Canon printer

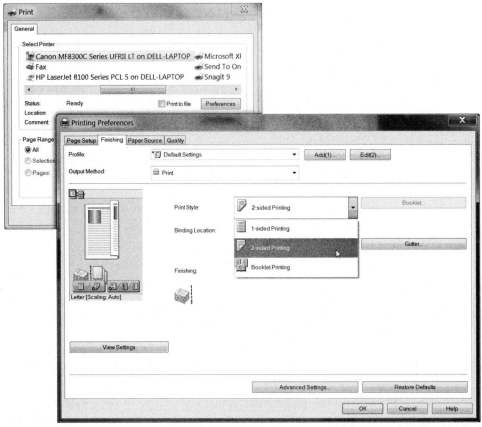

Source: Microsoft Windows 7

Figure 21-29 Printing on both sides of the paper

A+
220-801
1.11,
1.12,
4.2

Notes You might be expected to train a user how to install paper and envelopes in the various paper trays. Let the user know whom to contact if printer problems arise. You might also consider providing a means for the user to record problems with the printer that don't require immediate attention. For example, you can hang a clipboard and paper close to the printer for the user to write questions and comments that you can address at a later time.

MANAGING THE PRINTER QUEUE

Normally, when Windows receives a print job from an application, it places the job in a queue and prints from the queue, so that the application is released from the printing process as soon as possible. Several print jobs can accumulate in the queue, and the process is called **spooling**. (The word *spool* is an acronym for *simultaneous peripheral operations online*.) The print queue is sometimes called the **print spooler**. Most printing from Windows uses spooling.

To manage the printer queue, double-click the printer icon in the Windows 7 Devices and Printers window. The printer status window that appears for one printer is showing in Figure 21-30. Other printer status windows might be organized slightly differently. From this window, you can see the status and order of the print jobs. If the printer reports a problem with printing, it will be displayed as the status for the first job in the print queue. To cancel a single print job, right-click the job and select **Cancel** from the shortcut menu. See Figure 21-30. To cancel all print jobs, click **Printer** on the menu and select **Cancel All Documents**. If you still can't get the printer moving again, try pressing a Cancel or Reset button on the printer or turning the printer off and on. To verify that the problem with printing is solved, print a test page using the printer Properties box.

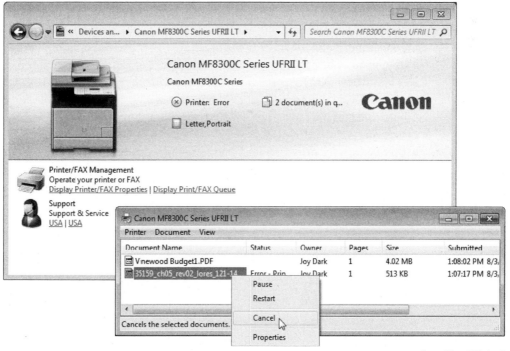

Source: Microsoft Windows 7

Figure 21-30 Manage the printer queue

21

A+
220-801
1.11,
1.12,
4.2

Notes If the printer queue is backed up, try deleting the first job in the queue (the one listed last.) If you are having a problem deleting all jobs in the queue, you can stop and restart the Windows print spooler service. How to do that is covered later in the chapter.

Now let's turn our attention to tasks you might be called on to do when maintaining and upgrading a printer.

PRINTER MAINTENANCE AND UPGRADES

A+
220-801
4.3

Printers generally last for years if they are properly used and maintained. To get the most out of a printer, it's important to follow the manufacturer's directions when using the device and to perform the necessary routine maintenance. For example, the life of a printer can be shortened if you allow the printer to overheat, don't use approved paper, or don't install consumable maintenance kits when they are required.

ONLINE SUPPORT FOR PRINTERS

The printer manufacturer's web site is an important resource when supporting printers. Here are some things to look for:

- ▲ *Online documentation.* Expect the printer manufacturer's web site to include documentation on installing, configuring, troubleshooting, using, upgrading, and maintaining the printer. Also look for information on printer parts and warranty, compatibility information, specifications and features of your printer, a way to register your printer, and how to recycle or dispose of a printer. You might also be able to download your printer manual in PDF format.
- ▲ *A knowledge base of common problems and what to do about them.* Some web sites offer a forum where you can communicate with others responsible for supporting a particular printer. Also look for an online chat link or email address for technical support.
- ▲ *Updated device drivers.* Sometimes you can solve printer problems by downloading and installing the latest drivers. Also, a manufacturer makes new features and options available through these drivers. Be sure you download files for the correct printer and OS.
- ▲ *Replacement parts.* When a printer part breaks, buy only parts made by or approved by the printer manufacturer. Manufacturers also sell consumable supplies such as toner and ink cartridges.
- ▲ *Printer maintenance kits.* The best practice is to buy everything you need for routine maintenance either from the printer manufacturer or an approved vendor. If you buy from a nonapproved vendor, you risk damaging the printer, voiding its warranty, or shortening its lifespan.
- ▲ *Firmware updates.* Some high-end printers have firmware that can be flashed to solve problems and add features. Be careful to download the correct update for your printer.

A+
220-801
4.3

For now, let's focus on how to protect yourself when working inside a printer. Some laser printer parts can get hot enough to burn you while in operation. So before you work inside a laser printer, turn it off, unplug it, and wait about 30 minutes for it to cool down. Printer parts that get hot might have one of the symbols in Figure 21-31 imprinted on or near them. Also notice in the figure other symbols that indicate danger. If you see these symbols on parts or in documentation, pay attention to them and stay safe.

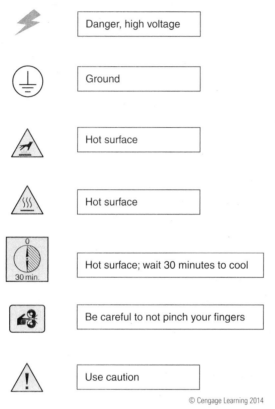

	Danger, high voltage
	Ground
	Hot surface
	Hot surface
	Hot surface; wait 30 minutes to cool
	Be careful to not pinch your fingers
	Use caution

© Cengage Learning 2014

Figure 21-31 Symbols imprinted on a device that indicate danger

Also know that a printer might still keep power even when the printer on/off switch is turned off. To ensure that the printer has no power, unplug it. Even when a laser printer is unplugged, internal components might still hold a dangerous electrical charge for some time. For your protection, laser printers use a laser beam that is always enclosed inside a protective case inside the printer. Therefore, when servicing a laser printer, you should never have to look at the laser beam, which can damage your eyes.

To protect memory modules and hard drives inside printers, be sure to use an antistatic ground bracelet to protect these sensitive components when installing them. It is not necessary or recommended that you wear the ground bracelet when exchanging consumables such as toner cartridges, fuser assembles, or image drums.

Here's one more tip to stay safe, but I don't want it to frighten you: When you work inside high-voltage equipment such as a laser printer, don't do it when no one else is around. If you have an emergency, someone needs to be close by to help you.

21

> **Notes** When working with laser printer toner cartridges, if you get toner dust on your clothes or hands while exchanging the cartridge, don't use hot water to clean it up. Remember that heat sets the toner. Go outdoors and use a can of compressed air to blow off the toner. Then use cold water to clean your hands and clothes. It's a good idea to wear a smock or apron when working on printers.

Figure 21-32 shows an ink cartridge being installed in an inkjet printer. To replace a cartridge, turn on the printer and open the front cover. The printer releases the cartridges. You can then open the latch on top of the cartridge and remove it. Install the new cartridge as shown in the figure.

© Cengage Learning 2014

Figure 21-32 Installing an ink cartridge in an inkjet printer

CLEANING A PRINTER

A printer gets dirty inside and outside as stray toner, ink, dust, and bits of paper accumulate. As part of routine printer maintenance, you need to regularly clean the printer. How often depends on how much the printer is used and the work environment. Some manufacturers suggest a heavily used printer be cleaned weekly, and others suggest you clean it whenever you exchange the toner, ink cartridges, or ribbon.

Clean the outside of the printer with a damp cloth. Don't use ammonia-based cleaners. Clean the inside of the printer with a dry cloth and remove dust, bits of paper, and stray toner. Picking up stray toner can be a problem. Don't try to blow it out with compressed air because you don't want the toner in the air. Also, don't use an antistatic vacuum cleaner. You can, however, use a vacuum cleaner designed to pick up toner, called a **toner vacuum**. This type of vacuum does not allow the toner that it picks up to touch any conductive surface. Some printer manufacturers also suggest you use an **extension magnet brush**. The long-handled brush is made of nylon fibers that are charged with static electricity and easily attract the toner like a magnet. For a laser printer, wipe the rollers from side to side with a dry cloth to remove loose dirt and toner. Don't touch the soft black roller (the transfer roller), or you might affect the print quality. You can find specific instructions for cleaning a printer on the printer manufacturer's web site.

A+
220-801
4.3

An inkjet printer might require **calibration** to align and/or clean the inkjet nozzles, which can solve a problem when colors appear streaked or out of alignment. To calibrate the printer, you might use the menu on the control panel of the printer or use software that came bundled with the printer. How to access these tools differs from one printer to another. See the printer manual to learn how to perform the calibration. For some printers, a Services tab is added to the printer Properties window. Other printer installations might put utility programs in the Start menu. The first time you turn on a printer after installing ink cartridges, it's a good idea to calibrate the printer.

If an inkjet printer still does not print after calibrating it, you can try to manually clean the cartridge nozzles. Check the printer manufacturer's web site for directions. For most inkjet printers, you are directed to use clean, distilled water and cotton swabs to clean the face of the ink cartridge, being careful not to touch the nozzle plate. To prevent the inkjet nozzles from drying out, don't leave the ink cartridges out of their cradle for longer than 30 minutes. Here are some general directions:

1. Following the manufacturer's directions, remove the inkjet cartridges from the printer and lay them on their sides on a paper towel.

2. Dip a cotton swab in distilled water (not tap water) and squeeze out any excess water.

3. Hold an ink cartridge so that the nozzle plate faces up and use the swab to wipe clean the area around the nozzle plate, as shown in Figure 21-33. Do not clean the plate itself.

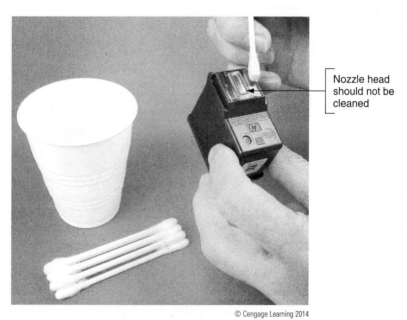

Nozzle head should not be cleaned

© Cengage Learning 2014

Figure 21-33 Clean the area around the nozzle plate with a damp cotton swab

4. Hold the cartridge up to the light and make sure that no dust, dirt, ink, or cotton fibers are left around the face of the nozzle plate. Make sure the area is clean.

5. Clean all the ink cartridges the same way and replace the cartridges in the printer.

6. Print a test page. If print quality is still poor, try calibrating the printer again.

7. If you still have problems, you need to replace the ink cartridges.

21

A+
220-801
4.3

Laser printers automatically calibrate themselves periodically. You can instruct a laser printer to calibrate at any time by using the controls on the front of the printer or the browser-based utility program that is included in the firmware of a network printer. To access the utility, enter the IP address of the printer in the browser address box.

PRINTER MAINTENANCE KITS

Manufacturers of high-end printers provide **printer maintenance kits,** which include specific printer components, step-by-step instructions for performing maintenance, and any special tools or equipment you need to do maintenance. For example, the maintenance plan for the HP Color LaserJet 4600 printer says to replace the transfer roller assembly after printing 120,000 pages and replace the fusing assembly after 150,000 pages. The plan also says the black ink cartridge should last for about 9,000 pages and the color ink cartridge for about 8,000 pages. HP sells the image transfer kit, the image fuser kit, and the ink cartridges designed for this printer.

> **A+ Exam Tip** The A+ 220-801 exam expects you to know about the importance of resetting the page count after installing a printer maintenance kit.

To find out how many pages a printer has printed so that you know if you need to do the maintenance, you need to have the printer give you the page count since the last maintenance. You can tell the printer to display the information or print a status report by using buttons on the front of the printer (see Figure 21-34) or you can use utility software from a computer connected to the printer. See the printer documentation to know how to get this report. For network printers that offer a browser-based utility, enter the IP address of the printer in your browser and use the utility to find the counters (Figure 21-35 shows such a utility for a Canon network printer).

After you have performed the maintenance, be sure to reset the page count so it will be accurate to tell you when you need to do the next routine maintenance. Keep a written record of the maintenance and other service done. If a printer gives problems, one of the first things you can do is check this service documentation to find out if maintenance is due. You can also check for a history of prior problems and how they were resolved.

© Cengage Learning 2014

Figure 21-34   Use buttons on the front of the printer to display information, including the page count

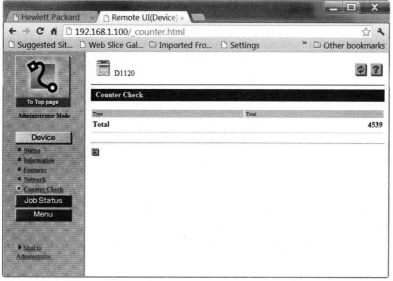

Source: Canon

Figure 21-35 Use the web-based printer utility to read the printer counters

As examples of replacing printer consumables, let's look at how to replace a toner cartridge, image drum, and fuser for the Oki Data color laser printer shown earlier in Figure 21-1.

> **A+ Exam Tip** The A+ 220-801 exam expects you to know how to replace a toner cartridge and apply a maintenance kit that can include an image drum or a fuser assembly.

A toner cartridge for this printer generally lasts for about 1,500 pages. Here are the steps to replace a color toner cartridge:

1. Turn off and unplug the printer. Press the cover release button on the top-left corner of the printer and open the printer cover (see Figure 21-36).

2. Figure 21-37 shows the cover up. Notice the four erase lamps on the inside of the cover. Look inside the printer for the four toner cartridges and the fuser assembly labeled in Figure 21-38. Pull the blue toner cartridge release button forward to release the cartridge from the image drum below it and to which it is connected (see Figure 21-39).

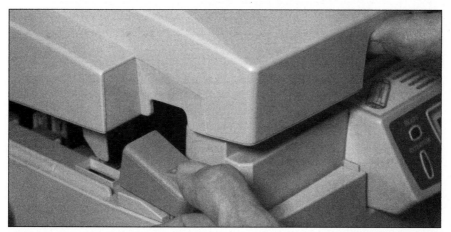

© Cengage Learning 2014

Figure 21-36 Open the printer cover

21

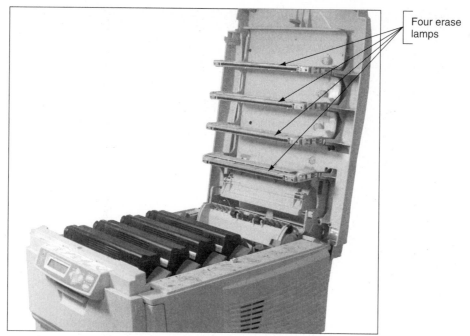

Figure 21-37 Cover lifted

© Cengage Learning 2014

Figure 21-38 Inside the Oki Data printer

© Cengage Learning 2014

3. Lift the cartridge out of the printer, lifting up on the right side first and then removing the left side (see Figure 21-40). Be careful not to spill loose toner.

4. Unpack the new cartridge. Gently shake it from side to side to loosen the toner. Remove the tape from underneath the cartridge, and place the cartridge in the printer by inserting the left side first and then the right side. Push the cartridge lever back into position to lock the cartridge in place. Close the printer cover.

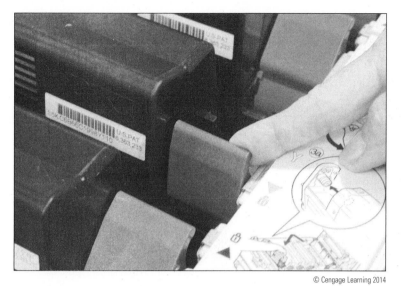

© Cengage Learning 2014

Figure 21-39 Push the blue lever forward to release the toner cartridge

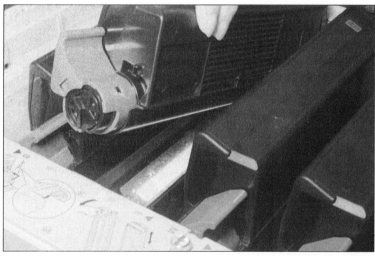

© Cengage Learning 2014

Figure 21-40 Remove the toner cartridge

The printer has four image drums, one for each color. The drums are expected to last for about 15,000 pages. When you purchase a new drum, the kit comes with a new color toner cartridge. Follow these steps to replace the cartridge and image drum. In these steps, we are using the yellow drum and cartridge:

1. Turn off and unplug the printer. Wait about 30 minutes after you have turned off the printer for it to cool down. Then open the printer cover. The toner cartridge is inserted into the image drum. Lift the drum together with the toner cartridge out of the printer (see Figure 21-41). Be sure to dispose of the drum and cartridge according to local regulations.

2. Unpack the new image drum. Peel the tape off the drum and remove the plastic film around it. As you work, be careful to keep the drum upright so as not to spill the toner. Because the drum is sensitive to light, don't allow the drum to be exposed to bright light or direct sunlight. Don't expose it to normal room lighting for longer than five minutes.

21

A+
220-801
4.3

Figure 21-41 Remove the image drum and toner cartridge as one unit

3. Place the drum in the printer. Install the new toner cartridge in the printer. Close the printer cover.

The fuser should last for about 45,000 pages. To replace the fuser, follow these steps:

1. Turn off and unplug the printer. Allow the printer to cool and open the cover.

2. Pull the two blue fuser levers forward to unlock the fuser (see Figure 21-42).

3. Lift the fuser out of the printer using the handle on the fuser, as shown in Figure 21-43.

4. Unpack the new fuser and place it in the printer. Push the two blue levers toward the back of the printer to lock the fuser in place.

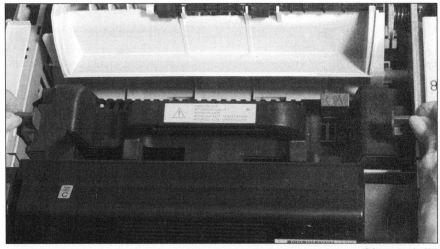

Figure 21-42 Pull the two fuser levers forward to release the fuser

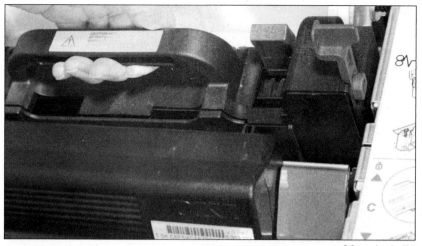

Figure 21-43 Remove the fuser

© Cengage Learning 2014

Whenever you service the inside of this printer, as a last step always carefully clean the LED erase lamps on the inside of the top cover (see Figure 21-44). The printer maintenance kits you've just learned to use all include a wipe to clean these strips.

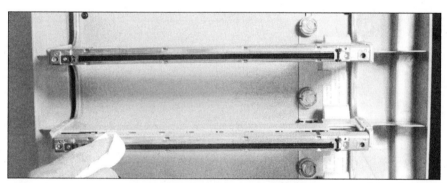

Figure 21-44 Clean the LED strips on the inside top cover

© Cengage Learning 2014

UPGRADE THE PRINTER MEMORY OR HARD DRIVE

Some printers have internal hard drives to hold print jobs and fonts, and printers might also give you the option to install additional memory in the printer. Extra memory can speed up memory performance, reduce print errors, and prevent Out of Memory errors. Check the user guide to determine how much memory the printer can support and what kind of memory to buy or what kind of internal hard drive the printer might support.

As you work with printer hardware, be sure you turn off the printer and disconnect it from the power source. Also, use an antistatic ground bracelet to protect memory modules from static electricity. Most likely, you will use a screwdriver to remove a cover plate on the printer to expose a cavity where memory or a drive can be installed. To access memory on one printer, you remove thumbscrews on the back of the printer and then pull out the formatter board shown in Figure 21-45. Memory modules are installed on this board (see Figure 21-46). You can also install a hard drive in one of the two empty bays on the board. The hard drive comes embedded on a proprietary board that fits in the bay.

21

© Cengage Learning 2014

Figure 21-45 Remove the formatter board from the printer

Two empty
DIMM slots

Two installed
DIMMs

Bays for hard
drives or other
components

© Cengage Learning 2014

Figure 21-46 Memory is installed on the formatter board

A+
220-801
4.3

After this equipment is installed, you must enable and configure it using the printer Properties window. For example, for the HP 8100 printer, use the Device Settings tab of the printer Properties box (see Figure 21-47). You can then set the hard drive as Installed or change the amount of Printer Memory that is installed. Some printers also give you the option to set the size of the hard drive.

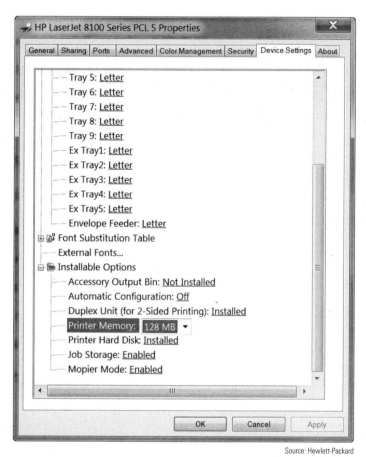

Source: Hewlett-Packard

Figure 21-47 Configure the printer for newly installed hardware

A+
220-801
4.2

A+
220-802
1.4

PRINT SERVERS AND THE PRINT MANAGEMENT TOOL

A **print server** is hardware or software that manages the print jobs sent to one or more printers on a network. The server receives print jobs from computers on the network and sends these jobs to the appropriate printer. A print server can be: (1) A dedicated hardware device, (2) software, such as Print Queue Manager by AMT Software, which is installed on a computer on the network, or (3) programs embedded in firmware on a printer, such as HP JetDirect, which is used by many HP printers.

Let's take a look at printer firmware used as a print server and at Print Management, a Windows 7 utility that you can use to manage printers on a network.

A+
220-801
4.2

A+
220-802
1.4

EMBEDDED FIRMWARE PRINT SERVER

Most high-quality printers offer a utility embedded in the firmware that you can use to manage print jobs, view the status of the printer, see a job history, and check counters, such as the number of pages printed. These utilities are accessed through a browser. For one Canon printer, when you enter the IP address of the printer in a browser window and log on to the firmware utility, the window in Figure 21-48 appears.

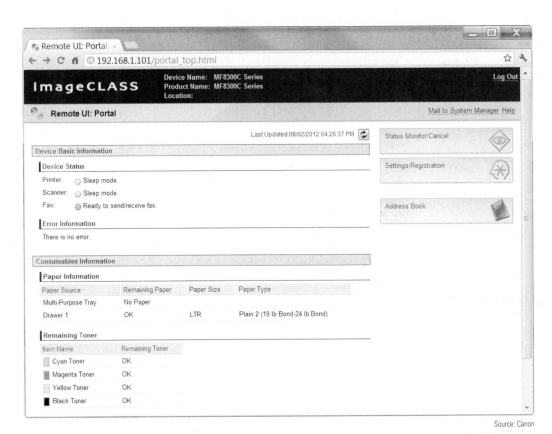

Source: Canon

Figure 21-48 Use the printer's web-based utility to view the printer status and manage print jobs

More advanced print server firmware programs allow you more control over how the printer is used. Using the print server, you can manage print protocols, start or stop jobs in the print queue, reorder jobs in the queue, cancel specific jobs coming from a particular computer on the network, and set up your email address so the printer alerts you by email when it has a problem.

WINDOWS PRINT MANAGEMENT

Windows 7/Vista professional and business editions offer the **Print Management** utility in the Administrative Tools group of Control Panel. (Home editions don't provide the Print Management tool.) You can use it to monitor and manage printer queues for all printers on the network. In Print Management, each computer on the network that shares a printer is considered a print server.

A+
220-801
4.2

A+
220-802
1.4

APPLYING │ CONCEPTS   LEARN TO USE PRINT MANAGEMENT

Follow these steps to learn to use Print Management:

1. In Control Panel, click **Administrative Tools** in the System and Security group. In the list of administrative tools, double-click **Print Management**. The Print Management window appears.

2. In the Print Servers group, drill down to your local computer and click **Printers**. The list of printers installed on your computer appears, as shown in Figure 21-49.

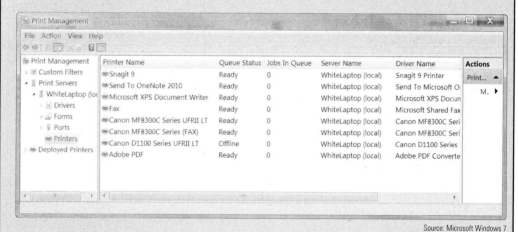

Source: Microsoft Windows 7

Figure 21-49   Use Print Management to monitor and manage printers on the network

3. To add other print servers to the list, right-click **Print Servers** in the left pane and click **Add/Remove Servers**. In the Add/Remove Servers box (see the left side of Figure 21-50), click **Browse**. Locate the computer (see the right side of Figure 21-50) and click **Select Server**. The computer is now listed under Add servers in the Add/Remove Servers box. Click **Add to List**. The computer is listed in the Print servers area. Click **OK** to close the Add/Remove Servers box.

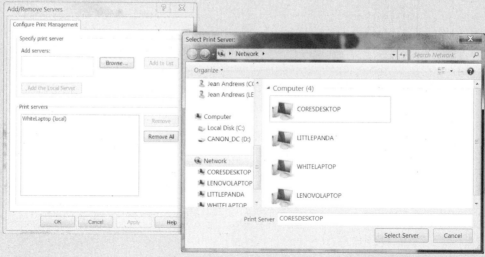

Source: Microsoft Windows 7

Figure 21-50   Select a print server to monitor and manage

A+
220-801
4.2

A+
220-802
1.4

4. The computer is now listed as a print server in the left pane of the Print Management window. Notice in Figure 21-51, you can view a computer on the network that has its printer offline and one job in the queue. Right-click this printer to see a menu with options shown in the figure that you can use to manage the printer and its printer queue.

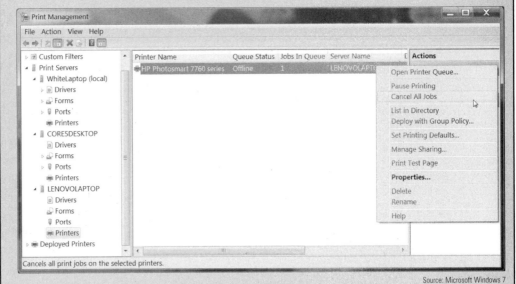

Source: Microsoft Windows 7

Figure 21-51   Manage print servers, printers, and printer queues on the network

TROUBLESHOOTING PRINTERS

A+
220-802
1.5, 4.9

In this part of the chapter, you'll learn some general and specific printer troubleshooting tips. If you need more help with a printer problem, turn to the manufacturer's web site for additional information and support.

APPLYING | CONCEPTS

Jill is the computer support technician responsible for supporting 10 users, their peer-to-peer network, printers, and computers. Everything was working fine when Jill left work one evening, but the next morning three users meet her at the door, complaining that they cannot print to the network printer and that important work must be printed by noon. What do you think are the first three things Jill should check?

As with all computer problems, begin troubleshooting by interviewing the user, finding out what works and doesn't work, and making an initial determination of the problem. When you think the problem is solved, ask the user to check things out to make sure he is satisfied with your work. And, after the problem is solved, be sure to document the symptoms of the problem and what you did to solve it.

PRINTER DOES NOT PRINT

When a printer does not print, the problem can be caused by the printer, the computer hardware or Windows, the application using the printer, the printer cable, or the network. Follow the steps in Figure 21-52 to isolate the problem.

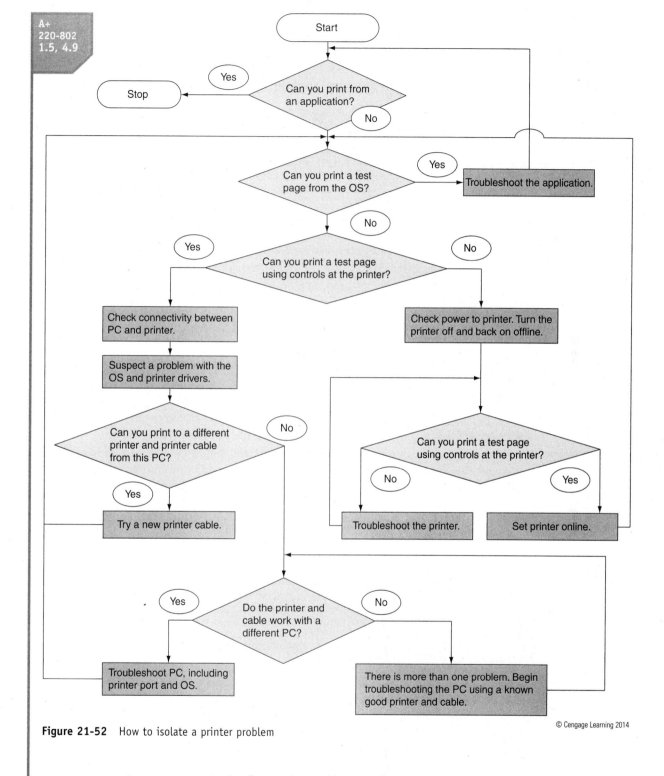

Figure 21-52 How to isolate a printer problem

© Cengage Learning 2014

As you can see in the figure, the problem can be isolated to one of the following areas:

- The printer itself
- Connectivity between the computer and its local printer
- Connectivity between the computer and a network printer
- The OS and printer drivers
- The application attempting to use the printer

21

A+
220-802
1.5, 4.9

In addition, if this is the first time you have tried to print after installing the printer, the printer drivers or the printer installation might be the problem. The following sections address printer problems caused by all of these categories, starting with hardware.

PROBLEMS WITH THE PRINTER ITSELF

To eliminate the printer as the problem, first check that the printer is on, and then print a **printer self-test page** by using controls at the printer. For directions to print a self-test page, see the printer's user guide. For example, you might need to hold down a button or buttons on the printer's front panel. If this test page prints correctly, then the printer is working.

A printer self-test page generally prints some text, some graphics, and some information about the printer, such as the printer resolution and how much memory is installed. Verify that the information on the test page is correct. For example, if you know that the printer should have 2 MB of onboard printer memory, but the test only reports 1 MB, then there is a problem with memory. If the information reported is not correct and the printer allows you to upgrade firmware on the printer, try doing that next.

If the self-test page does not print or prints incorrectly (for example, it has missing dots or smudged streaks through the page), then troubleshoot the printer until it prints correctly. When the printer self-test page does not print, check the following:

◢ Does the printer have paper? Is the paper installed correctly? Are the printer cover and rear access doors properly closed and locked? Is there a paper jam?

◢ If paper is jammed inside the printer, follow the directions in the printer documentation to remove the paper. Don't jerk the paper from the printer mechanism, but pull evenly on the paper, with care. You don't want to leave pieces of paper behind. Check for jammed paper from both the input tray and the output bin. Check both sides. An inkjet printer is likely to have a door in the back that you can open to gently remove the jammed paper, as shown in Figure 21-53.

© Cengage Learning 2014

Figure 21-53 Open the door on the back of an inkjet printer to remove jammed paper

A+
220-802
1.5, 4.9

- Is the paper not feeding? Remove the paper tray and check the metal plate at the bottom of the tray. Can it move up and down freely? If not, replace the tray. When you insert the tray in the printer, does the printer lift the plate as the tray is inserted? If not, the lift mechanism might need repair.

- Damp paper can cause paper jams or the printer to refuse to feed the paper or to wrinkle or crease the paper. Be sure to only use dry paper in a printer. Paper that is too thin can also crease or wrinkle in the printer.

- Look for an error message or error code in the control panel on the front of the printer. You might need to search the printer documentation or web site to find out the meaning of a code. For example, error codes in the 79.xx range for HP printers can indicate a variety of problems from a print job with characters it does not understand to a failed memory module in the printer.

- For some error codes, the problem might be with a print job the printer cannot process. Cancel all print jobs and disconnect the printer from the network. If the control panel reports "Ready," then you can assume the problem is with the network, computers, or print jobs, and not with the printer. If the error code is still displayed, the problem is with the printer. Follow the directions on the printer manufacturer's web site to address the error code.

- Try resetting the printer (for some printers, press the Reset button on the printer). Try powering down or unplugging the printer and starting it again. Check that power is getting to the printer. Try another power source.

- For an inkjet printer, check if nozzles are clogged. Sometimes, leaving the printer on for a while will heat up the ink nozzles and unclog them.

- For an impact printer, if the print head moves back and forth but nothing prints, check the ribbon. Is it installed correctly between the plate and print head? Is it jammed? If the ribbon is dried out, it needs to be replaced.

- Check the service documentation and printer page count to find out if routine maintenance is due or if the printer has a history of similar problems. Check the user guide for the printer and the printer manufacturer's web site for other troubleshooting suggestions.

If you still cannot get a printer to work, you might need to take the printer to a certified repair shop. Before you do, though, try contacting the manufacturer. You might also be able to open a chat session on the printer manufacturer's web site.

APPLYING | CONCEPTS

Now back to Jill and her company's network printer problem. Generally, Jill should focus on finding out what works and what doesn't work, always remembering to check the simple things first. Jill should first go to the printer and check that the printer is online and has no error messages, such as a Paper Out message. Then, Jill should ask, "Can anyone print to this printer?" To find out, she should go to the closest computer and try to print a Windows test page. If the test page prints, she should next go to one of the three computers that do not print and begin troubleshooting that computer's connection to the network. If the test page did not print at the closest computer, the problem is still not necessarily the printer. To eliminate the printer as the problem, the next step is to print a self-test page at the printer. If that self-test page prints, then Jill should check other computers on the network. Is the entire network down? Can one computer see another computer on the network? Perhaps part of the network is down (maybe because of a switch serving one part of the network).

21

A+
220-802
1.5, 4.9

PROBLEMS WITH A LOCAL PRINTER CABLE OR PORT

If the printer self-test did work, but the Windows printer test did not work, check for connectivity problems between the printer and the computer. For a local printer connected directly to a computer, the problem might be with the printer cable or the port the printer is using. Do the following:

- Check that the cable is firmly connected at both ends. For a USB port, try a different port. For some parallel ports, you can use a screwdriver to securely anchor the cable to the parallel port with two screws on each side of the port. If you suspect the cable is bad, you can use a multimeter to check the cable.
- Try a different cable. For older parallel cables, make sure the cable is no longer than 10 feet and verify that the cable is IEEE 1284-compliant.
- Try printing using the same printer and printer cable but a different computer.
- Use Device Manager to verify the port the printer is using is enabled and working properly. Try another device on the same port to verify the problem is not with the port.
- Use BIOS setup to check how the port is configured. Is it enabled? For a parallel port, is the port set to ECP or bidirectional?
- If you have access to a port tester device, test the port.

PROBLEMS WITH CONNECTIVITY FOR A NETWORK PRINTER OR SHARED PRINTER

If the self-test page prints but the Windows test page does not print and the printer is a network printer or shared printer, the problem might be with connectivity between the computer and the network printer or with the host computer that is sharing the printer.

> **A+ Exam Tip** The A+ 220-802 exam expects you to know how to determine if connectivity between the printer and the computer is the problem when troubleshooting printer issues.

Follow these steps to solve problems with network printers:

- Is the printer online?
- Turn the printer off and back on. Try rebooting the computer.
- Verify that the correct default printer is selected.
- Consider the IP address of the printer might have changed, which can happen if the printer is receiving a dynamic IP address. Using Windows, delete the printer, and then install the printer again. If this solves the problem, assign a static IP address to the printer to keep the problem from reoccurring.
- Can you print to another network printer? If so, there might be a problem with the printer. Look at the printer's configuration.
- Try pinging the printer. To do that, open a command prompt window and enter **ping 192.168.1.100** (substitute the IP address of your printer). If the printer replies (see Figure 21-54), the problem is not network connectivity.
- If pinging doesn't work, try using another network cable for the printer. Check status indicator lights on the printer network port and on the switch or router to which the printer connects.
- Use the printer's browser-based utility and check for status reports and error messages. Run diagnostic software that might be available on the utility menu.
- Try flashing the network printer's firmware.

A+
220-802
1.5, 4.9

```
Command Prompt

Microsoft Windows [Version 6.1.7601]
Copyright (c) 2009 Microsoft Corporation.  All rights reserved.

C:\Users\Jean Andrews>ping 192.168.1.100

Pinging 192.168.1.100 with 32 bytes of data:
Reply from 192.168.1.100: bytes=32 time=1ms TTL=255
Reply from 192.168.1.100: bytes=32 time=1ms TTL=255
Reply from 192.168.1.100: bytes=32 time=1ms TTL=255
Reply from 192.168.1.100: bytes=32 time=1ms TTL=255

Ping statistics for 192.168.1.100:
    Packets: Sent = 4, Received = 4, Lost = 0 (0% loss),
Approximate round trip times in milli-seconds:
    Minimum = 1ms, Maximum = 1ms, Average = 1ms

C:\Users\Jean Andrews>_
```

Source: Microsoft Windows 7

Figure 21-54   Use the ping command to determine if you have network connectivity with the printer

Even though you are using a network printer, the printer might have been installed as a shared printer. Let's look at an example of this situation. Figure 21-55 shows a Devices and Printers window with several installed printers. Notice the two installations of the HP LaserJet 8100 printer. The first installation was done installing the LaserJet 8100 as a network printer addressed by its IP address. The second installation was done by using a shared printer that was shared by another computer on the network named DELL-LAPTOP. When you print using the first installation of the LaserJet 8100, you print directly over the network to the printer. But when you print to the second installation of the LaserJet 8100, you print by way of the DELL-LAPTOP computer. If this computer is offline, the print jobs back up in the print queue until the computer is available.

When all users on a network are responsible for managing their own network resources, you should not install a network printer by using another computer on the network that has shared the printer. However, to get centralized control of a printer and its print queue, you can install a network printer on one computer, share it, and then install this shared printer on other computers on the network. Using this scenario, all print jobs must go through this one host computer, which becomes the print server for this printer. In this scenario, you can manage all print jobs to the printer from this one computer.

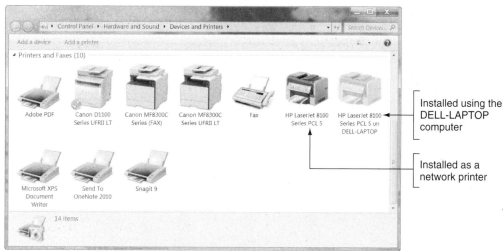

Source: Microsoft Windows 7

Figure 21-55   A network printer installed using two methods

21

A+
220-802
1.5, 4.9

When a computer has shared a local or network printer with others on the network, follow these steps to solve problems with these shared printers:

◢ Check that you can print a test page from the computer that has the printer attached to it locally or is sharing a network printer. If you cannot print from the host computer, solve the problem there before attempting to print from other computers on the network.

◢ Is enough hard drive space available on the client or host computer?

◢ Did you get an "Access denied" message when you tried to print from the remote computer? If so, you might not have access to the host computer. On the remote computer, go to Windows Explorer or the Network window and attempt to open shared folders on the printer's computer. Perhaps you have not entered a correct user account and password to access this computer; if so, you will be unable to use the computer's resources. Make sure you have a matching Windows user account and password on each computer.

◢ On the host computer, open the printer's Properties box and click the **Security** tab. Select **Everyone** and make sure Permissions for Everyone includes permission to print, as shown in Figure 21-56. Notice you can use this Security tab to control other things a user can do with the shared printer.

◢ Using Windows on the remote computer, delete the printer, and then install the printer again. Watch for and address any error messages that might appear.

PROBLEMS PRINTING FROM WINDOWS

If a self-test page works and you have already stepped through checking the printer connectivity, but you still cannot print a test page from Windows, try the following:

◢ The print spool might be stalled. Try deleting all print jobs in the printer's queue. Recall you can do that using the Windows 7 Devices and Printers window, the Vista Printers window, or the XP Printers and Faxes window. If the printer is still hung, try using buttons on the front of the printer to cancel print jobs. You can also power cycle the printer (turn it off and back on). Some printers have a Reset button for this purpose.

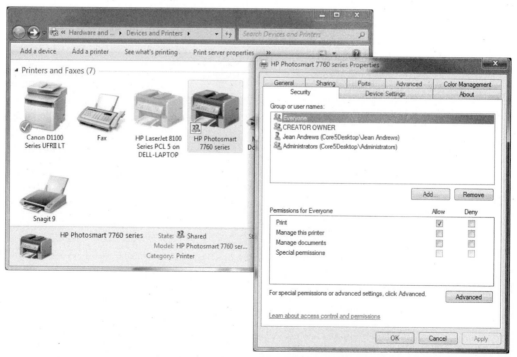

Figure 21-56   Give permission to everyone to print using this shared printer

Source: Microsoft Windows 7

A+ Exam Tip The A+ 220-802 exam expects you to know how to solve problems with the print spool.

◢ Verify that the correct printer is used.

◢ Verify that the printer is online. See the printer documentation for information on how to determine the status from the control panel of the printer. For many printers, "Ready" appears in this control panel.

◢ Verify that the printer cable or cable connections are solid.

◢ Stop and restart the Windows Print Spooler service. Windows uses the **Services console** to stop, start, and manage background services used by Windows and applications. Do the following:

　1. To stop the service, click **Start**, type **Services** in the search box, and press **Enter**. The Services console opens. Scroll down to and select **Print Spooler** (see Figure 21-57). Click **Stop** to stop the service.

　2. To delete any print jobs left in the queue, open Windows Explorer and delete all files in the C:\Windows\System32\spool\PRINTERS folder.

　3. Start the print spooler back up. To start up the print spooler, return to the Services console. With Print Spooler selected, click **Restart**. Close the Services console window.

◢ If you still cannot print, reboot the computer. Try deleting the printer and then reinstalling it.

◢ Check the printer manufacturer's web site for an updated printer driver. Download and install the correct driver.

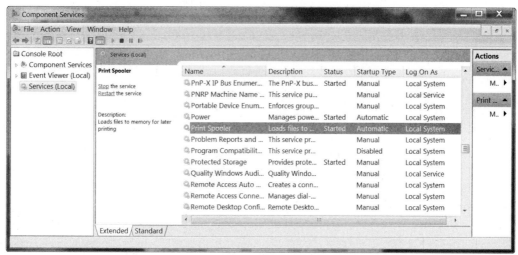

Source: Microsoft Windows 7

Figure 21-57　Use the Services console to stop and start the print spooler

◢ Try disabling printer spooling. On the printer's Properties dialog box, select the **Advanced** tab and then select **Print directly to the printer** (see Figure 21-58). Click **OK**. Spooling holds print jobs in a queue for printing, so if spooling is disabled, printing from an application can be slower.

◢ If you have trouble printing from an application, try to print to a file. For example, you can print to an XPS document by selecting **Microsoft XPS Document Writer** in the list of installed printers. Then you can double-click the .xps file, which opens in the XPS Viewer window, and you can print from this window.

◢ Verify that enough hard drive space is available for the OS to create temporary print files.

◢ Boot Windows into Safe Mode and attempt to print. If this step works, there might be a conflict between the printer driver and another driver or application.

◢ Run diagnostic software downloaded from the printer manufacturer's web site or diagnostic routines you can run from the printer's browser-based utility menu.

21

A+
220-802
1.5, 4.9

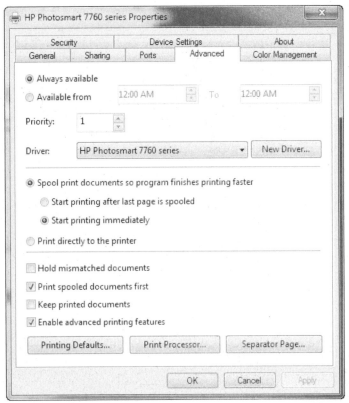

Figure 21-58 Disable printer spooling

Source: Hewlett-Packard

APPLYING | CONCEPTS SOLVING PROBLEMS WITH PRINTER INSTALLATIONS

Here are some steps you can take if the printer installation fails or installs with errors:

1. If you still have problems, consider that Windows might be using the wrong or corrupted printer drivers. Try removing the printer and then installing it again. To remove a printer, right-click the printer in the Devices and Printers window and click **Remove device** (refer to Figure 21-14). Try to install the printer again.

2. If the problem is still not solved, completely remove the printer drivers by using the printui command. The Printer User Interface command, **printui**, is used by administrators to manage printers and printer drivers on remote computers. You can also use it to delete drivers on the local computer. Follow these steps:

   a. If the printer is listed in the Devices and Printers window, remove it. (Sometimes Windows automatically puts a printer there when it finds printer drivers are installed.)

   b. Before you can delete printer drivers, you must stop the print spooler service. Open the Services console and use it to stop the Print Spooler (refer to Figure 21-57). To delete any print jobs left in the queue, open Windows Explorer and delete all files in the C:\Windows\System32\spool\PRINTERS folder.

   c. You can now start the print spooler back up. Because the printer is no longer listed in the Devices and Printers window, starting the spooler will not tie up these drivers.

> **Notes** If you ever have a problem clearing the printer queue, one thing you can do is stop and restart the print spooler.

d. Open an **elevated command prompt window**, which is a window used to enter commands that have administrator privileges. To open the window, click **Start**, **All Programs**, **Accessories**. Right-click **Command prompt** and click **Run as administrator**. Respond to the User Account Control box. To get past the UAC security box, you must be logged on as an administrator or enter an administrator password. The Administrator: Command Prompt window then opens, as shown on the left side of Figure 21-59.

e. At the command prompt, enter the command:

```
printui /s /t2
```

(In the command line, the /s causes the Print Server Properties box to open and the /t2 causes the Drivers tab to be the selected tab.)

f. The Print Server Properties box opens, as shown in the middle of Figure 21-59. Select the printer and click **Remove**. In the Remove Driver And Package box, select **Remove driver only** and click **OK**. It is not necessary to remove the driver package. (This driver package, also called the driver store, can be installed on this computer or a remote computer and holds a backup of the printer drivers.)

g. When a warning box appears, click **Yes**. Close all windows.

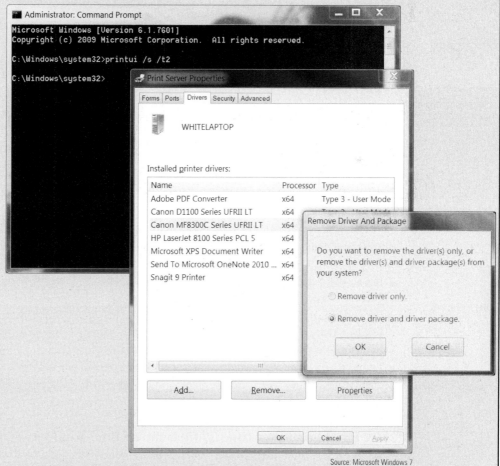

Source: Microsoft Windows 7

Figure 21-59   Use the printui command to delete printer drivers and possibly delete the driver package (driver store)

3. Try to install the printer again. Start the installation from the CD that came bundled with the printer or by using the printer setup program downloaded from the printer manufacturer's web site.

21

PROBLEMS PRINTING FROM APPLICATIONS

If you can print a Windows test page, but you cannot print from an application, try the following:

- Verify that the correct printer is selected in the application.
- Try printing a different file within the same application.
- Cancel all print jobs in the print queue and then reboot the computer. Reopen the application giving the print error and attempt to print again.
- Try creating data in a new file and printing it. Keep the data simple.
- Try printing from another application.
- If you can print from other applications, consider reinstalling the problem application.
- Close any applications that are not being used.
- Add more memory to the printer.

POOR PRINT QUALITY

Poor print quality can be caused by the printer drivers, the application, Windows, or the printer. Let's start by looking at what can cause poor print quality with laser printers and then move on to other problems that affect printouts.

> **A+ Exam Tip** The A+ 220-802 exam expects you to know how to resolve problems with streaks, faded prints, ghost images, garbled characters on a page, vertical lines, low memory errors, and wrong print colors. All these problems are covered in this part of the chapter.

POOR PRINT QUALITY FOR LASER PRINTERS

For laser printers, poor print quality, including faded, smeared, wavy, speckled, or streaked printouts, often indicates that the toner is low. All major mechanical printer components that normally create problems are conveniently contained within the replaceable toner cartridge. In most cases, the solution to poor-quality printing is to replace this cartridge.

Follow these general guidelines to fix poor print quality with laser printers:

- If you suspect the printer is overheated, unplug it and allow it to cool for 30 minutes.
- The toner cartridge might be low on toner or might not be installed correctly. Remove the toner cartridge and gently rock it from side to side to redistribute the toner. Replace the cartridge. To avoid flying toner, don't shake the cartridge too hard.
- If this doesn't solve the problem, try replacing the toner cartridge immediately.
- EconoMode (a mode that uses less toner) might be on; turn it off.
- The paper quality might not be high enough. Try a different brand of paper. Only use paper recommended for use with a laser printer. Also, some types of paper can receive print only on one side.
- The printer might need cleaning. Clean the inside of the printer with a dry, lint-free cloth. Don't touch the transfer roller, which is the soft, spongy black roller.
- If the transfer roller is dirty, the problem will probably correct itself after several sheets print. If not, take the printer to an authorized service center.
- Does the printer require routine maintenance? Check the web site of the printer's manufacturer for how often to perform the maintenance and to purchase the required printer maintenance kit.

Notes Extreme humidity can cause the toner to clump in the cartridge and give a Toner Low message. If this is a consistent problem in your location, you might want to invest in a dehumidifier for the room where your printer is located.

◢ Streaking is usually caused by a dirty developer unit or corona wire. The developer unit is contained in the toner cartridge. Replace the cartridge or check the printer documentation for directions on how to remove and clean the developer unit. Allow the corona wire to cool and clean it with a lint-free swab.

◢ Speckled printouts can be caused by the laser drum. If cleaning the printer and replacing the toner cartridge don't solve the problem, replace the laser drum.

Notes If loose toner comes out with your printout, the fuser is not reaching the proper temperature. Professional service is required.

◢ Distorted images can be caused by foreign material inside the printer that might be interfering with the mechanical components. Check for debris that might be interfering with the printer operation.

◢ If the page has a gray background or gray print, the image drum is worn out and needs to be replaced.

◢ A ghosted image appears a few inches below the actual darker image on the page. Ghosted images are usually caused by a problem with the image drum or toner cartridge. The drum is not fully cleaned in the cleaning stage, and toner left on it causes the ghost image. If the printer utility installed with the printer offers the option to clean the drum, try that first. The next solution is to replace the less expensive toner cartridge. If the problem is still not solved, replace the image drum.

POOR PRINT QUALITY FOR INKJET PRINTERS

Video
Replacing Ink Cartridges

To troubleshoot poor print quality for an inkjet printer, check the following:

1. Is the correct paper for inkjet printers being used?

   The quality of paper determines the final print quality, especially with inkjet printers. In general, the better the quality of the paper used with an inkjet printer, the better the print quality. Don't use less than 20-pound paper in any type of printer, unless the printer documentation specifically says that a lower weight is satisfactory.

2. Is the ink supply low, or is there a partially clogged nozzle?

3. Remove and reinstall the cartridge.

4. Follow the printer's documentation to clean each nozzle. Is the print head too close to or too far from the paper?

5. There is a little sponge in some printers near the carriage rest that can become clogged with ink. It should be removed and cleaned.

6. If you are printing transparencies, try changing the fill pattern in your application.

21

A+
220-802
4.9

7. Missing lines or dots on the printed page can be caused by the ink nozzles drying out, especially when the printer sits unused for a long time. Follow the directions given earlier in the chapter for cleaning inkjet nozzles.

8. Streaks or lines down the page can be caused by dust or dirt in the print head assemblage. Follow the manufacturer's directions to clean the inkjet nozzles.

POOR PRINT QUALITY FOR IMPACT PRINTERS

For an impact printer that is printing with poor print quality, do the following:

1. Begin with the ribbon. Does it advance normally while the carriage moves back and forth? If not, replace the ribbon. If the new ribbon still does not advance properly, check the printer's advance mechanism.

2. Adjust the print head spacing. Look for a lever adjustment you can use to change the distance between the print head and plate.

3. Check the print head for dirt. Make sure it's not hot before you touch it. If debris has built up, wipe each wire with a cotton swab dipped in alcohol or contact cleaner.

GARBLED CHARACTERS ON PAPER

If scrambled or garbled characters print on all or part of a page, the problem can be caused by the document being printed, the application, connectivity between the computer and the printer, or the printer. Follow these steps to zero in on the problem:

1. First, cancel all print jobs in the print queue. Then try printing a different document from the same application. If the second document prints correctly, the problem is with the original document.

2. Try printing using a different application. If the problem is resolved, try repairing or reinstalling the application.

3. For a USB printer, the problem might be with a USB hub, port, or cable. Is the USB cable securely connected at both ends? If you are using a USB hub, remove the hub, connecting the printer directly to the computer. Try a different USB cable or USB port.

4. Recycle the printer by powering it down and back up or pressing a Reset button.

5. Update the printer drivers. To do that, go to the web site of the printer manufacturer to find the latest drivers and follow their directions to install the drivers.

6. If the problem is still not solved, the printer might need servicing. Does the printer need maintenance? Search the web site of the printer manufacturer for other solutions.

LOW MEMORY ERRORS

For some printers, an error occurs if the printer does not have enough memory to hold the entire page. For other printers, only a part of the page prints. Some might signal this problem by flashing a light or displaying an error message on their display panels, such as "20 Mem Overflow," "Out of memory," or "Low Memory." The solution is to install more memory or to print only simple pages with few graphics. Print a self-test page to verify how much memory is installed. Some printers give you the option to install a hard drive in the printer to give additional printer storage space.

A+
220-802
4.9

WRONG PRINT COLORS

For a printer that is printing the wrong colors, do the following:

1. Some paper is designed to print on only one side. You might need to flip the paper in the printer.

2. Try adjusting the quality of print. How to do so varies by printer. For one color laser printer, open the **Printing Preferences** box and click the **Quality** tab (see the left side of Figure 21-60). You can try different selections on this box. To manually adjust the color, check **Manual Color Settings** and then click **Color Settings**. The box on the right side of Figure 21-60 appears.

3. For an inkjet printer, try cleaning the ink cartridges and calibrating the printer. One step in doing that prints a self-test page. If the self-test page shows missing or wrong colors, the problem is with the ink cartridges. Try cleaning the ink nozzles. If that doesn't work, replace the ink cartridges.

4. For a laser printer, try calibrating the printer.

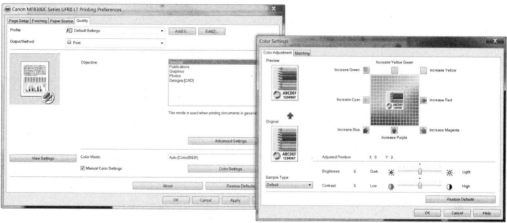

Source: Canon

Figure 21-60 Adjust printing quality and color

>> CHAPTER SUMMARY

Printer Types and Features

- ◢ The languages that Windows can use when it sends print jobs to a printer are PostScript, PCL, GDI, and XPS. In addition, Windows can send raw data to a printer. The printer converts the page into a bitmap, which it stores in the printer's memory before it prints.

- ◢ The two most popular types of printers are laser and inkjet. Other types of printers are thermal printers and impact printers (dot matrix). Laser printers produce the highest quality, followed by inkjet printers. Dot matrix printers have the advantage of being able to print multicopy documents.

- ◢ The seven steps that a laser printer performs to print are processing, charging, exposing, developing, transferring, fusing, and cleaning. The charging, exposing, developing, and cleaning steps take place inside removable cartridges, which makes the printer easier to maintain.

- ◢ Inkjet printers print by shooting ionized ink at a sheet of paper. The quality of the printout largely depends on the quality of paper used with the printer.

21

◢ Dot matrix printers are a type of impact printer. They print by projecting pins from the print head against an inked ribbon that deposits ink on the paper.

◢ Direct thermal printers use heat to burn dots into special paper, and thermal transfer printers melt the ribbon or foil during printing.

Using Windows to Install, Share, and Manage Printers

◢ A printer is installed as a local printer connected directly to a computer or a network printer that works as a device on the network. A computer can share a printer so that others can use it as a resource on the network.

◢ Windows 7 installs, manages, and removes a printer using the Devices and Printers windows; Vista uses the Printers window for these purposes, and XP uses the Printers and Faxes window. USB printers are installed automatically with Windows 7/Vista and by using the printer setup CD in XP.

◢ Under Windows 7/Vista/XP, you can also install a printer by launching a setup program on the CD that came bundled with the printer. The last step to install a printer is to print a printer test page.

◢ You can share an installed printer on the network so that other users can access the printer through the computer to which it connects. The host computer must be on and awake to serve up the printer.

◢ A printer can be shared in Windows so that others on the network can use it. To use a shared printer, the printer drivers must be installed on the remote computer.

◢ Network printers are usually identified on the network by their IP address.

◢ The Windows print queue is managed from the Windows 7 Devices and Printers window, the Vista Printers window, or the XP Printers and Faxes window.

Printer Maintenance and Upgrades

◢ An inkjet or laser printer can be calibrated to align the color on the page. The nozzles of an inkjet printer tend to clog or dry out, especially when the printer remains unused. The nozzles can be cleaned automatically by means of printer software or buttons on the front panel of the printer.

◢ Check the page count of the printer to know when service is due and you need to order the printer maintenance kit.

◢ Memory and a hard drive can be added to a printer to improve performance and prevent errors.

◢ Use a print server to manage printers on a network. Three types of print servers are a dedicated hardware device, software installed on a computer on the network, or programs embedded in firmware on a printer.

◢ The Print Management tool is a Windows Administrative Tool that can be used to manage printers and print servers on a network.

Troubleshooting Printers

◢ When troubleshooting printers, first isolate the problem. Narrow the source to the printer, connectivity between the computer and its local printer, the network, Windows, printer drivers, the application using the printer, or the printer installation. Test pages printed directly at the printer or within Windows can help narrow down the source of the problem.

▲ Poor print quality can be caused by the printer drivers, the application, Windows, or the printer. For a laser printer, consider that low toner can be the problem. For an inkjet printer, consider that the ink cartridges need cleaning or replacing. The quality of paper can also be a problem.

▲ A printer needs memory to render a print job. Low memory can cause part of the page not to print or a printer error.

>> KEY TERMS

For explanations of key terms, see the Glossary near the end of the book.

bitmap
calibration
default printer
Devices and Printers window
direct thermal printer
duplex printer
duplexing assembly
elevated command prompt window
Enhanced Parallel Port (EPP)
Extended Capabilities Port (ECP)
extension magnet brush
fuser assembly
GDI (Graphics Device Interface)
IEEE 1284
imaging drum
impact paper

impact printer
ink cartridge
inkjet printer
laser printer
local printer
LPT (Line Printer Terminal)
network printer
PCL (Printer Control Language)
pickup roller
PostScript
Print Management
Printers window
Printers and Faxes window
print head
print server
print spooler
printer maintenance kit
printer self test page

printui
raster line
raw data
REt (Resolution Enhancement technology)
separation pad
Services console
spooling
Standard Parallel Port (SPP)
thermal paper
thermal printer
thermal transfer printer
toner vacuum
tractor feed
transfer belt
transfer roller
XPS Document Writer
XPS (XML Paper Specification)

>> REVIEW QUESTIONS

1. Which type of printer works by placing toner on an electrically charged rotating drum (sometimes called the imaging drum) and then depositing the toner on paper as the paper moves through the system at the same speed the drum is turning?

    a) Inkjet

    b) Thermal

    c) Laser

    d) Impact

2. What final step in a printer installation process verifies the installation?

    a) Assign an IP address to the printer.

    b) Print a test page.

    c) Rename the printer to a recognizable name.

    d) Reboot the printer.

21

3. After a printer is installed, use ____ to manage printer features and hardware devices installed on the printer.

   a) Device Manager

   b) the Action center

   c) a printer maintenance kit

   d) the printer Properties box

4. A laser printer fuser should last for about ____ pages.

   a) 1,500

   b) 15,000

   c) 45,000

   d) 60,000

5. What can be done to eliminate a printer error message that indicates the printer does not have enough memory to hold the entire page?

   a) Print only simple pages with few graphics.

   b) Install a larger drum.

   c) Try creating data in a new file and printing it.

   d) Verify that enough hard drive space is available for the OS to create temporary print files.

6. True or false? If the printer specifications does NOT say PCL or PostScript, you can assume it is a GDI printer.

7. True or false? To install a local USB printer, all you have to do is plug in the USB printer and Windows 7/Vista installs the printer automatically.

8. True or false? If the printer self-test page does not print or prints incorrectly, then troubleshoot the startup BIOS until it prints correctly.

9. True or false? When all users on a network are responsible for managing their own network resources, you should install a network printer by using another computer on the network that has shared the printer.

10. True or false? For an impact printer that is printing with poor print quality, you should begin diagnosis by examining the ribbon.

11. The ____ assignments refer to the system resources a parallel port will use to manage a print job.

12. An inkjet printer might require ____ to align and/or clean the inkjet nozzles, which can solve a problem when colors appear streaked or out of alignment.

13. A(n) ____ printer connects directly to a computer by way of a USB port, parallel port, serial port, or wireless connection (Bluetooth, infrared, or Wi-Fi).

14. Several print jobs can accumulate in the queue, and the process is called ____.

15. A(n) ____ is hardware or software that manages the print jobs sent to one or more printers on a network.

Operating Systems Past and Present

As a PC support technician, you should be aware of the older and current operating systems and how they have evolved over the years.

DOS (DISK OPERATING SYSTEM)

In 1981, MS-DOS (also known as DOS) was introduced and quickly became the most popular OS among IBM computers and IBM-compatible computers using the Intel 8086 processors. DOS processed 16 bits at a time. Figure A-1 shows a computer screen using the DOS operating system. In those days, all computer screens used text and no graphics. As amazing as it might seem, old legacy applications that use the DOS operating system are still in use today. In fact, I still support one I wrote over 20 years ago that is used to track over a thousand entries in a huge annual horse show. The owners have the attitude, "If it ain't broke; don't fix it."

```
C:\>DIR \GAME

 Volume in drive C has no label
 Volume Serial Number is 0F52-09FC
 Directory of C:\GAME

 .              <DIR>       02-18-93      4:50a
 ..             <DIR>       02-18-93      4:50a
 CHESS          <DIR>       02-18-93      4:50a
 NUKE           <DIR>       02-18-93      4:51a
 PENTE          <DIR>       02-18-93      4:52a
 NETRIS         <DIR>       02-18-93      4:54a
 BEYOND         <DIR>       02-18-93      4:54a
        7 file(s)              0 bytes
                    9273344 bytes free

 C:\>
```

Source: Microsoft

Figure A-1   DOS provides a command-line prompt to receive user commands

DOS WITH WINDOWS 3.X

Early versions of Windows, including Windows 3.1 and Windows 3.2 (collectively referred to as Windows 3.x) didn't perform OS functions, but served as a user-friendly intermediate program between DOS, applications, and the user (see Figure A-2). Windows 3.x offered a graphical user interface, the Windows desktop, the windows concept, and the ability to keep more than one application open at the same time.

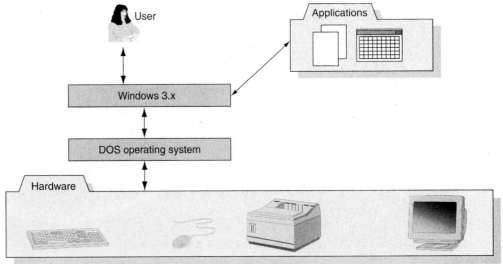

© Cengage Learning 2014

Figure A-2   Windows 3.x was layered between DOS and the user and applications to provide a graphics interface for the user and a multitasking environment for applications

WINDOWS 9X/ME

Windows 95, Windows 98, and Windows Me, collectively called Windows 9x/Me, used some DOS programs as part of the underlying OS (called a DOS core), and therefore had some DOS characteristics. However, these were true operating systems that could process 16 or 32 bits at a time and handle 16-bit and 32-bit applications.

WINDOWS NT AND WINDOWS 2000

Windows NT (New Technology) completely rewrote the OS core, totally eliminating the DOS core. Windows NT did all processing using 32 bits and was a major advance in OS architecture. Windows 2000 was an upgrade of Windows NT and offered several improvements, including a more stable environment, better network support, and features specifically targeting notebook computers. Microsoft didn't target Windows NT or 2000 to the home computer and game computer markets and did not make a commitment for Windows NT/2000 to be backward compatible with older software and hardware. Therefore, Windows 9x/Me lived on until Windows XP.

WINDOWS XP

Windows XP is an upgrade of Windows 2000 and attempted to integrate Windows 9x/Me and 2000, while providing added support for multimedia and networking technologies. Windows XP is the first Windows OS to allow multiple users to log on simultaneously to the OS, each with their own applications open. Although Windows XP was first released with some bugs, the second service pack (Service Pack 2) resolved most of these problems. XP underwent three service packs. It is an extremely stable OS and was popular in both the home and corporate markets. The Windows XP desktop (see Figure A-3) has a different look from the desktops for earlier Windows.

Source: Microsoft Windows XP

Figure A-3   The Windows XP desktop, Start menu, and Windows Media Player on the desktop

The two main editions were Windows XP Home Edition and Windows XP Professional, though other less significant editions included Windows XP Media Center Edition, Windows XP Tablet PC Edition, and Windows XP Professional x64 Edition.

Because many people and corporations decided to not upgrade from XP to Windows Vista, Microsoft was forced to extend support for XP long past their initial timeframe. Microsoft no longer provides mainstream support to individuals for XP, but is still providing extended support to corporations until April, 2014. This extended support includes technical advice and releasing new security patches.

> 💡 **A+ Exam Tip** The only operating systems covered on the A+ exams are Windows XP, Windows Vista, and Windows 7.

WINDOWS VISTA

Windows Vista, an upgrade to Windows XP, was the first Windows OS to use the Aero user interface. The Windows Vista desktop shown in Figure A-4 uses this interface. Notice the Vista **sidebar** on the right side of the desktop contains some Vista gadgets. A **gadget** is a mini-app that you can add or remove from the sidebar by clicking the + sign at the top left of the sidebar.

Source: Microsoft Windows Vista

Figure A-4 Windows Vista sidebar can be customized with Vista embedded gadgets or others you download from the web

Vista was not well received by consumers primarily because of the lack of compatibility with older hardware and software (called legacy hardware and software), the large amount of computer resources that Vista requires, and its slow performance. The first problem is partly caused by hardware manufacturers not providing Vista drivers for their devices that were originally sold with XP drivers. The second problem means that many low-end desktop and laptop computers can't run Vista. And the slow performance of Vista is partly due to the many unnecessary features (fluff) it offers; these features weigh heavy on system resources.

Vista comes in five versions: Windows Vista Home Basic, Home Premium, Business, Enterprise, and Ultimate. (Vista Starter is a sixth version available only to developing nations.) Also, Vista comes in 32-bit versions and 64-bit versions.

Vista underwent two service packs, and Microsoft no longer provides mainstream support for the OS. Microsoft is still providing extended support (advice and security patches) to corporations for Vista Business and Enterprise editions through April, 2017.

WINDOWS 7

Windows 7, the upgrade to Windows Vista, is the most current Windows desktop operating systems by Microsoft. Windows 7 solved many problems inherent in Vista: It performs better than Vista, is more compatible with legacy hardware and software, and provides a leaner and simpler user interface. Windows 7 introduced homegroups, the Action Center, and Windows XP Mode. Windows XP Mode is an environment useful for running legacy applications that work under XP but not under Windows 7.

WINDOWS 8

The next Microsoft desktop OS is code-named Windows 8, and is likely to be released by the time this book is in print. It has a tiled desktop designed especially for touch screens and a touch screen keyboard. Windows 8 is designed to work on a wide range of devices, from a powerful workstation to a smartphone. A **smartphone** is a mobile phone that has computing power, an installed operating system, and small applications called apps.

MAC OS

Currently, the Mac OS, which has its roots in the Unix OS, is available only on Macintosh computers from the Apple Corporation (*www.apple.com*). The Mac and the Mac OS were first introduced in 1984. The latest OS is Mac OS X (ten), which has had several releases. The latest release is called Mac OS X Lion. Figure A-5 shows the Mac OS X Lion desktop with a browser open.

> **Notes** Boot Camp software by Apple can be used to install Windows on a Mac computer as a dual boot with Mac OS X.

To keep from having to restart the Mac each time you want to switch from one OS to another, virtual machine software, such as VMWare (*www.vmware.com*), is used. The software creates a **virtual machine** (**VM**), which is a logical computer within a physical computer. The VM has its own virtual hard drive, and Windows can be installed in this virtual

A

Figure A-5 The Mac OS X Lion desktop and applications

Source: Apple, Inc. Photo © Cengage Learning 2014

environment on the VM's hard drive. A user can switch from the Mac OS to Windows by opening a VM window on the Mac OS desktop. You learn more about virtual machines in Chapter 7.

Currently, about 10 percent of personal computers sold today are Macs. Macs have been popular in the educational, graphics, and musical markets and are beginning to gain ground in both the corporate and home markets because Macs are stable and fun to use, costs are down, software is more available, and the iPad is acting like a magnet to bring more Macs into the corporate market.

> **Notes** You can learn more about the Mac OS by reading the content "Introducing the Mac OS" on this book's companion web site at *www.cengagebrain.com*. See the Preface for more information.

Linux is a variation of Unix that was created by Linus Torvalds when he was a student at the University of Helsinki in Finland. Versions of this OS are available for free, and all the underlying programming instructions (called source code) are also freely distributed. Like Unix, Linux is distributed by several different companies, whose versions of Linux are sometimes called **distributions**. Popular distributions of Linux include Ubuntu (*www.ubuntu.com*), Fedora (*fedoraproject.org*), RedHat (*www.redhat.com*), Puppy Linux (*puppylinux.org*), and Linux Mint (*linuxmint.com*).

> **A+ Exam Tip** The A+ exams do not cover Linux, the Mac OS, or server operating systems.

Linux is well suited to support various types of server applications such as a web server or email server. It is not as popular for a desktop OS because it is not easy to install or use and fewer Linux applications exist, as compared to those written for Windows or the Mac OS.

Linux is also used on netbooks because it requires fewer system resources than Windows. (A technician would say it has a small footprint.) Linux is an excellent training tool for learning UNIX.

A **shell** is the portion of an OS that relates to the user and to applications. The first Linux and UNIX shells consisted of commands entered at a command prompt. Two popular command-line shells for UNIX and Linux are the older Bourne shell and the newer Bourne-Again shell (BASH). But many users prefer a Windows-style GUI desktop. A typical Linux desktop is shown in Figure A-6.

Source: Canonical, Ltd. and Cengage Learning

Figure A-6 A desktop using the Ubuntu Unity shell and Ubuntu distribution of Linux

> **Notes** You can find out more about Linux by reading the content "Introducing Linux" on this book's companion web site at *www.cengagebrain.com*. See the Preface for more information.

OPERATING SYSTEMS USED ON MOBILE DEVICES

A major evolution of operating systems is the operating systems used on smartphones, handheld tablets, or other mobile devices. A **handheld tablet** is a computing device that has a touch screen, installed operating system that can support simple or complex apps, touch-screen keyboard, and wireless capability. Some handheld tablets are also smartphones. The operating system for a mobile device is installed at the factory. Here are the more popular ones:

- Android OS distributed by Google (*android.com*) is based on Linux and is used on various smartphones and tablets. Currently, Android is the most popular OS for smartphones.
- iOS by Apple (*apple.com*) is based on Mac OS X and is used on the iPhone and iPad by Apple.
- Blackberry OS by RIM (*rim.com*) is a proprietary OS used on devices built by RIM.
- Windows Phone by Microsoft (*microsoft.com*) is based on Windows and is used on devices made by Dell, Fujitsu, Nokia, Samsung, and others.
- The Symbian OS from the Symbian Foundation (*symbian.org*) is popular outside the United States and is used on devices made by multiple manufacturers, including Nokia, Samsung, Sony, and others.

A

Windows Vista

This appendix covers the major differences between Windows 7 and Windows Vista. The content here applies to several chapters in the book. After you learn about Windows 7 in a chapter, turn to this appendix to learn how Windows Vista differs.

A+ Exam Tip The A+ 220-802 exam covers Windows 7, Vista, and XP. Use this appendix to study for the Vista portions of this exam.

CHAPTER 3: INTRODUCING WINDOWS OPERATING SYSTEMS

Following are differences in Windows 7 and Windows Vista that are associated with content covered in Chapter 3.

USER ACCOUNT CONTROL BOX

In Vista, you have little control over when the User Account Control box appears except to completely disable it, but for security purposes, that is not recommended. However, if you do decide to disable it in Vista, here's how:

1. In **Control Panel**, click **User Accounts** in the User Accounts and Family Safety group. In the User Accounts window, click **Turn User Account Control on or off**. Respond to the UAC box.

2. In the dialog box that appears (see Figure B-1), uncheck **Use User Account Control (UAC) to help protect your computer**. Click **OK**. Close all windows.

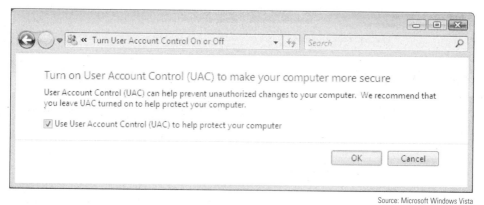

Source: Microsoft Windows Vista

Figure B-1   Using Vista, you can turn on or off the User Account Control box

CHAPTER 7: INSTALLING WINDOWS

Following are differences in Windows 7 and Windows Vista that are associated with content covered in Chapter 7.

HOW TO PREPARE FOR AND INSTALL WINDOWS VISTA

Recall that you can no longer purchase Windows Vista. However, you might be called on to reinstall Vista on an existing system. For the most part, if you know how to prepare for and install Windows 7, you can also install Vista.

EDITIONS AND VERSIONS OF VISTA

The Vista editions are Windows Vista Starter, Home Basic, Home Premium, Business, Enterprise, and Ultimate. All the editions are included on the Windows Vista setup DVD; the edition installed depends on the product key that you enter during the installation. The major features for all editions are listed in Table B-1.

A+
220-802
1.2

Feature	Starter	Home Basic	Home Premium	Business	Enterprise	Ultimate
Aero user interface			X	X	X	X
BitLocker Drive Encryption					X	X
Optional dual processors				X	X	X
Complete PC backup				X	X	X
Encrypting File System (EFS)				X	X	X
IE parental controls	X	X	X			X
Network and Sharing Center	X	X	X	X	X	X
Scheduled and network backups			X	X	X	X
Tablet PC			X	X	X	X
Windows DVD Maker			X			X
Windows Media Center			X			X
Windows Movie Maker			X			X
Windows SideShow			X	X	X	X
Shadow Copy backup				X	X	X
Join a domain				X	X	X
Group Policy				X	X	X
Processor: 32-bit or 64-bit		X	X	X	X	X
Remote Desktop				X	X	X
Windows Meeting Space			X	X	X	X

© Cengage Learning 2014

Table B-1   Vista editions and their features

As you can see from Table B-1, all Vista editions except the Starter edition came in a 32-bit or 64-bit version. Table B-2 lists the maximum memory supported by each edition. The recommended hardware requirements for Vista are the same as those for Windows 7, which are listed in Table 7-3 in Chapter 7.

Operating System	32-Bit Version	64-Bit Version
Vista Ultimate	4 GB	128 GB
Vista Enterprise	4 GB	128 GB
Vista Business	4 GB	128 GB
Vista Home Premium	4 GB	16 GB
Vista Home Basic	4 GB	8 GB
Vista Starter	1 GB	NA

© Cengage Learning 2014

Table B-2   Maximum memory supported by Vista editions

INSTALL VISTA AND CONFIGURE THE SYSTEM

An in-place upgrade, a clean install, and a dual boot installation of Vista begin and proceed the same way as do Windows 7 installations. The steps are not repeated here. After the Vista installation, you need to perform the same chores as described in Chapter 7 for Windows 7. These chores are also not repeated in this appendix.

B

A+
220-802
1.2

> **Notes** In Windows 7, you can view computers and their shared folders on the network by clicking Network in the left pane of Windows Explorer. In Vista, you can use this same method. In addition, you can click **Start**, **Network**. Windows Explorer opens showing the Network resources (see Figure B-2). Drill down to see these resources. The Network window on the Windows 7 Start menu is disabled by default, but you can add it using the Taskbar and Start Menu Properties box.

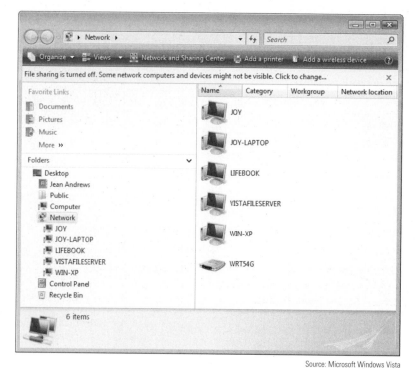

Source: Microsoft Windows Vista

Figure B-2   Use the Network window to access resources on your network

CHAPTER 10: MAINTAINING WINDOWS

Following are differences in Windows 7 and Windows Vista that are associated with content covered in Chapter 10.

A+
220-802
1.7

CREATE AND USE BACKUPS IN WINDOWS VISTA

Vista handles backups differently than does Windows 7 for the Windows volume, user data, and restore points. These differences are covered next.

BACK UP THE WINDOWS VISTA VOLUME

The backup of the Windows Vista volume is called the **Complete PC Backup**. The Complete PC backup can be saved to a local device such as an external hard drive or to DVDs. Don't back up the volume to another partition on the same hard drive. After the initial backup is made, Vista will automatically keep this backup current by making incremental backups.

> **Notes** Complete PC backup is not available in Vista Starter or Vista Home Editions.

A+
220-802
1.7

Follow these steps to create the initial Complete PC Backup:

1. Connect your backup device to your PC. If you're using an external hard drive, use Windows Explorer to verify you can access the drive.

2. From Control Panel, in the System and Maintenance group, click **Back up your computer**. The Backup and Restore Center window appears, as shown in Figure B-3.

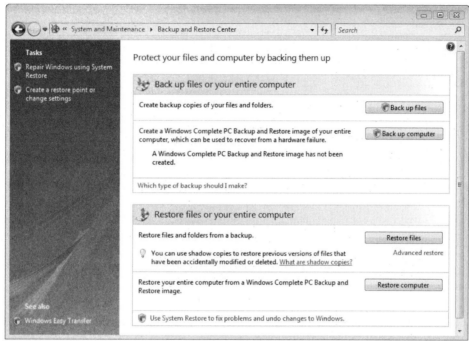

Source: Microsoft Windows Vista

Figure B-3 Windows Vista Backup and Restore Center

3. Click **Back up computer** and respond to the UAC dialog box. Vista displays a list of available backup devices. Select the backup media and click **Next**.

4. In the next window, Vista Backup shows you the Vista volume it will back up and gives you the opportunity to select other volumes it finds to include in the backup. Make your selections and click **Next**.

5. In the next window, the backup tells you the maximum amount of space expected for the backup. If you are backing up to DVDs, the backup tells you about how many DVDs are required. Click **Start backup** to begin the backup.

To use the Complete PC Backup image to restore a corrupted Vista volume, boot from the Vista setup DVD, launch the Windows Recovery Environment (Windows RE), and select **Windows Complete PC Restore** on the System Recovery Options menu. Chapter 14 covers more about using Windows RE.

BACK UP AND RESTORE USER DATA

The Windows Vista Backup and Restore Center limits your decisions about which user files and folders on a Vista system you can back up. In addition, you are forced to back up data for all users.

To set up a backup schedule of user data and settings, open the Backup and Restore Center window, shown earlier in Figure B-3, click **Back up files**, and respond to the UAC box. Following

A+
220-802
1.7

windows let you choose where to save the backup, the volumes to back up, and the type of files to back up. The window that allows you to select the type of files to back up is shown in Figure B-4. The next window lets you set the backup schedule.

Source: Microsoft Windows Vista

Figure B-4   Select the type of files to back up

To see the status of the last backup and change backup settings, click **Start, All Programs, Accessories, System Tools, Backup Status and Configuration**. The Backup Status and Configuration window opens, as shown in Figure B-5. If you change the settings, a new, full backup is created.

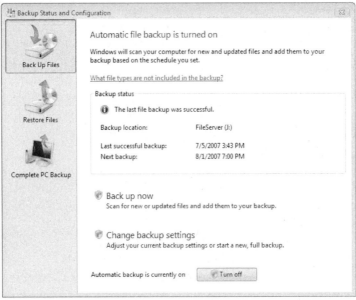

Source: Microsoft Windows Vista

Figure B-5   Backup Status and Configuration window

A+
220-802
1.7

To restore files from backup, on the Backup Status and Configuration window, click **Restore Files** and follow the directions on-screen to select a specific backup and specific folders or files to restore.

Because Windows Vista backup gives you so little control over the folders you choose to back up, many people turn to third-party backup utilities. If you use one of these utilities, besides the folders that contain your documents, spreadsheets, databases, and other data files, you also might want to back up these folders:

▲ *Your email messages and address book.* For Windows Mail, back up this folder: C:\Users*username*\AppData\Local\Microsoft\Windows Mail.

▲ *Your Internet Explorer favorites list.* To back up your IE favorites list, back up this folder: C:\Users*username*\Favorites.

BACK UP SYSTEM FILES

In Vista, System Protection creates restore points, and System Restore returns the system to a previous restore point the same as in Windows 7. The System Properties box for Vista is shown in Figure B-6. Make sure the drive on which Vista is installed is checked. To manually create a restore point, click **Create**. To apply a restore point, click **System Restore**. Incidentally, you can access this System Properties box in Vista by clicking **Create a restore point or change settings** in the left pane of the Backup and Restore Center window (refer to Figure B-3).

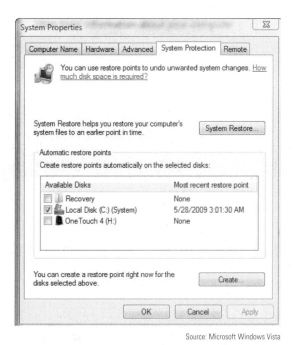

Source: Microsoft Windows Vista

Figure B-6 Make sure System Protection is turned on

B

CHAPTER 11: OPTIMIZING WINDOWS

Following are differences in Windows 7 and Vista that are associated with content covered in Chapter 11.

A+
220-802
1.4

WINDOWS VISTA SOFTWARE EXPLORER

Windows Vista uses the System Configuration utility to control startup programs just as does Windows 7. In addition, Vista offers **Software Explorer**, a user-friendly tool to control startup programs. Here is how to use Software Explorer:

1. To open Software Explorer, open Control Panel and click **Change startup programs**. The Windows Defender window opens. Under Category, select **Startup Programs** (see Figure B-7). A list of applications and services that are launched at startup appears.

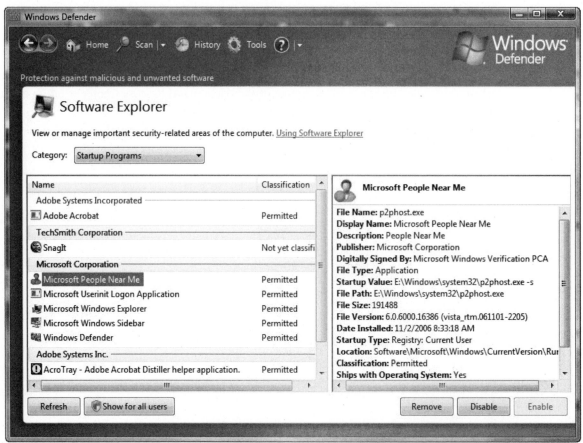

Source: Microsoft Windows Vista

Figure B-7 Use Software Explorer in Vista to find out what programs are launched at startup

2. Select a program on the left to see on the right side how the program is launched at startup. For example, in Figure B-7, the selected program is launched by way of a registry entry. If a startup program is launched by way of a startup folder, the path to the folder is given instead of the registry key.

3. To temporarily disable the selected startup program, click **Disable** at the bottom of the window.

VISTA RELIABILITY AND PERFORMANCE MONITOR

A+
220-802
1.4

The Windows Vista **Reliability and Performance Monitor (Perfmon.msc)** is an earlier version of three separate Windows 7 tools: Windows 7 Resource Monitor, Reliability Monitor, and Performance Monitor (Perfmon.msc). You can launch the Vista tool from the Computer Management Console or by entering **Perfmon.msc** in the Vista *Search* box. When you first open the monitor window (see Figure B-8), a resource overview appears that is similar to the Overview tab in the Windows 7 Resource Monitor window.

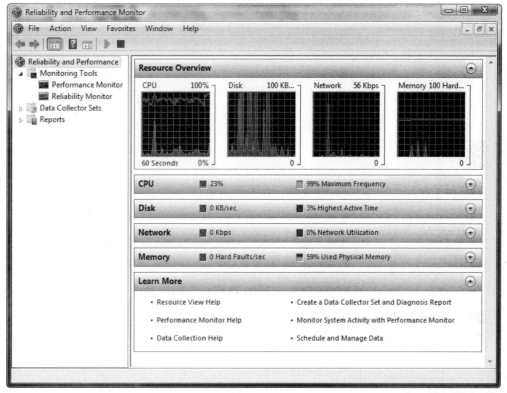

Source: Microsoft Windows Vista

Figure B-8 Reliability and Performance Monitor window shows the Resource Overview screen

Here is how to use the Reliability and Performance Monitor window:

◢ In the left pane, click **Performance Monitor** to see a real-time view of Windows performance counters, which are similar in function to the Windows 7 Performance Monitor. Just as in Windows 7, you can add and delete counters and use data collector sets.

◢ In the left pane, click **Reliability Monitor** to see a pane that gives information similar to the Windows 7 Reliability Monitor. To get detailed information about a problem, click a day that shows an error, and then click the plus sign beside the error's category. For example, in Figure B-9, there was a Windows failure indicated by a red X. When you click the red X or the day the failure occurred, a list of events on that day appears under the graph. Click a plus sign beside the event to see details about the event.

B

A+
220-802
1.4

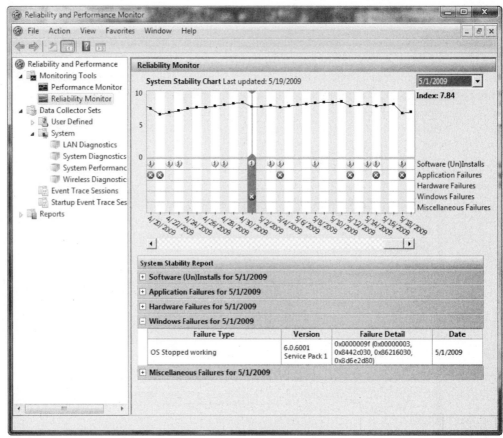

Figure B-9   Reliability Monitor shows a history of the system that can help identify problems with the stability of Windows

CHAPTER 15: CONNECTING TO AND SETTING UP A NETWORK

Following are differences in Windows 7 and Windows Vista that are associated with content covered in Chapter 15.

A+
220-802
1.5, 1.6

CONNECT TO A WIRED NETWORK IN VISTA

Follow these steps to connect a Vista computer to a wired network:

1. Open Control Panel, and click **Network and Sharing Center** in the Network and Internet group. In the Network and Sharing Center window (see the top part of Figure B-10), click **Connect to a network**.

2. When Vista recognizes available networks, they are listed in the Connect to a network box shown in the lower part of Figure B-10. If none are shown, click **Diagnose why Windows can't find any networks**. Then follow the recommendations that appear.

If you still do not have connectivity, follow these steps to verify and change TCP/IP settings:

1. In the left pane of the Network and Sharing Center, click **Manage network connections**. In the Network Connections window, right-click **Local Area Connection** and select **Properties** from the shortcut menu. Respond to the UAC box. The properties box appears (see the left side of Figure B-11).

Source: Microsoft Windows Vista

Figure B-10 Vista Network and Sharing Center manages network connections

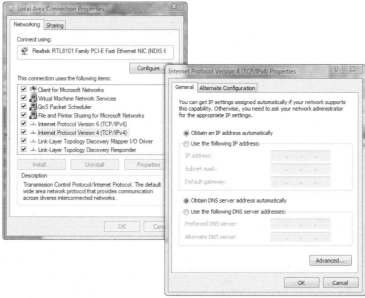

Source: Microsoft Windows Vista

Figure B-11 Verify and change TCP/IP settings

A+
220-802
1.5, 1.6

B

2. Select **Internet Protocol Version 4 (TCP/IPv4)** and click **Properties**. The properties box on the right side of Figure B-11 appears. Settings are correct for dynamic IP addressing.

3. To change the settings to static IP addressing, select **Use the following IP address**. Then enter the IP address, subnet mask, and default gateway.

4. If you have been given the IP addresses of DNS servers, check **Use the following DNS server addresses** and enter up to two IP addresses. If you have other DNS IP addresses, click **Advanced** and enter them on the **DNS** tab of the Advanced TCP/IP Settings box.

5. You can also enter settings for an alternate IP address by clicking the Alternate Configuration tab of the Properties box.

CONNECT TO A WIRELESS NETWORK IN VISTA

To connect a Vista computer to a wireless network, follow these steps:

1. Using your mouse, hover over or double-click the network icon in your notification area. Vista reports that wireless networks are available (see Figure B-12).

Source: Microsoft Windows Vista

Figure B-12 Windows reports that wireless networks are available

2. Click **Connect to a network**. A list of available networks appears (see Figure B-13).

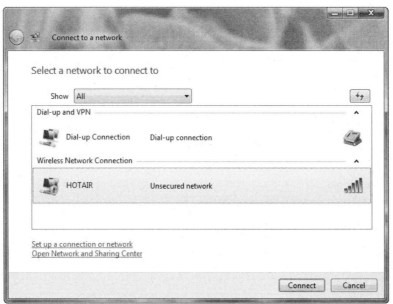

Source: Microsoft Windows Vista

Figure B-13 Select a wireless network

A+
220-802
1.5, 1.6

3. If you select an unsecured network, Vista warns you about sending information over it. Click **Connect Anyway**.

4. Vista reports the connection is made using the window in Figure B-14. If you are comfortable with Vista automatically connecting to this network in the future, check **Save this network**. Close the window. If you hover your mouse pointer over the network icon in the notification area or double-click it, you can see the network to which you are connected (see Figure B-15).

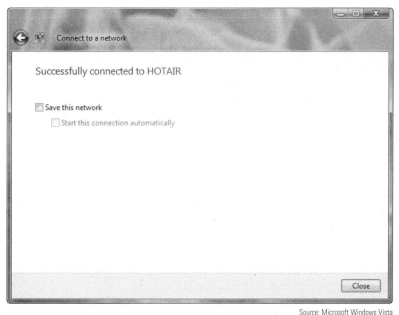

Source: Microsoft Windows Vista

Figure B-14   Decide if you want to save this network connection

Source: Microsoft Windows Vista

Figure B-15   Find out to which network you are connected

5. To verify firewall settings and check for errors, open the Network and Sharing Center window (see Figure B-16). Verify that Vista has configured the network as a public network and that Sharing and Discovery settings are all turned off. If Vista reports it has configured the network as a Private network, click **Customize** and change the setting to Public. In the figure, you can see there is a problem with the Internet connection from the HOTAIR network to the Internet.

B

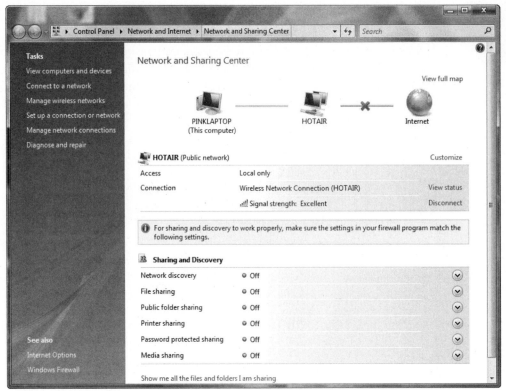

Source: Microsoft Windows Vista

Figure B-16 Verify that your connection is secure

6. Open your browser to test the connection. For some hotspots, a home page appears and you must enter a code or agree to the terms of use.

CHAPTER 17: WINDOWS RESOURCES ON A NETWORK

Following are differences in Windows 7 and Windows Vista that are associated with content covered in Chapter 17.

SUPPORT AND TROUBLESHOOT SHARED FOLDERS AND FILES

The Network and Sharing Center works a little differently in Vista than in Windows 7. If you have problems accessing a shared folder or file on a network, follow these steps using Windows Vista:

1. Open the Network and Sharing Center (see Figure B-17) and verify the following:

   ◢ **File sharing** is turned on.

   ◢ If you want to share the Public folder to the network, turn on **Public folder sharing**.

   ◢ If you want the added protection of requiring that all users on the network must have a valid user account and password on this computer, turn on **Password protected sharing**.

   ◢ If you want to share a printer connected to this PC with others on the network, turn on **Printer sharing**.

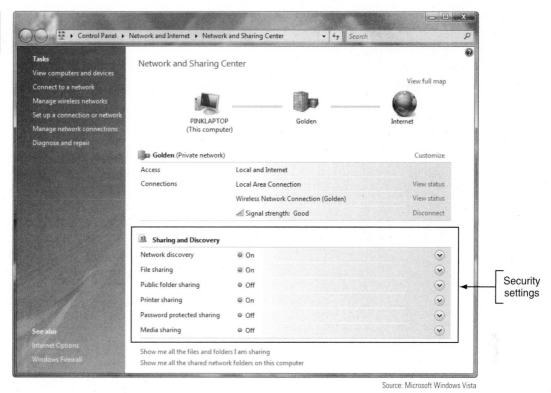

Source: Microsoft Windows Vista

Figure B-17 Use the Network and Sharing Center to verify the computer is set to share resources

2. In the Network and Sharing Center, click **Manage network connections**. In the Network Connections window, right-click the network connection icon, select **Properties** from the shortcut menu, and respond to the UAC box. In the Properties dialog box, verify that **File and Printer Sharing for Microsoft Networks** is checked.

CHAPTER 18: SECURITY STRATEGIES

Following are differences in Windows 7 and Windows Vista that are associated with content covered in Chapter 18.

CONFIGURE WINDOWS FIREWALL IN VISTA

For Windows Vista, to see how firewall protection is set for a public or private network, use the Network and Sharing Center window. Follow these steps:

1. Click **Start**, right-click **Network**, and select **Properties** from the shortcut menu. The Network and Sharing Center window opens.

2. For the window showing in Figure B-18, the computer is connected to a wired and wireless network. The wired network is set to Private, and the wireless network is set to Public. Because the computer is connected to a public network, the Sharing and Discovery settings at the bottom of the window are set for maximum protection. To change the security setting for the Public network, click **Customize**.

B

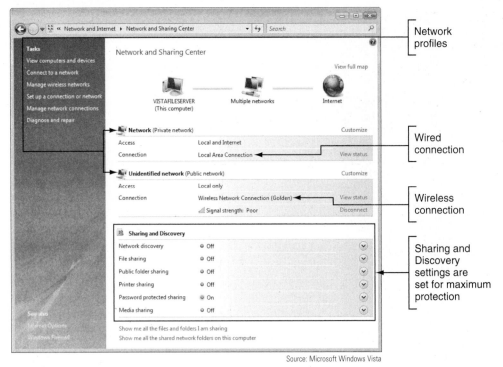

Network profiles

Wired connection

Wireless connection

Sharing and Discovery settings are set for maximum protection

Source: Microsoft Windows Vista

Figure B-18 Security is high when connected to a public network

3. The Set Network Location box appears (see Figure B-19). To allow for less security and more communication on the network, click **Private** and then click **Next**.

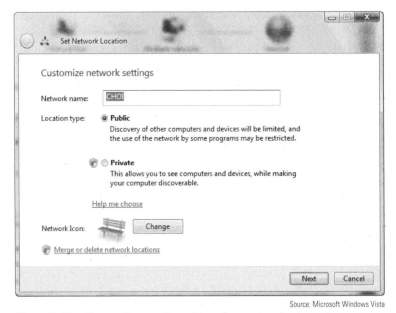

Source: Microsoft Windows Vista

Figure B-19 Change the security settings for a network

4. Sharing and Discovery settings are now less secure, allowing the PC to be seen on the network (Network discovery), files on the PC to be shared with others on the network (File sharing), and printers installed on this PC to be shared (Printer sharing). These are the standard settings for a private network. To change a setting under the Sharing and Discovery group, click the down arrow to the right of the item and turn the item on or off (see Figure B-20).

A+
220-802
1.5

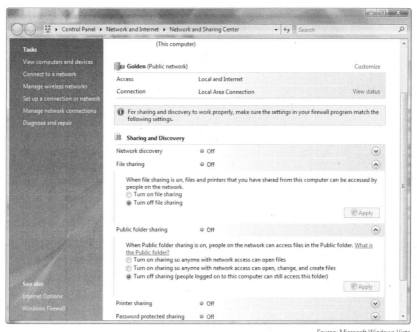

Source: Microsoft Windows Vista

Figure B-20 Change the setting of an item under the Sharing and Discovery group

To see how Windows Firewall is configured for Vista, follow these steps:

1. For Vista, in the left pane of the Network and Sharing Center window, click **Windows Firewall**. The Windows Firewall dialog box opens (see Figure B-21). No matter what type of network you are connected to, Windows Firewall should always be turned on unless you are using a third-party software firewall instead of Windows Firewall.

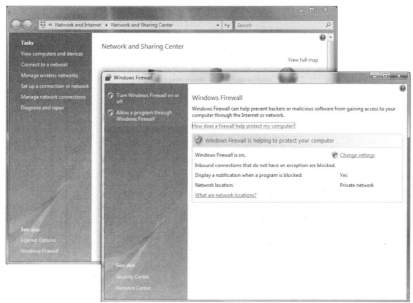

Source: Microsoft Windows Vista

Figure B-21 Windows Firewall is turned on

2. To see the details of how Windows Firewall is working, click **Change settings** and respond to the UAC box. The Windows Firewall Settings box opens (see Figure B-22).

B

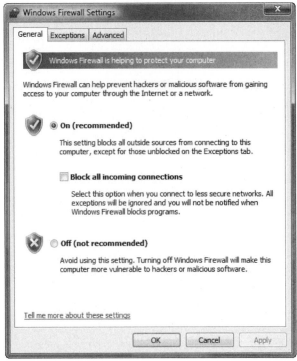

Source: Microsoft Windows Vista

Figure B-22 Windows Firewall is on but not working at its highest security level

3. Notice the check box for *Block all incoming connections*, which controls communication initiated from another computer. For a private network, Vista does not check this box. When connected to a public network, the box is checked. To see what incoming connections are allowed, click the **Exceptions** tab (as shown on the left side of Figure B-23).

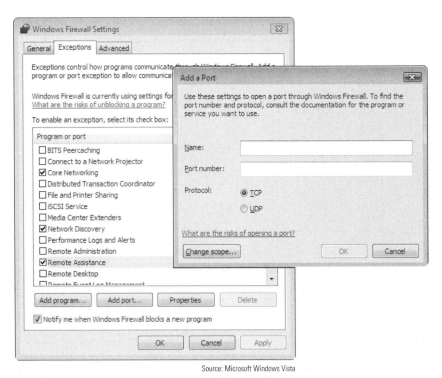

Source: Microsoft Windows Vista

Figure B-23 Exceptions allowed for incoming connections can be made by program or port

A+
220-802
1.5

4. You can change individual settings on this Exceptions tab by checking or unchecking items. For example, notice in Figure B-23 that File and Printer Sharing is not checked. If you want to allow another computer to initiate communication with this computer to access a shared file or printer, check this item. Recall that a computer uses a port number to control incoming activity from client applications or programs on the network. This Exceptions box controls these ports. Each item in the list is associated with one or more ports, which are opened or closed based on the settings on this tab.

5. If you want to make sure a specific port is open, such as when you use a nondefault port for a program, click **Add port**. In the Add a Port box (see the right side of Figure B-23), enter a name for the port and the port number and click **OK**.

6. After you have Windows Firewall configured the way you want it, click **OK** to close the Windows Firewall Settings window.

B

APPENDIX C

Windows XP

This appendix covers the major differences between Windows 7 and Windows XP. The content here applies to several chapters in the book. After you learn about Windows 7 in a chapter, turn to this appendix to learn how Windows XP differs.

CHAPTER 3: INTRODUCING WINDOWS OPERATING SYSTEMS

Following are differences in Windows 7 and Windows XP that are associated with content covered in Chapter 3.

DIFFERENCES IN THE WINDOWS XP DESKTOP AND THE WINDOWS 7 DESKTOP

The Windows XP desktop and Start menu are shown in Figure C-1. When you first install Windows 7 and Windows XP, only the Recycle Bin shows on the desktop by default. (Vista shows the Recycle Bin and the sidebar on the desktop.)

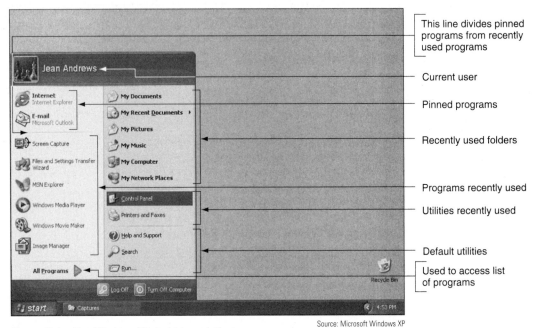

Source: Microsoft Windows XP

Figure C-1   The Windows XP desktop and Start menu

You can use the Display Properties box in XP to control the Start menu and taskbar. Right-click the desktop and select **Properties** from the shortcut menu. The left side of Figure C-2 shows the Display Properties box that appears with the Desktop tab selected. The right side of Figure C-2 shows the Desktop Items dialog box that appears when you click Customize Desktop. You can accomplish about the same things using the Windows 7 and Vista Personalization window and the XP Display Properties box, but they are organized differently.

When you first install Windows 7 and Windows XP, only the Recycle Bin shows on the desktop by default. (Vista shows the sidebar on the desktop.) In XP, you can add other shortcuts by using the Desktop Items box shown in Figure C-2. You can check My Documents, My Computer, My Network Places, and Internet Explorer to add these icons to the desktop. Also notice on this window the option to have Windows clean up your desktop by moving any shortcuts that you have not used in the last 60 days to a separate folder.

A+
220-802
1.1

Source: Microsoft Windows XP

Figure C-2 Windows XP Display Properties window lets you change settings for your desktop

CHAPTER 7: INSTALLING WINDOWS

Following are differences in Windows 7 and Windows XP that are associated with content covered in Chapter 7.

A+
220-802
1.1, 1.2

HOW TO PREPARE FOR AND INSTALL WINDOWS XP

Windows XP comes in these editions:

- **Windows XP Home Edition** targets the home computer market. It supports the FAT, FAT32, and NTFS file systems as do all the editions of XP. It is a 32-bit OS and can support up to 4 GB of memory.
- **Windows XP Professional** targets the business market. Features not in the Home Edition include the ability to join a domain, Group Policy, Offline Files and Folders, Encrypting File System, Remote Desktop, Automated System Recovery, multilingual capabilities, and support for multiple processors.
- **Windows XP Professional x64 Edition** (formally called Windows XP 64-Bit Edition) is a 64-bit operating system and can support up to 128 GB of memory. (All other editions of XP are 32-bit and can support up to 4 GB of memory.)
- **Windows XP Media Center Edition** is an enhanced edition of Windows XP Professional, and includes additional support for digital entertainment hardware such as video recording integrated with TV input.
- **Windows XP Tablet PC Edition** is designed for laptops and tablet PCs.

Table C-1 lists the minimum and recommended requirements for Windows XP Professional.

A+
220-802
1.1, 1.2

Component or Device	Minimum Requirement	Recommended Requirement
One or two CPUs	Pentium II 233 MHz or better	Pentium II 300 MHz or better
RAM	64 MB	128 MB up to 4 GB
Hard drive partition	2 GB	More than 2 GB
Free space on the hard drive partition	1.5 GB (bare bones)	2 GB or more

© Cengage Learning 2014

Table C-1   Minimum and Recommended Requirements for Windows XP Professional

Next we look at the steps to install Windows XP. Because the OS is so old and can no longer be purchased, the only situation you can expect to encounter is reinstalling XP when the current XP installation gets corrupted or installing XP on a new hard drive that has replaced a failed drive in an XP system.

> **Notes** For more detailed content on installing Windows XP, look on this textbook's companion web site for the content, "Installing Windows 2000/XP." See the Preface at the beginning of this book for how to access the web site.

Here are the general steps to install Windows XP:

1. As for any OS installation, back up data files and perform other tasks to prepare for an operating system installation. These steps are listed in Chapter 7 and are not repeated here.

> **Notes** An error might occur during the XP installation if files on the hard drive are using a path and filename that together exceed 256 characters. To get around this problem, if you have a path (folders and filenames) that exceeds 256 characters, before you begin the installation move these folders and files to another media such as a USB drive or another computer on the network. Later, you can restore the folders and files to the hard drive. After the installation, you might find these folders and files still on the hard drive although filenames might be truncated.

2. Start the XP installation using one of these methods:

   ◢ For any edition of Windows XP, boot from the Windows XP setup CD. A setup menu appears from which you can start a clean installation of XP (see Figure C-3). Press **Enter** to start the installation.

> **Notes** At the beginning of the Windows XP installation, if you need to use third-party drivers such as when your computer has multiple hard drives installed in a RAID array or uses SCSI or some SATA hard drives, press F6 when the blue screen appears. You can then install the XP RAID, SCSI, or SATA drivers that will be used by the XP setup process.

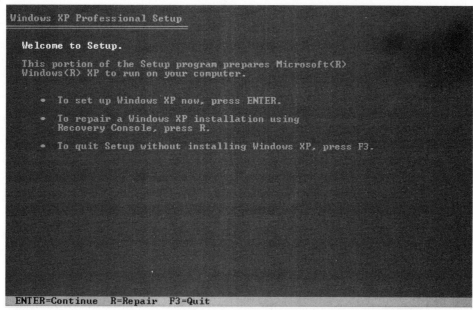

Source: Microsoft Windows XP

Figure C-3   Windows XP setup opening menu

▲ If you can start Windows, use the following command for any 32-bit installation of
Windows XP, substituting the drive letter of your CD drive for D in the command line:

```
D:\i386\Winnt32.exe
```

When you start the installation from within Windows, the Setup menu in Figure C-4
appears. Select **Install Windows XP**. On the next screen, under Installation Type, select
New Installation. The installation begins. (If you were upgrading an OS to Windows XP,
under New Installations, you would select Upgrade and then choose Express Upgrade or
Custom Upgrade.)

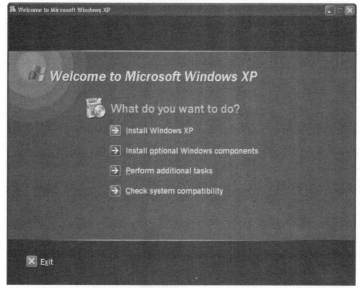

Source: Microsoft Windows XP

Figure C-4   Windows XP Setup menu

A+
220-802
1.1, 1.2

◢ When reinstalling Windows XP Professional x64 Edition, boot from the Windows setup CD. Alternately, you can start the installation using the following command line after Windows XP Professional x64 Edition has started:

```
D:\AMD64\Winnt32.exe
```

For 64-bit installations, the installation routine uses files stored in both the \AMD64 and \i386 folders.

3. Accept the End-User License agreement. Decide which partition and which file system to use for Windows. You can choose between FAT32 and NTFS. Choose NTFS unless the size of the volume is 2 GB or less. FAT32 does not use as much overhead as NTFS and is a better choice for these smaller volumes.

4. Select or assign values for your geographical location, your name, the name of your organization, and your product key. (The product key must be entered before the installation will continue.)

> **Notes** If you have lost the Windows XP product key and you can start the old installation of XP, you can use a utility to find out the product key. Use a search engine such as *Google.com* to search for a key finder utility such as Magical Jelly Bean Keyfinder. Download and run the keyfinder, but be careful to only download from reliable web sites you trust.

5. Enter the computer name and the password for the local Administrator account. Select the date, time, time zone, and network settings. (Most likely you need to install Client for Microsoft Networks and File and Printer Sharing, and select dynamic IP addresses.) Enter a workgroup or domain name. Expect the computer to reboot three or more times during the installation.

> **Notes** It is *very* important that you remember the Administrator password. You cannot log on to the system without it.

After you have installed XP, you need to do similar chores as you learned to do after installing Windows 7. Keep these differences in mind:

◢ *Windows XP uses the Network Setup Wizard.* To set up a new connection to the network, open Control Panel, and then click **Network and Internet Connections**. In the Network and Internet Connections window, click **Set up or change your home or small office network**. The Network Setup Wizard launches to step you through the process of connecting to the network.

◢ *Windows XP uses My Network Places.* To access the network, click **Start, My Network Places**. If you don't see network resources, try rebooting the PC. Use Device Manager to verify that the network card is installed and functioning with no errors. You might need to install device drivers for the network card or for the motherboard network port. To open Device Manager in XP, click **Start**, right-click **My Computer**, select **Properties** from the shortcut menu, and then select the **Hardware** tab from the System Properties window. Finally, click **Device Manager**.

A+
220-802
1.1, 1.2

> **💡 A+ Exam Tip** If you don't see My Network Places on the Start menu, you can add it. Right-click **Start** and select **Properties**. On the **Start menu** tab of the Taskbar and Start menu Properties box, click **Customize**. In the Customize Start Menu box, click the **Advanced** tab. Check **My Network Places** and click **OK** twice to close both boxes.

▲ *Windows XP uses the System Properties box to configure automatic updates.* Click **Start**, right-click **My Computer**, and select **Properties** from the shortcut menu. The System Properties box appears where you can see what service packs have been applied (see Figure C-5). Click the **Automatic Updates** tab to configure automatic updates.

Source: Microsoft Windows XP

Figure C-5 Use the System Properties box to find out what Windows XP service packs are installed

▲ *Windows XP uses the Add or Remove Programs applet to install and configure XP components.* To install an XP component that was not installed during the installation, open the Add or Remove Programs applet in Control Panel. Click **Add/Remove Windows Components**. Check a component you want to install and click **Next**.

▲ *Windows XP uses the Files and Settings Transfer Wizard.* This tool is used to transfer user data and settings from one XP installation to another when a domain is not involved. Instructions to use the tool can be found in XP Help and Support.

▲ *Windows XP uses the User Accounts applet to create user accounts.* To create a new account in Windows XP, open the **User Accounts** applet in Control Panel and click **Create a new account**. Enter an account name and click **Next**. For the privilege level of the account, select either Computer administrator or Limited. Click **Create Account**.

CHAPTER 10: MAINTAINING WINDOWS

Following are differences in Windows 7 and Windows XP that are associated with content covered in Chapter 10.

A+
220-802
1.7

CREATE AND USE BACKUPS IN WINDOWS XP

Backup procedures in Windows XP vary significantly from those in Windows 7. In this part of the appendix, we look at how to back up the entire Windows volume, Windows system files, and user data.

WINDOWS XP AUTOMATED SYSTEM RECOVERY

You can use the Windows XP **Automated System Recovery (ASR)** tool, which is part of the Windows XP Backup utility (Ntbackup.exe), to back up the entire volume on which Windows is installed, most likely drive C:.

> **Notes** By default, Windows XP Home Edition does not automatically install the Backup utility. To install it manually, go to the \VALUEADD\MSFT\NTBACKUP folder on your Windows XP setup CD and double-click **Ntbackup.msi**. The installation wizard will complete the installation.

The ASR backup process creates two items: a full backup of the drive on which Windows is installed and an ASR floppy disk on which information that will help Windows use Automated System Recovery is stored.

Follow these directions to create the backup and the ASR floppy disk:

1. Click **Start, All Programs, Accessories, System Tools,** and **Backup.** The Backup or Restore Wizard appears (see Figure C-6).

Source: Microsoft Windows XP

Figure C-6 Backup or Restore Wizard

A+
220-802
1.7

2. Click the **Advanced Mode** link. The Backup Utility window appears (see Figure C-7). On the Welcome tab, click **Automated System Recovery Wizard**. Then click **Next**.

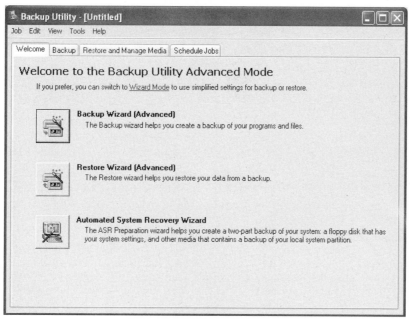

Source: Microsoft Windows XP

Figure C-7 Use the XP Backup Utility to create a backup of the Windows XP volume

3. Select the location of the backup and insert a disk into the floppy disk drive. This disk will become the ASR disk. Click **Next** and click **Finish**.

> **Notes** The ASR process assumes you have a floppy disk drive. If your computer does not have this drive, you can use an external floppy drive. If you don't have either, it's possible to skip the step of making the ASR disk at the time you make the ASR backup. However, you must make the ASR disk later before you can perform the ASR restore. And, a floppy disk drive is required to perform an ASR restore unless you use third-party software to get around this requirement. For an example of this software, see the Acronis web site at *www.acronis.com*.

4. The backup process shows its progress, as seen in Figure C-8. When the backup is finished, label the disk with the name "ASR Disk," the date it was created, and the computer's name, and put the disk in a safe place.

You will learn how to use the ASR backup to recover from a failed Windows volume later in this appendix.

> 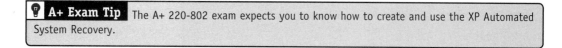 The A+ 220-802 exam expects you to know how to create and use the XP Automated System Recovery.

BACK UP WINDOWS XP SYSTEM FILES

Windows XP offers two tools for backing up its system files: System Restore, used to create restore points, and the XP Backup Utility.

A+
220-802
1.7

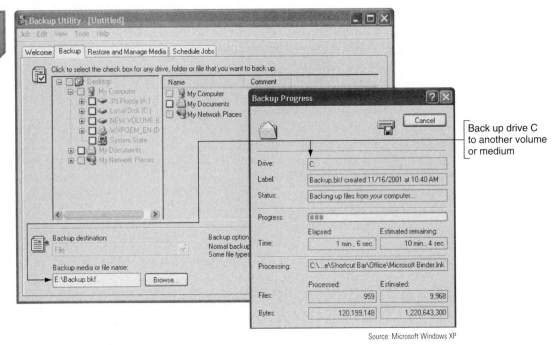

Back up drive C
to another volume
or medium

Source: Microsoft Windows XP

Figure C-8 The Backup utility can create a backup of drive C and an ASR disk to be used later for the Automated System Recovery utility

Use System Restore

Here is how to use XP System Restore:

◢ Click **Start**, right-click **My Computer**, and select **Properties**. The System Properties box opens. Click the **System Restore** tab (see Figure C-9). Using this box, you can turn on or off System Restore that creates restore points.

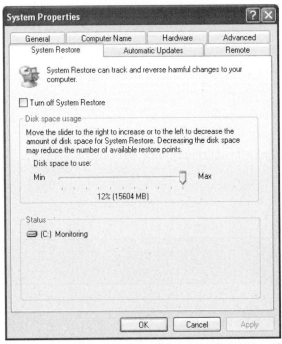

Source: Microsoft Windows XP

Figure C-9 Use the System Properties box to turn on or off System Restore that creates restore points

A+
220-802
1.7

◄ To manually create a restore point or apply a restore point, click **Start**, **All Programs**, **Accessories**, **System Tools**, and **System Restore**. In the System Restore dialog box, select **Create a restore point** or **Restore my computer to an earlier time**.

You can use the XP Backup utility to back up the **system state data**, which are the files critical to a successful operating system load. This backup includes all files necessary to boot the OS, the Windows XP registry, and all system files in the root directory of the Windows volume.

Back Up the System State

Here is how to back up the system state:

1. Click **Start**, **All Programs**, **Accessories**, **System Tools**, and **Backup**. The Backup or Restore Wizard appears (refer back to Figure C-6). Click **Advanced Mode**. On the Backup Utility window, click the **Backup** tab (see Figure C-10).

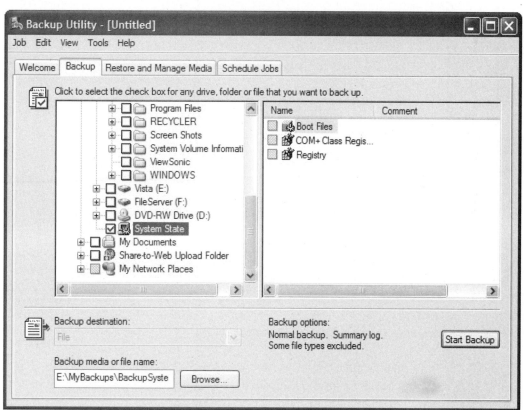

Source: Microsoft Windows XP

Figure C-10   Back up the Windows XP/2000 system state

2. Check the **System State** box in the list of items you can back up. Notice in Figure C-10 that the system state includes the boot files and the registry. It also includes the COM+ (Component Object Model) Class Registration Database, which contains information about applications and includes files in the Windows folders.

3. Click **Browse** to point to where you want the backup saved. You can back up to any media, including a second hard drive, USB drive, or network drive. Click **Start Backup**. A dialog box appears where you can decide to append the backup to the media or replace the data on the media with this backup. Make your selection, and click **Start Backup** again.

A+
220-802
1.7

> **Notes** When you back up the system state, the registry is also backed up to the folder C:\repair
> \RegBack. If you later have a corrupted registry, you can copy files from this folder to the registry folder,
> which is C:\System32\Config.

If Windows gives errors or the registry gets corrupted, you can restore the system to the state it was in when the last System State backup was made. To do that, open the Backup Utility window and select the **Restore and Manage Media** tab, which is shown in Figure C-11.

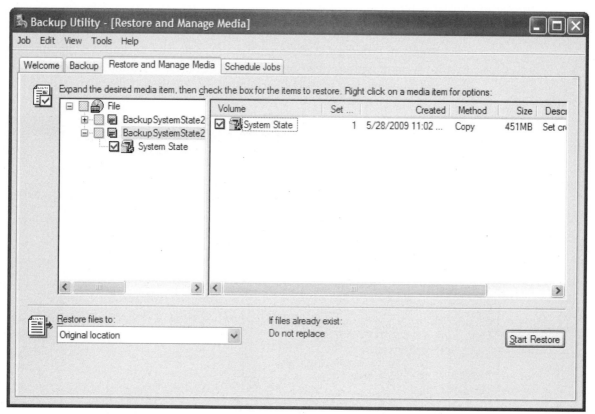

Source: Microsoft Windows XP

Figure C-11   Restore the system state from the Restore and Manage Media tab of the Backup dialog box

In the list of backup items, drill down to the System State and select it. In the lower-left corner, select the location to which the backup is to be restored. To restore the system state, select **Original location**. Click the **Start Restore** button in the lower-right corner. A warning box appears stating that you will overwrite the existing state. Click **OK** to start the process. Remember that you can restore the system state as a way of restoring the registry.

BACK UP USER DATA WITH WINDOWS XP

The Windows XP Backup utility (Ntbackup.exe) supports several types of scheduled backups:

▲ *Full backup (also called a normal backup).* All files selected for backup are copied to the backup media. Each file is marked as backed up by clearing its archive attribute. Later, if you need to recover data, this full backup is all you need. (After the backup, if a file is changed, its archive attribute is turned on to indicate the file has changed since its last backup.)

A+
220-802
1.7

▲ *Copy backup.* All files selected for backup are copied to the backup media, but files are not marked as backed up (meaning file archive attributes are not cleared). A Copy backup is useful if you want to make a backup apart from your regularly scheduled backups.

▲ *Incremental backup.* All files that have been created or changed since the last backup are backed up, and all files are marked as backed up (meaning file archive attributes are cleared). Later, if you need to recover data, you'll need the last full backup and all the incremental backups since this last full backup.

▲ *Differential backup.* All files that have been created or changed since the last full or incremental backup are backed up, and files are not marked as backed up. Later, if you need to recover data, you'll need the last full backup and the last differential backup.

▲ *Daily backup.* All files that have been created or changed on this day are backed up. Files are not marked as backed up. Later, if you need to recover data, you'll need the last full backup and all daily backups since this last full backup.

The two best ways to schedule backups are a combination of full backups and incremental backups, or a combination of full backups and differential backups. When using a full backup and incremental backups to restore all the data, you must use a full backup and all the incremental backups since the full backup was made. When using a full backup and differential backups, you only need the full backup and the last differential backup.

For a business with heavy data entry, suppose you decide you need to back up every night at 11:55 PM. To implement this backup plan, you might decide to schedule two backups: a full backup each Friday at 11:55 PM, and a differential backup each Monday, Tuesday, Wednesday, and Thursday at 11:55 PM.

To schedule a backup, do the following:

1. Open the backup utility and click the **Schedule Jobs** tab, as shown in Figure C-12. Select a date on which you want to schedule a backup, and then click the **Add Job** button.

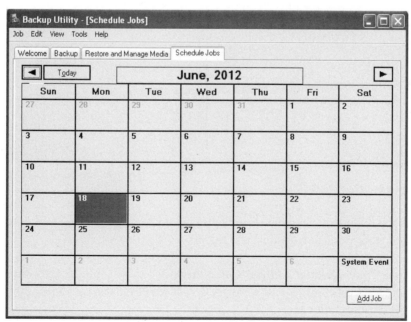

Source: Microsoft Windows XP

Figure C-12   The Schedule Jobs tab of the Windows XP Backup Utility window

A+
220-802
1.7

2. The Backup Wizard opens. Follow the directions on-screen to make these selections:

◢ Choose to back up files, drives, or network data that you select.

◢ Select the drives, folders, or files you want to back up.

◢ Select the storage device and folder to save the backup.

◢ Assign a name to the backup file.

◢ Select the type of backup (Normal, Copy, Incremental, Differential, or Daily). Recall that a Normal backup is a full backup.

◢ Decide whether you want to verify the data after the backup and compress the data.

◢ Decide whether you want to append the data to an existing backup or replace an existing backup.

◢ To choose to perform the backup later, select **Later** and give the job a name, as shown on the left side of Figure C-13.

◢ Decide how often the backup will occur (see the right side of Figure C-13 where the backup is scheduled for each Monday, Tuesday, Wednesday, and Thursday at 11:55 PM.

3. When the wizard completes, it gives you an on-screen report summarizing information about the backup.

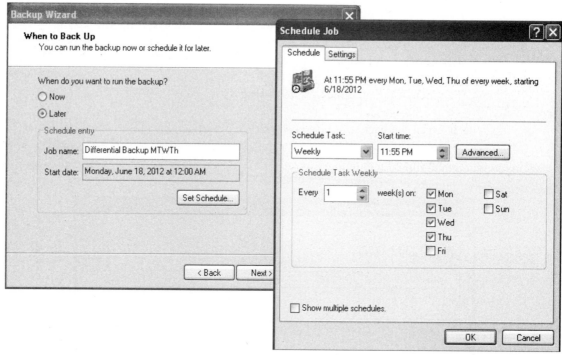

Source: Microsoft Windows XP

Figure C-13   Schedule repeated backups

Besides the folders that contain documents, spreadsheets, databases, and other data files, you also might want to back up these folders:

◢ *Email messages and address book.* For Outlook and Outlook Express, back up this folder: C:\Documents and Settings*username*\Local Settings\Application Data \Microsoft\Outlook.

◢ *Internet Explorer favorites list.* To back up an IE favorites list, back up this folder: C:\Documents and Settings*username*\Favorites.

To recover files, folders, or the entire drive from backup using the Windows XP Backup utility, click the **Restore and Manage Media** tab on the Backup Utility window, and then select the backup job to use for the restore. The Backup utility displays the folders and files that were backed up with this job. You can select the ones that you want to restore.

CHAPTER 11: OPTIMIZING WINDOWS

Following are differences in Windows 7 and Windows XP that are associated with content covered in Chapter 11.

TASK MANAGER IN WINDOWS XP

Windows 7/Vista Task Manager has six tabs: Applications, Processes, Services, Performance, Networking, and Users. Windows XP Task Manager does not have the Services tab (see Figure C-14). The Windows XP Users tab shows only when a system is set for Fast User Switching and lets you monitor other users logged onto the system. Figure C-14 shows the list of processes for a Windows XP system immediately after the installation was completed with no applications installed.

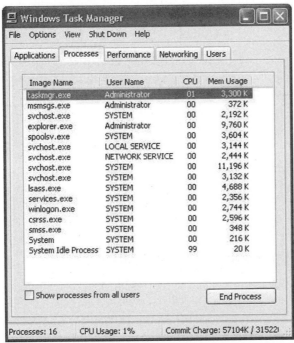

Source: Microsoft Windows XP

Figure C-14 This Processes tab of Windows XP Task Manager shows Windows processes before any applications are installed

WINDOWS XP PERFORMANCE MONITOR

Windows XP offers the Performance Monitor tool, also called the **System Monitor**. To open Performance Monitor, open **Control Panel**, and click **Administrative Tools** in the Performance and Maintenance group. Then double-click **Performance**. The Performance window is shown in Figure C-15.

A+
220-802
1.4

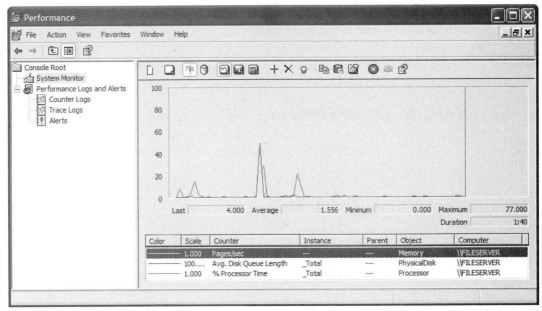

Figure C-15 Windows XP Performance Monitor (also called the System Monitor)

> 💡 **A+ Exam Tip** The A+ 220-802 exam expects you to be able to use the Control Panel in Classic View.

When you first open the window, System Monitor is selected and shows a graph presenting data collected by counters. This window and the counters work the same as the Windows 7/Vista Performance Monitor window. You can drill down into the Performance Logs and Alerts group in the left pane to start and stop groups of counters that work similarly to Windows 7/Vista data collector sets.

CHAPTER 14: TROUBLESHOOTING WINDOWS STARTUP PROBLEMS

Following are differences in Windows 7 and Windows XP that are associated with content covered in Chapter 14.

A+
220-802
1.3

WHAT HAPPENS WHEN WINDOWS XP STARTS UP

A Windows XP system has started up when the user has logged on, the Windows desktop is loaded, and the hourglass associated with the pointer has disappeared. Table C-2 outlines the steps in the boot sequence for Intel-based computers up to the point that the boot loader program, Ntldr, turns control over to the Windows core component program, Ntoskrnl.exe.

Step	Step Performed By	Description
1.	Startup BIOS	Startup BIOS runs the POST (power-on self test).
2.	Startup BIOS	Startup BIOS turns to the hard drive to find an OS. It first loads the MBR (Master Boot Record) and runs the master boot program within the MBR. (Recall that the master boot program is at the very beginning of the hard drive, before the partition table information.)

Table C-2 Steps in the Windows XP boot process for systems with Intel-based processors (continues)

A+
220-802
1.3

Step	Step Performed By	Description
3.	MBR program	The MBR program uses partition table information to find the active partition. It then loads the OS boot sector (also called the OS boot record) from the active partition and runs the program in this boot sector.
4.	Boot sector program	This boot sector program launches Ntldr (NT Loader).
5.	Ntldr, the Windows XP boot loader program	Ntldr launches the minifile system drivers so that files can be read from either a FAT system or an NTFS file system on the hard drive.
6.	Ntldr	Ntldr reads the Boot.ini file, a hidden text file that contains information about installed OSs on the hard drive. For a dual boot, Ntldr displays a boot loader menu for the user to select an OS to load.
7.	Ntldr	If the user chooses Windows XP, then the loader runs Ntdetect.com, a 16-bit real mode program that queries the computer for time and date (taken from CMOS RAM) and surveys hardware (buses, drives, mouse, ports). Ntdetect passes the information back to Ntldr. This information is used later to update the Windows XP registry concerning the Last Known Good hardware profile used.
8.	Ntldr	Ntldr then loads Ntoskrnl.exe, Hal.dll, and the System hive. Recall that the System hive is a portion of the registry that includes hardware information used to load the proper device drivers for the hardware that's present. Ntldr then loads these device drivers.
9.	Ntldr	Ntldr passes control to Ntoskrnl.exe; Ntoskrnl.exe continues to load the Windows desktop and the supporting Windows environment.

© Cengage Learning 2014

Table C-2 Steps in the Windows XP boot process for systems with Intel-based processors (continued)

FILES NEEDED TO START WINDOWS XP

The files needed to start Windows XP successfully are listed in Table C-3. Several of these system files form the core components of XP.

File	Location and Description
Ntldr	◢ Located in the root folder of the system partition (usually C:\) ◢ Boot loader program
Boot.ini	◢ Located in the root folder of the system partition (usually C:\) ◢ Text file contains boot parameters
Bootsect.dos	◢ Located in the root folder of the system partition (usually C:\) ◢ Used to load another OS in a dual-boot environment
Ntdetect.com	◢ Located in the root folder of the system partition (usually C:\) ◢ Real-mode program detects hardware present
Ntbootdd.sys	◢ Located in the root folder of the system partition (usually C:\) ◢ Required only if a SCSI boot device is used

© Cengage Learning 2014

Table C-3 Files needed to boot Windows XP successfully (continues)

A+
220-802
1.3

File	Location and Description
Ntoskrnl.exe	▲ Located in C:\Windows\system32* folder of the boot partition ▲ Core component of the OS executive and kernel services
Hal.dll	▲ Located in C:\Windows\system32 folder of the boot partition ▲ Hardware abstraction layer
Ntdll.dll	▲ Located in C:\Windows\system32 folder of the boot partition ▲ Intermediating service to executive services; provides many support functions
Win32k.sys Kernel32.dll Advapi32.dll User32.dll Gdi32.dll	▲ Located in C:\Windows\system32 folder of the boot partition ▲ Core components of the Win32 subsystem
System	▲ Located in C:\Windows\system32\config folder of the boot partition ▲ Registry hive that holds hardware configuration data, including which device drivers need loading at startup
Device drivers	▲ Multiple files located in C:\Windows\system32\drivers folder of the boot partition ▲ Windows and third-party drivers needed for startup
Pagefile.sys	▲ Located in the root folder of the system partition (usually C:\) ▲ Virtual memory swap file

*It is assumed that Windows is installed in the C:\Windows folder.

© Cengage Learning 2014

Table C-3 Files needed to boot Windows XP successfully (continued)

THE BOOT.INI FILE

One key file used by Windows XP startup is Boot.ini. Recall that the **Boot.ini** file is a hidden text file stored in the root directory of the active partition that Ntldr reads to see what operating systems are available and how to set up the boot. You can view and edit the Boot.ini file, which might be necessary when you are trying to solve a difficult boot problem. Figure C-16 shows an example of a Boot.ini file for Windows XP.

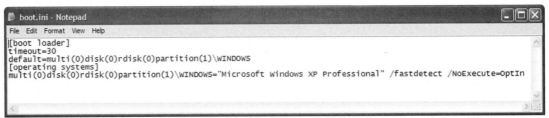

Source: Microsoft Windows XP

Figure C-16 A sample Windows XP Boot.ini file

Before you can view or edit the Boot.ini file using a text editor such as Notepad, you must first change the folder options to view hidden system files. To do so, open **Windows Explorer**, select the root directory, click **Tools** on the menu bar, click **Folder Options**, and then select the **View** tab. Uncheck the option to **Hide protected operating system files**.

There are two main sections in Boot.ini: the [boot loader] section and the [operating systems] section. The [boot loader] section contains the number of seconds the system gives the user to select an operating system before it loads the default operating system; this is called a timeout. In Figure C-16, the timeout is set to 30 seconds, the default value.

A+ 220-802 1.3

If the system is set for a dual boot, the path to the default operating system is also listed in the [boot loader] section.

The [operating systems] section of the Boot.ini file provides a list of operating systems that can be loaded, including the path to the boot partition of each operating system. Here is the meaning of each entry in Figure C-16:

- ▲ *Multi(0)*. Use the first hard drive controller.
- ▲ *Disk(0)*. Use only when booting from a SCSI hard drive.
- ▲ *Rdisk(0)*. Use the first hard drive.
- ▲ *Partition(1)*. Use the first partition on the drive.

Switches are sometimes used in the [operating systems] section. In Figure C-16, the first switch used in this Boot.ini file is /fastdetect, which causes the OS not to attempt to inspect any peripherals connected to a COM port (serial port) at startup.

The second switch is /NoExecute=OptIn. This switch is new with Windows XP Service Pack 2 and is used to configure Data Execution Prevention (DEP). DEP stops a program if it tries to use a protected area of memory, which some viruses attempt to do.

Although you can change the Boot.ini file by editing it, a better way to make changes is by using the System Properties box. To access it, right-click My Computer and select Properties from the shortcut menu. Several of the startup and recovery options that you can change in this box are recorded as changes to Boot.ini.

TROUBLESHOOT PROBLEMS WITH XP STARTUP

A+ 220-802 1.3, 4.6

When Windows XP startup fails, try to use options on the Advanced Options Menu, which can help fix problems with faulty device drivers or system services. To access the Advanced Options Menu, press **F8** near the beginning of the boot. The tools on this menu work as they do in Windows 7.

If the tools on this menu don't help, turn to the Emergency Repair Disk and then the Recovery Console. If XP still cannot start, use the Automated System Recovery to recover the XP installation.

WINDOWS XP EMERGENCY REPAIR DISK

A Windows XP **emergency repair disk** is a bootable floppy disk that can be used to boot the system bypassing the boot files stored in the root directory of drive C. If you boot from the disk and the Windows XP desktop loads successfully, then the problem is associated with damaged sectors or missing or damaged files in the root directory of drive C that are required to boot the OS. These sectors and files include the master boot program; the partition table; the OS boot record; the boot files named Ntldr file, Ntdetect.com file, and Ntbootdd.sys (if it exists); and the Boot.ini file. In addition, the problem can be caused by a boot sector virus. However, an emergency repair disk cannot be used to troubleshoot problems associated with unstable device drivers or any other system files stored in the \Windows folder or its subfolders.

You first create the boot disk by formatting the disk using a working Windows XP computer and then copying files to the disk. These files can be copied from a Windows XP setup CD or a Windows XP computer that is using the same version of Windows XP as the problem PC. Do the following to create the disk:

1. Obtain a floppy disk and format it on a Windows XP computer.

2. Using Explorer, copy Ntldr and Ntdetect.com from the i386 folder on the Windows XP setup CD or a Windows XP computer to the root of the floppy disk.

3. If your computer boots from a SCSI hard drive, then obtain a device driver (*.sys) for your SCSI hard drive, rename it **Ntbootdd.sys**, and copy it to the root of the floppy disk. (If you used an incorrect device driver, then you will receive an error after booting from the floppy disk. The error will mention a "computer disk hardware configuration problem" and that it "could not read from the selected boot disk." If this occurs, contact your computer manufacturer or hard drive manufacturer for the correct version of the SCSI hard drive device driver for your computer.)

4. Look at Boot.ini on the problem computer, and then obtain an identical copy from another known good computer (or create your own) and copy it to the root of the floppy disk.

5. If you can't find a good Boot.ini file to copy, you can use the following lines to create a Boot.ini file. These lines work for a Boot.ini file if the problem computer is booting from an IDE hard drive:

```
[boot loader]

timeout530

default5multi(0)disk(0)rdisk(0)partition(1)\WINDOWS

[operating systems]

multi(0)disk(0)rdisk(0)partition(1)\WINDOWS5"Microsoft
Windows XP Professional" /fastdetect
```

6. Write-protect the floppy disk so that it cannot become infected with a virus.

7. You have now created the Windows XP boot disk. Check BIOS setup to make sure the first boot device is set to the floppy disk, and then insert the boot disk and reboot your computer.

> **Notes** If you are creating your own Boot.ini file, be sure to enter a hard return after the /fastdetect switch in the last line of the file.

> **Notes** To learn more about the Windows XP boot disk, see the Microsoft Knowledge Base Articles 305595 and 314503 at the Microsoft web site *support.microsoft.com*.

If the Windows XP desktop loads successfully, then do the following to attempt to repair the Windows XP installation:

1. Load the Recovery Console and use the Fixmbr and Fixboot commands to repair the MBR and the OS boot sector.

2. Run antivirus software.

3. Use Disk Management to verify that the hard drive partition table is correct.

4. Defragment your hard drive.

5. Copy Ntldr, Ntdetect.com, and Boot.ini from your floppy disk to the root of the hard drive.

6. If you're using a SCSI hard drive, copy Ntbootdd.sys from your floppy disk to the root of the hard drive.

A+
220-802
1.3, 4.6

If the Windows XP desktop did not load by booting from the boot disk, then the next tool to try is the Recovery Console.

RECOVERY CONSOLE

Use **Recovery Console** when Windows XP does not start properly or hangs during the load. It works even when core Windows system files are corrupted. The Recovery Console is a command-driven operating system that does not use a GUI. With it, you can access the FAT16, FAT32, and NTFS file systems.

Using the Recovery Console, you can:

▲ Repair a damaged registry, system files, or file system on the hard drive
▲ Enable or disable a service or device driver
▲ Repair the MBR program on the hard drive or the boot sector on the system partition
▲ Repair a damaged Boot.ini file
▲ Recover data when the Windows installation is beyond repair

The Recovery Console software is on the Windows XP setup CD. You can launch the Recovery Console from the CD or manually install the Recovery Console on the hard drive and launch it from there.

To use the Recovery Console, insert the Windows XP setup CD in the CD drive and restart the system. When the Windows XP Setup opening menu appears (see Figure C-17), press **R** to load the Recovery Console.

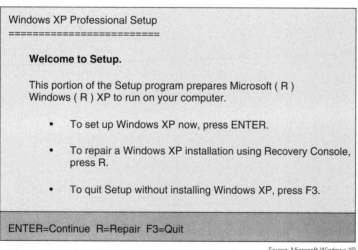

```
Windows XP Professional Setup
=========================

    Welcome to Setup.

    This portion of the Setup program prepares Microsoft ( R )
    Windows ( R ) XP to run on your computer.

      •  To set up Windows XP now, press ENTER.

      •  To repair a Windows XP installation using Recovery Console,
         press R.

      •  To quit Setup without installing Windows XP, press F3.


 ENTER=Continue  R=Repair  F3=Quit
```

Source: Microsoft Windows XP

Figure C-17 Windows XP Setup opening menu

You must enter the Administrator password in order to use the Recovery Console and access an NTFS volume. If the registry is so corrupted that the Recovery Console cannot read the password to validate it, you are not asked for the password, but you are limited in what you can do at the Recovery Console.

> **Notes** Here are two useful tips to help you when using the Recovery Console: To retrieve the last command entered, press **F3** at the command prompt. To retrieve the command one character at a time, press the **F1** key.

Many commands used at a command prompt window also work in the Recovery Console. These commands include attrib, cd, chkdsk, cls, copy, del, dir, disable, diskpart, enable, exit, format, help, listsvc, md, more, rd, and rename. (The Windows 7/Vista Bootsect, Bcdedit, and Bootrec commands will not work in XP.) Table C-4 lists some additional Recovery Console commands.

Command	Description	Examples

Expand	Expands compressed files and extracts files from cabinet files and copies the files to the destination folder.	**To extract File1 from the Drivers.cab file:**
		`C:\> Expand D:\i386\Drivers.cab -f:File1`
		To expand the compressed file, File1.cp_:
		`C:\> Expand File1.cp_`

Fixboot	Rewrites the OS boot sector on the hard drive. If a drive letter is not specified, the system drive is assumed.	**To repair the OS boot sector of drive C:** `C:\> Fixboot C:`
Fixmbr	Rewrites the Master Boot Record boot program.	**To repair the Master Boot Record boot program:** `C:\> Fixmbr`
Logon	Allows you to log onto an installation with the Administrator password. Use it to log onto a second installation of Windows in a dual-boot environment.	**When logged onto the first Windows installation, use this command to log onto the second installation:** `C:\> logon 2` **If you don't enter the password correctly after three tries, the system automatically reboots.**
Map	Lists all drive letters and file system types.	`C:\> Map`

Set	Displays or sets Recovery Console environmental variables.	**To turn off the prompt when you are overwriting files:**
		`C:\> Set nocopyprompt=true`
		To allow access to all files and folders on all drives:
		`C:\> Set allowallpaths=true`
		To allow copying any file to another media:
		`C:\> Set allowremovablemedia=true`

Systemroot	Sets the current directory to the directory where Windows XP is installed.	`C:\> Systemroot C:\WINDOWS>`

© Cengage Learning 2014

Table C-4   Commands available from the Recovery Console

Unless you first use the set command with certain parameters, you are not allowed into all folders, and you cannot copy files from the hard drive to a removable media.

The **Fixmbr** command restores the master boot program in the MBR, and the **Fixboot** command repairs the OS boot record. As you enter each command, you're looking for clues that might indicate at what point the drive has failed. For example, Figure C-18 shows the results of using the Fixmbr command, which appears to have worked without errors, but the Fixboot command has actually failed. This tells us that most likely the master boot program is healthy, but drive C is not accessible. After using these commands, if you don't see any errors, exit the Recovery Console and try to boot from the hard drive.

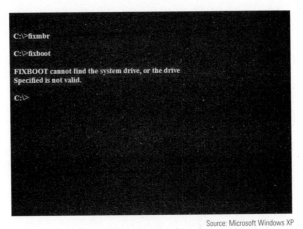

Source: Microsoft Windows XP

Figure C-18 Results of using the Fixmbr and Fixboot
commands in the Recovery Console

To exit the Recovery Console, type **Exit** and press **Enter**. The system will attempt to boot to the Windows desktop.

RESTORING THE SYSTEM USING AN AUTOMATED SYSTEM RECOVERY BACKUP

Recall that you can use the XP Backup or Restore Wizard to create an Automated System Recovery backup of the entire Windows volume. To restore the Windows volume to its state when the last ASR backup was made, do the following:

1. Boot the computer using the Windows XP setup CD.
2. A blue screen appears with the message "Press F6 to load RAID or SCSI drivers." If your system uses RAID, SCSI, or some SATA drives, press **F6**. If your system does not use these drives, ignore the message.
3. At the bottom of the blue screen, a message says, "Press F2 to run the Automated System Recovery process." Press **F2**.
4. The screen shown in Figure C-19 appears, instructing you to insert the ASR floppy disk. Insert the disk, and then press **Enter**. The entire Windows volume is reformatted and the volume is restored to the ASR backup.

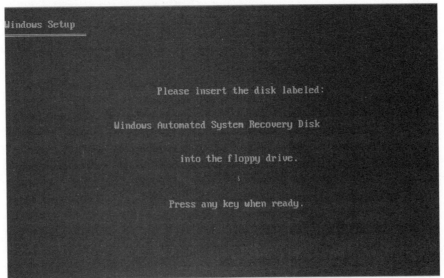

Source: Microsoft Windows XP

Figure C-19 Automatic System Recovery process must have the ASR floppy disk

CHAPTER 15: CONNECTING TO AND SETTING UP A NETWORK

Following are differences in Windows 7 and Windows XP that are associated with content covered in Chapter 15.

CONNECT TO A WIRED NETWORK IN XP

A+
220-802
1.5, 1.6

For Windows XP, to connect to a network or repair a connection, click **Start**, right-click **My Network Places**, and select **Properties** from the shortcut menu. The **Network Connections** window opens. See Figure C-20. To connect to a network, click **Create a new connection** in the left pane. To repair a wired network connection, right-click the **Local Area Connection** icon, and then select **Repair** from the shortcut menu.

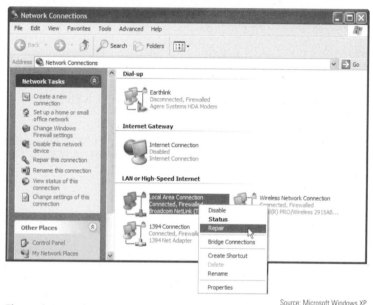

Figure C-20   Windows XP Network Connections window   Source: Microsoft Windows XP

You can also use the Control Panel to create and repair network connections. To open the Network Connections window, click **Network Connections** in Control Panel. To use a wizard to create a new network connection, click **Network Setup Wizard** in Control Panel and follow the directions to create the new connection.

VERIFY TCP/IP SETTINGS IN XP

To verify and change the TCP/IP settings for Windows XP, click **Start**, right-click **My Network Places**, and select **Properties** from the shortcut menu. The **Network Connections** window opens. Right-click the **Local Area Connection** icon, and then select **Properties** from the shortcut menu. Refer back to Figure C-20. The properties box opens. Select **Internet Protocol (TCP/IP)** and click **Properties**. Configure the TCP/IP properties the same as with Windows 7/Vista.

CONNECT TO A WIRELESS NETWORK IN XP

Here are the steps to connect to a public or private hot spot when using Windows XP:

1. Right-click **My Network Places** and select **Properties**. The Network Connections window opens. Right-click the **Wireless Network Connection** icon and select **View Available Wireless Networks** from the shortcut menu. The Wireless Network Connection window opens (see Figure C-21). Select an unsecured network from those listed and click **Connect**.

A+
220-802
1.5, 1.6

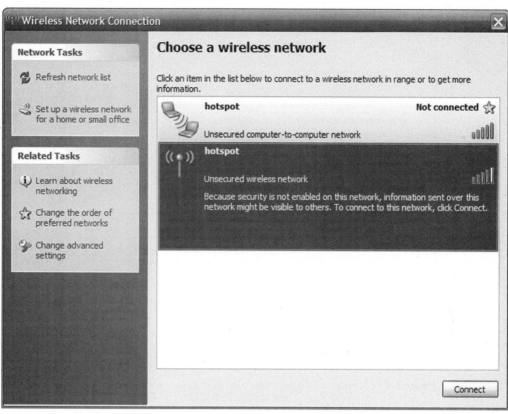

Source: Microsoft Windows XP

Figure C-21   Available wireless hot spots

2. When you select a secured network from the list, you must enter the key in a dialog box, as shown in Figure C-22.

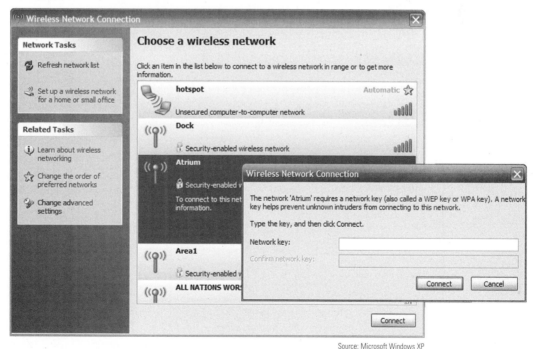

Source: Microsoft Windows XP

Figure C-22   To use a secured wireless network, you must know the encryption key

3. If you're having a problem making the connection and you know the SSID of the hot spot, you can enter the SSID. Click **Change advanced settings** in the Network Connections window. The Wireless Network Connection Properties dialog box opens. Click the **Wireless Networks** tab (see Figure C-23). Click **Add**.

A+
220-802
1.5, 1.6

Source: Microsoft Windows XP

Figure C-23 Manage wireless hot spots using the Wireless
Network Connection Properties box

4. The Wireless Network Properties window opens (see Figure C-24). Enter the SSID
of the network and make sure that Network Authentication is set to **Open** and Data
encryption is set to **Disabled**. Click **OK**. When a dialog box opens to warn you of the
dangers of disabling encryption, click **Continue Anyway**. Click **OK** to close the Wireless
Network Connection Properties dialog box. Try again to connect to the hot spot.

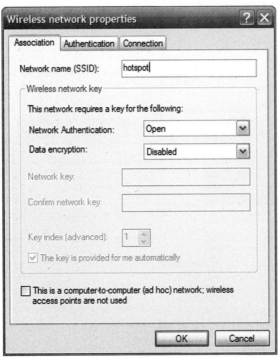

Source: Microsoft Windows XP

Figure C-24 Enter the SSID of a hot spot to which you
want to connect

CHAPTER 17: WINDOWS RESOURCES ON A NETWORK

Following are differences in Windows 7 and Windows XP that are associated with content covered in Chapter 17.

A+
220-802
1.8, 2.1

SHARE A FOLDER IN XP

To share a folder in Windows XP, follow these steps:

1. In Windows Explorer, right-click a folder and select **Sharing and Security** from the shortcut menu. The Properties box opens with the Sharing tab active (see Figure C-25). Click **If you understand the security risks but want to share files without running the wizard, click here.** The Enable File Sharing dialog box appears. Select **Just enable file sharing** and click **OK**. The Sharing tab on the Properties box now has the *Share this folder on the network* check box available, as shown in Figure C-25. You only need to enable file sharing once. After that, the check box is always available.

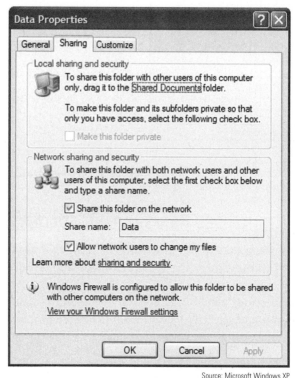

Source: Microsoft Windows XP

Figure C-25   A user on a network can share a folder with others on the network

2. Check **Share this folder on the network**. If you want to allow others to change the contents of the folder, check **Allow network users to change my files**. Click **Apply**, and close the window.

DISABLE SIMPLE FILE SHARING

Windows XP uses **simple file sharing** by default, which means you have no control over who has access to a shared folder or file. (By default, Windows 7/Vista does not use simple file sharing.) For Windows XP, to disable simple file sharing so that you have more control over access and can monitor that access, open the **Folder Options** applet in Control Panel and

A+
220-802
1.8, 2.1

click the **View** tab of the Folder Options box (see Figure C-26). Scroll down to the bottom of the **Advanced settings** list, uncheck **Use simple file sharing (Recommended)**, and click **Apply**. Close the window.

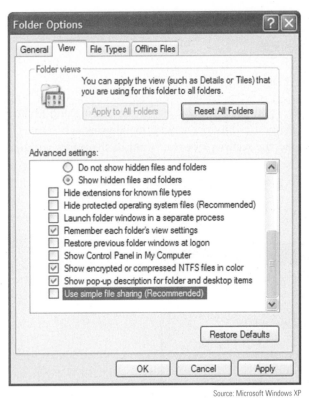

Source: Microsoft Windows XP

Figure C-26   Turn off Windows XP simple file sharing so that you have more control over access to files and folders

VERIFY XP COMPONENTS NEEDED FOR SHARING FOLDERS AND FILES

If you have a problem with sharing folders and files using Windows XP, do the following to verify that Windows components needed for sharing are installed and enabled:

1. Open the **Network Connections** window, right-click the connection icon (default name is **Local Area Connection**), and select **Properties** from the shortcut menu. The Local Area Connection Properties dialog box opens. See Figure C-27.

2. Verify **Client for Microsoft Networks** and **File and Printer Sharing for Microsoft Networks** are both checked. If you don't see these items in the list, click **Install** to install them. The Select Network Component Type box appears (see the left side of Figure C-27). Select **Client**, click **Add**, and follow the directions on-screen. When you're done, close all windows.

MAKE YOUR WINDOWS XP PERSONAL PROFILE PRIVATE

If you are using the NTFS file system with Windows XP, folders associated with your user account can be made private so that only you can access them. To make a user folder and all its subfolders private, in Windows Explorer, drill down to a folder that is part of your user profile under the Documents and Settings folder. Right-click the folder and select **Sharing and Security** from the shortcut menu. The folder Properties dialog box opens (see Figure C-28).

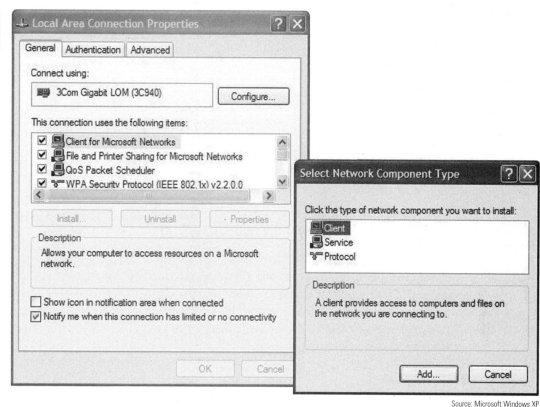

Source: Microsoft Windows XP

Figure C-27   Use the Network Connections applet to install a network client, service, or protocol for Windows XP

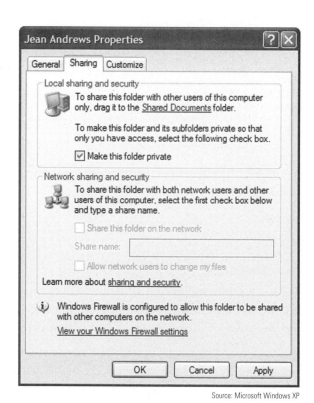

Source: Microsoft Windows XP

Figure C-28   A folder that belongs to a user profile in Windows XP can be made private

Check **Make this folder private** and click **Apply.** (If a folder is not part of a user profile in the Documents and Settings folder, this check box is dimmed.) When you make a personal folder private, be sure you have a password associated with your user account. If you don't have a password, anyone can log on as you and gain access to your private folders.

CHAPTER 18: SECURITY STRATEGIES

Following are differences in Windows 7 and Windows XP that are associated with content covered in Chapter 18.

HOW A USER LOGS ON IN WINDOWS XP

Using Windows XP, open **Control Panel,** and then open the **User Accounts** applet. Click **Change the way users log on or off.** The User Accounts window opens, as shown in Figure C-29. If you want to require users to press Ctrl-Alt-Delete to get a logon window, then uncheck **Use the Welcome screen.** If you want to allow only one user logged on at a time, then uncheck **Use Fast User Switching.** When you're done with your changes, click **Apply Options** to close the window.

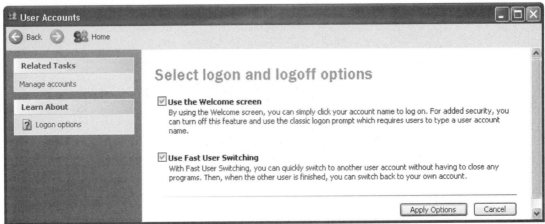

Source: Microsoft Windows XP

Figure C-29 Options to change the way Windows XP users log on or off

CONFIGURE WINDOWS FIREWALL IN WINDOWS XP

To view and change the Windows Firewall settings for Windows XP, use the Network Connections window. In the left pane, click **Change Windows Firewall settings.** The Windows Firewall window opens, as shown in Figure C-30. Verify that **On (recommended)** is selected.

A+
220-802
1.1, 1.4,
1.5, 1.6

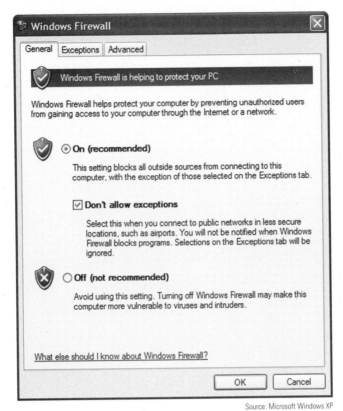

Source: Microsoft Windows XP

Figure C-30 Windows Firewall for Windows XP is set for
maximum protection

If you don't want to allow any communication to be initiated from remote computers, check **Don't allow exceptions**. This is the preferred setting when you're traveling or using public networks or Internet connections. If you are on a local network and need to allow others on the network to access your computer, uncheck **Don't allow exceptions**. Then click the **Exceptions** tab to select the exceptions to allow. For example, if you want to share files and folders on your local network, use the Exceptions tab to allow File and Printer Sharing activity.

Creating a Standard Image

To use the Windows Automated Installation Kit (AIK) to create a standard image, a system administrator uses one computer to set up the tools used to create the image (called the technician computer) and a second computer to build the image with all the Windows settings, drivers, and applications that will become part of the image (called the reference computer).

A+
220-802
1.2

This appendix contains the step-by-step process to create a standard image using the Windows AIK. For more information, see this link on the Microsoft web site: *technet .microsoft.com/en-us/library/ee523217(WS.10).aspx*. To create the image, you need two USB flash drives that are at least 8 GB in size and two computers. Designate one computer to be the technician computer and the other to be the reference computer. You also need a Windows 7 setup DVD. In these steps, we are using a 64-bit Windows 7 Professional DVD.

> **Notes** Before you begin creating a standard image, you might want to check out this video at the Microsoft Technet site: *technet.microsoft.com/en-us/windows/ee530017.aspx*.

PART 1: ON THE TECHNICIAN COMPUTER, INSTALL WINDOWS AIK

To install Windows AIK on the technician computer, follow these steps:

1. Go to the Microsoft Download Center (*www.microsoft.com/download*) and download the **Windows Automated Installation Kit (AIK) for Windows 7**, which is contained in an ISO file. At the time of this writing, the file is named KB3AIK_EN.iso. The download might take about two hours.

2. To burn the .iso file to a DVD, first insert a blank DVD-R into the optical drive. Right-click the .iso file and select **Burn disc image** from the shortcut menu. Follow the directions on-screen to burn the DVD.

3. Open the System window and find out if your OS installation is a 32-bit or 64-bit installation. On a separate sheet of paper, write the answer to this question:

   Are you using a 32-bit or 64-bit OS on the technician computer?

4. Using Windows Explorer, double-click one of the two setup programs on the DVD to install Windows AIK on your computer:

   ◢ If your OS is a 32-bit OS, double-click **wAIKX86.msi**.
   ◢ If your OS is a 64-bit OS, double-click **wAIKAMD64.msi**.

5. Follow the directions on-screen to install Windows AIK on your computer.

PART 2: ON THE TECHNICIAN COMPUTER, CREATE A BOOTABLE USB FLASH DRIVE (UFD)

Follow these steps on the technician computer to use Windows AIK to create a bootable UFD that contains the ImageX.exe program you will use to capture the image:

1. Click **Start**, **All Programs**, and **Microsoft Windows AIK**. In the Windows AIK group, right-click **Deployment Tools Command Prompt** and click **Run as administrator** (see Figure D-1). Respond to the UAC box. The Deployment Tools Command Prompt window opens.

2. Carefully enter one set of three commands to create an ISO folder on your hard drive with files in it that will later go on the bootable UFD:

   ◢ If the reference computer will hold a 32-bit installation of Windows, enter these three commands:

   • copype.cmd x86 C:\winpe_x86

   • copy C:\winpe_x86\winpe.wim C:\winpe_x86\ISO\sources\boot.wim

   • copy "C:\Program Files\Windows AIK\Tools\x86\ImageX.exe" C:\winpe_x86\ISO\

A+
220-802
1.2

Source: Microsoft Windows 7

Figure D-1 Opening the Deployment Tools Command Prompt window

Notes Note the space in **Program Files** and **Windows AIK** in the path to the ImageX.exe file.

◢ If the reference computer will hold a 64-bit installation of Windows, enter these three commands:

- copype.cmd amd64 C:\winpe_amd64

- copy C:\winpe_amd64\winpe.wim C:\winpe_amd64\ISO\sources\boot.wim

- copy "C:\Program Files\Windows AIK\Tools\amd64\ImageX.exe" C:\winpe_amd64\ISO\

3. Insert a USB flash drive in the USB port. Realize that all data on the drive will be deleted because you are about to format the drive. Open Windows Explorer and answer the following questions on a separate sheet of paper:

◢ What is the capacity of the UFD?
◢ How much of the UFD capacity is free space?
◢ What is the drive letter that Windows assigned to the UFD?

4. In the Deployment Tools Command Prompt window, enter the **diskpart** command. The Diskpart> prompt appears. Steps 5 through 13 use commands entered at the Diskpart> prompt.

5. To display a list of disks, enter **list disk**. A list of disks appears. On a separate sheet of paper, write the answer to this question:

◢ What is the number of the disk that is the UFD?

6. Verify you have the correct disk because you are about to erase everything on it. For example, in Figure D-2, the UFD I'm using has a capacity of 29 GB and is Disk 2 in the list of disks. On a separate sheet of paper, write the answer to this question:

▲ Does the capacity and free space recorded in Step 3 match what you see listed for your disk?

```
Administrator: Deployment Tools Command Prompt - diskpart

C:\winpe_amd64>copy "c:\Program Files\Windows AIK\Tools\amd64\ImageX.exe" C:\win
pe_amd64\ISO\
        1 file(s) copied.

C:\winpe_amd64>diskpart

Microsoft DiskPart version 6.1.7601
Copyright (C) 1999-2008 Microsoft Corporation.
On computer: BLUELIGHT

DISKPART> list disk

  Disk ###  Status         Size     Free     Dyn  Gpt
  --------  -------------  -------  -------   ---  ---
  Disk 0    Online          500 GB    48 GB
  Disk 1    Online         1038 GB   195 GB
  Disk 2    Online           29 GB     0 B

DISKPART> select disk 2

Disk 2 is now the selected disk.

DISKPART> _
```

Figure D-2 Identify the disk number for your UFD   Source: Microsoft Windows 7

7. Enter the command **select disk** *number*, substituting the number you recorded in Step 5 for *number* in the command line. The UFD is now the selected disk.

8. To delete all partition information on the UFD, enter the **clean** command.

9. To create a new primary partition, enter the command **create partition primary**.

10. To select this partition, enter the command **select partition 1**.

11. To format the partition, enter the command **format fs=fat32 quick**.

12. To make the partition the active partition, enter the command **active**.

13. To exit the Diskpart interface, enter the command **exit**. The C prompt in the Deployment Tools Command Prompt window appears.

14. To copy the ISO folder and its contents to the UFD, use one of the following commands, substituting the drive letter of your UFD for D in the command line:

▲ If the reference computer will hold a 32-bit installation of Windows, enter this command:
  xcopy /s C:\winpe_x86\ISO*.* D:

▲ If the reference computer will hold a 64-bit installation of Windows, enter this command:
  xcopy /s C:\winpe_amd64\ISO*.* D:

The UFD is now ready to capture the standard image that you create on the reference computer. Figure D-3 shows the root directory and the Properties box of the UFD.

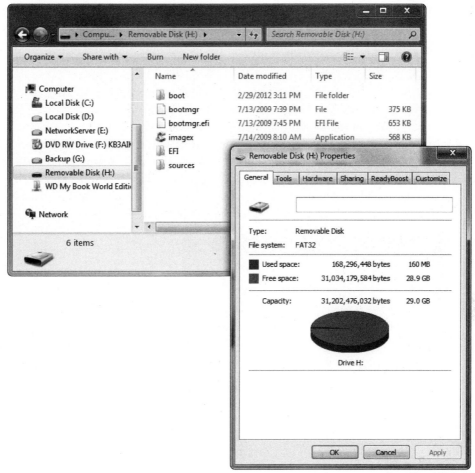

Source: Microsoft Windows 7

Figure D-3   Verify the files in the root directory of the UFD

PART 3: ON THE REFERENCE COMPUTER, INSTALL AND CUSTOMIZE WINDOWS 7

On the reference computer, follow these steps to install Windows 7 and all applications that go on the image:

1. Using a Windows 7 DVD or other media, install Windows 7. During the installation, enter a username, password, and other information as you would normally during a Windows installation. These items will later be deleted or cleaned from the installation. When asked for the product key, enter the product key as requested. If you are using a Volume Licensing version of Windows 7, enter the Volume Licensing product key. (You do not need to automatically activate Windows, but the product key is required.)

2. Install all Windows updates, device drivers, and applications that will be part of the image. Don't forget to install antivirus software. Configure all Windows settings as you want them in the standard image. Do not configure user settings because these settings will be lost when the image is cleaned.

3. Take care to verify you have all programs and settings as you want them because this is your last chance to change the image.

PART 4: ON THE REFERENCE COMPUTER, CLEAN THE IMAGE

In the steps that follow, you use the System Preparation utility (sysprep.exe) to restart the system in audit mode so you can delete the user profile and user account that were created during the Windows installation. Follow these steps:

1. To launch Sysprep, click **Start**, type **C:\Windows\System32\sysprep\sysprep.exe** in the Search box, and press **Enter**. The System Preparation Tool dialog box appears. In the System Cleanup Action area, select **Enter System Audit Mode**. Check **Generalize**. In the Shutdown Options area, select **Reboot** if it is not already selected. See Figure D-4. When you click **OK**, the system reboots into Audit Mode, which automatically logs you in using the built-in Administrator account so that you can delete the user profile that belongs to the user account you were using earlier when you installed applications and drivers in Step 2 of Part 3.

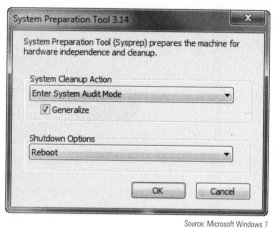

Source: Microsoft Windows 7

Figure D-4   Sysprep is ready to restart the system in audit mode

2. To delete the user profile you used in Step 2 of Part 3, click **Start**, type **user profile** in the Search box, and press **Enter**. In the User Profiles box (see Figure D-5), select the user profile. Click **Delete** and then click **Yes**. Close the User Profiles box.

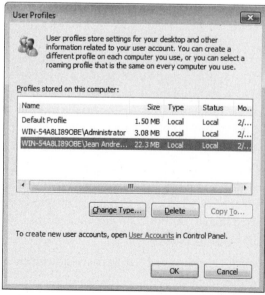

Source: Microsoft Windows 7

Figure D-5   Delete the user profile created during the Windows installation

A+
220-802
1.2

3. Using Control Panel or the Computer Management console, delete the user account (see Figure D-6). Close all open windows.

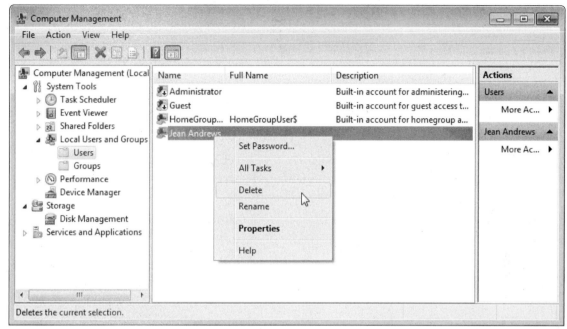

Source: Microsoft Windows 7

Figure D-6 Use the Computer Management console to delete the user account created during the Windows installation

PART 5: ON THE REFERENCE COMPUTER, GENERALIZE THE IMAGE

Next you use Sysprep again to remove any hardware-dependent information from the installation in a process called generalizing the image. Follow these steps:

1. On the reference computer, if the System Preparation Tool dialog box is not already open, launch sysprep to open it.

2. In the System Preparation Tool box, choose **Enter System Out-of-Box Experience (OOBE).** Check **Generalize.** In the Shutdown Options area, select **Shutdown** (see Figure D-7).

3. Click **OK.** Sysprep generalizes the system and the computer shuts down.

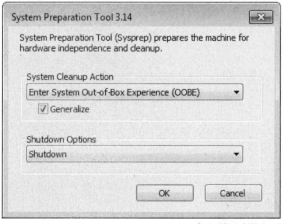

Source: Microsoft Windows 7

Figure D-7 Sysprep is set to remove hardware-dependent information from the Windows installation

A+
220-802
1.2

PART 6: ON THE REFERENCE COMPUTER, CAPTURE THE IMAGE

The ImageX.exe program on the UFD is used to capture the image. It stores the image on the UFD in the file Install.wim. Follow these steps to capture the image:

1. Boot the reference computer from the bootable UFD you created earlier. To boot from the UFD, you might need to access BIOS setup and change the order of boot devices to list a removable device first in the list of boot devices. When you boot from the UFD, Windows PE is launched and provides a command prompt window showing the command prompt as X:\windows\system32>.

2. Next you need to determine the drive letter for the volume on the hard drive that holds the Windows installation and the drive letter for the bootable UFD. Most likely, the Windows volume will be D:. Do the following:

   a. Enter the command **Dir D:**. If you see the Windows and Program Files folder listed, you have found the Windows volume. If not, try a different drive letter. On a separate sheet of paper, record the answer to this question:

      • What is the drive letter of the Windows volume?

   b. Enter the commands **Dir E:, Dir F:,** or **Dir G:** until you find the drive that holds the imagex.exe file. This drive is the bootable UFD. On a separate sheet of paper, record the answer to this question:

      • What is the drive letter of the bootable UFD?

   In our example, we use D: for the Windows volume and F: for the bootable UFD, but your results might be different.

3. In the command prompt window, enter this command to capture the image on the D: drive to the F: drive when Windows 7 Professional is installed:

   F:\imagex /compress fast /check /flags "Professional" /capture D: F:\install.wim "Windows 7 Professional" "Windows 7 Professional Custom"

   Here is the command to use when Windows 7 Home Premium is installed:

   F:\imagex /compress fast /check /flags "HomePremium" /capture D: F:\install.wim "Windows 7 Home Premium" "Windows 7 Home Premium Custom"

4. The install.wim file is now stored on the UFD. This install.wim file can be 3 GB or higher depending on the space needed for installed applications. Shut down the computer and remove the UFD.

> **Notes** A problem arises when the install.wim file is larger than 4 GB because the FAT32 file system on the UFD cannot handle a file that large. In this situation, you have a couple of options. You can format the UFD using the NTFS file system. However, know that some computers will not boot from a UFD that is using the NTFS file system. Another solution is to use a second UFD that is formatted with NTFS. Boot from the FAT32 UFD, switch to the NTFS UFD, and save the image to this second UFD.

5. Most UFDs don't have a write-on label. To help you remember what's stored on the UFD, you can create a Readme.txt file in the root, and include in it a description of the contents of the UFD.

> **Notes** When you restart the reference computer, the Set Up Windows screen appears where you can configure the time, currency, and keyboard settings, enter a computer name, user account, and product key, and accept the licensing agreement as you normally would during a Windows installation. The Windows desktop then appears.

D

PART 7: ON THE TECHNICIAN COMPUTER, PREPARE A SECOND UFD TO USE WHEN DEPLOYING THE IMAGE

Use the technician computer to prepare the deployment UFD. To do so, you format a second UFD using the FAT32 file system and make the UFD bootable. Then you copy all files on the Windows setup DVD to the UFD along with the install.wim file you captured. Follow these steps to prepare the deployment UFD:

1. On the technician computer, open the Deployment Tools Command Prompt window. You will use this window to enter the commands in this section.

2. Copy the Install.wim file from the UFD you used to capture the file to the hard drive of the technician computer using this command: **copy H:\install.wim C:\install.wim**. Substitute the drive letter of the UFD for H in the command line. You can now remove this UFD from the USB port.

3. Insert a second UFD in a USB port. Format it with the FAT32 file system and make it bootable. To do so, follow Steps 3 through 13 in Part 2 of this appendix. Note that these steps use the following commands: diskpart, list disk, select disk, clean, create partition primary, select partition, format, and active.

4. Insert the Windows 7 setup DVD in the optical drive. Enter this command to copy all files from the setup DVD to the UFD: **xcopy /s D:*.* E:*.***. In the command line, substitute the drive letter of your optical drive for D and substitute the drive letter of your UFD for E.

5. Use this command to copy the Install.wim file from the technician computer to the \Sources folder on the UFD, replacing the \Sources\install.wim file already there:

   Xcopy /r C:\install.wim E:\sources\install.wim

   Substitute the drive letter of your UFD for E in the command line.

6. Safely eject the UFD from the USB port. You might want to create a Readme.txt file in the root of the UFD with instructions and a description of the UFD contents.

To use the image on other computers, boot the computer from the UFD. Windows setup begins. Follow the instructions to install the OS. When the installation completes, all applications and Windows settings in the image are also installed. To make it easier to install the image on multiple computers, you might want to make several copies of the deployment UFD.

Keystroke Shortcuts in Windows

This appendix lists a few handy keystrokes to use when working with Windows, including the function keys you can use during startup. You can also use the mouse to do some of these same things, but keystrokes are sometimes faster. Also, in some troubleshooting situations, the mouse is not usable. At those times, knowing these keystrokes can get you out of a jam.

General Action	Keystrokes	Description
While loading Windows	F8	To display the Advanced Boot Options menu.
	Spacebar	To display the Windows boot menu.
Managing Windows and applications	F1	To display Help.
	Alt+Tab	To move from one loaded application to another.
	Ctrl+Tab and Ctrl+Shift+Tab	To move through tabbed pages in a dialog box.
	Alt+Esc	To cycle through items in the order they were opened.
	F6	To cycle through screen elements in a window or on the desktop.
	Win or Ctrl+Esc	Display Start menu. Use arrow keys to move over the menu. (The Win key is the one labeled with the Windows flag icon.)
	Win+E	Start Windows Explorer.
	Win+M	Minimize all windows.
	Win+Tab	Move through items on the taskbar.
	Win+R	Display the Run dialog box.
	Win+Break	Display the Windows 7/Vista System window or the XP System Properties window.
	F5	Refresh the contents of a window.
	Alt+F4	Close the active application window, or, if no window is open, shut down Windows.
	Ctrl+F4	Close the active document window.
	Alt+Spacebar	To display the System menu for the active window. To close this window, you can then use the arrow key to step down to Close.
	Alt+M	First, put the focus on the Start menu (use Win or Ctrl+Esc) and then press Alt+M to minimize all windows and move the focus to the desktop.
	F10 or Alt	Activate the menu bar in the active program.
	Ctrl+Alt+Del	Display the Task List, which you can use to switch to another application, end a task, or shut down Windows.
	Application	When an item is selected, display its shortcut menu. (The Application key is labeled with a box and an arrow.)
Working with text anywhere in Windows	Ctrl+C	Shortcut for Copy.
	Ctrl+V	Shortcut for Paste.
	Ctrl+A	Shortcut for selecting all text.
	Ctrl+X	Shortcut for Cut.
	Ctrl+Z	Shortcut for Undo.
	Ctrl+Y	Shortcut for Repeat/Redo.
	Shift+arrow keys	To select text, character by character.

General Action	Keystrokes	Description
Managing files, folders, icons, and shortcuts	Ctrl+Shift while dragging a file	Create a shortcut.
	Ctrl while dragging a file	Copy a file.
	Shift+Delete	Delete a file without placing it in the Recycle Bin.
	F2	Rename an item.
	Alt+Enter	Display an item's Properties window.
Selecting items	Shift+click	To select multiple entries in a list (such as file-names in Explorer), click the first item, hold down the Shift key, and click the last item you want to select in the list. All items between the first and last are selected.
	Ctrl+click	To select several nonsequential items in a list, click the first item to select it. Hold down the Ctrl key and click other items anywhere in the list. All items you click are selected.
Using menus	Alt	Press the Alt key to activate the menu bar.
	Alt, letter	After the menu bar is activated, press a letter to select a menu option. The letter must be under-lined in the menu.
	Alt, arrow keys, Enter	In a window, use the Alt key to make the menu bar active. Then use the arrow keys to move over the menu tree and highlight the correct option. Use the Enter key to select that option.
	Esc	Press Esc to exit a menu without making a selection.
Copying to the Clipboard	Print Screen	Copy the desktop to the Clipboard.
	Alt+Print Screen	Copy the active window to the Clipboard.

CompTIA A+ Acronyms

CompTIA provides a list of acronyms that you need to know before you sit for the A+ exams. You can download the list from the CompTIA web site at *www.comptia.org*. The list is included here for your convenience. However, CompTIA occasionally updates the list, so be sure to check the CompTIA web site for the latest version.

Acronym	Spelled Out
A/V	Audio Video
AC	alternating current
ACL	access control list
ACPI	advanced configuration power interface
ACT	activity
ADSL	asymmetrical digital subscriber line
AGP	accelerated graphics port
AMD	advanced micro devices
APIPA	automatic private internet protocol addressing
APM	advanced power management
ARP	address resolution protocol
ASR	automated system recovery
ATA	advanced technology attachment
ATAPI	advanced technology attachment packet interface
ATM	asynchronous transfer mode
ATX	advanced technology extended
BIOS	basic input/output system
BNC	Bayonet-Neill-Concelman or British Naval Connector
BTX	balanced technology extended
CAPTCHA	Completely Automated Public Turing Test To Tell Computers and Humans Apart
CCFL	Cold Cathode Fluorescent Lamp
CD	compact disc
CDFS	compact disc file system
CD-ROM	compact disc-read-only memory
CD-RW	compact disc-rewritable
CFS	Central File System, Common File System, Command File System
CMOS	complementary metal-oxide semiconductor
CNR	Communications and Networking Riser
COMx	communication port (x=port number)
CPU	central processing unit
CRIMM	Continuity Rambus Inline Memory Mode
CRT	cathode-ray tube
DAC	discretionary access control
DB-25	serial communications D-shell connector, 25 pins
DB-9	9 pin D shell connector
DC	direct current
DDOS	distributed denial of service
DDR	double data-rate
DDR RAM	double data-rate random access memory
DDR SDRAM	double data-rate synchronous dynamic random access memory

F

Acronym	Spelled Out
DFS	distributed file system
DHCP	dynamic host configuration protocol
DIMM	dual inline memory module
DIN	Deutsche Industrie Norm
DIP	dual inline package
DLP	digital light processing
DLT	digital linear tape
DMA	direct memory access
DMZ	demilitarized zone
DNS	domain name service or domain name server
DOS	denial of service
DRAM	dynamic random access memory
DSL	digital subscriber line
DVD	digital video disc or digital versatile disc
DVD-R	digital video disc-recordable
DVD-RAM	digital video disc-random access memory
DVD-ROM	digital video disc-read only memory
DVD-RW	digital video disc-rewritable
DVI	digital visual interface
ECC	error correction code
ECP	extended capabilities port
EEPROM	electrically erasable programmable read-only memory
EFS	encrypting file system
EIDE	enhanced integrated drive electronics
EMI	electromagnetic interference
EMP	electromagnetic pulse
EPP	enhanced parallel port
EPROM	erasable programmable read-only memory
ERD	emergency repair disk
ESD	electrostatic discharge
EVDO	evolution data optimized or evolution data only
EVGA	extended video graphics adapter/array
FAT	file allocation table
FAT12	12-bit file allocation table
FAT16	16-bit file allocation table
FAT32	32-bit file allocation table
FDD	floppy disk drive
Fn	Function (referring to the function key on a laptop)
FPM	fast page-mode
FQDN	fully qualified domain name

Acronym	Spelled Out
FRU	field replaceable unit
FSB	Front Side Bus
FTP	file transfer protocol
Gb	gigabit
GB	gigabyte
GDI	graphics device interface
GHz	gigahertz
GPS	global positioning system
GSM	global system for mobile communications
GUI	graphical user interface
HAL	hardware abstraction layer
HAV	Hardware Assisted Virtualization
HCL	hardware compatibility list
HDD	hard disk drive
HDMI	high definition media interface
HPFS	high performance file system
HTML	hypertext markup language
HTPC	Home Theater PC
HTTP	hypertext transfer protocol
HTTPS	hypertext transfer protocol over secure sockets layer
I/O	input/output
ICMP	internet control message protocol
ICR	intelligent character recognition
IDE	integrated drive electronics
IDS	Intrusion Detection System
IEEE	Institute of Electrical and Electronics Engineers
IIS	Internet Information Services
IMAP	internet mail access protocol
IP	internet protocol
IPCONFIG	internet protocol configuration
IPP	internet printing protocol
IPSEC	internet protocol security
IR	infrared
IrDA	Infrared Data Association
IRQ	interrupt request
ISA	industry standard architecture
ISDN	integrated services digital network
ISO	Industry Standards Organization
ISP	internet service provider
JBOD	just a bunch of disks

Acronym	Spelled Out
Kb	kilobit
KB	Kilobyte or knowledge base
LAN	local area network
LBA	logical block addressing
LC	Lucent connector
LCD	liquid crystal display
LDAP	lightweight directory access protocol
LED	light emitting diode
Li-on	lithium-ion
LPD/LPR	line printer daemon / line printer remote
LPT	line printer terminal
LVD	low voltage differential
MAC	media access control / mandatory access control
MAPI	messaging application programming interface
MAU	media access unit, media attachment unit
Mb	megabit
MB	megabyte
MBR	master boot record
MBSA	Microsoft Baseline Security Analyzer
MFD	multi-function device
MFP	multi-function product
MHz	megahertz
MicroDIMM	micro dual inline memory module
MIDI	musical instrument digital interface
MIME	multipurpose internet mail extension
MIMO	Multiple Input Multiple Output
MMC	Microsoft management console
MMX	multimedia extensions
MP3	Moving Picture Experts Group Layer 3 Audio
MP4	Moving Picture Experts Group Layer 4
MPEG	Moving Picture Experts Group
MSCONFIG	Microsoft configuration
MSDS	material safety data sheet
MUI	multilingual user interface
NAC	network access control
NAS	network-attached storage
NAT	network address translation
NetBEUI	networked basic input/output system extended user interface
NetBIOS	networked basic input/output system
NFS	network file system

Acronym	Spelled Out
NIC	network interface card
NiCd	nickel cadmium
NiMH	nickel metal hydride
NLX	new low-profile extended
NNTP	network news transfer protocol
NTFS	new technology file system
NTLDR	new technology loader
NTP	Network Time Protocol
OCR	optical character recognition
OEM	original equipment manufacturer
OLED	Organic Light Emitting Diode
OS	operating system
PAN	personal area network
PATA	parallel advanced technology attachment
PC	personal computer
PCI	peripheral component interconnect
PCIe	peripheral component interconnect express
PCIX	peripheral component interconnect extended
PCL	printer control language
PCMCIA	Personal Computer Memory Card International Association
PDA	personal digital assistant
PGA	pin grid array
PGA2	pin grid array 2
PII	Personally Identifiable Information
PIN	personal identification number
PKI	public key infrastructure
PnP	plug and play
POP3	post office protocol 3
PoS	Point of Sale
POST	power-on self test
POTS	plain old telephone service
PPP	point-to-point protocol
PPTP	point-to-point tunneling protocol
PRI	primary rate interface
PROM	programmable read-only memory
PS/2	personal system/2 connector
PSTN	public switched telephone network
PSU	power supply unit
PVC	permanent virtual circuit
PXE	preboot execution environment

Acronym	Spelled Out
QoS	quality of service
RAID	redundant array of independent (or inexpensive) discs
RAM	random access memory
RAS	remote access service
RDP	Remote Desktop Protocol
RDRAM	RAMBUS® dynamic random access memory
RF	radio frequency
RFI	radio frequency interference
RGB	red green blue
RIMM	RAMBUS® inline memory module
RIP	routing information protocol
RIS	remote installation service
RISC	reduced instruction set computer
RJ	registered jack
RJ-11	registered jack function 11
RJ-45	registered jack function 45
RMA	returned materials authorization
ROM	read only memory
RS-232 or RS-232C	recommended standard 232
RTC	real-time clock
S.M.A.R.T.	self-monitoring, analysis, and reporting technology
SAN	storage area network
SAS	Serial Attached SCSI
SATA	serial advanced technology attachment
SC	subscription channel
SCP	secure copy protection
SCSI	small computer system interface
SCSI ID	small computer system interface identifier
SD card	secure digital card
SDRAM	synchronous dynamic random access memory
SEC	single edge connector
SFC	system file checker
SFF	Small Form Factor
SGRAM	synchronous graphics random access memory
SIMM	single inline memory module
SLI	scalable link interface or system level integration or scanline interleave mode
SMB	server message block or small to midsize business
SMTP	simple mail transfer protocol
SNMP	simple network management protocol
SoDIMM	small outline dual inline memory module

Acronym	Spelled Out
SOHO	small office/home office
SP	service pack
SP1	service pack 1
SP2	service pack 2
SP3	service pack 3
SP4	service pack 4
SPDIF	Sony-Philips digital interface format
SPGA	staggered pin grid array
SRAM	static random access memory
SSH	secure shell
SSID	service set identifier
SSL	secure sockets layer
ST	straight tip
STP	shielded twisted pair
SVGA	super video graphics array
SXGA	super extended graphics array
TB	terabyte
TCP	transmission control protocol
TCP/IP	transmission control protocol/internet protocol
TDR	time domain reflectometer
TFTP	trivial file transfer protocol
TKIP	Temporal Key Integrity Protocol
TPM	trusted platform module
UAC	user account control
UART	universal asynchronous receiver transmitter
UDF	user defined functions or universal disk format or universal data format
UDMA	ultra direct memory access
UDP	user datagram protocol
UNC	universal naming convention
UPS	uninterruptible power supply
URL	uniform resource locator
USB	universal serial bus
USMT	user state migration tool
UTP	unshielded twisted pair
UXGA	ultra extended graphics array
VESA	Video Electronics Standards Association
VFAT	virtual file allocation table
VGA	video graphics array
VM	Virtual Machine
VoIP	voice over internet protocol

Acronym	Spelled Out
VPN	virtual private network
VRAM	video random access memory
WAN	wide area network
WAP	wireless application protocol
WEP	wired equivalent privacy
WIFI	wireless fidelity
WINS	windows internet name service
WLAN	wireless local area network
WPA	wireless protected access
WUXGA	wide ultra extended graphics array
XGA	extended graphics array
ZIF	zero-insertion-force
ZIP	zigzag inline package

F

Entry Points for Startup Processes

This appendix contains a summary of the entry points that can affect Windows 7/Vista startup. The entry points include startup folders, Group Policy folders, the Scheduled Tasks folder, and registry keys.

Programs and shortcuts to programs are stored in these startup folders:

▲ C:\Users*username*\AppData\Roaming\Microsoft\Windows\Start\Menu\
Programs\Startup
▲ C:\ProgramData\Microsoft\Windows\Start Menu\Programs\Startup

Startup and shutdown scripts used by Group Policy are stored in these folders:

▲ C:\Windows\System32\GroupPolicy\Machine\Scripts\Startup
▲ C:\Windows\System32\GroupPolicy\Machine\Scripts\Shutdown
▲ C:\Windows\System32\GroupPolicy\User\Scripts\Logon
▲ C:\Windows\System32\GroupPolicy\User\Scripts\Logoff

Scheduled tasks are stored in this folder:

▲ C:\Windows\System32\Tasks

To see a list of scheduled tasks, enter the **schtasks** command in a command prompt window.

These keys cause an entry to run once and only once at startup:

▲ HKLM\Software\Microsoft\Windows\CurrentVersion\RunOnce
▲ HKLM\Software\Microsoft\Windows\CurrentVersion\RunServiceOnce
▲ HKLM\Software\Microsoft\Windows\CurrentVersion\RunServicesOnce
▲ HKCU\Software\Microsoft\Windows\CurrentVersion\RunOnce

Group Policy places entries in the following keys to affect startup:

▲ HKCU\Software\Microsoft\Windows\CurrentVersion\Policies\Explorer\Run
▲ HKLM\Software\Microsoft\Windows\CurrentVersion\Policies\Explorer\Run

Windows loads many DLL programs from the following key, which is sometimes used by malicious software. Don't delete one unless you know it's causing a problem:

▲ HKLM\Software\Microsoft\Windows\CurrentVersion\ShellServiceObjectDelayLoad

Entries in the keys listed next apply to all users and hold legitimate startup entries. Don't delete an entry unless you suspect it to be bad:

▲ HKLM\Software\Microsoft\Windows\CurrentVersion\Run
▲ HKCU\Software\Microsoft\Windows NT\CurrentVersion\Windows
▲ HKCU\Software\Microsoft\Windows NT\CurrentVersion\Windows\Run
▲ HKCU\Software\Microsoft\Windows\CurrentVersion\Run

These keys and their subkeys contain entries that pertain to background services that are sometimes launched at startup:

▲ HKLM\Software\Microsoft\Windows\CurrentVersion\RunService
▲ HKLM\Software\Microsoft\Windows\CurrentVersion\RunServices

The following key contains a value named BootExecute, which is normally set to autochk. It causes the system to run a type of Chkdsk program to check for hard drive integrity when it was previously shut down improperly. Sometimes another program adds itself to this value, causing a problem. For more information about this situation, see the Microsoft Knowledge Base article 151376, "How to Disable Autochk If It Stops Responding During Reboot" at *support.microsoft.com*.

◢ HKLM\System\CurrentControlSet\Control\Session Manager

Here is an assorted list of registry keys that have all been known to cause various problems at startup. Remember, before you delete a program entry from one of these keys, research the program filename so that you won't accidentally delete something you want to keep:

◢ HKCU\Software\Microsoft\Command
◢ HKCU\Software\Microsoft\Command Processor\AutoRun
◢ HKCU\Software\Microsoft\Windows\CurrentVersion\RunOnce\Setup
◢ HKCU\Software\Microsoft\Windows NT\CurrentVersion\Windows\load
◢ HKLM\Software\Microsoft\Windows NT\CurrentVersion\Windows\AppInit_DLLs
◢ HKLM\Software\Microsoft\Windows NT\CurrentVersion\Winlogon\System
◢ HKLM\Software\Microsoft\Windows NT\CurrentVersion\Winlogon\Us
◢ HKCR\batfile\shell\open\command
◢ HKCR\comfile\shell\open\command
◢ HKCR\exefile\shell\open\command
◢ HKCR\htafile\shell\open\command
◢ HKCR\piffile\shell\open\command
◢ HKCR\scrfile\shell\open\command

Finally, check out the subkeys in the following key, which apply to 32-bit programs installed in a 64-bit version of Windows:

◢ HKLM\Software\Wow6432Node

Other ways in which processes can be launched at startup:

◢ Services can be set to launch at startup. To manage services, use the Services Console (services.msc).
◢ Device drivers are launched at startup. For a listing of installed devices, use Device Manager (devmgmt.msc) or the System Information Utility (msinfo32.exe).

Answers to Chapter Review Questions

This appendix provides the answers to the review questions found at the end of every chapter in the book. It's a good way for you to test your readiness for CompTIA's A+ 220-801 and 220-802 Certification exams. If you find you've missed several questions, review that content in the book until you feel you're ready for the real exam.

CHAPTER 1

1. b
2. a
3. d
4. c
5. c
6. True
7. False
8. True
9. False
10. False
11. form factors
12. Direct current (DC), DC, Direct current
13. C
14. System
15. Material Safety Data Sheet (MSDS), Material Safety Data Sheet, MSDS

CHAPTER 2

1. d
2. a
3. c
4. b
5. c
6. True
7. True
8. False
9. True
10. False
11. front panel
12. standoffs
13. heat sink
14. Thermal
15. Overclocking

CHAPTER 3

1. d
2. a
3. a
4. b
5. c
6. True
7. False
8. True
9. False
10. False
11. operating system (OS)
12. taskbar
13. service
14. file extension
15. library

CHAPTER 4

1. c
2. b
3. d
4. b
5. c
6. True
7. True
8. False
9. True
10. False
11. North Bridge
12. traces
13. PCI Express (PCIe), PCIe, PCI Express
14. CMOS (complementary metal-oxide semiconductors), CMOS, complementary metal-oxide semiconductor
15. Unified Extensible Firmware Interface (UEFI), Unified Extensible Firmware Interface, UEFI

CHAPTER 5

1. d
2. b
3. b
4. d
5. a
6. False
7. False
8. False
9. True
10. True
11. graphics processing unit (GPU), GPU, graphics processing unit
12. frequency
13. Centrino
14. BIOS
15. memory bank

CHAPTER 6

1. b
2. b
3. c
4. c
5. b
6. True
7. True
8. True
9. False
10. False
11. magnetic
12. host adapter
13. terminating resistor
14. autodetection
15. Fault tolerance

CHAPTER 7

1. a
2. d
3. d
4. c
5. a
6. False
7. True
8. False
9. True
10. False
11. custom
12. workgroup
13. Active Directory
14. domain
15. Device Manager

CHAPTER 8

1. c
2. a
3. b
4. d
5. c
6. True
7. False
8. False
9. True
10. True
11. biometric
12. stylus
13. touch screen
14. light-emitting diode (LED), LED, light-emitting diode
15. formatting

CHAPTER 9

1. c
2. b
3. d
4. a
5. b
6. False
7. True
8. True
9. False
10. False
11. expert
12. ticket
13. copyright
14. piracy
15. site license

CHAPTER 10

1. b
2. d
3. c
4. b
5. a
6. True
7. False
8. False
9. True
10. True
11. system image
12. file system
13. cmd.exe
14. mounted drive
15. basic

CHAPTER 11

1. a
2. c
3. b

4. b
5. a
6. False
7. False
8. True
9. True
10. True
11. process
12. registry
13. Windows Experience Index
14. memory leak
15. ReadyBoost

CHAPTER 12

1. c
2. d
3. a
4. c
5. b
6. True
7. False
8. False
9. True
10. False
11. Blue screen
12. System File Checker (SFC), SFC, System File Checker
13. 38
14. Taskkill
15. Default program

CHAPTER 13

1. b
2. d
3. a
4. c
5. b
6. True

7. False

8. True

9. True

10. False

11. chassis air guide (CAG)

12. artifacts

13. degauss

14. uninterruptible power supply (UPS)

15. zero-fill

CHAPTER 14

1. a

2. d

3. a

4. c

5. b

6. True

7. False

8. True

9. False

10. True

11. soft

12. WinLoad

13. F8

14. diskpart

15. recovery image

CHAPTER 15

1. c

2. a

3. d

4. b

5. d

6. True

7. False

8. False

9. True

10. True

11. C

12. subnet mask

13. SIM (Subscriber Identification Module), SIM, Subscriber Identification Module

14. filtering

15. multiple input/multiple output (MIMO), MIMO, multiple input/multiple output

CHAPTER 16

1. a

2. c

3. d

4. b

5. d

6. False

7. True

8. True

9. False

10. False

11. star

12. Full

13. hub

14. crimper

15. patch panel

CHAPTER 17

1. b

2. d

3. a

4. c

5. a

6. True

7. True

8. False

9. True

10. False

11. Wake on LAN (WoL), Wake on LAN, WoL

12. Share

13. Users

14. local shares

15. reverse lookup

CHAPTER 18

1. d
2. b
3. a
4. d
5. c
6. False
7. True
8. False
9. True
10. True
11. BitLocker Encryption
12. smart card
13. social engineering
14. Grayware
15. rootkit

CHAPTER 19

1. a
2. c
3. d
4. b
5. a
6. True
7. False
8. False
9. True
10. False
11. inverter
12. docking station
13. profile

14. DDR3

15. ghost

CHAPTER 20

1. d
2. a
3. b
4. a
5. a
6. False
7. False
8. True
9. True
10. True
11. Jailbreaking
12. multitouch
13. accelerometer
14. thin client
15. Type 1

CHAPTER 21

1. c
2. b
3. d
4. c
5. a
6. True
7. True
8. False
9. False
10. True
11. LPT (line printer terminal), LPT, line printer terminal
12. calibration
13. local
14. spooling
15. print server

GLOSSARY

This glossary defines terms related to managing and maintaining a personal computer.

100BaseT An Ethernet standard that operates at 100 Mbps and uses twisted-pair cabling up to 100 meters (328 feet). *Also called* Fast Ethernet. Variations of 100BaseT are 100BaseTX and 100BaseFX.

4G (Fourth Generation) The ability to use a cell phone to browse the web, stream music and video, play online games, and use instant messaging and video conferencing. 4G offers the fastest speed for cellular data.

4-pin motherboard auxiliary connector A connector on the motherboard used to provide additional power to the processor other than that provided by the P1 connector.

8-pin motherboard auxiliary connector A connector on the motherboard used to provide additional power to the processor other than that provided by the P1 connector or the earlier 4-pin auxiliary connector.

10-foot user interface Applications software used on large screens to control output display menus and other clickable items in fonts large enough to read at a distance of 10 feet.

20-pin P1 connector Used by an older ATX power supply and motherboard and provided +3.3 volts, +5 volts, +12 volts, –12 volts, and an optional and rarely used –5 volts.

24-pin P1 connector Used by ATX Version 2.2 power supply and motherboard and provides additional power for PCI Express slots.

25-pin SCSI connector A SCSI connector used by narrow SCSI that looks like a parallel port connector.

32-bit operating system Type of operating system that processes 32 bits at a time.

50-pin SCSI connector A type of SCSI connector, *also called* an A connector, used by narrow SCSI.

6TO4 In TCP/IP version 6, an older tunneling protocol being replaced by the more powerful Teredo or ISATAP protocols. Tunnels are used by IPv6 to transport IPv6 packets over an IPv4 network.

64-bit operating system Type of operating system that processes 64 bits at a time.

68-pin SCSI connector A type of SCSI connector, *also called* a P connector, used by wide SCSI.

1394a *See* FireWire 400.

1394b *See* FireWire 800.

802.11 a/b/g/n The collective name for the IEEE 802.11 standards for local wireless networking, which is the technical name for Wi-Fi.

A+ Certification A certification awarded by CompTIA (The Computer Technology Industry Association) that measures a PC technician's knowledge and skills.

AC adapter A device that converts AC to DC and can use regular house current to power a notebook computer.

Accelerated Graphics Port (AGP) A 32-bit wide bus standard developed specifically for video cards that includes AGP 1x, 2x, 3x, 4x, and 8x standards. AGP has been replaced by the PCI Express standards.

accelerometer A type of gyroscope used in mobile devices to sense the physical position of the device.

Action Center A tool in Windows 7 that lists errors and issues that need attention.

Active Directory A Windows server directory database and service that is used in managing a domain to allow for a single point of administration for all shared resources on a network, including files, peripheral devices, databases, web sites, users, and services.

active partition The primary partition on the hard drive that boots the OS. Windows calls the active partition the system partition.

ActiveX control A small app or add-on that can be downloaded from a web site along with a web page and is executed by a browser to enhance the web page.

adapter address *See* MAC (Media Access Control) address.

ad hoc mode A type of physical arrangement of the connection between computers where each wireless computer serves as its own wireless access point and is responsible for securing each connection.

administrative shares The folders that are shared by default on a network domain that administrator accounts can access.

Administrative tools A group of tools accessed through the Control Panel that you can use to manage the local computer or other computers on the network.

administrator account In Windows, a user account that grants to the administrator(s) rights and privileges to all hardware and software resources, such as the right to add, delete, and change accounts and to change hardware configurations.

Administrators group A type of user group. When a user account is assigned to this group, the account is granted rights that are assigned to an administrator account.

Advanced Configuration and Power Interface (ACPI) Standards used by system BIOS and other components that define power states for the system and processor used to conserve power when the system is not in full use.

Advanced Options menu A Windows menu that appears when you press F8 when Windows starts. The menu can be used to troubleshoot problems when loading Windows. In Windows 7/Vista, the menu is called the Advanced Boot Options menu.

adware Software installed on a computer that produces pop-up ads using your browser; the ads are often based on your browsing habits.

Aero Peek A Windows 7 feature that gives you a peek at the desktop when you move the mouse over the rectangle to the far-right side of the taskbar.

Aero Shake A Windows 7 feature that minimizes all other windows except the one you shake.

Aero Snap A Windows 7 feature that automatically maximizes a window when you drag it to the top of the desktop or snaps the window to the side of the screen when you drag it to a side.

Aero user interface The Windows 7/Vista 3D user interface that gives a glassy appearance. *Also called* Aero glass.

AES (Advances Encryption Standard) An encryption standard used by WPA2 and is currently the strongest encryption standard used by Wi-Fi.

airplane mode A setting within a mobile device that disables all three antennas so the device can neither transmit nor receive signals.

all-in-one computer A computer that has the monitor and computer case built together and uses components that are common to both a notebook and a desktop computer.

alternate IP address When configuring TCP/IP in Windows, the static IP address that Windows uses if it cannot lease an IP address from a DHCP server.

alternating current (AC) Current that cycles back and forth rather than traveling in only one direction. In the United States, the AC voltage from a standard wall outlet is normally between 110 and 115 V. In Europe, the standard AC voltage from a wall outlet is 220 V.

A Male connector A common type of USB connector that is flat and wide and connects an A Male USB port on a computer or USB hub.

amp A measure of electrical current.

Android An operating system used on mobile devices that is based on the Linux OS and supported by Google.

anonymous users User accounts that have not been authenticated on a computer.

ANSI (American National Standards Institute) A nonprofit organization dedicated to creating trade and communications standards.

answer file A text file that contains information that Windows requires in order to do an unattended installation.

antispyware software Software used to remove spyware and adware.

antistatic bags Static shielding bags that new computer components are shipped in.

antistatic gloves Gloves designed to prevent an ESD (electrostatic discharge) between you and a device, as you pick it up and handle it.

antistatic wrist strap *See* ground bracelet.

antivirus (AV) software Utility programs that prevent infection or scan a system to detect and remove viruses. McAfee Associates' VirusScan and Norton AntiVirus are two popular AV packages.

anycast address Using TCP/IP version 6, a type of IP address used by routers and identifies multiple destinations. Packets are delivered to the closest destination.

App Store The app on an Apple device (iPad, iPhone, or iPod touch) that can be used to download content from the iTunes Store web site (*itunes.apple.com*).

Apple ID A user account that uses a valid email address and password and is associated with a credit card number that allows you to download iOS updates and patches, apps, and multimedia content.

application proxy A program that is intended to work on a client computer when the complete application is on a server.

application virtualization Using this virtualization, a virtual environment is created in memory for an application to virtually install itself.

Application Virtualization (App-V) Software by Microsoft used for application virtualization.

artifacts Horizontally torn images on a computer screen.

ATAPI (Advanced Technology Attachment Packet Interface) An interface standard, part of the IDE/ATA standards, that allows tape drives, optical drives, and other drives to be treated like an IDE hard drive by the system.

ATA Secure Erase Standards developed by the American National Standard Institute (ANSI) that dictate how to securely erase data from solid-state devices such as a USB flash drive or SSD drive in order to protect personal privacy.

ATX (Advanced Technology Extended) The most common form factor for PC systems presently in use, originally introduced by Intel in 1995. ATX motherboards and cases make better use of space and resources than did the earlier AT form factor.

ATX12V power supply An ATX Version 2.1 power supply that provides a 12 V power cord with a 4-pin connector to be used by the auxiliary 4-pin power connector on motherboards used to provide extra power for processors.

Authenticated Users group All user accounts that have been authenticated to access the system except the Guest account. *Compare to* anonymous users.

Automated System Recovery (ASR) The Windows XP process that allows you to restore an entire hard drive volume or logical drive to its state at the time the backup of the volume was made.

Automatic Private IP Address (APIPA) In TCP/IP Version 4, IP address in the address range 169.254.x.y, used by a computer when it cannot successfully lease an IP address from a DHCP server.

auto-switching A function of a laptop computer AC adapter that is able to automatically switch between 110 V and 220 V AC power.

Backup Operator A type of Windows user account group. When a user account belongs to this group, it can back up and restore any files on the system regardless of its having access to these files.

ball grid array (BGA) A connection via a processor that is soldered to the motherboard, and the two are always purchased as a unit.

bandwidth In relation to analog communication, the range of frequencies that a communications channel or cable can carry. In general use, the term refers to the volume of data that can travel on a bus or over a cable stated in bits per second (bps), kilobits per second (Kbps), or megabits per second (Mbps). *Also called* data throughput or line speed.

barcode reader Used to scan barcodes on products at the points of sale or when taking inventory.

base station A fixed transceiver and antenna used to create one cell within a cellular network.

basic disk The term Windows uses that applies to a hard drive when the drive is a stand-alone drive in the system. *Compare to* dynamic disk.

batch file A text file containing a series of OS commands. Autoexec.bat is a batch file.

bcdedit A command used to manually edit the BCD.

Berg power connector A type of power connector used by a power cord to provide power to a floppy disk drive.

best-effort protocol *See* connectionless protocol.

biometric device An input device that inputs biological data about a person; the data can identify a person's fingerprints, handprints, face, voice, eyes, and handwriting.

BIOS (basic input/output system) Firmware that can control much of a computer's input/output functions, such as communication with the keyboard and the monitor.

BIOS setup The program in system BIOS that can change the values in CMOS RAM. *Also called* CMOS setup.

BitLocker Encryption A utility in Windows 7/Vista Ultimate and Enterprise editions that is used to lock down a hard drive by encrypting the entire Windows volume and any other volume on the drive.

bitmap A bunch of bits in rows and columns.

blue screen error *See* blue screen of death (BSOD).

blue screen of death (BSOD) A Windows error that occurs in kernel mode, is displayed against a blue screen, and causes the system to halt. The error might be caused by problems with devices, device drivers, or a corrupted Windows installation. *Also called* a stop error.

Bluetooth PIN code   A code that may be required to complete the Bluetooth connection in a pairing process.

Blu-ray Disc (BD)   An optical disc technology that uses the UDF version 2.5 file system and a blue laser beam, which is shorter than any red beam used by DVD or CD discs. The shorter blue laser beam allows Blu-ray discs to store more data than a DVD.

B Male connector   A USB connector that connects a USB 1.x or 2.0 device such as a printer.

BNC connector   A connector used with thin coaxial cable. Some BNC connectors are T-shaped and called T-connectors. One end of the T connects to the NIC, and the two other ends can connect to cables or end a bus formation with a terminator.

Boot Configuration Data (BCD) file   A Windows 7/Vista file structured the same as a registry file and contains configuration information about how Windows is started. The BCD file replaces the Boot.ini file used in Windows 2000/XP.

boot loader menu   A startup menu that gives the user the choice of which operating system to load, such as Windows XP or Windows 7, which are both installed on the same system, creating a dual boot.

boot partition   The hard drive partition where the Windows OS is stored. The system partition and the boot partition may be different partitions.

boot sector virus   An infectious program that can replace the boot program with a modified, infected version, often causing boot and data retrieval problems.

boot.ini   A Windows 2000/XP hidden text file that contains information needed to start the boot and build the boot loader menu.

booting   The process of starting up a computer and loading an operating system.

bootrec   A command used to repair the BCD and boot sectors.

bootsect   A command used to repair a dual boot system.

bridge   A device that stands between two segments of a network and manages network traffic between them.

Briefcase   A system folder in Windows 9x/Me that is used to synchronize files between two computers.

broadband   A transmission technique that carries more than one type of transmission on the same medium, such as voice and DSL on a regular telephone line.

brownouts   Temporary reductions in voltage, which can sometimes cause data loss. *Also called* sags.

bus   The paths, or lines, on the motherboard on which data, instructions, and electrical power move from component to component.

bus network   An older topology whereby all computers are connected in a sequential line.

cable Internet   A broadband technology that uses cable TV lines and is always connected (always up).

cable tester   A tool used to test a cable to find out if it is good or to find out what type of cable it is if the cable is not labeled.

calibration   The process of checking and correcting the graduations of an instrument or device such as an inkjet printer.

call tracking   A system that tracks the dates, times, and transactions of help-desk or on-site PC support calls, including the problem presented, the issues addressed, who did what, and when and how each call was resolved.

capacitive touch screen   A touch screen that uses electrodes that sense the conductive properties of skin. *Compare to* resistive touch screen.

CardBus   A PCMCIA specification that improved on the earlier PC Card standards. It improved I/O speed, increased the bus width to 32 bits, and supported lower-voltage PC Cards, while maintaining backward compatibility with earlier standards. CardBus has been replaced with ExpressCard specifications.

CAS Latency   A method of measuring access timing to memory, which is the number of clock cycles required to write or read a column of data off a memory module. CAS stands for Column Access Strobe. *Compare to* RAS Latency.

case fan   A fan inside a computer case used to draw air out of or into the case.

CAT-3 (Category 3)   A rating used for UTP cables that is less expensive than the more popular CAT-5 cables.

CAT-5 (Category 5)   A rating used for UTP cables. CAT-5 or higher cabling is required for Fast Ethernet.

CAT-6 (Category 6)   A rating used for UTP cables that has less crosstalk than CAT-5 or CAT-5e cables. CAT-6 cables contain a plastic cord down the center of the cable that helps to prevent crosstalk.

CAT-6a (Category 6a)   A rating used for UTP cables that is thicker than CAT-6 and used by 10GBase-T (10-Gigabit Ethernet).

CD (compact disc)   An optical disc technology that uses a red laser beam and can hold up to 700 MB of data.

CDFS (Compact Disc File System) The 32-bit file system for CD discs and some CD-R and CD-RW discs. *See also* Universal Disk Format (UDF).

CDMA (Code Division Multiple Access) A protocol standard used by cellular WANs and cell phones.

cellular network A network that can be used when a wireless network must cover a wide area. The network is made up of cells, each controlled by a base station. *Also called* a cellular WAN.

cellular WAN *See* cellular network.

central processing unit (CPU) *Also called* a micro-processor or processor. The component where almost all processing of data and instructions takes place. The CPU receives data input, processes information, and executes instructions.

Centrino A technology used by Intel whereby the processor, chipset, and wireless network adapter are all interconnected as a unit, which improves laptop performance.

Certificate of Authenticity A sticker that contains the Windows product key.

chain of custody Documentation that tracks evidence used in an investigation and includes exactly what, when, and from whom the evidence was collected, the condition of the evidence, and how the evidence was secured while in possession of a responsible party.

channel A specific radio frequency within a broader frequency.

chassis air guide (CAG) A round air duct that helps to pull and direct fresh air from outside a computer case to the cooler and processor.

child directories *See* subdirectory.

chipset A group of chips on the motherboard that controls the timing and flow of data and instructions to and from the CPU.

Class A A license for a range of IPv4 IP addresses that defines a single octet, which is the network portion of the IP addresses in that license. The last three octets can be used for the host address or for subnetting the network.

Class B A license for a range of IPv4 IP addresses that defines the first two octets, which is used for the network portion of the IP address. The last two octets can be used for the host address or for subnetting the network.

Class C A license for a range of IPv4 IP addresses that defines the first three octets, which is used for the network portion of the IP address.

Class C fire extinguisher A fire extinguisher rated to put out electrical fires.

classful subnet mask In TCP/IP Version 4, the default subnet mask that is used if a network is not divided into subnets. It is called a classful subnet mask because the network portion of the IP address aligns with the class license. For example, 11111111.11111111.11111111.00000000 or 255.255.255.0 is the classful subnet mask for a Class C license.

classless subnet mask In TCP/IP Version 4, the subnet mask takes some bits of the host portion of the IP address for the network ID and does not align the network portion of the IP address with the network octets assigned by the class license. The subnet mask can have a mix of zeroes and ones in one octet or can contain all ones in an octet that was not leased by the class license, for example, 11111111.111111 11.11110000.00000000 or 255.255.240.0.

clean install Used to overwrite the existing operating system and applications when installing Windows on a hard drive.

client/server Two computers communicating using a local network or the Internet. One computer takes on the role of making requests from the other computer. A computer making a request from another is called the client and the one answering the request is called the server.

client-side desktop virtualization Using this virtualization, software installed on a desktop or laptop manages virtual machines used by the local user.

client-side virtualization Using this virtualization, a personal computer provides multiple virtual environments for applications.

cloud computing A service where server-side virtualization is delegated to a third-party service, and the Internet is used to connect server and client machines.

cluster One or more sectors that constitute the smallest unit of space on a disk for storing data (also referred to as a file allocation unit). Files are written to a disk as groups of whole clusters.

CMOS (complementary metal-oxide semiconductor) The technology used to manufacture microchips. CMOS chips require less electricity, hold data longer after the electricity is turned off, and produce less heat than earlier technologies. The configuration or setup chip is a CMOS chip.

CMOS battery The battery on the motherboard used to power the CMOS chip that holds BIOS setup data so that the data is retained when the computer is unplugged.

CMOS RAM Memory contained on the CMOS configuration chip.

CMOS setup *See* BIOS setup.

coaxial cable A cable that has a single copper wire down the middle and a braided shield around it.

cold boot *See* hard boot.

CompactFlash (CF) card A flash memory device that allows for sizes up to 137 GB, although current sizes range up to 32 GB.

compatibility mode A group of settings that can be applied to older drivers or applications that might cause them to work in Windows using a newer version of Windows than the one the programs were designed to use.

Complete PC Backup A Vista utility that can make a backup of the entire volume on which Vista is installed and can also back up other volumes. *Compare to* system image.

Component Services (COM+) A Microsoft Management Console snap-in that can be used to register components used by installed applications.

composite video port A port used by television or by a video card that is designed to send output to a TV. A composite port is round and has only a single pin in the center of the port.

Compressed (zipped) Folder A folder with a .zip extension that contains compressed files. When files are put in the folder, they are compressed. When files are moved to a regular folder, the files are decompressed.

computer infestation *See* malicious software.

Computer Management (Compmgmt.msc) A Windows console that contains several administrative tools used by support technicians to manage the local computer or other computers on the network.

computer name *See* host name.

connectionless protocol A TCP/IP protocol such as UDP that works at the OSI Transport layer and does not guarantee delivery by first connecting and checking where data is received. It might be used for broadcasting, such as streaming video or sound over the web, where guaranteed delivery is not as important as fast transmission. *Also called* a best-effort protocol. *Also see* UDP (User Datagram Protocol).

connection-oriented protocol In networking, a TCP/IP protocol that confirms a good connection has been made before transmitting data to the other end, verifies data was received, and resends it if it is not. An example of a connection-oriented protocol is TCP.

console A window that consolidates several Windows administrative tools.

contrast ratio The contrast between true black and true white on a screen.

Control Panel A window containing several small utility programs called applets that are used to manage hardware, software, users, and the system.

cooler A cooling system that sits on top of a processor and consists of a fan and a heat sink.

copyright The right to copy the work that belongs to the creators of the works or others to whom the creator transfers this right.

C-RIMM (Continuity RIMM) A placeholder module that fills a memory slot on the motherboard when the slot does not hold a RIMM in order to maintain continuity.

crimper A tool used to attach a terminator or connector to the end of a cable.

crossover cable A cable used to connect two like devices such as a hub to a hub or a PC to a PC (to make the simplest network of all).

CRT (cathode-ray tube) monitor A type of monitor first used in older television sets.

custom installation In the Windows setup program, the option used to overwrite the existing operating system and applications, producing a clean installation of the OS. The main advantage is that problems with the old OS are not carried forward.

data bus Lines of the bus, a system of pathway used for communication on the motherboard, used for data.

data cartridge A full-sized cartridge that holds data and is used in a tape drive.

data collector set A utility within the Windows 7 Performance Monitor and the Windows Vista Reliability and Performance Monitor that is used to create a set of counters to collect data about the system to measure performance. The results can be saved to a report for future use.

data path size The number of lines on a bus that can hold data, for example, 8, 16, 32, and 64 lines, which can accommodate 8, 16, 32, and 64 bits at a time.

Data Sources Open Database Connectivity (ODBC) A tool in the Administrative Tools group of Control Panel that is used to allow data files to be connected to applications they normally would not use.

data throughput *See* bandwidth.

DB-15 port A 15-pin female port that transmits analog video.

DDR *See* Double Data Rate SDRAM.

dead pixel A pixel on an LCD monitor that is not working and can appear as a small white, black, or colored spots on the computer screen.

default gateway The gateway a computer on a network will use to access another network unless it knows to specifically use another gateway for quicker access to that network.

default printer The designated printer to which Windows prints unless another printer is selected.

default program A program associated with a file extension.

defragment To rewrite a file to a disk in one contiguous chain of clusters, thus speeding up data retrieval.

degauss button A button on some older CRT monitors used to eliminate accumulated or stray magnetic fields.

degausser A machine that exposes a storage device to a strong magnetic field to completely erase the data on a magnetic hard drive or tape drive.

desktop The initial screen that is displayed when an OS has a GUI interface loaded.

desktop case A computer case that lies flat and sometimes serves double-duty as a monitor stand.

device driver Small programs stored on the hard drive and installed in Windows that tell Windows how to communicate with a specific hardware device such as a printer, network, port on the motherboard, or scanner.

Device Manager Primary Windows tool for managing hardware.

Devices and Printers window A window used in Windows 7 to manage and uninstall printers.

DHCP (Dynamic Host Configuration Protocol) A protocol used by a server to assign a dynamic IP address to a computer when it first attempts to initiate a connection to the network and requests an IP address.

DHCP client A computer of other device (such as a network printer) that requests an IP address from a DHCP server.

digital certificate A code used to authenticate the source of a file or document or to identify and authenticate a person or organization sending data over a network. The code is assigned by a certificate authority such as VeriSign and includes a public key for encryption. *Also called* digital ID or digital signature.

digitizer *See* graphics tablet.

digitizing tablet *See* graphics tablet.

DIMM (dual inline memory module) A miniature circuit board installed on a motherboard to hold memory. DIMMs can hold up to 16 GB of RAM on a single module.

direct current (DC) Current that travels in only one direction (the type of electricity provided by batteries). Computer power supplies transform AC to low DC.

Direct Rambus DRAM A memory technology by Rambus and Intel that uses a narrow network-type system bus. Memory is stored on a RIMM module. *Also called* RDRAM, Rambus, or Direct RDRAM.

Direct RDRAM *See* Direct Rambus DRAM.

direct thermal printer A type of thermal printer that burns dots onto special coated paper as was done by older fax machines.

DirectX A Microsoft software development tool that software developers can use to write multimedia applications such as games, video-editing software, and computer-aided design software.

Disk Cleanup A Windows utility that enables you to delete temporary files to free up space on a drive.

disk cloning *See* drive imaging.

diskpart A Windows command to manage hard drives, partitions, and volumes.

DisplayPort A port that transmits digital video and audio (not analog transmissions) and is slowly replacing VGA and DVI ports on personal computers.

distribution server A file server holding Windows setup files used to install Windows on computers networked to the server.

distribution share The collective files in the installation that include Windows, device drivers, and applications. The package of files is served up by a distribution server.

distributions Versions of Linux or UNIX published by an individual or organization.

DMA (direct memory access) transfer mode A transfer mode used by devices, including the hard drive, to transfer data to memory without involving the CPU.

DMZ Stands for "demilitarized zone" and refers to removing firewall protection from a computer or network within an organization of protected computers and networks.

DNS (Domain Name System or Domain Name Service) A distributed pool of information (called the name space) that keeps track of assigned host names and domain names and their corresponding IP addresses. DNS also refers to the system that allows a host to locate information in the pool and the protocol the system uses.

DNS client When Windows queries the DNS server for a name resolution, which means to find an IP address for a computer when the fully qualified domain name is known.

DNS server A Doman Name Service server that uses a DNS protocol to find an IP address for a computer when the fully qualified domain name is known. An Internet Service Provider is responsible for providing access to one or more DNS servers as part of the service it provides for Internet access.

dock The area at the bottom of the Android screen where up to four apps can be pinned.

docking port A connector on the bottom of the notebook to connect to a port replicator or docking station.

docking station A device that receives a notebook computer and provides additional secondary storage and easy connection to peripheral devices.

domain In Windows, a logical group of networked computers, such as those on a college campus, that share a centralized directory database of user account information and security for the entire domain.

domain name A name that identifies a network and appears before the period in a website address such as *microsoft.com*. A fully qualified domain name is sometimes loosely called a domain name. *Also see* fully qualified domain name.

Double Data Rate SDRAM (DDR SDRAM) A type of memory technology used on DIMMs that runs at twice the speed of the system clock. *Also called* DDR SDRAM, SDRAM II, and DDR.

double-sided A DIMM feature whereby memory chips are installed on both sides of a DIMM.

drive imaging Making an exact image of a hard drive, including partition information, boot sectors, operating system installation, and application software to replicate the hard drive on another system or recover from a hard drive crash. *Also called* disk cloning or disk imaging.

driver store The location where Windows stores a copy of the driver software when first installing a device.

DSL (Digital Subscriber Line) A telephone line that carries digital data from end to end, and is used as a type of broadband Internet access.

dual boot The ability to boot using either of two different OSs, such as Windows XP and Windows 7. *Also called* multiboot.

dual channels A motherboard feature that improves memory performance by providing two 64-bit channels between memory and the chipset. DDR, DDR2, and DDR3 DIMMs can use dual channels.

dual processors Two processor sockets on a server motherboard.

dual ranked Double-sided DIMMs that provide two 64-bit banks. The memory controller accesses first one bank and then the other. Dual-ranked DIMMs do not perform as well as single-ranked DIMMs.

dual voltage selector switch A switch on the back of the computer case where you can switch the input voltage to the power supply to 115 V used in the United States or 220 V used in other countries.

dumb terminal *See* zero client.

duplexing assembly Used in a duplex printer, a duplexing assembly contains several rollers, turns the paper around, and draws it back through the print process to print on the back of the paper.

duplex printer A printer that is able to print on both sides of the paper.

DVD (digital versatile disc or digital video disc) A technology used by optical discs that uses a red laser beam and can hold up to 17 GB of data.

DVI-A A DVI (Digital Visual Interface) video port that only transmits analog data.

DVI-D A DVI (Digital Visual Interface) video port that works only with digital monitors.

DVI-I A DVI (Digital Visual Interface) video port that supports both analog and digital monitors.

DVI (Digital Video Interface) port A port that transmits digital or analog video.

dxdiag.exe A command used to display information about hardware and diagnose problems with DirectX.

dynamic disks A way to partition one or more hard drives so that the drives can work together to store data in order to increase space for data or to provide fault tolerance or improved performance. *Also see* RAID. *Compare to* basic disk.

dynamic IP address An IP address assigned by a DHCP server for the current session only, and is leased when the computer first connects to a network. When the session is terminated, the IP address is returned to the list of available addresses. *Compare to* static IP address.

dynamic RAM (DRAM) The most common type of system memory, it requires refreshing every few milliseconds.

dynamic volume A volume type used with dynamic disks by which you can create a single volume that uses space on multiple hard drives.

ECC (error-correcting code) A chipset feature on a motherboard that checks the integrity of data stored on DIMMs or RIMMs and can correct single-bit errors in a byte. More advanced ECC schemas can detect, but not correct, double-bit errors in a byte.

electrostatic discharge (ESD) Another name for static electricity, which can damage chips and destroy motherboards, even though it might not be felt or seen with the naked eye.

elevated command prompt window A Windows command prompt window that allows commands that require administrative privileges.

email hoax An email message that is trying to tempt you to give out personal information or trying to scam you.

Emergency Repair Disk (ERD) (1) In Windows 2000, a record of critical information about your system that can be used to fix a problem with the OS. The ERD enables restoration of the Windows 2000 registry on your hard drive. (2) In Windows XP, a bootable floppy disk that can boot the system, bypassing the boot files stored in the root of drive C.

Encrypted File System (EFS) A way to use a key to encode a file or folder on an NTFS volume to protect sensitive data. Because it is an integrated system service, EFS is transparent to users and applications.

enhanced CAT-5 (CAT-5e) A improved version of CAT-5 cable that reduces crosstalk.

Enhanced IDE (EIDE) PATA standard that supports the configuration of four IDE devices in a system.

Enhanced Parallel Port (EPP) A type of parallel port that transmits data in both directions.

escalate When a technician passes a customer's problem to higher organizational levels because he or she cannot solve the problem.

ESD gloves *See* antistatic gloves.

ESD mat *See* ground mat.

ESD strap *See* ground bracelet.

Ethernet port *See* network port.

Event Viewer (Eventvwr.msc) A Windows tool useful for troubleshooting problems with Windows, applications, and hardware. It displays logs of significant events such as a hardware or network failure, OS failure, OS error messages, a device or service that has failed to start, or General Protection Faults.

Everyone group In Windows, the Authenticated Users group as well as the Guest account. When you share a file or folder on the network, Windows, by default, gives access to the Everyone group.

executive services In Windows, a group of components running in kernel mode that interfaces between the subsystems in user mode and the HAL.

expansion card A circuit board inserted into a slot on the motherboard to enhance the capability of the computer.

expert system Software that uses a database of known facts and rules to simulate a human expert's reasoning and decision-making processes.

ExpressCard The latest PCMCIA standard for notebook I/O cards that uses the PCI Express and USB 2.0 data transfer standards. Two types of Express-Cards are ExpressCard/34 (34mm wide) and ExpressCard/54 (54mm wide).

Extended Capabilities Port (ECP) A type of parallel port that is faster than an EPP port.

extended partition The only partition on a hard drive that can contain more than one logical drive. In Windows, a hard drive can have only a single extended partition. *Compare to* primary partition.

extension magnet brush A long-handled brush made of nylon fibers that are charged with static electricity to pick up stray toner inside a printer.

external SATA (eSATA) A standard for external drives based on SATA that uses a special external shielded SATA cable up to 2 meters long. eSATA is up to six times faster than USB or FireWire.

Fast Ethernet *See* 100BaseT.

FAT (file allocation table) A table on a hard drive or floppy disk used by the FAT file system that tracks the clusters used to contain a file.

fault tolerance The degree to which a system can tolerate failures. Adding redundant components, such as disk mirroring or disk duplexing, is a way to build in fault tolerance.

F connector A connector used with an RG-6 coaxial cable and is used for connections to a TV and has a single copper wire.

FDISK A Windows 9x/Me command used to create and manage partitions on a hard drive.

ferrite clamp A clamp installed on a network cable to protect against electrical interference.

fiber optic A dedicated, leased line used for Internet access that uses fiber-optic cable from the ISP to a residence or place of business.

fiber-optic cable Cable that transmits signals as pulses of light over glass or plastic strands inside protected tubing.

field replaceable unit (FRU) A component in a computer or device that can be replaced with a new component without sending the computer or device back to the manufacturer. Examples: power supply, DIMM, motherboard, hard disk drive.

file allocation unit   *See* cluster.

file association   The association between a data file and an application that is determined by the file extension.

file attributes   The properties assigned to a file. Examples of file attributes are read-only and hidden status.

file extension   A portion of the name of a file that indicates how the file is organized or formatted, the type of content in the file, and what program uses the file. In command lines, the file extension follows the filename and is separated from it by a period, for example, Msd.exe, where exe is the file extension.

Files and Settings Transfer Wizard   A Windows XP tool used to copy user data and settings from one computer to another.

file server   A computer dedicated to storing and serving up data files and folders.

file system   The overall structure that an OS uses to name, store, and organize files on a disk. Examples of file systems are NTFS and FAT32. Windows is always installed on a volume that uses the NTFS file system.

File Transfer Protocol (FTP)   *See* FTP (File Transfer Protocol).

filename   The first part of the name assigned to a file, which does not include the file extension. In DOS, the filename can be no more than eight characters long and is followed by the file extension. In Windows, a filename can be up to 255 characters.

FireWire 400   A data transmission standard used by computers and peripherals (for example, a video camera) that transmits at 400 Mbps. *Also called* 1394a.

FireWire 800   A data transmission standard used by computers and peripherals (for example, a video camera) that transmits at 800 Mbps. *Also called* 1394b.

FireWire port   A port used for high-speed multimedia devices such as camcorders. *Also called* an IEEE 1394 port.

firmware   Software that is permanently stored in a chip. The BIOS on a motherboard is an example of firmware.

fixboot   A Windows 7/Vista command that repairs the boot sector of the system partition.

fixmbr   A Windows 7/Vista command to repair the MBR.

flashing BIOS   The process of upgrading or refreshing the programming stored on a firmware chip.

flat panel monitor   *See* LCD (Liquid Crystal Display) monitor.

flip-chip land grid array (FCLGA)   A type of socket used by processors that has blunt protruding pins on the socket that connect with lands or pads on the bottom of the processor. The chips in the processor package are flipped over so that the top of the chip makes contact with the socket.

flip-chip pin grid array (FCPGA)   A type of socket used by processors that has holes aligned in rows to receive pins on the bottom of the processor. The chips in the processor are flipped over so that the top of the chip makes contact with the socket.

floppy disk drive (FDD)   A drive that can hold either a 5½ inch or 3¼ inch floppy disk. *Also called* floppy drive.

floppy drive   *See* floppy disk drive (FDD).

folder   *See* subdirectory.

folder attributes   The properties assigned to a folder. Examples of folder attributes are read-only and hidden status.

formatting   *See* high-level formatting.

form factor   A set of specifications on the size, shape, and configuration of a computer hardware component such as a case, power supply, or motherboard.

formatting   Preparing a hard drive volume, logical drive, or USB flash drive for use by placing tracks and sectors on its surface to store information (for example, FORMAT D:).

fragmented file   A file that has been written to different portions of the disk so that it is not in contiguous clusters.

front panel connectors   A group of wires running from the front of the computer case to the motherboard.

front panel header   A group of pins on a motherboard that connect to wires that are connected to the front panel of the computer case.

Front Side Bus (FSB)   *See* system bus.

FTP (File Transfer Protocol)   A TCP/IP protocol and application that uses the Internet to transfer files between two computers.

full duplex   Communication that happens in two directions at the same time.

fully connected mesh topology   A network where each node connects to every node on the network.

fully qualified domain name (FQDN)   Identifies a computer and the network to which it belongs and includes the computer name and domain name. For example, *jsmith.amazon.com*. Sometimes loosely referred to as a domain name.

fuser assembly A component in laser printing that uses heat and pressure to fuse the toner to paper.

gadget A mini-app that appears on the Windows 7 desktop or Vista sidebar.

gateway Any device or computer that network traffic can use to leave one network and go to a different network.

GDI (Graphics Device Interface) A component of Windows that uses a less-sophisticated method of communicating with a printer than other methods. GDI draws and formats the page, converting it to bitmap form, and then sends the almost-ready-to-print bitmap to the printer.

geotracking A mobile device routinely reports its position to Apple or Google at least twice a day, which makes it possible for these companies to track your device's whereabouts.

ghost cursor A trail on the screen left behind when you move the mouse.

Gigabit Ethernet A version of Ethernet that supports rates of data transfer up to 1 gigabit per second.

gigahertz (GHz) One thousand MHz, or one billion cycles per second.

global account Sometimes called a domain user account or network account, the account is used at the domain level, created by an administrator, and stored in the SAM (security accounts manager) database on a Windows domain controller.

global address *See* global unicast address.

global unicast address In TCP/IP Version 6, an IP address that can be routed on the Internet. *Also called* global address.

Globally Unique Identifier Partition Table (GUID or GPT) A partitioning system installed on a hard drive that can support 128 partitions and is recommended for drives larger than 2 TB.

Gmail An email service provided by Google at *mail .google.com*.

Google account A user account, which is a valid email address, that is registered on the Google Play web site (*play.google.com*) and is used to download content to an Android device.

Google Play The official source for apps, *also called* the Android marketplace, at *play.google.com*.

GPS (Global Positioning System) receiver A receiver that uses the system of 24 or more satellites orbiting the earth. The receiver locates four or more of these satellites, and from these four locations calculates its own position in a process called triangulation.

graphical user interface (GUI) An interface that uses graphics as compared to a command-driven interface.

graphics processing unit (GPU) A processor that manipulates graphic data to form the images on a monitor screen. A GPU can be embedded on a video card or on the motherboard or integrated within the processor.

graphics tablet An input device that can use a stylus to hand draw. It works like a pencil on the tablet and uses a USB port.

grayware A program that AV software recognizes to be potentially harmful or potentially unwanted.

ground bracelet A strap you wear around your wrist that is attached to the computer case, ground mat, or another ground so that ESD is discharged from your body before you touch sensitive components inside a computer. *Also called* static strap, ground strap, ESD bracelet.

ground mat A mat that dissipates ESD and is commonly used by technicians who repair and assemble computers at their workbenches or in an assembly line.

Group Policy (gpedit.msc) A console available only in Windows professional and business editions that is used to control what users can do and how the system can be used.

GSM (Global System for Mobile Communications) An open standard for cellular WANs and cell phones that uses digital communication of data and is accepted and used worldwide.

Guests group A type of user group in Windows. User accounts that belong to this group have limited rights to the system and are given a temporary profile that is deleted after the user logs off.

gyroscope A device that contains a disc that is free to move and can respond to gravity as the device is moved.

HAL (hardware abstraction layer) The low-level part of Windows, written specifically for each CPU technology, so that only the HAL must change when platform components change.

half duplex Communication between two devices whereby transmission takes place in only one direction at a time.

handheld tablet A computing device with a touch screen that is larger than a smartphone and has functions similar to a smartphone.

hard boot Restart the computer by turning off the power or by pressing the Reset button. *Also called* a cold boot.

hard disk drive (HDD) *See* hard drive.

hard drive The main secondary storage device of a computer. Two technologies are currently used by hard drives: magnetic and solid state. *Also called* hard disk drive (HDD).

hardware address *See* MAC (Media Access Control) address.

hardware-assisted virtualization (HAV) A feature of a processor whereby it can provide enhanced support for hypervisor software to run virtual machines on a system. The feature must be enabled in BIOS setup.

hardware profile A group of settings that Windows keeps about a specific hardware configuration. A hardware profile can be manually configured in Windows XP, but Windows 7 and Vista automatically configure hardware profiles.

hardware RAID One of two ways to implement RAID. Hardware RAID is more reliable and better performing than software RAID, and is implemented using the BIOS on the motherboard or a RAID controller card.

HDMI (High Definition Multimedia Interface) port A digital audio and video interface standard currently used on televisions and other home theater equipment and expected to ultimately replace DVI.

HDMI connector A connector that transmits both digital video and audio and is used on most computers and televisions.

HDMI mini connector A smaller type of HDMI connector used for connecting some devices such as a smartphone to a computer.

heat sink A piece of metal, with cooling fins, that can be attached to or mounted on an integrated chip (such as the CPU) to dissipate heat.

hertz (Hz) Unit of measurement for frequency, calculated in terms of vibrations, or cycles per second. For example, for 16-bit stereo sound, a frequency of 44,000 Hz is used. *See also* megahertz.

hibernation A power-saving state that saves all work to the hard drive and powers down the system.

hidden share A folder whose folder name ends with a $ symbol. When you share the folder, it does not appear in the Network window or My Network Places window.

high-level formatting A process performed by the Windows Format program (for example, FORMAT C:/S), the Windows installation program, or the Disk Management utility. The process creates the boot record, file system, and root directory on a hard drive volume or logical drive, a floppy disk, or USB flash drive.

Also called formatting, OS formatting, or operating system formatting. *Compare to* low-level formatting.

high-touch using a standard image A strategy to install Windows that uses a standard image for the installation. A technician must perform the installation on the local computer. *Also see* standard image.

high-touch with retail media A strategy to install Windows where all the work is done by a technician sitting at the computer using Windows setup files. The technician also installs drivers and applications after the Windows installation is finished.

HKEY_CLASSES_ROOT (HKCR) A Windows registry key that stores information to determine which application is opened when the user double-clicks a file.

HKEY_CURRENT_CONFIG (HKCC) A Windows registry key that contains information about the hardware configuration that is used by the computer at startup.

HKEY_CURRENT_USER (HKCU) A Windows registry key that contains data about the current user. The key is built when a user logs on using data kept in the HKEY_USERS key and data kept in the Ntuser.dat file of the current user.

HKEY_LOCAL_MACHINE (HKLM) An important Windows registry key that contains hardware, software, and security data. The key is built using data taken from the SAM hive, the Security hive, the Software hive, and the System hive and from data collected at startup about the hardware.

HKEY_USERS (HKU) A Windows registry key that contains data about all users and is taken from the Default hive.

homegroup A type of peer-to-peer network where each computer shares files, folders, libraries, and printers with other computers in the homegroup. Access to the homegroup is secured using a homegroup password.

Home Theater PC (HTPC) A PC that is designed to play and possibly record music, photos, movies, and video on a television or extra-large monitor screen.

host adapter The circuit board that controls a SCSI bus supporting as many as seven or fifteen separate devices. The host adapter controls communication between the SCSI bus and the computer.

host name A name that identifies a computer, printer, or other device on a network, which can be used instead of the computer's IP address to address the computer on the network. The host name together with the domain name is called the fully qualified domain name. *Also called* computer name.

Hosts file   A file in the C:\Windows\System32\drivers\ etc folder that contains computer names and their associated IP addresses on the local network. The file has no file extension.

hot-plugging   Plugging in a device while the computer is turned on. The computer will sense the device and configure it without rebooting. In addition, the device can be unplugged without an OS error. *Also called* hot-swapping.

hot swappable   The ability to plug or unplug devices without first powering down the system. USB devices are hot swappable.

hot-swapping   Allows you to connect and disconnect a device while the system is running.

HTC Sense   A comprehensive user interface that incorporates the older TouchFLO technology used by mobile devices.

HTPC case   A case used to accommodate a home theater PC and must be small enough to fit on a shelf in an entertainment center.

HTTP (Hypertext Transfer Protocol)   The TCP/IP protocol used for the World Wide Web and used by web browsers and web servers to communicate.

HTTPS (HTTP secure)   The HTTP protocol working with a security protocol such as Secure Sockets Layer (SSL) or Transport Layer Security (TLS), which is better than SSL, to create a secured socket that includes data encryption.

hub   A network device or box that provides a central location to connect cables and distributes incoming data packets to all other devices connected to it. *Compare to* switch.

hybrid hard drive   A hard drive that uses both magnetic and SSD technologies. The bulk of storage uses the magnetic component, and a storage buffer on the drive is made of an SSD component. Windows ReadyDrive supports hybrid hard drives.

hybrid network   A network where a star network uses multiple switches in sequence, and the switches form a bus network.

Hyper-Threading   The Intel technology that allows each logical processor within the processor package to handle an individual thread in parallel with other threads being handled by other processors within the package.

HyperTransport   The AMD technology that allows each logical processor within the processor package to handle an individual thread in parallel with other threads being handled by other processors within the package.

hypervisor   *See* virtual machine manager (VMM).

I/O shield   A plate installed on the rear of a computer case that provides holes for I/O ports coming off the motherboard.

iCloud   A web site by Apple (*www.icloud.com*) used to sync content on Apple devices in order to provide a backup of the content.

IDE (Integrated Drive Electronics or Integrated Device Electronics)   A hard drive whose disk controller is integrated into the drive, eliminating the need for a controller cable and thus increasing speed, as well as reducing price. *See also* EIDE.

IEEE 1284   A standard for parallel ports and cables developed by the Institute for Electrical and Electronics Engineers and supported by hardware manufacturers.

IEEE1394 port   *See* FireWire port.

image deployment   Installing a standard image on a computer.

ImageX   A program included in the Windows Automated Installation Kit that is used to create and modify standard images.

imaging drum   An electrically charged rotating drum found in laser printers.

IMAP4 (Internet Message Access Protocol, version 4)   A protocol used by an email server and client that allows the client to manage email stored on the server without downloading the email. *Compare to* POP3.

impact paper   Paper used by impact printers and comes as a box of fanfold paper or in rolls (used with receipt printers).

impact printer   A type of printer that creates a printed page by using a mechanism that touches or hits the paper.

Infrared (IR)   An outdated wireless technology that has been mostly replaced by Bluetooth to connect personal computing devices.

Infrastructure as a Service (IaaS)   A cloud computing service that provides only the hardware, which can include servers, Network attached Storage (NAS) devices, and networks.

inherited permissions   Permissions assigned by Windows that are attained from a parent object.

initialization files Text files that keep hardware and software configuration information, user preferences, and application settings and are used by the OS when first loaded and when needed by hardware, applications, and users.

in-place upgrade A Windows installation that is launched from the Windows desktop. The installation carries forward user settings and installed applications from the old OS to the new one. A Windows OS is already in place before the installation begins.

ink cartridge Cartridge in inkjet printers that holds the different colors of ink for the printer.

inkjet printer A type of ink dispersion printer that uses cartridges of ink. The ink is heated to a boiling point and then ejected onto the paper through tiny nozzles.

interface In TCP/IP Version 6, a node's attachment to a link. The attachment can be a physical attachment (for example, when using a network adapter) or a logical attachment (for example, when using a tunneling protocol). Each interface is assigned an IP address.

interface ID In TCP/IP Version 6, the last 64 bits or 4 blocks of an IP address that identify the interface.

internal components The main components installed in a computer case.

Internet appliance A type of thin client that is designed to make it easy for a user to connect to the Internet, browse the web, use email, and perform other simple chores on the Internet.

Internet Options A dialog box used to manage Internet Explorer settings.

Internet Protocol version 4 (IPv4) A group of TCP/IP standards that uses IP addresses that have 32-bits.

Internet Protocol version 6 (IPv6) A group of TCP/IP standards that uses IP addresses that have 128 bits.

Internet Service Provider (ISP) A commercial group that provides Internet access for a monthly fee; AOL, Earthlink, and Comcast are large ISPs.

intranet Any private network that uses TCP/IP protocols. A large enterprise might support an intranet that is made up of several local networks.

inverter A device that converts DC to AC.

iOS The operating system owned and developed by Apple and used for their various mobile devices.

iPad A handheld tablet developed by Apple.

IP address A 32-bit or 128-bit address used to uniquely identify a device or interface on a network that uses TCP/IP protocols. The first numbers identify the network; the last numbers identify a host. An example of a 32-bit IP address is 206.96.103.114. An example of a 128-bit IP address is 2001:0000:B80::D3:9C5A:CC.

Ipconfig (IP configuration) A command that displays TCP/IP configuration information and can refresh TCP/IP assignments to a connection including its IP address.

iPhone A smartphone developed by Apple.

iPod touch A multimedia recorder and player developed by Apple.

ISATAP In TCP/IP Version 6, a tunneling protocol that has been developed for IPv6 packets to travel over an IPv4 network and stands for Intra-Site Automatic Tunnel Addressing Protocol.

ISDN (Integrated Services Digital Network) A broadband telephone line that can carry data at about five times the speed of regular telephone lines. Two channels (telephone numbers) share a single pair of wires. ISDN has been replaced by DSL.

ISO image A file format that has an .iso file extension and holds an image of all the data, including the file system that is stored on an optical disc. ISO stands for International Organization for Standardization.

iTunes Store The Apple web site at *itunes.apple.com* where apps, music, TV shows, movies, books, podcasts, and iTunes U content can be purchased and downloaded to Apple mobile devices.

iTunes U Content at the iTunes Store web site (*itunes.apple.com*) that contains lectures and even complete courses from many schools, colleges, and universities.

jailbreaking A process to break through the restrictions that only allow apps to an iOS device to be downloaded from the iTunes Store at *itunes.apple.com*. Gives the user root or administrative privileges to the operating system and the entire file system and complete access to all commands and features.

joule A measure of work or energy. One joule of energy produces one watt of power for one second.

jumper Two wires that stick up side by side on the motherboard or other device and are used to hold configuration information. The jumper is considered closed if a cover is over the wires and open if the cover is missing.

Jump List Appears when right-clicking an icon in the Windows 7 taskbar and provides access to some of the major functions of the program.

kernel The portion of an OS that is responsible for interacting with the hardware.

kernel mode A Windows "privileged" processing mode that has access to hardware components.

keyboard backlight A feature on some keyboards where the keys light up on the keyboard.

key fob A device, such as a type of smart card, that can fit conveniently on a key chain.

keylogger A type of spyware that tracks your keystrokes, including passwords, chat room sessions, email messages, documents, online purchases, and anything else you type on your PC. Text is logged to a text file and transmitted over the Internet without your knowledge.

keystone RJ-45 jack A jack that is used in an RJ-45 wall jack.

KVM (Keyboard, Video, and Mouse) switch A switch that allows you to use one keyboard, mouse, and monitor for multiple computers. Some KVM switches also include sound ports so that speakers and a microphone can be shared among multiple computers.

LAN (local area network) A computer network that covers only a small area, usually within one building.

land grid array (LGA) A feature of a CPU socket whereby pads, called lands, are used to make contact in uniform rows over the socket. *Compare to* pin grid array (PGA).

laptop *See* notebook.

laser printer A type of printer that uses a laser beam to control how toner is placed on the page and then uses heat to fuse the toner to the page.

Last Known Good Configuration In Windows, registry settings and device drivers that were in effect when the computer last booted successfully. These settings can be restored during the startup process to recover from errors during the last boot.

latency Delays in network transmissions resulting in slower network performance. Latency is measured by the round-trip time it takes for a data packet to travel from source to destination and back to source.

LC (local connector) connector A newer type of connector used by fiber-optic cables and can be used with either single-mode or multimode fiber-optic cables.

LCD (Liquid Crystal Display) monitor A monitor that uses LCD technology. LCD produces an image using a liquid crystal material made of large, easily polarized molecules. LCD monitors are flatter than CRT monitors and take up less desk space. *Also called* a flat-panel monitor.

LED (Light-Emitting Diode) A technology used in an LCD monitor that uses less mercury than earlier technologies.

Level 1 cache (L1 cache) Memory on the processor die used as a cache to improve processor performance.

Level 2 cache (L2 cache) Memory in the processor package but not on the processor die. The memory is used as a cache or buffer to improve processor performance. *Also see* Level 1 (L1) cache.

Level 3 cache (L3 cache) Cache memory further from the processor core than Level 2 cache but still in the processor package.

library In Windows 7, a collection of one or more folders that can be stored on different local drives or on the network.

license Permission for an individual to use a product or service. A manufacturer's method of maintaining ownership, while granting permission for use to others.

Lightweight Directory Access Protocol (LDAP) A protocol used by various client applications when the application needs to query a database.

limited account A type of Windows XP user group, also known as the Users group in Windows 2000. Accounts in this group have read-write access only on their own folders, read-only access to most system folders, and no access to other users' data. In Windows 7/Vista, a standard account is a limited account.

line-of-sight connectivity A connection used by satellites that requires no obstruction from mountains, trees, and tall buildings from the satellite dish to the satellite.

link In TCP/IP version 6, a local area network or wide area network bounded by routers. *Also called* local link.

link-local address *See* link-local unicast address.

link-local unicast address In TCP/IP Version 6, an IP address used for communicating among nodes in the same link and is allowed on the Internet. *Also called* local address and link-local address.

lite-touch, high-volume deployment A strategy that uses a deployment server on the network to serve up a Windows installation after a technician starts the process at the local computer.

Lithium Ion Currently the most popular type of battery popular with notebook computers that is more efficient than earlier types. Sometimes abbreviated as "Li-Ion" battery.

loadstate A command used by the User State Migration Tool (USMT) to copy user settings and data temporarily stored on a server or removable media to a new computer. *Also see* scanstate.

local account   A Windows user account that applies only to the local computer and cannot be used to access resources from other computers on the network. *Compare to* global account.

local area network (LAN)   A network bound by routers or other gateway devices.

local link   *See* link.

local printer   A printer connected to a computer by way of a port on the computer. *Compare to* network printer.

local shares   Folders on a computer that are shared with others on the network by using a folder's Properties box. Local shares are used with a workgroup and not with a domain.

logical drive   A portion or all of a hard drive extended partition that is treated by the operating system as though it were a physical drive or volume. Each logical drive is assigned a drive letter, such as drive F, and contains a file system. *Compare to* volume.

logical topology   The logical way computers connect on a network.

Logical Unit Number (LUN)   A number assigned to a logical device (such as a tray in a CD changer) that is part of a physical SCSI device, which is assigned a SCSI ID.

LoJack   A technology by Absolute Software used to track the whereabouts of a laptop computer and, if the computer is stolen, lock down access to the computer or erase data on it. The technology is embedded in the BIOS of many laptops.

loopback address   An IP address that indicates your own computer and is used to test TCP/IP configuration on the computer.

loopback plug   A device used to test a port in a computer or other device to make sure the port is working and might also test the throughput or speed of the port.

low-level formatting   A process (usually performed at the factory) that electronically creates the hard drive tracks and sectors and tests for bad spots on the disk surface.

LPT (Line Printer Terminal)   Assignments of system resources that are made to a parallel port and that are used to manage a print job. Two possible LPT configurations are referred to as LPT1: and LPT2:.

MAC (Media Access Control) address   A 48-bit (6-byte) hardware address unique to each NIC or onboard network controller that is assigned by the manufacturer at the factory and embedded on the device. The address is often printed on the adapter as hexadecimal numbers. An example is 00 00 0C 08 2F 35. *Also called* a physical address, an adapter address, or a hardware address.

magnetic hard drive   One of two technologies used by hard drives where data is stored as magnetic spots on disks that rotate at a high speed. The other technology is solid state drive (SSD).

main board   *See* motherboard.

malicious software   Any unwanted program that is transmitted to a computer without the user's knowledge and that is designed to do varying degrees of damage to data and software. Types of infestations include viruses, Trojan horses, worms, adware, spyware, keyloggers, browser hijackers, dialers, and downloaders. *Also called* malware, infestation, or computer infestation.

malware   *See* malicious software.

MAN (metropolitan area network)   A type of network that covers a large city or campus.

Master Boot Record (MBR)   The first sector on a hard drive, which contains the partition table and a program the BIOS uses to boot an OS from the drive.

master file table (MFT)   The database used by the NTFS file system to track the contents of a volume or logical drive.

Material Safety Data Sheet (MSDS)   A document that explains how to properly handle substances such as chemical solvents; it includes information such as physical data, toxicity, health effects, first aid, storage, disposal, and spill procedures.

megahertz (MHz)   One million Hz, or one million cycles per second. *See* hertz (Hz).

memory bank   The memory a processor addresses at one time. Today's desktop and notebook processors use a memory bank that is 64 bits wide.

Memory Diagnostics (mdsched.exe)   A Windows 7/ Vista utility used to test memory.

mesh network   Each node (a computer or other device) that uses the network is responsible for sending and receiving transmissions to any other node to which it wants to communicate with a central point of communication.

MicroATX (MATX)   A version of the ATX form factor. MicroATX addresses some new technologies that were developed after the original introduction of ATX.

Micro-A connector   A USB connector that has five pins and is smaller than the Mini-B connector. It is used on digital cameras, cell phones, and other small electronic devices.

Micro-B connector   A USB connector that has five pins and has a smaller height than the Mini-B connector. It is used on digital cameras, cell phones, and other small electronic devices.

microprocessor   *See* central processing unit (CPU).

Microsoft Assessment and Planning (MAP) Toolkit   Software that can be used by a system administrator from a network location to query hundreds of computers in a single scan to determine if a computer qualifies for a Windows upgrade.

Microsoft Exchange   A server application that can handle email, contacts, and calendars and is a popular application used by large corporations for employee email, contacts, and calendars.

Microsoft Management Console (MMC)   A Windows utility to build customized consoles. These consoles can be saved to a file with an .msc file extension.

MIDI (musical instrument digital interface)   A set of standards that are used to represent music in digital form. A MIDI port is a 5-pin DIN port that looks like a keyboard port, only larger.

Mini-B connector   A USB connector that has five pins and is often used to connect small electronic devices, such as a digital camera, to a computer.

MiniDin-6 connector   A 6-pin variation of the S-Video port and looks like a PS/2 connector used by a keyboard or mouse.

mini-HDMI connector   *See* HDMI mini connector.

Mini PCI   The PCI industry standard for desktop computer expansion cards, applied to a much smaller form factor for notebook expansion cards.

Mini PCI Express   A standard used for notebook internal expansion slots that follows the PCI Express standards applied to notebooks. *Also called* Mini PCIe.

Mini PCIe   *See* Mini PCI Express.

minicartridge   A tape drive cartridge that is only 3¼ × 2½ × ⅗ inches. It is small enough to allow two drives to fit into a standard 5 inch drive bay of a PC case.

mirrored volume   The term used by Windows for the RAID 1 level that duplicates data on one drive to another drive and is used for fault tolerance.

mirroring   A Windows XP technique to provide fault tolerance whereby one hard drive duplicates another hard drive.

modem port   A port used to connect dial-up phone lines to computers.

Molex power connector   A 4-pin power connector used to provide power to a PATA hard drive or optical drive.

motherboard   The main board in the computer, *also called* the system board. The CPU, ROM chips, DIMMs, RIMMs, and interface cards are plugged into the motherboard.

mount point   A folder that is used as a shortcut to space on another volume, which effectively increases the size of the folder to the size of the other volume. *Also see* mounted drive.

mounted drive   A volume that can be accessed by way of a folder on another volume so that the folder has more available space. *Also see* mount point.

mstsc   A command that allows you to start Remote Desktop Connection to remote in to your host computer using Remote Desktop.

MT-RJ (mechanical transfer registered jack) connector   A newer type of connector used by fiber-optic cables and can be used with either single-mode or multimode fiber-optic cables.

multiboot   *See* dual boot.

multicast address   In TCP/IP version 6, an IP address used when packets are delivered to all nodes on a network.

multicasting   In TCP/IP version 6, one host sends messages to multiple hosts, such as when the host transmits a video conference over the Internet.

multi-core processing   A processor technology whereby the processor housing contains two or more processor cores that operate at the same frequency but independently of each other.

Multimedia Messaging Service (MMS)   A technology that allows users to send text messages with photos, videos, or other multimedia content attached.

multimeter   A device used to measure the various attributes of an electrical circuit. The most common measurements are voltage, current, and resistance.

multiple input/multiple output (MIMO)   A feature of the IEEE 802.11n standard for wireless networking whereby two or more antennas are used at both ends of transmissions to improve performance.

multiplier   The factor by which the bus speed or frequency is multiplied to get the CPU clock speed.

multiprocessing   Two processing units installed within a single processor and first used by the Pentium processor.

multiprocessor platform A system that contains more than one processor. The motherboard has more than one processor socket and the processors must be rated to work in this multiprocessor environment.

multitouch A touch screen on a computer or mobile device that can handle a two-finger pinch.

name resolution The process of associating a character-based name with an IP address.

NAND flash memory The type of memory used in SSD drives. NAND stands for "Not AND" and refers to the logic used when storing a one or zero in the grid of rows and columns on the memory chip.

NAT (Network Address Translation) A TCP/IP protocol that substitutes the public IP address of the router for the private IP address of the other computer when these computers need to communicate on the Internet.

native resolution The actual (and fixed) number of pixels built into an LCD monitor. For the clearest display, always set the resolution to the native resolution.

navigation pane In Windows Explorer or the Computer window, pane on the left side of the window where devices, drives, and folders are listed. Double-click an item to drill down into the item.

nbtstat (NetBIOS over TCP/IP Statistics) A TCP/IP command that is used to display statistics about the NetBT protocol.

neighbors In TCP/IP version 6, two or more nodes on the same link.

netbook A low-end, inexpensive laptop with a small 9 or 10 inch screen and no optical drive that is generally used for Web browsing, email, and word processing by users on the go.

netstat (network statistics) A TCP/IP command that gives statistics about TCP/IP and network activity and includes several parameters.

net use A TCP/IP command that connects or disconnects a computer from a shared resource or can display information about connections.

net user A TCP/IP command used to manage user accounts.

network adapter *See* network interface card (NIC).

Network and Sharing Center The primary Windows 7/Vista utility used to manage network connections.

Network Attached Storage (NAS) A device that provides multiple bays for hard drives and an Ethernet port to connect to the network. The device is likely to support RAID.

network drive map Mounting a drive to a computer, such as drive E, that is actually hard drive space on another host computer on the network.

network interface card (NIC) An expansion card that plugs into a computer's motherboard and provides a port on the back of the card to connect a computer to a network. *Also called* a network adapter.

network multimeter A multifunctional tool that can test network connections, cables, ports, and network adapters.

network port A port used by a network cable to connect to the wired network.

network printer A printer that any user on the network can access, through its own network card and connection to the network, through a connection to a stand-alone print server, or through a connection to a computer as a local printer, which is shared on the network.

North Bridge That portion of the chipset hub that connects faster I/O buses (for example, the video bus) to the system bus. *Compare to* South Bridge.

notebook A portable computer that is designed for travel and mobility. Notebooks use the same technology as desktop PCs, with modifications for conserving voltage, taking up less space, and operating while on the move. *Also called* a laptop computer.

notification area An area to the right of the taskbar that holds the icons for running services; these services include the volume control and network connectivity. *Also called* the system tray or systray.

Nslookup (name space lookup) A TCP/IP command that lets you read information from the Internet name space by requesting information about domain name resolutions from the DNS server's zone data.

NTFS permissions A method to share a folder or file over a network and can apply to local users and network users. The folder or file must be on an NTFS volume. *Compare to* share permissions.

Ntldr The Windows XP program responsible for starting Windows XP, called the boot loader program.

octet In TCP/IP version 4, each of the four numbers that are separated by periods and make up a 32-bit IP address. One octet is 8 bits.

Offline Files A utility that allows users to work with files in the folder when the computer is not connected to the corporate network. When the computer is later connected, Windows syncs up the offline files and folders with those on the network.

ohm (Ω) The standard unit of measurement for electrical resistance. Resistors are rated in ohms.

OLED (Organic Light-emitting Diode) monitor A type of monitor that uses a thin LED layer or film between two grids of electrodes and does not use backlighting.

on-board ports Ports that are directly on the motherboard, such as a built-in keyboard port or on-board network port.

open source Operating system or application where the source code is available for free and anyone can modify and redistribute the source code.

operating system (OS) Software that controls a computer. An OS controls how system resources are used and provides a user interface, a way of managing hardware and software, and ways to work with files.

original equipment manufacturer (OEM) license A software license that only manufacturers or builders of personal computers can purchase to be installed only on a computer intended for sale.

OS boot record The first sector in the active partition. Windows XP uses this sector during the boot, but Windows 7/Vista does not.

overclocking Running a processor at a higher frequency than is recommended by the manufacturer, which can result in an unstable system, but is a popular thing to do when a computer is used for gaming.

packet A segment of data sent over a network as a unit that contains the data and information at the beginning of the segment that identifies the type of data, where it came from, and where it's going. *Also called* data packet or datagram.

pagefile.sys The Windows swap file that is used to hold the virtual memory that is used to enhance physical memory installed in a system.

pairing The process of two Bluetooth devices establishing connectivity.

PAN (personal area network) A small network consisting of personal devices at close range; the devices can include cell phones, PDAs, and notebook computers.

parallel ATA (PATA) An older IDE cabling method that uses a 40-pin flat or round data cable or an 80-conductor cable and a 40-pin IDE connector. *See also* serial ATA.

parallel port An outdated female 25-pin port on a computer that transmitted data in parallel, 8 bits at a time, and was usually used with a printer. The names for parallel ports are LPT1 and LPT2. Parallel ports have been replaced by USB ports.

parity An error-checking scheme in which a ninth, or "parity," bit is added. The value of the parity bit is set to either 0 or 1 to provide an even number of ones for even parity and an odd number of ones for odd parity.

parity error An error that occurs when the number of 1s in the byte is not in agreement with the expected number.

partition A division of a hard drive that can hold a volume. Using the MBR system, Windows can support up to four partitions on one hard drive.

partition table A table at the beginning of the hard drive that contains information about each partition on the drive. The partition table is contained in the Master Boot Record.

patch A minor update to software that corrects an error, adds a feature, or addresses security issues. *Also called* an update. *Compare to* service pack.

patch cable *See* straight-through cable.

patch panel A device that provides multiple network ports for cables that converge in one location such as an electrical closet or server room.

path A drive and list of directories pointing to a file such as C:\Windows\System32.

PC Card A card that uses a PC Card slot on a notebook and provides a port for peripheral devices or adds memory to the notebook. A PC Card is about the size of a credit card, but thicker.

PCI (Peripheral Component Interconnect) A bus common to desktop computers that uses a 32-bit wide or a 64-bit data path. Several variations of PCI exist. One or more notches on a PCI slot keep the wrong PCI cards from being inserted in the PCI slot.

PCI Express (PCIe) The latest evolution of PCI, which is not backward-compatible with earlier PCI slots and cards. PCIe slots come in several sizes, including PCIe x1, PCIe x4, PCIe x8, and PCIe x16.

PCL (Printer Control Language) A printer language developed by Hewlett-Packard that communicates to a printer how to print a page.

PCMCIA card Includes one or more variations of a PC Card to add memory to a notebook or provide ports for peripheral devices. For example, modem cards, network cards for wired or wireless network, sound cards, SCSI host adapters, FireWire controllers, USB controllers, flash memory adapter, TV tuner, and hard disks.

peer-to-peer (P2P) As applied to networking, a network of computers that are all equals, or peers. Each computer has the same amount of authority, and each can act as a server to the other computers.

Performance Information and Tools A Windows 7 utility that provides information to evaluate the performance of a system and to adjust Windows for best performance.

Performance Monitor A Microsoft Management Console snap-in that can track activity by hardware and software to measure performance.

permission propagation When Windows passes permissions from parent objects to child objects.

permissions Varying degrees of access assigned to a folder or file and given to a user account or user group. Access can include full control, write, delete, or read-only.

phishing (1) A type of identity theft where a person is baited into giving personal data to a web site that appears to be the web site of a reputable company with which the person has an account. (2) Sending an email message with the intent of getting the user to reveal private information that can be used for identify theft.

physical address *See* MAC (Media Access Control) address.

physical topology The physical arrangement of connections between computers.

pickup roller A part in a printer that pushes forward a sheet of paper from the paper tray.

Ping (packet internet groper) A TCP/IP command used to troubleshoot network connections. It verifies that the host can communicate with another host on the network.

pin grid array (PGA) A socket that has holes aligned in uniform rows around the socket to receive the pins on the bottom of the processor.

PIO (Programmed Input/Output) transfer mode A transfer mode that uses the CPU to transfer data from the hard drive to memory. PIO mode is slower than DMA mode.

pixel A small spot on a fine horizontal scan line. Pixels are illuminated to create an image on the monitor.

plasma monitor A type of monitor that provides high contrast with better color than LCD monitors. They work by discharging xenon and neon plasma on flat glass and don't contain mercury.

Platform as a Service (PaaS) A cloud computing service that provides the hardware and the operating system and is responsible for updating and maintaining both.

pointing stick *See* TrackPoint.

POP or POP3 (Post Office Protocol, version 3) The protocol that an email server and client use when the client requests the downloading of email messages. The most recent version is POP version 3. *Compare to* IMAP3.

port (1) As applied to services running on a computer, a number assigned to a process on a computer so that the process can be found by TCP/IP. *Also called* a port address or port number. (2) A physical connector, usually at the back of a computer, that allows a cable from a peripheral device, such as a printer, mouse, or modem, to be attached.

port address *See* port.

port filtering To open or close certain ports so they can or cannot be used. A firewall uses port filtering to protect a network from unwanted communication.

port forwarding A technique that allows a computer on the Internet to reach a computer on a private network using a certain port when the private network is protected by a firewall device using NAT. *Also called* tunneling.

port number *See* port.

port replicator A device designed to connect to a notebook computer in order to make it easy to connect the notebook to peripheral devices such as a full-sized monitor, keyboard, and AC power adapter.

port triggering When a firewall opens a port because a computer behind the firewall initiates communication on another port.

POST (power-on self test) A self-diagnostic program used to perform a simple test of the CPU, RAM, and various I/O devices. The POST is performed by startup BIOS when the computer is first turned on, and is stored in ROM-BIOS.

POST card A test card installed in a slot on the motherboard that is used to help discover and report computer errors and conflicts that occur when a computer is first turned on and before the operating system is launched.

POST diagnostic card *See* POST card.

PostScript A printer language developed by Adobe Systems that tells a printer how to print a page.

Power over Ethernet (PoE) A feature that might be available on high-end wired network adapters that allows power to be transmitted over Ethernet cable to remote devices.

power supply A box inside the computer case that receives power and converts it to provide power to the motherboard and other installed devices. Power supplies provide 3.3, 5, and 12 volts DC. *Also called* a power supply unit (PSU).

power supply tester A device that can test the output of each power cord coming from a power supply.

power supply unit (PSU) *See* power supply.

Power Users Group A type of user account group. Accounts assigned to this group can read from and write to parts of the system other than their own user profile folders, install applications, and perform limited administrative tasks.

Preboot eXecution Environment (PCE) Programming contained in the BIOS code on the motherboard used to start up the computer and search for a server on the network to provide a bootable operating system.

presentation virtualization Using this virtualization, a remote application running on a server is controlled by a local computer.

primary partition A hard disk partition that can contain only one volume. In Windows, a hard drive can have up to three primary partitions. *Compare to* extended partition.

principle of least privilege An approach where computer users are classified and the rights assigned are the minimum rights required to do their job.

print head The part in an inkjet or impact printer that moves across the paper, creating one line of the image with each pass.

Print Management A utility located in the Administrative Tool group in Windows 7/Vista professional and business editions that allows you to monitor and manage printer queues for all printers on the network.

print server Hardware or software that manages the print jobs sent to one or more printers on a network.

print spooler A queue for print jobs.

printer maintenance kit A kit purchased from a printer manufacturer that contains the parts, tools, and instructions needed to perform routine printer maintenance.

printer self-test page A test page that prints by using controls at the printer. The page allows you to eliminate a printer as a problem and usually prints test, graphics, and information about the printer such as the printer resolution and how much memory is installed.

Printers and Faxes window A window used in XP to manage and uninstall printers.

Printers window A window used in Windows Vista to manage and uninstall printers.

printui The Printer User Interface command used by administrators to manage printers on the local and remote computers.

privacy filter A device that fits over a monitor screen to prevent other people from viewing the monitor from a wide angle.

private IP address In TCP/IP version 4, an IP address that is used on a private network that is isolated from the Internet.

Problem Reports and Solutions A Windows utility that provides a list of current and past problems associated with a computer.

process A program that is running under the authority of the shell, together with the system resources assigned to it.

processor *See* central processing unit (CPU).

processor frequency The frequency at which the CPU operates. Usually expressed in GHz.

product activation The process that Microsoft uses to prevent software piracy. For example, once Windows 7 is activated for a particular computer, it cannot be legally installed on another computer.

Programs and Features A window within the Control Panel that lists the programs installed on a computer where you can uninstall, change, or repair programs.

projector Used to shine a light that projects a transparent image onto a large screen and is often used in classrooms or with other large groups.

protocol A set of rules and standards that two entities use for communication. For example, TCP/IP is a suite or group of protocols that define many types of communication on a TCP/IP network.

proxy server A computer that intercepts requests that a browser makes of a server and serves up the request from a cache it maintains in order to improve performance on a large network.

PS/2 port A round 6-pin port used by a keyboard or mouse.

public IP address In TCP/IP version 4, an IP address available to the Internet.

pull automation A Windows installation that requires the local user to start the process. *Compare to* push automation.

punchdown tool A tool used to punch individual wires from a network cable into their slots to terminate the cable.

push automation An installation where a server automatically pushes the installation to a computer when a user is not likely to be sitting at the computer. *Compare to* pull automation.

quad channels Technology used by a motherboard and DIMMs that allows the memory controller to access four DIMMS at the same time.

Quality of Service (QoS)   A feature used by Windows and network hardware devices to improve network performance for an application that is not getting the best network performance. VoIP requires a high QoS.

quarantined computer   A computer that is suspected of infection and is not allowed to use the network, is put on a different network dedicated to quarantined computers, or is allowed to access only certain network resources.

quick format   A format procedure, used to format a hard drive volume or other drive, that doesn't scan the volume or drive for bad sectors; use it only when a drive has been previously formatted and is in healthy condition.

QuickPath Interconnect   The technology used first by the Intel X58 chipset for communication between the chipset and the processor using 16 serial lanes similar to that used by PCI Express. Replaced the 64-bit wide Front Side Bus used by previous chipsets.

radio frequency (RF)   The frequency of waves generated by a radio signal, which are electromagnetic frequencies above audio and below light. For example, Wi-Fi 802.11n transmits using a radio frequency of 5 GHz and 2.4 GHz.

RAID (redundant array of inexpensive disks or redundant array of independent disks)   Several methods of configuring multiple hard drives to store data to increase logical volume size and improve performance, or to ensure that if one hard drive fails, the data is still available from another hard drive.

RAID 0   Using space from two or more physical disks to increase the disk space available for a single volume. Performance improves because data is written evenly across all disks. Windows calls RAID 0 a striped volume. *Also called* striping.

RAID 1   A type of drive imaging that duplicates data on one drive to another drive and is used for fault tolerance. Windows calls RAID 1 a mirrored volume.

RAID 1+0   *See* RAID 10.

RAID 10   A combination of RAID 1 and RAID 0 that requires at least four disks to work as an array of drives and provides the best redundancy and performance.

RAID 5   A technique that stripes data across three or more drives and uses parity checking, so that if one drive fails, the other drives can re-create the data stored on the failed drive. RAID 5 drives increase performance and provide fault tolerance. Windows calls these drives RAID-5 volumes.

RAID-5 volume   *See* RAID 5.

RAM (random access memory)   Memory modules on the motherboard containing microchips used to temporarily hold data and programs while the CPU processes both. Information in RAM is lost when the PC is turned off.

Rambus   *See* Direct Rambus DRAM.

RAS Latency   A method of measuring access timing to memory, which is the number of clock cycles required to write or read a row of data off a memory module. RAS stands for Row Access Strobe. *Compare to* CAS Latency.

raster line   A row in the bitmap that represents a page that has been rendered and is ready for printing.

raw data   Data sent to a printer without any formatting or processing.

RDRAM   *See* Direct Rambus DRAM.

read/write head   A sealed, magnetic coil device that moves across the surface of a disk in a hard disk drive (HDD) either reading data from or writing data to the disk.

ReadyBoost   A Windows 7/Vista utility that uses a flash drive or secure digital (SD) memory card to boost hard drive performance.

ReadyDrive   The Windows 7/Vista technology that supports a hybrid hard drive.

Recovery Console   In Windows XP, a lean bootable command-line operating system on the Windows XP setup CD that can be used to troubleshoot an XP boot problem.

recovery image   A backup of the Windows volume.

rectifier   An electrical device that converts AC to DC. A computer power supply contains a rectifier.

refresh rate   As applied to monitors, the number of times in one second the monitor can fill the screen with lines from top to bottom. *Also called* vertical scan rate.

registry   A database that Windows uses to store hardware and software configuration information, user preferences, and setup information.

Registry Editor (Regedit.exe)   The Windows utility used to edit the Windows registry.

Regsvr32   A utility that is used to register component services used by an installed application.

Reliability and Performance Monitor   A Vista utility (Perfmon.msc) that collects, records, and displays events, called Data Collector Sets, that can help track the performance and reliability of Windows. In Windows XP, this monitor is called the Performance Monitor or the System Monitor.

Reliability Monitor A Windows 7 utility that provides information about problems and errors that happen over time.

Remote Admin Gives an administrator access to the Windows folder on a remote computer.

RemoteApp and Desktop Connection A tool used to install a remote application on a client computer using either an application proxy file or a URL to the server application.

remote application An application that is installed and executed on a server and is presented to a user working at a client computer.

Remote Desktop A Windows tool that gives a user access to his or her Windows desktop from anywhere on the Internet.

Remote Desktop Protocol (RDP) The protocol used by Windows Remote Desktop and Remote Assistance utilities to connect to and control a remote computer.

Remote Desktop Services Software included in Windows 2008 and later that uses the RDP protocol to present a remote application and its data to the client. Prior to Windows 2008, the software was called Terminal Services.

remote network installation An automated installation where no user intervention is required.

remote wipe Remotely erases all contacts, email, photos, and other data from a device to protect your privacy.

resistive touch screen A touch screen that has two sheets of glass covered with a resistive coating. When pressure is placed on the top glass, the glass bends and makes contact with the lower glass. *Compare to* capacitive touch screen.

resolution The number of pixels on a monitor screen that are addressable by software (example: 1024 × 768 pixels).

Resource Monitor A Windows tool that monitors the performance of the processor, memory, hard drive, and network.

restore point A snapshot of the Windows system, usually made before installation of new hardware or applications.

REt (Resolution Enhancement technology) The term used by Hewlett-Packard to describe the way a laser printer varies the size of the dots used to create an image. This technology partly accounts for the sharp, clear image created by a laser printer.

retinal scanning As part of the authentication process, some systems use biometric data by scanning the blood vessels on the back of the eye and is considered the most reliable of all biometric data scanning.

reverse lookup To find the host name when you know a computer's IP address. The Nslookup command can perform a reverse lookup.

RFID badge A badge worn by an employee and is used to gain entrance into a locked area of a building. A Radio Frequency Identification token transmits authentication to the system when the token gets in range of a query device.

RG-59 coaxial cable An older and thinner coaxial cable once used for cable TV.

RG-6 coaxial cable A coaxial cable used for cable TV and replaced the older and thinner RG-59 coaxial cable.

RGB port *See* composite video port.

RIMM A type of memory module developed by Rambus, Inc.

ring network A type of network where nodes form a ring.

riser card A card that plugs into a motherboard and allows for expansion cards to be mounted parallel to the motherboard. Expansion cards are plugged into slots on the riser card.

RJ-11 *See* RJ-11 jack.

RJ-11 jack A phone line connection or port found on modems, telephones, and house phone outlets.

RJ-45 A port that looks like a large phone jack and is used by twisted-pair cable to connect to a wired network adapter or other hardware device. RJ stands for registered jack.

root directory The main directory, at the top of the top-down hierarchical structure of subdirectories, created when a hard drive or disk is first formatted. In Linux, it's indicated by a forward slash. In DOS and Windows, it's indicated by a backward slash.

rooting The process of obtaining root or administrator privileges to an Android device which then gives you complete access to the entire file system and all commands and features.

rootkit A type of malicious software that loads itself before the OS boot is complete and can hijack internal Windows components so that it masks information Windows provides to user-mode utilities such as Windows Explorer or Task Manager.

router A device that manages traffic between two or more networks and can help find the best path for traffic to get from one network to another.

RSA tokens A type of smart card that contains authentication information.

S1 state   On the BIOS power screen, one of the five S states used by ACPI power-saving mode to indicate different levels of power-savings functions. In the S1 state, the hard drive and monitor are turned off and everything else runs normally.

S2 state   On the BIOS power screen, one of the five S states used by ACPI power-saving mode to indicate different levels of power-savings functions. In S2 state, the hard drive and monitor are turned off and everything else runs normally. In addition, the processor is also turned off.

S3 state   On the BIOS power screen, one of the five S states used by ACPI power-saving mode to indicate different levels of power-savings functions. In S3 state, everything is shut down except RAM and enough of the system to respond to a wake-up. S3 is sleep mode.

S4 state   On the BIOS power screen, one of the five S states used by ACPI power-saving mode to indicate different levels of power-savings functions. In S4 state, everything in RAM is copied to a file on the hard drive and the system is shut down. When the system is turned on, the file is used to restore the system to its state before shut down. S4 is hibernation.

S5 state   On the BIOS power screen, one of the five S states used by ACPI power-saving mode to indicate different levels of power-savings functions. S5 state is the power off state after a normal shutdown.

sags   *See* brownouts.

SATA power connector   A 15-pin flat power connector that provides power to SATA drives.

SC (subscriber connector or standard connector) connector   A type of connector used by fiber-optic cables and can be used with either single-mode or multimode fiber-optic cables.

SCSI (Small Computer System Interface)   A fast interface between a host adapter and the CPU that can daisy chain as many as 7 or 15 devices on a single bus.

SCSI host adapter card   A card that manages the SCSI bus and serves as the gateway to the system bus. *Also called* the host adapter.

SCSI ID   A number from 0 to 15 assigned to each SCSI device attached to the daisy chain.

scanstate   A command used by the User State Migration Tool (USMT) to copy user settings and data from an old computer to a server or removable media. *Also see* loadstate.

screen orientation   The layout of the screen that is either portrait or landscape.

screen resolution   The number of dots or pixels on the monitor screen expressed as two numbers such as 1680×1050.

SDRAM II   *See* Double Data Rate SDRAM.

secondary logon   Using administrative privileges to perform an operation when you are not logged on with an account that has these privileges.

sector   On a hard disk drive or SSD, the smallest unit of bytes addressable by the operating system and BIOS. On hard disk drives, one sector equals 512 bytes; SSD drives might use larger sectors.

Secure Digital (SD) card   A type of memory card used in digital cameras, tablets, cell phones, MP3 players, digital camcorders, and other portable devices. The three standards used by SD cards are 1.x (regular SD), 2.x (SD High Capacity or SDHC), and 3.x (SD eXtended Capacity or SDXC).

Secure FTP (SFTP)   A TCP/IP protocol used to transfer files from an FTP server to an FTP client using encryption.

Secure Shell (SSH)   A protocol that is used to pass login information to a remote computer and control that computer over a network using encryption.

Security Center   A center in Vista where you can confirm Windows Firewall, Windows Update, anti-malware settings, including that of Windows Defender, and other security settings.

self-grounding   A method to safeguard against ESD that involves touching the computer case or power supply before touching a component in the computer case.

separation pad   A printer part that keeps more than one sheet of paper from moving forward.

sequential access   A method of data access used by tape drives, whereby data is written or read sequentially from the beginning to the end of the tape or until the desired data is found.

serial ATA (SATA)   An ATAPI interface standard that uses a narrower and more reliable cable than the 80-conductor cable and is easier to configure than PATA systems. *See also* parallel ATA.

serial port   A male 9-pin or 25-pin port on a computer system used by slower I/O devices such as a mouse or modem. Data travels serially, one bit at a time, through the port. Serial ports are sometimes configured as COM1, COM2, COM3, or COM4.

Server Message Block (SMB)   A protocol used by Windows to share files and printers on a network.

Service Set Identifier (SSID) The name of a wireless network.

server-side virtualization Using this virtualization, a server provides a virtual desktop or application for users on multiple client machines.

service A program that runs in the background to support or serve Windows or an application.

service pack A collection of several patches or updates that is installed as a single update to an OS or application.

Services console A console used by Windows to stop, start, and manage background services used by Windows and applications.

Service Set Identifier (SSID) The name of the access point for a wireless network.

setup BIOS Used to change motherboard settings. For example, you can use it to enable or disable a device on the motherboard, change the date and time that is later passed to the OS, and select the order of boot devices for startup BIOS to search when looking for an operating system to load.

shadow copy A copy of open files made so that open files are included in a backup.

share permissions A method to share a folder (not individual files) to remote users on the network, including assigning varying degrees of access to specific user accounts and user groups. Does not apply to local shares and can be used on an NTFS or FAT volume. *Compare to* NTFS permissions.

sheet battery A secondary battery that fits on the bottom of a notebook to provide additional battery charge time.

shell The portion of an OS that relates to the user and to applications.

shielded twisted pair (STP) cable A cable that is made of one or more twisted pairs of wires and is surrounded by a metal shield.

Short Message Service (SMS) A technology that allows users to send a test message using a smartphone.

shoulder surfing Where other people secretly peek at your monitor screen as you work to gain valuable information.

sidebar Located on the right side of the Vista desktop and displays Vista gadgets.

SIM (Subscriber Identity Module) card A small flash memory card that contains all the information a device needs to connect to a cellular network, including a password and other authentication information needed to access the network, encryption standards used, and the services that a subscription includes.

SIMM (single inline memory module) An outdated miniature circuit board used to hold RAM. SIMMs held 8, 16, 32, or 64 MB on a single module. SIMMs have been replaced by DIMMs.

simple file sharing A Windows XP technique to share folders or files with remote network users where you have no control over who has access to the shared folder or file.

Simple Network Management Protocol (SNMP) A TCP/IP protocol used to monitor network traffic.

simple volume A type of volume used on a single hard drive. *Compare to* dynamic volume.

single channel The memory controller on a motherboard that can access only one DIMM at a time. *Compare to* dual channel and triple channel.

single-sided A DIMM that has memory chips installed on one side of the module.

site license A license that allows a company to install multiple copies of software, or to allow multiple employees to execute the software from a file server.

slack Wasted space on a hard drive caused by not using all available space at the end of a cluster.

sleep mode A power-saving state for a computer used to save power when not using the computer. *Also see* S3 state.

sleep timers The number of minutes of inactivity before a computer goes into a power-saving state such as sleep mode.

S.M.A.R.T. (Self-Monitoring Analysis and Reporting Technology) A system BIOS and hard drive feature that monitors hard drive performance, disk spin up time, temperature, distance between the head and the disk, and other mechanical activities of the drive in order to predict when the drive is likely to fail.

smart card Any small device that contains authentication information that can be keyed into a logon window or read by a reader to authenticate a user on a network.

smart card reader A device that can read a smart card used to authenticate a person onto a network.

smartphone Primarily a cell phone and includes abilities to send text messages, text messages with photos, videos, or other multimedia content, surf the web, manage email, play games, take photos and videos, and download and use small apps.

SMTP (Simple Mail Transfer Protocol) A TCP/IP protocol used by email clients to send email messages to an email server and on to the recipient's email server. *Also see* POP and IMAP.

SMTP AUTH (SMTP Authentication) An improved version of SMTP and used to authenticate a user to an email server when the email client first tries to connect to the email server to send email. The protocol is based on the Simple Authentication and Security Layer (SASL) protocol.

snap-ins A Windows utility that can be installed in a console window by Microsoft Management Console.

social engineering The practice of tricking people into giving out private information or allowing unsafe programs into the network or computer.

SO-DIMM (small outline DIMM) A type of memory module used in notebook computers that uses DIMM technology. A DDR3 SO-DIMM has 204 pins. A DDR2 or DDR SO-DIMM has 200 pins. Older, outdated SO-DIMMs can have 72 pins or 144 pins.

soft boot To restart a PC without turning off the power, for example, in Windows 7, by clicking Start, pointing to Shut down, and clicking Restart. *Also called* warm boot.

Software as a Service (SaaS) A cloud computing service where the service is responsible for the hardware, the operating systems, and the applications installed.

Software Explorer A Vista tool used to control startup programs.

software piracy The act of making unauthorized copies of original software, which violates the Federal Copyright Act of 1976.

software RAID Using Windows to implement RAID. The setup is done using the Disk Management utility.

solid state device (SSD) An electronic device with no moving parts. A storage device that uses memory chips to store data instead of spinning disks (such as those used by magnetic hard drives and CD drives). Examples of solid state devices are jump drives (*also called* key drives or thumb drives), flash memory cards, and solid state disks used as hard drives in notebook computers designed for the most rugged uses. *Also called* solid state disk (SSD) or solid state drive (SSD).

solid state drive (SSD) A hard drive that has no moving parts. *Also see* solid state device (SSD).

South Bridge That portion of the chipset hub that connects slower I/O buses (for example, a PCI bus) to the system bus. *Compare to* North Bridge.

spacers *See* standoffs.

spanning Using a spanned volume to increase the size of a volume.

S/PDIF (Sony-Phillips Digital Interface) sound port A port that connects to an external home theater audio system, providing digital audio output and the nest signal quality.

spooling Placing print jobs in a print queue so that an application can be released from the printing process before printing is completed. Spooling is an acronym for simultaneous peripheral operations online.

spyware Malicious software that installs itself on your computer to spy on you. It collects personal information about you that it transmits over the Internet to web-hosting sites that intend to use your personal data for harm.

staggered pin grid array (SPGA) A feature of a CPU socket whereby the pins are staggered over the socket in order to squeeze more pins into a small space.

standard account The Windows 7/Vista user account type that can use software and hardware and make some system changes, but cannot make changes that affect the security of the system or other users.

standard image An image that includes Windows 7, drivers, and applications that are standard to all the computers that might use the image.

Standard Parallel Port (SPP) An outdated parallel port that allows data to flow in only one direction and is the slowest of the three types of parallel ports. *Also called* a Centronics port. *Compare to* EPP (Enhanced Parallel Port) and ECP (Extended Capabilities Port).

standby mode In Windows XP, standby mode is similar to Windows 7/Vista sleep mode where work is saved to memory and a trickle of power preserves that memory.

standoffs Round plastic or metal pegs that separate the motherboard from the case, so that components on the back of the motherboard do not touch the case.

startup BIOS Part of system BIOS that is responsible for controlling the computer when it is first turned on. Startup BIOS gives control over to the OS once it is loaded.

static IP address A permanent IP address that is manually assigned to a computer.

static RAM (SRAM) RAM chips that retain information without the need for refreshing, as long as the computer's power is on. They are more expensive than traditional DRAM.

ST (straight tip) connector A type of connector used by fiber-optic cables and can be used with either single-mode or multimode fiberoptic cables.

star network A network configuration that uses a centralized device such as a switch or hub to manage traffic on the network.

straight-through cable A cable used to connect a computer to a switch or other network device. *Also called* a patch cable.

striped volume A type of dynamic volume used for two or more hard drives that writes to the disks evenly rather than filling up allotted space on one and then moving on to the next. *Compare to* spanned volume.

striping *See* RAID 0.

strong password A password that is not easy to guess.

stylus A device that is included with a graphics tablet that works like a pencil on the tablet.

subdirectory A directory or folder contained in another directory or folder. *Also called* a child directory or folder.

subnet A group of local networks when several networks are tied together in a subsystem of the larger intranet. In TCP/IP Version 6, one or more links that have the same 64 bits in the first part of the IP address (called the prefix).

subnet ID In TCP/IP Version 6, the last block (16 bits) in the 64-bit prefix of an IP address. The subnet is identified using some or all of these 16 bits.

subnet mask In TCP/IP Version 4, 32 bits that include a series of ones followed by zeroes. For example, 11111111.11111111.11110000.00000000, which can be written as 255.255.240.0. The ones identify the network portion of an IP address, and the zeroes identify the host portion of an IP address. The subnet mask tells Windows if a remote computer is on the same or different network. *Also see* classless subnet mask and classful subnet mask.

suspend mode *See* sleep mode.

S-Video port A 4-pin or 7-pin round video port that sends two signals over the cable, one for color and the other for brightness, and is used by some high-end TVs and video equipment.

switch A device used to connect nodes on a network in a star network topology. It also segments the network to improve network performance by deciding which network segment is to receive a packet, on the basis of the packet's destination MAC address.

system BIOS (basic input/output system) BIOS located on the motherboard that is used to control essential devices before the OS is loaded.

system board *See* motherboard.

system bus The bus between the CPU and memory on the motherboard. The bus frequency in documentation is called the system speed, such as 400 MHz. *Also called* the memory bus, FrontSide Bus, local bus, or host bus.

system clock A line on a bus that is dedicated to timing the activities of components connected to it. The system clock provides a continuous pulse that other devices use to time themselves.

System Configuration Utility (Msconfig.exe) A Windows utility that can identify what processes are launched at startup and can temporarily disable a process from loading.

System File Checker (SFC) *See* SFC (System File Checker).

system image The backup of the entire Windows 7 volume and can also include backups of other volumes. The backup is made using the Windows 7 Backup and Restore utility.

System Information A Windows tool that provides details about a system, including installed hardware and software, the current system configuration, and currently running programs. The program file is Msinfo32.exe.

System Monitor The Windows XP Performance Monitor.

system partition The active partition of the hard drive containing the boot record and the specific files required to start the Windows launch.

System Protection A utility that automatically backs up system files and stores them in restore points on the hard drive at regular intervals and just before you install software or hardware.

system repair disc A disc you can create using Windows 7 that can be used to launch Windows RE.

System Restore A Windows utility used to restore the system to a restore point.

system state data In Windows 2000/XP, files that are necessary for a successful load of the operating system.

system tray *See* notification area.

System window A window that displays brief and important information about installed hardware and software and gives access to important Windows tools needed to support the system.

systray *See* notification area.

T568A Standards for wiring twisted-pair network cabling and RJ-45 connectors and have the green pair connected to pins 1 and 2 and the orange pair connected to pins 3 and 6.

T568B Standards for wiring twisted-pair network cabling and RJ-45 connectors and have the orange pair using pins 1 and 2 and the green pair connected to pins 3 and 6.

tailgating When someone who is unauthorized follows the employee through a secured entrance to a room or building.

Task Manager (Taskmgr.exe) A Windows utility that lets you view the applications and processes running on your computer as well as information about process and memory performance, network activity, and user activity.

Task Scheduler A Windows tool that can set a task or program to launch at a future time, including at startup.

taskbar A bar normally located at the bottom of the Windows desktop, displaying information about open programs and providing quick access to others.

Taskkill A command that uses the process PID to kill a process.

Tasklist A command that returns the process identifier (PID), which is a number that identifies each running process.

TCP (Transmission Control Protocol) The protocol in the TCP/IP suite of protocols that works at the OSI Transport layer and establishes a session or connection between parties and guarantees packet delivery.

TCP/IP (Transmission Control Protocol/Internet Protocol) The group or suite of protocols used for almost all networks, including the Internet. Fundamentally, TCP is responsible for error checking transmissions, and IP is responsible for routing.

technical documentation The technical reference manuals, included with software packages and hardware, that provide directions for installation, usage, and troubleshooting. The information extends beyond that given in user manuals.

Telnet A TCP/IP protocol used by the Telnet client/server applications to allow an administrator or other user to control a computer remotely.

Teredo In TCP/IP Version 6, a tunneling protocol named after the Teredo worm that bores holes in wood. IPv6 addresses intended to be used by this protocol always begin with the same 32-bit prefix. Teredo IP addresses begin with 2001, and the prefix is written as 2001::/32.

Terminal Services *See* Remote Desktop Services.

terminating resistor The resistor added at the end of a SCSI chain to dampen the voltage at the end of the chain.

thermal compound A creamlike substance that is placed between the bottom of the cooler heatsink and the top of the processor to eliminate air pockets and to help to draw heat off the processor.

thermal paper Special coated paper used by thermal printers.

thermal printer A type of line printer that uses wax-based ink, which is heated by heat pins that melt the ink onto paper.

thermal transfer printer A type of thermal printer that uses a ribbon that contains wax-based ink. The heating element melts the ribbon onto special thermal paper so that it stays glued to the paper as the feeder assembly moves the paper through the printer.

thick client A regular desktop computer or laptop that is sometimes used as a client by a virtualization server.

thin client A computer that has an operating system, but has little computer power and might only need to support a browser used to communicate with a virtualization server.

thread Each process that the CPU is aware of; a single task that is part of a longer task or request from a program.

Thunderbolt A port that transmits both video and data on the same port and cable. The port is shaped the same as the DisplayPort and is compatible with DisplayPort devices.

ticket An entry in a call-tracking system made by whoever receives a call for help and used to track and document actions taken. The ticket stays open until the issue is resolved.

TKIP (Temporal Key Integrity Protocol) A type of encryption protocol used by WPA to secure a wireless Wi-Fi network. *Also see* WPA (WiFi Protected Access).

tone probe A two-part kit that is used to find cables in the walls of a building. *Also called* a toner probe.

toner probe *See* tone probe.

toner vacuum A vacuum cleaner designed to pick up toner used in laser printers and does not allow it to touch any conductive surface.

topology The physical arrangement of the connections between computers in a network.

TouchFLO A multi-touch technology developed by High Tech Computer (HTC) and widely used by mobile devices.

touchpad A common pointing device on a notebook computer.

touch screen An input device that uses a monitor or LCD panel as a backdrop for user options. Touch screens can be embedded in a monitor or LCD panel or installed as an add-on device over the monitor screen.

tower case The largest type of personal computer case. Tower cases stand vertically and can be as high as two feet tall. They have more drive bays and are a good choice for computer users who anticipate making significant upgrades.

TPM (Trusted Platform Module) chip A chip on a motherboard that holds an encryption key required at startup to access encrypted data on the hard drive. Windows 7/Vista BitLocker Encryption can use the TPM chip.

Tracert (trace route) A TCP/IP command that enables you to resolve a connectivity problem when attempting to reach a destination host such as a web site.

traces A wire on a circuit board that connects two components or devices.

track One of many concentric circles on the surface of a hard disk drive or floppy disk.

TrackPoint Similar to a touchpad, a unique and popular pointing device embedded in the keyboard of some IBM and Lenovo ThinkPad notebooks.

tractor feed A continuous feed within an impact printer that feeds fanfold paper through the printer rather than individual sheets, making them useful for logging ongoing events or data.

transfer belt A laser printer component that completes the transferring step in the printer.

transfer roller A soft, black roller in a laser printer that puts a positive charge on the paper. The charge pulls the toner from the drum onto the paper.

transformer An electrical device that changes the ratio of current to voltage. A computer power supply is basically a transformer and a rectifier.

trip hazard Loose cables or cords in a traffic area where people can trip over them.

triple channels When the memory controller accesses three DIMMs at the same time. DDR3 DIMMs support triple channeling.

Trojan A type of malware that tricks you into opening it by substituting itself for a legitimate program.

TV tuner card An adapter card that receives a TV signal and displays TV on the computer screen.

twisted-pair cabling Cabling, such as a network cable, that uses pairs of wires twisted together to reduce crosstalk.

Type 1 hypervisor Software to manage virtual machines that is installed before any operating system is installed.

Type 2 hypervisor Software to manage virtual machines that is installed as an application in an operating system.

UDF (Universal Disk Format) file system A file system for optical media used by all DVD discs and some CD-R and CD-RW discs.

UDP (User Datagram Protocol) A connectionless TCP/IP protocol that works at the OSI Transport layer and does not require a connection to send a packet or guarantee that the packet arrives at its destination. The protocol is commonly used for broadcasting to multiple nodes on a network or the Internet. *Compare to* TCP (Transmission Control Protocol).

ultra-thin client *See* zero client.

unattended installation A Windows installation that is done by storing the answers to installation questions in a text file or script that Windows calls an answer file so that the answers do not have to be typed in during the installation.

unicast address Using TCP/IP version 6, an IP address assigned to a single node on a network.

Unified Extensible Firmware Interface (UEFI) An interface between firmware on the motherboard and the operating system and improves on legacy BIOS processes for booting, handing over the boot to the OS, and loading device drivers and applications before the OS loads.

uninterruptible power supply (UPS) A device that raises the voltage when it drops brownouts.

unique local address (ULA) *See* unique local unicast address.

unique local unicast address In TCP/IP Version 6, an address used to identify a specific site within a large organization. It can work on multiple links within the same organization. The address is a hybrid between a global unicast address that works on the Internet and a link-local unicast address that works on only one link. *Also called* unique local address (ULA).

unshielded twisted pair (UTP) cable The most popular cabling method for local networks and is the least expensive and is commonly used on LANs. The cable is made of twisted pairs of wires and is not surrounded by shielding.

upgrade paths A qualifying OS required by Microsoft in order to perform an in-place upgrade.

USB 3.0 B-Male connector A USB connector used by SuperSpeed USB 3.0 devices such as printers or scanners.

USB 3.0 Micro-B connector   A small USB connector used by SuperSpeed USB 3.0 devices. The connectors are not compatible with regular Micro-B connectors.

USB (Universal Serial Bus) port   A type of port designed to make installation and configuration of I/O devices easy, providing room for as many as 127 devices daisy-chained together.

User Account Control (UAC) dialog box   A Windows 7/Vista security feature that displays a dialog box when an event requiring administrative privileges is about to happen.

User group   The group of standard user accounts.

user mode   In Windows, a mode that provides an interface between an application and the OS, and only has access to hardware resources through the code running in kernel mode.

user profile   A collection of files and settings about a user account that enables the user's personal data, desktop settings, and other operating parameters to be retained from one session to another.

user profile namespace   The group of folders and subfolders in the C:\Users folder that belong to a specific user account and contain the user profile.

User State Migration Tool (USMT)   A Windows utility that helps you migrate user files and preferences from one computer to another to help a user make a smooth transition from one computer to another.

VGA (Video Graphics Adapter) port   A 15-pin analog video port popular for many years.

VGA mode   Standard VGA settings, which include a resolution of 640 × 480.

video capture card   An adapter card that captures video input and saves it to a file on the hard drive.

video memory   Memory used by the video controller. The memory might be contained on a video card or be part of system memory. When part of system memory, the memory is dedicated by Windows to video.

Virtual Desktop Infrastructure (VDI)   A presentation of a virtual desktop made to a client computer by a server that is serving up a virtual machine.

virtual machine (VM)   One or more logical machines created within one physical machine.

virtual machine manager (VMM)   Software that creates and manages virtual machines on a server or on a local computer. *Also called* hypervisor.

virtual memory   A method whereby the OS uses the hard drive as though it were RAM. *Also see* pagefile.sys.

virtual private network (VPN)   A security technique that uses encrypted data packets between a private network and a computer somewhere on the Internet.

virtualization   When one physical machine hosts multiple activities that are normally done on multiple machines.

virtualization server   A computer that serves up virtual machines to multiple client computers and provides a virtual desktop for users on these client machines.

virtual machine (VM)   One or more logical machines created within one physical machine.

virus   A program that often has an incubation period, is infectious, and is intended to cause damage. A virus program might destroy data and programs or damage a disk drive's boot sector.

virus definition   A set of distinguishing characteristics of a virus and used by antivirus software to identify new viruses as they get into the wild. *Also called* virus signatures.

virus encyclopedia   A database about viruses that is kept on the Internet.

virus signature   *See* virus definition.

VoIP (Voice over Internet Protocol)   A TCP/IP protocol and an application that provides voice communication over a network. *Also called* Internet telephone.

VoIP phone   A telephone that connects to a network and uses the VoIP TCP/IP protocol for voice communication over the network or the Internet.

volume   A primary partition that has been assigned a drive letter and can be formatted with a file system such as NTFS. *Compare to* logical drive.

volt   A measure of potential difference in an electrical circuit. A computer ATX power supply usually provides five separate voltages: +12 V, −12 V, +5 V, −5 V, and +3.3 V.

wait state   A clock tick in which nothing happens, used to ensure that the microprocessor isn't getting ahead of slower components. A 0-wait state is preferable to a 1-wait state. Too many wait states can slow down a system.

Wake on LAN   Configuring a computer so that it will respond to network activity when the computer is in a sleep state.

WAN (wide area network)   A network or group of networks that span a large geographical area.

warm boot   *See* soft boot.

watt The unit of electricity used to measure power. A typical computer may use a power supply that provides 500W.

WEP (Wired Equivalent Privacy) An encryption protocol used to secure transmissions on a Wi-Fi wireless network; however, it is no longer considered secure because the key used for encryption is static (it doesn't change).

Wi-Fi (Wireless Fidelity) The common name for standards for a local wireless network as defined by IEEE 802.11. *Also see* 802.11 a/b/g/n.

Wi-Fi Protected Setup (WPS) A method used to secure a wireless network from an outside attack and was designed to make it easier for users to connect their computers to a wireless network when a hard-to-remember SSID and security key are used.

wildcard An * or ? character used in a command line that represents a character or group of characters in a filename or extension.

Windows 7 Enterprise A Windows operating system that includes additional features over Windows 7 Professional. The major additional features include BitLocker Drive Encryption used to encrypt an entire hard drive and support for multiple languages. The edition does not include Windows DVD Maker. Multiple site licenses are available.

Windows 7 Home Basic A Windows operating system that has limited features and is available only in underdeveloped countries and can only be activated in these countries.

Windows 7 Home Premium A Windows operating system that is similar to Windows 7 Home Basic but includes additional features.

Window 7 Professional A Windows operating system that is intended for business users. You can purchase multiple site licenses (*also called* volume licensing) using this edition.

Windows 7 Starter A Windows operating system that has the most limited features and is intended to be used on netbooks or in developing nations. In the United States, it can only be obtained preinstalled by the manufacturer on a new netbook computer. Windows Starter comes only in the 32-bit version. All other editions of Windows 7 are available in either the 32-bit or 64-bit version.

Windows 7 Ultimate A Windows operating system that includes every Windows 7 feature. Multiple licenses are not available with this edition.

Windows Automated Installation Kit (AIK) The Windows AIK for Windows 7 contains a group of tools used to deploy Windows 7 in a large organization and contains the User State Migration Tool (USMT).

Windows Boot Loader (WinLoad.exe) One of two programs that manage the loading of Windows 7/Vista. The program file is stored in C:\ Windows\ System32, and it loads and starts essential Windows processes.

Windows Boot Manager (BootMgr) The Windows 7/Vista program that manages the initial startup of Windows. The BootMgr program file is stored in the C:\ root directory and has no file extension.

Windows Defender Antispyware utility included in Windows 7/Vista.

Windows Easy Transfer A Windows tool used to transfer Windows 7/Vista/XP user data and preferences to the Windows 7/Vista/XP installation on another computer.

Windows Experience Index A Windows 7/Vista feature that gives a summary index designed to measure the overall performance of a system on a scale from 1.0 to 7.9.

Windows Firewall A personal firewall that protects a computer from intrusion and is automatically configured when you set your network location in the Network and Sharing Center.

Windows Preinstallation Environment (Windows PE) A minimum operating system used to start the Windows installation.

Windows Recovery Environment (Windows RE) A lean operating system installed on the Windows 7/Vista setup DVD and also on a Windows 7 hard drive that can be used to troubleshoot problems when Windows refuses to start.

Windows Vista Business The Vista edition designed for business users and includes support for a domain, Group Policy, and Encrypted File System, and does not include consumer features such as Movie Maker.

Windows Vista Enterprise The Vista edition that expands on Windows Vista Business, adding security features such as BitLocker Encryption.

Windows Vista Home Basic The Vista edition that is designed for low-cost home systems that don't require full security and networking features. It does not include the Aero glass interface.

Windows Vista Home Premium The Vista edition that includes more features than Windows Vista Home Basic, including the Aero user interface, DVD Maker, Media Center, SideShow, and backups.

Windows Vista Starter   The Vista edition with the most limited features and intended to be used in developing nations.

Windows Vista Ultimate   The Vista edition that includes every Windows Vista feature. Multiple licensing is not available.

Windows XP Home Edition   The XP edition that does not include Remote Desktop, multilingual capabilities, roaming profiles, and support for high-end processors.

Windows XP Media Center Edition   This XP edition is an enhanced version of XP Professional that includes support for digital entertainment hardware.

Windows XP Mode   A Windows XP environment installed in Windows 7 that can be used to support older applications.

Windows XP Professional   The XP edition that includes Remote Desktop, roaming profiles, multilingual capabilities and enhanced security features.

Windows XP Professional x64 Edition (formally called Windows XP 64-Bit Edition)   A 64-bit operating system and can support up to 128 GB of memory. (All other editions of XP are 32-bit and can support up to 4 GB of memory.)

Windows XP Tablet PC Edition   The XP edition designed for notebooks and tablet PCs.

wireless access point   A wireless device that creates a wireless network.

wireless access point   A wireless device that is used to create and manage a wireless network.

wireless LAN (WLAN)   A type of LAN that does not use wires or cables to create connections, but instead transmits data over radio or infrared waves.

wireless locator   A tool that can locate a Wi-Fi hotspot and tell you the strength of the RF signal.

wireless wide area network (WWAN)   A cellular network for computers and mobile devices using broadband. *Also called* a cellular network.

wire stripper   A tool used when terminating a cable. The tool cuts away the plastic jacket or coating around the wires in a cable so that a connector can be installed on the end of the cable.

workgroup   In Windows, a logical group of computers and users in which administration, resources, and security are distributed throughout the network, without centralized management or security.

worm   An infestation designed to copy itself repeatedly to memory, on drive space, or on a network, until little memory, disk space, or network bandwidth remains.

WPA (WiFi Protected Access)   A data encryption method for wireless networks that use the TKIP (Temporal Key Integrity Protocol) encryption method and the encryption keys are changed at set intervals while the wireless LAN is in use. WPA is stronger than WEP.

WPA2 (WiFi Protected Access 2)   A data encryption standard compliant with the IEEE802.11i standard that uses the AES (Advanced Encryption Standard) protocol. WPA2 is currently the strongest wireless encryption standard.

x86 processor   An older processor that first used the number 86 in the model number and processes 32 bits at a time.

x86-64 bit processor   Hybrid processors that can process 32 bits or 64 bits.

xD-Picture Card   A type of flash memory device that has a compact design and currently holds up to 8 GB of data.

XPS (XML Paper Specification)   A standard introduced with Windows Vista and designed to ultimately replace GDI as the method Windows uses to render a printed page before sending it to the printer.

XPS Document Writer   A Windows 7/Vista feature that creates a file with an .xps file extension. The file is similar to a .pdf file and can be viewed, edited, printed, faxed, emailed, or posted on Web sites.

zero client   A client computer that does not have an operating system and merely provides an interface between the user and the server.

zero insertion force (ZIF) socket   A socket that uses a small lever to apply even force when you install the processor into the socket.

zero-fill utility   A hard drive utility that fills every sector on the drive with zeroes.

zero-touch, high volume deployment   An installation strategy that does not require the user to start the process. Instead a server pushes the installation to a computer when a user is not likely to be sitting at it.

INDEX